Educational Psychology

SEVENTH EDITION

John W. Santrock
University of Texas at Dallas

EDUCATIONAL PSYCHOLOGY

Published by McGraw Hill LLC, 1325 Avenue of the Americas, New York, NY 10121. Copyright © 2021 by McGraw Hill LLC. All rights reserved. Printed in the United States of America. No part of this publication may be reproduced or distributed in any form or by any means, or stored in a database or retrieval system, without the prior written consent of McGraw Hill LLC, including, but not limited to, in any network or other electronic storage or transmission, or broadcast for distance learning.

Some ancillaries, including electronic and print components, may not be available to customers outside the United States.

This book is printed on acid-free paper.

1 2 3 4 5 6 7 8 9 LWI 24 23 22 21 20

ISBN 978-1-260-57130-1
MHID 1-260-57130-0

Cover Image: *Paul Bradbur/age footstock*

All credits appearing on page or at the end of the book are considered to be an extension of the copyright page.

The Internet addresses listed in the text were accurate at the time of publication. The inclusion of a website does not indicate an endorsement by the authors or McGraw Hill LLC, and McGraw Hill LLC does not guarantee the accuracy of the information presented at these sites.

mheducation.com/highered

For the educators in my family: My wife, Mary Jo, a teacher; my father, John F. Santrock, Jr., a teacher, principal, and superintendent of schools; my mother, Ruth Smith Santrock, an administrative assistant; my grandmother, Della Karnes Santrock, who taught all grades in a one-room school; and my grandfather, John F. Santrock, Sr., a principal.

About the Author

John Santrock with his grandchildren Luke, Alex, and Jordan
Courtesy of Dr. John Santrock

John Santrock received his Ph.D. from the University of Minnesota. He taught at the University of Charleston and the University of Georgia before joining the Program in Psychology at the University of Texas at Dallas, where he currently teaches a number of undergraduate courses and was recently given the University's Effective Teaching Award. In 2010, he created the UT-Dallas Santrock undergraduate scholarship, an annual award that is given to outstanding undergraduate students majoring in developmental psychology to enable them to attend research conventions.

John has been a member of the editorial boards of *Child Development* and *Developmental Psychology*. His research on father custody is widely cited and used in expert witness testimony to promote flexibility and alternative considerations in custody disputes. John also has authored these exceptional McGraw-Hill texts: *Children* (13th edition), *Adolescence* (16th edition), *A Topical Approach to Life-Span Development* (8th edition), and *Essentials of Life-Span Development* (5th edition).

For many years, John was involved in tennis as a player, teaching professional, and coach of professional tennis players. At the University of Miami (FL), the tennis team on which he played still holds the NCAA Division I record for most consecutive wins (137) in any sport. John's wife, Mary Jo, has a master's degree in special education and has worked as a teacher and a Realtor. He has two daughters—Tracy, who worked for a number of years as a technology marketing specialist, and Jennifer, who has been a medical sales specialist. However, recently both have followed in their mother's footsteps and are now Realtors. He has one granddaughter, Jordan, age 24, who works for the accounting firm Ernst & Young, and two grandsons, Alex, age 11, and Luke, age 10. In the last two decades, John also has spent time painting expressionist art.

Brief Contents

CHAPTER 1	Educational Psychology: A Tool for Effective Teaching 1
CHAPTER 2	Cognitive and Language Development 28
CHAPTER 3	Social Contexts and Socioemotional Development 70
CHAPTER 4	Individual Variations 113
CHAPTER 5	Sociocultural Diversity 144
CHAPTER 6	Learners Who Are Exceptional 184
CHAPTER 7	Behavioral and Social Cognitive Approaches 219
CHAPTER 8	The Information-Processing Approach 255
CHAPTER 9	Complex Cognitive Processes 295
CHAPTER 10	Social Constructivist Approaches 334
CHAPTER 11	Learning and Cognition in the Content Areas 356
CHAPTER 12	Planning, Instruction, and Technology 392
CHAPTER 13	Motivation, Teaching, and Learning 427
CHAPTER 14	Managing the Classroom 467
CHAPTER 15	Standardized Tests and Teaching 503
CHAPTER 16	Classroom Assessment and Grading 536

Contents

Preface xx

CHAPTER 1

Educational Psychology: A Tool for Effective Teaching 1

Exploring Educational Psychology 2
- Historical Background 2
- Teaching: Art and Science 4

Effective Teaching 6
- Professional Knowledge and Skills 6
- Commitment, Motivation, and Caring 11

> **SELF-ASSESSMENT 1** *The Best and Worst Characteristics of My Teachers* 13

Research In Educational Psychology 15
- Why Research Is Important 15
- Research Methods 16
- Program Evaluation Research, Action Research, and the Teacher-As-Researcher 21
- Quantitative And Qualitative Research 22

> **CONNECTING WITH THE CLASSROOM: CRACK THE CASE** *The Classroom Decision* 24

Connecting with Learning: Reach Your Learning Goals 25

Key Terms 27

Portfolio Activities 27

Jamie Grill/Getty Images

CHAPTER 2

Cognitive and Language Development 28

An Overview of Child Development 29
- Exploring What Development Is 29
- Processes and Periods 29
- Developmental Issues 31
- Development and Education 33

Cognitive Development 35
- The Brain 35
- Piaget's Theory 40
- Vygotsky's Theory 50

> **SELF-ASSESSMENT 1** *Applying Piaget and Vygotsky in My Classroom* 54

Ariel Skelley/Blend Images LLC

Contents vii

Language Development 58
- What Is Language? 58
- Biological and Environmental Influences 59
- How Language Develops 59

  CONNECTING WITH THE CLASSROOM: CRACK THE CASE *The Book Report* 66

Connecting with Learning: Reach Your Learning Goals 66

Key Terms 69

Portfolio Activities 69

Omgimages/iStockphoto/Getty Images

CHAPTER 3

Social Contexts and Socioemotional Development 70

Contemporary Theories 71
- Bronfenbrenner's Ecological Theory 71
- Erikson's Life-Span Development Theory 73

Social Contexts of Development 77
- Families 77
- Peers 82
- Schools 85

Socioemotional Development 92
- The Self and Identity 92

  SELF-ASSESSMENT 1 *Where Are You Now? Exploring Your Identity* 96

- Moral Development 97
- Emotional Development 104

  CONNECTING WITH THE CLASSROOM: CRACK THE CASE *The Fight* 108

Connecting with Learning: Reach Your Learning Goals 109

Key Terms 111

Portfolio Activities 112

Science Photo Library/Alamy Stock Photo

CHAPTER 4

Individual Variations 113

Intelligence 114
- What Is Intelligence? 114
- Intelligence Tests 115
- Theories of Multiple Intelligences 117

  SELF-ASSESSMENT 1 *Evaluating Myself on Gardner's Eight Types of Intelligence* 122

- The Neuroscience of Intelligence 124
- Controversies And Issues In Intelligence 125

Learning and Thinking Styles 132
- Impulsive/Reflective Styles 132
- Deep/Surface Styles 133
- Optimistic/Pessimistic Styles 134
- Criticisms of Learning and Thinking Styles 134

Personality and Temperament 136
Personality 136
Temperament 137

CONNECTING WITH THE CLASSROOM: CRACK THE CASE
Workshops 140

Connecting with Learning: Reach Your Learning Goals 141

Key Terms 143

Portfolio Activities 143

CHAPTER 5

Sociocultural Diversity 144

Ariel Skelley/Blend Images/Getty Images

Culture and Ethnicity 145
Culture 146
Socioeconomic Status 147
Ethnicity 151
Second-Language Learning and Bilingual Education 154

Multicultural Education 158
Empowering Students 160
Culturally Relevant Teaching 161
Issues-Centered Education 162
Improving Relationships Among Children from Different Ethnic Groups 162

Gender 168
Exploring Gender Views 168
Gender Stereotyping, Similarities, and Differences 169
Gender Controversy 172
Gender-Role Classification 172
Gender in Context 173

SELF-ASSESSMENT 1 *What Gender-Role Orientation Will I Present to My Students?* 174

Eliminating Gender Bias 175

CONNECTING WITH THE CLASSROOM: CRACK THE CASE
These Boys 180

Connecting with Learning: Reach Your Learning Goals 180

Key Terms 182

Portfolio Activities 183

CHAPTER 6

Learners Who Are Exceptional 184

Faithhoca/Getty Images

Children with Disabilities 185
Learning Disabilities 186
Attention Deficit Hyperactivity Disorder 189
Intellectual Disability 193

Contents ix

    Physical Disorders   196
    Sensory Disorders   196
    Speech and Language Disorders   197
    Autism Spectrum Disorders   198
    Emotional and Behavioral Disorders   199

    SELF-ASSESSMENT 1 *Evaluating My Experiences with People Who Have Various Disabilities and Disorders*   201

Educational Issues Involving Children with Disabilities   204
    Legal Aspects   204
    Technology   207

Children Who Are Gifted   208
    Characteristics   208
    Nature/Nurture And Domain-Specific Giftedness   209
    Educating Children Who Are Gifted   210

    CONNECTING WITH THE CLASSROOM: CRACK THE CASE *Now What?*   214

Connecting with Learning: Reach Your Learning Goals   215

Key Terms   218

Portfolio Activities   218

Monkey Business Images/Shutterstock

CHAPTER 7

Behavioral and Social Cognitive Approaches   219

What Is Learning?   220
    What Learning Is and Is Not   220
    Approaches to Learning   221

Behavioral Approaches to Learning   222
    Classical Conditioning   223
    Operant Conditioning   225

Applied Behavior Analysis in Education   228
    What Is Applied Behavior Analysis?   228
    Increasing Desirable Behaviors   228
    Decreasing Undesirable Behaviors   231
    Evaluating Operant Conditioning And Applied Behavior Analysis   235

Social Cognitive Approaches to Learning   237
    Bandura's Social Cognitive Theory   237
    Observational Learning   238

    SELF-ASSESSMENT 1 *Models and Mentors in My Life and My Students' Lives*   241

    Cognitive-Behavioral Approaches and Self-Regulation   242

    SELF-ASSESSMENT 2 *Self-Monitoring*   246

    Evaluating the Social Cognitive Approaches   249

    CONNECTING WITH THE CLASSROOM: CRACK THE CASE *Consequences*   250

Connecting with Learning: Reach Your Learning Goals   251

Key Terms   253

Portfolio Activities   254

Ariel Skelley/Blend Images LLC

CHAPTER 8

The Information-Processing Approach 255

The Nature of the Information-Processing Approach 256
  The Information-Processing Approach 256
  Cognitive Resources: Capacity and Speed of Processing Information 257
  Mechanisms Of Change 258

Attention 259
  What Is Attention? 259
  Developmental Changes 260

Memory 264
  What Is Memory? 264
  Encoding 264
  Storage 267
  Retrieval And Forgetting 272

Expertise 277
  Expertise And Learning 277

  SELF-ASSESSMENT 1 How Effective Are My Memory and Study Strategies? 282

  Acquiring Expertise 283
  Expertise and Teaching 283

Metacognition 285
  Developmental Changes 285
  The Good Information-Processing Model 287
  Strategies and Metacognitive Regulation 288

  CONNECTING WITH THE CLASSROOM: CRACK THE CASE The Test 291

Connecting with Learning: Reach Your Learning Goals 291

Key Terms 293

Portfolio Activities 294

Rachel Frank/Fancy/Corbis/Glow Images

CHAPTER 9

Complex Cognitive Processes 295

Conceptual Understanding 296
  What Are Concepts? 296
  Promoting Concept Formation 297

Thinking 302
  What Is Thinking? 302
  Executive Function 302
  Reasoning 304
  Critical Thinking 305
  Decision Making 310
  Creative Thinking 313

  SELF-ASSESSMENT 1 How Good Am I at Thinking Creatively? 314

Problem Solving 319
  Steps in Problem Solving 319
  Obstacles to Solving Problems 321

Contents   xi

  Developmental Changes   321
  Problem-Based Learning and Project-Based Learning   322
  SELF-ASSESSMENT 2 *How Effective Are My Thinking and Problem-Solving Strategies?*   324

Transfer   326
  What Is Transfer   326
  Types of Transfer   326
  CONNECTING WITH THE CLASSROOM: CRACK THE CASE *The Statistics Test*   330

Connecting with Learning: Reach Your Learning Goals   331

Key Terms   333

Portfolio Activities   333

Kali Nine LLC/iStock/Getty Images

CHAPTER 10

Social Constructivist Approaches   334

Social Constructivist Approaches to Teaching   335
  Social Constructivism in the Broader Constructivist Context   335
  Situated Cognition   337

Teachers and Peers as Joint Contributors to Students' Learning   338
  Scaffolding   338
  Cognitive Apprenticeship   338
  Tutoring   338
  Cooperative Learning   342

Structuring Small-Group Work   348
  Composing The Group   348
  Team-Building Skills   349
  Structuring Small-Group Interaction   349

  SELF-ASSESSMENT 1 *Evaluating My Social Constructivist Experiences*   351

  CONNECTING WITH THE CLASSROOM: CRACK THE CASE *The Social Constructivist Classroom*   353

Connecting with Learning: Reach Your Learning Goals   353

Key Terms   355

Portfolio Activities   355

Hill Street Studios/Blend Images/Getty Images

CHAPTER 11

Learning and Cognition in the Content Areas   356

Expert Knowledge and Pedagogical Content Knowledge   357

Reading   358
  A Developmental Model of Reading   359
  Approaches to Reading   360
  Cognitive Approaches   361
  Social Constructivist Approaches   362

Writing 365
Developmental Changes 366
Cognitive Approaches 367
Social Constructivist Approaches 368

SELF-ASSESSMENT 1 *Evaluating My Reading and Writing Experiences* 370

Mathematics 372
Developmental Changes 373
Controversy in Math Education 374
Cognitive Processes 374
Some Constructivist Principles 375
Technology and Math Instruction 376

Science 379
Science Education 379
Constructivist Teaching Strategies 380

Social Studies 382
What Is Social Studies? 382
Constructivist Approaches 384

Technology Resources 385

CONNECTING WITH THE CLASSROOM: CRACK THE CASE *The Constructivist Math Curriculum* 387

Connecting with Learning: Reach Your Learning Goals 388

Key Terms 391

Portfolio Activities 391

LWA/Dann Tardif/Blend Images/Corbis

CHAPTER 12

Planning, Instruction, and Technology 392

Planning 393
Instructional Planning 393
Time Frames and Planning 394

Teacher-Centered Lesson Planning and Instruction 397
Teacher-Centered Lesson Planning 397
Direct Instruction 399
Teacher-Centered Instructional Strategies 401
Evaluating Teacher-Centered Instruction 406

Learner-Centered Lesson Planning and Instruction 407
Learner-Centered Principles 407
Some Learner-Centered Instructional Strategies 408
Evaluating Learner-Centered Strategies 410

Technology and Education 414
The Technology Revolution and the Internet 414
Standards for Technology-Literate Students 416
Teaching, Learning, and Technology 417

SELF-ASSESSMENT 1 *Evaluating My Technology Skills and Attitudes* 421

CONNECTING WITH THE CLASSROOM: CRACK THE CASE *The Big Debate* 423

Contents   xiii

Connecting with Learning: Reach Your Learning Goals 424

Key Terms 426

Portfolio Activities 426

CHAPTER 13

Motivation, Teaching, and Learning 427

Wavebreakmedia/Shutterstock

Exploring Motivation 428
- What Is Motivation? 429
- Perspectives on Motivation 429

Achievement Processes 432
- Extrinsic and Intrinsic Motivation 432
- Attribution 437
- Mastery Motivation And Mindset 438
- Self-Efficacy 441
- Goal Setting, Planning, And Self-Monitoring 442
- Expectations 443
- Delay of Gratification 444
- Values and Purpose 445

Motivation, Relationships, and Sociocultural Contexts 449
- Social Motives 449
- Social Relationships 449
- Sociocultural Contexts 452

Exploring Achievement Difficulties 454
- Students Who Are Low Achieving and Have Low Expectations for Success 454
- Students Who Protect Their Self-Worth By Avoiding Failure 455
- Students Who Procrastinate 456
- Students Who are Perfectionists 457
- Students With High Anxiety 457
- Students Who are Uninterested or Alienated 458

  SELF-ASSESSMENT 1 *Evaluating My Motivation 461*

  CONNECTING WITH THE CLASSROOM: CRACK THE CASE *The Reading Incentive Program 462*

Connecting with Learning: Reach Your Learning Goals 462

Key Terms 466

Portfolio Activities 466

Ariel Skelley/Blend Images LLC

CHAPTER 14

Managing the Classroom 467

Why Classrooms Need to be Managed Effectively 468
- Management Issues in Elementary and Secondary School Classrooms 469
- The Crowded, Complex, and Potentially Chaotic Classroom 470
- Getting off to the Right Start 471
- Emphasizing Instruction and a Positive Classroom Climate 472
- Management Goals and Strategies 474

Designing the Physical Environment of the Classroom 476
Principles of Classroom Arrangement 476
Arrangement Style 477

Creating a Positive Environment for Learning 479
General Strategies 480
Creating, Teaching, and Maintaining Rules and Procedures 480
Getting Students to Cooperate 483
Classroom Management and Diversity 484

Being a Good Communicator 486
Speaking Skills 486
Listening Skills 488
Nonverbal Communication 489

> **SELF-ASSESSMENT 1** *Evaluating My Communication Skills* 490

Dealing with Problem Behaviors 492
Management Strategies 492
Dealing with Aggression 495

> **CONNECTING WITH THE CLASSROOM: CRACK THE CASE** *The Chatty Student* 499

Connecting with Learning: Reach Your Learning Goals 500

Key Terms 502

Portfolio Activities 502

Ocean/Comstock Images/Corbis

CHAPTER 15

Standardized Tests and Teaching 503

The Nature of Standardized Tests 504
Standardized Tests and Their Purposes 504
Criteria for Evaluating Standardized Tests 505

Aptitude and Achievement Tests 509
Comparing Aptitude and Achievement Tests 509
Types of Standardized Achievement Tests 510
High-Stakes State Standards-Based Tests 510
Standardized Tests of Teacher Candidates 517

The Teacher's Roles 520
Preparing Students to Take Standardized Tests 520
Understanding And Interpreting Test Results 521

> **SELF-ASSESSMENT 1** *Evaluating My Knowledge of and Skills in Computing Measures of Central Tendency and Variability* 525

Using Standardized Test Scores to Plan and Improve Instruction 527

Issues in Standardized Tests 529
Standardized Tests, Alternative Assessments, and High-Stakes Testing 530
Diversity And Standardized Testing 530

> **CONNECTING WITH THE CLASSROOM: CRACK THE CASE** *The Standardized Test Pressure* 531

Connecting with Learning: Reach Your Learning Goals 532

Key Terms 535

Portfolio Activities 535

Contents xv

CHAPTER 16

Classroom Assessment and Grading 536

FatCamera/E+/Getty Images

The Classroom as an Assessment Context 537
Assessment as an Integral Part of Teaching 537
Making Assessment Compatible with Contemporary Views of Learning and Motivation 540
Creating Clear, Appropriate Learning Targets 541
Establishing High-Quality Assessments 542
Current Trends 544

Traditional Tests 547
Selected-Response Items 547
Constructed-Response Items 549

Alternative Assessments 552
Trends in Alternative Assessment 552
Performance Assessment 553
Portfolio Assessment 558

SELF-ASSESSMENT 1 *Planning My Classroom Assessment Practices* 562

Grading and Reporting Performance 563
The Purposes of Grading 563
The Components of a Grading System 564
Reporting Students' Progress and Grades to Parents 566
Some Issues in Grading 566

CONNECTING WITH THE CLASSROOM: CRACK THE CASE *The Case of the Project* 569

Connecting with Learning: Reach Your Learning Goals 570

Key Terms 572

Portfolio Activities 572

Glossary G-1
Praxis™ Practice Answer Key P-1
InTASC I-1
References R-1
Name Index I-1
Subject Index I-10

List of Features

SELF-ASSESSMENT

The Best and Worst Characteristics of My Teachers	13
Applying Piaget and Vygotsky in My Classroom	54
Where Are You Now? Exploring Your Identity	96
Evaluating Myself on Gardner's Eight Types of Intelligence	122
What Gender-Role Orientation Will I Present to My Students?	174
Evaluating My Experiences with People Who Have Various Disabilities and Disorders	201
Models and Mentors in My Life and My Students' Lives	241
Self-Monitoring	246
How Effective Are My Memory and Study Strategies?	282
How Good Am I at Thinking Creatively?	314
How Effective Are My Thinking and Problem-Solving Strategies?	324
Evaluating My Social Constructivist Experiences	351
Evaluating My Reading and Writing Experiences	370
Evaluating My Technology Skills and Attitudes	421
Evaluating My Motivation	461
Evaluating My Communication Skills	490
Evaluating My Knowledge of and Skills in Computing Measures of Central Tendency and Variability	525
Planning My Classroom Assessment Practices	562

CONNECTING WITH THE CLASSROOM: CRACK THE CASE

The Classroom Decision	24
The Book Report	66
The Fight	108
Workshops	140
These Boys	180
Now What?	214
Consequences	250
The Test	291
The Statistics Test	330
The Social Constructivist Classroom	353
The Constructivist Math Curriculum	387
The Big Debate	423
The Reading Incentive Program	462
The Chatty Student	499
The Standardized Test Pressure	531
The Case of the Project	569

CONNECTING WITH TEACHERS

Margaret Metzger	2
Donene Polson	29
Keren Abra	71
Shiffy Landa	114
Margaret Longworth	145
Verna Rollins Hayes	185
Ruth Sidney Charney	220
Laura Bickford	256
Marilyn Whirry	296
Chuck Rawls	335
Wendy Nelson Kauffman	357
Lois Guest and Kevin Groves	393
Jaime Escalante	428
Adriane Lonzarich	468
Barbara Berry	504
Vicky Farrow	537

THROUGH THE EYES OF STUDENTS

"You Are the Coolest"	12
A Good Teacher	13
Identity Exploring	97
Jewel Cash, Teen Dynamo	102
It's Okay to Be Different	196
Eyes Closed	197
Children Who Are Gifted Speak	210
"Watch Her, Mom"	229
The Cobwebs of Memory	266
The Thinking Room	302
The 12-Year-Old Filmmaker and Oozy Red Goop	318
Writing Self-Evaluations	368
Hari Prabhakar, Student on a Path to Purpose	445
First Week of School	471
Forensics Teacher Tommie Lindsey's Students	488
It's as if a Test Score is All There Is to a Person	513
Accepting Responsibility	565

CONNECTING WITH STUDENTS: BEST PRACTICES

Strategies for Becoming an Effective Teacher	14
Strategies for Becoming an Effective Teacher-Researcher	23
Strategies for Working with Preoperational Thinkers	44
Strategies for Working with Concrete Operational Thinkers	46
Strategies for Working with Formal Operational Thinkers	47
Strategies for Applying Piaget's Theory to Children's Education	51
Strategies for Applying Vygotsky's Theory to Children's Education	55
Strategies for Vocabulary Development at Different Developmental Levels	64
Strategies for Educating Children Based on Bronfenbrenner's Theory	73
Strategies for Educating Children Based on Erikson's Theory	76
Strategies for Forging School-Family-Community Linkages	82
Strategies for Improving Children's Social Skills	84
Strategies for Improving Children's Self-Esteem	95
Strategies for Increasing Children's Prosocial Behavior	101
Strategies for Interpreting Intelligence Test Scores	117
Strategies for Implementing Each of Gardner's Multiple Intelligences	121
Strategies for the Use of Tracking	130
Strategies for Working with Impulsive Children	132
Strategies for Helping Surface Learners Think More Deeply	133
Strategies for Teaching Children with Different Temperaments	138
Strategies for Working with Children in Poverty	151
Strategies for Working with Linguistically and Culturally Diverse Children	156
Best Practices and Strategies for Multicultural Education	165
Strategies for Working with Children Who Have Learning Disabilities	190
Strategies for Working with Children Who Have ADHD	193
Strategies for Working with Children Who Have an Intellectual Disability	195
Strategies for Working with Children Who Have a Hearing Impairment	198
Strategies for Working with Children with Disabilities as a Regular Classroom Teacher	206

Feature	Page
Strategies for Working with Children Who Are Gifted	212
Strategies for Using Time-Out	233
Best Practices and Strategies for Effectively Using Observational Learning	243
Strategies for Encouraging Students to Be Self-Regulated Learners	248
Strategies for Helping Students Pay Attention	262
Strategies for Helping Students Improve Their Memory	274
Guidelines for Helping Students Use Strategies	289
Strategies for Helping Students Form Concepts	300
Strategies for Improving Children's Thinking	309
Strategies for Making Competent Decisions for Yourself and Your Students	312
Strategies for Guiding Students to Think More Creatively	316
Strategies for Improving Students' Problem Solving	323
Strategies for Helping Students Transfer Information	328
Best Practices and Strategies for Using Peer Tutoring	343
Strategies for Developing Students' Team-Building Skills	350
Strategies for Incorporating Writing into the Curriculum	371
Strategies for Teaching Mathematics	377
Best Practices and Strategies for Teaching Science	380
Strategies for Lecturing	402
Strategies for the Effective Use of Questions	402
Strategies for Using Learner-Centered Instruction	412
Strategies for Choosing and Using Technology in the Classroom	422
Strategies for Student Self-Determination and Choice	433
Strategies for Helping Students Achieve Flow	434
Strategies for Improving Students' Self-Efficacy	442
Strategies for Helping Students Conquer Procrastination	456
Strategies for Helping Students Overcome Their Perfectionist Tendencies	457
Strategies to Reach Uninterested or Alienated Students	458
Strategies for a Good Beginning of the School Year	471
Strategies for Increasing Academic Learning Time	472
Strategies for Designing a Classroom Arrangement	478
Strategies for Being an Effective Classroom Manager	481
Strategies for Establishing Classroom Rules and Procedures	482
Strategies for Guiding Students to Share and Assume Responsibility	484
Strategies for Reducing Bullying	497
Strategies for Improving Students' Test-Taking Skills	523
Strategies for Communicating Test Results to Parents	528
Strategies for Writing Multiple-Choice Items	548
Strategies for Scoring Essay Questions	550
Strategies for Developing Scoring Rubrics	557
Best Strategies for Parent-Teacher Conferences Related to Grades and Assessment	567

Expert Consultants for **Educational Psychology**

Educational psychology has become an enormous, complex field and no single author, or even several authors, can possibly keep up with the rapidly changing content in the main areas of the field. To solve this problem, author John Santrock sought the input of leading experts about content in many different areas of educational psychology. The experts provided detailed evaluations and recommendations for chapter(s) or content in their area(s) of expertise.

The following individuals are among those who served as expert consultants for one or more of the previous editions of this text:

Albert Bandura   *Stanford University*
Robert Siegler   *Carnegie Mellon University*
Carolyn Evertson   *Vanderbilt University*
Michael Pressley   *Michigan State University*
Karen Harris   *Arizona State University*
Kenji Hakuta   *Stanford University*
Joyce Epstein   *Johns Hopkins University*
James Kauffman   *University of Virginia*
Barbara McCombs   *University of Denver*
Donna Ford   *Vanderbilt University*
Eric Anderman   *Ohio State University*
Micki Chi   *Arizona State University*
Daniel Hallahan   *University of Virginia*
Susan Goldman   *University of Illinois at Chicago*
Allan Wigfield   *University of Maryland*
Steven Yussen   *University of Minnesota*

The biographies and photographs of the experts for the Seventh Edition of Educational Psychology, who literally are a Who's Who in the field of educational psychology, follow.

Courtesy of Dr. Carol Dweck

Carol Dweck Dr. Dweck is widely recognized as one of the world's leading experts on motivation and achievement. She is Professor of Psychology at Stanford University, having previously been a professor of psychology at Columbia University. Dr. Dweck obtained her Ph.D. in psychology from Yale University. Her research explores the mindsets individuals use to understand themselves and guide their behavior. Dr. Dweck's studies examine the origins of these mindsets, their role in motivation and self-regulation, and their influence on achievement and interpersonal relationships. Dr. Dweck has received numerous awards, including the Thorndike Career Achievement Award in Educational Psychology, the James McKeen Cattell Lifetime Achievement Award, and the Wilbur Cross Medal from Yale University. Her book *Mindset* also has been given many awards and is widely considered to be a major contribution to the field of motivation. Photo courtesy of Carol Dweck

"John Santrock's chapter on motivation is excellent. He presents the different aspects of motivation in a compelling way with lots of practical tips based on state-of-the-art research." –Dr. Carol Dweck

Courtesy of Dr. Richard Mayer

Richard Mayer Dr. Mayer is widely recognized as one of the leading experts on the application of cognitive psychology to children's education. He is Professor of Psychology at the University of California, Santa Barbara (UCSB), where he has served since 1975. Dr. Mayer obtained his Ph.D. in Psychology from the University of Michigan. His current research interests focus on the intersection of cognition, instruction, and technology with a special focus on multimedia learning and computer-supported learning. He has been President of the Division of Educational Psychology of the American Psychological Association, editor of *Educational Psychologist,* co-editor of *Instructional Science,* Chair of the UCSB Department of Psychology, and a recipient of the E. L. Thorndike Award for career achievement in educational psychology. Dr. Mayer has been awarded the Distinguished Contribution of Applications of Psychology to Education and Training Award from the American Psychological Association and has been ranked as the most productive educational psychologist by *Contemporary Educational Psychology.* He has been Vice President for Division C (Learning and Instruction) of the American Educational Research Association and is on the editorial boards of 12 journals, mainly in educational psychology. He has been the Principal Investigator or co-PI on more than 30 grants. Dr. Mayer has served on a local school board in Goleta, California, since 1981. He is the author or editor of more than 500 publications, including 30 books, such as *Computer Games for Learning, Multimedia Learning* (2nd ed.), *Handbook of Learning and Instruction* (2nd ed.) (with Patricia Alexander), *E-Learning and the Science of Instruction* (with R. Clark), *Cambridge Handbook of Multimedia Learning,* and *Applying the Science of Learning.* Photo courtesy of Richard Mayer

"I enjoyed reading the chapters and appreciate the coverage given to cognitive topics in the book. Dr. Santrock's book is recognized as a leading educational psychology textbook. . . . The coverage of the topics is appropriate and up-to-date, the writing style is clear and friendly, and the book makes good connections to practical educational issues." –Dr. Richard Mayer

Courtesy of Dr. Kirsten Butcher

Kirsten Butcher A leading expert on technology and education, Dr. Butcher is Director of the Center for the Advancement of Technology in Education in the Department of Education at the University of Utah. Dr. Butcher also is Director of the Instructional Design and Educational Technology program at the University of Utah and a professor in the Department of Educational

Psychology the University. She obtained her Ph.D. from the University of Colorado–Boulder. Dr. Butcher's work focuses on how well-designed, interactive technologies can support students' higher-level cognitive processing of information in areas such as integration, inference, and transfer. Photo courtesy of Kristen R. Butcher

"This text provides an excellent overview of the concepts and concerns essential to modern educators. Dr. Santrock moves seamlessly between theory and practice for a thorough introduction to contemporary instruction. His text covers the essential concepts and approaches to effective instruction for 21st century educators." –Dr. Kirsten Butcher

Courtesy of Dr. Dale Schunk

Dale Schunk Dr. Schunk is one of the world's leading experts on children's learning and motivation in educational settings. He is Dean of Education and Professor of Curriculum at the University of North Carolina–Greensboro. Dr. Schunk obtained his Ph.D. from Stanford University and previously was on the faculty at the University of Houston, University of North Carolina–Chapel Hill, and Purdue University (where he was head of the Department of Educational Studies). He has published over 100 articles and chapters, is the author of *Learning Theories: An Educational Perspective* (7th ed.), co-author of *Academic Self-Efficacy* (with Maria DiBenedetto), and co-author of *Motivation in Education* (4th ed.) (with Judith Meece and Paul Pintrich). Photo courtesy of Dale Schunk

"John Santrock's text provides excellent coverage of major motivational theories and applications to educational contexts. Student activities (such as Praxis® questions, self-reflections) and reviews are very helpful . . . strong section on motivation. . . . Very clearly written—will be easily understood by undergraduates. The chapter on motivation, teaching, and learning reviews current theories and research on key motivational topics with high relevance to education. . . . There are lots of specific applications to different types of students, which students will appreciate. It is nice to see the coverage of social motivation, as this topic often is minimized in favor of motivation for academic learning." –Dr. Dale Schunk

Courtesy of Dr. Kathryn Wentzel

Kathryn Wentzel Dr. Wentzel is a leading expert on the social aspects of motivation and achievement. She is Professor of Human Development in the Department of Human Development, Learning, and Quantitative Methods at the University of Maryland. Dr. Wentzel obtained her Ph.D. in Psychological Studies in Education at Stanford University, after which she held post-doctoral positions at Stanford and the University of Illinois. Her research focuses on the social aspects of children's and adolescents' motivation and achievement. She has published more than 100 articles and book chapters and co-edited a number of books, including *Handbook of Motivation at School* (2nd ed.) and *Handbook of Social Influences in School Contexts*. Dr. Wentzel is currently editor of *Educational Psychology* and past editor of *Journal of Applied Developmental Psychology*. Photo courtesy of Dr. Kathryn Wentzel

"I enjoyed reading the chapters (3, Social Contexts and Socioemotional Development, and 13, Motivation, Teaching, and Learning) and think they are in great shape. My comments are mostly for 'fine tuning'. . . . This is a well-written and comprehensive introductory chapter on social contexts and socioemotional development as they pertain to schooling. The chapter on motivation does a very good job of covering current work in the field. . . . I especially liked the teachers' quotes throughout." –Kathryn Wentzel

Courtesy of William Howe

Bill Howe Dr. Howe is a leading expert on diversity and multicultural education. He has been education consultant for multicultural education, gender equity, and civil rights at the Connecticut State Department of Education. He is Past President of the National Association for Multicultural Education. Dr. Howe is the founder of the New England Conference on Multicultural Education. He serves on the boards of a number of organizations, including the STEM National Advisory Board, Advisory Board for Native Village, Asian Pacific American Coalition of CT (APAC), and Advisory Board for International Educational Resources at Yale University. In recent years, Dr. Howe has trained more than 15,000 educators in multicultural education. Dr. Howe recently co-authored *Becoming a Multicultural Educator* (2nd ed.). Photo courtesy of William Howe

"No topics covered should be omitted. . . . I enjoyed reading this text and learned a lot from reading it. . . . I like the format. I like the practical suggestions as they pertain to teaching and learning. . . . Above all, I like the writing style. It is user-friendly. . . . I find this text helpful in that it has many great applicable suggestions." –Dr. Bill Howe

Courtesy of James McMillan

James McMillan A leading expert on educational assessment, Dr. McMillan is Professor of Educational Foundations at Virginia Commonwealth University. Dr. McMillan obtained his Ph.D. at Northwestern University. He has authored a number of books on educational assessment, including *Fundamentals of Education Research* (7th ed.) and *Classroom Assessment* (6th ed.). Dr. McMillan has published extensively in leading educational journals, including *Educational Psychology, Educational Measurement,* and *American Educational Research Journal*. His current research focuses on how students' mistakes and learning errors can facilitate motivation, self-regulation, study skills, and subsequent achievement. Dr. McMillan recently was given his university's School of Education teaching award. He also has been active in Virginia's state testing and accountability program. Photo courtesy of James McMillan

"The strength of these chapters (1, Introduction, 15, Standardized Tests and Teaching, and 16, Classroom Assessment and Grading) is on identifying issues that can be used for further research and discussion. There is good coverage of essential topics. The connection to Praxis is excellent. I also like the portfolio section at the end of each chapter." –Dr. James McMillan

Preface

It is gratifying that the first six editions of *Educational Psychology* have been so well received. One of the goals for each edition has been to write a book that students say this about:

"I love this book."

"I am using many of the ideas from my educational psychology text in my teaching and they are working great!"

"I teach in the inner city and my educational psychology text is a great resource for me. The focus on diversity and technology have been extremely useful. I am enriched by the book."

These comments come from Jennifer Holliman-McCarthy, Richard Harvell, and Greg Hill, who have used this text in their educational psychology course and gone on to become public school teachers.

Another goal for each edition of *Educational Psychology* has been to write a book that instructors say this about:

"I wasn't prepared to like this text. In general, ed psych texts are all too predictable. While people claim to be innovative, in the end they are not. In contrast, John Santrock's text is a big WOW! His book is different. It is written for the prospective teacher and not the future educational psychologist."

"Those who are not using Santrock have not seen it. Please communicate my sincere enjoyment of this quality text to John Santrock."

These comments come from educational psychology instructors Randy Lennon, University of Northern Colorado, and Robert Brown, Florida Atlantic University-Boca Raton.

CONNECTING THEORY AND PRACTICE

A major goal of this text is to make meaningful connections between theory and practice. Students are more engaged when they understand how the concepts and strategies they are learning can be used to teach effectively, understand developmental changes in their students, and foster positive relationships between students and parents.

Four aspects of the text that emphasize this connection are: (1) Connecting with Teachers, (2) Connecting with Students: Best Practices, (3) Connecting with Development, and (4) Connecting with the Classroom: Crack the Case.

Connecting with Teachers

Engaging chapter openers detail experiences of real teachers on topics such as establishing a community of learners, encouraging students to think, and staying ahead of technology in the classroom. Many of these stories were written especially for this text by outstanding teachers.

Connecting with Students: Best Practices

Each chapter includes strategies—many provided by award-winning teachers—on a variety of topics including how to help students improve their memory and tips for preparing engaging lectures.

Connecting with Development

Prospective teachers want to better understand developmental changes in students and the best way to teach students at the grade level at which they will teach. To better understand developmental changes in students across all grade-levels, a number of outstanding early childhood, elementary, middle, and high school teachers provided recommendations that relate to chapter topics. Their comments appear multiple times within chapters.

> Might social media such as Facebook serve as an amplification tool for adolescent egocentrism? In a clever experimental study, researchers found that Facebook usage does indeed increase self-interest (Chiou et al., 2014).
>
> Some teachers were recently asked to describe how they apply Piaget's cognitive stages to their classroom. Following are their comments:
>
> **EARLY CHILDHOOD** When I teach songs to preschool students who are in the preoperational stage, I use PowerPoint slides projected on the board. The slides have either all the words of the song included, or just key words. I also include corresponding clip art and pictures on the page borders.
> —CONNIE CHRISTY, *Aynor Elementary School (Preschool Program)*
>
> **ELEMENTARY SCHOOL: GRADES K–5** In my second-grade science class, I use the following method to help students move from concrete thinking to more abstract thinking: Children are given tasks and asked to discuss what happened (for example, the object sank or floated; when something is added to a system, the outcome changes). Then a theory or idea is developed from the actual observations. When children observe an occurrence and explain what was seen, they can more easily move from the concrete to the more abstract. Although these methods and others like it work well with my students, I need to repeat them often.
> —JANINE GUIDA POUTRE, *Clinton Elementary School*
>
> **MIDDLE SCHOOL: GRADES 6–8** I challenge my seventh-grade students to share examples of how they've applied our classroom lessons to the real world. They can earn extra credit for doing so, but seem to care less about the points than they do about the opportunity to share their accomplishments. For example, after completing a unit on Progressivism, a student shared how he had gone online on his home computer and donated money to help Darfur refugees. He had previously planned to use this money to buy himself a new guitar. This student took the theory of social activism from the Progressive era 100 years ago and applied it to his life today. This student's actions clearly demonstrate Piaget's formal operational stage in action.
> —MARK FODNESS, *Bemidji Middle School*
>
> **HIGH SCHOOL: GRADES 9–12** My high school art students take part in creativity competitions in which they build, create, explore, problem solve, and perform solutions to challenges presented to them. The competition—"Destination Imagination"—has challenged my students to brainstorm ideas and solutions to seemingly impossible tasks. As a result of their participation in this event, they have won regional and state titles along with the world championship.
> —DENNIS PETERSON, *Deer River High School*

Connecting with the Classroom: Crack the Case

Each chapter concludes with a relevant case study. These real life teaching examples provide students an opportunity to reflect and think critically about what they have learned in the chapter. At the end of the case study, students are asked a series of questions—in some cases, PRAXIS-type multiple-choice items—that encourage them to reflect on and think critically about the case.

> **Connecting with the Classroom: Crack the Case**
>
> **The Book Report**
>
> Mr. Johnson assigned his high school senior American government students to read two books during the semester that had "something, anything to do with government or political systems" and to write a brief report about each of their chosen books.
>
> One student in the class, Cindy, chose to read *1984* and *Animal Farm*, both by George Orwell. *1984* is a book about what could happen in "the future" year of 1984, given certain earlier political decisions. In essence, the world turns into a terrible place in which "Big Brother" monitors all of one's actions via two-way television-like screens. Infractions of minor rules are punished severely. *Animal Farm* is a brief novel about political systems in which the characters are portrayed as various farm animals such as pigs and dogs. Cindy enjoyed both books and completed them both before mid-term. Her reports were insightful, reflecting on the symbolism contained in the novels and the implications for present-day government.
>
> Cindy's friend, Lucy, had put off reading her first book until the last minute. She knew Cindy enjoyed reading about government and had finished her reports. Lucy asked Cindy if she knew of a "skinny book" she could read to fulfill the assignment. Cindy gladly shared her copy of *Animal Farm* with her friend, but as Lucy began reading the book she wondered why Cindy had given her this book. It didn't seem to fit the requirements of the assignment at all.
>
> The day before the first reports were due, Mr. Johnson overheard the girls talking. Lucy complained to Cindy, "I don't get it. It's a story about pigs and dogs."
>
> Cindy responded, "They aren't really supposed to be farm animals. It's a story about the promises of communism and what happened in the Soviet Union once the communists took over. It's a great story! Don't you see? The pigs symbolize the communist regime that overthrew the czars during the Russian Revolution. They made all kinds of promises about equality for everyone. The people went along with them because they were sick and tired of the rich and powerful running everything while they starved. Once the czars were eliminated, the communists established a new government but didn't keep any of their promises, controlled everything. Remember in the book when the pigs moved into the house and started walking on two legs? That's supposed to be like when the communist leaders began acting just like the czars. They even created a secret police force—the dogs in the story. Remember how they bullied the other animals? Just like the secret police in the Soviet Union."
>
> Lucy commented, "I still don't get it. How can a pig or a dog be a communist or a cop? They're just animals."
>
> Cindy looked at her friend, dumbfounded. How could she *not* understand this book? It was so obvious.
>
> 1. Drawing on Piaget's theory, explain why Cindy understood the book.
> 2. Based on Piaget's theory, explain why Lucy didn't understand the book.
> 3. What could Mr. Johnson do to help Lucy understand?
> 4. How could Mr. Johnson have presented this assignment differently, so that Lucy did not need to rush through a book?
> 5. At which stage of cognitive development would Piaget say that Cindy is operating?
>   a. sensorimotor
>   b. preoperational
>   c. concrete operational
>   d. formal operational
>   *Explain your choice.*
> 6. At which stage of cognitive development would Piaget say that Lucy is operating?
>   a. sensorimotor
>   b. preoperational
>   c. concrete operational
>   d. formal operational
>   *Explain your choice.*

THE LEARNING SYSTEM

Now more than ever, students struggle to find the main ideas in their courses, especially in courses like educational psychology that include so much material. *Educational Psychology* provides extensive learning connections throughout the chapter.

The learning system connects the chapter opening outline, learning goals for the chapter, mini-chapter maps that open each main section of the chapter, a *Review,*

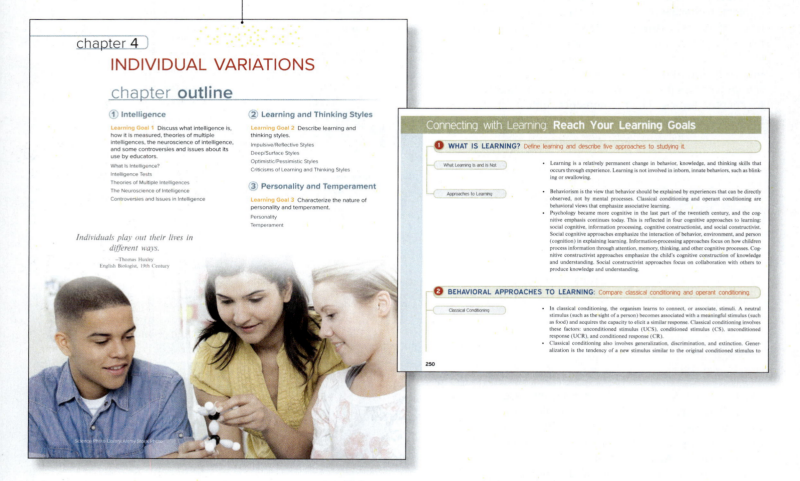

Reflect, and Practice feature at the end of each main section, and a chapter summary at the end of each chapter—*Connecting with Learning: Reach Your Learning Goals:*

| Chapter Outline | Chapter Learning Goals | Mini-Chapter Maps | Review, Reflect, and Practice | Reach Your Learning Goals |

The learning system keeps the key ideas in front of the student from the beginning to the end of the chapter. Each chapter has no more than five main headings and corresponding learning goals, which are presented in the chapter-opening spread. Mini-chapter maps that link up with the learning goals are presented at the beginning of each major section in the chapter. Then, at the end of each main section of a chapter, the learning goal is repeated in the "Review, Reflect, and Practice" feature, which prompts students to review the key topics in the section and poses a question to encourage them to think critically about what they have read, and as indicated earlier, in many cases how they will incorporate the material into their own teaching. At the end of the chapter, under the heading "Reach Your Learning Goals," the learning goals guide students through the bulleted chapter review, connecting with the chapter outline at the beginning of the chapter and the "Review, Reflect, and Practice" feature at the end of major chapter sections.

At the end of each chapter, Portfolio Activities related to the chapter's content are presented. They are organized into three categories for instructors' ease of use: Independent Reflection, Research/Field Experience, and Collaborative Work. Each Portfolio Activity is coded to a specific INTASC standard.

MAIN CHAPTER-BY-CHAPTER CHANGES

The seventh edition of *Educational Psychology* includes dozens of new and updated references to ensure students are provided with the most up-to-date research on the topics covered in this book. Here are the biggest changes to the new edition as they relate to each chapter of the book.

Chapter 1:

New emphasis on shaping caring and motivated teachers including mindfulness practice and updated research on students' perceptions of the characteristics of outstanding teachers.

Discussion of the controversy surrounding student test scores as an indicator of teacher effectiveness.

Chapter 2:

Distinction between phenotype and genotype.

New discussion on "reasoned risk behavior" in adolescents.

Chapter 3:

An updated section details new research on how school friendships promote prosocial behavior among adolescents and protect against substance abuse and aggression.

New research on what inspires motivation in middle school students.

Summary of a new guide "Preventing Dropout in Secondary Schools" that provides recommendations for increasing graduation rates.

Expanded discussion of what might trigger some students to cheat across different education levels.

New section on the social justice imperative as it relates to caring for students who have been exposed to traumatic experiences.

Chapter 4:

Enhanced discussion on the negative effects of stereotype threat is illustrated with examples of women in professional spaces and African-American adolescents at school.

Added example of a between-class grouping that involves dividing students into a college preparatory track and a general track.

Chapter 5:

Extended discussion of culturally relevant pedagogy and its characteristics. New discussion of Ijeoma Oluo's book, *So You Want to Talk about Race* in which she lays out basic rules for determining whether something is about race.

Extended discussion on gender gaps in science, technology, engineering, and mathematics (STEM), including recommendations for increasing female's interest in STEM.

Discussion about a recent meta-analysis of research on the bystander effect breaks down the likelihood of helping based on different factors.

Chapter 6:

Updated section on Learning Disabilities includes the new recommendations associated with the reauthorization of IDEA for identifying students with learning disabilities including the Response to Intervention process.

Chapter 8:

New discussion of the different types of cognitive load theory and the strategies teachers can use to avoid extraneous cognitive load.

Enhanced discussion of PQ4R explains its foundational principles and its global reach.

New discussion of a study that evaluated the effects of meta-strategic knowledge training on eighth-graders, especially low-achieving students.

Chapter 9:

New discussion of the importance of considering the cultural differences of our students in order to avoid contributing to systemic racism.

Chapter 12:

Added example of a problem-based learning project involving students exploring the impact of environmental conditions on their community.

Chapter 14:

New discussion of the five essential components of culturally responsive classroom management.

Enhanced discussion of bullying and the differences between bystanders, outsiders, reinforcers, and assistants.

Chapter 15:

Added discussion on how state tests are used as standards-based tests required for states to receive federal education funds.

Enhanced section on the inadequacies of high-stakes tests and the controversies surrounding the use of value-added models.

New strategies for preparing and encouraging students ahead of standardized tests.

New explanation of how to choose the measure of central tendency when evaluating ordinal versus ranked data.

Chapter 16:

Added examples of open-ended activities to be used during performance assessment.

New discussion of "Passportfolios" or "proficiency portfolios" as a means for demonstrating competence and readiness for the next level or work.

In "Connecting with Students," new examples for communicating a child's progress and grades to their parents.

ACKNOWLEDGEMENTS

I would especially like to thank Alysia Roehrig of Florida State University (FSU) for all of her editing and support in completing this revision. She is Professor of Educational Psychology at FSU, where she is the Graduate Program Coordinator. She is also and Director of PURPOSE (Partners United for Research Pathways Oriented to Social Justice in Education), an Institute of Education Sciences funded Pathways to the Education Science Training Program intended to increase the diversity of the doctorate in education. She earned her Ph.D. from the University of Notre Dame, where her advisor was Michael Pressley. Her research focuses on effective teaching. She is dedicated to making educational research accessible through projects like curating evidence-based practice briefs for educators, preparing the next generation of researchers to do culturally relevant research in collaboration with school stakeholders, and updating this book for future educators. Alysia's outstanding contributions and insights were essential in developing the 7th edition.

I am deeply indebted to many people at McGraw-Hill who have provided outstanding guidance and support for this text. I especially thank Marketing Manager Nancy Baudean, for the guidance and support she has provided; Product Development Manager Francesca King who did excellent work in coordinating many aspects of editing for this project; and also Content Project Manager, Danielle Clement and Content Licensing Specialist, Carrie Burger. Nicole Bridge, Reshmi Rajeesh, and the ansrsource team, who handled developmental editing for this edition of the book, have been terrific to work with and did an excellent job in guiding and editing the revision of the manuscript. SPi Global did an excellent job of copyediting the manuscript. I thank Nancy DeFrates-Densch, Northern Illinois University, whose experience and understanding of translating theory into practice clearly came through in the examples she created for "Teaching Connections: Best Practices and Strategies for . . ." in every chapter in the text. Nancy also contributed extensively to the book by writing the case studies, the PRAXIS™ Practice items, and creating many examples of Best Practices. I Thank you also to the reviewers of this edition: Reva Fish, SUNY Buffalo State; Albee Mendoza, Wesley College; Christopher Maglio, Truman State University; Paul Yoder, Truman State University; Ann Selleck, Lansing Community College; David D. Timony, Delaware Valley University; Yan Yang, University of West Georgia; Nicole Williams, University of Findlay.

On pages xix–xx of the preface the numerous expert content and research consultants for the book are profiled. As stated earlier, their feedback was invaluable in helping me to make the book's content superior to what I could have accomplished alone.

Peer Reviewers from Previous Editions

In developing the prior editions of *Educational Psychology,* we asked a number of educational psychology instructors to provide us with detailed information about the best ways to improve the text. Their recommendations were extremely helpful. Special thanks go to the following peer reviewers of previous editions.

Frank Adams, *Wayne State College*
Irene Aiken, *The University of North Carolina at Pembroke*
Eric Anderman, *University of Kentucky*
James M. Applefield, *University of North Carolina–Wilmington*
Elizabeth C. Arch, *Pacific University*
Robert R. Ayres, *Western Oregon University*
Bambi Bailey, *Midwestern State University*
Jeffrey Baker, *Rochester Institute of Technology*
Melissa Lorenson Barstow, *Community College of Rhode Island*
Dorothy A. Battle, *Georgia Southern University*
Douglas Beed, *University of Montana, Missoula*
Richard Benedict, *Madonna University*
John T. Binfet, *California State University–San Bernadino*
Lyanne Black, *Indiana University of PA*
Christopher S. Boe, *Pfeiffer University*
Joseph Braun, *California State University–Dominguez Hills*
Roger Briscoe, *Indiana University of Pennsylvania*
Jonathan Brown, *Clarion University*
Kathy Brown, *University of Central Oklahoma*
Randy Brown, *University of Central Oklahoma*
Robert G. Brown, *Florida Atlantic University*
Alison Bryant, *University of Missouri–Columbia*
Kay Bull, *Oklahoma State University*
Mary D. Burbank, *University of Utah*
Melva M. Burke, *East Carolina University*
Russell N. Carney, *Southwest Missouri State University*
Chuck Catania, *Miami University of Ohio*
John Newman Clark, *University of South Alabama*
Sheryl Needle Cohn, *University of Central Florida*
Ellen Contopidis, *Keuka College*
Suzy Cox, *Utah Valley University*
Dorothy Valcarcel Craig, *Middle Tennessee University*
Rhoda Cummings, *University of Nevada–Reno*
Reagan Curtis, *Northwestern State University*

David Dalton, Kent State University
Nancy Defrates-Densch, Northern Illinois University
Rayne Sperling Dennison, Penn State
Gypsy Denzine, Northern Arizona University
Carlos F. Diaz, Florida Atlantic University
Jesse Diaz, Central Washington University
Ronna Dillon, Southern Illinois University–Carbondale
Joseph DiMauro, DeSales University
Peter Doolittle, Virginia Polytechnic University
Jayne Downey, Montana State University
Ruth Doyle, Casper College
Ronald Dugan, The College of St. Rose
David Dungan, Emporia State University
Kenneth Durgans, Xavier University
Audrey Edwards, Eastern Illinois University
Gordon Eisenmann, Augusta State University
Howard Epstein, Miami University of Ohio
Lena Ericksen, Western Washington University
Tsile Evers, Miami University–Oxford
Vicky Farrow, Lamar University
Daniel Fasko, Bowling Green State University
Sheryl Feinstein, Augusta College
Aubrey Fine, California Polytechnic University
Jaclyn Finkel, Anne Arundel Community College
Ericka Fisher, College of the Holy Cross
William R. Fisk, Clemson University
William L. Franzen, University of Missouri–St. Louis
Beth Gallihue, Towson University
M. Arthur Garmon, Western Michigan University
Patsy Garner, Crowder College
Laura Gaudet, Chadron State College
Susan Goldman, Vanderbilt University
Alyssa Gonzalez, Florida Atlantic University
Caroline Gould, Eastern Michigan University
Charles R. Grah, Austin Peay State University
Kim Grilliot, Bowling Green State University
Joyce Grohman, Atlantic Cape Community College
Lynne A. Hammann, University of Akron
Felicia Hanesworth, Medaille College
Andrew Hanson, California State University–Chico
Walter Hapkiewicz, Michigan State University
Gregory Harper, State University of New York–Fredonia
Diane J. Harris, San Francisco State University
Algea Harrison, Oakland University
Jan Hayes, Middle Tennessee State University
William E. Herman, State University of New York–Potsdam
David Holliway, Marshall University
Alice S. Honig, Syracuse University
Sherri Horner, University of Memphis
Mara Huber, State University of New York–Fredonia
John H. Hummel, Valdosta State University
Judith Hughey, Kansas State University
Mona Ibrahim, Concordia College
Emilie Johnson, Lindenwood University
Steven Kaatz, Bethel College
Deborah Kalkman, Northern Illinois University

Susan Kelley, Lycoming College
Lee Kem, Murray State University
Elizabeth Kirk, Miami University of Ohio
Elaine Kisisel, Calumet College of Saint Joseph
Beverly Klecker, Morehead State University
Nancy Knapp, University of Georgia
Robert L. Kohn, University of Kansas
Becky Ladd, Illinois State University
William Lan, Texas Tech University
Marvin Lee, Shenandoah University
Randy Lennon, University of Northern Colorado
Bernie Les, Wayne State University
Edward Levinson, Indiana University
Dov Liberman, University of Houston
Kathryn W. Linden, emeritus, Purdue University
Kim Loomis, Kennesaw State University
Barbara F. Maestas, Towson University
P. Y. Mantzicopoulos, Purdue University
Julia M. Matuga, Bowling Green State University
Richard E. Mayer, University of California–Santa Barbara
Catherine McCartney, Bemidji State University
John R. McClure, Northern Arizona University
Rita McKenzie, Northern Arizona University
James H. McMillan, Virginia Commonwealth University
Sharon McNeely, Northeastern Illinois University
Lisa Mehlig, Northern Illinois University
John K. Meis, Flager College
Dorothy D. Miles, Saint Louis University
Barbara Milligan, Middle Tennessee State University
Connie M. Moss, Duquesne University
Beverly Moore, Auburn University
Ronald Mulson, Hudson Valley Community College
Peter Myerson, University of Wisconsin–Oshkosh
Joseph D. Nichols, Indiana-Purdue University
Ernest Owen, Western Kentucky University
David Oxendine, University of North Carolina–Pembroke
Ann Pace, University of Missouri
Karen Menke Paciorek, Eastern Michigan University
Nita A. Paris, Kennesaw State University
Peggy Perkins, University of Nevada–Las Vegas
Jim Persinger, Emporia State University
Joseph Pizzillo, Rowan University
Catherine Polydore, Eastern Illinois University
Barbara M. Powell, Eastern Illinois University
Geoff Quick, Lansing Community College
Barbara L. Radigan, Community College of Allegheny County
Sandra Nagel Randall, Saginaw Valley State University
Nan Bernstein Ratner, University of Maryland–College Park
Marla Reese-Weber, Illinois State University
Robert Rice, Western Oregon University
Lynda Robinson, University of the Ozarks
James Rodriquez, San Diego State University
Susan Rogers, Columbus State Community College
Lawrence R. Rogien, Columbus State Community College
Paul Rosenberg, Muhlenberg College
Deborah Salih, University of Northern Iowa

Jill Salisbury-Glennon, *Auburn University*
Ala Samarapungavan, *Purdue University*
Charles Jeff Sandoz, *University of Louisiana*
Rolando A. Santos, *California State University–Los Angeles*
Susan Sawyer, *Southeastern Louisiana University*
Gilbert Sax, *University of Washington*
Gayle Schou, *Grand Canyon University*
Dale Schunk, *University of North Carolina–Greensboro*
Thomas Sepe, *Community College of Rhode Island*
Marvin Seperson, *Nova Southeastern University*
Lisa Sethre-Hofstad, *Concordia College*
Alison Shook, *Albright College*
Jenny Singleton, *University of Illinois–Urbana-Champaign*
Michael Slavkin, *University of Southern Indiana*
Patricia Slocum, *College of DuPage*
Brian G. Smith, *Moorhead State University*
Michael Smith, *Weber State University*
Judith Stechly, *West Liberty State University*
Michael Steiff, *University of California–Davis*
Daniel Stuempfig, *California State University–Chico*
O. Suthern Sims, Jr., *Mercer University*
Gabriele Sweidel, *Kutztown University of Pennsylvania*
David E. Tanner, *California State University–Fresno*
Sara Tannert, *Miami University of Ohio*
David Tarver, *Angelo State University*
Karen Thierry, *Rutgers University*
Yuma I. Tomes, *Virginia Commonwealth University*
Donna Townsend, *Southwestern Assemblies of God University*
Julie Turner, *University of Notre Dame*
Kenneth Tyler, *University of Kentucky*
Atilano Valencia, *California State University–Fresno*
Eva G. Vandergiessen, *Fairmont State College*
David Vawter, *Wintrhop University*
Linda Veronie, *Slippery Rock University*
Libby Vesilind, *Bucknell University*
Penny Warner, *Winona State University*
Linda Weeks, *Lamar University*
Earl F. Wellborn, Jr., *Missouri Valley College*
David Wendler, *Martin Luther College*
Patricia Whang, *California State University–Monterey Bay*
Allan Wigfield, *University of Maryland–College Park*
Ryan Wilke, *Florida State University*
Glenda Wilkes, *University of Arizona*
Patricia Willems, *Florida Atlantic University*
Tony L. Williams, *Marshall University*
Victor Willson, *Texas A&M University*
Ann K. Wilson, *Buena Vista University*
Steven R. Wininger, *Western Kentucky University*
Betsy Wisner, *State University of New York–Cortland*
Elizabeth F. Wisner, *Florida Community College at Jacksonville*
Jina Yoon, *Wayne State University*
Michael Young, *University of Connecticut*
Peter Young, *Southern Oregon University*

Steven Yussen, *University of Minnesota*
Samuel Zimmerman, *Pace University*

Early Childhood, Elementary School, and Secondary School Teachers

Following are the outstanding teachers who provided descriptions of their real-world experiences in the classroom for the Developmental Focus feature that appears one or more times in each chapter.

Keren Abra, *School of the Sacred Heart, San Francisco, CA*
Connie Christy, *Aynor Elementary School (Preschool Program), Aynor, SC*
Maureen "Missy" Dangler, *Suburban Hills School, Chatham, NJ*
Mark Fodness, *Bemidji Middle School, Bemidji, MN*
Elizabeth J. Frascella, *Clinton Elementary, Chatham, NJ*
Susan M. Froelich, *Clinton School, Maplewood, NJ*
Valerie Gorham, *Kiddie Quarters, Union, NJ*
Jennifer Heiter, *Bremen High School, Bremen, IN*
Craig Jensen, *Cooper Mountain Elementary, Portland, OR*
Heidi Kaufman, *MetroWest YMCA Child Care and Educational Program, Framingham, MA*
Esther Lindbloom, *Cooper Mountain Elementary, Beaverton, OR*
Casey Maass, *Edison Middle School, West Orange, NJ*
Karen L. Perry, *Cooper Mountain Elementary, Portland, OR*
Dennis Peterson, *Deer River High School, Bemidji, MN*
Felicia Peterson, *Pocantico Hills School, Sleepy Hollow, NY*
Janine Guida Poutre, *Clinton Elementary, Chatham, NJ*
Shane Schwarz, *Clinton Elementary, South Orange, NJ*
Sandy Swanson, *Menomonee Falls High School, Menomonee Falls, WI*
Heather Zoldak, *Ridge Wood Elementary School, Northville, MI*

Expert Consultants From Previous Editions

A number of leading experts in the field of educational psychology provided detailed comments about chapters and topics in their areas of expertise. Special thanks go to the following expert consultants who contributed to previous editions.

Albert Bandura, *Stanford University*
Gary Bitter, *Arizona State University*
Joyce Epstein, *Johns Hopkins University*
Carlos Diaz, *Florida Atlantic University*
Eva Essa, *University of Nevada, Reno*
Carolyn Evertson, *Vanderbilt University*
Kenji Hakuta, *Stanford University*
Daniel Hallahan, *University of Virginia*
James Kauffman, *University of Virginia*
Richard Mayer, *University of California–Santa Barbara*
Barbara McCombs, *University of Denver*
James McMillan, *Virginia Commonwealth University*
Valerie Pang, *San Diego State University*
Michael Pressley, *University of Notre Dame*
Dale Schunk, *University of North Carolina–Greensboro*

Robert Siegler, *Carnegie Mellon University*
Karen Swan, *Kent State University*

Panel of Early Childhood, Elementary, Middle, and High School Teachers

A large panel of individuals who teach at the early childhood, elementary, middle, and high school levels provided me with the material about special teaching moments that they have experienced. These moments appear in the Teaching Stories and Best Practices boxes throughout the text. I owe these teachers a great deal of thanks for sharing the real world of their teaching experiences.

Karen Abra, *School of the Sacred Heart, San Francisco, CA*
Mrs. Lou Aronson, *Devils Lake High School, Devils Lake, ND*
Daniel Arnoux, *Lauderhill Middle Community School, Broward, FL*
Lynn Ayres, *East Middle School, Ypsilanti, MI*
Fay Bartley, *Bright Horizon Childrens Center, Bronx, NY*
Barbara M. Berry, *Ypsilanti High School, Ypsilanti, MI*
Kristen Blackenship, *Salem Church Elementary, Midlothian, VA*
Wendy Bucci, *Sugar Creek Elementary School, Verona, WI*
Stella Cohen, *Hackley School, Tarrytown, NY*
Connie Christy, *Aynor Elementary, Aynor, SC*
Julie Curry, *Hubbard Elementary School, Forsyth, GA*
Alina Durso, *PS 59-Beekman Hill International School, New York, NY*
Andrea Fenton, *Cortez High School, Glendale Union, AZ*
Mark Fodness, *Bemidji Middle School, Bemidji, MN*
Kathy Fuchser, *St. Francis High School, Humphrey, NE*
Lawren Giles, *Baechtel Grove Middle School, Bibb County, GA*
Jerri Hall, *Miller Magnet Middle School, Bibb County, GA*
Jenny Heiter, *Bremen High School, Bremen, IN*
Anita Marie Hitchcock, *Holley Navarre Primary, Santa Rosa Schools, FL*
Laura Johnson-Brickford, *Nordhoff High School, Ojai, CA*
Heidi Kaufman, *Associate Executive Director of Childcare, MetroWest YMCA, Framingham, MA*
Juanita Kerton, *Gramercy School/New York League for Early Learning, New York, NY*
Chaille Lazar, *Hedgecoxe Elementary, Plano, TX*
Margaret Longworth, *St. Lucie West Middle School, St. Lucie, FL*
Adriane Lonzarich, *Heartwood, San Mateo, CA*
RoseMary Moore, *Angelo State University, Angelo, TX*
Therese Olejniczak, *Central Middle School, East Grand Forks, MN*
Dennis Peterson, *Deer River High School, Bemidji, MN*
Chuck Rawls, *Appling Middle School, Bibb County, GA*
Verna Brown Rollins, *West Middle School, Ypsilanti, MI*
Donna L. Shelhorse, *Short Pump Middle School, Henrico County, VA*
Michele Siegal, *Brockton High School, Brockton, MA*
Jason Stanley, *Syracuse Dunbar Avoca, Syracuse, NE*
Vicky Stone, *Cammack Middle School, Huntington, VA*
Sandy Swanson, *Menomonee Falls High School, Menomonee Falls, WI*
Tamela Varney, *Central City Elementary, Cabell County, WV*
Marlene Wendler, *St. Paul's Lutheran School, New Ulm, MN*
William Willford, *Perry Middle School, Perry, GA*
Yvonne Wilson, *North Elementary School, Deer River, MN*
Susan Youngblood, *Weaver Middle School, Bibb County, GA*
Heather Zoldak, *Ridge Wood Elementary, Northville, MI*

McGraw-Hill Connect

The 7th edition of *Educational Psychology* is now available online with Connect, McGraw-Hill Education's integrated assignment and assessment platform. Connect also offers SmartBook for the new edition, which is the first adaptive reading experience proven to improve grades and help students study more effectively. All of the title's ancillary content is also available through Connect, including:

- Test Bank with almost 1,000 questions specifically related to the main text, including multiple-choice, short-answer, critical thinking, and essay questions, many of which are applied assessment
- PowerPoint slides covering every chapter and concept presented in the text
- Instructor's Manual with teaching suggestions, learning objectives, extended chapter outlines, lecture/discussion suggestions, video and film recommendations
- The PRAXIS™ II study guide
- Bibliography Builder for easy and accurate citations and references

FOR INSTRUCTORS

You're in the driver's seat.

Want to build your own course? No problem. Prefer to use our turnkey, prebuilt course? Easy. Want to make changes throughout the semester? Sure. And you'll save time with Connect's auto-grading too.

65%
Less Time Grading

Laptop: McGraw-Hill; Woman/dog: George Doyle/Getty Images

They'll thank you for it.

Adaptive study resources like SmartBook® 2.0 help your students be better prepared in less time. You can transform your class time from dull definitions to dynamic debates. Find out more about the powerful personalized learning experience available in SmartBook 2.0 at **www.mheducation.com/highered/connect/smartbook**

Make it simple, make it affordable.

Connect makes it easy with seamless integration using any of the major Learning Management Systems—Blackboard®, Canvas, and D2L, among others—to let you organize your course in one convenient location. Give your students access to digital materials at a discount with our inclusive access program. Ask your McGraw-Hill representative for more information.

Padlock: Jobalou/Getty Images

Solutions for your challenges.

A product isn't a solution. Real solutions are affordable, reliable, and come with training and ongoing support when you need it and how you want it. Our Customer Experience Group can also help you troubleshoot tech problems—although Connect's 99% uptime means you might not need to call them. See for yourself at **status.mheducation.com**

Checkmark: Jobalou/Getty Images

FOR STUDENTS

Effective, efficient studying.

Connect helps you be more productive with your study time and get better grades using tools like SmartBook 2.0, which highlights key concepts and creates a personalized study plan. Connect sets you up for success, so you walk into class with confidence and walk out with better grades.

Study anytime, anywhere.

Download the free ReadAnywhere app and access your online eBook or SmartBook 2.0 assignments when it's convenient, even if you're offline. And since the app automatically syncs with your eBook and SmartBook 2.0 assignments in Connect, all of your work is available every time you open it. Find out more at **www.mheducation.com/readanywhere**

"I really liked this app—it made it easy to study when you don't have your textbook in front of you."

- Jordan Cunningham, Eastern Washington University

No surprises.

The Connect Calendar and Reports tools keep you on track with the work you need to get done and your assignment scores. Life gets busy; Connect tools help you keep learning through it all.

Calendar: owattaphotos/Getty Images

Learning for everyone.

McGraw-Hill works directly with Accessibility Services Departments and faculty to meet the learning needs of all students. Please contact your Accessibility Services office and ask them to email accessibility@mheducation.com, or visit **www.mheducation.com/about/accessibility** for more information.

Top: Jenner Images/Getty Images, Left: Hero Images/Getty Images, Right: Hero Images/Getty Images

chapter 1

EDUCATIONAL PSYCHOLOGY: A TOOL FOR EFFECTIVE TEACHING

chapter outline

1 Exploring Educational Psychology

Learning Goal 1 Describe some basic ideas about the field of educational psychology.

Historical Background
Teaching: Art and Science

2 Effective Teaching

Learning Goal 2 Identify the attitudes and skills of an effective teacher.

Professional Knowledge and Skills
Commitment, Motivation, and Caring

3 Research in Educational Psychology

Learning Goal 3 Discuss why research is important to effective teaching and how educational psychologists and teachers can conduct and evaluate research.

Why Research Is Important
Research Methods
Program Evaluation Research, Action Research, and the Teacher-as-Researcher
Quantitative and Qualitative Research

I touch the future. I teach.
—Christa McAuliffe
American Educator and Astronaut, 20th Century

Jamie Grill/Getty Images RF

Connecting with **Teachers** Margaret Metzger

Effective teachers know that principles of educational psychology and educational research will help them guide students' learning. Margaret Metzger has been an English teacher at Brookline High School, in Massachusetts, for more than 25 years. She gave the following advice to a student teacher she was supervising, and it conveys her understanding of basic principles of educational psychology, such as teaching how to learn and the need to apply educational research to teaching practice:

> Emphasize *how* to learn, rather than what to learn. Students may never know a particular fact, but they always will need to know how to learn. Teach students how to read with a genuine comprehension, how to shape an idea, how to master difficult material, how to use writing to clarify thinking. A former student, Anastasia Korniaris, wrote to me, "Your class was like a hardware store. All the tools were there. Years later I'm still using that hardware store that's in my head. . . ."
>
> Include students in the process of teaching and learning. Every day ask such basic questions as, "What did you think of this homework? Did it help you learn the material? Was the assignment too long or too short? How can we make the next assignment more interesting? What should the criteria for assessment be?" Remember that we want students to take ownership of their learning. . . .
>
> Useful research has been conducted lately on learning styles and frames of intelligence. Read that research. The basic idea to keep in mind is that students should think for themselves. Your job is to teach them how to think and to give them the necessary tools. Your students will be endlessly amazed at how intelligent they are. You don't need to show them how intelligent you are. . . .
>
> In the early years of teaching you must expect to put in hours and hours of time. You would invest similarly long hours if you were an intern in medical school or an associate in a law firm. Like other professionals, teachers work much longer hours than outsiders know. . . .
>
> You have the potential to be an excellent teacher. My only concern is that you not exhaust yourself before you begin. Naturally, you will want to work very hard as you learn the craft.

(Source: Metzger, 1996, pp. 346–351.)

Preview

In the quotation that opens this chapter, twentieth-century teacher and astronaut Christa McAuliffe commented that she touched the future through her chosen profession of teaching. As a teacher, you will touch the future because children are the future of any society. In this chapter, we explore what the field of educational psychology is all about and how it can help you make a positive contribution to children's futures.

LG 1 Describe some basic ideas about the field of educational psychology.

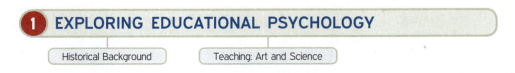

1 EXPLORING EDUCATIONAL PSYCHOLOGY

Historical Background | Teaching: Art and Science

Psychology is the scientific study of behavior and mental processes. **Educational psychology** is the branch of psychology that specializes in understanding teaching and learning in educational settings. Educational psychology is a vast landscape that will take us an entire book to describe.

HISTORICAL BACKGROUND

The field of educational psychology was founded by several pioneers in psychology just before the start of the twentieth century. Three pioneers—William James, John Dewey, and E. L. Thorndike—stand out in the early history of educational psychology.

William James Soon after launching the first psychology textbook, *Principles of Psychology* (1890), William James (1842–1910) gave a series of lectures called "Talks to Teachers" (James, 1899/1993) in which he discussed the applications of psychology to educating children. James argued that laboratory psychology experiments often can't tell us how to teach children effectively. He emphasized the importance of observing teaching and learning in classrooms for improving education. One of his

educational psychology The branch of psychology that specializes in understanding teaching and learning in educational settings.

William James

John Dewey

E. L. Thorndike

James, Dewey, and Thorndike created and shaped the field of educational psychology. *What were their ideas about educational psychology?*
(*Left to Right*) ©Paul Thompson/FPG/Getty Images; ©Hulton Archive/Getty Images; The Popular Science Monthly, 1912

recommendations was to start lessons at a point just beyond the child's level of knowledge and understanding to stretch the child's mind.

John Dewey A second major figure in shaping the field of educational psychology was John Dewey (1859–1952), who became a driving force in the practical application of psychology. In 1894 at the University of Chicago, Dewey established the first major educational psychology laboratory in the United States. Later, at Columbia University, he continued his innovative work. We owe many important ideas to John Dewey. First, we owe to him the view of the child as an active learner. Before Dewey, it was believed that children should sit quietly in their seats and passively learn in a rote manner. In contrast, Dewey (1933) argued that children learn best by doing. Second, we owe to Dewey the idea that education should focus on the whole child and emphasize the child's adaptation to the environment. Dewey reasoned that children should not be just narrowly educated in academic topics but should learn how to think and adapt to a world outside school. He especially thought that children should learn how to be reflective problem solvers. Third, we owe to Dewey the belief that all children deserve to have access to education. This democratic ideal was not in place at the beginning of Dewey's career in the latter part of the nineteenth century, when quality education was reserved for a small portion of children, especially boys from wealthy families. Dewey pushed for a quality education for all children—girls and boys—as well as children from different socioeconomic and ethnic groups.

E. L. Thorndike A third pioneer was E. L. Thorndike (1874–1949), who focused on assessment and measurement and promoted the scientific underpinnings of learning. Thorndike argued that one of schooling's most important tasks is to hone children's reasoning skills, and he excelled at conducting detailed scientific studies of teaching and learning. Thorndike especially promoted the idea that educational psychology must have a scientific base and should focus strongly on measurement.

Diversity and Early Educational Psychology The most prominent figures in the early history of educational psychology, as in most disciplines, were mainly White males such as James, Dewey, and Thorndike. Prior to changes in civil rights laws and policies in the 1960s, only a few dedicated non-White individuals obtained the necessary degrees and broke through racial exclusion barriers to take up research in the field (Spring, 2014; Webb & Metha, 2017).

Two pioneering African American psychologists, Mamie and Kenneth Clark, conducted research on African American children's self-conceptions and identity (Clark & Clark, 1939). In 1971, Kenneth Clark became the first African American president

DIVERSITY

Mamie and Kenneth Clark

Like other disciplines, educational psychology had few individuals who were ethnic minorities or women involved in its early history. The individuals shown here were among the few from such backgrounds to overcome barriers and contribute to the field. In celebrating their contributions, it is important to note that those who are ethnic minorities and/or female are still underrepresented in many areas of higher education and research.

Courtesy of Kate C. Harris

of the American Psychological Association. In 1932, Latino psychologist George Sanchez conducted research showing that intelligence tests were culturally biased against ethnic minority children.

Like ethnic minorities, women also faced barriers in higher education and therefore have only gradually become prominent contributors to psychological research. One often overlooked person in the history of educational psychology is Leta Hollingworth. She was the first individual to use the term *gifted* to describe children who attained exceptionally high scores on intelligence tests (Hollingworth, 1916).

The Behavioral Approach Thorndike's approach to the study of learning guided educational psychology through the first half of the twentieth century. In American psychology, B. F. Skinner's (1938) view, which built on Thorndike's ideas, strongly influenced educational psychology in the middle of the century. Skinner's behavioral approach involved attempts to precisely determine the best conditions for learning. Skinner argued that the mental processes proposed by psychologists such as James and Dewey were not observable and therefore could not be appropriate subject matter for a scientific study of psychology, which he defined as the science of observable behavior and its controlling conditions. In the 1950s, Skinner (1954) developed the concept of *programmed learning,* which involved reinforcing the student after each of a series of steps until the student reached a learning goal. In an early technological effort, he created a teaching machine to serve as a tutor and reinforce students for correct answers (Skinner, 1958).

The Cognitive Revolution The objectives spelled out in the behavioral approach to learning did not address many of the actual goals and needs of classroom educators (Hilgard, 1996). In reaction, as early as the 1950s, Benjamin Bloom created a taxonomy of cognitive skills that included remembering, comprehending, synthesizing, and evaluating, which he suggested teachers should help students develop and use. The cognitive revolution in psychology began to take hold by the 1980s and ushered in an era of enthusiasm for applying the concepts of cognitive psychology—memory, thinking, reasoning, and so on—to help students learn. Thus, toward the latter part of the twentieth century, many educational psychologists returned to an emphasis on the cognitive aspects of learning advocated by James and Dewey at the beginning of the century. Both cognitive and behavioral approaches—especially cognitive—continue to be a part of educational psychology today (Fuchs et al., 2016; Wang et al., 2016). There will be much more about these approaches later in this text. More recently, educational psychologists have increasingly focused on the socioemotional aspects of students' lives. For example, they are analyzing the school as a social context and examining the role of culture in education (Gauvain, 2016; Koppelman, 2017; Rowe et al., 2016; Wentzel & Ramani, 2016). We explore the socioemotional aspects of teaching and learning in many chapters of this text.

TEACHING: ART AND SCIENCE

RESEARCH

How scientific can teachers be in their approach to teaching? Both science and the art of skillful, experienced practice play important roles in a teacher's success. Educational psychology draws much of its knowledge from broader theory and research in psychology (Graham & Taylor, 2016; Ryan & Deci, 2016). For example, the theories of Jean Piaget and Lev Vygotsky were not created in an effort to inform teachers about ways to educate children, but in other chapters you will see that both of these theories have many applications that can guide your teaching. The field also draws from theory and research created and conducted directly by educational psychologists, and from teachers' practical experiences. For example, you will read about Dale Schunk's (2016) classroom-oriented research on self-efficacy (the belief that one can master a situation and produce positive outcomes). Educational psychologists also recognize that teaching sometimes must depart from scientific recipes, requiring improvisation and spontaneity (Borich, 2017; Parkay, 2016).

> **Thinking Back/Thinking Forward**
>
> Self-efficacy plays an important role in motivation. Connect to "Motivation, Teaching, and Learning."

As a scientific discipline, educational psychology aims to provide you with research knowledge that you can effectively apply to teaching situations and with research skills that will enhance your understanding of the factors that influence student learning (Glesne, 2016). But your teaching will still remain an art. In addition to what you can learn from research, you will also continually make important judgments in the classroom based on your personal skills and experiences as well as the accumulated wisdom shared with you by other teachers (Estes & Mintz, 2016).

Informed by formal and informal data about her students, this teacher selects evidence-based teaching practices to implement in her classroom. With a fine balance of self-reflection and classroom monitoring, she is often successful in engaging students from diverse backgrounds and skill levels in collaborative problem solving. *To what extent is her teaching likely art, science, or both?*
Kali9/E+/Getty Images

Review, Reflect, and Practice

(1) Describe some basic ideas about the field of educational psychology.

REVIEW
- How is educational psychology defined? Who were some key thinkers in the history of educational psychology, and what were their ideas?
- How would you describe the roles of art and science in the practice of teaching?

REFLECT
- John Dewey argued that children should not sit quietly in their seats and learn in a rote manner. Do you agree with Dewey? Why or why not?

PRAXIS™ PRACTICE
1. Mr. Smith believes that all children are entitled to an education and that this education should focus on the whole child. His views are most consistent with those of
   a. Benjamin Bloom
   b. John Dewey
   c. B. F. Skinner
   d. E. L. Thorndike

2. Four teachers are discussing the influences that contribute to effective teaching. Which of the following four statements is likely to be most accurate?
   a. Applying information from scientific research is the most important factor in being an effective teacher.
   b. You can't beat a teacher's own personal experiences for becoming an effective teacher.
   c. Being an effective teacher is influenced by scientific research knowledge, teaching skills, and personal experiences.
   d. A teacher's innate skills trump all other factors in being an effective teacher.

Please see answer key at end of book . . . .

LG 2 Identify the attitudes and skills of an effective teacher.

2 EFFECTIVE TEACHING
- Professional Knowledge and Skills
- Commitment, Motivation, and Caring

Because of the complexity of teaching and individual variation among students, effective teaching is not achievable through a "one size fits all" prescription. Teachers must master a variety of perspectives and strategies and be flexible in their application. This requires the following key ingredients: (1) professional knowledge and skills, and (2) commitment, motivation, and caring.

PROFESSIONAL KNOWLEDGE AND SKILLS

Effective teachers have good command of their subject matter and a solid core of teaching skills (Mayer & Alexander, 2017). They have excellent instructional strategies supported by methods of goal setting, instructional planning, and classroom management. They know how to motivate, communicate, and work effectively with students who have different levels of skills and come from culturally diverse backgrounds. Effective teachers also understand how to use appropriate levels of technology in the classroom.

Subject-Matter Competence In their lists of the characteristics of effective teachers characteristics, secondary school students have consistently mentioned teachers' knowledge of the subject (NASSP, 1997; Williams et al., 2012). Having a thoughtful, flexible, conceptual understanding of subject matter is indispensable for being an effective teacher (Hamilton & Duschi, 2017). Of course, knowledge of subject matter includes more than just facts, terms, and general concepts. It also includes knowledge about organizing ideas, connections among ideas, ways of thinking and arguing, patterns of change within a discipline, beliefs about a discipline, and the ability to carry ideas from one discipline to another. Clearly, having a deep understanding of the subject matter is an important aspect of being a competent teacher (Anderman & Klassen, 2016; Burden & Byrd, 2016; Guillaume, 2016).

Instructional Strategies At a broad level, two major approaches characterize how teachers teach: constructivist and direct instruction. The constructivist approach was at the center of James' and Dewey's philosophies of education. The direct instruction approach has more in common with Thorndike's view.

The **constructivist approach** is a learner-centered approach that emphasizes the importance of individuals actively constructing their knowledge and understanding with guidance from the teacher. In the constructivist view, teachers should not attempt to simply pour information into children's minds. Rather, children should be encouraged to explore their world, discover knowledge, reflect, and think critically with careful monitoring and meaningful guidance from the teacher (Robinson-Zanartu et al., 2015; Van de Walle et al., 2016). Constructivists argue that for too long children have been required to sit still, be passive learners, and rotely memorize irrelevant as well as relevant information (Parkay, 2016).

Today, constructivism may include an emphasis on *collaboration*—children working with each other in their efforts to know and understand (Gauvain, 2016). A teacher with a constructivist instructional philosophy would not have children memorize information rotely but would give them opportunities to meaningfully construct knowledge and understand the material while guiding their learning (Bendixen, 2016).

By contrast, the **direct instruction approach** is a structured, teacher-centered approach characterized by teacher direction and control, high teacher expectations for students' progress, maximum time spent by students on academic tasks, and efforts by the teacher to keep negative affect to a minimum. An important goal in the direct instruction approach is maximizing student learning time (Borich, 2017; Joyce et al., 2015).

constructivist approach A learner-centered approach to learning that emphasizes the importance of individuals actively constructing knowledge and understanding with guidance from the teacher.

direct instruction approach A structured, teacher-centered approach characterized by teacher direction and control, high teacher expectations for students' progress, maximum time spent by students on academic tasks, and efforts by the teacher to keep negative affect to a minimum.

Some experts in educational psychology emphasize that many effective teachers use both a constructivist *and* a direct instruction approach rather than relying exclusively on one or the other (Darling-Hammond & Bransford, 2005). Further, some circumstances may call for a constructivist approach, others for a direct instruction approach. For example, experts increasingly recommend an explicit, intellectually engaging direct instruction approach when teaching students who have a reading or a writing disability (Berninger et al., 2015). Whether you teach more from a constructivist approach or more from a direct instruction approach, you can be an effective teacher.

What characterizes constructivist and direct instruction approaches to educating students?
Ariel Skelley/Blend Images LLC

Thinking Skills Effective teachers model and communicate good thinking skills. Among the most important thinking skills for teachers to engage in and guide their students in developing are **critical thinking** skills, which involve thinking reflectively and productively and evaluating evidence. Getting students to think critically is not easy; many students develop a habit of passively learning material and rotely memorizing concepts rather than thinking deeply and reflectively (Sternberg & Sternberg, 2017). Thinking critically also means being open-minded and curious on the one hand, yet being careful to avoid making mistakes in interpreting something.

Throughout this text, we will encourage you to think critically about topics and issues. At the end of each main section in a chapter, you will encounter "Reflect" questions related to a topic that you have just read about. In the chapter, "Complex Cognitive Processes," you will read more extensively about critical thinking and other higher-level thinking processes such as reasoning, decision making, and creative thinking, and you will learn how to encourage your students' critical thinking by building it into your lessons.

Goal Setting and Instructional Planning Whether they take a constructivist or more traditional approach, effective teachers don't just "wing it" in the classroom. They set high goals for their teaching and organize plans for reaching those goals (Senko, 2016). They also develop specific criteria for success. They spend considerable time in instructional planning, organizing their lessons to maximize students' learning (Burden & Byrd, 2016). As they plan, effective teachers reflect and think about how they can make learning both challenging and interesting. Good planning requires consideration of the kinds of information, demonstrations, models, inquiry opportunities, discussion, and practice students need over time to understand particular concepts and develop particular skills. Although research has found that all of these features can support learning, the process of instructional design requires that teachers figure out which things students should do when, in what order, and how (Darling-Hammond et al., 2005). The growing emphasis on blended and online learning, particularly in high schools, highlights the role of teachers as instructional designers (Gyabak et al., 2015).

> **Thinking Back/Thinking Forward**
>
> In planning, teachers need to figure out which things students should do, when, in what order, and how. Connect to "Planning, Instruction, and Technology."

Developmentally Appropriate Teaching Practices Competent teachers have a good understanding of children's development and know how to create instructional materials appropriate for their developmental levels (Bredekamp, 2017; Morrison, 2017). U.S. schools are organized by grade and to some degree by age, but these are not always good predictors of children's development.

At any grade level, there is usually a two- or three-year span of ages with an even wider span of skills, abilities, and developmental stages. Understanding developmental pathways and progressions is extremely important for teaching in ways that are optimal for each child (Feeney et al., 2016).

Throughout this text, your attention will be drawn to developmental aspects of educating children and examples of teaching and learning that take into account a child's

DEVELOPMENT

critical thinking Thinking reflectively and productively and evaluating the evidence.

developmental level. Two chapters are devoted exclusively to development: "Cognitive and Language Development" and "Social Contexts and Socioemotional Development."

Classroom Management Skills An important aspect of being an effective teacher is keeping the class as a whole working together and oriented toward classroom tasks (Emmer & Evertson, 2017). Effective teachers establish and maintain an environment in which learning can occur. To create this optimal learning environment, teachers need a repertoire of strategies for establishing rules and procedures, organizing groups, monitoring and pacing classroom activities, and handling misbehavior (Evertson & Emmer, 2017; Jones & Jones, 2016; see also "Managing the Classroom" chapter in this book).

Motivational Skills Effective teachers have good strategies for helping students become self-motivated and take responsibility for their learning (Kitsantas & Cleary, 2016; Soloman & Anderman, 2017; Wentzel & Miele, 2016). Educational psychologists increasingly stress that this is best accomplished by providing real-world learning opportunities of optimal difficulty and novelty for each student. Students are motivated when they can make choices in line with their personal interests. Effective teachers give them the opportunity to think creatively and deeply about projects.

In addition to guiding students to become self-motivated learners, it is essential to establish high expectations for students' achievement (Schunk & DiBenedetto, 2016). High expectations for children's achievement need to come from teachers and parents. Too often children are rewarded for inferior or mediocre performance, and as a result they do not reach their full potential. When high expectations are created, a key aspect of education is to provide children—especially low-achieving children—effective instruction and support to meet these expectations. The chapter, "Motivation, Teaching, and Learning," covers the topic of motivation in detail.

> **Thinking Back/Thinking Forward**
> The best teachers have very few discipline problems, not because they are great disciplinarians but because they are great teachers. Connect to "Managing the Classroom."

Communication Skills Also indispensable to teaching are skills in speaking, listening, overcoming barriers to verbal communication, tuning in to students' nonverbal communication, and constructively resolving conflicts (Beebe et al., 2017; Zarefsky, 2017). Communication skills are critical not only in teaching but also in interacting with parents. Effective teachers use good communication skills when they talk "with" rather than "to" students, parents, administrators, and others; keep criticism at a minimum; and have an assertive rather than aggressive, manipulative, or passive communication style. Effective teachers work to improve students' communication skills as well. This is especially important because communication skills have been rated as the skills most sought after by today's employers. More on this in "Managing the Classroom" chapter in this book.

Paying More Than Lip Service to Individual Variations Virtually every teacher knows that it is important to take individual variations into account when teaching, but this is not always easy to do. Your students will have varying levels of intelligence, and have different learning preferences, temperaments, and personality traits (Bryce, et al., 2018; Sternberg, 2016). You also are likely to have some gifted students and others with disabilities of various types (Van Tassell-Baska, 2015).

Consider Amber Larkin's challenges and experiences as a beginning teacher (Wong Briggs, 2007). Her classroom was housed in a trailer, and her students included children who were homeless, non–English speaking, had disabilities, or were refugees who had never worn shoes or experienced any type of formal education. After four years of teaching, she was named one of *USA Today*'s National All-Star Teachers. Almost all of her students pass state-mandated No Child Left Behind tests, but she is just as pleased about her students' socioemotional growth. Her principal described her in the following manner: "There's an unspoken

Amber Larkin helps fifth-grade student Miya Kpa improve his academic skills. *What are some strategies for paying more than lip service to individual variation in students?*
Davis Turner

aura that great things are going to happen, and that's how she goes about her day" (Wong Briggs, 2007, p. 6D).

Effectively teaching students with such diverse characteristics requires much thought and effort. **Differentiated instruction** involves recognizing individual variations in students' knowledge, readiness, interests, and other characteristics, and taking these differences into account in planning curriculum and engaging in instruction (Taylor, 2015). Differentiated instruction emphasizes tailoring assignments to meet students' needs and abilities. It is unlikely that a teacher can generate 20 to 30 different lesson plans to address the needs of each student in a classroom. However, differentiated instruction advocates discovering "zones" or "ballparks" in which students in a classroom cluster, thus providing three or four types/levels of instruction rather than 20 to 30. Response to Intervention (RTI) can support this process of differentiation to meet students' needs. In the chapters titled "Individual Variations" and "Learners Who Are Exceptional" we provide strategies to help you guide students with different levels of skills and different characteristics to learn effectively.

DIVERSITY

Working Effectively with Students from Culturally Diverse Backgrounds Today, one of every five children in the United States is from an immigrant family, and by 2040 it is estimated that one of every three U.S. children will fit this description. Nearly 80 percent of the new immigrants are people of color from Latin America, Asia, and the Caribbean. Approximately 75 percent of the new immigrants are of Spanish-speaking origin, although children speaking more than 100 different languages are entering U.S. schools. In today's world of increasing intercultural contact, effective teachers are knowledgeable about people from different cultural backgrounds and are sensitive to their needs (Bucher, 2015; Koppelman, 2017). Effective teachers encourage students to have positive personal contact with diverse students and think of ways to create such settings. They guide students in thinking critically about cultural and ethnic issues, forestall or reduce bias, cultivate acceptance, and serve as cultural mediators (Gollnick & Chinn, 2017). Effective teachers also consider culturally relevant education, which is "committed to collective empowerment and social justice" (Aronson & Laughter, 2016, p. 164). An effective teacher also needs to be a broker, or middle person, between the culture of the school and the culture of certain students, especially those who are unsuccessful academically (Sarraj et al., 2015).

What are some strategies effective teachers use regarding diversity issues?
Blend Images/SuperStock

Here are cultural questions that competent teachers ask themselves (Pang, 2005):

- Do I recognize the power and complexity of cultural influences on students?
- Are my expectations for my students culturally based or biased?
- Am I doing a good job of seeing life from the perspective of students who come from cultures different from my own?
- Am I teaching the skills students may need to develop in order to talk in class if their culture is one in which they have little opportunity to practice "public" talking?
- Are my assessments fair and unbiased?

Assessment Knowledge and Skills Competent teachers also have good assessment knowledge and skills. There are many aspects to effectively using assessment in the

> **Thinking Back/Thinking Forward**
>
> Teachers can follow a number of guidelines for effective multicultural teaching. Connect to "Sociocultural Diversity."

differentiated instruction Involves recognizing individual variations in students' knowledge, readiness, interests, and other characteristics, and taking these differences into account when planning curriculum and engaging in instruction.

> **Thinking Back/Thinking Forward**
>
> An important aspect of assessment is to make it compatible with contemporary views of learning and motivation. Connect to "Classroom Assessment and Grading."

classroom (Brookhart & Nitko, 2015; Popham, 2017). You will need to decide what types of assessments you want to use to document your students' performance after instruction. You also will need to use assessment effectively before and during instruction (Chappuis et al., 2017). For example, before teaching a unit on plate tectonics, you might decide to assess whether your students are familiar with terms like *continent, earthquake,* and *volcano.*

During instruction, you might want to use ongoing observation and monitoring to determine whether your instruction is at a level that challenges students and to detect students who need your individual attention (Veenman, 2017). You will need to grade students to provide feedback about their achievement.

Other aspects of assessment you will be involved with include state-mandated tests to assess students' achievement and teachers' knowledge and skills (Popham, 2017). The federal government's No Child Left Behind (NCLB) legislation required states to test students annually in mathematics, English/language arts, and science, and holds states accountable for the success and failure of their students (McMillan, 2014). Then, in 2009, the Common Core State Standards Initiative was endorsed by the National Governors Association in an effort to implement more rigorous state guidelines for educating students. The Common Core Standards specify what students should know and the skills they should develop at each grade level in various content areas (Common Core State Standards Initiative, 2016).

The most recent initiative in U.S. education is the *Every Student Succeeds Act (ESSA)* that was passed into law in December 2015. As of 2019, every state's plan to implement ESSA has been approved, and the majority have begun implementing the changes (Klein, 2019). The law replaced *No Child Left Behind,* in the process modifying but not completely eliminating standardized testing. ESSA retains annual testing for reading and writing success in grades 3 to 8, then once more in high school. The new law also allows states to scale back the role that tests have played in holding schools accountable for student achievement. And schools must use at least one nonacademic factor—such as student engagement—when tracking schools' success.

Other aspects of the new law include continuing to require states and districts to improve their lowest-performing schools and to ensure that they improve their work with historically underperforming students, such as English-language learners, students who are ethnic minorities, and students with a disability. Also, states and districts are required to put in place challenging academic standards, although they can opt out of state standards involving Common Core.

Because of NCLB, and more recently the Common Core State Standards Initiative and EssA, the extent to which instruction should be tied to standards, or what is called *standards-based instruction,* has become a major issue in educational psychology and U.S. classrooms. The focus is on establishing standards of excellence and determining what it takes to get students to pass external, large-scale tests. Many educational psychologists stress that the challenge is to teach creatively within the structure imposed by the legislation (McMillan, 2014). Much more information about No Child Left Behind, the Common Core State Standards Initiative, and the Every Student Succeeds Act is provided in the chapter, "Standardized Tests and Teaching."

Before you become a teacher, your subject-matter knowledge and teaching skills are also likely to be assessed by the state in which you plan to teach. A large majority of states now use the PRAXIS™ test to determine whether prospective teachers are qualified to teach. Because of the increasing use of the PRAXIS™ test, this text includes a number of resources to help you prepare for this test.

Technological Skills Technology alone does not necessarily improve students' ability to learn, but it can support learning (Maloy et al., 2017; Roblyer, 2016). Conditions that support the effective use of technology in education include vision and support from educational leaders; teachers skilled in using technology for learning; content standards and curriculum resources; assessment of effectiveness of technology for learning; and an emphasis on the child as an active, constructive learner (ISTE, 2007).

Students benefit from teachers who increase their technology knowledge and integrate computers appropriately into classroom learning (Lever-Duffy & McDonald, 2015; Maloy et al., 2017). This integration should match up with students' learning needs, including the need to prepare for tomorrow's jobs, many of which will require technological expertise and computer-based skills (Aleven et al., 2017). In addition, effective teachers are knowledgeable about various assistive devices to support the learning of students with disabilities (Marchel et al., 2015).

TECHNOLOGY

Recently the International Society for Technology in Education (ISTE, 2016) updated technology standards for students. These standards involve being a(n):

- *Empowered Learner.* Students actively use technology to reach learning goals.
- *Digital Citizen.* Students demonstrate responsibility and are ethical in their use of technology.
- *Knowledge Constructor.* Students use a variety of resources and digital tools to construct knowledge, become more creative, and engage in meaningful learning.
- *Innovative Designer.* Students use various technologies to solve problems and craft useful and imaginative solutions to these problems.
- *Computational Thinker.* Students develop strategies in using technology to create solutions and test them.
- *Creative Communicator.* Students communicate effectively and think creatively in their use of digital tools to attain goals.
- *Global Collaborator.* Students use technology to widen their perspectives and enhance their learning by connecting with others locally and globally.

Further, there is considerable concern about the enormous number of hours children and adolescents spend in screen time—how much time is spent watching television or DVDs, playing video games, and using computers or mobile media such as iPhones—and how this time can influence their school success as well as their health (Branscum & Crowson, 2016; Calvert, 2015; Wu et al., 2016). There is also concern about the huge increase in media multitasking and how this might impair children and adolescents' ability to focus on an academic task while connected to some form of media unrelated to their schoolwork (Cain et al., 2016; Courage et al., 2015). Considerable concern also surrounds the extensive time students spend on social media and how it might influence aspects of their academic and socioemotional development, such as being a perpetrator or target of cyberbullying (Fisher et al., 2016; Marino et al., 2016; Selkie et al., 2015). Much more about these aspects of technology will be discussed in the chapter, "Planning, Instruction, and Technology."

COMMITMENT, MOTIVATION, AND CARING

Being an effective teacher also requires commitment, motivation, and caring. This includes having a good attitude and caring about students (Gasser et al., 2018).

What are some important aspects of incorporating technology in the classroom?
BananaStock/age fotostock

THROUGH THE EYES OF STUDENTS

"You Are the Coolest"

I just want to thank you for all the extra time you took to help me. You didn't have to do that but you did and I want to thank you for it. Thanks also for being straight up with me and not beating around the bush and for that you are the coolest. I'm sorry for the hard times I gave you. You take so much junk but through all that you stay calm and you are a great teacher.

Jessica
Seventh-Grade Student
Macon, Georgia
Letter to Chuck Rawls, Her Teacher, at the End of the School Year

---

Beginning teachers often report that the investment of time and effort needed to be an effective teacher is huge. Some teachers, even experienced ones, say they have "no life" from September to June. Even putting in hours on evenings and weekends, in addition to all of the hours spent in the classroom, might still not be enough to get things done.

In the face of these demands, it is easy to become frustrated or to get into a rut and develop a negative attitude. Commitment and motivation help get effective teachers through the tough moments of teaching. Effective teachers have confidence in their own self-efficacy, refuse to let negative emotions diminish their motivation, and bring a positive attitude and enthusiasm to the classroom (Anderman & Klassen, 2016; Fives & Buehl, 2016). These qualities are contagious and help make the classroom a place where students want to be. Recent research on mindfulness practices have shown that self-care interventions also can have beneficial effects for teachers and their students (Hwang et al., 2019).

So, what is likely to nurture your own positive attitudes and continued enthusiasm for teaching? As in all fields, success breeds success. It's important to become aware of times when you've made a difference in an individual student's life. Consider the words of one of the expert consultants for this book, Carlos Diaz, now a professor of education at Florida Atlantic University, about Mrs. Oppel, his high school English teacher:

> To this day, whenever I see certain words *(dearth, slake)* I recognize them fondly as some of Mrs. Oppel's vocabulary words. As a teacher, she was very calm and focused. She also was passionate about the power of language and the beauty of literature. I credit her, at least partially, for my determination to try to master the English language and become a professor and writer. I wish I could bottle these characteristics and implant them in all of my students.

The better teacher you become, the more rewarding your work will be. And the more respect and success you achieve in the eyes of your students, the better you will feel about your commitment to teaching. With that in mind, stop for a moment and think about the images you have of your own former teachers. Some of your teachers likely were outstanding and left you with a very positive image. In a national survey of almost a thousand students 13 to 17 years of age, having a good sense of humor, making the class interesting, and having knowledge of the subject matter were the characteristics students listed as the most important for teachers to have (NASSP, 1997). Even more recently, secondary students identified similar traits of outstanding teachers: friendly/relates/bonds/cares, enjoys subject/knowledgeable/can teach, and classroom management/respect (Williams et al., 2012). Characteristics secondary school students most frequently attributed to their worst teachers were having a boring class, not explaining things clearly, and showing favoritism. These characteristics and others that reflect students' images of their best and worst teachers are shown in Figure 1.

Characteristics of best teachers	% Total
1. Have a sense of humor	79.2
2. Make the class interesting	73.7
3. Have knowledge of their subjects	70.1
4. Explain things clearly	66.2
5. Spend time to help students	65.8
6. Are fair to their students	61.8
7. Treat students like adults	54.4
8. Relate well to students	54.2
9. Are considerate of students' feelings	51.9
10. Don't show favoritism toward students	46.6

Characteristics of worst teachers	% Total
1. Are dull/have a boring class	79.6
2. Don't explain things clearly	63.2
3. Show favoritism toward students	52.7
4. Have a poor attitude	49.8
5. Expect too much from students	49.1
6. Don't relate to students	46.2
7. Give too much homework	44.2
8. Are too strict	40.6
9. Don't give help/individual attention	40.5
10. Lack control	39.9

FIGURE 1 STUDENTS' IMAGES OF THEIR BEST AND WORST TEACHERS
Source: Mood of American Youth 1996 survey, National Association of Secondary School Principals.

SELF-ASSESSMENT 1
The Best and Worst Characteristics of My Teachers

When you studied Figure 1, were you surprised by any of the characteristics listed by students to describe their best and worst teachers? Which of the top five characteristics students listed for the best teachers surprised you the most? Which of the top five characteristics of the worst teachers surprised you the most?

Now think about the top five characteristics of the best and the worst teachers you have had. In generating your lists, don't be constrained by the characteristics described in Figure 1. Also, after you have listed each characteristic, write down one or more examples of situations that reflected the characteristic.

FIVE CHARACTERISTICS OF THE BEST TEACHERS I HAVE HAD

Characteristics | Examples of Situations That Reflected the Characteristic

1. _____
2. _____
3. _____
4. _____
5. _____

FIVE CHARACTERISTICS OF THE WORST TEACHERS I HAVE HAD

Characteristics | Examples of Situations That Reflected the Characteristic

1. _____
2. _____
3. _____
4. _____
5. _____

Think about the roles that a good sense of humor and your own genuine enthusiasm are likely to play in your long-term commitment as a teacher. Also, notice other characteristics in Figure 1 that relate to the caring nature of outstanding teachers. Effective teachers care for their students, often referring to them as "my students." They really want to be with the students and are dedicated to helping them learn. At the same time, they keep their role as a teacher distinct from student roles. Beyond their own caring, effective teachers also look for ways to help their students consider others' feelings and care about each other.

To think about the best and worst characteristics of the teachers you have had, complete *Self-Assessment 1*. Use the self-assessment to further explore the attitudes behind your commitment to become a teacher.

THROUGH THE EYES OF STUDENTS

A Good Teacher

Mike, Grade 2:
A good teacher is a teacher that does stuff that catches your interest. Sometimes you start learning and you don't even realize it. A good teacher is a teacher that does stuff that makes you think (Nikola-Lisa & Burnaford, 1994).

CONNECTING WITH STUDENTS: Best Practices
Strategies for Becoming an Effective Teacher

1. *Effective teaching requires teachers to wear many different hats.* It's easy to fall into the trap of thinking that if you have good subject-matter knowledge, excellent teaching will follow. Being an effective teacher requires many diverse skills. In *Through the Eyes of Teachers* you can read about how Susan Bradburn, who teaches grades 4 and 6 at West Marian Elementary School in North Carolina, brings many different skills to create effective lessons.

THROUGH THE EYES OF TEACHERS
The "Turtle Lady"

Susan Bradburn teaches grades 4 to 6 at West Marian Elementary School in North Carolina. She created a school museum in which students conduct research and create exhibitions. She has put her school-museum concept "on wheels" by having students take carts to other classes and into the community, and she has used award money to spread the use of mobile museums to other North Carolina schools. Nicknamed "the turtle lady" because of her interest in turtles and other animals, Susan takes students on three-day field trips to Edisto Island, South Carolina, to search for fossils and study coastal ecology. Her students sell calendars that contain their original poetry and art, and they use the proceeds to buy portions of a rain forest so it won't be destroyed.

Susan Bradburn (*left*) with several students at West Marian Elementary School.
Alan Marler/AP Images

2. *Engage in perspective taking.* You want to be the very best teacher you can possibly be. Think about what your students need from you to improve their academic and life skills. Also reflect on how you perceive your students and how they perceive you.

3. *Keep the list of characteristics of effective teachers we have discussed in this chapter with you through your teaching career.* Looking at the list and thinking about the different areas of effective teaching can benefit you as you go through your student teaching, your days as a beginning teacher, and even your years as an experienced teacher. By consulting it from time to time, you might realize that you have let one or two areas slip and need to spend time improving yourself.

4. *Stay committed and motivated.* Being an effective teacher requires being committed and motivated to learn even in the face of difficult and adverse circumstances (Anderman & Klassen, 2016). Work through your frustrations and develop good coping skills to face the tough times that come in any career. Remember that a positive attitude and a deep commitment to caring for children are key aspects to becoming a good teacher.

Review, Reflect, and Practice

2 Identify the attitudes and skills of an effective teacher.

REVIEW
- What professional knowledge and skills are required to be an effective teacher?
- Why is it important for teachers to be committed and motivated?

REFLECT
- What is most likely to make teaching rewarding for you in the long run?

PRAXIS™ PRACTICE
1. Suzanne spends a considerable amount of time writing lesson plans, developing criteria for student success, and organizing materials. Which professional skill is she demonstrating?
   a. classroom management
   b. communication

Review, Reflect, and Practice

   c. developmentally appropriate teaching practices
   d. goal setting and instructional management
2. Mr. Marcinello, who is midway through his first year of teaching, feels frustrated with his job. He is developing a negative attitude, and it is carrying over in his teaching. Which of the following areas does Mr. Marcinello need to work on the most at this point to become an effective teacher?
   a. classroom management and communication
   b. commitment and motivation
   c. technology and diversity
   d. subject-matter competence and individual variations

Please see answer key at end of book . . . .

3 RESEARCH IN EDUCATIONAL PSYCHOLOGY

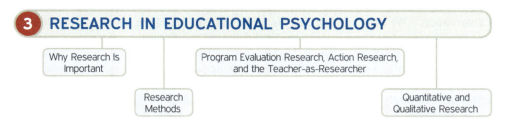

LG 3 Discuss why research is important to effective teaching and how educational psychologists and teachers can conduct and evaluate research.

Research can be a valuable source of information about teaching. We will explore why research is important and how it is done, including how you can be a teacher-researcher.

WHY RESEARCH IS IMPORTANT

It sometimes is said that experience is the best teacher. Your own experiences and experiences that other teachers, administrators, and experts share with you will make you a better teacher. However, by providing you with valid information about the best ways to teach children, research also can make you a better teacher (Smith & Davis, 2016).

RESEARCH

We all get a great deal of knowledge from personal experience. We generalize from what we observe and frequently turn memorable encounters into lifetime "truths." But how valid are these conclusions? Sometimes we err in making these personal observations or misinterpret what we see and hear. Chances are, you can think of many situations in which you thought other people read you the wrong way, just as they might have felt that you misread them. When we base information only on personal experiences, our conclusions can be biased because we sometimes make judgments that protect our ego and self-esteem.

We get information not only from personal experiences but also from authorities or experts. In your teaching career, you will hear many authorities and experts spell out a "best way" to educate students. The authorities and experts, however, don't always agree, do they? You might hear one expert one week tell you about a reading instruction method that is absolutely the best, yet the next week hear another expert tout a different method. One experienced teacher might tell you to do one thing with your students, while another experienced teacher tells you to do the opposite. How can you decide which one to believe? One way to clarify the situation is to look closely at research on the topic.

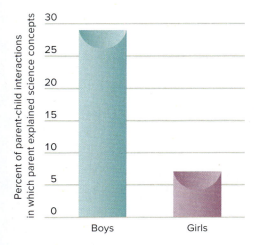

FIGURE 2 PARENTS' EXPLANATIONS OF SCIENCE TO SONS AND DAUGHTERS AT A SCIENCE MUSEUM

In a naturalistic observation study at a children's science museum, parents were three times more likely to explain science to boys than girls (Crowley et al., 2001). The gender difference occurred regardless of whether the father, the mother, or both parents were with the child, although the gender difference was greatest for fathers' science explanations to sons and daughters.

laboratory A controlled setting from which many of the complex factors of the real world have been removed.

naturalistic observation Observation conducted in the real world rather than in a laboratory.

participant observation Observation conducted while the teacher-researcher is actively involved as a participant in the activity or setting.

RESEARCH METHODS

Collecting information (or data) is an important aspect of research. When educational psychology researchers want to find out, for example, whether regularly playing video games detracts from student learning, eating a nutritious breakfast improves alertness in class, or getting more recess time decreases absenteeism, they can choose from many methods of gathering research information (Gliner et al., 2017; Trochim et al., 2016).

The three basic methods used to gather information in educational psychology are descriptive, correlational, and experimental.

Descriptive Research Descriptive data collection involves observing and recording behavior. For example, an educational psychologist might observe the extent to which children are aggressive in a classroom or interview teachers about their attitudes toward a specific teaching strategy. By itself, descriptive research cannot prove what causes some phenomenon, but it can reveal important information about people's behavior and attitudes (Boynton, 2017).

Observation We look at things all the time. Casually watching two students interacting, however, is not the same as making the type of observation used in scientific studies. Scientific observation is highly systematic. In the context of quantitative research, it requires knowing what you are looking for, trying to conduct observations in an unbiased manner, accurately recording and categorizing what you see, and effectively communicating your observations (Jackson, 2016; Salkind, 2017).

A common way to record observations is to write them down, often using shorthand or symbols. In addition, tape recorders, video cameras, special coding sheets, one-way mirrors, and computers increasingly are being used to make observation more accurate, reliable, and efficient. Observations can be made in laboratories or in naturalistic settings (Babbie, 2017). A **laboratory** is a controlled setting from which many of the complex factors of the real world have been removed. Some educational psychologists conduct research in laboratories at the colleges or universities where they work and teach. Although laboratories often help researchers gain more control in their studies, they have been criticized as being artificial.

In **naturalistic observation**, behavior is observed in the real world. Educational psychologists conduct naturalistic observations of children in classrooms, at museums, on playgrounds, in homes, in neighborhoods, and in other settings. Naturalistic observation was used in one study that focused on conversations between parents and children in a children's science museum (Crowley et al., 2001). Parents were three times as likely to engage boys as girls in explanatory talk while visiting different exhibits at the science museum (see Figure 2). In another study, Mexican American parents who had completed high school used more explanations with their children as they were observed at a science museum than Mexican American parents who had not completed high school (Tennebaum et al., 2002).

Participant observation occurs when the observer-researcher is actively involved as a participant in the activity or setting (McMillan, 2016). The participant observer will often participate in a context and observe, then take notes on what he or she has viewed. The observer usually makes these observations and writes down notes over a period of days, weeks, or months and looks for patterns in the observations. For example, to study a student who is doing poorly in the class without apparent reason, the teacher might develop a plan to observe the student from time to time and record observations of the student's behavior and what is going on in the classroom at the time.

Following are strategies recommended by teachers at different grade levels regarding how they use participant observation in their classrooms.

EARLY CHILDHOOD We take notes, observe, and record the activities of our young children throughout the day. Taking notes on children at the preschool level can be challenging because when children first notice that you are intently watching and taking notes, they may become curious and ask many questions, or become overly anxious and say things like, "Look at me!" to the teacher. As the year goes by, however, children get used to the recordings, and the questions are less frequent, allowing for a more accurate assessment of a child's needs.

—**VALARIE GORHAM,** *Kiddie Quarters, Inc.*

ELEMENTARY SCHOOL: GRADES K–5 I meet with leveled reading groups, typically ranging from three to five students. Materials and texts that are at the group's instructional level are used. As the lesson and activities are carried out, I take quick notes as I see the group or individuals grasping concepts, struggling in any way, or if a "teachable moment" presents itself. These notes help me later in my planning to make decisions about whether to reteach a certain lesson/concept, move on to new concepts/materials, or go to something other than originally planned because of a teachable moment or connection that has been discovered.

—**SUSAN FROELICH,** *Clinton Elementary School*

MIDDLE SCHOOL: GRADES 6–8 I once had a student who often came to class unprepared and late. Over time, I observed the student, took notes, and created a chart for myself that listed the times the student did not come to class prepared or on time. Because I kept good records, I was able to find out that when the student had a physical education class just before my class, he was late. I then worked with the student and phys. ed. teacher to come up with a solution so that the student had time to get to my class with the necessary classroom materials.

—**CASEY MAASS,** *Edison Middle School*

HIGH SCHOOL: GRADES 9–12 In the lab portion of my class, I have a chart that identifies when students are off-task and a notation for what they are doing instead of the task, such as listening to an iPod, talking to their friends, and so on. After a pattern develops, I talk with the student and show them their pattern on the chart. High school students tend to understand graphs and data better than being reminded while they are being off-task. For me, charting provides a more positive environment than an interruption or reprimand.

—**SANDY SWANSON,** *Menomonee Falls High School*

Interviews and Questionnaires Sometimes the quickest and best way to get information about students and teachers is to ask them for it. Educational psychologists use interviews and questionnaires (surveys) to find out about children's and teachers' experiences, beliefs, and feelings. Most interviews take place face-to-face, although they can be done in other ways, such as over the phone or the Internet. Questionnaires usually are given to individuals in written form. They, too, can be transmitted in many ways, such as directly by hand, by mail, or via the Internet.

Good interviews and surveys in quantitative research involve concrete, specific, and unambiguous questions and some means of checking the authenticity of the respondents' replies (Leary, 2017). Interviews and surveys, however, are not without problems. One crucial limitation is that many individuals give socially desirable answers, responding in a way they think is most socially acceptable and desirable rather than expressing how they truly think or feel. Skilled interviewing techniques and questions that increase forthright responses are crucial to obtaining accurate information (Kazdin, 2017). Another problem with interviews and surveys is that the respondents sometimes simply are untruthful.

Standardized Tests **Standardized tests** have uniform procedures for administration and scoring. They assess students' aptitudes or skills in different domains. Many standardized tests allow a student's performance to be compared with the performance of other students at the same age or grade level, in many cases on a national basis. Students might take a number of standardized tests, including tests that assess their intelligence, achievement, personality, career interests, and other skills (Gregory, 2016; Mills & Gay, 2016). These tests can provide outcome measures for research studies, information that helps psychologists and educators make decisions about an individual student, and comparisons of students' performance across schools, states, and countries.

Standardized tests also play an important role in a major contemporary educational psychology issue—*accountability,* which involves holding teachers and students responsible for student performance (Popham, 2017). As we indicated earlier, both students and teachers increasingly are being given standardized tests in the accountability effort. The U.S. government's No Child Left Behind Act is at the centerpiece of accountability; it mandated that in 2005 every state had to give standardized tests to students in grades 3 through 8 in language arts and math, with testing for science achievement added in 2007. Controversially, many states used these student test scores to calculate teacher effectiveness scores that were linked to bonuses and continuing employment (Pressley et al., 2018). School grades, based partially on student test scores, were also linked to school funding and take-over.

Physiological Measures Researchers are increasingly using physiological measures when they study children's and adolescents' development (Johnson, 2016). A physiological measure that is increasingly being used is neuroimaging, especially *functional magnetic resonance imaging* (fMRI) that uses electromagnetic waves to construct images of a person's brain tissue and biochemical activity (de Haan & Johnson, 2016; Galvan & Tottenham, 2016). Heart rate has been used as an indicator of children's development of perception, attention, and memory (Kim et al., 2015). Further, heart rate has been used as an index of different aspects of emotional development, such as inhibition, anxiety, and depression (Blood et al., 2015).

Researchers also are assessing levels of hormones when they study children's and adolescents' development. *Cortisol* is a hormone produced by the adrenal gland that is linked to the body's stress level and has been measured in studies of temperament, emotional reactivity, peer relations, and child psychopathology (Jacoby et al., 2016). As puberty unfolds, the blood levels of certain hormones increase. To determine the nature of these hormonal changes, researchers analyze blood samples from adolescent volunteers.

Further, there has been a major increase in the study of genetic and environmental influences on children's and adolescent development (Hill & Roth, 2016). As researchers have become more capable of assessing actual genes, they increasingly are examining how specific genes or combinations of genes might influence such education-related topics as intelligence, ADHD, autism, and many other areas (Grigorenko et al., 2016). We will have much more to say about the topic of genetic/environmental interaction in the "Physical and Cognitive Development" chapter and in a number of other chapters as well.

Case Studies A **case study** is an in-depth look at an individual. Case studies often are used when unique circumstances in a person's life cannot be duplicated, for either practical or ethical reasons. For example, consider the case study of Brandi Binder (Nash, 1997). She developed such severe epilepsy that surgeons had to remove the right side of her brain's cerebral cortex when she was 6 years old. Brandi lost virtually

standardized tests Tests with uniform procedures for administration and scoring. They assess students' performance in different domains and allow a student's performance to be compared with the performance of other students at the same age or grade level on a national basis.

case study An in-depth look at an individual.

all control over the muscles on the left side of her body, the side controlled by the right side of her brain. At age 17, however, after years of therapy ranging from leg lifts to mathematics and music training, Brandi is an A student. She loves music and art, which usually are associated with the right side of the brain. Her recuperation is not 100 percent—for example, she has not regained the use of her left arm—but her case study shows that if there is a way to compensate, the human brain will find it. Brandi's remarkable recovery also provides evidence against the stereotype that the left side (hemisphere) of the brain is solely the source of logical thinking and the right hemisphere exclusively the source of creativity. Brains are not that neatly split in terms of most functioning, as Brandi's case illustrates.

Although case studies provide dramatic, in-depth portrayals of people's lives, we need to exercise caution when interpreting them. The subject of a case study is unique, with a genetic makeup and set of experiences that no one else shares. For these reasons, the findings often do not lend themselves to statistical analysis and may not generalize to other people.

Ethnographic Studies An **ethnographic study** consists of in-depth description and interpretation of behavior in an ethnic or a cultural group that includes direct involvement with the participants (Jachyra et al., 2015). This type of study might include observations in naturalistic settings as well as interviews. Many ethnographic studies are long-term projects.

In one ethnographic study, the purpose was to examine the extent to which schools were enacting educational reforms for language minority students (U.S. Office of Education, 1998). In-depth observations and interviews were conducted in a number of schools to determine whether they were establishing high standards and restructuring the way education was being delivered. Several schools were selected for intensive evaluation, including Las Palmas Elementary School in San Clemente, California. The study concluded that this school, at least, was making the necessary reforms for improving the education of language minority students.

Focus Groups *Focus groups* involve interviewing people in a group setting, in most cases to obtain information about a particular topic or issue (Nel et al., 2015). Focus groups typically consist of five to nine people in which a group facilitator asks a series of open-ended questions. Focus groups can be used to assess the value of a product, service, or program, such as a newly developed school Web site or the benefits of a recently instituted after-school program for middle school students.

Personal Journals and Diaries Individuals can be asked to keep personal journals or diaries to document quantitative aspects of their activities (such as how often the individual uses the Internet) or qualitative aspects of their lives (such as their attitudes and beliefs about a particular topic or issue). Increasingly, researchers are providing digital audio or video recorders to participants in a study rather than have them write entries in a personal journal or diary.

Correlational Research In **correlational research**, the goal is to describe the strength of the relationship between two or more events or characteristics. Correlational research is useful because the more strongly two events are correlated (related or associated), the more effectively we can predict one from the other (Gravetter & Wallnau, 2017; Levin et al., 2015). For example, if researchers find that low-involved, permissive teaching is correlated with a student's lack of self-control, it suggests that low-involved, permissive teaching might be one source of the lack of self-control.

Correlation by itself, however, does not equal causation (Heiman, 2015; Howell, 2017). The correlational finding just mentioned does not mean that permissive teaching necessarily causes low student self-control. It could mean that, but it also could mean that the students' lack of self-control caused the teachers to throw up their arms in despair and give up trying to control the out-of-control class. It also could be that

Brandi Binder is evidence of the brain's hemispheric flexibility and resilience. Despite having the right side of her cortex removed because of a severe case of epilepsy, Brandi at the age of 17 engaged in many activities often portrayed as only "right-brain" activities. She loved music and art and is shown here working on one of her paintings.
Brandi Binder

ethnographic study In-depth description and interpretation of behavior in an ethnic or a cultural group that includes direct involvement with the participants.

correlational research Research that describes the strength of the relation between two or more events or characteristics.

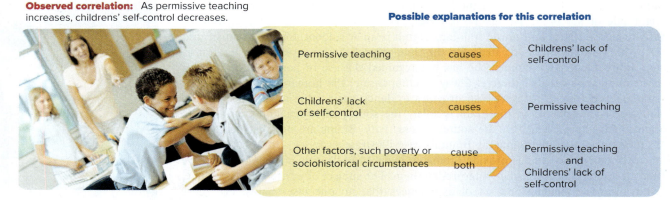

FIGURE 3 POSSIBLE EXPLANATIONS OF CORRELATIONAL DATA

An observed correlation between two events cannot be used to conclude that one event caused the other. Some possibilities are that the second event caused the first event or that a third, unknown event caused the correlation between the first two events.

BananaStock/age fotostock

other factors, such as poverty or cultural expectations/biases, caused the correlation between permissive teaching and low student self-control. Figure 3 illustrates these possible interpretations of correlational data.

Experimental Research

Experimental research allows educational psychologists to determine the causes of behavior. Educational psychologists accomplish this task by performing an *experiment,* a carefully regulated procedure in which one or more of the factors believed to influence the behavior being studied is manipulated and all other factors are held constant (McMillan, 2016). If the behavior under study changes when a factor is manipulated, we say that the manipulated factor causes the behavior to change. *Cause* is the event that is being manipulated. *Effect* is the behavior that changes because of the manipulation. Experimental research is the most valid method of establishing cause and effect. Because correlational research does not involve manipulation of factors, it is not an accurate way to isolate cause (Gravetter & Forzano, 2016).

Experiments involve at least one independent variable and one dependent variable. The **independent variable** is the manipulated, influential, experimental factor. The label *independent* indicates that this variable can be changed independently of any other factors. For example, suppose we want to design an experiment to study the effects of peer tutoring on student achievement. In this example, the amount and type of peer tutoring could be an independent variable.

The **dependent variable** is the factor that is measured in an experiment. It can change as the independent variable is manipulated. The label *dependent* is used because the values of this variable depend on what happens to the participants in the experiment as the independent variable is manipulated. In the peer tutoring study, achievement is the dependent variable. This might be assessed in a number of ways. Let's say in this study it is measured by scores on a nationally standardized achievement test.

In experiments, the independent variable consists of differing experiences given to one or more experimental groups and one or more control groups. An **experimental group** is a group whose experience is manipulated. A **control group** is a comparison group that is treated in every way like the experimental group except for the manipulated factor. The control group serves as the baseline against which the effects of the manipulated condition can be compared. In the peer tutoring study, we need to have one group of students who get peer tutoring (experimental group) and one group of students who don't receive it (control group).

Another important principle of experimental research is **random assignment**: Researchers assign participants to experimental and control groups by chance.

---

experimental research Research that allows the determination of the causes of behavior and involves conducting an experiment, which is a carefully regulated procedure in which one or more of the factors believed to influence the behavior being studied is manipulated and all others are held constant.

independent variable The manipulated, influential, experimental factor in an experiment.

dependent variable The factor that is measured in an experiment.

experimental group The group whose experience is manipulated in an experiment.

control group In an experiment, a group whose experience is treated in every way like the experimental group except for the manipulated factor.

random assignment In experimental research, the assignment of participants to experimental and control groups by chance.

This practice reduces the likelihood that the experiment's results will be due to any preexisting differences between the groups. In our study of peer tutoring, random assignment greatly reduces the probability that the two groups will differ on such factors as age, family status, initial achievement, intelligence, personality, health, and alertness.

To summarize the experimental study of peer tutoring and student achievement, each student is randomly assigned to one of two groups. One group (the experimental group) is given peer tutoring; the other (the control group) is not. The independent variable consists of the differing experiences (tutoring or no tutoring) that the experimental and control groups receive. After the peer tutoring is completed, the students are given a nationally standardized achievement test (dependent variable). Figure 4 illustrates the experimental research method applied to time management and students' grades.

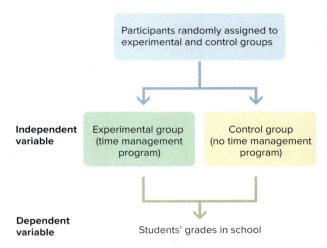

FIGURE 4 EXPERIMENTAL RESEARCH STRATEGY APPLIED TO THE STUDY OF THE EFFECTS OF TIME MANAGEMENT ON STUDENTS' GRADES

PROGRAM EVALUATION RESEARCH, ACTION RESEARCH, AND THE TEACHER-AS-RESEARCHER

In discussing research methods so far, we have mainly covered methods used to improve our knowledge and understanding of general educational practices. The same methods also can be applied to research whose aim is more specific, such as determining how well a particular educational strategy or program is working. This more narrowly targeted work often includes program evaluation research, action research, and the teacher-as-researcher.

Program Evaluation Research **Program evaluation research** is research designed to make decisions about the effectiveness of a particular program related to its implementation and outcomes. It often focuses on a specific location or type of program. Because program evaluation research often is directed at answering a question about a specific school or school system, its results are not intended to be generalized to other settings. A program evaluation researcher might ask questions like these:

- Has a gifted program started two years ago been implemented as proposed?
- What challenges to implementing a new technology program were faced and how were they addressed?
- What differences in students' reading skills are observed when comparing those who participated in the two different reading program used by the school system?

Action Research **Action research** is used to solve a specific classroom or school problem, improve teaching and other educational strategies, or make a decision at a specific location (Hendricks, 2017; Kayaoglu, 2015; Rowell et al., 2015). The goal of action research is to improve educational practices immediately in one or two classrooms, at one school, or at several schools. Action research is carried out by teachers and administrators rather than educational psychology researchers. The practitioners, however, might follow many of the guidelines of scientific research described earlier, such as trying to make the research and observations as systematic as possible to avoid bias and misinterpretation (Hendricks, 2017). Action research can be carried out school-wide or in more limited settings by a smaller group of teachers and administrators; it can even be accomplished in a single classroom by an individual teacher.

The Teacher-as-Researcher The concept of **teacher-as-researcher** (also called "teacher-researcher") is the idea that classroom teachers can conduct their own studies to improve their teaching practices. To obtain information, the teacher-researcher uses methods such as participant observation, interviews, and case studies. One widely used technique is the clinical interview, in which the teacher makes the student feel

program evaluation research Research designed to make decisions about the effectiveness of a particular program.

action research Research used to solve a specific classroom or school problem, improve teaching and other educational strategies, or make a decision at a specific location.

teacher-as-researcher Also called teacher-researcher, this concept involves classroom teachers conducting their own studies to improve their teaching practice.

comfortable, shares beliefs and expectations, and asks questions in a nonthreatening manner. Before conducting a clinical interview with a student, the teacher usually will put together a targeted set of questions to ask. Clinical interviews not only can help you obtain information about a particular issue or problem but also can provide you with a sense of how children think and feel.

In addition to participant observation, the teacher might conduct several clinical interviews with a student, discuss the student's situation with the child's parents, and consult with a school psychologist about the student's behavior. Based on this work as teacher-researcher, the teacher may be able to create an intervention strategy that improves the student's behavior.

Thus, learning about educational research methods not only can help you understand the research that educational psychologists conduct but also has another practical benefit. The more knowledge you have about research in educational psychology, the more effective you will be in the increasingly popular teacher-researcher role (Thomas, 2005).

QUANTITATIVE AND QUALITATIVE RESEARCH

Now that a wide range of research methods has been described, let's look at an increasingly common way of categorizing these methods: quantitative research and qualitative research (Glesne, 2016; McMillan, 2016). **Quantitative research** uses numerical calculations to discover information about a particular topic. Experimental and correlational research designs reflect quantitative research. So do many of the descriptive measures that were described earlier, such as observations, interviews, surveys, and standardized tests, when statistics are used to analyze the data collected. **Qualitative research** involves obtaining information using descriptive measures such as interviews, case studies, ethnographic studies, focus groups, and personal journals and diaries, that usually generate textual data that can be analyzed thematically rather than statistically.

Recently, educational psychologists have recognized the potential benefits of conducting **mixed methods research**, which blends different research designs or methods (McMillan, 2016). For example, researchers might use both quantitative and qualitative research methods. They might use an experimental design and statistically analyze the data (quantitative) and also use a focus group or case study (qualitative) to obtain greater breadth and depth of information about a particular topic.

Now that we have explored many aspects of research designs and measures, let's examine how research might influence the strategies teachers use in the classroom. To find out, I asked the following teachers at different grade levels to describe how their teaching had been influenced by research:

EARLY CHILDHOOD Brain research has demonstrated the amazing amount of learning that takes place during the early years of life, in addition to the significant impact of high-quality early childhood education and care on the academic and long-term success of a child. Given the age of the children at our center—toddlers through pre-K—I find this research extremely motivating.

—HEIDI KAUFMAN, *MetroWest YMCA Child Care and Educational Program*

ELEMENTARY SCHOOL: GRADES K–5 When adopting our new kindergarten reading curriculum, we conducted local assessments and collected data, read relevant research of best practices, and worked cooperatively to come up with the policies and practices that will work in collaboration with our state expectations as well as our school vision and mission.

—HEATHER ZOLDAK, *Ridge Wood Elementary School*

quantitative research Employs numerical calculations in an effort to discover information about a particular topic.

qualitative research Involves obtaining information using descriptive measures such as interviews, case studies, personal journals and diaries, and focus groups, as well as using thematic analysis rather than statistics to analyze textual data.

mixed methods research Involves research that blends different research designs or methods.

MIDDLE SCHOOL: GRADES 6–8 I attend Learning and the Brain conferences and read associated research papers and books. These materials have helped me understand brain development in middle school children, especially the considerable changes in early adolescence. This understanding has influenced my classroom management, enabled me to provide differentiated instruction, and helped me to appreciate and work with a range of students' learning styles and needs.

—KEREN ABRA, *Convent of the Sacred Heart School*

HIGH SCHOOL: GRADES 9–12 The person who has most influenced my teaching is Nancie Atwell, a teacher who teaches teachers about teaching. Her lessons on how to get students to love reading are pragmatic and simple, yet extremely effective: Read what the students are reading, "sell" the books by talking about them to students, let students see you reading, read when they read, give time in class to read, make books easily available to students, and be excited and energetic when discussing new books in class. At the beginning of the year, nonreaders (who comprise the majority of the class) groan and roll their eyes when I say it is reading time. However, in just a few short weeks, students beg for daily reading time.

—JENNIFER HEITER, *Bremen High School*

CONNECTING WITH STUDENTS: Best Practices
Strategies for Becoming an Effective Teacher-Researcher

1. *As you plan each week's lessons, think about your students and which ones might benefit from your role as a teacher-researcher.* As you reflect on the past week's classes, you might notice that one student seemed to be sliding downhill in her performance and that another student seemed to be especially depressed. As you think about such students, you might consider using your participant observer or clinical interview skills in the following week to find out why they are having problems.

2. *Take a course in educational research methods.* This can improve your understanding of how research is conducted.

3. *Use the library or Internet resources to learn more about teacher-researcher skills.* This might include locating information about how to be a skilled clinical interviewer and a systematic, unbiased observer.

4. *Ask someone else (such as another teacher) to observe your class and help you develop some strategies for the particular research problem that you want to solve.*

Review, Reflect, and Practice

3 Discuss why research is important to effective teaching and how educational psychologists and teachers can conduct and evaluate research.

REVIEW
- Why is research important in educational psychology?
- What are some types of research? What is the difference between correlational research and experimental research?
- What are some kinds of research that relate directly to effective classroom practices? What tools might a teacher use to do classroom research?
- What characterizes quantitative and qualitative research?

continued

Review, Reflect, and Practice

REFLECT

- In your own K–12 education, can you remember a time when one of your teachers might have benefited from conducting action research regarding the effectiveness of his or her own teaching methods? What action research questions and methods might have been useful to the teacher?

PRAXIS™ PRACTICE

1. Which of the following is more scientific?
   a. systematic observation
   b. personal experience
   c. one person's opinion
   d. a book written by a journalist

2. Mr. McMahon wants to know how much time his students spend off-task each day. To determine this, he carefully watches the students in class, keeping a record of off-task behavior. Which research approach has he used?
   a. case study
   b. experiment
   c. laboratory experiment
   d. naturalistic observation

3. Ms. Simon has been hired to determine how effective a school's health education program has been in reducing adolescent pregnancies. Which type of research will she conduct?
   a. action research
   b. experimental research
   c. program evaluation
   d. teacher-as-researcher

4. Mr. Nugerian wants to use qualitative research to discover why one of his students is slacking off in their homework. Which of the following techniques is he likely to use to find out information about this problem?
   a. experimental research
   b. correlational research
   c. case study
   d. observation with statistical analysis of the data

Please see answer key at end of book . . . .

Connecting with the Classroom: Crack the Case

The Classroom Decision

Ms. Huang teaches fourth grade at King Elementary School. Her class comprise 26 students: 16 girls and 10 boys. They are an ethnically and economically diverse group. They are also diverse in terms of their achievement levels. She has two students who have been identified as being gifted and three students with diagnosed learning disabilities. Overall, they are a cooperative group with a desire to learn.

Ms. Huang's school district recently purchased a new math curriculum that emphasizes conceptual understanding and application of mathematical principles to real-life situations. While Ms. Huang appreciates the new curriculum, she also has some concerns. Many of Ms. Huang's students have not yet mastered their basic math facts. Ms. Huang fears that without knowing their basic math facts very well, understanding mathematical principles will be useless and her students still won't be able to apply these principles. She also worries that this will cause her students undue frustration and may decrease their interest and motivation in math.

In the past, Ms. Huang has had her students work on developing mastery of math facts using drill-and-practice methods such as flashcards, worksheets filled with fact problems, and a computer game that is essentially an electronic version of flashcards with graphics. She is comfortable with this method and says that it has helped prior students to develop the mastery she believes they need.

She voices her concern to her principal, who responds that the publisher's representative provided the district with evidence that the new program also helps students to develop mastery of basic facts. However, Ms. Huang is still skeptical. She wants very badly to do the right thing for her students, but she isn't sure what that is. First, she checks the What Works Clearinghouse and finds the program has not yet been reviewed. She decides that she needs to conduct some classroom research to determine which will benefit her students more—the new curricular approach or her more traditional approach.

1. What issues would need to be considered in conducting such a study?
2. What type of research would be most appropriate?
   a. case study
   b. correlational research
   c. experimental research
   d. naturalistic observation
3. Why?
4. If she compared the two different curricula and their outcomes, what would the independent variable be?
   a. student achievement relative to basic math facts
   b. the control group
   c. the experimental group
   d. which curricular approach was used
5. If Ms. Huang decided to conduct an experimental study in which she compared the two different curricula and their outcomes, what would the dependent variable be?
   a. student achievement relative to basic math facts
   b. the control group
   c. the experimental group
   d. which curricular approach was used
6. How should Ms. Huang go about conducting her study?

Connecting with Learning: Reach Your Learning Goals

 EXPLORING EDUCATIONAL PSYCHOLOGY: Describe some basic ideas about the field of educational psychology.

Historical Background

- Educational psychology is the branch of psychology that specializes in understanding teaching and learning in educational settings.
- William James and John Dewey were important pioneers in educational psychology, as was E. L. Thorndike. William James emphasized the importance of classroom observation to improve education. Among the important concepts in educational psychology that we owe to Dewey are these: the child as an active learner, education of the whole child, emphasis on the child's adaptation to the environment, and the democratic ideal that all children deserve a quality education. Thorndike, a proponent of the scientific foundation of learning, argued that schools should sharpen children's reasoning skills.
- There were few individuals from ethnic minority groups and few women in the early history of educational psychology because of ethnic and gender barriers.
- Further historical developments included Skinner's behaviorism in the mid-twentieth century and the cognitive revolution that had taken hold by the 1980s. Also in recent years, there has been expanded interest in the socioemotional aspects of children's lives, including cultural contexts.

Teaching: Art and Science

- Teaching is linked to both science and art. In terms of art, skillful, experienced practice contributes to effective teaching. In terms of science, information from psychological research can provide valuable ideas.

continued

2 EFFECTIVE TEACHING: Identify the attitudes and skills of an effective teacher.

Professional Knowledge and Skills

- Effective teachers have subject-matter competence, use effective instructional strategies, engage in good thinking skills and guide students in developing these thinking skills, pay more than lip service to individual variations, work with diverse ethnic and cultural groups, and have skills in the following areas: goal setting and planning, developmentally appropriate teaching practices, classroom management, motivation, communication, assessment, and technology.

Commitment, Motivation, and Caring

- Being an effective teacher requires commitment and motivation. This includes having a good attitude and caring about students. It is easy for teachers to get into a rut and develop a negative attitude, but students pick up on this and it can harm their learning.

3 RESEARCH IN EDUCATIONAL PSYCHOLOGY: Discuss why research is important to effective teaching and how educational psychologists and teachers can conduct and evaluate research.

Why Research Is Important

- Personal experiences and information from experts can help you become an effective teacher.
- The information you obtain from research also is extremely important. It will help you sort through various strategies and determine which are most and least effective. Research helps to eliminate errors in judgment that are based only on personal experiences.

Research Methods

- Numerous methods can be used to obtain information about various aspects of educational psychology. Research data-gathering methods can be classified as descriptive, correlational, and experimental.
- Descriptive methods include observation, interviews and questionnaires, standardized tests, physiological measures, case studies, ethnographic studies, focus groups, and personal journals and diaries.
- In correlational research, the goal is to describe the strength of the relation between two or more events or characteristics. An important research principle is that correlation does not equal causation.
- Experimental research allows the causes of behavior to be determined and is the most valid method of establishing cause and effect. Conducting an experiment involves examining the influence of at least one independent variable (the manipulated, influential, experimental factor) on one or more dependent variables (the measured factor). Experiments involve the random assignment of participants to one or more experimental groups (the groups whose experience is being manipulated) and one or more control groups (comparison groups treated in every way like the experimental group except for the manipulated factor).

Program Evaluation Research, Action Research, and the Teacher-as-Researcher

- Program evaluation research is designed to assess the effectiveness of a particular program.
- Action research is used to solve a specific classroom or social problem, improve teaching strategies, or make a decision at a specific location.
- The teacher-as-researcher (teacher-researcher) conducts classroom studies to improve his or her educational practices.

Quantitative and Qualitative Research

- Quantitative research employs numerical calculations in an effort to discover information about a particular topic. Experimental and correlational research designs reflect quantitative research.
- Qualitative research involves obtaining information using descriptive methods such as interviews, case studies, and ethnographic studies, with thematic analysis of textual data rather than statistical analyses.
- Mixed methods research blends different research designs or methods.

KEY TERMS

action research 21
case study 18
constructivist approach 6
control group 20
correlational research 19
critical thinking 7

dependent variable 20
differentiated instruction 9
direct instruction approach 6
educational psychology 2
ethnographic study 19
experimental group 20

experimental research 20
independent variable 20
laboratory 16
mixed methods research 22
naturalistic observation 16
participant observation 16

program evaluation research 21
qualitative research 22
quantitative research 22
random assignment 20
standardized tests 18
teacher-as-researcher 21

PORTFOLIO ACTIVITIES

Now that you have a good understanding of this chapter, complete these exercises to expand your thinking.

Independent Reflection

1. **Positive Perspectives on Teaching.** At the beginning of the chapter, you read teacher-astronaut Christa McAuliffe's quote: "I touch the future. I teach." Put on your creative thinking hat and come up with one or more brief quotes that describe positive aspects of teaching.

2. **Your Goals as a Teacher.** After some thinking, write a personal response to the following questions: What kind of teacher do you want to become? What strengths do you want to have? What kinds of potential weaknesses might you need to overcome? Either place the statement in your portfolio or seal it in an envelope that you will open after your first month or two of teaching.

3. **Preparing for Challenges.** Think about the grade level you are planning to teach. Consider at least one way your classroom at that grade level is likely to be challenging. Write about how you will cope with these challenges.

Research/Field Experience

4. **Comparing Articles in Scholarly and Mass Market Publications.** Information about educational psychology appears in research journals and in magazines and newspapers. Find an article in a research or professional journal (such as *Contemporary Educational Psychologist, Educational Psychologist, Educational Psychology Review, Journal of Educational Psychology,* or *Phi Delta Kappan*) and an article in a newspaper or magazine on the same topic. How does the research/professional article differ from the newspaper or magazine account? What can you learn from this comparison? Write down your conclusions and keep copies of the articles.

chapter 2

COGNITIVE AND LANGUAGE DEVELOPMENT

chapter outline

① An Overview of Child Development

Learning Goal 1 Define development and explain the main processes, periods, and issues in development, as well as links between development and education.

Exploring What Development Is
Processes and Periods
Developmental Issues
Development and Education

② Cognitive Development

Learning Goal 2 Discuss the development of the brain and compare the cognitive developmental theories of Jean Piaget and Lev Vygotsky.

The Brain
Piaget's Theory
Vygotsky's Theory

③ Language Development

Learning Goal 3 Identify the key features of language, biological and environmental influences on language, and the typical growth of the child's language.

What Is Language?
Biological and Environmental Influences
How Language Develops

*Ah! What would the world be to us
If the children were no more?
We should dread the desert behind us
Worse than the dark before.*

—Henry Wadsworth Longfellow
American Poet, 19th Century

Connecting with Teachers   Donene Polson

In this chapter, you will study Lev Vygotsky's sociocultural cognitive theory of development. Donene Polson's classroom reflects Vygotsky's emphasis on the importance of collaboration among a community of learners. Donene teaches at Washington Elementary School in Salt Lake City, an innovative school that emphasizes the importance of people learning together (Rogoff et al. 2001). Children as well as adults plan learning activities. Throughout the day at school, students work in small groups.

Donene loves working in a school in which students, teachers, and parents work as a community to help children learn (Polson, 2001). Before the school year begins, Donene meets with parents at each family's home to prepare for the upcoming year, getting acquainted and establishing schedules to determine when parents can contribute to classroom instruction. At monthly teacher-parent meetings, Donene and the parents plan the curriculum and discuss children's progress. They brainstorm about community resources that can be used to promote children's learning.

Many students come back to tell Donene that experiences in her classroom made important contributions to their development and learning. For example, Luisa Magarian reflected on how her experience in Donene's classroom helped her work with others in high school:

> From having responsibility in groups, kids learn how to deal with problems and listen to each other or try to understand different points of view. They learn how to help a group work smoothly and how to keep people interested in what they are doing. . . . As coeditor of the student news magazine at my high school, I have to balance my eagerness to get things done with patience to work with other students. (Rogoff et al., 2001, pp. 84–85)

As Donene Polson's story shows, theories of cognitive development can form the basis of innovative instructional programs.

Preview

Examining the shape of children's development allows us to understand it better. This chapter—one of two on development—focuses on children's cognitive and language development. Before we delve into these topics, though, we need to explore some basic ideas about development.

LG 1 Define development and explain the main processes, periods, and issues in development, as well as links between development and education.

Twentieth-century Spanish-born American philosopher George Santayana once reflected, "Children are on a different plane. They belong to a generation and way of feeling properly their own." Let's explore what that plane is like.

EXPLORING WHAT DEVELOPMENT IS

Why study children's development? As a teacher, you will be responsible for a new wave of children each year in your classroom. The more you learn about children's development, the more you can understand at what level it is appropriate to teach them.

Just what do psychologists mean when they speak of a person's "development"? **Development** is the pattern of biological, cognitive, and socioemotional changes that begins at conception and continues through the life span. Most development involves growth, although it also eventually involves decay (dying).

PROCESSES AND PERIODS

The pattern of child development is complex because it is the product of several processes: biological, cognitive, and socioemotional. Development also can be described in terms of periods.

development The pattern of biological, cognitive, and socioemotional processes that begins at conception and continues through the life span. Most development involves growth, although it also eventually involves decay (dying).

Children are the legacy we leave for the time we will not live to see.

—Aristotle
Greek Philosopher, 4th Century B.C.

Biological, Cognitive, and Socioemotional Processes *Biological processes* produce changes in the child's body and underlie brain development, height and weight gains, motor skills, and puberty's hormonal changes. Genetic inheritance plays a large part.

Cognitive processes involve changes in the child's thinking, intelligence, and language. Cognitive developmental processes enable a growing child to memorize a poem, imagine how to solve a math problem, come up with a creative strategy, or speak meaningfully connected sentences.

Socioemotional processes involve changes in the child's relationships with other people, changes in emotion, and changes in personality. Parents' nurturance toward their child, a boy's aggressive attack on a peer, a girl's development of assertiveness, and an adolescent's feelings of joy after getting good grades all reflect socioemotional processes in development.

Biological, cognitive, and socioemotional processes are intertwined. Consider a child smiling in response to a parent's touch. This response depends on biological processes (the physical nature of the touch and responsiveness to it), cognitive processes (the ability to understand intentional acts), and socioemotional processes (the act of smiling often reflects a positive emotional feeling and smiling helps to connect us in positive ways with other human beings). Two rapidly emerging fields are exploring connections across biological, cognitive, and socioemotional processes:

- *developmental cognitive neuroscience,* which explores links between development, cognitive processes, and the brain (de Haan & Johnson, 2016). For example, later in this chapter you will learn about connections between developmental changes in regions of the brain and children's thinking.
- *developmental social neuroscience,* which examines connections between socioemotional processes, development, and the brain (Decety & Cowell, 2016; Monahan et al., 2016). Later in this chapter you will read about developmental changes in the brain and adolescents' risk-taking behavior and peer relations.

DEVELOPMENT

Periods of Development For the purposes of organization and understanding, we commonly describe development in terms of periods. In the most widely used system of classification, the developmental periods are infancy, early childhood, middle and late childhood, adolescence, early adulthood, middle adulthood, and late adulthood.

Infancy extends from birth to 18 to 24 months. It is a time of extreme dependence on adults. Many activities are just beginning, such as language development, symbolic thought, sensorimotor coordination, and social learning.

Early childhood (sometimes called the "preschool years") extends from the end of infancy to about 5 years. During this period, children become more self-sufficient, develop school readiness skills (such as learning to follow instructions and identify letters), and spend many hours with peers. First grade typically marks the end of early childhood.

Middle and late childhood (sometimes called the "elementary school years") extends from about 6 to 11 years of age. Children master the fundamental skills of reading, writing, and math, achievement becomes a more central theme, and self-control increases. In this period, children interact more with the wider social world beyond their family.

Adolescence is the development period that goes from childhood to adulthood, beginning around ages 10 to 12 and ending in the late teens. Adolescence starts with rapid physical changes, including height and weight gains and development of sexual functions. Adolescents intensely pursue independence and seek their own identity. Their thought becomes more abstract, logical, and idealistic.

In the 21st century, a transitional period—*emerging adulthood,* which occurs from approximately 18 to 25 years of age—has been described (Arnett, 2006, 2012, 2015). Experimentation and exploration characterize the emerging adult. At this point in

Periods of Development

Prenatal period (conception to birth)

Infancy (birth to 18–24 months)

Early childhood (2–5 years)

Middle and late childhood (6–11 years)

Adolescence (10–12 to 18–21 years)

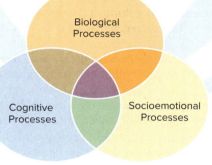

Processes of Development

FIGURE 1 PERIODS AND PROCESSES OF DEVELOPMENT

Development moves through the infancy, early childhood, middle and late childhood, and adolescence periods. These periods of development are the result of biological, cognitive, and socioemotional processes.

(*Left to Right*) Steve Allen/Brand X Pictures/Getty Images; Cohen/Ostrow/Digital Vision/Getty Images; Laurence Mouton/PhotoAlto/Getty Images; George Doyle/Stockbyte/Getty Images; SW Productions/Brand X Pictures/Getty Images

---

their development, many individuals are still exploring which career path they want to follow, what they want their identity to be, and which lifestyle they want to adopt (for example, being single, cohabiting, or getting married).

Adult developmental periods have been described, but this discussion is confined to the periods most relevant for children's and adolescents' education. The child and adolescent periods of human development are shown in Figure 1 along with the processes of development (biological, cognitive, and socioemotional). The interplay of these processes produces the periods of human development.

DEVELOPMENTAL ISSUES

Despite all of the knowledge that developmentalists have acquired, debate continues about the relative importance of factors that influence the developmental processes and about how the periods of development are related. The most important issues in the study of children's development include nature and nurture, continuity and discontinuity, and early and later experience.

Nature and Nurture The **nature-nurture issue** involves the debate about whether development is primarily influenced by nature or by nurture (Belsky & Pluess, 2016). *Nature* refers to an organism's biological inheritance, *nurture* to its environmental experiences. Almost no one today argues that development can be explained by nature or nurture alone. But some ("nature" proponents) claim that the most important

nature-nurture issue Nature refers to an organism's biological inheritance, nurture to environmental influences. The "nature" proponents claim biological inheritance is the most important influence on development; the "nurture" proponents claim environmental experiences are the most important.

Children are busy becoming something they have not quite grasped yet, something which keeps changing.

—Alastair Reid
American poet, 20th century

influence on development is biological inheritance, and others ("nurture" proponents) claim that environmental experiences are the most important influence.

According to the nature proponents, the range of environments can be vast, but an evolutionary and genetic blueprint produces commonalities in growth and development (Audesirk et al., 2017; Buss, 2015). We walk before we talk, speak one word before two words, grow rapidly in infancy and less so in early childhood, and experience a rush of sexual hormones in puberty. Extreme environments—those that are psychologically barren or hostile—can stunt development, but nature proponents emphasize the influence of tendencies that are genetically wired into humans.

By contrast, other psychologists emphasize the importance of nurture, or environmental experiences, in development (Burt et al., 2016). Experiences run the gamut from the individual's biological environment (nutrition, exercise, medical care, drugs, and physical accidents) to the social environment (family, peers, schools, community, media, and culture) (Gonzales et al., 2016; Pianta, 2016).

The **epigenetic view** states that development is the result of an ongoing, bidirectional interchange between heredity and the environment. Let's look at an example that reflects the epigenetic view. A baby inherits genes from both parents at conception. During childhood, environmental experiences such as nutrition, stress, learning, child care, and encouragement can modify genetic activity and the activity of the nervous system that directly underlies behavior. Heredity and environment thus operate together—or collaborate—to produce a child's intelligence, temperament, health, ability to read, and so on (Moore, 2015). While a genotype reflects a person's genetic make up, a phenotype is the observable result of the interaction of the genotype and environment.

Thus, if an attractive, popular, intelligent girl is elected president of her high school senior class, is her success due to heredity or to environment? Of course, the answer is "both." The relative contributions of heredity and environment are not quantifiable. That is, we can't say that such-and-such a percentage of nature and such-and-such a percentage of experience make us who we are. Nor is it accurate to say that full genetic expression happens once, at the time of conception or birth, after which we carry our genetic legacy into the world to see how far it takes us. Genes produce proteins throughout the life span, in many different environments. Or they don't produce these proteins, depending in part on how harsh or nourishing those environments are.

In developmental psychologist David Moore's (2013, 2015) view, the biological systems that generate behaviors are extremely complex but too often these systems have been described in overly simplified ways that can be misleading. Thus, although genetic factors clearly contribute to behavior and psychological processes, they don't determine these phenotypes independently from the contexts in which they develop. From Moore's (2013, 2015) perspective, it is misleading to talk about "genes for" eye color, intelligence, achievement, personality, or other characteristics. Moore commented that in retrospect we should not have expected to be able to make the giant leap from DNA's molecules to a complete understanding of human behavior any more than we should anticipate being able to easily link air molecules in a concert hall with a full-blown appreciation of a symphony's wondrous experience.

Imagine for a moment that there is a cluster of genes that are somehow associated with youth violence. (This example is hypothetical because we don't know of any such combination.) The adolescent who carries this genetic mixture might experience a world of loving parents, regular nutritious meals, lots of books, and a series of competent teachers. Or the adolescent's world might include parental neglect, a neighborhood in which gunshots and crime are everyday occurrences, and inadequate schooling. In which of these environments are the adolescent's genes likely to manufacture the biological underpinnings of criminality?

epigenetic view Development is seen as an ongoing, bidirectional interchange between heredity and the environment.

Are children completely at the mercy of their genes and environment as they develop? Their genetic heritage and environmental experiences are pervasive influences on their development (Raeff, 2017). However, children not only are the outcomes of their heredity and the environment they experience, but they also can author a unique developmental path by changing the environment.

> In reality, we are both the creatures and creators of our worlds. We are . . . the products of our genes and environments. Nevertheless, . . . the stream of causation that shapes the future runs through our present choices. . .
>
> Mind matters . . . Our hopes, goals, and expectations influence our future. (Myers, 2010, p. 168)

Continuity and Discontinuity The **continuity-discontinuity issue** focuses on the extent to which development involves gradual, cumulative change (continuity) or distinct stages (discontinuity). For the most part, developmentalists who emphasize nurture usually describe development as a gradual, continuous process, like the seedling's growth into an oak. Those who emphasize nature often describe development as a series of distinct stages, like the change from caterpillar to butterfly.

Consider continuity first. A child's first word, though seemingly an abrupt, discontinuous event, is actually the result of weeks and months of growth and practice. Puberty, another seemingly abrupt, discontinuous occurrence, is actually a gradual process occurring over several years.

Viewed in terms of discontinuity, each person is described as passing through a sequence of stages in which change is qualitatively rather than quantitatively different. A child moves at some point from not being able to think abstractly about the world to being able to. This is a qualitative, discontinuous change in development, not a quantitative, continuous change.

Early and Later Experience The **early-later experience issue** focuses on the degree to which early experiences (especially in infancy) or later experiences are the key determinants of the child's development. That is, if infants experience harmful circumstances, can those experiences be overcome by later, positive ones? Or are the early experiences so critical—possibly because they are the infant's first, prototypical experiences—that they cannot be overridden by a later, better environment?

The early-later experience issue has a long history and continues to be hotly debated among developmentalists (Kuhn & Lindenberger, 2016). Some developmentalists argue that unless infants experience warm, nurturing care during the first year or so of life, their development will never quite be optimal (O'Connor, 2016). In contrast, later-experience advocates argue that children are malleable throughout development and that later sensitive caregiving is just as important as earlier sensitive caregiving (Masten, 2016).

Evaluating the Developmental Issues Most developmentalists recognize that it is unwise to take an extreme position on the issues of nature and nurture, continuity and discontinuity, and early and later experiences. Development is not all nature or all nurture, not all continuity or all discontinuity, and not all early or later experiences. However, there is still spirited debate about how strongly development is influenced by each of these factors (Grigorenko et al., 2016).

DEVELOPMENT AND EDUCATION

The introductory chapter briefly described the importance of engaging in developmentally appropriate teaching practices. Here we expand on this important topic and discuss the concept of splintered development.

Developmentally appropriate teaching takes place at a level that is neither too difficult and stressful nor too easy and boring for the child's developmental level

continuity-discontinuity issue The issue regarding whether development involves gradual, cumulative change (continuity) or distinct stages (discontinuity).

early-later experience issue Involves the degree to which early experiences (especially infancy) or later experiences are the key determinants of the child's development.

> **Thinking Back/Thinking Forward**
>
> New guidelines exist for developmentally appropriate education Connect to "Social Contexts and Socioemotional Development."

(NAEYC, 2009). One of the challenges of developmentally appropriate teaching is that you likely will have students with an age range of several years and a range of abilities and skills in the classes you teach. Competent teachers are aware of these developmental differences. Rather than characterizing students as "advanced," "average," and "slow," they recognize that their development and ability are complex, and children often do not display the same competence across different skills.

Splintered development refers to the circumstances in which development is uneven across domains (Horowitz et al., 2005). One student may have excellent math skills but poor writing skills. Within the area of language, another student may have excellent verbal language skills but not have good reading and writing skills. Yet another student may do well in science but lack social skills.

Cognitively advanced students whose socioemotional development is at a level expected for much younger children present a special challenge. For example, a student may excel at science, math, and language but be immature emotionally. Such a child may not have any friends and be neglected or rejected by peers. This student will benefit considerably from having a teacher who helps him or her learn how to manage emotions and behave in more socially appropriate ways.

As we discuss development in this chapter and the next, keep in mind how the developmental changes we describe can help you understand the optimal level for teaching and learning. For example, it is not a good strategy to try to push children to read before they are developmentally ready—but when they are ready, reading materials should be presented at the appropriate level.

Review, Reflect, and Practice

 Define development and explain the main processes, periods, and issues in development, as well as links between development and education.

REVIEW
- What is the nature of development?
- What three broad processes interact in a child's development? What general periods do children go through between birth and the end of adolescence?
- What are the main developmental issues? What conclusions can be reached about these issues?
- What implications does the concept of development have for the notion of "appropriate" learning?

REFLECT
- Imagine you are working with a Tim, who is a second grader struggling with reading comprehension. How might his academic challenges impact his feelings about reading and himself as a reader? Now imagine you are working with Alex, an eighth grader who is picked on by her peers. How might her negative interactions with peers impact her ability to work with others and learn in small groups?

PRAXIS™ PRACTICE
1. Mr. Huxtaby is giving a talk on development to a parent-teacher organization. In his talk, which of the following is he most likely to describe as not being an example of development?
   a. pubertal change
   b. improvement in memory
   c. change in friendship
   d. an inherited tendency to be shy

splintered development The circumstances in which development is uneven across domains.

Review, Reflect, and Practice

2. Ms. Halle teaches third grade. Which period of development is likely to be of most interest to her?
   a. infancy
   b. early childhood
   c. middle childhood and late childhood
   d. adolescence

3. Piaget argued that children progress through a series of cognitive development stages. In contrast, Skinner stressed that individuals simply learn more as time goes on. Which developmental issue is highlighted in their disagreement?
   a. continuity and discontinuity
   b. early and later experience
   c. nature and nurture
   d. biological and socioemotional development

4. Alexander's scores on standardized mathematics achievement tests are always very high—among the highest in the nation. In contrast, his scores on reading achievement tests indicate that he is about average. This is an example of
   a. developmentally appropriate teaching
   b. early versus later development
   c. nature versus nurture
   d. splintered development

Please see answer key at end of book . . . .

2 COGNITIVE DEVELOPMENT

LG 2 Discuss the development of the brain and compare the cognitive developmental theories of Jean Piaget and Lev Vygotsky.

Twentieth-century American poet Marianne Moore said that the mind is "an enchanting thing." How this enchanting thing develops has intrigued many psychologists. First, we explore increasing interest in the development of the brain and then turn to two major cognitive theories—Piaget's and Vygotsky's.

THE BRAIN

Not long ago, scientists thought that our genes primarily determine how our brains are "wired" and that the cells in the brain responsible for processing information just develop on their own with little or no input from environmental experiences. According to that view, whatever brain your genes have provided to you, you are essentially stuck with it. That view of the brain, however, turned out to be wrong. Instead, it is clear that the brain has plasticity and its development depends on contexts and experiences children engage in (de Haan & Johnson, 2016; Goddings & Mills, 2017).

In the increasingly popular **neuroconstructivist view**, (a) biological processes (genes, for example) and environmental experiences (enriched or impoverished, for example) influence the brain's development; (b) the brain has plasticity (the ability to change) and depends on experience; and (c) development of the brain is linked closely with cognitive development. These factors constrain or advance the construction of cognitive skills (Karmiloff-Smith, 2017; Monahan et al., 2016). In other words, what children do can change the development of their brains.

neuroconstructivist view Emphasizes that brain development is influenced by both biological processes and environmental experiences; the brain has plasticity and depends on experience; and brain development is linked closely with cognitive development.

36 Chapter 2 Cognitive and Language Development

Development of Neurons and Brain Regions The number and size of the brain's nerve endings continue to increase at least into adolescence. Some of the brain's growth in size also is due to **myelination**, the process of encasing many cells in the brain with a myelin sheath (see Figure 2). This increases the speed at which information travels through the nervous system (Fields, 2015). Myelination in brain areas important in focusing attention is not complete until about 10 years of age. The implications for teaching are that children will have difficulty focusing their attention and maintaining it for very long in early childhood, but their attention will improve as they move through the elementary school years. The most extensive increase in myelination, which occurs in the brain's frontal lobes where reasoning and thinking occur, takes place during adolescence (Galvan & Tottenham, 2016).

Another important aspect of the brain's development at the cellular level is the dramatic increase in connections between neurons (nerve cells). *Synapses* are tiny gaps between neurons where connections between neurons are made. Researchers have discovered an interesting aspect of synaptic connections. Nearly twice as many of these connections are made than will ever be used (Huttenlocher & Dabholkar, 1997). The connections that are used become stronger and survive, whereas the unused ones are replaced by other pathways or disappear. In the language of neuroscience, these connections are "pruned." Figure 3 vividly shows the dramatic growth and later pruning of synapses in the visual, auditory, and prefrontal cortex areas of the brain. These areas are critical for higher-order cognitive functioning such as learning, memory, and reasoning. Notice that in the **prefrontal cortex** (where higher-level thinking and self-regulation take place) it is not until middle to late adolescence that the adult density of the synapses is achieved.

Figure 4 shows the location of the brain's four lobes. As just indicated, growth in the prefrontal cortex (the front region of the frontal lobes) continues through adolescence. Rapid growth in the temporal lobes (language processing) and parietal lobes (spatial location) occurs from age 6 through puberty.

Brain Development in Middle and Late Childhood Total brain volume stabilizes by the end of middle and late childhood, but significant changes in various structures and regions of the brain continue to occur as brain growth tapers off (Wendelken et al., 2016).

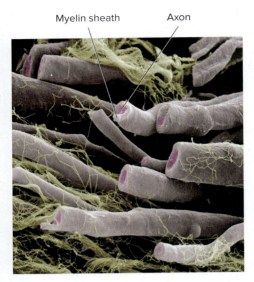

FIGURE 2 MYELINATED NEURON FIBER

The myelin sheath, shown in grey, encases the axon (pink). This image was produced by an electron microscope that magnified the nerve fiber 12,000 times. *What role does myelination play in the brain's development?*

Steve Gschmeissner/Science Photo Library/Getty Images

DEVELOPMENT

myelination The process of encasing many cells in the brain with a myelin sheath that increases the speed at which information travels through the nervous system.

prefrontal cortex The front region of the frontal lobes; involved in reasoning, decision making, and self-control.

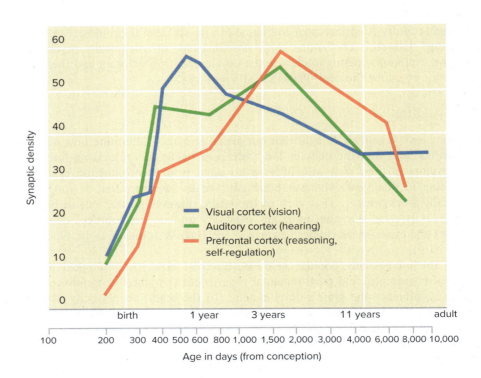

FIGURE 3 SYNAPTIC DENSITY IN THE HUMAN BRAIN FROM INFANCY TO ADULTHOOD

The graph shows the dramatic increase and then pruning of synaptic density for three regions of the brain: visual cortex, auditory cortex, and prefrontal cortex. Synaptic density is believed to be an important indication of the extent of connectivity between neurons.

In particular, the brain pathways and circuitry involving the prefrontal cortex continue to increase in middle and late childhood. These advances in the prefrontal cortex are linked to children's improved attention, reasoning, and cognitive control (Monahan et al., 2016).

Leading researchers in developmental cognitive neuroscience have proposed that the prefrontal cortex likely orchestrates the functions of many other brain regions during development (de Haan & Johnson, 2016). As part of this organizational role, the prefrontal cortex may provide an advantage to neural networks and connections that include the prefrontal cortex. In this view, the prefrontal cortex coordinates which neural connections are the most effective for solving a problem.

Links between the changing brain and children's cognitive development involve activation of some brain areas, with some areas increasing in activation while others decrease (de Haan & Johnson, 2016). One shift in activation that occurs as children develop in middle and late childhood is from diffuse, larger areas to more focal, smaller areas. This shift is characterized by synaptic pruning in which areas of the brain not being used lose synaptic connections and those being used gain additional connections. The increased focal activation is linked to improved cognitive performance, especially in *cognitive control,* which involves flexible and effective control in a number of areas (Durston et al., 2006). These areas include controlling attention, reducing interfering thoughts, inhibiting motor actions, and flexibility in switching between competing choices (Casey, 2015).

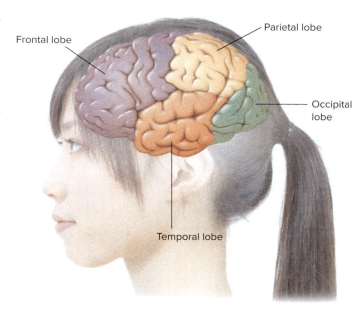

FIGURE 4 THE BRAIN'S FOUR LOBES

Shown here are the locations of the brain's four lobes: frontal, occipital, temporal, and parietal.
Takayuki/Shutterstock

Brain Development in Adolescence Along with the rest of the body, the brain is changing in adolescence. As noted earlier, the connections between neurons are "pruned" as children and adolescents develop. As a result of this pruning, by the end of adolescence individuals have "fewer, more selective, more effective connections between neurons than they did as children" (Kuhn, 2009). And this pruning means that the activities adolescents engage in and don't engage in influence which neural connections will be strengthened and which will disappear.

Using fMRI brain scans, scientists have recently discovered that adolescents' brains undergo significant structural changes (Crone, 2017; Monahan et al., 2016). The **corpus callosum**, where fibers connect the brain's left and right hemispheres, thickens in adolescence, and this improves adolescents' ability to process information (Chavarria et al., 2014). Earlier we discussed advances in the development of the prefrontal cortex in childhood. However, the prefrontal cortex doesn't finish maturing until the emerging adult years, approximately 18 to 25 years of age, or later (Steinberg, 2015a, b).

At a lower, subcortical level, the **limbic system**, which is the seat of emotions and where rewards are experienced, matures much earlier than the prefrontal cortex and is almost completely developed in early adolescence (Monahan et al., 2016). The limbic system structure that is especially involved in emotion is the **amygdala**. Figure 5 shows the locations of the corpus callosum, prefrontal cortex, limbic system, and amygdala.

Leading researcher Charles Nelson (2011) points out that although adolescents are capable of very strong emotions, their prefrontal cortex hasn't adequately developed to the point at which they can control these passions. This means that the brain region for putting the brakes on risky, impulsive behavior is still under construction during adolescence. Or consider this interpretation of the development of emotion and cognition in adolescence: "early activation of strong 'turbo-charged' feelings with a relatively unskilled set of 'driving skills' or cognitive abilities to modulate strong emotions and motivations" (Dahl, 2004, p. 18). This developmental disjunction may account for increased risk taking and other problems in adolescence (Steinberg, 2015a, b).

> **Thinking Back/Thinking Forward**
>
> A surge of interest surrounds identification of the aspects of the brain that are involved in intelligence. Connect to "Individual Variations."

corpus callosum The brain region where fibers connect the left and right hemispheres.

limbic system Brain region that is the seat of emotions and in which rewards are experienced.

amygdala The seat of emotions in the brain.

38 Chapter 2 Cognitive and Language Development

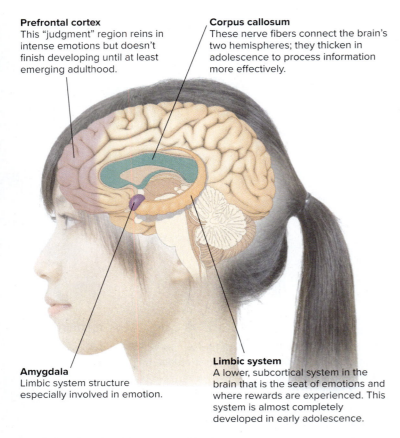

Prefrontal cortex
This "judgment" region reins in intense emotions but doesn't finish developing until at least emerging adulthood.

Corpus callosum
These nerve fibers connect the brain's two hemispheres; they thicken in adolescence to process information more effectively.

Amygdala
Limbic system structure especially involved in emotion.

Limbic system
A lower, subcortical system in the brain that is the seat of emotions and where rewards are experienced. This system is almost completely developed in early adolescence.

FIGURE 5 THE CHANGING ADOLESCENT BRAIN: PREFRONTAL CORTEX, LIMBIC SYSTEM, AMYGDALA, AND CORPUS CALLOSUM
Takayuki/Shutterstock

lateralization Specialization of functions in each hemisphere of the brain.

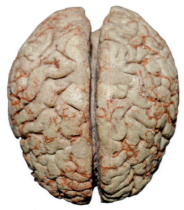

FIGURE 6 THE HUMAN BRAIN'S TWO HEMISPHERES
The two halves (hemispheres) of the human brain are clearly seen in this photograph.
IgorZD/Shutterstock

Lateralization The cerebral cortex (the outer surface of the brain that is at the highest level of the central nervous system) is divided into two halves, or hemispheres (see Figure 6). **Lateralization** is the specialization of functions in each hemisphere of the brain (Francks, 2016). In individuals with an intact brain, there is a specialization of function in some areas.

The most extensive research on the brain's two hemispheres involves language. In most individuals, speech and grammar are localized to the left hemisphere. However, not all language processing is carried out in the brain's left hemisphere (Moore et al., 2014). For example, understanding such aspects of language as appropriate use of language in different contexts, evaluation of the emotional expressiveness of language, and much of humor involves the right hemisphere (Godfrey & Grimshaw, 2016). Also, when individuals lose much of their left hemisphere because of an accident, surgery for epilepsy, or other reasons, the right hemisphere in many cases can reconfigure itself for increased language processing (Xing et al., 2016).

Because of the differences in functioning of the brain's two hemispheres, people commonly use the phrases "left-brained" and "right-brained" to suggest that one hemisphere is dominant. Unfortunately, much of this talk is greatly exaggerated. For example, laypeople and the media commonly exaggerate hemispheric specialization by claiming that the left brain is logical and the right brain is creative. However, most complex functioning—such as logical and creative thinking—in normal people involves communication between both sides of the brain. Scientists who study the brain are typically very cautious when using terms such as *left-brained* and *right-brained* because the brain is more complex than those terms suggest.

Plasticity As we have seen, the brain has plasticity (de Haan & Johnson, 2016; Nagel & Scholes, 2017). Children's experiences can affect how their brains develop. By engaging students in optimal learning environments, you can stimulate brain development.

The remarkable case of Michael Rehbein illustrates the brain's plasticity. When Michael was 4½, he began to experience uncontrollable seizures—as many as 400 a day. Doctors said that the only solution was to remove the left hemisphere of his brain, where the seizures were occurring. Michael had his first major surgery at age 7 and another at age 10. Although recovery was slow, his right hemisphere began to reorganize and eventually took over functions, such as speech, that normally occur in the brain's left hemisphere (see Figure 7). Individuals like Michael are living proof of the growing brain's remarkable plasticity and ability to adapt and recover from a loss of brain tissue.

The Brain and Children's Education Unfortunately, too often statements about the implications of brain science for children's education have been speculative at best and often far removed from what neuroscientists know about the brain (Busso & Pollack, 2015; Gleichgerrcht et al., 2015). We don't have to look any further than the hype about "left-brained" individuals being more logical and "right-brained" individuals being more creative to see that links between neuroscience and brain education are incorrectly made (Sousa, 1995).

Another commonly promoted link between neuroscience and brain education is that there is a critical, or sensitive, period—a biological window of opportunity—when learning is easier, more effective, and more easily retained than later in development. However, some experts on the development of the brain and learning conclude that the critical period view is exaggerated. One leading neuroscientist even told educators that although children's brains acquire a great deal of information during the early years, most learning likely takes place after synaptic formation stabilizes, which is after the age of 10 (Goldman-Rakic, 1996).

A major issue involving the development of the brain is which comes first, biological changes in the brain or experiences that stimulate these changes (Lerner et al., 2008)? Consider a study in which the prefrontal cortex thickened and more brain connections formed when adolescents resisted peer pressure (Paus et al., 2008). Scientists have yet to determine whether the brain changes come first or whether the brain changes are the result of experiences with peers, parents, and others. Once again, we encounter the nature/nurture issue that is so prominent in examining children's and adolescents' development.

Given all of the hype about brain education in the media, what can we conclude about the current state of knowledge in applying the rapidly increasing research on the brain's development to education? Based on the current state of knowledge:

- *Both early and later experiences, including educational experiences, are very important in the brain's development.* Significant changes continue to occur at the cellular and structural level in the brain through adolescence.

- *Synaptic connections between neurons can change dramatically as a consequence of the learning experiences children and adolescents have.* Connections between neurons that are used when children focus their attention, remember, and think as they are reading, writing, and doing math are strengthened; those that aren't used are replaced by other pathways or disappear.

- *Development at the highest level of the brain—the prefrontal cortex, where such important cognitive processes as thinking, reasoning, and decision making primarily occur—continues at least through the emerging adult years* (Monahan et al., 2016). This development in the prefrontal cortex moves from being more diffuse to more focal and involves increased efficiency of processing information (de Haan & Johnson, 2016). As activation in the prefrontal cortex becomes more focused, cognitive control increases. This is exemplified in children being able to focus their attention more effectively and ignore distractions while they are learning as they become older.

- *Despite the increased focal activation of the prefrontal cortex as children grow older, changes in the brain during adolescence present a challenge to increased cognitive control.* In adolescence, the earlier maturation of the limbic system and the amygdala, which are involved in processing of emotions, and the more drawn-out development of the prefrontal cortex, provide an explanation of the difficulty adolescents have in controlling their emotions and their tendency to engage in risk-taking behavior (Monahan et al., 2016).

- *Brain functioning occurs along specific pathways and involves integration of function.* According to leading experts Kurt Fischer and Mary Helen Immordino-Yang (2008),

    One of the lessons of educational neuroscience, even at this early point in its development, is that children learn along specific pathways, but they do not act or think in compartments. . . . On the one hand, they develop their learning along specific pathways defined by particular content, such as mathematics or history, but on the other hand they make connections between those pathways.

Reading is an excellent example of how brain functioning occurs along specific pathways and is integrated. Consider a child who is asked by a teacher to read aloud to the class. Input from the child's eyes is transmitted to the child's brain, then passed through many brain systems, which translate the patterns of black and white into codes for letters, words, and associations. The output occurs in the form of messages to the child's lips and tongue. The child's own gift of speech is possible because brain systems are organized in ways that permit language processing.

(a)

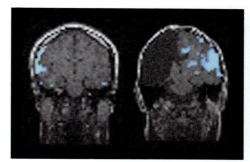

(b)

FIGURE 7 PLASTICITY IN THE BRAIN'S HEMISPHERES

(a) Michael Rehbein at 14 years of age. (b) Michael's right hemisphere (*top*) has reorganized to take over the language functions normally carried out by corresponding areas in the left hemisphere of an intact brain (*bottom*). However, the right hemisphere is not as efficient as the left, and more areas of the brain are recruited to process speech.
Courtesy of The Rehbein Family

What are some applications of research on brain development to children's education?
Corbis/age fotostock

These conclusions suggest that education throughout the childhood and adolescent years can benefit children's and adolescents' learning and cognitive development (Monahan et al., 2016). Where appropriate throughout the rest of the book, we will discuss research involving the development of the brain and children's education.

PIAGET'S THEORY

Poet Noah Perry once asked, "Who knows the thoughts of a child?" More than anyone, the famous Swiss psychologist Jean Piaget (1896–1980) knew.

Cognitive Processes What processes do children use as they construct their knowledge of the world? Piaget stressed that these processes are especially important in this regard: schemas, assimilation and accommodation, organization, and equilibration.

Schemas Piaget (1954) said that as the child seeks to construct an understanding of the world, the developing brain creates **schemas**. These are actions or mental representations that organize knowledge. In Piaget's theory, behavioral schemas (physical activities) characterize infancy, and mental schemas (cognitive activities) develop in childhood. A baby's schemas are structured by simple actions that can be performed on objects, such as sucking, looking, and grasping. Older children have schemas that include strategies and plans for solving problems. For example, a 6-year-old might have a schema that involves the strategy of classifying objects by size, shape, or color. By the time we have reached adulthood, we have constructed an enormous number of diverse schemas, ranging from how to drive a car, to how to balance a budget, to the concept of fairness.

Assimilation and Accommodation To explain how children use and adapt their schemas, Piaget offered two concepts: assimilation and accommodation. **Assimilation** occurs when children incorporate new information into their existing schemas. **Accommodation** occurs when children adjust their schemas to fit new information and experiences.

Consider an 8-year-old girl who is given a hammer and nail to hang a picture on the wall. She has never used a hammer, but from observing others do this she realizes that a hammer is an object to be held, that it is swung by the handle to hit the nail, and that it usually is swung a number of times. Recognizing each of these things, she fits her behavior into this schema she already has (assimilation). But the hammer is heavy, so she holds it near the top. She swings too hard and the nail bends, so she adjusts the pressure of her strikes. These adjustments reflect her ability to slightly alter her conception of the world (accommodation). Just as both assimilation and accommodation are required in this example, so are they required in many of the child's thinking challenges (see Figure 8).

Organization To make sense out of their world, said Piaget, children cognitively organize their experiences. **Organization** in Piaget's theory is the grouping of isolated behaviors and thoughts into a higher-order system. Continual refinement of this organization is an inherent part of development. A boy with only a vague idea about how to use a hammer also may have a vague idea about how to use other tools. After learning how to use each one, he relates these uses, organizing his knowledge.

Equilibration and Stages of Development **Equilibration** is a mechanism that Piaget proposed to explain how children shift from one stage of thought to the next. The shift occurs as children experience cognitive conflict, or disequilibrium, in trying to understand the world. Eventually, they resolve the conflict and reach a balance, or equilibrium, of thought. Piaget pointed out that there is considerable movement between states of cognitive

schemas In Piaget's theory, actions or mental representations that organize knowledge.

assimilation Piagetian concept of the incorporation of new information into existing knowledge (schemas).

accommodation Piagetian concept of adjusting schemas to fit new information and experiences.

organization Piaget's concept of grouping isolated behaviors into a higher-order, more smoothly functioning cognitive system; the grouping or arranging of items into categories.

equilibration A mechanism that Piaget proposed to explain how children shift from one stage of thought to the next. The shift occurs as children experience cognitive conflict, or disequilibrium, in trying to understand the world. Eventually, they resolve the conflict and reach a balance, or equilibrium, of thought.

equilibrium and disequilibrium as assimilation and accommodation work in concert to produce cognitive change. For example, if a child believes that the amount of a liquid changes simply because the liquid is poured into a container with a different shape—for instance, from a container that is short and wide into a container that is tall and narrow—she might be puzzled by such issues as where the "extra" liquid came from and whether there is actually more liquid to drink. The child will eventually resolve these puzzles as her thinking becomes more advanced. In the everyday world, the child is constantly faced with such counterexamples and inconsistencies.

Assimilation and accommodation always take the child to a higher ground. For Piaget, the motivation for change is an internal search for equilibrium. As old schemas are adjusted and new schemas are developed, the child organizes and reorganizes the old and new schemas. Eventually, the organization is fundamentally different from the old organization; it is a new way of thinking.

Thus, the result of these processes, according to Piaget, is that individuals go through four stages of development. A different way of understanding the world makes one stage more advanced than another. Cognition is *qualitatively* different in one stage compared with another. In other words, the way children reason at one stage is different from the way they reason at another stage.

Piagetian Stages Each of Piaget's stages is age-related and consists of distinct ways of thinking. Piaget proposed four stages of cognitive development: sensorimotor, preoperational, concrete operational, and formal operational (see Figure 9).

Assimilation occurs when people incorporate new information into their existing schematic knowledge. *How might this 8-year-old girl first attempt to use the hammer and nail, based on her preexisting schematic knowledge about these objects?*

Accommodation occurs when people adjust their knowledge schemas to new information. *How might the girl adjust her schemas regarding hammers and nails during her successful effort to hang the picture?*

FIGURE 8   ASSIMILATION AND ACCOMMODATION

Sensorimotor Stage

The infant constructs an understanding of the world by coordinating sensory experiences with physical actions. An infant progresses from reflexive, instinctual action at birth to the beginning of symbolic thought toward the end of the stage.

Birth to 2 Years of Age

Preoperational Stage

The child begins to represent the world with words and images. These words and images reflect increased symbolic thinking and go beyond the connection of sensory information and physical action.

2 to 7 Years of Age

Concrete Operational Stage

The child can now reason logically about concrete events and classify objects into different sets.

7 to 11 Years of Age

Formal Operational Stage

The adolescent reasons in more abstract, idealistic, and logical ways.

11 Years of Age Through Adulthood

FIGURE 9   THE FOUR PIAGETIAN STAGES OF COGNITIVE DEVELOPMENT

(*Left to Right*) Stockbyte/Getty Images; Jacobs Stock Photography/BananaStock/Getty Images; Fuse/image100/Corbis; Purestock/Getty Images

DEVELOPMENT

The Sensorimotor Stage The **sensorimotor stage**, which lasts from birth to about 2 years of age, is the first Piagetian stage. In this stage, infants construct an understanding of the world by coordinating their sensory experiences (such as seeing and hearing) with their motor actions (reaching, touching)—hence the term *sensorimotor*. At the beginning of this stage, infants show little more than reflexive patterns to adapt to the world. By the end of the stage, they display far more complex sensorimotor patterns.

The Preoperational Stage The **preoperational stage** is the second Piagetian stage. Lasting approximately from about 2 to 7 years of age, it is more symbolic than sensorimotor thought but does not involve operational thought. However, it is egocentric and intuitive rather than logical.

Preoperational thought can be subdivided into two substages: symbolic function and intuitive thought. The **symbolic function substage** occurs roughly between 2 and 4 years of age. In this substage, the young child gains the ability to represent mentally an object that is not present. This stretches the child's mental world to new dimensions. Expanded use of language and the emergence of pretend play are other examples of an increase in symbolic thought during this early childhood substage. Young children begin to use scribbled designs to represent people, houses, cars, clouds, and many other aspects of the world. Possibly because young children are not very concerned about reality, their drawings are fanciful and inventive (Winner, 1986). One 3½-year-old looked at the scribble he had just drawn and described it as a pelican kissing a seal (see Figure 10a). In the elementary school years, children's drawings become more realistic, neat, and precise (see Figure 10b).

Even though young children make distinct progress in this substage, their preoperational thought still has an important limitation: egocentrism. *Egocentrism* is the inability to distinguish between one's own perspective and someone else's perspective. Piaget and Barbel Inhelder (1969) initially studied young children's egocentrism by devising the three mountains task (see Figure 11). The child walks around the model of the mountains and becomes familiar with what the mountains look like from different perspectives. The child also can see that there are different objects on the mountains. The child then is seated on one side of the table on which the mountains are placed. The experimenter moves a doll to different locations around the table. At each location, the child is asked to select from a series of photos the one that most accurately reflects the view the doll is seeing. Children in the preoperational stage often pick the view that reflects where they are sitting rather than the doll's view.

What further cognitive changes take place in the preoperational stage? The **intuitive thought substage** is the second substage of preoperational thought, starting at about 4 years of age and lasting until about 7 years of age. At this substage, children begin to use primitive reasoning and want to know the answers to all sorts of questions. Piaget called this substage "intuitive" because children seem so sure about their knowledge and understanding yet are unaware of how they know what they know. That is, they say they know something but know it without the use of rational thinking.

Many of these preoperational examples show a characteristic of thought called **centration**, which involves focusing (or centering) attention on one characteristic to the exclusion of all others. Centration is most clearly present in preoperational children's lack of **conservation**, the idea that some characteristic of an object stays the same even though the object might change in appearance. For example, to

sensorimotor stage The first Piagetian stage, lasting from birth to about 2 years of age, when infants construct an understanding of the world by coordinating sensory experiences with motor actions.

preoperational stage The second Piagetian stage, lasting from about 2 to 7 years of age, when symbolic thought increases and operational thought is not yet present.

symbolic function substage The first substage of preoperational thought, occurring between about 2 and 4 years of age; the ability to represent an object not present develops a symbolic thinking increases; egocentrism is present.

intuitive thought substage The second substage of preoperational thought, lasting from about 4 to 7 years of age. Children begin to use primitive reasoning and want to know the answer to all sorts of questions. They seem sure about their knowledge in this substage but are unaware of how they know what they know.

centration Focusing, or centering, attention on one characteristic to the exclusion of all others; characteristic of preoperational thinking.

conservation The idea that some characteristic of an object stays the same even though the object might change in appearance; a cognitive ability that develops in the concrete operational stage, according to Piaget.

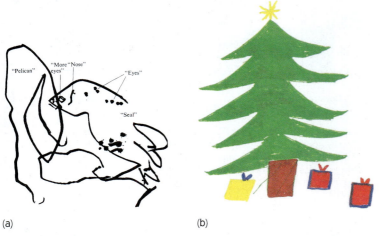

FIGURE 10 COGNITIVE DEVELOPMENTAL CHANGES IN CHILDREN'S DRAWINGS

(a) A 3½-year-old's symbolic drawing. Halfway into this drawing, the 3½-year-old artist said it was "a pelican kissing a seal." (b) This 11-year-old's drawing is neater and more realistic but also less inventive.

Wolf, D. P. *Drawing from the symbolic drawings of young children.*

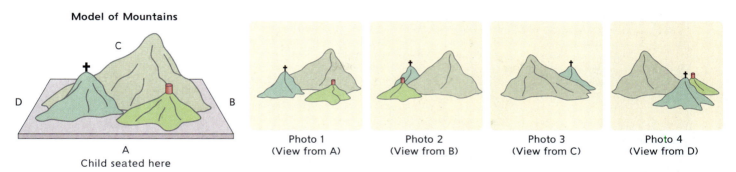

FIGURE 11 PIAGET'S THREE MOUNTAINS TASK

The mountain model on the far left shows the child's perspective from view A, where he or she is sitting. The four squares represent photos showing the mountains from four different viewpoints of the model—A, B, C, and D. The experimenter asks the child to identify the photo in which the mountains look as they would from position B. To identity the photo correctly, the child has to take the perspective of a person sitting at spot B. Invariably, a child who thinks in a preoperational way cannot perform this task. When asked what a view of the mountains looks like from position B, the child selects Photo 1, taken from location A (the child's own view at the time) instead of Photo 2, the correct view.

adults it is obvious that a certain amount of liquid stays the same regardless of a container's shape. But this is not obvious at all to young children. Rather, they are struck by the height of the liquid in the container. In this type of conservation task (Piaget's most famous), a child is presented with two identical beakers, each filled to the same level with liquid (see Figure 12). The child is asked if the beakers have the same amount of liquid. The child usually says yes. Then the liquid from one beaker is poured into a third beaker, which is taller and thinner. The child now is asked if the amount of liquid in the tall, thin beaker is equal to the liquid that remains in the second original beaker. Children younger than 7 or 8 usually say no. They justify their answer by referring to the differing height or width of the beakers. Older children usually answer yes. They justify their answers appropriately: If you poured the liquid back, the amount would still be the same.

In Piaget's view, failing the conservation of liquid task indicates that the child is at the preoperational stage of thinking. Passing the test suggests the child is at the concrete operational stage of thinking.

According to Piaget, preoperational children also cannot perform what he called *operations*. In Piaget's theory, operations are mental representations that are reversible.

As in the beaker task, preschool children have difficulty understanding that reversing an action brings about the original conditions from which the action began. These two examples should further help you understand Piaget's concepts of operations. A young child might know that $4 + 2 = 6$ but not understand that the reverse, $6 - 2 = 4$, is true. Or let's say a preschooler walks to his friend's house each day but always gets a ride home. If asked to walk home from his friend's house, he probably would reply that he didn't know the way because he never had walked home before.

Some developmentalists do not believe Piaget was entirely correct in his estimate of when conservation skills emerge. For example, Rochel Gelman (1969) trained preschool children to attend to relevant aspects of the conservation task. This improved their conservation skills.

Further, children show considerable variation in attaining conservation skills. Researchers have found that 50 percent of children develop conservation of mass at 6 to 9 years of age, 50 percent demonstrate conservation of length at 4 to 9 years of age, 50 percent show conservation of area at 7 to 9 years of age, and 50 percent of children don't attain conservation of weight until 8 to 10 years of age (Horowitz et al., 2005; Sroufe et al., 1992).

Yet another characteristic of preoperational children is that they ask a lot of questions. The barrage begins around age 3. By about 5, they have just about exhausted

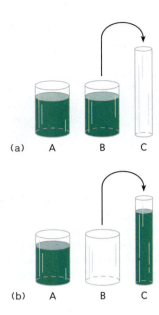

FIGURE 12 PIAGET'S CONSERVATION TASK

The beaker test is a well-known Piagetian test to determine whether a child can think operationally—that is, can mentally reverse actions and show conservation of the substance. (a) Two identical beakers are presented to the child. Then, the experimenter pours the liquid from B into C, which is taller and thinner than A or B. (b) The child is asked if these beakers (A and C) have the same amount of liquid. The preoperational child says "no." When asked to point to the beaker that has more liquid, the preoperational child points to the tall, thin beaker.

Tony Freeman/PhotoEdit

the adults around them with "Why?" "Why" questions signal the emergence of the child's interest in figuring out why things are the way they are. Following is a sampling of 4- to 6-year-olds' questions (Elkind, 1976):

"What makes you grow up?"
"Who was the mother when everybody was a baby?"
"Why do leaves fall?"
"Why does the sun shine?"

CONNECTING WITH STUDENTS: Best Practices
Strategies for Working with Preoperational Thinkers

As you have just read, young children think on a different plane from older children. Following are some effective strategies for advancing young children's thinking.

1. *Ask children to make comparisons.* These might involve such concepts as bigger, taller, wider, heavier, and longer.
2. *Give children experience in ordering operations.* For example, have children line up in rows from tall to short and vice versa. Bring in various examples of animal and plant life cycles, such as several photographs of butterfly development or the sprouting of beans or kernels of corn.
3. *Have children draw scenes with perspective.* Encourage them to make the objects in their drawings appear to be at the same location as in the scene they are viewing. For example, if they see a horse at the end of a field, they should place the horse in the same location in the drawing.
4. *Construct an inclined plane or a hill.* Let children roll marbles of various sizes down the plane. Ask them to compare how quickly the different-size marbles reach the bottom. This should help them understand the concept of speed.
5. *Ask children to justify their answers when they draw conclusions.* For example, when they say that pouring a liquid from a short, wide container into a tall, thin container makes the liquid change in volume, ask, "Why do you think so?" or "How could you prove this to one of your friends?"

The Concrete Operational Stage The **concrete operational stage**, the third Piagetian stage of cognitive development, lasts from about 7 to about 11 years of age. Concrete operational thought involves using operations. Logical reasoning replaces intuitive reasoning, but only in concrete situations. Classification skills are present, but abstract problems go unsolved.

A concrete operation is a reversible mental action pertaining to real, concrete objects. Concrete operations allow the child to coordinate several characteristics rather than focus on a single property of an object. At the concrete operational level, children can do mentally what they previously could do only physically, and they can reverse concrete operations.

An important concrete operation is classifying or dividing things into different sets or subsets and considering their interrelationships. Reasoning about a family tree of four generations reveals a child's concrete operational skills (Furth & Wachs, 1975). The family tree shown in Figure 13 suggests that the grandfather (A) has three children (B, C, and D), each of whom has two children (E through J), and one of these children (J) has three children (K, L, and M). Concrete operational thinkers understand the classification. For example, they can reason that person J can at the same time be father, brother, and grandson. A preoperational thinker cannot.

Some Piagetian tasks require children to reason about relations between classes. One such task is **seriation**, the concrete operation that involves ordering stimuli along some quantitative dimension (such as length). To see if students can serialize, a teacher might place eight sticks of different lengths in a haphazard way on a table. The teacher then asks the student to order the sticks by length. Many young children end up with two or three small groups of "big" sticks or "little" sticks rather than a correct ordering of all eight sticks. Another mistaken strategy they use is to evenly line up the tops of the sticks but ignore the bottoms. The concrete operational thinker simultaneously understands that each stick must be longer than the one that precedes it and shorter than the one that follows it.

Transitivity involves the ability to reason about and logically combine relationships. If a relation holds between a first object and a second object, and also holds between the second object and a third object, then it also holds between the first and third objects. For example, consider three sticks (A, B, and C) of differing lengths. A is the longest, B is intermediate in length, and C is the shortest. Does the child understand that if A is longer than B, and B is longer than C, then A is longer than C? In Piaget's theory, concrete operational thinkers do; preoperational thinkers do not.

The Formal Operational Stage The **formal operational stage**, which emerges at about 11 to 15 years of age, is Piaget's fourth and final cognitive stage. At this stage, individuals move beyond reasoning only about concrete experiences and think in more abstract, idealistic, and logical ways.

The abstract quality of formal operational thinking is evident in verbal problem solving. The concrete operational thinker needs to see the concrete elements A, B, and C to make the logical inference that if A = B and B = C, then A = C. In contrast, the formal operational thinker can solve this problem when it is verbally presented. Accompanying the abstract nature of formal operational thought are the abilities to idealize and imagine possibilities. At this stage, adolescents engage in extended speculation about the ideal qualities they desire in themselves and others. These idealistic thoughts may be expressed in fantasy. Many adolescents become impatient with their newfound ideals and the problems of how to live them out.

At the same time that adolescents are thinking more abstractly and idealistically, they also are beginning to think more logically. As formal operational thinkers, they

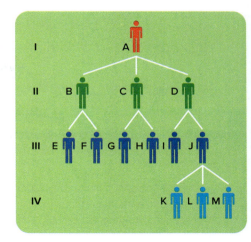

FIGURE 13 CLASSIFICATION
A family tree of four generations (*I to IV*): The preoperational child has trouble classifying the members of the four generations; the concrete operational child can classify the members vertically, horizontally, and obliquely (up and down and across). For example, the concrete operational child understands that a family member can be a son, a brother, and a father, all at the same time.

concrete operational stage Piaget's third cognitive developmental stage, occurring between about 7 and 11 years of age. At this stage, the child thinks operationally, and logical reasoning replaces intuitive thought but only in concrete situations; classification skills are present, but abstract problems present difficulties.

seriation A concrete operation that involves ordering stimuli along some quantitative dimension.

transitivity The ability to reason and logically combine relationships.

formal operational stage Piaget's fourth cognitive developmental stage, which emerges between about 11 and 15 years of age; thought becomes more abstract, idealistic, and logical.

CONNECTING WITH STUDENTS: Best Practices
Strategies for Working with Concrete Operational Thinkers

As you have just learned, for most of elementary school, children think at a concrete operational level. Their thought process is different from the thinking of young children as well as that of adolescents. Following are some effective strategies for advancing the thinking of children who are at the concrete operational level:

1. *Encourage students to discover concepts and principles.* Ask relevant questions about what is being studied to help them focus on some aspect of their learning. Refrain from telling students the answers to their questions outright. Try to get them to reach the answers through their own thinking.
2. *Involve children in operational tasks.* These include adding, subtracting, multiplying, dividing, ordering, seriating, and reversing. Use concrete materials for these tasks, possibly introducing math symbols later.
3. *Plan activities in which students practice the concept of ascending and descending classification hierarchies.* Have students list the following in order of size (such as largest to smallest): city of Atlanta, state of Georgia, country of United States, Western Hemisphere, and planet Earth.
4. *Include activities that require conservation of area, weight, and displaced volume.* Realize that there is considerable variation in children's attainment of conservation across different domains.
5. *Continue to ask students to justify their answers when they solve problems.* Help them to check the validity and accuracy of their conclusions.

think more like scientists. They devise plans to solve problems and systematically test solutions. Piaget's term **hypothetical-deductive reasoning** embodies the concept that adolescents can develop hypotheses (best hunches) about ways to solve problems and systematically reach a conclusion. Formal operational thinkers test their hypotheses with judiciously chosen questions and tests. In contrast, concrete operational thinkers often fail to understand the relation between a hypothesis and a well-chosen test of it, stubbornly clinging to ideas that already have been discounted.

hypothetical-deductive reasoning Piaget's formal operational concept that adolescents can develop hypotheses to solve problems and systematically reach a conclusion.

Might adolescents' ability to reason hypothetically and to evaluate what is ideal versus what is real lead them to engage in demonstrations, such as this protest related to improving education. *What other causes might be attractive to adolescents' newfound cognitive abilities of hypothetical-deductive reasoning and idealistic thinking?*
Sheila Fitzgerald/Shutterstock

A form of egocentrism also emerges in adolescence (Elkind, 1978). *Adolescent egocentrism* is the heightened self-consciousness reflected in adolescents' beliefs that others are as interested in them as they themselves are. Adolescent egocentrism also includes a sense of personal uniqueness. It involves the desire to be noticed, visible, and "on stage."

Egocentrism is a normal adolescent occurrence, more common in the middle school than in high school years. However, for some individuals, adolescent egocentrism can contribute to reckless behavior, including suicidal thoughts, drug use, and failure to use contraceptives during sexual intercourse. Egocentricity may lead some adolescents to think that they are invulnerable.

However, reason to question the accuracy of the invulnerability aspect of the personal fable is provided by research that reveals many adolescents don't consider themselves invulnerable (Fischoff et al., 2010). Some research studies suggest that rather than perceiving themselves to be invulnerable, adolescents tend to portray themselves as vulnerable to experiencing a premature death (Reyna & Rivers, 2008). A recent study highlights "that a significant proportion of adolescent risk behavior may actually be strategic and planned in advance (reasoned risk behavior)" and associated with sensation seeking and perceptions of the risk behavior as beneficial more than risky (Maslowsky et al., 2019, p. 243).

What characterizes adolescent egocentrism?
Moodboard/Cultura/Getty Images

RESEARCH

CONNECTING WITH STUDENTS: Best Practices
Strategies for Working with Formal Operational Thinkers

As you have just learned, adolescents think on a different plane from children. Following are some effective strategies for working with adolescents who are formal operational thinkers.

1. *Realize that many adolescents are not full-fledged formal operational thinkers.* Thus, many of the teaching strategies discussed earlier regarding the education of concrete operational thinkers still apply to many young adolescents. As discussed next in *Through the Eyes of Teachers,* Jerri Hall, a math teacher at Miller Magnet High School in Georgia, emphasizes that when a curriculum is too formal and too abstract, it will go over students' heads.

THROUGH THE EYES OF TEACHERS
Piaget as a Guide

I use Piaget's developmental theory as a guide in helping children learn math. In the sixth, seventh, and eighth grades, children are moving from the concrete to the abstract stage in their cognitive processes; therefore, when I teach, I try to use different methods to aid my students to understand a concept. For example, I use fraction circles to help students understand how to add, subtract, multiply, and divide fractions, and the students are allowed to use these until they become proficient with the algorithms. I try to incorporate hands-on experiences in which students discover the rules themselves, rather than just teaching the methods and having the students practice them with drill. It is extremely important for students to understand the why behind a mathematical rule so they can better understand the concept.

Jerri Hall. A math teacher at Miller Magnet High School in Georgia.

2. *Propose a problem and invite students to form hypotheses about how to solve it.* For example, a teacher might say, "Imagine that a girl has no friends. What should she do?"
3. *Present a problem and suggest several ways it might be approached.* Then ask questions that stimulate students to evaluate the approaches. For example, describe several ways to investigate a robbery, and ask students to evaluate which is best and why.
4. *Develop projects and investigations for students to carry out.* Periodically ask them how they are going about collecting and interpreting the data.
5. *Encourage students to create hierarchical outlines when you ask them to write papers.* Make sure they understand how to organize their writing in terms of general and specific points. The abstractness of formal operational thinking also means that teachers with students at this level can encourage them to use metaphors.

Might social media such as Facebook serve as an amplification tool for adolescent egocentrism? In a clever experimental study, researchers found that Facebook usage does indeed increase self-interest (Chiou et al., 2014).

Some teachers were recently asked to describe how they apply Piaget's cognitive stages to their classroom. Following are their comments:

EARLY CHILDHOOD When I teach songs to preschool students who are in the preoperational stage, I use PowerPoint slides projected on the board. The slides have either all the words of the song included, or just key words. I also include corresponding clip art and pictures on the page borders.

—CONNIE CHRISTY, *Aynor Elementary School (Preschool Program)*

ELEMENTARY SCHOOL: GRADES K-5 In my second-grade science class, I use the following method to help students move from concrete thinking to more abstract thinking: Children are given tasks and asked to discuss what happened (for example, the object sank or floated; when something is added to a system, the outcome changes). Then a theory or idea is developed from the actual observations. When children observe an occurrence and explain what was seen, they can more easily move from the concrete to the more abstract. Although these methods and others like it work well with my students, I need to repeat them often.

—JANINE GUIDA POUTRE, *Clinton Elementary School*

MIDDLE SCHOOL: GRADES 6-8 I challenge my seventh-grade students to share examples of how they've applied our classroom lessons to the real world. They can earn extra credit for doing so, but seem to care less about the points than they do about the opportunity to share their accomplishments. For example, after completing a unit on Progressivism, a student shared how he had gone online on his home computer and donated money to help Darfur refugees. He had previously planned to use this money to buy himself a new guitar. This student took the theory of social activism from the Progressive era 100 years ago and applied it to his life today. This student's actions clearly demonstrate Piaget's formal operational stage in action.

—MARK FODNESS, *Bemidji Middle School*

HIGH SCHOOL: GRADES 9-12 My high school art students take part in creativity competitions in which they build, create, explore, problem solve, and perform solutions to challenges presented to them. The competition—"Destination Imagination"—has challenged my students to brainstorm ideas and solutions to seemingly impossible tasks. As a result of their participation in this event, they have won regional and state titles along with the world championship.

—DENNIS PETERSON, *Deer River High School*

TECHNOLOGY

Piaget, Constructivism, and Technology The basic idea of *constructivism* is that students learn best when they are actively constructing information and knowledge. Piaget's theory is a strongly constructivist view. Early in the application of technology to children's learning, Seymour Papert (1980), who studied with Piaget for five years, created the Logo programming language for computers that was based on Piaget's constructivist view. A small robot labeled the "Logo Turtle" guided children in constructing solutions to problems. Today, a wide variety of programs claim constructivism as their foundation and are used in schools worldwide. Examples include robotic kits for students at different grade levels: Bee-Bots (www.bee-bot.us/) can be programmed for autonomous movement, even by very young children; Dash (www.makewonder.com/dash) and Finch (www.finchrobot.com/) pair with programming apps and languages; Cubelets (www.modrobotics.com/cubelets) are sensor-based blocks that can be programmed to respond to light, sound, motion, and other environmental cues; and Arduino (www.arduino.cc/) is appropriate for older children to create robotics that use sensors.

Other technologies that support constructive thinking include Scratch (http://scratch.mit.edu/), which is an online programming and communication space for children, and the Computer Clubhouse Network (theclubhousenetwork.org), which is an international consortium of computer clubs linked over the Internet for 10- to 18-year-olds from low-income communities that provides a creative and safe out-of-school learning environment with adult mentors. An important development in this area is the computational thinking movement, which emphasizes that students need to understand how computers work in order to function in the 21st century. (For more ideas on how to integrate technology in teaching and learning, check out the blog from the International Society for Technology in Education [ISTE]: https://www.iste.org/explore/articleDetail?articleid=152.)

Children can design games and solve problems by learning to code. Learners can creatively use technology to explore their ideas and develop their skills.
Hero Images/Getty Images

Evaluating Piaget's Theory   What were Piaget's main contributions? Has his theory withstood the test of time?

Contributions   Piaget is a giant in the field of developmental psychology. We owe to him the present field of children's cognitive development. We owe to him a long list of masterful concepts including assimilation and accommodation, object permanence, egocentrism, conservation, and hypothetical-deductive reasoning. Along with William James and John Dewey, we also owe to Piaget the current vision of children as active, constructive thinkers.

Piaget also was a genius when it came to observing children. His careful observations showed us inventive ways to discover how children act on and adapt to their world. Piaget showed us some important things to look for in cognitive development, such as the shift from preoperational to concrete operational thinking. He also showed us how children need to make their experiences fit their schemas (cognitive frameworks) yet simultaneously adapt their schemas to experience.

Criticisms   Piaget's theory has not gone unchallenged. Over the years, people have challenged Piaget's theory because research evidence has provided little support for his proposal of discrete and immutable developmental stages. Questions have been raised in the following areas:

- *Estimates of children's competence.* Some cognitive abilities emerge earlier than Piaget thought, others later (Monahan et al., 2016; Quinn & Bhatt, 2016). Conservation of number has been

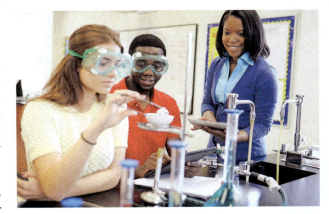

Having an outstanding teacher and gaining a good education in the logic of science and mathematics are important cultural experiences that promote the development of operational thought. *Might Piaget have underestimated the roles of culture and schooling in children's cognitive development?*
Monkey Business Images/Shutterstock

demonstrated as early as age 3, although Piaget did not think it emerged until age 7. Young children are not as uniformly "pre-" this and "pre-" that (pre-causal, preoperational) as Piaget thought (Flavell et al., 2002). Other cognitive abilities can emerge later than Piaget thought. Many adolescents still think in concrete operational ways or are just beginning to master formal operations (Kuhn, 2009).

- *Stages.* Cognitive development is not as stage-like as Piaget envisioned (Müller & Kerns, 2015). Piaget conceived of stages as unitary structures of thought. Some concrete operational concepts, however, do not appear at the same time. For example, children do not learn to conserve at the same time as they learn to cross-classify.
- *Training children to reason at a higher level.* Some children who are at one cognitive stage (such as preoperational) can be trained to reason at a higher cognitive stage (such as concrete operational). However, Piaget argued that such training is only superficial and ineffective, unless the child is at a maturational transition point between the stages (Gelman & Opfer, 2004).
- *Culture and education.* Culture and education exert stronger influences on children's development than Piaget envisioned (Gauvain, 2016). For example, the age at which children acquire conservation skills is related to the extent to which their culture provides relevant practice (Cole, 2006). An outstanding teacher can guide students' learning experiences that will help them move to a higher cognitive stage.

Still, some developmental psychologists reason we should not throw out Piaget altogether. These **neo-Piagetians** argue that Piaget got some things right but that his theory needs considerable revision. In their revision of Piaget, neo-Piagetians emphasize how children process information through attention, memory, and strategies (Case, 2000). They especially stress that a more accurate vision of children's thinking requires more knowledge of strategies, how quickly and how automatically children process information, the particular cognitive task involved, and the division of cognitive problems into smaller, more precise steps (Fazio et al., 2016).

Despite such criticism, Piaget's theory is a very important one. As we see next, there are many ways to apply his ideas to educating children.

VYGOTSKY'S THEORY

In addition to Piaget's theory, another major developmental theory that focuses on children's cognition was developed in Russia by Lev Vygotsky. In Vygotsky's theory children's cognitive development is shaped by the cultural context in which they live (Gauvain, 2016; Holzman, 2017; Yasnitsky & Van der Veer, 2016).

DEVELOPMENT

The Zone of Proximal Development Vygotsky's belief in the importance of social influences, especially instruction, on children's cognitive development is reflected in his concept of the zone of proximal development. **Zone of proximal development (ZPD)** is Vygotsky's term for the range of tasks that are too difficult for the child to master alone but that can be learned with guidance and assistance from adults or more-skilled children. Thus, the lower limit of the ZPD is the level of skill reached by the child working independently. The upper limit is the level of additional responsibility the child can accept with the assistance of an able instructor (see Figure 14). The ZPD captures the child's cognitive skills that are in the process of maturing and can be accomplished only with the assistance of a more-skilled person.

Teaching in the zone of proximal development reflects the concept of developmentally appropriate teaching is described earlier in the chapter. It involves being aware of "where students are in the process of their development and taking

> **Thinking Back/Thinking Forward**
>
> The information-processing approach emphasizes that children develop a gradually increasing capacity for processing information. Connect to "The Information-Processing Approach."

neo-Piagetians Developmental psychologists who believe that Piaget got some things right but that his theory needs considerable revision; they emphasize information processing through attention, memory, and strategies.

zone of proximal development (ZPD) Vygotsky's term for the range of tasks that are too difficult for children to master alone but can be mastered with guidance and assistance from adults or more-skilled children.

CONNECTING WITH STUDENTS: Best Practices
Strategies for Applying Piaget's Theory to Children's Education

Earlier in this chapter, you learned about applying Piaget's theory to teaching children at different stages of cognitive development. Following are five general Piaget-based strategies for educating children:

1. *Take a constructivist approach.* Piaget emphasized that children learn best when they are active and seek solutions for themselves. Piaget opposed teaching methods that treat children as passive receptacles. The educational implication of Piaget's view is that in all subjects students learn best by making discoveries, reflecting on them, and discussing them, rather than blindly imitating the teacher or doing things by rote.

2. *Facilitate rather than direct learning.* Effective teachers design situations that allow students to learn by doing. These situations promote students' thinking and discovery. Teachers listen, watch, and question students to help them gain better understanding. They ask relevant questions to stimulate students' thinking and ask them to explain their answers. As described in *Through the Eyes of Teachers,* Suzanne Ransleben creates imaginative classroom situations to facilitate students' learning.

THROUGH THE EYES OF TEACHERS
Stimulating Students' Thinking and Discovery

Suzanne Ransleben teaches ninth- and tenth-grade English in Corpus Christi, Texas. She designs classroom situations that stimulate students' reflective thinking and discovery. Suzanne created Grammar Football to make diagramming sentences more interesting for students and has students decipher song lyrics to help them better understand how to write poetry. When students first encounter Shakespeare, "they paint interpretations of their favorite line from Romeo and Juliet" (Source: Wong Briggs, 2004, p. 7D).

3. *Consider the child's knowledge and level of thinking.* Students do not come to class with empty heads. They have many ideas about the physical and natural world including concepts of space, time, quantity, and causality. These ideas differ from the ideas of adults. Teachers need to interpret what a student is saying and respond with discourse close to the student's level.

Suzanne Ransleben, teaching English.
Billy Calzada

4. *Promote the student's intellectual health.* When Piaget came to lecture in the United States, he was asked, "What can I do to get my child to a higher cognitive stage sooner?" He was asked this question so often here compared with other countries that he called it the American question. Piaget believed that maturation in children's learning should occur naturally and that children should not be pushed into achieving too much too early in their development.

5. *Turn the classroom into a setting of exploration and discovery.* What do actual classrooms look like when the teachers adopt Piaget's views? Several first- and second-grade math classrooms provide some good examples (Kamii, 1985, 1989). The teachers emphasize students' own exploration and discovery. The classrooms are less structured than what we think of as a typical classroom. Workbooks and predetermined assignments are not used. Rather, the teachers observe the students' interests and natural participation in activities to determine what the course of learning will be. For example, a math lesson might be constructed around counting the day's lunch money or dividing supplies among students. Often games are prominently used in the classroom to stimulate mathematical thinking.

advantage of their readiness. It is also about teaching to enable developmental readiness, not just waiting for students to be ready" (Horowitz et al., 2005, p. 105).

Scaffolding   Closely linked to the idea of the ZPD is the concept of scaffolding developed by Jerome Bruner (Wood et al., 1976). **Scaffolding** means changing the level of support. Over the course of a teaching session, a more-skilled person

scaffolding A technique that involves changing the level of support for learning. A teacher or more advanced peer adjusts the amount of guidance to fit the student's current performance.

FIGURE 14 VYGOTSKY'S ZONE OF PROXIMAL DEVELOPMENT

Vygotsky's zone of proximal development has a lower limit and an upper limit. Tasks in the ZPD are too difficult for the child to perform alone. They require assistance from an adult or a more-skilled child. As children experience the verbal instruction or demonstration, they organize the information in their existing mental structures so that they can eventually perform the skill or task alone.

Roberto Westbrook/Getty Images

(a teacher or more advanced peer) adjusts the amount of guidance to fit the child's current performance (Wilkinson & Gaffney, 2016). When the student is learning a new task, the skilled person may use direct instruction. As the student's competence increases, less guidance is given. Scaffolding is often used to help students attain the upper limits of their zone of proximal development.

Asking probing questions is an excellent way to scaffold students' learning and help them to develop more sophisticated thinking skills. A teacher might ask a student such questions as "What would an example of that be?" "Why do you think that is so?" "Now, what's the next thing you need to do?" and "How can you connect those?" Over time, students should begin internalizing these kinds of probes and improve monitoring of their own work (Horowitz et al., 2005).

Many teachers who successfully use scaffolding circulate around the classroom, giving "just-in-time" assistance to individuals or detecting a class-wide misconception and then leading a discussion to correct the problem. They also give children "time to grapple with problems" and guide them when they observe that the child can no longer make progress (Horowitz et al., 2005, pp. 106–107).

Language and Thought In Vygotsky's view, language plays an important role in a child's development. According to Vygotsky, children use speech not only for social communication, but also to help them solve tasks. Vygotsky (1962) further argued that young children use language to plan, guide, and monitor their behavior. This use of language for self-regulation is called *private speech*. For example, young children talk aloud to themselves about such things as their toys and the tasks they are trying to complete. Thus, when working on a puzzle, a child might say, "This piece doesn't fit; maybe I'll try that one." A few minutes later she utters, "This is hard." For Piaget private speech is egocentric and immature, but for Vygotsky it is an important tool of thought during the early childhood years (Alderson-Day & Fernyhough, 2014).

Vygotsky said that language and thought initially develop independently of each other and then merge. He emphasized that all mental functions have external, or social, origins. Children must use language to communicate with others before they can focus inward on their own thoughts. Children also must communicate externally and use language for a long period of time before they can make the transition from external to internal speech. This transition period occurs between 3 and 7 years of age and involves talking to oneself. After a while, the self-talk becomes second nature to children, and they can act without verbalizing. When this occurs, children have internalized their egocentric speech in the form of *inner speech,* which becomes their thoughts.

Vygotsky argued that children who use private speech are more socially competent than those who don't. He argued that private speech represents an early transition in becoming more socially communicative. For Vygotsky, when young children talk to themselves, they are using language to govern their behavior and guide themselves.

Piaget held that self-talk is egocentric and reflects immaturity. However, researchers have found support for Vygotsky's view that private speech plays a positive role in children's development (Winsler et al., 2000). Researchers have revealed that children use private speech more when tasks are difficult, after they make mistakes, and when they are not sure how to proceed (Berk, 1994). They also have found that children who use private speech are more attentive and improve their performance more than children who do not use private speech (Berk & Spuhl, 1995).

Teachers were recently asked how they apply Vygotsky's theory to their classroom. After reading their responses about Vygotsky, you might want to compare these responses with teachers' descriptions of how they apply Piaget's theory in their classrooms.

EARLY CHILDHOOD In teaching music to preschoolers, I use private speech to help children learn unfamiliar rhythms. When my young students are learning a new

rhythm pattern on the African drums, for example, they don't count the eighth and quarter notes, because that is too difficult. Instead, I suggest certain words for them to repeat in rhythmic patterns to learn the beat, or they can come up with their own words to match the new rhythm. My guidance allows children to improve their understanding of musical rhythm.

—CONNIE CHRISTY, *Aynor Elementary School (Preschool Program)*

ELEMENTARY SCHOOL: GRADES K–5 One way to maximize students' zone of proximal development is by flexible grouping. In flexible grouping, groups change often based on need, interest, and so on. I use different group styles—for example, whole class, small group, homogenous groups, and heterogeneous groups. Variance in

group members and group styles allows all students to be instructed within their zone of proximal development. This may be on grade level in one area, above grade level in another, and below grade level in still another. The point is that flexible grouping allows me to give students of varying levels the instruction necessary to learn.

—SUSAN FROELICH, *Clinton Elementary School*

MIDDLE SCHOOL: GRADES 6–8 When I teach my students a new skill, it is important that I stay close to them while they are working. This way if they need my assistance, I am there to help them master the new skill with some guidance. This practice works especially well when we are working on multistep projects.

—CASEY MAASS, *Edison Middle School*

HIGH SCHOOL: GRADES 9–12 Advanced art students and independent-study students have always been an active part of my classroom, especially when it comes to helping other students maximize their zone of proximal development (and grow in their own skills as artists as well). In my ceramics class, for example, I have several

advanced students—who have especially strong knowledge and skills on the ceramic wheel—help my first-year students, who are attempting to work on the wheel for the first time. This additional assistance from the advanced students allows me to help other students who need further instruction.

—DENNIS PETERSON, *Deer River High School*

We have discussed a number of ideas about both Piaget's and Vygotsky's theories and how the theories can be applied to children's education. To reflect on how you might apply their theories to your own classroom, complete *Self-Assessment 1*.

Evaluating Vygotsky's Theory How does Vygotsky's theory compare with Piaget's? Although both theories are constructivist, Vygotsky's is a **social constructivist approach**, which emphasizes the social contexts of learning and the construction of knowledge through social interaction.

In moving from Piaget to Vygotsky, the conceptual shift is from the individual to collaboration, social interaction, and sociocultural activity (Holzman, 2017; Yasnitsky & Van der Veer, 2016). The endpoint of cognitive development for Piaget is formal operational thought. For Vygotsky, the endpoint can differ, depending on which skills are considered to be the most important in a particular culture. For Piaget, children construct knowledge by transforming, organizing, and reorganizing previous knowledge. For Vygotsky, children construct knowledge through social

> **Thinking Back/Thinking Forward**
> Collaborative learning and cognitive apprenticeships reflect Vygotsky's social constructivist approach. Connect to "Social Constructivist Approaches."

social constructivist approach Emphasizes the social contexts of learning and that knowledge is mutually built and constructed; Vygotsky's theory exemplifies this approach.

SELF-ASSESSMENT 1
Applying Piaget and Vygotsky in My Classroom

The grade level at which I plan to teach is _____

PIAGET
The concepts in Piaget's theory that should help me the most in understanding and teaching children at this grade level are

Concept	Example
_____	_____
_____	_____
_____	_____

VYGOTSKY
The concepts in Vygotsky's theory that should help me the most in understanding and teaching children at this grade level are

Concept	Example
_____	_____
_____	_____
_____	_____

CONNECTING WITH STUDENTS: Best Practices
Strategies for Applying Vygotsky's Theory to Children's Education

Vygotsky's theory has been embraced by many teachers and has been successfully applied to education (Adams, 2015; Hmelo-Silver & Chinn, 2016). Here are some ways in which educators can apply Vygotsky's theory:

1. *Assess the child's ZPD.* Like Piaget, Vygotsky did not think that formal, standardized tests are the best way to assess children's learning. Rather, Vygotsky argued that assessment should focus on determining the child's zone of proximal development. The skilled helper presents the child with tasks of varying difficulty to determine the best level at which to begin instruction.

2. *Use the child's zone of proximal development in teaching.* Teaching should begin toward the zone's upper limit, so that the child can reach the goal with help and move to a higher level of skill and knowledge. Offer just enough assistance. You might ask, "What can I do to help you?" Or simply observe the child's intentions and attempts and provide support when needed. When the child hesitates, offer encouragement. And encourage the child to practice the skill. You may watch and appreciate the child's practice or offer support when the child forgets what to do. In *Through the Eyes of Teachers,* you can read about John Mahoney's teaching practices that reflect Vygotsky's emphasis on the importance of the zone of proximal development.

THROUGH THE EYES OF TEACHERS
Using Dialogue and Reframing Concepts to Find the Zone of Proximal Development

John Mahoney teaches mathematics at a high school in Washington, D.C. In Mahoney's view, guiding students' success in math is both collaborative and individual. He encourages dialogue about math during which he reframes concepts that help students subsequently solve problems on their own. Mahoney also never gives students the answers to math problems. As one student commented, "He's going to make you think." His tests always include a problem that students have not seen but for which they have enough knowledge to figure out the solution (Source: Wong Briggs, 2005).

CONNECTING WITH STUDENTS: Best Practices
Strategies for Applying Vygotsky's Theory to Children's Education

3. *Use more-skilled peers as teachers.* Remember that it is not just adults who are important in helping children learn. Children also benefit from the support and guidance of more-skilled children (Gredler, 2009). For example, pair a child who is just beginning to read with one who is a more advanced reader.

4. *Monitor and encourage children's use of private speech.* Be aware of the developmental change from externally talking to oneself when solving a problem during the preschool years to privately talking to oneself in the early elementary school years. In the elementary school years, encourage children to internalize and self-regulate their talk to themselves.

5. *Place instruction in a meaningful context.* Educators today are moving away from abstract presentations of material, instead providing students with opportunities to experience learning in real-world settings. For example, instead of just memorizing math formulas, students work on math problems with real-world implications.

6. *Transform the classroom with Vygotskian ideas.* Tools of the Mind is a curriculum that is grounded in Vygotsky's (1962) theory, with special attention given to cultural tools and developing self-regulation, the zone of proximal development, scaffolding, private speech, shared activity, and play as important activity (Hyson et al. 2006). Figure 15 illustrates how scaffolding was used in Tools of the Mind to improve a young child's writing skills. The Tools of the Mind curriculum was created by Elena Bodrova and Deborah Leong (2007) and has been implemented in more than 200 classrooms. Most of the children in the Tools of the Mind programs are considered at risk for school failure because of their living circumstances, which in many instances involve poverty and other difficult conditions such as being homeless and having parents with drug problems.

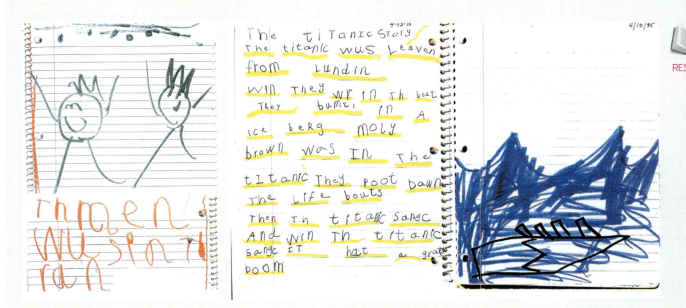

FIGURE 15 WRITING PROGRESS OF A 5-YEAR-OLD BOY OVER TWO MONTHS USING THE SCAFFOLDING PROCESS IN TOOLS OF THE MIND

Source: "*Tools of the Mind: A Case Study of Implementing the Vygotskian Approach in American Early Childhood and Primary Classrooms*" (pp. 36–38), by E. Bodrova and D.J. Leong, 2001, International Bureau of Education.

interaction. The implication of Piaget's theory for teaching is that children need support to explore their world and discover knowledge. The main implication of Vygotsky's theory for teaching is that students need many opportunities to learn with the teacher and more-skilled peers. In both Piaget's and Vygotsky's theories, teachers serve as facilitators and guides, rather than as directors and molders of learning. Figure 16 compares Vygotsky's and Piaget's theories.

What are some contributions and criticisms of Vygotsky's theory?
Beau Lark/Fancy/Glow Images

Criticisms of Vygotsky's theory also have surfaced. Some critics point out that Vygotsky was not specific enough about age-related changes (Gauvain, 2016). Another criticism focuses on Vygotsky not adequately describing how changes in socioemotional capabilities contribute to cognitive development (Gauvain, 2016). Yet another criticism is that he overemphasized the role of language in thinking. Also, his emphasis on collaboration and guidance has potential pitfalls. Might facilitators be too helpful in some cases, as when a parent becomes too overbearing and controlling? Further, some children might become lazy and expect help when they might have done something on their own.

In our coverage of cognitive development, we have focused on the views of two giants in the field: Piaget and Vygotsky. However, information processing also has emerged as an important perspective in understanding children's cognitive development (Fazio et al., 2016; Fuchs et al., 2016). It emphasizes how information enters the mind, how it is stored and transformed, and how it is retrieved to perform mental activities such as problem solving and reasoning. It also focuses on how automatically and quickly children process information. Because information processing will be covered extensively in other chapters, we mention it only briefly here.

	Vygotsky	Piaget
Sociocultural Context	Strong emphasis	Little emphasis
Constructivism	Social constructivist	Cognitive constructivist
Stages	No general stages of development proposed	Strong emphasis on stages (sensorimotor, preoperational, concrete operational, and formal operational)
Key Processes	Zone of proximal development, language, dialogue, tools of the culture	Schema, assimilation, accommodation, operations, conservation, classification
Role of Language	A major role; language plays a powerful role in shaping thought	Language has a minimal role; cognition primarily directs language
View on Education	Education plays a central role, helping children learn the tools of the culture	Education merely refines the child's cognitive skills that have already emerged
Teaching Implications	Teacher is a facilitator and guide, not a director; establish many opportunities for children to learn with the teacher and more-skilled peers	Also views teacher as a facilitator and guide, not a director; provide support for children to explore their world and discover knowledge

FIGURE 16 COMPARISON OF VYGOTSKY'S AND PIAGET'S THEORIES

(*Left*) A.R. Lauria/Dr. Michael Cole, Laboratory of Human Cognition, University of California, San Diego; (*right*) Bettmann/Getty Images

Review, Reflect, and Practice

❷ Discuss the development of the brain and compare the cognitive developmental theories of Jean Piaget and Lev Vygotsky.

REVIEW
- How does the brain develop, and what implications does this development have for children's education?
- What four main ideas did Piaget use to describe cognitive processes? What stages did he identify in children's cognitive development? What are some criticisms of his view?
- What is the nature of Vygotsky's theory? How can Vygotsky's theory be applied to education and his theory compared to Piaget's? What is a criticism of Vygotsky's theory?

REFLECT
- Do you consider yourself to be a formal operational thinker? Do you still sometimes feel like a concrete operational thinker? Give examples.

PRAXIS™ PRACTICE

1. Sander is a 16-year-old boy who takes many risks, such as driving fast and drinking while driving. Recent research on the brain indicates that a likely reason for this risk-taking behavior is that Sander's:
   a. hippocampus is damaged
   b. prefrontal cortex is still developing
   c. brain lateralization is incomplete
   d. myelination is complete

2. Mrs. Gonzales teaches first grade. Which of the following teaching strategies of Mrs. Gonzales would Piaget most likely endorse?
   a. demonstrating how to perform a math operation and having students imitate her
   b. creating flash cards to teach vocabulary
   c. using a standardized test to assess students' reading skills
   d. designing contexts that promote students' thinking and discovery

3. Mr. Gould's fourth-grade students are learning about the relations among percentages, decimals, and fractions. Mr. Gould distributes an assignment requiring students to convert fractions to decimals and then to percentages. Christopher can do this assignment without help from Mr. Gould or his classmates. What would Vygotsky say about this task for Christopher?
   a. This task is appropriate for Christopher because it is within his zone of proximal development.
   b. This task is inappropriate for Christopher because it is above his zone of proximal development.
   c. This task is inappropriate for Christopher because it is below his zone of proximal development.
   d. This task is inappropriate for Christopher because it is within his zone of proximal development.

Please see answer key at end of book . . . .

LG 3 Identify the key features of language, biological, and environmental influences on language, and the typical growth of the child's language.

3 LANGUAGE DEVELOPMENT

- What Is Language?
- Biological and Environmental Influences
- How Language Develops

Take a moment to think about how important language is in children's everyday lives. They need language to speak with others, listen to others, read, and write. Their language enables them to describe past events in detail and to plan for the future. Language lets us pass down information from one generation to the next and create a rich cultural heritage.

WHAT IS LANGUAGE?

Language is a form of communication—whether spoken, written, or signed—that is based on a system of symbols. Language consists of the words used by a community (vocabulary) and the rules for varying and combining them (grammar and syntax).

All human languages have some common characteristics (Clark, 2017; Hoff, 2015). These include infinite generativity and organizational rules. *Infinite generativity* is the ability to produce an endless number of meaningful sentences using a finite set of words and rules.

When we say "rules," we mean that language is orderly and that rules describe the way language works (Berko Gleason & Ratner, 2009). Language involves five systems of rules: phonology, morphology, syntax, semantics, and pragmatics.

Phonology Every language is made up of basic sounds. **Phonology** is the sound system of a language, including the sounds used and how they may be combined (Del Campo et al., 2015). For example, English has the sounds *sp, ba,* and *ar,* but the sound sequences *zx* and *qp* do not occur.

A *phoneme* is the basic unit of sound in a language; it is the smallest unit of sound that affects meaning. A good example of a phoneme in English is /k/, the sound represented by the letter *k* in the word *ski* and the letter *c* in the word *cat.* The /k/ sound is slightly different in these two words, and in some languages such as Arabic these two sounds are separate phonemes.

Morphology **Morphology** refers to the units of meaning involved in word formation. A *morpheme* is a minimal unit of meaning; it is a word or a part of a word that cannot be broken into smaller meaningful parts. Every word in the English language is made up of one or more morphemes. Some words consist of a single morpheme (e.g., *help*), whereas others are made up of more than one morpheme (e.g., *helper,* which has two morphemes, *help + er,* with the morpheme *-er* meaning "one who," in this case "one who helps"). Thus, not all morphemes are words by themselves—for example, *pre-, -tion,* and *-ing* are morphemes.

Just as the rules that govern phonology describe the sound sequences that can occur in a language, the rules of morphology describe the way meaningful units (morphemes) can be combined in words (Clark, 2017). Morphemes have many jobs in grammar, such as marking tense (e.g., *she walks* versus *she walked*) and number (*she walks* versus *they walk*).

Syntax **Syntax** involves the way words are combined to form acceptable phrases and sentences (Los, 2015). If someone says to you, "Bob slugged Tom" or "Bob was slugged by Tom," you know who did the slugging and who was slugged in each case because you have a syntactic understanding of these sentence structures. You also understand that the sentence "You didn't stay, did you?" is a grammatical sentence but that "You didn't stay, didn't you?" is unacceptable and ambiguous.

---

language A form of communication, whether spoken, written, or signed, that is based on a system of symbols.

phonology A language's sound system.

morphology Refers to the units of meaning involved in word formation.

syntax The ways that words must be combined to form acceptable phrases and sentences.

Semantics Semantics refers to the meaning of words and sentences. Every word has a set of semantic features, or required attributes related to meaning. *Girl* and *woman,* for example, share many semantic features, but they differ semantically in regard to age.

Words have semantic restrictions on how they can be used in sentences (Clark, 2017; Duff et al., 2015). The sentence, *The bicycle talked the boy into buying a candy bar,* is syntactically correct but semantically incorrect. The sentence violates our semantic knowledge that bicycles don't talk.

Pragmatics A final set of language rules involves **pragmatics**, the appropriate use of language in different contexts (Clark, 2014). Pragmatics covers a lot of territory. When you take turns speaking in a discussion, you are demonstrating knowledge of pragmatics. You also apply the pragmatics of English when you use polite language in appropriate situations (e.g., when talking to a teacher) or tell stories that are interesting.

Pragmatic rules can be complex, and they differ from one culture to another. If you were to study the Japanese language, you would come face-to-face with many pragmatic rules about conversing with individuals of various social levels and with various relationships to you.

BIOLOGICAL AND ENVIRONMENTAL INFLUENCES

Famous linguist Noam Chomsky (1957) argued that humans are prewired to learn language at a certain time and in a certain way. Some language scholars view the remarkable similarities in how children acquire language all over the world, despite the vast variation in language input they receive, as strong evidence that language has a biological basis (Hickok & Small, 2016).

Despite the influence of biology, children clearly do not learn language in a social vacuum (Pace et al., 2016). Children are neither exclusively biological linguists nor exclusively social architects of language. No matter how long you converse with a dog, it won't learn to talk, because it doesn't have the human child's biological capacity for language. Unfortunately, though, some children fail to develop good language skills even in the presence of very good role models and interaction. An interactionist view emphasizes the contributions of both biology and experience in language development. That is, children are biologically prepared to learn language as they and their caregivers interact (Harley, 2017). In or out of school, encouragement of language development—not drill and practice—is the key. Language development is not simply a matter of being rewarded for saying things correctly and imitating a speaker. Children benefit when their parents and teachers actively engage them in conversation, ask them questions, and emphasize interactive rather than directive language (Hirsh-Pasek et al., 2015; Pace et al., 2016).

Both biological and environmental influences play important roles in children's language development.
Hill Street Studios/Blend Images LLC

HOW LANGUAGE DEVELOPS

What are some of the key developmental milestones in language development? We will examine these milestones in infancy, early childhood, middle and late childhood, and adolescence.

DEVELOPMENT

Infancy Language acquisition advances past a number of milestones in infancy (Cartmill & Goldin-Meadow, 2016). Because the main focus of this text is on children and adolescents rather than infants, only several of the many language milestones in

semantics The meaning of words and sentences.

pragmatics The appropriate use of language in different contexts.

infancy will be highlighted. Babbling occurs in the middle of the first year and infants usually utter their first word at about 10 to 13 months. By 18 to 24 months, infants usually have begun to string two words together. In this two-word stage, they quickly grasp the importance of language in communication, creating phrases such as "Book there," "My candy," "Mama walk," and "Give Papa."

Early Childhood   As children leave the two-word stage, they move rather quickly into three-, four-, and five-word combinations. The transition from simple sentences expressing a single proposition to complex sentences begins between 2 and 3 years of age and continues into the elementary school years (Bloom, 1998).

RESEARCH

Rule Systems of Language   Let's explore the changes in the five rules systems we described earlier—phonology, morphology, syntax, semantics, and pragmatics—during early childhood. In terms of phonology, most preschool children gradually become sensitive to the sounds of spoken words. They notice rhymes, enjoy poems, make up silly names for things by substituting one sound for another (such as *bubblegum, bubblebum, bubbleyum*), and clap along with each syllable in a phrase.

As children move beyond two-word utterances, there is clear evidence that they know morphological rules. Children begin using the plural and possessive forms of nouns (*dogs* and *dog's*); putting appropriate endings on verbs (*-s* when the subject is third-person singular, *-ed* for the past tense, and *-ing* for the present progressive tense); and using prepositions (*in* and *on*), articles (*a* and *the*), and various forms of the verb *to be* ("I *was going* to the store"). In fact, they *overgeneralize* these rules, applying them to words that do not follow the rules. For example, a preschool child might say "foots" instead of "feet" or "goed" instead of "went."

Children's understanding of morphological rules was the subject of a classic experiment by children's language researcher Jean Berko (1958). Berko presented preschool and first-grade children with cards like the one shown in Figure 17. Children were asked to look at the card while the experimenter read the words on it aloud. Then the children were asked to supply the missing word. This might sound easy, but Berko was interested not just in the children's ability to recall the right word but also in their ability to say it "correctly" with the ending that was dictated by morphological rules. *Wugs* is the correct response for the card in Figure 17. Although the children's responses were not perfectly accurate, they were much better than chance would dictate. Moreover, they demonstrated their knowledge of morphological rules not only with the plural forms of nouns ("There are two wugs") but also with the possessive forms of nouns and with the third-person singular and past-tense forms of verbs. Berko's study demonstrated not only that the children relied on rules, but also that they had *abstracted* the rules from what they had heard and could apply them to novel situations.

Preschool children also learn and apply rules of syntax (Clark, 2017). After advancing beyond two-word utterances, the child shows a growing mastery of complex rules for how words should be ordered. Consider *wh-* questions, such as "Where is Daddy going?" or "What is that boy doing?" To ask these questions properly, the child must know two important differences between *wh-* questions and affirmative statements (for instance, "Daddy is going to work" and "That boy is waiting on the school bus"). First, a *wh-* word must be added at the beginning of the sentence. Second, the auxiliary verb must be inverted—that is, exchanged with the subject of the sentence. Young children learn quite early where to put the *wh-* word, but they take much longer to learn the auxiliary-inversion rule. Thus, preschool children might ask, "Where Daddy is going?" and "What that boy is doing?"

The speaking vocabulary of a 6-year-old child ranges from 8,000 to 14,000 words. Assuming that word learning began when the child was 12 months old, this translates into a rate of five to eight new word meanings a day between the ages of 1 and 6.

What are some important aspects of how word learning optimally occurs? Kathy Hirsh-Pasek and Roberta Golinkoff (Harris et al., 2011; Hirsh-Pasek &

FIGURE 17   STIMULI IN BERKO'S STUDY OF YOUNG CHILDREN'S UNDERSTANDING OF MORPHOLOGICAL RULES

In Jean Berko's (1958) study, young children were presented cards such as this one with a "wug" on it. Then the children were asked to supply the missing word and say it correctly. "Wugs" is the correct response here.

Gleason, J. B. (1958). "The child's learning of English morphology." *Word*, 14, 154. Copyright ©1958 by Jean Berko Gleason. By permission of the author.

Golinkoff, 2016) emphasize six key principles in young children's vocabulary development:

1. *Children learn the words they hear most often.* They learn the words they encounter when interacting with parents, teachers, siblings, peers, and also from books. They especially benefit from encountering words that they do not know.
2. *Children learn words for things and events that interest them.* Parents and teachers can direct young children to experience words in contexts that interest the children; playful peer interactions are especially helpful in this regard.
3. *Children learn words better in responsive and interactive contexts than in passive contexts.* Children who experience turn-taking opportunities, joint focusing experiences, and positive, sensitive socializing contexts with adults encounter the scaffolding necessary for optimal word learning. They learn words less effectively when they are passive learners.
4. *Children learn words best in contexts that are meaningful.* Young children learn new words more effectively when new words are encountered in integrated contexts rather than as isolated facts.
5. *Children learn words best when they access clear information about word meaning.* Children whose parents and teachers are sensitive to words the children might not understand and provide support and elaboration with hints about word meaning learn words better than children whose parents and teachers quickly state a new word and don't monitor whether the child understands its meaning.
6. *Children learn words best when grammar and vocabulary are considered.* Children who experience a large number of words and diversity in verbal stimulation develop a richer vocabulary and better understanding of grammar. In many cases, vocabulary and grammar development are connected.

What are some effective strategies for using technology to support children's vocabulary? Computers can be used to support children's vocabulary development. Book apps and eBooks often feature a "read aloud" function that can be helpful for young or struggling readers. Further, using a computer for listening to and watching stories can be part of a student's reading center rotations, reading assignment, or an option during choice time. Learning new words can be enhanced if teachers plan a way for students to keep track of new words. For example, students can record new words in a portfolio for future reference.

TECHNOLOGY

Teachers also can use iPods, tablets, or classroom computer stations to create listening centers that support vocabulary development. Audiobooks also can be used to supplement printed materials, allow students to listen to dramatization of stories, and pique students' interest. Audiobooks may especially benefit students with special needs. Technology gives teachers access to an incredible number of strategies for teaching reading and writing. For example, an important resource provided by the National Council of Teachers of English is their READ WRITE THINK website at http://www.readwritethink.org/.

In addition to the remarkable advances young children make in semantics, substantial changes in pragmatics also occur during early childhood. A 6-year-old is simply a much better conversationalist than a 2-year-old. What are some of the changes in pragmatics that are made in the preschool years? At about 3 years of age, children improve in their ability to talk about things that are not physically present. That is, they improve their command of the characteristic of language known as *displacement.* Children become increasingly removed from the "here and now" and are able to talk about things not physically present, as well as things that happened in the past or may happen in the future. Preschoolers can tell you what they want for lunch tomorrow, something that would not have been possible at the two-word stage in infancy. Preschool children also become increasingly able to talk in different ways to different people.

> **Thinking Back/Thinking Forward**
>
> Teachers can guide students in adopting a number of cognitive strategies for becoming better readers and writers. Connect to "Learning and Cognition in the Content Areas."

RESEARCH

Early Literacy Concern about U.S. children's ability to read and write has led to a careful examination of preschool and kindergarten children's experiences, with the hope that a positive orientation toward reading and writing can be developed early in life (Beaty & Pratt, 2015). Parents and teachers need to provide young children with a supportive environment for the development of literacy skills (Vukelich et al., 2016). Children should be active participants in a wide range of interesting listening, talking, writing, and reading experiences (Tompkins, 2015).

Instruction should be built on what children already know about oral language, reading, and writing. Further, early precursors of literacy and academic success include language skills, phonological and syntactic knowledge, letter identification, and enjoyment of books.

What are some strategies for using books effectively with preschool children? Ellen Galinsky (2010) emphasized these strategies:

- *Use books to initiate conversation with young children.* Ask them to put themselves in the book characters' places and imagine what they might be thinking or feeling.
- *Use what and why questions.* Ask young children to describe what they think is going to happen next in a story and then to see if it occurs.
- Encourage children to ask questions about stories.
- *Choose some books that play with language.* Creative books on the alphabet, including those with rhymes, often interest young children.

In the chapter on planning, instruction, and teaching we will further discuss children's literacy development.

Middle and Late Childhood Children gain new skills as they enter school that make it possible to learn to read and write. These include increased use of language to talk about things that are not physically present, learning what a word is, and learning how to recognize and talk about sounds. They also learn the *alphabetic principle,* which means that the letters of the alphabet represent sounds of the language.

Vocabulary development continues at a breathtaking pace for most children during the elementary school years. After five years of word learning, the 6-year-old child does not slow down. According to some estimates, elementary school children in the United States are moving along at the awe-inspiring rate of 22 words a day! The average U.S. 12-year-old has developed a speaking vocabulary of approximately 50,000 words.

During middle and late childhood, changes occur in the way mental vocabulary is organized. When asked to say the first word that comes to mind when they hear a word, preschool children typically provide a word that often follows the word in a sentence. For example, when asked to respond to *dog* the young child may say "barks," or to the word *eat* respond with "lunch." At about 7 years of age, children begin to respond with a word that is the same part of speech as the stimulus word. For example, a child may now respond to the word *dog* with "cat" or "horse." To *eat,* they now might say "drink." This is evidence that children now have begun to categorize their vocabulary by parts of speech.

The process of categorizing becomes easier as children increase their vocabulary. Children's vocabulary increases from an average of about 14,000 words at age 6 to an average of about 40,000 words by age 11.

Children make similar advances in grammar. During the elementary school years, children's improvement in logical reasoning and analytical skills helps them understand such constructions as the appropriate use of comparatives *(shorter, deeper)* and

What are some effective early literacy experiences that parents can provide young children?
JGI/Tom Grill/Blend Images LLC

subjectives ("If you were president . . ."). During the elementary school years, children become increasingly able to understand and use complex grammar, such as the following sentence: *The boy who kissed his mother wore a hat.* They also learn to use language in a more connected way, producing connected discourse. They become able to relate sentences to one another to produce descriptions, definitions, and narratives that make sense. Children must be able to do these things orally before they can be expected to deal with them in written assignments.

These advances in vocabulary and grammar during the elementary school years are accompanied by the development of **metalinguistic awareness**, which is knowledge about language, such as knowing what a preposition is or being able to discuss the sounds of a language. Metalinguistic awareness allows children "to think about their language, understand what words are, and even define them" (Berko Gleason, 2009, p. 4). It improves considerably during the elementary school years. In elementary school, defining words also becomes a regular part of classroom discourse and children increase their syntax as they study and talk about the components of sentences, such as subjects and verbs.

Children also make progress in understanding how to use language in culturally appropriate ways—pragmatics. By the time they enter adolescence, most children know the rules for the use of language in everyday contexts—that is, what is appropriate and inappropriate to say.

What are some advances in language that children make during middle and late childhood?
Ariel Skelley/Blend Images/Corbis

Adolescence Language development during adolescence includes increasingly sophisticated use of words (Berko Gleason, 2009). As they develop abstract thinking, adolescents become much better than children at analyzing the function a word performs in a sentence.

Adolescents also develop more subtle abilities with words. They make strides in understanding *metaphor,* which is an implied comparison between unlike things. For example, individuals "draw a line in the sand" to indicate a nonnegotiable position; a political campaign is said to be a marathon, not a sprint. And adolescents become better able to understand and to use *satire,* which is the use of irony, derision, or wit to expose folly or wickedness. Caricatures are an example of satire. More advanced logical thinking also allows adolescents, from about 15 to 20 years of age, to understand complex literary works.

Most adolescents are also much better writers than children are. They are better at organizing ideas before they write, at distinguishing between general and specific points as they write, at stringing together sentences that make sense, and at organizing their writing into an introduction, body, and concluding remarks.

Some teachers recently shared about the strategies they use to expand or advance children's and adolescents' language development in class. Following are their responses:

EARLY CHILDHOOD My preschool students often listen to a piece of music and then describe what they heard in their own words. I use this opportunity to broaden their music vocabulary by expanding on what they've said. For example, a child listening to a recording might say, "I heard a low sound." I then respond by saying, "So what instrument do you think could have made that low *pitch*?"

—CONNIE CHRISTY, *Aynor Elementary School (Preschool Program)*

metalinguistic awareness Knowledge of language.

DEVELOPMENT

ELEMENTARY SCHOOL: GRADES K-5 I often tell my fifth-grade students rich, vivid stories about my childhood experiences growing up in eastern Oregon. It is during these teaching moments that my students pay the most attention. I sometimes write these stories on a computer and project them onto a screen in the classroom. Then the students and I discuss the stories and the language used—for example, similes, metaphors, figures of speech. We revise and edit the stories as a group and discuss strengths and weaknesses. The students are then assigned a similar topic to write about. This transfer of knowledge is amazing as the students are entertained, exposed to a new way of writing as it happens—and they see how something can be improved on the spot.

—CRAIG JENSEN, *Cooper Mountain Elementary School*

MIDDLE SCHOOL: GRADES 6-8 During classroom discussions with my seventh-grade students, I intentionally incorporate unfamiliar words that will encourage them to ask, "What does that mean?" For example, when talking about John D. Rockefeller in class recently, I asked, "How many of you would like to become a philanthropist?" I urge students to use their newly learned word at home and to tell the class how they worked it into a conversation. This is a simple way to make vocabulary fun!

—MARK FODNESS, *Bemidji Middle School*

HIGH SCHOOL: GRADES 9-12 My high school students often use slang words that I am unfamiliar with. When this happens, I ask the students what the word means and politely tell them that I want to expand my vocabulary. This dialogue often results in conversations about more appropriate words that the students can use in the workplace, classroom, or at home (and I learn something too!).

—SANDY SWANSON, *Menomonee Falls High School*

CONNECTING WITH STUDENTS: Best Practices
Strategies for Vocabulary Development at Different Developmental Levels

In the section on semantic development, we discussed the impressive gains in vocabulary that many children make as they go through the early childhood, middle and late childhood, and adolescent years. However, there are significant individual variations in children's vocabulary, and a good vocabulary contributes in important ways to school success (Pan & Uccelli, 2009). In addition to ideas described earlier on using technology to improve children's vocabulary, here are other strategies to use in the classroom:

Preschool and Kindergarten

1. *Explain new vocabulary in books that you read to young children.*
2. *Name and describe all of the things in the classroom.*
3. *In everyday conversation with children, introduce and elaborate on words that children are unlikely to know about.* This activity can also be used at higher grade levels.

Elementary, Middle, and High School

1. *If students have severe deficits in vocabulary knowledge, provide intense vocabulary instruction.*
2. *As a rule, don't introduce more than 10 words at a time.*
3. *Give students an opportunity to use words in a variety of contexts.* These contexts might include read-aloud, fill-in-the-blank sentences, and read-and-respond activities (students read short, information articles about a topic that includes targeted vocabulary words and then respond to questions about the articles).
4. *Writing can help students process word meanings actively.* For example, assign students a topic to write about using assigned vocabulary words.

Source: Curtis & Longo, 2001.

Review, Reflect, and Practice

③ Identify the key features of language, biological and environmental influences on language, and the typical growth of the child's language.

REVIEW
- What is language? Describe these five features of spoken language: phonology, morphology, syntax, semantics, and pragmatics.
- What evidence supports the idea that humans are "prewired" for learning language? What evidence supports the importance of environmental factors?
- What milestones does a child go through in the course of learning language, and what are the typical ages of these milestones?

REFLECT
- How have teachers encouraged or discouraged your own mastery of language? What experiences have done the most to expand your language skills?

PRAXIS™ PRACTICE
1. Josh has developed a large vocabulary. Which of the following language systems does this reflect?
   a. semantics
   b. pragmatics
   c. syntax
   d. morphology
2. Children raised in isolation from human contact often show extreme, long-lasting language deficits that are rarely entirely overcome by later exposure to language. This evidence supports which aspect of language development?
   a. biological
   b. environmental
   c. interactionist
   d. pragmatic
3. Tamara is discussing the birds she saw flying over her neighborhood. She says, "We saw a flock of gooses." If Tamara's language development is normal for her age, how old is Tamara likely to be?
   a. 2 years old
   b. 4 years old
   c. 6 years old
   d. 8 years old

Please see answer key at end of book . . . .

Connecting with the Classroom: Crack the Case

The Book Report

Mr. Johnson assigned his high school senior American government students to read two books during the semester that had "something, anything to do with government or political systems" and to write a brief report about each of their chosen books.

One student in the class, Cindy, chose to read *1984* and *Animal Farm*, both by George Orwell. *1984* is a book about what could happen in "the future" year of 1984, given certain earlier political decisions. In essence, the world turns into a terrible place in which "Big Brother" monitors all of one's actions via two-way television-like screens. Infractions of minor rules are punished severely. *Animal Farm* is a brief novel about political systems in which the characters are portrayed as various farm animals such as pigs and dogs. Cindy enjoyed both books and completed them both before mid-term. Her reports were insightful, reflecting on the symbolism contained in the novels and the implications for present-day government.

Cindy's friend, Lucy, had put off reading her first book until the last minute. She knew Cindy enjoyed reading about government and had finished her reports. Lucy asked Cindy if she knew of a "skinny book" she could read to fulfill the assignment. Cindy gladly shared her copy of *Animal Farm* with her friend, but as Lucy began reading the book she wondered why Cindy had given her this book. It didn't seem to fit the requirements of the assignment at all.

The day before the first reports were due, Mr. Johnson overheard the girls talking. Lucy complained to Cindy, "I don't get it. It's a story about pigs and dogs."

Cindy responded, "They aren't really supposed to be farm animals. It's a story about the promises of communism and what happened in the Soviet Union once the communists took over. It's a great story! Don't you see? The pigs symbolize the communist regime that overthrew the czars during the Russian Revolution. They made all kinds of promises about equality for everyone. The people went along with them because they were sick and tired of the rich and powerful running everything while they starved. Once the czars were eliminated, the communists established a new government but didn't keep any of their promises, controlled everything. Remember in the book when the pigs moved into the house and started walking on two legs? That's supposed to be like when the communist leaders began acting just like the czars. They even created a secret police force—the dogs in the story. Remember how they bullied the other animals? Just like the secret police in the Soviet Union."

Lucy commented, "I still don't get it. How can a pig or a dog be a communist or a cop? They're just animals."

Cindy looked at her friend, dumbfounded. How could she *not* understand this book? It was so obvious.

1. Drawing on Piaget's theory, explain why Cindy understood the book.
2. Based on Piaget's theory, explain why Lucy didn't understand the book.
3. What could Mr. Johnson do to help Lucy understand?
4. How could Mr. Johnson have presented this assignment differently, so that Lucy did not need to rush through a book?
5. At which stage of cognitive development would Piaget say that Cindy is operating?
   a. sensorimotor
   b. preoperational
   c. concrete operational
   d. formal operational
   Explain your choice.
6. At which stage of cognitive development would Piaget say that Lucy is operating?
   a. sensorimotor
   b. preoperational
   c. concrete operational
   d. formal operational
   Explain your choice.

Connecting with Learning: Reach Your Learning Goals

 AN OVERVIEW OF CHILD DEVELOPMENT: Define development and explain the main processes, periods, and issues in development, as well as links between development and education.

Exploring What Development Is

- Development is the pattern of biological, cognitive, and socioemotional changes that begins at conception and continues through the life span. Most development involves growth, but it also eventually includes decay (dying).
- The more you learn about children's development, the better you will understand the level at which to appropriately teach them. Childhood provides a foundation for the adult years.

Processes and Periods
- Child development is the product of biological, cognitive, and socioemotional processes, which often are intertwined.
- Periods of development include infancy, early childhood, middle and late childhood, and adolescence.

Developmental Issues
- The main developmental issues are nature and nurture, continuity and discontinuity, and early and later experience.
- The nature-nurture issue focuses on the extent to which development is mainly influenced by nature (biological influence) or nurture (environmental influence). Although heredity and environment are pervasive influences on development, humans can author a unique developmental path by changing the environment.
- Some developmentalists describe development as continuous (gradual, cumulative change), others describe it as discontinuous (a sequence of abrupt stages).
- The early-later experience issue focuses on whether early experiences (especially in infancy) are more important in development than later experiences.
- Most developmentalists recognize that extreme positions on the nature-nurture, continuity-discontinuity, and early-later experience issues are unwise. Despite this consensus, these issues continue to be debated.

Development and Education
- Developmentally appropriate teaching takes place at a level that is neither too difficult and stressful nor too easy and boring for the child's developmental level.
- Splintered development occurs when there is considerable unevenness in development across domains.

2 COGNITIVE DEVELOPMENT: Discuss the development of the brain and compare the cognitive developmental theories of Jean Piaget and Lev Vygotsky.

The Brain
- An especially important part of growth is the development of the brain and nervous system.
- Myelination involving hand-eye coordination is not complete until about 4 years of age, and myelination involving focusing attention is not finished until about 10.
- Substantial synaptic pruning of the brain connections takes place, and the adult level of density of synaptic connections is not reached until some point in adolescence.
- Different regions of the brain grow at different rates. Changes in the brain in middle and late childhood include advances in functioning in the prefrontal cortex, which are reflected in improved attention, reasoning, and cognitive control. During middle and late childhood, less diffusion and more focal activation occurs in the prefrontal cortex, a change that is associated with an increase in cognitive control. However, the prefrontal cortex doesn't finish maturing until the emerging adult years.
- Researchers have recently found a developmental disjunction between the early development of the limbic system and the amygdala, which are responsible for emotion, and the later development of the prefrontal cortex, which is responsible for reasoning and thinking. They argue that these changes in the brain may help to explain the risk-taking behavior and lack of mature judgment in adolescents. Changes in the brain during adolescence also involve the thickening of the corpus callosum.
- Lateralization in some verbal and nonverbal functions occurs, but in many instances functioning is linked to both hemispheres.
- There is considerable plasticity in the brain, and the quality of learning environments children experience influence the development of their brain.
- Too often links between neuroscience and education have been overstated. Based on recent research, what we do know indicates that educational experiences throughout childhood and adolescence can influence the brain's development.

Piaget's Theory
- Jean Piaget proposed a major theory of children's cognitive development that involves these important processes: schemas, assimilation and accommodation, organization, and equilibration.

continued

- In Piaget's theory, cognitive development unfolds in a sequence of four stages: sensorimotor (birth to about age 2), preoperational (about 2 to 7 years), concrete operational (about 7 to 11 years), and formal operational (about 11 to 15 years). Each stage is a qualitative advance.
- In the sensorimotor stage, infants construct an understanding of the world by coordinating their sensory experiences with their motor actions.
- Thought is more symbolic at the preoperational stage, although the child has not yet mastered some important mental operations. Preoperational thought includes symbolic function and intuitive thought substages. Egocentrism and centration are constraints.
- At the concrete operational stage, children can perform operations, and logical thought replaces intuitive thought when reasoning can be applied to specific or concrete examples. Classification, seriation, and transitivity are important concrete operational skills.
- At the formal operational stage, thinking is more abstract, idealistic, and logical. Hypothetical-deductive reasoning becomes important. Adolescent egocentrism characterizes many young adolescents.
- We owe to Piaget a long list of masterful concepts as well as the current vision of the child as an active, constructivist thinker. Criticisms of his view focus on his low estimates of children's competence, overly discreet stages, discouraging the training of children to reason at a higher cognitive level, and the neo-Piagetian criticism of not being precise enough about how children learn.

Vygotsky's Theory

- Lev Vygotsky proposed another major theory of cognitive development. Vygotsky's view emphasizes that cognitive skills need to be interpreted developmentally, are mediated by language, and have their origins in social relations and culture.
- Zone of proximal development (ZPD) is Vygotsky's term for the range of tasks that are too difficult for children to master alone but that can be learned with the guidance and assistance of adults and more-skilled children.
- Scaffolding is an important concept in Vygotsky's theory. He also argued that language plays a key role in guiding cognition.
- Applications of Vygotsky's ideas to education include using the child's zone of proximal development and scaffolding, using more-skilled peers as teachers, monitoring and encouraging children's use of private speech, and accurately assessing the zone of proximal development. These practices can transform the classroom and establish a meaningful context for instruction.
- Like Piaget, Vygotsky emphasized that children actively construct their understanding of the world. Unlike Piaget, he did not propose stages of cognitive development, and he emphasized that children construct knowledge through social interaction. In Vygotsky's theory, children depend on tools provided by the culture, which determines which skills they will develop. Some critics say that Vygotsky overemphasized the role of language in thinking.

③ LANGUAGE DEVELOPMENT: Identify the key features of language, biological, and environmental influences on language, and the typical growth of the child's language.

What Is Language?

- Language is a form of communication, whether spoken, written, or signed, that is based on a system of symbols.
- Human languages are infinitely generative. All human languages also have organizational rules of phonology, morphology, syntax, semantics, and pragmatics. Phonology is the sound system of a language; morphology refers to the units of meaning involved in word formation; syntax involves the ways that words must be combined to form acceptable phrases and sentences; semantics refers to the meaning of words and sentences; and pragmatics describes the appropriate use of language in different contexts.

Biological and Environmental Influences

- Children are biologically prepared to learn language as they and their caregivers interact. Some language scholars argue that the strongest evidence for the biological basis of language is that children all over the world reach language milestones at about the same age despite vast differences in their environmental experiences.

How Language Develops

- However, children do not learn language in a social vacuum. Children benefit when parents and teachers actively engage them in conversation, ask them questions, and talk with—not just to—them. In sum, biology and experience interact to produce language development.
- Language acquisition advances through stages. Babbling occurs at about 3 to 6 months, the first word at 10 to 13 months, and two-word utterances at 18 to 24 months.
- As children move beyond two-word utterances, they can demonstrate that they know some morphological rules, as documented in Jean Berko's study. Children also make advances in phonology, syntax, semantics, and pragmatics in early childhood.
- Young children's early literacy experiences enhance the likelihood children will have the language skills necessary to benefit from schooling.
- Vocabulary development increases dramatically during the elementary school years, and by the end of elementary school most children can apply appropriate rules of grammar. Metalinguistic awareness also advances in the elementary school years.
- In adolescence, language changes include more effective use of words; improvements in the ability to understand metaphor, satire, and adult literary works; and writing.

KEY TERMS

accommodation 40
amygdala 37
assimilation 40
centration 42
concrete operational stage 45
conservation 42
continuity-discontinuity issue 33
corpus callosum 37
development 29
early-later experience issue 33
epigenetic view 32
equilibration 40
formal operational stage 45
hypothetical-deductive reasoning 46
intuitive thought substage 42
language 58
lateralization 38
limbic system 37
metalinguistic awareness 63
morphology 58
myelination 36
nature-nurture issue 31
neo-Piagetians 50
neuroconstructivist view 35
organization 40
phonology 58
pragmatics 59
prefrontal cortex 36
preoperational stage 42
scaffolding 51
schemas 40
semantics 59
sensorimotor stage 42
seriation 45
social constructivist approach 53
splintered development 34
symbolic function substage 42
syntax 58
transitivity 45
zone of proximal development (ZPD) 50

PORTFOLIO ACTIVITIES

Now that you have a good understanding of this chapter, complete these exercises to expand your thinking.

Independent Reflection

1. **Communicating with Children.** Select the general age of the child you expect to teach one day. Make a list of that child's characteristic ways of thinking according to Piaget's theory of cognitive development. List other related characteristics of the child based on your own childhood. Then make a second list of your own current ways of thinking. Compare the lists. In what important cognitive ways do you and the child differ? What adjustments in thinking will you need to make when you set out to communicate with the child? Summarize your thoughts in a brief essay.

2. **Benefits of Formal Operational Thinking.** How might thinking in formal operational ways rather than concrete operational ways help students develop better study skills?

3. **Language Development.** What is the most useful idea related to children's language development that you read about in this chapter? Write the idea down in your portfolio and explain how you will implement this idea in your classroom.

Research/Field Experience

4. **Whole-Brained Thinking.** Find an education article in a magazine or on the Internet that promotes "left-brained" and "right-brained" activities for learning. In a brief report, criticize the article based on what you read in this chapter about neuroscience and brain education.

chapter 3

SOCIAL CONTEXTS AND SOCIOEMOTIONAL DEVELOPMENT

chapter outline

① Contemporary Theories

Learning Goal 1 Describe two contemporary perspectives on socioemotional development: Bronfenbrenner's ecological theory and Erikson's life-span development theory.

Bronfenbrenner's Ecological Theory
Erikson's Life-Span Development Theory

② Social Contexts of Development

Learning Goal 2 Discuss how the social contexts of families, peers, and schools are linked with socioemotional development.

Families
Peers
Schools

③ Socioemotional Development

Learning Goal 3 Explain these aspects of children's socioemotional development: self-esteem, identity, moral development, and emotional development.

The Self and Identity
Moral Development
Emotional Development

In the end, the power behind development is life.

—Erik Erikson.
European-born American Psychotherapist, 20th Century

Connecting with Teachers Keren Abra

The socioemotional contexts of children's lives influence their ability to learn. Keren Abra teaches fifth grade in San Francisco. A student in her class, Julie, was very quiet—so quiet that in classroom discussions she whispered her responses. Her parents, who had gone through a bitter divorce, agreed that Julie needed a good therapist.

Julie was significantly underachieving, doing minimal work and scoring low on tests. A crisis of low grades and incomplete work brought her mother to school one evening, and her father to school the next morning, to talk with Keren. Later that week, Keren spoke with Julie, who looked terrified. Following are Keren's comments about her talk with Julie:

> I kept some objectives in mind. This child needed to know that she was a good student, that she was loved, that adults could be consistent and responsible, and that she didn't have to hide and keep secrets. I told her that her parents had come in because we all were concerned about her and knew we needed to help her. I told her that her parents loved her very much and asked if she knew this (she and I agreed that nobody's perfect, least of all adults with their own problems). I explained that a tutor was going to help her with her work.... I talked with Julie about how much I liked her and about coming forward more in class.

Change did not happen overnight with Julie, but she did begin to increasingly look me in the eye with a more confident smile. She spoke out more in class, and improved her writing efforts. Her best months were when she was seeing both a therapist and a tutor, although her grades remained a roller coaster. At the end of the school year, she commented that she and her mother both noticed that her best work was when she felt supported and confident. For an 11-year-old, that is a valuable insight.

Quote by Keren Abra.

Preview

Divorce is just one of the many aspects of children's social contexts that can have profound effects on children's performance in school. Later in the chapter, we will examine the topic of divorce and provide teaching strategies for helping students cope with the divorce of their parents. We will explore how parents cradle children's lives as well as how children's development is influenced by successive waves of peers, friends, and teachers. Children's small worlds widen as they become students and develop relationships with many new people. In this second chapter on development, we will study these social worlds and examine children's socioemotional development.

1 CONTEMPORARY THEORIES

Bronfenbrenner's Ecological Theory | Erikson's Life-Span Development Theory

LG 1 Describe two contemporary perspectives on socioemotional development: Bronfenbrenner's ecological theory and Erikson's life-span development theory.

A number of theories address children's socioemotional development. In this chapter, we will focus on two main theories: Bronfenbrenner's ecological theory and Erikson's life-span development theory. These two theories were chosen for the comprehensive way they address the social contexts in which children develop (Bronfenbrenner) and major changes in children's socioemotional development (Erikson). Later in this text we will discuss other theories (behavioral and social cognitive) that also are relevant to socioemotional development.

Thinking Back/Thinking Forward

Bandura's social cognitive theory also emphasizes the importance of social contexts. Connect to "Behavioral and Social Cognitive Approaches."

BRONFENBRENNER'S ECOLOGICAL THEORY

The ecological theory developed by Urie Bronfenbrenner (1917–2005) primarily focuses on the social contexts in which children live and the people who influence their development.

DEVELOPMENT

Five Environmental Systems Bronfenbrenner's (1995, Bronfenbrenner & Morris, 2006) **ecological theory** identifies five environmental systems that range from close interpersonal interactions to broad-based influences of culture. The five systems are the microsystem, mesosystem, exosystem, macrosystem, and chronosystem (see Figure 1).

ecological theory Bronfenbrenner's theory that development is influenced by five environmental systems: microsystem, mesosystem, exosystem, macrosystem, and chronosystem.

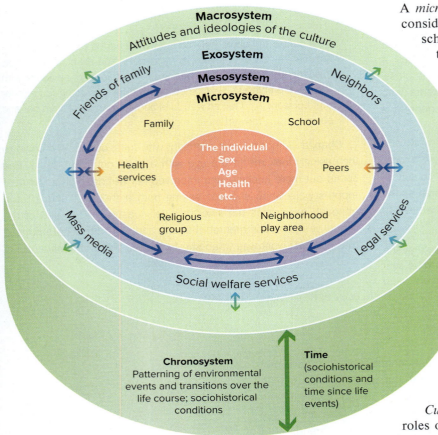

FIGURE 1 BRONFENBRENNER'S ECOLOGICAL THEORY OF DEVELOPMENT

Bronfenbrenner's ecological theory describes five environmental systems: microsystem, mesosystem, exosystem, macrosystem, and chronosystem.

A *microsystem* is a setting in which the individual spends considerable time, such as the student's family, peers, school, and neighborhood. Within these microsystems, the individual has direct interactions with parents, teachers, peers, and others. For Bronfenbrenner, the student is not a passive recipient of experiences but is someone who reciprocally interacts with others and helps to construct the microsystem.

The *mesosystem* involves linkages between microsystems. Examples are the connections between family experiences and school experiences and between family and peers. We will have more to say about family-school connections later in the chapter.

The *exosystem* is at work when experiences in another setting (in which the student does not have an active role) influence what students and teachers experience in the immediate context. For example, consider the school and park supervisory boards in a community. They have strong roles in determining the quality of schools, parks, recreation facilities, and libraries, which can help or hinder a child's development.

The *macrosystem* involves the broader culture. *Culture* is a very broad term that encompasses the roles of ethnicity and socioeconomic factors in children's development. It's the broadest context in which students and teachers live, reinforcing the society's values and customs (Shiraev & Levy, 2010). For example, some cultures (such as rural China and Iran) emphasize traditional gender roles.

The *chronosystem* includes the sociohistorical conditions of students' development. For example, the lives of children today differ in many ways from what their parents and grandparents experienced as children (Schaie & Willis, 2016). Today's children are more likely to be in child care, use computers, and grow up in new kinds of dispersed, deconcentrated cities that are not quite urban, rural, or suburban.

Evaluating Bronfenbrenner's Theory Bronfenbrenner's theory has gained popularity in recent years. It provides one of the few theoretical frameworks for systematically examining social contexts on both micro and macro levels, bridging the gap between behavioral theories that focus on small settings and anthropological theories that analyze larger settings. His theory has been instrumental in showing how different contexts of children's lives are interconnected. As we have just discussed, teachers often need to consider not just what goes on in the classroom but also what happens in students' families, neighborhoods, and peer groups.

It should be mentioned that Bronfenbrenner (2000) added biological influences to his theory and subsequently described it as a *bioecological* theory. Nonetheless, ecological, environmental contexts still predominate in Bronfenbrenner's theory (Haines et al., 2015; Orrock & Clark, 2016).

Bronfenbrenner's theory has been criticized for paying too little attention to biological and cognitive factors in children's development and not addressing the step-by-step developmental changes that are the focus of theories such as Piaget's and Erikson's.

DIVERSITY

CONNECTING WITH STUDENTS: Best Practices
Strategies for Educating Children Based on Bronfenbrenner's Theory

1. *Think about the child as embedded in a number of environmental systems and influences.* These include schools and teachers, parents and siblings, the community and neighborhood, peers and friends, the media, religion, and culture.
2. *Pay attention to the connection between schools and families.* Build these connections through formal and informal outreach.
3. *Recognize the importance of the community, socioeconomic status, and culture in the child's development.* These broader social contexts can have powerful influences on the child's development (Gonzales et al., 2016; Zusho et al., 2016). In *Through the Eyes of Teachers,* Juanita Kirton, an assistant principal at Gramercy Preschool in New York City, describes the community's value for her students.

THROUGH THE EYES OF TEACHERS
The Community Is Full of Learning Opportunities and Supports for Students

Use of the community is very important. New York City is full of opportunities. I have been able to work closely with the Disabled Library in the neighborhood. They have been great at supplying the school with audiobooks for the children and lending special equipment for their use. The local fire department has been used for numerous trips. The firemen have been especially attentive to the students because of their various disabilities. The fire department has also come to visit the school, which was very exciting for the children. It was amazing to see how patient the firefighters were with the students. I am also encouraged to see many colleges and universities sending items and student teachers visiting the school. Donations from the Hasbro toy company during the holidays make a big difference in the way some students and families get to spend their holiday vacation. Our students are very visible in the New York City community, where we are located. This helps our neighbors get to know the staff and children and creates a safer environment.

Juanita Kirton

ERIKSON'S LIFE-SPAN DEVELOPMENT THEORY

Complementing Bronfenbrenner's analysis of the social contexts in which children develop and the people who are important in their lives, the theory of Erik Erikson (1902–1994) presents a developmental view of people's lives in stages. Let's take a journey through Erikson's view of the human life span.

Eight Stages of Human Development In Erikson's (1968) theory, eight stages of development unfold as people go through the human life span (see Figure 2). Each stage consists of a developmental task that confronts individuals with a crisis. For Erikson, each crisis is not catastrophic but a turning point of increased vulnerability and enhanced potential. The more successfully an individual resolves each crisis, the more psychologically healthy the individual will be. Each stage has both positive and negative aspects.

Trust versus mistrust is Erikson's first psychosocial stage. It occurs in the first year of life. The development of trust requires warm, nurturing caregiving. The positive outcome is a feeling of comfort and minimal fear. Mistrust develops when infants are treated negatively or ignored.

Autonomy versus shame and doubt is Erikson's second psychosocial stage. It occurs in late infancy and the toddler years. After gaining trust in their caregivers, infants begin to discover that their behavior is their own. They assert their independence and realize their will. If infants are restrained too much or punished too harshly, they develop a sense of shame and doubt.

Initiative versus guilt is Erikson's third psychosocial stage. It corresponds to early childhood, about 3 to 5 years of age. As young children experience a widening social

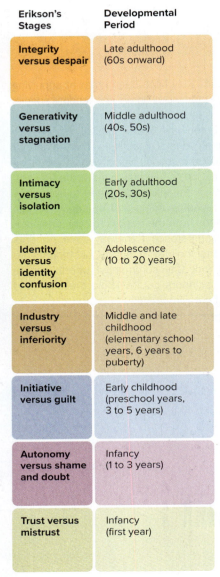

FIGURE 2 ERIKSON'S EIGHT STAGES OF THE HUMAN LIFE SPAN

What are the implications of saying that people go through stages of development?

Erik Erikson with his wife, Joan, an artist. Erikson generated one of the most important developmental theories of the twentieth century. *Which stage of Erikson's theory are you in? Does Erikson's description of this stage characterize you?*

Jon Erikson/Science Source

world, they are challenged more than they were as infants. To cope with these challenges, they need to engage in active, purposeful behavior that involves initiative. Children develop uncomfortable guilt feelings if they are irresponsible or are made to feel too anxious.

Industry versus inferiority is Erikson's fourth psychosocial stage. It corresponds approximately with the elementary school years, from 6 years of age until puberty or early adolescence. As children move into the elementary school years, they direct their energy toward mastering knowledge and intellectual skills. The danger in the elementary school years is developing a sense of inferiority, unproductiveness, and incompetence.

Identity versus identity confusion is Erikson's fifth psychosocial stage. It corresponds to the adolescent years. Adolescents try to find out who they are, what they are all about, and where they are going in life. They are confronted with many new roles and adult statuses (such as vocational and romantic). Adolescents need to be allowed to explore different paths to attain a healthy identity. If adolescents do not adequately explore different roles and don't carve out a positive future path, they can remain confused about their identity.

Intimacy versus isolation is Erikson's sixth psychosocial stage. It corresponds to the early adult years, the twenties and thirties. The developmental task is to form positive close relationships with others. The hazard of this stage is that one will fail to form an intimate relationship with a romantic partner or friend and become socially isolated.

Generativity versus stagnation is Erikson's seventh psychosocial stage. It corresponds to the middle adulthood years, the forties and fifties. Generativity means transmitting something positive to the next generation. This can involve such roles as parenting and teaching, through which adults assist the next generation in developing useful lives. Erikson described stagnation as the feeling of having done nothing to help the next generation.

Integrity versus despair is Erikson's eighth and final psychosocial stage. It corresponds to the late adulthood years, the sixties until death. Older adults review their lives, reflecting on what they have done. If the retrospective evaluations are positive, they develop a sense of integrity. That is, they view their life as positively integrated and worth living. In contrast, older adults become despairing if their backward glances are mainly negative.

Several teachers were asked how they apply Erikson's life-span theory in their classrooms. Following are their comments.

EARLY CHILDHOOD The initiative versus guilt stage of Erikson's theory characterizes my classroom as students are expected to become more responsible throughout the year. Children are assigned "jobs" to do for the day, such as being the door-holder, line leader, or messenger. The children are also expected to follow through with classroom and school rules. Uncomfortable, guilty feelings may arise if the children feel irresponsible as a result of breaking classroom rules or not fulfilling their responsibilities.

—MISSY DANGLER, *Suburban Hills School*

ELEMENTARY SCHOOL: GRADES K–5 The industry versus inferiority stage of Erikson's theory most applies to my second-grade students. As children enter this stage, there is an energy to learn; however, the dangers at this stage are that children may feel incompetent if they are unsuccessful in their work. As a teacher of students at this developmental stage, it is important to give students opportunities to be successful. For example, if a second-grader is reading at a kindergarten level, and second-grade-level materials are given to this student, the student will develop feelings of incompetence. I use leveled reading materials in my classroom in reading and spelling. Each student is reading and being instructed with material at his or her reading level, which fosters feelings of confidence.

—SUSAN FROELICH, *Clinton Elementary School*

MIDDLE SCHOOL: GRADES 6–8 Erikson's identity versus identity confusion stage is evident in my sixth-grade students. At this stage, so many of my students experience a decline in self-esteem. To address these negative feelings, I often have them become the teacher. That is, under my guidance, a student will conduct different classroom activities. Many times I select students who need to be recognized by their peers to be teacher for a day. Other times, I ask students—especially those most reluctant to participate in class—to have lunch with me. During lunch, I give them steps on how to overcome any fears or apprehensions they may have about taking part in class.

—MARGARET REARDON, *Pocantico Hills School*

HIGH SCHOOL: GRADES 9–12 As high school teachers dealing with students in the identity versus identity confusion stage, we need to especially value adolescents as human beings. I know of so many teachers who roll their eyes at their students' petty squabbles and emotional curves. However, we need to remember that we went through the very same things, and these struggles helped to define who we are as adults. This came to me so vividly during my student teaching. The building was so similar in design to my own school. As I walked in the door, I immediately experienced every pimple on my chin and every tear shed in the girls' bathroom. Suddenly, I was the insecure girl listening to Lionel Richie at the dance, longing for John to ask me out.

—JENNIFER HEITER, *Bremen High School*

Evaluating Erikson's Theory Erikson's theory captures some of life's key socioemotional tasks and places them in a developmental framework (Kroger, 2015). His concept of identity is especially helpful in understanding older adolescents and college students. His overall theory was a critical force in forging our current view of human development as lifelong rather than being restricted only to childhood.

Erikson's theory is not without its critics (Cote, 2015). Some experts point out that his stages are too rigid. Life-span development pioneer Bernice Neugarten (1988) says that identity, intimacy, independence, and many other aspects of socioemotional development are not like beads on a string that appear in neatly packaged age intervals. Rather, they are important issues throughout most of our lives. Although much research has been conducted on some of Erikson's stages (identity versus identity confusion, in particular), the overall scope of his theory (such as whether the eight stages always occur in the order and timetable he proposed) has not been scientifically documented. For example, for some individuals (especially females), intimacy concerns precede identity or develop simultaneously.

CONNECTING WITH STUDENTS: Best Practices
Strategies for Educating Children Based on Erikson's Theory

1. *Encourage initiative in young children.* Children in preschool and early childhood education programs should be given a great deal of freedom to explore their world. They should be allowed to choose some of the activities they engage in. If their requests for doing certain activities are reasonable, the requests should be honored. Provide exciting materials that will stimulate their imagination. Children at this stage love to play. It not only benefits their socioemotional development but also is an important medium for their cognitive growth. Especially encourage social play with peers and fantasy play. Help children assume responsibility for putting toys and materials back in place after they have used them. Criticism should be kept to a minimum so that children will not develop high levels of guilt and anxiety. Structure activities and environment for successes rather than failures by giving them developmentally appropriate tasks; for example, don't frustrate young children by having them sit for long periods of time doing academic paper-and-pencil tasks.

2. *Promote industry in elementary school children.* Teachers have a special responsibility for children's development of industry. It was Erikson's hope that teachers could provide an atmosphere in which children become passionate about learning. In elementary school, children thirst to know. Most arrive at elementary school steeped in curiosity and a motivation to master tasks. In Erikson's view, it is important for teachers to nourish this motivation for mastery and curiosity. Challenge students, but don't overwhelm them. Be firm in requiring students to be productive, but don't be overly critical. Especially be tolerant of honest mistakes and make sure that every student has opportunities for many successes.

3. *Stimulate identity exploration in adolescence.* Recognize that the student's identity is multidimensional. Ask adolescents to write essays about such dimensions, including vocational goals, intellectual achievement, and interests in hobbies, sports, music, and other areas, exploring who they are and what they want to do with their lives. Have people from different careers come and talk with your students about their work regardless of the grade you teach. Encourage adolescents to think independently and to freely express their views by listening to and reading about debates on religious, political, and ideological issues. This will stimulate them to examine different perspectives.

4. *Examine your life as a teacher through the lens of Erikson's eight stages.* Your successful career as a teacher could be a key aspect of your overall identity. Develop positive relationships with a partner, one or more friends, and with other teachers or mentors, all of which can be very rewarding and enhance your identity as a teacher.

5. *Benefit from the characteristics of some of Erikson's other stages.* Competent teachers trust, show initiative, are industrious and model a sense of mastery, and are motivated to contribute something meaningful to the next generation. In your role as a teacher, you will actively meet the criteria for Erikson's concept of generativity.

In *Through the Eyes of Teachers,* Therese Olejniczak, a teacher at Central Middle School in East Grand Forks, Minnesota, describes how she encourages students to think about their identity on the first day of school.

THROUGH THE EYES OF TEACHERS
Using Art to Explore Adolescents' Identities

My seventh-grade art students come to class the first day expecting to read a list of classroom rules. I surprise them by passing out sheets of art paper, old magazines, and glue with the verbal directions to tell me about themselves—build a self-portrait—with torn paper. The students are inventive, enthusiastic, and excited to focus on their identities, and waste no time beginning. . . . After the opening project, my students are at ease knowing their creative expression is allowed and encouraged, and I am better able to understand their many changing attitudes and need to express them.

Therese Olejniczak

Review, Reflect, and Practice

1 Describe two contemporary perspectives on socioemotional development: Bronfenbrenner's ecological theory and Erikson's life-span development theory.

REVIEW
- What are Bronfenbrenner's five environmental systems? What are some criticisms of his theory?
- What are the eight Eriksonian stages? What are some criticisms of his theory?

Review, Reflect, and Practice

REFLECT
- How well do you think your own socioemotional development can be described using Erikson's theory?

PRAXIS™ PRACTICE
1. Which of the following is the best example of the mesosystem?
   a. Ike's parents monitor his behavior closely. They know where he is and with whom at all times.
   b. Ike's parents express concern about his grades. They attend parent-teacher conferences and belong to the PTA, as does John's teacher. They chaperone field trips.
   c. Ike attends church regularly, goes to religious school each week, and is preparing for his confirmation.
   d. Ike is quite adept with technology. His parents often ask him to program their electronic devices because of their lack of experience with these things when they were children.
2. Ms. Rogers teaches fourth grade. Understanding that it is important for her students to do well on the state-mandated achievement tests, she has high expectations for their daily work. Often her lessons frustrate some of her students because they don't understand the material. Rather than helping them to understand, she forges ahead. She is then frustrated by their performance on homework, often making caustic remarks on their papers. How would Ms. Rogers' teaching style be described from Erikson's perspective?
   a. Ms. Rogers' teaching style is closely aligned with the need to promote industry in elementary school children. Her high expectations will motivate the children to succeed.
   b. Ms. Rogers' teaching style is closely aligned with elementary-school-age children's need to discover who they are and establish an identity.
   c. Ms. Rogers' teaching style is unlikely to promote industry in elementary-school-age children. Instead, it is likely to make them feel inferior.
   d. Ms. Rogers' teaching style is likely to increase students' initiative. They will respond to her high expectations by taking initiative in their work.

Please see answer key at end of book ....

2 SOCIAL CONTEXTS OF DEVELOPMENT

LG 2 Discuss how the social contexts of families, peers, and schools are linked with socioemotional development.

In Bronfenbrenner's theory, the social contexts of children's lives are important influences on their development. Let's explore three of the contexts in which children spend much of their time: families, peers, and schools.

FAMILIES

Although children grow up in diverse families, in virtually every family parents play an important role in supporting and stimulating children's academic achievement and attitudes toward school (Rowe et al., 2016). The value parents place on education can determine whether children do well in school. Parents not only influence children's in-school achievement, but they also make decisions about children's out-of-school activities. Whether children participate in such activities as sports, music, and other activities is heavily influenced by the extent to which parents sign up children for such activities and encourage their participation (Wigfield et al., 2015).

Parenting Styles There might be times when it is helpful for you to understand how parents are rearing their children and the effects this has on the children. Is there a best way to parent? Diana Baumrind (1971, 1996), a leading authority on parenting, thinks so. She states that parents should be neither punitive nor aloof. Rather, they should develop rules for children while at the same time being supportive and nurturing. Hundreds of research studies, including her own, support her view (Steinberg, 2014). Baumrind says that parenting styles fall into four main categories:

- **Authoritarian parenting** is restrictive and punitive. Authoritarian parents exhort children to follow their directions and respect them. They place firm limits and controls on their children and allow little verbal exchange. For example, an authoritarian parent might say, "Do it my way or else. There will be no discussion!" Children of authoritarian parents often behave in socially incompetent ways. They tend to be anxious about social comparison, fail to initiate activity, and have poor communication skills.

- **Authoritative parenting** encourages children to be independent but still places limits and controls on their actions. Extensive verbal give-and-take is allowed, and parents are nurturant and supportive. Children whose parents are authoritative often behave in socially competent ways. They tend to be self-reliant, delay gratification, get along with their peers, and show high self-esteem. Because of these positive outcomes, Baumrind strongly endorses authoritative parenting.

- **Neglectful parenting** is a parenting style in which parents are uninvolved in their children's lives. Children of neglectful parents develop the sense that other aspects of their parents' lives are more important than they are. Children of neglectful parents often behave in socially incompetent ways. They tend to have poor self-control, don't handle independence well, and aren't motivated to achieve.

- **Indulgent parenting** is a parenting style in which parents are highly involved with their children but place few limits or restrictions on their behaviors. These parents often let their children do whatever they want because they believe the combination of nurturant support and lack of restraints will produce a creative, confident child. The result is that these children usually don't learn to control their own behavior. Indulgent parents do not take into account the development of the whole child.

Do the benefits of authoritative parenting transcend the boundaries of ethnicity, socioeconomic status, and household composition? Although some exceptions have been found, research links authoritative parenting with competence on the part of the child across a wide range of ethnic groups, social strata, cultures, and family structures (Steinberg, 2014).

Nonetheless, researchers have found that in some ethnic groups, aspects of the authoritarian style may be associated with more positive child outcomes than Baumrind predicts. Elements of the authoritarian style may take on different meanings and have different effects depending on the cultural context (Clarke-Stewart & Parke, 2014).

For example, Asian American parents often adhere to aspects of traditional Asian child-rearing practices that are sometimes described as authoritarian. Many Asian American parents exert considerable control over their children's lives. However, Ruth Chao (2005, 2007) argues that the style of parenting used by many Asian American

authoritarian parenting A restrictive and punitive parenting style in which there is little verbal exchange between parents and children; this style is associated with children's social incompetence.

authoritative parenting A positive parenting style that encourages children to be independent but still places limits and controls on their actions, allows extensive verbal give-and-take, and is associated with children's social competence.

neglectful parenting A parenting style of uninvolvement in which parents spend little time with their children; associated with children's social incompetence.

indulgent parenting A parenting style that includes parental involvement but places few limits or restrictions on children's behavior; linked with children's social incompetence.

parents is distinct from the domineering control of the authoritarian style. Instead, Chao argues that the control reflects concern and involvement in children's lives and is best conceptualized as a type of training. The high academic achievement of Asian American children may be a consequence of the "training" provided by their parents.

Parent Involvement in Children's Schooling and Achievement Do students do better in school when parents are involved in various aspects of their schooling and achievement? In a recent study of more than 15,000 fifth-grade students, a higher level of parental school-based involvement and higher parental educational expectations were linked to adolescents' higher cumulative grade point average and also to higher educational attainment approximately eight years after their high school graduation (Benner et al., 2016). Also in this study, parental school-based involvement was especially beneficial for students in low-socioeconomic-status (SES) families, while a higher level of parental academic advice was linked to greater academic success for students in higher-SES families.

DIVERSITY

Coparenting *Coparenting* is the support that parents provide one another in jointly raising a child. Poor coordination between parents, undermining of the other parent, lack of cooperation and warmth, and disconnection by one parent are conditions that place children at risk for problems (Galdiolo & Roskam, 2016; Goldberg & Carlson, 2015).

The Changing Family in a Changing Society Increasing numbers of children are being raised in divorced families, stepparent families, and families in which both parents work outside the home. As divorce has become epidemic, a staggering number of children have been growing up in single-parent families. The United States has a higher percentage of single-parent families than virtually any other industrialized country (see Figure 3). Today, about one in every four children in the United States has been part of a stepfamily by age 18. Also, more than two of every three mothers with a child from 6 to 17 years of age are in the labor force.

Working Parents Work can produce positive and negative effects on parenting (O'Brien et al., 2014; Veira et al., 2016). Recent research indicates that the nature of parents' work has a stronger influence on children's development than whether one or both parents work outside the home (Clarke-Stewart & Parke, 2014). Ann Crouter (2006) recently described how parents bring their experiences at work into their homes. She concluded that parents who have poor working conditions, such as long hours, overtime work, stressful work, and lack of autonomy at work, are likely to be more irritable at home and engage in less effective parenting than their counterparts who have better working conditions. A consistent finding is the children (especially girls) of working mothers engage in less gender stereotyping and have more egalitarian views of gender roles (Goldberg & Lucas-Thompson, 2008).

Children in Divorced Families Children from divorced families show poorer adjustment (related to academic achievement, behavior, anxiety, and depression) than their counterparts in nondivorced families (Arkes, 2015; Weaver & Schofield, 2015). Nonetheless, keep in mind that a majority of children in divorced families do not have significant adjustment problems (related to academic achievement, behavior, anxiety, and depression) (Ahrons, 2007).

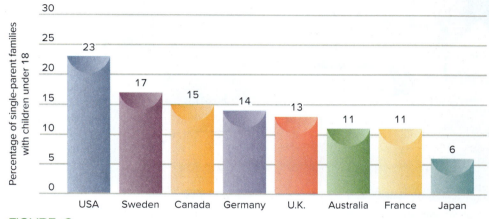
FIGURE 3 PERCENTAGE OF SINGLE-PARENT FAMILIES IN VARIOUS COUNTRIES

What are some concerns about children in divorced families?
Purestock/Getty Images

Note that marital conflict may have negative consequences for children in the context of marriage or divorce (Cummings & Miller, 2015; Cummings & Valentino, 2015; Davies et al., 2016; Jouriles et al., 2016). Indeed, many of the problems children from divorced homes experience begin during the predivorce period, a time when parents are often in active conflict with each other. Thus, when children from divorced homes show problems, the problems may not be due only to the divorce but also to the marital conflict that led to it (Brock & Kochanska, 2016).

The effects of divorce on children are complex, depending on such factors as the child's age, the child's strengths and weaknesses at the time of the divorce, the type of custody, socioeconomic status, and postdivorce family functioning (Demby, 2016; Elam et al., 2016). The use of support systems (relatives, friends, housekeepers), an ongoing positive relationship between the custodial parent and the ex-spouse, the ability to meet financial needs, and quality schooling help children adjust to the stressful circumstances of divorce (Alba-Fisch, 2016; Lansford, 2013). A recent study found that cooperative coparenting between divorced spouses was linked to children having fewer adjustment problems (Lamela et al., 2016).

E. Mavis Hetherington's (1995, 2006) research documents the importance of schools when children grow up in a divorced family. Throughout elementary school, children in divorced families had the highest achievement and fewest problems when both the parenting environment and the school environment were authoritative (according to Baumrind's categorization). In the divorced families, when only one parent was authoritative, an authoritative school improved the child's adjustment. The most negative parenting environment occurred when neither parent was authoritative. The most negative school environment was chaotic and neglecting.

School-Family Linkages Even though parents typically spend less time with their children as the children go through elementary and secondary school, they continue to have a strong influence on children's development (Clark et al., 2015). Parents can serve as gatekeepers and provide guidance as children assume more responsibility for themselves (Kobak & Kerig, 2015). Parents especially play an important role in supporting and stimulating children's academic achievement (Rowe et al., 2016). The value parents place on education can influence children's performance in school. Parents not only influence children's in-school achievement, but they also make decisions about children's out-of-school activities (Vandell et al., 2015), like music and sports (Wigfield et al., 2015).

Experienced teachers understand the importance of getting parents involved in children's education (Chang et al., 2015). All parents, even those with considerable education, need yearly guidance from teachers in how to remain productively involved in their children's education. For one thing, education expert Joyce Epstein (2001, 2009) explains that almost all parents want their children to succeed in school, but parents need clear and useful information from their children's teachers and from other school and district leaders on how to help their children reach their full potential. For example, sometimes parents ask their child, "How was school today?" We know that may end with the child responding, "Fine" or "Okay" and

What are some important parental influences on children's schooling and achievement?
Digital Vision/Getty Images

not much more. Parents should be guided, instead, to ask their child, "Would you read to me something you wrote today?" or "Could you show me something you learned in math today?" or similar direct questions about work and projects in other content areas. Conversations or homework assignments that enable students to share ideas and celebrate successes are likely to promote positive school-related parent-child interactions.

For ways to develop effective school-family-community partnerships and programs, see the Web site of at safesupportivelearning.ed.gov/training-technical-assistance/education-level/early-learning/family-school-community-partnerships. Also, teachers can use various technologies to keep parents connected with their children's education and activities. These include using an online blog, posting on Twitter or Instagram, as well as using e-mail or personal text messages to communicate with parents. These all can be good options to ensure that parents stay informed and involved with their children's schooling.

Teachers at different levels of schooling were asked to provide suggestions about how to get parents/guardians involved in the schooling of their child. Following are their responses.

EARLY CHILDHOOD Parents are an integral part of our classroom community; teachers cannot be successful without parental cooperation and participation. We engage parents through ongoing conversation, home phone calls when needed, weekly newsletters, e-mails, parent-teacher conferences, and workshops every month where dinner is served.

—VALARIE GORHAM, *Kiddie Quarters, Inc*

ELEMENTARY SCHOOL: GRADES K-5 Not all parents are available to volunteer in the classroom. For that reason, I provide alternative ways for parents to participate in their child's schooling. For example, I sometimes ask parents to prepare materials at home that will be used in a classroom lesson. Additionally, each month we have a monthly homework calendar that parents complete with their child and fill out a response form on the back letting me know what the parent learned about their child, as well as how they helped their child complete the tasks.

—HEATHER ZOLDAK, *Ridge Wood Elementary School*

MIDDLE SCHOOL: GRADES 6-8 My team uses technology to communicate with parents daily. We post grades, homework, and daily announcements online. We also require our students to use planners to write down assignments, missing work, and so on. We contact parents if there are concerns, but we also contact parents with positive news about their child.

—MARK FODNESS, *Bemidji Middle School*

HIGH SCHOOL: GRADES 9-12 I teach 15 miles from my home in a small community, but I make it a point to be visible—this may mean shopping at the grocery or drugstore in my school's community rather than frequenting the one closer to my home. When I shop within the vicinity of the school, I often see my students working and parents shopping, which makes me more approachable. I also try to go to school plays, competitions, and athletic events so that when parent-teacher conferences roll around, parents who have grown familiar with my face may be more inclined to attend the conference.

—JENNIFER HEITER, *Bremen High School*

CONNECTING WITH STUDENTS: Best Practices
Strategies for Forging School-Family-Community Linkages

Joyce Epstein has identified six types of involvement that can be implemented to develop comprehensive school, family, and community partnerships in any elementary, middle, or high school. These goal-oriented and age-appropriate activities include the following:

1. *Provide assistance to families.* Schools can provide parents with information about child-rearing skills, the importance of family support, child and adolescent development, and home contexts that enhance learning at each grade level. Teachers are an important contact point between schools and families and can become aware of whether the family is meeting the child's basic physical and health needs.

2. *Communicate effectively with families about school programs and their child's progress.* This involves both school-to-home and home-to-school communication. Encourage parents to attend parent-teacher conferences and other school functions. Set up times for parent meetings that are convenient for them to attend.

3. *Encourage parents to be volunteers.* Try to match the skills of volunteers to classroom needs. In some schools parents are extensively involved in educational planning and in assisting teachers. Parents have different talents and abilities, just like children, which is reflected in comments by Heather Zoldak, a teacher at Ridge Wood Elementary School in Michigan, in *Through the Eyes of Teachers.*

4. *Involve families with their children in learning activities at home.* This includes homework and other curriculum-linked activities and decisions. Epstein (1998) coined the term *interactive homework* and designed a program that encourages students to go to their parents for help. In one elementary school that uses Epstein's approach, a weekly letter from the teacher informs parents about the objective of each assignment, gives directions, and asks for comments.

5. *Include families as participants in school decisions.* Parents can be invited to join PTA/PTO boards, various committees, councils, and other parent organizations. At Antwa Elementary School in a rural area of Wisconsin, potluck supper parent-teacher organization meetings involve discussions with parents about school and district educational goals, age-appropriate learning, child discipline, and testing performance.

6. *Coordinate community collaboration.* Help interconnect the work and resources of community businesses, agencies, colleges and universities, and other groups to strengthen school programs, family practices, and student learning (Epstein, 2009). Schools can alert families to community programs and services that will benefit them.

THROUGH THE EYES OF TEACHERS
Encouraging Parent Involvement

Understanding that parents come with different levels of comfort with the school environment is important when encouraging parent support for the classroom. Prepare a variety of opportunities for parents to become involved inside the classroom and to support the classroom in other ways. Due to busy schedules, work restrictions, or comfort level based on their own experiences with school, some parents may be more involved if they can help outside the classroom on field trips or even prepare items at home for an upcoming project. Taking steps to build the comfort level and relationship with parents is a key factor in encouraging parents to be volunteers.

Heather Zoldak

PEERS

In addition to families and teachers, *peers*—children of about the same age or maturity level—also play powerful roles in children's development and schooling (Kindermann, 2016; Wentzel & Muenks, 2016). For example, researchers have found that children who play well with others and have at least one close friend adjust better in the transition to first grade, achieve more in school, and have better mental health (Ladd et al., 1999). One of the most important functions of the peer group is to provide a source of information and comparison about the world outside of the family.

DEVELOPMENT

Peer Statuses Developmentalists have pinpointed five types of peer status: popular children, average children, neglected children, rejected children, and controversial children.

Many children worry about whether or not they are popular. *Popular children* are frequently nominated as a best friend and are rarely disliked by their peers. Popular children give out reinforcements, listen carefully, maintain open lines of

What are some statuses that children have with their peers?
Paul/Getty Images

communication with peers, are happy, act like themselves, show enthusiasm and concern for others, and are self-confident without being conceited (Hartup, 1983). *Average children* receive an average number of both positive and negative nominations from their peers. *Neglected children* are infrequently nominated as a best friend but are not disliked by their peers. *Rejected children* are infrequently nominated as someone's best friend and are often actively disliked by their peers. *Controversial children* are frequently nominated both as someone's best friend and as being disliked. (Learn more about the characteristics of children with different statuses and the accuracy of ratings for identifying statuses in research by McKown et al., 2011.)

Rejected children often have more serious adjustment problems than do neglected children, especially when rejected children are highly aggressive (Rubin et al., 2016). A social-skills intervention program was successful in increasing social acceptance and self-esteem and decreasing depression and anxiety in peer-rejected children (DeRosier & Marcus, 2005). Students participated in the program once a week (50 to 60 minutes) for eight weeks. The program included instruction in how to manage emotions, how to improve prosocial skills, how to become better communicators, and how to compromise and negotiate.

A special peer relations problem involves bullying (Espelage & Colbert, 2016). In the chapter on managing the classroom we will discuss strategies for dealing with bullies.

Friendship Friendships influence children's attitudes toward school and how successful they are in the classroom (Wentzel & Muenks, 2016). The importance of friendship was underscored in a two-year longitudinal study (Wentzel et al., 2004). Sixth-grade students who did not have a friend engaged in less prosocial behavior (cooperation, sharing, helping others), had lower grades, and were more emotionally distressed (depression, low well-being) than students who had at least one friend, and they continued to have higher levels of emotional distress in eighth grade.

More recently, researchers have found that school friendships and perceptions of belongingness helped protect middle school students against substance use and aggression (Forster et al., 2015). And a meta-analysis synthesizing the results of 22 studies found that working together with a friend and having a friend were positively related to cognitive (linguistic skills, scientific reasoning, etc.) and performance outcomes (test scores, grades, etc.) (Wentzel et al., 2018). How we define and understand

CONNECTING WITH STUDENTS: Best Practices
Strategies for Improving Children's Social Skills

In every class you teach, some children will likely have weak social skills. One or two might be rejected children. Several others might be neglected. Here are some good strategies for improving children's social skills:

1. *Help rejected children learn to listen to peers and "hear what they say" instead of trying to dominate peers.*
2. *Help neglected children attract attention from peers in positive ways and hold their attention.* They can do this by asking questions, listening in a warm and friendly way, and saying things about themselves that relate to the peers' interests. Also work with neglected children on entering groups more effectively.
3. *Provide children low in social skills with knowledge about how to improve these skills.* In one study of sixth- and seventh-graders, knowledge of both appropriate and inappropriate strategies for making friends was related positively to peer acceptance (Wentzel & Erdley, 1993).

Knowledge of Appropriate Strategies Includes Knowing:

- How to initiate interaction, such as asking someone about his or her favorite activities and asking the other child to do things together
- That it is important to be nice, kind, and considerate
- That it is necessary to show respect for others by being courteous and listening to what others have to say

Knowledge of Inappropriate Strategies Includes Knowing:

- That it is not a good idea to be aggressive, show disrespect, be inconsiderate, hurt others' feelings, gossip, spread rumors, embarrass others, or criticize others

What are some appropriate and inappropriate strategies for improving social skills?
Cathy Yeulet/Stockbroker/123RF

- Not to present yourself negatively, be self-centered, care only about yourself, or be jealous, grouchy, or angry all the time
- Not to engage in antisocial behavior, such as fighting, yelling at others, picking on others, making fun of others, being dishonest, breaking school rules, or taking drugs

4. *Read and discuss appropriate books on peer relations with students, and devise supportive games and activities.* Include these books as thematic units in your curriculum for young children. Make books on peer relations and friendship available to older children and adolescents.

TECHNOLOGY

friendships has become even more complex if we also consider how we can use of technology to connect with each other.

Given the prolific growth in social media use by adolescents over the last decade, it is important to consider the potential impacts of how often and how they use it. A study of European teens found that "socializing, following people not known in real life, and online shopping are significantly related to conduct problems" and "playing games and posting content such as videos on social media are significantly related to compulsive Internet use" (De Calheiros Velozo & Stauder, 2018, "Highlights" section). Despite the many concerns that have been raised about the negative impacts of social media use, there may be some benefits. For example, Dutch adolescents' use of social media (frequency of usage of social network sites like Facebook and instant messaging with applications like WhatsApp) was related to improvements in empathy, including their ability to understand peers' feelings and to "feel with" their peers (Vossen & Valkenburg, 2016).

Having friends can be a developmental advantage, but keep in mind that friendships are not all alike. Having friends who are academically oriented, socially skilled, and supportive is a developmental advantage (Choukas-Bradley & Prinstein, 2016), but having certain types of friends also can be a developmental disadvantage. For example, a recent study revealed that having friends who engage in delinquent behavior is associated with early onset and more persistent delinquency (Evans et al., 2016).

SCHOOLS

In school, children spend many years as members of a small society that exerts a tremendous influence on their socioemotional development. How does this social world change as children develop?

Schools' Changing Social Developmental Contexts Social contexts vary through the early childhood, elementary school, and adolescent years (Minuchin & Shapiro, 1983). The early childhood setting is a protected environment whose boundary is the classroom. In this limited social setting, young children interact with one or two teachers, usually female, who are powerful figures in their lives. Young children also interact with peers in dyads or small groups.

The classroom still is the main context in elementary school, although it is more likely to be experienced as a social unit than is the early childhood classroom. The teacher symbolizes authority, which establishes the climate of the classroom, the conditions of social interaction, and the nature of group functioning. Peer groups are more important now, and students have an increased interest in friendship.

As children move into middle and junior high school, the school environment increases in scope and complexity (Wigfield et al., 2016). The social field is now the whole school rather than the classroom. Adolescents interact with teachers and peers from a broader range of cultural backgrounds on a broader range of interests. More of the teachers are male. Adolescents' social behavior becomes weighted more strongly toward peers, extracurricular activities, clubs, and the community (Vandell et al., 2015). Secondary school students are more aware of the school as a social system and might be motivated to conform to it or challenge it.

DEVELOPMENT

Early Childhood Education There are many variations in how young children are educated (Burchinal et al., 2015). However, an increasing number of education experts advocate that this education be developmentally appropriate (Feeney et al., 2016; Morrison, 2017).

Developmentally Appropriate Education In previous chapters we described the importance of engaging in developmentally appropriate teaching practices. Here we expand on the topic of developmentally appropriate practice (DAP) in our discussion of developmentally appropriate educational practices for children from birth to 8 years of age. **Developmentally appropriate education** is based on knowledge of the typical development of children within an age span (age-appropriateness) as well as the uniqueness of the child (individual-appropriateness). DAP in education emphasizes the importance of creating settings that encourage children to be active learners and reflect children's interests and capabilities. Desired outcomes for DAP include thinking critically, working cooperatively, solving problems, developing self-regulatory skills, and enjoying learning. The emphasis in DAP is on the process of learning rather than its content (Bredekamp, 2017). The most recent developmentally appropriate guidelines provided by the National Association for the Education of Young Children (NAEYC) were issued in 2009 and are currently being revised.

Do developmentally appropriate educational practices improve young children's development? Some researchers have found that young children in developmentally appropriate classrooms are likely to have less stress, have better work habits, be more creative, and be more skilled socially than children in developmentally inappropriate classrooms (Hart et al., 2003; Stipek et al., 1995). However, not all studies show significant positive

> **Thinking Back/Thinking Forward**
>
> Developmentally appropriate practice (DAP) takes place at a level that is neither too difficult and stressful nor too easy and boring for the child's developmental level. Connect with "Educational Psychology: A Tool for Effective Teaching."

RESEARCH

developmentally appropriate education Education that focuses on the typical developmental patterns of children (age appropriateness) and the uniqueness of each child (individual appropriateness).

benefits for developmentally appropriate education (Hyson et al., 2006). Among the reasons it is difficult to generalize about research on developmentally appropriate education is that individual programs often vary, and developmentally appropriate education is an evolving concept. Recent changes in the concept have given more attention to sociocultural factors, to the teacher's active involvement, and to how academic skills should be emphasized and how they should be taught (NAEYC, 2009).

The Montessori Approach Montessori schools are patterned after the educational philosophy of Maria Montessori (1870–1952), an Italian physician-turned-educator who crafted a revolutionary approach to young children's education at the beginning of the twentieth century. Her approach has been widely adopted in private schools, especially those with early childhood programs, in the United States.

The **Montessori approach** is a philosophy of education in which children are given considerable freedom and spontaneity in choosing activities. They are allowed to move from one activity to another as they desire. The teacher acts as a facilitator rather than a director. The teacher shows the child how to perform intellectual activities, demonstrates interesting ways to explore curriculum materials, and offers help when the child requests it (Cossentino, 2008; Lillard, 2017). A special emphasis in Montessori schools is to encourage children to make decisions at an early age and become self-regulated problem solvers who manage time effectively (Hyson et al., 2006). The number of Montessori schools in the United States has expanded dramatically in recent years, from one school in 1959 to 355 schools in 1970 to approximately 4,500 in 2016 with estimates of Montessori schools worldwide at approximately 20,000 in 2016 (North American Montessori Teachers' Association, 2016).

Some developmentalists favor the Montessori approach, but others hold that it neglects children's social development. For example, although Montessori fosters independence and the development of cognitive skills, it deemphasizes verbal interaction between the teacher and child and between peers. Montessori's critics also argue that it restricts imaginative play and that its heavy reliance on self-corrective materials may not adequately allow for creativity or accommodate a variety of learning styles (Goffin & Wilson, 2001).

Controversy in Early Childhood Education A current controversy in early childhood education involves the curriculum (Bredekamp, 2017; Feeney et al., 2016). On one side are those who advocate a child-centered, constructivist approach much like that

Montessori approach An educational philosophy in which children are given considerable freedom and spontaneity in choosing activities and are allowed to move from one activity to another as they desire.

Larry Page and Sergey Brin, founders of the highly successful Internet search engine Google, said that their early years at Montessori schools were a major factor in their success (International Montessori Council, 2006). During an interview with Barbara Walters, they said they learned how to be self-directed learners and self-starters at Montessori (ABC News, 2005). They commented that Montessori experiences encouraged them to think for themselves and allowed them the freedom to develop their own interests.
Kim Kulish/Corbis/Getty Images

emphasized by the National Association for the Education of Young Children (NAEYC), along the lines of developmentally appropriate practice. On the other side are those who advocate an academic, direct instruction approach.

In reality, many high-quality early childhood education programs include both academic and constructivist approaches. Many education experts like Lilian Katz (1999), though, worry about academic approaches that place too much pressure on young children to achieve and don't provide any opportunities to actively construct knowledge. Competent early childhood programs also should focus on cognitive development *and* socioemotional development, not exclusively on cognitive development (NAEYC, 2009).

Early Childhood Education for Children from Low-Income Families Beginning in the 1960s, Project Head Start was designed to provide young children from low-income families opportunities to acquire the skills and experiences that are important for success in school. Funded by the federal government, Project Head Start continues to serve children who are disadvantaged today. Project Head Start is the largest federally funded program for U.S. children.

DIVERSITY

In high-quality Head Start programs, parents and communities are involved in positive ways. The teachers are knowledgeable about children's development and use developmentally appropriate practices.

However, mixed results have been found for Head Start (Miller et al., 2016). A recent study found that one year of Head Start was linked to higher performance in early math, early reading, and receptive vocabulary (Miller et al., 2014). In another recent study, the best results occurred for Head Start children who had low initial cognitive ability, whose parents had low levels of education, and who attended Head Start more than 20 hours a week (Lee et al., 2014). It is not unusual to find early gains and then see them go away in elementary school.

RESEARCH

The Transition to Elementary School

As children make the transition to elementary school, they interact and develop relationships with new and significant others. School provides them with a rich source of ideas to shape their sense of self.

A special concern about early elementary school classrooms is that they not proceed primarily on the basis of negative feedback. I (your author) vividly remember

As children make the transition to elementary school, they interact and develop relationships with new and significant others. School provides them with a rich source of new ideas to shape their sense of self. *What is a current concern about the transition to elementary school?*
Ariel Skelley/Blend Images/Getty Images

my first-grade teacher. Unfortunately, she never smiled; she was a dictator in the classroom, and learning (or lack of learning) progressed more on the basis of fear than of enjoyment and passion. Fortunately, I experienced some warmer, more student-friendly teachers later on.

Children's self-esteem is higher when they begin elementary school than when they complete it (Blumenfeld et al., 1981). Is that because they experienced so much negative feedback and were criticized so much along the way? We will say more in other chapters about the roles of reinforcement and punishment in children's learning and about managing the classroom.

Teachers play an important role at every level of schooling, including elementary schools (Borich, 2017; Wentzel, 2016). In a series of studies from infancy through third grade, positive teacher-child relationships were linked to a number of positive child outcomes (Howes & Ritchie, 2002). In this research, even when children evidenced a lack of trust in prior caregivers, a positive current relationship with a teacher could compensate for earlier negative relationships. Children who have warm, positive relationships with their teachers have a more positive attitude toward school, are more enthusiastic about learning, and achieve more in school (Martin & Collie, 2016).

TECHNOLOGY

Recently, there has been a dramatic increase in the number of "educational apps" that are marketed to help children learn and achieve. In a recent analysis, Kathy Hirsh-Pasek and her colleagues (2015) provided the following advice that can help teachers and parents choose apps that will benefit children:

- Choose apps that provide support for sustained engagement in the educational task rather than apps with lots of bells and whistles that distract children.
- Select apps that use guided exploration to encourage children to discover information themselves rather than just giving children the information and telling them what to know.
- Search for apps that are likely to lead to social interaction through conversation and discussion rather than apps that limit interacting with others.

The Schooling of Adolescents Three special concerns about adolescent schooling are (1) the transition to middle or junior high school, (2) effective schooling for young adolescents, and (3) the quality of high schools. How might the transition to middle or junior high school be difficult for many students?

RESEARCH

The Transition to Middle or Junior High School This transition can be stressful because it coincides with many other developmental changes (Wigfield et al., 2015). Students are beginning puberty and have increased concerns about their body image. The hormonal changes of puberty stimulate increased interest in sexual matters. Students are becoming more independent from their parents and want to spend more time with peers. They must make the change from a smaller, more personalized classroom to a larger, more impersonal school. Achievement becomes more serious business, and getting good grades becomes more competitive.

As students move from elementary to middle or junior high school, they experience the *top-dog phenomenon*. This refers to moving from the top position (in elementary school, being the oldest, biggest, and most powerful students in the school) to the lowest position (in middle or junior high school, being the youngest, smallest, and least powerful students in the school). Schools that provide more support, less anonymity, more stability, and less complexity improve student adjustment during this transition (Fenzel et al., 1991).

There can also be positive aspects to the transition to middle or junior high school. Recent research suggests middle school students' perceptions of their school context (i.e., clear expectations, choice, relevance, and emotional support at the beginning of seventh-grade) positively influence their academic motivation, and in turn, their school engagement (Wang & Eccles, 2013). Students are more likely to feel grown up, have more subjects from which to select, have more opportunities to spend time with peers and locate compatible friends, and enjoy increased independence from direct parental monitoring. They also may be more challenged intellectually by academic work.

Effective Schools for Young Adolescents Educators and psychologists worry that junior high and middle schools have become watered-down versions of high schools, mimicking their curricular and extracurricular schedules. Critics argue that these schools should offer activities that reflect a wide range of individual differences in biological and psychological development among young adolescents. Near the end of the twentieth century, the Carnegie Foundation (1989) issued an extremely negative evaluation of U.S. middle schools. It concluded that most young adolescents attended massive, impersonal schools; were taught from irrelevant curricula; trusted few adults in school; and lacked access to health care and counseling. It recommended that the nation develop smaller "communities" or "houses" to lessen the impersonal nature of large middle schools, have lower student-to-counselor ratios (10 to 1 instead of several hundred to 1), involve parents and community leaders in schools, develop new curricula, have teachers team teach in more flexibly designed curriculum blocks that integrate several disciplines, boost students' health and fitness with more in-school programs, and help students who need public health care to get it. Three decades later, experts are still finding that U.S. middle schools need a major redesign if they are to be effective in educating adolescents (Roeser, 2016; Soloman & Anderman, 2017).

Comstock/PictureQuest/Getty Images

Improving America's High Schools Just as there are concerns about U.S. middle school education, so are there concerns about U.S. high school education (Eccles & Roeser, 2015; Simpkins et al., 2015). Critics stress that in many high schools expectations for success and standards for learning are too low. Critics also argue that too often high schools foster passivity and that schools should create a variety of pathways for students to achieve an identity. Many students graduate from high school with inadequate reading, writing, and mathematical skills—including many who go on to college and have to enroll in remediation classes there. Other students drop out of high school and do not have skills that will allow them to obtain decent jobs, much less to be informed citizens.

The transition to high school can have problems, just as the transition to middle school can. These problems may include the following (Eccles & Roeser, 2015): high schools are often even larger, more bureaucratic, and more impersonal than middle schools are; there isn't much opportunity for students and teachers to get to know each other, which can lead to distrust; and teachers too infrequently make content relevant to students' interests. Such experiences likely undermine the motivation of students.

Robert Crosnoe's (2011) book, *Fitting In, Standing Out,* highlighted another major problem with U.S. high schools: how the negative social aspects of adolescents' lives undermine their academic achievement. In his view, adolescents become immersed in complex peer group cultures that demand conformity. High school is supposed to be about getting an education, but in reality for many youth it is more about navigating the social worlds of peer relations that may or may not value education and academic achievement. The adolescents who fail to fit in, especially those who are obese or gay, become stigmatized. Crosnoe recommends increased school counseling services, expanded extracurricular activities, and improved parental monitoring to reduce such problems.

In the last half of the twentieth century and the first decade of the twenty-first century, U.S. high school dropout rates declined (National Center for Education Statistics, 2016). In the 1940s, more than half of U.S. 16- to 24-year-olds had dropped out of school; by 1990, this rate had dropped to 12 percent. In 2016, this figure had decreased further to 6.1 percent. The dropout rate of Latinx adolescents remains high, although it has been decreasing considerably in the twenty-first century (from 28 percent in 2000 to 15 percent in 2010 to 8.6 percent in 2016 and varies greatly by Hispanic subpopulation and immigration status). The lowest dropout rate in 2016 occurred for Asian American adolescents (2.9 percent), followed by non-Latinx

DIVERSITY

RESEARCH

White adolescents (5.2 percent), African American adolescents (6.2 percent), Latinx adolescents (8.6 percent), and American Indian/Alaska Native adolescents (18.2 percent) (McFarland et al., 2018). The difference in the White and Black dropout rates was not significantly different for the first time in 2016.

Gender differences characterize U.S. dropout rates, with males more likely to drop out than females in 2016 (7.1 versus 5.1 percent) (McFarland et al., 2018). The gender gap in dropout rates was observed for White, Black, and Latinx 16- to 24-year-olds.

The average U.S. high school dropout rates just described mask some very high dropout rates in low-income areas of inner cities. For example, in cities such as Detroit, Cleveland, and Chicago, dropout rates are higher than 50 percent. Also, the percentages cited earlier are for 16- to 24-year-olds. When dropout rates are calculated in terms of students who do not graduate from high school within four years, the percentage is also much higher. Thus, in considering high school dropout rates, it is important to examine age, the number of years it takes to complete high school, and various contexts including ethnicity, gender, and school location.

Students drop out of school for many reasons (Dupere et al., 2015). In one study, almost 50 percent of the dropouts cited school-related reasons for leaving school, such as not liking school or being expelled or suspended (Rumberger, 1995). Such adverse situations within the school environment are characterized as school push out factors that lead to dropping out (Doll et al., 2013). Twenty percent of the dropouts (but 40 percent of the Latinx students) cited economic reasons for leaving school. One-third of the female students dropped out for personal reasons such as pregnancy or marriage (i.e., "pull out" factors related to dropout).

A recent What Works Clearinghouse practice guide, Preventing Dropout in Secondary Schools (https://ies.ed.gov/ncee/wwc/PracticeGuide/24) provides evidence-based recommendations for reducing dropout and increasing graduation rates. There is strong evidence to support engaging "students by offering curricula and programs that connect schoolwork with college and career success and that improve students' capacity to manage challenges in and out of school" (Rumberger et al., 2017, p. 5). There is moderate evidence to support the following two strategies: "Provide intensive, individualized support to students who have fallen off track and face significant challenges to success" and "For schools with many at-risk students, create small, personalized communities to facilitate monitoring and support" (Rumberger et al., 2017, p. 5). The guide provides suggestions on how to implement the strategies and overcome potential obstacles.

Early detection of children's school-related difficulties, and getting children engaged with school in positive ways, are important strategies for reducing high school dropout rates (Crosnoe et al., 2015). The Bill and Melinda Gates Foundation (2008, 2016) funds efforts to reduce the dropout rate in schools where dropout rates are high. One strategy that is being emphasized in programs sponsored by the Gates Foundation is keeping students who are at risk for dropping out of school with the same teachers through their high school years. The hope is that the teachers will get to know these students much better, that their relationship with the students will improve, and that they will be able to monitor and guide the students toward graduating from high school. Recent initiatives by the Gates Foundation (2016) involve creating a new generation of courseware that adapts to students' learning needs and blending face-to-face instruction with digital tools that help students to learn independently.

Comstock Images/Alamy Stock Photo

Participation in extracurricular activities also is linked to reduced school dropout rates (Eccles & Roeser, 2015). Adolescents in U.S. schools usually have a wide array of extracurricular activities from which to choose. These adult-sanctioned activities typically occur in the after-school hours and can be sponsored either by the school or the community. They include such diverse activities as sports, academic clubs, band, drama, and service groups. In addition to lower school dropout rates, researchers have found that participation in extracurricular activities is linked to higher grades, greater school engagement, improved likelihood of going to college, higher self-esteem, and lower rates of depression, delinquency, and substance abuse (Simpkins et al., 2015). Adolescents benefit from participating in a range of extracurricular activities more than from focusing on a single extracurricular activity. Also, the more years adolescents spend in extracurricular activities, the stronger the link is with positive developmental outcomes (Mahoney et al., 2010). A recent study revealed that immigrant adolescents who participated in extracurricular activities improved their academic achievement and increased their school engagement (Camacho & Fuligni, 2015).

Of course, the quality of the extracurricular activities matters. High-quality extracurricular activities that are likely to promote positive adolescent development offer competent and supportive adult mentors, opportunities for increasing school connectedness, challenging and meaningful activities, and opportunities for improving skills (Mahoney et al., 2010).

Comstock Images/SuperStock

Review, Reflect, and Practice

2 Discuss how the social contexts of families, peers, and schools are linked with socioemotional development.

REVIEW
- What four parenting styles did Baumrind propose, and which style is likely to be the most effective? How do aspects of families such as working parents, divorce, and stepfamilies affect children's development and education? In what ways can school-family linkages be strengthened?
- How are peers defined, and what are the five peer statuses? What risks are attached to certain peer statuses? How do friendships matter?
- What are some characteristics and key aspects of schools at different levels of education—early childhood education, the transition to elementary school, and the schooling of adolescents?

REFLECT
- What parenting style(s) have you witnessed and experienced? What effects did they have?

PRAXIS™ PRACTICE
1. Which of the following teachers is most likely to encourage appropriate parental involvement in children's education?
   a. Mr. Bastian sends home weekly progress notes to the parents who request them. He invites each parent to a conference at the end of the first grading period, and contacts parents if a child is in serious trouble at school.
   b. Ms. Washington contacts parents before the school year begins. She holds a meeting for parents to discuss her expectations for both children and parents and to answer questions. She requests volunteers to help in the classroom and chaperone field trips. She sends home weekly progress reports that include academic and social information.
   c. Ms. Jefferson tells parents that their children need to develop independence, which won't happen if they hover around at school and interfere with the educational process.
   d. Ms. Hernandez holds two parent-teacher conferences each year and e-mails parents if children fall behind in their work or present any problems in class. She occasionally e-mails a parent when a child has made marked improvement or accomplished something special.

continued

Review, Reflect, and Practice

2. Samuel is in fourth grade. He is large for his age, but not very mature. He is extremely sensitive to any kind of criticism—constructive or not. He cries when somebody teases him, which happens often. Samuel often elicits teasing from his peers by engaging in it himself. Which peer status is most likely for Samuel?
   a. controversial
   b. neglected
   c. popular
   d. rejected

3. Which of the following is the best example of a developmentally appropriate unit on pioneer life for third-graders?
   a. Mr. Johnson's class has read about the daily lives of pioneers and is now constructing log cabins that demonstrate their understanding of the typical cabin of the period. Mr. Johnson moves around the room, giving help when needed, asking students why they are including certain features, and ensuring that all stay on task.
   b. In Ms. Lincoln's class, each student has read a different book about pioneer life and is now writing a book report. The students work quietly at their desks on their reports. She occasionally chastises students for talking or for daydreaming.
   c. Mr. Roosevelt's class is taking turns reading aloud a book about pioneer life. Each student reads a paragraph of the book in turn. When they are finished with the book, they will be tested on the content.
   d. Ms. Silver is lecturing to her students about pioneer life. She has gone over reasons for the westward migration, modes of transportation, and clearing the land and building a cabin. She will give them a test about pioneer life on Friday.

Please see answer key at end of book . . . .

LG 3 Explain these aspects of children's socioemotional development: self-esteem, identity, moral development, and emotional development.

The living self has one purpose only: to come into its own fullness of being, as a tree comes into full blossom, or a bird into spring beauty, or a tiger into lustre.

—D. H. Lawrence
British author, 20th Century

RESEARCH

self-esteem Also called *self-image* and *self-worth,* the individual's overall conception of herself or himself.

3 SOCIOEMOTIONAL DEVELOPMENT

The Self and Identity | Moral Development | Emotional Development

So far we have discussed three important social contexts that influence students' socioemotional development: families, peers, and schools. In this section, we focus more on the individual students themselves as we explore the development of the self and identity, morality, and emotions.

THE SELF AND IDENTITY

According to twentieth-century Italian playwright Ugo Betti, when children say "I," they mean something unique, not to be confused with any other. Psychologists often refer to that "I" as the self. Two important aspects of the self are self-esteem and identity.

Self-Esteem Self-esteem refers to an individual's overall view of himself or herself. Self-esteem also is referred to as *self-worth,* or *self-image.* For example, a child with high self-esteem might perceive that she is not just a person but a *good* person.

For many students, periods of low self-esteem come and go. But for some students, persistent low self-esteem translates into other, more serious problems. Persistent low self-esteem is linked with low achievement, depression, eating disorders, and delinquency (Harter, 2016). A New Zealand longitudinal study assessed self-esteem at 11, 13, and 15 years of age and adjustment and competence of the same individuals when they were 26 years old (Trzesniewski et al., 2006). The results revealed that adults characterized by poorer mental and physical health, worse economic prospects, and higher levels of criminal behavior were more likely to have had low self-esteem in adolescence than their better-adjusted, more competent adult counterparts.

The seriousness of the problem depends not only on the nature of the student's low self-esteem but on other conditions as well. When low self-esteem is compounded by difficult school transitions (such as the transition to middle school) or family problems (such as divorce), the student's problems can intensify.

Researchers have found that self-esteem changes as children develop (Harter, 2016). In one study, both boys and girls had high self-esteem in childhood but their self-esteem dropped considerably in early adolescence (Robins et al., 2002). The self-esteem of girls dropped about twice as much as that of boys during adolescence (see Figure 4). Other studies have also found that female adolescents had lower self-esteem than male adolescents, and their lower self-esteem was associated with less healthy adjustment (McLean & Breen, 2009). However, note in Figure 4 that despite the drop in self-esteem among adolescent girls, their average self-esteem score (3.3) was still higher than the neutral point on the scale (3.0).

Variations in self-esteem are related to many aspects of development (Hill, 2015; Park & Park, 2015). For example, one study found that self-esteem may affect the life-span trajectories of affect and depression, relationship and job satisfaction, and health. However, much of the research on self-esteem is *correlational* rather than experimental. Keep in mind that correlation does not equal causation. Thus, if a correlational study finds an association between children's low self-esteem and low academic achievement, low academic achievement could cause the low self-esteem as much as low self-esteem causes low academic achievement, or some other factor may cause both.

In fact, there are only moderate correlations between school performance and self-esteem, and these correlations do not suggest that high self-esteem produces better school performance (Baumeister et al., 2003). Efforts to increase students' self-esteem have not always led to improved school performance (Davies & Brember, 1999).

Students' self-esteem often varies across different domains, such as academic, athletic, physical appearance, social skills, and so on (Harter, 2016). Thus, a student might have high self-esteem in regard to his or her schoolwork but have low self-esteem in the areas of athletic skills, physical appearance, and social skills. Even within the academic domain, a student might have high self-esteem in some subjects (math, for example) and low self-esteem in others (English, for example).

Some teachers were recently asked to share what strategies they use to promote self-esteem in their classrooms. Following are their recommendations.

EARLY CHILDHOOD Our preschoolers feel really great when they receive stickers, stamps, and reward certificates for good behavior and work. In addition, each week children are asked to come to school with one special item from home to discuss in class and say why the item is important to them.

—MISSY DANGLER, *Suburban Hills School*

ELEMENTARY SCHOOL: GRADES K–5 To help my second-graders improve self-esteem I focus on what they are doing correctly as opposed to what they are doing incorrectly. I steer them to the correct answer rather than saying, "No, that's not right." Repeating or rephrasing the question also gives them another chance to try again in a nonthreatening environment. I also get on their eye level physically, sitting or bending down, so I can look them straight in the eyes, not down over them. These strategies help my young students feel important, valued, and part of the class, not just as a learner, but as a person.

—JANINE GUIDA POUTRE, *Clinton Elementary School*

How is school performance linked to children's self-esteem?

Fabrice Lerouge/Onoky/SuperStock

DEVELOPMENT

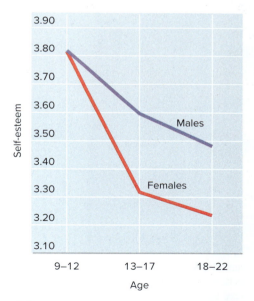

FIGURE 4 THE DECLINE OF SELF-ESTEEM IN ADOLESCENCE

In one study the self-esteem of both boys and girls declined during adolescence, but it declined considerably more for girls than boys (Robins et al., 2002). The self-esteem scores represent the mean self-esteem scores on a 5-point scale, with higher scores reflecting higher self-esteem.

MIDDLE SCHOOL: GRADES 6–8 I once had a student that did poorly on tests and quizzes. Every time there was a test, he would break down and start calling himself names because he could not answer the questions. However, this student was very good at drawing, and I used that skill to bolster his self-esteem. For example, I made sure that every time I needed some kind of diagram for a class assignment, I called on him for help. I would tell him that he had amazing artistic ability and tell him that everyone has strengths and weaknesses, and that it was important to work on his test-taking issues in order to improve them. I also told him about a few of my own weaknesses and what I do to improve them, and I created review games that included drawing to help him study for quizzes. This did not help his self-esteem overnight, but over the course of the school year he became prouder of his work and did not put himself down as much.

—CASEY MAASS, *Edison Middle School*

HIGH SCHOOL: GRADES 9–12 With my high school students, I make praise loud and clear, and I love to take the kids who have been labeled "loser" and relabel them as "reader" or "grammar princess" or "best arguer in the school." Although these labels may seem silly, my high school students blossom under the praise. I also remember that the praise I give to one of my students may be the only praise that he or she has heard—indeed, that student may not get any praise at home. Praise not only improves self-esteem for students' in-class performance, but it also gives them *permission* to succeed and do well in general.

—JENNIFER HEITER, *Bremen High School*

Identity Development Another important aspect of the self is identity. As noted earlier in the chapter, Erik Erikson (1968) argued that the most important issue in adolescence involves identity development—searching for answers to questions like these: Who am I? What am I all about? What am I going to do with my life? Not usually considered during childhood, these questions become nearly universal concerns during the high school and college years (Waterman, 2015).

Identity Statuses Canadian researcher James Marcia (1980, 1998) analyzed Erikson's concept of identity and concluded that it is important to distinguish between exploration and commitment. *Exploration* involves examining meaningful alternative identities. *Commitment* means showing a personal investment in an identity and staying with whatever that identity implies.

The extent of an individual's exploration and commitment is used to classify him or her according to one of four identity statuses (see Figure 5).

- **Identity diffusion** occurs when individuals have not yet experienced a crisis (that is, they have not yet explored meaningful alternatives) or made any commitments. Not only are they undecided about occupational and ideological choices, but they are also likely to show little interest in such matters.
- **Identity foreclosure** occurs when individuals have made a commitment but have not yet experienced a crisis. This occurs most often when parents hand down commitments to their adolescents, more often than not in an authoritarian manner. In these circumstances, adolescents have not had adequate opportunities to explore different approaches, ideologies, and vocations on their own.
- **Identity moratorium** occurs when individuals are in the midst of a crisis, but their commitments are either absent or only vaguely defined.

identity diffusion The identity status in which individuals have neither explored meaningful alternatives nor made a commitment.

identity foreclosure The identity status in which individuals have made a commitment but have not explored meaningful alternatives.

identity moratorium The identity status in which individuals are in the midst of exploring alternatives but have not yet made a commitment.

CONNECTING WITH STUDENTS: Best Practices
Strategies for Improving Children's Self-Esteem

A current concern is that too many of today's children and adolescents grow up receiving empty praise and as a consequence have inflated self-esteem (Graham, 2005; Stipek, 2005). Too often they are given praise for mediocre or even poor performances. They may have difficulty handling competition and criticism.

However, it is possible to raise children's self-esteem constructively. Consider the following four strategies (Bednar et al., 1995; Harter, 2006):

1. *Identify the causes of low self-esteem and the areas of competence important to the self.* This is critical. Is the child's low self-esteem due to poor school achievement? Family conflict? Weak social skills? Students have the highest self-esteem when they perform competently in areas that they themselves feel are important. Thus, find out from students with low self-esteem what areas of competence they value.

2. *Provide emotional support and social approval.* Virtually every class has children who have received too many negative evaluations. These children might come from an abusive and demeaning family that constantly puts them down, or they might have been in prior classrooms that delivered too much negative feedback. Your emotional support and social approval can make a big difference in helping them value themselves more. In *Through the Eyes of Teachers,* Judy Logan, a middle school teacher in San Francisco, underscores the importance of providing emotional support.

3. *Help children achieve.* Achieving can improve children's self-esteem. Straightforward teaching of real academic skills often improves children's achievement, and subsequently their self-esteem. Often it is not enough to tell children they can achieve something; you also have to help them develop their academic skills.

4. *Develop children's coping skills.* For students with low self-esteem, their unfavorable self-evaluations trigger denial, deception, and avoidance. This type of self-generated disapproval makes a student feel personally inadequate. But when children face a problem and cope with it realistically, honestly, and nondefensively, it can help raise their self-esteem.

THROUGH THE EYES OF TEACHERS
Listening, Explaining, and Supporting

I believe that a good teacher should passionately be on the side of her students. That does not mean I support them in everything they do. It means I demand the best of them and am willing to help them be their best selves. It means I listen, explain, support, and allow without judgment, sarcasm, or the need to impose the truth from the outside. The passage from childhood to adulthood we call adolescence is a very vulnerable journey. It is often a difficult time for students and for their families. It is an adolescent's "job" to rebel at times and to question the family environment that was such a comfortable cocoon during childhood. No matter how wonderful the parents, how loving the family, each adolescent needs to have other adults in whom to confide.

Source: *Teaching Stories,* by J. Logan, 1997, Kodansha International.

- **Identity achievement** occurs when individuals have undergone a crisis and have made a commitment.

To further consider identity, complete *Self-Assessment 1*. There you will be able to apply Marcia's identity statuses to a number of different areas of identity in your own life.

DIVERSITY

Position on Occupation and Ideology	Identity Diffusion	Identity Foreclosure	Identity Moratorium	Identity Achievement
Crisis	Absent	Absent	Present	Present
Commitment	Absent	Present	Absent	Present

FIGURE 5 MARCIA'S FOUR STATUSES OF IDENTITY

identity achievement The identity status in which individuals have explored meaningful alternatives and made a commitment.

SELF-ASSESSMENT 1
Where Are You Now? Exploring Your Identity

Your identity is made up of many different parts, and so too will your students' identities be composed of many different dimensions. By completing this checklist, you should gain a better sense of your own identity and the different aspects of your future students' identities. For each component, check your identity status as diffused, foreclosed, in a moratorium, or achieved.

Identity Component	IDENTITY STATUS			
	Diffused	Foreclosed	Moratorium	Achieved
Vocational identity				
Religious identity				
Achievement/intellectual identity				
Political identity				
Sexual identity				
Gender identity				
Relationship identity				
Lifestyle identity				
Ethnic and cultural identity				
Personality characteristics				
Interests				

If you checked "Diffused" or "Foreclosed" for any areas, take some time to think about what you need to do to move into a "Moratorium" identity status in those areas, and write about this in your portfolio.

RESEARCH

DEVELOPMENT

Ethnic Identity *Ethnic identity* is an enduring aspect of the self that includes a sense of membership in an ethnic group, along with the attitudes and feelings related to that membership. The immediate contexts in which ethnic minority youth live also influence their identity development (Azmitia, 2015). In the United States, many ethnic minority youth live in pockets of poverty, are exposed to drugs, gangs, and crime, and interact with youth and adults who have dropped out of school or are unemployed. Support for developing a positive identity is scarce. In such settings, programs for youth can make an important contribution to positive identity development.

Researchers are also increasingly finding that a positive ethnic identity is related to positive outcomes for ethnic minority adolescents (Ikram et al., 2016; Updegraff & Umana-Taylor, 2015). In a recent study, having pride in one's ethnic group and a strong ethnic identity were linked to lower substance use in adolescents

(Grindal & Nieri, 2016). And in another recent study, strong ethnic group affiliation and connection served a protective function in reducing risk for psychiatric problems (Anglin et al., 2016).

MORAL DEVELOPMENT

As children develop a sense of self and an identity, they also develop a sense of morality. **Moral development** concerns rules and conventions about just interactions between people. First we will discuss Lawrence Kohlberg's cognitive developmental theory of moral development, and then we will explore the more recently proposed domain theory of moral development.

Kohlberg's Theory Lawrence Kohlberg (1976, 1986) stressed that moral development primarily involves moral reasoning and occurs in stages. Kohlberg arrived at his theory after interviewing children, adolescents, and adults (primarily males) about their views on a series of moral dilemmas. A key concept in understanding progression through the levels and stages is that their morality becomes more internal or mature. That is, their reasons for their moral decisions or values begin to go beyond the external or superficial reasons they gave when they were younger. Let's further examine Kohlberg's stages.

THROUGH THE EYES OF STUDENTS

Identity Exploring

One adolescent girl, 16-year-old Michelle Chin, made these comments about ethnic identity development: "My parents do not understand that teenagers need to find out who they are, which means a lot of experimenting, a lot of mood swings, a lot of emotions and awkwardness. Like any teenager, I am facing an identity crisis. I am still trying to figure out whether I am a Chinese American or an American with Asian eyes."

Michelle Chin

Red Chopsticks/Getty Images

Kohlberg's Level 1: Preconventional Reasoning **Preconventional reasoning** is the lowest level of reasoning in Kohlberg's theory and consists of two stages: Punishment and obedience orientation (stage 1) and individualism, instrumental purpose, and exchange (stage 2).

- Stage 1. *Punishment and obedience orientation* is the first Kohlberg stage of moral development. At this stage, moral thinking is often tied to punishment. For example, children and adolescents obey adults because adults tell them to obey.
- Stage 2. *Individualism, instrumental purpose, and exchange* is the second stage of Kohlberg's theory. At this stage, individuals pursue their own interests but also let others do the same. Thus, what is right involves an equal exchange. People are nice to others so that others will be nice to them in return.

Kohlberg's Level 2: Conventional Reasoning **Conventional reasoning** is the second, or intermediate, level in Kohlberg's theory of moral development. Individuals abide by certain standards (internal), but they are the standards of others (external), such as parents or the laws of society. The conventional reasoning level consists of two stages: mutual interpersonal expectations, relationships, and interpersonal conformity (stage 3) and social systems morality (stage 4).

- Stage 3. *Mutual interpersonal expectations, relationships, and interpersonal conformity* is Kohlberg's third stage of moral development. At this stage, individuals value trust, caring, and loyalty to others as a basis of moral judgments. Children and adolescents often adopt their parents' moral standards at this stage, seeking to be thought of by their parents as a "good girl" or a "good boy."
- Stage 4. *Social systems morality* is the fourth stage in Kohlberg's theory of moral development. At this stage, moral judgments are based on understanding

moral development Development with respect to the rules and conventions of just interactions between people.

preconventional reasoning The lowest level in Kohlberg's theory. At this level, morality is often focused on reward and punishment. The two stages in preconventional reasoning are punishment and obedience orientation (stage 1) and individualism, instrumental purpose, and exchange (stage 2).

conventional reasoning The second, or intermediate, level in Kohlberg's theory of moral development. At this level, individuals abide by certain standards (internal), but they are the standards of others such as parents or the laws of society (external). The conventional level consists of two stages: mutual interpersonal expectations, relationships, and interpersonal conformity (stage 3) and social systems morality (stage 4).

98 Chapter 3 Social Contexts and Socioemotional Development

Lawrence Kohlberg, the architect of a provocative cognitive developmental theory of moral development. *What is the nature of his theory?*
Harvard University Archives, UAV 605.295.8, Box 7, Kohlberg

RESEARCH

postconventional reasoning The third and highest level in Kohlberg's theory of moral development. At this level, morality is more internal. The postconventional level consists of two stages: social contract or utility and individual rights (stage 5) and universal ethical principles (stage 6).

the social order, law, justice, and duty. For example, adolescents may say that, for a community to work effectively, it needs to be protected by laws that are adhered to by its members.

Kohlberg's Level 3: Postconventional Reasoning **Postconventional reasoning** is the third and highest level in Kohlberg's theory. At this level, morality is more internal. The postconventional level of morality consists of two stages: social contract or utility and individual rights (stage 5) and universal ethical principles (stage 6).

- Stage 5. *Social contract or utility and individual rights* is the fifth Kohlberg stage. At this stage, individuals reason that values, rights, and principles undergird or transcend the law. A person evaluates the validity of actual laws and examines social systems in terms of the degree to which they preserve and protect fundamental human rights and values.
- Stage 6. *Universal ethical principles* is the sixth and highest stage in Kohlberg's theory of moral development. At this stage, the person has developed a moral standard based on universal human rights. When faced with a conflict between law and conscience, the person will follow conscience, even though the decision might involve personal risk.

A summary of Kohlberg's three levels and six stages, along with examples of each of the stages, is presented in Figure 6. In studies of Kohlberg's theory, longitudinal data show a relation of the stages to age, although few people ever attain the two highest stages, especially stage 6 (Colby et al., 1983). Before age 9, most children reason about moral dilemmas at a preconventional level. By early adolescence, they are more likely to reason at the conventional level.

Kohlberg stressed that underlying changes in cognitive development promote more advanced moral thinking. He also said that children construct their moral thoughts as they pass through the stages—that they do not just passively accept a cultural norm for morality. Kohlberg argued that a child's moral thinking can be advanced through discussions with others who reason at the next higher stage. Kohlberg thought that the mutual give-and-take of peer relations promotes more advanced moral thinking because of the role-taking opportunities they provide children.

LEVEL 1 Preconventional Level No Internalization	LEVEL 2 Conventional Level Intermediate Internalization	LEVEL 3 Postconventional Level Full Internalization
Stage 1 Punishment and obedience orientation *Children obey because adults tell them to obey. People base their moral decisions on fear of punishment.*	**Stage 3** Mutual Interpersonal Expectations, Relationships, and Interpersonal Conformity *Individuals value trust, caring, and loyalty to others as a basis for moral judgments.*	**Stage 5** Social Contract or Utility and Individual Rights *Individuals reason that values, rights, and principles undergird or transcend the law.*
Stage 2 Individualism, Instrumental Purpose, and Exchange *Individuals pursue their own interests but let others do the same. What is right involves equal exchange.*	**Stage 4** Social Systems Morality *Moral judgments are based on understanding of the social order, law, justice, and duty.*	**Stage 6** Universal Ethical Principles *The person has developed moral judgments that are based on universal human rights. When faced with a dilemma between law and conscience, a personal, individualized conscience is followed.*

FIGURE 6 KOHLBERG'S THREE LEVELS AND SIX STAGES OF MORAL DEVELOPMENT
Kohlberg argued that people everywhere develop their moral reasoning by passing through these age-based stages.

Kohlberg's Critics Kohlberg's provocative theory has not gone unchallenged (Narváez, 2015, 2016; Roseth, 2016; Turiel, 2015). One criticism centers on the idea that moral thoughts don't always predict moral behavior. The criticism is that Kohlberg's theory places too much emphasis on moral thinking and not enough on moral behavior. Moral reasons sometimes can be a shelter for immoral behavior. Bank embezzlers and U.S. presidents endorse the loftiest of moral virtues, but their own behavior can prove to be immoral. No one wants a nation of stage-6 Kohlberg thinkers who know what is right yet do what is wrong.

Another line of criticism is that Kohlberg's theory is too individualistic. Carol Gilligan (1982, 1998) distinguishes between the justice perspective and the care perspective. Kohlberg's is a **justice perspective** that focuses on the rights of the individual, who stands alone and makes moral decisions. The **care perspective** views people in terms of their connectedness. Emphasis is placed on relationships and concern for others. According to Gilligan, Kohlberg greatly underplayed the care perspective—possibly because he was a male, most of his research was on males, and he lived in a male-dominant society.

In extensive interviews with girls from 6 to 18 years of age, Gilligan and her colleagues (Gilligan, 1992; Gilligan et al., 2003) found that girls consistently interpret moral dilemmas in terms of human relationships and base these interpretations on watching and listening to other people. Some researchers concluded that girls' moral orientations are somewhat more likely to focus on care for others but that overall gender differences in moral thinking are small (Blakemore et al., 2009).

Kohlberg argued that emotion has negative effects on moral reasoning. However, increasing evidence indicates that emotions play an important role in moral thinking. Researchers have found that individuals who have damage to a particular region in the brain's prefrontal cortex lose the ability to integrate emotions into their moral judgments (Damasio, 1994). Losing their intuitive feelings about what is right or wrong, they can't adequately decide which actions to take and have trouble making choices involving moral issues. Research with healthy individuals also has shown that the moral decisions individuals make are linked to the intensity and activation of emotion in the prefrontal cortex and the amygdala (Shenhav & Greene, 2014).

Carol Gilligan. What is Gilligan's view of moral development?
Courtesy of Dr. Carol Gilligan

Domain Theory The **domain theory of moral development** states that there are different domains of social knowledge and reasoning. In this theory, an especially important distinction is between moral and social conventional domains. In domain theory, children's and adolescents' moral and social conventional domains emerge from their attempts to understand and deal with different forms of social experience (Killen & Smetana, 2015; Turiel, 2015).

Social conventional reasoning focuses on conventional rules that have been established by social consensus to control behavior and maintain the social system. The rules themselves are arbitrary, such as raising your hand in class before speaking, using one staircase at school to go up and the other to go down, not cutting in front of someone standing in line to buy movie tickets, and stopping at a stop sign when driving. There are sanctions if we violate these conventions, although the rules can be changed by consensus.

In contrast, moral reasoning focuses on ethical issues and rules of morality. Unlike conventional rules, moral rules are not arbitrary. They are obligatory, widely accepted, and somewhat impersonal (Turiel, 2015). Rules pertaining to lying, cheating, stealing, and physically harming another person are moral rules because violation of these rules affronts ethical standards that exist apart from social consensus and convention. Moral judgments involve concepts of justice, whereas social conventional judgments are concepts of social organization. Violating moral rules is usually more serious than violating conventional rules.

Domain theory is a serious challenge to Kohlberg's approach because Kohlberg argued that social conventions are a stop-over on the road to higher moral sophistication. For domain theory advocates, social conventional reasoning is not lower than postconventional reasoning but rather something that needs to be disentangled from the moral thread (Killen & Smetana, 2015).

justice perspective A moral perspective that focuses on the rights of the individual; Kohlberg's theory is a justice perspective.

care perspective A moral perspective that focuses on connectedness and relationships among people; Gilligan's approach reflects a care perspective.

domain theory of moral development Theory that moral development includes the domains of social knowledge and reasoning.

social conventional reasoning Focuses on conventional rules that have been established by social consensus to control behavior and maintain the social system.

Why do students cheat? What are some strategies teachers can adopt to prevent cheating?
Christopher Robbins/Image Source

Cheating
A moral development concern of teachers is whether students cheat and how to handle the cheating if it is discovered (Ding et al., 2014). Academic cheating can take many forms, including plagiarism, using "cheat sheets" during an exam, copying from a neighbor during a test, purchasing papers, and falsifying lab results. A 2006 survey revealed that 60 percent of secondary school students said they had cheated on a test in school during the past year and one-third of the students reported that they had plagiarized information from the Internet in the past year (Josephson Institute of Ethics, 2006). More recently, 93% of high school students from upper middle class communities admitted to cheating at least once (Galloway, 2012).

Why do students cheat? Among the reasons students give for cheating include pressure to get high grades, time pressures, a self-perception that one doesn't have the ability to succeed, poor teaching, lack of interest, and perceiving a low likelihood of being caught and punished for cheating (Stephens, 2008). In terms of pressure to get high grades, students are more likely to cheat if their goal is simply to get a high grade; they are less likely to cheat if their goal is to master the material being studied. In terms of having a self-perception that one doesn't have the ability to succeed, their doubts about their ability and failure-related anxiety may lead them to cheat. In terms of perceiving a low likelihood of being caught and punished for cheating, students may weigh the risk of getting a good grade by cheating as less costly than getting a failing grade by not cheating (Anderman & Anderman, 2010). In terms of poor teaching, students are more likely to cheat when they perceive their teacher to be incompetent, unfair, and uncaring (Stephens, 2008).

A long history of research also implicates the power of the situation in determining whether students cheat or not (Hartshorne & May, 1928-1930; Anderman & Anderman, 2010). For example, even high achieving students may be more inclined to cheat when they feel stressed and pressured about grades, there is more discrepancy between their academic performance and their school's overall level of achievement, social comparison and competition are emphasized in the classroom, they have heavy school workloads, or they feel they have to maintain their status (Miller et al., 2017). At the college level, students at elite military academies are also more apt to become cheaters when more of their peers are cheaters (Carrell et al., 2008).

Among the strategies for decreasing academic cheating are preventive measures such as making sure students are aware of what constitutes cheating and what the consequences will be if they cheat, closely monitoring students' behavior while they are taking tests, and emphasizing the importance of being a moral, responsible individual who engages in academic integrity. In promoting academic integrity, many colleges have instituted an honor code policy that emphasizes self-responsibility, fairness, trust, and scholarship. However, few secondary schools have developed honor code policies. The International Center for Academic Integrity (https://academicintegrity.org/) has extensive materials available to help schools develop academic integrity policies.

Prosocial Behavior
Caring about the welfare and rights of others, feeling concern and empathy for them, and acting in a way that benefits others are all components of prosocial behavior. *Prosocial behavior* involves transcending narrow self-interest and valuing the perspectives of others. The purest forms of prosocial behavior are motivated by **altruism**, an unselfish interest in helping another person (Eisenberg et al., 2015).

Learning to share is an important aspect of prosocial behavior. It is important that children develop a belief that sharing is an obligatory part of a social relationship and involves a question of right and wrong. Children and the people they interact with also benefit from experiencing **gratitude**, a feeling of thankfulness and appreciation, especially in response to someone doing something kind or helpful.

Gender differences characterize prosocial behavior, which may be due to gender-specific socialization pressures in adolescence (Van der Graaf et al., 2018).

Learning to share is an important aspect of altruism. What are some ways teachers can encourage students to be more altruistic?
John Slater/Photodisc/Getty Images

altruism An unselfish interest in helping another person.

gratitude A feeling of thankfulness and appreciation, especially in response to someone doing something kind or helpful.

CONNECTING WITH STUDENTS: Best Practices
Strategies for Increasing Children's Prosocial Behavior

Parents and teachers can play important roles in promoting prosocial behavior in children by modeling it and providing children with opportunities to engage in it. For example, teachers can do the following (Eisenberg et al., 2006; Eisenberg et al., 2016; Eisenberg & Spinrad, 2016; Eisenberg et al., 2015; Wittmer & Honig, 1994):

1. *Encourage children to be accountable for their own behavior and to treat others with kindness and respect.*
2. *Model being helpful, cooperative, and showing concern for others, and encourage these behaviors in children.* For example, a teacher who comforts a child in times of stress is likely to observe other children imitating her comforting behavior.
3. *Valuing and emphasizing consideration of others' needs encourages children to engage in more helping behaviors.*
4. *Tell the child after he or she has engaged in prosocial behavior how pleased you are with the child's prosocial action.* Go beyond just saying, "That's good" or "That's nice." Be specific in identifying prosocial behaviors. You might say, "You are being helpful." Or, you might say, "You shared because you like to help others."
5. *Develop class and school projects that foster altruism.* Let children come up with examples of projects they can do that will help others. These projects might include cleaning up the schoolyard, writing to children in troubled lands, collecting toys or food for individuals in need, and making friends with older adults during visits to a nursing home.

What can teachers do to encourage prosocial behavior, such as this girl providing assistance?
Rhienna Cutler/E+/Getty Images

Females view themselves as more prosocial and empathic, and they also engage in more prosocial behavior than males do (Eisenberg & Spinrad, 2016; Eisenberg et al., 2015). Longitudinal research demonstrates that "growth in prosocial behavior starts earlier for girls than for boys, and, in accordance with gender role intensification theory, gender differences increase between early and mid-adolescence" (Van der Graaf et al., 2018, p. 1096).

Moral Education Is there a best way to educate students so they will develop better moral values? Moral education is hotly debated in educational circles (Narváez, 2014; Roseth, 2016; Turiel, 2015). We will study one of the earliest analyses of moral education, then turn to some contemporary views.

The Hidden Curriculum John Dewey was one of educational psychology's pioneers. Dewey (1933) recognized that even when schools do not have specific programs in moral education, they provide moral education through a "hidden curriculum." The **hidden curriculum**—conveyed by the moral atmosphere that is a part of every school—is created by school and classroom rules, the moral orientation of teachers and school administrators, and text materials. Teachers serve as models of ethical or unethical behavior (Sanger, 2008). Classroom rules and peer relations at school transmit attitudes about cheating, lying, stealing, and showing consideration for others. Through its rules and regulations, the school administration infuses the school with a value system.

hidden curriculum Dewey's concept that every school has a pervasive moral atmosphere even if it does not have a program of moral education.

character education A direct approach to moral education that involves teaching students basic moral literacy to prevent them from engaging in immoral behavior and doing harm to themselves or others.

values clarification An approach to moral education that emphasizes helping people clarify what their lives are for and what is worth working for; students are encouraged to define their own values and understand the values of others.

cognitive moral education An approach to moral education based on the belief that students should value things such as democracy and justice as their moral reasoning develops; Kohlberg's theory has served as the foundation for many cognitive moral education efforts.

service learning A form of education that promotes social responsibility and service to the community.

THROUGH THE EYES OF STUDENTS

Jewel Cash, Teen Dynamo

Jewel Cash (seated next to her mother) participates in a crime watch meeting at a community center.
Matthew J Lee/The Boston Globe/Getty Images

Jewel Cash was raised in one of Boston's housing projects by her mother, a single parent. As a high school student at Boston Latin Academy, Jewel was a member of the Boston Student Advisory Council, mentored children, volunteered at a women's shelter, managed and danced in two troupes, and was a member of a neighborhood watch group—among other activities. Jewel told an interviewer from the *Boston Globe*, "I see a problem and I say, 'How can I make a difference?' . . . I can't take on the world, even though I can try. . . . I'm moving forward but I want to make sure I'm bringing people with me" (Silva, 2005, pp. B1, B4). Today, as an emerging adult, Jewel works with a public consulting group and continues to help others as a mentor and community organizer.

Jewel Cash, Boston Globe, 2005

Character Education Currently, "30 states and District of Columbia already have statutes and regulations that encourage or require SEL [social and emotional learning] or character education programs in schools", but only 15 states mandate such programs (Gabriel et al., 2019). Character education is a direct approach to moral education that involves teaching students basic moral literacy to prevent them from engaging in immoral behavior and doing harm to themselves or others (Annas et al., 2016). https://www.childtrends.org/state-laws-promoting-social-emotional-and-academic-development-leave-room-for-improvement The argument is that behaviors such as lying, stealing, and cheating are wrong, and that students should be taught this throughout their education (Narváez, 2015, 2016). According to the character education approach, every school should have an explicit moral code that is clearly communicated to students. Any violations of the code should be met with sanctions. Instruction in moral concepts with respect to specific behaviors, such as cheating, can take the form of example and definition, class discussions and role-playing, or rewards to students for proper behavior. More recently, an emphasis on the importance of encouraging students to develop a care perspective has been accepted as a relevant aspect of character education (Noddings, 2008). Rather than just instructing adolescents to refrain from morally deviant behavior, a care perspective advocates educating students in the importance of engaging in prosocial behaviors, such as considering others' feelings, being sensitive to others, and helping others. Critics argue that some character education programs encourage students to be too passive and noncritical.

Values Clarification **Values clarification** means helping people to clarify what their lives are for and what is worth working for. In this approach, students are encouraged to define their own values and to understand others' values. Values clarification differs from character education in not telling students what their values should be. In values clarification exercises, there are no right or wrong answers. The clarification of values is left up to the individual student. Advocates of values clarification say it is value-free. Critics, however, argue that its controversial content offends community standards. They also say that because of its relativistic nature, values clarification undermines accepted values and fails to stress morally correct behavior.

Cognitive Moral Education **Cognitive moral education** is an approach based on the belief that students should learn to value ideals such as democracy and justice as their moral reasoning develops. Kohlberg's theory has been the basis for a number of cognitive moral education programs. In a typical program, high school students meet in a semester-long course to discuss a number of moral issues. The instructor acts as a facilitator rather than as a director of the class. The hope is that students will develop more advanced notions of such concepts as cooperation, trust, responsibility, and community (Enright et al., 2008).

Toward the end of his career, Kohlberg (1986) recognized that the moral atmosphere in schools is more important than he initially envisioned. For example, in one study, a semester-long moral education class based on Kohlberg's theory was successful in advancing moral thinking in three democratic schools but not in three authoritarian schools (Higgins et al., 1983).

Service Learning **Service learning** is a form of education that promotes social responsibility and service to the community. In service learning, students engage in activities such as tutoring, helping older adults, working in a hospital, assisting at a child-care center, or cleaning up a vacant lot to make a play area. An important goal of service learning is for students to become less self-centered and more strongly motivated to help others (Eisenberg, et al., 2015; Roseth, 2016). Service learning is often more effective when two conditions are met (Nucci, 2006): (1) giving students some degree of choice in the service activities in which they participate, and (2) providing students opportunities to reflect about their participation.

Service learning takes education out into the community. Adolescent volunteers tend to be extraverted, committed to others, and have a high level of self-understanding (Eisenberg et al., 2015).

Researchers have found that service learning benefits adolescents in a number of ways (Hart et al., 2014). These improvements in adolescent development related to service learning include higher grades in school, increased goal setting, higher self-esteem, an improved sense of being able to make a difference for others, and an increased likelihood of serving as volunteers in the future (Benson et al., 2006; Celio et al., 2011). A study of more than 4,000 high school students revealed that those who worked directly with individuals in need were better adjusted academically, whereas those who worked for organizations had better civic outcomes (Schmidt et al., 2007). And in a study, students themselves saw the benefit of participating in service learning programs—74 percent of African American and 70 percent of Latinx adolescents said that service learning programs could have a "fairly or very big effect" on keeping students from dropping out of school (Bridgeland et al., 2008).

RESEARCH

What strategies do teachers use to advance their students' moral development, values, and prosocial behavior with their classmates? Following are their recommendations.

EARLY CHILDHOOD One prosocial rule that we establish with our preschoolers is zero tolerance for fighting. However, this is a difficult concept to teach some young children because when they are angry, the first thing they want to do is hit. A way to address hitting is to constantly teach children self-control. For example, we say things to children like "When we are walking in the hallway, we have control of own body and can make it walk a certain way." Our goal is to make self-control second nature in our children.

—VALARIE GORHAM, *Kiddie Quarters, Inc.*

ELEMENTARY SCHOOL: GRADES K–5 My fifth-graders take on at least two community-service projects a year. This year, we went on a field trip to the Oregon Food Bank. My students learned about hungry families in Oregon, what each child can do to help, and were given a task to do at the food bank. We bagged around 1,600 pounds of carrots, and this equated to feeding about 57 families. It was hard work, but my students saw the results and felt good about themselves.

—CRAIG JENSEN, *Cooper Mountain Elementary School*

MIDDLE SCHOOL: GRADES 6–8 As my seventh-graders study history, I like to present them with discussion questions in the form of moral dilemmas: "What would you do if . . . " types of questions. A teacher can ask an endless number of ques-tions that relate to a student's everyday life. For instance, Robert E. Lee had to decide if he would be loyal to his state or his country. In this lesson, I ask students questions such as: "Is your loyalty ever tested? If so, how did you make your decision?" These questions make for great discussions and get students thinking about their own values and morals.

—MARK FODNESS, *Bemidji Middle School*

HIGH SCHOOL: GRADES 9–12 I sometimes discuss my own moral dilemmas with my students and tie them to classroom topics so that they have a role model. For example, I once told them the story of when my infant daughter and I were in Walmart and she somehow grabbed a jar of baby food off the shelf and tucked it into her car seat. I didn't notice the jar until I lifted her out of the car when we arrived home. Although the value of the jar of food was only 37 cents, I returned it to the store. I share this story with my students when we discuss plagiarism and Modern Language Association (MLA) citation style to emphasize the importance of being honest.

—JENNIFER HEITER, *Bremen High School*

EMOTIONAL DEVELOPMENT

Imagine your life without emotion. Emotion is the color and music of life, as well as the tie that binds people together. **Emotions** refer to feelings, or affect, that occur when an individual is in a state or an interaction that is important to him or her, especially to his or her well-being.

When we think about emotions, a few dramatic feelings such as rage or glorious joy spring to mind. But emotions can be subtle as well, such as uneasiness in a new situation or the contentment a mother feels when she holds her baby. Psychologists classify the broad range of emotions in many ways, but almost all classifications designate an emotion as either positive or negative. Positive emotions include enthusiasm, joy, and love. Negative emotions include anxiety, anger, guilt, and sadness.

Development of Emotions Let's now explore how emotional development unfolds and how teachers can guide and support the positive development of students' emotions.

Early Childhood Between 2 and 4 years of age, children considerably increase the number of terms they use to describe emotions (Lewis, 2016). During this time, they are also learning about the causes and consequences of feelings.

When children are 4 to 5 years of age, they show an increased ability to reflect on emotions. They also begin to understand that the same event can elicit different feelings in different people. Moreover, they show a growing awareness that they need to manage their emotions to meet social standards (Eisenberg et al., 2016). And, by 5 years of age, most children can accurately identify emotions that are produced by challenging circumstances and describe strategies they might call on to cope with everyday stress (Blair et al., 2016; Cole, 2016).

One program that is designed to improve young children's emotional understanding is the Emotion-Based Prevention Program (EBP) (Izard et al., 2008). This program consists of a teacher-conducted emotions course in the classroom, emotion tutoring and coaching teacher dialogues, and weekly parent messages that reinforce the lessons taught in the classroom. In the classroom component, teachers ask children to label or demonstrate emotional expressions, share ideas about what causes them to feel the emotions they described, compare expressions of different emotions and their intensities, and draw out or act out emotion expressions for their classmates. A recent study found that EBP was effective in improving Head Start children's emotion knowledge and the children who participated in the program showed a decrease in their expression of negative emotions and internalizing behaviors (Finion et al., 2015).

Middle and Late Childhood During middle and late childhood, many children show marked improvement in understanding and managing their emotions (Calkins & Perry, 2016). However, in some instances, as when they experience stressful circumstances, their coping abilities may be challenged. Here are some important

emotions Feelings, or affect, that occur when an individual is engaged in an interaction that is important to him or her, especially to his or her well-being.

What are some important aspects of emotional development in middle and late childhood?
(*Left*) Phil Date/Wavebreak Media Ltd/123RF; (*right*) Hero Images/Getty Images

developmental changes in emotions during the middle and late childhood years (Denham et al., 2015; Kuebli, 1994; Thompson, 2015):

- During the elementary school years, children show marked improvement in their ability to suppress or conceal negative emotional reactions. Children now sometimes intentionally hide their emotions. Although a boy may feel sad that a friend does not want to play with him, he may decide not to share those feelings with his parents.
- In this time frame, children also use self-initiated strategies for redirecting feelings. In the elementary school years, children reflect more about emotional experiences and develop strategies to cope with their emotional lives. Children can more effectively manage their emotions by cognitive means, such as using distracting thoughts. A boy may be excited about his birthday party that will take place later in the afternoon, but still be able to concentrate on his schoolwork during the day.
- Also in middle and late childhood, children develop a capacity for genuine empathy. For example, two girls may see another child in distress on the playground and run to the child and ask if they can help.

Adolescence Adolescence has long been described as a time of emotional turmoil (Hall, 1904). Adolescents are not constantly in a state of "storm and stress," but emotional highs and lows do increase during early adolescence (Rosenblum & Lewis, 2003). Young adolescents can be on top of the world one moment and down in the dumps the next. In some instances, the intensity of their emotions seems out of proportion to the events that elicit them (Morris et al., 2013). Young adolescents might sulk a lot, not knowing how to adequately express their feelings. With little or no provocation, they can blow up at their parents or siblings, a response that might reflect the defense mechanism of displacing their feelings onto another person. For some adolescents, such emotional swings can reflect serious problems. Girls are especially vulnerable to depression in adolescence (Nolen-Hoeksema, 2011). But it is important for adults to recognize that moodiness is a normal aspect of early adolescence and to understand that most adolescents make it through these moody times to become competent adults.

Social-Emotional Education Programs An increasing number of social-emotional educational programs have been developed to improve many aspects of children's and adolescents' lives. Two such programs are the Second Step program created by the Committee for Children (2016) and the Collaborative for Academic, Social, and Emotional Learning (CASEL, 2016). Many social-emotional education programs only target young children, but Second Step can be implemented in pre-K through eighth grade and CASEL can be used with pre-K through twelfth-grade students.

- *Second Step* focuses on the following aspects of social-emotional learning from pre-K through the eighth grade: (1) pre-K: self-regulation and executive function skills that improve their attention and help them control their behavior; (2) K-grade 5: making friends, self-regulation of emotion, and solving problems; and (3) communication skills, coping with stress, and decision making to help them avoid engaging in problem behaviors.
- *CASEL* targets five core social and emotional learning domains: (1) self-awareness (recognizing one's emotions and how they affect behavior, for example); (2) self-management (self-control, coping with stress, and impulse control, for example); (3) social awareness (perspective taking and empathy, for example); (4) relationship skills (developing positive relationships and communicating effectively with individuals from diverse backgrounds, for example); and (5) responsible decision making (engaging in ethical behavior and understanding the consequences of one's actions, for example).

Coping with Stress In service learning and integrative ethical education, an important theme is getting students to help others. There are times, though, when students need help, especially when they experience stressful events (Brenner, 2016; Masten, 2016). As children get older, they more accurately appraise a stressful situation and determine how much control they have over it. Older children generate more coping alternatives to stressful conditions and use more cognitive coping strategies (Saarni et al., 2006). They are better than younger children at intentionally shifting their thoughts to something that is less stressful and at reframing, or changing one's perception of a stressful situation. For example, a younger child may be very disappointed that a teacher did not say hello when the child arrived in the classroom. An older child may reframe the situation and think, "My teacher may have been busy with other things and just forgot to say hello."

DEVELOPMENT

By 10 years of age, most children are able to use these cognitive strategies to cope with stress (Saarni, 1999; Zimmer-Gembeck & Skinner, 2011). However, in families that have not been supportive and are characterized by turmoil or trauma, children may be so overwhelmed by stress that they do not use such strategies (Frydenberg, 2008).

What are some effective strategies teachers can use to help children cope with traumatic events such as the terrorist attacks on the United States on 9/11/2001 and Hurricane Katrina in August 2005?

(*Left*) Spencer Platt/Getty Images; (*right*) Michael Rieger/FEMA

Disasters can especially harm children's development and produce adjustment problems. Children who experience disasters often display acute stress reactions, depression, panic disorder, and post-traumatic stress disorder (Sullivan & Simonson, 2016). Proportions of children developing these problems following a disaster depend on such factors as the nature and severity of the disaster, as well as the support available to the children. The terrorist attacks on the World Trade Center in New York City and the Pentagon in Washington, D.C., on September 11, 2001, and the mass shooting of elementary school students and teachers in Sandy Hook, Connecticut, in December 2012 raised special concerns about how to help children cope with such stressful events. Children who have developed a number of coping techniques have the best chance of adapting and functioning competently in the face of disasters and trauma (Ungar, 2015).

Following are some strategies teachers can use to help students cope with stressful events (Gurwitch et al., 2001, pp. 4–11):

- Reassure children (numerous times, if necessary) of their safety and security.
- Allow children to retell events and be patient in listening to them.
- Encourage children to talk about any disturbing or confusing feelings, reassuring them that such feelings are normal after a stressful event.
- Protect children from re-exposure to frightening situations and reminders of the trauma—for example, by limiting discussion of the event in front of the children.
- Help children make sense of what happened, keeping in mind that children may misunderstand what took place. For example, young children "may blame themselves, believe things happened that did not happen, believe that terrorists are in the school, etc. Gently help children develop a realistic understanding of the event" (p. 10).

Given that students, and disproportionately those from low-income, minority communities, can be exposed to numerous traumatic experiences, a school-wide trauma-informed care approach has been called a social justice imperative. In a trauma-informed care approach, you might undergo staff training to learn to recognize the signs and symptoms of trauma in your students and to help you "to respond appropriately to the academic and behavioral manifestations of trauma symptoms" (Ridgard et al., 2015, p. 12). This is a relatively new approach. Though more research is needed, initial studies suggest that tiered, school-wide approaches to addressing trauma may improve students' achievement and behavior and reduce symptoms of post-traumatic stress disorder and depression (Berger, 2019).

We have examined how students develop, focusing mainly on the general pattern. In the chapter on individual variations, we will explore how students vary in regard to intelligence and other personal characteristics.

Review, Reflect, and Practice

3 Explain these aspects of children's socioemotional development: self-esteem, identity, moral development, and emotional development.

REVIEW

- What is self-esteem, and what are some ways to increase students' self-esteem?
- What is the nature of identity development, and what are the four statuses of identity?
- What is moral development? What levels of moral development were identified by Kohlberg, and what are three criticisms of his theory? Contrast the justice and care

continued

> ### Review, Reflect, and Practice
>
> perspectives. How can the domain theory of moral development be described? What characterizes academic cheating? What are some forms of moral education?
> - What are emotions? How does emotion develop? How can children be helped to cope with stress?
>
> **REFLECT**
> - What is the level of moral development likely to be among the children you intend to teach? How might this affect your approach to how you manage students' relations with others in the class?
>
> **PRAXIS™ PRACTICE**
> 1. Teachers can have the most positive impact on students' self-esteem and achievement by
>   a. making academic tasks easy
>   b. having children who often receive negative feedback from peers work in groups with these peers to foster social approval
>   c. helping children succeed by teaching them appropriate learning strategies
>   d. intervening in children's problems so that they don't get frustrated
> 2. Marika sees Jamal take Yosuke's snack. Soon afterward, she sees Yosuke retaliate by taking Jamal's favorite pen. Marika does not report these incidents to the teacher, because they involve equal exchanges. According to Kohlberg, which stage of moral development has Marika reached?
>   a. stage 1
>   b. stage 2
>   c. stage 3
>   d. stage 4
> 3. Ms. Delgado teaches third grade in a community in which a gunman opened fire on the patrons of a store in the local mall. Her students are understandably upset by the news and by the fact that the gunman has not yet been apprehended. According to Gurwitch and colleagues (2001), which of the following would be the *least* appropriate thing for Ms. Delgado to do?
>   a. Allow her students to talk about what happened and their fears that it could happen at the school.
>   b. Disallow conversation about the shootings so that the students do not get upset.
>   c. Reassure her students that they are safe at school, including a brief discussion of appropriate emergency procedures.
>   d. Listen to the students' accounts to ensure that they have no misconceptions regarding having caused the shootings.
>
> *Please see answer key at end of book . . . .*

Connecting with the Classroom: Crack the Case

The Fight

Many schools, including the one in which Miss Mahoney teaches, emphasize character education as a strategy for preventing violence. The basic idea is to promote empathy among students and to disallow behaviors such as teasing, name-calling, and threats of any kind. Miss Mahoney has included character education in the curriculum of her fifth-grade class. However, many of her students, especially the

boys, continue to display the very behaviors she is trying to eliminate.

Two students in Miss Mahoney's class, Santana and Luke, are on the same club soccer team and often get into verbal conflicts with each other, although they appreciate each other's talents on the field. Tuesday night at practice, in violation of the team's rules, Santana tells Luke that he "sucks." Luke decides to let it go. He doesn't want Santana to suffer a one-game suspension, recognizing Santana's value to the team in light of facing a tough opponent that weekend.

Thursday in class, Luke accuses Santana of stealing the cards he was using to organize a project. Luke is very angry. Santana also gets infuriated, claiming he did not steal them. He then finds them on the floor and hands them to Luke. "Here's your dumb cards, Luke," he says. "See, I didn't steal them."

In anger, Luke says, "Fine. Then how come they're all crinkled? You know, I could beat you up and maybe I just will."

"Yeah, right. You and who else?" asks Santana with a sneer.

Two other boys working nearby overhear the altercation and begin contributing their perspectives.

"Yeah, Santana, Luke would kick your rear," says Grant.

"I think Santana would win," chimes in Peter.

"Meet me at the park tomorrow after school and let's just see!" demands Santana.

"No problem," retorts Luke.

Thursday evening, they are both at soccer practice. Nothing is said about the fight that was to take place the next day after school.

Friday morning, Santana's mother calls Miss Mahoney to tell her that Santana is afraid to come to school because Luke has threatened to beat him up. Obviously, Miss Mahoney is concerned and realizes she must address the situation. Luke's mother also talks to the principal about the situation. However, all Santana's mother told either of them is that Luke had threatened to beat up her son. She didn't know why and did not think the reason mattered in the least. She wanted her son protected and the other boy punished.

That morning, Luke's mother was in the school for another purpose. The principal stopped her to talk about the situation, telling her that Santana had told his mother he was afraid to come to school because Luke was going to beat him up. Luke's mother asked for more information. On hearing Santana's side of the story, which was simply that Luke had threatened him, she told the principal that this didn't sound right—that Luke was impulsive enough that if he'd wanted to beat up Santana, he probably would have just hit him, not planned a fight for a later date. She wanted to talk to Luke before she jumped to any conclusions and asked that Miss Mahoney and the principal talk to both of the boys and any other children involved.

Both Miss Mahoney and the principal did as Luke's mother asked. The story that came out is the one you read. They decided that Luke should serve an in-school suspension the following day and miss recess all week "because it is the third 'incident' we've had with him this year." Santana received no punishment and walked away from the meeting grinning.

- What are the issues in this case?
- At what stage of moral development would you expect these boys to be, based on the information you have? What predictions can you make regarding each boy's sense of self and emotional development?
- What can you say about the boys' mothers?
- What do you think about the punishment that Luke received? How would you have handled this situation?
- What impact do you think this will have on the boys' future relationship? How is it likely to affect their attitudes toward school?

Connecting with Learning: Reach Your Learning Goals

1 CONTEMPORARY THEORIES: Describe two contemporary perspectives on socioemotional development: Bronfenbrenner's ecological theory and Erikson's life-span development theory.

Bronfenbrenner's Ecological Theory

Erikson's Life-Span Development Theory

- Bronfenbrenner's ecological theory seeks to explain how environmental systems influence children's development. Bronfenbrenner described five environmental systems that include both micro and macro inputs: microsystem, mesosystem, exosystem, macrosystem, and chronosystem. Bronfenbrenner's theory is one of the few systematic analyses that includes both micro and macro environments. Critics say the theory lacks attention to biological and cognitive factors. They also point out that it does not address step-by-step developmental changes.

- Erikson's life-span development theory proposes eight stages, each centering on a particular type of challenge or dilemma: trust versus mistrust, autonomy versus shame and doubt, initiative versus guilt, industry versus inferiority, identity versus identity confusion, intimacy versus isolation, generativity versus stagnation, and integrity versus despair. Erikson's theory has made important contributions to understanding socioemotional development, although some critics say the stages are too rigid and that their sequencing lacks research support.

continued

② SOCIAL CONTEXTS OF DEVELOPMENT: Discuss how the social contexts of families, peers, and schools are linked with socioemotional development.

Families

- Baumrind described four parenting styles: authoritarian, authoritative, neglectful, and indulgent. Authoritative parenting is associated with children's social competence and is likely to be the most effective style of parenting.
- Children benefit when parents engage in coparenting. The nature of parents' work can affect their parenting quality.
- A number of factors are linked to children's adjustment in divorced families.
- An important aspect of school-family linkages focuses on parental involvement. Fostering school-family partnerships involves providing assistance to families, communicating effectively with families about school programs and student progress, encouraging parents to be volunteers, involving families with their children in learning activities at home, including families in school decisions, and coordinating community collaboration.

Peers

- Peers are children of about the same age or maturity level. Parents influence their children's peer worlds in a number of ways. Peer relations are linked to children's competent socioemotional development.
- Children can have one of five peer statuses: popular, average, rejected, neglected, or controversial. Rejected children often have more serious adjustment problems than do neglected children.
- Friendship is an important aspect of students' social relations. Students who have friends engage in more prosocial behavior, have higher grades, and are less emotionally distressed.

Schools

- Schools involve changing social developmental contexts from preschool through high school. The early childhood setting is a protected environment with one or two teachers, usually female. Peer groups are more important in elementary school. In middle school, the social field enlarges to include the whole school, and the social system becomes more complex.
- Controversy characterizes early childhood education curricula. On one side are the advocates of developmentally appropriate, child-centered, constructivist programs; on the other are those who advocate an instructivist, academic approach. An increasingly popular early childhood program is the Montessori approach.
- Head Start has provided early childhood education for children from low-income families. High-quality Head Start programs are effective educational interventions, but up to 40 percent of these programs may be ineffective.
- The transition to middle or junior high is stressful for many students because it coincides with so many physical, cognitive, and socioemotional changes. It involves going from the top-dog position to the lowest position in a school hierarchy.
- A number of recommendations for improving U.S. middle schools have been made. An increasing number of educational experts also believe that substantial changes need to be made in U.S. high school education.
- Participation in extracurricular activities has a number of positive outcomes for adolescents.

③ SOCIOEMOTIONAL DEVELOPMENT: Explain these aspects of children's socioemotional development: self-esteem, identity, moral development, and emotional development.

The Self and Identity

- Self-esteem, also referred to as *self-worth* or *self-image,* is the individual's overall conception of himself or herself. Self-esteem often varies across domains and becomes more differentiated in adolescence. Four keys to increasing students' self-esteem are to (1) identify the causes of low self-esteem and the domains of competence important to the student, (2) provide

- emotional support and social approval, (3) help students achieve, and (4) develop students' coping skills.
- Marcia proposed that adolescents have one of four identity statuses (based on the extent to which they have explored or are exploring alternative paths and whether they have made a commitment): identity diffusion, identity foreclosure, identity moratorium, identity achievement.
- Ethnic identity is an important dimension of identity for students and teachers to consider, especially when working toward equity in schools.

Moral Development

- Moral development concerns rules and conventions about just interactions between people.
- Kohlberg stressed that the key to understanding moral development is moral reasoning and that it unfolds in stages. Kohlberg developed a provocative theory of moral reasoning. He argued that development of moral reasoning consists of three levels—preconventional, conventional, and postconventional—and six stages (two at each level). Kohlberg reasoned that these stages were age related. Two main criticisms of Kohlberg's theory are (1) Kohlberg did not give enough attention to moral behavior, and (2) Kohlberg's theory gave too much power to the individual and not enough to relationships with others. In this regard, Gilligan argues that Kohlberg's theory is a male-oriented justice perspective. She argues that what is needed in moral development is a female-oriented care perspective.
- The domain theory of moral development states that there are different domains of social knowledge and reasoning. In this theory, an especially important distinction is made between moral and social conventional reasoning.
- Academic cheating is pervasive and can occur in many ways. A long history of research indicates the power of the situation in influencing whether students cheat or not. An important aspect of prosocial behavior is altruism, an unselfish interest in helping another person. Sharing and gratitude are two aspects of prosocial behavior. The hidden curriculum is the moral atmosphere that every school has. Three types of moral education are character education, values clarification, and cognitive moral education. Service learning is becoming increasingly important in schools.

Emotional Development

- Emotions refer to feelings, or affect, that occur when an individual is in a state or an interaction that is important to him or her, especially his or her well-being. Significant changes in emotional understanding unfold across the early childhood, middle and late childhood, and adolescent years.
- As children get older, they use a greater variety of coping strategies and more cognitive strategies. Teachers can help students develop effective strategies for coping with stressful events such as terrorist attacks and hurricanes by offering reassurance, encouraging children to talk about disturbing feelings, and helping children make sense of what happened.

KEY TERMS

altruism 100
authoritarian parenting 78
authoritative parenting 78
care perspective 99
character education 102
cognitive moral education 102
conventional reasoning 97
developmentally appropriate education 85

domain theory of moral development 99
ecological theory 71
emotions 104
gratitude 100
hidden curriculum 101
identity achievement 95
identity diffusion 94

identity foreclosure 94
identity moratorium 94
indulgent parenting 78
justice perspective 99
Montessori approach 86
moral development 97
neglectful parenting 78
postconventional reasoning 98

preconventional reasoning 98
self-esteem 92
service learning 102
social conventional reasoning 99
values clarification 102

PORTFOLIO ACTIVITIES

Now that you have a good understanding of this chapter, complete these exercises to expand your thinking.

Independent Reflection

1. **Meeting the Socioemotional Needs of Students.** Think about the age of students you intend to teach. Which of Erikson's stages is likely to be central for them? What, if anything, does Bronfenbrenner's theory suggest about important resources for students at that age? Does his system suggest particular challenges to students or ways that you as a teacher might facilitate their success? Write down your ideas in your portfolio.

Research/Field Experience

2. **Family-School Linkages.** Interview several teachers from local schools about how they foster family-school linkages. Try to talk with a kindergarten teacher, an elementary teacher, a middle school teacher, and a high school teacher. Summarize your discoveries.

Collaborative Work

3. **The Role of Moral Education in Schools.** Which approach to moral education (character education, values clarification, or cognitive moral education) do you like the best? Why? Should schools be in the business of providing specific moral education programs? Get together with several other students in this class and discuss your perspectives. Then write a brief statement that reflects your own perspective on moral education.

chapter 4

INDIVIDUAL VARIATIONS

chapter outline

① Intelligence

Learning Goal 1 Discuss what intelligence is, how it is measured, theories of multiple intelligences, the neuroscience of intelligence, and some controversies and issues about its use by educators.

What Is Intelligence?
Intelligence Tests
Theories of Multiple Intelligences
The Neuroscience of Intelligence
Controversies and Issues in Intelligence

② Learning and Thinking Styles

Learning Goal 2 Describe learning and thinking styles.

Impulsive/Reflective Styles
Deep/Surface Styles
Optimistic/Pessimistic Styles
Criticisms of Learning and Thinking Styles

③ Personality and Temperament

Learning Goal 3 Characterize the nature of personality and temperament.

Personality
Temperament

Individuals play out their lives in different ways.

—Thomas Huxley
English Biologist, 19th Century

Science Photo Library/Alamy Stock Photo

Connecting with Teachers Shiffy Landa

Shiffy Landa, a first-grade teacher at H. F. Epstein Hebrew Academy in St. Louis, Missouri, uses the multiple-intelligences approach of Howard Gardner (1983, 1993) in her classroom. Gardner argues that there is not just one general type of intelligence but at least eight specific types.

Landa (2000, pp. 6–8) believes that the multiple-intelligences approach is the best way to reach children because they have many different kinds of abilities. In Landa's words:

> My role as a teacher is quite different from the way it was just a few years ago. No longer do I stand in front of the room and lecture to my students. I consider my role to be one of a facilitator rather than a frontal teacher. The desks in my room are not all neatly lined up in straight rows . . . students are busily working in centers in cooperative learning groups, which gives them the opportunity to develop their interpersonal intelligences.

Shiffy Landa

Students use their "bodily-kinesthetic intelligence to form the shapes of the letters as they learn to write. . . . They also use this intelligence to move the sounds of the vowels that they are learning, blending them together with letters, as they begin to read."

Shiffy Landa, H. F. Epstein Hebrew Academy

Landa states that "intrapersonal intelligence is an intelligence that often is neglected in the traditional classroom." In her classroom, students "complete their own evaluation sheets after they have concluded their work at the centers. They evaluate their work and create their own portfolios," in which they keep their work so they can see their progress.

As she was implementing the multiple-intelligences approach in her classroom, Landa recognized that she needed to educate parents about it. She created "a parent education class called the Parent-Teacher Connection," which meets periodically to view videos, talk about multiple intelligences, and discuss how they are being introduced in the classroom. She also sends a weekly newsletter to parents, informing them about the week's multiple-intelligences activities and students' progress.

Preview

Shiffy Landa's classroom techniques build on Howard Gardner's multiple-intelligences theory, one of the theories of intelligence that we will explore in this chapter. You will see that there is spirited debate about whether people have a general intelligence or a number of specific intelligences. Intelligence is but one of several main topics in this chapter. We also will examine learning and thinking styles, as well as personality and temperament. For each of these topics, an important theme is students' individual variations and the best strategies for teachers to use related to these variations.

LG 1 Discuss what intelligence is, how it is measured, theories of multiple intelligences, the neuroscience of intelligence, and some controversies and issues about its use by educators.

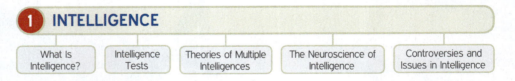

1 INTELLIGENCE

- What Is Intelligence?
- Intelligence Tests
- Theories of Multiple Intelligences
- The Neuroscience of Intelligence
- Controversies and Issues in Intelligence

Intelligence is one of our most prized possessions. However, even the most intelligent people have not been able to agree on how to define and measure the concept of intelligence.

WHAT IS INTELLIGENCE?

What does the term *intelligence* mean to psychologists? Some experts describe intelligence as the ability to solve problems. Others describe it as the capacity to adapt and learn from experience. Still others argue that intelligence includes characteristics such as creativity and interpersonal skills.

The problem with intelligence is that—unlike height, weight, and age—intelligence cannot be directly measured. We can't peel back a person's scalp and see how much intelligence he or she has. We can evaluate intelligence only *indirectly* by studying and comparing the intelligent acts that people perform.

The primary components of intelligence are similar to the cognitive processes of memory and thinking that are discussed in other chapters. The differences in how these cognitive processes are described, and how we will discuss intelligence, lie in the concepts of individual differences and assessment. *Individual differences* are the stable, consistent ways in which people are different from one another. Individual differences in intelligence generally have been measured by intelligence tests designed to tell us whether a person can reason better than others who have taken the test.

We will use as our definition of **intelligence** the ability to solve problems and to adapt and learn from experiences. But even this broad definition doesn't satisfy everyone. As you will see shortly, Robert Sternberg (2012, 2016a, b) proposes that practical know-how should be considered part of intelligence. In his view, intelligence involves weighing options carefully and acting judiciously, as well as developing strategies to improve shortcomings. Sternberg (2014) also recently described intelligence as the ability to adapt to, shape, and select environments. In adapting to the environment, if individuals find the environment suboptimal, they can change it to make it more suitable for their skills and desires. By contrast, a definition of intelligence based on a theory such as Lev Vygotsky's would have to include the ability to use the tools of the culture with help from more-skilled individuals. Because intelligence is such an abstract, broad concept, it is not surprising that there are different ways to define it.

INTELLIGENCE TESTS

In this section, we will first describe individual intelligence tests, and then we will examine group intelligence tests.

Individual Intelligence Tests The two main intelligence tests that are administered to children on an individual basis today are the Stanford-Binet test and the Wechsler scales. As you will see next, an early version of the Binet was the first intelligence test that was created.

The Binet Tests In 1904, the French Ministry of Education asked psychologist Alfred Binet to devise a method of identifying children who were unable to learn in school. School officials wanted to reduce crowding by placing in special schools students who would not benefit from regular classroom teaching. Binet and his student Theophile Simon developed an intelligence test to meet this request. The test is called the 1905 Scale. It consisted of 30 questions, ranging from the ability to touch one's ear to the abilities to draw designs from memory and define abstract concepts.

Binet developed the concept of **mental age (MA)**, an individual's level of mental development relative to others. In 1912, William Stern created the concept of **intelligence quotient (IQ)**, which refers to a person's mental age divided by chronological age (CA), multiplied by 100. That is, IQ = MA/CA × 100.

If mental age is the same as chronological age, then the person's IQ is 100. If mental age is above chronological age, then the person's IQ is greater than 100. For example, a 6-year-old with a mental age of 8 would have an IQ of 133. If mental age is below chronological age, then the person's IQ is less than 100. For example, a 6-year-old with a mental age of 5 would have an IQ of 83.

The Binet test has been revised many times to incorporate advances in the understanding of intelligence and intelligence testing. These revisions are called the *Stanford-Binet tests* (because the revisions were made at Stanford University). By administering the test to large numbers of people of different ages from different backgrounds, researchers have found that scores on a Stanford-Binet test approximate a normal distribution (see Figure 1). As described more fully in the chapter on standardized tests and teaching, a **normal distribution** is symmetrical, with a majority of the scores falling in the middle of the possible range of scores and far fewer scores appearing toward the extremes of the range.

> **Thinking Back/Thinking Forward**
>
> Vygotsky's social-constructivist approach emphasizes that intelligence is constructed through interactions with more-skilled individuals, which is reflected in his concept of the zone of proximal development. Connect with "Cognitive and Language Development."

Alfred Binet constructed the first intelligence test after being asked to create a measure to determine which children would benefit from instruction in France's schools.
Universal History Archive/Getty Images

> **Thinking Back/Thinking Forward**
>
> The most common way of classifying a child as gifted is that the child scores 130 or higher on an intelligence test. Connect to "Learners Who Are Exceptional."

intelligence Problem-solving skills and ability to adapt to and learn from experiences.

mental age (MA) An individual's level of mental development relative to others.

intelligence quotient (IQ) A person's mental age (MA) divided by chronological age (CA), multiplied by 100.

normal distribution A "bell-shaped curve" in which most of the scores are clustered around the mean and scores that are far above or below the mean are rare.

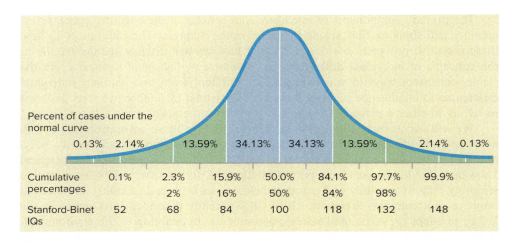

FIGURE 1 THE NORMAL CURVE AND STANFORD-BINET IQ SCORES

The distribution of IQ scores approximates a normal curve. Most of the population falls in the middle range of scores. Notice that extremely high and extremely low scores are very rare. Slightly more than two-thirds of the scores fall between 84 and 116. Only about 1 in 50 individuals has an IQ higher than 132, and only about 1 in 50 individuals has an IQ lower than 68.

The current Stanford-Binet test is administered individually to people aged 2 through adult. It includes a variety of items, some of which require verbal responses, others nonverbal responses. For example, items that reflect a typical 6-year-old's level of performance on the test include the verbal ability to define at least six words, such as *orange* and *envelope*, as well as the nonverbal ability to trace a path through a maze. Items that reflect an average adult's level of performance include defining such words as *disproportionate* and *regard*, explaining a proverb, and comparing idleness and laziness.

The current version of the Stanford-Binet is the fifth edition. An important addition to the fourth edition that has been continued and expanded on in the fifth edition is analysis of five aspects of cognitive ability (fluid reasoning, knowledge, quantitative reasoning, visual-spatial reasoning, and working memory) and two aspects of intelligence (Bart & Peterson, 2008). The five aspects of cognitive ability are fluid reasoning (abstract thinking), knowledge (conceptual information), quantitative reasoning (math skills), visual-spatial reasoning (understanding visual forms and spatial layouts), and working memory (recall of new information). The two aspects of intelligence assessed by the fifth edition of the Stanford-Binet are verbal intelligence and nonverbal intelligence. A general composite score is still obtained to reflect overall intelligence. The Stanford-Binet continues to be one of the most widely used tests to assess students' intelligence.

The Wechsler Scales Another set of tests widely used to assess students' intelligence is called the *Wechsler scales,* developed by psychologist David Wechsler. They include the Wechsler Preschool and Primary Scale of Intelligence–Fourth Edition (WPPSI-IV) to test children from 2 years 6 months to 7 years 3 months of age; the Wechsler Intelligence Scale for Children–Fifth Edition (WISC-V) for children and adolescents 6 to 16 years of age; and the Wechsler Adult Intelligence Scale–Fourth Edition (WAIS-IV).

The Wechsler scales not only provide an overall IQ score and scores on a number of subtests but also yield several composite indexes (for example, the Verbal Comprehension Index, the Working Memory Index, and the Processing Speed Index). The subtest and composite scores allow the examiner to quickly determine the areas in which the child is strong or weak. Three of the Wechsler subscales are shown in Figure 2.

Intelligence tests such as the Stanford-Binet and Wechsler are given on an individual basis. A psychologist approaches an individual assessment of intelligence as a structured interaction between the examiner and the student. This provides the psychologist with an opportunity to sample the student's behavior. During the testing, the examiner observes

Verbal Subscales

Similarities

A child must think logically and abstractly to answer a number of questions about how things might be similar.

Example: "In what way are a lion and a tiger alike?"

Comprehension

This subscale is designed to measure an individual's judgment and common sense.

Example: "What is the advantage of keeping money in a bank?"

Nonverbal Subscales

Block Design

A child must assemble a set of multicolored blocks to match designs that the examiner shows.
Visual-motor coordination, perceptual organization, and the ability to visualize spatially are assessed.

Example: "Use the four blocks on the left to make the pattern on the right."

FIGURE 2 SAMPLE SUBSCALES OF THE WECHSLER INTELLIGENCE SCALE FOR CHILDREN–FIFTH EDITION (WISC-V)

Simulated items similar to those in the Wechsler Intelligence Scale for Children–Fifth Edition. The Wechsler includes 11 subscales—6 verbal and 5 nonverbal. Three of the subscales are shown here.

Source: Wechsler Intelligence Scale for Children. NCS Pearson, Inc.

CONNECTING WITH STUDENTS: Best Practices
Strategies for Interpreting Intelligence Test Scores

Psychological tests are tools (Anastasi & Urbino, 1997). Like all tools, their effectiveness depends on the user's knowledge, skill, and integrity. A hammer can be used to build a beautiful kitchen cabinet or to break down a door. Similarly, psychological tests can be well used or badly abused. Here are some cautions about IQ that can help teachers avoid using information about a student's intelligence in negative ways:

1. *Avoid unwarranted stereotypes and negative expectations about students based on IQ scores.* Too often, sweeping generalizations are made on the basis of an IQ score. Imagine that you are in the teachers' lounge on the second day of school in the fall. You mention one of your students, and another teacher remarks that she had him in her class last year. She says that he was a real dunce and that he scored 83 on an IQ test. How hard is it to ignore this information as you go about teaching your class? Probably difficult. But it is important that you not develop the expectation that because Johnny scored low on an IQ test, it is useless to spend much time teaching him (Weinstein, 2004). An IQ test should always be considered a measure of current performance. It is not a measure of fixed potential. Maturational changes and enriched environmental experiences can advance a student's intelligence.

2. *Don't use IQ tests as the main or sole characteristic of competence.* A high IQ is not the ultimate human value. Teachers need to consider not only students' intellectual competence in areas such as verbal skills, but also their creative and practical skills.

3. *Especially be cautious in interpreting the meaningfulness of an overall IQ score.* It is wiser to think of intelligence as consisting of a number of domains. Many educational psychologists stress that it is important to consider the student's strengths and weaknesses in different areas of intelligence. Intelligence tests such as the Wechsler scales can provide information about those strengths and weaknesses.

the ease with which rapport is established, the student's enthusiasm and interest, whether anxiety interferes with the student's performance, and the student's degree of tolerance for frustration.

Group Intelligence Tests Students also may be given an intelligence test in a group setting. Group intelligence tests include the Lorge-Thorndike Intelligence Tests and the Otis-Lennon School Ability Test (OLSAT). Group intelligence tests are more convenient and economical than individual tests, but they do have their drawbacks. When a test is given to a large group, the examiner cannot establish rapport, determine the student's level of anxiety, and so on. In a large-group testing situation, students might not understand the instructions or might be distracted by other students.

Because of such limitations, when important decisions are made about students, a group intelligence test should always be supplemented with other information about the student's abilities. For that matter, the same strategy holds for an individual intelligence test, although it usually is wise to have less confidence in the accuracy of group intelligence test scores. Many students take tests in large groups at school, but a decision to place a student in a class for students with intellectual disabilities or a class for students who are gifted should not be based on a group test alone. In such instances, an extensive amount of relevant information about the student's abilities should be obtained outside the testing situation.

THEORIES OF MULTIPLE INTELLIGENCES

Is it more appropriate to think of a student's intelligence as a general ability or as a number of specific abilities? Psychologists have thought about this question since early in the twentieth century and continue to debate the issue.

Sternberg's Triarchic Theory According to Robert J. Sternberg's (1986, 2004, 2010, 2012, 2013, 2014, 2015a, 2016a, b) **triarchic theory of intelligence**, intelligence comes in three forms: analytical, creative, and practical. Analytical intelligence involves the ability to analyze, judge, evaluate, compare, and contrast. Creative intelligence

triarchic theory of intelligence Sternberg's view that intelligence comes in three main forms: analytical, creative, and practical.

Robert J. Sternberg, who developed the triarchic theory of intelligence.
Courtesy of Dr. Robert Sternberg

consists of the ability to create, design, invent, originate, and imagine. Practical intelligence focuses on the ability to use, apply, implement, and put into practice.

To understand what analytical, creative, and practical intelligence mean, let's look at examples of people who reflect these three types of intelligence:

- Consider Latisha, who scores high on traditional intelligence tests such as the Stanford-Binet and is a star analytical thinker. Latisha's *analytical intelligence* approximates what has traditionally been called intelligence and what is commonly assessed by intelligence tests.
- Todd does not have the best test scores but has an insightful and creative mind. Sternberg calls the type of thinking at which Todd excels *creative intelligence.*
- Finally, consider Emanuel, a person whose scores on traditional IQ tests are low but who quickly identifies solutions to real-life problems. He easily picks up knowledge about how the world works. Emanuel's "street smarts" and practical know-how are what Sternberg calls *practical intelligence.*

Sternberg (2015a, 2016a, b) says that students with different triarchic patterns look different in school. Students with high analytic ability tend to be favored in conventional schools. They often do well in classes in which the teacher lectures and gives objective tests. These students typically get good grades, do well on traditional IQ tests and the SAT, and later gain admission to competitive colleges.

Students high in creative intelligence often are not in the top rung of their class. Creatively intelligent students might not conform to teachers' expectations about how assignments should be done. They give unique answers, for which they might get reprimanded or marked down.

Like students high in creative intelligence, students who are practically intelligent often do not relate well to the demands of school. However, these students frequently do well outside the classroom's walls. Their social skills and common sense may allow them to become successful managers or entrepreneurs, despite undistinguished school records.

Sternberg (2015a, 2016a, b) stresses that few tasks are purely analytic, creative, or practical. Most tasks require some combination of these skills. For example, when students write a book report, they might analyze the book's main themes, generate new ideas about how the book could have been written better, and think about how the book's themes can be applied to people's lives. Sternberg argues that it is important for classroom instruction to give students opportunities to learn through all three types of intelligence.

Sternberg (2016c) argues that *wisdom* is linked to both practical and academic intelligence. In his view, academic intelligence is a necessary but in many cases insufficient requirement for wisdom. Practical knowledge about the realities of life also is needed for wisdom. For Sternberg, balance between self-interest, the interests of others, and context produces a common good. Thus, wise individuals don't just look out for themselves—they also need to consider others' needs and perspectives, as well as the particular context involved. Sternberg assesses wisdom by presenting problems to individuals that require solutions which highlight various intrapersonal, interpersonal, and contextual interests. He also emphasizes that such aspects of wisdom should be taught in schools (Sternberg, 2016c).

Gardner's Eight Frames of Mind As we indicated in the *Connecting with Teachers* introduction to this chapter, Howard Gardner (1983, 1993, 2002) argues that there are many specific types of intelligence, or frames of mind. They are described here along with examples of the occupations in which they are reflected as strengths (Campbell et al., 2004):

- *Verbal skills:* The ability to think in words and to use language to express meaning (authors, journalists, and speakers)
- *Mathematical skills:* The ability to carry out mathematical operations (scientists, engineers, and accountants)
- *Spatial skills:* The ability to think three-dimensionally (architects, artists, and sailors)

- *Bodily-kinesthetic skills:* The ability to manipulate objects and be physically adept (surgeons, craftspeople, dancers, and athletes)
- *Musical skills:* A sensitivity to pitch, melody, rhythm, and tone (composers, musicians, and music therapists)
- *Intrapersonal skills:* The ability to understand oneself and effectively direct one's life (theologians and psychologists)
- *Interpersonal skills:* The ability to understand and effectively interact with others (teachers and mental health professionals)
- *Naturalist skills:* The ability to observe patterns in nature and understand natural and human-made systems (farmers, botanists, ecologists, and landscapers)

Gardner argues that each form of intelligence can be destroyed by a different pattern of brain damage, that each involves unique cognitive skills, and that each shows up in unique ways in both the gifted and idiot savants (individuals who have an intellectual disability but also have an exceptional talent in a particular domain, such as drawing, music, or numerical computation).

At various times, Gardner has considered including *existential intelligence,* which involves concern and reasoning about meaning in life, as a ninth intelligence (McKay, 2008). However, he has not yet added it as a different form of intelligence.

Although Gardner has endorsed the application of his model to education, he has also witnessed some misuses of the approach. Here are some cautions he gives about using it (Gardner, 1998):

- There is no reason to assume that every subject can be effectively taught in eight different ways to correspond to the eight intelligences, and attempting to do this is a waste of effort.
- Don't assume that it is enough just to apply a certain type of intelligence. For example, in terms of bodily-kinesthetic skills, random muscle movements have nothing to do with cultivating cognitive skills.
- There is no reason to believe that it is helpful to use one type of intelligence as a background activity while children are working on an activity related to a different type of intelligence. For example, Gardner points out that playing music in the background while students solve math problems is a misapplication of his theory.

Howard Gardner, shown here working with young adolescents, developed the view that intelligence includes eight kinds of skills: verbal, mathematical, spatial, bodily-kinesthetic, musical, intrapersonal, interpersonal, and naturalist.
Steve Hansen/The Life Images Collection/Getty Images and

Technology can be used to facilitate learning in each area of intelligence (Dickinson, 1998, pp. 1–3):

- *Verbal skills.* "Computers encourage students to revise and rewrite compositions; this should help them to produce more competent papers. Many aspects of computer-mediated communication, such as e-mail, chat, and text messaging, provide students with opportunities to practice and expand their verbal skills." Web publishing, blogging, cloud-based tools, video production, and videocasting also can be helpful for writing and revising documents and presentations.
- *Logical/mathematical skills.* "Students of every ability can learn effectively through interesting software programs that provide immediate feedback and go far beyond drill-and-practice exercises." Formula manipulation software such as *Mathematica* (www.wolfram.com/products/mathematica/index.html) and math apps for mobile devices that are available on iTunes and the Android play store can help students improve their logical/mathematics skills. Look for apps that provide useful feedback on errors and those that target conceptual knowledge in addition to providing procedural practice.
- *Spatial skills.* Computers allow students to see and manipulate material. Virtual-reality technology can also provide students with opportunities to exercise their visual-spatial skills. Google Cardboard is an inexpensive way to integrate virtual-reality technology into a classroom. 3D printing also is becoming increasingly available—not always at an individual school, but sometimes through districts or local libraries and colleges. 3D printing allows physical manipulation to support spatial reasoning.

- *Bodily-kinesthetic skills.* "Computers rely mostly on eye-hand coordination for their operation—keyboarding and the use of a mouse or touch-screen. This kinesthetic activity . . . makes the student an active participant in the learning." The Oculus (www.oculus.com) makes virtual-reality gaming headsets and controllers that can be used to improve students' bodily-kinesthetic skills.
- *Musical skills.* Apple Computer's GarageBand (www.apple.com/mac/garageband/) software is a good way to practice musical skills. There also are numerous apps for Apple and Android that allow music to be created, recorded, and played back for students.
- *Interpersonal skills.* "When students use computers in pairs or small groups, their comprehension and learning are facilitated and accelerated. Positive learning experiences can result as students share discoveries, support each other in solving problems, and work collaboratively on projects."
- *Intrapersonal skills.* "Technology offers the means to explore a line of thought in great depth." There are many apps and websites that provide tools, videos, and guidance to support intrapersonal skills like self-regulated learning and emotion regulation with self-monitoring techniques.
- *Naturalist skills.* Electronic technologies can "facilitate scientific investigation, exploration, and other naturalist activities." For example, National Geographic Online allows students to go on virtual expeditions with famed explorers and photographers. Also, there are some attractive science projects that let students collect data in their local environment and contribute to science by submitting their data/findings online. Examples include Project Feederwatch (http://feederwatch.org/), Bumble Bee Watch (www.bumblebeewatch.org), and Globe at Night campaign (www.globeatnight.org/) More citizen-science projects can be found at www.nationalgeographic.org/idea/citizen-science-projects/.

How do practicing teachers apply Gardner's theory of multiple intelligences in their classrooms? Following are their recommendations.

EARLY CHILDHOOD Since each one of my preschoolers is different, I recognize that they have different skills and different needs. For example, we had a child who was very good at physical activities, such as bouncing a ball and tossing it into a net, but who struggled with learning how to count. To improve her counting skills, we had her count the number of times she bounced the ball and how many times the ball went into the net.

—HEIDI KAUFMAN, *Metro West YMCA Child Care and Educational Program*

ELEMENTARY SCHOOL: GRADES K–5 Students need choices. Some need to move around regularly in the classroom, sit on the floor, or write on the board. Some need a nondistracting, edge of the room seat. If instruction is given, or a question is asked, partner-talk can help to reinforce learning, but some students need a quiet, personal prompt from the teacher. I also provide choices for final assignments—for example, oral presentation, graphic representation, an essay or poem, and PowerPoint slides.

—KEREN ABRA, *Convent of the Sacred Heart Elementary School*

MIDDLE SCHOOL: GRADES 6–8 Group projects offer great opportunities to incorporate Gardner's theory into the classroom. I try to develop group projects that  require participants to read, do artwork, do math, think creatively, speak in public, and so on. By including these various skills, group members are able to express their knowledge in a way that meets their individual style of learning.

—CASEY MAASS, *Edison Middle School*

CONNECTING WITH STUDENTS: Best Practices
Strategies for Implementing Each of Gardner's Multiple Intelligences

Gardner's theory of multiple intelligences continues to be applied to children's education. Following are some strategies that teachers can use related to Gardner's eight types of intelligence (Campbell et al., 2004):

1. *Verbal skills.* Read to children and let them read to you, visit libraries and bookstores with children, and have children summarize and retell a story they have read.
2. *Mathematical skills.* Play games of logic with children, be on the lookout for situations that can inspire children to think about and construct an understanding of numbers, and take children on field trips to computer labs, science museums, and electronics exhibits.
3. *Spatial skills.* Have a variety of creative materials for children to use, take children to art museums and hands-on children's museums, and go on walks with children. When they are back in the classroom, ask them to visualize where they have been and then draw a map of their experiences.
4. *Bodily-kinesthetic skills.* Provide children with opportunities for physical activity and encourage them to participate, provide areas where children can play indoors and outdoors, and encourage children to participate in dance activities.
5. *Musical skills.* Give children an opportunity to play musical instruments, create opportunities for children to make music and rhythms together using voices and instruments, and take children to concerts.
6. *Intrapersonal skills.* Encourage children to have hobbies and interests, listen to children's feelings and give them sensitive feedback, and have children keep a journal or scrapbook of their ideas and experiences.
7. *Interpersonal skills.* Encourage children to work in groups, help children to develop communication skills, and provide group games for children to play.
8. *Naturalist skills.* Create a naturalist learning center in the classroom, engage children in outdoor naturalist activities, such as taking a nature walk or adopting a tree, and have children make collections of flora or fauna and classify them. In *Through the Eyes of Teachers,* Joanna Smith, a high school English teacher, describes how she implements Gardner's multiple intelligences into her classroom.

THROUGH THE EYES OF TEACHERS
Giving Students a Choice of Which Type of Intelligence They Want to Use for a Project

I try to draw on Gardner's eight frames of mind throughout the year by giving a variety of assignments. My students sometimes have a choice about which "type of intelligence" to use, depending on their project. For example, at the end of the first semester, students do an outside reading project based on a self-selected book. They create a project based on the book's themes and characters. For example, students might give a monologue from a character's perspective, create a family tree, make a CD of thematic songs, or give a "tour" of the book's setting live or on tape. This type of project is always successful because it allows students to choose in what mode, in what frame of mind, they will present their knowledge.

Joanna Smith

HIGH SCHOOL: GRADES 9–12 I often give my students the power of choice when it comes to how a project can be completed. For example, they can complete a project as an artistic piece, a written project, or a demonstration so that students can choose the mode that best fits their comfort level.

—JENNIFER HEITER, *Bremen High School*

We have discussed a number of ideas about Gardner's concept of multiple intelligences. To evaluate your strengths and weaknesses on his eight types of intelligence, see *Self-Assessment 1.*

Emotional Intelligence Both Gardner's and Sternberg's theories include one or more categories related to the ability to understand oneself and others and to get along in the world. In Gardner's theory, the categories are interpersonal intelligence and intrapersonal intelligence; in Sternberg's theory, practical intelligence. Other theorists who emphasize interpersonal, intrapersonal, and practical aspects of intelligence focus on what is called *emotional intelligence,* which was popularized by Daniel Goleman (1995) in his book *Emotional Intelligence.*

SELF-ASSESSMENT 1
Evaluating Myself on Gardner's Eight Types of Intelligence

Read these items and rate yourself on a 4-point scale. Each rating corresponds to how well a statement describes you: 1 = not like me at all, 2 = somewhat unlike me, 3 = somewhat like me, and 4 = a lot like me.

Verbal Thinking

1. I do well on verbal tests, such as the verbal part of the SAT.
2. I am a skilled reader and read prolifically.
3. I love the challenge of solving verbal problems.

Logical/Mathematical Thinking

4. I am a very logical thinker.
5. I like to think like a scientist.
6. Math is one of my favorite subjects.

Spatial Skills

7. I am good at visualizing objects and layouts from different angles.
8. I have the ability to create maps of spaces and locations in my mind.
9. If I had wanted to be, I think I could have been an architect.

Bodily-Kinesthetic Skills

10. I have great hand-eye coordination.
11. I excel at sports.
12. I am good at using my body to carry out an expression, as in dance.

Musical Skills

13. I play one or more musical instruments well.
14. I have a good "ear" for music.
15. I am good at making up songs.

Insightful Skills for Self-Understanding

16. I know myself well and have a positive view of myself.
17. I am in tune with my thoughts and feelings.
18. I have good coping skills.

Insightful Skills for Analyzing Others

19. I am very good at "reading" people.
20. I am good at collaborating with other people.
21. I am a good listener.

Naturalist Skills

22. I am good at observing patterns in nature.
23. I excel at identifying and classifying objects in the natural environment.
24. I understand natural and human-made systems.

SELF-ASSESSMENT 1

SCORING AND INTERPRETATION

Total your score for each of the eight types of intelligence and place the total in the blank that follows the label for each kind of intelligence. Which areas of intelligence are your strengths? In which are you the least proficient? It is highly unlikely that you will be strong in all eight areas or weak in all eight areas. By being aware of your strengths and weaknesses in different areas of intelligence, you can get a sense of which areas of teaching students will be the easiest and most difficult for you. If I (your author) had to teach musical skills, I would be in big trouble because I just don't have the talent. However, I do have reasonably good movement skills and spent part of my younger life playing and coaching tennis. If you are not proficient in some of Gardner's areas and you have to teach students in those areas, consider getting volunteers from the community to help you. For example, Gardner says that schools need to do a better job of calling on retired people, most of whom likely would be delighted to help students improve their skills in the domain or domains in which they are competent. This strategy also helps to link communities and schools with a sort of "intergenerational glue."

The concept of emotional intelligence was initially developed by Peter Salovey and John Mayer (1990). They conceptualize **emotional intelligence** as the ability to perceive and express emotion accurately and adaptively (such as taking the perspective of others), to understand emotion and emotional knowledge (such as understanding the roles that emotions play in friendship and other relationships), to use feelings to facilitate thought (such as being in a positive mood, which is linked to creative thinking), and to manage emotions in oneself and others (such as being able to control one's anger).

There continues to be considerable interest in the concept of emotional intelligence (Boyatzis et al., 2015; Conn et al., 2016; Fernandez-Berrocal & Checa, 2016). A recent study revealed that emotional intelligence abilities were linked to academic achievement above and beyond cognitive and personality factors (Lanciano & Curci, 2014). However, critics argue that emotional intelligence broadens the concept of intelligence too far and has not been adequately assessed and researched (Hogeveen et al., 2016; Humphrey et al., 2007).

emotional intelligence The ability to perceive and express emotion accurately and adaptively, to understand emotion and emotional knowledge, to monitor one's own and others' emotions and feelings, to discriminate among them, and to use this information to guide one's thinking and action.

Do Children Have One Intelligence or Many Intelligences? Figure 3 provides a comparison of Gardner's, Sternberg's, and Salovey/Mayer's views. Notice that Gardner includes a number of types of intelligence not addressed by the other views, and that Sternberg is unique in emphasizing creative intelligence. These theories of multiple intelligences have much to offer. They have stimulated us to think more broadly about what makes up people's intelligence and competence (Moran & Gardner, 2006). And they have motivated educators to develop programs that instruct students in different domains (Winner, 2006).

Theories of multiple intelligences also have many critics. They conclude that the research base to support these theories has not yet been developed. In particular, some argue that Gardner's classification seems arbitrary. For example, if musical skills represent a type of intelligence, why don't we also refer to chess intelligence, prizefighter intelligence, and so on? A number of psychologists still support the concept of g (general intelligence) (Burkhart et al., 2016; Checa & Fernandez-Berrocal, 2015; Shakeshaft et al., 2015). For example, one expert on intelligence, Nathan Brody (2007) argues that people who excel at one type of intellectual task

Gardner	Sternberg	Salovey/Mayer
Verbal Mathematical	Analytical	
Spatial Movement Musical	Creative	
Interpersonal Intrapersonal	Practical	Emotional
Naturalistic		

FIGURE 3 COMPARISONS OF STERNBERG'S, GARDNER'S, AND SALOVEY/MAYER'S VIEWS OF INTELLIGENCE

are likely to excel at other intellectual tasks. Thus, individuals who do well at memorizing lists of digits are also likely to be good at solving verbal problems and spatial layout problems. This general intelligence includes abstract reasoning or thinking, the capacity to acquire knowledge, and problem-solving ability.

Advocates of the concept of general intelligence point to its success in predicting school and job success (Deary et al., 2007). For example, scores on tests of general intelligence are substantially correlated with school grades and achievement test performance, both at the time of the test and years later (Cucina et al., 2016; Kyllonen, 2016; Strentze, 2007). For example, a recent meta-analysis of 240 independent samples and more than 100,000 individuals found a correlation of +0.54 between intelligence and school grades (Roth et al., 2015).

Intelligence tests are moderately correlated with job performance (Lubinski, 2009). Individuals with higher scores on tests designed to measure general intelligence tend to get higher-paying, more prestigious jobs (Lubinski, 2009). However, general IQ tests predict only about one-fourth of the variation in job success, with most variation being attributable to other factors such as motivation and education (Wagner & Sternberg, 1986). Further, the correlations between IQ and achievement decrease the longer people work at a job, presumably because as they gain more job experience they perform better (Hunt, 1995).

RESEARCH

Some experts who argue for the existence of general intelligence conclude that individuals also have specific intellectual abilities (Brody, 2007). In sum, controversy still characterizes whether it is more accurate to conceptualize intelligence as a general ability, specific abilities, or both (Sternberg, 2016a, b). Sternberg (2016a, b) actually accepts that there is a *g* for the kinds of analytical tasks that traditional IQ tests assess but thinks that the range of tasks those tests measure is far too narrow.

THE NEUROSCIENCE OF INTELLIGENCE

In the current era of extensive research on the brain, interest in the neurological underpinnings of intelligence has increased (Deary, 2012; Santarnecchi et al., 2015). Among the questions about the brain's role in intelligence that are being explored are these: Is having a bigger brain linked to higher intelligence? Is intelligence located in certain brain regions? Is the speed at which the brain processes information linked to intelligence?

Are individuals with bigger brains more intelligent than those with smaller brains? Studies using MRI scans to assess total brain volume indicate a moderate correlation (about .3 to .4) between brain size and intelligence (Carey, 2007; Luders et al., 2009).

Might intelligence be linked to specific regions of the brain? Early consensus was that the frontal lobes (see purple portion in Figure 4) are the likely location of intelligence. Today, some experts continue to emphasize that high-level thinking skills involved in intelligence are linked to the prefrontal cortex, which covers the front part of the frontal lobe (Santarnecchi et al., 2015; Sternberg & Sternberg, 2016). However, other researchers recently have found that intelligence is distributed more widely across brain regions (Lee et al., 2012). The most prominent finding from brain-imaging studies is that a distributed neural network involving the frontal and parietal lobes (the yellow portion in Figure 4) is related to higher intelligence (Margolis et al., 2013). A recent study revealed that the frontoparietal network (connecting the frontal and parietal lobes) is responsible for cognitive control and connectivity to brain regions outside the network (Cole et al., 2012). Albert Einstein's total brain size was average, but a region of his brain's parietal lobe that is very active in processing math and spatial information was 15 percent larger than average (Witelson

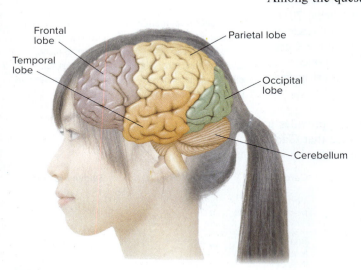

FIGURE 4 INTELLIGENCE AND THE BRAIN

Researchers recently have found that a higher level of intelligence is linked to a distributed neural network in the frontal and parietal lobes. To a lesser extent than the frontal/parietal network, the temporal and occipital lobes, as well as the cerebellum, also have been found to have links to intelligence. The current consensus is that intelligence is likely to be distributed across brain regions rather than being localized in a specific region such as the frontal lobes.
Takayuki/Shutterstock

et al., 1999). Other brain regions that have been linked to higher intelligence (although at a lower level of significance than the frontal/parietal lobe network) include the temporal (the orange region in Figure 4) and occipital lobes (the green region in Figure 4), as well as the cerebellum (the striped, lower right region in Figure 4; Luders et al., 2009).

Researchers recently have found that a higher level of intelligence is linked to a distributed neural network in the frontal and parietal lobes. To a lesser extent than the frontal/parietal network, the temporal and occipital lobes, as well as the cerebellum, also have been found to have links to intelligence. The current consensus is that intelligence is likely to be distributed across brain regions rather than being localized in a specific region such as the frontal lobes.

Examining the neuroscience of intelligence has also led to study of the role that neurological speed might play in intelligence (Waiter et al., 2009). Research results have not been consistent for this possible link, although a recent study found that children who are gifted show faster processing speed and more accurate processing of information than children who are not gifted (Duan et al., 2013).

As technological advances allow closer study of the brain's functioning in coming decades, we are likely to see more specific conclusions about the brain's role in intelligence. As this research proceeds, keep in mind that both heredity and environment likely contribute to links between the brain and intelligence, including the connections we discussed between brain size and intelligence. Also, Robert Sternberg (2014) recently concluded that research on the brain's role in intelligence has been more effective in answering some questions (such as "What aspects of the brain are involved in learning a list of words?") than in answering others (such as "Why do some individuals consider shaking hands socially intelligent but others do not?").

CONTROVERSIES AND ISSUES IN INTELLIGENCE

The topic of intelligence is surrounded by controversy. Is nature or nurture more important in determining intelligence? Are intelligence tests culturally biased? Should IQ tests be used to place children in particular schooling tracks?

Nature and Nurture The **nature-nurture issue** involves the debate about whether development is primarily influenced by nature or by nurture. *Nature* refers to a person's biological inheritance, *nurture* to environmental experiences.

"Nature" proponents argue that intelligence is primarily inherited and that environmental experiences play only a minimal role in its manifestation. The emerging view of the nature-nurture issue is that many complicated qualities, such as intelligence, probably have some genetic loading that gives each person a propensity for a particular developmental trajectory, such as low, average, or high intelligence. The actual development of intelligence, however, requires more than just heredity.

Most experts today agree that the environment also plays an important role in intelligence (Grigorenko et al., 2016; Sternberg, 2016 a, b). This means that improving children's environments can raise their intelligence. It also means that enriching children's environments can improve their school achievement and promote the acquisition of skills needed for employment. Craig Ramey and his associates (1988) found that high-quality early educational child care (through 5 years of age) significantly raised the tested intelligence of young children from impoverished backgrounds. Positive effects of this early intervention were still evident in the intelligence and achievement of these students when they were 13 and 21 years of age (Ramey et al., 2009). And research by Richard Nisbett and his colleagues (2012) supported the influence of environment on intelligence: A 12- to 18-point increase in IQ was found when children are adopted from low-income families into middle- and upper-income families.

Another argument for the influence of environment on intelligence involves the increasing scores on IQ tests around the world. Scores on these tests have been rising so fast that a high percentage of people regarded as having average intelligence in

> **Thinking Back/Thinking Forward**
> The nature-nurture issue is one of developmental psychology's main issues. Connect to "Cognitive and Language Development."

RESEARCH

nature-nurture issue Nature refers to an organism's biological inheritance, nurture to environmental influences. The "nature" proponents claim biological inheritance is the most important influence on development; the "nurture" proponents claim environmental experiences are the most important.

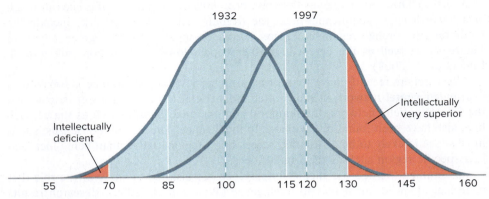

FIGURE 5 THE FLYNN EFFECT

As measured by the Stanford-Binet intelligence test, American children seem to be getting smarter. Scores of a group tested in 1932 fell along a bell-shaped curve with half below 100 and half above. Studies show that if children took that same test today, half would score above 120 on the 1932 scale. Very few of them would score in the "intellectually deficient" end, on the left side, and about one-fourth would rank in the "very superior" range.

the early 1900s would be considered below average in intelligence today (Flynn, 1999, 2007, 2011, 2013) (see Figure 5). If a representative sample of today's children took the Stanford-Binet test used in 1932, about one-fourth would be defined as very superior, a label usually accorded to less than 3 percent of the population. Because the increase has taken place in a relatively short period of time, it can't be due to heredity but instead might result from such environmental factors as the explosion in information people are exposed to and the much higher percentage of the population receiving education. A recent meta-analysis of 53 studies conducted since 1972 found that IQ scores have been rising about 3 points per decade since that year and that the increase in IQ scores does not seem to be diminishing (Trahan et al., 2014). This worldwide increase in intelligence test scores over a short time frame is called the *Flynn effect* after the researcher who discovered it—James Flynn.

Studies of schooling also reveal effects on intelligence (Sternberg et al., 2009). The biggest effects occur when large groups of children are deprived of formal education for an extended period, resulting in lower intelligence.

One analysis of studies on schooling and intelligence concluded that schooling and intelligence influence each other (Ceci & Williams, 1997). For example, individuals who finish high school are more intelligent than those who drop out of school. This might be because brighter individuals stay in school longer, or because the environmental influence of schooling contributes to their intelligence.

Researchers increasingly are interested in manipulating the early environment of children who are at risk for impoverished intelligence (Duncan et al., 2015; Wadsworth et al., 2016). The emphasis is on prevention rather than remediation. Many low-income parents have difficulty providing an intellectually stimulating environment for their children. Programs that educate parents to be more sensitive caregivers and better teachers, as well as support services such as quality child-care programs, can make a difference in a child's intellectual development (Bredekamp, 2017; Morrison, 2017).

It is extremely difficult to tease apart the effects of nature or nurture, so much so that psychologist William Greenough (1997, 2000) says that asking which is more important is like asking what's more important to a rectangle, its length or its width. We still do not know what, if any, specific genes actually promote or restrict a general level of intelligence. If such genes exist, they certainly are found both in children whose families and environments appear to promote the development of children's abilities and in children whose families and environments do not appear to be as supportive. Regardless of one's genetic background, growing up "with all the

DEVELOPMENT

advantages" does not guarantee high intelligence or success, especially if those advantages are taken for granted. Nor does the absence of such advantages guarantee low intelligence or failure, especially if the family and child can make the most of whatever opportunities are accessible to them.

Ethnicity and Culture Are there ethnic differences in intelligence? Are conventional tests of intelligence biased, and if so, can we develop culture-fair tests?

DIVERSITY

Ethnic Comparisons In the United States, children from African American and Latinx families score below children from White families on standardized intelligence tests (Yeung, 2012). On average, African American school children score 10 to 15 points lower on standardized intelligence tests than White American school children do (Brody, 2000). These are *average scores,* however. About 15 to 25 percent of African American school children score higher than half of White school children do, and many Whites score lower than most African Americans. The reason is that the distribution of scores for African Americans and Whites overlap.

As African Americans have gained social, economic, and educational opportunities, the gap between African Americans and Whites on standardized intelligence tests has begun to narrow (Ogbu & Stern, 2001). A recent research review concluded that the IQ gap between African Americans and non-Latinx Whites has been reduced considerably in recent years (Nisbett et al., 2012). This gap especially narrows in college, where African American and White students often experience more similar environments than in the elementary and high school years (Myerson et al., 1998). Also, when children from disadvantaged African American families are adopted into more-advantaged middle-socioeconomic-status families, their scores on intelligence tests more closely resemble national averages for middle-socioeconomic-status children than for lower-socioeconomic-status children (Scarr & Weinberg, 1983). Further, a recent study using the Stanford-Binet Intelligence Scales found no differences in overall intellectual ability between non-Latinx White and African American preschool children when the children were matched on age, gender, and parental education level (Dale et al., 2014). Nonetheless, a recent analysis concluded that the underrepresentation of African Americans in STEM (science, technology, engineering, and math) subjects and careers is linked to practitioners' expectations that they have less innate talent than non-Latinx Whites (Leslie et al., 2015).

Cultural Bias and Culture-Fair Tests Many of the early tests of intelligence were culturally biased, favoring urban children over rural children, children from middle-income families over children from low-income families, and White children over minority children (Miller-Jones, 1989). The standards for the early tests were almost exclusively based on non-Latinx White, middle-socioeconomic-status children. Contemporary intelligence tests attempt to reduce such cultural bias (Merenda, 2004).

One potential influence on intelligence test performance is **stereotype threat**, the anxiety that one's behavior might confirm a negative stereotype about one's group (Pennington et al., 2016; Scott & Rodriquez, 2015; Steele & Aronson, 2004; Spencer et al., 2016; Suad Nasir et al., 2016). For example, when African Americans take an intelligence test, they may experience anxiety about confirming the old stereotype that Blacks are "intellectually inferior." Some studies have confirmed the existence of stereotype threat (Appel & Kronberger, 2012; Wasserberg, 2014). For example, African American students do more poorly on standardized tests if they perceive that they are being evaluated. If they think the test doesn't count, they perform as well as White students (Aronson, 2002). Brief and simple interventions pointing out role models (e.g., reading a story about a woman who did well in a difficult math course) or writing a self-affirmation can protect against the negative effects of stereotype threat (Shapiro et al., 2013).

RESEARCH

In contrast, brief and simple interventions pointing out role models or writing a self-affirmation can protect against the negative effects of stereotype threat.

stereotype threat Anxiety regarding whether one's behavior might confirm a negative stereotype about one's group.

How might stereotype threat be involved in ethnic minority students' performance on standardized tests?
Ocean/Comstock Images/Corbis

For example "women exposed to examples of successful women—such as reading about women with impressive achievements in architecture or invention, or women students who have excelled in science, technology, engineering, and math (STEM) fields—performed better on a diagnostic test of math ability" (Shapiro et al., 2013, p. 279). African American seventh-graders who completed a self-affirmation exercise that involved writing only one paragraph about why a value they identified as important (e.g., being good at art, relationships with friends) was important to themselves had better end of term grades than those who wrote about why that value might be important to others (Cohen et al., 2006). Geoffrey Cohen and his colleagues (2006) found "having students reaffirm their sense of personal adequacy or 'self-integrity' . . . significantly improved the grades of African American students and reduced the racial achievement gap by 40%" (p. 1307). Critics, on the other hand, argue that the extent to which stereotype threat explains the testing gap has been exaggerated (Sackett et al., 2009).

Culture-fair tests are intelligence tests that aim to avoid cultural bias. Two types of culture-fair tests have been developed. The first includes questions familiar to people from all socioeconomic and ethnic backgrounds. For example, a child might be asked how a bird and a dog are different, on the assumption that virtually all children are familiar with birds and dogs. The second type of culture-fair test contains no verbal questions. One widely used culture-fair test is the Raven's Progressive Matrices Test. Even though tests such as the Raven's Progressive Matrices are designed to be culture-fair, people with more education still score higher than those with less education do.

Why is it so hard to create culture-fair tests? Most tests tend to reflect what the dominant culture thinks is important (Zhang & Sternberg, 2012). If tests have time limits, that will bias the test against groups not concerned with time. If languages differ, the same words might have different meanings for different language groups. Even pictures can produce bias because some cultures have less experience with drawings and photographs. Within the same culture, different groups could have different attitudes, values, and motivation, and this could affect their performance on intelligence tests. Because of such difficulties in creating culture-fair tests, Robert Sternberg concludes that there are no culture-fair tests, only *culture-reduced tests.*

Ability Grouping and Tracking
Another controversial issue is whether it is beneficial to use students' scores on an intelligence test to place them in ability groups. Two types of ability grouping have been used in education: between-class and within-class.

Between-Class Ability Grouping (Tracking) **Between-class ability grouping (tracking)** consists of grouping students based on their ability or achievement. A typical between-class grouping involves dividing students into a college preparatory track and a general track. Within the two tracks, further ability groupings might be made, such as two levels of math instruction for college preparatory students. Another form of tracking takes place when a student's abilities in different subject areas are taken into account. For example, the same student might be in a high-track math class and a middle-track English class.

Tracking has long been used in schools as a way to organize students, especially at the secondary level. The positive view of tracking is that it narrows the range of

culture-fair tests Tests of intelligence that are intended to be free of cultural bias.

between-class ability grouping (tracking) Grouping students based on their ability or achievement.

skill in a group of students, making it easier to teach them. Tracking is said to prevent less-able students from "holding back" more talented students.

Critics of tracking argue that it stigmatizes students who are consigned to low-track classes (Banks, 2014). For example, students can get labeled as "low-track" or "the dummy group." Critics also say that low-track classrooms often have less-experienced teachers, fewer resources, and lower expectations. Further, critics stress that tracking is used to segregate students according to ethnicity and socioeconomic status because higher tracks have fewer students from ethnic minority and impoverished backgrounds (Banks, 2014). In this way, tracking can actually replay segregation within schools. The detractors of tracking also argue that average and above-average students do not get substantial benefits from being grouped together.

Does research support the critics' contention that tracking is harmful to students? Researchers have found that tracking harms the achievement of low-track students (Kelly, 2008). However, tracking seems to benefit high-track students (such as those in a gifted program). Also, researchers have found that "students who are 'tracked-up' or who are exposed to a more rigorous curriculum learn more than the same ability students who are 'tracked-down' or offered a less challenging course of study. . ." (Banks et al., 2005, p. 239).

These students participate in the Advancement Via Individual Determination (AVID) program in San Diego. Rather than being placed in a low track, they are enrolled in rigorous courses and provided support to help them achieve success. *What types of support are they provided?*
John Fletcher/The Asheville Citizen-Times/AP Images

One variation of between-class ability grouping is the **nongraded (cross-age) program**, in which students are grouped by their ability in particular subjects regardless of their age or grade level (Fogarty, 1993). This type of program is used far more in elementary than in secondary schools, especially in the first three grades. For example, a math class might be composed of first-, second-, and third-graders grouped together because of their similar math ability. The **Joplin plan** is a standard nongraded program for instruction in reading. In the Joplin plan, students from second, third, and fourth grade might be placed together because of their similar reading level.

RESEARCH

As noted earlier, tracking has negative effects on low-track students. When tracks are present, it is especially important to give low-achieving students an opportunity to improve their academic performance and thus change tracks. In the San Diego County Public Schools, the Advancement Via Individual Determination (AVID) program provides support for underachieving students. Instead of being placed in a low track, they are enrolled in rigorous courses but are not left to achieve on their own. A comprehensive system of support services helps them succeed. For example, a critical aspect of the program is a series of workshops that teach students note-taking skills, question-asking skills, thinking skills, and communication skills. The students also are clustered into study groups and urged to help each other clarify questions about assignments. College students, many of them AVID graduates, serve as role models, coaches, and motivators for the students. At each AVID school, a lead teacher oversees a team of school counselors and teachers from every academic discipline. In recent years, the dropout rate in AVID schools has declined by more than one-third, and an amazing 99 percent of the AVID graduates have enrolled in college. A number of AVID programs have been created in U.S. schools, and researchers have found that the programs have a positive influence on students' high school and college achievement (Griffen, 2013; Huerta & Watt, 2015; Huerta et al., 2013).

In sum, tracking is a controversial issue, especially because of the restrictions it places on low-track students. Too often, scores on a single, group IQ test are used to

nongraded (cross-age) program A variation of between-class ability grouping in which students are grouped by their ability in particular subjects, regardless of their age or grade level.

Joplin plan A standard nongraded program for instruction in reading.

CONNECTING WITH STUDENTS: Best Practices
Strategies for the Use of Tracking

As you have read, if tracking is used, a number of cautions need to be exercised. Following are some strategies teachers can adopt if tracking is implemented in the school in which they teach.

1. *Use other measures of student knowledge and potential in particular subject areas to place students in ability groups rather than a group-administered IQ test.*
2. *Avoid labeling groups as "low," "middle," and "high."* Also avoid comparisons of groups.
3. *Don't form more than two or three ability groups.* You won't be able to give a larger number of groups adequate attention and instruction.
4. *Consider the students' placements in various ability groups as subject to review and change.* Carefully monitor students' performance, and if a low-track student progresses adequately, move the student to a higher group. If a high-track student is doing poorly, evaluate whether the high track is the right one for the student and decide what supports the student might need to improve performance.
5. *Especially consider alternatives to tracking for low-achieving students.* Throughout this book, we will discuss instructional strategies and support services for low-achieving students, such as those being used in the AVID program.

place students in a particular track. Researchers have found that group IQ tests are not good predictors of how well students will do in a particular subject area (Garmon et al., 1995).

Within-Class Ability Grouping **Within-class ability grouping** involves placing students in two or three groups within a class to take into account differences in students' abilities. A typical within-class ability grouping occurs when elementary school teachers place students in several reading groups based on their reading skills. A second-grade teacher might have one group using a third-grade, first-semester reading program; another using a second-grade, first-semester program; and a third group using a first-grade, second-semester program. Such within-class grouping is far more common in elementary than in secondary schools. The subject area most often involved is reading, followed by math. Although many elementary school teachers use some form of within-class ability grouping, there is no clear research support for this strategy.

within-class ability grouping Placing students in two or three groups within a class to take into account differences in students' abilities.

Review, Reflect, and Practice

 Discuss what intelligence is, how it is measured, theories of multiple intelligences, the neuroscience of intelligence, and some controversies and issues about its use by educators.

REVIEW
- What does the concept of intelligence mean?
- What did Binet and Wechsler contribute to the field of intelligence? What are some pros and cons of individual versus group tests of intelligence?
- What is Sternberg's triarchic theory of intelligence? What is Gardner's system of "frames of mind"? What is Mayer, Salovey, and Goleman's concept of emotional intelligence? How is each theory relevant to education? What are some aspects of the controversy about whether intelligence is better conceptualized as general intelligence or multiple intelligences?
- How is the brain linked to intelligence?
- What are three controversies related to intelligence?

Review, Reflect, and Practice

REFLECT
- Suppose that you were about to teach a particular group of children for the first time and were handed intelligence test scores for every child in the class. Would you hesitate to look at the scores? Why or why not?

PRAXIS™ PRACTICE
1. Which of the following is the best indicator of high analytical intelligence according to Sternberg?
   a. scoring 135 on an IQ test
   b. reciting the Gettysburg Address from memory
   c. not making the same mistakes twice when given the opportunity to repeat a task after receiving feedback
   d. earning high grades
2. Susan took the Otis-Lennon School Ability Test to determine if she qualified for her school's gifted program. Based on her score of 125, she did not qualify for the program. Which of the following is a valid statement regarding this screening procedure?
   a. Because this was an individual test, the psychologist was able to ensure that rapport had been established and that anxiety did not interfere with her performance. Thus, the decision should stand.
   b. Because this was a group test, the psychologist was unable to ensure that rapport had been established and anxiety did not interfere with her performance. Thus, the decision should not stand. More information is needed.
   c. Because her score was well above average, she should be included in the gifted program.
   d. Because her score is just average, she should not be included in the gifted program.
3. Which of these students best exemplifies Sternberg's practical intelligence?
   a. Jamal, who writes wonderful science fiction stories
   b. Chandra, who is able to understand *The Great Gatsby's* symbolism at a complex level
   c. Mark, who is the most talented athlete in the school
   d. Susan, who gets along well with others and is good at "reading" others' emotions
4. Which of these statements best reflects what is currently known about the brain's role in intelligence?
   a. The total size of a child's brain is strongly correlated with intelligence.
   b. Intelligence is likely distributed widely across brain regions.
   c. Intelligence is located almost entirely in the brain's prefrontal lobe.
   d. The most consistent finding about the brain and intelligence is that higher intelligence is linked to a lower volume of gray matter.
5. Which of these statements is most consistent with current research on the nature-nurture issue in intelligence?
   a. Because intelligence in mainly inherited, there is little room to improve students' intelligence.
   b. Because intelligence is influenced by both heredity and environment, providing students with an enriched classroom environment might have a positive influence on their intelligence.
   c. Students who delay schooling tend to score higher on intelligence tests than those who do not, which suggests that environment is more important for intelligence than heredity.
   d. Recent steep increases in intelligence indicate that intelligence is mainly determined by heredity.

Please see answer key at end of book . . . .

LG 2 Describe learning and thinking styles.

2 LEARNING AND THINKING STYLES

Intelligence refers to ability. **Learning and thinking styles** are not abilities but, rather, preferred ways of using one's abilities (Sternberg, 2015c). In fact, teachers will tell you that children approach learning and thinking in an amazing variety of ways. Teachers themselves also vary in their styles of learning and thinking. None of us has just a single learning and thinking style; each of us has a profile of many styles, which may vary by subject matter. Individuals vary so much that literally hundreds of learning and thinking styles have been proposed by educators and psychologists.

The following coverage of learning and thinking styles is not meant to be exhaustive but introduces three sets of styles (impulsive/reflective, deep/surface, and optimistic/pessimistic) and some criticisms that have been made of the concept of learning and thinking styles.

IMPULSIVE/REFLECTIVE STYLES

Impulsive/reflective styles, also referred to as *conceptual tempo*, involve a student's tendency either to act quickly and impulsively or to take more time to respond and reflect on the accuracy of an answer (Kagan, 1965). Impulsive students often make more mistakes than reflective students.

Research on impulsivity/reflection shows that reflective students are more likely than impulsive students to do well at the following tasks (Jonassen & Grabowski, 1993): remembering structured information; reading comprehension and text interpretation; and problem solving and decision making. However, critics suggest that the effects of impulsivity/reflection are better explained by cognitive processes and personality (An & Carr, 2017).

Reflective students also are more likely than impulsive students to set their own learning goals and concentrate on relevant information. Reflective students usually have higher standards for performance. The evidence is strong that reflective students learn more effectively and do better in school than impulsive students.

In thinking about impulsive and reflective styles, keep in mind that although most children learn better when they are reflective rather than impulsive, some children are simply fast, accurate learners and decision makers. Reacting quickly is a bad

> **Thinking Back/Thinking Forward**
>
> Self-regulation, which involves self-generation and self-monitoring of thoughts, feelings, and behaviors to reach a goal, is increasingly recognized as a key aspect of learning. Connect to "Behavioral and Social Cognitive Approaches."

learning and thinking styles Individuals' preferences in how they use their abilities.

impulsive/reflective styles Involves a student's tendency either to act quickly and impulsively or to take more time to respond and reflect on the accuracy of the answer.

CONNECTING WITH STUDENTS: Best Practices
Strategies for Working with Impulsive Children

You are likely to have some children in your classroom who are impulsive. You can help them become less impulsive by adopting the following strategies.

1. *Monitor students in the class to determine which ones are impulsive.*
2. *Talk with impulsive students about taking their time to think through an answer before they respond.*
3. *Encourage students to label new information as they work with it.*
4. *Model the reflective style as a teacher.*
5. *Help students set high standards for their performance.*
6. *Recognize when impulsive students start to take more time to reflect.* Compliment them on their improvement.
7. *Guide students in creating their own plan to reduce impulsivity.*

CONNECTING WITH STUDENTS: Best Practices
Strategies for Helping Surface Learners Think More Deeply

In addition to having children in your classroom who are impulsive, you also are likely to teach children who are surface learners. Following are some effective strategies for turning surface learners into learners who think more deeply.

1. *Monitor students to determine which ones are surface learners.*
2. *Discuss with students the importance of going beyond rote memorization.* Encourage them to connect what they are learning now with what they have learned in the past.
3. *Ask questions and give assignments that require students to fit information into a larger framework.* For example, instead of just asking students to name the capital of a particular state, ask them if they have visited the capital and what their experiences were, what other cities are located in that section of the United States, or how large or small the city is.
4. *Be a model who processes information deeply rather than just scratching the surface.* Explore topics in depth, and talk about how the information you are discussing fits within a larger network of ideas.
5. *Avoid asking questions that require pat answers.* Instead, ask questions that require students to deeply process information. Connect lessons more effectively with children's existing interests. In *Through the Eyes of Teachers,* East Grand Forks, Minnesota, middle school teacher Therese Olejniczak describes how she gets students to slow down so they won't gloss over important material.

THROUGH THE EYES OF TEACHERS
Paying Attention to the Details

Seventh-graders are in a hurry, no matter which intelligences they favor or use. I often teach study skills to students to help them slow down and gather details they might miss in their haste to complete assignments.

One method I use is to have the entire class silently read an article on a topic I've selected with their interests in mind. Then I ask the students to list details of the article on the blackboard. I call on students one at a time as they raise their hands enthusiastically, and each student—in his or her adolescent need to belong—participates by contributing details to the list. Afterward, the students and I review the details, marveling at the depth of information they have found. Unplanned peer-tutoring occurs when students discover obscure items that others have skimmed past, revealing to one another their need to slow down. Small groups then create final reports that include a written summary and illustration.

Therese Olejniczak

---

strategy only if you come up with wrong answers. Also, some reflective children ruminate forever about problems and have difficulty finishing tasks. Teachers can encourage these children to retain their reflective orientation but arrive at more timely solutions. In the chapter on behavioral and social cognitive approaches we will discuss a number of other strategies for helping students self-regulate their behavior.

DEEP/SURFACE STYLES

Deep/surface styles involve how students approach learning materials. Do they do this in a way that helps them understand the meaning of the materials (deep style) or as simply what needs to be learned (surface style) (Marton et al., 1984)? Students who approach learning with a surface style fail to tie what they are learning into a larger conceptual framework. They tend to learn in a passive way, often rotely memorizing information. Deep learners are more likely to actively construct what they learn and give meaning to what they need to remember. Thus, deep learners take a constructivist approach to learning. Deep learners also are more likely to be self-motivated to learn, whereas surface learners are more likely to be motivated to learn because of external rewards, such as grades and positive feedback from the teacher (Snow et al., 1996). These approaches to studying and learning have been found to explain the effects of personality on achievement (Swanberg & Martinsen, 2010).

Several teachers were recently asked to identify the strategies they use to influence their students' learning and thinking styles. Following are their recommendations.

> **Thinking Back/Thinking Forward**
> In one view of memory, deeper processing of information is predicted to produce better memory than shallow processing of information. Connect to "The Information-Processing Approach."

deep/surface styles Involve the extent to which students approach learning materials in a way that helps them understand the meaning of the materials (deep style) or as simply what needs to be learned (surface style).

EARLY CHILDHOOD Preschoolers can be very eager to answer a question or take part in an activity, which means they often talk over others so that they can be heard by the teacher. While we are always happy to have enthusiastic students, we also teach them to wait to be called on and to take their time before answering a question.

—MISSY DANGLER, *Suburban Hills School*

ELEMENTARY SCHOOL: GRADES K–5 We use a "think time" procedure in which students think and respond to a question on signal after an adequate time for reflection. And we incorporate a think-pair-share procedure that gives all students an opportunity to think about a question, pair up with a partner, and then share their ideas. I also ask students what their partner said to encourage listening skills.

—HEATHER ZOLDAK, *Ridge Wood Elementary School*

MIDDLE SCHOOL: GRADES 6–8 I try to provide differentiated learning opportunities to suit all of my students' learning styles. For example, the students who are gifted can work on extensive independent research projects, and students who enjoy technology are allowed to complete a research project using a PowerPoint presentation. I give hands-on projects to students who enjoy drawing or developing creative projects.

—FELICIA PETERSON, *Pocantico Hills School*

HIGH SCHOOL: GRADES 9–12 As an art teacher, I foster an attitude of openness and acceptance in my classroom, which helps to promote my students' learning. When students feel that their ideas will be respected and heard, they are not afraid to try something different.

—DENNIS PETERSON, *Deer River High School*

OPTIMISTIC/PESSIMISTIC STYLES

Optimistic/pessimistic styles involve having either a positive (optimistic) or negative (pessimistic) outlook on the future. In *The Optimistic Child,* Martin Seligman (2007) described how parents, teachers, and coaches can instill optimism in children, which he argues helps to make them more resilient, less likely to become depressed, and more likely to succeed academically.

A study of adolescents found that having an optimistic style of thinking predicted a reduction in suicidal ideation for individuals who had experienced negative and potentially traumatic life events (Hirsch et al., 2009). Another study revealed that adolescents with an optimistic thinking style had a lower risk of developing depressive symptoms than their pessimistic counterparts (Patton et al., 2011).

Interest has been directed toward applying the concept of *academic optimism* to teaching (Sezgin & Erdogan, 2015). This concept emphasizes that positive academic outcomes will occur if teachers (1) believe they can make a difference in their students' academic achievement; (2) trust students and parents to cooperate in this objective; and (3) believe in their ability to overcome problems and be resilient in the face of difficulties (Hoy et al., 2008). Researchers have found that academic optimism is linked to students' academic success (Fahey et al., 2010; Gurol & Kerimgil, 2010; Hoy et al., 2006).

CRITICISMS OF LEARNING AND THINKING STYLES

Criticisms have been leveled at the concept of learning and thinking styles. A survey of researchers in the field of learning and thinking styles revealed that the three most common criticisms of these styles involve (1) low reliability of the styles (lack of

optimistic/pessimistic styles Involves having either positive (optimistic) or negative (pessimistic) expectations for the future.

consistency when they are assessed); (2) low validity of the styles (whether the tests that are used actually measure the styles purportedly being assessed); and (3) confusion in the definitions of styles (Peterson et al., 2009). Two recent research reviews supported these criticisms, finding that scientific support for learning style theories is lacking (Cuevas, 2015; Willingham et al., 2015). Moreover, there is strong evidence that matching instruction to students' learning styles or preferences does NOT improve learning (Reiner & Willingham, 2010).

Nonetheless, some educators believe that the concept of learning and thinking styles is valuable. The three sets of styles discussed here—impulsive and reflective, deep and surface, and optimistic and pessimistic—were selected because they likely have more meaningful applications to helping students learn more effectively than do other styles.

Review, Reflect, and Practice

 Describe learning and thinking styles.

REVIEW
- What is meant by learning and thinking styles?
- Describe impulsive/reflective styles.
- How can deep/surface styles be characterized?
- What are optimistic/pessimistic styles?
- How have learning and thinking styles been criticized?

REFLECT
- Describe yourself or someone else you know well in terms of the learning and thinking styles presented in this section.

PRAXIS™ PRACTICE

1. Ms. Garcia has her students read passages from a novel and then gives them 30 minutes to describe the gist of what they have read. Which students are likely to do well on this task?
   a. students with an impulsive style of thinking
   b. students with a reflective style of thinking
   c. students with practical intelligence
   d. students with average intelligence

2. Which question encourages a deep style of thinking?
   a. What is the inverse of one-half?
   b. What is the lowest prime number?
   c. How much flour would you use to make half of the cookie recipe?
   d. What does it mean to say that addition is the opposite of subtraction?

3. Which of the following teachers is likely to have the most positive results with his or her students?
   a. Mrs. Hoyle, who believes in her ability to be resilient when facing difficult circumstances
   b. Mr. Winkle, who is not very confident that he can make a difference in his students' outcomes
   c. Ms. Overton, who does not think it is a good idea to trust parents to cooperate with her objectives
   d. Mr. Constantine, who is uncertain that he can overcome problems he faces in the classroom

Please see answer key at end of book . . . .

LG 3 Characterize the nature of personality and temperament.

3 PERSONALITY AND TEMPERAMENT

We have seen that it is important to be aware of individual variations in children's cognition. It also is important to understand individual variations in their personality and temperament.

PERSONALITY

We make statements about personality all the time and prefer to be around people with certain types of personality. Let's examine just what the term *personality* means.

Personality refers to distinctive thoughts, emotions, and behaviors that characterize the way an individual adapts to the world. Think about yourself for a moment. What is your personality like? Are you outgoing or shy? Considerate or caring? Friendly or hostile? These are some of the characteristics involved in personality.

How stable are personality traits in adolescence? Some researchers have found that personality is not as stable in adolescence as in adulthood (Roberts et al., 2008). The greater degree of change in personality during adolescence may be linked to the exploration of new identities.

DEVELOPMENT

The "Big Five" Personality Factors As with intelligence, psychologists are interested in identifying the main dimensions of personality (Engler, 2009). Some personality researchers argue that they have identified the **"Big Five" factors of personality**, the "supertraits" thought to describe personality's main dimensions: openness, conscientiousness, extraversion, agreeableness, and neuroticism (emotional stability) (see Figure 6). (Notice that if you create an acronym from these trait names, you get the word *OCEAN*.)

Evidence for the importance of the Big Five factors indicates that they are related to such important aspects of children's, adolescents', and adults' lives as health, intelligence and cognitive functioning, achievement and work, and relationships (Hill & Roberts, 2016).

RESEARCH

A major finding in the study of the Big Five factors in childhood and adolescence is the emergence of conscientiousness as a key predictor of adjustment and competence (Hill & Roberts, 2016). Indeed, research supports that conscientiousness is the most important personality predictor of academic achievement (Poropat, 2016). For example, a recent study revealed that conscientiousness at age 16 predicted academic achievement at age 19 (Rosander & Backstrom, 2014). Also, in a study, students high in conscientiousness were less likely to avoid or delay studying (Klimstra et al., 2012). Further, in another recent study conscientiousness at age 7 was linked to being less likely to smoke at 50 years of age (Pluess & Bartley, 2015).

personality Distinctive thoughts, emotions, and behaviors that characterize the way an individual adapts to the world.

Big Five factors of personality Openness, conscientiousness, extraversion, agreeableness, and neuroticism (emotional stability).

FIGURE 6 THE "BIG FIVE" FACTORS OF PERSONALITY

Each column represents a broad "supertrait" that encompasses more narrow traits and characteristics. Using the acronym OCEAN can help you to remember the Big Five personality factors (openness, conscientiousness, and so on).

The second strongest personality predictor of academic achievement is openness to experience (Poropat, 2016). Conscientiousness and openness to experience are more highly correlated with academic achievement in secondary school than in elementary school while openness to experience is more strongly associated with academic success in elementary school (Poropat, 2016).

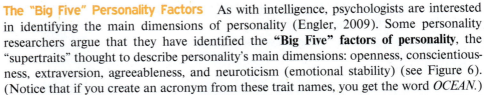

Openness	**C**onscientiousness	**E**xtraversion	**A**greeableness	**N**euroticism (emotional stability)
• Imaginative or practical	• Organized or disorganized	• Sociable or retiring	• Softhearted or ruthless	• Calm or anxious
• Interested in variety or routine	• Careful or careless	• Fun-loving or somber	• Trusting or suspicious	• Secure or insecure
• Independent or conforming	• Disciplined or impulsive	• Affectionate or reserved	• Helpful or uncooperative	• Self-satisfied or self-pitying

The Big Five factors can give you a framework for thinking about your students' personality traits. Your students will differ in their levels of emotional stability, extraversion or introversion, openness to experience, agreeableness, and conscientiousness.

Person-Situation Interaction In discussing learning and thinking styles, we indicated that a student's style can vary according to the subject matter the student is learning or thinking about. The same is true for personality characteristics. According to the concept of **person-situation interaction**, the best way to characterize an individual's personality is not in terms of personal traits or characteristics alone, but also in terms of the situation involved. Researchers have found that students choose to be in some situations and avoid others (Carver & Scheier, 2017).

Suppose you have an extravert and an introvert in your class. According to the theory of person-situation interaction, you can't predict which one will show the best adaptation unless you consider the situation they are in. The theory of person-situation interaction predicts that the extravert will adapt best when asked to collaborate with others and that the introvert will adapt best when asked to carry out tasks independently. Similarly, the extravert likely will be happier when socializing with lots of people at a party, the introvert when in a more private setting alone or with a friend.

An adolescent with a high level of conscientiousness organizes his daily schedule and plans how to use his time effectively. What are some characteristics of conscientiousness? How is it linked to adolescents' competence?
Westend61/Getty Images

In sum, don't think of personality traits as always dooming a student to behave in a particular way across all situations. The context or situation matters (Friedman & Schustack, 2016). Monitor situations in which students with varying personality characteristics seem to feel most comfortable and provide them with opportunities to learn in those situations. If a particular personality trait is detrimental to the student's school performance (perhaps one student is so introverted that he or she fears working in a group), think of ways you can support the student's efforts to change.

TEMPERAMENT

Temperament is closely related to personality and to learning and thinking styles. **Temperament** is a person's behavioral style and characteristic ways of responding. Some students are active; others are calm. Some respond warmly to people; others fuss and fret. Such descriptions involve variations in temperament.

Another way of describing temperament is in terms of predispositions toward emotional reactivity and self-regulation (Bates & Pettit, 2015). *Reactivity* involves the speed and intensity with which an individual responds to situations involving positive or negative emotions. *Self-regulation* involves the extent to which an individual controls his or her emotions.

Temperament Classifications Scientists who study temperament seek to find the best ways to classify temperaments. The most well-known classification was proposed by Alexander Chess and Stella Thomas (Chess & Thomas, 1977; Thomas & Chess, 1991). They conclude that there are three basic styles, or clusters, of temperament:

- An **easy child** is generally in a positive mood, quickly establishes regular routines in infancy, and adapts easily to new experiences.
- A **difficult child** reacts negatively and cries frequently, engages in irregular daily routines, and is slow to accept change.
- A **slow-to-warm-up child** has a low activity level, is somewhat negative, and displays a low intensity of mood.

In their longitudinal investigation, Chess and Thomas found that 40 percent of the children they studied could be classified as easy, 10 percent as difficult, and

person-situation interaction The view that the best way to conceptualize personality is not in terms of personal traits or characteristics alone, but also in terms of the situation involved.

temperament A person's behavioral style and characteristic ways of responding.

easy child A temperament style in which the child is generally in a positive mood, quickly establishes regular routines, and easily adapts to new experiences.

difficult child A temperament style in which the child tends to react negatively, cries frequently, engages in irregular routines, and is slow to accept new experiences.

slow-to-warm-up child A temperament style in which the child has a low activity level, is somewhat negative, and displays a low intensity of mood.

CONNECTING WITH STUDENTS: Best Practices
Strategies for Teaching Children with Different Temperaments

Here are some teaching strategies related to students' temperaments (Keogh, 2003; Sanson & Rothbart, 1995):

1. *Show attention to and respect for individuality* (Sanson & Rothbart, 1995). Teachers need to be sensitive to each student's signals and needs. The goal of good teaching might be accomplished in one way with one student, in another way with another student, depending on the students' temperaments.

2. *Consider the structure of the students' environment* (Sanson & Rothbart, 1995). Crowded, noisy classrooms often pose greater problems for a "difficult" child than for an "easy" child. Fearful, withdrawn students often benefit from slower entry into new contexts.

3. *Be aware of problems that can emerge from labeling a child "difficult" and applying packaged programs for "difficult children"* (Sanson & Rothbart, 1995). Acknowledging that some children are harder to teach than others often is helpful. Advice on how to handle a particular temperament also can be useful. However, whether a particular characteristic is truly "difficult" depends on its fit with the environment, so the problem does not necessarily rest with the child. As with labeling a child as more or less intelligent, labeling the child as "difficult" has the danger of becoming a self-fulfilling prophecy. Also keep in mind that temperament can be modified to some degree (Sanson & Rothbart, 2002).

Here are some effective strategies for dealing with difficult children in the classroom (Keogh, 2003):

- Try to avoid confrontations and power struggles by anticipating problem situations for the student; if the student engages in disruptive behavior, intervene at the first instance of the disruption.
- Evaluate the physical context of the classroom, such as where the difficult child sits, who sits near him or her, and so on for clues about ways to reduce disruptive behavior.
- Minimize delay times between activities and time spent standing in line, which gives a difficult child less time to be disruptive.

4. *Use effective strategies with shy and slow-to-warm-up students.* Keep in mind that it is easy to overlook shy, slow-to-warm-up children because they are unlikely to cause problems in the classroom. Following are some strategies for helping these children (Keogh, 2003):

- Don't place this type of student immediately into group activities, and let the student become involved in groups at his or her own pace initially. If over time, shy students are still reluctant to actively participate in groups, encourage them but don't push them.
- Assign students' work partners with their temperaments in mind; for example, don't pair an intense, difficult child with a shy, slow-to-warm-up child.
- Help shy, slow-to-warm-up students get started on activities that they appear hesitant about beginning and be available to provide help during these activities.

5. *Help children with problems controlling their emotions to regulate their behavior.* In this regard, you can:

- Control your emotions when interacting with students. By observing how you handle difficult situations, students may model your calm behavior.
- Recognize that you are an important person in being able to guide children to regulate their emotions. Instruct children to talk to themselves in ways that may help to reduce their frustration and arousal. For example, if children have difficulty controlling their anger, they can learn to distract themselves from arousing events or stop and take a series of deep breaths.

15 percent as slow to warm up. Notice that 35 percent did not fit any of the three patterns. Researchers have found that these three basic clusters of temperament are moderately stable across the childhood years. A difficult temperament, or a temperament that reflects a lack of control, can place a student at risk for problems.

Another way of classifying temperament focuses on the differences between a shy, subdued, timid child and a sociable, extraverted, bold child. Jerome Kagan (2002, 2010, 2013) regards shyness with strangers (peers or adults) as one feature of a broad temperament category called *inhibition to the unfamiliar.*

Mary Rothbart and John Bates (2006) emphasize that three broad dimensions best represent what researchers have found to characterize the structure of temperament. Here are descriptions of these three temperament dimensions (Rothbart, 2004, p. 495):

- *Extraversion/surgency* includes approach, pleasure, activity, smiling, and laughter. Kagan's uninhibited children fit into this category.

- *Negative affectivity* consists of "fear, frustration, sadness, and discomfort." These children are easily distressed; they may fret and cry often. Kagan's inhibited children fit this category.
- *Effortful control* (self-regulation) is an important dimension of temperament. Infants who are high in effortful control show an ability to keep their arousal from getting too intense and have strategies for soothing themselves. By contrast, children who are low in effortful control are often unable to control their arousal; they are easily agitated and become intensely emotional. A study of school-age children in the United States and China revealed that in both cultures low effortful control was linked to externalizing problems, such as lying, cheating, being disobedient, and being overly aggressive (Zhou et al., 2009). Also, a recent study revealed that effortful control was a strong predictor of academic success skills in kindergarten children from low-income families (Morris et al., 2013).

Individual differences emerge in the development of children's temperament styles, such as effortful control (Bates, 2012a, b). For example, although maturation of the brain's prefrontal lobes must occur for any child's attention to improve and the child to achieve effortful control, some children develop effortful control while others do not. These individual differences in children are at the heart of what characterizes temperament (Bates & Pettit, 2015).

An important point about temperament classifications such as Chess and Thomas' and Rothbart and Bates' is that children should not be pigeonholed as having only one temperament dimension, such as "difficult" or "negative affectivity." A good strategy when attempting to classify a child's temperament is to think of temperament as consisting of multiple dimensions (Bates, 2012a, b). For example, one child might be extraverted, show little emotional negativity, and have good self-regulation. Another child might be introverted, show little emotional negativity, and have a low level of self-regulation.

DEVELOPMENT

Goodness of Fit   The match between an individual's temperament and the environmental demands the individual must cope with, called **goodness of fit**, can be important to his or her adjustment. In general, the temperament characteristics of effortful control, manageability, and agreeableness reduce the effects of adverse environments, whereas negative emotionality increases their effects (Bates & Pettit, 2015).

Review, Reflect, and Practice

③ Characterize the nature of personality and temperament.

REVIEW
- What is meant by the concept of personality?
- What are the Big Five factors of personality?
- What does the idea of person-situation interaction suggest about personality?
- How is temperament different from personality?
- Describe an easy child, a difficult child, and a slow-to-warm-up child.
- What are other categorizations of temperament?
- What are some good teaching strategies related to children's temperament?

REFLECT
- Describe yourself in terms of the Big Five personality factors. In your K–12 education, how aware do you think your teachers were of your personality strengths and weaknesses? Might things have been different if they had known you better?

continued

goodness of fit The match between a child's temperament and the environmental demands the child must cope with.

Review, Reflect, and Practice

PRAXIS™ PRACTICE

1. Maria is an outgoing, agreeable, fun-loving child. According to the concept of person-situation interaction, which of the following is likely to characterize Maria?
   a. Maria enjoys working independently on detail-oriented tasks.
   b. Maria likes to work on tasks that involve interaction with other students.
   c. Maria prefers to read by herself in a corner.
   d. Maria needs to be taught to control her impulses.
2. Stanton has been a challenging student. His frustration tolerance is low, and when he gets frustrated he often disrupts the class with angry outbursts. His teacher has difficulty handling him. What advice is most likely to help her deal with Stanton?
   a. She should show her frustration in dealing with him because once he realizes the impact of his behavior on others, he will learn to control his behavior.
   b. She should be calm with Stanton so he can observe a more adaptive response to frustration.
   c. She should send him out of the classroom every time he gets angry.
   d. She should separate him from his classmates and make him do his classwork by himself so that the other students don't imitate his behavior.

Please see answer key at end of book . . . .

Connecting with the Classroom: Crack the Case

Workshops

Mr. Washington and his colleague, Ms. Rosario, had just attended a workshop on adapting instruction to children's learning styles. Ms. Jacobson and her colleague, Mr. Hassan, had just attended a workshop on adapting instruction to cover multiple intelligences. The four met in the teachers' workroom and were discussing what they had learned.

"Well," said Mr. Washington, "this certainly explains why some students seem to want to sit and listen to me talk, while others like to be more actively involved. Joe's obviously an executive type. He likes lectures. Martha, on the other hand, must be legislative. She just loves to work on projects and can't stand it when I tell her how to do things."

"No, I don't think so," Ms. Jacobson replies. "I think Joe's high in verbal intelligence. That's why he can make sense out of your lectures. He writes well, too. Martha likes to do things with her hands. She's higher in spatial and bodily-kinesthetic intelligence."

Mr. Washington responds, "No, no, no. Learning styles explain their differences much better. Here, look at this."

At this point, Mr. Washington shows Ms. Jacobson the handouts from the workshop he and Ms. Rosario had attended. Mr. Hassan gets out the handouts from the workshop he and Ms. Jacobson had attended as well. They begin comparing notes. They all recognize students in each of the schemes in the handouts. In fact, they can recognize the same student in both sets of handouts.

At this point, two other teachers—Mrs. Peterson and Mrs. Darby—walk into the room. They are very excited about a graduate class they are taking at a nearby university.

Mrs. Peterson says, "You know, I never thought about personality when considering teaching methods. It's no wonder Martha doesn't behave terribly well in my class. She's just too impulsive for the kind of structure I have."

Ms. Jacobson is dismayed. "You mean they're telling you we have to adapt our classrooms to the students' personalities now, too?" she asks.

Mr. Hassan is also upset. "Gee," he says, "just when I thought I had it all figured out. Used to be we just had to consider IQ. Now all this. We have 25 kids in our classes. How can we possibly adapt to all these differences? What are we supposed to do, have 25 different lesson plans? Maybe we should do some kind of profile on them and then group them by profile. What do you think, guys?"

1. What are the issues in this case?
2. To what extent should teachers adapt their instruction to the strengths, learning styles, and personalities of their students? Why?

3. What will you do in your classroom to accommodate individual differences such as students' strengths, learning styles, and personalities?
4. What other individual differences do you think you might have to accommodate? How will you do this?
5. On which theory is Ms. Jacobson basing her comments regarding Joe and Martha?
   a. Gardner's eight frames of mind
   b. general intelligence
   c. Sternberg's triarchic theory of intelligence
   d. Vygotsky's sociocultural theory

Connecting with Learning: Reach Your Learning Goals

1 INTELLIGENCE: Discuss what intelligence is, how it is measured, theories of multiple intelligences, the neuroscience of intelligence, and some controversies and issues about its use by educators.

What Is Intelligence?
- Intelligence consists of problem-solving skills and the ability to adapt to and learn from experiences. Interest in intelligence often focuses on individual differences and assessment.

Intelligence Tests
- Binet and Simon developed the first intelligence test. Binet developed the concept of mental age, and Stern created the concept of IQ as MA/CA × 100. The Stanford-Binet scores approximate a normal distribution.
- The Wechsler scales also are widely used to assess intelligence. They yield an overall IQ plus scores on a number of subscales and composite indexes.
- Group tests are more convenient and economical to administer than individual tests, but group tests have a number of drawbacks (lack of opportunities for the examiner to establish rapport, distraction from other students). A group intelligence test should always be supplemented with other relevant information when decisions are made about students. This also holds for an individual intelligence test.

Theories of Multiple Intelligences
- According to Sternberg's triarchic theory of intelligence, intelligence comes in three forms: analytical, creative, and practical.
- Gardner argues there are eight types of intelligence, or frames of mind: verbal, mathematical, spatial, bodily-kinesthetic, musical, intrapersonal, interpersonal, and naturalist.
- The concept of emotional intelligence was initially developed by Salovey and Mayer. Goleman popularized the concept of emotional intelligence in his book, *Emotional Intelligence*. Mayer, Salovey, and Goleman stress that emotional intelligence is an important aspect of being a competent person.
- All of these approaches have much to offer, stimulating teachers to think more broadly about what makes up a student's competencies. However, they have been criticized for including some skills that should not be classified as intelligence and for lack of a research base to support the approaches. Also, advocates of the general concept of intelligence argue that general intelligence is a reasonably good predictor of school and job performance.

The Neuroscience of Intelligence
- Advances in brain imaging have increased interest in discovering links between the brain and intelligence. A moderate correlation has been found between overall brain size and intelligence. Recent research has revealed a link between a distributed neural network in the frontal and parietal lobes and intelligence.

Controversies and Issues in Intelligence
- Three controversies and issues related to intelligence are (1) the nature-nurture question of how heredity and environment interact to produce intelligence; (2) the fairness with which intelligence testing applies across cultural and ethnic groups; and (3) whether students should be grouped according to ability (tracking). It is especially important to recognize that intelligence tests are an indicator of current performance rather than fixed potential.

continued

2 LEARNING AND THINKING STYLES: Describe learning and thinking styles.

Impulsive/Reflective Styles
- Styles are not abilities but, rather, preferred ways of using abilities. Each individual has a number of learning and thinking styles.
- Impulsive/reflective styles also are referred to as *conceptual tempo*. This dichotomy involves a student's tendency to act quickly and impulsively or to take more time to respond and reflect on the accuracy of an answer. Impulsive students typically make more mistakes than reflective students do.

Deep/Surface Styles
- Deep/surface styles involve the extent to which students approach learning in a way that helps them understand the meaning of materials (deep style) or as simply what needs to be learned (surface style). Deep learners are more likely to be self-motivated to learn and take a constructivist approach to learning; surface learners are more likely to be motivated to learn because of external rewards.
- Optimistic/pessimistic styles involve having either a positive (optimistic) or negative (pessimistic) outlook on the future. Being optimistic is linked to being more resilient, less depressed, and more academically successful than being pessimistic. Interest also has developed in the concept of academic optimism, which also is linked to students' academic achievement.

Criticisms of Learning and Thinking Styles
- Criticisms involve (1) low reliability of styles, (2) low validity of styles, and (3) confused definition of styles.

3 PERSONALITY AND TEMPERAMENT: Characterize the nature of personality and temperament.

Personality
- Personality refers to distinctive thoughts, emotions, and behaviors that characterize the way an individual adapts to the world.
- Psychologists have identified the Big Five personality factors as openness, conscientiousness, extraversion, agreeableness, and neuroticism (emotional stability). The Big Five factors give teachers a framework for thinking about a student's personality characteristics. The Big Five factor of conscientiousness has increasingly been shown to be an important factor in children's and adolescents' development.
- The concept of person-situation interaction states that the best way to characterize an individual's personality is not in terms of traits alone but in terms of both the traits and the situations involved.
- Temperament refers to a person's behavioral style and characteristic way of responding.

Temperament
- Chess and Thomas maintain that there are three basic temperament styles, or clusters: an easy child (generally in a positive mood), a difficult child (reacts negatively and cries easily), and a slow-to-warm-up child (low activity level, somewhat negative). A difficult temperament places a child at risk for problems.
- Other temperament categorizations have been proposed by Kagan (inhibition to the unfamiliar) and Rothbart and Bates (extraversion/surgency, negative affectivity, and effortful control [self-regulation]).
- In education involving students' temperaments, teachers can show attention to, and respect for, individuality; consider the structure of a student's environment; be aware of the problems involved in labeling a student as "difficult"; and use effective classroom strategies with difficult children, shy and slow-to-warm up children, and children who have difficulty regulating their emotions.

KEY TERMS

between-class ability grouping (tracking) 128
Big Five factors of personality 136
culture-fair tests 128
deep/surface styles 133
difficult child 137
easy child 137
emotional intelligence 123
goodness of fit 139
impulsive/reflective styles 132
intelligence 115
intelligence quotient (IQ) 115
Joplin plan 129
learning and thinking styles 132
mental age (MA) 115
nature-nurture issue 125
nongraded (cross-age) program 129
normal distribution 115
optimistic/pessimistic styles 134
personality 136
person-situation interaction 137
slow-to-warm-up child 137
stereotype threat 127
temperament 137
triarchic theory of intelligence 117
within-class ability grouping 130

PORTFOLIO ACTIVITIES

Now that you have a good understanding of this chapter, complete these exercises to expand your thinking.

Independent Reflection

1. Evaluate your own intelligence profile according to Gardner. In what frames of mind do you come out strongest? In which of Sternberg's three areas do you feel you are the strongest? Write about your self-evaluation. (INTASC: Principles *1, 2*)

Research/Field Experience

2. Interview several teachers about students' different learning and thinking styles. Ask them what teaching strategies they use to accommodate these differences in students. Write a synopsis of your interviews. (INTASC: Principles *1, 2, 3, 8, 9*)

3. Form a group of five or six students from your class, and have one person identify his or her personality and temperament traits. Have other members do the same, in turn. After all have presented, discuss how the individuals in your group are similar or different. How will your personalities and temperaments translate into teaching styles? Write about this experience. (INTASC: Principles *1, 2*)

chapter 5

SOCIOCULTURAL DIVERSITY

chapter outline

① Culture and Ethnicity

Learning Goal 1 Discuss how variations in culture, socioeconomic status, and ethnic background need to be taken into account in educating children.

Culture
Socioeconomic Status
Ethnicity
Second-Language Learning and Bilingual Education

② Multicultural Education

Learning Goal 2 Describe some ways to promote multicultural education.

Empowering Students
Culturally Relevant Teaching
Issues-Centered Education
Improving Relationships Among Children from Different Ethnic Groups

③ Gender

Learning Goal 3 Explain various facets of gender, including similarities and differences in boys and girls; discuss gender issues in teaching.

Exploring Gender Views
Gender Stereotyping, Similarities, and Differences
Gender Controversy
Gender-Role Classification
Gender in Context
Eliminating Gender Bias

We need every human gift and cannot afford to neglect any gift because of artificial barriers of sex or race or class or national origin.

—Margaret Mead
American Anthropologist, 20th Century

Ariel Skelley/Blend Images/Getty Images

Connecting with Teachers Margaret Longworth

Margaret Longworth taught high school for a number of years and was a Teacher of the Year. She recently moved to the middle school level and currently teaches language arts at West Middle School in St. Lucie, Florida. In thinking about sociocultural diversity, she believes it is important for teachers to make schools "user friendly" for parents. In her words:

> Many parents—especially ethnic minority parents of color—are very intimidated by schools. They think teachers know everything. Principals know everything. And God forbid that they ever would need to approach the school board. To combat this intimidation, I became "user friendly." Many students and parents center their lives around the church in my community. So, to break the barriers between school and home, my Haitian paraprofessional began setting up meetings for me at the Haitian churches. The churches gave me their Sunday evening services. After they completed their preliminaries, they turned the service over to me. Through the assistance of an interpreter, I presented opportunities to help parents develop academic and life skills through education. I talked with them about special education classes, gifted classes, language programs, and scholarships, and encouraged them to keep their children in school. In turn, they felt confident enough to ask me about different happenings at school. Because of the parent-school-church connections that I was able to build up, I rarely had a discipline problem. If I did have to call parents, they would leave work or whatever they were doing and show up in my classroom. Many of these parents developed a relationship with the principal and guidance counselor and felt free to talk with school officials.

Margaret Longworth believes that the key to improving children's interethnic relations in the classroom is to strive for understanding. She comments:

> Understanding other persons' points of view requires spending time with them and getting to know them—how they think and feel. As students talk with each other and begin to appreciate each other, they soon learn that in many ways they aren't that different after all.

Margaret Longworth

Preview

Ours is a multicultural world of diverse backgrounds, customs, and values. Margaret Longworth's story shows how teachers can improve students' lives and educational orientation by building bridges to their community. In this chapter, we will explore many ways teachers have found to educate children from diverse cultural, socioeconomic, and ethnic backgrounds, including ways to make the classroom relevant for these children. We will also examine gender in schools, including ways in which teachers interact differently with boys and girls.

1 CULTURE AND ETHNICITY
— Culture — Socioeconomic Status — Ethnicity — Second-Language Learning and Bilingual Education

LG 1 Discuss how variations in culture, socioeconomic status, and ethnic background need to be taken into account in educating children.

The students in the schools of Fairfax County, Virginia, near Washington, D.C., come from 182 countries and speak more than two hundred languages. Although the Fairfax County schools are a somewhat extreme example, they are harbingers of what is coming to America's schools. In many schools, a majority of students are now from ethnic minority backgrounds, challenging the current definition of the term "ethnic minority."

In this section, we will explore diversity in terms of cultures, socioeconomic status, and ethnicity. We'll also examine language issues with a focus on second-language learning and bilingual education.

DIVERSITY

RESEARCH

CULTURE

Culture refers to the behavior patterns, beliefs, and all other products of a particular group of people that are passed on from generation to generation. These products result from the interactions among groups of people and their environments over many years (Samovar et al., 2017). A cultural group can be as large as the United States or as small as an isolated Amazon tribe. Whatever its size, the group's culture influences the behavior of its members (Cole & Tan, 2015; Holloway & Jonas, 2016; Matsumoto & Juang, 2017).

Psychologist Donald Campbell and his colleagues (Brewer & Campbell, 1976; Campbell & LeVine, 1968) found that people in all cultures often believe that what happens in their culture is "natural" and "correct" and what happens in other cultures is "unnatural" and "incorrect," behave in ways that favor their cultural group, and feel hostility toward other cultural groups.

Psychologists and educators who study culture often are interested in comparing what happens in one culture with what happens in one or more other cultures (Qu & Pomerantz, 2015; Rowe et al., 2016). In many countries, males have far greater access to educational opportunities, more freedom to pursue a variety of careers, and fewer restrictions on sexual activity than do females (UNICEF, 2016). **Cross-cultural studies** involve such comparisons, providing information about the degree to which people are similar and to what degree certain behaviors are specific to certain cultures (Chen & Liu, 2016). For example, one study found that from the beginning of the seventh grade through the end of the eighth grade, U.S. students valued academics less and their motivation for school success decreased (Wang & Pomerantz, 2009). By contrast, the value placed on academics by Chinese adolescents did not change across this time frame and their motivation for academic success was sustained.

> **Thinking Back/Thinking Forward**
>
> Students in China, Japan, and Taiwan consistently outperform U.S. students in math achievement. Students in Singapore and Hong Kong recently had far greater gains in reading achievement than did U.S. students. Connect to "Standardized Tests and Teaching."

What are some differences in individualistic and collectivistic cultures? What are some teaching strategies for working with students from these cultures?
Andersen Ross/Blend Images/Getty Images

Individualistic and Collectivistic Cultures One way that differences in cultures have been described involves individualism and collectivism (Kormi-Nouri et al., 2015). **Individualism** refers to a set of values that give priority to personal goals rather than to group goals. Individualistic values include feeling good, gaining personal distinction, and establishing independence. **Collectivism** consists of a set of values that support the group. Personal goals are subordinated to preserve group integrity, interdependence of the group's members, and harmonious relationships (Masumoto & Juang, 2017). Many Western cultures such as those of the United States, Canada, Great Britain, and the Netherlands are described as individualistic. Many Eastern cultures such as those of China, Japan, India, and Thailand are labeled collectivistic. Mexican culture also has stronger collectivistic characteristics than U.S. culture does. However, the United States has many collectivistic subcultures, such as Chinese American and Mexican American. A recent study conducted from 1970 to 2008 found that although China still is characterized by collectivistic values, the frequency of words used in China to index individualistic values increased across this time period (Zeng & Greenfield, 2015).

A recent analysis proposed four values that reflect parents' beliefs in individualistic cultures about what is required for children's effective development of autonomy: (1) *personal choice,* (2) *intrinsic motivation,* (3) *self-esteem,* and (4) *self-maximization,* which consists of achieving one's full potential (Tamis-LeMonda et al., 2008). The analysis also proposed that three values reflect parents' beliefs in collectivistic cultures: (1) *connectedness to the family and other close relationships,* (2) *orientation to*

culture The behavior patterns, beliefs, and all other products of a particular group of people that are passed on from generation to generation.

cross-cultural studies Studies that compare what happens in one culture with what happens in one or more other cultures; they provide information about the degree to which people are similar and to what degree behaviors are specific to certain cultures.

individualism A set of values that give priority to personal rather than to group goals.

collectivism A set of values that support the group.

the larger group, and (3) *respect and obedience.* The contrast is striking: the values of parents in individualistic cultures emphasize individual characteristics, choice, and outcomes while those in collectivist cultures prioritize relationships, connections, and respect for others.

Critics of the concept of individualistic and collectivistic cultures argue that these terms are too broad and simplistic, especially as globalization increases (Kagitcibasi, 2007). Regardless of their cultural background, people need both a positive sense of self and connectedness to others to develop fully as human beings. The analysis by Carolyn Tamis-LeMonda and her colleagues (2008, p. 204) emphasizes that in many families, children are not reared in environments that uniformly endorse individualistic or collectivistic values, thoughts, and actions. Rather, in many families, children are "expected to be quiet, assertive, respectful, curious, humble, self-assured, independent, dependent, affectionate, or reserved depending on the situation, people present, children's age, and social-political and economic circles."

Cross-Cultural Comparisons of Adolescents' Time Use In addition to examining whether cultures are individualistic or collectivistic, another important cross-cultural comparison involves how children and adolescents spend their time (Larson, 2014; Larson & Dawes, 2015; Larson et al., 2009). Reed Larson and Suman Verma (1999) studied how adolescents in the United States, Europe, and East Asia spend their time in work, play, and developmental activities such as school. U.S. adolescents spent about 60 percent as much time on schoolwork as East Asian adolescents did, mainly because U.S. adolescents did less homework. U.S. adolescents also spent more time in paid work than their counterparts in most developed countries. Also, U.S. adolescents had more free time than adolescents in other industrialized countries. About 40 to 50 percent of U.S. adolescents' waking hours (not counting summer vacations) was spent in discretionary activities, compared with 25 to 35 percent in East Asia and 35 to 45 percent in Europe. Whether this additional discretionary time is a liability or an asset for U.S. adolescents, of course, depends on how they use it.

How do East Asian and U.S. adolescents spend their time differently?
JGI/Tom Grill/Blend Images LLC

The largest amounts of U.S. adolescents' free time were spent using the media and engaging in unstructured leisure activities, often with friends. U.S. adolescents spent more time in voluntary structured activities—such as sports, hobbies, and organizations—than East Asian adolescents did.

According to Reed Larson (2007, 2014), U.S. adolescents may have too much unstructured time for optimal development. When adolescents are allowed to choose what they do with their time, they typically engage in unchallenging activities such as hanging out and watching TV. Although relaxation and social interaction are important aspects of adolescence, it seems unlikely that spending large numbers of hours per week in unchallenging activities fosters development. Structured voluntary activities may provide more promise for adolescent development than unstructured time, especially if adults give responsibility to adolescents, challenge them, and provide competent guidance in these activities (Larson & Dawes, 2015).

 DEVELOPMENT   RESEARCH

 TECHNOLOGY

SOCIOECONOMIC STATUS

Socioeconomic status (SES) refers to the grouping of people with similar occupational, educational, and economic characteristics. Socioeconomic status implies certain inequalities. Generally, members of a society have (1) occupations that vary in prestige, and some individuals have more access than others to higher-status occupations; (2) different levels of educational attainment, and some individuals have more access than others to better education; (3) different economic resources; and (4) different levels of power to influence a community's institutions. These differences in the ability to control resources and to participate in society's rewards

> **Thinking Back/Thinking Forward**
>
> Comparisons of U.S. and East Asian students reveal differences in math education, including time spent on learning tasks. Connect to "Planning, Instruction, and Technology."

socioeconomic status (SES) A grouping of people with similar occupational, educational, and economic characteristics.

RESEARCH

produce unequal opportunities (McLoyd et al., 2015; Roche, 2016; Wadsworth et al., 2016). Socioeconomic differences are a "proxy for material, human, and social capital within and beyond the family" (Huston & Ripke, 2006, p. 425). In the United States, SES has important implications for education. Low-SES individuals often have less education, less power to influence a community's institutions (such as schools), and fewer economic resources.

A parent's SES is linked to the neighborhoods in which children live and the schools they attend (Murry et al., 2015). Such variations can influence children's school success and adjustment (Crosnoe & Benner, 2015).

So far we have focused on the challenges that many students from low-income families face. However, research by Suniya Luthar and her colleagues (Ansary et al., 2012, 2016; Luthar, 2006; Luthar et al., 2015) has found that adolescents from affluent families also face challenges. Adolescents in the affluent families Luthar has studied are vulnerable to high rates of substance abuse. In addition, her research has found that adolescent males from such families have more adjustment difficulties than do females, with affluent female adolescents being more likely to attain superior levels of academic success. Luthar and her colleagues (Luthar et al., 2013) also have found that youth in upwardly mobile, upper-middle-SES families are more likely to engage in drug use and have more internalized and externalized problems than their counterparts in middle-SES families.

Vonnie McLoyd (*right*) has conducted a number of important investigations of the roles of poverty, ethnicity, and unemployment in children's and adolescents' development. She has found that economic stressors often diminish children's and adolescents' belief in the utility of education and their achievement strivings.
Courtesy of Vonnie McLoyd

The Extent of Poverty in America In a report on the state of America's children, the Children's Defense Fund (1992) described what life is like for too many children. When sixth-graders in a poverty-stricken area of St. Louis were asked to describe a perfect day, one boy said that he would erase the world, then sit and think. Asked if he wouldn't rather go outside and play, the boy responded, "Are you kidding, out there?"

Children who grow up in poverty represent a special concern (Duncan et al., 2015; Tran et al., 2016; Wadsworth et al., 2016). In 2014, 21.1 percent of U.S. children under 18 years of age were living in families with incomes below the poverty line, with African American and Latinx families with children having especially high rates of poverty (more than 30 percent) (DeNavas-Walt & Proctor, 2015). In 2014, 12.7 percent of non-Latinx White children were living in poverty. Compared with non-Latinx White children, ethnic minority children are more likely to experience persistent poverty over many years and to live in isolated poor neighborhoods where social supports are minimal and threats to positive development abundant.

The U.S. statistic of 21 percent of children living in poverty is much higher than those from other industrialized nations. For example, Canada has a child poverty rate of 9 percent and Sweden has a rate of 2 percent. Moreover, the U.S. statistic of 21 percent represents an increase from 2001 (16 percent) but reflects a slight drop from a peak of 23 percent in 1993.

Poverty is demarcated along educational lines. In 2014, for adults 25 years and older, 29 percent of those with no high school diploma, 14 percent with a high school diploma but no college, 10 percent with some college, no degree, and 5 percent with a bachelor's degree or higher lived in poverty in the United States.

Educating Students from Low-SES Backgrounds Children in poverty often face problems at home and at school that compromise their learning (Gardner et al., 2016; Tran et al., 2016). A review of the environment of childhood poverty concluded that compared with their economically more-advantaged counterparts, poor children experience the following adversities (Evans, 2004): more family conflict, violence, chaos, and separation from their families; less social support; less intellectual stimulation; more TV viewing; inferior schools and child-care facilities, as well as parents who are less involved in their school activities; more pollution and crowded, noisy homes; and more dangerous, deteriorating neighborhoods (see Figure 1). Children living in rural poverty are exposed to similar stressors (Vernon-Feagans et al., 2012), and the cumulative effects of exposure to such risks can negatively impact mental health into young adulthood (Evans & Cassells, 2014).

The schools that children from impoverished backgrounds attend often have fewer resources than schools in higher-income neighborhoods. In low-income areas, students tend to have lower achievement test scores, lower graduation rates, and lower rates of college attendance. School buildings and classrooms are often old, crumbling, and poorly maintained. They are also more likely to be staffed by young teachers with less experience than schools in higher-income neighborhoods. Schools in low-income areas also are more likely to encourage rote learning, whereas schools in higher-income areas are more likely to work with children to improve their thinking skills. In sum, far too many schools in low-income neighborhoods provide students with environments that are not conducive to effective learning.

In *Savage Inequalities,* Jonathan Kozol (1991) vividly described some of the problems that children of poverty face in their neighborhood and at school. For example, Kozol observed that in East St. Louis, Illinois, which is 98 percent African American, there were no obstetric services, no regular trash collection, and few jobs. Blocks upon blocks of housing consist of dilapidated, skeletal buildings. Residents breathe the chemical pollution of nearby Monsanto Chemical Company. Raw sewage repeatedly backs up into homes. Child malnutrition is common. Fear of violence is real. The problems of the streets spill over into the schools, where sewage also backs up from time to time. Classrooms and hallways are old and unattractive, athletic facilities inadequate. Teachers run out of chalk and paper, and the science labs are 30 to 50 years out of date.

Kozol says that anyone who visits places like East St. Louis, even for a brief time, comes away profoundly shaken. Kozol also notes that although children in low-income neighborhoods and schools experience many inequities, these children and their families also have many strengths, including courage. Parents in such impoverished circumstances may intensely pursue ways to get more effective teachers and better opportunities for their children.

There is increasing interest in developing two-generation educational interventions to improve the academic success of children living in poverty (Gardner et al., 2016; Sommer et al., 2016). For example, a recent large-scale effort to help children escape from poverty is the Ascend two-generation educational intervention being conducted by the Aspen Institute (2013; King et al., 2015). The focus of the intervention emphasizes education (increasing postsecondary education for mothers and improving the quality of their children's early childhood education), economic support (housing, transportation, financial education, health insurance, and food assistance), and social capital (peer support including friends and neighbors; participation in community and faith-based organizations; school and work contacts).

A downward trajectory is not inevitable for children and adolescents living in poverty (Philipsen et al., 2009). One potential positive path for youth who live in low-income circumstances is to become involved with a caring mentor. The Quantum Opportunities Program, funded by the Ford Foundation, was a four-year, year-round

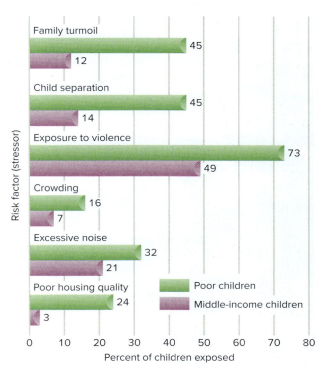

FIGURE 1 EXPOSURE TO SIX STRESSORS AMONG POOR AND MIDDLE-INCOME CHILDREN

Source: "The Environment of Poverty," by G. W. Evans and G. W. English, 2002, *Child Development, 73,* pp. 1238–1248.

What are some of the challenges faced by children growing up in the South Bronx?
Andy Levin/Science Source

In *The Shame of the Nation*, Jonathan Kozol (2005) criticized the inadequate quality and lack of resources in many U.S. schools, especially those in the poverty areas of inner cities that have high concentrations of ethnic minority children. Kozol praises teachers like Angela Lively, who keeps a box of shoes in her Indianapolis classroom for students in need.
Michael Conroy/AP Images

Children participating in the Quantum Opportunities Program at the Carver Center in Washington, D.C.
Zuma Press Inc/Alamy Stock Photo

RESEARCH

mentoring effort (Carnegie Council on Adolescent Development, 1995). The students were entering the ninth grade at a high school with high rates of poverty, were minorities, and came from families that received public assistance. Each day for four years, mentors provided sustained support, guidance, and concrete assistance to their students.

The Quantum program required students to participate in three types of activities: (1) academic-related activities outside school hours, including reading, writing, math, science, and social studies, peer tutoring, and computer skills training; (2) community-service projects, including tutoring elementary school students, cleaning up the neighborhood, and volunteering in hospitals, nursing homes, and libraries; and (3) cultural enrichment and personal development activities, including life skills training, and college and job planning. In exchange for their commitment to the program, students were offered financial incentives that encouraged participation, completion, and long-range planning. An evaluation of the Quantum project compared the mentored students with a nonmentored control group. Sixty-three percent of the mentored students graduated from high school, but only 42 percent of the control group did; 42 percent of the mentored students were currently enrolled in college, but only 16 percent of the control group were. Furthermore, control-group students were twice as likely as the mentored students to receive food stamps or welfare, and they had more arrests. Such programs clearly have the potential to overcome the intergenerational transmission of poverty and its negative outcomes.

The original Quantum Opportunities Program no longer exists, but the Eisenhower Foundation (2010) is replicating the Quantum program in Alabama, South Carolina, New Hampshire, New Mexico, Virginia, Massachusetts, Mississippi, Oregon, Maryland, Washington, D.C., and Wisconsin. In a recent evaluation of the Quantum Opportunities program, students in the program had higher grade point averages and were more likely to graduate from high school and be accepted into college in comparison with a control group of students not enrolled in the program (Curtis & Bandy, 2016).

A recent study assessed the effects of the Positive Action program in 14 urban, low-income Chicago schools across 6 years from grades 3 to 8 (Lewis et al., 2013). The Positive Action program is a K-12 curriculum that focuses on self-concept, self-control and responsibility, physical and mental health, honesty, getting along with others, and continually striving for self-improvement. The program includes teacher, counselor, family, and community training and activities to improve school-wide atmosphere. In comparison with control group schools that did not implement the Positive Action program, students in the program engaged in a lower rate of violence-related behavior and received fewer disciplinary referrals and suspensions from school.

In yet another recent study, more than 500 ninth- to twelfth-grade students living in low-income settings in Los Angeles were chosen through a random admissions lottery to attend high-performing public charter schools (Wong et al., 2014). Compared with a control group of students who did not get to attend the high-performing charter schools, the students attending the charter schools had better scores on math and English standardized tests and were less likely to drop out of school.

CONNECTING WITH STUDENTS: Best Practices
Strategies for Working with Children in Poverty

Jill Nakamura is enjoying her home visit with her student, Ashley Jordan.

The Jordan Family and Courtesy of Jill Nakamura

As we have seen, children living in poverty face challenges in school. Following are some effective strategies for working with children living in poverty.

1. *Improve thinking and language skills.* If you teach in a school in a low-income neighborhood, adopt the goal of helping children improve their thinking and language skills. As you will see in *Through the Eyes of Teachers,* this is an important goal in the classroom of Jill Nakamura, a first-grade teacher in Fresno, California.

THROUGH THE EYES OF TEACHERS
Daily After-School Reading Club for Students in a High-Poverty School

Jill Nakamura teaches in a school located in a high-poverty area. She visits students at home early in the school year in an effort to connect with them and develop a partnership with their parents. "She holds daily after-school reading clubs for students reading below grade level . . . ; those who don't want to attend must call parents to tell them." In a recent school year (2004), she "raised the percent of students reading at or above grade level from 29 percent to 76 percent" (Wong Briggs, 2004, p. 6D).

2. *Don't overdiscipline.* Where poverty and other factors make it difficult to maintain safety and discipline, strive for a workable tradeoff between discipline and children's freedom. We will say more about classroom discipline in the chapter on managing the classroom.

3. *Make student motivation a high priority.* Because many children from low-income backgrounds might come to your class not having experienced high parental standards for achievement, and thus might lack the motivation to learn, pay special attention to motivating these children to learn. We will address this topic further in the chapter on motivation, teaching, and learning.

4. *Think about ways to support and collaborate with parents.* Recognize that many parents in poor areas are not able to provide much academic supervision or assistance to their children. Look for ways to support the parents who can be trained and helped to do so.

5. *Look for ways to involve talented people from impoverished communities.* Recognize that parents in poor areas can be quite talented, caring, responsive people in ways that teachers might not expect. Most impoverished communities have people whose wisdom and experience defy stereotypes. Find these people and ask them to volunteer their services to help support children's learning in your classroom, accompany children on field trips, and make the school more attractive.

6. *Observe the strengths of children from low-income backgrounds.* Many children from these circumstances come to school with considerable untapped knowledge, and teachers can access such richness. For example, these children may have substantial knowledge about how to use mass transit, whereas children in higher-income families are transported in cars.

ETHNICITY

The word *ethnic* comes from the Greek word that means "nation." **Ethnicity** refers to a shared pattern of characteristics such as cultural heritage, nationality, race, religion, and language. Everyone is a member of one or more ethnic groups, and relations between people from different ethnic backgrounds, not just in the United States but in virtually every corner of the world, are often charged with bias and conflict. This conflict is evident in the recent controversies surrounding immigration

DIVERSITY

ethnicity A shared pattern of characteristics such as cultural heritage, nationality, race, religion, and language.

and detention centers across the US–Mexico border, where thousands of families and children have come from across Latin America to immigrate or seek asylum in the United States.

Immigration Nowhere is the changing tapestry of American culture more apparent than in the changing ethnic balances among America's citizens (Gollnick & Chinn, 2017; Schaefer, 2015). Relatively high rates of minority immigration have contributed to the growth in the proportion of ethnic minorities in the U.S. population. In 2014, 62 percent of children 18 years and younger were non-Latinx White; by 2060, this figure is projected to decrease to 44 percent (Colby & Ortman, 2015). In 2014 in the United States, 17 percent were Latinx but in 2060 that figure is projected to increase to 29 percent. Asian Americans are expected to be the fastest-growing ethnic group of children: In 2014, 5 percent were Asian American and that figure is expected to grow to 9 percent in 2060. The percent of African American children is anticipated to increase slightly from 2014 to 2016 (12.4 to 13 percent).

While the ethnic minority school population is growing rapidly, a large majority of public school teachers are non-Latinx White. In 2011–2012, 82 percent of these teachers were non-Latinx White, 8 percent were Latinx, and 7 percent were African American (Maxwell, 2014).

Do ethnic minority students have more academic success when they are taught by a member of their ethnic minority group? A recent study found that when African American and non-Latinx White students in grades 3 through 10 were assigned to teachers of their own ethnicity in reading and when African American, Asian American, and non-Latinx White students were assigned to teachers of their own ethnicity in math, small but positive effects in reading and math were attained (Egalite et al., 2015). Lower-performing African American and non-Latinx White students especially benefited from having a teacher who matched their ethnicity.

An important point about any ethnic group is that it is diverse (Koppelman, 2017). There are many ready examples: Mexican Americans and Cuban Americans are Latinxs, but they had different reasons for immigrating to the United States, come from varying socioeconomic backgrounds, partake in different customs, and experience different rates and types of employment in the United States. Individuals born in Puerto Rico are distinguished from Latinx individuals who have immigrated to the United States in that they are born U.S. citizens and are therefore not immigrants, regardless of where they live in the United States. Similarly, the U.S. government currently recognizes 511 different Native American tribes, each having a unique ancestral background with differing values and characteristics.

(*Top*) Immigrant children from 12 countries participating in a U.S. citizenship ceremony in Queens, New York, on June 11, 2009. *What are some characteristics of immigrant children in the United States?* (*Bottom*) Latinx immigrants in the Rio Grande Valley, Texas. *What are some cultural adaptations and educational challenges these immigrant children from Guadalajara, Mexico, might face in the United States?*

(*Top*) Mario Tama/Getty Images; (*bottom*) Alison Wright/National Geographic Creative/Alamy Stock Photo

Asian Americans include individuals of Chinese, Japanese, Filipino, Korean, and Southeast Asian origin, each group having distinct ancestries and languages. The diversity of Asian Americans is reflected in their educational attainment. Some achieve a high level of education; many others have little education. For example, 90 percent of Korean American males graduate from high school, but only 71 percent of Vietnamese males do. Such diversity in Asian Americans is often overlooked because many Asian Americans are very successful in school achievement, don't take health risks, and don't engage in delinquent behavior. Because of these characteristics, they have been referred to as the "model minority." However, many Asian American students experience adjustment problems that include loneliness, anxiety, and depression (Sue et al., 2016, 2017).

Many of the families that have immigrated in recent decades to the United States, such as Asian Americans and Mexican Americans, come from collectivistic cultures in which family obligation and duty to one's family are strong (Fuligni & Tsai, 2015). The family obligation and duty may take the form of assisting parents in their occupations and contributing to the family's welfare. This often occurs in service and manual labor jobs, such as those in construction, gardening, cleaning, and restaurants. Many immigrant students serve as translators and negotiators for their families with the outside English-speaking world. Asian American and Latinx families place a greater emphasis on family duty and obligation than do non-Latinx White families.

Ethnicity and Schools Educational segregation is still a reality for children of color in the United States (Banks, 2014). Almost one-third of African American and Latinx students attend schools in which 90 percent or more of the students are from minority groups, typically their own minority group. The school experiences of students from different ethnic groups also depart in other ways (Banks, 2015). For example, African American and Latinx students are much less likely than non-Latinx White or Asian American students to be enrolled in academic, college preparatory programs and much more likely to be enrolled in remedial and special education programs. Asian American students are far more likely than students from other ethnic minority groups to take advanced math and science courses in high school. African American students are twice as likely as Latinxs, Native Americans, or Whites to be suspended from school. Ethnic minorities of color constitute the majority of students in the largest school districts in the United States. However, 90 percent of the teachers in America's schools are non-Latinx White, and the percentage of minority teachers is projected to be even lower in coming years.

Further, just as the schools of students from low-income backgrounds have fewer resources than those of students from higher-income backgrounds, so too do the schools of students from ethnic minority backgrounds have fewer resources than the schools of their counterparts from largely non-Latinx White backgrounds (Zusho et al., 2016). For example, studies have found that students in California's predominantly minority schools had less access to every instructional resource surveyed, including textbooks, supplies, and computers, and were five times more likely to have uncertified teachers than students in predominantly non-Latinx White schools (Oakes & Saunders, 2002; Shields et al., 2001).

In *The Shame of the Nation,* Jonathan Kozol (2005) described his visits to 60 U.S. schools in low-income areas of cities in 11 states. He saw many schools in which the minority population was 80 to 90 percent, concluding that school segregation is still present for many poor minority students. Kozol saw many of the inequities just summarized—unkempt classrooms, hallways, and restrooms; inadequate textbooks and supplies; and lack of resources. He also saw teachers mainly instructing students to rotely memorize material, especially as preparation for mandated tests, rather than engage in higher-level thinking. Kozol also frequently observed teachers using threatening disciplinary tactics to control the classroom.

Prejudice, Discrimination, and Bias The negative schooling experiences of many ethnic minority children that Kozol described may involve prejudice, discrimination, and bias (Marks et al., 2015). **Prejudice** is an unjustified negative attitude toward an individual because of the individual's membership in a group. The group toward which the prejudice is directed might be defined by ethnicity, sex, age, or virtually any other detectable difference. Our focus here is prejudice against ethnic groups of color.

People who oppose prejudice and discrimination often have contrasting views. Some value and praise the strides made in civil rights in recent years. Others criticize American schools and other institutions because they conclude that many forms of discrimination and prejudice still exist (Bucher, 2015).

prejudice An unjustified negative attitude toward an individual because of the individual's membership in a group.

Diversity and Differences Historical, economic, and social experiences produce both prejudicial and legitimate differences among various ethnic groups. Individuals who live in a particular ethnic or cultural group adapt to that culture's values, attitudes, and stresses. Their behavior might be different from one's own yet be functional for them. Recognizing and respecting these differences is an important aspect of getting along in a diverse, multicultural world. Recall also the point made earlier that another important dimension of every ethnic group is its diversity. Not only is U.S. culture diverse—so is every ethnic group within the U.S. culture.

SECOND-LANGUAGE LEARNING AND BILINGUAL EDUCATION

Are there sensitive periods in learning a second language? That is, if individuals want to learn a second language, how important is the age at which they begin to learn it? What is the best way for U.S. schools to teach children who come from homes in which English is not the primary language?

DIVERSITY

DEVELOPMENT

Second-Language Learning For many years, it was claimed that if individuals did not learn a second language prior to puberty they would never reach native-language learners' proficiency in the second language (Johnson & Newport, 1991). However, recent research indicates a more complex conclusion: There are sensitive periods for learning a second language. Additionally, these sensitive periods likely vary across different areas of language systems (Thomas & Johnson, 2008). For example, late language learners, such as adolescents and adults, may learn new vocabulary more easily than new sounds or new grammar (Neville, 2006). Also, children's ability to pronounce words with a native-like accent in a second language typically decreases with age, with an especially sharp drop occurring after the age of about 10 to 12. Adults tend to learn a second language faster than children, but their level of second-language mastery is not as high as children's. And the way children and adults learn a second language differs somewhat. Compared with adults, children are less sensitive to feedback, less likely to use explicit strategies, and more likely to learn a second language from large amounts of input (Thomas & Johnson, 2008).

Students in the United States are far behind their counterparts in many developed countries in learning a second language. For example, in Russia, schools have 10 grades, called *forms,* which roughly correspond to the 12 grades in American schools. Russian children begin school at age 7 and begin learning English in the third form. Because of this emphasis on teaching English, most Russian citizens under the age of 40 today are able to speak at least some English. The United States is the only technologically advanced Western nation that does not have a national foreign language requirement at the high school level, even for students in rigorous academic programs.

Benefits of Bilingualism U.S. students who do not learn a second language may be missing more than the chance to acquire a skill. *Bilingualism*—the ability to speak two languages—has a positive effect on children's cognitive development (Tompkins, 2015). Children who are fluent in two languages perform better than their single-language counterparts on tests of control of attention, concept formation, analytical reasoning, cognitive flexibility, and cognitive complexity (Bialystok, 2001, 2007, 2011, 2014, 2015). They also are more conscious of the structure of spoken and written language and better at noticing errors of grammar and meaning, skills that benefit their reading ability (Bialystok, 2014, 2015).

Research indicates that bilingual children do have a smaller vocabulary in each language than monolingual children do (Bialystok, 2011). Most children who learn two languages are not exposed to the same

Children in many countries learn more than one language. Shown here is author John Santrock observing a preschool in Fes, Morocco, in 2015. The young children sang songs in three different languages—Arabic, French, and English. *Do you think children in the United States should learn more than one language?*
Dr. John Santrock

quantity and quality of each language. However, bilingual children do not show delays in the rate at which they acquire language overall (Hoff, 2016). In a recent study, by 4 years of age children who continued to learn Spanish and English languages had a total vocabulary growth that was greater than that of monolingual children (Hoff et al., 2014).

Overall, bilingualism is linked to positive outcomes for children's language and cognitive development. An especially important developmental question that many parents of infants and young children have is whether it would be useful or confusing to teach them two languages simultaneously. The answer is that teaching infants and young children two languages simultaneously (as when the mother's native language is English and the father's is Spanish) has numerous benefits and few drawbacks (Bialystok, 2014, 2015).

In the United States, many immigrant children go from being monolingual in their home language to bilingual in that language and in English, only to end up as monolingual speakers of English. This is called *subtractive bilingualism,* and it can have negative effects on children, who often become ashamed of their home language.

Bilingual Education A current controversy related to bilingualism involves the millions of U.S. children who come from homes in which English is not the primary language (Echevarria et al., 2015). What is the best way to teach these English language learners (ELLs)?

ELLs have been taught in one of two main ways: (1) instruction in English only, or (2) a *dual-language* (used to be called *bilingual*) approach that involves instruction in their home language and English. In a dual-language approach, instruction is given in both the ELL child's home language and English for varying amounts of time at certain grade levels. One of the arguments for the dual-language approach is the research discussed earlier demonstrating that bilingual children have more advanced information-processing skills than monolingual children do.

A first- and second-grade bilingual English-Cantonese teacher instructing students in Chinese in Oakland, California.
Elizabeth Crews

If a dual-language strategy is used, too often it has been thought that immigrant children need only one or two years of this type of instruction. However, in general it takes immigrant children approximately three to five years to develop speaking proficiency and seven years to develop reading proficiency in English (Hakuta et al., 2000). Also, immigrant children vary in their ability to learn English. Children who come from lower socioeconomic backgrounds have more difficulty than those from higher socioeconomic backgrounds (Hakuta, 2001). Thus, especially for immigrant children from low socioeconomic backgrounds, more years of dual-language instruction may be needed than they currently are receiving.

What have researchers found regarding outcomes of ELL programs? Drawing

A Latinx teacher works with students in a bilingual class on science.
Big Cheese Photo LLC/Alamy Stock Photo

conclusions about the effectiveness of ELL programs is difficult because of variations across programs in the number of years they are in effect, type of instruction, quality of schooling other than ELL instruction, teachers, children, and other factors. Further, no effective experiments have been conducted that compare dual-language education with English-only education in the United States (Snow & Kang, 2006). Some experts have concluded that the quality of instruction is more important in determining outcomes than the language in which it is delivered (Lesaux & Siegel, 2003).

RESEARCH

Nonetheless, other experts, such as Kenji Hakuta (2001, 2005), support the combined home language and English approach because (1) children have difficulty learning a subject when it is taught in a language they do not understand; and (2) when both languages are integrated in the classroom, children learn the second language more readily and participate more actively. In support of Hakuta's view, most large-scale studies have found that the academic achievement of ELLs is higher in dual-language programs than English-only programs (Genesee & Lindholm-Leary, 2012).

CONNECTING WITH STUDENTS: Best Practices
Strategies for Working with Linguistically and Culturally Diverse Children

Here are some classroom recommendations from the National Association for the Education of Young Children (NAEYC, 1996) for working with linguistically and culturally diverse children:

1. "Recognize that all children are cognitively, linguistically, and emotionally connected to the language and culture of their home" (NAEYC, 1996, p. 3).
2. "Acknowledge that children can demonstrate their knowledge and capacity in many ways" (NAEYC, 1996, p. 3). Whatever language children speak, they should be able to show their capabilities and feel appreciated and valued.
3. "Understand that without comprehensible input, second-language learning can be difficult" (NAEYC, 1996, p. 4). It takes time to be linguistically competent in any language.
4. "Model appropriate use of English, and provide the child with opportunities to use newly acquired vocabulary and language" (NAEYC, 1996, p. 7). Learn at least a few words in the child's first language to demonstrate respect for the child's culture.
5. "Actively involve parents and families in the early learning program and setting" (NAEYC, 1996, p. 4). Encourage and assist parents in becoming knowledgeable about the value for children of knowing more than one language. Provide parents with strategies to support and maintain home language learning.
6. "Recognize that children can and will acquire the use of English even when their home language is used and respected" (NAEYC, 1996, p. 6). In Through the Eyes of Teachers, Daniel Arnoux, a middle school English teacher in Broward, Florida, describes how he seeks to make a difference in the lives of students whose first language is not English.

THROUGH THE EYES OF TEACHERS
Giving Students a Sense of Pride

For the past seven years, I have been teaching ESOL (English for speakers of other languages) in addition to other middle-school subjects. I believe that I've made a difference in my students' lives by giving them a sense of pride in their heritage and by providing a learning environment in which they can grow.

To achieve equality, the educational system must recognize students' ethnic background and gender. The student's home culture isn't to be discarded but instead used as a teaching tool. What works best in improving children's interethnic problems is to confront the problem head-on. I create lessons that teach empathy and tolerance toward others. I've used my free time to talk to classes about human rights and prejudice toward students of different nationalities and cultures—in particular Haitian students, who are continually harassed and sometimes beaten in school. Try always to know your students as human beings, and they will surely open up to you and learn. Tell them that you believe in them. If you believe they can achieve, they will.

Daniel Arnoux

7. Collaborate with other teachers "to learn more about working with linguistically and culturally diverse children" (NAEYC, 1996, p. 7).

Review, Reflect, and Practice

❶ Discuss how variations in culture, socioeconomic status, and ethnic background need to be taken into account in educating children.

REVIEW
- What is culture? How do individualistic and collectivistic cultures differ? How do U.S. adolescents spend their time compared with adolescents in Europe and East Asia?
- What is socioeconomic status? In what ways are children from impoverished backgrounds likely to have difficulty in school?
- How is ethnicity involved in children's schooling? What is the nature of second language learning? What characterizes bilingual education?

REFLECT
- In the context of education, are all ethnic differences negative? Come up with some differences that might be positive in U.S. classrooms.

PRAXIS™ PRACTICE

1. Mr. Austin, who grew up in the midwestern United States, teaches math in a high school with students who have immigrated from Mexico, Korea, Vietnam, India, Pakistan, Poland, and the Czech Republic. He often uses competitive games as class activities, many of which involve individual races to solve problems on the whiteboard at the front of the classroom. Some of his students seem to immensely enjoy the games, but some students get upset because they are unable to solve a problem. They become even more upset when Mr. Austin constructively criticizes them during the game. The most plausible explanation is that students who do *not* enjoy the games
   a. are not good athletes
   b. have low self-esteem
   c. grew up in a collectivist culture
   d. grew up in an individualist culture

2. Sally is a third-grade student at an economically diverse school. Sally lives in poverty, as do about one-fourth of her class. Another one-fourth of the class come from upper-middle-income families, and another half come from middle-income families. Sally's teacher, Ms. Roberts, has assigned a diorama (a scenic representation with sculpted figures and lifelike objects) project in lieu of a standard book report on *Charlotte's Web*.

   Kanesha, one of the more affluent children in the class, has created an elaborate diorama in a large shoe box. She placed plastic animals and small dolls in the diorama. The inside of her box is paneled with craft sticks to look like barn siding, and she used fine fishing line to create a web.

   Although Sally read, understood, and enjoyed the book, her diorama does not compare favorably to Kanesha's. First, she did not have a shoe box to use, so she used an old box she found at a grocery store. She made her animals out of paper because she could not afford plastic animals. She made her web out of an old shoelace.

   When Sally looked at her diorama next to Kanesha's, she almost cried. She did cry when Ms. Roberts gushed over how lovely Kanesha's diorama looked. What should Ms. Roberts have done differently?
   a. She should have explained the income differences to the students before they began their project.
   b. She should have had the students write traditional book reports.
   c. She should have provided the materials and then had the students create the dioramas.
   d. She should have praised Sally's diorama more than Kanesha's.

continued

Review, Reflect, and Practice

3. Robert teaches at an ethnically diverse elementary school. Since he decided to become a teacher, his goal has been to teach in a school like this one because he wants to help ethnic minority children. In his class, he makes considerable effort to ensure that all of his students are successful and feel part of the larger group. He is warm and caring toward his students, sometimes even providing lunch for those who forget to bring one or don't have enough money for the cafeteria. He often praises minority students for work that he would find only average from his majority students. What is Robert doing wrong?
   a. He is substituting nurturance for academic standards.
   b. He should provide a more nurturing environment for all students.
   c. He should provide lunch for all of his students or none of them.
   d. He is setting standards for minority students that are too high.

4. Mr. Williams teaches first grade and thinks his students will benefit from learning a second language, so he labels many of the items in his classroom in both English and Spanish. He chose Spanish because that is the second most common language in the area in which he teaches. What research supports Mr. Williams' approach?
   a. First-graders are the right age to learn to read a second language but aren't too old to learn to speak a second language.
   b. Because students in most countries do not learn to read a second language, Mr. Williams is giving his students an important advantage.
   c. Children learn a second language better and more easily at this age than they will when they get older.
   d. Mr. Williams should select a second language that is unfamiliar to most of his class.

Please see answer key at end of book . . . .

LG 2 Describe some ways to promote multicultural education.

2 MULTICULTURAL EDUCATION

Empowering Students | Culturally Relevant Teaching | Issues-Centered Education | Improving Relationships Among Children from Different Ethnic Groups

The hope is that multicultural education can contribute to making the United States more like what the late civil rights leader Martin Luther King, Jr., dreamed of: a nation where children will be judged not by the color of their skin but by the content of their character.

Multicultural education is education that values diversity and includes the perspectives of a variety of cultural groups on a regular basis. Its proponents believe that children of color should be empowered and that multicultural education benefits all students (Banks, 2014, 2015). An important goal of multicultural education is equal educational opportunity for all students. This includes closing the gap in academic achievement between mainstream students and students from underrepresented groups.

Multicultural education grew out of the civil rights movement of the 1960s and the call for equality and social justice for women and people of color (Gollnick & Chinn, 2017). As a field, multicultural education includes issues related to socioeconomic status, ethnicity, and gender. An increasing trend in multicultural education, though, is not to make ethnicity a focal point but to also include socioeconomic status, religion, disability, gender, sexual orientation, and other forms of differences (Koppelman, 2017). Another important point about contemporary multicultural education is that many individuals think that it is reserved for students of color. However, all students, including non-Latinx White students, can benefit from multicultural education.

DIVERSITY

multicultural education Education that values diversity and includes the perspectives of a variety of cultural groups on a regular basis.

Because social justice is one of the foundational values of multicultural education, prejudice reduction and equity pedagogy are core components (Banks, 2014, 2015). *Prejudice reduction* refers to activities teachers can implement in the classroom to eliminate negative and stereotypical views of others. *Equity pedagogy* refers to the modification of the teaching process to incorporate materials and learning strategies appropriate to both boys and girls and to various ethnic groups.

You and your students will benefit if you take a course or have some type of preparation involving multicultural education. For example, a study of math and science teachers revealed that their students' achievement was enhanced when their "teachers had a degree in the field in which they were teaching *and* had had preparation regarding multicultural education, special education, and English language development (Wenglinksy, 2002)" (Banks et al., 2005, p. 233). Professional organizations also have put together a number of resources you can use to address diversity in your classroom (e.g., http://www.nea.org/tools/resources-addressing-multicultural-diversity-issues-in-your-classroom.htm; http://www.ascd.org/research-a-topic/multicultural-education-resources.aspx).

Multicultural education expert James Banks (2014) described what characterizes a multicultural school. Following are some characteristics he thinks should be present if a school practices multicultural education:

- *The school staff's attitudes, beliefs, and actions.* The school's staff has high expectations for all students and are passionate about helping them learn.
- *The curriculum.* Multicultural education reforms the course of study so that students perceive events, concepts, and issues from the diverse views of different ethnic and socioeconomic groups.
- *Instructional materials.* Many biases are present in textbooks and learning materials. Among these biases are marginalizing the experiences of people of color, second-language minorities, women, and low-income individuals. In a multicultural school, instructional materials represent the backgrounds and experiences of people from diverse ethnic and cultural groups.
- *The school culture and the hidden curriculum.* The hidden curriculum is the curriculum that is not explicitly taught but that nevertheless is present and learned by students. The school's attitudes toward diversity can appear in subtle ways, such as the types of photographs that are present on school bulletin boards, the ethnic composition of the school's staff, and the fairness with which students from diverse backgrounds are disciplined or suspended. In a multicultural school, the school's contexts are revised so that the hidden curriculum's message reflects positive aspects of diversity.
- *The counseling program.* A multicultural school's counseling program guides students from diverse backgrounds toward effective career choices and helps students take the appropriate courses that will enable them to pursue these choices. The school's counselors challenge diverse students to dream and provide them with strategies to reach those dreams.

What should be present if a school practices multicultural education?
Hill Street Studios/Blend Images/Getty Images

Teachers were recently asked how they promote diversity and acceptance of others in the classroom. Following are their responses.

EARLY CHILDHOOD In all areas of my classroom, multicultural books in several languages, posters, and other items—for example, garments, dolls, and music—that speak to diversity are displayed. The foods served to children during meal and snack times come from various cuisines and ethnic groups. At story time, books are read in different languages by parents and interpreted for the children to understand. Our philosophy is that we don't have to teach diversity, it already exists.

—VALARIE GORHAM, *Kiddie Quarters, Inc.*

ELEMENTARY SCHOOL: GRADES K–5 I teach the second-grade integrated ESL (English as a second language) class. At the beginning of the school year, as we are establishing our classroom community, we take time to recognize each student by creating a bulletin board with a poster of the world at the center. The display is entitled: "We are the children . . . We are the World." Each child's photo is taken and then displayed with a string designating his or her country of origin. We use this map throughout the year as a springboard for many geography and social studies lessons as we explore and learn about the world and each other's cultural backgrounds.

—ELIZABETH FRASCELLA, *Clinton Elementary School*

MIDDLE SCHOOL: GRADES 6–8 I sometimes hear students call each other names in the halls and in the cafeteria. Instead of ignoring this behavior, I make sure I use these incidents as teaching moments and explain to the students why it is wrong to call others names. I also use my classroom time to educate students on the beliefs and customs of different religions and cultural groups. And I am the advisor of our school's Unity Club, which celebrates the diversity within our school by showcasing different cultures. For example, the club recently created a special bulletin board displaying the flags from each country represented within our school.

—CASEY MAASS, *Edison Middle School*

HIGH SCHOOL: GRADES 9–12 One-third of my school's population is Native American. As an art teacher, I present information on Native American art forms including pottery, beading, birchbark baskets, quillwork, and black ash baskets. All students learn what a Native American medicine wheel is (a circle of life) and what the various symbols—colors, directions, and animals—mean. Students make a medicine wheel for themselves and their own personal culture, whether they are Native American or not. Each piece is unique, which speaks to the diversity within the school.

—DENNIS PETERSON, *Deer River High School*

EMPOWERING STUDENTS

The term **empowerment** refers to providing people with the intellectual and coping skills to succeed and create a more just world. In the 1960s to 1980s, multicultural education was concerned with empowering students and better representing minority and cultural groups in curricula and textbooks. Empowerment continues to be an important theme of multicultural education today (Gollnick & Chinn, 2017). In this view, schools should give students the opportunity to learn about the experiences, struggles, and visions of many different ethnic and cultural groups (Koppelman, 2017). The hope is that this will raise minority students' self-esteem, reduce prejudice, and provide more-equal educational opportunities. The hope also is that it will help White students become more knowledgeable about minority groups and that both

empowerment Providing people with intellectual and coping skills to succeed and make this a more just world.

White students and students of color will develop multiple perspectives within their curricula.

Banks (2014) suggests that future teachers can benefit from writing a brief essay about a situation in which they felt marginalized (excluded) by another group. Virtually everyone, whether from a minority or majority group, has experienced this type of situation at some point. Banks emphasizes that you should be in a better position to understand the issues of sociocultural diversity after writing such an essay.

CULTURALLY RELEVANT TEACHING

Culturally relevant teaching is an important aspect of multicultural education (Gollnick & Chinn, 2017). It seeks to make connections with the learner's cultural background.

What is involved in empowering students?
Monkey Business Images/Shutterstock

Multicultural education experts stress that effective teachers are aware of and integrate culturally relevant teaching into the curriculum because it makes teaching more effective (Koppelman, 2017). Ladson-Billings (1995), based on her research on effective teaching for African American students, suggests that in culturally relevant teaching: "a) students must experience academic success; b) students must develop and/or maintain cultural competence; and c) students must develop a critical consciousness through which they challenge the status quo of the current social order" (p. 160). For example, we should

DIVERSITY

1. create learning opportunities that are neither too hard nor too easy for students,
2. rather than replace students' Black English Vernacular (BVE), provide them with opportunities to use BVE in poetry and celebrate their cultural heritage, and
3. help students consider how the structures of our society may maintain the achievement gap and other by products of structural racism and how we can change them.

As we rethink education for minoritized students, she also recommends that we reconsider reframing `gaps', which are laced with deficit connotations, as a byproduct of education debt. The debt analogy suggests deficiencies in student performance can be traced back to the capitalization of historical, economic, sociopolitical, and moral injustices to which these students, and their ancestors, were subjected (Ladson-Billings, 2006). This is aligned with Gay's (2013) call for educators to teach "to" and "through" cultural lenses by bridging school with students' lived experiences, creating community among individuals, and developing student agency.

Culturally relevant teaching is an important aspect of multicultural education. One aspect of culturally relevant teaching involves going into the community where parents live and work. Here a teacher visits a home of students who attend the Susan B. Anthony Elementary School in Sacramento.
Renee C. Byer

Going into the community where your students live and their parents work can improve your understanding of their ethnic and cultural backgrounds (Banks, 2014; Gollnick & Chinn, 2017). The *funds of knowledge approach* emphasizes that teachers should visit students' households and develop social relationships with their students' family members to learn more about their cultural and ethnic background so that they can incorporate this knowledge into their teaching (Moll & González, 2004). Through this approach, teachers can learn more about the occupations, interests, and community characteristics of their students' families. Examples of the funds of knowledge approach include guiding students to understand how their parents' carpentry skills relate to geometry and how the type of language students encounter outside of the classroom might help teachers in teaching students in English classes in school. Researchers have found that when the funds of knowledge approach is used, Latinx students' academic performance improves (González et al., 2005). The funds of knowledge approach acts as a bridge between the student's school and community.

Teachers need to have high achievement expectations for students from ethnic minority and low-income backgrounds and engage them in rigorous academic programs (Zusho et al., 2016). When high achievement expectations and rigorous academic programs are combined with culturally relevant teaching and community connections, students from ethnic minority and low-income backgrounds benefit enormously. In one study of California students, a four-year evaluation found that Latinx students who participated in a rigorous academic program that included community-based writing and study, academic advising, and time with community leaders were almost twice as likely to apply to and attend universities as their counterparts who did not participate in the program (Gandara, 2002).

ISSUES-CENTERED EDUCATION

DIVERSITY

Issues-centered education also is an important aspect of multicultural education. In this approach, students are taught to systematically examine issues that involve equity and social justice. They not only clarify their values but also examine alternatives and consequences if they take a particular stance on an issue. Issues-centered education is closely related to moral education, which we discussed in the chapter on social contexts and socioemotional development.

> **Thinking Back/Thinking Forward**
>
> Values clarification is one of several approaches to moral education. Connect to "Social Contexts and Socioemotional Development."

Consider the circumstance when some students were concerned with the lunch policy at their high school (Pang, 2005). The students who were on federally subsidized programs were forced to use a specific line in the cafeteria, which "labeled" them poor. Many of these low-income students felt humiliated and embarrassed to the point that they went without lunch. The students alerted teachers to what had happened to them, and together, the students and teachers developed a plan of action. They presented the plan to the school district, which revised its lunch line policy at the ten high schools affected by it.

IMPROVING RELATIONSHIPS AMONG CHILDREN FROM DIFFERENT ETHNIC GROUPS

A number of strategies and programs are available to improve relationships among children from different ethnic groups. To begin, we will discuss one of the most powerful strategies.

DIVERSITY

The Jigsaw Classroom When social psychologist Elliot Aronson was a professor at the University of Texas at Austin, the school system contacted him for ideas to reduce the increasing racial tension in classrooms. Aronson (1986) developed the concept of the **jigsaw classroom**, which involves having students from different cultural backgrounds cooperate by doing different parts of a project to reach a common goal. Aronson used the term *jigsaw* because he saw the technique as much like a group of students cooperating to put different pieces together to complete a jigsaw puzzle.

jigsaw classroom A classroom in which students from different cultural backgrounds cooperate by doing different parts of a project to reach a common goal.

How might this work? Consider a class of students, some White, some African American, some Latinx, some Native American, and some Asian American. The lesson concerns the life of Joseph Pulitzer. The class might be broken up into groups of six students each, with the groups being as equally mixed as possible in terms of ethnic composition and achievement level. The lesson about Pulitzer's life is divided into six parts, and one part is assigned to each member of each six-person group. The parts might be passages from Pulitzer's biography, such as how the Pulitzer family came to the United States, Pulitzer's childhood, his early work, and so on. All students in each group are given an allotted time to study their parts. Then the groups meet, and each member works to teach his or her part to the group. Learning depends on the students' interdependence and cooperation in reaching the same goal.

What are some features of a jigsaw classroom?
Ariel Skelley/Blend Images LLC

Sometimes the jigsaw classroom strategy is described as creating a superordinate goal or common task for students. Team sports, drama productions, and music performances are additional examples of contexts in which students cooperatively and often very enthusiastically participate to reach a superordinate goal.

Positive Personal Contact with Others from Different Cultural Backgrounds

Contact by itself does not always improve relationships. For example, busing ethnic minority students to predominantly non-Latinx White schools, or vice versa, has not reduced prejudice or improved interethnic relations (Frankenberg & Orfield, 2007). What matters is what happens after students arrive at a school.

Relations improve when students talk with each other about their personal worries, successes, failures, coping strategies, interests, and so on. When students reveal personal information about themselves, they are more likely to be perceived as individuals than simply as members of a group. Sharing personal information frequently produces this discovery: People from different backgrounds share many of the same hopes, worries, and feelings. Sharing personal information can help break down in-group/out-group and we/they barriers.

Perspective Taking

Exercises and activities that help students see other people's perspectives can improve interethnic relations. In one exercise, students learn certain proper behaviors of two distinct cultural groups (Shirts, 1997). Subsequently, the two groups interact with each other in accordance with those behaviors. As a result, they experience feelings of anxiety and apprehension. The exercise is designed to help students understand the culture shock that comes from being in a cultural setting with people who behave in ways that are very different from what one is used to. Students also can be encouraged to write stories or act out plays that involve prejudice or discrimination. In this way, students "step into the shoes" of students who are culturally different from themselves and feel what it is like to not be treated as an equal.

Studying people from different parts of the world also encourages students to understand different perspectives. In social studies, students can be asked why people in certain cultures have customs different from their own. Teachers can also encourage students to read books on many different cultures.

Global Lab Project

TECHNOLOGY

Technology Connections with Students Around the World Traditionally, students have learned within the walls of their classroom and interacted with their teacher and other students in the class. Technology can expand the reach of classroom activities through such activities as video conferencing (Skype, Google Hangouts, for example), social media (Twitter, Instagram), and online collaboration tools (Google Drive). Also, with advances in telecommunications, students can learn with and from teachers and students around the world.

For example, in the Global Student Laboratory Project (https://globallab.org/en/#.V70dyfkrLRY), an international, telecommunication-based project, students have investigated local and global environments (Globallab, 2016; Schrum & Berenfeld, 1997). More than 130 projects are available, involving topics such as world currencies, managing a travel agency, natural pH indicators, ways to make our world better, and "waste: danger or opportunity?" In one activity, students shared their findings and then collaboratively identified various aspects of environments, discussed research plans, and conducted distributed studies using the same methods and procedures. Students participated from such diverse locations as Moscow, Russia; Warsaw, Poland; Kenosha, Wisconsin; San Antonio, Texas; Pueblo, Colorado; and Aiken, South Carolina. As their data collection and evaluation evolved, students continued to communicate with their peers worldwide and to learn more, not only about science, but also about the global community.

The First Lego League (www.firstinspires.org/robotics/fll) is a global competition for children 9 to 14 years of age focused on science and robotics challenges as well as learning collaborative learning skills. Many schools sponsor teams of learners to participate in local competitions where students have an opportunity to advance to national and international events.

New advances in telecommunications make it possible for students around the world to communicate through videoconferencing over the Internet. For example, at the Research Center for Educational Technology (RCET) at Kent State University, Ohio, elementary students and their teachers are collaborating with their peers at the Instituto Thomas Jefferson in Mexico City on a variety of projects including studies of plant biology, climate, and biography, using both Internet-based videoconferencing and e-mail (Swan et al., 2006). RCET (www.kent.edu/rcet) researchers have found that projects that share common understandings but highlight local differences are especially productive.

Videoconferencing is an excellent way that diverse students can communicate and collaborate. For example, an increasing number of schools are also using Internet-based videoconferencing for foreign language instruction. Instead of simulating a French café in a typical French language class, American students might talk with French students in a real café in France. Also, Mystery Skype is an enjoyable activity for elementary school classrooms (https://education.microsoft.com/skype-in-the-classroom/mystery-skype). And Microsoft sponsors a page where you can find guest speakers for your classroom via videoconference (https://education.microsoft.com/skype-in-the-classroom/find-guest-speakers).

Such global technology projects can go a long way toward reducing students' ethnocentric beliefs. The active building of connections around the world through telecommunications gives students the opportunity to experience others' perspectives, better understand other cultures, and reduce prejudice.

Students in the Research Center for Educational Technology's AT&T classroom at Kent State University, studying plant biology with students at the Instituto Thomas Jefferson in Mexico City.
Research Center for Educational Technology, Kent State University

Reducing Bias Children especially benefit if they learn early in their lives to show respect for individuals from ethnic groups other than their own. For example, in early childhood, teachers need to directly confront any hint of racism or discrimination in children's interactions.

Louise Derman-Sparks and the Anti-Bias Curriculum Task Force (1989) created a number of tools to help young children reduce, handle, or even eliminate their biases.

These are some of the antibias strategies recommended for teachers:

- Display images of children from a variety of ethnic and cultural groups. Select books for students that also reflect this diversity.
- Choose play materials and activities that encourage ethnic and cultural understanding. Use dramatic play to illustrate nonstereotypic roles and families from diverse backgrounds.
- Talk with students about stereotyping and discriminating against others. Make it a firm rule that no child can be teased or excluded because of his or her ethnicity or race.
- Engage parents in discussions of how children develop prejudice, and inform parents about your efforts to reduce ethnic bias in your classroom.

Increasing Tolerance Development of tolerance and respect for individuals from diverse ethnic groups is an important aspect of multicultural education (Gollnick & Chinn, 2017). The "Teaching Tolerance Project" provides schools with resources and materials to improve intercultural understanding and relationships between White children and children of color (Heller & Hawkins, 1994). The biannual magazine *Teaching Tolerance* is distributed to every public and private school in the United States (you can obtain a free copy by contacting Teaching Tolerance through www.tolerance.org/magazine/subscribe). The magazine's purpose is to share views on and provide resources for teaching tolerance. For elementary school teachers, the "Different and Same" videos and materials (available through www.fredrogers.org) can help children become more tolerant.

The School and Community as a Team Yale psychiatrist James Comer (1988, 2006, 2010) stresses that a community team approach is the best way to educate children. Three important aspects of the Comer Project for Change are (1) a governance and management team that develops a comprehensive school plan, assessment strategy, and staff development program; (2) a mental health or school support team; and (3) a parents' program. The Comer program emphasizes a no-fault approach (the focus should be on solving problems, not blaming), no decisions except by consensus, and no paralysis (that is, no naysayer can stand in the way of a strong majority decision). Comer says the entire school community should have a cooperative rather than an adversarial attitude. The Comer program has been implemented successfully in over 1000 schools around the world (Teare, 2018).

In the book *Leave No Child Behind,* Comer (2004) agreed with the increased emphasis on higher standards and accountability in U.S. schools but argued that the emphasis on test scores and curriculum alone is inadequate. Comer says that children's socioemotional development and relationships with caregivers also need to be improved if educational reform is to be successful.

James Comer (*left*) is shown with some inner-city African American students who attend a school where Comer has implemented his community team approach.
Chris Volpe Photography

CONNECTING WITH STUDENTS: Best Practices
Best Practices and Strategies for Multicultural Education

We already have discussed many ideas that will benefit children's relations with people from different ethnic and cultural backgrounds. Further guidelines for multicultural teaching include these recommendations from leading multicultural education expert James Banks (2006, 2008):

1. *Be sensitive to racist content in materials and classroom interactions.* A good source for learning more about racism addressing a White audience is Paul Kivel's (2017) book, *Uprooting Racism: How White People Can Work for Racial Justice.* For the perspective of a Black woman about how to

continued

CONNECTING WITH STUDENTS: Best Practices
Best Practices and Strategies for Multicultural Education

talk about race, see Ijeoma Oluo's (2018) book, *So You Want to Talk about Race*. She sets the stage by laying out basic rules for determining whether something is about race:

- "It is about race if a person of color thinks it is about race" (Oluo, p. 15).
- "It is about race if it disproportionately or differently affects people of color" (Oluo, p. 15).
- "It is about race if it fits into a broader pattern of events that disproportionately or differently affect people of color" (Oluo, p. 15).

2. *Learn more about different ethnic groups.* According to diversity expert Carlos Diaz (2005), only when you consider yourself "multiculturally literate" will you likely encourage students to think deeply and critically about diversity. Otherwise, says Diaz, teachers tend to see diversity as a "can of worms" that they don't want to open because they lack the background to explain it. To increase your multicultural literacy, read at least one major book on the history and culture of American ethnic groups. One of Banks' books that includes historical descriptions of these groups is *Cultural Diversity and Education* (2015).

3. *Be aware of students' ethnic attitudes.* Respond to students' cultural views in sensitive ways. In *Through the Eyes of Teachers*, Kathy Fucher, a high school teacher in Humphrey, Nebraska, describes some strategies for reducing students' prejudice.

THROUGH THE EYES OF TEACHERS
Seeking to Reduce Prejudice Toward Latinx Students in Nebraska

The meatpacking industry in Nebraska has brought many Latinos to our area. I find my students have a definite negative attitude toward them, usually as a result of their parents' influence. My effort to help them realize their prejudice is to teach David Gutterson's *Snow Falling on Cedars* to senior-level students. Though the fictional novel takes place off Puget Sound and deals with Japanese immigrants during World War II, I take students through discussion questions that provide striking similarity to their prejudice against Latinos. I have no way to measure the degree of prejudice, but I feel that education and awareness are key steps in decreasing the problem.

Kathy Fucher

4. *Use trade books, films, videotapes, and recordings to portray ethnic perspectives.* Banks' (2003) book, *Teaching Strategies for Ethnic Studies*, describes a number of these. In *Through the Eyes of Teachers*, Marlene Wendler, a fourth-grade teacher in New Ulm, Minnesota, describes her teaching strategies in this regard.

THROUGH THE EYES OF TEACHERS
Using Literature to Show How Minorities Have Been Treated

I use literature to help students understand other people and how they have sometimes been treated unfairly. During January, I focus on the southeastern United States in our social studies class and integrate language arts by having the whole class read *Meet Addy* and *Mississippi Bridge*. On Martin Luther King Day we read his biography. We get a little overview of how the Jews were treated in World War II through *Number the Stars*. We also get interested in learning more about Anne Frank. When the children read how these minorities were treated, they understand more fully that all people are more similar to them than different.

Marlene Wendler

5. *Take into account your students' developmental status when you select various cultural materials.* In early childhood and elementary school classrooms, make the learning experience specific and concrete. Banks stresses that fiction and biographies are especially good choices for introducing cultural concepts to these students. Students at these levels can study such concepts as similarities, differences, prejudice, and discrimination but are not developmentally ready to study concepts such as racism.

6. *Perceive all students in positive ways and have high expectations for them regardless of their ethnicity.* All students learn best when their teachers have high achievement expectations for them and support their learning efforts. We will have much more to say about the importance of high expectations for students' achievement in the chapter on motivation, teaching, and learning.

7. *Recognize that most parents, regardless of their ethnicity, are interested in their children's education and want them to succeed in school.* However, understand that many parents of color have mixed feelings about schools because of their own experiences with discrimination. Think of positive ways to get parents of color more involved in their children's education and view them as partners in their children's learning.

Review, Reflect, and Practice

 Describe some ways to promote multicultural education.

REVIEW
- What is multicultural education? What is the aim of "empowering" students?
- What is culturally relevant teaching?
- What is issues-centered education?
- How can teachers improve relationships among children from different ethnic groups?

REFLECT
- In terms of multicultural education, what do you hope to do as a teacher differently from what your former teachers did?

PRAXIS™ PRACTICE

1. Which of these is the best educational practice for empowering students?
   a. avoiding discussion of prejudice and discrimination
   b. teaching a second language to all non-Latinx White students
   c. having separate weekly classes on multicultural topics
   d. encouraging all students to study culture critically

2. Which teacher's practice best exemplifies the concept of culturally relevant education?
   a. Mr. Lincoln, who does not allow any discussion of race or ethnicity in his class, deeming it irrelevant to his students' education
   b. Mr. Peters, who has differing expectations of his students based on gender, ethnicity, and SES
   c. Mr. Welch, who displays favoritism to members of ethnic minority groups
   d. Mr. Patterson, who recognizes that he comes from a different background from his students but spends time in the community to better understand their culture

3. Which of the following is the best example of issues-centered education?
   a. As Mr. DeRosa's students study their history text, they look at events in terms of fairness to all groups and long-term social impact.
   b. Ms. Pang's students discuss historical facts and their impact on mainstream culture.
   c. Ms. Broadhouse's students are encouraged to debate issues, but debate winners always share the same views as Ms. Broadhouse.
   d. Mr. Taha's students are having a culture fair this Friday.

4. Middlesborough High School is an ethnically diverse school with considerable racial tension and conflict. When possible, the students self-select single-ethnicity groups. When forced to work in ethnically diverse groups, the students often argue and fail to cooperate. Several racially motivated violent episodes have occurred during this school year. Based on information in the text, which of these practices is most likely to improve relationships among the students from different ethnic groups?
   a. Assign the students to read books about various ethnic groups' history and contributions and discuss them in class in mixed ethnic groups.
   b. Keep putting students of mixed ethnicity together in classes and project groups so that they get to know each other and the conflict will decrease.
   c. Allow the students to stay in single-ethnicity groups because they are old enough to make these choices for themselves.
   d. Ignore ethnicity altogether so that students gradually become less aware of ethnic differences.

Please see answer key at end of book . . . .

LG 3 Explain various facets of gender, including similarities and differences in boys and girls; discuss gender issues in teaching.

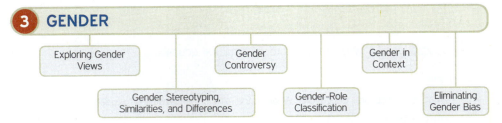

3 GENDER

- Exploring Gender Views
- Gender Stereotyping, Similarities, and Differences
- Gender Controversy
- Gender-Role Classification
- Gender in Context
- Eliminating Gender Bias

Gender is a term that is used extensively throughout our everyday lives, including schools and education. What are some different views of gender?

EXPLORING GENDER VIEWS

Gender refers to the characteristics of people as males and females. **Gender roles** are sets of expectations that prescribe how females or males should think, act, and feel. **Gender typing** refers to acquisition of a traditional masculine or feminine role. For example, aggression is more characteristic of a traditional masculine role and nurturing is more characteristic of a traditional feminine role.

There are various ways to view gender development (Leaper, 2015). Some views stress the influence of biological factors on the behavior of males and females; others emphasize social or cognitive factors. Even gender experts with a strong environmental orientation acknowledge that girls and boys are treated differently because of their physical differences and their different roles in reproduction.

Social views of gender especially highlight the various social contexts in which children develop, such as families, peers, school, and the media. Many parents encourage boys and girls to engage in different types of play and activities (Leaper & Farkas, 2015). Girls are more likely to be given dolls and, when old enough, are more likely to be assigned baby-sitting duties. Girls are encouraged to be more nurturing than boys. Fathers are more likely to engage in aggressive play with their sons than with their daughters. Parents allow their adolescent sons to have more freedom than their adolescent daughters.

Peers also reward and punish gender-related behavior (Rubin et al., 2015). After extensive observations of elementary school classrooms, two researchers characterized the play settings as "gender school" (Luria & Herzog, 1985). In elementary school, boys usually hang out with boys and girls with girls. It is easier for "tomboy" girls to join boys' groups than for "feminine" boys to join girls' groups, because of our society's greater sex-typing pressure on boys. Developmental psychologist Eleanor Maccoby (1998, 2007), who has studied gender for a number of decades, concludes that peers play an especially important gender-socializing role, teaching each other what is acceptable and unacceptable gender behavior.

Schools and teachers have important gender-socializing influences on boys and girls. Shortly, we will explore such topics as the gender differences related to schools and students' interactions with teachers, educational achievement, and gender bias in classrooms.

The media also play a gender-socializing role, portraying females and males in particular gender roles (Senden et al., 2015). Even with the onset of more diverse programming in recent years, researchers still find that television presents males as more competent than females (Starr, 2015).

In addition to biological and social factors, cognitive factors also contribute to children's gender development (Martin & Ruble, 2010). **Gender schema theory**, currently the most widely accepted cognitive theory of gender, states that gender-typing emerges as children gradually develop gender schemas of what is gender-appropriate and gender-inappropriate in their culture. A *schema* is a cognitive structure, a network of associations that guides an individual's perceptions. A *gender schema* organizes the world in terms of female and male. Children are internally motivated to perceive the

gender The characteristics of people as males and females.

gender role A set of expectations that prescribes how females or males should think, act, and feel.

gender typing Acquisition of a traditional masculine or feminine role.

gender schema theory States that gender typing emerges as children gradually develop gender schemas of what is gender-appropriate and gender-inappropriate in their culture.

The playground in elementary school is like going to "gender school," as boys prefer to interact with boys and girls choose to interact with girls.
Yellow Dog Productions/Digital Vision//Getty Images

> **Thinking Back/Thinking Forward**
>
> Schema theories of memory state that when children reconstruct memory they fit it into information that already exists in their minds. Connect to "The Information-Processing Approach."

world and to act in accordance with their developing schemas. Bit by bit, children pick up what is gender-appropriate and gender-inappropriate in their culture, and develop gender schemas that shape how they perceive the world and what they remember. Children are motivated to act in ways that conform with these gender schemas (Martin et al., 2013).

GENDER STEREOTYPING, SIMILARITIES, AND DIFFERENCES

What are the real differences between boys and girls? Before attempting to answer that question, let's consider the problem of gender stereotypes.

Gender Stereotypes **Gender stereotypes** are broad categories that reflect impressions and beliefs about what behavior is appropriate for females and males. All stereotypes—whether they relate to gender, ethnicity, or other categories—refer to an image of what the typical member of a category is like. Many stereotypes are so general that they become ambiguous. Consider the categories of "masculine" and "feminine." Diverse behaviors can be assigned to each category, such as scoring a touchdown or growing facial hair for "masculine," playing with dolls or wearing lipstick for "feminine." Stereotyping students as "masculine" or "feminine" can have significant consequences (Best, 2010). Labeling a male "feminine" or a female "masculine" can diminish his or her social status and acceptance in groups.

Recent research continues to find that gender stereotyping is pervasive. Researchers have found that boys' gender stereotypes are more rigid than girls' (Blakemore et al., 2009).

Gender stereotyping changes developmentally (Zosuls et al., 2008). By the time children enter elementary school, they have considerable knowledge about which activities are linked with being male or female.

RESEARCH

Gender Similarities and Differences in Academically Relevant Domains Many aspects of students' lives can be examined to determine how similar or different girls and boys are.

DEVELOPMENT

The Brain Does gender affect brain structure and activity? Human brains are much alike, whether the brain belongs to a male or a female (Hyde, 2014). However, researchers have found some differences. Some of the differences that have been discovered are described below:

- Female brains are smaller than male brains, but female brains have more folds; the larger folds (called *convolutions*) allow more surface brain tissue within the skulls of females than in males (Luders et al., 2009).
- An area of the parietal lobe that functions in visuospatial skills tends to be larger in males than in females (Frederikse et al., 2000).
- The areas of the brain involved in emotional expression tend to show more metabolic activity in females than in males (Gur et al., 1995).

Similarities and differences in the brains of males and females could be due to evolution and heredity as well as social experiences.

Physical Performance Because physical education is an integral part of U.S. educational systems, it is important to address gender similarities and differences in physical performance. In general, boys outperform girls in athletic skills such as running, throwing, and jumping. In the elementary school years, the differences often are not large; they become more dramatic in the middle school years. The hormonal changes of puberty result in increased muscle mass for boys and increased body fat for girls. This leads to an advantage for boys in activities related to strength, size, and power. Nonetheless, environmental factors are involved in physical performance even after puberty. Girls are less likely to participate in activities that promote the motor skills necessary to do well in sports.

gender stereotypes Broad categories that reflect impressions and beliefs about what behavior is appropriate for females and males.

Activity level is another area of physical performance in which gender differences occur. From very early in life, boys are more active than girls are in terms of gross motor movements (Blakemore et al., 2009). In the classroom, this means that boys are more likely than girls to fidget and move around the room, and they are less likely to pay attention. In physical education classes, boys expend more energy through movement than girls do.

Intelligence No gender differences occur in overall intellectual ability, but gender differences do appear in some cognitive areas, such as math and verbal skills (Halpern, 2012).

Math and Science Skills Are there gender differences in mathematical abilities? A very large-scale study of more than 7 million U.S. students in grades 2 through 11 revealed no differences in math scores for boys and girls (Hyde et al., 2008). Also, in the most recent National Assessment of Educational Progress (2015) reports, there were virtually no gender differences in math scores at the fourth- and eighth-grade levels. However, since its initial assessment in 1972 through 2015, males have scored higher on the math section of the SAT than females—in 2015, the average scores were 527 for males and 496 for females (College Board, 2015).

One area of math that has been examined for possible gender differences is visuospatial skills, which include being able to rotate objects mentally and determine what they would look like when rotated. These types of skills are important in courses such as plane and solid geometry and geography. A research review revealed that boys have better visuospatial skills than girls (Halpern, 2012). For example, despite equal participation in the National Geography Bee, in most years all ten finalists are boys (Liben, 1995). However, some experts argue that the gender difference in visuospatial skills is small (Hyde, 2007).

What about science? Are there gender differences? In the 2009 National Assessment of Educational Progress, for high school graduates who had earned credits in specific science courses (advanced biology, chemistry, and physics) males had higher scores than females (Cunningham et al., 2015). In this study, male high school graduates also reported that they liked science better than their female counterparts did. In another study focused on eighth- and tenth-graders, boys scored higher than girls on science tests, especially among average- and high-ability students (Burkham et al., 1997). In science classes that emphasized hands-on lab activities, girls' science test scores improved considerably. This suggests the importance of active involvement of students in science classrooms, which may promote gender equity.

The gender gaps observed in science, technology, engineering, and mathematics (STEM) scores and careers can be explained by a number of "environmental factors that influence ability, preferences, and the rewards for those choices" (Kahn & Ginther, 2017, p. ii). For example, parents' and female teachers' math anxiety are related to students' math anxiety, as well as girls' beliefs that "boys are good at math and girls good at reading" and their lower math achievement (Kahn & Ginther, 2017, p. 13). Researchers Shulamit Kahn and Donna Ginther, in their literature review, explained how stereotypes, culture and interest, among other factors, contribute to the STEM gap, which begins in childhood and solidifies in middle school. Another review of literature review on this topic adds that societal beliefs and expectation about gender ability differences and "cultural pressures to pursue traditionally masculine or feminine interests (e.g., 'boys don't play with dolls'), are far more likely than biology alone to impact career decisions" (Wang & Degol, 2017, p. 129). Authors Ming-Te Wang and Jessica Degol made the following research-informed suggestions to help increase the females' interest in STEM:

- "Intervene early to cultivate interest in math and science" (p. 130).
- "Break down stereotypes about women and STEM" (p. 131).
- "Emphasize effort and hard work instead of talent" (p. 131).
- "Add more storytelling to stem learning" (p. 131).

- "Communicate the relevance of a STEM degree to real-world applications" (p. 132).
- "Provid[e] more female role models for girls and women" (p. 132).

Verbal Skills A major review of gender similarities and differences conducted in the 1970s concluded that girls have better verbal skills than boys do (Maccoby & Jacklin, 1974). During the elementary and secondary school years, girls outperform boys in reading and writing. In a recent study of U.S. students, girls had higher reading achievement than boys in grades 4 and 8 (National Assessment of Educational Progress, 2015). However, for SAT scores, just as in the math section, males have scored higher than females on the reading section for many years, although the difference is much smaller (in 2015, the average for males was 497 and for females it was 493) (College Board, 2015).

Girls also have performed substantially better than boys in grades 4 and 8 in writing skills (National Assessment of Educational Progress, 2007). For the writing section of the SAT, since its inception in 2006, females have scored higher than males—in 2015, the average female score was 490, the average male score 478 (College Board, 2015).

Educational Attainment In regard to school achievement, girls earn better grades and complete high school at a higher rate than boys do (Halpern, 2012). Boys are more likely than girls to be assigned to special/remedial education classes. Girls are more likely to be engaged with academic material, be attentive in class, put forth more academic effort, and participate more in class than boys are (DeZolt & Hull, 2001).

Keep in mind that measures of achievement in school or scores on standardized tests in math, science, reading, and writing may reflect many factors besides cognitive ability. For example, performance in school may in part reflect attempts to conform to gender roles or differences in motivation, self-regulation, or other socioemotional characteristics (Klug et al., 2016; Wentzel & Miele, 2016; Wigfield et al., 2015).

Relationship Skills Researchers have found that girls are more "people oriented" and boys are more "things oriented" (Galambos et al., 2009). In a recent research review, this conclusion was supported by findings that girls spend more time in relationships, while boys spend more time alone, playing video games, and playing sports; that girls work at part-time jobs that are people-oriented such as waitressing and baby-sitting, while boys are more likely to take part-time jobs that involve manual labor and using tools; and that girls are interested in careers that are more people-oriented, such as teaching and social work, while boys are more likely to be interested in object-oriented careers, such as mechanics and engineering (Perry & Pauletti, 2011). Also, researchers have found that adolescent girls engage in more self-disclosure (communication of intimate details about themselves) in close relationships, are better at actively listening in a conversation than are boys, and emphasize affiliation or collaboration (Leaper, 2013, 2015). Adolescent girls, in particular, are more likely to engage in self-disclosure and to provide emotional support in friendship than are boys (Leaper, 2013, 2015). By contrast, boys are more likely to value self-assertion and dominance than are girls in their interactions with friends and peers (Leaper, 2013, 2015).

Prosocial Behavior Are there gender differences in prosocial behavior? Girls view themselves as more prosocial and empathic than boys do (Eisenberg et al., 2015). Across childhood and adolescence, girls engage in more prosocial behavior (Hastings et al., 2015). The biggest gender difference occurs for kind and considerate behavior, with a smaller difference in sharing.

Aggression One of the most consistent gender differences is that boys are more physically aggressive than girls (Underwood, 2011). The difference is especially pronounced when children are provoked—this difference occurs across all cultures and appears very early in children's development (Ostrov et al., 2004). Both biological

> **Thinking Back/Thinking Forward**
>
> Teachers can play important roles in promoting children's prosocial behavior and providing them with opportunities to engage in prosocial behavior. Connect to "Social Contexts and Socioemotional Development."

> **Thinking Back/Thinking Forward**
>
> Serious, persistent problems in aggression can lead to children being classified as having an emotional and behavioral disorder. Connect to "Learners Who Are Exceptional."

What gender differences characterize aggression?
Fuse/Corbis RF/Getty Images

and environmental factors have been proposed to account for differences in physical aggression. Biological factors include heredity and hormones; environmental factors include cultural expectations, adult and peer models, and the rewarding of physical aggression in boys.

Although boys are consistently more physically aggressive than girls, might girls show as much or more verbal aggression, such as yelling, than boys? When verbal aggression is examined, gender differences typically either disappear or are sometimes even more pronounced in girls (Eagly & Steffen, 1986).

Recently, increased interest has been shown in *relational aggression*, which involves harming someone by manipulating a relationship (Blakely-McClure & Ostrov, 2016; Busching & Krahe, 2015; Mulvey & Killen, 2016; Orpinas et al., 2015). Relational aggression includes such behaviors as trying to make others dislike a certain individual by spreading malicious rumors about the person or ostracizing him or her. Mixed findings have characterized research on whether girls show more relational aggression than boys, but one consistent finding is that relational aggression comprises a greater percentage of girls' overall aggression than it does for boys (Putallaz et al., 2007). And a research review revealed that girls engage in more relational aggression than boys in adolescence but not in childhood (Smith et al., 2010).

Emotion and Its Regulation Gender differences occur in some aspects of emotion (Deng et al., 2016; Leaper, 2015). Recent research reviews have found that overall gender differences in children's emotional expression were small, with girls showing more positive emotions (sympathy, for example) and more internalized emotions (sadness and anxiety, for example) (Chaplin, 2015; Chaplin & Aldao, 2013). In this analysis, the gender difference in positive emotions became more pronounced with age as girls more strongly expressed positive emotions than boys in middle and late childhood and in adolescence.

An important skill is the capacity to regulate and control one's emotions and behavior (Thompson, 2015). Boys usually show less self-regulation of their emotions than girls do, and this low self-control can translate into behavior problems (Pascual et al., 2012).

GENDER CONTROVERSY

The previous sections revealed some substantial differences in physical performance, writing skills, aggression, self-regulation, and prosocial behavior but small or nonexistent differences in communication, math, and science. Controversy swirls about such similarities and differences. Evolutionary psychologists such as David Buss (2012, 2015) argue that gender differences are extensive and caused by the adaptive problems faced across evolutionary history. Alice Eagly (2012, 2013) also concludes that gender differences are substantial but reaches a very different conclusion about their cause. She emphasizes that gender differences are due to social conditions that have resulted in women having less power and controlling fewer resources than men.

By contrast, Janet Shibley Hyde (2014) concludes that gender differences have been greatly exaggerated, especially fueled by popular books such as John Gray's (1992) *Men Are from Mars, Women Are from Venus* and Deborah Tannen's (1990) *You Just Don't Understand*. She argues that the research shows that females and males are similar on most psychological factors.

GENDER-ROLE CLASSIFICATION

Not very long ago, it was accepted that boys should grow up to be masculine and girls to be feminine. In the 1970s, however, as both females and males became dissatisfied with the burdens imposed by their stereotypic roles, alternatives to femininity and masculinity were proposed. Instead of describing masculinity and femininity as a continuum in which more of one means less of the other, it was proposed that individuals could have both masculine and feminine traits.

This thinking led to the development of the concept of **androgyny**, the presence of positive masculine and feminine characteristics in the same person (Bem, 1977; Spence & Helmreich, 1978). The androgynous boy might be assertive (masculine) and nurturant (feminine). The androgynous girl might be powerful (masculine) and sensitive to others' feelings (feminine). Studies have confirmed that societal changes are leading girls to be more assertive (Spence & Buckner, 2000) and that sons are more androgynous than their fathers (Guastello & Guastello, 2003).

Gender experts such as Sandra Bem argue that androgynous individuals are more flexible, competent, and mentally healthy than their masculine or feminine counterparts. To some degree, though, which gender-role classification is best depends on context. For example, in close relationships, feminine and androgynous orientations might be more desirable. One study found that children high in femininity showed a stronger interest in caring than did children high in masculinity (Karniol et al., 2003). However, masculine and androgynous orientations might be more desirable in traditional academic and work settings because of the achievement demands in these contexts.

Despite talk about the "sensitive male," William Pollack (1999) argues that little has been done to change traditional ways of raising boys. He says that the "boy code" tells boys that they should show little if any emotion and should act tough. Boys learn the boy code in many contexts, especially peer contexts—sandboxes, playgrounds, schoolrooms, camps, hangouts. The result, according to Pollack, is a "national crisis of boyhood." Pollack and others suggest that boys would benefit from being socialized to express their anxieties and concerns and to better regulate their aggression. To think about your gender-role classification, see *Self-Assessment 1*.

GENDER IN CONTEXT

Earlier we said that the concept of gender-role classification involves categorizing people in terms of personality traits. However, recall from our discussion of personality in the chapter on individual variations that it is beneficial to think of personality in terms of person-situation interaction rather than personality traits alone. Let's now further explore gender in context.

Helping Behavior and Emotion   The stereotype is that females are better than males at helping, but the likelihood of engaging in helping behavior depends on the context. Females are more likely than males to volunteer their time to help children with personal problems and engage in caregiving behavior. However, in situations where males feel a sense of competence or those that involve danger, males are more likely to help (Eagly & Crowley, 1986). For example, a male is more likely than a female to stop and help a person stranded by the roadside with a flat tire. A recent meta-analysis of research on the bystander effect ("the phenomenon that an individual's likelihood of helping decreases when passive bystanders are present in a critical situation") that analyzed studies from 1968 to 2008, showed that the bystander effect decreases when (1) bystanders know one another, (2) they are real instead of passive confederates, and (3) they can provide more physical support (Fischer et al., 2011, p. 517). The authors hypothesized that "because of their greater physical strength, male bystanders should be able to provide more physical support in case of intervention than female bystanders" (p. 522). Their results suggest that males are more likely to intervene in dangerous situations.

She is emotional; he is not. That's the master emotional stereotype. However, like helping behavior, emotional differences in males and females depend on the particular emotion involved and the context in which it is displayed (Chaplin, 2015; Shields, 1991). Males are more likely to show anger toward strangers, especially male strangers, when they feel they have been challenged. Males also are more likely to

androgyny The presence of positive masculine and feminine characteristics in the same individual.

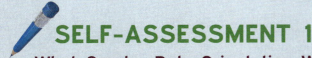

SELF-ASSESSMENT 1
What Gender-Role Orientation Will I Present to My Students?

The items below inquire about what kind of person you think you are. Place a check mark in the column that best describes you for each item: 1 = Not like me at all, 2 = Somewhat unlike me, 3 = Somewhat like me, and 4 = Very much like me.

Item	1	2	3	4
1. I'm independent.	___	___	___	___
2. My emotional life is important to me.	___	___	___	___
3. I provide social support to others.	___	___	___	___
4. I'm competitive.	___	___	___	___
5. I'm a kind person.	___	___	___	___
6. I'm sensitive to others' feelings.	___	___	___	___
7. I'm self-confident.	___	___	___	___
8. I'm self-reflective.	___	___	___	___
9. I'm patient.	___	___	___	___
10. I'm self-assertive.	___	___	___	___
11. I'm aggressive.	___	___	___	___
12. I'm willing to take risks.	___	___	___	___
13. I like to tell secrets to my friends.	___	___	___	___
14. I like to feel powerful.	___	___	___	___

SCORING AND INTERPRETATION

Items 1, 4, 7, 10, 11, 12, 14 are masculine items. Items 2, 3, 5, 6, 8, 9, and 13 are feminine items. Look at the pattern of your responses. If you mainly checked 3 and 4 for the masculine items and mainly 1 and 2 for the feminine items, you likely are characterized by masculinity. If you mainly checked 3 and 4 for the feminine items and 1 and 2 for the masculine items, you likely are characterized by femininity. If you mainly checked 3 and 4 for both the masculine items and the feminine items, you likely are characterized by androgyny. If you mainly checked 1 and 2 for both the masculine and feminine items, your gender-role classification is likely undifferentiated.

turn their anger into aggressive action. Emotional differences between females and males often show up in contexts that highlight social roles and relationships. For example, females are more likely to discuss emotions in terms of relationships. They also are more likely to express fear and sadness.

DIVERSITY

Culture The importance of considering gender in context is most apparent when examining what is culturally prescribed behavior for females and males in different countries around the world (Matsumoto & Juang, 2017). In the United States, there is now more acceptance of similarities in male and female behavior, but in many other countries roles have remained gender-specific (Best, 2010). For example, in many Middle Eastern countries the division of labor between males and females is dramatic. In Iraq and Iran, males primarily are socialized and schooled to work in the public sphere; females are mainly socialized to remain in the private world of home and child rearing. Any deviations from this traditional masculine and feminine behavior are severely disapproved of. Likewise, in rural China, although women have made some strides, the male role is still dominant.

Cultural and ethnic backgrounds also influence how boys and girls will be socialized in the United States. One study indicated that Latino and Latina adolescents were socialized differently as they were growing up (Raffaelli & Ontai, 2004). Latinas experienced far greater restrictions than Latinos in curfews, interacting with members of the other sex, getting a driver's license, getting a job, and involvement in after-school activities.

ELIMINATING GENDER BIAS

How gendered are social interactions between teachers and students? What can teachers do to reduce or eliminate gender bias in their classrooms?

Teacher-Student Interaction   Gender bias is present in classrooms. Teachers interact more with boys than with girls at all levels of schooling (Blakemore et al., 2009). What evidence is there that this interaction is biased against boys? Here are some factors to consider (DeZolt & Hull, 2001):

- Complying with instructions, following rules, and being neat and orderly are valued and reinforced in many classrooms. These are behaviors that are typically associated with girls rather than boys.
- A large majority of teachers are females, especially in the elementary school. This may make it more difficult for boys than for girls to identify with their teachers and model their teachers' behavior.
- Boys are more likely than girls to be identified as having learning problems.
- Boys are more likely than girls to be criticized.
- School personnel tend to stereotype boys' behavior as problematic.
- Since the mid-1970s, girls have outnumbered boys in gifted programs (Freeman & Garces-Bascal, 2015).

A school in the Middle East with boys only. Many adolescents in the Middle East are not allowed to interact with the other sex, even in school. Although in the United States there now is more acceptance of similarities in schooling and work opportunities for males and females, many countries around the world remain more gender-specific.
Yvan Cohen/LightRocket/Getty Images

What evidence is there that the classroom is biased against girls? Consider the following factors (Sadker, 2016; Sadker & Sadker, 1994, 2005):

- In a typical classroom, girls are more compliant, boys more rambunctious. Boys demand more attention; girls are more likely to quietly wait their turn. Educators worry that girls' tendency to be compliant and quiet comes at a cost: diminished assertiveness.
- In many classrooms, teachers spend more time watching and interacting with boys, whereas girls work and play quietly on their own. Most teachers don't intentionally favor boys by spending more time with them, yet somehow the classroom frequently ends up with this type of gendered profile.
- Boys get more instruction than girls and more help when they have trouble with a question. Teachers often give boys more time to answer a question, more hints at the correct answer, and further tries if they give the wrong answer.
- Girls and boys enter first grade with roughly equal levels of self-esteem, yet by the middle school years, girls' self-esteem is significantly lower than boys' (Robins et al., 2002).

Thus, there is evidence of gender bias against both boys and girls in schools (Leaper & Brown, 2015). Many school personnel are not aware of their gender-biased attitudes. These attitudes are deeply entrenched in, and supported by, the general culture. Increasing awareness of gender bias in schools is clearly an important strategy in reducing such bias.

Might single-sex education be better for children than coed education? The argument for single-sex education is that it eliminates distraction from the other sex and reduces sexual harassment. Single-sex public education has increased dramatically in recent years. In 2002, only 12 public schools in the United States provided single-sex education; during the 2011–2012 school year, 116 public schools were single-sex and an additional 390 provided such experiences (NASSPE, 2012).

The increase in single-sex education has especially been fueled by its inclusion in the No Child Left Behind legislation as a means of improving the educational

What are some recent changes in single-sex education in the United States? What does research say about whether same-sex education is beneficial?
Jim Weber/ZUMAPRESS/Newscom

experiences and academic achievement of low-income students of color. It appears that many of the public schools offering single-sex education have a high percentage of such youth (Klein, 2012). However, three recent research reviews concluded that there have been no documented benefits of single-sex education, especially in the highest-quality studies (Goodkind, 2013; Halpern et al., 2011; Pahlke et al., 2014). One review, titled "The Pseudoscience of Single-Sex Schooling," by Diane Halpern and her colleagues (2011) concluded that single-sex education is highly misguided, misconstrued, and unsupported by any valid scientific evidence. They emphasize that among the many arguments against single-sex education, the strongest is its reduction of opportunities for boys and girls to work together in a supervised, purposeful environment. Other leading experts on gender also have recently argued that the factors that benefit students' education and development are more likely to be found in coeducational rather than single-sex schools (Bigler et al., 2014; Huston, 2015; Liben, 2015).

There has been a special call for single-sex public education for one group of adolescents—African American boys—because of their historically poor academic achievement and high dropout rate from school (Mitchell & Stewart, 2013). In 2010, Urban Prep Academy for Young Men became the first all-male, all African American public charter school. One hundred percent of its first graduates enrolled in college, despite the school's location in a section of Chicago where poverty, gangs, and crime predominate. Because so few public schools focus solely on educating African American boys, it is too early to tell whether this type of single-sex education can be effective across a wide range of participants (Barbarin et al., 2014).

Curriculum Content and Athletics Content Schools have made considerable progress in reducing sexism and sex stereotyping in books and curriculum materials, largely in response to Title IX of the Educational Amendment Act of 1972, which states that schools must treat females and males equally. As a result, today's textbooks and class materials are more gender-neutral. Also, schools now offer girls far more opportunities to take vocational educational courses and participate in athletics than was the case when their parents and grandparents went to school. In 1972, 7 percent of high school athletes were girls. In 2013, that figure had risen to 57 percent (Child Trends Data Bank, 2015). In 2013, the percentages of secondary school students participating in athletics were as follows: eighth grade: 66 percent males, 62 percent females; tenth grade: 65 percent males, 58 percent females; and twelfth grade:

66 percent males, 52 percent females. In addition, schools no longer can expel or deny services to pregnant adolescents.

Nonetheless, bias is still present at the curricular level. For example, school text adoptions occur infrequently, and therefore many students have continued to use outdated, gender-biased books.

How do teachers try to prevent gender bias in their classrooms? Following are their responses.

EARLY CHILDHOOD The books we have in the classroom showcase men and women in various roles—for example, some of our books have female doctors and male nurses. We also encourage boys to cook and girls to build. However, we often have concern from parents when their son expresses interest in playing with dolls or playing "dress up" with the girls. We had a parent workshop about these concerns in which we told parents that at this developmental stage, children are experimenting with roles and working out situations through play. This was a difficult workshop because although they listened, parents were not interested in breaking traditions.

—Valarie Gorham, *Kiddie Quarters, Inc.*

ELEMENTARY SCHOOL: GRADES K–5 To get my fifth-grade students to recognize gender bias, I do a short unit using old books I've collected over the years that are very gender biased. We talk about the historical aspect of these books and how roles have changed for both men and women. In addition to discussing how women's roles have changed, I also point out that men now have opportunities they didn't have in the past such as being nurses and early childhood education teachers.

—Craig Jensen, *Cooper Mountain Elementary School*

MIDDLE SCHOOL: GRADES 6–8 To prevent my sixth-grade students from sitting together by gender—that is, boys with boys and girls with girls—I have them sit in mixed, cooperative groups with each group consisting of two boys and two girls. Another strategy I use in class is to never randomly pick students to participate. Instead, I go down my class list so that everyone gets a chance or I choose students in a boy-girl order.

—Casey Maass, *Edison Middle School*

HIGH SCHOOL: GRADES 9–12 I love to do exactly the opposite of what is traditional in my class when it comes to gender. For example, I ask girls to help me move heavy books, or boys to help clean up a spill. Recently, I was telling my students how to address formal business letters, and we were talking about using "Miss," "Mr.,"

"Mrs.," or "Ms." I told them that I think it is silly that women are defined by marital status, whereas men are "Mr." regardless. Several students, boys and girls alike, had a faraway look that said, "I hadn't thought of that before." I may have planted a seed that will grow into their questioning the traditions that have very little merit in our modern world.

—Jennifer Heiter, *Bremen High School*

Sexual Harassment and Abuse Girls can encounter sexual harassment in many different forms—ranging from sexist remarks and covert physical contact (patting, brushing against bodies) to blatant propositions and sexual assaults. Literally millions of girls experience such sexual harassment each year in educational settings. A study of 12- to 18-year-old U.S. girls revealed that 90 percent of the girls reported having been sexually harassed at least once, with the likelihood increasing with age

(Leaper & Brown, 2008). Further, a recent national survey on adolescent relationships found the following percentages of adolescents who were involved in various types of relationship abuse (perpetration and victimization) (Taylor & Mumford, 2016):

- Psychological abuse: 65.5 percent said they had been the victims of psychological abuse (insulting behavior, excessive tracking, spreading rumors, for example) and 62 percent said they had perpetrated such abuse.
- Sexual abuse: 18 percent reported being the victims of sexual abuse and 12 percent said they had perpetrated such abuse.
- Physical abuse: 17.5 percent reported being the victims of physical abuse and 11.9 percent said they had perpetrated such abuse.

Overall, the majority of 12-18 year olds in Taylor and Mumford's (2016) sample reported experiencing some form of adolescent relationship abuse (ARA) with a significant other, either as a victim, a perpetrator, or both. They found that ARA victimization rates (69%) did not differ across boys and girls. In all but one case (girls were more likely to perpetrate physical abuse), rates of perpetration did not vary by gender either. Rates tended to vary by age rather than gender. Among 12-14 year olds, more boys than girls reported being victims of moderate threats or physical violence, while the opposite trend was found in 15-18 year olds. Younger adolescents also were less likely to be victims of sexual abuse.

The U.S. Office for Civil Rights (2016) publishes a guide on sexual harassment. In this guide, a distinction is made between quid pro quo and hostile environment sexual harassment:

- **Quid pro quo sexual harassment** occurs when a school employee threatens to base an educational decision (such as a grade) on a student's submission to unwelcome sexual conduct. For example, a teacher gives a student an *A* for allowing the teacher's sexual advances, or the teacher gives the student an *F* for resisting the teacher's approaches.
- **Hostile environment sexual harassment** occurs when students are subjected to unwelcome sexual conduct that is so severe, persistent, or pervasive that it limits the students' ability to benefit from their education. Such a hostile environment is usually created by a series of incidents, such as repeated sexual overtures.

Quid pro quo and hostile environment sexual harassment are illegal in educational settings, but potential victims are often not given access to a clear reporting and investigation mechanism where they can make a complaint.

Sexual harassment is a form of power and dominance of one person over another, which can result in harmful consequences for the victim. Sexual harassment can be especially damaging when the perpetrators are teachers who have considerable power and authority over students.

quid pro quo sexual harassment Occurs when a school employee threatens to base an educational decision (such as a grade) on a student's submission to unwelcome sexual conduct.

hostile environment sexual harassment Occurs when students are subjected to unwelcome sexual conduct that is so severe, persistent, or pervasive that it limits the students' ability to benefit from their education.

Review, Reflect, and Practice

❸ Explain various facets of gender, including similarities and differences in boys and girls; discuss gender issues in teaching.

REVIEW
- What is gender, and what do the concepts of gender roles and gender-typing mean? How have psychologists attempted to explain gender from biological, social, and cognitive perspectives?
- What are gender stereotypes? What problems are created by gender stereotypes? How are boys and girls similar and different?
- What characterizes gender-role classification?

Review, Reflect, and Practice

- How might looking at behaviors in context reduce gender stereotyping?
- What evidence is there of gender bias in the classroom? What progress have schools made in reducing bias?

REFLECT
- From your own K–12 education, come up with at least one instance in which your school or teacher favored either boys or girls. As a teacher, how would you try to correct that gender bias?

PRAXIS™ PRACTICE

1. In Jack's family, the person who does the cooking does not do the dishes. Since Jack's mother generally cooks, his father generally does the dishes. One day in the "housekeeping" area of his kindergarten class, Jack was pretending to be the father of the family. His "wife" Emily pretended to cook dinner on the toy stove. After the family ate, Emily started to pretend to wash the dishes. Jack gasped and protested, "Hey, I'm the dad!"

   This example best supports which perspective of gender development?
   a. biological
   b. gender schema
   c. gender socialization
   d. psychoanalytic

2. Which teacher's opinion about gender differences is best supported by current research?
   a. Mr. Kain, who believes that girls are more talkative than boys
   b. Ms. Nash, who believes that boys are better at math than girls
   c. Ms. Kim, who believes that boys are more physically aggressive than girls
   d. Ms. Walter, who believes that boys are generally fairer and more law-abiding than girls

3. Which student would best be described as androgynous?
   a. Alex, who is sensitive to others' feelings, shares secrets with friends, and provides social support to others
   b. Chris, who is independent, competitive, patient, self-reflective, and provides social support to others
   c. Pat, who is kind, sensitive, self-reflective, and likes to tell secrets to friends
   d. Terry, who is independent, competitive, self-confident, aggressive, and willing to take risks

4. A male is most likely to display helping behavior in which situation?
   a. A friend's car battery has died and needs a jump.
   b. A small child needs help writing a poem for language arts class.
   c. A family member is ill and needs someone to provide care.
   d. A friend needs advice about a personal problem.

5. Ms. Vandt teaches fifth grade. Her class is composed of approximately equal numbers of boys and girls. She often wonders why the boys can't behave more like the girls. The girls sit quietly, follow rules, and work well together. The boys have problems sitting still. They are rowdy and loud. Ms. Vandt tries to treat all of her students the same, but she often needs to reprimand the boys. What should she do?
   a. Allow the children time and space to move around and blow off steam. This will help the boys to attend better in class and the girls to socialize.
   b. Continue to reprimand the boys when they behave inappropriately. They will learn to sit quietly and be compliant.
   c. Divide the children into gender-specific groups so that the boys don't interfere with the girls' work.
   d. Point out the girls' compliant behavior as a model for the boys, so that they will understand what is expected of them.

Please see answer key at end of book . . . .

Connecting with the Classroom: Crack the Case

These Boys

Imagine that Larry is a 9-year-old boy in the fourth-grade class in which you are student teaching. You have heard him and a number of other students complaining about gender bias on the part of their teacher, Mrs. Jones. One day you overhear Larry being reprimanded by Mrs. Jones for an altercation he had with Annie, a female classmate.

"It isn't fair, Mrs. Jones," Larry says. "Annie took my homework and ripped it, and I get in trouble for taking it back."

"Now, Larry," admonishes Mrs. Jones. "You know Annie would never do that. You go apologize to her. I'll see you after school."

Larry walks away with a very angry look on his face, muttering, "The girls *never* get in trouble. It's always the boys."

You have heard this from students of Mrs. Jones in the past but have never really believed it. Over the course of the next three weeks you pay much closer attention to Mrs. Jones' behavior with a special sensitivity to gender bias. You notice that girls receive higher grades than do boys, except in math. Boys are required to stay after school several times, girls not at all. When Mrs. Jones is on recess duty and there are altercations between boys and girls on the playground, the boys end up standing against the wall, while the girls walk away, smiling. In class, the girls are used as models of behaviors much more frequently than the boys. Their work receives more praise as well. You examine what students have been reading over the course of the year. Their required reading thus far consists of *Little House on the Prairie*, *Charlotte's Web*, and *Little Women*.

The only thing you notice that appears to favor the boys is that they receive more of Mrs. Jones' attention. On further examination, however, you see that much of the attention is disciplinary in nature.

At one point, you overhear Mrs. Jones as she is walking down the hall, saying to a colleague, "These boys, I just don't know what I am going to do with them."

1. What are the issues in this case?
2. Based on the ideas and information presented in your text to this point, discuss what you believe to be happening in this classroom and the possible influences on Mrs. Jones' ideas of gender. Cite research and theories of gender development.
3. What influence do you believe Mrs. Jones's behavior will have on her students? Why?
4. What should Mrs. Jones do at this point? Why? What sort of outside assistance might help her?
5. If you were a student teacher in this classroom, what, if anything, would you do? Why?
6. What will you do in your own classroom to minimize gender bias?

Connecting with Learning: Reach Your Learning Goals

1 CULTURE AND ETHNICITY: Discuss how variations in culture, socioeconomic status, and ethnic background need to be taken into account in educating children.

Culture
- Culture refers to the behavior patterns, beliefs, and all other products of a particular group of people that are passed on from generation to generation. The products result from the interaction among groups of people and their environment over many years.
- Cultures have been classified as individualistic (having a set of values that give priority to personal goals rather than group goals) and collectivistic (having a set of values that support the group). Many Western cultures are individualistic, many Eastern cultures collectivistic.
- U.S. adolescents spend less time in school and doing homework, more time in paid work, and have more discretionary time than their counterparts in Europe and East Asia. Concern has been expressed about what U.S. adolescents do with all of the discretionary time many of them have.

Socioeconomic Status
- Socioeconomic status (SES) is the categorization of people according to economic, educational, and occupational characteristics. The most emphasis is given to distinctions between

Ethnicity

- individuals with low and middle socioeconomic status. Low-SES individuals usually have less education, less power to influence schools and other community institutions, and fewer economic resources than higher-SES individuals.
- Currently more than 21 percent of America's children under the age of 18 live in poverty. Children in poverty face problems at home and at school that present barriers to their learning. Schools in low-income neighborhoods often have fewer resources and less-experienced teachers, and they are more likely to encourage rote learning rather than activities that expand their thinking skills.

- The school population increasingly consists of children of color. School segregation is still a factor in the education of children of color. African American and Latinx students are less likely than non-Latinx White and Asian American students to be enrolled in college preparatory courses.
- Historical, economic, and social experiences produce legitimate differences among ethnic groups, and it is important to recognize these differences. However, too often the differences are viewed as deficits on the part of the minority group when compared with the mainstream non-Latinx White group. It is important to recognize the extensive diversity that exists within each cultural group.

Second-Language Learning and Bilingual Education

- Researchers have found that learning two languages simultaneously as an infant or young child has cognitive benefits. Success in learning a second language is greater in childhood than in adolescence.
- The term *dual-language education* is used to describe programs and classes for students whose native language is not English. Dual-language education programs vary in terms of whether English-language learners (ELL) are taught primarily in English or with a combination of English and their native language. Becoming proficient in English for ELL students is usually a very lengthy process.

2 MULTICULTURAL EDUCATION: Describe some ways to promote multicultural education.

Empowering Students

- Multicultural education values diversity and includes the perspectives of a variety of cultural groups on a regular basis.
- Empowerment, which consists of providing people with the intellectual and coping skills to succeed and make this a more just world, is an important aspect of multicultural education today. It involves giving students the opportunity to learn about the experiences, struggles, and visions of many different ethnic and cultural groups. The hope is that empowerment will raise minority students' self-esteem, reduce prejudice, and provide more-equal educational opportunities.

Culturally Relevant Teaching

- Culturally relevant teaching is an important aspect of multicultural education. It seeks to make connections with the learner's cultural background.

Issues-Centered Education

- Issues-centered education also is an important aspect of multicultural education. In this approach, students are taught to systematically examine issues that involve equity and social justice.

Improving Relationships Among Children from Different Ethnic Groups

- Among the strategies/related ideas for improving relationships between children from different ethnic groups are the jigsaw classroom (having students from different cultural backgrounds cooperate by doing different parts of a project to reach a common goal), positive personal contact, perspective taking, reduced bias, increased tolerance, and development of the school and community as a team.

continued

3 GENDER: Explain various facets of gender, including similarities and differences in boys and girls; discuss gender issues in teaching.

Exploring Gender Views
- Gender refers to the characteristics of people as males and females. Among the components of gender are gender roles and gender typing.
- Biological, social, and cognitive views of gender have been proposed. Some views stress biological factors; other views emphasize social or cognitive factors. The most widely accepted cognitive view today is gender schema theory.

Gender Stereotyping, Similarities, and Differences
- Gender stereotypes are broad categories that reflect impressions and beliefs about what behavior is appropriate for females and males. All stereotypes involve an image of what the typical member of a category is like. Some gender stereotypes can be harmful for children.
- Psychologists have studied gender similarities and differences in physical performance, the brain, math and science skills, verbal skills, school attainment, relationship skills, aggression/self-regulation, and prosocial behavior.

Gender Controversy
- Gender differences in some areas are substantial (physical performance, reading and writing skills, school attainment, physical aggression, and prosocial behavior); in others they are small or nonexistent (intelligence, as well as math and science ability in elementary and secondary school). Controversy swirls about the magnitude and causes of such similarities and differences. Some psychologists trace gender differences to adaptive problems faced across evolutionary history, while others point to social conditions that have caused women to have less power than men. Still others argue that differences between females and males have been greatly exaggerated.

Gender-Role Classification
- Gender-role classification focuses on how masculine, feminine, or androgynous an individual is. In the past, competent males were supposed to be masculine (powerful, for example), females feminine (nurturant, for example). The 1970s brought the concept of androgyny, the idea that the most competent individuals have both masculine and feminine positive characteristics. A special concern involves adolescents who adopt a strong masculine role.

Gender in Context
- Evaluation of gender-role categories and gender similarities and differences in areas such as helping behavior and emotion suggest that the best way to think about gender is not in terms of personality traits but instead in terms of person-situation interaction (gender in context).
- Although androgyny and multiple gender roles are often available for American children to choose from, many countries around the world still are male-dominant.

Eliminating Gender Bias
- There is gender bias in schools against boys and girls. Many school personnel are unaware of these biases. An important teaching strategy is to attempt to eliminate gender bias.
- Schools have made considerable progress in reducing sexism and sex stereotyping in books and curriculum materials, but some bias still exists.
- Sexual harassment is a special concern in schools and is more pervasive than was once believed. Recently, a distinction has been made between quid pro quo sexual harassment and hostile environment sexual harassment.

KEY TERMS

androgyny 173
collectivism 146
cross-cultural studies 146
culture 146
empowerment 160
ethnicity 151
gender 168
gender role 168
gender schema theory 168
gender stereotypes 169
gender typing 168
hostile environment sexual harassment 178
individualism 146
jigsaw classroom 162
multicultural education 158
prejudice 153
quid pro quo sexual harassment 178
socioeconomic status (SES) 147

PORTFOLIO ACTIVITIES

Now that you have a good understanding of this chapter, complete these exercises to expand your thinking.

Independent Reflection

1. **Fostering Cultural Understanding in the Classroom.** Imagine that you are teaching a social studies lesson about the westward movement in U.S. history and a student makes a racist, stereotyped statement about Native Americans, such as "The Indians were hot-tempered and showed their hostility toward the White settlers." How would you handle this situation? (Banks, 1997). Describe the strategy you would adopt. (INTASC: Principles *1, 4, 5, 7, 8*)

Research/Field Experience

2. **Equity in Action.** Observe lessons being taught in several classrooms that include boys and girls and students from different ethnic groups. Did the teachers interact with females and males differently? If so, how? Did the teachers interact with students from different ethnic groups in different ways? If so, how? Describe your observations. (INTASC: Principles *2, 9*)

Collaborative Work

3. **Planning for Diversity.** With three or four other students in the class, come up with a list of specific diversity goals for your future classrooms. Also brainstorm and come up with some innovative activities to help students gain positive diversity experiences, such as the inclusive map discussed in this chapter. Summarize the diversity goals and activities. (INTASC: Principles *2, 3, 5, 8*)

chapter 6

LEARNERS WHO ARE EXCEPTIONAL

chapter outline

① Children with Disabilities

Learning Goal 1 Describe the various types of disabilities and disorders.

Learning Disabilities
Attention Deficit Hyperactivity Disorder
Intellectual Disability
Physical Disorders
Sensory Disorders
Speech and Language Disorders
Autism Spectrum Disorders
Emotional and Behavioral Disorders

② Educational Issues Involving Children with Disabilities

Learning Goal 2 Explain the legal framework and technology advances for children with disabilities.

Legal Aspects
Technology

③ Children Who Are Gifted

Learning Goal 3 Define what gifted means and discuss some approaches to teaching children who are gifted.

Characteristics
Nature/Nurture and Domain-Specific Giftedness
Educating Children Who Are Gifted

Only the educated are free.
—Epicurus.
Greek Philosopher, 4th Century B.C.

Faithhoca/Getty Images

Connecting with Teachers Verna Rollins Hayes

Verna Rollins Hayes taught language arts in the Ypsilanti Community School system in Ypsilanti, Michigan, and developed a reputation for working successfully with so-called hard to teach or difficult students. She found that the best strategy to use with these students was to find out what they need, decide how to provide it, provide it, and constantly evaluate whether it is working. A challenge for many regular education classroom teachers is how to effectively teach children with disabilities. In many instances, the education of children with disabilities in the regular education classroom is carried out in coordination with a special education teacher or staff. Here is Verna Rollins Hayes description of her contribution in the coordinated effort to teach a student with a severe disability:

> Jack was in a special education classroom for children with physical disabilities. He has twisted legs, cerebral palsy, seizures, and some other brain damage from birth. He also has a comparatively short attention span. Since he drools, speaks in a loud monotone, stutters when he is excited, and has so little motor control that his penmanship is unreadable, people often think he has an intellectual disability.
>
> My strategies included making sure that he had all the equipment he needed to succeed. I gave him tissues for the drooling and mutually agreed-upon reminders to wipe his mouth. I found that he could speak softly and without stuttering if he calmed down. We developed a signaling plan in which I would clear my throat when he talked too loudly and I would prompt him with the phrase "slow speech" when he was too excited to speak in a smooth voice.
>
> He used a computer to take quizzes and needed a little more time to complete any task, but he was so excited about being "out in the real world" that his attention span improved, as did his self-worth. In fact, his mother wrote a letter to me expressing her gratitude for the "most positive influence you have been on him! You have re-instilled and greatly increased his love of reading and writing. You have given my child a wonderful gift."

Zuma Press Inc/Alamy Stock Photo

Preview

Verna Rollins Hayes was challenged to find the best way to teach a child with multiple disabilities in her classroom and to coordinate this teaching with Jack's special education teacher. Like Verna Rollins Hayes, you will likely work with children who are differently-abled if you teach in a regular classroom. In the past, public schools did little to educate these children. Today, however, children with disabilities must have a free, appropriate education—and increasingly they are educated in regular classrooms. In this chapter, we will study children with many different types of disabilities, as well as another group of children who are exceptional—those who are gifted.

LG 1 Describe the various types of disabilities and disorders.

Of all children in the United States, 12.9 percent from 3 to 21 years of age received special education or related services in 2012-2013, an increase of 3 percent since 1980-1981 (Condition of Education, 2015). Figure 1 shows the five largest groups of students with a disability who were served by federal programs during the 2012-2013 school year (National Center for Education Statistics, 2016).

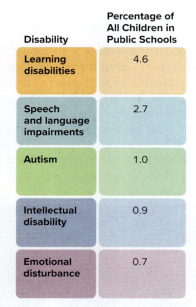

FIGURE 1 U.S. CHILDREN WITH A DISABILITY WHO RECEIVE SPECIAL EDUCATION SERVICES

Figures are for the 2012–2013 school year and represent the five categories with the highest numbers and percentages of children. Both learning disability and attention deficit hyperactivity disorder are combined in the learning disabilities category.

Source: "The Conditions of Education 2017," by National Center for Education Statistics, 2017, *The Condition of Education 2017*, U.S. Office of Education.

learning disability Difficulty in learning that involves understanding or using spoken or written language; the difficulty can appear in listening, thinking, reading, writing, and spelling. A learning disability also may involve difficulty in doing mathematics. To be classified as a learning disability, the learning problem is not primarily the result of visual, hearing, or motor disabilities; intellectual disability; emotional disorders; or due to environmental, cultural, or economic disadvantage.

Educators increasingly speak of "children with disabilities" or "children who are differently-abled" rather than "disabled children" to emphasize the person, not the disability. Also, children with disabilities are no longer referred to as "handicapped," although the term *handicapping conditions* is still used to describe the impediments to the learning and functioning of individuals with a disability that have been imposed by society. For example, when children who use a wheelchair do not have adequate access to a bathroom, transportation, and so on, this is referred to as a handicapping condition.

LEARNING DISABILITIES

Bobby's second-grade teacher complains that his spelling is awful. Eight-year-old Tim says reading is really hard for him, and a lot of times the words don't make much sense. Alisha has good oral language skills but has considerable difficulty in computing correct answers to arithmetic problems. Each of these students has a learning disability.

Characteristics and Identification The U.S. government created a definition of learning disabilities in 1997 and then reauthorized the definition with a few minor changes in 2004. Following is a description of the government's definition of what determined whether a child should be classified as having a learning disability. A child with a **learning disability** has difficulty in learning that involves understanding or using spoken or written language, and the difficulty can appear in listening, thinking, reading, writing, and spelling. A learning disability also may involve difficulty in doing mathematics. To be classified as a learning disability, the learning problem is not primarily the result of visual, hearing, or motor disabilities; intellectual disability; emotional disorders; or due to environmental, cultural, or economic disadvantage.

From the mid-1970s through the early 1990s, there was a dramatic increase in the percentage of U.S. students receiving special education services (from 1.8 percent in 1976–1977 to 12.2 percent in 1994–1995) (National Center for Education Statistics, 2008). Some experts say that the dramatic increase reflected poor diagnostic practices and overidentification. They argue that teachers sometimes are too quick to label children with the slightest learning problem as having a learning disability, instead of recognizing that the problem may rest in their ineffective teaching. Other experts say the increase in the number of children being labeled with a "learning disability" is justified (Hallahan et al., 2015).

About three times as many boys as girls are classified as having a learning disability. Among the explanations for this gender difference are a greater biological vulnerability among boys and *referral bias* (that is, boys are more likely to be referred by teachers for treatment because of their behavior).

Most learning disabilities are lifelong. Compared with children who do not have a learning disability, children with a learning disability are more likely to show poor academic performance, high dropout rates, and poor employment and postsecondary education records (Berninger, 2006). Children with a learning disability who are taught in the regular classroom without extensive support rarely achieve the level of competence of children without a disability, even those who are low achieving (Hocutt, 1996). Still, despite the problems they encounter, many children with a learning disability grow up to lead normal lives and engage in productive work (Heward, Alber et al., 2017).

Diagnosing whether a child has a learning disability is often a difficult task (Smith et al., 2016). Because federal guidelines are just that—guidelines—it is up to each state, or in some cases school systems within a state, to determine how to define and implement diagnosis of learning disabilities. The same child might be diagnosed as having a learning disability in one school system and receive services but not be diagnosed and not receive services in another school system. In such cases, parents sometimes will move to a different school district to either obtain or avoid the diagnosis.

Initial identification of a possible learning disability usually is made by the classroom teacher. If a learning disability is suspected, the teacher calls on specialists. An interdisciplinary team of professionals is best suited to verify whether a student has a learning disability. Individual psychological evaluations (of intelligence) and educational assessments (such as current level of achievement) are required (Hallahan et al., 2015). In addition, tests of visual-motor skills, language, and memory may be used.

It is important to note that the reauthorization of IDEA also included some new recommendations as to how students are identified as having learning disabilities. The Response to Intervention (RTI) process as introduced as a way to help reduce over-identification of learning disabilities by making sure that quality instruction and interventions have first been applied. RTI also "can provide (1) data for more effective and earlier identification of students with LD and (2) a systematic way to ensure that students experiencing educational difficulties receive more timely and effective support" (National Joint Committee on Learning Disabilities, 2005, p. 249). Additionally, RTI was recommended as a way to identify those with learning disabilities (to replace the discrepancy model for identification), though this part of the recommendation is implemented less often, with many schools still using the identification processes described previously in this chapter.

RTI is a tiered system implemented in districts and schools across the United States, but with a wide range of fidelity. In Tier 1, evidenced-based practices for general classroom instruction are implemented to prevent failure of about 80% of students. At Tier 2, about 15% of students, who lag behind peers while receiving the general classroom instruction, receive more frequent progress monitoring and intensive, individualized interventions (sometimes in small groups) to help them make gains. Students who fail to make gains in Tier 2 (about 5% of students) will receive more intensive, systematic, specialized intervention, which can include special education services. A learning disability would be identified using the RTI model if a student, receiving quality instruction and remedial services, is still unable to make satisfactory progress. (See this user-friendly Special Education Guide for more information: https://www.specialeducationguide.com/pre-k-12/response-to-intervention/.)

Reading, Writing, and Math Difficulties   The most common academic areas in which children with a learning disability have problems are reading, writing, and math.

Dyslexia   Among children with a learning disability, 80 percent have trouble with reading. Such children have difficulty with phonological skills, which involve being able to understand how sounds and letters match up to make words, and also can have problems in comprehension. **Dyslexia** is a category reserved for individuals with a severe impairment in their ability to read and spell (Hulme & Snowling, 2015; Thompson et al., 2015).

Dysgraphia   **Dysgraphia** is a learning disability that involves difficulty in handwriting (Berninger et al., 2015; Dohla & Heim, 2016). Children with dysgraphia may write very slowly, their writing products may be virtually illegible, and they may make numerous spelling errors because of their inability to match up sounds and letters (Berninger et al., 2015). One study revealed that boys were more impaired in handwriting than were girls (Berninger et al., 2008).

Dyscalculia   **Dyscalculia**, also known as developmental arithmetic disorder, is a learning disability that involves difficulty in math computation (Kucian & von Aster, 2015; Rapin, 2016). It is estimated to characterize 2 to 6 percent of U.S. elementary school children (National Center for Learning Disabilities, 2006). Researchers have found that children with difficulties in math computation often have cognitive and neuropsychological deficits, including poor performance in working memory, visual perception, and visuospatial abilities (Mammarella et al., 2015). A child may have

> **Thinking Back/Thinking Forward**
>
> An increasing number of experts conclude that direct instruction in phonological training is a key aspect of learning to read. Connect to "Learning and Cognition in the Content Areas."

RESEARCH

dyslexia A severe impairment in the ability to read and spell.

dysgraphia A learning disability that involves difficulty in handwriting.

dyscalculia Also known as developmental arithmetic disorder, this learning disability involves difficulty in math computation.

RESEARCH

both a reading and a math disability, and there are cognitive deficits that characterize both types of disabilities, such as poor working memory (Siegel, 2003).

Causes and Intervention Strategies The precise causes of learning disabilities have not yet been determined. However, some possible causes have been proposed. Learning disabilities tend to occur in families where one parent has a disability such as dyslexia or dyscalculia, although the specific genetic transmission of learning disabilities is not known. Also, some learning disabilities are likely caused by problems during prenatal development or delivery. For example, researchers have found that learning disabilities are more prevalent in children who were low birth weight and preterm infants (Jarjour, 2015).

Researchers also use brain-imaging techniques, such as magnetic resonance imaging (MRI), to reveal any regions of the brain that might be involved in learning disabilities (Shaywitz et al., 2008) (see Figure 2). This research indicates that it is unlikely learning disabilities reside in a single, specific brain location. More likely, learning disabilities are due to problems with integrating information from multiple brain regions or subtle difficulties in brain structures and functions (National Institutes of Health, 1993).

Interventions with children who have a learning disability often focus on improving reading ability (Bursuck & Damer, 2015; Reid et al., 2009). Intensive instruction over a period of time by a competent teacher can help many children (Del Campo et al., 2015). Improvement in children's reading skills and changes in brain regions involved in reading often require early intervention and/or intensive instruction in reading (Lyytinen et al., 2015).

Some teachers were recently asked how they work with students with a learning disability. Following are their responses.

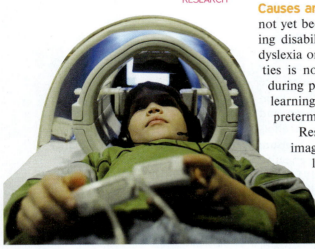

FIGURE 2 BRAIN SCANS AND LEARNING DISABILITIES
An increasing number of studies are using MRI brain scans to examine the brain pathways involved in learning disabilities. Shown here is 9-year-old Patrick Price, who has dyslexia. Patrick is going through an MRI scanner disguised by drapes to look like a child-friendly castle. Inside the scanner, children must lie virtually motionless as words and symbols flash on a screen and they are asked to identify them by clicking different buttons.
Manuel Balce Ceneta/AP Images

RESEARCH

EARLY CHILDHOOD To accommodate our children with learning disabilities, we have them sit close to teachers during work time at craft tables, use more transition warnings so all students clearly know when we are moving to a different activity, and prepare lessons that are visual and hands-on. Having children of different abilities in our school not only benefits the learning of children with disabilities, but it immensely helps their "typically" developing peers to accept others who are not like them.

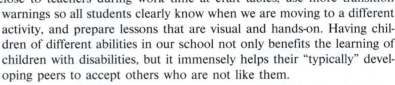

—Valarie Gorham, *Kiddie Quarters, Inc.*

ELEMENTARY SCHOOL: GRADES K–5 Learning disabilities come in all shapes and sizes and require adaptations to ensure that all students reach their full potential. An adaptation that helps a student with ADHD is not an adaptation that will help a student with dyslexia. Some of the adaptations and modifications I use in my class are visuals, modeling, graphic organizers, and mnemonic devices. Many students with learning disabilities have trouble learning information through one sense. Therefore, the more senses you engage while teaching, the more likely the children will learn.

—Shane Schwarz, *Clinton Elementary School*

MIDDLE SCHOOL: GRADES 6–8 When working with students with learning disabilities, I offer assistance with organization (by providing a notebook with color-coded individual folders for each subject); provide a structured classroom setting with high expectations; have private, open discussions concerning specific disabilities with the student; maintain a consistent classroom routine and schedule (students with learning challenges often have difficulty with change); and provide a daily overview of the day.

—Felicia Peterson, *Pocantico Hills School*

HIGH SCHOOL: GRADES 9-12 With high school students, I find it extremely effective to pair the student with a learning disability with a concerned, helpful peer. Sometimes it is necessary to let the peer know what to expect or how to help the other student. However, there is a fine line to walk as you do not want other students to be aware of the student's disability. I also find that books on tape help students with a learning disability master information, as does providing extra time to complete tests and quizzes.

—SANDY SWANSON, *Menomonee Falls High School*

ATTENTION DEFICIT HYPERACTIVITY DISORDER

Matthew has attention deficit hyperactivity disorder, and the outward signs are fairly typical. He has trouble attending to the teacher's instructions and is easily distracted. He can't sit still for more than a few minutes at a time, and his handwriting is messy. His mother describes him as very fidgety.

Characteristics **Attention deficit hyperactivity disorder (ADHD)** is a disability in which children consistently show one or more of these characteristics over a period of time: (1) inattention, (2) hyperactivity, and (3) impulsivity. For an ADHD diagnosis, onset of these characteristics early in childhood is required, and the characteristics must be debilitating for the child.

Inattentive children have difficulty focusing on any one thing and may get bored with a task after only a few minutes. One study found that problems in sustaining attention were the most common type of attentional problem in children with ADHD (Tsal et al., 2005). Hyperactive children show high levels of physical activity, almost always seeming to be in motion. Impulsive children have difficulty curbing their reactions and don't do a good job of thinking before they act. Depending on the characteristics that children with ADHD display, they can be diagnosed as (1) ADHD with predominantly inattention, (2) ADHD with predominantly hyperactivity/impulsivity, or (3) ADHD with both inattention and hyperactivity/impulsivity.

> **Thinking Back/Thinking Forward**
>
> Sustained attention is the ability to maintain attention over a period of time. Sustained attention is a very important aspect of cognitive development. Connect to "The Information-Processing Approach."

DEVELOPMENT

Diagnosis and Developmental Status The number of children diagnosed and treated for ADHD has increased substantially, by some estimates doubling in the 1990s. The American Psychiatric Association (2013) reported in the DSM-V Manual that 5 percent of children have ADHD, although estimates are higher in community samples. For example, the Centers for Disease Control and Prevention (2016) estimates that ADHD has continued to increase in 4- to 17-year-old children, going from 8 percent in 2003 to 9.5 percent in 2007 and to 11 percent in 2016. According to the Centers for Disease Control and Prevention, 13.2 percent of U.S. boys and 5.6 of U.S. girls have ever been diagnosed with ADHD.

There is controversy about the increased diagnosis of ADHD, however (Lewis et al., 2017; Turnbull et al., 2016). Some experts attribute the increase mainly to heightened awareness of the disorder. Others are concerned that many children are being diagnosed without undergoing extensive professional evaluation based on input from multiple sources.

Unlike learning disabilities, ADHD is not supposed to be diagnosed by school teams because ADHD is a disorder that appears in the classification of psychiatric disorders (called DSM-V) with specific diagnostic criteria. Although some school teams may diagnose a child as having ADHD, this is incorrectly done and can lead to legal problems for schools and teachers. One reason that is given as to why a school team should not do the diagnosis for ADHD is that ADHD is difficult to differentiate from other childhood disorders, and accurate diagnosis requires evaluation by a specialist in the disorder, such as a child psychiatrist.

attention deficit hyperactivity disorder (ADHD) A disability in which children consistently show one or more of the following characteristics over a period of time: (1) inattention, (2) hyperactivity, and (3) impulsivity.

CONNECTING WITH STUDENTS: Best Practices
Strategies for Working with Children Who Have Learning Disabilities

1. *Take the needs of the child with a learning disability into account during instructional time.* Clearly state the objective of each lesson. Present it visually on the board or with an overhead projector as well. Be sure directions are explicit. Explain them orally. Use concrete examples to illustrate abstract concepts.

2. *Provide accommodations for testing and assignments.* This refers to changing the academic environment so that these children can demonstrate what they know. An accommodation usually does not involve altering the amount of learning the child has to demonstrate. Common accommodations include reading instructions aloud to children, highlighting important words (such as *underline,* or *answer two of the three questions*), using/giving untimed tests, and providing extra time on assignments.

3. *Make modifications.* This strategy changes the work itself, making it different from other children's work in an effort to encourage children's confidence and success. Asking a child with dyslexia to give an oral report while other children give written reports is an example of a modification.

4. *Improve organizational and study skills.* Many children with learning disabilities do not have good organizational skills. Teachers and parents can encourage them to keep long-term and short-term calendars and create "to-do" lists each day. Projects should be broken down into their elements, with steps and due dates for each part.

5. *Work with reading and writing skills.* As indicated earlier, the most common type of learning disability involves reading problems. Children with a reading problem often read slowly, so give them more advance notice of outside reading assignments and more time for in-class reading. Many children with a learning disability that involves writing deficits find that using a computer helps them compose their writing projects more quickly and competently, so make sure to provide them the opportunity to use a computer for their assignments. In *Through the Eyes of Teachers,* you can read about the unique strategy a second-grade teacher created for working with children who have a learning disability.

Kathryn Cantrell, Courtesy of Nancy Downing

phonics, sign language, and lively jingles to make learning fun for students. She developed the character Uey Long (a "uey" is the sign over a short vowel) to demonstrate vowel rules.

6. *Challenge children with a learning disability to become independent and reach their full potential.* It is important not only to provide support and services for children with a learning disability but also to guide them toward becoming responsible and independent. Teachers need to challenge children with a learning disability to become all they can be. We will have more to say about the importance of challenging children with disabilities to reach their potential later in this chapter.

7. *Become familiar with applications for mobile devices that offer strategies for children with a learning disability, and recommend these to the children's parents.* These include:

   - https://www.specialeducationguide.com/pre-k-12/tools-and-research/7-apps-to-use-as-assistive-technology/. This site lists seven assistive applications that can be used with mobile devices.

   - www.readingrockets.org/article/assistive-technology-kids-learning-disabilities-overview. Parents of students with a learning disability can use this site to find applications related to their child's disability.

THROUGH THE EYES OF TEACHERS
Creating a Character Named Uey Long

Nancy Downing, a teacher at Don R. Roberts Elementary School in Little Rock, Arkansas, takes a multisensory approach to education, which she developed while working with her own child, who has learning difficulties. She created Downfeld Phonics using

The seven teaching strategies we have described are not meant to give children with a learning disability an unfair advantage over other students, just to provide them with an equal chance to learn. Balancing the needs of children with learning disabilities and the needs of other students is a challenging task.

TECHNOLOGY

Although signs of ADHD are often present in the preschool years, children with ADHD are not usually classified until the elementary school years. The increased academic and social demands of formal schooling, as well as stricter standards for behavioral control, often illuminate the problems of the child with ADHD. Elementary school teachers typically report that this type of child has difficulty in working independently, completing seat work, and organizing work. Restlessness and distractibility also are often noted. These problems are more likely to be observed when doing repetitive or difficult tasks, or tasks the child perceives to be boring (such as completing worksheets or doing homework).

It used to be thought that children with ADHD improved during adolescence, but now it appears this often is not the case. Estimates suggest symptoms of ADHD decrease in only about one-third of adolescents. Increasingly, it is being recognized that these problems may continue into adulthood (Fritz & O'Connor, 2016; Marshall et al., 2016).

Causes and Treatment Definitive causes of ADHD have not been found. However, a number of causes have been proposed (Turnbull et al., 2016). Some children likely inherit a tendency to develop ADHD from their parents (Gallo & Posner, 2016). Other children likely develop ADHD because of damage to their brain during prenatal or postnatal development (Chiang et al., 2015). Among early possible contributors to ADHD are cigarette and alcohol exposure, as well as a high level of maternal stress during prenatal development and low birth weight (Obel et al., 2016; Say et al., 2016).

As with learning disabilities, the development of brain-imaging techniques is leading to a better understanding of the brain's role in ADHD (Berger et al., 2015; Wolfers et al., 2016). One study revealed that peak thickness of the cerebral cortex occurred three years later (10.5 years) in children with ADHD than in children without ADHD (peak at 7.5 years) (Shaw et al., 2007). The delay was more prominent in the prefrontal regions of the brain that especially are important in attention and planning (see Figure 3). Researchers also are exploring the roles that various neurotransmitters, such as serotonin and dopamine, might play in ADHD (Zhong et al., 2016). A recent study found that the dopamine transporter gene DAT 1 was involved in decreased cortical thickness in the prefrontal cortex of children with ADHD (Fernandez-Jaen et al., 2015).

Many children with ADHD show impulsive behavior, such as this child who is throwing a paper airplane at other children. *How would you handle this situation if you were a teacher and this were to happen in your classroom?*
Jupiterimages/Photos.com/Getty Images

The delays in brain development just described are in areas linked to executive function. An increasing focus of interest in the study of children with ADHD is their difficulty performing tasks involving executive function, such as behavioral inhibition when necessary, use of working memory, and effective planning (Craig et al., 2016; Dovis et al., 2015). Researchers also have found deficits in theory of mind in children with ADHD (Mary et al., 2016).

Stimulant medication such as Ritalin or Adderall (which has fewer side effects than Ritalin) is effective in improving the attention of many children with ADHD, but it usually does not improve their attention to the same level as children who do not have ADHD (Brams et al., 2009). Researchers have often found that combining medication (such as Ritalin) with behavior management improves the behavior of children with ADHD better than medication alone or behavior

DEVELOPMENT

RESEARCH

RESEARCH

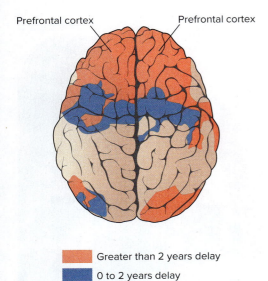

FIGURE 3 DEVELOPMENT OF THE BRAIN IN CHILDREN WITH ADHD SHOWS A DELAYED PEAK IN THICKNESS OF THE CEREBRAL CORTEX

Note: The greatest delays occurred in the prefrontal cortex.

management alone, although not in all cases (Centers for Disease Control and Prevention, 2016).

Teachers play an important role in monitoring whether ADHD medication has been prescribed at the right dosage level. For example, it is not unusual for a student on ADHD medication to complete academic tasks in the morning, but in the afternoon, when the dosage has worn off, to be inattentive or hyperactive.

Critics argue that many physicians are too quick to prescribe stimulants for children with milder forms of ADHD. Also, in 2006, the U.S. government issued a warning about the cardiovascular risks of using stimulant medication to treat ADHD.

Recently, researchers have been exploring the possibility that three types of brain, cognitive, and physical training exercises might reduce ADHD symptoms. First, *neurofeedback* can improve the attention of children with ADHD (Zuberer et al., 2015). Neurofeedback trains individuals to become more aware of their physiological responses so they can attain better control over their brain's prefrontal cortex, where executive control primarily occurs.

Second, *mindfulness training* also has been found to reduce ADHD symptoms of children with ADHD (Anderson & Guthery, 2015). Mindfulness training especially focuses on getting individuals to focus on moment-to-moment experiences, and can include such activities as yoga, meditation, and tai chi. A recent meta-analysis concluded that mindfulness training significantly improved the attention of children with ADHD (Cairncross & Miller, 2016).

Third, *exercise* is being investigated as a possible treatment for children with ADHD (Pan et al., 2016). In a recent study, a higher physical activity level in adolescence was linked with a lower incidence of ADHD in emerging adulthood (Rommel et al., 2015). Also, a recent meta-analysis concluded that short-term aerobic exercise is effective in reducing symptoms such as inattention, hyperactivity, and impulsivity (Cerillo-Urbina et al., 2015). Another recent meta-analysis indicated that exercise is associated with better executive function in children with ADHD (Vysniauske et al., 2016).

RESEARCH

When teachers were asked how they work with students who have been diagnosed with ADHD, they provided the following recommendations.

EARLY CHILDHOOD Our preschoolers who have been diagnosed with ADHD work well within a very structured environment. Although our ADHD students are treated just like any other student in the classroom, we take care to give them ample physical activity and sometimes receive extra time to gather their thoughts and calm down by taking a few deep breaths. If necessary, medication is given as prescribed by a pediatrician.

—Missy Dangler, *Suburban Hills School*

ELEMENTARY SCHOOL: GRADES K–5 I find that frequent breaks (such as asking the student to bring something to the school secretary or to put something away) helps give the child an opportunity to move a bit and then refocus. In second grade, we play a lot of singing and movement games (such as "Simon Says") in the room between lessons, or when I see a lot of "itchiness." All of these games/songs allow standing up, moving, and singing or laughing and provide stretching and body awareness, which can help a child with ADHD to focus. Also, I don't have a problem with a child lying on the floor to work or standing at a desk, if that is how the child needs to focus. This is okay as long as the child is not bothering anyone else and is completing the task at hand.

—Janine Guida Poutre, *Clinton Elementary School*

MIDDLE SCHOOL: GRADES 6–8 Working with ADHD students requires organization and planning. My ADHD students sit in a strategic location in the room. I usually pick a spot that allows them freedom to get up and move around if necessary. I also make sure that these students sit where I can easily access them. And I give directions clearly and ask the ADHD students to repeat the directions to me to make sure that they not only are listening but also understand.

—CASEY MAASS, *Edison Middle School*

HIGH SCHOOL: GRADES 9–12 One of my biggest challenges in teaching is working with untreated ADHD students. One thing I do with my ADHD students is to sit them in the front row. I may touch the student's shoulder as I walk by or gently knock on the desk to refocus the student's attention. When I am walking about the room, I will "loop" back to the student's desk or quietly ask for directions to be repeated back to me. I often check their assignment books to make sure that homework assignments are written down correctly. Of course, communication with parents also is very important.

—JENNIFER HEITER, *Bremen High School*

INTELLECTUAL DISABILITY

Increasingly, children with an intellectual disability are being taught in the regular classroom. The most distinctive feature of intellectual disability is inadequate intellectual functioning (Kaderavek, 2015). Long before formal tests were developed to assess intelligence, individuals with an intellectual disability were identified by a lack of age-appropriate skills in learning and in caring for themselves. Once intelligence tests were created, numbers were assigned to indicate how mild or severe the intellectual disability was. A child might have a mild intellectual disability and be able to learn in the regular classroom or have a severe intellectual disability and be unable to learn in that setting.

> **Thinking Back/Thinking Forward**
>
> The Stanford-Binet Test and the Wechsler Scales are the two most widely used individually administered intelligence tests. Connect to "Individual Variations."

CONNECTING WITH STUDENTS: Best Practices
Strategies for Working with Children Who Have ADHD

1. Monitor whether the child's stimulant medication is working effectively.
2. Repeat and simplify instructions about in-class and homework assignments.
3. Involve a special education resource teacher.
4. State clear expectations and give the child immediate feedback.
5. *Use proven, effective behavior management strategies, such as providing positive feedback for progress.* We will discuss these approaches in considerable detail in the chapter on behavioral and social cognitive approaches.
6. *Provide structure and teacher-direction.* In many instances, a structured learning environment benefits children with ADHD. In *Through the Eyes of Teachers* Joanna Smith, a high school English teacher, describes how she arranges her classroom to accommodate students with ADHD.

THROUGH THE EYES OF TEACHERS
Structuring the Classroom to Benefit Students with ADHD

I have found success with these students when I seat them in the front row, make instructions explicit, break down larger tasks into smaller ones, write necessary information on the board and point out exactly where it is, allow extra time on tests (as specified on his or her plan), and check in with the students frequently. This frequent contact allows me to know how the student is doing, how much he understands, and gives him a welcomed opportunity to chat.

Joanna Smith

7. *Provide opportunities for students to get up and move around.*
8. *Break assignments into shorter segments.*

Type of Intellectual Disability	IQ Range	Percentage
Mild	55–70	89
Moderate	40–54	6
Severe	25–39	4
Profound	Below 25	1

FIGURE 4 CLASSIFICATION OF INTELLECTUAL DISABILITY BASED ON IQ

In addition to low intelligence, deficits in adaptive behavior and early onset also are included in the definition of intellectual disability (Green et al., 2016). Adaptive skills include skills needed for self-care and social responsibility such as dressing, toileting, feeding, self-control, and peer interaction. By definition, **intellectual disability** is a condition with an onset before age 18 that involves low intelligence (usually below 70 on a traditional individually administered intelligence test) and difficulty in adapting to everyday life. For an individual to be given a diagnosis of intellectual disability, the low IQ and low adaptiveness should be evident in childhood, not following a long period of normal functioning that is interrupted by an accident or other type of assault on the brain.

Classification and Types of Intellectual Disability As indicated in Figure 4, intellectual disability is classified as mild, moderate, severe, or profound. Approximately 89 percent of students with intellectual disability fall into the mild category. By late adolescence, individuals with mild intellectual disability can be expected to develop academic skills at approximately the sixth-grade level. In their adult years, many can hold jobs and live on their own with some supportive supervision or in group homes. Individuals with more severe intellectual disability require more support.

If you have a student with an intellectual disability in your classroom, the degree of impairment is likely to be mild. Children with severe intellectual disability are more likely to also show signs of other neurological complications, such as cerebral palsy, epilepsy, hearing impairment, visual impairment, or other metabolic birth defects that affect the central nervous system (Terman et al., 1996).

Most school systems still use the classifications mild, moderate, severe, and profound. However, because these categorizations based on IQ ranges aren't perfect predictors of functioning, a newer classification system is based on the degree of support children require to function at their highest level (Hallahan et al., 2015). As shown in Figure 5, the categories used are intermittent, limited, extensive, and pervasive.

Determinants Genetic factors, brain damage, and environmental factors are key determinants of intellectual disability. Let's explore genetic causes first.

DEVELOPMENT

Intermittent	Supports are provided "as needed." The individual may need episodic or short-term support during life-span transitions (such as job loss or acute medical crisis). Intermittent supports may be low- or high-intensity when provided.
Limited	Supports are intense and relatively consistent over time. They are time-limited but not intermittent. Require fewer staff members and cost less than more-intense supports. These supports likely will be needed for adaptation to the changes involved in the school-to-adult period.
Extensive	Supports are characterized by regular involvement (for example, daily) in at least some setting (such as home or work) and are not time-limited (for example, extended home-living support).
Pervasive	Supports are constant, very intense, and are provided across settings. They may be of a life-sustaining nature. These supports typically involve more staff members and intrusiveness than the other support categories.

FIGURE 5 CLASSIFICATION OF INTELLECTUAL DISABILITY BASED ON LEVELS OF SUPPORT

Source: *Intellectual Disability: Definition, Classification, and Systems of Supports* (p. 26), by DL. Coulter, 1992, American Association on Intellectual Developmental Disabilities.

intellectual disability A condition with an onset before age 18 that involves low intelligence (usually below 70 on a traditional individually administered intelligence test) and difficulty in adapting to everyday life.

Genetic Factors The most commonly identified form of intellectual disability is **Down syndrome**, which is genetically transmitted. Children with Down syndrome have 47 chromosomes instead of 46 (Lewanda et al., 2016). They have a round face, a flattened skull, an extra fold of skin over the eyelids, a protruding tongue, short limbs, and motor and mental disabilities. It is not known why the extra chromosome is present, but the health of the male sperm or female ovum might be involved. Women between the ages of 18 and 38 are far less likely than younger or older women to give birth to a child with Down syndrome. Down syndrome appears in about 1 in every 700 live births. African American children are rarely born with Down syndrome.

With early intervention and extensive support from the child's family and professionals, many children with Down syndrome can grow into independent adults (Skotko et al., 2016). Children with Down syndrome can fall into the mild to severe categories of intellectual disability.

Brain Damage and Environmental Factors Brain damage can result from seizures, infections, and environmental hazards (Pisani & Spagnoli, 2016). Infections in the pregnant mother-to-be, such as rubella (German measles), syphilis, herpes, and AIDS, can cause intellectual disability in children. Meningitis and encephalitis are infections that can develop in childhood. They cause inflammation in the brain and can produce intellectual disability. Environmental hazards that can result in intellectual disability include blows to the head, malnutrition, poisoning (e.g., lead), birth injury, and alcoholism or heavy drinking on the part of the pregnant woman. For more information see the following webpages: https://www.thearc.org/what-we-do/resources/fact-sheets/causes-and-prevention and https://www.cdc.gov/ncbddd/developmentaldisabilities/facts.html).

A child with Down syndrome. *What causes a child to develop Down syndrome?*
Realistic Reflections

DEVELOPMENT

Down syndrome A genetically transmitted form of intellectual disability due to an extra (47th) chromosome.

CONNECTING WITH STUDENTS: Best Practices
Strategies for Working with Children Who Have an Intellectual Disability

During the school years, the main goals of teaching children with an intellectual disability are to provide them with basic educational skills such as reading and mathematics, as well as vocational skills (Boyles & Contadino, 1997). Here are some positive teaching strategies for giving children who have an intellectual disability the best learning experience:

1. *Help children who have an intellectual disability to practice making personal choices and to engage in self-determination when possible.*

2. *Always keep in mind the child's level of mental functioning.* Children who have an intellectual disability will be at a considerably lower level of mental functioning than most other students in your class. If you start at one level of instruction and the child is not responding effectively, move to a lower level.

3. *Individualize your instruction to meet the child's needs.*

4. *As with other children with a disability, make sure that you give concrete examples of concepts.* Make your instructions clear and simple.

5. *Give children opportunities to practice what they have learned.* Have them repeat steps a number of times and overlearn a concept to retain it.

6. *Have positive expectations for the child's learning.* It is easy to fall into the trap of thinking that a child with an intellectual disability cannot achieve academically. Set a goal to maximize his or her learning.

7. *Look for resource support.* Use teacher aides and recruit volunteers such as sensitive retirees to help you educate children with an intellectual disability. They can assist you in increasing the amount of one-on-one instruction the child receives.

8. *Consider using applied behavior analysis strategies.* Some teachers report that these strategies improve children's self-maintenance, social, and academic skills. If you are interested in using these strategies, consult a resource such as *Applied Behavior Analysis for Teachers* by Paul Alberto and Anne Troutman (2017). The precise steps involved in applied behavior analysis can help you use positive reinforcement effectively with children who have an intellectual disability.

PHYSICAL DISORDERS

Physical disorders in children include orthopedic impairments, such as cerebral palsy, and seizure disorders. Many children with physical disorders require special education and related services, such as transportation, physical therapy, school health services, and psychological services.

Orthopedic Impairments **Orthopedic impairments** involve restricted movement or lack of control over movement due to muscle, bone, or joint problems. The severity of problems ranges widely. Orthopedic impairments can be caused by prenatal or perinatal problems, or they can be due to disease or accident during the childhood years. With the help of adaptive devices and medical technology, many children with orthopedic impairments function well in the classroom (Lewis et al., 2017).

Cerebral palsy is a disorder that involves a lack of muscular coordination, shaking, or unclear speech. The most common cause of cerebral palsy is lack of oxygen at birth. Special computers especially can help children with cerebral palsy to learn.

orthopedic impairments Restricted movements or lack of control of movements, due to muscle, bone, or joint problems.

cerebral palsy A disorder that involves a lack of muscle coordination, shaking, or unclear speech.

epilepsy A neurological disorder characterized by recurring sensorimotor attacks or movement convulsions.

Seizure Disorders The most common seizure disorder is **epilepsy**, a neurological disorder characterized by recurring sensorimotor attacks or movement convulsions (Berg et al., 2014). Children who experience seizures are usually treated with one or more anticonvulsant medications, which often are effective in reducing the seizures but do not always eliminate them (Mudigoudar et al., 2016).

When they are not having a seizure, students with epilepsy show normal behavior. If you have a child in your class who has a seizure disorder, become well acquainted with the procedures for monitoring and helping the child during a seizure.

SENSORY DISORDERS

Sensory disorders include visual and hearing impairments. Visual impairments include the need for corrective lenses, low vision, and being educationally blind. Children who are hearing impaired can be born deaf or experience a loss in hearing as they develop.

Visual Impairments A small portion of students (about 1 in every 1,000 students) have very serious visual problems and are classified as visually impaired. This includes students who have low vision and students who are blind. Children with *low vision* have a visual acuity of between 20/70 and 20/200 (on the familiar Snellen scale, in which 20/20 vision is normal) with corrective lenses. Children with low vision can read large-print books or regular books with the aid of a magnifying glass. Children who are *educationally blind* cannot use their vision in learning and must rely on their hearing and touch to learn. Approximately 1 in every 3,000 children is educationally blind.

Many children who are educationally blind have normal intelligence and function very well academically with appropriate supports and learning aids. 3-D printing provides an important technology support for students

TECHNOLOGY

THROUGH THE EYES OF STUDENTS

It's Okay to Be Different

Why me? I often ask myself, why did I have to be the one? Why did I get picked to be different? It took more than ten years for me to find answers and to realize that I'm not more different than anyone else. My twin sister was born with no birth defects, but I was born with cerebral palsy.

People thought I was stupid because it was hard for me to write my own name. So when I was the only one in the class to use a typewriter, I began to feel I was different. It got worse when the third-graders moved on to the fourth grade and I had to stay behind. I got held back because the teachers thought I'd be unable to type fast enough to keep up. Kids told me that was a lie and the reason I got held back was because I was a retard. It really hurt to be teased by those I thought were my friends. . . .

I have learned that no one was to blame for my disability. I realize that I can do things and that I can do them very well. Some things I can't do, like taking my own notes in class or running in a race, but I will have to live with that. . . .

There are times when I wish I had not been born with cerebral palsy, but crying isn't going to do me any good. I can only live once, so I want to live the best I can. . . . Nobody else can be the Angela Marie Erickson who is writing this. I could never be, or ever want to be, anyone else.

—*Angie Erickson*
Ninth-Grade Student
Wayzata, Minnesota

with visual impairments. Also, haptic devices (involving the sense of touch) have been found to increase the learning and exploration of students with a visual impairment (Nam et al., 2012; Pawluk et al., 2015).

An important task in working with a child who has visual impairments is to determine the modality (such as touch or hearing) through which the child learns best. Seating in the front of the class often benefits the child with a visual impairment.

Hearing Impairments A hearing impairment can make learning very difficult for children. Children who are born deaf or experience a significant hearing loss in the first several years of life usually do not develop normal speech and language. You also might have some children in your class who have hearing impairments that have not yet been detected. If you have students who turn one ear toward a speaker, frequently ask to have something repeated, don't follow directions, or frequently complain of earaches, colds, and allergies, consider having the student's hearing evaluated by a specialist, such as an audiologist.

Many children with hearing impairments receive supplementary instruction beyond the regular classroom. There are two categories of educational approaches to help students with hearing impairments: oral and manual. *Oral approaches* include using lip reading, speech reading (a reliance on visual cues to teach reading), and whatever hearing the student has. *Manual approaches* involve sign language and finger spelling. Sign language is a system of hand movements that symbolize words. Finger spelling consists of "spelling out" each word by signing.

SPEECH AND LANGUAGE DISORDERS

Speech and language disorders include a number of speech problems (such as articulation disorders, voice disorders, and fluency disorders) and language problems (difficulties in receiving information and expressing thoughts) (Owens et al., 2015).

Approximately 21 percent of all children who receive special education services have a speech or language impairment (Condition of Education, 2015).

Articulation Disorders **Articulation disorders** are problems in pronouncing sounds correctly (Bauman-Waengler, 2016). A child's articulation at 6 or 7 years is still not always error-free, but it should be by age 8. A child with an articulation problem might find communicating with peers and the teacher difficult or embarrassing. As a result, the child might avoid asking questions, participating in discussions, or communicating with peers. Articulation problems can usually be improved or resolved with speech therapy, though the process might take months or years (Bernthal et al., & Flipsen, 2017).

Voice Disorders **Voice disorders** are reflected in speech that is hoarse, harsh, too loud, too high-pitched, or too low-pitched. Children with cleft palate often have a voice disorder that makes their speech difficult to understand. If a child speaks in a way that is consistently difficult to understand, refer the child to a speech therapist.

Fluency Disorders **Fluency disorders** often involve what is commonly called "stuttering." Stuttering occurs when a child's speech has a spasmodic hesitation,

THROUGH THE EYES OF STUDENTS

Eyes Closed

In kindergarten, children truly begin to appreciate, not fear or think strange, each other's differences. A few years ago, a child in my kindergarten class was walking down the hall with his eyes closed and ran into the wall. When I asked him what he was doing, he said, "I was just trying to do like Darrick. How come he does it so much better?" Darrick is his classmate who is legally blind. He wanted to experience what it was like to be blind. In this case, imitation truly was the greatest form of flattery.

—*Anita Marie Hitchcock*
Kindergarten Teacher
Holle Navarre Primary
Santa Rosa County, Florida

Speech therapist Sharla Peltier, helping a young child improve his language and communication skills. *What are some different types of speech problems children can have?*
Courtesy of Sharla Peltier

speech and language disorders A number of speech problems (such as articulation disorders, voice disorders, and fluency disorders) and language problems (difficulties in receiving information and expressing language).

articulation disorders Problems in pronouncing sounds correctly.

voice disorders Disorders producing speech that is hoarse, harsh, too loud, too high-pitched, or too low-pitched.

fluency disorders Disorders that often involve what is commonly referred to as "stuttering."

CONNECTING WITH STUDENTS: Best Practices
Strategies for Working with Children Who Have a Hearing Impairment

1. *Be patient.*
2. *Speak normally (not too slowly or too quickly).*
3. *Don't shout, because this doesn't help.* Speaking distinctly is more helpful.
4. *Reduce distractions and background noises.*
5. *Face the student to whom you are speaking, because the student needs to read your lips and see your gestures.*
6. *Check into obtaining recorded texts.* For over half a century, recorded textbooks from Learning Ally have contributed to the educational progress of students with visual, perceptual, or other disabilities. More than 90,000 volumes of these audio and computerized books are available at no charge (https://learningally.org/).

---

prolongation, or repetition. The anxiety many children feel because they stutter often just makes their stuttering worse. Speech therapy is recommended (Bernthal et al., 2017).

Language Disorders **Language disorders** include a significant impairment in a child's receptive or expressive language. **Receptive language** involves the reception and understanding of language. **Expressive language** involves using language for expressing one's thoughts and communicating with others. Language disorders can result in significant learning problems (Owens et al., 2015). Treatment by a language therapist generally produces improvement in the child with a language disorder, but the problem usually is not eradicated. Language disorders include difficulties in phrasing questions properly to get the desired information, following oral directions, following conversation, especially when it is rapid and complex, and understanding and using words correctly in sentences.

Specific language impairment (SLI) involves language development problems with no other obvious physical, sensory, or emotional difficulties (Kaderavek, 2015; Swanson, 2016). In some cases, the disorder is referred to as *developmental language disorder*.

Children with SLI have problems in understanding and using words in sentences. One indicator of SLI in 5-year-old children is their incomplete understanding of verbs. They typically drop the –*s* from verb tenses (such as "She walk to the store" instead of "She walks to the store") and ask questions without "be" or "do" verbs (rather than saying "Does he live there?" the child will say "He live there?"). These characteristics make children with specific language impairment sound like children who are approximately two years younger than they are.

Early identification of SLI is important and can usually be accurately accomplished by 5 years of age and in some cases earlier. Intervention includes modeling correct utterances, rephrasing the child's incorrect utterances during conversation, and reading instruction. Parents may also wish to send a child with SLI to a speech or language pathologist.

AUTISM SPECTRUM DISORDERS

Autism spectrum disorders (ASD), also called pervasive developmental disorders, range from the more severe disorder called *autistic disorder* to the milder disorder called *Asperger syndrome* or high-functioning autism. Autism spectrum disorders

---

Thinking Back/Thinking Forward

Syntax is the language system that involves the way words are combined to form acceptable phrases and sentences. Connect to "Cognitive and Language Development."

---

language disorder Significant impairments in a child's receptive or expressive language.

receptive language The reception and understanding of language.

expressive language The ability to use language to express one's thoughts and communicate with others.

specific language impairment (SLI) Involves problems in language development that are not accompanied by other obvious physical, sensory, or emotional problems; in some cases, the disorder is called developmental language disorder.

autism spectrum disorders (ASD) Also called pervasive developmental disorders, they range from the severe disorder labeled autistic disorder to the milder disorder called Asperger syndrome. Children with these disorders are characterized by problems in social interaction, verbal and nonverbal communication, and repetitive behaviors.

are characterized by problems in social interaction, problems in verbal and nonverbal communication, and repetitive behaviors (Bernier & Dawson, 2016; Boutot, 2017; Wheeler et al., 2015). Children with these disorders may also show atypical responses to sensory experiences (National Institute of Mental Health, 2016). Autism spectrum disorders can often be detected in children as young as 1 to 3 years of age.

Recent estimates of the prevalence of autism spectrum disorders indicate that they are dramatically increasing in occurrence or are increasingly being detected. Once thought to affect only 1 in 2,500 children decades ago, they were estimated to be present in about 1 in 150 children in 2002 (Centers for Disease Control and Prevention, 2007) and 1 in 88 children in 2008 (Centers for Disease Control and Prevention, 2012). In the most recent survey, autism spectrum disorders were identified five times more often in boys than in girls, and 8 percent of individuals aged 3 to 21 with these disorders were receiving special education services (Condition of Education, 2015).

Autistic disorder is a severe developmental autism spectrum disorder that has its onset during the first three years of life and includes deficiencies in social relationships; abnormalities in communication; and restricted, repetitive, and stereotyped patterns of behavior.

Asperger syndrome is a relatively mild autism spectrum disorder in which the child has relatively good verbal language skills, milder nonverbal language problems, and a restricted range of interests and relationships (Boutot, 2017; Helles et al., 2015). Children with Asperger syndrome often engage in obsessive, repetitive routines and preoccupations with a particular subject. For example, a child may be obsessed with baseball scores or YouTube videos.

What causes autism spectrum disorders? The current consensus is that autism is a brain dysfunction characterized by abnormalities in brain structure and neurotransmitters (Conti et al., 2015). Recent interest has focused on a lack of connectivity between brain regions as a key factor in autism (Fakhoury, 2015). Genetic factors also likely play a role in the development of autism spectrum disorders (Ning et al., 2015), but there is no evidence that family socialization causes autism. Intellectual disability is present in some children with autism, while others show average or above-average intelligence (Memari et al., 2012).

Children with autism benefit from a well-structured classroom, individualized instruction, and small-group instruction (Simmons et al., 2014). Behavior modification techniques are sometimes effective in helping autistic children learn (Wheeler, et al., 2015; Zirpoli, 2016).

What characterizes autism spectrum disorders?
Realistic Reflections

RESEARCH

EMOTIONAL AND BEHAVIORAL DISORDERS

Most children have emotional problems sometime during their school years. A small percentage have problems so serious and persistent that they are classified as having an emotional or a behavioral disorder (Hallahan et al., 2015). **Emotional and behavioral disorders** consist of serious, persistent problems that involve relationships, aggression, depression, fears associated with personal or school matters, and other inappropriate socioemotional characteristics. Approximately 6 percent of children who have a disability and require an individualized education plan fall into this classification (Condition of Education, 2015). Boys are three times as likely as girls to have these disorders.

Various terms have been used to describe emotional and behavioral disorders, including *emotional disturbances, behavior disorders,* and *maladjusted children.* The term *emotional disturbance (ED)* recently has been used to describe children with these types of problems for whom it has been necessary to create individualized

autistic disorder A severe developmental autism spectrum disorder that has its onset in the first three years of life and includes deficiencies in social relationships, abnormalities in communication, and restricted, repetitive, and stereotyped patterns of behavior.

Asperger syndrome A relatively mild autism spectrum disorder in which the child has relatively good verbal language, milder nonverbal language problems, a restricted range of interests and relationships, and often engages in repetitive routines.

emotional and behavioral disorders Serious, persistent problems that involve relationships, aggression, depression, fears associated with personal or school matters, and other inappropriate socioemotional characteristics.

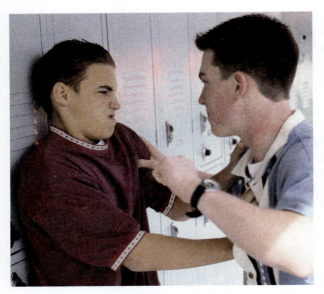

What are some characteristics of students who show aggressive, out-of-control behaviors?
SW Productions/Photodisc/Getty Images

learning plans. However, critics argue that this category has not been clearly defined.

Aggressive, Out-of-Control Behaviors Some children classified as having a serious emotional disturbance engage in disruptive, aggressive, defiant, or dangerous behaviors and are removed from the classroom. These children are much more likely to be boys than girls and more likely to come from low-income than from middle- or high-income families (Powers et al., 2016). When these children are returned to the regular classroom, both the regular classroom teacher and a special education teacher or consultant must spend a great deal of time helping them adapt and learn effectively.

In the chapter on social contexts and socioemotional development we discussed rejected students and improving students' social skills. Many of the comments and recommendations we made there apply to children with a serious emotional disturbance. In other chapters we will discuss more strategies and plans for effectively dealing with children who show emotional and behavioral problems.

Depression, Anxiety, and Fears Some children turn their emotional problems inward. Their depression, anxiety, or fears become so intense and persistent that their ability to learn is significantly compromised. All children feel depressed from time to time, but most get over their despondent, down mood in a few hours or a few days. For some children, however, the negative mood is more serious and longer lasting. *Depression* is a type of mood disorder in which the individual feels worthless, believes that things are unlikely to get better, and behaves lethargically for a prolonged period of time. When children show these signs for two weeks or longer, they likely are experiencing depression. Having a poor appetite and not being able to sleep well also can be associated with depression.

Depression is much more likely to appear in adolescence than in childhood and has a much higher incidence in girls than in boys (Salk et al., 2016). Experts on depression say that this gender difference is likely due to a number of factors. Females tend to ruminate on their depressed mood and amplify it, whereas males tend to distract themselves from the negative mood; girls' self-images are often more negative than those of boys during adolescence; and societal bias against female achievement might be involved (Schwartz-Mette & Rose, 2016).

Because it is turned inward, depression is far more likely to go unnoticed than aggressive, acting-out behaviors. If you think that a child has become depressed, have the child meet with the school counselor (Kauffman & Landrum, 2009).

Anxiety involves a vague, highly unpleasant feeling of fear and apprehension. It is normal for children to be concerned or worried when they face life's challenges, but some children have such intense and prolonged anxiety that it substantially impairs their school performance (Griffiths & Fazel, 2016). Some children also have personal or school-related fears that interfere with their learning. If a child shows marked or substantial fears that persist, have the child see the school counselor. More information about anxiety appears in the chapter on motivation, teaching, and learning.

At this point, we have explored many different disabilities and disorders. To evaluate your experiences with people who have these disabilities and disorders, complete *Self-Assessment 1*.

Thinking Back/Thinking Forward

Rejected children are infrequently nominated as someone's best friend and also actively disliked by their peers. Connect to "Social Contexts and Socioemotional Development."

Teachers can use effective strategies to deal with fighting, bullying, and hostility toward the teacher. Connect to "Managing the Classroom."

Thinking Back/Thinking Forward

A number of programs have been developed to reduce students' high anxiety levels. Connect to "Motivation, Teaching, and Learning."

DEVELOPMENT

SELF-ASSESSMENT 1
Evaluating My Experiences with People Who Have Various Disabilities and Disorders

Read each of these statements and place a check mark next to the ones that apply to you.

1. **Learning Disabilities**
   _____ I know someone who has a learning disability and have talked with her or him about the disability.
   _____ I have observed students with learning disabilities in the classroom and talked with teachers about their strategies for educating them.
   _____ I have a learning disability and have used strategies to help me be successful in school.

2. **Attention Deficit Hyperactivity Disorder**
   _____ I know someone with ADHD and have talked with him or her about the disability.
   _____ I have observed students with ADHD in the classroom and talked with teachers about their strategies for educating them.
   _____ I have ADHD and have used strategies to help me to be successful in school.

3. **Intellectual Disability**
   _____ I know someone who has an intellectual disability and have talked with her or his parents about their child's disability.
   _____ I have observed students with an intellectual disability in the classroom and talked with their teachers about their strategies for educating them.
   _____ I have an intellectual disability and have used strategies to help me be successful in school.

4. **Physical Disorders**
   _____ I know someone with a physical disorder and have talked with him or her about the disability.
   _____ I have observed students with physical disorders in the classroom and talked with their teachers about strategies for educating them.
   _____ I have a physical disorder and have used technology/tools to help me be successful in school.

5. **Sensory Disorders**
   _____ I know someone with a sensory disorder and have talked with her or him about the disability.
   _____ I have observed students with sensory disorders in the classroom and talked with their teachers about their strategies for educating them.
   _____ I have a sensory disorder and have used technology/tools to help me be successful in school.

6. **Speech and Language Disorders**
   _____ I know someone with a speech and language disorder and have talked with him or her about the disability.
   _____ I have observed students with a speech and language disorder in the classroom and talked with their teachers about strategies for educating them.
   _____ I have a speech and language disorder and have used strategies to help me be successful in school.

7. **Autism Spectrum Disorders**
   _____ I know someone with an autism spectrum disorder.
   _____ I have observed students with an autism spectrum disorder in the classroom and talked with their teachers about strategies for educating them.
   _____ I have an autism spectrum disorder and have used strategies to help me be successful in school.

8. **Emotional and Behavioral Disorders**
   _____ I know someone with an emotional and behavioral disorder and have talked with her or him about the disorder.
   _____ I have observed students with emotional and behavioral disorders and talked with their teachers about strategies for educating them.
   _____ I have an emotional and behavioral disorder and have used strategies to help me be successful.

For those disabilities that you did not place a check mark beside, make it a point to get to know and talk with someone who has the disability and observe students with the disability in the classroom. Then talk with their teachers about their strategies for educating them.

Review, Reflect, and Practice

 Describe the various types of disabilities and disorders.

REVIEW
- What is the definition of a learning disability? What are some common learning disabilities? How are they identified? How are they best treated?
- What is attention deficit hyperactivity disorder? What are some important aspects of attention deficit hyperactivity disorder for teachers to know?
- What is the nature of intellectual disability?
- What types of physical disorders in children are teachers likely to see?
- What are some common visual and hearing sensory disorders in children?
- What are the differences among articulation, voice, fluency, and language disorders?
- What characterizes autism spectrum disorders?
- What are the main types of emotional and behavioral disorders?

REFLECT
- Considering the age group of children and the subject that you plan to teach, which of the disabilities that we have discussed do you think will present the most difficulty for your teaching? Where should you focus your attention in learning more about this disability?

PRAXIS™ PRACTICE

1. Marty is in the fourth grade. Intelligence tests indicate that he is of average to above-average intelligence. However, his grades in reading, social studies, spelling, and science are very low. His math grades, on the other hand, are quite high and his writing skills are adequate. Achievement tests indicate that he reads at the first-grade level. When he reads aloud, it is apparent that he has difficulty matching sounds and letters. Marty most likely has
   a. ADHD
   b. dyscalculia
   c. dyslexia
   d. dysgraphia

2. Which of the following classroom environments is most likely to help students with ADHD achieve?
   a. Ms. Caster's class, which is very loosely structured so that students will only have to attend to something for a short period of time.
   b. Ms. Dodge's class, which is tightly structured and has explicit expectations. Student learning is often supplemented with computer games and physical activity.
   c. Ms. Ebert's class, in which students are expected to sit still for extended periods of time, working independently on seatwork.
   d. Ms. Fish's class, in which students work at their own pace on self-selected tasks and receive sporadic feedback regarding their progress and behavior.

3. Marci is a White non-Latinx student with mild intellectual disability. In addition to cognitive deficits, she has poor motor skills. Her legs and arms are shorter than average. She has a round face, with an extra fold of skin over her eyelids. Her tongue protrudes. What is most likely the cause of Marci's intellectual disability?
   a. Down syndrome
   b. fetal alcohol spectrum disorders
   c. fragile X syndrome
   d. maternal illness during pregnancy

Review, Reflect, and Practice

4. Mark is a middle school student in Ms. Walsh's language-arts class. She observes that Mark often stares out the window. Sometimes calling his name redirects his attention to her; at other times he continues to stare out the window for several seconds and appears oblivious to Ms. Walsh's reprimands. Mark's grades are suffering as a result of his inattention. What is the most likely explanation for Mark's inattention?
   a. ADHD
   b. absence seizure disorder
   c. tonic-clonic epilepsy
   d. cerebral palsy

5. Amiel's first-grade teacher notices that he squints a lot and holds books close to his face. Amiel most likely has which of the following disorders?
   a. physical disorder
   b. speech and language disorder
   c. sensory disorder
   d. autism spectrum disorder

6. Carrie's third-grade teacher, Ms. Brown, often gets frustrated when Carrie tries to answer questions in class. Carrie takes a long time to answer. Her sentence structure is not as good as that of other students in her class, and she often presents ideas in what sounds like a random manner. Ms. Brown should suspect that Carrie has
   a. articulation disorder
   b. expressive language disorder
   c. receptive language disorder
   d. specific language impairment

7. Mike is a seventh-grade boy of above-average intelligence. He has good language skills but does not interact well with other young adolescents. He has one friend and responds well to his mother and to the aide who works with him, although he shies away from contact with other people. He does fairly well in school, as long as his routine is not disrupted. He especially enjoys math and anything to do with numbers. He has memorized the batting averages of the starting line-up of all major league baseball teams. Mike most likely has
   a. autistic disorder
   b. Asperger syndrome
   c. behavioral disorder
   d. specific language disorder

8. Which middle school student is at greatest risk of developing a serious emotional disturbance?
   a. Jill, the most popular girl in the seventh grade, who sometimes says demeaning things to less popular girls
   b. Kevin, an eighth-grader who gets good grades in most subjects, has difficulty interacting with classmates, and has memorized all of Shakespeare's sonnets
   c. Harriet, a sixth-grade girl whose ADHD symptoms are controlled well by medication
   d. Mark, a seventh-grade boy who gets poor grades in many classes and frequently acts out in angry, violent ways

Please see answer key at end of book . . . .

LG 2 Explain the legal framework and technology advances for children with disabilities.

2 EDUCATIONAL ISSUES INVOLVING CHILDREN WITH DISABILITIES

- Legal Aspects
- Technology

Public schools are legally required to serve all children with disabilities in the least restrictive environment possible. We will explore the legal aspects of working with children who have a disability and examine the role of technology in educating children with a disability.

LEGAL ASPECTS

Beginning in the mid-1960s to mid-1970s, legislatures, the federal courts, and the U.S. Congress laid down special educational rights for children with disabilities. Prior to that time, most children with disabilities were either refused enrollment or inadequately served by schools. In 1975, Congress enacted **Public Law 94-142**, the Education for All Handicapped Children Act, which required that all students with disabilities be given a free, appropriate public education and which provided the funding to help implement this education.

Individuals with Disabilities Education Act (IDEA) In 1990, Public Law 94-142 was recast as the **Individuals with Disabilities Education Act (IDEA)**. IDEA was amended in 1997 and then reauthorized in 2004 and renamed the Individuals with Disabilities Education Improvement Act. IDEA spells out broad mandates for services to all children with disabilities (Heward et al., 2017). These include evaluation and eligibility determination, appropriate education and an individualized education plan (IEP), and education in the least restrictive environment (LRE) (Smith et al., 2016).

Children who are thought to have a disability are evaluated to determine their eligibility for services under IDEA. Schools are prohibited from planning special education programs in advance and offering them on a space-available basis. In other words, schools must provide appropriate education services to all children who are determined to need them (Turnbull et al., 2016).

Children must be evaluated and diagnosed with a disability before a school can begin providing special education services. However, because an assessment can take a long time, variations of pre-referral interventions are in place in many schools. Parents must be invited to participate in the evaluation process. Reevaluation is required at least every three years (sometimes every year), when requested by parents, or when conditions suggest a reevaluation is needed. A parent who disagrees with the school's evaluation can obtain an independent evaluation, which the school is required to consider in providing special education services. If the evaluation finds that the child has a disability and requires special services, the school must provide the child with appropriate services.

IDEA requires that students with disabilities have an **individualized education plan (IEP)**. An IEP is a written statement that spells out a program specifically tailored for the student with a disability. In general, the IEP should be (1) related to the child's learning capacity, (2) specially constructed to meet the child's individual needs and not merely a copy of what is offered to other children, and (3) designed to provide educational benefits.

Increasingly, children with disabilities are being taught in the regular classroom, as is this child with mild intellectual disability. *What are some legal aspects of educating children with disabilities?*
E.D. Torial/Alamy Stock Photo

Public Law 94-142 The Education for All Handicapped Children Act, which required that all students with disabilities be given a free, appropriate public education and also provided the funding to help implement this education.

Individuals with Disabilities Education Act (IDEA) This act spells out broad mandates for services to all children with disabilities, including evaluation and determination of eligibility, appropriate education and an individualized education plan (IEP), and education in the least restrictive environment (LRE).

individualized education plan (IEP) A written statement that spells out a program specifically tailored for the student with a disability.

IDEA has many other specific provisions that relate to the parents of a child with a disability. These include requirements that schools send notices to parents of proposed actions, that parents be allowed to attend meetings regarding the child's placement or individualized education plan, and that parents have the right to appeal school decisions to an impartial evaluator.

Amendments were made to IDEA in 1997. Two of these involve positive behavioral support and functional behavioral assessment.

Positive behavioral support focuses on culturally appropriate application of positive behavioral interventions to attain important behavior changes in children. "Culturally appropriate" refers to considering the unique and individualized learning histories of children (social, community, historical, gender, and so on). Positive behavioral support especially emphasizes supporting desirable behaviors rather than punishing undesirable behaviors in working with children with a disability or disorder.

Functional behavioral assessment involves determining the consequences (what purpose the behavior serves), antecedents (what triggers the behavior), and setting events (contexts in which the behavior occurs). Functional behavioral assessment emphasizes understanding behavior in the context in which it is observed and guiding positive behavioral interventions that are relevant and effective.

A major aspect of the 2004 reauthorization of IDEA involved aligning it with the government's No Child Left Behind (NCLB) legislation, which was designed to improve the educational achievement of all students, including those with disabilities. Both IDEA and NCLB mandate that most students with disabilities be included in general assessments of educational progress. This alignment includes requiring most students with disabilities to take standardized tests of academic achievement and to achieve at a level equal to that of students without disabilities. Whether this expectation is reasonable is an open question (Hallahan et al., 2015). Alternative assessments for students with disabilities and funding to help states improve instruction, assessment, and accountability for educating students with disabilities are included in the 2004 reauthorization of IDEA.

Least Restrictive Environment (LRE) Under IDEA, the child with a disability must be educated in the **least restrictive environment (LRE)**. This means a setting as similar as possible to the one in which children who do not have a disability are educated. And schools must make an effort to educate children with a disability in the regular classroom. The term **inclusion** means educating a child with special educational needs full-time in the regular classroom. In a recent school year (2014), 61 percent of U.S. students with a disability spent more than 80 percent of their school day in a general classroom (compared with only 33 percent in 1990 (Condition of Education, 2015).

What is least restrictive likely depends to some degree on the child's disability (Smith et al., 2016). Some children with a learning disability or a speech impairment can be educated in the regular classroom, but children with severe hearing or vision impairments may need to be educated in separate classes or schools (Lewis et al., 2017).

In the last two decades, collaborative teaming has been increasingly advocated in educating children with disabilities (Hallahan et al., 2015). In *collaborative teaming,* people with diverse expertise interact to provide services for children. Researchers have found that collaborative teaming often results in gains for children, as well as improved skills and attitudes for teachers (Snell & Janney, 2005).

Ideally, collaborative teaming encourages shared responsibility in planning and decision making. It also enables educators with diverse expertise to construct effective alternatives to traditional educational approaches. When collaborative teaming is used, many children remain in the regular classroom, and the regular classroom teacher is actively involved in planning the child's education.

Many legal changes regarding children with disabilities have been extremely positive. Compared with several decades ago, far more children today are receiving competent, specialized services. For many children, inclusion in the regular classroom, with modifications or supplemental services, is appropriate (Heward et al., 2017).

> **Thinking Back/Thinking Forward**
> No Child Left Behind is the federal government's legislation that requires states to test students annually in various subjects. Connect to "Educational Psychology: A Tool for Effective Teaching" and "Standardized Tests and Teaching."

least restrictive environment (LRE) A setting that is as similar as possible to the one in which children who do not have a disability are educated.

inclusion Educating children with special education needs full-time in the regular classroom.

However, some leading experts on special education argue that the effort to use inclusion to educate children with disabilities has become too extreme in some cases. For example, James Kauffman and his colleagues (Kauffman et al., 2015; Kauffman et al., 2004) state that inclusion too often has meant making accommodations in the regular classroom that do not always benefit children with disabilities. They advocate a more individualized approach that does not always involve full inclusion but rather allows for options such as special education outside the regular classroom. Kauffman and his colleagues (2004, p. 620) acknowledge that children with disabilities "*do* need the services of specially trained professionals to achieve their full potential. They *do*

CONNECTING WITH STUDENTS: Best Practices
Strategies for Working with Children with Disabilities as a Regular Classroom Teacher

1. *Carry out each child's individualized education plan (IEP).*
2. *Encourage your school to provide increased support and training in how to teach children with disabilities.* In *Through the Eyes of Teachers,* Michelle Evans, a sixth-grade teacher, describes her relationship with resource personnel and some strategies that worked for her students.

THROUGH THE EYES OF TEACHERS
Strategies for Working with Children Who Have a Disability

Support and resource personnel are invaluable. Communication with parents, students, and with anyone involved is essential. Make certain that you communicate with your entire class, too. . . . Because I want each student to feel successful, I create different levels of mastery or participation in learning objectives.

One student with cerebral palsy had difficulty standing, mental impairments, and other problems. She had little and often no short-term memory. As we sat together and talked, I found that her strength was that she loved to copy words, stories, and other things. Her hands were weak, but writing helped them. Her parents wanted her to do anything she could. By capitalizing on her fondness for copying and writing, she eventually learned math facts and spelling words. I assigned a poem about having a positive attitude as a memorization for everyone in the class. A few kids complained that the poem would be too hard to memorize when I presented it. She copied that poem so many times that three days after the assignment she stood and delivered it flawlessly to the class. I could see the complainers melt away as we all realized that she was the first to recite the poem. Her parents came to witness her accomplishment. There wasn't a dry eye in the room by the time she finished. She taught us a great deal.

Michelle Evans

3. *Become more knowledgeable about the types of children with disabilities in your classroom.* Read education journals, such as *Exceptional Children, Teaching Exceptional Children,* and *Journal of Learning Disabilities,* to keep up-to-date on the latest information about these children. Look into taking a class at a college or university or a continuing education course on topics such as exceptional children, intellectual disabilities, learning disabilities, and emotional and behavioral disorders.

4. *Be cautious about labeling children with a disability.* It is easy to fall into the trap of using the label as an explanation for the child's learning difficulties. For example, a teacher might say, "Well, Larry has trouble with reading because he has a learning disability" when in fact the reason Larry is having trouble with reading is unknown or not yet identified. Also, labels have a way of remaining after the child has improved considerably. Remember that terms such as *intellectual disability* and *learning disability* are descriptive labels for disorders. Always think of children with disabilities in terms of what the best conditions are for improving their learning and how they can be helped to make progress rather than in terms of unchanging labels.

5. *Remember that children with disabilities benefit from many of the same teaching strategies that benefit children without disabilities and vice versa.* These include being caring, accepting, and patient; having positive expectations for learning; helping children with their social and communication skills as well as academic skills; and challenging children with disabilities to reach their full potential.

6. *Help children without a disability to understand and accept children with a disability.* Provide children without a disability information about children with a disability and create opportunities for them to interact with each other in positive ways. Peer tutoring and cooperative learning activities can be used to encourage positive interaction between children without a disability and children with a disability. We will discuss these activities further in the chapter on social constructivist approaches.

sometimes need altered curricula or adaptations to make their learning possible. However, we sell students with disabilities short when we pretend that they are not different from typical students. We make the same error when we pretend that they must *not* be expected to put forth extra effort if they are to learn to do some things—or learn to do something in a different way." Like general education, an important aspect of special education should be to challenge students with disabilities "to become all they can be."

One concern about special education involves disproportionate representation of students from minority backgrounds in special education programs and classes. The U.S. Department of Education (2000) has three concerns about the overrepresentation of minority students in special education programs and classes: (1) students may be unserved or receive services that do not meet their needs; (2) students may be misclassified or inappropriately labeled; and (3) placement in special education classes may be a form of discrimination.

TECHNOLOGY

Nico Calabria, who was born without a hip and right leg, dribbles the ball during soccer practice in Concord, Massachusetts. He already has become one of the top wrestlers in the state in his weight class and has successfully climbed the top of Africa's highest mountain.
Matt Stone/Boston Herald/AP Images

The Individuals with Disabilities Education Act (IDEA), including its 1997 amendments, requires that technology devices and services be provided to students with disabilities if they are necessary to ensure a free, appropriate education (Dell et al., 2017).

Two types of technology that can be used to improve the education of students with disabilities are instructional technology and assistive technology. *Instructional technology* includes various types of hardware and software, combined with innovative teaching methods, to accommodate students' learning needs in the classroom (Luiselli & Fischer, 2016). Examples of instructional technology that are being used with students with a disability today are software, Web sites, and apps for mobile devices (Butcher & Jameson, 2016).

Assistive technology consists of various services and devices designed to help students with disabilities function within their environment (Marchel et al., 2015). Examples include communication aids, alternative computer keyboards, and adaptive switches. Following are excellent Web sites on assistive technologies:

- www.unicef.org/disabilities/files/Assistive-Tech-Web.pdf
- www.edutopia.org/article/assistive-technology-resources

The Edutopia site has a valuable set of resources for children with physical and learning disabilities.

TECHNOLOGY

Review, Reflect, and Practice

2 Explain the legal framework and technology advances for children with disabilities.

REVIEW
- What is IDEA? How is it related to IEPs and LREs? What is the current thinking about inclusion?
- What is the difference between instructional and assistive technology?

REFLECT
- What do you think will present the greatest challenges to you in teaching children with a disability?

PRAXIS™ PRACTICE

1. Jenny has a moderate learning disability. She is educated in the special education classroom of her school, as she has been for the past two years. She and her classmates eat lunch in the resource room as well. Each of the students in the resource room

continued

Special input devices can help students with physical disabilities use computers more effectively. Many students with physical disabilities such as cerebral palsy cannot use a conventional keyboard and mouse but can use alternative keyboards effectively.
Wendy Maeda/The Boston Globe/Getty Images

Review, Reflect, and Practice

works on different things, due to their very different abilities and disabilities. This placement was made because the regular education teachers in Jenny's school do not have the necessary skills to teach Jenny. Therefore, she was placed in the resource room with the school's sole special educator. What is the legal issue with this placement?
  a. Jenny's IEP does not specify a diagnosis.
  b. Jenny is not being educated in the least restrictive environment.
  c. Jenny's placement needs to be reconsidered at least every six months.
  d. The functional behavior assessment did not consider the use of technology.

2. Azel has cerebral palsy. His teacher has found an alternative computer keyboard to facilitate his learning. What type of technology is the teacher using?
  a. instructional technology
  b. computer-assisted instruction
  c. assistive technology
  d. complex hypermedia

Please see answer key at end of book . . . .

LG 3 Define what gifted means and discuss some approaches to teaching children who are gifted.

3 CHILDREN WHO ARE GIFTED

Characteristics — Nature/Nurture and Domain-Specific Giftedness — Educating Children Who Are Gifted

The final type of exceptionality we will discuss is quite different from the disabilities and disorders that we have described so far. **Children who are gifted** have above-average intelligence (usually defined as an IQ of 130 or higher) and/or superior talent in some domain such as art, music, or mathematics. Admissions standards for children who are gifted in schools are typically based on intelligence and academic aptitude (Molinero et al., 2016). However, there is an increasing call to widen the criteria to include such factors as creativity and commitment (Ambrose & Sternberg, 2016a, b). The U.S. government has described five areas of giftedness: intellectual, academic, creative, visual and performing arts, and leadership.

Some critics argue that too many children in "gifted programs" aren't really gifted in a particular area but are just somewhat bright, usually cooperative, and, usually, non-Latinx White. They say the mantle of brilliance is cast on many children who are not that far from simply being "smart normal" (Winner, 2014).

General intelligence as defined by an overall IQ score continues to be a key criterion in many states' decision of whether a child should be placed in a gifted program, but changing conceptions of intelligence increasingly include ideas such as Gardner's multiple intelligences and creativity. As a result, placement decisions may move away from an IQ criterion in the future (Ambrose & Machek, 2015; Olszewski-Kubilius & Thomson, 2015).

Thinking Back/Thinking Forward

Robert J. Sternberg argues that creative thinking should be considered a different form of intelligence than the intelligence measured by traditional standardized tests of intelligence. Connect to "Individual Variations" and "Complex Cognitive Processes."

CHARACTERISTICS

Ellen Winner (1996), an expert on creativity and giftedness, described three criteria that characterize children who are gifted:

1. *Precocity.* Children who are gifted are precocious when given the opportunity to use their gift or talent. They begin to master an area earlier than their peers. Learning in their domain is more effortless for them than for children who are

children who are gifted Children with above-average intelligence (usually defined as an IQ of 130 or higher) and/or superior talent in some domain such as art, music, or mathematics.

not gifted. In most instances, children who are gifted are precocious because they have an inborn high ability in a particular domain or domains, although this inborn precocity has to be identified and nourished.

2. *Marching to their own drummer.* Children who are gifted learn in a qualitatively different way than children who are not gifted. One way they march to a different drummer is that they require less support, or scaffolding, from adults to learn than their nongifted peers do. Often they resist explicit instruction. They also often make discoveries on their own and solve problems in unique ways within their area of giftedness. They can be normal or below normal in other areas.

3. *A passion to master.* Children who are gifted are driven to understand the domain in which they have high ability. They display an intense, obsessive interest and an ability to focus. They are not children who need to be pushed by their parents. They frequently have a high degree of internal motivation.

A fourth area in which children who are gifted excel involves information-processing skills. Researchers have found that children who are gifted learn at a faster pace, process information more rapidly, are better at reasoning, use more effective strategies, and monitor their understanding better than their nongifted counterparts (Ambrose & Sternberg, 2016a).

Research also supports the conclusion that gifted people tend to be more mature than others, have fewer emotional problems than others, and grow up in a positive family climate. For example, a recent study revealed that parents and teachers identified elementary school children who are not gifted as having more emotional and behavioral risks than children who are gifted (Eklund et al., 2015). In this study, when children who are gifted did have problems, they were more likely to be internalized problems, such as anxiety and depression, than externalized problems, such as acting out and high levels of aggression.

NATURE/NURTURE AND DOMAIN-SPECIFIC GIFTEDNESS

Two important issues in the education of children are: (1) What roles do nature and nurture play in giftedness? (2) To what extent is giftedness domain-specific?

Nature/Nurture Is giftedness a product of heredity or environment? Likely both (Duggan & Friedman, 2014). Individuals who are gifted recall that they had signs of high ability in a particular area at a very young age, prior to or at the beginning of formal training. This suggests the importance of innate ability in giftedness. However, researchers have also found that individuals with world-class status in the arts, mathematics, science, and sports all report strong family support and years of training and practice (Bloom, 1985). Deliberate practice is an important characteristic of individuals who become experts in a particular domain. For example, in one study, the best musicians engaged in twice as much deliberate practice over their lives as did the least successful ones (Ericsson et al., 1993).

Domain-Specific Giftedness Individuals who are highly gifted are typically not gifted in many domains, and research on giftedness is increasingly focused on domain-specific developmental trajectories (Winner, 2014). During the childhood years, the domain in which individuals are gifted usually emerges. Thus, at some point in the childhood years the child who is to become a gifted artist or the child who is to become a gifted mathematician begins to show expertise in that domain. Regarding domain-specific giftedness, software genius Bill Gates (1998), the founder of Microsoft and one of the world's richest persons, commented that when you are good at something you may have to resist the urge to think that you will be good at everything. Gates says that because he has been so successful at software development, people expect him to be brilliant about other domains in which he is far from being a genius.

At 2 years of age, art prodigy Alexandra Nechita colored in coloring books for hours and took up pen and ink. She had no interest in dolls or friends. By age 5 she was using watercolors. Once she started school, she would start painting as soon as she got home. At the age of 8, in 1994, she saw the first public exhibit of her work. In succeeding years, working quickly and impulsively on canvases as large as 5 feet by 9 feet, she has completed hundreds of paintings, some of which sell for close to $100,000 apiece. Shown here as a teenager, Alexandra has continued to paint—relentlessly and passionately. It is, she says, what she loves to do. *What are some characteristics of children who are gifted?*
Koichi Kamoshida/Newsmakers/Hulton Archive/Getty Images

RESEARCH

DEVELOPMENT

EDUCATING CHILDREN WHO ARE GIFTED

Increasingly, experts argue that the education of children who are gifted in the United States requires a significant overhaul (Ambrose & Sternberg, 2016a, b; Winner, 2014). Underchallenged children who are gifted can become disruptive, skip classes, and lose interest in achieving. Sometimes these children just disappear into the woodwork, becoming passive and apathetic toward school. Teachers need to challenge children who are gifted to establish and reach high expectations.

Four program options for children who are gifted follow (Hertzog, 1998):

- *Special classes.* Historically, this has been a common way to educate children who are gifted. The special classes during the regular school day are called "pullout" programs. Some special classes also are held after school, on Saturdays, or in the summer.
- *Acceleration and enrichment in the regular classroom setting.* This could include early admission to kindergarten, grade skipping (also known as double promotion), telescoping (completing two grades in one year), advanced placement, subject-matter acceleration, and self-paced instruction (Cloud, 2007). Curriculum compacting is a variation of acceleration in which teachers skip over aspects of the curriculum that they believe children who are gifted do not need.
- *Mentor and apprenticeship programs.* These are important, underutilized ways to motivate, challenge, and effectively educate children who are gifted.
- *Work/study and/or community-service programs.* Educational reform has brought into the regular classroom many strategies that once were the domain of separate gifted programs. These include an emphasis on problem-based learning, having children do projects, creating portfolios, and critical thinking. Combined with the increasing emphasis on educating all children in the regular classroom, many schools now try to challenge and motivate children who are gifted in the regular classroom. Some schools also include after-school or Saturday programs or develop mentor apprenticeship, work/study, or community-service programs. Thus, an array of in-school and out-of-school opportunities is provided.

The Schoolwide Enrichment Model (SEM), developed by Joseph Renzulli (1998), is a program for children who are gifted that focuses on total school improvement. Renzulli says that when enrichment has a school-wide emphasis, positive outcomes are likely to occur, not only for children who are gifted but also for children who are not gifted and for classroom and resource teachers. When school-wide enrichment is emphasized, "us" versus "them" barriers often decrease, and classroom teachers are more willing to use curriculum compacting with their children who are most gifted. Instead of feeling isolated, resource teachers begin to feel more like members of a team, especially when they work with regular classroom teachers on enriching the entire classroom. Thus, important goals of SEM are to improve outcomes for both students who are gifted and those who are not gifted and to improve the contributions and relationships of classroom and resource teachers (Reis & Renzulli, 2014).

A number of experts argue that too often children who are gifted are socially isolated and underchallenged in the classroom (Winner, 2014). It is not unusual for them to be ostracized

---

THROUGH THE EYES OF STUDENTS

Children Who Are Gifted Speak

James Delisle (1987) interviewed hundreds of elementary school children who are gifted. Here are some of their comments.

In response to "Describe Your Typical School Day":

Oh what a bore to sit and listen,
To stuff we already know.
Do everything we've done and done again,
But we must still sit and listen.
Over and over read one more page
Oh bore, oh bore, oh bore.

    Girl, Age 9, New York

I sit there pretending to be reading along when I'm really six pages ahead. When I understand something and half the class doesn't, I have to sit there and listen.

    Girl, Age 10, Connecticut

In response to "What Makes a Teacher a Gifted Teacher?":

She is capable of handling our problems and has a good imagination to help us learn.

    Girl, Age 10, Louisiana

Will challenge you and let the sky be your limit.

    Boy, Age 11, Michigan

Opens your mind to help you with your life.

    Boy, Age 11, New Jersey

Source: *Gifted Kids Speak Out*, by J.R. Delisle, 1987, Free Spirit Publishing.

and labeled "nerds" or "geeks." A child who is truly gifted often is the only child in the room who does not have the opportunity to learn with students of like ability. Many eminent adults report that school was a negative experience for them, that they were bored and sometimes knew more than their teachers (Bloom, 1985). Winner (2006) points out that American education will benefit when standards are raised for all children. When some children are still underchallenged, she recommends that they be allowed to attend advanced classes in their domain of exceptional ability, such as allowing some especially precocious middle school students to take college classes in their area of expertise. For example, Bill Gates, founder of Microsoft, took college math classes and hacked a computer security system at 13; Yo-Yo Ma, famous cellist, graduated from high school at 15 and attended Juilliard School of Music in New York City.

Some educators conclude that the inadequate education of children who are gifted has been compounded by the federal government's No Child Left Behind policy that seeks to raise the achievement level of students who are not doing well in school at the expense of enriching the education of children who are gifted (Clark, 2008). In the era of No Child Left Behind policy, some individuals who are concerned about the neglect of students who are gifted argue that schools spend far more time identifying students' deficiencies than cultivating students' talents (Cloud, 2007). For example, U.S. schools spend approximately $8 billion a year educating students with an intellectual disability and only $800 million educating students who are gifted. In many cases, say the critics, U.S. education squanders the potential contributions of America's most talented young minds (Cloud, 2007).

A final concern is that African American, Latinx, and Native American children are underrepresented in gifted programs (Ford, 2012, 2014, 2015a, b; Mills, 2015). Much of the underrepresentation involves the lower test scores for these children compared with non-Latinx White and Asian American children, which may be due to reasons such as test bias and fewer opportunities to develop language skills such as vocabulary and comprehension (Ford, 2012, 2014, 2015a, b).

How do teachers work with students who are gifted? Following are their responses.

EARLY CHILDHOOD Our preschoolers who are considered gifted are given more challenging projects to complete and given more responsibilities throughout the day. Parents are also contacted and given strategies and suggestions about extracurricular activities that will stimulate their child's strengths.

—MISSY DANGLER, *Suburban Hills School*

ELEMENTARY SCHOOL: GRADES K–5 When working with students who are gifted, it is important to remember that they don't need *more* work, but they do need work that will challenge them. Also, no matter how gifted students are, their work needs to always be checked to make sure that they haven't misunderstood something.

—ESTHER LINDBLOOM, *Cooper Mountain Elementary School*

MIDDLE SCHOOL: GRADES 6–8 It is important that you not bore students who are gifted in your classroom. For example, if children who are gifted are learning about the causes and effects of the Civil War and they already know the information being covered, I would have them apply what they already know by having them create a journal about someone who lived during that time period.

—CASEY MAASS, *Edison Middle School*

HIGH SCHOOL: GRADES 9–12 Students who are gifted have a unique set of issues. They need to be challenged at a higher level, but they also need to accept the fact that other students who are not as gifted as they are also have worth. My homeroom is a prime example. Among the 18 students I have, one is the number-one student who never found a math or science problem that he couldn't solve; one is learning disabled with a seizure disorder; and three students have missed school time for jail. In the three years that we have been together, we have worked on respecting differences in each other and on teamwork activities, and have won homeroom competitions. Relationships are key in getting students of all abilities to work together and feel part of a school or classroom community. Teachers need to build trust in order for this to happen.

—SANDY SWANSON, *Menomonee Falls High School*

CONNECTING WITH STUDENTS: Best Practices
Strategies for Working with Children Who Are Gifted

Here are some recommended strategies for working with children who are gifted (Colangelo et al., 2004, pp. 49–50):

1. *Recognize that the child is academically advanced.*
2. *Guide the child to new challenges and ensure that school is a positive experience.* To read about some ways talented teacher Margaret (Peg) Cagle accomplishes this, see *Through the Eyes of Teachers.*

THROUGH THE EYES OF TEACHERS
Passionate About Teaching Math to Students Who Are Gifted

Margaret (Peg) Cagle teaches gifted seventh- and eighth-grade math students at Lawrence Middle School in Chatsworth, California. She especially advocates challenging students who are gifted to take intellectual risks. To encourage collaboration, she often has students work together in groups of four, and frequently tutors students during lunch hour. As 13-year-old Madeline Lewis commented, "If I don't get it one way, she'll explain it another and talk to you about it and show you until you do get it." Peg says it is important to be passionate about teaching math and open up a world for students that shows them how beautiful learning math can be.

Source: Wong Briggs, 2007, p. 6D

Margaret (Peg) Cagle with some of the gifted seventh- and eighth-grade math students she teaches at Lawrence Middle School in Chatsworth, California.
Scott Buschman

3. *Remember that giftedness is usually domain-specific.* Don't expect a student to be gifted across most domains.
4. *Monitor the accurate evaluation of the child's readiness to be accelerated.*
5. *Discuss with parents ways to appropriately challenge the child.*
6. *Learn about and use resources for children who are gifted.* Among these are the National Research Center on Gifted and Talented Education at the University of Connecticut and the Belin-Blank Center at the University of Iowa; *Gifted Child Quarterly* and *Gifted Child Today* journals; and books on children who are gifted, such as *Giftedness and Talent in the 21st Century* (Ambrose & Sternberg, 2016a).

Review, Reflect, and Practice

3 Define what gifted means and discuss some approaches to teaching children who are gifted.

REVIEW
- What is the definition of being gifted? What are some criticisms of gifted programs? What characteristics does Winner ascribe to children who are gifted?

Review, Reflect, and Practice

- What roles do nature/nurture, developmental changes, and domain specificity play in giftedness?
- What are some options for educating students who are gifted?

REFLECT
- Suppose that you had several students in your class who were strikingly gifted. Might this lead to problems? Explain. What might you do to prevent such problems from developing?

PRAXIS™ PRACTICE

1. Ms. Larson has a student in her kindergarten class who continuously surprises her. He requested that she allow him to play with a puzzle of the United States that no children had played with in years. She observed him expertly put each state in place, saying its name as he did so. Soon he was teaching the other students in the class each state's name, its capital, and where it belonged in the puzzle. On a recent trip to the school learning center, he asked to check out a book of international flags that was written at an eighth-grade level. Her first instinct was to deny his request, but instead she asked him about the book. He told her, "I know I can't read *all* of it, but I can read the names of the countries, and I want to learn more flags. See how many I already know?" He then flipped through the book, correctly identifying most of the flags. Which characteristics of giftedness is this student showing?
   a. numerical ability, highly developed social skills, and precocity
   b. verbal ability, intensity, and a passion to master
   c. high reading level, marching to his own drummer, and stubbornness
   d. precocity, marching to his own drummer, and a passion to master

2. Roberto is gifted in math but not in social studies and English. These characteristics of Roberto's giftedness are best described as
   a. due more to nature than nurture
   b. domain-specific
   c. reflecting deliberate practice
   d. domain-general

3. The kindergarten student in Ms. Larson's class (item 1) continued to progress in school. In fourth grade, he finished third in his K–8 school's geography bee. He finished first in the next two years. In seventh grade, he finally took his first course in geography. He received *C*'s. He often complained to his parents that he already knew the material being taught, that he wanted to learn "new stuff, not just listen to the same old junk." His teacher put a great deal of emphasis on completing map worksheets, which he completed very quickly and sloppily. He often became disruptive in class. How should the geography teacher handle this situation?
   a. The teacher should punish the student for disrupting class. The student should continue to do the same assignments as the other students, because he needs to understand that not all work is fun.
   b. The teacher should consider curriculum compacting, because the student has already mastered the course content. Once he is challenged, his disruptive behavior is likely to diminish.
   c. The teacher should ask this student to become a co-teacher.
   d. The teacher should use the student's sloppy work as a negative example to the rest of the class.

Please see answer key at end of book . . . .

Connecting with the Classroom: Crack the Case

Now What?

Before the school year starts, Ms. Inez always holds a "get acquainted meeting" with the parents of her incoming kindergartners. She does this so that she can explain what the children will be doing in kindergarten, her educational philosophy and expectations, and the procedure for dropping students off at school the first day. She encourages parents to ask questions and share any concerns they might have. Inevitably, parents do have concerns and questions they would like addressed.

Here are some typical things she hears from parents:

"Joey still naps in the afternoon; can we have him changed to the morning class?"

"Ashley has severe asthma. She will need to have her nebulizer close in case she has an asthma attack. Do you know how to use one?"

"I just know that Steve won't be able to sit still for very long. Do you let the kids move around a lot?"

"I hope you give the kids lots of active time. Bill won't be able to sit still for long either."

"Alex is very advanced for his age. What can you do to challenge him?"

"Amanda is advanced, too." "So is my Timmy." "Well, Peter seems to be behind. He doesn't speak very well."

Ms. Inez listens respectfully to each concern or question and assures the parents, "I'll do everything I can to ensure your children have a good year in my class. All children are different and learn at different rates, so don't be too worried about your child being a little bit behind or ahead. I think we'll all do fine together." As she is leaving for the evening, she chuckles at the number of parents who think their children are very advanced. It's the same every year—about a third of the parents are convinced that their child is the next Einstein.

The school year begins uneventfully. Ms. Inez uses the children's free-play time to observe them. Although there are obvious differences between the children, she doesn't notice that any of the children are truly exceptional, except perhaps for Harman and Rowan. Their lack of attention and inability to sit still during story time is beginning to be a bit disruptive. Ms. Inez makes a note to herself to talk to their parents about the possibility that they might have ADHD and recommend testing. Some other students might be candidates for this as well, including Alex. Although Ms. Inez has learned how to use Ashley's nebulizer, she hasn't needed to use it thus far.

Each day at the beginning of class, Ms. Inez marks off the day of the month on the calendar with a large X. She then writes a statement on the blackboard, describing the day's weather. On the tenth day of school she writes on the board, "Today is sunny and hot." She then reads the statement to the students so that they can begin to make word associations. "Today is sunny and warm." Alex shouts out, "That isn't what you wrote. You wrote today is sunny and hot." Ms. Inez is astounded. Later, during free-play time she asks Alex to sit with her. Alex looks longingly at the puzzles, but grudgingly complies. "Alex, will you read this book to me?"

"Sure," replies Alex, and he does so flawlessly.

Ms. Inez queries, "Do you have this book at home?"

Alex: "Yep. Lots of others, too."

Ms. Inez: "How about this one? Do you have it?"

Alex: "Nope."

Ms. Inez: "Well, then, suppose you try to read this one to me."

Alex: "Okay, but then can I go play with the puzzles?"

Ms. Inez: "Certainly."

Alex reads the book to Ms. Inez, missing only a few words, and then rushes off to play with the puzzles, build towers of blocks and knock them down, and play with trucks. The next day during calendar time, Ms. Inez asks the class, "If today is the fifteenth day of the month and there are thirty days in the month, how could we find out how many days are left?"

The children call out, "We could count the days that don't have X's on them."

"Very good," replies Ms. Inez.

Alex looks puzzled. "What's wrong, Alex?" asks Ms. Inez.

"Why don't we just subtract?" he asks.

1. What are the issues in this case?
2. Why do you suppose Ms. Inez makes light of parents' perceptions of their children's strengths?
3. How should Ms. Inez approach the parents of the students she thinks might have ADHD?
4. Is it appropriate for Ms. Inez or the schools team to make a diagnosis of ADHD? Why or why not?
5. If Alex can already read and subtract, are there other skills he has likely mastered? If so, what might they be? How might this impact his experiences in kindergarten? How should Ms. Inez address this?
6. Which of the following is most likely true about Alex?

    a. Alex has a fluency disorder.
    b. Alex has a learning disability.
    c. Alex has ADHD.
    d. Alex is gifted.

Connecting with Learning: Reach Your Learning Goals

1 CHILDREN WITH DISABILITIES: Describe the various types of disabilities and disorders.

Learning Disabilities

- An estimated 13 percent of U.S. children between 3 and 21 years of age receive special education or related services. The term "children with disabilities" is now used rather than "disabled children," and children with disabilities are no longer referred to as handicapped children.
- The greatest number of children served by special education are those with a learning disability. A child with a learning disability has difficulty in learning that involves understanding or using spoken or written language, and the difficulty can appear in listening, thinking, reading, writing, and spelling. A learning disability also may involve difficulty in doing mathematics.
- To be classified as a learning disability, the learning problem is not primarily the result of visual, hearing, or motor disabilities; intellectual disability; emotional disorders; or due to environmental, cultural, or economic disadvantage. About three times as many boys as girls have a learning disability.
- The most common academic problems for children with a learning disability are reading, writing, and math. Dyslexia is a severe impairment in the ability to read and spell. Dysgraphia is a learning disability that involves having difficulty in handwriting. Dyscalculia is a learning disability that involves difficulties in math computation.
- Controversy surrounds the "learning disability" category; some critics believe it is overdiagnosed; others argue that it is not. Diagnosis is difficult, especially for mild forms. Initial identification of children with a possible learning disability often is made by the classroom teacher, who then asks specialists to evaluate the child. Various causes of learning disabilities have been proposed. Many interventions for learning disabilities focus on reading ability and include such strategies as improving decoding skills. The success of even the best-designed interventions depends on the training and skills of the teacher.

Attention Deficit Hyperactivity Disorder

- Attention deficit hyperactivity disorder (ADHD) is a disability in which children consistently show problems in one or more of these areas: inattention, hyperactivity, and impulsivity. For an ADHD diagnosis, the characteristics must appear early in childhood and be debilitating for the child. Although signs of ADHD may be present in early childhood, diagnosis of ADHD often doesn't occur until the elementary school years.
- Many experts recommend a combination of academic, behavioral, and medical interventions to help students with ADHD learn and adapt. ADHD is not supposed to be diagnosed by school teams because accurate diagnosis requires evaluation by a specialist, such as a psychiatrist. It is important for teachers to monitor whether ADHD medication has been prescribed at the right dosage, to involve a special education resource teacher, to use behavior management strategies, to supply immediate feedback to the child for clearly stated expectations, and to provide structure and teacher-direction. Other recent efforts to reduce ADHD symptoms involve neurofeedback, mindfulness training, and exercise.

Intellectual Disability

- Intellectual disability is a condition with an onset before age 18 that involves low intelligence (usually below 70 on an individually administered intelligence test) and difficulty in adapting to everyday life.
- Intellectual disability has been classified in terms of four categories based mainly on IQ scores: mild, moderate, severe, and profound. More recently, a classification system has been advocated that is based on degree of support required. Determinants of intellectual disability include genetic factors (as in Down syndrome), brain damage (which can result from many different infections, including AIDS), and environmental hazards.

Physical Disorders

- Among the physical disorders that students might have are orthopedic impairments (such as cerebral palsy) and seizure disorders (such as epilepsy).

continued

Sensory Disorders
- Sensory disorders include visual and hearing impairments.
- Visual impairments include having low vision and being educationally blind. A child with low vision can read large-print books or regular books with a magnifying glass. An educationally blind child cannot use vision in learning, instead relying on hearing and touch. An important task is to determine which modality (such as touch or hearing) the student who is visually impaired learns best in. A number of technological devices help these students learn.
- Educational strategies for students with hearing impairments fall into two main categories: oral and manual. Increasingly, both approaches are used with the same student in a total-communication approach.

Speech and Language Disorders
- Speech and language disorders include a number of speech problems (such as articulation disorders, voice disorders, and fluency disorders) and language problems (difficulties in receiving and expressing language). Articulation disorders are problems in pronouncing words correctly. Voice disorders are reflected in speech that is too hoarse, loud, high-pitched, or low-pitched. Children with cleft palate often have a voice disorder. Fluency disorders often involve what we commonly call "stuttering."
- Language disorders involve significant impairments in children's receptive or expressive language. Receptive language involves the reception and understanding of language. Expressive language involves using language for expressing one's thoughts and communicating with others. Specific language impairment (SLI) is another type of speech and language disorder that children may have and involves problems in understanding and using words in sentences.

Autism Spectrum Disorders
- Autism spectrum disorder (ASD) is an increasingly popular term that refers to a broad range of autism disorders including the classical, severe form of autism, as well as Asperger syndrome.
- Autism is a severe autism spectrum disorder with an onset in the first three years of life, and it involves abnormalities in social relationships and communications. It also is characterized by repetitive behaviors. The current consensus is that autism involves an organic brain dysfunction.

Emotional and Behavioral Disorders
- Emotional and behavioral disorders consist of serious, persistent problems that involve relationships, aggression, depression, fears associated with personal or school matters, and other inappropriate socioemotional characteristics.
- The term emotional disturbance (ED) recently has been used to describe this category of disorders, although the use of this term has been criticized. In severe instances of aggressive, out-of-control behaviors, students are removed from the classroom. These problems are far more characteristic of boys than of girls. Problems involving depression, anxiety, and fear, involving turning problems inward, are much more likely to appear in girls than in boys.

❷ EDUCATIONAL ISSUES INVOLVING CHILDREN WITH DISABILITIES: Explain the legal framework and technology advances for children with disabilities.

Legal Aspects
- The educational rights for children with disabilities were laid down in the mid-1960s. In 1975, Congress enacted Public Law 94-142, the Education for All Handicapped Children Act, which mandated that all children be given a free, appropriate public education. Public Law 94-142 was recast in 1990 as the Individuals with Disabilities Education Act (IDEA), which spells out broad requirements for services to all children with disabilities. Children who are thought to have a disability are evaluated to determine their eligibility for services.
- The IDEA has many provisions that relate to the parents of children with disabilities. IDEA was amended in 1997 and then reauthorized in 2004 and renamed the Individuals with Disabilities Education Improvement Act. The 2004 version especially focuses on its alignment with No Child Left Behind legislation, which has raised questions about whether students

- with disabilities can be expected to meet the same general education standards and achievement as students without disabilities.
- The IEP is a written plan of the program specifically tailored for the child with a disability. The plan should (1) relate to the child's learning capacity; (2) be individualized and not a copy of a plan that is offered to other children; and (3) be designed to provide educational benefits.
- The concept of least restrictive environment (LRE) is contained in the IDEA. It states that children with disabilities must be educated in a setting that is as similar as possible to the one in which children without disabilities are educated. This provision of IDEA has given a legal basis to making an effort to educate children with disabilities in the regular classroom. The term *inclusion* means educating children with disabilities full-time in the regular classroom. The trend is toward using inclusion more. Children's academic and social success is affected more by the quality of instruction they receive than by where they are placed.

Technology

- Instructional technology includes various types of hardware and software, combined with innovative teaching methods, to accommodate children's needs in the classroom. Assistive technology consists of various services and devices to help children with disabilities function within their environment.

3 CHILDREN WHO ARE GIFTED: Define what gifted means and discuss some approaches to teaching children who are gifted.

Characteristics

- Children who are gifted have above-average intelligence (usually defined as an IQ of 130 or higher) and/or superior talent in some domain, such as art, music, or mathematics. Some critics argue that gifted programs include too many children who are just somewhat bright, usually cooperative, and usually non-Latinx White. Winner described children who are gifted as having three main characteristics: precocity, marching to the tune of a different drummer, and a passion to master.

Nature/Nurture and Domain-Specific Giftedness

- Giftedness is likely a consequence of both heredity and environment. Developmental changes characterize giftedness. Deliberate practice is often important in the achievement of the gifted. Increasingly the domain-specific aspect of giftedness is emphasized.

Educating Children Who Are Gifted

- Educational programs available for children who are gifted include special classes ("pullout" programs), acceleration, enrichment, mentor and apprenticeship programs, as well as work/study or community-service programs. Debate focuses on whether acceleration or enrichment programs most benefit children who are gifted.
- Children who are gifted increasingly are being educated in the regular classroom. Some experts recommend that increasing the standards in the regular classroom will help children who are gifted, although programs such as mentoring and additional instruction might be needed for children who are still underchallenged. One concern is that the No Child Left Behind legislation has harmed the education of students who are gifted by focusing attention on students' deficiencies.

KEY TERMS

articulation disorders 197
Asperger syndrome 199
attention deficit hyperactivity disorder (ADHD) 189
autism spectrum disorders (ASD) 198
autistic disorder 199
cerebral palsy 196
children who are gifted 208
Down syndrome 195
dyscalculia 187
dysgraphia 187
dyslexia 187
emotional and behavioral disorders 199
epilepsy 196
expressive language 198
fluency disorders 197
inclusion 205
individualized education plan (IEP) 204
Individuals with Disabilities Education Act (IDEA) 204
intellectual disability 194
language disorders 198
learning disability 186
least restrictive environment (LRE) 205
orthopedic impairments 196
Public Law 94-142 204
receptive language 198
specific language impairment (SLI) 198
speech and language disorders 197
voice disorders 197

PORTFOLIO ACTIVITIES

Now that you have a good understanding of this chapter, complete these exercises to expand your thinking.

Independent Reflection

1. **Fostering Positive School-Home Linkages for Children with Disabilities.** Place yourself in the role of a parent. Imagine that the school has just notified you that your child has a learning disability. Write down answers to these questions: (1) What feelings are you likely to be having as a parent? (2) As a parent, what questions do you want to ask the teacher? (3) Now put yourself in the role of the teacher. How would you respond to these questions? (INTASC: Principles 2, 10)

Research/Field Experience

2. **Inclusion in Action.** Interview elementary school, middle school, and high school teachers about their impressions of inclusion and other aspects of educating children with disabilities. Ask them what their most successful strategies are in working with children who have disabilities. Also ask what the biggest challenges are. Write a summary of the interviews. (INTASC: Principle 9)

Collaborative Work

3. **Technology Resources for Gifted Students.** Together with three or four other students in your class, come up with a list and description of software programs that you think would benefit gifted children. One good source of information on such software is the *Journal of Electronic Learning*. Write down the list and descriptions. (INTASC: Principles 2, 8, 9)

chapter 7
BEHAVIORAL AND SOCIAL COGNITIVE APPROACHES

chapter outline

1 What Is Learning?

Learning Goal 1 Define learning and describe five approaches to studying it.

What Learning Is and Is Not
Approaches to Learning

2 Behavioral Approaches to Learning

Learning Goal 2 Compare classical conditioning and operant conditioning.

Classical Conditioning
Operant Conditioning

3 Applied Behavior Analysis in Education

Learning Goal 3 Apply behavior analysis to education.

What Is Applied Behavior Analysis?
Increasing Desirable Behaviors
Decreasing Undesirable Behaviors
Evaluating Operant Conditioning and Applied Behavior Analysis

4 Social Cognitive Approaches to Learning

Learning Goal 4 Summarize social cognitive approaches to learning.

Bandura's Social Cognitive Theory
Observational Learning
Cognitive-Behavioral Approaches and Self-Regulation
Evaluating the Social Cognitive Approaches

To learn is a natural pleasure.
—Aristotle
Greek Philosopher, 4th Century B.C.

Monkey Business Images/Shutterstock

Connecting with Teachers Ruth Sidney Charney

Ruth Sidney Charney has been a teacher for more than 35 years. She has developed the responsive classroom approach to teaching and learning, a method that emphasizes positive reinforcement of students' good behavior. Following are some of her thoughts about reinforcing students' learning (Charney, 2005):

> We reinforce children when we notice. We notice the personal detail our children bring to school and we notice their efforts to behave and learn. . . . We applaud the five correct answers on the math paper (when last week there were only two), the extra sentence in writing, the crisp adjectives, the ten minutes of fair play in a game. . . .
>
> We reinforce by noticing the positive attempts children make to follow the rules and meet class expectations. We reinforce when children are practicing new skills or when they demonstrate behaviors recently modeled. . . .
>
> Examples of noticing and reinforcing students include:
> - "Today's the day, isn't it?" the teacher whispers to Hector. He smiles at her and they share a quick high-five salute, acknowledging Hector's impending solo performance in the church choir.
> - "Snazzy new boots?" the teacher asks Leila as she struts into class. . . .
> - "Thanks for helping Tessa with her spelling. I notice you gave her good hints so she could spell some of the words herself."
> - "I noticed it took much less time today to get in line. What did you notice . . . ?"
> - "I noticed you got your math done this morning with no interruption. That took lots of concentration. . . ."
> - "Thank you for your very efficient clean-up today. I noticed caps back on markers, pencils with points down in cans, paper off the floor. . . ."
> - "You really found an interesting way to solve the problem and complete the project together."

Source: *Using Language to Encourage and Empower Children*, Part 2: Exploring the First "R": To Reinforce, by R.S. Charney, 2005, EducatioWorld (https://www.educationworld.com/a_curr/columnists/charney/charney004b.shtml).

Preview

Virtually everyone agrees that helping students learn is an important function of schools. However, not everyone agrees on the best way to learn. We begin this chapter by examining just what learning involves, then turn to the main behavioral approaches to learning. Next, we explore how behavioral principles are applied to educating students. In the final section, we will discuss the social cognitive approaches to learning.

LG 1 Define learning and describe five approaches to studying it.

1 WHAT IS LEARNING?

Learning is a central focus of educational psychology. When people are asked what schools are for, a common reply is "To help children learn."

WHAT LEARNING IS AND IS NOT

When children learn how to use a computer, they might make some mistakes along the way, but at a certain point they will get the knack of the behaviors required to use the computer effectively. The children will change from being individuals who cannot operate a computer into being individuals who can. Once they have learned how, they don't lose those skills. It's like learning to drive a car. Once you have learned how, you don't have to learn all over again each time you get behind the steering wheel. Thus, **learning** can be defined as a relatively permanent influence on behavior, knowledge, and thinking skills, which comes about through experience.

Not everything we know is learned. We inherit some capacities—they are inborn or innate, not learned. For example, we don't have to be taught to swallow, to flinch at loud noises, or to blink when an object comes too close to our eyes. Most human behaviors, however, do not involve heredity alone. When children use a computer in a new way, work harder at solving problems, ask better questions, explain an answer in a more logical way, or listen more attentively, the experience of learning is at work.

learning A relatively permanent influence on behavior, knowledge, and thinking skills, which comes about through experience.

The scope of learning is broad (Powell et al., 2017). It involves academic behaviors and nonacademic behaviors. It occurs in schools and everywhere else that children experience their world.

APPROACHES TO LEARNING

A number of approaches to learning have been proposed. Next we explore behavioral and cognitive approaches to learning.

Behavioral The learning approaches that we discuss in the first part of this chapter are called *behavioral*. **Behaviorism** is the view that behavior should be explained by observable experiences, not by mental processes. For the behaviorist, behavior is everything that we do, both verbal and nonverbal, that can be directly seen or heard: a child creating a poster, a teacher explaining something to a child, one student picking on another student, and so on. **Mental processes** are defined by psychologists as the thoughts, feelings, and motives that each of us experiences but that cannot be observed by others. Although we cannot directly see thoughts, feelings, and motives, they are no less real. Mental processes include children thinking about ways to create the best poster, a teacher feeling good about children's efforts, and children's inner motivation to control their behavior.

For the behaviorist, these thoughts, feelings, and motives are not appropriate subject matter for a science of behavior because they cannot be directly observed. Behaviorists don't deny that thoughts, feelings, and motives exist; rather, they say these mental processes are not needed to explain behavior. Classical conditioning and operant conditioning, two behavioral views that we will discuss shortly, adopt this stance. Both of these views emphasize **associative learning**, which consists of learning that two events are connected or associated (Domjan, 2015). For example, associative learning occurs when a student associates a pleasant event with learning something in school, such as the teacher smiling when the student asks a good question.

Cognitive *Cognition* means "thought," and psychology became more cognitive or began focusing more on thought in the last part of the twentieth century. The cognitive emphasis continues today and is the basis for numerous approaches to learning (Ashcraft & Radvansky, 2016; Sternberg, 2016a, b). We discuss four main cognitive approaches to learning in this book: social cognitive; information-processing; cognitive constructivist; and social constructivist. The *social cognitive* approaches, which emphasize how behavior, environment, and person (cognitive) factors interact to influence learning, will be covered later in this chapter (Bandura, 2012, 2015). The second set of approaches, *information-processing*, which is addressed in a later chapter, focuses on how children process information through attention, memory, thinking, and other cognitive processes (Siegler, 2016a, b). The third set of approaches, *cognitive constructivist*, emphasizes the child's cognitive construction of knowledge and understanding (Grenell & Carlson, 2016). The fourth set of cognitive approaches, *social constructivist*, focuses on collaboration with others to produce knowledge and understanding (Gauvain, 2016).

Adding these four cognitive approaches to the behavioral approaches, we arrive at five main approaches to learning that we discuss in this book: behavioral, social cognitive, information-processing, cognitive constructivist, and social constructivist. All contribute to our understanding of how children learn. A summary of the five approaches is presented in Figure 1.

As you read about learning and cognition, keep in mind that students are more likely to learn in optimal ways in appropriate learning environments. Students learn best when learning environments are tailored to specific learning goals, to the students' backgrounds and prior knowledge, and to the contexts in which learning will occur. Thus, teachers not only need to understand the basic principles of

---

Thinking Back/Thinking Forward

Piaget's theory is a cognitive constructivist approach. Vygotksy's theory is a social constructivist approach. Connect with "Cognitive and Language Development" and "Social Constructivist Approaches."

---

behaviorism The view that behavior should be explained by observable experiences, not by mental processes.

mental processes Thoughts, feelings, and motives that cannot be observed by others.

associative learning Learning that two events are connected (associated).

Behavioral	Social Cognitive	Information-Processing	Cognitive Constructivist	Social Constructivist
Emphasis on experiences, especially reinforcement and punishment as determinants of learning and behavior	Emphasis on interaction of behavior, environment, and person (cognitive) factors as determinants of learning	Emphasis on how children process information through attention, memory, thinking, and other cognitive processes	Emphasis on the child's cognitive construction of knowledge and understanding	Emphasis on collaboration with others to produce knowledge and understanding

FIGURE 1 APPROACHES TO LEARNING

learning but must also know how to use them to meet diverse learning goals in contexts where students' needs differ (Bransford et al., 2005; Yasnitsky & Van der Veer, 2016).

Review, Reflect, and Practice

① Define learning and describe five approaches to studying it.

REVIEW
- What is learning? Are there any behaviors that don't reflect learning?
- What essentially is behaviorism? What are four main cognitive approaches to learning?

REFLECT
- How do you learn? Think of a behavior you engage in and describe how you learned it.

PRAXIS™ PRACTICE
1. According to the psychological definition of learning, all of the following are examples of learning *except*
    a. writing
    b. sneezing
    c. swimming
    d. washing dishes
2. Mr. Zeller does not believe his students have learned anything unless they demonstrate it to him. This demonstration could be through assignments they turn in to him, answering questions in class, or the way they behave. Which approach to learning is most consistent with Mr. Zeller's ideas?
    a. cognitive
    b. behavioral
    c. social cognitive
    d. conditioning

Please see answer key at end of book . . . .

LG 2 Compare classical conditioning and operant conditioning.

② BEHAVIORAL APPROACHES TO LEARNING

The behavioral approaches emphasize the importance of children making connections between experiences and behavior. The first behavioral approach we will examine is classical conditioning.

CLASSICAL CONDITIONING

Classical conditioning is a type of learning in which an organism learns to connect, or associate, stimuli. In classical conditioning, a neutral stimulus (such as the sight of a person) becomes associated with a meaningful stimulus (such as food) and acquires the capacity to elicit a similar response. Classical conditioning was the brainchild of Ivan Pavlov (1927). To fully understand Pavlov's theory of classical conditioning, we need to understand two types of stimuli and two types of responses: unconditioned stimulus (UCS), unconditioned response (UCR), conditioned stimulus (CS), and conditioned response (CR).

Figure 2 summarizes the way classical conditioning works. An *unconditioned stimulus (UCS)* is a stimulus that automatically produces a response without any prior learning. Food was the UCS in Pavlov's experiments. An *unconditioned response (UCR)* is an unlearned response that is automatically elicited by the UCS. In Pavlov's experiments, the dog's salivation in response to food was the UCR. A *conditioned stimulus (CS)* is a previously neutral stimulus that eventually elicits a conditioned response after being associated with the UCS. Among the conditioned stimuli in Pavlov's experiments were various sights and sounds that occurred prior to the dog's actually eating the food, such as the sound of the door closing before the food was placed in the dog's dish. A *conditioned response (CR)* is a learned response to the conditioned stimulus that occurs after UCS-CS pairing.

Classical conditioning can be involved in both positive and negative experiences of children in the classroom. Among the things in the child's schooling that produce pleasure because they have become classically conditioned are a favorite song and feelings that the classroom is a safe and fun place to be. For example, a song could

classical conditioning A form of associative learning in which a neutral stimulus becomes associated with a meaningful stimulus and acquires the capacity to elicit a similar response.

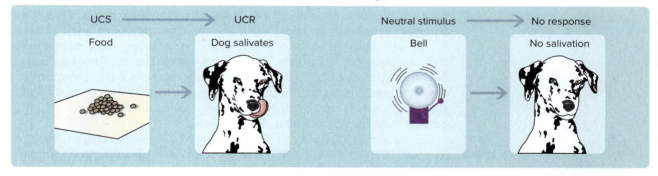

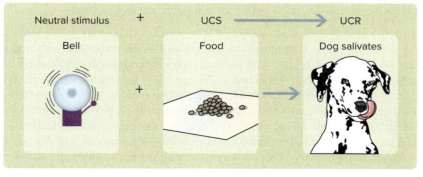

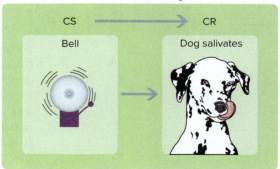

FIGURE 2 PAVLOV'S CLASSICAL CONDITIONING

In one experiment, Pavlov presented a neutral stimulus (bell) just before an unconditioned stimulus (food). The neutral stimulus became a conditioned stimulus by being paired with the unconditioned stimulus. Subsequently, the conditioned stimulus (bell) by itself was able to elicit the dog's salivation.

be neutral for the child until the child joins in with other classmates to sing it with accompanying positive feelings.

Children can develop fear of the classroom if they associate the classroom with criticism, so the classroom becomes a CS for fear. Classical conditioning also can be involved in test anxiety. For example, a child fails and is criticized, which produces anxiety; thereafter, the child associates tests with anxiety, so they then can become a CS for anxiety (see Figure 3).

Some children's health problems also might involve classical conditioning (Chance, 2014). Certain physical complaints—asthma, headaches, and high blood pressure—might be partly due to classical conditioning. We usually say that such health problems can be caused by stress. Often what happens, though, is that certain stimuli, such as a parent's or teacher's heavy criticism, are conditioned stimuli for physiological responses. Over time, the frequency of the physiological responses can produce a health problem. A teacher's persistent criticism of a student can cause the student to develop headaches, muscle tension, and so on. Anything associated with the teacher, such as classroom learning exercises and homework, might trigger the student's stress and subsequently be linked with headaches or other physiological responses.

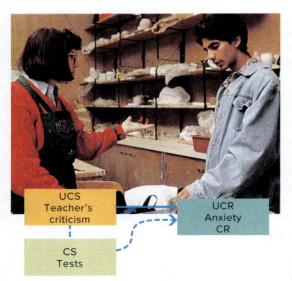

FIGURE 3 CLASSICAL CONDITIONING INVOLVED IN TEACHERS' CRITICISM OF CHILDREN AND TESTS
Elizabeth Crews

Generalization, Discrimination, and Extinction In studying a dog's responses to various stimuli, Pavlov rang a bell before giving meat powder to the dog. By being paired with the UCS (meat), the bell became a CS and elicited the dog's salivation. After a time, Pavlov found that the dog also responded to other sounds, such as a whistle. The more bell-like the noise, the stronger the dog's response. *Generalization* in classical conditioning involves the tendency of a new stimulus similar to the original conditioned stimulus to produce a similar response. Let's consider a classroom example. A student is criticized for poor performance on a biology test. When the student begins to prepare for a chemistry test, she also becomes very nervous because these two subjects are closely related in the sciences. Thus, the student's anxiety generalizes from taking a test in one subject to taking a test in another.

Discrimination in classical conditioning occurs when the organism responds to certain stimuli but not others. To produce discrimination, Pavlov gave food to the dog only after ringing the bell, not after any other sounds. Subsequently, the dog responded only to the bell. In the case of the student taking tests in different classes, she doesn't become nearly as nervous about taking an English test or a history test because they are very different subject areas.

Extinction in classical conditioning involves the weakening of the conditioned response (CR) in the absence of the unconditioned stimulus (UCS). In one session, Pavlov rang the bell repeatedly but did not give the dog any food. Eventually the dog stopped salivating at the sound of the bell. Similarly, if the student who gets nervous while taking tests begins to do much better on tests, her anxiety will fade.

Systematic Desensitization Sometimes the anxiety and stress associated with negative events can be eliminated by classical conditioning. **Systematic desensitization** is a method based on classical conditioning that reduces anxiety by getting the individual to associate deep relaxation with successive visualizations of increasingly anxiety-producing situations. Imagine that you have a student in your class who is extremely nervous about talking in front of the class. The goal of systematic desensitization is to get the student to associate public speaking with relaxation, such as walking on a quiet beach, rather than anxiety. Using successive visualizations (e.g., choosing a topic, drafting a speech, practicing, giving the speech), the student might practice systematic desensitization two weeks before the talk, then a week before, four days before, two days before, the day before, the morning of the talk, on entering the room where the talk is to be given, on the way to the podium, and during the talk.

systematic desensitization A method based on classical conditioning that reduces anxiety by getting the individual to associate deep relaxation with successive visualizations of increasingly anxiety-provoking situations.

Desensitization involves a type of counterconditioning (Rajiah & Saravanan, 2014). The relaxing feelings that the student imagines (UCS) produce relaxation (UCR). The student then associates anxiety-producing cues (CS) with the relaxing feelings. Such relaxation is incompatible with anxiety. By initially pairing a weak anxiety-producing cue with relaxation and gradually working up the hierarchy (from two weeks before the talk to walking up to the podium to give the talk), all of the anxiety-producing cues should generate relaxation (CR).

Chances are you will have students who fear speaking in front of the class or have other anxieties, and there may be circumstances in your own life where you might benefit from replacing anxiety with relaxation. For example, it is not unusual for some teachers to feel comfortable when talking in front of their students but to get very nervous if asked to give a presentation at a teaching conference. Counselors and mental health professionals have been very successful at getting individuals to overcome their fear of public speaking using systematic desensitization. Should you be interested in adopting this strategy, do it with the help of a school psychologist rather than on your own.

Evaluating Classical Conditioning Classical conditioning helps us understand some aspects of learning better than others (Domjan, 2015). It excels in explaining how neutral stimuli become associated with unlearned, involuntary responses (Poulos & Thompson, 2015). It is especially helpful in understanding students' anxieties and fears. However, it is not as effective in explaining voluntary behaviors, such as why a student studies hard for a test or likes history better than geography. For these areas, operant conditioning is more relevant.

OPERANT CONDITIONING

Operant conditioning (also called *instrumental conditioning*) is a form of learning in which the consequences of behavior produce changes in the probability that the behavior will occur. Operant conditioning is at the heart of B. F. Skinner's (1938) behavioral view. Consequences—rewards and punishments—are contingent on the organism's behavior.

Reinforcement and Punishment **Reinforcement (reward)** is a consequence that increases the probability that a behavior will occur. In contrast, **punishment** is a consequence that decreases the probability a behavior will occur. For example, you might tell one of your students, "Congratulations. I'm really proud of the story that you wrote." If the student works harder and writes an even better story the next time, your positive comments are said to reinforce, or reward, the student's writing behavior. If you frown at a student for talking in class and the student's talking decreases, your frown is said to punish the student's talking.

To reinforce behavior means to strengthen the behavior (Domjan, 2015). Two forms of reinforcement are positive reinforcement and negative reinforcement. In **positive reinforcement**, the frequency of a response increases because it is followed by a rewarding stimulus, as in the example in which the teacher's positive comments increased the student's writing behavior. Similarly, complimenting parents on being at a parent-teacher conference might encourage them to come back again.

Conversely, in **negative reinforcement**, the frequency of a response increases because it is followed by the removal of an aversive (unpleasant) stimulus. For example, a father nags at his son to do his homework. He keeps nagging. Finally, the son gets tired of hearing the nagging and does his homework. The son's response (doing his homework) removed the unpleasant stimulus (nagging).

One way to remember the distinction between positive and negative reinforcement is that in positive reinforcement something is added. In negative reinforcement, something is subtracted, or removed. It is easy to confuse negative reinforcement and

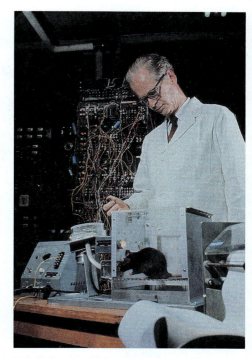

B. F. Skinner conducting an operant conditioning study in his behavioral laboratory. The rat being studied is in a Skinner box.
Nina Leen/The LIFE Picture Collection/Getty Images

operant conditioning A form of learning in which the consequences of behavior produce changes in the probability that the behavior will occur.

reinforcement (**reward**) A consequence that increases the probability that a behavior will occur.

punishment A consequence that decreases the probability that a behavior will occur.

positive reinforcement Reinforcement based on the principle that the frequency of a response increases because it is followed by a rewarding stimulus.

negative reinforcement Reinforcement based on the principle that the frequency of a response increases because an aversive (unpleasant) stimulus is removed.

Positive Reinforcement

Behavior:
Student asks a good question

Consequence:
Teacher praises student

Future behavior:
Student asks more good questions

Negative Reinforcement

Behavior:
Student turns homework in on time

Consequence:
Teacher stops criticizing student

Future behavior:
Student increasingly turns homework in on time

Punishment

Behavior:
Student interrupts teacher

Consequence:
Teacher verbally reprimands student

Future behavior:
Student stops interrupting teacher

FIGURE 4 REINFORCEMENT AND PUNISHMENT
Remember that reinforcement comes in positive and negative forms. In both forms, the consequences increase behavior. In punishment, behavior is decreased.
(*Left to right*) Daniel Laflor/Vetta/Getty Images; Hero/Corbis/Fancy/Glow Images; Westend61/zerocreatives/Getty Images

punishment. To keep these terms straight, remember that negative reinforcement *increases* the probability a response will occur, whereas punishment *decreases* the probability it will occur. Figure 4 summarizes and presents examples of the concepts of positive reinforcement, negative reinforcement, and punishment.

Generalization, Discrimination, and Extinction In our coverage of classical conditioning, we discussed generalization, discrimination, and extinction. These processes also are important dimensions of operant conditioning (Miltenberger, 2016). Remember that in classical conditioning, generalization is the tendency of a stimulus similar to the conditioned stimulus to produce a response similar to the conditioned response. *Generalization* in operant conditioning means giving the same response to a stimulus similar to the one for which it was originally reinforced. Especially of interest is the extent to which behavior generalizes from one situation to another. For example, if a teacher praises the student for asking good questions related to English, will this generalize to harder work in history, math, and other subjects?

Remember that in classical conditioning, discrimination means responding to certain stimuli but not others. *Discrimination* in operant conditioning involves differentiating among stimuli or environmental events. For example, a student knows that the tray on the teacher's desk labeled "Math" is where she is supposed to place today's math work, whereas another tray labeled "English" is where today's English assignments are to be put. This might sound overly simple, but it is important because students' worlds are filled with such discriminative stimuli. Around school these discriminative stimuli might include signs that say "Stay Out," "Form a Line Here," and so on.

In operant conditioning, *extinction* occurs when a previously reinforced response is no longer reinforced and the response decreases. In the classroom, the most common use of extinction is for the teacher to withdraw attention from a behavior that the attention is maintaining. For example, in some cases a teacher's attention inadvertently reinforces a student's disruptive behavior, as when a student pinches another student and the teacher immediately talks with the perpetrator. If this happens on a regular basis, the student might learn that pinching other students is a good way to get the teacher's attention. If the teacher withdraws his or her attention, the pinching might extinguish.

Review, Reflect, and Practice

 Compare classical conditioning and operant conditioning.

REVIEW
- What is classical conditioning? What are the UCS, UCR, CS, and CR? In the context of classical conditioning, what are generalization, discrimination, extinction, and systematic desensitization?
- What is operant conditioning? Explain the different types of reinforcement and punishment. In the context of operant conditioning, what are generalization, discrimination, and extinction?

REFLECT
- Do you think that your emotions are the result of classical conditioning, operant conditioning, or both? Explain.

PRAXIS™ PRACTICE
1. Sylvia is participating in a class spelling bee. The teacher asks her to spell the word *mortgage*. "Don't forget the *t*, don't forget the *t*," Sylvia says to herself. "M-O-R-T-A-G-E," says Sylvia. "I'm sorry, that's incorrect, Sylvia," says her teacher. One of the students in the back of the class snickers and comments, "Gee, about time Miss Smarty-pants got one wrong. See, she's not so smart." Some other students join in the laughter. Sylvia begins to cry and runs out of the room. After that, Sylvia becomes very anxious about spelling bees. According to classical conditioning theory, what is the conditioned stimulus in this scenario?
   a. the teacher telling her she is incorrect
   b. the other students' laughter
   c. the word *mortgage*
   d. spelling bees
2. Tyler is a fourth-grade student. He loves to crack jokes, often at his teacher's expense. One day he called his teacher, Ms. Bart, "Ms. Fart." Ms. Bart quickly admonished him for his behavior and told him that name-calling was unacceptable. She made him stay after school to discuss his behavior. The other students in the class thought Tyler's nickname for Ms. Bart was hilarious, laughing along with Tyler and later telling him what a good name that was for Ms. Bart. The next day, Tyler again called Ms. Bart by the insulting nickname. According to operant conditioning theory, Tyler continued to use this name in spite of having to stay after school the day before because
   a. the behavior had continued for a lengthy period of time
   b. he was positively reinforced by his classmates for the behavior
   c. he was negatively reinforced by his teacher for his behavior
   d. he was punished by his teacher for his behavior

Please see answer key at end of book . . . .

LG 3 Apply behavior analysis to education.

Many applications of operant conditioning have been made outside of research laboratories in the wider worlds of classrooms, homes, businesses, psychotherapy, hospitals, and other real-world settings (Spiegler, 2016). This section describes how teachers can use applied behavior analysis to improve students' behavior and learning.

WHAT IS APPLIED BEHAVIOR ANALYSIS?

Applied behavior analysis involves applying the principles of operant conditioning to change human behavior. Three uses of applied behavior analysis are especially important in education: increasing desirable behavior, using prompts and shaping, and decreasing undesirable behavior (Alberto & Troutman, 2017). Applications of applied behavior analysis often use a series of steps. These often begin with some general observations and then turn to determining the specific target behavior that needs to be changed, as well as observing its antecedent conditions. Behavioral goals are then set, particular reinforcers or punishers are selected, a behavior management program is carried out, and the success or failure of the program is evaluated (Miltenberger, 2016).

INCREASING DESIRABLE BEHAVIORS

Six operant conditioning strategies can be used to increase a child's desirable behaviors: choose effective reinforcers; make reinforcers contingent and timely; select the best schedule of reinforcement; consider contracting; use negative reinforcement effectively; and use prompts and shaping.

Choose Effective Reinforcers Not all reinforcers are the same for every child. Applied behavior analysts recommend that teachers find out what reinforcers work best with which children—that is, individualize the use of particular reinforcers. For one student it might be praise, for another it might be getting to spend more time participating in a favorite activity, for another it might involve being a hall monitor for a week, and for yet another it could be getting to surf the Internet. To find out the most effective reinforcers for a child, you can examine what has motivated the child in the past (reinforcement history), what the student wants but can't easily or frequently get, and the child's perception of the reinforcer's value. Some applied behavior analysts recommend asking children which reinforcers they like best. Another recommendation is to consider novel reinforcers to reduce the child's boredom. Natural reinforcers such as praise and privileges are generally recommended over material rewards such as candy, stars, and money.

Activities are some of the most common reinforcers that teachers use. Named after psychologist David Premack, the **Premack principle** states that a high-probability activity can serve as a reinforcer for a low-probability activity. The Premack principle is at work when an elementary school teacher tells a child, "When you complete your writing assignment, you can play a game on the computer" (but only effective if playing games on a computer is more desirable for the student than writing). The Premack principle also can be used with the entire class. A teacher might tell the class, "If all of the class gets their homework done by Friday, we will take a field trip next week."

> **Thinking Back/Thinking Forward**
>
> Applied behavior analysis can be used as part of managing the classroom effectively. Connect to "Managing the Classroom."

applied behavior analysis Application of the principles of operant conditioning to change human behavior.

Premack principle The principle that a high-probability activity can serve as a reinforcer for a low-probability activity.

Make Reinforcers Contingent and Timely For a reinforcer to be effective, the teacher must give it only after the child performs the particular behavior. Applied behavior analysts often recommend that teachers make "If . . . then" statements to children—for example, "Tony, if you finish ten math problems, then you can go out to play." This makes it clear to Tony what he has to do to get the reinforcer. Applied behavior analysts say that it is important to make the reinforcer contingent on the child's behavior. That is, the child has to perform the behavior to get the reward. If Tony does not complete ten math problems and the teacher still lets him go out to play, the contingency has not been established.

Reinforcers are more effective when they are given in a timely way, as soon as possible after the child performs the target behavior. This helps children see the contingency connection between the reward and their behavior. If the child completes the target behavior (such as doing ten math problems by midmorning) and the teacher doesn't give the child playtime until late afternoon, the child might have trouble making the contingency connection.

Select The Best Schedule of Reinforcement Most of the examples given so far assume continuous reinforcement—that is, the child is reinforced every time he or she makes a response. In continuous reinforcement, children learn very rapidly, but when the reinforcement stops (the teacher stops praising), extinction also occurs rapidly. In the classroom, continuous reinforcement is rare. A teacher with a classroom of 25 or 30 students can't praise a child every time he or she makes an appropriate response.

Partial reinforcement involves reinforcing a response only part of the time. Skinner (1957) developed the concept of **schedules of reinforcement**, which are partial reinforcement timetables that determine when a response will be reinforced. The four main schedules of reinforcement are fixed-ratio, variable-ratio, fixed-interval, and variable-interval.

On a *fixed-ratio schedule,* a behavior is reinforced after a set number of responses. For example, a teacher might praise the child only after every fourth correct response, not after every response. On a *variable-ratio schedule,* a behavior is reinforced on an unpredictable basis like in gambling. For example, a teacher's praise might be given after the second correct response, after eight more correct responses, after the next seven correct responses, and after the next three correct responses.

Interval schedules are determined by the amount of time elapsed since the last behavior was reinforced. On a *fixed-interval schedule,* the first appropriate response after a fixed amount of time is reinforced. For example, a teacher might praise a child for the first good question the child asks after two minutes have elapsed or give a quiz every week. On a *variable-interval schedule,* a response is reinforced after a variable amount of time has elapsed. On this schedule, the teacher might praise the child's question-asking after three minutes have gone by, then after fifteen minutes have gone by, after seven minutes have gone by, and so on. Giving a pop quiz at uneven intervals is another example of a variable-interval schedule.

What is the effect of using these schedules of reinforcement with children? Initial learning is usually faster with continuous rather than partial reinforcement. In other words, when students are first learning a behavior, continuous reinforcement works better. However, partial reinforcement produces greater persistence and greater resistance to extinction than continuous reinforcement does. Thus, once children master a response, partial reinforcement works better than continuous reinforcement.

Children on fixed schedules show less persistence and faster response extinction than children on variable schedules. Children show the most persistence on a variable-interval schedule. This schedule produces slow, steady responding because children don't know when the reward will come. As we mentioned earlier, giving pop quizzes

> **THROUGH THE EYES OF STUDENTS**
>
> **"Watch Her, Mom"**
>
> One year a third-grade teacher at Salem Church Elementary School in Chesterfield County, Virginia, had an especially loud, active group of third-graders. The teacher, Kristen Blankenship, used a combination of individual and group positive reinforcement as a management strategy.
>
> Not having a cafeteria, students ate their lunches in the classroom. While joining her son for lunch one day, Daniel's mother pulled Kristen aside, smiled, and said that he had just whispered to her, "Watch her, Mom. She never yells, but she sure knows how to keep them in line."

schedules of reinforcement Partial reinforcement timetables that determine when a response will be reinforced.

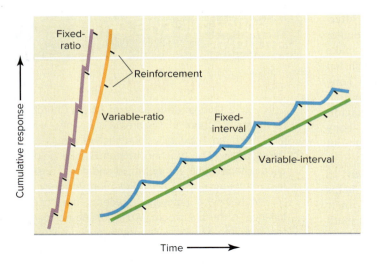

FIGURE 5 SCHEDULES OF REINFORCEMENT AND DIFFERENT PATTERNS OF RESPONDING

In this figure, each hash mark indicates the delivery of reinforcement. Notice that ratio schedules (reinforcement is linked with number of responses) produce higher rates of responding than interval schedules (reinforcement is linked with the amount of time elapsed). The predictability of a reward also is important in that a predictable (fixed) schedule produces a higher response rate than an unpredictable (variable) schedule.

contracting Putting reinforcement contingencies into writing.

prompt An added stimulus or cue that is given just before a response that increases the likelihood the response will occur.

at uneven intervals is a good example of the variable-interval schedule. If the teacher starts making the quizzes more predictable (for example, once a week on Fridays), children will begin to show the stop-start work pattern that characterizes the fixed-interval schedule. That is, they won't work hard for most of the week; then toward the end of the week they will start cramming for the quiz. Thus, if your goal as a teacher is to increase children's persistence after the behavior has been established, variable schedules work best, especially the variable-interval schedule. Figure 5 shows the different response patterns associated with the different schedules of reinforcement.

Consider Contracting **Contracting** involves putting reinforcement contingencies in writing. If problems arise and children don't uphold their end of the bargain, the teacher can refer the children to the contract they agreed to. Applied behavior analysts suggest that a classroom contract should be the result of input from both the teacher and the student. Classroom contracts have "If . . . then" statements and are signed by the teacher and child, then dated. A teacher and child might agree on a contract that states that the child agrees to be a good citizen by doing _____, _____, and _____. As part of the contract, the teacher agrees to _____ if the student behaves in this manner. In some instances, the teacher asks another child to sign the contract as a witness to the agreement.

Use Negative Reinforcement Effectively Remember that in *negative reinforcement,* the frequency of response increases because the response removes an aversive (unpleasant) stimulus (Alberto & Troutman, 2017). A teacher who says, "Thomas, because you were off task earlier, now you have to stay in your seat and finish writing your story before you join the other students in making a poster," is using punishment (staying in seat) to reduce off-task behavior. Then, when Thomas finishes his work, negative reinforcement is being used as the punishing consequence (staying in seat) is removed with the goal of increasing future on-task behavior.

Using negative reinforcement has some drawbacks. Sometimes when teachers try to use this behavioral strategy, children throw a tantrum, run out of the room, or destroy materials. These negative outcomes happen most often when children don't have the skills or capabilities to do what the teacher asks of them.

Use Prompts and Shaping Earlier in our discussion of operant conditioning, we indicated that discrimination involves differentiating among stimuli or environmental events. Students can learn to discriminate among stimuli or events through differential reinforcement. Two differential reinforcement strategies available to teachers are prompts and shaping (Alberto & Troutman, 2017).

Prompts A **prompt** is an added stimulus or cue that is given just before a response that increases the likelihood that the response will occur. A reading teacher who holds up a card with the letters *w-e-r-e* and says, "Not was, but . . . " is using a verbal prompt. An art teacher who places the label "Watercolors" on one group of paints and "Oils" on another also is using prompts. Prompts help get behavior going. Once the students consistently show the correct responses, the prompts are no longer needed.

Instructions can be used as prompts (Alberto & Troutman, 2017). For example, as the art period is drawing to a close, the teacher says, "Let's get started on reading." If the students keep doing art, the teacher adds the prompt, "Okay, put away your art materials and come with me over to the reading area." Some prompts come in the form of hints, as when the teacher tells students to line up "quietly." Bulletin boards are common locations for prompts, frequently displaying reminders of class rules, due dates for projects, the location of a meeting, and so on. Some prompts are presented visually, as when the teacher places her hand on her ear when a student is not speaking loudly enough.

Shaping When teachers use prompts, they assume that students can perform the desired behaviors. But sometimes students do not have the ability to perform them. In this case, shaping is required. **Shaping** involves teaching new behaviors by reinforcing successive approximations to a specified target behavior. Initially, you reinforce any response that in some way resembles the target behavior. Subsequently, you reinforce a response that more closely resembles the target, and so on until the student performs the target behavior, and then you reinforce it.

Suppose you have a student who has never completed 50 percent or more of her math assignments. You set the target behavior at 100 percent, but you reinforce her for successive approximations to the target. You initially might provide a reinforcer (some type of privilege, for example) when she completes 60 percent, then the next time only when she completes 70 percent, then 80, then 90, and finally 100 percent.

Shaping can be an important tool for the classroom teacher because most students need reinforcement along the way to reaching a learning goal (Chance, 2014). Shaping can be especially helpful for learning tasks that require time and persistence to complete. However, when using shaping, remember to implement it only if the other types of positive reinforcement and prompts are not working. Also remember to be patient. Shaping can require the reinforcement of a number of small steps en route to a target behavior, and these might take place only over an extended period of time.

DECREASING UNDESIRABLE BEHAVIORS

When teachers want to decrease children's undesirable behaviors (such as teasing, hogging a class discussion, or smarting off to the teacher), what are their options? Applied behavior analysts Paul Alberto and Anne Troutman (2017) recommend using these steps in this order:

1. Use differential reinforcement.
2. Terminate reinforcement (extinction).
3. Remove desirable stimuli.
4. Present aversive stimuli (punishment).

shaping Teaching new behaviors by reinforcing successive approximations to a specified target behavior.

Thus, the teacher's first option should be differential reinforcement. Punishment should be used only as a last resort and always in conjunction with providing the child with information about appropriate behavior.

Use Differential Reinforcement In *differential reinforcement,* the teacher reinforces behavior that is more appropriate or that is incompatible with what the child is doing. For example, the teacher might reinforce a child for doing learning activities on a computer rather than playing games with it, for being courteous rather than interrupting, for being seated rather than running around the classroom, or for completing homework on time rather than late.

Terminate Reinforcement (Extinction) The strategy of terminating reinforcement involves withdrawing positive reinforcement from a child's inappropriate behavior. Many inappropriate behaviors are inadvertently maintained by positive reinforcement, especially the teacher's attention. Applied behavior analysts point out that this can occur even when the teacher gives attention to an inappropriate behavior by criticizing, threatening, or yelling at the student. Many teachers find it difficult to determine whether they are giving too much attention to inappropriate behavior. A good strategy is to get someone to observe your classroom on several occasions and chart the patterns of reinforcement you use with your students (Alberto & Troutman, 2017). If you become aware that you are giving too much attention to a student's inappropriate

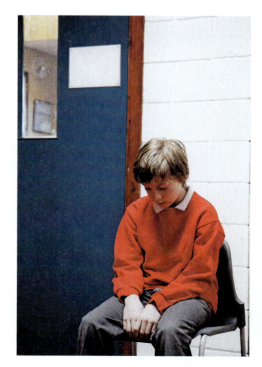

This student has been placed in "time-out" for misbehaving. *What is the nature of time-out?*
Ableimages/DigitalVision/Getty Images

behavior, ignore that behavior and give attention to the student's appropriate behavior. Always combine taking attention away from inappropriate behavior with giving attention to appropriate behavior. For instance, when a student stops monopolizing the conversation in a group discussion after you withdraw your attention, compliment the student on the improved behavior.

Remove Desirable Stimuli Suppose you have tried the first two options, and they haven't worked. A third option is to remove desirable stimuli from the student. Two strategies for accomplishing this are "time-out" and "response cost."

Time-Out The most widely used strategy that teachers use to remove desirable stimuli is **time-out**. In other words, take the student away from positive reinforcement. For example, a teacher might use time-out with a student who won't stay in his seat or engages in loud confrontations with the teacher.

Response Cost A second strategy for removing desirable stimuli involves **response cost**, which refers to taking a positive reinforcer away from a student, as when the student loses certain privileges. For example, after a student misbehaves, the teacher might take away 10 minutes of recess time or the privilege of being a class monitor. Response cost typically involves some type of penalty or fine. As with time-out, response cost should always be used in conjunction with strategies for increasing the student's positive behaviors.

How do teachers use applied behavior analysis in their classrooms? Following are their responses.

EARLY CHILDHOOD We use applied behavior analysis with our preschoolers by giving time-out to students who are misbehaving. For example, if a child throws a toy across the room during free play, hits another student, or speaks disrespectfully, we explain why this behavior is inappropriate and give time-out. The child has to sit in a chair, away from other students, and misses five minutes of free-play time. As a result, the child learns that negative behavior will not be tolerated.

—Missy Dangler

ELEMENTARY SCHOOL: GRADES K–5 For my second-grade students, tangible or implied (a smile from me or attention) rewards work best. I also find that a com-bination of individual and group rewards work well in my classroom. For example, I give each student a "Compliment Sheet" at the beginning of the school year. When I see behavior that I want to encourage, I tell the student publicly that he or she may have a compliment. The student fills in one of the circles on the compliment page, and the others in the class—seeing that this student's particular behavior has been rewarded—imitate the student's behavior almost immediately. The rules are that no compliment may be removed and that a student may not ask for a compliment. When the Compliment Sheet is completed, a big deal is made of it, and the student can go the prize box and choose a small token such as stickers. At first this is an external way of conditioning behavior, but the children seem to move rapidly from wanting the "thing" to wanting the compliment to wanting the positive attention to doing the right thing.

—Janine Guida Poutre

MIDDLE SCHOOL: GRADES 6–8 I'm not big on rewards for my sixth-grade students. I think students who act inappropriately in class need to learn how to cope and deal with controlling their behavior without expecting to receive something in return. Instead of rewards, I give students who turn from negative behavior to positive

time-out Removing an individual from positive reinforcement.

response cost Taking a positive reinforcer away from an individual.

CONNECTING WITH STUDENTS: Best Practices
Strategies for Using Time-Out

In using time-out, you have several options:

1. *Keep the student in the classroom, but deny the student access to positive reinforcement.* This strategy is most often used when a student does something minor. The teacher might ask the student to put his or her head down on the desk for a few minutes or might move the student to the periphery of an activity so the student can still observe other students experiencing positive reinforcement. In *Through the Eyes of Teachers,* kindergarten teacher Rosemary Moore describes an innovative use of time-out.

THROUGH THE EYES OF TEACHERS
The Peace Place

Resolving conflicts is always difficult for children. When my kindergartners engaged in power struggles, they often turned to me to referee. I thought it would be much more beneficial if they could arrive at their own compromise. Ownership of the plan would make it more acceptable to all parties. To accomplish this, I put two small chairs in a corner of the room. Above the chairs was a sign that said, "Peace Place." Then when I heard a struggle begin, I would send the parties to this corner. There they sat facing each other with their knees almost touching. Their task was to negotiate a "peace plan." When the plan was agreed upon, they were to come to me. I would listen to their plan and either approve it or send them back for another try. Initially, this took some time, but as the children began to realize that the time they spent arguing was time away from the activity they were arguing about, they arrived at their plan much more quickly. It was a pleasure to watch them grow in their negotiating abilities.

Rosemary Moore

2. *For time-out to be effective, the setting from which the student is removed has to be positively reinforcing, and the setting in which the student is placed has to lack positive reinforcement.* For example, if you seat a student in the hall outside your classroom and students from other classes come down the hall and talk with the student, the time-out is clearly not going to serve its intended purpose.

3. *If you use time-out, be sure to identify the student's behaviors that resulted in time-out.* For example, say to the student, "You tore up Corey's paper, so go to time-out right now for five minutes." Don't get into an argument with the student or accept lame excuses as to why the student should not get a time-out. If necessary, take the student to the time-out location. If the misbehavior occurs again, identify the behavior once again and repeat the time-out. If the student starts yelling, knocking over furniture, and so on, when you assign time-out, add time to time-out. Be sure to let the student out of time-out when the designated time away from positive reinforcement is up. Don't comment on how well the student behaved during time-out; just return the student to the prior activity.

4. *Positively reinforce the student's positive behavior when he or she is not in time-out.* Reinforce positive behavior during regular class time. For example, if a student got time-out for disruptive behavior, the teacher can praise the student for quietly working on an assignment during class.

5. *Keep records of each time-out session, especially if a time-out room is used.* This will help you monitor effective and ethical use of time-outs.

behavior more responsibility in the classroom. For example, students who engage in good behavior are given classroom jobs—for example, handing out pencils and paper, checking my mail box in the main office, and turning on/shutting off computers. Students love responsibility and are happy when I depend on them to perform important duties in the classroom.

—FELICIA PETERSON

HIGH SCHOOL: GRADES 9–12 I set clear expectations for my high school students. For example, it is a classroom expectation that students are in my classroom, ready to work, when the bell rings. Students soon learn that walking in late results in not knowing what is going on in class and may lower their grade if they cannot complete an activity. It is important to start class on time and not let the stragglers determine when class will start.

—SANDY SWANSON

What are some effective strategies for using reprimands?
Chris Schmidt/E+/Getty Images

> **Thinking Back/Thinking Forward**
>
> Authoritarian parenting is restrictive and punitive, and so is an authoritarian classroom management style. Both are less effective styles than authoritative (rather than authoritarian) parenting and an authoritative classroom management style. Connect with "Social Contexts and Socioemotional Development" and "Managing the Classroom."

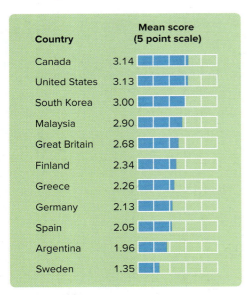

Country	Mean score (5 point scale)
Canada	3.14
United States	3.13
South Korea	3.00
Malaysia	2.90
Great Britain	2.68
Finland	2.34
Greece	2.26
Germany	2.13
Spain	2.05
Argentina	1.96
Sweden	1.35

FIGURE 6 ATTITUDES ABOUT CORPORAL PUNISHMENT IN DIFFERENT COUNTRIES

A 5-point scale was used to assess attitudes toward corporal punishment, with scores closer to 1 indicating an attitude against its use and scores closer to 5 suggesting an attitude favoring its use.

Present Aversive Stimuli (Punishment) Most people associate the presentation of aversive (unpleasant) stimuli with punishment, as when a teacher yells at a student or a parent spanks a child. However, in accordance with the definition of punishment given earlier in the chapter, an aversive stimulus is punishment only if it decreases the undesirable behavior. All too often, though, aversive stimuli are not effective punishments, in that they do not decrease the unwanted behavior and indeed sometimes increase the unwanted behavior over time.

The most common types of aversive stimuli that teachers use are verbal reprimands. These are more effectively used when the teacher is near the student rather than across the room and when used together with a nonverbal reprimand such as a frown or eye contact. Reprimands are more effective when they are given immediately after unwanted behavior and when they are short and to the point. Such reprimands do not have to involve yelling and shouting, which often just raise the noise level of the classroom and present the teacher as an uncontrolled model for students. Instead, a firmly stated "stop doing that" with eye contact is often sufficient to stop unwanted behavior. Another strategy is to take the student aside and reprimand the student in private rather than in front of the entire class.

Many countries, such as Sweden, have banned the physical punishment of schoolchildren (which usually involves school paddling) by principals and teachers. However, in 2015, 19 U.S. states still allowed it with the greatest prevalence in southern states. Research on college students in 11 countries found that the United States and Canada have more favorable attitudes toward corporal punishment than many other countries (Curran et al., 2001; Hyman et al., 2001) (see Figure 6). Use of corporal punishment by parents is legal in every state in America, and it is estimated that 70 to 90 percent of American parents have spanked their children (Straus, 1991). A national survey of U.S. parents with 3- and 4-year-old children found that 26 percent of parents reported spanking their children frequently, and 67 percent of the parents reported yelling at their children frequently (Regalado et al., 2004).

In U.S. schools, male minority students from low-income backgrounds are the most frequent recipients of physical punishment. Many psychologists and educators argue that physical punishment of students should not be used in any circumstance.

Physical or otherwise, numerous problems are associated with using aversive stimuli as intended punishment:

- Especially when you use intense punishment such as yelling or screaming, you are presenting students with an out-of-control model for handling stressful situations.
- Punishment can instill fear, rage, or avoidance in students. Skinner's biggest concern was this: What punishment teaches is how to avoid something. For example, a student who experiences a punitive teacher might show a dislike for the teacher and not want to come to school.
- When students are punished, they might become so agitated and anxious that they can't concentrate clearly on their work for a long time after the punishment has been given.
- Punishment tells students what not to do rather than what to do. If you make a punishing statement, such as "No, that's not right," always accompany it with positive feedback, such as "but why don't you try this."
- What is intended as punishment can turn out to be reinforcing. A student might learn that misbehaving will not only get the teacher's attention but put the student in the limelight with classmates as well.
- Punishment can be abusive. When parents discipline their children, they might not intend to be abusive, but they might become so upset and angry when they are punishing the child that they become abusive. Teachers in all 50 states are legally required to report even reasonable suspicions of child abuse to the police

or local child protective services. Teachers should learn about their state's laws and their school district's policy regarding the reporting of child abuse.

Debate about the effects of punishment on children's development continues (Ferguson, 2013; Gershoff, 2013; Gershoff & Grogan-Kaylor, 2016; Laible et al., 2015; Theunissen et al., 2015). One debate about punishment that is ongoing involves a distinction between mild punishment and more intense punishment. A research review of 26 studies concluded that only severe or predominant use of spanking, not mild spanking, compared unfavorably with alternative discipline practices with children (Larzelere & Kuhn, 2005). Indeed, there are few longitudinal studies of punishment and few studies that distinguish adequately between moderate and heavy use of punishment. In a recent meta-analysis in which physical punishment that was not abusive was distinguished from physical abuse, physical punishment was linked to detrimental child outcomes (Gershoff & Grogan-Kaylor, 2017).

RESEARCH

However, research on punishment is correlational in nature, making it difficult to discover causal factors. Also, consider the concept of reciprocal socialization that emphasizes bidirectional child and parent influences. Researchers have found links between children's early behavioral problems and parents' greater use of physical punishment over time (Laible et al., 2015). Nonetheless, a large majority of leading experts on parenting conclude that physical punishment has harmful effects on children and should not be used.

In a recent research review, a leading expert on punishment, Elizabeth Gershoff (2013), concluded that the defenders of spanking have not produced any evidence that spanking produces positive outcomes for children and that negative outcomes of spanking have been replicated in many studies. Also, one thing that is clear is that when physical punishment involves abuse, it can be very harmful to children's development, as discussed later in this chapter (Cicchetti & Toth, 2015, 2016).

A final lesson related to using punishment less often is to spend more class time monitoring what students do right rather than what they do wrong. Too often disruptive behavior, not competent behavior, grabs a teacher's attention. Every day make it a point to scan your classroom for positive student behaviors that you ordinarily would not notice and give students attention for them.

Thinking Back/Thinking Forward

The new trend in classroom management places more emphasis on guiding students toward self-discipline and less on externally controlling the student. Connect to "Managing the Classroom."

EVALUATING OPERANT CONDITIONING AND APPLIED BEHAVIOR ANALYSIS

Operant conditioning and applied behavior analysis have made contributions to teaching practice (Alberto & Troutman, 2017). Reinforcing and punishing consequences are part of teachers' and students' lives. Teachers give grades, praise and reprimand, smile and frown. Learning about how such consequences affect students' behavior improves your capabilities as a teacher. Used effectively, behavioral techniques can help you manage your classroom. Reinforcing certain behaviors can improve some students' conduct and—used in conjunction with the time-out—can increase desired behaviors in some incorrigible students.

Critics of operant conditioning and applied behavior analysis argue that the whole approach places too much emphasis on external control of students' behavior—a better strategy is to help students learn to control their own behavior and become internally motivated. Some critics argue that it is not the reward or punishment that changes behavior but, rather, the belief or expectation that certain actions will be rewarded or punished (Schunk, 2016). In other words, the behavioral theories do not give adequate attention to cognitive processes involved in learning (Ashcraft & Radvansky, 2016). Critics also point to potential ethical problems when operant conditioning is used inappropriately, as when a teacher immediately resorts to punishing students instead of first considering reinforcement strategies, or punishes a student without also

When used effectively, what are ways that operant conditioning and applied behavior analysis can help teachers manage the classroom? What are some criticisms that have been leveled at these approaches?
Fuse/Corbis/Getty Images

giving the student information about appropriate behavior. Another criticism is that when teachers spend a lot of time using applied behavior analysis, they might focus too much on student conduct and not enough on academic learning. We will have much more to say about student conduct in the chapter on managing the classroom.

Review, Reflect, and Practice

 Apply behavior analysis to education.

REVIEW
- What is applied behavior analysis?
- What are six ways to increase desirable behaviors?
- What are four ways to decrease undesirable behaviors?
- What are some effective and ineffective uses of operant conditioning and applied behavior analysis?

REFLECT
- Come up with your own example in an educational setting for each of the six ways to increase desirable behavior.

PRAXIS™ PRACTICE
1. The uses of applied behavior analysis in education include all of the following *except*
   a. asking a child to reflect about undesirable behavior
   b. increasing desirable behavior
   c. using prompts and shaping
   d. decreasing undesirable behavior

2. Ms. Sanders wants her students to be quiet and ready to learn as soon as possible after coming in from recess. Sometimes the children are so excited that they have difficulty quieting down. To help remind them that it is time to be quiet and listen, Ms. Sanders flicks the light switch on and off several times. The children immediately quiet and listen to her instructions. According to applied behavioral analysis, what is Ms. Sanders doing when she turns the lights on and off?
   a. prompting
   b. punishing
   c. coercing
   d. shaping

3. Sid is a real handful in class. He talks when he should be working quietly. He gets out of his seat without permission. He often disrupts class. His third-grade teacher, Ms. Marin, sends him out into the hall when he misbehaves as a form of time-out. However, Sid continues to misbehave. At one point, Ms. Marin checks on Sid in the hall and finds him quietly tossing a ball back and forth with a child from another class. Why has time-out been ineffective with Sid?
   a. Ms. Marin did not present an aversive enough stimulus to Sid.
   b. Ms. Marin did not use differential reinforcement effectively.
   c. Sid finds being in class to be reinforcing.
   d. Sid finds being in the hallway to be reinforcing.

4. Critics of applied behavior analysis techniques often point out that when these techniques are used in the classroom they
   a. lead to physical abuse of students
   b. do not work effectively
   c. take time away from academics
   d. emphasize external control of behavior

Please see answer key at end of book . . . .

4 SOCIAL COGNITIVE APPROACHES TO LEARNING

LG 4 Summarize social cognitive approaches to learning.

Because students' thoughts affect their behavior and learning, a number of cognitive approaches to learning have been proposed. In this section, we will explore several social cognitive approaches, beginning with social cognitive theory. This theory evolved out of behavioral theories but has become increasingly more cognitive (Spiegler, 2016).

BANDURA'S SOCIAL COGNITIVE THEORY

Social cognitive theory states that social and cognitive factors, as well as behavior, play important roles in learning. Cognitive factors might involve the students' expectations for success; social factors might include students' observing their parents' achievement behavior. Social cognitive theory is an increasingly important source of classroom applications (Schunk, 2016).

Albert Bandura (1986, 1997, 2001, 2009, 2012, 2015) is the main architect of social cognitive theory. He says that when students learn, they can cognitively represent or transform their experiences. Recall that in operant conditioning, connections occur only between environmental experiences and behavior.

Bandura developed a *reciprocal determinism model* that consists of three main factors: behavior, person/cognitive, and environment. As shown in Figure 7, these factors can interact to influence learning: Environmental factors influence behavior, behavior affects the environment, person (cognitive) factors influence behavior, and so on. Bandura uses the term *person*, but I have modified it to *person/cognitive* because so many of the person factors he describes are cognitive. The person factors Bandura describes that do not have a cognitive bent are mainly personality traits and temperament. Such factors might include being introverted or extraverted, active or inactive, calm or anxious, and friendly or hostile. Cognitive factors include expectations, beliefs, attitudes, strategies, thinking, and intelligence. Affective and emotional factors such as emotional self-regulation or temperament also are included in person/cognitive factors.

Consider how Bandura's model might work in the case of the achievement behavior of a high school student we will call Sondra:

- *Cognition influences behavior.* Sondra develops cognitive strategies to think more deeply and logically about how to solve problems. The cognitive strategies improve her achievement behavior.
- *Behavior influences cognition.* Sondra's studying (behavior) has led her to achieve good grades, which in turn produces positive expectancies about her abilities and gives her self-confidence (cognition).
- *Environment influences behavior.* The school Sondra attends recently developed a pilot study-skills program to help students learn how to take notes, manage their time, and take tests more effectively. The study-skills program improves Sondra's achievement behavior.
- *Behavior influences environment.* The study-skills program is successful in improving the achievement behavior of many students in Sondra's class. The students' improved achievement behavior stimulates the school to expand the program so that all students in the high school participate in it.
- *Cognition influences environment.* The expectations and planning of the school's principal and teachers made the study-skills program possible in the first place.

Albert Bandura, who developed social cognitive theory.
Courtesy of Dr. Albert Bandura

Thinking Back/Thinking Forward

The Big Five Personality Factors are openness, conscientiousness, extraversion, agreeableness, and neuroticism (emotional stability). Connect to "Individual Variations."

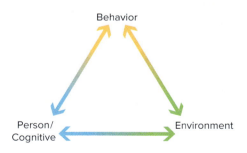

FIGURE 7 BANDURA'S SOCIAL COGNITIVE THEORY

Bandura's social cognitive theory emphasizes reciprocal influences of behavior, environment, and person/cognitive factors.

social cognitive theory Bandura's theory that social and cognitive factors, as well as behavior, play important roles in learning.

- *Environment influences cognition.* The school establishes a resource center where students and parents can go to check out books and materials on improving study skills. The resource center also makes study-skills tutoring services available to students. Sondra and her parents take advantage of the center's resources and tutoring. These resources and services improve Sondra's thinking skills.

In Bandura's learning model, person/cognitive factors play important roles. The person/cognitive factor that Bandura (2009, 2015) has emphasized the most in recent years is **self-efficacy**, the belief that one can master a situation and produce positive outcomes. Bandura (2009, 2010c) says that self-efficacy has a powerful influence over behavior. For example, a student who has low self-efficacy might not even try to study for a test because he doesn't believe it will do him any good. We will have much more to say about self-efficacy in the chapter on motivation, teaching, and learning.

Next, we discuss the important learning process of observational learning, which is another of Bandura's main contributions. As you read about observational learning, note how person/cognitive factors are involved.

> **Thinking Back/Thinking Forward**
>
> Your self-efficacy as a teacher will have an important impact on the quality of learning your students experience. Connect to "Motivation, Teaching, and Learning."

OBSERVATIONAL LEARNING

Observational learning is learning that involves acquiring skills, strategies, and beliefs by observing others. Observational learning involves imitation but is not limited to it. What is learned typically is not an exact copy of what is modeled but rather a general form or strategy that observers often apply in creative ways. The capacity to learn behavior patterns by observation eliminates tedious trial-and-error learning. In many instances, observational learning takes less time than operant conditioning.

Processes in Observational Learning Bandura (1986) describes four key processes in observational learning: attention, retention, production, and motivation (see Figure 8):

- *Attention.* Before students can produce a model's actions, they must attend to what the model is doing or saying. Attention to the model is influenced by a host of characteristics. For example, warm, powerful, atypical people command more attention than do cold, weak, typical people. Students are more likely to be attentive to high-status models than to low-status models. In most cases, teachers are high-status models for students.

FIGURE 8 BANDURA'S MODEL OF OBSERVATIONAL LEARNING

In Bandura's model of observational learning, four processes need to be considered: attention, retention, production, and motivation. *How might these processes be involved in this classroom situation in which a teacher is demonstrating how to tell time?*
Jeffry W. Myers/Corbis Documentary/Getty Images

- *Retention.* To reproduce a model's actions, students must code the information and keep it in memory so that they can retrieve it. A simple verbal description or a vivid image of what the model did assists students' retention. For example, the teacher might say, "I'm showing the correct way to do this. You have to do this step first, this step second, and this step third," as she models how to solve a math problem. A video with a colorful character demonstrating the importance of considering other students' feelings might be remembered better than if the teacher just tells the students to do this. Such colorful characters are at the heart of the popularity of *Sesame Street* with children. Students' retention will be improved when teachers give vivid, logical, and clear demonstrations.
- *Production.* Children might attend to a model and code in memory what they have seen—but, because of limitations in their motor ability, not be able to

> **Thinking Back/Thinking Forward**
>
> Four types of attention are selective, divided, sustained, and executive. Connect to "The Information-Processing Approach."

self-efficacy The belief that one can master a situation and produce positive outcomes.

observational learning Learning that involves acquiring skills, strategies, and beliefs by observing others.

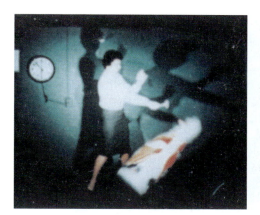 

FIGURE 9 BANDURA'S CLASSIC BOBO DOLL STUDY: THE EFFECTS OF OBSERVATIONAL LEARNING ON AGGRESSION

(*Left*) An adult model aggressively attacks the Bobo doll. (*Right*) A kindergarten-age girl who has observed the model's aggressive actions follows suit. *In Bandura's experiment, under what conditions did the children reproduce the model's aggressive actions?*

(Both) Dr. Albert Bandura

reproduce the model's behavior. A 13-year-old might watch basketball player Lebron James and golfer Michelle Wie execute their athletic skills to perfection, or observe a famous pianist or artist, but not be able to reproduce their motor actions. Teaching, coaching, and practice can help children improve their motor performances.

- *Motivation.* Often children attend to what a model says or does, retain the information in memory, and possess the motor skills to perform the action but are not motivated to perform the modeled behavior. This was demonstrated in Bandura's (1965) classic Bobo doll study when children who saw the model being punished did not reproduce the punished model's aggressive actions (see Figure 9). However, when they subsequently were given a reinforcement or incentive (stickers or fruit juice), they did imitate the model's behavior.

Bandura argues that reinforcement is not always necessary for observational learning to take place. But if the child does not reproduce the desired behaviors, four types of reinforcement can help do the trick: (1) reward the model; (2) reward the child for approximating the behavior; (3) instruct the child to make self-reinforcing statements such as "Good, I did it!" or "Okay, I've done a good job of getting most of this right; now if I keep trying I will get the rest"; or (4) show how the behavior leads to reinforcing outcomes.

> **Thinking Back/Thinking Forward**
>
> For memory to work, students have to take information in (encoding), store it or represent it (storage), and retrieve it for some purpose later (retrieval). Connect to "The Information-Processing Approach."

Models in the Classroom   As you can see, you will be an important model in students' lives. Your students will be observing your behavior countless times every day of the school year. An intentional way that teachers can use observational learning is through *modeled demonstrations,* in which the teacher describes and shows students how to solve problems and successfully complete academic tasks. For example, a teacher might demonstrate how to create an outline for a paper or do a PowerPoint presentation. Also students can become more reflective and think more critically by observing models.

In addition to observing and learning from your behavior in the classroom, students learn from observing many other models, including parents, mentors, and peers. Students especially are likely to attend to and attempt to learn the behaviors of individuals who are competent and have prestige (Schunk, 2016). For example, a teacher might invite a well-known professional athlete to come to her class and talk about how important it is to read and do well in school. Because of the athlete's prestige, the students are likely to attend to what the athlete says and be motivated to adopt the behaviors he or she recommends.

Peers also can be important models in the classroom (Wentzel & Muenks, 2016). When a student observes peers successfully doing school tasks, especially peers that a student likes or admires, the student's self-efficacy for performing well in school likely increases.

Ken Brisco is a mentor in Aurora, Colorado. Here he is mentoring an eighth grade student who is considered at risk for potential gang involvement.
Helen H. Richardson/The Denver Post/Getty Images

DIVERSITY

RESEARCH

One concern about the models that children and adolescents observe and interact with in the classroom is the lack of ethnic and gender diversity. As students in U.S. schools have become more ethnically diverse in recent decades, their teachers are still overwhelmingly non-Latinx White females. In 2012, approximately 18 percent of U.S. public school students were African American, but only 7 percent of their teachers were African American (National Center for Education Statistics, 2015). Only a small percentage of the African American teachers were males. In the same year, Latinxs made up 24 percent of U.S. public school students, but only 8 percent of their teachers were Latinx. A majority of U.S. public schools still do not have any ethnic minority teachers.

In 2012, 76 percent of public elementary and secondary school teachers were female, 24 percent male (National Center for Education Statistics, 2015). Men comprise about 10 percent of elementary school teachers but comprise nearly half of middle and high school teachers (many of whom are lured by additional incentives for coaching athletic teams). Also, only 1.8 percent of elementary and secondary school teachers were African American males and only 1.6 percent of the teachers were Latinx in a recent year (Toldson & Lewis, 2012).

Regardless of your ethnic background, look around the community for possible mentors for students, especially students who come from low-income backgrounds and who lack positive role models. For example, the aim of the 3-to-1 mentoring program is to surround each ethnic minority male student with three positive ethnic minority role models. The program began when several African American men were challenged by a sermon delivered by Zach Holmes at St. Luke's Methodist Church in Dallas. In the sermon, Reverend Holmes urged his congregation to become more involved with children, both their own and children in the community who don't have good role models. The 3-to-1 mentoring program has signed up more than 200 men and 100 boys (ages 4 to 18). That's far short of the goal of three mentors for each boy, but the men are working on increasing the number of mentors in the program. Some of the men in the mentoring program have their own children, like Dr. Leonard Berry, a physician, who has two sons and a daughter. He heeded the minister's challenge and regularly participates in the mentoring program, which involves academic tutoring as well as outings to activities such as sporting and cultural events. The mentors also take the students to visit the Johnson Space Center in Houston. To evaluate the roles that models and mentors have played in your own life and can play in your students' lives, complete *Self-Assessment 1*.

SELF-ASSESSMENT 1
Models and Mentors in My Life and My Students' Lives

Having positive role models and mentors can make an important difference in whether individuals develop optimally and reach their full potential. First, evaluate the influence of role models and mentors who have played an important part in your life. Second, think about the type of role model you want to be for your students. Third, give some thought to how you will incorporate other models and mentors into your students' lives. Fourth, explore who your education mentor might be.

MY MODELS AND MENTORS

List the most important role models and mentors in your life. Then describe what their positive modeling and mentoring have meant to your development.

Role Models and Mentors   *Their Contributions*

1. _____   _____
2. _____   _____
3. _____   _____
4. _____   _____
5. _____   _____

The Type of Role Model I Want to Be for My Students

Describe which characteristics and behaviors you believe are the most important for you to model for your students.

1. _____   _____
2. _____   _____
3. _____   _____
4. _____   _____
5. _____   _____

How Will I Incorporate Models and Mentors in My Classroom?

Describe a systematic plan for bringing models and mentors into your students' lives in one or more domain(s) you plan to teach, such as math, English, science, and music.

_____
_____

Who Will Be My Education Mentor? What Would My Ideal Education Mentor Be Like?

Do you have someone in mind who might serve as an education mentor when you become a teacher? If so, describe the person.

_____

What would your ideal education mentor be like?

_____
_____

Several teachers were asked how they use observational learning in the classroom. Following are their responses.

EARLY CHILDHOOD Preschool children spend a lot of time doing informal observation and may try to imitate what someone else has done to see if they can get similar results. For example, when a teacher tells a group of children to walk down the hall instead of running and praises those students who are walking, children who are running often slow down and walk, hoping they will be praised by the teacher.

—Heidi Kaufman

ELEMENTARY SCHOOL: GRADES K–5 My basic assumption with my elementary school students is that they learn appropriate behavior by observation and experience. Class rules are established and agreed upon at the beginning of the school year. I model effective learning behaviors, identify them when students use them, teach study skills, and end every class by stating one or two behavioral skills that were done well.

—Keren Abra

MIDDLE SCHOOL: GRADES 6–8 I use observational learning with my sixth-grade students all the time. I make sure that they understand my expectations by not only discussing them but also showing them what I expect. For example, I create checklists for my students at the beginning of the year so they can assess their work and monitor their progress. We then go over the checklists one-on-one and as a group and discuss ways that they can improve their work or behavior in order to reach their desired goals.

—Casey Maass

HIGH SCHOOL: GRADES 9–12 As a high school art teacher, I am fortunate to work in an area that is visual, hands-on, and creative. Through one-on-one demonstrations, small-group and sometimes total class lectures/demonstrations, my students observe and learn artistic skills.

—Dennis Peterson

TECHNOLOGY   DEVELOPMENT

Models in the Media—the Example of Sesame Street Children are exposed to an extensive number of models in the media, so it is especially important that these experiences be positive. The television show *Sesame Street* is a very effective educational program that in includes many positive observational learning opportunities for young children. The program began in 1969 and is still going strong. A fundamental message of *Sesame Street* is that learning and entertainment work well. On *Sesame Street*, learning is exciting and entertaining. A recent meta-analysis of studies in 14 countries found that watching the TV show *Sesame Street* produced positive outcomes in three areas: cognitive skills, learning about the world, and social reasoning and attitudes toward outgroups (Mares & Pan, 2013).

COGNITIVE-BEHAVIORAL APPROACHES AND SELF-REGULATION

Operant conditioning spawned applications in real-world settings, and the interest in cognitive-behavioral approaches has also produced such applications. In the fifth century B.C., the Chinese philosopher Confucius said, "If you give a man a fish, you feed him for a day. If you teach a man to fish, you feed him for a lifetime." As you read about the cognitive-behavioral approaches and self-regulation, you will discover that they reflect Confucius' simple observation.

What educational lessons can be learned from Sesame Street?

Scott J. Ferrell/Congressional Quarterly/Alamy Stock Photo

CONNECTING WITH STUDENTS: Best Practices
Best Practices and Strategies for Effectively Using Observational Learning

1. *Think about what type of model you will present to students.* Every day, hour after hour, students will watch and listen to what you say and do. Just by being around you, students will absorb a great deal of information. They will pick up your good or bad habits, your expectations for their high or low achievement, your enthusiastic or bored attitude, your controlled or uncontrolled manner of dealing with stress, your learning style, your gender attitudes, and many other aspects of your behavior. A good strategy, then, is that you behave as you want your students to behave.

2. *Demonstrate and teach new behaviors.* Demonstrating means that you, the teacher, are a model for your students' observational learning. Demonstrating how to do something, from solving a math problem, reading, writing, thinking, to controlling anger or performing physical skills, is a common technique used by teachers. For example, a teacher might model how to diagram a sentence, develop a strategy for solving algebraic equations, or shoot a basketball. When demonstrating how to do something, you need to call students' attention to the relevant details of the learning situation. Your demonstrations also should be clear and follow a logical sequence.

3. *Think about ways to use peers as effective models.* The teacher is not the only model in the classroom. As with teachers, children can pick up their peers' good and bad habits, high or low achievement orientations, and so on, through observational learning. Remember that students are often motivated to imitate high-status models. Older peers usually have higher status than same-age peers. Thus, a good strategy is to have older peers from a higher grade model how to engage in the behaviors you want your students to perform. For students with low abilities or who are not performing well, a low-achieving student who struggles but puts considerable effort into learning and ultimately performs the behaviors can be a good model. More will be said about peer collaboration and peers as tutors in the chapter on social constructivist approaches.

4. *Think about ways that mentors can be used as models.* Students and teachers benefit from having a mentor—someone they look up to and respect, someone who serves as a competent model, someone who is willing to work with them and help them achieve their goals. Just spending a few hours a week with a mentor can make a difference in a student's life, especially if the student's parents have not been good role models. As a teacher, a potential mentor for you is a more experienced teacher, possibly someone who teaches down the hall and has had a number of years of experience in dealing with some of the same problems and issues you will have to cope with.

5. *Evaluate which classroom guests will provide good models for students.* To change the pace of classroom life for you and your students, invite guests who have something meaningful to talk about or demonstrate. Recall Gardner's theory of multiple intelligences: There likely are some domains (physical, musical, artistic, or other) in which you don't have the skills to serve as a competent model for your students. When you need to have such skills demonstrated to your students, spend some time locating competent models in the community. Invite them to come to your classroom to demonstrate and discuss their skills. If this can't be arranged, set up field trips in which you take students to see them where they are working or performing. In *Through the Eyes of Teachers,* fourth-grade teacher Marlene Wendler describes a positive role model her school brings to teachers' classrooms.

THROUGH THE EYES OF TEACHERS
Here Comes the Judge

Our local judge has taken a proactive role in trying to eliminate teen behavioral problems. With a half dozen adults from the community, he comes to the fourth-grade classrooms in our areas and puts on skits about bullying. They show the whole group picking on a student in a bus situation. Then they do the skit again with someone in the group stopping the bullying. The students then role-play bullying situations, learning what to do if they are bullied and how to help someone who is bullied. Having the judge come to our school has made a lasting impression on our students.

Marlene Wendler

6. *Consider the models children observe on television, videos, and digital content.* Students observe models when they watch television programs, videos, or films, or when they experience digital content in your classroom and on computers and mobile devices. The principles of observational learning we described earlier apply to these media. For example, the extent to which the students perceive the media models as high or low in status, intriguing or boring, and so on will influence the extent of their observational learning.

TECHNOLOGY

Cognitive-Behavioral Approaches In the **cognitive-behavioral approaches**, the emphasis is on getting students to monitor, manage, and regulate their own behavior rather than letting it be controlled by external factors. In some circles, this has been called *cognitive behavior modification* (Spiegler, 2016). Cognitive-behavioral approaches stem from both cognitive psychology, with its emphasis on the effects of thoughts on behavior, and behaviorism, with its emphasis on techniques for changing behavior. Cognitive-behavioral approaches try to change students' misconceptions, strengthen their coping skills, increase their self-control, and encourage constructive self-reflection (Miltenberger, 2016).

Self-instructional methods are cognitive-behavioral techniques aimed at teaching individuals to modify their own behavior. Self-instructional methods help people alter what they say to themselves.

Imagine a situation in which a high school student is extremely nervous about taking standardized tests, such as the SAT. The student can be encouraged to talk to himself in positive ways. Following are some self-talk strategies that students and teachers can use to cope more effectively with such stressful situations (Meichenbaum et al., 1975):

- Prepare for anxiety or stress. "What do I have to do?" "I'm going to develop a plan to deal with it." "I'll just think about what I have to do." "I won't worry. Worry doesn't help anything." "I have a lot of different strategies I can use."
- Confront and handle the anxiety or stress. "I can meet the challenge." "I'll keep on taking just one step at a time." "I can handle it. I'll just relax, breathe deeply, and use one of the strategies." "I won't think about my stress. I'll just think about what I have to do."
- Cope with feelings at critical moments. "What is it I have to do?" "I knew my anxiety might increase. I just have to keep myself in control." "When the anxiety comes, I'll just pause and keep focusing on what I have to do."
- Use reinforcing self-statements. "Good, I did it." "I handled it well." "I knew I could do it." "Wait until I tell other people how I did it!"

In many instances, the strategy is to replace negative self-statements with positive ones. For example, a student might say to herself, "I'll never get this work done by tomorrow." This can be replaced with positive self-statements such as these: "This is going to be tough, but I think I can do it." "I'm going to look at this as a challenge rather than a stressor." "If I work really hard, I might be able to get it done." Or in having to participate in a class discussion, a student might replace the negative thought "Everyone else knows more than I do, so what's the use of saying anything?" with positive self-statements such as these: "I have as much to say as anyone else." "My ideas may be different, but they are still good." "It's okay to be a little nervous; I'll relax and start talking." Figure 10 shows posters that students in one fifth-grade class developed to help them remember how to talk to themselves while listening, planning, working, and checking.

Talking positively to oneself can help teachers and students reach their full potential. Uncountered negative thinking has a way of becoming a self-fulfilling prophecy. You think you can't do it, and so you don't. If negative self-talk is a problem for you, at random times during the day ask yourself, "What am I saying to myself right now?" Moments that you expect will be potentially stressful are excellent times to examine your self-talk. Also monitor your students' self-talk. If you hear students saying, "I can't do this" or "I'm so slow that I'll never get this done," spend some time getting them to replace their negative self-talk with positive self-talk.

Cognitive behaviorists recommend that students improve their performance by monitoring their own behavior (Schunk, 2016). This can involve getting students to keep charts or records of their behavior. When I (your author) wrote this book, I had a chart on my wall with each of the chapters listed. I planned how long it would take me to do each of the chapters, and then as I completed each one I checked it off and wrote down the date of completion. Teachers can get students to do some similar monitoring of their own progress by getting them to keep records of how many

---

cognitive-behavioral approaches Changing behavior by getting individuals to monitor, manage, and regulate their own behavior rather than letting it be controlled by external factors.

self-instructional methods Cognitive-behavioral techniques aimed at teaching individuals to modify their own behavior.

assignments they have finished, how many books they have read, how many homework papers they have turned in on time, how many days in a row they have not interrupted the teacher, and so on. In some cases, teachers place these self-monitoring charts on the walls of the classroom. Alternatively, if the teacher thinks that negative social comparison with other students will be highly stressful for some students, then a better strategy might be to have students keep private records (in a notebook, for example) that are periodically checked by the teacher.

Self-monitoring is an excellent strategy for improving learning, and one that you can help students learn to do effectively. By completing *Self-Assessment 2,* you should get a sense of the benefits of self-monitoring for your students.

Self-Regulatory Learning Educational psychologists increasingly advocate the importance of self-regulatory learning (Kitsantas & Cleary, 2016). **Self-regulatory learning** consists of the self-generation and self-monitoring of thoughts, feelings, and behaviors in order to reach a goal. These goals might be academic (improving comprehension while reading, becoming a more organized writer, learning how to do multiplication, asking relevant questions) or they might be socioemotional (controlling one's anger, getting along better with peers) (McClelland et al.; McClelland et al., 2016).

As children become older, their capacity for self-regulation increases (Miele & Scholer, 2016). The increased capacity for self-regulation is linked to developmental advances in the brain's prefrontal cortex (Blair et al., 2016).

What are some of the characteristics of self-regulated learners? Self-regulatory learners do the following things (Winne, 2001, 2005):

- Set goals for extending their knowledge and sustaining their motivation
- Are aware of their emotional makeup and have strategies for managing their emotions
- Periodically monitor their progress toward a goal
- Fine-tune or revise their strategies based on the progress they are making
- Evaluate obstacles that may arise and make the necessary adaptations

Self-regulation is an important aspect of school readiness (Blair & Raver, 2015). In the Chicago School Readiness Project that involved 35 Head Start programs, the positive achievement outcomes for children occur through improvement in teacher-child relationships and children's increased self-regulation (Jones et al., 2013).

Researchers also have found that high-achieving students are often self-regulatory learners (Schunk, 2016). For example, compared with low-achieving students, high-achieving students set more specific learning goals, use more strategies to learn, self-monitor their learning more, and more systematically evaluate their progress toward a goal.

Self-regulation also plays an important role in helping children and adolescents be more conscientious, not just in childhood and adolescence, but later in life. For example, research indicates self-regulation fosters conscientiousness, both directly and through its link to academic motivation/success and internalized compliance with norms (Eisenberg et al., 2014).

Teachers, tutors, mentors, counselors, and parents can help students become self-regulatory learners. Barry Zimmerman, Sebastian Bonner, and Robert Kovach (1996) developed a model for turning low-self-regulatory students into students who engage in these multistep strategies: (1) self-evaluation and monitoring, (2) goal setting and strategic planning, (3) putting a plan into action and monitoring it, and (4) monitoring outcomes and refining strategies (see Figure 11).

Zimmerman and colleagues describe a seventh-grade student who is doing poorly in history and apply their self-regulatory model to her situation. In step 1, she self-evaluates her studying and test preparation by keeping a detailed record of them. The teacher gives her some guidelines for keeping these records. After several weeks, the student turns the records in and traces her poor test performance to low comprehension of difficult reading material.

Poster 1
While listening
1. Does this make sense?
2. Am I getting this?
3. I need to ask a question before I forget.
4. Pay attention.
5. Can I do what the teacher is saying to do?

Poster 2
While planning
1. Do I have everything together?
2. Do I have my friends tuned out so I can get this done?
3. I need to get organized first.
4. What order can I do this in?
5. I know this stuff.

Poster 3
While working
1. Am I working fast enough?
2. Stop staring at my girlfriend (boyfriend) and get back to work.
3. How much time is left?
4. Do I need to stop and start all over?
5. This is hard for me but I can manage it.

Poster 4
While checking
1. Did I finish everything?
2. What do I need to recheck?
3. Am I proud of this work?
4. Did I write all of the words?
5. I think I'm finished. I organized myself. Did I daydream too much, though?

FIGURE 10 SOME POSTERS DEVELOPED BY A FIFTH-GRADE CLASS TO HELP THEM REMEMBER HOW TO EFFECTIVELY TALK TO THEMSELVES

Source: "Four Posters Developed by a Fifth Grade Class," by B.H. Manning and B.D. Payne, in *Self-Talk for Teachers and Students,* 1996, Pearson Education, Inc.

RESEARCH

self-regulatory learning The self-generation and self-monitoring of thoughts, feelings, and behaviors in order to reach a goal.

SELF-ASSESSMENT 2
Self-Monitoring

Self-monitoring can benefit you as well as your students. Many successful learners regularly self-monitor their progress to see how they are doing in their effort to complete a project, develop a skill, or perform well on a test or other assessment. For the next month, self-monitor your study time for this course you are taking in educational psychology. To achieve high grades, most instructors recommend that students spend two or three hours out of class studying, doing homework, and working on projects for every hour they are in class in college (Santrock & Halonen, 2009). The experience of self-monitoring your own study time should give you a sense of how important such skills are for your students to develop. You might adapt this form for students' homework, for example. Remember from our discussion of Bandura's social cognitive theory that self-efficacy involves your belief that you can master a situation and produce positive outcomes. One way to evaluate self-efficacy is your expectancy for attaining a particular score on an upcoming quiz or test. Determine what score or grade you want to achieve on your next quiz or test. Then each day you study, rate your self-efficacy for achieving the score you desire on a 3-point scale: 1 = not very confident, 2 = moderately confident, and 3 = very confident.

FORM FOR SELF-MONITORING STUDY TIME

		STUDY CONTEXT					
Date	Assignment	Time Started	Time Finished	Where?	With Whom?	Distractions	Self-Efficacy

In step 2, the student sets a goal, in this case of improving reading comprehension, and plans how to achieve the goal. The teacher assists her in breaking the goal into components, such as locating main ideas and setting specific goals for understanding a series of paragraphs in her textbook. The teacher also provides the student with strategies, such as focusing initially on the first sentence of each paragraph and then scanning the others as a means of identifying main ideas. Another support the teacher might offer the student is adult or peer tutoring in reading comprehension if it is available.

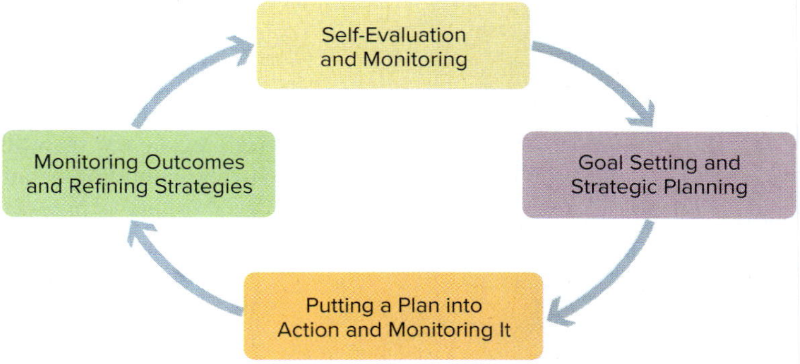

In step 3, the student puts the plan into action and begins to monitor her progress. Initially, she may need help from the teacher or tutor in identifying main ideas in the reading. This feedback can help her monitor her reading comprehension more effectively on her own.

In step 4, the student monitors her improvement in reading comprehension by evaluating whether it has had any impact on her learning outcomes. Most importantly, has her improvement in reading comprehension led to better performance on history tests?

Self-evaluations reveal that the strategy of finding main ideas has only partly improved her comprehension, and only when the first sentence contained the paragraph's main idea, so the teacher recommends further strategies. Figure 12 describes how teachers can apply the self-regulatory model to homework.

FIGURE 11 A MODEL OF SELF-REGULATORY LEARNING

(Cycle: Self-Evaluation and Monitoring → Goal Setting and Strategic Planning → Putting a Plan into Action and Monitoring It → Monitoring Outcomes and Refining Strategies → back to Self-Evaluation and Monitoring)

1. Self-evaluation and monitoring

- The teacher distributes forms so that students can monitor specific aspects of their studying.
- The teacher gives students daily assignments to develop their self-monitoring skills and a weekly quiz to assess how well they have learned the methods.
- After several days, the teacher begins to have students exchange their homework with their peers. The peers are asked to evaluate the accuracy of the homework and how effectively the student engaged in self-monitoring. Then the teacher collects the homework for grading and reviews the peers' suggestions.

2. Goal setting and strategic planning

- After a week of monitoring and the first graded exercise, the teacher asks students to give their perceptions of the strengths and weaknesses of their study strategies. The teacher emphasizes the link between learning strategies and learning outcomes.
- The teacher and peers recommend specific strategies that students might use to improve their learning. Students may use the recommendations or devise new ones. The teacher asks students to set specific goals at this point.

3. Putting a plan into action and monitoring it

- The students monitor the extent to which they actually enact the new strategies.
- The teacher's role is to make sure that the new learning strategies are openly discussed.

4. Monitoring outcomes and refining strategies

- The teacher continues to give students opportunities to gauge how effectively they are using their new strategies.
- The teacher helps students summarize their self-regulatory methods by reviewing each step of the self-regulatory learning cycle. She also discusses with students the hurdles the students had to overcome and the self-confidence they have achieved.

FIGURE 12 APPLYING THE SELF-REGULATORY MODEL TO HOMEWORK

The development of self-regulation is influenced by many factors, among them modeling and self-efficacy (Bandura, 2012, 2015). Consider Zimmerman's four-phase model and how modeling can be an effective strategy for building self-regulatory skills and self-efficacy in improving reading and writing (Schunk & Zimmerman, 2006). Among the self-regulatory skills that models can engage in are planning and managing time effectively, attending to and concentrating, organizing and coding information strategically, establishing a productive work environment, and using social resources. For example, students might observe a teacher engage in an effective time management strategy and verbalize appropriate principles. By observing such models, students can come to believe that they also can plan and manage time effectively, which creates a sense of self-efficacy for academic self-regulation and motivates students to engage in those activities.

Self-efficacy can influence a student's choice of tasks, effort expended, persistence, and achievement (Bandura, 2012, 2015). Compared with students who doubt their learning capabilities, those with high self-efficacy for acquiring a skill or performing a task participate more readily, work harder, persist longer in the face of difficulty, and achieve at a higher level. Self-efficacy can have a strong effect on achievement, but it is not the only influence. High self-efficacy will not result in competent performance when requisite knowledge and skills are lacking. We will further explore self-efficacy, goal setting, planning, and self-regulation in the chapter on motivation, teaching, and learning.

Teachers who encourage students to be self-regulatory learners convey the message that students are responsible for their own behavior, for becoming educated, and for becoming contributing citizens to society. Another message conveyed by self-regulatory learning is that learning is a personal experience that requires active and dedicated

CONNECTING WITH STUDENTS: Best Practices
Strategies for Encouraging Students to Be Self-Regulated Learners

Following are some effective strategies for guiding students to engage in self-regulated learning:

1. *Gradually guide students to become self-regulated learners.* Helping students become self-regulated learners takes time and requires considerable monitoring, guidance, and encouragement on your part. High-achieving students are more likely to already be self-regulated learners than low-achieving students. All students can benefit from practicing their self-regulated learning skills, but recognize that low-achieving students will need more instruction and time to develop these skills.

2. *Make the classroom learning experience challenging and interesting for students.* When students are bored and uninterested in learning, they are less likely to become self-regulated learners. Instead of giving students one particular book to read, providing students with a variety of interesting books is likely to encourage their motivation to read. Giving students choices increases students' personal investment in their learning and increases their self-regulation.

3. *Provide tips about thoughts and actions that will help students engage in self-regulation.* These might include giving specific guidelines as needed, such as "Planning for 30 minutes will help you . . ." and "Every day stop and monitor where you are in what you want to accomplish." Other suggestions include encouraging students to reflect on their strengths and weaknesses in a learning situation and encouraging them to search for help and ways to use help effectively (All Kinds of Minds, 2009).

4. *Give students opportunities to experience the type of activities recommended by Zimmerman and his colleagues (1996).* That is, create projects for students in which they self-evaluate their current learning, set a goal to improve their learning and plan how to reach the goal, put the plan into action and monitor their progress toward the goal, and monitor the outcome and refine their strategies. Monitor students' progress through these steps and encourage their ability to engage in these learning activities independently.

5. *Model self-regulated learning.* Verbalize effective self-regulation strategies for students, and tell students how you use self-regulation in your learning.

6. *Make sure that students don't just self-regulate but combine self-regulation with effective strategies for learning.* Students can self-regulate all they want, but if they don't have the "know-how" their self-regulation is unlikely to be beneficial.

participation by the student. The following Web site offers an app for iPads that children can use to improve their self-regulation: www.selfregulationstation.com/sripad-app/

EVALUATING THE SOCIAL COGNITIVE APPROACHES

The social cognitive approaches have made important contributions to educating children (Bandura, 2012, 2015; Spiegler, 2016). While keeping the behaviorists' scientific flavor and emphasis on careful observation, they significantly expanded the emphasis of learning to include social and cognitive factors. Considerable learning occurs through watching and listening to competent models and then imitating what they do. The emphasis in the cognitive-behavioral approach on self-instruction, self-talk, and self-regulatory learning provides an important shift from learning that is controlled by others to taking responsibility for one's own learning (Miltenberger, 2016). These self-enacted strategies can significantly improve students' learning.

Critics of the social cognitive approaches come from several camps. Some cognitive theorists point out that the approaches still focus too much on overt behavior and external factors and not enough on the details of how cognitive processes such as thinking, memory, and problem solving actually take place. Some developmentalists criticize them for being nondevelopmental in the sense that they don't specify age-related, sequential changes in learning. It is true that social cognitive theory does not address development in great depth because it is mainly a theory of learning and social behavior. But labeling it as nondevelopmental is not accurate. Also, humanistic theorists fault social cognitive theorists for not placing enough attention on self-esteem and caring, supportive relationships. All of these criticisms also have been leveled at the behavioral approaches, such as Skinner's operant conditioning.

TECHNOLOGY

What are some contributions of the social cognitive approaches to educating children? What are some criticisms of these approaches?
Rebecca Emery/Photodisc/Getty Images

Review, Reflect, and Practice

4 Summarize social cognitive approaches to learning.

REVIEW
- How does Figure 7 help to summarize Bandura's social cognitive theory? What does he mean by self-efficacy?
- What is Bandura's model of observational learning?
- What is the focus of self-instructional methods? What does self-regulatory learning involve?
- What are some contributions and criticisms of the social cognitive approaches?

REFLECT
- Give some examples of how you use self-instructional and self-regulatory methods in your personal life. How effective are these methods? Should you use them more than you do? Explain.

PRAXIS™ PRACTICE
1. Macy sits staring at her math homework. She has not attempted a single problem. "What's the use?" she sighs. "I'll never get it right." According to Bandura's social cognitive theory, what is the most plausible explanation for Macy's response?
   a. Macy does not have the requisite language skills to do her homework.
   b. Macy has low self-efficacy.
   c. Macy has too much math anxiety.
   d. Macy's teacher has not provided enough negative feedback about her math homework.

continued

Review, Reflect, and Practice

2. Matt is the star of his high school's basketball team. The team is doing very well this year, in large part because of Matt's performance. This makes him a very popular student. About halfway through basketball season, Matt decides to shave his head. Soon other members of the basketball team shave their heads. Then the trend spreads to the rest of the school. By the end of February, 30 percent of the male students in the school have shaved heads. According to Bandura's social cognitive theory, what is the most plausible explanation for the students' behavior?
   a. Matt is a high-status role model.
   b. Matt was not punished.
   c. Matt was positively reinforced.
   d. Matt's self-efficacy was raised.

3. Marsha, a junior in high school, has debilitating test anxiety. She is particularly anxious about high-stakes tests, such as final exams. She often becomes so anxious that she "blanks out" and forgets everything that she has studied. What would a teacher using a cognitive behavior modification approach do to help her with her test anxiety?
   a. Help Marsha to develop anxiety management strategies and use self-instructions.
   b. Give her a study-skills book to read.
   c. Encourage her to think more about the consequences if she does do better on the tests.
   d. Tell Marsha to study until she has overlearned the material.

4. An important way in which social cognitive theory builds on behavioral theory is its emphasis on
   a. personality
   b. self-efficacy
   c. attitudes
   d. careful observation

Please see answer key at end of book . . . .

Connecting with the Classroom: Crack the Case

Consequences

Adam, a student in Mr. Potter's fourth-grade class, is disruptive from time to time, although he is very bright. One day during language arts, Adam began talking loudly to other students in his area. He was also laughing and telling jokes. Mr. Potter chose to ignore Adam's behavior, hoping he would stop on his own. But Adam didn't stop. Instead, his behavior became more raucous. Still Mr. Potter ignored it. Soon Adam was making enough noise that Mr. Potter was afraid that students in the neighboring classrooms would be disturbed, so he verbally reprimanded Adam.

Adam was a bit quieter for the next few minutes. After that, however, he once again became loud and disruptive. Again Mr. Potter verbally reprimanded him. This time he also told Adam that if he continued with his disruptive behavior, he would have to go to the office. Adam's behavior became even more disruptive, so

Mr. Potter sent him to the office. When Adam arrived at the office it was full of people—teachers getting their mail and making copies, volunteers signing in, students who were ill, students sent on errands, and other students who had been sent for disciplinary reasons. The school secretary told Adam to have a seat, which he did. He conversed with every person who entered the office as well as those who were there when he arrived. Half an hour after his arrival, he was sent back to class. He behaved quite well for the rest of the day, to Mr. Potter's relief.

The next day when students were assigned to write a paragraph, Adam once again became disruptive. He loudly told jokes to his classmates, laughed until tears were streaming down his face, and threw a paper airplane across the room. Mr. Potter reprimanded him and asked him to stop. When Adam didn't comply, Mr. Potter sent him to the office, which was once again bustling with activity.

Over the course of the next two weeks, Adam was sent to the office for disrupting class each day, always during a writing assignment. Mr. Potter was perplexed. Even more perplexing was that within three school days other children were becoming disruptive as well, requiring that they too be sent to the office.

Answer the following questions using principles of behavioral learning theories and correct terminology.

1. What are the issues in this case?
2. Why did Adam continue to disrupt class despite the consequences?
3. What has Adam learned?
4. Why did the other students join Adam in his disruptive behavior?
5. What should Mr. Potter do now?
6. What was Mr. Potter most likely trying to do when he initially ignored Adam's disruptive behavior?
   a. He was trying to extinguish the behavior by not reinforcing it.
   b. He was trying to negatively reinforce the behavior.
   c. He was trying to positively reinforce the behavior.
   d. He was trying to punish the behavior.
7. If Adam's goal was to escape writing assignments, which of the following best explains the consequences in operant conditioning terms?
   a. Adam was negatively reinforced for his behavior. An aversive stimulus was removed.
   b. Adam was positively reinforced for his behavior. A pleasant stimulus was presented.
   c. Adam was punished for his behavior. A pleasant stimulus was removed.
   d. Adam was punished for his behavior. An aversive stimulus was presented.

Connecting with Learning: Reach Your Learning Goals

1 WHAT IS LEARNING? Define learning and describe five approaches to studying it.

What Learning Is and Is Not

- Learning is a relatively permanent change in behavior, knowledge, and thinking skills that occurs through experience. Learning is not involved in inborn, innate behaviors, such as blinking or swallowing.

Approaches to Learning

- Behaviorism is the view that behavior should be explained by experiences that can be directly observed, not by mental processes. Classical conditioning and operant conditioning are behavioral views that emphasize associative learning.
- Psychology became more cognitive in the last part of the twentieth century, and the cognitive emphasis continues today. This is reflected in four cognitive approaches to learning: social cognitive, information processing, cognitive constructionist, and social constructivist. Social cognitive approaches emphasize the interaction of behavior, environment, and person (cognition) in explaining learning. Information-processing approaches focus on how children process information through attention, memory, thinking, and other cognitive processes. Cognitive constructivist approaches emphasize the child's cognitive construction of knowledge and understanding. Social constructivist approaches focus on collaboration with others to produce knowledge and understanding.

2 BEHAVIORAL APPROACHES TO LEARNING: Compare classical conditioning and operant conditioning.

Classical Conditioning

- In classical conditioning, the organism learns to connect, or associate, stimuli. A neutral stimulus (such as the sight of a person) becomes associated with a meaningful stimulus (such as food) and acquires the capacity to elicit a similar response. Classical conditioning involves these factors: unconditioned stimulus (UCS), conditioned stimulus (CS), unconditioned response (UCR), and conditioned response (CR).
- Classical conditioning also involves generalization, discrimination, and extinction. Generalization is the tendency of a new stimulus similar to the original conditioned stimulus to produce a

continued

similar response. Discrimination occurs when the organism responds to certain stimuli and not to others. Extinction involves the weakening of the CR in the absence of the UCS.
- Systematic desensitization is a method based on classical conditioning that reduces anxiety by getting the individual to associate deep relaxation with successive visualizations of increasingly anxiety-producing situations. Classical conditioning is better at explaining involuntary behavior than voluntary behavior.

Operant Conditioning

- In operant conditioning (also called instrumental conditioning), the consequences of behavior produce changes in the probability that the behavior will occur. Operant conditioning's main architect was B. F. Skinner.
- Reinforcement (reward) is a consequence (either positive or negative) that increases the probability that a behavior will occur; punishment is a consequence that decreases the probability that a behavior will occur. In positive reinforcement, a behavior increases because it is followed by a rewarding stimulus (such as praise). In negative reinforcement, a behavior increases because the response removes an aversive (unpleasant) stimulus.
- Generalization, discrimination, and extinction also are involved in operant conditioning. Generalization means giving the same response to stimuli similar to those previously reinforced. Discrimination is differentiating among stimuli or environmental events. Extinction occurs when a previously reinforced response is no longer reinforced and the response decreases.

③ APPLIED BEHAVIOR ANALYSIS IN EDUCATION: Apply behavior analysis to education.

What Is Applied Behavior Analysis?

- Applied behavior analysis involves applying the principles of operant conditioning to change human behavior.

Increasing Desirable Behaviors

- Strategies to increase desirable behaviors include choosing effective reinforcers, making reinforcers timely and contingent, selecting the best schedule of reinforcement, contracting, using negative reinforcement effectively, and using prompts and shaping. Find out which reinforcers work best with which students.
- The Premack principle states that a high-probability activity can be used to reinforce a low-probability activity. Applied behavior analysts recommend that a reinforcement be contingent—that is, be given in a timely manner and only if the student performs the behavior. "If . . . then" statements can be used to make it clear to students what they have to do to get a reward.
- Skinner described a number of schedules of reinforcement. Most reinforcement in the classroom is partial. Skinner described four schedules of partial reinforcement: fixed-ratio, variable-ratio, fixed-interval, and variable-interval. Contracting involves putting reinforcement contingencies in writing. Although negative reinforcement can increase some students' desirable behavior, exercise caution with students who don't have good self-regulatory skills. A prompt is an added stimulus or cue that increases the likelihood that a stimulus will produce a desired response. Shaping involves teaching new behaviors by reinforcing successive approximations to a specified target behavior.

Decreasing Undesirable Behaviors

- Strategies for decreasing undesirable behaviors include using differential reinforcement, terminating reinforcement, removing desirable stimuli, and presenting aversive stimuli.
- In differential reinforcement, the teacher might reinforce behavior that is more appropriate or that is incompatible with what the student is doing.
- Terminating reinforcement (extinction) involves taking reinforcement away from a behavior. Many inappropriate behaviors are maintained by teacher attention, so taking away the attention can decrease the behavior.
- The most widely used strategy for removing desirable stimuli is time-out. A second strategy for removing desirable stimuli involves response cost, which occurs when a positive reinforcer, such as a privilege, is taken away from the student.
- An aversive stimulus becomes a punishment only when it decreases behavior. The most common form of punishment in the classroom is verbal reprimands. Punishment should be used

Evaluating Operant Conditioning and Applied Behavior Analysis

- only as the last option and in conjunction with reinforcement of desired responses. Physical punishment should not be used in the classroom.

- Used effectively, behavioral techniques can help you manage your classroom. Critics say that these approaches place too much emphasis on external control and not enough on internal control. They also argue that ignoring cognitive factors leaves out much of the richness of students' lives. Critics warn about potential ethical problems when operant conditioning is used inappropriately. And some critics say that teachers who focus too much on managing the classroom with operant techniques may place too much emphasis on conduct and not enough on academic learning.

4 SOCIAL COGNITIVE APPROACHES TO LEARNING: Summarize social cognitive approaches to learning.

Bandura's Social Cognitive Theory

- Albert Bandura is the main architect of social cognitive theory. His reciprocal determinism model of learning includes three main factors: person/cognition, behavior, and environment. The person (cognitive) factor given the most emphasis by Bandura in recent years is self-efficacy, the belief that one can master a situation and produce positive outcomes.

Observational Learning

- Observational learning is learning that involves acquiring skills, strategies, and beliefs by observing others. Bandura describes four key processes in observational learning: attention, retention, production, and motivation. Observational learning is involved in many aspects of children's lives, including the classroom and the media.

Cognitive-Behavioral Approaches and Self-Regulation

- Self-instructional methods are cognitive-behavioral techniques aimed at teaching individuals to modify their own behavior. In many cases, it is recommended that students replace negative self-statements with positive ones. Cognitive behaviorists argue that students can improve their performance by monitoring their behavior.
- Self-regulatory learning consists of the self-generation and self-monitoring of thoughts, feelings, and behaviors to reach a goal. High-achieving students are often self-regulatory learners. One model of self-regulatory learning involves these components: self-evaluation and monitoring, goal setting and strategic planning, putting a plan into action, and monitoring outcomes and refining strategies. Self-regulation is an important aspect of school readiness. An important aspect of self-regulatory learning is that it gives students responsibility for their learning.

Evaluating the Social Cognitive Approaches

- The social cognitive approaches have significantly expanded the scope of learning to include cognitive and social factors in addition to behavior. A considerable amount of learning occurs by watching and listening to competent models and then imitating what they do.
- The cognitive-behavioral emphasis on self-instruction, self-talk, and self-regulatory learning provides an important shift from learning controlled by others to self-management of learning.
- Critics of the social cognitive approaches say that they still place too much emphasis on overt behavior and external factors and not enough on the details of how cognitive processes such as thinking occur. These approaches also are criticized for being nondevelopmental (although social cognitive advocates argue this label is not justified) and not giving enough attention to self-esteem and warmth.

KEY TERMS

applied behavior analysis 228
associative learning 221
behaviorism 221
classical conditioning 223
cognitive-behavioral approaches 244
contracting 230
learning 220
mental processes 221
negative reinforcement 225
observational learning 238
operant conditioning 225
positive reinforcement 225
Premack principle 228
prompt 230
punishment 225
reinforcement (reward) 225
response cost 232
schedules of reinforcement 229
self-efficacy 238
self-instructional methods 244
self-regulatory learning 245
shaping 231
social cognitive theory 237
systematic desensitization 224
time-out 232

PORTFOLIO ACTIVITIES

Now that you have a good understanding of this chapter, complete these exercises to expand your thinking.

Independent Reflection

1. **Design a Self-Regulation Plan.** Letitia is a high school student who doesn't have adequate self-regulatory skills, and this is causing her to have serious academic problems. She doesn't plan or organize, has poor study strategies, and uses ineffective time management. Using Zimmerman's four-step strategy, design an effective self-regulation program for Letitia. (INTASC: Principle *3*)

Research/Field Experience

2. ***Sesame Street* and Social Cognitive Learning.** *Sesame Street* uses many effective techniques to increase children's attention and help them learn. Watch an episode. Analyze the show. How were these techniques used on the show you watched? Describe any additional techniques you observed that you might be able to use in your classroom. (INTASC: Principles *1, 7, 9*)

Collaborative Work

3. **Decreasing Undesirable Behaviors.** Together with three or four other students in your class, consider the following students' undesirable behaviors. You want to decrease the behaviors. What is the best strategy for each? Discuss and compare your strategies with the group.
   a. Andrew, who likes to utter profanities every now and then
   b. Sandy, who tells you to quit bugging her when you ask her questions
   c. Matt, who likes to mess up other students' papers
   d. Rebecca, who frequently talks with other students around her while you are explaining or demonstrating something.
   (INTASC: Principles *1, 5*)

chapter 8
THE INFORMATION-PROCESSING APPROACH

chapter outline

① The Nature of the Information-Processing Approach

Learning Goal 1 Describe the information-processing approach.

The Information-Processing Approach

Cognitive Resources: Capacity and Speed of Processing Information

Mechanisms of Change

② Attention

Learning Goal 2 Characterize attention and summarize how it changes during development.

What Is Attention?

Developmental Changes

③ Memory

Learning Goal 3 Discuss memory in terms of encoding, storage, and retrieval.

What Is Memory?

Encoding

Storage

Retrieval and Forgetting

④ Expertise

Learning Goal 4 Draw some lessons about learning from the way experts think.

Expertise and Learning

Acquiring Expertise

Expertise and Teaching

⑤ Metacognition

Learning Goal 5 Explain the concept of metacognition and identify some ways to improve children's metacognition.

Developmental Changes

The Good Information-Processing Model

Strategies and Metacognitive Regulation

The mind is an enchanting thing.

—Marianne Moore
American Poet, 20th Century

Ariel Skelley/Blend Images LLC

Connecting with Teachers Laura Bickford

Laura Bickford chairs the English Department at Nordoff High School in Ojai, California. She recently spoke about how she encourages students to think:

> I believe the call to teach is a call to teach students how to think. In encouraging critical thinking, literature itself does a good bit of work for us, but we still have to be guides. We have to ask good questions. We have to show students the value in asking their own questions, in having discussions and conversations. In addition to reading and discussing literature, the best way to move students to think critically is to have them write. We write all the time in a variety of modes: journals, formal essays, letters, factual reports, news articles, speeches, or other formal oral presentations. We have to show students where they merely scratch the surface in their thinking and writing. I call these moments "hits and runs." When I see this "hit and run" effort, I draw a window on the paper. I tell them it is a "window of opportunity" to go deeper, elaborate, and clarify. Many students don't do this kind of thinking until they are prodded to do so.
>
> I also use metacognitive strategies all the time—that is, helping students know about knowing. These include asking students to comment on their learning after we have finished particular pieces of projects and asking them to discuss in advance what we might be seeking to learn as we begin a new project or activity. I also ask them to keep reading logs so they can observe their own thinking as it happens. For example, they might copy a passage from a reading selection and comment on it. Studying a passage from J. D. Salinger's *The Catcher in the Rye*, a student might write: "I've never thought about life the way that Holden Caulfield does. Maybe I see the world differently than he does. He always is so depressed. I'm not depressed. Salinger is good at showing us someone who is usually depressed. How does he manage to do that?" In addition, I ask students to comment on their own learning by way of grading themselves. This year a student gave me one of the most insightful lines about her growth as a reader that I have ever seen from a student. She wrote, "I no longer think in a monotone when I'm reading." I don't know if she grasps the magnitude of that thought or how it came to be that she made that change. It is magic when students see themselves growing like this.

Courtesy of Laura Johnson Bickford

Preview

In the opening story, teacher Laura Bickford tells how she uses metacognitive strategies, one of the important aspects of cognitive learning and a major topic of this chapter. In addition to metacognition, we'll explore what it means to take an information-processing approach in teaching and examine three important aspects of cognition: attention, memory, and expertise.

LG 1 Describe the information-processing approach.

1 THE NATURE OF THE INFORMATION-PROCESSING APPROACH

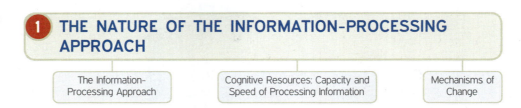

How capable are children? Proponents of the information-processing approach to learning believe they are highly capable. Children attend to information being presented and tinker with it. They develop strategies for remembering. They form concepts. They reason and solve problems. These important skills are the topics of this section.

THE INFORMATION-PROCESSING APPROACH

The **information-processing approach** emphasizes that children manipulate information, monitor it, and strategize about it. Central to this approach are cognitive processes such as attention, memory, and thinking (Bauer & Larkina, 2016; Casey &

information-processing approach A cognitive approach in which children manipulate information, monitor it, and strategize about it. Central to this approach are cognitive processes such as attention, memory, and thinking.

others, 2016; Reynolds & Romano, 2016). According to the information-processing approach, children develop a gradually increasing capacity for processing information, which allows them to acquire increasingly complex knowledge and skills (Mayer & Alexander, 2017; Siegler, 2016a, b; Siegler & Braithwaite, 2017).

Behaviorism and its associative model of learning was a dominant force in psychology until the 1950s and 1960s, when many psychologists began to acknowledge that they could not explain children's learning without referring to mental processes such as memory and thinking. The term *cognitive psychology* became a label for approaches that sought to explain behavior by examining mental processes (Gluck et al., 2016). Although a number of factors stimulated the growth of cognitive psychology, none was more important than the development of computers. The first modern computer, developed by John von Neumann in the late 1940s, showed that inanimate machines could perform logical operations. This suggested that some mental operations might be carried out by computers, possibly telling us something about the way human cognition works. Cognitive psychologists often draw analogies to computers to help explain the relation between cognition and the brain. The physical brain is compared with the computer's hardware, cognition with its software. Although computers and software aren't perfect analogies for brains and cognitive activities, nonetheless, the comparison contributed to our thinking about the child's mind as an active information-processing system.

COGNITIVE RESOURCES: CAPACITY AND SPEED OF PROCESSING INFORMATION

As children grow and mature, and as they experience the world, their information-processing abilities increase. These changes are likely influenced by increases in both capacity and speed of processing. These two characteristics are often referred to as *cognitive resources*, which are proposed to have an important influence on memory and problem solving.

Both biology and experience contribute to growth in cognitive resources. Changes in the brain provide a biological foundation for increased cognitive resources. As children grow and mature, important biological developments occur both in brain structures, such as changes in the frontal lobes, and at the level of neurons, such as the blooming and pruning of connections between neurons that produces fewer but stronger connections (de Haan & Johnson, 2016). Also, myelination (the process that covers the axon with a myelin sheath) increases the speed of electrical impulses in the brain. Myelination continues into emerging adulthood (Monahan et al., 2016).

Most information-processing psychologists argue that an increase in capacity also improves processing of information (Ashcraft & Radvansky, 2016; Siegler, 2016a, b). For example, as children's information-processing capacity increases, they likely can hold in mind several dimensions of a topic or problem simultaneously, whereas younger children are more prone to focus on only one dimension. Adolescents can discuss how the varied experiences of the Founding Fathers influenced the Declaration of Independence and Constitution. Elementary-age children are more likely to focus on simple facts about the founders' lives.

What is the role of processing speed? How fast children process information often influences what they can do with that information. If an adolescent is trying to add up mentally the cost of items he is buying at the grocery store, he needs to be able to compute the sum before he has forgotten the price of the individual items. Children's speed in processing information is linked with their competence in thinking (Chevalier et al., 2015). For example, how fast children can articulate a series of words affects how many words they can store and remember. Generally, fast processing is linked with good performance on cognitive tasks. However, some compensation for slower processing speed can be achieved through effective strategies.

Researchers have devised a number of ways to assess processing speed. For example, it can be assessed through a *reaction-time task* in which individuals are asked

> **Thinking Back/Thinking Forward**
>
> Nearly twice as many synaptic connections between neurons are made as will ever be used. Connections that are used become strengthened and survive; unused ones become replaced by other pathways or disappear. Connect to "Cognitive and Language Development."

> **Thinking Back/Thinking Forward**
>
> The information processing perspective of development can be applied to explain the observed changes highlighted in Piaget's stages. Connect to "Cognitive and Language Development."

DEVELOPMENT

to push a button as soon as they see a stimulus such as a light. Or individuals might be asked to match letters or numbers with symbols on a computer screen.

There is abundant evidence that the speed with which such tasks are completed improves dramatically across the childhood years (Ferrer et al., 2013). For example, a study of 8- to 13-year-old children revealed that processing speed increased with age, and further that the developmental change in processing speed preceded an increase in working memory capacity (Kail, 2007).

There is controversy about whether the increase in processing speed is due to experience or biological maturation. Experience clearly plays an important role. Think how much faster you could process the answer to a simple arithmetic problem as an adolescent than as a child. Also think about how much faster you can process information in your native language than in a second language. The influence of biological maturation likely involves myelination.

MECHANISMS OF CHANGE

According to Robert Siegler (1998, 2016a, b), three mechanisms work together to create changes in children's cognitive skills: encoding, automaticity, and strategy construction.

Encoding is the process by which information gets stored in memory. Changes in children's cognitive skills depend on increased skill at encoding relevant information and ignoring irrelevant information. For example, to a 4-year-old, an *s* in cursive writing is a shape very different from an *s* that is printed. But a 10-year-old has learned to encode the relevant fact that both are the letter *s* and to ignore the irrelevant differences in their shape.

Automaticity refers to the ability to process information with little or no effort. Practice allows children to encode increasing amounts of information automatically. For example, once children have learned to read well, they do not think about each letter in a word as a letter; instead, they encode whole words. Once a task is automatic, it does not require conscious effort. As a result, as information processing becomes more automatic, we can complete tasks more quickly and handle more than one task at a time. Imagine how long it would take you to read this page if you did not encode words automatically but instead focused your attention on each letter in each word.

Strategy construction is the creation of new procedures for processing information. For example, children's reading benefits when they develop the strategy of stopping periodically to take stock of what they have read so far. Developing an effective repertoire of strategies and selecting the best one to use on a learning task is a critical aspect of becoming an effective learner (Bjorklund, 2012).

In addition to these mechanisms of change, children's information processing is characterized by *self-modification* (Siegler, 1998, 2016a, b). That is, children learn to use what they have learned in previous circumstances to adapt their responses to a new situation. For example, a child who is familiar with dogs and cats goes to the zoo and sees lions and tigers for the first time. She then modifies her concept of "animal" to include her new knowledge. Part of this self-modification draws on **metacognition,** which means "knowing about knowing" (Flavell, 2004; Guerten et al., 2016; Sobel & Letourneau, 2016). One example of metacognition is what children know about the best ways to remember what they have read. Do they know that they will remember what they have read better if they can relate it to their own lives in some way? Thus, in Siegler's application of information processing to development, children play an active role in their cognitive development when they develop metacognitive strategies.

What two characteristics of cognitive resources have an important influence on memory and problem solving?
Beau Lark/Glow Images

Thinking Back/Thinking Forward

The information processing perspective of development can be applied to explain Piaget's concept of accommodation, which describes a change in children's thinking similar to self-modification. Connect to "Cognitive and Language Development."

encoding The process by which information gets into memory.

automaticity The ability to process information with little or no effort.

strategy construction Creation of a new procedure for processing information.

metacognition Cognition about cognition, or "knowing about knowing."

Review, Reflect, and Practice

1 Describe the information-processing approach.

REVIEW
- What is the information-processing approach?
- What are two important cognitive resources and how do they contribute to developmental changes in children's information processing?
- What are some key mechanisms of change in the information-processing approach?

REFLECT
- In terms of your ability to learn, are there ways that you wish you were more like a computer? Or are you better than any computer in all aspects of processing information? Explain.

PRAXIS™ PRACTICE

1. Information processing is most closely aligned with
   a. behaviorism
   b. cognitive psychology
   c. social cognitive theory
   d. ecological theory
2. According to the information-processing approach, a 15-year-old can compute faster than a 10-year-old because the
   a. 15-year-old's brain has had more time to develop, and the 15-year-old has had more experience working with numbers
   b. 15-year-old has had more experiences of both positive and negative reinforcement
   c. 15-year-old's brain has lost many of its original connections and undergone demyelinization
   d. 15-year-old has had much more time to develop rote memory skills
3. Ms. Parks wants her students to know their basic math facts without having to stop to think about them. Therefore, Ms. Parks plays many math games with her second-grade students, such as addition and subtraction bingo, math bees, and card games. What is Ms. Parks' goal in playing these games with her students?
   a. to develop automaticity for math facts
   b. to encourage strategy construction
   c. to foster encoding skills
   d. to improve metacognitive skills, such as self-awareness

Please see answer key at end of book . . . .

2 ATTENTION

LG 2 Characterize attention and summarize how it changes during development.

The world holds a lot of information that we need to perceive. What is attention and what effect does it have? How does it change developmentally?

WHAT IS ATTENTION?

Attention is the focusing of mental resources. Attention improves cognitive processing for many tasks, from hitting a baseball to reading a book or adding numbers (Rothbart & Posner, 2015). At any one time, though, children, like adults, can pay attention to only a limited amount of information. They allocate their attention in different ways

attention The focusing of mental resources.

What attentional demands does multitasking place on children and adolescents?
Alberto Pomares/Apomares/E+/Getty Images

(Reynolds & Romano, 2016). Psychologists have labeled these types of allocation as selective attention, divided attention, sustained attention, and executive attention.

- **Selective attention** is focusing on a specific aspect of experience that is relevant while ignoring others that are irrelevant. Focusing on one voice among many in a crowded room or a noisy restaurant is an example of selective attention.
- **Divided attention** involves concentrating on more than one activity at the same time. If you are listening to music while you are reading this, you are engaging in divided attention.
- **Sustained attention** is the ability to maintain attention over an extended period of time. Sustained attention is also called vigilance. Staying focused on reading this chapter from start to finish without interruption is an example of sustained attention. A recent study found that sustained attention in preschoolers was linked to a greater likelihood of completing college by 25 years of age (McClelland et al., 2013).
- **Executive attention** involves planning actions, allocating attention to goals, detecting and compensating for errors, monitoring progress on tasks, and dealing with novel or difficult circumstances. An example of executive attention is effectively deploying attention to carry out the aforementioned cognitive tasks while writing a 10-page paper for a history course.

RESEARCH

One trend involving divided attention is children's and adolescents' multitasking, which in some cases involves not just dividing attention between two activities, but even three or more (Courage, 2015). A major influence on the increase in multitasking is availability of multiple electronic media. Many children and adolescents have a range of electronic media at their disposal. It is not unusual for adolescents to divide their attention by working on homework while engaging in an instant messaging conversation, surfing the Web, and looking at an iTunes playlist. Is this multitasking beneficial or harmful? A recent research review concluded that at a general level, digital technologies (surfing the Internet, texting someone) while engaging in a learning task (reading, listening to a lecture) distract learners and result in impaired performance on many tasks (Courage et al., 2015).

DEVELOPMENT

Sustained and executive attention also are very important aspects of cognitive development. As children and adolescents are required to engage in larger, increasingly complex tasks that require longer time frames to complete, their ability to sustain attention is critical for succeeding on the tasks. An increase in executive attention supports the rapid increase in effortful control required to effectively engage in these complex academic tasks (Rothbart & Posner, 2015).

DEVELOPMENTAL CHANGES

Some important changes in attention occur during childhood (Ristic & Enns, 2015). The length of time children can pay attention increases as they get older. The toddler wanders around, shifts attention from one activity to another, and seems to spend little time focused on any one object or event. In contrast, the preschool child might watch television for half an hour at a time.

Preschool children's ability to control and sustain their attention is related to school readiness and achievement later in childhood (Rothbart & Posner, 2015). For example, a study of more than 1,000 children revealed that their ability to sustain their attention at 54 months of age (4.5 years) was linked to their school readiness (which included achievement and language skills) (NICHD Early Child Care Research Network, 2005). In another study, the ability to focus attention better at age 5 was linked to a higher level of school achievement at age 9 (Razza et al., 2012). Sustained attention improves rapidly from 5 to 10 years of age, and this increased attention is linked to better performance on cognitive tasks (Betts et al., 2006). A recent study also found that sustained attention continues to improve during adolescence; this improvement in sustained attention in adolescence was linked to maturation of the brain's frontal lobes (Thillay et al., 2015).

selective attention Focusing on a specific aspect of experience that is relevant while ignoring others that are irrelevant.

divided attention Concentrating on more than one activity at a time.

sustained attention Maintaining attention over an extended period of time; also called vigilance.

executive attention Involves planning actions, allocating attention to goals, detecting and compensating for errors, monitoring progress on tasks, and dealing with novel or difficult circumstances.

Control over attention shows important changes during childhood (Ristic & Enns, 2015). External stimuli are likely to determine the target of the preschooler's attention; what is salient, or obvious, grabs the preschooler's attention. For example, suppose a flashy, attractive clown presents the directions for solving a problem. Preschool children are likely to pay attention to the clown and ignore the directions, because they are influenced strongly by the salient features of the environment. After the age of 6 or 7, children pay more attention to features relevant to performing a task or solving a problem, such as the directions. Thus, instead of being controlled by the most striking stimuli in their environment, older children can direct their attention to more important stimuli. This change reflects a shift to *cognitive control* of attention, so that children act less impulsively and reflect more.

Attention to relevant information increases steadily through the elementary and secondary school years. Processing of irrelevant information decreases in adolescence.

As children grow up, their abilities both to direct selective attention and to divide attention also improve. Older children and adolescents are better than younger children at tasks that require shifts of attention. For example, writing a good story requires shifting attention among many competing tasks—spelling the words, composing grammar, structuring paragraphs, and conveying the story as a whole. Children also improve in their ability to do two things at once. For example, in one investigation, 12-year-olds were markedly better than 8-year-olds and slightly worse than 20-year-olds at allocating their attention in a situation involving two tasks (divided attention) (Manis et al., 1980). These improvements in divided attention might be due to an increase in cognitive resources (through increased processing speed or capacity), automaticity, or increased skill at directing resources.

Individual variations also characterize children, with some children having such significant attention problems that they are classified as having attention deficit hyperactivity disorder (ADHD). One study revealed that such attention problems in childhood are linked to information-processing difficulties in late adolescence (Friedman et al., 2007). In this study, 7- to 14-year-old children with attention problems (including inattention, disorganization, impulsivity, and hyperactivity) had difficulties with working memory and inhibiting responses at 17 years of age.

Several teachers were recently asked what they do to help students focus their attention in class. Following are their responses.

Thinking Back/Thinking Forward

Researchers have found increased focal activation in the prefrontal cortex from 7 to 30 years of age. Connect to "Cognitive and Language Development."

DEVELOPMENT

RESEARCH

Thinking Back/Thinking Forward

The number of children diagnosed and treated for ADHD has increased substantially, by some estimates doubling. Review details on the diagnosis of and treatments for ADHD in the section on Attention Deficit Hyperactivity Disorder. Connect to "Learners who are Exceptional."

EARLY CHILDHOOD   Very young children are just developing their attention span. To help them along, we often use songs or instruments for transitions from play time to work time. When material is introduced, we call out the children's names and ask questions, thus engaging them with the newly introduced item. During story time, we use exaggerated physical gestures and take on the voices of characters in the book to keep children motivated and listening.

—VALARIE GORHAM, *Kiddie Quarters, Inc.*

ELEMENTARY SCHOOL: GRADES K–5   One strategy I use to keep my fourth-grade students focused is to get into a role. For example, when I read *Bubba, the Cowboy Prince,* I put on a cowboy hat and create an accent. I also find that saying, "You will see this on your homework tonight" and "This will be on your test" also grab their attention.

—SHANE SCHWARZ, *Clinton Elementary School*

MIDDLE SCHOOL: GRADES 6–8   My students especially stay focused when I let them teach each other—that is, I let them take turns playing the role of teacher.

—CASEY MAASS, *Edison Middle School*

HIGH SCHOOL: GRADES 9-12 High school students stay more focused when they know how events and information presented in class relate to their own lives. For example, the topic of food-borne illness is boring to most of my students, but when I tell them about how I got salmonella poisoning from a plate of chicken salad at a local restaurant, and the intense suffering I went through for many days, they become more intrigued with the topic of salmonella, its causes, prevention, and symptoms.

—SANDY SWANSON, *Menomonee Falls High School*

CONNECTING WITH STUDENTS: Best Practices
Strategies for Helping Students Pay Attention

With so many classroom tasks to complete and so many children in a class, it is easy to overlook working with children to improve their information-processing skills, such as attention. Follow are some effective strategies to adopt in improving children's attention.

1. *Encourage students to pay close attention and minimize distraction.* Talk with children about how important it is to pay attention when they need to remember something. Give them exercises with opportunities to give their undivided attention to something. For example, in countries such as Hungary, kindergarten children participate in exercises designed to improve their attention (Mills & Mills, 2000; Posner & Rothbart, 2007). In one such exercise, the teacher sits in the center of a circle of children, and each child is required to catch the teacher's eye before being permitted to leave the group. In other exercises, teachers have children participate in stop-go activities during which they have to listen for a specific signal, such as a drumbeat or an exact number of rhythmic beats, before stopping the activity.

2. *Use cues or gestures to signal that something is important.* This might involve raising your voice, repeating something with emphasis, and writing the concept on the board or on a transparency. (For a behavioral explanation for why cues/prompts are effective, see the section on "Increasing Desirable Behaviors" in the chapter "Behavioral and Social Cognitive Approaches.")

3. *Help students generate their own cue or catch phrase for when they need to pay attention.* Possibly vary this from month to month. Give them a menu of options to select from, such as "Alert," "Focus," or "Zero in." Teach them to say their word or pet phrase quietly but firmly to themselves when they catch their minds wandering.

4. *Make learning interesting.* Boredom can set in quickly for students, and when it does their attention wanes. Relating ideas to students' interests increases their attention; in other words, what we teach should be relevant to students' lives. (Relevance is also an important aspect of the culturally relevant teaching approach addressed in the chapter on sociocultural diversity.) Infuse the classroom with novel, unusual, or surprising exercises. Start off a biology exercise on heredity and aging with a question such as "Can you live to be 100?" or "Might someone be able to live to be even 400 someday?" Think of relevant questions such as these to introduce various topics, as students will be more likely to pay attention to material that they can relate to.

5. *Use media and technology effectively as part of your effort to vary the pace of the classroom.* Video and television programs have built-in attention-getting formats, such as zooming in on an image; flashing a vivid, colorful image on the screen; and switching from one setting to another. Look for relevant videos and television programs that can help you vary the classroom's pace and increase students' attention. Unfortunately, too many teachers show videos only to keep students quiet, which does not promote learning. However, if the curriculum is dull, it doesn't matter what kinds of "tricks" or "splashes" the teacher uses—students will not learn effectively. Make sure that the media and technology you use captures students' attention in meaningful ways that promote effective learning. Also, new technology tools make it easier to embed questions and gather students' responses (see, for example, EdPuzzle: https://edpuzzle.com/ and PlayPosit: www.playposit.com/

TECHNOLOGY

Computer exercises recently have been developed to improve children's attention (Rothbart & Posner, 2015). For example, one study found that the attention exercises in Captain's Log (Braintrain), a commercially available program, were effective in reducing first-grade students' attention problems (Rabiner et al., 2010). Ten attention exercises that focus on training auditory and

RESEARCH

CONNECTING WITH STUDENTS: Best Practices
Strategies for Helping Students Pay Attention

visual attention were used in the study. In one exercise, a student has to press the space bar on a computer each time a symbol appears that matches one already on the screen. Other tasks require students to remember the locations of objects that recently have been presented. To advance through the program, students had to sustain their attention longer as tasks became more difficult.

6. *Focus on active learning to make learning enjoyable.* A different exercise, a guest, a field trip, and many other activities can be used to make learning more enjoyable, reduce student boredom, and increase attention. In *Through the Eyes of Teachers,* middle school English and drama teacher Lynn Ayres describes how games can add interest at all grade levels.

THROUGH THE EYES OF TEACHERS
Turning Boring Exercises into Active Learning Games

I have found that the most boring exercises (such as the kind you find on worksheets and textbooks) can be turned into an active learning game. One favorite game in my seventh-grade English class was "sit-set, rise-raise." I'd put two students in chairs next to tables and place a book on each table. If I said "rise," they were to stand. If I said "raise," they were to raise the book. They were to seat themselves if I said "sit," and they were to place the book on the table if I said "set." If I said "rise," and one of them stood up and the other student lifted the book, the student with the book held up was out and was replaced by a teammate. Or if they both stood up, the one who stood up first stayed, and the other student was replaced by a teammate. The students loved that game, and they really learned the difference between those two commonly confused pairs of verbs in the process.

That game taught me the effectiveness of getting students physically involved. I developed dozens of other games involving bells and timers and teams that had students running around the room, ringing bells, trying to beat a member of the opposing team in telling me if a word was a noun or an adjective. Almost any workbook or textbook exercise can be turned into a physical activity game if you put some thought into it, and middle school students learn so much more from doing an exercise that is both physical and mental.

Lynn Ayres

7. *Don't overload students with too much information.* We live in an "information overload" society. Students who are given too much information too fast often have difficulty focusing their attention.

8. *Be aware of individual differences in students' attentional skills.* Some students have severe problems in paying attention. You will need to take this into account when presenting material. Before you begin an exercise, look around the room for potential distractions, such as an open window to a playground where students are being noisy. Close the window and draw the shade to eliminate the distraction.

Review, Reflect, and Practice

 Characterize attention and summarize how it changes during development.

REVIEW
- What is attention? What are four ways attention can be allocated?
- How does attention develop in childhood and adolescence?

REFLECT
- Imagine that you are an elementary school teacher and a child is having difficulty sustaining attention on a learning task. What strategies would you try to use to help the child sustain attention?

PRAXIS™ PRACTICE
1. Ms. Samson teaches first grade. Often while she is working with one group of children, she must monitor the behavior of the rest of the class, occasionally intervening in some manner. Sometimes she has three or four students at her desk, each needing something different from her. This does not seem to faze her in the least. She can talk

continued

> **Review, Reflect, and Practice**
>
> to one student while tying another's shoes and monitoring the behavior of the rest with no problem. What skill has Ms. Samson mastered?
> a. divided attention
> b. selective attention
> c. sustained attention
> d. personal attention
>
> 2. Mark shifts his attention very quickly from one thing to another. The more colorful and noisy the thing, the more likely it is to draw his attention. He rarely attends to any one thing for more than a few minutes. From this description, Mark is most likely to be a
> a. toddler
> b. preschooler
> c. elementary-school-age child
> d. adolescent
>
> *Please see answer key at end of book....*

LG 3 Discuss memory in terms of encoding, storage, and retrieval.

3 MEMORY

What Is Memory? | Encoding | Storage | Retrieval and Forgetting

Twentieth-century playwright Tennessee Williams once commented that life is all memory except for that one present moment that goes by so quickly that you can hardly catch it going. But just what is memory?

WHAT IS MEMORY?

Memory is the retention of information over time. Educational psychologists study how information is initially placed or encoded into memory, how it is retained or stored after being encoded, and how it is found or retrieved for a certain purpose later. Memory anchors the self in continuity. Without memory you would not be able to connect what happened to you yesterday with what is going on in your life today. Today, the emphasis is not on how children add something to memory but rather on how children actively construct their memory (Howe, 2015).

The main body of our discussion of memory will focus on encoding, storage, and retrieval. Thinking about memory in terms of these processes should help you to understand it better (see Figure 1). For memory to work, children have to take information in, store it or represent it, and then retrieve it for some purpose later.

As you learned earlier, *encoding* is the process by which information gets into memory. *Storage* is the retention of information over time. *Retrieval* means taking information out of storage. Let's now explore each of these three important memory activities in greater detail.

memory The retention of information over time, which involves encoding, storage, and retrieval.

FIGURE 1 PROCESSING INFORMATION IN MEMORY

As you read about the many aspects of memory in this chapter, think about the organization of memory in terms of these three main activities: encoding, storage, and retrieval.

Encoding
Getting information into memory

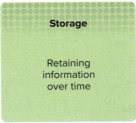

Storage — Retaining information over time

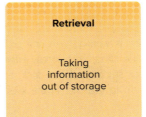

Retrieval — Taking information out of storage

ENCODING

Attention is a key aspect of the encoding process (Schneider, 2015). By focusing their attention, as children listen to a teacher, do homework, write a paper, read a book, watch a movie, listen to music, or talk with a friend, they can encode the information into memory. In addition to attention, encoding consists of a number of processes: rehearsal, deep processing, elaboration, constructing images, and organization.

Rehearsal Rehearsal is the conscious repetition of information over time to increase the length of time information stays in memory. For example, when you make a date to meet your best friend for lunch, you are likely to repeat, or rehearse, the date and time: "OK—Wednesday at 1:30." Rehearsal works best when you need to encode and remember a list of items for a brief period of time. When you must retain information over long periods of time, as when you are studying for a test you won't take until next week, other strategies usually work better than rehearsal. Rehearsal does not work well for retaining information over the long term because it often involves just rote repetition of information without imparting any meaning to it. When you construct your memory in meaningful ways, you remember better. As we will see next, you also remember better when you process material deeply and elaborate it.

Deep Processing Following the discovery that rehearsal is not an efficient way to encode information for long-term memory, Fergus Craik and Robert Lockhart (1972) proposed that we can process information at a variety of levels. Their **levels of processing theory** states that the processing of memory occurs on a continuum from shallow to deep, with deeper processing producing better memory. Shallow processing means analyzing the sensory, or physical, features of a stimulus at a shallow level. This might involve detecting the lines, angles, and contours of a printed word's letters or a spoken word's frequency, duration, and loudness. At an intermediate level of processing, you recognize the stimulus and give it a label. For example, you identify a four-legged, barking object as a dog. Then, at the deepest level, you process information semantically, in terms of its meaning. For example, if a child sees the word *boat*, at the shallow level she might notice the shapes of the letters, at the intermediate level she might think of the characteristics of the word (for instance, that it rhymes with *coat*), and at the deepest level she might think about the last time she went fishing with her dad on a boat and the kind of boat it was. Note, a child living in poverty in a landlocked area might never have seen a boat, so it is important to consider your students' individual differences to help them create meaningful connections. Researchers have found that individuals remember information better when they process it at a deep level (Abbassi et al., 2015; Soravia et al., 2016).

Elaboration Cognitive psychologists soon recognized, however, that there is more to good encoding than just depth of processing. They discovered that when individuals use elaboration in their encoding of information, their memory benefits (Ashcraft & Radvansky, 2016). **Elaboration** is the extensiveness of information processing involved in encoding. Thus, when you present the concept of democracy to students, they likely will remember it better if they come up with good examples of it. Thinking of examples is a good way to elaborate information. For instance, self-reference is an effective way to elaborate information. If you are trying to get students to remember the concept of fairness, the more they can generate personal examples of inequities and equities they have personally experienced, the more likely they are to remember the concept.

The use of elaboration changes developmentally (McDonnell et al., 2016). Adolescents are more likely to use elaboration spontaneously than children are. Elementary school children can be taught to use elaboration strategies on a learning task, but they are less likely than adolescents to use the strategies on other learning tasks in

THROUGH THE EYES OF STUDENTS

The Cobwebs of Memory

I think the point of having memories is to share them, especially with close friends or family. If you don't share them, they are just sitting inside your brain getting cobwebs. If you have a great memory of Christmas and no one to share it with, what's the point of memories?

Quote by a Seventh-Grade Student
West Middle School, Ypsilanti, Michigan

RESEARCH

DEVELOPMENT

rehearsal The conscious repetition of information over time to increase the length of time information stays in memory.

levels of processing theory The theory that processing of memory occurs on a continuum from shallow to deep, with deeper processing producing better memory.

elaboration The extensiveness of information processing involved in encoding.

the future. Nonetheless, verbal elaboration can be an effective memory strategy even with young elementary school children. In one study, the experimenter told second- and fifth-grade children to construct a meaningful sentence for a keyword (such as "The postman carried a letter in his cart" for the keyword *cart*) (Pressley et al., 1980). Both second- and fifth-grade children remembered the keywords better when they constructed a meaningful sentence containing the word than when the keyword and its definition were told to the child.

One reason elaboration works so well in encoding is that it adds to the distinctiveness of memory code (Hofmeister & Vasishth, 2014). To remember a piece of information, such as a name, an experience, or a fact about geography, students need to search for the code that contains this information among the mass of codes in their long-term memory. The search process is easier if the memory code is unique. The situation is not unlike searching for a friend at a crowded airport—if your friend is 6 feet 3 inches tall and has flaming red hair, it will be easier to find him in the crowd than if he has more common features. Also, as a student elaborates information, more information is stored. And as more information is stored, it becomes easier to differentiate the memory from others. It is also easier to access the memory later because there are more connections made to facilitate retrieval.

Constructing Images When we construct an image of something, we are elaborating the information. For example, how many windows are there in the apartment or house where your family has lived for a substantial part of your life? Few of us ever memorize this information, but you probably can come up with a good answer, especially if you reconstruct a mental image of each room.

RESEARCH

Allan Paivio (1971, 1986, 2013) argues that memories are stored in one of two ways: as verbal codes or as image codes. For example, you can remember a picture by a label (*The Last Supper*, a verbal code) or by a mental image. Paivio says that the more detailed and distinctive the image code is, the better your memory of the information will be.

Researchers have found that encouraging children to use imagery to remember verbal information works better for older children than for younger children (Schneider, 2004). In one study, experimenters presented 20 sentences to first- through sixth-grade children to remember (such as "The angry bird shouted at the white dog" and "The policeman painted the circus tent on a windy day") (Pressley et al., 1987). Children were randomly assigned to an imagery condition (make a picture in your head for each sentence) and a control condition (children were told just to try hard). The imagery instructions improved memory more for the older children (grades 4 through 6) than for the younger children (grades 1 through 3). Researchers have found that young elementary school children can use imagery to remember pictures better than they can use it to remember verbal materials such as sentences (Schneider & Pressley, 1997).

Organization If students organize information when they are encoding it, their memory benefits (Schneider, 2015). To understand the importance of organization in encoding, complete the following exercise: Recall the 12 months of the year as quickly as you can. How long did it take you? What was the order of your recall? Your answers are probably a few seconds and in natural order (January, February, March, and so on). Now try to remember the months in alphabetical order. Did you make any errors? How long did it take you? There is a clear distinction between recalling the months in natural order and recalling alphabetically. This exercise is a good one to use with your students to help them understand the importance of organizing their memories in meaningful ways.

When you present information in an organized way, your students are more likely to remember it. This is especially true if you organize information hierarchically or outline it. Also, if you simply encourage students to organize information, they often will remember it better than if you give them no instructions about organizing (Mandler, 1980).

Chunking is a beneficial organizational memory strategy that involves grouping, or "packing," information into "higher-order" units that can be remembered as single units. Chunking works by making large amounts of information more manageable and more meaningful. For example, consider this simple list of words: *hot, city, book, forget, tomorrow, smile.* Try to hold these in memory for a moment, and then write them down. If you recalled all six words, you succeeded in holding 30 letters in your memory. But it would have been much more difficult to try to remember those 30 letters. Chunking them into words made them meaningful.

STORAGE

After children encode information, they need to retain, or store, the information. Children remember some information for less than a second, some for about half a minute, and other information for minutes, hours, years, even a lifetime. The three types of memory, which correspond to these different time frames, are *sensory memory* (which lasts a fraction of a second to several seconds); *short-term memory* (lasts about 30 seconds); and *long-term memory* (which lasts up to a lifetime).

Sensory Memory
Sensory memory holds information from the world in its original sensory form for only an instant, not much longer than the brief time a student is exposed to the visual, auditory, and other sensations.

Students have a sensory memory for sounds for up to several seconds, similar to a brief echo. However, their sensory memory for visual images lasts only for about one-fourth of a second. Because sensory information lasts for only a fleeting moment, an important task for the student is to attend to the sensory information that is important for learning quickly, before it fades.

Short-Term Memory
Short-term memory is a limited-capacity memory system in which information is retained for as long as 30 seconds, unless the information is rehearsed or otherwise processed further, in which case it can be retained longer. Compared with sensory memory, short-term memory is limited in capacity but relatively longer in duration. Its limited capacity intrigued George Miller (1956), who described this in a paper with a catchy title: "The Magical Number Seven, Plus or Minus Two." Miller pointed out that on many tasks, students are limited in how much information they can keep track of without external aids. Usually the limit is in the range of 7 ± 2 items.

The most widely cited example of the 7 ± 2 phenomenon involves **memory span,** the number of digits an individual can report back without error from a single presentation. How many digits individuals can report back depends on how old they are. In one study, memory span increased from two digits in 2-year-olds, to five digits in 7-year-olds, to six to seven digits in 12-year-olds (Dempster, 1981) (see Figure 2). Many college students can handle lists of eight or nine digits. Keep in mind that these are averages and that individuals differ. For example, many 7-year-olds have a memory span of fewer than six or seven digits; others have a memory span of eight or more digits.

Related to short-term memory, British psychologist Alan Baddeley (2000, 2007, 2012, 2013) proposed that **working memory** is a three-part system that temporarily holds information as people perform tasks. Working memory is a kind of mental "workbench" where information is manipulated and assembled to help us make decisions, solve problems, and comprehend written and spoken language. Notice that working memory is not like a passive storehouse with shelves to store information until it moves to long-term memory. Rather, it is a very active memory system (Logie & Cowan, 2015).

Figure 3 shows Baddeley's view of working memory and its three components: phonological loop, visuospatial working memory, and central executive. Think of them as an executive (central executive) with two assistants (phonological loop and visuospatial working memory) to help do your work.

DEVELOPMENT

chunking Grouping, or "packing," information into "higher-order" units that can be remembered as single units.

sensory memory Memory that holds information from the world in its original form for only an instant.

short-term memory A limited-capacity memory system in which information is retained for as long as 30 seconds, unless the information is rehearsed, in which case it can be retained longer.

memory span The number of digits an individual can report back without error in a single presentation.

working memory A three-part system that holds information temporarily as a person performs a task. A kind of "mental workbench" that lets individuals manipulate, assemble, and construct information when they make decisions, solve problems, and comprehend written and spoken language.

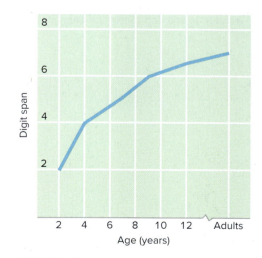

FIGURE 2 DEVELOPMENTAL CHANGES IN MEMORY SPAN

In one study, memory span increased from two digits at 2 years of age to five digits at 7 years of age (Dempster, 1981). By 12 years of age, memory span had increased on average another one and a half digits.

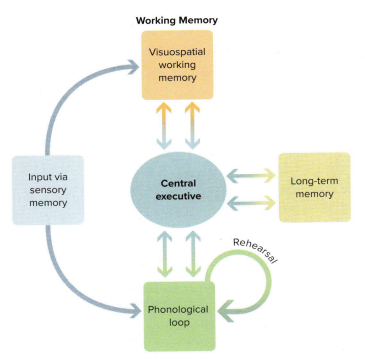

FIGURE 3 BADDELEY'S WORKING MEMORY MODEL

In Baddeley's working memory model, working memory consists of three main components: the phonological loop, visuospatial working memory, and the central executive. The phonological loop and visuospatial working memory serve as assistants, helping the central executive do its work. Input from sensory memory goes to the phonological loop, where information about speech is stored and rehearsal takes place, and to visuospatial working memory, where visual and spatial information, including imagery, is stored. Working memory is a limited-capacity system, and information is stored there for only a brief time. Working memory interacts with long-term memory, drawing information from long-term memory and transmitting information to long-term memory for longer storage.

- The *phonological loop* is specialized to briefly store speech-based information about the sounds of language. The phonological loop contains two separate components: an acoustic code, which decays in a few seconds, and rehearsal, which allows individuals to repeat the words in the phonological store.
- *Visuospatial working memory* stores visual and spatial information, including visual imagery. Like the phonological loop, visuospatial working memory has a limited capacity. The phonological loop and visuospatial working memory function independently. You could rehearse numbers in the phonological loop while making spatial arrangements of letters in visuospatial working memory.
- The *central executive* integrates information not only from the phonological loop and visuospatial working memory but also from long-term memory. In Baddeley's view, the central executive plays important roles in attention, planning, and organizing behavior. The central executive acts much like a supervisor who determines which information and issues deserve attention and which should be ignored. It also selects which strategies to use to process information and solve problems. As with the other two components of working memory—the phonological loop and visuospatial working memory—the central executive has a limited capacity.

Working memory develops gradually. Even by 8 years of age, children can only hold in memory half the items that adults can remember (Kharitonova et al., 2015). Working memory is linked to many aspects of children's development (Bigorra et al., 2016; Gerst et al., 2016). For example, children who have better working memory are more advanced in reading comprehension, math skills, and problem solving than their counterparts with less effective working memory (Swanson, 2016).

The following recent studies reflect the strength of working memory to improve children's performance in these areas:

RESEARCH

- Verbal working memory played a key role in 7- to 11-year-old children's ability to follow instructions over extended periods of activity (Jaroslawska et al., 2016).
- Children with better working memory had higher academic achievement in math fluency, calculation, reading fluency, and passage comprehension (Blankenship et al., 2015).
- Children's verbal working memory was linked to these aspects of language acquisition in both first- and second-language learners: morphology, syntax, and grammar (Verhagen & Leseman, 2016). However, their verbal working memory was not related to vocabulary development.
- A working memory training program (CogMed) implemented when students were in the fourth grade was linked to higher achievement in math and reading two years later in the sixth grade than a control group of children who received education as usual (Soderqvist & Bergman, 2015). To learn more about the CogMed working memory training program for children and how it can be used in classrooms, go to www.cogmed.com/educators
- A working memory training program improved the arithmetic problem-solving skills of 8- to 10-year-olds (Cornoldi et al., 2015).
- A working memory training program improved the listening comprehension skills of first-grade children (Peng & Fuchs, 2016).

Is the working memory of adolescents better than the working memory of children? One study found that it was (Swanson, 1999). Investigators examined the performance of children and adolescents on both verbal and visuospatial working memory tasks. Working memory increased substantially from 8 through 24 years of age no matter what the task. Thus, the adolescent years are likely to be an important developmental period for improvement in working memory.

Long-Term Memory Long-term memory is a type of memory that holds enormous amounts of information for a long period of time in a relatively permanent fashion. A typical human's long-term memory capacity is staggering, and the efficiency with which individuals can retrieve information is impressive. It often takes only a moment to search through this vast storehouse to find the information we want. Think about your own long-term memory. Who wrote the Gettysburg Address? Who was your first-grade teacher? You can answer thousands of such questions instantly. Of course, not all information is retrieved so easily from long-term memory.

A Model of the Three Memory Stores

This three-stage concept of memory we have been describing was developed by Richard Atkinson and Richard Shiffrin (1968). According to the **Atkinson-Shiffrin model,** memory involves a sequence of sensory memory, short-term memory, and long-term memory stages (see Figure 4). As we have seen, much information makes it no further than the sensory memories of sounds and sights. This information is retained only for a brief instant. However, some information, especially that to which we pay attention, is transferred to short-term memory, where it can be retained for about 30 seconds (or longer with the aid of rehearsal). Atkinson and Shiffrin claimed that the longer information is retained in short-term memory through the use of rehearsal, the greater its chance is of getting into long-term memory. Notice in Figure 4 that information in long-term memory also can be retrieved back into short-term memory.

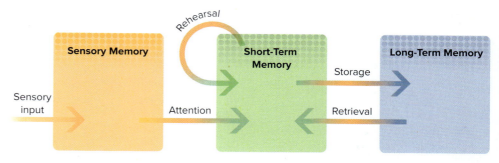

FIGURE 4 ATKINSON AND SHIFFRIN'S MODEL OF MEMORY

In this model, sensory input goes into sensory memory. Through the process of attention, information moves into short-term memory, where it remains for 30 seconds or less, unless it is rehearsed. When the information goes into long-term memory storage, it can be retrieved throughout a person's lifetime.

Some contemporary experts on memory believe that the Atkinson-Shiffrin model is too simple (Bartlett, 2015). They argue that memory doesn't always work in a neatly packaged three-stage sequence, as Atkinson and Shiffrin proposed. For example, these contemporary experts stress that *working memory* uses long-term memory's contents in more flexible ways than simply retrieving information from it. Despite these problems, the model is useful in providing an overview of some components of memory.

Long-Term Memory's Contents Just as different types of memory can be distinguished by how long they last, memory can be differentiated on the basis of its contents. For long-term memory, many contemporary psychologists accept the hierarchy of contents described in Figure 5 (Bartlett, 2015). In this hierarchy, long-term memory is divided into the subtypes of declarative and procedural memory. Declarative memory is subdivided into episodic memory and semantic memory.

Declarative and Procedural Memory **Declarative memory** is the conscious recollection of information, such as specific facts or events that can be verbally communicated. Declarative memory has been called "knowing that" and more recently has been labeled "explicit memory." Demonstrations of students' declarative memory could include recounting an event they have witnessed or describing a basic principle of math. However, students do not need to be talking in order to use declarative memory. If students simply sit and reflect on an experience, their declarative memory is involved.

long-term memory A type of memory that holds enormous amounts of information for a long period of time in a relatively permanent fashion.

Atkinson-Shiffrin model A model of memory that involves a sequence of three stages: sensory memory, short-term memory, and long-term memory.

declarative memory The conscious recollection of information, such as specific facts or events that can be verbally communicated.

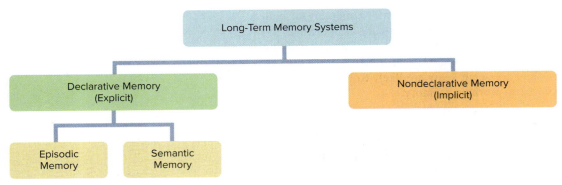

FIGURE 5 CLASSIFICATION OF LONG-TERM MEMORY'S CONTENTS

Procedural memory is nondeclarative knowledge in the form of skills and cognitive operations. Procedural memory cannot be consciously recollected, at least not in the form of specific events or facts. This makes procedural memory difficult, if not impossible, to communicate verbally. Procedural memory is sometimes called "knowing how," and it also has been described as "implicit memory." When students apply their abilities to perform a dance, ride a bicycle, or type on a computer keyboard, their procedural memory is at work. It also is at work when they speak grammatically correct sentences without having to think about how to do it.

Episodic and Semantic Memory Cognitive psychologist Endel Tulving (2000) distinguishes between two subtypes of declarative memory: episodic and semantic. **Episodic memory** is the retention of information about the where and when of life's happenings. Students' memories of the first day of school, whom they had lunch with, or the guest who came to talk with their class last week are all episodic.

Semantic memory is a student's general knowledge about the world. It includes the following:

- Knowledge of the sort learned in school (such as knowledge of geometry)
- Knowledge in different fields of expertise (such as knowledge of chess, for a skilled 15-year-old chess player)
- "Everyday" knowledge about meanings of words, famous people, important places, and common things (such as what the word *pertinacious* means or who Nelson Mandela is)

Semantic memory is independent of the person's identity with the past. For example, students might access a fact—such as "Lima is the capital of Peru"—and not have the foggiest idea when and where they learned it. Figure 6 compares the characteristics of episodic and semantic memory.

Representing Information in Memory How do students represent information in their memory? Three main theories have addressed this question: network, schema, and fuzzy trace.

Network Theories **Network theories** describe how information in memory is organized and connected. They emphasize nodes in the memory network. The nodes stand for labels or concepts. Consider the concept "bird." One of the earliest network theories described memory representation as hierarchically arranged, with more-concrete concepts ("canary," for example) nestled under more abstract concepts (such as "bird"). However, it soon became clear that such hierarchical networks are too neat to accurately portray how memory representation really works. For example, students take longer to answer the question "Is an ostrich a bird?" than to answer the question "Is a canary a bird?" Thus, today memory researchers envision the memory network as more irregular and distorted (Ashcraft & Radvansky, 2016). A typical bird, such as a canary, is closer to the node, or center, of the category "bird" Figure 7 than is the atypical ostrich.

procedural memory Nondeclarative knowledge in the form of skills and cognitive operations. Procedural memory cannot be consciously recollected, at least not in the form of specific events or facts.

episodic memory The retention of information about the where and when of life's happenings.

semantic memory An individual's general knowledge about the world, independent of the individual's identity with the past.

network theories Theories that describe how information in memory is organized and connected; they emphasize nodes in the memory network.

Characteristic	Episodic Memory	Semantic Memory
Units	Events, episodes	Facts, ideas, concepts
Organization	Time	Concepts
Emotion	More important	Less important
Retrieval process	Deliberate (effortful)	Automatic
Retrieval report	"I remember"	"I know"
Education	Irrelevant	Relevant
Intelligence	Irrelevant	Relevant
Legal testimony	Admissible in court	Inadmissible in court

FIGURE 6 SOME DIFFERENCES BETWEEN EPISODIC & SEMANTIC MEMORY

These characteristics have been proposed as the main ways to differentiate episodic from semantic memory.

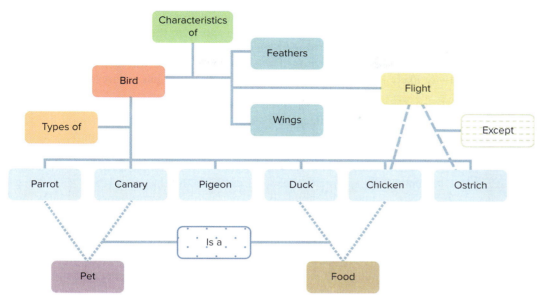

FIGURE 7 MEMORY NETWORK FOR THE CONCEPT OF BIRD

Schema Theories Long-term memory has been compared with a library of books. The idea is that our memory stores information just as a library stores books. In this analogy, the way students retrieve information is said to be similar to the process they use to locate and check out a book. The process of retrieving information from long-term memory, however, is not as precise as the library analogy suggests. When we search through our long-term memory storehouse, we don't always find the exact "book" we want, or we might find the "book" we want but discover that only "several pages" are intact—we have to reconstruct the rest.

Schema theories state that when we reconstruct information, we fit it into information that already exists in our mind. A **schema** is information—concepts, knowledge, information about events—that already exists in a person's mind. Unlike network theories, which assume that retrieval involves specific facts, schema theory claims that long-term memory searches are not very exact. We often don't find precisely what we want. When asked to retrieve information, we frequently fill in the gaps between our fragmented memories with a variety of accuracies and inaccuracies.

We have schemas for all sorts of information (Gluck et al., 2016). If you tell virtually any story to your class and then ask the students to write down what the story was about, you likely will get many different versions. That is, your students won't remember every detail of the story you told and will reconstruct the story with their own particular stamp on it. Suppose you tell your class a story about two men and two women who were involved in a train crash in France. One student might reconstruct the story by saying the characters died in a plane crash, another might describe three men and three women, another might say the crash was in Germany, and so on. The reconstruction and distortion of memory is nowhere more apparent than in the memories given by courtroom witnesses. In criminal court trials, the variations in people's memories of what happened underscores how we reconstruct the past rather than take an exact photograph of it.

In sum, schema theory accurately predicts that people don't always coldly store and retrieve bits of data in a computer-like fashion. The mind can distort an event as it encodes and stores impressions of reality.

A **script** is a schema for an event. Scripts often have information about physical features, people, and typical occurrences. This kind of information is helpful when teachers and students need to figure out what is happening around them. In a script

schema theories Theories that when we construct information, we fit it into information that already exists in our mind.

schema Information—concepts, knowledge, information about events—that already exists in a person's mind.

script A schema for an event.

for an art activity, students likely will remember that you will instruct them on what to draw, that they are supposed to put on smocks over their clothes, that they must get the art paper and paints from the cupboard, that they are to clean the brushes when they are finished, and so on. For example, a student who comes in late to the art activity likely knows much of what to do because he has an art activity script.

Fuzzy Trace Theory Another variation of how individuals reconstruct their memories is **fuzzy trace theory,** which states that when individuals encode information it creates two types of memory representations: (1) a *verbatim memory trace,* which consists of precise details; and (2) a *fuzzy trace,* or gist, which is the central idea of the information (Brainerd et al., 2006, 2015; Brainerd & Reyna, 2014). For example, consider a child who is presented with information about a pet store that has 10 birds, 6 cats, 8 dogs, and 7 rabbits. Then the child is asked two different types of questions: (1) verbatim questions, such as "How many cats are in the pet store, 6 or 8?" and (2) gist questions, such as "Are there more cats or more dogs in the pet store?" Researchers have found that preschool children tend to remember verbatim information better than gist information, but elementary-school-aged children are more likely to remember gist information (Brainerd & Reyna, 2014). Thus, in fuzzy trace theory, the increased use of gist information by elementary-school-aged children accounts for their improved memory, because fuzzy traces are less likely to be forgotten than verbatim traces.

RETRIEVAL AND FORGETTING

After students have encoded information and then represented it in memory, they might be able to retrieve some of it but might also forget some of it. What factors influence whether students can retrieve information?

fuzzy trace theory States that memory is best understood by considering two types of memory representations: (1) verbatim memory trace and (2) fuzzy trace, or gist. In this theory, older children's better memory is attributed to the fuzzy traces created by extracting the gist of information.

serial position effect The principle that recall is better for items at the beginning and the end of a list than for items in the middle.

Retrieval When we retrieve something from our mental "data bank," we search our store of memory to find the relevant information. Just as with encoding, this search can be automatic or it can require effort. For example, if you ask your students what month it is, the answer will immediately spring to their lips. That is, the retrieval will be automatic. But if you ask your students to name the guest speaker who came to the class two months earlier, the retrieval process likely will require more effort.

An item's position on a list also affects how easy or difficult it will be to remember it. In the **serial position effect,** recall is better for items at the beginning and end of a list than for items in the middle. Suppose that when you give a student directions about where to go to get tutoring help, you say, "Left on Mockingbird, right on Central, left on Balboa, left on Sandstone, and right on Parkside." The student likely will remember "Left on Mockingbird" and "Right on Parkside" better than "Left on Balboa." The *primacy effect* is that items at the beginning of a list tend to be remembered. The *recency effect* is that items at the end of the list also tend to be remembered.

Figure 8 shows a typical serial position effect with a slightly stronger recency effect than primacy effect. The serial position effect applies not only to lists but also to events. If you spread out a history lesson over a week and then ask students about it the following Monday, they likely will have the best memory for what you told them on Friday of last week and the worst memory for what you told them on Wednesday of last week.

Another factor that affects retrieval is the nature of the cues people use to prompt their memory (Schneider, 2015; van Lamsweerde et al., 2016). Students can learn to create effective cues. For example, if a student has a "block" about remembering the name of the guest who came to class two months ago, she might go through the alphabet, generating names with each letter. If she manages to stumble across the right name, she likely will recognize it.

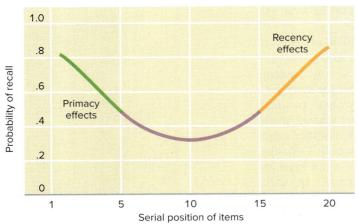

FIGURE **8** THE SERIAL POSITION EFFECT
When a person is asked to memorize a list of words, the words memorized last usually are recalled best, those at the beginning next best, and those in the middle least efficiently.

Another consideration in understanding retrieval is the **encoding specificity principle,** which says that associations formed at the time of encoding or learning tend to be effective retrieval cues. For example, imagine that a 13-year-old child has encoded this information about Mother Teresa: She was born in Albania, lived most of her life in India, became a Roman Catholic nun, was saddened by seeing people sick and dying in Calcutta's streets, and won a Nobel Prize for her humanitarian efforts to help the poor and suffering. Later, when the child tries to remember details about Mother Teresa, she can use words such as *Nobel Prize, Calcutta,* and *humanitarian* as retrieval cues. The concept of encoding specificity is compatible with our earlier discussion of elaboration: The more elaboration children use in encoding information, the better their memory of the information will be. Encoding specificity and elaboration reveal how interdependent encoding and retrieval are.

Yet another aspect of retrieval is the nature of the retrieval task itself. *Recall* is a memory task in which individuals must retrieve previously learned information, as students must do for fill-in-the-blank or essay questions. *Recognition* is a memory task in which individuals only have to identify ("recognize") learned information, as is often the case on multiple-choice tests. Many students prefer multiple-choice items because they provide good retrieval cues, which fill-in-the-blank and essay items don't do.

Forgetting One form of forgetting involves the cues we just discussed. **Cue-dependent forgetting** is retrieval failure caused by a lack of effective retrieval cues. The notion of cue-dependent forgetting can explain why a student might fail to retrieve a needed fact for an exam even when he is sure he "knows" the information. For example, if you are studying for a test in this course and are asked a question about a distinction between recall and recognition in retrieval, you likely will remember the distinction better if you possess the cues "fill-in-the-blank" and "multiple-choice," respectively.

The principle of cue-dependent forgetting is consistent with **interference theory,** which states that we forget not because we actually lose memories from storage but rather because other information gets in the way of what we are trying to remember. For a student who studies for a biology test, then studies for a history test, and then takes the biology test, the information about history will interfere with remembering the information about biology. Thus, interference theory implies that, if you have more than one test to study for, you should study last what you are going to be tested on next. That is, the student taking the biology test would have benefited from studying history first and studying biology afterward. This strategy also fits with the recency effect we described earlier.

Another source of forgetting is memory decay. According to **decay theory,** new learning involves the creation of a neurochemical "memory trace," which will eventually disintegrate. Thus, decay theory suggests that the passage of time is responsible for forgetting.

Memories decay at different speeds. Some memories are vivid and last for long periods of time, especially when they have emotional ties. We can often remember these "flashbulb" memories with considerable accuracy and vivid imagery. For example, consider a car accident you were in or witnessed, the night of your high school graduation, an early romantic experience, and where you were when you heard that Donald Trump had been elected president. Chances are, you will be able to retrieve this information many years after the event occurred.

Teachers were asked how they help their students improve their memory skills. Following are their responses.

EARLY CHILDHOOD Repetition often helps preschoolers remember. For example, as a weekly theme, we focus on a letter of the week. Children are asked to write the same letter throughout the week. They also hear stories related to just that one letter and are asked to bring in something for "show and tell" that starts with the letter being highlighted that week.

—MISSY DANGLER

encoding specificity principle The principle that associations formed at the time of encoding or learning tend to be effective retrieval cues.

cue-dependent forgetting Retrieval failure caused by a lack of effective retrieval cues.

interference theory The theory that we forget not because we actually lose memories from storage but because other information gets in the way of what we are trying to remember.

decay theory The theory that new learning involves the creation of a neurochemical "memory trace," which will eventually disintegrate. Thus, decay theory suggests that the passage of time is responsible for forgetting.

ELEMENTARY SCHOOL: GRADES K-5 One strategy that works well with my students is to play the game *Jeopardy!* and use categories like math, grammar, science, social studies, and famous stories. The game keeps them excited and focused on the topics. Students receive bonus points for correct answers, which they can trade in for certain classroom privileges.

—CRAIG JENSEN

MIDDLE SCHOOL: GRADES 6-8 I use self-tests to help my seventh-graders improve their memory. Based on notes taken in class, students create their own quizzes and tests. Questions are on one side of the paper, answers on the other. When they study, they are seeing the questions, not the answers. This approach not only helps them remember, but also helps eliminate test anxiety for many students because they know what the test looks like before they get to class.

—MARK FODNESS

HIGH SCHOOL: GRADES 9-12 I find that mnemonic devices, silly little rhymes, and dances work best when helping my students remember information. Amazingly, as goofy as this may sound, my high school students remember information using these techniques.

—JENNIFER HEITER

CONNECTING WITH STUDENTS: Best Practices
Strategies for Helping Students Improve Their Memory

As with attention, students benefit when teachers work with them to improve their memory skills. Following are some effective strategies teachers can use to enhance children's memory skills.

1. *Motivate children to remember material by understanding it rather than by memorizing it.* Children will remember information better over the long term if they understand the information rather than just rehearse and memorize it. Rehearsal works well for encoding information into short-term memory, but when children need to retrieve the information from long-term memory, it is much less efficient. For most information, encourage children to understand it, give it meaning, elaborate on it, and personalize it. Give children concepts and ideas to remember and then ask them how they can relate the concepts and ideas to their own personal experiences and meanings. Give them practice on elaborating a concept so they will process the information more deeply.

2. *Repeat with variation on the instructional information and link early and often.* Memory development research expert Patricia Bauer (2009) recommends improving children's consolidation and reconsolidation of the information they are learning by two methods: Providing variations on a lesson theme to increase the number of associations in memory storage, and linking, to expand the network of associations in memory storage. Both strategies expand the routes for retrieving information from storage.

3. *Assist students in organizing what they put into their memory.* Children will remember information better if they organize it hierarchically. Give them some practice arranging and reworking material that requires some structuring. Graphic organizers are great for this. Lots of resources for supporting elaboration, connections, and organization of information can be found online: http://www.theteachertoolkit.com/index.php/tool/graphic-organizers https://www.teachervision.com/lesson-planning/graphic-organizer

4. *Teach mnemonic strategies. Mnemonics* are memory aids for remembering information. Mnemonic strategies can involve imagery and words (Homa, 2008). Different types of mnemonics include:

   - *Method of loci.* In the *method of loci*, children develop images of items to be remembered and mentally store them in familiar locations. Rooms of a house and stores on

CONNECTING WITH STUDENTS: Best Practices
Strategies for Helping Students Improve Their Memory

a street are common locations used in this memory strategy. In *Through the Eyes of Teachers,* teacher Rosemary Moore describes a similar idea for teaching spelling words.

THROUGH THE EYES OF TEACHERS
Seeing Words in the Mind's Eye

Many children memorize spelling words quite easily, but a few struggle with this. I wanted to help these students as much as I could, so I would write the spelling words on index cards and place them in random order and various positions (vertically, diagonally, upside-down, across the front of the room). As we did spelling assignments, exercises, and games throughout the week, the words were there for the students to refer to if they got "stuck." The index cards were taken down before the test on Friday, but as I called out each of the spelling words I would notice students turning their eyes to the place where the particular word had been displayed. I believe they were seeing the word in their "mind's eye." My students' spelling scores improved dramatically.

Rosemary Moore

FIGURE 9 THE KEYWORD METHOD

To help children remember the state capitals, the keyword method was used. A special component of the keyword method is the use of mental imagery. For example, to help children remember that Annapolis is the capital of Maryland, they were encouraged to envision two apples being married, thus associating apple with Annapolis and marry with Maryland.

- *Rhymes.* Examples of mnemonic rhymes are the spelling rule "*i* before *e* except after *c*," the month rule, "Thirty days hath September, April, June, and November," the bolt-turning rule "Right is tight, left is loose," and the alphabet song.
- *Acronyms.* This strategy involves creating a word from the first letters of items to be remembered. For example, *HOMES* can be used as a cue for remembering the five Great Lakes in North America: *Huron, Ontario, Michigan, Erie,* and *Superior.*
- *Keyword method.* Another mnemonic strategy that involves imagery is the *keyword method,* in which vivid imagery is attached to important words. This method has been used to practical advantage in teaching students how to rapidly master new information such as foreign vocabulary words, the states and capitals of the United States, and the names of U.S. presidents. For example, in teaching children that Annapolis is the capital of Maryland, you could ask them to connect vivid images of Annapolis and Maryland, such as two apples getting married (Levin, 1980) (see Figure 9).
5. *Embed memory-relevant language when instructing children.* Teachers vary considerably in how much they use memory-relevant language that encourages students to remember information. In research that involved extensive observations of a number of first-grade teachers in the classroom, Peter Ornstein and his colleagues (Ornstein et al., 2007; Ornstein et al., 2010) found that in the time segments observed, the teachers rarely used strategy suggestions or metacognitive (thinking about thinking) questions. In this research, when lower-achieving students were placed in classrooms in which teachers were categorized as "high-mnemonic teachers" who frequently embedded memory-relevant information in their teaching, their achievement increased (Ornstein et al., 2007).

RESEARCH

6. *Guide students to use distributed practice,* which involves creating a schedule of practice that spreads out study activities over time. Students tend to postpone much of their study until just before they take a test. Cramming is better than not studying at all, but students benefit from spreading out their study of the content for an exam (Dunlosky et al., 2013).
7. *Give students practice tests and encourage them to test themselves.* Practice testing can include having students ask themselves questions about the content to see if they can answer them, getting students to answer questions or test items at the end of each chapter in textbooks, and having students do practice tests that teachers have created or retrieved from electronic supplements for texts (Dunlosky et al., 2013).
8. Encourage students to engage in *elaborative interrogation,* which involves generating an explanation for why some fact or piece of information is accurate or true (Dunlosky et al., 2013). Students benefit from asking themselves "Why?" questions when they are studying and learning.

In a recent research review, John Dunlosky and his colleagues (2013) found that distributed practice and practice testing had high utility in helping students learn and remember content. They also discovered that elaborative interrogation had moderate utility benefitting students' learning and remembering. In this research review, highlighting and underlining, summarizing, rereading, using the keyword method, and using imagery for text learning had low utility.

Review, Reflect, and Practice

③ Discuss memory in terms of encoding, storage, and retrieval.

REVIEW
- What is memory? What is necessary for it to work?
- How are these five processes—rehearsal, deep processing, elaboration, constructing images, and organization—involved in encoding?
- What are the three time frames of memory? How are long-term memory's contents described? What are three theories about how these long-term contents might be represented in memory? What makes a memory easier or harder to retrieve? What are some theories about why we forget?

REFLECT
- Which principles and strategies in our discussion of memory are likely to be useful for the subjects and grade levels at which you plan to teach?

PRAXIS™ PRACTICE

1. Natalie is playing a game called "memory" at a birthday party. A covered tray with 15 objects is brought into the room. The cover is removed, and the children have 30 seconds to memorize the objects. They will then write down the objects they remember. The child who correctly remembers the most objects wins the game. Natalie notices that five of the objects are hair-related items—a comb, a brush, shampoo, a barrette, and a ponytail holder. She notices that another five objects are school supplies—a pencil, a pen, a ruler, a marker, and a glue stick. The final five objects appear to be random. Natalie has no problem remembering the items that she was able to group by type. She only remembers two of the other items. What memory strategy is Natalie using?
   a. chunking
   b. constructing images
   c. elaboration
   d. rehearsal

2. To test his students' memory skills, Mr. Watkins reads lists of nonsense words to them and asks them to recall as many as they can. Veronica can recall five words. If she performs as is expected for her age, how old is Veronica most likely to be?
   a. 4
   b. 7
   c. 12
   d. 17

3. When asked to describe in detail how to make a peanut-butter-and-jelly sandwich, Maria skips several steps. When asked to make a sandwich, Maria does so flawlessly. Why is it that although Maria knows how to make a sandwich, she is unable to describe the process in detail?
   a. It is difficult to translate procedural memory into words.
   b. Maria has not encoded the process into long-term memory.
   c. It is difficult to translate episodic memory into semantic memory.
   d. Maria's episodic memory is faulty.

4. Mr. Madison wants his students to know the names of all of the states in the United States. To help them remember, he teaches them a song in which each state name is sung in alphabetical order. Most of his students learn the song with relative ease. They even sing the song to themselves when he gives them a quiz that requires them to write down the name of each state. However, when he gives them blank U.S. maps to

Review, Reflect, and Practice

fill in with state names, his students cannot complete them successfully. Why were they able to remember the names of the states, but not their locations?
a. Mnemonic devices, such as the song Mr. Madison taught his students, are not effective for memorizing material.
b. Mnemonic devices, such as the song Mr. Madison taught his students, increase the likelihood of cue-dependent forgetting.
c. Mnemonic devices, such as the song Mr. Madison taught his students, increase the serial position effect.
d. Mnemonic devices, such as the song that Mr. Madison taught his students, involve rote memorization and do not generalize to other memory tasks.

Please see answer key at end of book . . . .

4 EXPERTISE

LG 4 Draw some lessons about learning from the way experts think.

In the last section, we considered various aspects of memory. Our ability to remember new information about a subject depends considerably on what we already know about it. For example, a student's ability to recount what she saw when she was at the library is largely governed by what she already knows about libraries, such as where books on certain topics are likely to be shelved and how to check books out. If she knew little about libraries, the student would have a much harder time recounting what was there.

The contribution of prior content knowledge to our ability to remember new material is especially evident when we compare the memories of experts and novices in a particular knowledge domain (Ericsson, 2014; Ericsson et al., 2016; Gong et al., 2015). An expert is the opposite of a novice (someone who is just beginning to learn a content area). Experts demonstrate especially impressive memory in their areas of expertise (Baer, 2015). One reason that children remember less than adults is that they are far less expert in most areas.

EXPERTISE AND LEARNING

Studying the behavior and mental processes of experts can give us insights about how to guide students in becoming more effective learners (Cianciolo & Sternberg, 2016; Neumann et al., 2016). What is it, exactly, that experts do? According to the National Research Council (1999), experts are better than novices at the following:

- Detecting features and meaningful patterns of information
- Accumulating more content knowledge and organizing it in a manner that shows an understanding of the topic
- Retrieving important aspects of knowledge with little effort
- Adapting an approach to new situations
- Using effective strategies

In this section, we will consider various ways that you can help your students learn and apply the skills that experts use so effortlessly.

RESEARCH

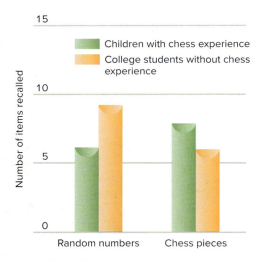

FIGURE 10 MEMORY FOR NUMBERS AND CHESS PIECES

Detecting Features and Meaningful Patterns of Organization Experts are better at noticing important features of problems and contexts that novices may ignore (Bransford et al., 2006). Thus, the attentional advantage of experts starts them off at a more advantageous level than novices in a learning context. Experts also have superior recall of information in their area of expertise. The process of chunking, which we discussed earlier, is one way they accomplish this superior recall. For example, "Chess masters perceive chunks of meaningful information, which affects their memory of what they see. . . . Lacking a hierarchical, highly organized structure for the domain, novices cannot use this chunking strategy" (National Research Council, 1999, p. 21).

In areas where children are knowledgeable and competent, their memory is often extremely good. In fact, it often exceeds that of adults who are novices in that content area. This was documented in a study of 10-year-old chess experts (Chi, 1978). These children were excellent chess players but not especially brilliant in other ways. As with most 10-year-olds, their memory spans for digits were shorter than an adult's. However, they remembered the configurations of chess pieces on chessboards far better than did college students who were novices at chess (see Figure 10).

Expert teachers recognize features and patterns that are not noticed by novice teachers (National Research Council, 1999, pp. 21, 25). For example, in one study, expert and novice teachers had a very different understanding of the events in a videotaped classroom lesson, in which three screens showed simultaneous events taking place throughout the classroom (left, center, and right areas) (Sabers et al., 1991). One expert teacher said, "On the left monitor, the students' note taking indicates that they have seen sheets like this before; it's fairly efficient at this point because they're used to the format they are using." One novice teacher sparsely responded, "It's a lot to watch."

Organization and Depth of Knowledge Experts' knowledge is organized around important ideas or concepts more than novices' knowledge is (National Research Council, 1999). This provides experts with a much deeper understanding of knowledge than novices have (Bransford et al., 2006). This textbook supports your development of organized, deep knowledge of educational psychology by helping you make connections between ideas covered via the Thinking Back/Thinking Forward boxes.

Experts in a particular area usually have far more elaborate networks of information about that area than novices do (see Figure 11). The information they represent in memory has more nodes, more interconnections, and better hierarchical organization.

The implications for teaching are that too often a curriculum is designed in a way that makes it difficult for students to organize knowledge in meaningful ways. This especially occurs when there is only superficial coverage of facts before moving on to the next topic. In this context, students have little time to explore the topic in depth and get a sense of what the important, organizing ideas are. This type of

FIGURE 11 AN EXAMPLE OF HOW INFORMATION IS ORGANIZED IN THE MIND OF EXPERT AND A NOVICE

(a) An expert's knowledge is based on years of experience in which small bits of information have been linked with many other small pieces, which together are placed in a more general category. This category is in turn placed in an even more general category of knowledge. The dotted lines are used as pointers, associations between specific elements of knowledge that connect the lower branches and provide mental shortcuts in the expert's mind.
(b) The novice's knowledge shows far fewer connections, shortcuts, and levels than an expert's knowledge.

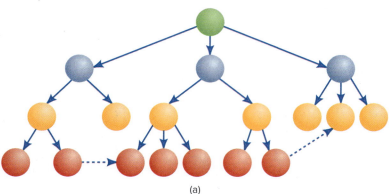
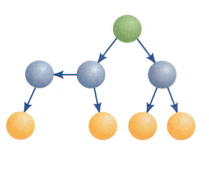

(a) (b)

shallow presentation can occur in any subject area but is common in history and science texts that emphasize facts (National Research Council, 1999).

Fluent Retrieval   Retrieval of relevant information can range from taking a lot of effort to being fluent and almost effortless. Experts retrieve information in an almost effortless, automatic manner, whereas novices expend a great deal of effort in retrieving information (Ericsson & Moxley, 2013).

Effortless retrieval places fewer demands on conscious attention. Since the amount of information a student can attend to at one time is limited, ease of processing information in some aspects of a task frees up capacity to attend to other aspects of a task.

Consider expert and novice readers. Expert readers can quickly scan the words of a sentence and paragraph, which allows them to devote attention to understanding what they are reading. However, novice readers' ability to decode words is not yet fluent, so they have to allocate considerable attention and time to this task, which restricts the time they can give to understanding a passage. An important aspect of teaching is to help students develop the fluency they need to competently perform cognitive tasks.

Students' fluency or automaticity is an important issue for teachers to attend to when designing instructional tasks. This is due to cognitive load or the amount of working memory used to complete a task (Sweller, 2012). Given the limited capacity of working memory and the variability in attention required to successfully complete different tasks, cognitive load theory suggests that there are three kinds of cognitive load teachers should consider that may impact whether the student learns the material or not. These are intrinsic load (related to the complexity of the task/material), germane load (related to the working memory resources needed to learn the material), and extrinsic load (related to the load imposed by the instructional procedures). To help students be successful, the extraneous load (like noise in the classroom, unclear directions, not breaking up the task into smaller steps) should be reduced. This would help students to put more of their finite resources toward learning and completing the task. Ways to reduce extraneous load include the following:

- Provide novice students with worked examples that show how to solve problems before students complete practice problems, rather than just having students practice doing problems
- Reduce split-attention by integrating elements of the solution to example problems into diagrams
- Present verbal information in a spoken rather than written format, which allows learners to take advantage of the separate auditory and visual processing systems rather than overloading the visual system
- Remove redundancy
- Ask students to imagine a concept or procedure to help develop schema (though this technique may be effective only for those with some expertise in an area already)

Adaptive Expertise   An important aspect of expertise "is whether some ways of organizing knowledge are better" than others for helping people to be "flexible and adaptive to new situations" (National Research Council, 1999, p. 33). Adaptive experts are able to approach new situations flexibly rather than always responding in a rigid, fixed routine (Ericsson, 2014). An important theme in the book *Preparing Teachers for a Changing World* (Darling-Hammond & Bransford, 2005, p. 3) was to "help teachers become 'adaptive experts' who are prepared for effective lifelong learning that allows them to continually add to their knowledge and skills." Thus, teachers characterized by adaptive expertise are flexible and open to rethinking important ideas and practices to improve their students' learning.

Indeed, innovation *and* efficiency are the two main dimensions of one model of adaptive expertise (Bransford et al., 2006). Experts characterized by *efficiency* can quickly retrieve and apply information in skillful ways to explain something or solve a problem. Experts characterized by *innovation* are able to move away from efficiency, at least on a short-term basis, and unlearn previous routines. Innovation occurs when individuals "let go" and rethink their routine way of doing something.

In this model, adaptive experts possess a balance of efficiency and innovation (Bransford et al., 2006). For example, efficiency is at work when a teacher teaches students to speedily complete math computations, but this efficiency may limit the students' competence when they face new math problems. When this efficiency-oriented teacher adapts and adds teaching for understanding and application, innovation is taking place. The new skills she teaches are likely to increase the students' competence when they encounter new math problems.

Adaptive experts are motivated to learn from others. This may not be that difficult when the learning involves making a teacher's existing routines and practices more efficient. However, as we just indicated, adaptive expertise also includes innovation that requires sometimes replacing or transforming prior routines and practices, which is often not easy to do. Your teaching likely will benefit if you seek feedback from other competent teachers, even if their approaches are different than yours. This might occur when you watch a videotape of your teaching with other teachers who provide feedback about your teaching or invite a colleague to come to your classroom to observe your teaching.

In sum, adaptive expertise is a critical aspect of being an outstanding teacher. Teachers who are knowledgeable and adept at adapting different methods, practices, and strategies to meet the needs of different students are most likely to guide students to higher levels of learning and achievement.

Strategies Experts use effective strategies in understanding the information in their area of expertise and in advancing it (Ericsson et al., 2016; Gong et al., 2015). Earlier in the chapter we described a number of strategies that students can use to remember information, and later in the chapter we will further examine strategies in our discussion of metacognition.

Patricia Alexander (2003) uses the label *acclimation* to describe the initial stage of expertise in a particular domain (such as English, biology, or mathematics). At this stage, students have limited and fragmented knowledge that restricts their ability to detect the difference between accurate and inaccurate and relevant and tangential information. To help students move beyond the acclimation stage, teachers need to guide students in determining what content is central and what is peripheral, as well as what is accurate and well supported and what is inaccurate and unsupported. In Alexander's (2003) view, students don't come to the classroom equipped with the strategies they need to move beyond the acclimation stage. Teachers must help students learn effective strategies and practice them in relevant situations before students can experience their value. Students also need to be encouraged to change and combine strategies to solve the problem at hand.

Spreading Out and Consolidating Learning Students' learning benefits when teachers talk with them about the importance of regularly reviewing what they learn. Children who have to prepare for a test will benefit from distributing their learning over a longer period rather than cramming for the test at the last minute. Cramming tends to produce short-term memory that is processed in a shallow rather than deep manner. A final, concentrated tune-up before the test is better than trying to learn everything at the last minute.

Asking Themselves Questions When children ask themselves questions about what they have read or about an activity, they expand the number of associations with the information they need to retrieve. At least as early as the middle of elementary school, the self-questioning strategy can help children to remember. For example, as children read, they can be encouraged to stop periodically and ask themselves questions such as "What is the meaning of what I just read?" "Why is this important?" and "What is an example of the concept

What are some good study strategies?
Ingram Publishing/SuperStock

I just read?" Students can use the same self-questioning strategy when they listen to you conduct a lesson, hear a guest give a talk, or watch a video. If you periodically remind children to generate questions about their experiences, they are more likely to remember the experiences. A literature review on the research of testing the effects of self-questioning on reading comprehension found that self-questioning strategies used during reading improve reading comprehension by enabling students to monitor their comprehension and learn independently (Joseph et al., 2015).

Taking Good Notes Taking good notes from either a lecture or a text benefits learning (Halonen & Santrock, 2013). When children are left to take notes without being given any strategies, they tend to take notes that are brief and disorganized. When they do write something down, it often is a verbatim record of what they have just heard. Give children some practice in taking notes and then evaluate their note taking. Encourage children not to write down everything they hear when they take notes. It is impossible to do this, anyway, and it can prevent them from getting the big picture of what the speaker is saying. Here are some good note-taking strategies:

- *Summarizing.* Have the children listen for a few minutes and then write down the main idea that a speaker is trying to get across in that time frame. Then have the child listen for several more minutes and write down another idea, and so on.
- *Outlining.* Show the children how to outline what a speaker is saying, using first-level heads as the main topics, second-level heads as subtopics under the first-level heads, and third-level heads under the second-level heads.
- *Using concept maps.* Help the children practice drawing concept maps, which are similar to outlines but visually portray information in a more spiderlike format (see the chapter on complex cognitive processes).

All three note-taking strategies described so far—summarizing, outlining, and using concept maps—help children evaluate which ideas are the most important to remember. Outlining and concept maps also help children arrange the material hierarchically, which underscores an important theme of learning: It works best when it is organized.

Using a Study System Various systems have been developed to help people to remember information that they are studying from a book. One of the earliest systems was called *SQ3R,* which stands for *Survey, Question, Read, Recite,* and *Review.* A more recently developed system is called *PQ4R,* which stands for *Preview, Question, Read, Reflect, Recite,* and *Review.* Thus, the PQ4R system adds an additional step, "Reflect," to the SQ3R system. PQ4R is based on a number of the well-established principles of learning and cognition. While it has been argued that this technique may be more rigid and sequential than actual, expert metacognition in practice (Donndelinger, 2005), it provides a useful heuristic for learners to scaffold their own deeper comprehension. It is used throughout the world, where its effectiveness has been tested in diverse contexts. For example, a number of recent experiments demonstrated achievement benefits for secondary students in a number of different subjects in countries throughout the Middle East (Al-Qawabeh & Aljazi, 2018).

From the later elementary school years on, students will benefit from practicing the PQ4R system. The system benefits students by getting them to meaningfully organize information, ask questions about it, reflect on it, and review it. Here are more details about the steps in the PQ4R system:

- *Preview.* Tell your students to briefly survey the material to get a sense of the overall organization of ideas—to look at the headings to see the main topics and subtopics that will be covered.
- *Question.* Encourage the children to ask themselves questions about the material as they read it.
- *Read.* Now tell the children to read the material. Encourage your students to be active readers—to immerse themselves in what they are reading and strive to

SELF-ASSESSMENT 1
How Effective Are My Memory and Study Strategies?

Teachers who themselves practice using good memory and study strategies are more likely to model and communicate these to their students than teachers who don't use such strategies. Candidly respond to these items about your own memory and study strategies. Rate yourself on this scale: 1 = never, 2 = some, 3 = moderate, 4 = almost, or 5 = always. Then total your points.

1. I'm a good time manager and planner.
2. I'm good at focusing my attention and minimizing distractions.
3. I try to understand material rather than rotely memorizing it.
4. I ask myself questions about what I have read or about class activities.
5. I take good notes in class and from textbooks.
6. I regularly review my notes.
7. I use mnemonic strategies.
8. I'm very organized in the way I encode information.
9. I spread out my studying to consolidate my learning.
10. I use good retrieval cues.
11. I use the PQ4R method or a similar study method.

1	2	3	4	5

SCORING AND INTERPRETATION

If you scored 50–55 total points, you likely use good memory and study strategies. If you scored 45–49 points, you likely have some reasonably good memory and study strategies. If you scored below 45, spend some time working on improving your memory and study strategies.

If you would like to learn more about effective memory and study strategies, one resource is a book called *Your Guide to College Success* (Santrock & Halonen, 2009). Also, to gain more experience in developing good memory and study strategies, contact the study-skills center at your college or university; specialists there likely will be able to help you.

understand what the author is saying. This helps students to avoid being empty readers whose eyes just track the lines of text but whose minds fail to register anything important.

- *Reflect.* By occasionally stopping and reflecting on the material, students increase its meaningfulness. Encourage the children to be analytic at this point in studying. After they have read something, challenge them to break open the ideas and scratch beneath their surface. This is a good time for them to think out applications and interpretations of the information, as well as connecting it with other information already in their long-term memory.
- *Recite.* This involves children self-testing themselves to see if they can remember the material and reconstruct it. At this point, encourage the children to make up a series of questions about the material and then try to answer them.
- *Review.* Tell your students to go over the material and evaluate what they know and don't know. At this point, they should reread and study the material they don't remember or understand well.

To evaluate the extent to which you use good memory and study strategies, complete *Self-Assessment 1*.

ACQUIRING EXPERTISE

What determines whether or not someone becomes an expert? Can motivation and practice bring someone to expert status? Or does expertise also require a great deal of talent?

Practice and Motivation One perspective is that a particular kind of practice—*deliberate practice*—is required to become an expert. Deliberate practice involves practice that is at an appropriate level of difficulty for the individual, provides corrective feedback, and allows opportunities for repetition (Ericsson, 2014).

In one study of violinists at a music academy, the extent to which students engaged in deliberate practice distinguished novices and experts (Ericsson et al., 1993). The top violinists averaged 7,500 hours of deliberate practice by age 18, the good violinists only 5,300 hours. Many individuals give up on becoming an expert because they won't put forth the effort required to engage in extensive deliberate practice over a number of years.

RESEARCH

Such extensive practice requires considerable motivation. Students who are not motivated to practice for long hours are unlikely to become experts in a particular area. For example, a student who complains about all of the work, doesn't persevere, and doesn't extensively practice solving math problems over a number of years is not going to become an expert in math.

Talent A number of psychologists who study expertise stress that it requires not only deliberate practice and motivation but also talent (Hunt, 2006; Sternberg & Sternberg, 2016).

A number of abilities—music and athletic, for example—seem to have a heritable component (Santos et al., 2016; Seesjarvi et al., 2016). For example, is it likely that Mozart could have become such an outstanding musical composer just because he practiced long hours? Is it likely that LeBron James became such a fantastic basketball player just because he was motivated to do so? Many talented individuals have attempted to become as great as Mozart or James but have given up trying after only mediocre performances. Clearly, heredity matters. Nonetheless, Mozart and James would not have developed expertise in their fields without being highly motivated and engaging in extensive deliberate practice. Talent alone does not make an expert.

EXPERTISE AND TEACHING

Being an expert in a particular domain—such as physics, history, or math—does not mean that the expert is good at helping others learn it (Bransford et al., 2006). Indeed, "expertise can sometimes hurt teaching because many experts forget what is easy and what is difficult for students" (National Research Council, 1999, p. 32).

Pedagogical Content Knowledge Some educators have distinguished between the content knowledge required for expertise and the pedagogical content knowledge necessary to effectively teach it. *Pedagogical content knowledge* includes ideas about common difficulties that students have as they try to learn a content area; typical paths students must take to understand the area; and strategies for helping students overcome the difficulties they experience.

Expert teachers are good at monitoring students' learning and assessing students' progress. They also know what types of difficulties students are likely to encounter, are aware of students' existing knowledge, and use this awareness to teach

An expert teacher monitoring students' learning. *What are some characteristics of expert teachers?*
Russell Illig/Photodisc/Getty Images

at the right level and to make new information meaningful. Some educational psychologists argue that in the absence of expert pedagogical awareness of their own students, inexpert teachers simply rely on textbook publishers' materials, which, of course, contain no information about the particular pedagogical needs of students in the teacher's classroom (Brophy, 2004).

Review, Reflect, and Practice

4 Draw some lessons about learning from the way experts think.

REVIEW
- What do experts do that novices often don't do in the process of learning?
- What does it take to become an expert?
- Is subject experience enough to make a good teacher? What else is needed?

REFLECT
- Choose an area in which you feel you are at least somewhat of an expert. Compare your ability to learn in that field with the ability of a novice.

PRAXIS™ PRACTICE

1. The case studies in this text are designed to help educational psychology students learn the material and begin to develop expertise. The first question of each case study asks students to identify the issues in the case. The author most likely included this question for each case because he understood that
   a. it is important for students to consolidate their learning
   b. it is important for students to learn to determine what content is central and what is peripheral
   c. in learning, it is important to strike a balance between efficiency and innovation
   d. students need a great deal of help in developing fluid retrieval skills

2. Ryan is the best player on his soccer team. His coach thinks of him as a coach's dream player because he works so hard. It is rare for Ryan to perform a skill better than his teammates when it is initially introduced, but by the time the next practice comes, he will have mastered the skill. At one point, Ryan decided that he wanted to be able to score from a corner kick. He gathered up all the soccer balls he could find and kicked them one after another from the corner, trying to curl them into the goal. When he had finished, he gathered the balls and did it again. He continued this for an entire afternoon, and thereafter for at least an hour after school each day. His coach was very happily surprised when, in the next game, Ryan scored a goal from a corner kick. Why has Ryan developed expertise in soccer?
   a. He engages in extensive deliberative practice.
   b. He is relying on an inborn talent.
   c. He has an excellent teacher in his coach.
   d. He uses the PQ4R method.

3. Mr. Williams is a former college history professor who is now teaching high school American history. He discusses his research and writing with his students and tries to make history come alive by telling them about how historians find out about the past. After a month of teaching, he finds that his students seem confused during class discussions and perform poorly on tests of factual knowledge. The most likely explanation is that Mr. Williams lacks
   a. content expertise
   b. pedagogical content knowledge
   c. metacognition
   d. cue-dependent knowledge

Please see answer key at end of book . . . .

5 METACOGNITION

LG 5 Explain the concept of metacognition and identify some ways to improve children's metacognition.

So far in this chapter, we have examined a number of ways you can help students improve their ability to process information as they learn, including ways to improve their attention and memory, as well as strategies that can increase the likelihood that they will make the transition from being a novice to being an expert. Another way that you can help children process information more effectively is by encouraging them to examine what they know about how their mind processes information (Sobel & Letourneau, 2015). As you read at the beginning of this chapter, this involves *metacognition,* which involves cognition about cognition, or "knowing about knowing" (Flavell, 2004). A distinction can be made between metacognitive knowledge and metacognitive activity. *Metacognitive knowledge* involves monitoring and reflecting on one's current or recent thoughts. This includes both factual knowledge, such as knowledge about the task, one's goals, or oneself, and strategic knowledge, such as how and when to use specific procedures to solve problems. *Metacognitive activity* occurs when students consciously adapt and manage their thinking strategies during problem solving and purposeful thinking.

Metacognition helps children to perform many academic tasks more effectively (Lai et al., 2015). Metacognitive skills also have been taught to students to help them solve problems (Koenig et al., 2015). In one study, eighth-grade students were trained in meta-strategic knowledge (MSK) or explicit knowledge about higher order thinking strategies related to controlling variables (Zohar & Ben David, 2008). In this experiment, students were randomly assigned to treatment or control conditions during a 12-lesson biology unit on reproduction. Students in both conditions participated for the same amount of time in inquiry tasks that required them to control variables (i.e., "compare between at least two cases while keeping all variables constant except the target variable;" Zohar & Ben David, 2008, p. 64). Only students in the experimental condition received explicit MSK instruction that included the following: the name of the strategy ("control of variables"), the "why" regarding the need to control variables to draw valid causal inferences, the "how" regarding how to use (and how not to use) the strategy, and the "when" regarding understanding what type of tasks require the use of the strategy (when we want to establish a causal relationship). The researchers found that MSK-trained students' strategic and meta-strategic thinking improved dramatically following instruction, and the benefit was maintained 3 months later. In particular, there was a strong effect of MSK training on low achieving students.

One expert on children's thinking, Deanna Kuhn (2009), argues that metacognition should be a stronger focus of efforts to help children become better critical thinkers, especially at the middle school and high school levels. She distinguishes between first-order cognitive skills, which enable children to know about the world (and have been the main focus of critical-thinking programs), and second-order cognitive skills—meta-knowing skills—which involve knowing about one's own (and others') knowing.

DEVELOPMENTAL CHANGES

How does metacognition change in childhood? Are there further changes in metacognition during adolescence?

Childhood Many studies have focused on children's metamemory, or knowledge of how memory works. In the last several decades, there has been extensive interest in children's theories about how the human mind works.

DEVELOPMENT

Metamemory By 5 or 6 years of age, children usually know that familiar items are easier to learn than unfamiliar ones, that short lists are easier than long ones, that recognition is easier than recall, and that forgetting becomes more likely over time (Lyon & Flavell, 1993). In other ways, however, young children's metamemory is limited. They don't understand that related items are easier to remember than unrelated ones or that remembering the gist of a story is easier than remembering information verbatim (Kreutzer & Flavell, 1975). By fifth grade, students understand that gist recall is easier than verbatim recall.

Preschool children also have an inflated opinion of their memory abilities. For example, in one study, a majority of preschool children predicted that they would be able to recall all 10 items on a list of 10 items. When tested, none of the young children managed this feat (Flavell, et al., 1970). As they move through the elementary school years, children give more realistic evaluations of their memory skills (Schneider & Pressley, 1997).

Preschool children also have little appreciation for the importance of memory cues, such as "It helps when you can think of an example of it." By 7 or 8 years of age, children better appreciate the importance of cueing for memory. In general, children's understanding of their memory abilities and their skill in evaluating their performance on memory tasks is relatively poor at the beginning of the elementary school years but improves considerably by age 11 or 12 (Bjorklund & Rosenblum, 2000).

Theory of Mind Even young children are curious about the nature of the human mind (Hughes & Devine, 2015; Lane et al., 2016; Wellman, 2015). They have a **theory of mind**, which refers to awareness of one's own mental processes and the mental processes of others. Studies of theory of mind view the child as "a thinker who is trying to explain, predict, and understand people's thoughts, feelings, and utterances" (Harris, 2006, p. 847). Researchers are increasingly discovering that children's theory of mind is linked to cognitive processes and disabilities. For example, theory of mind competence at age 3 is related to a higher level of metamemory at age 5 (Lockl & Schneider, 2007). Researchers also have found that autistic children have difficulty in developing a theory of mind, especially in understanding others' beliefs and emotions (Kana et al., 2015). Recent research also has documented that children with attention deficit hyperactivity disorder (Mohammadzadeh et al., 2016) and specific language disorder (Nilsson & de Lopez, 2016) have theory of mind deficits.

Language development likely plays a prominent role in the increasingly reflective nature of theory of mind as children go through the childhood years (Meins et al., 2013). Researchers have found that differences in children's language skills predict performance on theory of mind tasks (Hughes & Devine, 2015).

Among other factors that influence children's theory of mind development are advances in prefrontal cortex functioning (Powers et al., 2015), engaging in make-believe play (Kavanaugh, 2006), and various aspects of social interaction (Hughes & Devine, 2015). Among the social interaction factors that advance children's theory of mind are being securely attached to parents who engage children in mental state talk ("That's a good thought you have" or "Can you tell what he's thinking?") (Laranjo et al., 2010) and having older siblings and friends who engage in mental state talk (Hughes et al., 2010).

Children's theory of mind changes as they go through childhood and adolescence:

- *Two to Three Years of Age.* In this time frame, children begin to understand three mental states: (1) perceptions, (2) emotions, and (3) desires. *Perceptions:* The child realizes that another person sees what is in front of her eyes and not necessarily what is in front of the child's eyes. *Emotions:* The child can distinguish between positive (for example, happy) and negative (for example, sad) emotions. A child might say, "Tommy feels bad." *Desires:* The child understands that if someone wants something, he or she will try to get it. A child

theory of mind Awareness of one's own mental processes and the mental processes of others.

might say, "I want my mommy." Children refer to desires earlier and more frequently than they refer to cognitive states such as thinking, knowing, and beliefs (Rakoczy et al., 2007). Two- to three-year-olds understand the way that desires are related to actions and to simple emotions (Harris, 2006). For example, they understand that people will search for what they want and that if they obtain it, they are likely to feel happy, but if they don't get it, they will keep searching for it and are likely to feel sad or angry.

- *Four to Five Years of Age.* Children come to understand that the mind can represent objects and events accurately or inaccurately. The realization that people can have *false beliefs*—beliefs that are not true—develops in a majority of children by the time they are 5 years old (Wellman et al., 2001). In one study of false beliefs, young children were shown a Band-Aids box and asked what was inside (Jenkins & Astington, 1996). To the children's surprise, the box actually contained pencils. When asked what a child who had never seen the box would think was inside, 3-year-olds typically responded "pencils." However, the 4- and 5-year-olds, grinning at the anticipation of the false beliefs of other children who had not seen what was inside the box, were more likely to say "Band-Aids." Children's understanding of thinking has some limitations in early childhood (Bianco et al., 2016). They often underestimate when mental activity is likely occurring. For example, they fail to attribute mental activity to someone who is sitting quietly, reading, or talking (Flavell et al., 1995).

RESEARCH

- *Middle and Late Childhood.* It is only beyond the early childhood years that children have a deepening appreciation of the mind itself rather than just an understanding of mental states (Wellman, 2011, 2015). Not until middle and late childhood do children see the mind as an active constructor of knowledge or a processing center (Flavell et al., 1998). In middle and late childhood, children move from understanding that beliefs can be false to understanding that beliefs and mind are "interpretive," exemplified in an awareness that the same event can be open to multiple interpretations (Carpendale & Chandler, 1996).
- *Adolescence.* Important changes in metacognition also take place during adolescence (Kuhn, 2009). Compared with children, adolescents have an increased capacity to monitor and manage cognitive resources to effectively meet the demands of a learning task. This increased metacognitive ability results in more effective cognitive functioning and learning.

Adolescents have more resources available to them than children (through increased processing speed, capacity, and automaticity), and they are more skilled at directing the resources. Further, adolescents have a better meta-level understanding of strategies—that is, knowing the best strategy to use and when to use it in performing a learning task (Kuhn, 2009). Next, we examine a model that places a high importance on students' use of strategies as an effective way to improve school success.

THE GOOD INFORMATION-PROCESSING MODEL

Michael Pressley and his colleagues (Pressley et al., 1989; Schneider & Pressley, 1997) developed a metacognitive model called the *Good Information-Processing model.* It emphasizes that competent cognition results from a number of interacting factors. These include strategies, content knowledge, motivation, and metacognition. They argue that children become good at cognition in three main steps:

1. *Children are taught by parents or teachers to use a particular strategy.* With practice, they learn about its characteristics and advantages for learning *specific knowledge.* The more intellectually stimulating children's homes and schools are, the greater the number of specific strategies they will encounter and learn to use.

2. *Teachers may demonstrate similarities and differences in multiple strategies in a particular domain, such as math, which motivates students to see shared features of different strategies.* This leads to better *relational knowledge*.
3. *At this point, students recognize the general benefits of using strategies, which produces general strategy knowledge.* They learn to attribute successful learning outcomes to the efforts they make in evaluating, selecting, and monitoring strategy use *(metacognitive knowledge and activity)*.

STRATEGIES AND METACOGNITIVE REGULATION

In the view of Pressley and his colleagues (Pressley, 1983, 2007; Pressley & Harris, 2006; Pressley & Hilden, 2006), the key to education is helping students learn a rich repertoire of strategies that produce solutions to problems. Good thinkers routinely use strategies and effective planning to solve problems. Good thinkers also know when and where to use strategies (metacognitive knowledge about strategies). Understanding when and where to use strategies often results from the learner's monitoring of the learning situation.

Pressley and his colleagues argue that when students are given instruction about effective strategies, they often can apply strategies that they previously have not used on their own. They emphasize that students benefit when the teacher models the appropriate strategy and overtly verbalizes its steps. Then, students subsequently practice the strategy, guided and supported by the teacher's feedback until the students can use it autonomously. When instructing students about employing a strategy, it also is a good idea to explain to them how using the strategy will benefit them. However, there are some developmental limitations to this approach. For instance, young children often cannot use mental imagery competently.

Just having students practice the new strategy is usually not enough for them to continue to use the strategy and transfer it to new situations. For effective maintenance and transfer, encourage students to monitor the effectiveness of the new strategy relative to their use of old strategies by comparing their performance on tests and other assessments (Harris et al., 2008). Pressley says that it is not enough to say, "Try it, you will like it"; instead, you need to say, "Try it and compare."

An important aspect of metacognition is monitoring how well one is performing on a task (Fiorella & Mayer, 2015). This might involve becoming aware that one has not studied enough for a test or needs to reread a particular section of a chapter to understand it better. Mismonitoring is common. For example, elementary school students often think they are better prepared for a test than they actually are and think they understand text material better than they do. One strategy is to encourage students who mismonitor to create practice tests and questions to assess how complete their understanding is.

Learning how to use strategies effectively often takes time. Initially, it takes time to learn to execute the strategies, and it requires guidance and support from the teacher. With practice, students learn to execute strategies faster and more competently. *Practice* means that students use the effective strategy over and over again until they perform it automatically. To execute the strategies effectively, they need to have the strategies in long-term memory, and extensive practice makes this possible. Learners also need to be motivated to use the strategies. Thus, an important implication for helping students develop strategies such as organization is that once a strategy is learned, students usually need more time before they can use it efficiently. Further, it is important for teachers to be aware that students may drop an effective strategy or continue to use a strategy that does not help them.

Do children use one strategy or multiple strategies in memory and problem solving? They often use more than one strategy. Most children benefit from generating a variety of alternative strategies and experimenting with different approaches to a problem and discovering what works well, when, and where. This is especially true for children from the middle elementary school grades on, although some cognitive psychologists argue that even young children should be encouraged to practice varying strategies (Siegler, 2016a, b).

> **Thinking Back/Thinking Forward**
> Self-monitoring is also a key step in the self-regulation process. Connect to "Behavioral and Social Cognitive Approaches."

What are some strategies for improving metacognitive regulation?
Monkey Business Images/Shutterstock

Pressley and his colleagues (Pressley et al., 2001, 2003, 2004) have spent considerable time observing strategy instruction by teachers and strategy use by students in elementary and secondary school classrooms. They conclude that teachers' use of strategy instruction is far less complete and intense than what is needed for students to learn how to use strategies effectively. They argue that education needs to be restructured so that students are provided with more opportunities to become competent strategic learners.

A final point about strategies is that many strategies depend on prior knowledge. For example, students can't apply organizational strategies to a list of items unless they know the correct categories into which the items fall. The point about the importance of prior knowledge in strategy use coincides with the emphasis in our earlier discussion of how experts use more effective strategies than novices.

CONNECTING WITH STUDENTS: Best Practices
Guidelines for Helping Students Use Strategies

Following are some effective ways that teachers can guide students to develop and use strategies (Pressley, 1983, 2007; Pressley & McCormick, 2007):

1. *Recognize that strategies are a key aspect of solving problems.* Monitor students' knowledge and awareness of strategies for effective learning outcomes. Many students do not use good strategies and are unaware that strategies can help them learn. And after students learn a strategy, they tend to shorten and reduce it, in the process losing important components. Thus, be sure to monitor students who modify strategies in ways that make the strategies less effective.

2. *Model effective strategies for students.*

3. *Give students many opportunities to practice the strategies.* As students practice the strategies, provide guidance and support to the students. Give them feedback until they can use the strategies independently. As part of your feedback, inform them about where and when the strategies are most useful.

4. *Encourage students to monitor the effectiveness of their new strategy in comparison with the effectiveness of old strategies.*

5. *Remember that it takes students a considerable amount of time to learn how to use an effective strategy.* Be patient and give students continued support during this tedious learning experience. Keep encouraging students to use the strategy over and over again until they can use it automatically.

6. *Understand that students need to be motivated to use the strategies.* Students are not always going to be motivated to use the strategies. Especially important to students' motivation is their expectations that the strategies will lead to successful learning outcomes. It can also help if students set goals for learning effective strategies. And when students attribute their learning outcomes to the effort they put forth, their learning benefits. The chapter on motivation, teaching, and learning provides numerous recommendations for guiding students to become more motivated, which you can link to helping students become motivated to use strategies.

7. *Encourage children to use multiple strategies.* Most children benefit from experimenting with multiple strategies, finding out what works well, when, and where.

8. *Read more about strategy instruction.* Two good resources are *Best Practices in Literacy Instruction* (Gambrell et al., 2007) and a chapter by Michael Pressley and Karen Harris (2006) titled "Cognitive strategies instruction: From basic research to classroom instruction," both of which include numerous helpful ideas about how to improve children's use of strategies. Especially good online sources are (1) https://iris.peabody.vanderbilt.edu/module/srs/#content (a free online interactive tutorial on strategy instruction), and (2) http://cehs.unl.edu/secd/teaching-strategies/ (Robert Reid's excellent Web site that is devoted to strategy instruction).

9. *Ask questions that help to guide students' thinking in various content areas.* These might include "How can proofreading help me in writing a paper?" "Why is it important periodically to stop when I'm reading and try to understand what is being said so far?" and "What is the purpose of learning this formula?"

10. *Recognize that low-achieving students and students with disabilities often need more support and time to become effective in independently using strategies.*

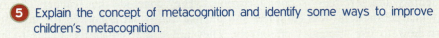

Review, Reflect, and Practice

5 Explain the concept of metacognition and identify some ways to improve children's metacognition.

REVIEW
- How do young children compare with older children in their metacognitive abilities?
- According to Pressley and colleagues' Good Information-Processing model, competent cognition results from what interacting factors?
- How can children be helped to learn metacognitive strategies and self-regulation?

REFLECT
- How might the three steps in the Good Information-Processing model be part of teaching a topic to children? Select a topic that you might teach one day and try working through it as an example.

PRAXIS™ PRACTICE

1. Sharmala's uncle has just played a trick on her. He presented her with a can that looked like a can of peanuts. However, when she opened the can, a cloth snake sprang out at her. Sharmala thought the trick was very funny and could hardly wait to play it on her brother. When her uncle asked her what she thought her brother would expect to be in the can, she giggled and responded, "Peanuts, but won't he be surprised." This is an example of Sharmala's development of
   a. the ability to allocate attention to different aspects of a problem
   b. problem-solving expertise
   c. metamemory skills
   d. theory of mind

2. Marvel has learned to use strategies to solve math problems but does not use them to study for history exams or spelling quizzes. According to the Good Information-Processing model, the next step for Marvel's metacognitive development would most likely be to
   a. ask his teacher for specific strategies for studying history
   b. ask his parents about the benefits of using strategies for math
   c. understand shared features of many different strategies
   d. learn to attribute successful learning to use of strategies

3. Mr. Quinton has taught his students the PQ4R strategy for reading textbooks, in hopes that it will help them on their next history test. The majority of his class improves their scores. Mr. Quinton is disappointed when in spite of improved performance, many of his students don't continue using the PQ4R strategy. What is the most plausible explanation for the students' behavior?
   a. They did not compare the results of using the PQ4R with their prior strategies.
   b. They don't have the requisite background knowledge to use the PQ4R strategy effectively.
   c. They have not had enough practice to use the strategy effectively.
   d. They have not yet developed expertise in using the strategy.

Please see answer key at end of book . . . .

Connecting with the Classroom: Crack the Case

The Test

George has a test next week in his eighth-grade history class. He is having considerable difficulty remembering terms, names, and facts. On his last test, he identified General Sherman as a Vietnam War hero and Saigon as the capital of Japan. Historical dates are so confusing to him that he does not even try to remember them. In addition, George has difficulty spelling.

The test will consist of 50 objective test items (multiple-choice, true/false, and fill-in-the-blank) and two essay items. In general, George does better on essay items. He purposely leaves out any names about which he is uncertain and always omits dates. Sometimes he mixes up his facts, though, and often loses points for misspelled words. On objective items he has real problems. Usually, more than one answer will appear to be correct to him. Often he is "sure" he is correct, only to discover later that he was mistaken.

Before the last test, George tried to design some mnemonic devices to help him remember information. He used acronyms, such as *HOMES* (for *H*uron, *O*ntario, *M*ichigan, *E*rie, and *S*uperior). Although he remembered his acronyms quite well, he could not recall what each letter stood for. The result was a test paper filled with acronyms. Another time a classmate suggested that George try using concept maps. This classmate lent George the concept maps she had designed for her own use. George looked at them and found them to be very busy and confusing—he couldn't figure out what they even meant. They were not at all useful to him.

George has decided he is in need of some serious help if he is to pass this class. He has asked you to help him learn the material.

1. What are the issues in this case?
2. With what type of learning is George having difficulty?
3. What type of learning is easier for George?
4. Design a study-skills program for George drawing on principles of the cognitive information-processing approach.

Connecting with Learning: Reach Your Learning Goals

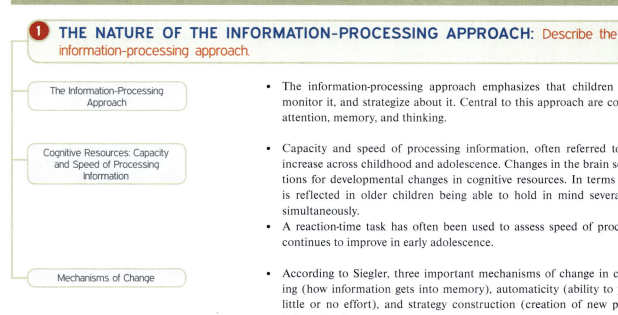

1 THE NATURE OF THE INFORMATION-PROCESSING APPROACH: Describe the information-processing approach.

- The Information-Processing Approach

  - The information-processing approach emphasizes that children manipulate information, monitor it, and strategize about it. Central to this approach are cognitive processes such as attention, memory, and thinking.

- Cognitive Resources: Capacity and Speed of Processing Information

  - Capacity and speed of processing information, often referred to as cognitive resources, increase across childhood and adolescence. Changes in the brain serve as biological foundations for developmental changes in cognitive resources. In terms of capacity, the increase is reflected in older children being able to hold in mind several dimensions of a topic simultaneously.
  - A reaction-time task has often been used to assess speed of processing. Processing speed continues to improve in early adolescence.

- Mechanisms of Change

  - According to Siegler, three important mechanisms of change in cognitive skills are encoding (how information gets into memory), automaticity (ability to process information with little or no effort), and strategy construction (creation of new procedures for processing information).
  - Children's information processing is characterized by self-modification, and an important aspect of this self-modification involves metacognition—that is, knowing about knowing.

continued

2 ATTENTION: Characterize attention and summarize how it changes during development.

What Is Attention?

- Attention involves focusing mental resources. Four ways that children and adolescents can allocate their attention are selective attention (focusing on a specific aspect of experience that is relevant while ignoring others that are irrelevant), divided attention (concentrating on more than one activity at the same time), sustained attention (maintaining attention over an extended period of time), and executive attention (planning actions, allocating attention to goals, detecting and compensating for errors, monitoring progress on tasks, and dealing with novel or difficult circumstances).
- Multitasking is an example of divided attention, and it can have harmful effects on children's and adolescents' attention when they are engaging in a challenging task.

Developmental Changes

- Salient stimuli tend to capture the attention of the preschooler. After 6 or 7 years of age, there is a shift to more cognitive control of attention. Selective attention improves through childhood and adolescence.

3 MEMORY: Discuss memory in terms of encoding, storage, and retrieval.

What Is Memory?

- Memory is the retention of information over time and involves encoding, storage, and retrieval.

Encoding

- In everyday language, encoding has much to do with attention and learning. Rehearsal, deep processing, elaboration, constructing images, and organization are processes involved in encoding, which is the mechanism by which information gets into memory. Rehearsal increases the length of time that information stays in memory. In deep processing, information is processed semantically, in terms of its meaning. Elaboration involves extensiveness of information processing. Constructing images helps to elaborate the information, and when information is presented in an organized way, it is easier to remember.

Storage

- One way that memory varies involves its time frames: sensory memory, short-term memory, and long-term memory. There is increasing interest in working memory, which is a kind of mental workbench.
- The Atkinson-Shiffrin model states that memory involves a sequence of three stages: sensory, short-term, and long-term memory. Long-term memory includes different types of content.
- Many contemporary psychologists accept this hierarchy of long-term memory's contents: division into declarative and procedural memory, with declarative memory further subdivided into episodic and semantic memory. Declarative memory (explicit memory) is the conscious recollection of information, such as specific facts or events. Procedural memory (implicit memory) is knowledge of skills and cognitive operations about how to do something; it is hard to communicate this knowledge verbally. Episodic memory is the retention of information about the where and when of life's happenings; semantic memory is a general knowledge about the world.
- Three major approaches to how information is represented are network theories (which focus on how information is organized and connected, with emphasis on nodes in the memory network); schema theories (which stress that students often reconstruct information and fit it into an existing schema); and fuzzy trace theory (which states that memory is best understood by considering two types of memory representation: 1. verbatim memory trace and 2. fuzzy trace, or gist). In fuzzy trace theory, older children's better memory is attributed to the fuzzy traces created by extracting the gist of information. A script is a schema for an event.

Retrieval and Forgetting

- Retrieval is influenced by the serial position effect (memory is better for items at the beginning and end of a list than for items in the middle), the effectiveness of retrieval cues, encoding specificity, and the retrieval task (such as recall versus recognition).
- Forgetting can be explained in terms of cue-dependent forgetting (failure to use effective retrieval cues), interference theory (because information gets in the way of what we are trying to remember), and decay (losing information over time).

4 EXPERTISE: Draw some lessons about learning from the way experts think.

Expertise and Learning

- Five important characteristics of experts are that they (1) notice features and meaningful patterns of information that novices don't; (2) have acquired a great deal of content knowledge that is organized in a manner that reflects deep understanding of the subject; (3) can retrieve important aspects of their knowledge with little effort; (4) are adaptive in their approach to new situations; and (5) use effective strategies.

Acquiring Expertise

- Becoming an expert usually requires deliberate practice, motivation, and talent.

Expertise and Teaching

- Being an expert in a particular area does not mean that the expert is good at helping others learn it. Pedagogical content knowledge is required to effectively teach a subject.

5 METACOGNITION: Explain the concept of metacognition and identify some ways to improve children's metacognition.

Developmental Changes

- Children's metamemory improves considerably through the elementary school years. At 5 years of age, a majority of children understand that people can have false beliefs, and in middle and late childhood they understand that people actively construct knowledge. Adolescents have an increased capacity to monitor and manage resources to effectively meet the demands of a learning task, although there is considerable individual variation in metacognition during adolescence.

The Good Information-Processing Model

- Developed by Michael Pressley and his colleagues, the Good Information-Processing model stresses that competent cognition results from several interacting factors including strategies, content knowledge, motivation, and metacognition.

Strategies and Metacognitive Regulation

- In the view of Pressley and his colleagues, the key to education is helping students learn a rich repertoire of strategies that produce solutions to problems. Most children benefit from using multiple strategies and exploring which ones work well, when, and where. For example, teachers can model strategies for students and ask questions that help guide students' thinking in various content areas.

KEY TERMS

Atkinson-Shiffrin model 269
attention 259
automaticity 258
chunking 267
cue-dependent forgetting 273
decay theory 273
declarative memory 269
divided attention 260
elaboration 265

encoding 258
encoding specificity principle 273
episodic memory 270
executive attention 260
fuzzy trace theory 272
information-processing approach 256
interference theory 273
levels of processing theory 265

long-term memory 269
memory 264
memory span 267
metacognition 258
network theories 270
procedural memory 270
rehearsal 265
schema 271
schema theories 271
script 271

selective attention 260
semantic memory 270
sensory memory 267
serial position effect 272
short-term memory 267
strategy construction 258
sustained attention 260
theory of mind 286
working memory 267

PORTFOLIO ACTIVITIES

Now that you have a good understanding of this chapter, complete these exercises to expand your thinking.

Independent Reflection

1. **Developing Expert Knowledge.** Think about the experts you know. Are your parents or instructors considered experts in their fields? How do you think they came to become experts and how long did it take? Based on what you know about how experts process information, which strategies do you think these experts use to organize, remember, and utilize their knowledge and skills? (INTASC: Principles *1, 8, 9*)

Research/Field Experience

2. **Capturing Students' Attention.** Observe a kindergarten, elementary, middle school, and high school classroom and focus on how the teacher maintains students' attention. How effective are each teacher's strategies? Would you do things differently to capture the students' attention? (INTASC: Principles *1, 9*)

Collaborative Work

3. **Strategies to Enhance Memory.** Get together with three or four other students in the class and brainstorm about the best ways to guide students in developing better memory and study strategies. Discuss how you might do this differently for children and adolescents at different grade levels. For example, at what age should students start learning effective note-taking strategies? For children too young to be taking elaborate notes, are there gamelike activities that might help them begin to learn the concept and value of taking notes or keeping running records of some event? Write your conclusions. (INTASC: Principles *1, 8*)

chapter 9

COMPLEX COGNITIVE PROCESSES

chapter outline

① Conceptual Understanding

Learning Goal 1 Discuss conceptual understanding and strategies for teaching concepts.

What Are Concepts?
Promoting Concept Formation

② Thinking

Learning Goal 2 Describe several types of thinking and ways that teachers can foster them.

What Is Thinking?
Executive Function
Reasoning
Critical Thinking
Decision Making
Creative Thinking

③ Problem Solving

Learning Goal 3 Take a systematic approach to problem solving.

Steps in Problem Solving
Obstacles to Solving Problems
Developmental Changes
Problem-Based Learning and Project-Based Learning

④ Transfer

Learning Goal 4 Define transfer and explain how to enhance it as a teacher.

What Is Transfer?
Types of Transfer

I think, therefore I am.

—René Descartes
French Philosopher and Mathematician, 17th Century

Connecting with Teachers   Marilyn Whirry

Marilyn Whirry is a twelfth-grade English teacher at Mira Costa High School in Manhattan Beach, California. In 1999, she was named Teacher of the Year in the United States and honored at a White House reception. The following description of Marilyn's teaching appeared in a report by the Council of Chief State School Officers (2005, pp. 1–3).

> Marilyn's enthusiasm for life carries over into the classroom. Marilyn says about her life: "It is a canvas with swirling brush strokes that depict the motifs of my experience." According to Marilyn, teachers may never know how many students' lives they changed for the better because of their sense of responsibility and excitement for life.
>
> Marilyn's teaching philosophy centers around embracing and celebrating the act of learning. She says that teachers need to help students become motivated to search for knowledge and to discover answers to questions of why and how. One of Marilyn's most important goals as a teacher is to get students to think deeply as they read and write. . . . Her teaching strategies include getting students to become aware of writing techniques in literary works that "promote dialogue and debate in group discussions."
>
> One of Marilyn's former students, Mary-Anna Rae, said that Marilyn's "intellectual engagement and her passion for life make her a powerful role model for students. In everything she does, she makes it clear that she is listening, attending to the students' deepest thinking." Mary-Anna, who now teaches herself, adds that Marilyn "enriched and expanded her world." Mary-Anna also says that Marilyn helped her to "grow more confident in what I had to say, finding my writer's voice and discovering that I could give my life purpose."

Marilyn Whirry, teaching in her 12th grade classroom.
Ken Lubas/Los Angeles Times/Getty Images

Preview

One of Marilyn Whirry's major goals is to get her students to think deeply, an important emphasis in this chapter. In addition to exploring many aspects of thinking, we examine how teachers can guide students to engage in these other complex cognitive processes: understanding concepts, solving problems, and transferring what they learn to other settings.

LG 1 Discuss conceptual understanding and strategies for teaching concepts.

1 CONCEPTUAL UNDERSTANDING

What Are Concepts?   Promoting Concept Formation

Conceptual understanding is a key aspect of learning. An important teaching goal is to help students understand the main concepts in a subject rather than just memorize isolated facts. In many cases, conceptual understanding is enhanced when teachers explore a topic in depth and give appropriate, interesting examples of the concepts involved. As you will see, concepts are the building blocks of thinking.

WHAT ARE CONCEPTS?

Concepts group objects, events, and characteristics on the basis of common properties. Concepts help us to simplify, summarize, and organize information (Quinn, 2016; Quinn & Bhatt, 2016).

Imagine a world in which we had no concepts: We would see each object as unique and would not be able to make any generalizations. If we had no concepts, we would find the most trivial problems difficult to formulate and impossible to solve. Indeed, concepts help students make sense of the world. Consider the concept of "book." If a student were not aware that a book is made of sheets of paper of uniform size, all bound together along one edge, and full of printed words and pictures in some meaningful order, each time the student encountered a new book she would have to figure out what it was. In a way, then, concepts keep us from "reinventing

concepts Ideas that group objects, events, and characteristics on the basis of common properties.

the wheel" each time we come across a new piece of information.

Concepts also aid the process of remembering, making it more efficient. When students group objects to form a concept, they can remember the concept and then retrieve the concept's characteristics. Thus, when you assign math homework, you probably won't have to go through the details of what math is or what homework is. Students will have embedded in their memory a number of appropriate associations. In ways such as this, concepts not only help to jog memory but also make communication more efficient. If you say, "It's time for art," students know what you mean. You don't have to go into a lengthy explanation of what art is. Thus, concepts help students to simplify and summarize information, as well as improve the efficiency of their memory, communication, and use of time.

Students form concepts through direct experiences with objects and events in their world. For example, in constructing a sophisticated concept of "cartoons," children might initially experience TV cartoon shows, then read comic strips, and eventually look at some political caricatures. Students also form concepts through experience with symbols (things that stand for, or represent, something else). For example, words are symbols. So are math formulas, graphs, and pictures.

Some concepts are relatively simple, clear, and concrete, whereas others are more complex, fuzzy, and abstract. The former are easier to agree on. For example, most people can agree on the meaning of "baby." But we have a harder time agreeing on what is meant by "young"

What features make these all chairs?
Vectors Bang/Shutterstock

or "old." We agree on whether something is an apple more readily than on whether something is a fruit. Some concepts are especially complex, fuzzy, and abstract, like the concepts involved in theories of economic collapse or string theory in physics.

PROMOTING CONCEPT FORMATION

Teachers can guide students to recognize and form effective concepts in a number of ways. The process begins with becoming aware of the features of a given concept.

Learning About the Features of Concepts An important aspect of concept formation is learning the key features, attributes, or characteristics of the concept (Quinn & Bhatt, 2016). These are the defining elements of a concept, the dimensions that make it different from another concept. For example, in our earlier example of the concept of "book," the key features include sheets of paper, being bound together along one edge, and being full of printed words and pictures in some meaningful order. Other characteristics such as size, color, and length are not key features that define the concept of "book." Consider also these critical features of the concept of "dinosaur": extinct and reptilian. Thus, in the case of the concept of "dinosaur," the feature "extinct" is important.

Defining Concepts and Providing Examples An important aspect of teaching concepts is to clearly define them and give carefully chosen examples. The *rule-example strategy* is an effective way to do this (Tennyson & Cocchiarella, 1986). The strategy consists of four steps:

1. *Define the concept.* As part of defining it, link it to a superordinate concept and identify its key features or characteristics. A *superordinate* concept is a larger class into which it fits. Thus, in specifying the key features of the concept of *dinosaur,* you might want to mention the larger class into which it fits: reptiles.

2. *Clarify terms in the definition.* Make sure that the key features or characteristics are well understood. Thus, in describing the key features of the concept of *dinosaur*, it is important for students to know what a reptile is—usually an egg-laying vertebrate that has an external covering of scales or horny plates and breathes by means of lungs.
3. *Give examples to illustrate the key features or characteristics.* With regard to dinosaurs, one might give examples and descriptions of different types of dinosaurs, such as a triceratops, an apatosaur, and a stegosaur. The concept can be further clarified by giving examples of other reptiles that are not dinosaurs, such as snakes, lizards, crocodiles, and turtles. Indeed, giving nonexamples of a concept as well as examples is often a good strategy for teaching concept formation. More examples are required when you teach complex concepts and when you work with less-sophisticated learners.
4. *Provide additional examples.* Ask students to categorize concepts, explain their categorization, or have them generate their own examples of the concept (Rawson et al., 2015). Give examples of other dinosaurs, such as *Tyrannosaurus, Ornitholestes,* and *Dimetrodon,* or ask students to find more examples themselves. Also ask them to think up other nonexamples of dinosaurs, such as dogs, cats, and whales.

Hierarchical Categorization and Concept Maps Categorization is important because once a concept is categorized it can take on characteristics and features from being a member of a category (Sloutsky, 2015). For example, students can infer that a triceratops is a reptile even if they have never been told that fact as long as they know that dinosaurs are reptiles and a triceratops is a dinosaur. Knowing that a triceratops is a type of dinosaur lets students infer that a triceratops assumes the characteristics of dinosaurs (it is a reptile).

A **concept map** is a visual presentation of a concept's connections and hierarchical organization. Getting students to create a map of a concept's features or characteristics can help them to learn the concept (Jin & Wong, 2015). The concept map also might embed the concept in a superordinate category and include examples and nonexamples of the concept (Tzeng, 2014). The visual aspects of the concept map relate to the use of imagery in memory. You might create a concept map with students' help, or let them try to develop it individually or in small groups. Figure 1 shows an example of a concept map for the concept of "reptile."

> **Thinking Back/Thinking Forward**
>
> When students construct an image of something, they elaborate the information, which helps them to remember it. Connect to "The Information-Processing Approach."

concept map A visual presentation of a concept's connections and hierarchical organization.

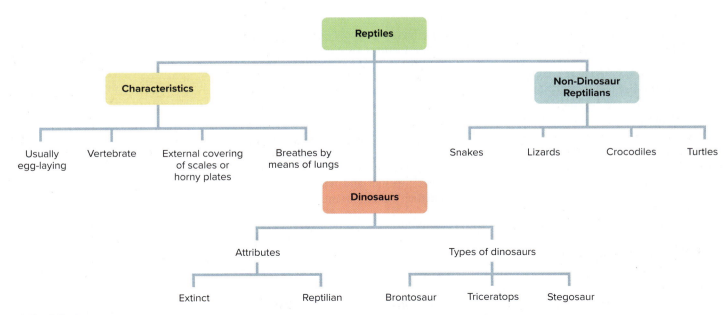

FIGURE 1 EXAMPLE OF A CONCEPT MAP FOR THE CONCEPT OF "REPTILE"

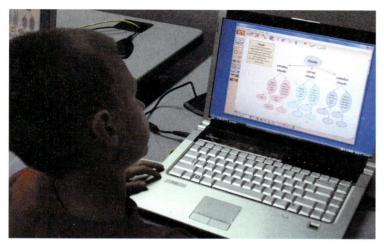

A student in the Research Center for Educational Technology's AT&T Classroom at Kent State University displaying the concept map he made in Kidspiration.
Research Center for Educational Technology, Kent State University

Teachers can access a number of concept mapping software programs to use in the classroom. Inspiration and Kidspiration (www.inspiration.com) are good ones. Wikipedia also has a linked list of concept mapping software that teachers can use: https://en.wikipedia.org/wiki/List_of_concept-_and_mind-mapping_software.

Hypothesis Testing *Hypotheses* are specific assumptions and predictions that can be tested to determine their accuracy. Students benefit from the practice of developing hypotheses about what a concept is and is not. One way to develop a hypothesis is to come up with a rule about why some objects fall within a concept and others do not. Here is an example of how you can give your students practice in developing such hypotheses: Present your students with the picture of geometric forms shown in Figure 2. Then silently select the concept of one of those geometric forms (such as "circle" or "green circle") and ask your students to develop hypotheses about what concept you have selected. They zero in on your concept by asking you questions related to the geometric forms and eliminating nonexamples. You might also let the students take turns selecting a concept and answering questions from the other students. Work with your students on developing the most efficient strategies for identifying the correct concept.

Prototype Matching In **prototype matching**, individuals decide whether an item is a member of a category by comparing it with the most typical item(s) of the category (Rosch, 1973). The more similar the item is to the prototype, the more likely it is that the individual will say the item belongs in the category; the less similar, the more

TECHNOLOGY

Thinking Back/Thinking Forward

In addition to outlining and constructing concept maps, summarizing is a good strategy for learning and remembering information. Connect to "The Information-Processing Approach."

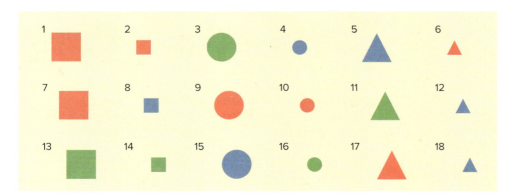

FIGURE 2 GETTING STUDENTS TO GENERATE HYPOTHESES ABOUT A CONCEPT

prototype matching Deciding whether an item is a member of a category by comparing it with the most typical item(s) of the category.

The concept of birds includes many different types of birds. *Which of these birds is likely to be viewed as the most typical bird?*
(*Left*) Digital Zoo/Digital Vision/Getty Images; (*Middle*) Design Pics Inc./Alamy Stock Photo; (*Right*) Digital Zoo/Digital Vision/Getty Images

likely the person will judge that it doesn't belong in the category. For example, a student's concept of a football player might include being big and muscular like an offensive lineman. But some football players, such as many field goal kickers, are not so big and muscular. An offensive lineman is a more prototypical example of a football player than a field goal kicker. When students consider whether someone belongs in the category "football player," they are more likely to think of someone who looks like an offensive lineman than to think of someone who looks like a field goal kicker. Similarly, robins are viewed as being more typical birds than ostriches or penguins. Nonetheless, members of a category can vary greatly and still have qualities that make them a member of that category.

CONNECTING WITH STUDENTS: Best Practices
Strategies for Helping Students Form Concepts

1. *Use the rule-example strategy.* Remember that this involves four steps: (a) define the concept; (b) clarify the terms in the definition; (c) give examples to illustrate the key features or characteristics; and (d) provide additional examples and ask students to categorize these and explain their categorization, or have students generate their own examples of the concepts.

2. *Help students learn not only what a concept is but also what it is not.* Let's return to the concept "cartoon." Students can learn that even though they are humorous, jokes, clowns, and funny poems are not cartoons. If you are teaching the concept of "triangle," ask students to list the characteristics of "triangle" such as "three-sided," "geometric shape," "can be of any size," "can be of any color," "sides can vary in length," "angles can be different," and so on; also ask them to list examples of things that are not triangles, such as circles, squares, and rectangles.

3. *Make concepts as clear as possible and give concrete examples.* Spend some time thinking about the best way to present a new concept, especially an abstract one. Make it as clear as possible. If you want students to understand the concept "vehicle," ask them to come up with examples of it. They probably will say "car" and maybe "truck" or "bus." Show them photographs of other vehicles, such as a sled and a boat, to illustrate the breadth of the concept.

CONNECTING WITH STUDENTS: Best Practices
Strategies for Helping Students Form Concepts

4. *Help students relate new concepts to concepts they already know.* In the chapter on the information-processing approach we discussed the strategy of outlining for taking notes. Once students have learned this procedure, it is easier for them to learn how to construct concept maps, because you can show them how concept maps are linked with outlining in terms of hierarchical organization.

5. *Encourage students to create concept maps.* Getting students to map out the hierarchical organization of a concept can help them understand the concept's characteristics from more general to more specific. Hierarchical organization benefits memory.

6. *Ask students to generate hypotheses about a concept.* Generating hypotheses encourages students to think and develop strategies. Work with students on developing the most efficient strategies for determining what a concept is.

7. *Give students experience in prototype matching.* Think of different concepts and then ask students what the prototypes of the concepts are. Then ask them for nonprototypical examples of the concept.

8. *Check for students' understanding of a concept and motivate them to apply the concept to other contexts.* Make sure that students don't just memorize a concept, but ask them how the concept can be applied in different contexts. For example, in learning the concept of fairness, ask students how fairness can make life smoother, not only at school but also at play, at home, and at work.

Review, Reflect, and Practice

 Discuss conceptual understanding and strategies for teaching concepts.

REVIEW
- What are concepts and why are they indispensable to thinking?
- What are some ways that students can be guided to construct effective concepts?

REFLECT
- What might the concept "art" mean to a 3-year-old? To a 10-year-old? To a 16-year-old? To a professional artist? How do such changes come about?

PRAXIS™ PRACTICE

1. Which of the following is the best example of a superordinate concept?
   a. collie
   b. dog
   c. German shepherd
   d. poodle

2. Ms. Peloti wants her students to learn about the concept "bird." She discusses the characteristics of birds with her students, including a defining characteristic: feathers. She then discusses irrelevant characteristics, such as flying—insects and bats fly too, but they are not birds; ostriches don't fly, but they are birds. Finally, the class discusses what a typical bird looks like. They finally agree that the most typical bird is a robin. Ms. Peloti then gives the children a list of animals and asks them to determine whether they are birds by comparing them to the robin. What strategy of concept formation does this task represent?
   a. concept mapping
   b. hypothesis testing
   c. prototype matching
   d. relating concepts

Please see answer key at end of book . . . .

LG 2 Describe several types of thinking and ways that teachers can foster them.

2 THINKING

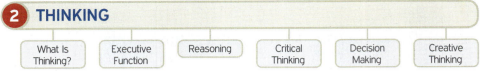

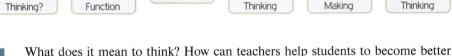

What does it mean to think? How can teachers help students to become better thinkers? In this section, we will attempt to answer these important questions.

WHAT IS THINKING?

Thinking involves manipulating and transforming information in memory. We think to conceptualize, reason, critique, decide, create, and solve problems. Students can think about concrete subjects, such as a vacation at the beach or how to win at a video game. They can also think about more abstract subjects, such as the meaning of freedom or identity. They can think about the past (such as what happened to them last month) and the future (what their life will be like in the year 2030). They can think about reality (such as how to do better on their next math test) and fantasy (what it would be like to meet Barack Obama or land a spacecraft on Mars).

EXECUTIVE FUNCTION

Recently, increasing interest has surrounded the development of children's **executive function**, an umbrella-like concept that encompasses a number of higher-level cognitive processes linked to the development of the brain's prefrontal cortex (Cassidy, 2016; Groppe & Elsner, 2016; Moriguchi et al., 2016). Executive function involves managing one's thoughts to engage in goal-directed behavior and exercise self-control (Griffin et al., 2015; Muller & Kerns, 2015). In the chapter on the information-processing approach, we described the recent interest in *executive attention* and *working memory*, which both come under the umbrella of executive function.

In early childhood, executive function especially involves developmental advances in cognitive inhibition (such as inhibiting a strong tendency that is incorrect), cognitive flexibility (such as shifting attention to another item or topic), goal-setting (such as sharing a toy or mastering a skill like catching a ball), and delay of gratification (the ability to forego an immediate pleasure or reward for a more desirable one later) (Casey et al., 2016). During early childhood, the relatively stimulus-driven toddler is transformed into a child capable of flexible, goal-directed problem solving that characterizes executive function (Zelazo & Muller, 2011).

Researchers have found that advances or impairments in executive function in the preschool years are linked to math skills, language development, and school readiness (Blair & Raver, 2015). A recent study revealed that executive function skills predicted mathematical gains in kindergarten (Fuhs et al., 2014). Another recent study of young children documented that executive function was associated with their emergent literacy and vocabulary development (Becker et al., 2014). And yet another recent study found that young children who showed delayed development of executive function had a lower level of school readiness (Willoughby et al., 2016).

How might executive function change in the middle and late childhood years and be linked to children's success in school? Adele Diamond and Kathleen Lee (2011) recently highlighted the following dimensions of executive function that they conclude are the most important for 4- to 11-year-old children's cognitive development and school success:

- *Self-control/inhibition.* Children need to develop self-control that will allow them to concentrate and persist on learning tasks, to inhibit their tendencies to

---

THROUGH THE EYES OF STUDENTS

The Thinking Room

I recently talked with my granddaughter, Jordan Bowles, who is just beginning the second grade in Apex, North Carolina. I asked her what her classes were like this year.

She responded, "The usual stuff. Well, there is this one new class that I go to once a week. It's in the thinking room."

I then asked her what she was supposed to learn there.

Jordan said, "They are going to teach me not to jump to conclusions, and my mom is happy about that."

RESEARCH

thinking Manipulating and transforming information in memory, which often is done to form concepts, reason, think critically, make decisions, think creatively, and solve problems.

executive function An umbrella-like concept that encompasses a number of higher-level cognitive processes linked to the development of the brain's prefrontal cortex. Executive function involves managing one's thoughts to engage in goal-directed behavior and exercise self-control.

repeat incorrect responses, and to resist the impulse to do something now that they later would regret.
- *Working memory.* Children need an effective working memory to efficiently process the masses of information they will encounter as they go through school and beyond.
- *Flexibility.* Children need to be flexible in their thinking to consider different strategies and perspectives.

A number of diverse activities and factors have been found to increase children's executive function, such as computerized training that uses games to improve working memory (CogMed, 2013); some aspects of language, including vocabulary size, verbal labeling, and bilingualism (Nesbitt et al., 2015); aerobic exercise (Hillman et al., 2014); scaffolding of self-regulation (the Tools of the Mind program is one example) (Bodrova & Leong, 2015); mindfulness training (Gallant, 2016); imagination (Carlson & White, 2013); and some types of school curricula (the Montessori curriculum, for example) (Diamond, 2013).

Parents, teachers, and peers play important roles in the development of executive function. Ann Masten and her colleagues (Masten, 2013, 2014a, b, 2016; Masten & Cicchetti, 2016; Masten & Labella, 2016; Masten et al., 2008) have found that executive function and parenting skills are linked to homeless children's success in school. Masten believes that executive function and good parenting skills are related. She says that when we see children with good executive function, we often see adults around them that are good self-regulators. Parents model, they support, and they scaffold these skills. And a recent study revealed that experiencing peer problems (such as victimization and rejection) beginning in early childhood is linked to lower executive function later in childhood (Holmes et al., 2016). Also in this study, better executive function reduced the likelihood of experiencing peer problems later in childhood.

Deanna Kuhn (2009), a leading expert on adolescent cognitive development, argues that the most important cognitive change in adolescence is improvement in executive function. She especially thinks that a key aspect of such change is an increase in *cognitive control,* which involves effective control in a number of areas, including controlling attention, reducing interfering thoughts, and being cognitively flexible (Carlson et al., 2013). Cognitive control continues to increase in adolescence and emerging adulthood (Casey, 2015; Casey et al., 2016).

Think about all the times adolescents need to engage in cognitive control, such as the following situations (Galinsky, 2010):

- making a real effort to stick with a task, avoiding being distracted by interfering thoughts or environmental events, and instead doing what is most effective;
- stopping and thinking before acting to avoid blurting out a comment that a minute or two later they wish they hadn't said;
- continuing to work on something that is important but boring when there is something a lot more fun to do, inhibiting their behavior and doing the boring but important task, saying to themselves, "I have to show the self-discipline to finish this."

Controlling attention is a key aspect of learning and thinking in adolescence. Distractions that can interfere with attention in adolescence come from the external environment (other students talking while the student is trying to listen to a teacher, or the student turning on a laptop or tablet PC during class and looking at a new friend request on Facebook, for example) or intrusive distractions from competing thoughts in the individual's mind. Self-oriented thoughts, such as worrying, self-doubt, and intense, emotionally laden thoughts may especially interfere with focusing attention on thinking tasks.

REASONING

Reasoning is logical thinking that uses induction and deduction to reach a conclusion (Ricco, 2015). We begin by focusing on inductive reasoning.

Inductive Reasoning **Inductive reasoning** involves reasoning from the specific to the general. That is, it consists of drawing conclusions (forming concepts) about all members of a category based on observing only some of its members (Hawkins et al., 2016). Researchers have found that inductive reasoning skill is often a good predictor of academic achievement (Cracolice & Busby, 2015; Murawska & Zollman, 2015).

RESEARCH

What are some examples of the use of inductive reasoning in classrooms? When a student in English class reads only a few Emily Dickinson poems and is asked to draw conclusions from them about the general nature of Dickinson's poems, inductive reasoning is being requested. When a student is asked whether a concept in a math class applies to other contexts, such as business or science, again, inductive reasoning is being called for. Educational psychology research is inductive when it studies a sample of participants to draw conclusions about the population from which the sample is drawn. It is also inductive in that scientists rarely take a single study as strong evidence to reach a conclusion about a topic, instead requiring a number of studies on the same topic to have more confidence in a conclusion.

RESEARCH

Indeed, an important aspect of inductive reasoning is repeated observation. Through repeated observation, information about similar experiences accumulates to the point that a repetitive pattern can be detected and a more accurate conclusion drawn about it. To study this aspect of inductive reasoning, researchers have examined whether inductive inferences are justified based on evidence about a single instance of two co-occurring events (Kuhn et al., 2004). When two events occur together in time and space, we often conclude that one has caused the other, despite the possibility that other factors are involved. For example, a parent might conclude, "Harry is a bad influence on my daughter; Sharon didn't drink before she met him." The boy might be the cause, but the event may have been a coincidence. Of course, if there is repeated evidence (for example, every girl Harry has ever gone out with develops a drinking problem), then the argument becomes more persuasive.

Anthony Harvie/Getty Images

Consider also a child who observes a black snake and concludes "All snakes are black." The child's cousin sends him an e-mail about a pet snake she recently bought, and the child concludes that the pet snake must be black. However, the child clearly has not observed all of the snakes in the world—actually only one in this case—so he has seen only a small sample of the world's snake population. Of course, he would be forced to change his mind if he saw a gray snake or a white snake. The conclusions drawn as a result of inductive reasoning are never absolutely certain, only more or less probable. But induction can provide conclusive *negative* results—for example, seeing a yellow snake proves that the assertion "All snakes are black" is *false*.

Notice that inductive conclusions are never entirely certain—that is, they may be inconclusive. An inductive conclusion may be very likely, but there always is a chance that it is wrong, just as a sample does not perfectly represent its population (Kuhn, 2009). Teachers can help students improve their inductive reasoning by encouraging them to consider that the conclusion they reach depends on the quality and the quantity of the information available. Students often overstate a conclusion, making it more definitive than the evidence indicates.

Let's now consider another aspect of inductive reasoning: It is basic to analogies. An **analogy** is a correspondence between otherwise dissimilar things. Analogies can be used to improve students' understanding of new concepts by comparing them with already learned concepts.

inductive reasoning Reasoning from the specific to the general.

analogy A correspondence in some respects between otherwise dissimilar things.

One type of analogy involves formal reasoning and has four parts, with the relation between the first two parts being the same as, or very similar to, the relation between the last two. For example, solve this analogy: Beethoven is to music as Picasso is to _____. To answer correctly ("art"), you had to induce the relation between Beethoven and music (the former created the latter) and apply this relationship to Picasso (what did he create?).

How good are children and adolescents at inductive reasoning? Adolescents are better at many aspects of inductive reasoning than are children, including analogies and false inclusion when generalizing from a single event, but not as good as young adults (Kuhn, 2009).

Deductive Reasoning In contrast with inductive reasoning, **deductive reasoning** is reasoning from the general to the specific. Figure 3 provides a visual representation of the difference between inductive and deductive reasoning.

When you solve puzzles or riddles, you are engaging in deductive reasoning. When you learn about a general rule and then understand how it applies in some situations but not others, you are engaging in deductive reasoning (Johnson-Laird, 2008). Deductive reasoning is always certain in the sense that if the initial rules or assumptions are true, then the conclusion will be correct. When educators and psychologists use theories and intuitions to make predictions, and then evaluate these predictions by making further observations, they are using deductive reasoning.

Many aspects of deductive reasoning have been studied, including the occasions when knowledge and reasoning conflict. During adolescence, individuals are increasingly able to reason deductively even when the premises being reasoned about are false (Kuhn, 2009). Consider this deductive inference problem:

All basketball players are motorcycle drivers. All motorcycle drivers are women.

Assuming that these two statements are true, decide whether the following statement is true or false:

All basketball players are women.

Children rarely conclude that such conclusions are valid deductions from the premises. From early adolescence through early adulthood, individuals improve in their ability to make accurate conclusions when knowledge and reasoning conflict. That is, they can "reason independently of the truth status of the premises" (Kuhn & Franklin, 2006).

CRITICAL THINKING

Currently, psychologists and educators are showing considerable interest in critical thinking, although it is not an entirely new idea (Bonney & Sternberg, 2017). **Critical thinking** involves thinking reflectively and productively and evaluating the evidence. Many of the "Reflect" questions that appear in every section of this book call for critical thinking.

Mindfulness According to Ellen Langer (1997, 2005), mindfulness is a key to critical thinking. **Mindfulness** means being alert, mentally present, and cognitively flexible while going through life's everyday activities and tasks. Mindful students maintain an active awareness of the circumstances in their lives (Bostic et al., 2015; Roeser, 2016).

Mindful students create new ideas, are open to new information, and are aware of more than one perspective. In contrast, mindless students are entrapped in old ideas, engage in automatic behavior, and operate from a single perspective. Mindless students accept what they read or hear without questioning the accuracy of the information. Mindless students become trapped in rigid mindsets, not taking into account possible variations in contexts and perspectives. Langer emphasizes that asking good questions is an important aspect of mindful thinking. She also stresses that it is important to focus on the process of learning rather than the outcome. For example, Trisha didn't do well on her math test earlier this week. All she can think about is how poorly she did. If she were engaging in mindfulness, Trisha would evaluate why she did so poorly and think about what changes she could make to do better on the next test.

Recently, Robert Roeser and his colleagues (Roeser, 2016; Roeser & Eccles, 2015; Roeser et al., 2014; Roeser & Zelazo, 2012; Zelazo & Lyons, 2012) have proposed

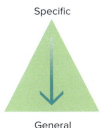

FIGURE 3 INDUCTIVE AND DEDUCTIVE REASONING

The pyramid at the top represents inductive reasoning—going from specific to general. The upside-down pyramid at the bottom represents deductive reasoning—going from general to specific.

DEVELOPMENT

deductive reasoning Reasoning from the general to the specific.

critical thinking Thinking reflectively and productively and evaluating the evidence.

mindfulness Being alert, mentally present, and cognitively flexible while going through life's everyday activities and tasks. Mindful students maintain an active awareness of the circumstances in their lives.

RESEARCH

that mindfulness training could be implemented in schools through practices such as using age-appropriate activities that increase children's reflection on moment-to-moment experiences and result in improved self-regulation (Roeser, 2016; Roeser & Eccles, 2015). For example, in a recent study, a training program on mindfulness and caring for others was effective in improving the cognitive control of fourth- and fifth-graders (Schonert-Reichl et al., 2015). In other recent research, mindfulness training has been found to improve preschool children's attention and self-regulation (Poehlmann-Tynan et al., 2016), elementary school children's achievement (Singh & others, 2016), elementary school students' coping strategies in stressful situations (Dariotis & others, 2016), and adolescents' mood and achievement (Bennett & Dorjee, 2016). Also, in two recent studies, mindfulness-based intervention improved the lives of public school teachers, reducing their stress, improving their mood at school and at home, and providing better sleep (Crain et al., 2016; Taylor et al., 2016).

In addition to mindfulness, activities such as yoga, meditation, and tai chi have been suggested as candidates for improving children's cognitive and socioemotional development. Together these activities are being grouped under the topic of *contemplative science,* a cross-disciplinary term that involves the study of how various types of mental and physical training might enhance children's development (Roeser & Eccles, 2015; Zelazo & Lyons, 2012).

Critical Thinking in Schools In addition to mindfulness training, following are some ways teachers can consciously build critical thinking into their lesson plans:

- Ask not only what happened but also "how" and "why."
- Examine supposed "facts" to determine whether there is evidence to support them.
- Argue in a reasoned way rather than through emotions.
- Recognize that there is sometimes more than one good answer or explanation.
- Compare various answers to a question and judge which is really the best answer.
- Evaluate and possibly question what other people say rather than immediately accepting it as the truth.
- Ask questions and speculate beyond what you already know to create new ideas and new information.

Jacqueline and Martin Brooks (1993, 2001) lament that few schools really teach students to think critically. In their view, schools spend too much time on getting students to give a single correct answer in an imitative way rather than encouraging students to expand their thinking by coming up with new ideas and rethinking earlier conclusions. They believe that too often teachers ask students to recite, define, describe, state, and list rather than to analyze, infer, connect, synthesize, criticize, create, evaluate, think, and rethink.

One way to encourage students to think critically is to present them with controversial topics or articles that present both sides of an issue to discuss. Some teachers shy away from having students engage in these types of critical-thinking debates or discussions because it is not "polite" or "nice" (Winn, 2004). However, critical thinking is promoted when students encounter conflicting accounts of arguments and debates, which can motivate them to delve more deeply into a topic and attempt to resolve an issue (Kuhn, 2009). In these circumstances, students often benefit when teachers refrain from stating their own views, allowing students to more freely explore different sides of issues and multiple perspectives on topics.

Also, a recent meta-analysis concluded that in trying to increase students' general critical-thinking skills, dialogue (discussion) was helpful, especially when the teacher posed questions and there were both whole-class teacher-led discussions and smaller-group teacher-led discussions (Abrami et al., 2015). Also in this meta-analytic review, students' general critical-thinking skills improved when they experienced authentic or situated problems and examples, especially when thinking was applied to problem solving.

Getting students to think critically is not always an easy task (Bonney & Sternberg, 2016). Many students come into a class with a history of passive learning, having been encouraged to recite the correct answer to a question rather than put forth the intellectual effort to think in more complex ways. By assigning more tasks that require students to focus on an issue, a question, or a problem, rather than just reciting facts, teachers stimulate students' ability to think critically.

Critical Thinking in Adolescence If a solid base of fundamental skills (such as literacy and math skills) is not developed during childhood, critical-thinking skills are unlikely to mature in adolescence. For those adolescents who lack fundamental skills, potential gains in adolescent thinking are not likely. For other adolescents, this time is an important transitional period in the development of critical thinking (Kuhn, 2009). Several cognitive changes occur during adolescence that facilitate improvements in critical thinking, including the following (Keating, 1990):

- Increased speed, automaticity, and capacity of information processing, which frees cognitive resources for other purposes
- More knowledge in a variety of domains
- An increased ability to construct new combinations of knowledge
- A greater range and more spontaneous use of strategies or procedures such as planning, considering alternatives, and cognitive monitoring

Technology and Critical Thinking An increasing number of technology applications are available to improve students' critical-thinking skills. David Jonassen (2006, 2010) argues that one of the best uses of technology in education involves computer applications that encourage students to think critically about the content they are studying. He calls such applications "mindtools" and sees them as constructivist tools that scaffold student creation of knowledge and reasoning about subject content. Jonassen distinguishes several categories of mindtools, including semantic organization tools, dynamic modeling tools, information interpretation tools, and conversation and collaboration tools.

TECHNOLOGY

Semantic organization tools, such as databases and concept mapping tools, help students organize, analyze, and visualize information they are studying. For example, students studying climate can query global databases to test their hypotheses concerning links between climate and population. Inspiration and Kidspiration are concept mapping tools for K–12 students that are relatively inexpensive and easy to use (see www.inspiration.com). One advantage of these concept mapping tools is that they offer visual mapping for students who are not yet strong readers or who are English language learners. These tools are available as software for laptops or desktop computers, and they also can be purchased as iPhone or iPad apps for schools/teachers with those devices.

Dynamic modeling tools help students explore connections between concepts. These include spreadsheets, expert systems, systems modeling tools, and microworlds. For example, spreadsheets have been used in mathematics classes to help students explore mathematical relations between numbers. Microworlds simulate real-world phenomena, such as genetic combinations. PhET simulations are helpful for simulating phenomena and exploring relationships (see https://phet.colorado.edu/en/simulations).

Information interpretation tools help learners access and interpret information. They include visualization and knowledge construction tools. For example, visualization tools are visual models of complex phenomena that make the phenomena more comprehensible. Knowledge construction tools, such as web development, online tools, video editing, or web design programs, scaffold student construction of knowledge in various forms. Here are some good examples of knowledge construction tools:

- Taking and annotating pictures to demonstrate concepts/knowledge
- Creating video animations using online tools (for example, iKITMovie or Moovly)

Students in the Research Center for Educational Technology's AT&T classroom at Kent State University studying energy by designing an energy-efficient home using *Better Homes and Gardens Home Designer software*.
Research Center for Educational Technology, Kent State University

Kindergarten students in the Research Center for Educational Technology's AT&T classroom at Kent State University exploring patterns by programming the Logo Robotic Turtle.
Research Center for Educational Technology, Kent State University

- Web site development using online programs such as Weebly for Education or Google sites such as Google Apps for Education
- Stop Action movies that combine hands-on construction and digital capture (for example, HUE animation software or the MyCreate app)

Finally, various digital *conversation and collaboration tools,* such as e-mail, online discussion, chat, videoconferencing, and blogs, allow students to interact and collaborate with experts and other students around the world. For example, students studying foreign languages can converse with native speakers using computer-mediated communication.

How do teachers help their students improve their critical-thinking skills? Following are their responses.

EARLY CHILDHOOD One of the techniques we use to develop our preschoolers' critical-thinking skills is to have them put a favorite item into a mystery box. The child then tells the class three clues about what is in the box, and the rest of the class guesses until they figure out what is inside the box. This game is rotated so that each child has a chance to put something in the box.

—MISSY DANGLER, *Suburban Hills School*

ELEMENTARY SCHOOL: GRADES K–5 One trait that is essential to critical thinking is intellectual courage. I teach this trait by asking my second-graders to consider such questions as "If everyone around you believes in 'such and such,' why is it hard to disagree?" or "When is it good to disagree?" or "Why do people get mad when they are questioned or doubted?" These questions help my students to think outside the box.

—ELIZABETH FRASCELLA, *Clinton Elementary School*

MIDDLE SCHOOL: GRADES 6–8 I always have the question: "What is the significance . . . ?" written on the classroom whiteboard. When we are covering any topic in sixth-grade social studies class, I point to that question. I also have students write in a journal reflecting on a historical event and have them discuss what would be different today if the event never took place.

—CASEY MAASS, *Edison Middle School*

HIGH SCHOOL: GRADES 9–12 We have our psychology students compile a "personality scrapbook" that includes completed personality tests along with reflective journals about the results as they relate to the student. Students then write a final paper entitled: "Who am I?" in which they "rethink" their own assumptions about themselves and their personality development. Students can also criticize and evaluate the effectiveness of personality tests in general.

—JOSEPH MALEY, *South Burlington High School*

CONNECTING WITH STUDENTS: Best Practices
Strategies for Improving Children's Thinking

Twentieth-century German dictator Adolf Hitler once remarked that it was fortunate for people in power that most people do not think. Education should help students become better thinkers. Every teacher would agree with that goal, but the means for reaching it are not always in place in schools. Here are some guidelines for helping students to become better thinkers.

1. *Be a guide in helping students to construct their own thinking.* You can't—and shouldn't—do students' thinking for them. However, you can and should be an effective guide in helping students construct their own thinking. Here are some guidelines teachers can follow to help students construct their own thinking (Brooks & Brooks, 1993, 2001):

Do
- Highly value students' questions
- View students as thinkers with emerging theories about the world
- Seek students' points of view
- Seek elaboration of students' initial responses
- Nurture students' intellectual curiosity

Don't
- View students' minds as empty or see the role of a teacher as simply pouring information into students' minds
- Rely too heavily on textbooks and workbooks
- Simply seek the correct answer to validate student learning

2. *Use thinking-based questions.* One way to analyze your teaching strategies is to make sure you're using thinking-based questioning in addition to a lecture-based approach and fact-based questioning (Sternberg & Spear-Swirling, 1996). In the lecture-based approach, the teacher presents information in the form of a lecture. This is a helpful approach for quickly presenting a body of information, such as factors that led to the French Revolution. In fact-based questioning, the teacher asks questions primarily designed to get students to describe factual information. This is best used for reinforcing newly acquired information or testing students' content knowledge. For example, the teacher might ask, "When did the French Revolution occur? Who were the king and queen of France at that time?" In thinking-based questioning, the teacher asks questions that stimulate thinking and discussion. For example, the teacher might say, "Compare the French and American revolutions. How were they similar? How were they different?"

Strive to include thinking-based questions in your teaching. They will help your students construct a deeper understanding of a topic. In *Through the Eyes of Teachers*, Alan Haskvitz describes how he challenges students to think more independently and creatively.

THROUGH THE EYES OF TEACHERS
Challenging Students to Be Intellectual Risk-Takers

Alan Haskvitz, who teaches social studies at Suzanne Middle School in Walnut, California, believes in learning by doing and the importance of motivating students to improve the community. His students have rewritten voting instructions adopted by Los Angeles County, lobbied for a law requiring state government buildings to have drought-resistant landscaping, and created measures to

continued

CONNECTING WITH STUDENTS: Best Practices
Strategies for Improving Children's Thinking

reduce the city's graffiti. Alan has posted links to thousands of teacher resources at www.reacheverychild.com. He challenges students to be independent thinkers and intellectual risk-takers. He has students create an ideal island and discuss what everything from government to geography would be like on the island. (Sources: Briggs, 1999; Educational Cyber Playground, 2006).

3. *Provide positive role models for thinking.* Look around your community for positive role models who can demonstrate effective thinking, and invite them to visit your classroom and talk with your students. Also think about contexts in the community, such as museums, colleges and universities, hospitals, and businesses, where you can take students and they can observe and interact with competent thinkers.

4. *Be a thinking role model for your students.* Have an active and inquiring mind yourself. Examine what we have said about thinking in this chapter. Work on being a positive thinking model for students by practicing these strategies.

5. *Keep up-to-date on the latest developments in thinking.* Continue to learn actively about new developments in teaching students to become more effective thinkers after you have become a teacher. Over the next decade, there likely will be new technology programs that can improve students' thinking skills. Go to libraries to read educational journals and attend professional conferences that include information about thinking. For example, be alert to new developments in mindfulness training, both for teachers and students. Recently, a new journal called *Mindfulness* was created that can provide you with the latest information about this topic. Also, a recent book, *Mindfulness for Teachers: Simple Skills for Peace and Productivity in the Classroom* by Patricia Jennings (2015), provides excellent classroom strategies.

Alan Haskvitz with middle school students Simon Alarcon and Tracy Blozis, examining bones and trying to figure out where in the animal kingdom they belong.
Alan Haskvitz

6. *Embrace technology as a context for improving students' thinking skills.* Various aspects of technology, online publishing, and social media can be used as tools for teaching 21st-century learners to interact and communicate more effectively with the world.

THROUGH THE EYES OF TEACHERS
Making Learning and Technology Meaningful for Students

Kathy Cassidy is a first-grade teacher in Moose Jaw, Saskatchewan, Canada, who has taken full advantage of available technology to enhance her students' learning. Among the technologies she uses are blogging, Skype, and Twitter. In addition to teaching, she has written several books, including a recently written ebook (*Connected from the Start*), and speaks regularly at conferences. For a closer look at her extensive use of technology in the classroom, see http://kathycassidy.com

Kathy Cassidy using technology in her first-grade classroom.
Kathy Cassidy

DECISION MAKING

Think of all the decisions you have to make in your life. Which grade level and subject should I teach? Should I go to graduate school right after college or get a job first? Should I establish myself in a career before settling down to have a family? Should I buy a house or rent? **Decision making** is thinking that involves evaluating alternatives and choosing among them.

In deductive reasoning, people use clear-cut rules to draw conclusions. When we make decisions, the rules are seldom clear-cut and we may have limited knowledge about the consequences of various decisions. In addition, important information might be missing, and we might not trust all of the information we have.

decision making Evaluating alternatives and making choices among them.

Biases and Flaws in Decision Making

Another fruitful category of decision-making research involves the biases and flawed heuristics (rules of thumb) that affect the quality of decisions. In many cases, our decision-making strategies are well adapted to deal with a variety of problems. However, we are prone to certain flaws in our thinking (Stanovich, 2013). Common flaws involve confirmation bias, belief perseverance, overconfidence bias, and hindsight bias. Decision making is improved when we become aware of these potential flaws.

> **Thinking Back/Thinking Forward**
>
> The prefrontal cortex of the brain, which is an important region in higher-level thinking such as decision making, is not fully developed in adolescence. Connect to "Cognitive and Language Development."

Confirmation Bias **Confirmation bias** is the tendency to search for and use information that supports our ideas rather than refutes them. Thus, in making a decision, a student might have an initial belief that a certain approach is going to work. He tests out the approach and finds out that it does work some of the time. He concludes that his approach is right rather than further exploring the fact that in a number of cases it doesn't work.

We tend to seek out and listen to people whose views confirm our own rather than listen to dissenting views. Thus, you might have a particular teaching style, such as lecturing, that you like to use. If so, you probably have a tendency to seek advice from other teachers who use that style rather than from teachers who prefer other styles, such as collaborative problem solving by students.

Belief Perseverance Closely related to confirmation bias, **belief perseverance** is the tendency to hold on to a belief in the face of contradictory evidence. People have a difficult time letting go of an idea or a strategy once they have embraced it (Stanovich, 2013). Consider Madonna. We might have a hard time thinking of her in a maternal role because of the belief perseverance that she is a wild, fun-loving rock star.

Another example of belief perseverance gives some college students trouble. They may have gotten good grades in high school by using the strategy of cramming for tests the night before. The ones who don't adopt a new strategy—spacing their study sessions more evenly through the term—often do poorly in college.

Overconfidence Bias **Overconfidence bias** is the tendency to have more confidence in judgments and decisions than we should have, based on probability or past experience. People are overconfident about how long those with a fatal disease will live, which businesses will go bankrupt, whether a defendant is guilty in a court trial, and which students will do well in college. People consistently have more faith in their judgments than predictions based on statistically objective measures indicate they should.

In one study, college students were asked to make predictions about themselves in the coming academic year (Vallone et al., 1990). They were asked to predict whether they would drop any courses, vote in an election, and break up with their girlfriend or boyfriend. At the end of the year, the accuracy of their predictions was examined. The results: They were more likely to drop a class, not vote in an election, and break up with a girlfriend or a boyfriend than they had predicted.

RESEARCH

Hindsight Bias People not only are overconfident about what they predict will happen in the future (overconfidence bias), but also tend to overrate their past performances at prediction. **Hindsight bias** is our tendency to falsely report, after the fact, that we accurately predicted an event.

When baseball season is just beginning, lots of people in different cities are predicting that their teams are going to make it to the World Series. Come October, after almost all of the teams have fallen by the wayside, many of the same people will say, "I told you our team wasn't going to have a good season."

Decision Making in Adolescence Adolescence is a time of increased decision making—which friends to choose, which person to date, whether to have sex, whether

confirmation bias The tendency to search for and use information that supports our ideas rather than refutes them.

belief perseverance The tendency to hold on to a belief in the face of contradictory evidence.

overconfidence bias The tendency to have more confidence in judgments and decisions than we should have, based on probability or past experience.

hindsight bias The tendency to falsely report, after the fact, having accurately predicted an event.

How do emotions and social contexts influence adolescents' decision making?
Rubberball Productions/Brand X Pictures/Getty Images

DEVELOPMENT

dual-process model States that decision-making is influenced by two systems—one analytical and one experiential—that compete with each other; in this model, it is the experiential system—monitoring and managing actual experiences—that benefits adolescent decision making.

to seek immediate satisfaction or delay gratification in exchange for a positive outcome, whether to go to college, and so on (Reyna & Zayas, 2014). How competent are adolescents at making decisions? Older adolescents often make better decisions than younger adolescents, who in turn, make better decisions than children.

Most individuals make better decisions when they are calm rather than emotionally aroused, which may especially be true for adolescents (Steinberg, 2015a, b). Thus, the same adolescent who makes a wise decision when calm may make an unwise decision when emotionally aroused.

Social contexts play a key role in adolescent decision-making. For example, adolescents' are more likely to make risky choices in contexts where substances and other temptations are readily available (Steinberg, 2015a, b). Recent research reveals that the presence of peers in risk-taking situations increases the likelihood that adolescents will make risky decisions (Silva et al., 2016). In one study of risk-taking involving a simulated driving task, the presence of peers increased an adolescent's decision to engage in risky driving by 50 percent but had no effect on adults (Gardner & Steinberg, 2005). One view is that the presence of peers activates the brain's reward system, especially dopamine pathways (Monahan et al., 2016; Smith et al., 2015).

One proposal to explain adolescent decision making is the **dual-process model**, which states that decision making is influenced by two cognitive systems—one analytical and one experiential, which compete with each other (Reyna et al., 2015). The dual-process model emphasizes that it is the experiential system—monitoring and managing actual experiences—that benefits adolescents' decision making, not the analytical system. In this view, adolescents don't benefit from engaging in reflective, detailed, higher-level cognitive analysis about a decision, especially in

CONNECTING WITH STUDENTS: Best Practices
Strategies for Making Competent Decisions for Yourself and Your Students

1. *Weigh the costs and benefits of various outcomes.* You will encounter many circumstances in which you will benefit from pursuing this strategy. For example, will your students benefit from examining a particular topic in a small-group format or a lecture format?

2. *Avoid confirmation bias.* Do you tend to only seek out people to talk with whose views confirm your own? Does a particular student avoid people with dissenting views and, if so, how can you help him or her?

3. *Resist belief perseverance.* Are you holding on to some beliefs that might be outdated and need to be changed? Do students have beliefs based on their past experiences that they are clinging to which don't fit their current situation? If so, how can you help them?

4. *Don't engage in overconfidence bias.* Do you have more confidence in your decisions than you should, based on probability or your past experience? Might one of your future students gloss over the fact that he or she did poorly on the previous test in your class and be overconfident and not put in extra hours of study?

5. *Avoid hindsight bias.* Be aware that people have a tendency to falsely report, after the fact, that they were able to predict an event.

6. *If you plan to teach in middle or high school, spend some time reading about and thinking further about how adolescents make decisions and the factors that influence their decision making.* Younger adolescents need to occupy their time with positive activities to limit their opportunities to engage in risk-taking behavior.

high-risk, real-world contexts. In such contexts, adolescents just need to know that there are some circumstances that are so dangerous that they need to be avoided at all costs. However, some experts on adolescent cognition argue that in many cases adolescents benefit from both analytical and experiential systems (Kuhn, 2009).

CREATIVE THINKING

An important aspect of thinking is to be able to think creatively (Ambrose & Sternberg, 2016; Renzulli, 2017; Sternberg, 2017; Sternberg & Sternberg, 2016). **Creativity** is the ability to think about something in novel and unusual ways and come up with unique solutions to problems.

J. P. Guilford (1967) distinguished between **convergent thinking**, which produces one correct answer and is characteristic of the kind of thinking required on conventional intelligence tests, and **divergent thinking**, which produces many answers to the same question and is more characteristic of creativity. For example, a typical convergent item on a conventional intelligence test is "How many quarters will you get in return for 60 dimes?" The question has only one right answer. In contrast, divergent questions have many possible answers. For example, consider these questions: "What image comes to mind when you think of sitting alone in a dark room?" and "What are some unique uses for a paper clip?"

Are intelligence and creativity related? Although most creative students are quite intelligent (as measured by high scores on conventional intelligence tests), the reverse is not necessarily true. Many highly intelligent students are not very creative (Ambrose & Sternberg, 2016; Barbot & Tinio, 2015).

Steps in the Creative Process The creative process is often described as a five-step sequence:

1. *Preparation.* Students become immersed in a problem issue that interests them and their curiosity is aroused.
2. *Incubation.* Students churn ideas around in their heads and are likely to make some unusual connections in their thinking.
3. *Insight.* Students experience the "Aha!" moment when all pieces of the puzzle seem to fit together.
4. *Evaluation.* Now students must decide whether the idea is valuable and worth pursuing. They need to think, "Is the idea novel or is it obvious?"
5. *Elaboration.* This final step often covers the longest span of time and involves the hardest work. This step is what famous twentieth-century American inventor Thomas Edison was thinking about when he said that creativity is 1 percent inspiration and 99 percent perspiration.

Mihaly Csikszentmihalyi (pronounced ME-high CHICK-sent-me-high-ee) (1996) argues that this five-step sequence provides a helpful framework for thinking about how to develop creative ideas. However, he emphasizes that creative people don't always go through the steps in a linear sequence. For example, elaboration is often interrupted by periods of incubation. Fresh insights may appear during incubation, evaluation, and elaboration. And insight might take years or only a few hours. Sometimes the creative idea consists of one deep insight. At other times, it is a series of small insights. To evaluate your creative thinking skills, see *Self-Assessment 1*.

Teaching and Creativity An important teaching goal is to help students become more creative (Beghetto & Kaufman, 2017; Renzulli, 2017). Teachers need to recognize that students will show more creativity in some domains than others (Sternberg, 2017). A student who shows creative-thinking skills in mathematics may not exhibit these skills in art, for example.

> **Thinking Back/Thinking Forward**
>
> In Sternberg's view, creative thinking is quite different from the analytical thinking that is at the core of traditional intelligence tests. Connect to "Individual Variations."

creativity The ability to think about something in novel and unusual ways and come up with unique solutions to problems.

convergent thinking Thinking with the aim of producing one correct answer. This is usually the type of thinking required on conventional intelligence tests.

divergent thinking Thinking with the aim of producing many answers to the same question. This is characteristic of creativity.

SELF-ASSESSMENT 1
How Good Am I at Thinking Creatively?

Rate each of these activities as they apply to you in terms of how often you engage in them: 1 = never, 2 = rarely, 3 = sometimes, and 4 = a lot.

	1	2	3	4
1. I come up with new and unique ideas.				
2. I brainstorm with others to creatively find solutions to problems.				
3. I am internally motivated.				
4. I'm flexible about things and like to play with my thinking.				
5. I read about creative projects and creative people.				
6. I'm surprised by something and surprise others every day.				
7. I wake up in the morning with a mission.				
8. I search for alternative solutions to problems rather than giving a pat answer.				
9. I have confidence in my ability to create something innovative and worthwhile.				
10. I delay gratification and persist until I have developed creative ideas and products.				
11. I take risks in developing creative thoughts.				
12. I spend time around creative people.				
13. I spend time in settings and activities that stimulate me to be creative.				

Examine your overall pattern of responses. What are your strengths and weaknesses in creativity? Keep practicing your strengths and work on improving your weaknesses to provide students with a creative role model.

RESEARCH

A special concern today is that the creative thinking of children in the United States appears to be declining. A study of approximately 300,000 U.S. children and adults found that creativity scores rose until 1990, but since then have been steadily declining (Kim, 2010). Among the likely causes of this decline are the amount of time U.S. children spend watching TV and playing video games instead of engaging in creative activities, as well as the lack of emphasis on creative-thinking skills in schools (Gregorson et al., 2013). In some countries, though, there has been increasing emphasis on creative thinking in schools. For example, historically, creative thinking has typically been discouraged in Chinese schools. However, Chinese educators are now encouraging teachers to spend more classroom time on creative activities (Plucker, 2010).

Your students also will greatly benefit if you are a creative thinker and engage in creative thinking in the course of your everyday teaching. Mihaly Csikszentmihalyi (1996) has recommended a number of strategies for becoming more creative that might help you become a more creative thinker. He interviewed 90 leading figures in art, business, government, education, and science to learn how creativity works. He discovered that creative people regularly experience a state he calls *flow,* a heightened state of pleasure experienced when we are engaged in mental and physical challenges that absorb us. Csikszentmihalyi (2000) points out that everyone is capable of achieving flow. Based on his interviews with some of the most creative people in the world, the first step toward a more creative life is cultivating your curiosity and interest. Here are some ways to do this:

- *Try to be surprised by something every day.* Maybe it is something you see, hear, or read about. Become absorbed in a lecture or a book. Be open to what the world is telling you. Life is a stream of experiences. Swim widely and deeply in it, and your life will be richer.

- *Try to surprise at least one person every day.* In a lot of things you do, you have to be predictable and patterned. Do something different for a change. Ask a question you normally would not ask. Invite someone to go with you to a museum you never have visited.
- *Write down each day what surprised you and how you surprised others.* Most creative people keep a diary, notes, or lab records to ensure that their experiences are not fleeting or forgotten. Start with a specific task. Each evening record the most surprising event that occurred that day and your most surprising action. After a few days, reread your notes and reflect on your past experiences. After a few weeks, you might see a pattern of interest emerging in your notes, one that might suggest an area you can explore in greater depth.
- *When something sparks your interest, follow it.* Usually when something captures your attention, it is short-lived—an idea, a song, a flower. Too often we are too busy to explore the idea, song, or flower further. Or we think these areas are none of our business because we are not experts about them. Yet the world is our business. We can't know which part of it is best suited to our interests until we make a serious effort to learn as much as we can about as many aspects of it as possible.
- *Wake up in the morning with a specific goal to look forward to.* Creative people wake up eager to start the day. Why? Not necessarily because they are cheerful, enthusiastic types but because they know that there is something meaningful to accomplish each day, and they can't wait to get started.
- *Spend time in settings that stimulate your creativity.* In Csikszentmihalyi's (1996) research, he gave people an electronic pager and beeped them randomly at different times of the day. When he asked them how they felt, they reported the highest levels of creativity when walking, driving, or swimming. I (your author) do my most creative thinking when I'm jogging. These activities are semiautomatic in that they take a certain amount of attention while leaving some time free to make connections among ideas.

Recall that a current concern is the education of children who are gifted in the face of standards-based education designed to meet requirements of legislation such as the Every Student Succeeds Act. There is also mounting concern that this legislation has harmed the development of students' creative thinking by pressuring them to memorize information in order to do well on standardized tests.

Some teachers were recently asked how they help their students develop creative-thinking skills. Following are their responses.

This is the setting where Mihaly Csikszentmihalyi (pictured above) gets his most creative thoughts. *When and where do you get your most creative thoughts? Do you think any of Csikszentmihalyi's recommendations would help you to become a more creative thinker?*
Dr. Mihaly Csikszentmihalyi

> **Thinking Back/Thinking Forward**
>
> Experts argue that the education of gifted students in the United States requires a significant overhaul. Connect to "Learners Who Are Exceptional."

EARLY CHILDHOOD When teaching music to my preschool students, I have them suggest an instrument from our instrument library to make the sound of a character in the book. Students also have to give a reason for why they selected the particular instrument.

—CONNIE CHRISTY, *Aynor Elementary School (Preschool Program)*

ELEMENTARY SCHOOL: GRADES K–5 When I teach social studies, I have my students construct a mock travel agency. We start out by talking about traveling around the world, which emphasizes geography. We then discuss the business of travel agencies. The students brainstorm about what the travel agent's job entails and what would be found at a real travel agency. Students then become the travel agent, create travel brochures, book trips, and so on. This social studies project is fun and involves reading, writing, research, art, and marketing.

—CRAIG JENSEN, *Cooper Mountain Elementary School*

MIDDLE SCHOOL: GRADES 6-8 When telling stories to my students, I often leave the last part of the story blank and have them create an ending. There is no right or wrong answer—just an opportunity for students to expand their creative thinking.

—MARGARET REARDON, *Pocantico Hills School*

HIGH SCHOOL: GRADES 9-12 By providing an environment of freedom and safety, teachers can foster students' creative thinking. In particular, I find that having students brainstorm about various topics makes the creative juices flow.

—DENNIS PETERSON, *Deer River High School*

CONNECTING WITH STUDENTS: Best Practices
Strategies for Guiding Students to Think More Creatively

An important teaching goal is to guide students to become better creative thinkers (Ambrose & Sternberg, 2016). Following are some effective strategies for helping students improve their creative-thinking skills:

Engage in Creative Thinking During the Course of Everyday Teaching.

Students' creative thinking benefits when they are around teachers who think creatively and give the students opportunities to observe them thinking in creative ways. Periodically revisit Csikszentmihalyi's recommendations for becoming a creative thinker to improve your creative-thinking skills.

Encourage Creative Thinking on a Group and Individual Basis

Brainstorming is a technique in which people are encouraged to come up with creative ideas in a group, play off each other's ideas, and say practically whatever comes to mind that seems relevant to a particular issue. Participants are usually told to hold off from criticizing others' ideas at least until the end of the brainstorming session.

Provide Environments That Stimulate Creativity

Some classrooms nourish creativity, while others inhibit it (Beghetto & Kaufman, 2017; Renzulli, 2017). Teachers who encourage creativity often rely on students' natural curiosity (Gottlieb et al., 2017; Skiba et al., 2017). They provide exercises and activities that stimulate students to find insightful solutions to problems, rather than ask a lot of questions that require rote answers. Teachers also encourage creativity by taking students on field trips to locations where creativity is valued. Howard Gardner (1993) emphasizes that science, discovery, and children's museums offer rich opportunities to stimulate creativity. The design of schools and classrooms may influence the creativity of students (Baer, 2016). School environments that encourage independent work, are stimulating but not distracting, and make resources readily available are likely to encourage students' creativity (Runco, 2016).

Don't Overcontrol Students

Teresa Amabile (1993) says that telling students exactly how to do things leaves them feeling that originality is a mistake and exploration is a waste of time. If, instead of dictating which activities they should engage in, you let your students select their interests and you support their inclinations, you will be less likely to destroy their natural curiosity. Amabile also emphasizes that when teachers hover over students all of the time, they make them feel that they are constantly being watched while they are working. When students are under constant surveillance, their creative risk-taking and adventurous spirit diminish.

Encourage Internal Motivation

Excessive use of prizes, such as gold stars, money, or toys, can stifle creativity by undermining the intrinsic pleasure students derive from creative activities. Creative students' motivation is the satisfaction generated by the work itself. Competition for prizes and formal evaluations often undermine intrinsic motivation and creativity (Hennessey, 2011, 2017). However, material rewards need not be ruled out altogether. We will say more about internal and external motivation in the chapter on motivation, teaching, and learning.

CONNECTING WITH STUDENTS: Best Practices
Strategies for Guiding Students to Think More Creatively

Guide Students to Help Them Think in Flexible Ways

Creative thinkers show flexibility by approaching problems in many different ways rather than getting locked into rigid patterns of thought. Give students opportunities to exercise this flexibility in their thinking (Ambrose & Sternberg, 2016).

Build Students' Self-Confidence

To expand students' creativity, it helps when teachers encourage students to believe in their own ability to create something innovative and worthwhile. Building students' confidence in their creative skills aligns with Bandura's (2012, 2015) concept of *self-efficacy*, the belief that one can master a situation and produce positive outcomes. We will have much more about self-efficacy in the chapter on motivation, teaching, and learning.

THROUGH THE EYES OF STUDENTS
The 12-Year-Old Filmmaker and Oozy Red Goop

Steven was 12 years old when he got his filmmaking badge in the Boy Scouts. He started imagining what he needed to do to make a movie, and his father bought him a Super-8 movie camera. Steven made a film called *The Last Gunfight*. His mother gave him free rein of the house, letting him virtually turn it into a movie studio. When he was 16 years old and was making a movie called *The Firelight*, he needed some "red, bloody-looking goop to ooze from the kitchen cabinets," so he persuaded his mother to buy 30 cans of cherries. Steven dumped the cherries into a pressure cooker and produced an "oozy red goop."

Steven is Steven Spielberg, whose mother supported his imagination and passion for filmmaking. Of course, Spielberg went on to become one of Hollywood's greatest directors, gaining worldwide recognition with such films as *E.T., Jurassic Park,* and *Schindler's List*. (Source: Goleman et al., 1993, p. 70.)

Guide Students to Be Persistent and Delay Gratification

Most highly successful creative products take years to develop. Most creative individuals work on ideas and projects for months and years without being rewarded for their efforts (Ambrose & Sternberg, 2016; Sternberg, 2017). Children don't become experts at sports, music, or art overnight. It usually takes many years working at something to become an expert at it; so it is with being a creative thinker who produces a unique, worthwhile product.

Encourage Students to Take Risks

Creative individuals take risks and seek to discover or invent something never before discovered or invented (Sternberg, 2017). They risk spending a lot of time on an idea or project that may not work. Creative people are not afraid of failing or getting something wrong. They often see failure as an opportunity to learn. They might go down 20 dead-end streets before they come up with a successful innovation.

Introduce Students to Creative People

A good strategy is to identify the most creative people in your community and ask them to come to your class and describe what helps them become creative or to demonstrate their creative skills. A writer, a poet, a craftsperson, a musician, a scientist, and many others can bring their props and productions to your class.

Connect with Technology

An increasing number of Internet sites provide excellent resources for enhancing students' creative thinking. Some of these sites are listed below:

- **Doodlecast for Kids.** This app lets children bring their artwork to life. They narrate as they draw, then play the animated sketch back as a video.
- **Strip Designer** and **ComicBook** are excellent apps for helping students create comic strips.
- **Digital Storytelling and Writing.** Puppet Pals scaffolds characters and settings so that even young children can record stories. For actual book creation, the My Story Book Creator app is good for young children and the Book Creator app lets students and teachers create attractive, polished books that can be published as iBooks or exported as PDFs.
- **GarageBand** can be used by older children to record various musical pieces, and **Toca Band** is a similar app that younger children can use.

Review, Reflect, and Practice

2 Describe several types of thinking and ways that teachers can foster them.

REVIEW
- What is thinking?
- How is executive function defined, how does it change developmentally, and what influences its development?
- How do inductive and deductive reasoning differ?
- What is the focus of critical thinking? Do most schools teach students to think critically?
- What is decision making? What are some flaws that can hinder effective decision making?
- What is creative thinking? How can teachers foster creative thinking?

REFLECT
- Some experts lament that few schools teach students to think critically. Does your own experience support this view? If you agree with the experts, why is critical thinking not more widely or effectively taught?

PRAXIS™ PRACTICE
1. Mr. Sampson wants to improve his students' executive function skills. Which of the following activities is most likely to help him accomplish this goal?
   a. work with students on memorizing a poem
   b. give students tips on multitasking efficiently
   c. create opportunities for students to manage their thoughts and set goals
   d. have students do computational math problems

2. Ms. McDougal has a pet rabbit in her classroom. One day while Amari is petting the rabbit, it bites her. Amari decides that all rabbits are mean. This is an example of what kind of reasoning?
   a. analogy
   b. critical thinking
   c. deductive
   d. inductive

3. Which teaching strategy is most likely to foster the development of critical-thinking skills in social studies?
   a. having students create timelines of important historical dates
   b. presenting students with worksheets that require them to recall the facts presented in their textbooks
   c. presenting students with statements such as "Lincoln was our greatest president" to defend or refute
   d. giving a multiple-choice test

4. Many students enter their educational psychology courses believing that when an authority figure presents an aversive stimulus to a child and the child's misbehavior diminishes, the authority figure has negatively reinforced the child's behavior. Of course, we know that the authority figure has punished the child's behavior. Many of the students who entered your class with this misconception will get questions incorrect that test this idea on the final exam and will still have this misconception when they leave the class. What is the best explanation for this phenomenon?
   a. belief perseverance
   b. confirmation bias
   c. hindsight bias
   d. none of the above

Review, Reflect, and Practice

5. All fifth-grade classes at Central School have just read *The Jungle Book*. Which assignment is most likely to foster creativity?
   a. The students write a story about how their lives would have been different if they had grown up in the wild like Mowgli.
   b. The students complete a story diagram, in which they describe the setting, characters, plot, climax, and theme of the book.
   c. The students create models of the temple where the monkeys lived, following a prototype that the teacher constructed.
   d. The students complete worksheets containing questions about the plot and characters of the book.

Please see answer key at end of book . . . .

3 PROBLEM SOLVING

LG 3 Take a systematic approach to problem solving.

Let's examine problem solving as a cognitive process, including the steps it involves, the obstacles to it, and how best to teach it.

Problem solving involves finding an appropriate way to attain a goal. Consider these tasks that require students to engage in problem solving: creating a project for a science fair, writing a paper for an English class, getting a community to be more environmentally responsive, and giving a talk on the factors that cause people to be prejudiced. Although these tasks seem quite different, each involves a similar series of steps.

problem solving Finding an appropriate way to attain a goal.

STEPS IN PROBLEM SOLVING

Efforts have been made to specify the steps that individuals go through in effectively solving problems. Following are four such steps (Bransford & Stein, 1993):

1. **Find and Frame Problems** Before you can solve a problem, you must recognize that it exists. In the past, most problem-solving exercises in school involved well-defined problems that lent themselves to specific, systematic operations that produced a well-defined solution. Today, educators increasingly recognize the need to teach students the real-world skill of identifying problems instead of just offering clear-cut problems to be solved (Ashcraft & Radvansky, 2016).

   Consider a student whose broad goal is to create a science-fair project. What branch of science would it be best for her to present—biology, physics, computer science, psychology? After making that decision, she'll have to narrow the problem even more. For example, which domain within psychology will she explore—perception, memory, thinking, personality? Within the domain of memory, she might pose this question: How reliable are people's memories of traumatic events they have experienced? Thus, it may take considerable exploration and refinement for the student to narrow the problem enough to generate specific solutions. Exploring such alternatives is an important part of problem solving.

2. **Develop Good Problem-Solving Strategies** Once students find a problem and clearly define it, they need to develop strategies for solving it

An important first step in solving many problems is finding and framing the various problems within the main problem. For example, in creating a science-fair project, certain problems have to be defined and solved before arriving at the final solution of a finished project.
Ariel Skelley/Blend Images/Getty Images

(Ericsson et al., 2016). Among the effective strategies are setting subgoals and using algorithms, heuristics, and means-end analysis.

Subgoaling involves setting intermediate goals that put students in a better position to reach the final goal or solution. Students might do poorly in solving problems because they don't generate subproblems or subgoals. Let's return to the science-fair project on the reliability of people's memory for traumatic events they have experienced. What might be some subgoaling strategies? One might be locating the right books and research journals on memory; another might be interviewing people who have experienced traumas in which basic facts have been recorded. At the same time that the student is working on this subgoaling strategy, she likely will benefit from establishing further subgoals in terms of what she needs to accomplish along the way to her final goal of a finished science project. If the science project is due in three months, she might set the following subgoals: finishing the first draft of the project two weeks before the project is due; having the research completed a month before the project is due; being halfway through the research two months before the project is due; having three trauma interviews completed two weeks from today; and starting library research tomorrow.

Notice that in establishing the subgoals, we worked backward in time. This is often a good strategy. Students first create a subgoal closest to the final goal and then work backward to the subgoal closest to the beginning of the problem-solving effort.

Algorithms are strategies that guarantee a solution to a problem. Algorithms come in different forms, such as formulas, instructions, and tests of all possible solutions.

When students solve a multiplication or long division problem by following a set procedure, they are using an algorithm. When they follow the directions for diagramming a sentence, they are using an algorithm. Algorithms are helpful in solving clear-cut problems. But since many real-world problems aren't so straightforward, looser strategies also are needed.

Heuristics are strategies or rules of thumb that can suggest a solution to a problem without guaranteeing that it will work. Heuristics help us to narrow down the possible solutions and help us find one that works. Suppose that you go out on a day hike and find yourself lost in the mountains. A common heuristic for getting "unlost" is simply to head downhill and pick up the nearest tiny stream. Small streams lead to larger ones, and large streams often lead to people. Thus, this heuristic usually works, although it could bring you out on a desolate beach.

In the face of a multiple-choice test, several heuristics could be useful. For example, if you are not sure about an answer, you could start by trying to eliminate the answers that look most unlikely and then guessing among the remaining ones. Also, for hints about the answer to one question, you could examine the statements or answer choices for other questions on the test.

A **means-end analysis** is a heuristic in which one identifies the goal (end) of a problem, assesses the current situation, and evaluates what needs to be done (means) to decrease the difference between the two conditions. Another name for means-end analysis is *difference reduction*. Means-end analysis also can involve the use of subgoaling, which was described earlier. Means-end analysis is commonly used in solving problems. Consider our previous example of a student who wants to do a science-fair project (the end) but has not yet found a topic. Using means-end analysis, she could assess her current situation, in which she is just starting to think about the project. Then she could map out a plan to reduce the difference between her current state and the goal (end). Her "means" might include talking to several scientists in the community about potential projects, going to the library to study the topic she chooses, and exploring the Internet for potential projects and ways to carry them out.

3. **Evaluate Solutions** Once we think we have solved a problem, we might not know whether our solution is effective unless we evaluate it. It helps to have in mind

subgoaling The process of setting intermediate goals that place students in a better position to reach the final goal or solution.

algorithms Strategies that guarantee a solution to a problem.

heuristics Strategies or rules of thumb that can suggest a solution to a problem but don't ensure that it will work.

means-end analysis A heuristic in which one identifies the goal (end) of a problem, assesses the current situation, and evaluates what needs to be done (means) to decrease the difference between the two conditions.

a clear criterion for determining the effectiveness of the solution. For example, what will be the student's criterion for effectively solving the science-fair problem? Will it be simply getting it completed? Receiving positive feedback about the project? Winning an award? Winning first place? Gaining the self-satisfaction of having set a goal, planned for it, and reached it?

4. **Rethink and Redefine Problems and Solutions over Time** An important final step in problem solving is to continually rethink and redefine problems and solutions over time. People who are good at problem solving are motivated to improve on their past performances and to make original contributions. Thus, the student who completed the science-fair project can look back at the project and think about ways the project could have been improved. The student might use feedback from judges or others who attended the fair in order to fine-tune the project for presentation again in some future venue.

OBSTACLES TO SOLVING PROBLEMS

Some common obstacles to solving problems are fixation and a lack of motivation and persistence. We'll also discuss inadequate emotional control, which is another stumbling block to effective problem solving.

Fixation It is easy to fall into the trap of becoming fixated on a particular strategy for solving a problem. **Fixation** involves using a prior strategy and failing to look at a problem from a fresh, new perspective. *Functional fixedness* is a type of fixation in which an individual fails to solve a problem because he or she views the elements involved solely in terms of their usual functions. A student who uses a shoe to hammer a nail has overcome functional fixedness to solve a problem.

A **mental set** is a type of fixation in which an individual tries to solve a problem in a particular way that has worked in the past. I (your author) had a mental set about using a typewriter rather than a computer to write my books. I felt comfortable with a typewriter and had never lost any sections I had written. It took a long time for me to break out of this mental set. Once I did, I found that books are much easier to write using a computer. You might have a similar mental set against using the new computer and video technology available for classroom use. A good strategy is to keep an open mind about such changes and monitor whether your mental set is keeping you from trying out new technologies that could make the classroom more exciting and more productive.

Lack of Motivation and Persistence Even if your students already have great problem-solving abilities, that hardly matters if they are not motivated to use them. It is especially important for students to be internally motivated to tackle a problem and persist at finding a solution. Some students avoid problems or give up too easily.

An important task for teachers is to devise or steer students toward problems that are meaningful to them and to encourage and support them in finding solutions. Students are far more motivated to solve problems that they can relate to their personal lives than textbook problems that have no personal meaning for them. Problem-based learning takes this real-world, personal approach.

Inadequate Emotional Control Emotion can facilitate or restrict problem solving. At the same time that they are highly motivated, good problem solvers are often able to control their emotions and concentrate on finding a solution to a problem. Too much anxiety or fear can especially restrict a student's ability to solve a problem. Individuals who are competent at solving problems are usually not afraid of making mistakes.

DEVELOPMENTAL CHANGES

Young children have some drawbacks that prevent them from solving many problems effectively. Especially notable is their lack of planning, which improves during the

> **Thinking Back/Thinking Forward**
> Motivation involves behavior that is energized, directed, and sustained. Connect to "Motivation, Teaching, and Learning."

fixation Using a prior strategy and thereby failing to examine a problem from a fresh, new perspective.

mental set A type of fixation in which an individual tries to solve a problem in a particular way that has worked in the past.

DEVELOPMENT

elementary and secondary school years. Among the reasons for the poor planning skills of young children is their tendency to try to solve problems too quickly at the expense of accuracy and their inability to inhibit an activity. Planning often requires inhibiting a current behavior to stop and think; preschool children often have difficulty inhibiting an ongoing behavior, especially if it is enjoyable. Another drawback of young children's problem-solving ability is that even though they may know a rule they may fail to use it.

Other reasons that older children and adolescents become better problem solvers than young children involve *knowledge* and *strategies*. The problems that older children and adolescents must solve are often more complex than those young children face, and solving these problems accurately usually requires accumulated knowledge. The more children know about a particular topic, the better able they will be to solve a problem related to the topic. The increase in accumulated knowledge about a topic ties in with our discussion of experts and novices in the chapter on the information-processing approach.

Older children and adolescents also are more likely than young children to have effective strategies that help them solve problems. Recall our extensive discussion of metacognition and strategies in the chapter on the information-processing approach, in which we discussed how children's use of strategies improves as they get older. Especially important in using strategies to solve problems is to have a range of strategies from which to select, and students' repertory of strategies increases during the elementary and secondary school years. Adolescents also have an increased capacity to monitor and manage their resources to effectively meet the demands of a problem-solving task, and they are better at screening out information irrelevant to solving a problem.

PROBLEM-BASED LEARNING AND PROJECT-BASED LEARNING

Now that we have discussed many aspects of problem solving, we turn our attention to two types of learning involving problems. First, we will discuss problem-based learning and then we will discuss project-based learning.

Problem-Based Learning **Problem-based learning** emphasizes solving authentic problems like those that occur in daily life. Problem-based learning is used in a program called YouthALIVE! at the Children's Museum of Indianapolis. There, students solve problems related to conceiving, planning, and installing exhibits; designing videos; creating programs to help visitors understand and interpret museum exhibits; and brainstorming about strategies for reaching the wider community.

Unlike direct instruction in which the teacher presents ideas and demonstrates skills, in problem-based learning teachers orient students to a problem or problems and get students to explore and discover solutions on their own (Lozano et al., 2015; Winfrey Avant & Bracy, 2015). Problem-based learning is especially effective in helping students develop confidence in generating their own thinking skills.

The general flow of problem-based learning consists of five phases: (1) orient students to the problem; (2) organize students for study; (3) assist with independent and group investigations; (4) develop and present artifacts and exhibits; and (5) analyze and evaluate work (Arends, 2004). Figure 4 provides more detailed information about the five phases of problem-based learning. We will further discuss problem-based learning in the chapter on planning, instruction, and technology.

Project-Based Learning In **project-based learning**, students work on real, meaningful problems and create tangible products (Tobias et al.,

problem-based learning Learning that emphasizes authentic problems like those that occur in daily life.

project-based learning Learning in which students work on real, meaningful problems and create tangible products.

Phases	Teacher's Roles
Phase 1: Orient the student to the problem	Communicate clearly the goals of the lesson, inform students what is expected of them, and guide students to become motivated to engage in self-directed problem solving.
Phase 2: Organize students for study	Help students define and organize study tasks related to the problem.
Phase 3: Assist independent and group investigation	Encourage students to obtain appropriate information, conduct experiments, and search for explanations and solutions.
Phase 4: Develop and present artifacts and exhibits	Guide students' planning and creation of appropriate artifacts such as reports and videos, and help them to share their work with others.
Phase 5: Analyze and evaluate the problem-solving process	Encourage students to reflect on their investigations and the strategies and steps they used.

FIGURE 4 FIVE PHASES OF PROBLEM-BASED LEARNING

CONNECTING WITH STUDENTS: Best Practices
Strategies for Improving Students' Problem Solving

1. *Give students extensive opportunities to solve real-world problems.* Make this a part of your teaching. Develop problems that are relevant to your students' lives. Such real-world problems are often referred to as "authentic," in contrast with textbook problems that too often do not have much meaning for students.

2. *Monitor students' effective and ineffective problem-solving strategies.* Keep the four problem-solving steps in mind when you give students opportunities to solve problems. Also keep in mind such obstacles to good problem solving as becoming fixated, harboring biases, not being motivated, and not persisting. In *Through the Eyes of Teachers,* Lawren Giles, who teaches at Baechtel Grove Middle School in Willits, California, describes the different strategies she encourages students to use.

THROUGH THE EYES OF TEACHERS
A Toolbox of Strategies

In teaching math, I use such problem-solving strategies as working backward, making a similar but simpler problem, drawing a diagram, making a table, and looking for patterns. We talk about what strategies make the most sense with different types of problems. When students successfully solve a problem, we look to see what methods were used, often finding more than one. I talk about multiple strategies in terms of carpenters having more than one kind of hammer in their toolboxes.

Lawren Giles

3. *Involve parents in children's problem solving.* The University of California at Berkeley has developed a program called *Family Math* (*Matematica Para la Familia* in Spanish) that helps parents experience math with their children in a positive, supportive way (Schauble et al., 1996). In the program, Family Math classes are usually taught by grade levels (K–2, 3–5, and 6–8). Many of the math activities require teamwork and communication between parents and children, who come to better understand not only the math but also each other. Family Math programs have served more than 400,000 parents and children in the United States.

4. *Work with children and adolescents to improve their use of rules, knowledge, and strategies in solving problems.* Recognize that young children may know a rule that enables them to solve a problem but not use it, so you may need to encourage them to use the rules they know. Encourage children to build up their knowledge base and to improve their knowledge of effective strategies that will help them solve problems.

5. *Use technology effectively.* Be motivated to incorporate multimedia programs into your classroom. Such programs can significantly improve your students' thinking and problem-solving skills.

2015). Project-based learning and problem-based learning are sometimes treated as synonymous. However, while still emphasizing the process of learning in a constructivist manner, project-based learning gives more attention to the end product than problem-based learning does. The types of problems explored in project-based learning are similar to those studied by scientists, mathematicians, historians, writers, and other professionals (Langbeheim, 2015).

Project-based learning environments are characterized by five main features (Krajcik & Blumenfeld, 2006):

1. *A driving question.* The learning process begins with a key question or problem that needs to be solved.
2. *Authentic, situated inquiry.* As students examine the key question, they learn about the problem-solving process engaged in by experts in the discipline in relevant contexts.
3. *Collaboration.* Students, teachers, and community participants collaborate to find solutions to the problem.
4. *Scaffolding.* Learning technologies are used to challenge students to go beyond what they normally would do in a problem-solving context.
5. *End product.* Students create tangible end products that address the key question.

To evaluate your thinking and problem-solving skills, complete Self-Assessment 2.

SELF-ASSESSMENT 2
How Effective Are My Thinking and Problem-Solving Strategies?

Teachers who practice good thinking and problem-solving strategies themselves are more likely to model and communicate these to their students than teachers who don't use such strategies. Candidly respond to these items about your own thinking and problem-solving strategies. Rate yourself: 1 = very much unlike me; 2 = somewhat unlike me; 3 = somewhat like me; and 4 = very much like me; then total your points.

1	2	3	4

1. I am aware of effective and ineffective thinking strategies.
2. I periodically monitor the thinking strategies I use.
3. I am good at reasoning.
4. I use good strategies for forming concepts.
5. I am good at thinking critically and deeply about problems and issues.
6. I construct my own thinking rather than just passively accepting what others think.
7. I like to use technology as part of my effort to think effectively.
8. I have good role models for thinking.
9. I keep up-to-date on the latest educational developments in thinking.
10. I use a system for solving problems, such as the four-step system described in the text.
11. I am good at finding and framing problems.
12. I make good decisions and monitor biases and flaws in my decision making.
13. When solving problems, I use strategies such as subgoaling and working backward in time.
14. I don't fall into problem-solving traps such as fixating, lacking motivation or persistence, and not controlling my emotions.
15. When solving problems, I set criteria for my success and evaluate how well I have met my problem-solving goals.
16. I make a practice of rethinking and redefining problems over an extended period of time.
17. I love to work on problem-solving projects.
18. I am good at creative thinking.
19. Total _____

SCORING AND INTERPRETATION

If you scored 66–72 points, your thinking strategies likely are very good. If you scored 55–65 points, you likely have moderately good thinking strategies. If you scored below 54 points, you likely would benefit from working on your thinking strategies.

Review, Reflect, and Practice

 Take a systematic approach to problem solving.

REVIEW
- What is problem solving? What are the main steps in problem solving?
- What are three obstacles to problem solving?
- What are some developmental changes in problem solving?
- What is problem-based learning? What is project-based learning?

REFLECT
- When you tackle a difficult problem, do you follow the four steps we described? What might you do to become a better model of a problem solver for your students?

PRAXIS™ PRACTICE

1. Which of the following is the best example of the use of a heuristic?
   a. Betina needs to compute the average of a series of numbers. First she determines their sum and then divides the sum by the number in the series.
   b. Anders becomes separated from his mother at the store. He goes to a cashier and tells her that he is lost. The cashier takes him to the service counter and his mother is paged.
   c. Samarie needs to remember all five of the Great Lakes. He uses the acronym HOMES.
   d. Marjorie needs to know how much carpet she needs to cover the floor of her room. She uses the formula for the area of a rectangle and converts square feet to square yards.

2. Which of the following is the best example of functional fixedness?
   a. Zack needs to tighten a screw, but he has no screwdriver. He has some change in his pocket, but he does not try to use a dime instead of a screwdriver.
   b. Xavier continues to use the strategy of adding a number multiple times rather than learning his multiplication facts.
   c. Maria uses the formula for the area of a rectangle when solving a problem requiring her to find the area of a triangle.
   d. Sol is lost in the woods. He remembers his mother telling him that if he gets lost like this, he should "hug a tree." He stays in one spot and within 30 minutes his family finds him.

3. Jackson is 16 years old and is much better at problem solving than when he was younger. Which of the following is most likely to explain his improved problem solving as a teenager?
   a. His hormones are settling down better since he is no longer in puberty.
   b. He is better at monitoring the demands of a problem-solving task.
   c. He is more stimulus-driven, and that helps him to sort through more stimuli when he is given a problem to solve.
   d. He uses a minimum number of strategies that he knows well.

4. Which of the following is the best example of problem-based learning?
   a. Ms. Christian's science students use a shoebox to protect a raw egg from breaking when dropped off the school roof.
   b. Ms. Kohler's students solve word problems to help them see the application of math facts to everyday life.
   c. Ms. Kringle's students solve a series of addition and multiplication problems of increasing difficulty.
   d. Ms. Randall's students answer the questions at the end of the chapter in their history book.

Please see answer key at end of book . . . .

LG 4 Define transfer and explain how to enhance it as a teacher.

4 TRANSFER

- What Is Transfer?
- Types of Transfer

An important complex cognitive goal is for students to be able to apply what they learn in one situation to new situations. An important goal of schooling is that students learn things that they can apply outside the classroom. Schools are not functioning effectively if students do well on tests in language arts but can't write a competent letter as part of a job application. Schools also are not effectively educating students if the students do well on math tests in the classroom but can't solve arithmetic problems on a job.

WHAT IS TRANSFER?

Transfer occurs when a person applies previous experiences and knowledge to learning or problem solving in a new situation. Thus, if a student learns a concept in math and then uses this concept to solve a problem in science, transfer has occurred. It also has occurred if a student reads and studies about the concept of fairness in school and subsequently treats others more fairly outside the classroom.

Some experts argue that the best way to ensure transfer is to "teach for it" (Schwartz et al., 2005). They stress that transfer problems virtually are eliminated when teaching occurs in contexts where individuals need to perform. By preparing students so that the problems they are likely to encounter in real life are at worst near-transfer problems, the gap between students' present learning level and learning goals is significantly reduced (Bransford et al., 2005). Some other strategies that can improve transfer include giving two or more examples of a concept because one often is not enough; giving students representations or models, such as matrices, that help them structure a problem-solving activity; and encouraging students to generate more information themselves, which increases the likelihood they will remember what needs to be transferred (Sears, 2008). Yet another strategy to increase transfer is to give students well-structured contrasting cases and have them try to invent solutions for them before being given a lecture on the expert solution. The idea is that by first inventing a solution, students bring their prior knowledge to bear on the problem and make connections to the features of the problem. When they see the expert solution and how it relates the key features to each other, the students should be able to better understand how it works and thus transfer it more effectively in the future.

TYPES OF TRANSFER

What are some different types of transfer? Transfer can be characterized as (1) near or far, and (2) low-road or high-road (Schunk, 2016).

Near or Far Transfer **Near transfer** occurs when the classroom learning situation is similar to the one in which the initial learning took place. For example, if a geometry teacher instructs students in how to logically prove a concept and then tests the students on this logic in the same setting in which they learned the concept, near transfer is involved.

Far transfer means the transfer of learning to a situation very different from the one in which the initial learning took place. For instance, if a student gets a part-time job in an architect's office and applies what he learned in geometry class to helping the architect analyze a spatial problem different from any problem the student encountered in geometry class, far transfer has occurred.

Low-Road or High-Road Transfer Gabriel Salomon and David Perkins (1989) distinguished between low-road and high-road transfer. **Low-road transfer** occurs when previous learning automatically, often unconsciously, transfers to another situation.

transfer Applying previous experiences and knowledge to learning or problem solving in a new situation.

near transfer The transfer of learning to a situation that is similar to the one in which the initial learning took place.

far transfer The transfer of learning to a situation that is very different from the one in which the initial learning took place.

low-road transfer The automatic, often unconscious, transfer of learning to another situation.

This occurs most often with highly practiced skills in which there is little need for reflective thinking. For example, when competent readers encounter new sentences in their native language, they read them automatically.

By contrast, **high-road transfer** is conscious and effortful. Students consciously establish connections between what they learned in a previous situation and the new situation they now face. High-road transfer is mindful—that is, students have to be aware of what they are doing and think about the connection between contexts. High-road transfer implies abstracting a general rule or principle from previous experience and then applying it to the new problem in the new context. For example, students might learn about the concept of subgoaling (setting intermediate goals) in math class. Several months later, one of the students thinks about how subgoaling might help him complete a lengthy homework assignment in history. This is high-road transfer.

Salomon and Perkins (1989) subdivide high-road transfer into forward-reaching and backward-reaching transfer. **Forward-reaching transfer** occurs when students think about how they can apply what they have learned to new situations (from their current situation, they look "forward" to apply information to a new situation ahead). For forward-reaching transfer to take place, students have to know something about the situations to which they will transfer learning. **Backward-reaching transfer** occurs when students look back to a previous ("old") situation for information that will help them solve a problem in a new context.

To better understand these two types of high-road transfer, imagine a student sitting in English class who has just learned some writing strategies for making sentences and paragraphs come alive and "sing." The student begins to reflect on how she could use those strategies to engage readers next year, when she plans to become a writer for the school newspaper. That is forward-reaching transfer. Now consider a student who is at his first day on the job as editor of the school newspaper. He is trying to figure out how to construct the layout of the pages. He reflects for a few moments and thinks about some geography and geometry classes he has previously taken. He draws on those past experiences for insights into constructing the layout of the student newspaper. That is backward-reaching transfer.

Cultural Practices and Transfer

Cultural practices may be involved in how easy or difficult transfer is. Prior knowledge includes the kind of knowledge that learners acquire through cultural experiences, such as those involving ethnicity, socioeconomic status, and gender (National Research Council, 1999). In some cases, this cultural knowledge can support children's learning and facilitate transfer, but in others it may interfere.

DIVERSITY

For children from some cultural backgrounds, there is a minimal fit or transfer between what they have learned in their home communities and what is required or taught by the school. For example, consider the language skill of storytelling. Euro-American children use a linear style that more closely approximates the linear expository style of writing and speaking taught in most schools (Lee & Slaughter-Defoe, 1995). This may involve recounting a series of events in a rigidly chronological sequence. By contrast, in some ethnic groups—such as Asian/Pacific Islander or Native American—a nonlinear, holistic/circular style is more common in telling a story, and non-Latinx White teachers may consider their discourse to be disorganized (Clark, 1993). Also, in African American children, a nonlinear, topic-associative storytelling approach is common (Michaels, 1986).

Methods of argumentation in support of certain beliefs also differ across cultures. Chinese speakers prefer to present supporting evidence first, leading up to a major point or claim (in contrast with a topic sentence followed by supporting details). Non-Chinese listeners sometimes judge this style as "beating around the bush" (Tsang, 1989). Rather than perceiving such variations in communication styles as being chaotic or as necessarily inferior to Euro-American styles, teachers need to be responsive to them and aware of cultural differences. This is especially important in the early elementary school grades when students are making the transition from the home environment to the school environment.

high-road transfer Applying information from one situation to another in a way that is conscious and effortful.

forward-reaching transfer Occurs when the individual looks for ways to apply learned information to a future situation.

backward-reaching transfer Occurs when the individual looks back to a previous situation for information to solve a problem in a new context.

If we fail to consider how the cultural differences of our students may be inconsistent with the traditional Euro-American school system, do not respect the cultural capital of our students, and are not responsive to culture in our teaching, then we contribute to the systemic racism that maintains the status quo. This includes the achievement gaps described in the chapter on sociocultural diversity. Without discussions about race, it will be difficult to change school practices that widen the equity gap between white students and students of color (Chapman, 2013).

What are some ways teachers help their students transfer classroom knowledge to the outside world? Following are their responses.

EARLY CHILDHOOD One way that we connect classroom knowledge with the outside world is to have instruments in class that make sounds similar to the music children hear when they are at home. For example, we have children from different cultures, and the music they and their families listen to features congas, steel drums, and guitars; we have these instruments in class and encourage children to play them.

—Valarie Gorham, *Kiddie Quarters, Inc.*

ELEMENTARY SCHOOL: GRADES K–5 When discussing immigration with my second-graders, I begin by asking them to think of a time when they moved to a new place, such as a new classroom or school, a new house or community, or a new country. I then ask them how they felt (for example, happy, sad, nervous) when they moved to this new place and why they felt this way. Then I ask them to take these thoughts and draw a picture of this time in their lives. This exercise helps students transfer information they have learned in class about immigration to similar experiences in their own lives.

—Elizabeth Frascella, *Clinton Elementary School*

MIDDLE SCHOOL: GRADES 6–8 When teaching social studies, I often have my students read newspaper articles about a particular topic and then write their own newspaper article that responds to what they have read. This gets them more personally involved in the topic.

—Casey Maass, *Edison Middle School*

HIGH SCHOOL: GRADES 9–12 High school students, especially juniors and seniors, are particularly interested in future careers. As a career and technical education teacher, I find that my students especially enjoy the unit on career awareness in which they identify personal skills and interests and identify careers in which those skills and interests would be best served.

—Sandy Swanson, *Menomonee Falls High School*

CONNECTING WITH STUDENTS: Best Practices
Strategies for Helping Students Transfer Information

1. *Think about what your students need for success in life.* We don't want students to finish high school with a huge data bank of content knowledge but no idea how to apply it to the real world. One strategy for thinking about what students need to know is to use the "working-backward" problem-solving strategy we discussed earlier in this chapter. For example, what do employers want high school and college graduates to be able to do? In a national survey of employers of college students, the three skills that employers most wanted graduates to have were (1) oral communication skills, (2) interpersonal skills, and (3) teamwork skills (Collins, 1996). The employers

CONNECTING WITH STUDENTS: Best Practices
Strategies for Helping Students Transfer Information

also wanted students to be proficient in their field, have leadership abilities, have analytical skills, be flexible, and be able to work with computers. In addition to these skills, which remain important in more recent surveys of employers, problem solving, critical thinking, and decision making often rank highly (Hart, 2006; NACE, 2013, 2015, 2017, 2018). By thinking about and practicing the competencies that your students will need in the future and working with them to improve these skills, you will be guiding them for positive transfer.

2. *Give students many opportunities for real-world learning.* Too often, learning in schools has been artificial, with little consideration for transfer beyond the classroom or textbook. This will be less true for your students if you give them as many real-world problem-solving and thinking challenges as possible. You can bring the real world into your classroom by inviting people from varying walks of life to come and talk with your students. Also, technology can be used to lower barriers for community participation and include experts and guests from near and far. Or you can take your students to the real world by incorporating visits to museums, businesses, colleges, and so on in the curriculum. Technology also can be used for digital field trips. For example, the National Gallery of Art provides open digital access to more than 45,000 images (https://images.nga.gov/en/page/show_home_page.html). In *Through the Eyes of Teachers,* you can read about Chris Laster, an outstanding teacher who instructs students in ways that help them transfer what they learn to the world outside the classroom.

Chris Laster working with a student on the flight deck of the space shuttle that Laster and other teachers built.
Michael A. Schwarz

THROUGH THE EYES OF TEACHERS
Bringing Science Alive and Connecting Students to the Community

Chris Laster's students say that he brings science alive. Among Laster's innovative real-world teaching strategies that help students transfer their knowledge and understanding beyond the classroom are the following:

- **Science Blasters.** Students write, direct, and produce short videos for the school's closed-circuit TV station.
- **Sci-Tech Safari.** Over the summer, students get hands-on experience on field trips to intriguing places such as the Okefenokee Swamp.
- **Intrepid.** Students engage in vigorous training to prepare for a simulated 27-hour space mission aboard a realistic-looking space shuttle built by Laster and other teachers with parts from local businesses and a nearby air force base (Copeland, 2003).

3. *Root concepts in applications.* The more you attempt to pour information into students' minds, the less likely it is that transfer will occur. When you present a concept, first define it (or get students to help you define it) and then ask students to generate examples. Challenge them to apply the concept to their personal lives or to other contexts.

4. *Teach for depth of understanding and meaning.* Teaching for understanding and meaning transfers more effectively than does teaching for the retention of facts. And students' understanding improves when they actively construct meaning and try to make sense out of material.

5. *Use prompts to encourage students to engage in self-explanation.* Researchers have found that generating explanations for oneself increases transfer. For example, one study revealed that encouraging third- to fifth-grade students engaging in math problem-solving exercises to explain how they arrived at their answers was linked with improved transfer to new types of math problems (Rittle-Johnson, 2006).

6. *Teach strategies that will generalize.* Transfer involves not only skills and knowledge but also strategies (Schunk, 2016). Too often students learn strategies but don't understand how to apply them in other contexts. They might not understand that the strategy is appropriate for other situations, might not know how to modify it for use in another context, or might not have the opportunity to apply it (Pressley, 2007).

One model for teaching strategies that will generalize consists of three phases for improving transfer (Phye & Sanders, 1994).

continued

CONNECTING WITH STUDENTS: Best Practices
Strategies for Helping Students Transfer Information

In an initial acquisition phase, students are given information about the importance of the strategy and how to use it as well as opportunities to rehearse and practice using it. In the second phase, called retention, students get more practice in using the strategy, and their recall of how to use the strategy is checked out. In the third phase, transfer, students are given new problems to solve. These problems require them to use the same strategy, but on the surface the new problems appear to be different.

> **Thinking Back/Thinking Forward**
> Teachers can engage in a number of strategies in helping students use more effective learning strategies. Connect to "The Information-Processing Approach."

Review, Reflect, and Practice

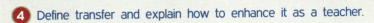

④ Define transfer and explain how to enhance it as a teacher.

REVIEW
- What is transfer? Why should teachers think about it?
- What are some different types of transfer?

REFLECT
- Are there experiences from your own formal education that don't seem to transfer to your life outside of school? What do you think is going on in such situations?

PRAXIS™ PRACTICE
1. Which of the following is *not* an example of transfer?
   a. Maria reads a novel written in the eighteenth century and uses the information she gleans about marriage customs to answer a question in history class.
   b. Frank studies hard and learns an algorithm in math class.
   c. Danielle learns about endangered amphibians in science class and uses the information to research a science-fair project.
   d. Emma learns to use a dictionary in language-arts class and uses it to look up a social studies term.
2. Which of the following is the best example of far transfer?
   a. Cory uses the techniques she was taught in statistics class to analyze the data for a research project.
   b. Debbie drives her sister's car with little thought because of her experience driving her own car.
   c. Jason uses the trouble-shooting process that he was taught with regard to computers to successfully diagnose the problem with his car.
   d. Mike is able to read the Spanish word for television (televisión) because it looks like the English word.

Please see answer key at end of book . . . .

Connecting with the Classroom: Crack the Case

The Statistics Test

Cassandra has a test in her math class this Friday. She has spent the last several evenings studying the statistical formulas for measures of central tendency and variability, as she knows they will be covered on the test. To do this she has quizzed herself repeatedly. In the beginning, she got the two concepts confused, but after repeated tries she can now recite the formulas for each without fail. She is certain that she will have no problems on the test.

When she receives her test on Friday, the first thing she does is write down all of the formulas before she can forget them, certain that this will ensure that she does well on the exam. After writing down the formulas, she begins reading the test. The first question gives a list of scores and asks for the mean, median, mode, variance, and standard deviation.

Cassandra anxiously looks at her list of formulas. She knows which formula goes with which measure—for instance, she knows that the formula for the mean is Sx/n. The problem is that she doesn't know what Sx means. She is reasonably sure that "$/n$" means she is to divide by n, but what is n? When looking at the rest of the formulas, she realizes that she has similar problems. She stares at the test in dismay. After all that studying and careful memorization, she can't complete a single problem on the test.

1. What are the issues in this case?
2. What went wrong for Cassandra?
3. What should she do differently if she wants to do better on her next test?
4. If you were the teacher of Cassandra's class, how would you help your students to prepare for this type of test?
5. Which of the following strategies is most likely to help Cassandra on her next statistics test?
   a. Concentrate on learning only one formula at a time.
   b. Forget about memorizing the formulas.
   c. Learn the definitions of *mean, median, mode, variance,* and *standard deviation*.
   d. Work practice problems of each type.
6. Which of the following teaching strategies would be most likely to help students to do well on this type of test?
   a. Make certain that students understand what the formulas mean by working many example problems in class.
   b. Quiz students on the definitions of *mean, median, mode, variance,* and *standard deviation*.
   c. Quiz students on the formulas.
   d. Teach students a mnemonic device to help them remember the formulas.

Connecting with Learning: Reach Your Learning Goals

1 CONCEPTUAL UNDERSTANDING: Discuss conceptual understanding and strategies for teaching concepts.

What Are Concepts?
- Concepts group objects, events, and characteristics on the basis of common properties. Concepts help us to simplify, summarize, and organize information. Concepts improve memory, communication, and time use.

Promoting Concept Formation
- In teaching concept formation to children, it is helpful to discuss with them the key features of concepts, definitions and examples of concepts (using the rule-example strategy), hierarchical categorization and concept maps, hypothesis testing, and prototype matching.

2 THINKING: Describe several types of thinking and ways that teachers can foster them.

What Is Thinking?
- Thinking involves manipulating and transforming information in memory. Types of thinking include forming concepts, reasoning, thinking critically, making decisions, thinking creatively, and solving problems.

Executive Function
- Executive function is an umbrella-like concept that involves a number of higher-level cognitive processes linked to the development of the brain's prefrontal cortex.
- Executive function involves managing one's thoughts to engage in goal-directed behavior and exercise self-control.
- In early childhood, executive function includes advances in cognitive inhibition, cognitive flexibility, goal-setting, and delay of gratification. In middle and late childhood, advances occur in self-control/inhibition, working memory, and flexibility. In adolescence, cognitive control increases.
- Among the factors that contribute to executive function are a number of diverse activities, including computerized training, aerobic exercise, scaffolding, mindfulness, parenting, and teaching.

continued

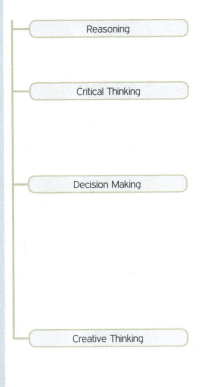

- Inductive reasoning involves reasoning from the specific to the general. Analogies draw on inductive reasoning. Deductive reasoning is reasoning from the general to the specific. Both inductive and deductive reasoning improve during adolescence.

- Critical thinking involves thinking reflectively and productively and evaluating evidence. Mindfulness is a concept that reflects critical thinking. Brooks and Brooks argue that too few schools teach students to think critically and deeply. They stress that too often schools give students a correct answer instead of encouraging them to expand their thinking by coming up with new ideas.

- Decision making is thinking that involves evaluating alternatives and making choices among them. One type of decision making involves weighing the costs and benefits of various outcomes. Numerous biases (confirmation bias, belief perseverance, overconfidence bias, and hindsight bias) can interfere with good decision making.
- Older adolescents make better decisions than younger adolescents, who in turn are better at this than children are. Adolescents often make better decisions when they are calm than when they are emotionally aroused. Social contexts, especially the presence of peers, influence adolescent decision making. The dual process model has been advanced to explain the nature of adolescent decision making.

- Creativity is the ability to think about something in novel and interesting ways and come up with unique solutions to problems.
- Guilford distinguished between convergent thinking (which produces one correct answer and is characteristic of the type of thinking required on conventional intelligence tests) and divergent thinking (which produces many answers to the same question and is characteristic of creativity).
- Although most creative students are quite intelligent, the reverse is not necessarily true.
- The creative process often involves five steps, although they don't always follow the same sequence.
- Here are some ways teachers can foster creativity in students: encourage creative thinking on a group and individual basis, provide environments that stimulate creativity, don't overcontrol students, encourage internal motivation, foster flexible thinking, build students' self-confidence, encourage students to take risks, guide students to be persistent and delay gratification, and introduce students to creative people.

3 PROBLEM SOLVING: Take a systematic approach to problem solving.

- Problem solving involves finding an appropriate way to attain a goal. Four steps in problem solving are (1) finding and framing problems; (2) developing good problem-solving strategies (such as using subgoaling, heuristics, algorithms, and means-end analysis); (3) evaluating solutions; and (4) rethinking and redefining problems and solutions over time.

- Obstacles to solving problems include fixedness (functional fixedness and mental set), lack of motivation and persistence, and not controlling one's emotions.

- Developmental changes in problem solving occur. Accumulated knowledge and effective use of strategies improve older children's and adolescents' problem-solving ability.

- Problem-based learning emphasizes solving authentic problems like those that occur in daily life. In project-based learning, students work on real, meaningful problems and create tangible products.

④ TRANSFER: Define transfer and explain how to enhance it as a teacher.

What Is Transfer?
- Transfer occurs when a person applies previous experiences and knowledge to learning or problem solving in a new situation. Students especially benefit when they can apply what they learn in the classroom to situations in their lives outside of the classroom.

Types of Transfer
- Types of transfer include near and far and low-road and high-road. Near transfer occurs when situations are similar; far transfer occurs when situations are very different. Low-road transfer occurs when previous learning automatically transfers to another situation. High-road transfer is conscious and effortful. High-road transfer can be subdivided into forward-reaching and backward-reaching transfer.
- Cultural practices also are an important consideration in transfer.

KEY TERMS

algorithms 320
analogy 304
backward-reaching transfer 327
belief perseverance 311
concept map 298
concepts 296
confirmation bias 311
convergent thinking 313
creativity 313
critical thinking 305
decision making 310
deductive reasoning 305
divergent thinking 313
dual-process model 312
executive function 302
far transfer 326
fixation 321
forward-reaching transfer 327
heuristics 320
high-road transfer 327
hindsight bias 311
inductive reasoning 304
low-road transfer 326
means-end analysis 320
mental set 321
mindfulness 305
near transfer 326
overconfidence bias 311
problem solving 319
problem-based learning 322
project-based learning 322
prototype matching 299
subgoaling 320
thinking 302
transfer 326

PORTFOLIO ACTIVITIES

Now that you have a good understanding of this chapter, complete these exercises to expand your thinking.

Independent Reflection

1. **Evaluate Your Decision-Making Skills.** Reflect on the ways that you make decisions. Are you able to make good-quality decisions regardless of opposition from others? Discuss to what extent your decisions are influenced by confirmation bias, belief perseverance, overconfidence bias, and hindsight bias. What can you do to strengthen your decision-making skills? (INTASC: Principles *8, 9*)

Research/Field Experience

2. **Creativity Research.** Read work by one of the leading researchers in the field of creativity, such as Teresa Amabile or Mark Runco. What are the key findings about creativity discussed in the research? To what extent can this research be implemented in the classroom? (INTASC: Principles *8, 9*)

Collaborative Work

3. **Create a Problem-Based Learning Project.** Thinking creatively, get together with three or four other students in the class and devise a problem-solving adventure in a subject area other than math, such as science, social science, or literature. Write it down. (INTASC: Principles *4, 8*)

chapter 10
SOCIAL CONSTRUCTIVIST APPROACHES

chapter outline

① Social Constructivist Approaches to Teaching

Learning Goal 1 Compare the social constructivist approach with other constructivist approaches.

Social Constructivism in the Broader Constructivist Context

Situated Cognition

② Teachers and Peers as Joint Contributors to Students' Learning

Learning Goal 2 Explain how teachers and peers can jointly contribute to children's learning.

Scaffolding

Cognitive Apprenticeship

Tutoring

Cooperative Learning

③ Structuring Small-Group Work

Learning Goal 3 Discuss effective decisions in structuring small-group work.

Composing the Group

Team-Building Skills

Structuring Small-Group Interaction

The human being is by nature a social animal.
—Aristotle
Greek Philosopher, 4th Century B.C.

Kali Nine LLC/iStock/Getty Images

Connecting with Teachers   Chuck Rawls

Chuck Rawls teaches language arts at Appling Middle School in Macon, Georgia. He provides this teaching story about peer tutoring, a social constructivist approach to instruction:

> I was tricked into trying something different my first year of teaching. It was peer teaching in the guise of a schoolwide activity known as "Switch Day." This consists of having selected students switch places with members of the faculty and staff. Each student who wants to switch is required to choose a faculty or staff member and then write an essay explaining why he or she wants to switch with that particular person. To my surprise, Chris wrote a very good essay and was selected to switch with me.
>
> It worked wonderfully. Chris delivered the lesson very professionally, and the students were engaged because it was something new and different. It was a riot to watch because Chris, both intentionally and unintentionally, used many of my pet phrases and mannerisms. He really did know his stuff, though, and demonstrated this as he helped students with their seatwork.
>
> As the saying goes, "I didn't know he had it in him." Chris became my resident expert on subject-verb agreement, as that was the topic of the lesson and the students remembered what he taught them. I learned two lessons that day: (1) don't be afraid to try something different, and (2) peer tutoring works. However, it has to be the right student teaching the right material in the right setting.

Preview

Children do some of their thinking by themselves, but because we are social beings, as Chuck Rawls' teaching story indicates, effective learning can also take place when children collaborate. Because of emphasis in the U.S. on the individual rather than the group, collaborative thinking has only recently emerged as an important theme in American education. This chapter focuses on the collaborative thinking advocated by social constructivist approaches.

1 SOCIAL CONSTRUCTIVIST APPROACHES TO TEACHING

LG 1 Compare the social constructivist approach with other constructivist approaches.

The social constructivist approaches involve a number of innovations in classroom learning. Before we study these innovations, let's first consolidate our knowledge about various constructivist perspectives and where the social constructivist approaches fit within the overall constructivist framework.

SOCIAL CONSTRUCTIVISM IN THE BROADER CONSTRUCTIVIST CONTEXT

Recall that *constructivism* emphasizes how individuals actively construct knowledge and understanding. Early in this text, we described Piaget's and Vygotsky's theories of development, both of which are constructivist. In other chapters, our main focus was on the information-processing approaches to learning, which included some ideas about how the individual child uses information-processing skills to think in constructivist ways. According to all of these constructivist approaches, students author their own knowledge.

In general, a **social constructivist approach** emphasizes the social contexts of learning and says that knowledge is mutually built and constructed. Involvement with others creates opportunities for students to evaluate and refine their understanding as they are exposed to the thinking of others and as they participate in creating shared understanding (Gauvain, 2016; Hmelo-Silver & Chinn, 2016; Sinha et al.,

> **Thinking Back/Thinking Forward**
>
> One of the main debates about educating students focuses on whether a constructivist or direct instruction approach is the better strategy. Connect with "Educational Psychology: A Tool for Effective Teaching" and "Planning, Instruction, and Technology."

social constructivist approach Emphasizes the social contexts of learning and that knowledge is mutually built and constructed; Vygotsky's theory exemplifies this approach.

What is the social constructivist approach to education?
Monkeybusinessimages/iStock/Getty Images

2015). In this way, experiences in social contexts provide an important mechanism for the development of students' thinking (Adams, 2015).

Vygotsky's social constructivist theory is especially relevant for the current chapter. Vygotsky's model is a social child embedded in a sociohistorical context. Moving from Piaget to Vygotsky, the conceptual shift is from the individual to collaboration, social interaction, and sociocultural activity. In Piaget's cognitive constructivist approach, students construct knowledge by transforming, organizing, and reorganizing previous knowledge and information. Vygotsky's social constructivist approach emphasizes that students construct knowledge through social interactions with others. The content of this knowledge is influenced by the culture in which the student lives, which includes language, beliefs, and skills (Yasnitsky & Van der Veer, 2016).

Piaget emphasized that teachers should provide support for students to explore and develop understanding. Vygotsky emphasized that teachers should create many opportunities for students to learn by co-constructing knowledge along with the teacher and with peers (Gauvain, 2016). In both Piaget's and Vygotsky's models, teachers serve as facilitators and guides rather than as directors and molders of children's learning.

Notice that we speak about emphasis rather than a clear-cut distinction. Often there are no clear-cut distinctions between social constructivist and other constructivist approaches. For example, when teachers serve as guides for students in discovering knowledge, there are social dimensions to the construction. And the same is true for processing information. If a teacher creates a brainstorming session for students to come up with good memory strategies, social interaction is clearly involved.

Thinking Back/Thinking Forward

Teachers can use a number of strategies linked to Vygotsky's theory in educating students. Connect to "Cognitive and Language Development."

Some sociocultural approaches, such as Vygotsky's, emphasize the importance of culture in learning—for example, culture can determine what skills are important (such as computer skills, communication skills, and teamwork skills) (Gauvain, 2016). Other approaches focus more exclusively on the immediate social circumstances of the classroom, as when students collaborate to solve a problem.

In one study of collaborative learning, pairs of children from two U.S. public schools worked together (Matusov et al., 2001). One member of each pair was from a traditional school that provided only occasional opportunities for children to work together as they learned. The other member of the pair was from a school that emphasized collaboration throughout the school day. The children with the collaborative schooling background more often built on the partner's ideas in a collaborative way than the children with traditional schooling experience. The traditional school children predominantly used a "quizzing" form of guidance based on asking known-answer questions and withholding information to test the partner's understanding. Collaborative learning often works best in classrooms with well-specified learning goals.

RESEARCH

TECHNOLOGY

An increasing number of efforts are being made to connect collaborative learning and technology in the classroom (Huang, 2015; Wardlow & Harm, 2015). For example, one approach, Computer-Supported Collaborative Learning (CSCL), attempts to increase peer interaction and joint construction of knowledge through technology (Howland et al., 2015; Jeong & Hmelo-Silver, 2016; Xiong et al., 2015).

SITUATED COGNITION

Situated cognition is an important assumption in the social constructivist approaches. It refers to the idea that thinking is located (situated) in social and physical contexts, not within an individual's mind. In other words, knowledge is embedded in, and connected to, the context in which the knowledge developed (Gomez & Lee, 2015; Malinin, 2016). If this is so, it makes sense to create learning situations that are as close to real-world circumstances as possible. For example, to expand students' knowledge and understanding of volcanoes, some students are placed in the role of scientists studying an active volcano, while other students are given the task of reporting what to expect to an emergency evacuation team (PSU, 2006). Using Internet resources, the "scientist" students examine news stories about active volcanos; the "evacuation team" students search for information about the impact that volcanos have on inhabitants and how people can be removed from the danger of an erupting volcano. Our discussion of problem-based learning and project-based learning in the chapter on complex cognitive processes demonstrated a similar emphasis on situated cognition.

TECHNOLOGY

> **Thinking Back/Thinking Forward**
>
> Problem-based learning emphasizes solving authentic problems like those that occur in everyday life. Project-based learning involves students working on real, meaningful problems and creating tangible products. Connect to "Complex Cognitive Processes."

Review, Reflect, and Practice

 Compare the social constructivist approach with other constructivist approaches.

REVIEW
- Although they overlap, what is the basic difference between Piaget's and Vygotsky's approaches?
- What is situated cognition?

REFLECT
- From what you learned in the chapter on cognitive and language development, do you think you would feel more at home with Piaget or Vygotsky? How might that be reflected in your own approach to classroom teaching?

PRAXIS™ PRACTICE
1. Which of the following is an example of a social constructivist approach?
   a. In Mr. Hanratty's class, students work together on social studies projects.
   b. In Ms. Baker's class, students work independently to discover basic principles of science.
   c. In Ms. Rinosa's class, students are assigned one hour of homework a day.
   d. In Mr. Francois' class, students engage in silent reading of their self-chosen books.
2. Which of the following best reflects situated cognition?
   a. Students read a book about the role of a justice of the peace in the legal system.
   b. The teacher arranges for students to visit a local justice of the peace office, talk with the justice of the peace, and observe a justice of the peace session.
   c. Students are given an assignment to collaborate with each other and write a report on the role of the justice of the peace in the legal system.
   d. The teacher assigns students the task of searching for articles about what a justice of the peace does and to do an oral report on what they have found.

Please see answer key at end of book . . . .

situated cognition The idea that thinking is located (situated) in social and physical contexts, not within an individual's mind.

LG 2 Explain how teachers and peers can jointly contribute to children's learning.

2 TEACHERS AND PEERS AS JOINT CONTRIBUTORS TO STUDENTS' LEARNING

Scaffolding | Cognitive Apprenticeship | Tutoring | Cooperative Learning

Social constructivist approaches emphasize that teachers and peers can contribute to students' learning. Four tools for making this happen are scaffolding, cognitive apprenticeship, tutoring, and cooperative learning.

SCAFFOLDING

In the chapter on cognitive and language development we described *scaffolding* as the technique of changing the level of support over the course of a teaching session; a more-skilled person (teacher or more-advanced peer of the child) adjusts the amount of guidance to fit the student's current performance. When a student is learning a new task, the teacher might use direct instruction. As the student's competence increases, the teacher provides less guidance. Think of scaffolding in learning like the scaffolding used to build a bridge. The scaffolding provides support when needed, but it is gradually removed as the bridge approaches completion. Researchers have found that when teachers and peers use scaffolding in collaborative learning, students' learning benefits (Molenaar et al., 2014).

Look for opportunities to use scaffolding in the classroom. For instance, good tutoring involves scaffolding, as we will see shortly. Also, scaffolding is increasingly used when technology is involved in learning (Jung & Suzuki, 2015). Strive to offer just the right amount of assistance. Don't do for students what they can do for themselves. But do monitor their efforts and give them needed support and assistance. A good technology tool for creating personalized learning paths for students is available at Oppia.org. Teachers also can create adapted instruction through the use of Web pages and videos.

COGNITIVE APPRENTICESHIP

Developmental psychologist Barbara Rogoff (2003, 2015) stresses that an important tool of education is **cognitive apprenticeship**, a technique in which an expert stretches and supports a novice's understanding and use of a culture's skills. The term *apprenticeship* underscores the importance of active learning and highlights the situated nature of learning (Peters-Burton et al., 2015). In a cognitive apprenticeship, teachers often model strategies for students. Then, teachers or more-skilled peers support students' efforts at doing the task. Finally, they encourage students to continue their work independently.

To illustrate the importance of cognitive apprenticeships in learning, Rogoff describes the contrasting experiences of students from middle-income and poverty backgrounds. Many middle- and upper-income American parents involve their children in cognitive apprenticeships long before they go to kindergarten or elementary school. They read picture books with young children and bathe their children in verbal communication. In contrast, American parents living in poverty are less likely to engage their children in a cognitive apprenticeship that involves books, extensive verbal communication, and scaffolding (Bradley et al., 2001).

Cognitive apprenticeships are important in the classroom. Researchers have found that students' learning benefits from teachers who think of their relationship with a student as a cognitive apprenticeship, using scaffolding and guided participation to help the student learn (Grindstaff & Richmond, 2008).

> **Thinking Back/Thinking Forward**
> Scaffolding is closely linked to Vygotsky's concept of the zone of proximal development. Connect with "Cognitive and Language Development."

RESEARCH

cognitive apprenticeship A relationship in which an expert stretches and supports a novice's understanding and use of a culture's skills.

TUTORING

Tutoring is basically cognitive apprenticeship between an expert and a novice. Tutoring can take place between and adult and a child or between a more-skilled child and a less-skilled child. Individual tutoring is an effective strategy that benefits many students, especially those who are not doing well in a subject (Slavin et al., 2009).

Classroom Aides, Volunteers, and Mentors It is frustrating to find that some students need more individual help than you as their teacher can give them while still meeting the needs of the class as a whole. Classroom aides, volunteers, and mentors can help reduce some of this frustration. Monitor and evaluate your class for students who might benefit from one-on-one tutoring. Scour the community for individuals with skills in the areas in which these students need more individual attention than you are able to give. Some parents, college students, and retirees might be interested in filling your classroom tutoring needs.

Several individual tutoring programs have been developed. The Reading Recovery program offers daily half-hour one-on-one tutorial sessions for students who are having difficulty learning to read after one year of formal instruction (Serry et al., 2014). A recent analysis of the Reading Recovery program, with strict criteria for research support, in 147 schools revealed that Reading Recovery had positive outcomes on the general reading achievement of struggling first-grade readers (What Works Clearinghouse, 2014).

DEVELOPMENT

RESEARCH

Another program that uses tutoring is Success for All (SFA). Developed by Robert Slavin and his colleagues (1996; Slavin et al., 2009), this comprehensive program includes the following elements:

- *A systematic reading program* that emphasizes phonics, vocabulary development, and storytelling and retelling in small groups
- *A daily 90-minute reading period* with students in the first through third grades being regrouped into homogeneous cross-age ability groups
- *One-on-one tutoring in reading* by specially trained certified teachers who work individually with students who are reading below grade level
- *Assessments every eight weeks to* determine students' reading progress, adjust reading group placement, and assign tutoring if needed
- *Professional development for teachers and tutors,* which includes three days of in-service training and guidelines at the beginning of the school year, and follow-up training throughout the year
- *A family support team* designed to provide parenting education and support family involvement in the school

Participants in the Success for All middle school program. *What is the nature of the Success for All program?*
Success For All Foundation

In an earlier analysis, research indicated that Success for All had positive effects on students' alphabetic skills, such as phonological awareness (What Works Clearinghouse, 2009); however, a more recent analysis concluded that although there is strong evidence of a positive effect on alphabetics, the majority of the research conducted on Success for All did not meet rigorous scientific guidelines (What Works Clearinghouse, 2017).

RESEARCH

Mentors can play an important role in improving some students' learning (Weiler et al., 2016). Usually viewed as older and wiser, mentors guide, teach, and support younger individuals, who are sometimes called *mentees* or *protégés*.

The guidance is accomplished through demonstration, instruction, challenge, and encouragement on a more or less regular basis over an extended period of time. In the course of this process, the mentor and the young person develop a special bond of mutual commitment. In addition, the younger person's relationship to the mentor takes on an emotional character of respect, loyalty, and identification (Hamilton & Hamilton, 2004).

The majority of mentoring programs operate outside the school setting and include such organizations as Big Brothers and Big Sisters, the largest formal mentoring program in the United States, as well as Boys and Girls Clubs of America and

Thinking Back/Thinking Forward

Mentoring involves serving as a positive model for a student. There is a lack of male and minority role models and mentors in children's education. Connect to "Behavioral and Social Cognitive Approaches."

Mentoring provides students with role models and benefits students' academic achievement.

Jim West/Alamy Stock Photo

Thinking Back/Thinking Forward

Peers play an important role in many aspects of children's education. Connect to "Social Contexts and Socioemotional Development," "Planning, Instruction, and Technology," and "Motivation, Teaching, and Learning."

RESEARCH

Giving Back is a nonprofit organization that involves having individuals 50+ years of age serve as mentors for children to help them develop cognitive and interpersonal skills. Shown here is a mentor from Giving Back Mentoring working with a young girl to improve her cognitive skills.

Giving Back, Inc.

YMCA and YWCA. However, schools have been the location of an increasing number of mentoring efforts, both for students and for beginning teachers who are mentored by experienced teachers (What Works Clearinghouse, 2009). The mentor comes to the school and works with the student, in many cases for an hour each week. Schools can be helpful in identifying students who might benefit from mentoring. A good strategy is to select for mentoring students who are placed at risk for underachieving, as well as other students. Also, some mentoring relationships are more effective than others, and the matching of a student with a mentor requires careful selection and monitoring (Rhodes & Lowe, 2009).

Peer Tutors Fellow students also can be effective tutors (Clarke et al., 2015; Wilkinson & Gaffney, 2016). In peer tutoring, one student teaches another. In *cross-age peer tutoring,* the peer is older. In *same-age peer tutoring,* the peer is a classmate. Cross-age peer tutoring usually works better than same-age peer tutoring. An older peer is more likely to be skilled than a same-age peer, and being tutored by a same-age classmate is more likely to embarrass a student and lead to negative social comparison.

Peer tutoring engages students in active learning and allows the classroom teacher to guide and monitor student learning as she or he moves around the classroom. Researchers have found that peer tutoring often benefits students' achievement. In a recent study, peer tutoring improved the receptive language and print knowledge of English language learners (Xu, 2015). Also, a meta-analysis concluded that peer tutoring benefits students' achievement (Leung, 2015). In this meta-analysis, students in secondary schools improved the most, followed by college students, elementary school students, and kindergarten students.

In some instances, the tutoring benefits the tutor as well as the tutee, especially when the older tutor is a low-achieving student. Teaching something to someone else is one of the best ways to learn, although researchers have found that tutees' learning benefits more than tutors' learning (Roscoe & Chi, 2008).

In a study that won the American Educational Research Association's award for best research study, the effectiveness of a class-wide peer tutoring program in reading was evaluated for three learner types: low-achieving students with and without disabilities and average-achieving students (Fuchs et al., 1997). Twelve elementary and middle schools were randomly assigned to experimental (peer tutoring) and control (no peer tutoring) groups. The peer tutoring program was conducted in 35-minute sessions during regularly scheduled reading instruction three days a week. It lasted for 15 weeks. The training of peer tutors emphasized helping students get practice in reading aloud from narrative text, reviewing and sequencing information read, summarizing large amounts of reading material, stating main ideas, predicting and checking story outcomes, and using other reading strategies. Pretreatment and posttreatment reading achievement data were collected. Irrespective of the type of learner, students in the peer tutoring classrooms showed greater reading progress over the 15 weeks than their counterparts who did not receive peer tutoring.

Peer-Assisted Learning Strategies (PALS) The peer tutoring program used in the study just described is called Peer-Assisted Learning Strategies (PALS). PALS was created by the John F. Kennedy Center and the Department of Special Education at Peabody College at Vanderbilt University. In PALS, teachers identify which children require help on specific skills and who the most appropriate children are to help other children learn those skills. Using this information, teachers pair children in the class so that partners work simultaneously and productively on different activities that address the problems they are experiencing. Pairs are changed regularly so that as students work on a variety of skills, all students have the opportunity of being "coaches" and "players."

PALS is a 25- to 35-minute activity that is used two to four times a week. Typically it creates 13 to 15 pairs in a classroom. It has been designed for use in the areas of reading and mathematics for kindergarten through sixth grade. It is not designed to replace existing curricula.

In PALS Math, students work on a sheet of problems in a skill area, such as adding, subtracting, number concepts, or charts and graphs. PALS Math involves pairing students as a coach and a player. The coach uses a sheet with a series of questions designed to guide the player and provides feedback to the player. Students then exchange papers and score each other's practice sheets. Students earn points for cooperating and constructing good explanations during coaching and for doing problems correctly during practice. PALS Math and PALS Reading are effective in developing students' mathematical and reading skills (Fuchs et al., 2000; Mathes et al., 2001).

Students participating in the PALS program.
Larry Wilson, PALS Tutoring Program, Vanderbilt Kennedy Center, Vanderbilt University

The PALS program is highly effective with students placed at risk, especially students in the early elementary grades, ethnic minority students, and students in urban schools (Rohrbeck et al., 2003). In one study, the reading comprehension of third- through sixth-grade native Spanish-speaking English language learners improved more when they were taught in a PALS format than in other reading instruction formats (Saenz et al., 2005). An analysis involving strict criteria for evidence of research support revealed that PALS has potentially positive outcomes for alphabetic knowledge in beginning readers (What Works Clearinghouse, 2012).

RESEARCH

Two other peer tutoring programs are Reciprocal Peer Tutoring (RPT) and Class Wide Peer Tutoring (CWPT) (Ginsburg-Block, 2005). RPT was initially developed for use with low-achieving urban elementary school students and provides opportunities for students to alternate in tutor and tutee roles. CWPT includes tutor training, reciprocal teaching, and motivational strategies such as team competition (Bowman-Perrott, 2009). A study found that over a three-year period CWPT was effective in improving middle school students' grades on weekly quizzes (Kamps et al., 2008).

DIVERSITY

The Valued Youth program is another effective peer tutoring program. In 24 cities in the United States and Brazil, the Valued Youth program (now jointly sponsored by the Intercultural Development Research Association and Coca-Cola, and called the Coca-Cola Valued Youth program) gives secondary school students who are not achieving well or are at risk for school-related problems the responsibility of tutoring elementary school children (IDRA, 2013; Simons et al., 1991). The Valued Youth program began in 1984 and continues to expand today, with more than 650,000 students having participated in the program. The hope is that the tutoring experience will improve not only the achievement of the students being tutored but also the achievement of the tutors. Over the course of the program's existence, only 1 percent of students in the United States and 2.2 percent in Brazil who participated in the Valued Youth program dropped out of school (IDRA, 2013).

One of the Valued Youth program tutors said, "Tutoring makes me want to come to school because I have to come and teach the younger kids." He

Students in the Coca-Cola Valued Youth program. *What are some characteristics and outcomes of the program?*
IDRA Coca-Cola Valued Youth Program

also said that he did not miss many days of school, as he used to, because when he had been absent the elementary school children always asked him where he was and told him that they missed him. He said that he really liked the kids he taught, and that if he had not been a tutor he probably would have dropped out of school already.

TECHNOLOGY

Online Peer Tutoring Online peer tutoring is increasingly being used in elementary schools, secondary schools, and colleges. Online peer tutoring usually begins with the teacher engaging students in online peer tutoring. Then, as students gain more experience in working together online, some of the online tutoring activities are conducted by trained, knowledgeable students. Of course, as with face-to-face tutoring, students will need training and guidance to become successful collaborators and peer tutors. One program, Microsoft Peer Coaching, combines technology with peer coaching for teachers themselves (Barron et al., 2009). An important emphasis in the Microsoft program is having teachers coach other teachers in using technology to improve student learning. Also, any online video conferencing program (for example, Skype or Google Hangouts) can be used to facilitate online peer tutoring.

Several teachers recently were asked how they use peer tutors and mentors in their classrooms. Following are their responses.

EARLY CHILDHOOD We often have children lead various activities in the classroom—such as "show and tell"—giving them the opportunity to learn from each other.

—MISSY DANGLER, *Suburban Hills School*

ELEMENTARY SCHOOL: GRADES K–5 I use peer tutors in a variety of ways with my second-graders: "Buddy Readers" pairs strong readers with struggling readers; "Resident Experts" gives students showing full understanding of new skills in math, science, and social studies the opportunity to work with students who need extra help in these areas. In "Ask Three, Before Me," students who finish a writing task are expected to confer with three other students about their work (and make revisions as suggested) before sharing with me.

—ELIZABETH FRASCELLA, *Clinton Elementary School*

MIDDLE SCHOOL: GRADES 6–8 We first identify students who likely will be successful peer tutors and students who likely would benefit from having a tutor. We then have peer tutors go through a training session; without this training, tutoring is much less likely to be successful. Tutoring not only helps the student who needs extra help, but also benefits the tutor because one of the best ways to learn a concept is by teaching it to someone else.

—MARK FODNESS, *Bemidji Middle School*

HIGH SCHOOL: GRADES 9–12 Students in my food service class are mentors to first-graders at the elementary school next door. My students do reading activities, including acting out and making "Stone Soup" with the younger children. While these activities help the first-graders, it also reinforces important social skills for my high school students.

—SANDY SWANSON, *Menomonee Falls High School*

COOPERATIVE LEARNING

cooperative learning Learning that occurs when students work in small groups to help each other learn.

Cooperative learning occurs when students work in small groups to help each other learn. Cooperative learning groups vary in size, although four is a typical number of

CONNECTING WITH STUDENTS: Best Practices
Best Practices and Strategies for Using Peer Tutoring

Here are some suggestions for how to best use peer tutoring (Goodlad & Hirst, 1989; Jenkins & Jenkins, 1987):

1. *Spend time training tutors.* For peer tutoring to be successful, you will have to spend some time training the tutors. To get peer tutors started off right, discuss competent peer tutoring strategies. Demonstrate how scaffolding works. Give the tutors clear, organized instructions and invite them to ask questions about their assignments. Divide the group of peer tutors into pairs and let them practice what you have just demonstrated. Let them alternately be tutor and tutee.

2. *Use cross-age tutoring rather than same-age tutoring when possible.* In Through the Eyes of Teachers you can read about the use of cross-age peer tutoring at a zoo.

3. *Let students participate in both tutor and tutee roles.* This helps students learn that they can both help and be helped. Pairing of best friends often is not a good strategy because they have trouble staying focused on the learning assignment.

THROUGH THE EYES OF TEACHERS
Cross-Age Peer Teaching at a Zoo

In Lincoln, Nebraska, several high school science teachers use the Folsom Children's Zoo and Botanical Gardens as a context for guiding students' learning. The science classes are taught in two trailers at the zoo. The teachers emphasize the partnership of students, teachers, zoo, and community. One highlight of the program is the "Bug Bash," when the high school students teach fourth-grade students about insects.

4. *Don't let tutors give tests to tutees.* This can undermine cooperation between the students.

5. *Don't overuse peer tutoring.* It is easy to fall into the trap of using high-achieving students as peer tutors too often. Be sure that these students get ample opportunities to participate in challenging intellectual tasks themselves.

6. *Let parents know that their child will be involved in peer tutoring.* Explain to them the advantages of this learning strategy and invite them to visit the classroom to observe how the peer tutoring works.

---

students. In some cases, cooperative learning is done in dyads (two students). When students are assigned to work in a cooperative group, the group usually stays together for weeks or months, but cooperative groups usually occupy only a portion of the student's school day or year. In a cooperative learning group, each student typically learns a part of a larger unit and then teaches that part to the group (Akcay, 2016; Jurkowski & Hanze, 2015). When students teach something to others, they tend to learn it more deeply.

Research on Cooperative Learning Researchers have found that cooperative learning can be an effective strategy for improving achievement (Han, 2015). In a recent meta-analysis of 26 studies, cooperative learning had a positive effect on math achievement and attitude toward math (Capar & Tarim, 2015). In a recent study of fifth-graders, the cooperative learning teaching method improved the achievement and satisfaction of students more than the lecture teaching method (Mohammadjani & Tonkaboni, 2015). And in another study, cooperative learning increased the vocabulary skills of fourth-grade students more than a traditional method of teaching (Bilen & Tavil, 2015).

RESEARCH

Two conditions that are important to implement in cooperative learning are (Slavin, 1995, 2015):

- *Group rewards are generated.* Some type of recognition or reward is given to the group so that the group members can sense that it is in their best interest to help each other learn.

- *Individuals are held accountable.* Some method of evaluating a student's individual contribution, such as an individual quiz or report, needs to be used. Without this individual accountability, some students might do some "social loafing" (let other students do their work), and some might be left out because others believe that they have little to contribute.

When the conditions of group rewards and individual accountability are met, cooperative learning improves achievement across different grades and in tasks that range from basic skills to problem solving (Johnson & Johnson, 2002).

RESEARCH

Motivation Increased motivation to learn is common in cooperative groups (Gambrari et al., 2015; Johnson et al., 2014). In one study, fifth- and sixth-grade Israeli students were given a choice of continuing to do schoolwork or going out to play (Sharan & Shaulov, 1990). Only when students were in cooperative groups were they likely to forgo going out to play. Positive peer interaction and positive feelings about making their own decisions were motivating factors behind students' choice to participate in the cooperative groups. In another study, high school students made greater gains and expressed more intrinsic motivation to learn algebraic concepts when they were in cooperative rather than individualistic learning contexts (Nichols & Miller, 1994).

Interdependence and Teaching One's Peers Cooperative learning also promotes increased interdependence and connection with other students (Johnson & Johnson, 2015; Johnson et al., 2014). In one study, fifth-graders were more likely to move to a correct strategy for solving decimal problems if their partners clearly explained their ideas and considered each other's proposals (Ellis et al., 1994).

Types of Tasks in Which Cooperative Learning Works Best Do some types of tasks work better in cooperative, collaborative efforts and others better on an individual basis? Researchers have found that cooperative learning implemented without rewards has little benefit on simple tasks such as rote learning, memorization, or basic mathematics but produces better results with more complex tasks (Sears, 2006).

Cooperative Learning Approaches A number of cooperative learning approaches have been developed. They include STAD (Student-Teams-Achievement Divisions), the jigsaw classroom (I and II), learning together, group investigation, and cooperative scripting. To read about these approaches, see Figure 1.

Creating a Cooperative Community The school community is made up of faculty, staff, students, parents, and people in the neighborhood. More broadly, the school community also includes central administrators, college admissions officers, and future employers. To create an effective learning community, David and Roger Johnson (2002, pp. 144–146) conclude that cooperation and positive interdependence needs to occur at a number of different levels.

- *Class cooperation.* There are many ways to create cooperation and interdependence for the whole class. Class goals can be generated and class rewards given. This can be accomplished by adding bonus points to all class members' academic scores when all class members attain a goal "or by giving nonacademic rewards, such as extra free time, extra recess time, stickers, food, T-shirts, or a class party." Classroom cooperation can be promoted by "putting teams in charge of daily class cleanup, running a class bank or business, or engaging in other activities that benefit the class as a whole. Classroom interdependence may also be structured through dividing resources, such as having the class publish a newsletter in which each cooperative group contributes one article . . . one class was studying geography." The ceiling was turned into a large world map. "The class was divided into eight cooperative groups. Each group was assigned a geographical location on which to do a report. The class then planned an itinerary for a trip to visit all eight places. Yarn was used to

STAD (Student-Teams-Achievement Divisions)

STAD involves team recognition and group responsibility for learning in mixed-ability groups (Slavin, 1995). Rewards are given to teams whose members improve the most over their past performances. Students are assigned to teams of four or five members. The teacher presents a lesson, usually over one or two class periods. Next, students study worksheets based on material presented by the teacher. Students monitor their team members' performance to ensure that all members have mastered their material.

Teams practice working on problems together and study together, but the members take quizzes individually. The resulting individual scores contribute to the team's overall score. An individual's contribution to the team score is based on that individual's improvement, not on an absolute score, which motivates students to work hard because each contribution counts. In some STAD classrooms, a weekly class newsletter is published that recognizes both team and individual performances.

The STAD approach has been used in a variety of subjects (including math, reading, and social studies) and with students at different grade levels. It is most effective for learning situations that involve well-defined objectives or problems with specific answers or solutions. These include math computation, language use, geography skills, and science facts.

The Jigsaw Classroom

In the chapter on sociocultural diversity, we described the jigsaw classroom, which involves having students from different cultural backgrounds cooperate by doing different parts of a project to reach a common goal. Here we elaborate on the concept.

Developed by Elliot Aronson and his colleagues (1978), *jigsaw I* is a co-operative learning approach in which six-member teams work on material that has been broken down into parts. Each team member is responsible for a part. Members of different teams who have studied the same part convene, discuss their part, and then return to their teams, where they take turns teaching their part to other team members.

Robert Slavin (1995) created *jigsaw II*, a modified version of *jigsaw I*. Whereas *jigsaw I* consists of teams of six, *jigsaw II* usually has teams of four or five. All team members study the entire lesson rather than one part, and individual scores are combined to form an overall team score, as in STAD. After they have studied the entire lesson, students become expert on one aspect of the lesson; then students with the same topics meet in expert groups to discuss them. Subsequently, they return to their teams and help other members of the team learn the material.

Learning Together

Created by David and Roger Johnson (1994), this approach has four components: (1) face-to-face interaction, (2) positive interdependence, (3) individual accountability, and (4) development of interpersonal group skills. Thus, in addition to Slavin's interest in achievement, the Johnsons' cooperative learning approach also focuses on socioemotional development and group interaction. In learning together, students work in four- or five-member heterogeneous groups on tasks with an emphasis on discussion and team building (Johnson & Johnson, 2009).

Group Investigation

Developed by Shlomo Sharan (1990; Sharan & Sharan, 1992), this approach involves a combination of independent learning and group work in two- to six-member groups, as well as a group reward for individual achievement. The teacher chooses a problem for the class to study, but students decide what they want to study in exploring the problem. The work is divided among the group's members, who work individually. Then the group gets together, integrating, summarizing, and presenting the findings as a group project. The teacher's role is to facilitate investigation and maintain cooperative effort. Students collaborate with the teacher to evaluate their effort. In Sharan's view, this is the way many real-world problems are solved in communities around the world.

Cooperative Scripting

Students work in reciprocal pairs, taking turns summarizing information and orally presenting it to each other (Dansereau, 1988; McDonald et al. 1985). One member of the pair presents the material. The other member listens, monitors the presentation for any mistakes, and gives feedback. Then the partner becomes the teacher and presents the next set of material while the first member listens and evaluates it.

FIGURE 1 COOPERATIVE LEARNING APPROACHES

mark their journey. As they arrived at each spot, the appropriate group presented its report" about the location.

- *Interclass cooperation.* An interdisciplinary team of teachers may organize their classes into a "neighborhood" or "school within a school" in which classes work together on joint projects.
- *School-wide cooperation.* Cooperation at the level of the entire school can be attained in a number of ways. "The school mission statement may articulate the mutual goals shared by all members of the school and be displayed on the

school walls" and highlighted on a school Web page. "Teachers can work in a variety of cooperative teams . . . and faculty/staff can meet weekly in teaching teams and/or study groups. . . . Teachers may be assigned to task forces to plan and implement solutions to school-wide issues. . . . Finally, school interdependence may be highlighted in a variety of school-wide activities, such as the weekly student-produced school news broadcast, . . . all-school projects, and regular school assemblies."

- *School-parent cooperation.* Cooperation is promoted between the school and parents "by involving parents in establishing mutual goals and strategic plans to attain the goals, . . . in sharing resources to help the school achieve its goals," and in creating activities that improve the likelihood that parents will develop a positive attitude toward the school.

- *School-neighborhood cooperation.* If the school is embedded in a neighborhood, a positive interdependence between the school and the neighborhood can benefit both. The school's mission "can be supported by neighborhood merchants who provide resources and financing for various events. Classes can perform neighborhood service projects, such as cleaning up a park."

Evaluating Cooperative Learning Among the positive aspects of cooperative learning are increased interdependence and interaction with other students, enhanced motivation to learn, and improved learning by teaching material to others (Johnson & Johnson, 2015; Slavin, 2015). The possible drawbacks of cooperative learning are that some students prefer to work alone; low-achieving students may slow down the progress of high-achieving students; a few students may do most or all of the cognitive work while others do little (called "social loafing"); some students may become distracted from the group's task because they enjoy socializing; and many students lack the skills needed to collaborate effectively with others, engage in productive discussions, and explain their ideas or evaluate others' ideas effectively (Blumenfeld et al., 2006). Teachers who implement cooperative learning in their classrooms need to be attentive to these drawbacks and work to reduce them.

How do teachers use cooperative learning in their classrooms? Following are their responses.

EARLY CHILDHOOD We often have our preschoolers work together by creating art projects or by cooking together. In these tasks, children are assigned different responsibilities and learn how to work together to reach a common goal.

—Missy Dangler, *Suburban Hills School*

ELEMENTARY SCHOOL: GRADES K-5 I use base groups with learning partners on an ongoing basis in my classroom. These groups consist of four children who have established a feeling of trust with each other, work well together, and are balanced by gender, ability, and interest. The idea of learning partners is introduced as struggling readers are placed in these groups with students who are able to be supportive readers and empathetic to their classmates' needs.

—Elizabeth Frascella, *Clinton Elementary School*

MIDDLE SCHOOL: GRADES 6-8 The best group projects have a role for every participant; they all need to feel like they bring something to the table. I develop group projects that require participants to read, do artwork, think creatively, speak in public, and so on. By including these skills, group members should be able to express their knowledge in a way that meets their style of learning.

—Mark Fodness, *Bemidji Middle School*

HIGH SCHOOL: GRADES 9–12 I have learned that it is better not to have groups in which students select who will be included. Instead, I use a deck of cards for random groups and change them for each project. Also, many students have had experiences with cooperative learning—and unfortunately some have learned to sit back and let others in the group do all the work. Teachers need to monitor the groups to make sure all students make an effort to contribute in the group.

—SANDY SWANSON, *Menomonee Falls High School*

Review, Reflect, and Practice

 Explain how teachers and peers can jointly contribute to children's learning.

REVIEW
- What is scaffolding?
- What is a cognitive apprenticeship?
- Is tutoring effective? What are some alternative sources of tutors?
- What is cooperative learning and how might it benefit students? What are some ways to structure it?

REFLECT
- How would you handle the situation if parents became angry that, because of time allotted to cooperative learning, their children were being allowed less time to learn on an individual basis?

PRAXIS™ PRACTICE
1. Which of the following is the best example of scaffolding?
   a. Steve gives his friend Vlade the answers to today's homework.
   b. Steve helps his friend Vlade complete today's homework by giving him the least amount of assistance he needs for each question.
   c. Steve helps his friend Vlade complete today's homework by giving him hints to each answer.
   d. Steve tells his friend Vlade that he has to do his homework on his own.
2. Which of the following is an example of a cognitive apprenticeship?
   a. Ms. Notwitzki asks her students lots of questions. If a student does not know the answer to a question, she moves on to another student because she does not want her students to be embarrassed.
   b. Ms. Edgar pays attention to both the verbal and nonverbal cues her students give her regarding their understanding of her lessons. If she asks a student a question, she can determine if the student is thinking or confused. She often gives her students hints to help them answer.
   c. Ms. Lindell asks her students lots of questions. If a student does not respond immediately to her query, she gives the student the correct answer.
   d. Ms. Samuel lectures her class and they take notes. She answers any questions that they have at the end of the lesson.
3. Which teacher is using peer tutoring in the most positive way for both the tutor and the student?
   a. Ms. Gasol uses sixth-grade students to tutor her third-grade students in math for 30 minutes, four times each week. She gives each tutor explicit instructions.
   b. Ms. Mathews uses the buddy system in her class. Children choose who they would like to tutor them and what they would like to learn. Generally, they pick a close friend.

continued

Review, Reflect, and Practice

c. Ms. Rankowski selects lower-achieving students from the higher grades to come to her class at least once per week to work with her students. She generally has them do things such as administer spelling tests.
d. Ms. Taylor likes to use peer tutoring with her students, especially in math. She has found that often other students can explain things to her students more easily than she can. Therefore, she uses more advanced students in her class to teach those who are struggling with math concepts.

4. Mr. Kotter has assigned the students to work cooperatively on a project about the Civil War. He puts the students into heterogeneous groups of four and gives each group the project guidelines. They are to turn in one project on which they will receive a group grade. He is surprised when some students contribute little to their group's effort. What is Mr. Kotter doing *wrong*?
   a. Mr. Kotter did not include any individual accountability in his assessment.
   b. Mr. Kotter should not give the students a group grade.
   c. Mr. Kotter should not have used heterogeneous groups.
   d. Mr. Kotter should not use cooperative learning in history.

Please see answer key at end of book . . . .

LG 3 Discuss effective decisions in structuring small-group work.

3 STRUCTURING SMALL-GROUP WORK

Composing the Group · Team-Building Skills · Structuring Small-Group Interaction

We have seen that group work has many benefits for students. It requires careful planning on the teacher's part, however. When you structure students' work in small groups, you have to make decisions about how to compose the group, build team skills, and structure group interaction.

COMPOSING THE GROUP

Teachers often ask how they should assign students to small groups in their class. The cooperative learning approaches featured in Figure 1 generally recommend heterogeneous groups with diversity in ability, ethnic background, socioeconomic status, and gender. The reasoning behind heterogeneous grouping is that it maximizes opportunities for peer tutoring and support, improves cross-gender and cross-ethnic relations, and ensures that each group has at least one student who can do the work.

Heterogeneous Ability One of the main reasons for using heterogeneous ability groups is that they benefit low-ability students, who can learn from higher-ability students. However, some critics argue that such heterogeneous groupings hold back high-ability students. In most studies, though, high-achieving students perform equally well on achievement tests after working in heterogeneous groups or homogeneous groups (e.g., Hooper et al., 1989; Saleh et al., 2005). In heterogeneous groups, high-ability students often assume the role of "teacher" and explain concepts to other students. In homogeneous groups, high-ability students are less likely to assume this teaching role.

One problem with heterogeneous groups is that when high-ability, low-ability, and medium-ability students are included, the medium-ability students get left out to some extent; high-ability and low-ability students form teacher-student relationships, excluding medium-ability students from group interaction. Medium-ability students might perform better in groups where most or all of the students have medium abilities.

Ethnic, Socioeconomic, and Gender Heterogeneity One of the initial reasons that cooperative learning groups were formed was to improve interpersonal relations among students from different ethnic and socioeconomic backgrounds. The hope was that interaction under conditions of equal status in cooperative groups would reduce prejudice. However, getting students to interact on the basis of equal status has been more difficult than initially envisioned.

DIVERSITY

When forming ethnically and socioeconomically heterogeneous groups, it is important to pay attention to a group's composition. One recommendation is to not make the composition too obvious. Thus, you might vary different social characteristics (ethnicity, socioeconomic status, and gender) simultaneously, such as grouping together a middle-income African American female, a non-Latinx White male from a low-income family, and so on. In this way, for example, the White males would not all be from high-income families. Another recommendation is to avoid forming groups that have only one minority student, if at all possible; this avoids calling attention to the student's "solo status."

In mixed-gender groups, males tend to be more active and dominant. Thus, when mixing females and males, an important task for teachers is to encourage girls to speak up and boys to allow girls to express their opinions and contribute to the group's functioning. A general strategy is to have an equal number of girls and boys.

TEAM-BUILDING SKILLS

Good cooperative learning in the classroom requires that time be spent on team-building skills. This involves thinking about how to start team building at the beginning of the school year, helping students become better listeners, giving students practice in contributing to a team product, getting students to discuss the value of a team leader, and working with team leaders to help them deal with problem situations.

STRUCTURING SMALL-GROUP INTERACTION

One way to facilitate students' work in small groups is to assign students different roles. For example, consider these roles that students can assume in a group (Kagan, 1992):

- Encourager—brings out reluctant students and is a motivator
- Gatekeeper—equalizes participation of students in the group
- Coach—helps with academic content
- Checker—makes sure the group understands the material
- Taskmaster—keeps the group on task
- Recorder—writes down ideas and decisions
- Quiet captain—monitors the group's noise level
- Materials monitor—obtains and returns supplies

Such roles help groups to function more smoothly and give all members of the group a sense of importance. Note that although we just described nine different roles that can be played in groups, most experts, as we noted earlier, recommend that groups not exceed five or six members to function effectively. Some members can fill multiple roles, and all roles do not always have to be filled.

Another way roles can be specialized is to designate some students as "summarizers" and others as "listeners." Researchers have consistently found that summarizing benefits learning more than listening, so if these roles are used, all members should get opportunities to be summarizers (Dansereau, 1988).

CONNECTING WITH STUDENTS: Best Practices
Strategies for Developing Students' Team-Building Skills

Here are some guidelines for helping students develop team-building skills (Aronson & Patnoe, 1997):

1. *Don't begin the year with cooperative learning on a difficult task.* Teachers report that academic cooperative learning often works best when students have previously worked together on team-building exercises. A short period each day for several weeks is usually adequate for this team building. Many students have not had much experience in working in cooperative groups, so having them engage in team-building exercises helps them to learn how to interact with each other effectively before they begin to work on a difficult group project.

2. *Do team building at the level of the cooperative group (two to six students) rather than at the level of the entire class.* Some students on the team will be more assertive; others will be more passive. The team-building goal is to give all members some experience in being valuable team members, as well as to get them to learn that being cooperative works more effectively than being competitive.

3. *In team building, work with students to help them become better listeners.* Ask students to introduce themselves by name all at the same time to help them see that they have to take turns and listen to each other instead of hogging a conversation. You also can ask students to come up with behavioral descriptions of how they can show others that they are listening. These might include looking directly at the speaker, rephrasing what she just said, summarizing her statement, and so on.

4. *Give students some practice in contributing to a common product as part of team building.* Ask each student to participate in drawing a group picture by passing paper and pen from student to student. Each student's task is to add something to the picture as it circulates several times through the team. When the picture is finished, discuss each student's contribution to the team. Students will sense that the product is not complete unless each member's contribution is recognized. In *Through the Eyes of Teachers,* you can read about how a ninth-grade history teacher uses this strategy effectively.

THROUGH THE EYES OF TEACHERS
An Eye-Level Meeting of the Minds

Jimmy Furlow has groups of students summarize textbook sections and put them on transparencies to help the entire class prepare for a test. Furlow lost both legs in Vietnam but he rarely stays in one place, moving his wheelchair around the room and communicating with students at eye level. When the class completes their discussion of all the points on the overhead, Furlow edits their work to demonstrate concise, clear writing and help students zero in on an important point (Marklein, 1998).

Ninth-grade history teacher Jimmy Furlow converses with a student in his class.
Todd Lillard

Jimmy Furlow

5. *During team building, you may want to discuss the value of having a group leader.* You can ask students to discuss the specific ways a leader should function to maximize the group's performance. Their brainstorming might come up with such characteristics as "helps get the group organized," "keeps the group on task," "serves as liaison between the teacher and the group," "shows enthusiasm," "is patient and polite," and "helps the group deal with disagreements and conflicts." The teacher may select the group leader or students may be asked to elect one.

6. *Work with team leaders to help them deal with problem situations.* For example, some members might rarely talk, one member might dominate the group, members might call each other names, some members might refuse to work, one member might want to work alone, and everyone might talk at once. You can get group leaders together and get them to role-play such situations and discuss effective strategies for handling the problem situation.

To evaluate your attitudes about social constructivist approaches and whether you are likely to use such strategies when you teach, complete Self-Assessment 1.

SELF-ASSESSMENT 1
Evaluating My Social Constructivist Experiences

What experiences have you already had with social constructivist thinking and learning? You may have had such experiences in school or in other settings. For each of these settings that you have experienced, record at least one instance in which you can look back and see social constructivist principles at work.

1. Your family:
   _____
   _____

2. A club or program such as the Scouts:
   _____
   _____

3. Your K–12 school experience:
   _____
   _____

4. College:
   _____
   _____

How do those experiences shape your judgment regarding these ideas for classroom teaching?

1. That thinking should be viewed as located (situated) in social and physical contexts, not only within an individual's mind:
   _____
   _____

2. Vygotsky's sociocultural cognitive theory:
   _____
   _____

3. Scaffolding:
   _____
   _____

4. Peer tutoring:
   _____
   _____

5. Cooperative learning:
   _____
   _____

6. Small-group work:
   _____
   _____

Review, Reflect, and Practice

 Discuss effective decisions in structuring small-group work.

REVIEW
- What are some important considerations in placing students in small groups?
- What can teachers do to build team skills within groups?
- What types of role assignments can improve a group's structure?

REFLECT
- Suppose you and five other students have decided to form a group to study for a final exam in educational psychology. How would you structure the group? What roles would you want the group to assign?

PRAXIS™ PRACTICE
1. Which of the following represents the best practice for forming work groups?
   a. one non-Latina White, high-achieving girl; three African American, middle-achieving boys
   b. one African American, high-achieving boy; two non-Latina White, middle-achieving girls; one Asian American, low-achieving boy
   c. two Asian American, high-achieving boys; two non-Latino White, low-achieving boys
   d. two African American, high-achieving girls; one African American, middle-achieving boy; one African American, low-achieving girl

2. Mr. Fandango decides to work on team building at the beginning of the school year. To this end, he takes his entire class outside and has them create a human knot. They then must work together to untie the "knot." Several students become frustrated and angry during the activity. Mr. Fandango intervenes by encouraging the students to elect a leader and to listen to each other. According to *Best Practices: "Strategies for Developing Students' Team-Building Skills,"* what did Mr. Fandango do *incorrectly*?
   a. He did not emphasize the importance of listening skills.
   b. He did not have enough students in the group.
   c. He did not use heterogeneous grouping.
   d. He started with the whole class and a difficult task.

3. George, John, Paul, Cassie, and Mackenzie are working together on a group project involving the Civil War. George is the resident expert on the Civil War. As the group works on the project, George answers the other students' questions. John volunteers to get all the supplies that the group needs. The project goes smoothly, and each of the students participates, because Cassie reminds them that everyone's contribution is valuable. During one group work session, the group starts discussing last weekend's football game. Paul says, "Hey, guys, we're supposed to be working on this project, you know." After this, the group gets back on task. They become so engrossed in their discussion that they become rather noisy. At this point, Mackenzie reminds her peers to quiet down. Which student took the gatekeeper role?
   a. George
   b. John
   c. Mackenzie
   d. Cassie

Please see answer key at end of book . . . .

Connecting with the Classroom: Crack the Case

The Social Constructivist Classroom

Mariana is a new second-grade teacher who is full of enthusiasm about her job. She believes that students should be very active in constructing their own knowledge and that they should work together in doing this. To that end, she has decided that she wants her classroom to be a social constructivist classroom and has made some decisions about some things she wants to do this year with her students.

First, she knows that she will have to provide students with scaffolding when material is new and gradually adjust the amount of help her students receive. She wants to use peer tutoring for this in her class because she believes that children can often learn more from each other than they can from an adult. So she sets up a system in which the more-advanced students in her class help those who are less advanced.

Mariana also likes the idea of cooperative learning. She creates student groups so that they are heterogeneous with regard to ability, gender, ethnicity, and SES. She then assigns roles to each student in a group. Sometimes these roles are things such as coach, encourager, checker, taskmaster, recorder, and materials monitor. She uses this approach for many content areas. Sometimes she uses a jigsaw approach in which each student is responsible for becoming an expert in a particular area and then sharing that expertise with his or her group members. She uses this approach in science and in social studies.

In math, Mariana feels very fortunate that her school has adopted the Everyday Mathematics curriculum. This program makes connections with the real world that she thinks is so important in math instruction. Group work is also stressed.

Mariana hopes that her students and their parents will share her excitement as they "all learn together." However, she soon becomes disappointed. When she groups students, she hears groans of "Not again." "Why do I have to work with her? She doesn't know anything." "He's too bossy." "I always have to be with him, and then I end up doing everything." "She never lets me do anything but sit there and watch." Parents have gotten in on the act too. She has received calls and letters from parents who don't understand what she's trying to do. They all seem concerned about test scores and grades rather than what their children are learning together. One parent asked that her child no longer be grouped with another child who is "holding back" her child's learning.

1. What are the issues in this case?
2. What do you think Mariana did incorrectly?
3. What should she do now to recover her constructivist classroom?
4. How can she elicit the cooperation of the parents?
5. Which of the following suggestions would you make to Mariana regarding peer tutoring?
    a. Allow children to choose their partners.
    b. Insist that the more-advanced students help those who are less advanced, regardless of parental feelings.
    c. Use cross-age peer tutoring rather than same-age peer tutoring.
    d. Use peer tutors who don't like each other so they won't be tempted to goof around instead of working.
6. Which of the following suggestions would you make to Mariana regarding her use of student groups?
    a. Compose gender-segregated groups to make students more comfortable.
    b. Compose racially segregated groups to make students more comfortable.
    c. Give leadership roles to students who are shy to help draw them out.
    d. Mix up the group composition from time to time, so that middle-ability-level students don't get left out.

Connecting with Learning: Reach Your Learning Goals

 SOCIAL CONSTRUCTIVIST APPROACHES TO TEACHING: Compare the social constructivist approach with other constructivist approaches.

Social Constructivism in the Broader Constructivist Context

- Piaget's and Vygotsky's theories are constructivist. Piaget's theory is a cognitive constructivist theory, whereas Vygotsky's is social constructivist.
- The implication of Vygotsky's model for teaching is to establish opportunities for students to learn through social interactions with others—with the teacher and peers—in constructing knowledge and understanding. In Piaget's view, students construct knowledge by transforming, organizing, and reorganizing previous knowledge and information.

continued

Situated Cognition

- In both Piaget's and Vygotsky's models, teachers are facilitators, not directors. Distinctions between cognitive and social constructivist approaches are not always clear-cut. All social constructivist approaches emphasize that social factors contribute to students' construction of knowledge and understanding.

- Situated cognition is the idea that thinking is located (situated) in social and physical contexts, not within an individual's mind.

2 TEACHERS AND PEERS AS JOINT CONTRIBUTORS TO STUDENTS' LEARNING: Explain how teachers and peers can jointly contribute to children's learning.

Scaffolding

- Scaffolding is the technique of providing changing levels of support over the course of a teaching session, with a more-skilled individual—a teacher or a more-advanced peer of the child—providing guidance to fit the student's current performance.

Cognitive Apprenticeship

- A cognitive apprenticeship involves a novice and an expert, who stretches and supports the novice's understanding of and use of a culture's skills.

Tutoring

- Tutoring involves a cognitive apprenticeship between an expert and a novice. Tutoring can take place between an adult and a child or a more-skilled child and a less-skilled child.
- Individual tutoring is effective. Classroom aides, volunteers, and mentors can serve as tutors to support teachers and classroom learning.
- Reading Recovery and Success for All are examples of effective tutoring programs. In many cases, students benefit more from cross-age tutoring than from same-age tutoring. Tutoring can benefit both the tutee and the tutor.

Cooperative Learning

- Cooperative learning occurs when students work in small groups to help each other learn. Researchers have found that cooperative learning can be an effective strategy for improving students' achievement, especially when group goals and individual accountability are instituted.
- Cooperative learning works better for complex than simple tasks. Cooperative learning often improves intrinsic motivation, encourages student interdependence, and promotes deep understanding.
- Cooperative learning approaches include STAD (Student Teams Achievement Divisions), the jigsaw classroom (I and II), learning together, group investigation, and cooperative scripting.
- Cooperative learning approaches generally recommend heterogeneous groupings with diversity in ability, ethnicity, socioeconomic status, and gender. Creating a cooperative community involves developing positive interdependence at a number of levels: a small group within a classroom, the class as a whole, between classrooms, the entire school, between parents and the school, and between the school and the neighborhood.
- Cooperative learning has a number of strengths, but there also are some potential drawbacks to its use.

3 STRUCTURING SMALL-GROUP WORK: Discuss effective decisions in structuring small-group work.

Composing the Group

- Two strategies in composing a small group are to assign children to heterogeneous groups and to have the group membership reflect diversity in ability, ethnic background, socioeconomic status, and gender.

- Structuring small-group work also involves attention to team-building skills. A good strategy is to spend several weeks at the beginning of the school year on building team skills, helping students become better listeners, and giving them practice in contributing to a team product. Assigning one student in each small group to be a team leader can help to build the team.

- A group also can benefit when students are assigned different roles—for example, encourager, gatekeeper, taskmaster, quiet captain, and materials monitor—that are designed to help the group function more smoothly.

KEY TERMS

cognitive apprenticeship 338   cooperative learning 342   situated cognition 337   social constructivist approach 335

PORTFOLIO ACTIVITIES

Now that you have a good understanding of this chapter, complete these exercises to expand your thinking.

Independent Reflection

1. **Evaluating Social Constructivist Experiences.** To what extent have you experienced various social constructivist approaches in your education? Think about your different levels of schooling (early childhood, elementary, middle, high school, and college), and evaluate your experience (or lack of experience) with scaffolding, cognitive apprenticeship, tutoring, and cooperative learning. (INTASC: Principles *1, 3, 8, 9*)

Collaborative Work

2. **Balancing Individual and Group Activities.** With four or five other students in the class, discuss how much of the curriculum should include group activities and how much should involve individual activities at the early childhood, elementary, middle, high school, and college levels. Describe your group's thoughts. Also discuss whether some subject areas might lend themselves better than others to group activities. (INTASC: Principles *2, 3, 4, 8*)

chapter 11
LEARNING AND COGNITION IN THE CONTENT AREAS

chapter outline

① Expert Knowledge and Pedagogical Content Knowledge

Learning Goal 1 Distinguish between expert knowledge and pedagogical content knowledge.

② Reading

Learning Goal 2 Explain how reading develops and discuss some useful approaches to teaching reading.

A Developmental Model of Reading
Approaches to Reading
Cognitive Approaches
Social Constructivist Approaches

③ Writing

Learning Goal 3 Describe how writing develops and discuss some useful approaches to teaching writing.

Developmental Changes
Cognitive Approaches
Social Constructivist Approaches

④ Mathematics

Learning Goal 4 Characterize how mathematical thinking develops and identify some issues related to teaching mathematics.

Developmental Changes
Controversy in Math Education
Cognitive Processes
Some Constructivist Principles
Technology and Math Instruction

⑤ Science

Learning Goal 5 Identify some challenges and strategies related to teaching children how to think scientifically.

Science Education
Constructivist Teaching Strategies

⑥ Social Studies

Learning Goal 6 Summarize how learning in social studies is becoming more constructivist.

What Is Social Studies?
Constructivist Approaches

⑦ Technology Resources

Learning Goal 7 Identify online resources for implementing constructivist approaches to content area teaching.

Meaning is not given to us but by us.

—Eleanor Duckworth
Contemporary teacher, teacher educator, and educational theorist

Hill Street Studios/Blend Images/Getty Images

Connecting with Teachers Wendy Nelson Kauffman

Wendy Nelson Kauffman teaches social studies to tenth- and twelfth-grade students at a Bloomfield, Connecticut, high school. Wendy turned to teaching after a career in journalism that left her feeling unfulfilled. To improve the thinking and writing skills of her students, she has them do various activities such as the following:

- Writing autobiographies each fall
- Keeping journals all year and writing position papers on historical questions
- Participating in dramatic role-playing
- Carrying out debates and holding "town meetings" to discuss contentious issues such as racial problems
- Interpreting political cartoons and songs
- Making posters
- Engaging in real-world learning experiences—these have included a visit to Ellis Island, after which students acted out immigrant experiences in a school-wide performance, and interviews with retirement home residents about the Great Depression and World War II for an oral history book

In Wendy's words, "Certain skills they have to learn: writing, critical thinking, class participation. If you mix that with something that's fun for them and plays to their strengths, I think it makes it easier for them to do the hard work in class." Wendy also mentors new teachers, about whom she says, "I want them to feel safe, I want them to take risks, I want them to become who they want to be."

(Source: "USA Today's 2003 All-USA Teacher Team," by W. N. Kauffman, October 16, 2003, *USA Today*.)

Stace Rowe, Courtesy of Metropolitan Learning Center

Preview

In previous chapters, we described the basic principles of children's learning and cognition. In this chapter, we will apply these principles to learning and cognition in five content areas: reading, writing, mathematics, science, and social studies. We begin the chapter by revisiting the concept of expertise and exploring the distinction between expert knowledge and pedagogical content knowledge, the kind of knowledge that teachers like Wendy Nelson Kauffman use to teach effectively.

EXPERT KNOWLEDGE AND PEDAGOGICAL CONTENT KNOWLEDGE

LG 1 Distinguish between expert knowledge and pedagogical content knowledge.

In the chapter on the information-processing approach we discussed the distinction between experts and novices. We saw that sometimes individuals who are experts in the content of a particular area, such as mathematics or biology, aren't good at teaching it in ways that help others learn it effectively. These individuals have *expert knowledge* but lack *pedagogical content knowledge*. Let's examine the difference between the two types of knowledge.

Expert knowledge, sometimes referred to as *subject matter knowledge,* means excellent knowledge about the content of a particular discipline (Ericsson et al., 2016). Clearly, expert knowledge is important—how can teachers teach students something that they don't understand themselves (Burden & Byrd, 2016)? However, some individuals with expert knowledge about a particular subject area, such as reading, math, or science, have difficulty understanding the subject matter in a way that allows them to teach it effectively to others. The term *expert blind spots* has been used to describe the gap between what an expert knows and what students know (Nathan & Petrosino, 2003). Too often experts (teachers) don't communicate all of the information and steps

expert knowledge Also called *subject matter knowledge;* means excellent knowledge about the content of a particular discipline.

What is pedagogical content knowledge? How is it different from expert knowledge?
Rebecca Emery/Photodisc/Getty Images

necessary for students (novices) to learn something about the content of a particular discipline (Bransford et al., 2005).

What teachers need in addition to expert knowledge is **pedagogical content knowledge**—knowledge about how to effectively teach a particular discipline. Both expert knowledge and pedagogical content knowledge are required for being an expert teacher. *Expert teachers* know the structure of their disciplines, and this knowledge gives them the ability to create cognitive road maps that guide the assignments they give to students, the assessments they use to evaluate students' progress, and the types of questions and answers they generate in class (National Research Council, 2005). Being an expert teacher in a particular discipline also involves being aware of which aspects of the discipline are especially difficult or easy for students to learn (Mayer & Alexander, 2017).

In previous chapters, we explored general teaching strategies that are effective across all disciplines. For example, a good teacher in any discipline asks questions that stimulate students' curiosity, encourages students to go beyond the surface of a topic and gain a depth of understanding about a topic, and pays attention to individual variations in students' learning. However, pedagogical content knowledge about particular disciplines goes beyond these general teaching strategies (Cunningham, 2017; Mayer & Alexander, 2017; Van de Walle et al., 2016). We will examine five content areas—reading, writing, mathematics, science, and social studies—and describe effective teaching strategies in each one.

> **Thinking Back/Thinking Forward**
> Teachers can guide students in learning a number of effective strategies and metacognitive strategies for learning. Connect to "The Information-Processing Approach."

Review, Reflect, and Practice

1 Distinguish between expert knowledge and pedagogical content knowledge.

REVIEW
- How is expert knowledge different from pedagogical content knowledge?

REFLECT
- Have you ever had a teacher who was clearly an expert in his or her discipline but not a good teacher? What pedagogical content knowledge was missing?

PRAXIS™ PRACTICE

1. Maria is frustrated with her calculus teacher, a former university math professor. He knows his math but has a difficult time communicating his knowledge to his students. In fact, half the time in class, Maria has no idea what he is talking about. When she asks for help, he is willing to meet with her, but his explanations are no clearer than they are in class. Which statement best characterizes Maria's calculus teacher?
    a. He has both expert knowledge in calculus and pedagogical content knowledge.
    b. He has expert knowledge in calculus but lacks pedagogical content knowledge.
    c. He lacks expert knowledge in calculus but has pedagogical content knowledge.
    d. He lacks both expert knowledge in calculus and pedagogical content knowledge.

Please see answer key at end of book . . . .

LG 2 Explain how reading develops and discuss some useful approaches to teaching reading.

2 READING

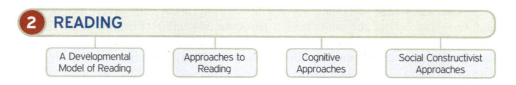

A Developmental Model of Reading | Approaches to Reading | Cognitive Approaches | Social Constructivist Approaches

pedagogical content knowledge Knowledge about how to effectively teach a particular discipline.

Reading expert Steve Stahl (2002) argues that the three main goals of reading instruction should be to help children (1) automatically recognize words, (2) comprehend text, and (3) become motivated to read and appreciate reading. These goals are interrelated.

If children cannot recognize words automatically, their comprehension suffers. If they cannot comprehend the text, they are unlikely to be motivated to read it.

Analyses by Rich Mayer (2004, 2008) focused on the cognitive processes a child needs to go through in order to read a printed word. In his view, the three processes are as follows:

1. *Being aware of sound units in words,* which consists of recognizing phonemes
2. *Decoding words,* which involves converting printed words to sounds
3. *Accessing word meaning,* which consists of finding a mental representation of a word's meaning

How do children develop the reading skills that Stahl and Mayer describe? What is the best way to teach children to read? How can children construct their reading skills? These are among the main questions that we will examine in our coverage of reading. As we discuss these questions, you will see that teachers play a key role in the development of children's reading skills (Fisher & Frey, 2016).

A DEVELOPMENTAL MODEL OF READING

In one view, reading skills develop in five stages (Chall, 1979). The age boundaries are approximate and do not apply to every child. For example, some children learn to read before they enter first grade. Nonetheless, Chall's stages convey a general sense of the developmental changes involved in learning to read:

DEVELOPMENT

- *Stage 0.* From birth to first grade, children master several prerequisites for reading. Many learn the left-to-right progression and order of reading, how to identify the letters of the alphabet, and how to write their names. Some learn to read words that commonly appear on signs. As a result of watching TV shows such as *Sesame Street* and attending preschool and kindergarten programs, many children today develop greater knowledge about reading at younger ages than in the past.
- *Stage 1.* In first and second grade, many children begin to read. They do so by learning to sound out words (that is, translate individual letters or groups of letters into sounds and blend sounds into words). During this stage, they also complete their learning of letter names and sounds.
- *Stage 2.* In second and third grade, children become more fluent at retrieving individual words and other reading skills. However, at this stage, reading is still not used much for learning. The mechanical demands of learning to read are so taxing at this point that children have few resources left over to process the content.
- *Stage 3.* In fourth through eighth grade, children become increasingly able to obtain new information from print. The change from stage 2 to stage 3 involves a shift from "learning to read" to "reading to learn." In stage 3, children still have difficulty understanding information presented from multiple perspectives within the same story. For children who haven't yet learned to read, a downward spiral begins that leads to serious difficulties in many academic subjects.
- *Stage 4.* In the high school years, many students become fully competent readers. They develop the ability to understand material written from many different perspectives. This allows some students to engage in more sophisticated discussions of literature, history, economics, and politics. It is no accident that great novels are not presented to students until high school, because understanding the novels requires advanced reading skills.

Keep in mind that the age boundaries in Chall's model are approximate and do not apply to every child. However, the stages convey a sense of the developmental changes involved in becoming a competent reader.

What are some developmental changes in reading?
Comstock/Stockbyte/Getty Images

This teacher is helping a student sound out words. Researchers have found that phonics instruction is a key aspect of teaching students to read, especially beginning readers and students with weak reading skills.
Gideon Mendel/Corbis/Getty Images

phonics approach An approach that emphasizes that reading instruction should teach phonics and its basic rules for translating written symbols into sounds; early reading instruction should use simplified materials.

whole-language approach An approach that stresses that reading instruction should parallel children's natural language learning. Reading materials should be whole and meaningful.

Reading takes time and effort. *What can you do as a teacher to encourage children to read more books?*
FatCamera/Getty Images

As the previous discussion has implied, *reading* is the ability to understand written discourse. Children cannot be said to read if all they can do is respond to flash cards. Good readers have mastered the basic language rules of phonology, morphology, syntax, and semantics that we discussed in the chapter on cognitive and language development.

APPROACHES TO READING

What are some approaches to teaching children how to read? Education and language experts continue to debate how children should be taught to read.

One debate has focused on the phonics approach versus the whole-language approach. The **phonics approach** emphasizes that reading instruction should focus on phonics and basic rules for translating written symbols into sounds. Early reading instruction should involve simplified materials. Only after learning the correspondence rules that relate spoken phonemes to the alphabet letters that represent them should children be given complex reading materials, such as books and poems (Leu & Kinzer, 2017).

By contrast, the **whole-language approach** stresses that reading instruction should parallel children's natural language learning. Reading materials should be whole and meaningful. That is, children should be given material in its complete form, such as stories and poems, so that they begin to understand language's communicative function. Reading should be connected with listening and writing skills. Although there are variations in whole-language programs, most share the premise that reading should be integrated with other skills and subjects, such as science and social studies, and that it should focus on real-world material. Thus, a class might read newspapers, magazines, or books and then write about and discuss them. In some whole-language classes, beginning readers are taught to recognize whole words or even entire sentences and to use the context of what they are reading to guess at unfamiliar words.

Which approach is better? Children can benefit from both approaches, but instruction in phonics needs to be emphasized especially in kindergarten and the first grade (Bear et al., 2016; Cunningham, 2017).

Conclusions reached by the National Reading Panel (2000) suggest that children benefit from *guided oral* reading—that is, from reading aloud with guidance and feedback. A recent study found that both individualized and small-group guided reading interventions improved the reading comprehension and attitude of struggling readers (Oostdam et al., 2015). Learning strategies for reading comprehension—such as monitoring one's own reading progress and summarizing—also benefit children's reading progress (Allyn, 2016; Cunningham & Allington, 2016).

In one study, Michael Pressley and his colleagues (2001) examined literacy instruction in five U.S. classrooms. In the most effective classrooms, teachers exhibited excellent classroom management based on positive reinforcement and cooperation; balanced teaching of skills, literature, and writing; scaffolding and matching of task demands to students' skill levels; encouragement of student self-regulation; and forming strong connections across subject areas. In general, the extensive observations did not support any particular reading approach (such as whole-language or phonics); rather, excellent instruction involved multiple, well-integrated components. An important point in this study is that effective reading instruction involves more than using a specific teaching approach—it also includes effective classroom management, encouragement of self-regulation, and other components.

Reading, like other important skills, takes time and effort to master (Allington, 2015). In a national assessment, children in the fourth grade had higher scores on a national reading test when they read 11 or more pages daily for school and homework (National Assessment of Educational Progress, 2000) (see Figure 1). Teachers who required students to read a great deal on a daily basis had students who were more proficient at reading than teachers who required little reading by their students.

COGNITIVE APPROACHES

Cognitive approaches to reading emphasize decoding and comprehending words, applying prior knowledge, and developing expert reading strategies.

Decoding and Comprehending Words At the beginning of our discussion of reading, we described Mayer's (2008) view that decoding words is a key cognitive process in learning to read. Cognitive approaches emphasize the cognitive processes involved in decoding and comprehending words (Allyn, 2016; Fox & Alexander, 2017; Oakhill et al., 2016). Important in this regard are certain metacognitive skills and increasing automaticity that is characterized by fluency (Cunningham & Allington, 2016).

Metacognition is involved in reading in the sense that good readers develop control of their own reading skills and understand how reading works (Allyn, 2016). For example, good readers know that it is important to comprehend the "gist" of what an author is saying.

Teachers can help students develop good metacognitive strategies for reading by getting them to monitor their own reading, especially when they run into difficulties in their reading (Fox & Alexander, 2017; Kostons & van der Werf, 2015). Here are some metacognitive strategies that teachers can encourage their students to use for improving their reading skills (Pressley & Harris, 2006):

- Overview text before reading.
- Look for important information while reading and pay more attention to it than other information; ask yourself questions about the important ideas or relate them to something you already know.
- Attempt to determine the meaning of words not recognized (use the words around a word to figure out its meaning, use a dictionary, or temporarily ignore the unfamiliar word and wait for further clarification).
- Monitor text comprehension.
- Understand relationships between parts of text.
- Recognize when you might need to go back and reread a passage (you didn't understand it the first time, you want to clarify an important idea, the material seemed important to remember, or you need to underline or summarize important points for later review).
- Adjust pace of reading depending on the difficulty of the material.

When students process information automatically, they do so with little or no conscious effort (Tompkins, 2016). When word recognition occurs rapidly, comprehension of meaning often follows in a rapid fashion. By contrast, many beginning or poor readers do not recognize words automatically. Their processing capacity is consumed by the demands of word recognition, so they have less capacity to devote to comprehension of groupings of words as phrases or sentences. As their processing of words and passages becomes more automatic, it is said that their reading becomes more fluent (Calet et al., 2015). In a recent study of fourth-grade students, oral

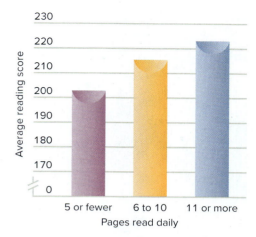

FIGURE 1 THE RELATION OF READING ACHIEVEMENT TO NUMBER OF PAGES READ DAILY

In an analysis of reading in the fourth grade conducted by the National Assessment of Educational Progress (2000), reading more pages daily in school and as part of homework assignments was related to higher scores on a reading test in which scores ranged from 0 to 500.

What characterizes the cognitive approaches to reading?
Comstock/Getty Images

reading fluency (but not silent reading fluency) was linked to better reading comprehension (Price et al., 2016).

Students' fluency often improves when they do the following (Mayer, 2008): (1) hear others read a passage before and after they read it, which is called assisted practice; (2) spend considerable time reading various passages; and (3) speak with appropriate expression and rhythm in oral reading.

Prior Knowledge Another principle involved in cognitive approaches to reading is that students' prior knowledge about a topic is related to what they remember from reading about the topic and their ability to make correct inferences about the material they read (Mayer, 2008). If teachers detect that students don't have adequate knowledge about a topic they are going to read about, what should be done? First, teachers need to evaluate whether the reading material is too difficult for students. If so, passages that are more appropriate for the students' reading level can be chosen. Also, teachers can provide prereading activities related to the topic.

Developing Expert Reading Strategies In cognitive approaches, researchers have searched for the underlying cognitive processes that explain reading. This search has led to an interest in strategies, especially the strategies of expert readers compared with those of novice readers (Cunningham & Allington, 2016). Researchers advise teachers to guide students in developing good reading strategies.

Michael Pressley and his colleagues (1992) developed the **transactional strategy instruction approach**, a cognitive approach to reading that emphasizes instruction in strategies (especially metacognitive strategies). In their view, strategies control students' abilities to remember what they read. It is especially important to teach students metacognitive strategies to monitor their reading progress. Summarizing is also thought to be an important reading strategy. In the strategy approach, authors of teachers' manuals for subjects other than reading are encouraged to include information about the importance of reading strategies, how and when to use particular strategies, and prompts to remind students about using strategies.

SOCIAL CONSTRUCTIVIST APPROACHES

The social constructivist approaches bring the social aspects of reading to the forefront (Hiebert & Raphael, 1996). The contribution of the social context in helping children learn to read includes such factors as how much emphasis the culture places on reading, the extent to which parents have exposed their children to books before they enter formal schooling, the teacher's communication skills, the extent to which teachers give students opportunities to discuss what they have read, and the district-mandated reading curriculum. Whereas cognitive constructivists emphasize the student's construction of meaning, social constructivists stress that meaning is *socially negotiated*. In other words, meaning involves not only the reader's contribution but also the social context and the purpose for reading. Social constructivist approaches emphasize the importance of giving students opportunities for engaging in meaningful dialogue about their reading. One way to do this is through reciprocal teaching.

Reciprocal Teaching **Reciprocal teaching** involves students taking turns leading a small-group discussion. Reciprocal teaching also can involve a teacher and a student. In reciprocal teaching, teachers initially explain the strategies and model how to use them to make sense of the text. Then they ask students to demonstrate the strategies, offering support as students learn the strategies. As in scaffolding, the teacher gradually assumes a less active role, letting the student take more initiative. For example,

> **Thinking Back/Thinking Forward**
>
> Social constructivist approaches emphasize the social contexts of learning and the idea that knowledge is mutually constructed. Connect to "Social Constructivist Approaches."

transactional strategy instruction approach A cognitive approach to reading that emphasizes instruction in strategies, especially metacognitive strategies.

reciprocal teaching A learning arrangement in which students take turns leading a small-group discussion; can also involve teacher-scaffolded instruction.

Annemarie Palincsar and Ann Brown (1984) used reciprocal teaching to improve students' abilities to enact certain strategies to improve their reading comprehension. In this teacher-scaffolded instruction, teachers worked with students to help them generate questions about the text they had read, clarify what they did not understand, summarize the text, and make predictions.

Research on reciprocal teaching suggests that it is a very effective strategy for improving reading comprehension (Webb & Palincsar, 1996). For example, one study examined the influence of reading strategies (summarizing, questioning, clarifying, and predicting) in reciprocal teaching within small groups, pairs, and instructor-guided small groups (Sporer et al., 2009). Compared with a control group of students who received traditional instruction, students who received strategy instruction achieved higher scores in reading comprehension. Further, students who practiced reciprocal teaching in small groups scored higher on a standardized reading achievement test than students in instructor-guided and traditional instruction groups. Also, in a recent overview of research, it was concluded that a number of studies provide support for the benefits of reciprocal teaching in improving students' reading skills (McAllum, 2014).

Students engaged in a reciprocal teaching group. *What characterizes reciprocal teaching in reading?*
Global Education Systems Ltd/Connectors reading series (www.globaled.co.nz)

RESEARCH

School/Family/Community Connections From the social constructivist perspective, schools are not the only sociocultural context that is important in reading. Families and communities are also important.

Of special concern are the language experiences of students from low-income families (Navsaria & Sanders, 2015). In one research study, on average, young children in families who were receiving public assistance heard about 600 words an hour, whereas young children whose parents were professionals heard about 2,100 words an hour (Hart & Risley, 1995). Also, children in the low-income families received only half as much language experience in their early years as children in middle-income families. The researchers also found that children in high-income families received twice as much language experience as children in middle-income families.

At-risk students who do not read outside of school fall further behind as they go through the elementary school years. Many parents of at-risk students have their own reading difficulties, as well as problems in obtaining books.

Given the contextual influences on children's language and reading development, how can teachers help students to read more effectively? Following are some teachers' responses.

EARLY CHILDHOOD With very young children, it is essential to have a print-rich environment in which they can see words and phrases everywhere. Our classroom is filled with storybooks, picture dictionaries, magazines, and so on. Also, every object in the classroom is labeled—for example, doors,

What are some important aspects of social contexts that influence children's reading?
Paul Burns/Corbis/Getty Images

chairs, windows, and bookshelves, so children associate the word printed on the label with the object. And children's names are printed in many places so that they get used to seeing it in print.

—VALARIE GORHAM, *Kiddie Quarters, Inc.*

ELEMENTARY SCHOOL: GRADES K–5 I help my second-graders read more effectively by stressing reading for comprehension. That said, I incorporate prereading, during-reading, and postreading comprehension strategies. In prereading, I state the purpose of the reading and preview pictures, titles, headings, boldface words, and so on. During reading we check the selection for meaning (Does it make sense? Any confusing words?) and reread for understanding. In postreading, we check to see if we know what was read, summarize, and reflect.

—ELIZABETH FRASCELLA, *Clinton Elementary School*

MIDDLE SCHOOL: GRADES 6–8 One of the best ways to become a better reader is to read! Every time I cover a historical era with my seventh-graders, I also make them aware of the related books that are available in our school library. Our librarian will pull corresponding books off the shelves and display them for students. Even the most ardent "nonreader" has a book he or she likes; the trick is to find the right book!

—MARK FODNESS, *Bemidji Middle School*

HIGH SCHOOL: GRADES 9–12 With the way we teach reading in America, it is no wonder many students hate it. We teachers make reading so painful and serious— for example, we pick apart novels, we quiz and test to death. Teachers need to show students that reading is fun—they should read what students are reading; "sell" the books to students by talking about the most interesting parts; let students see them reading; and be excited and energetic when discussing new books in class.

—JENNIFER HEITER, *Bremen High School*

Review, Reflect, and Practice

 Explain how reading develops and discuss some useful approaches to teaching reading.

REVIEW
- What happens at each stage in Chall's developmental model of reading?
- What are some differences between the whole-language approach and the phonics approach to teaching reading? Which approach is better?
- What are the key ideas in cognitive approaches to reading?
- What are the important features of social constructivist approaches to reading?

REFLECT
- What would be some of the key considerations in a balanced view of teaching reading?

PRAXIS™ PRACTICE
1. Kareem is reading his science text. He is taking notes as he reads to help him remember the information. He has learned much about science from his text this year. For instance, he learned that there are many different kinds of rocks that vary in how

Review, Reflect, and Practice

they were formed, their hardness, and their color. However, when presented with conflicting views on a scientific matter, Kareem is easily confused. Which of Chall's (1979) developmental stages of reading best characterizes Kareem?
   a. stage 1
   b. stage 2
   c. stage 3
   d. stage 4

2. Which of the following is the best example of the use of the whole-language approach in teaching reading?
   a. Ms. Tillman uses flash cards to help her students develop their sight vocabulary.
   b. Ms. Muhammad's students are immersed in literature. They read various types of literature and write about what they have read.
   c. Ms. Orton uses a phonics workbook to help her students develop their decoding skills.
   d. Ms. Wade's students use a computer game to practice their reading skills. A character says a word, and the student clicks on the correct printed word.

3. Which of the following is the best example of a teacher using a cognitive approach to help students improve their reading skills?
   a. Ms. Beckham uses flash cards to help students learn new words and reinforces them with candy for correct responses.
   b. Ms. Gomes has her students choose from a variety of books to read. Those students who read a particular book then meet to discuss the book on a regular basis.
   c. Ms. Owen emphasizes the importance of using context clues to help determine the meaning of new words.
   d. Ms. Ronaldo has her students write each word they miss on a spelling pretest five times to help them remember the word.

4. Which of the following is the best example of a teacher using a social constructivist approach to teach reading?
   a. Ms. Beckham uses flash cards to help students learn new words and rewards them with candy for correct responses.
   b. Ms. Gomes has her students choose from a variety of books to read. Those students who read a particular book then meet to discuss the book on a regular basis.
   c. Ms. Owen emphasizes the importance of using context clues to help determine the meaning of new words.
   d. Ms. Ronaldo has her students write each word they miss on a spelling pretest five times to help them remember the word.

Please see answer key at end of book....

LG 3 Describe how writing develops and discuss some useful approaches to teaching writing.

RESEARCH

There are increasing concerns about students' current writing competence (Graham, 2017; Graham et al., 2017; Tompkins, 2015, 2016). One study revealed that 70 to 75 percent of U.S. students in grades 4 through 12 are low-achieving writers (Persky et al., 2003). College instructors report that 50 percent of high school graduates are not prepared for college-level writing (Achieve, Inc., 2005).

RESEARCH

One study of U.S. language arts, social studies, and science high school teachers raised concerns about the quality of writing instruction in U.S. high schools (Kluhara et al., 2009). The teachers in this study reported that their college teacher education program did not adequately prepare them to teach writing in high school. The study also revealed that writing assignments infrequently involved analysis and interpretation and that almost 50 percent of teachers did not assign any multi-paragraph writing assignments in the span of one month. Two-thirds of U.S. students also indicate that their writing assignments total less than one hour per week (Applebee & Langer, 2006).

DEVELOPMENT

As with reading, teachers play a critical role in students' development of writing skills (De La Paz & McCutchen, 2017; Fisher & Frey, 2016; Rouse & Graham, 2017). The observations of classrooms made by Michael Pressley and his colleagues (2007) revealed that students became good writers when teachers spent considerable time on writing instruction and were passionate about teaching students to write. Their observations also indicated that classrooms with students who scored high on writing assessments had walls that overflowed with examples of effective writing, whereas it was much harder to find such examples on the walls of classrooms that had many students who scored low on writing assessments.

Our further coverage of writing focuses on these questions: How do writing skills develop? What are cognitive and social constructivist approaches to writing?

DEVELOPMENTAL CHANGES

Children's writing emerges out of their early scribbles, which appear at around 2 to 3 years of age. In early childhood, children's motor skills usually become well enough developed for them to begin printing letters and their name. In the United States, most 4-year-olds can print their first name. Five-year-olds can reproduce letters and copy several short words. As they develop their printing skills, children gradually learn to distinguish between the distinctive characteristics of letters, such as whether the lines are curved or straight, open or closed, and so on. Through the early elementary grades, many children continue to reverse letters such as *b* and *d* and *p* and *q*. At this point in development, if other aspects of the child's development are normal, these letter reversals are not a predictor of literacy problems.

As children begin to write, they often invent spellings of words. They usually do this by relying on the sounds of words they hear as clues for how to spell. Teachers and parents should encourage children's early writing without being overly concerned about the proper formation of letters or correct conventional spelling. Such errors should be viewed as a natural part of the young child's growth, not scrutinized and criticized. Spelling and printing corrections can be made in positive ways and judiciously enough to avoid dampening early enjoyment and spontaneity in writing.

Like becoming a good reader, becoming a good writer takes many years and lots of practice (De La Paz & McCutchen, 2017; Graham & Harris, 2016, 2017). Children should be given many writing opportunities during the elementary and secondary school years (Cunningham & Allington, 2016). As their language and cognitive skills improve with good instruction, so will their writing skills. For example, developing a more sophisticated understanding of syntax and grammar serves as an underpinning for better writing. So do such cognitive skills as organization and logical reasoning.

Through elementary, middle, and high school, students develop increasingly sophisticated methods of organizing their ideas. In early elementary school, they narrate and describe or write short poems. In late elementary and middle school, they move to projects such as book reports that combine narration with more reflection and analysis. In high school, they become more skilled at forms of exposition that do not depend on narrative structure (Conley, 2008).

RESEARCH

A meta-analysis (use of statistical techniques to combine the results of studies) revealed that the following interventions were the most effective in improving the writing quality of fourth- through twelfth-grade students: (1) strategy instruction, (2) summarization, (3) peer assistance, and (4) setting goals (Graham & Perin, 2007).

COGNITIVE APPROACHES

Cognitive approaches to writing emphasize many of the same themes that we discussed in regard to reading, such as constructing meaning and developing strategies (De La Paz & McCutchen, 2017; Graham & Harris, 2016, 2017). Planning, problem solving, revising, and metacognitive strategies are thought to be especially important in improving students' writing.

Planning Planning, which includes outlining and organizing content information, is an important aspect of writing (Tompkins, 2016). Teachers should show students how to outline and organize a paper and give feedback about their efforts. Figure 2 provides a model for helping students plan their compositions to meet a deadline.

Problem Solving Much of the instruction in writing in schools involves teaching students how to write sentences and paragraphs properly. However, there is more to writing than avoiding run-on sentences or making sure that paragraphs support topic sentences (Graham et al., 2017). More fundamentally, writing is a broader sort of problem solving. One psychologist called the problem-solving process in writing "the making of meaning" (Kellogg, 1994).

As problem solvers, writers need to establish goals and work to attain them (Graham & Harris, 2017; Harris & Graham, 2016). It also is helpful to think of writers as constrained by their need for integrated understanding of the subject, knowledge of how the language system works, and the writing problem itself. The writing problem includes the purpose of the paper, the audience, and the role of the writer in the paper to be produced (Flower & Hayes, 1981). A student who is struggling with writing may be having difficulty with any one of these aspects of writing. Identifying the specific difficulty is the first step in helping the student become a better writer.

Revising Revising is a major component of successful writing. Revising involves writing multiple drafts, getting feedback from individuals who are knowledgeable about writing, and learning how to use the critical feedback to improve the writing. It also includes detecting and correcting errors. Researchers have found that older and more-skilled writers are more likely to revise their writing than younger and less-skilled writers (Hayes & Flower, 1986).

Metacognition and Strategies Emphasizing knowledge of writing strategies moves into the area of metacognition, which we discussed in the chapter on the information-processing approach. Monitoring one's writing progress is especially important in becoming a good writer (Fidalgo et al., 2016; Graham et al., 2017; Harris et al., 2017). This includes being receptive to feedback and applying what one learns in writing one paper to making the next paper better (McKeown & Beck, 2010). In a recent study, the Self-Regulated Strategy Development (SRSD) was implemented with second-grade teachers and their students who were at risk for writing failure (Harris et al., 2015). The students were taught a general planning strategy, general writing strategies (creating a catchy opening, using effective vocabulary, following a clear system of organization, and including an effective ending). The intervention produced positive results for genre elements, story writing quality, motivation, and effort, as well as meaningful generalization to personal writing.

A research review indicated that the following writing strategies should be taught to secondary school students (Graham & Perin, 2007):

- *Prewriting.* A good strategy is to have students engage in prewriting activities that involve generating or organizing ideas for their composition.
- *Planning, revising, and editing.* These are critical skills in becoming a good writer, and students need considerable practice in developing and using them.

One to two months before the deadline	Select topic. Map ideas. Develop writing plan. Begin to develop a thesis statement. Start research.
Two weeks before the deadline	Develop individual sections of paper. Revise with vigor. Complete research. Finalize thesis statement.
The week before the deadline	Polish the individual sections of the paper. Create an interesting title. Check references for accuracy. Get some feedback.
The night before the deadline	Combine the parts of the paper. Print the final draft. Proofread the paper. Assemble the paper.

FIGURE 2 A SAMPLE TIMETABLE FOR A WRITING DEADLINE

Source: *Your Guide to College Success: Strategies for Achieving Your Goals* (2nd ed., p. 225), by J. W. Santrock and J. S. Halonen, 2002, Wadsworth.

> **Thinking Back/Thinking Forward**
> Metacognition involves cognition about cognition, or knowing about knowing. Connect to "The Information-Processing Approach."

RESEARCH

- *Summarization.* Teachers need to explicitly and systematically teach students how to summarize the text they write.
- *Sentence combining.* Students need to practice constructing more complex, sophisticated sentences.

SOCIAL CONSTRUCTIVIST APPROACHES

As in reading, social constructivist approaches emphasize that writing is best understood as being culturally embedded and socially constructed rather than being internally generated.

The Social Context of Writing
The social constructivist perspective focuses on the social context in which writing is produced. Students need to participate in a writing community to understand author/reader relationships and learn to recognize how their perspective might differ from that of others (Hiebert & Raphael, 1996).

Some students bring to the classroom a rich background of writing experiences and encouragement to write; others have little writing experience and have not been encouraged to write extensively. In some classrooms the teacher places a high value on writing; in others the teacher treats writing as being less important. One study revealed that in a school in which students showed high achievement in writing and reading, language arts were given a high priority by the principal and teachers (Pressley et al., 2007). The principal directed resources toward reading and writing instruction, including a considerable expansion of the number of books in the school's library and encouragement of field trips related to language arts.

Meaningful Writing and Student-Teacher Writing Conferences
According to social constructivist approaches, students' writing should include opportunities to create "real" texts, in the sense of writing about personally meaningful situations. For example, consider Anthony, whose teacher frequently asks students to write about personal experiences. He wrote about his grandmother's life and death, and his teacher gave him considerable support for writing about this emotional experience. Student-teacher writing conferences play an important support role in helping students become better writers.

Peer Collaboration and Editing
While working in groups, writers experience the processes of inquiry, clarification, and elaboration that are important in good writing (Webb & Palincsar, 1996). Also, students often benefit when they edit other students' writing. Online tools for collaborative writing such as Google docs make it easy for students to collaborate, give and receive feedback on specific text, and track individual contributions.

Students often bring diverse experiences to bear when they collaborate and coauthor papers. Such rich, shared collaboration can produce new insights into what to write about. By contrast, writing simply to meet the teacher's expectations often produces constrained, imitative, and conforming results. In peer writing groups, teacher expectations are often less apparent. In addition to benefiting from the dynamics of peer collaboration, students' writing often improves when they edit other students' writing.

THROUGH THE EYES OF STUDENTS

Writing Self-Evaluations

San Francisco fifth-grade teacher Keren Abra periodically asks her students to evaluate their writing for their writing portfolios. Here are several of her students' comments toward the end of the school year.

Michelle: I am in fifth grade right now and I love writing. Anytime that I get to write I will; as far as I can remember I have loved writing. I feel that my writing has developed since fourth grade and I am pleased with my writing. Some authors might not like their writing, unlike me; I have never thrown away any of my writing. I love to share my writing and give and get ideas from other writers. . . . If I could describe myself as a writer I would say (not to brag) that I was a descriptive, imaginative, captivating writer.

Sarah: I think writing a story is easy because there is so much to write about and if I have to write about a certain thing there are also more things to do with the story. . . . If someone read my writing they would think I probably am a happy and energetic kid. They will think this because most of my stories are upbeat.

Janet: I feel that when I'm writing I could do better. I could do better especially on spelling. When I was in kindergarten we did not do a lot of writing. When I was in third grade I did not like writing. It was scary learning new things about writing. I'm in fifth grade and I love to write but sometimes it annoys me that I can't spell that well. One thing I like about my writing is the way I put action into all of my work because I love to get excited! I think that if someone were to read my writing uncorrected they would not be able to read it. If it was corrected I think the person would really like my story.

School-Community Connections Social constructivist approaches emphasize connecting students' experiences at school with the world outside the classroom. A good strategy is to involve the writing community in your class. Look around your community and think about expert writers who might be willing to visit your classroom to discuss their work. Most communities have such experts, such as journalists and other authors and editors. One of the four most successful middle schools in the United States identified by Joan Lipsitz (1984) built a special Author's Week into its curriculum. Based on students' interests, availability, and diversity, authors are invited to discuss their craft with students. Students sign up to meet individual authors. Before they meet an author, they are required to read at least one of the author's books. Students prepare questions for their author sessions. In some cases, authors come to the class for several days to work with students on their writing projects.

In the course of our discussion of reading and writing, we have described a number of ideas that can be used in the classroom. To evaluate your reading and writing experiences, complete *Self-Assessment 1*.

How do teachers help students improve their writing skills? Following are several teachers' responses.

EARLY CHILDHOOD Gradually, preschoolers learn to write. They start with scribbling, then move on to drawing shapes, and then move to writing basic letters. It is important to encourage and support (not correct) children while they learn and practice.

—HEIDI KAUFMAN, *Metro West YMCA Child Care and Educational Program*

ELEMENTARY SCHOOL: GRADES K-5 One way I help my fifth-graders become better writers is to compose a story myself. I start by showing them how I brainstorm writing ideas and go all the way through to writing the final copy. As I do this, I talk out loud, letting students hear my thought process and thus learn effective writing strategies.

—CRAIG JENSEN, *Cooper Mountain Elementary School*

MIDDLE SCHOOL: GRADES 6-8 Peer editing is an important part of teaching writing skills. I find it especially important to have my students edit each other's work so that they can pick up any writing errors in a classmate's paper, while learning from studying another student's writing style.

—CASEY MAASS, *Edison Middle School*

HIGH SCHOOL: GRADES 9-12 Although state standards describe which genres of writing to teach, it is up to the teacher to decide how best to teach them. I take my students through the basic writing phases: brainstorming, prewriting, outlining, first draft, revision, and final draft. I also get my students to think about style by showing them how to replace boring verbs with vivid verbs, or by deleting unnecessary adverbs and adjectives.

—JENNIFER HEITER, *Bremen High School*

SELF-ASSESSMENT 1
Evaluating My Reading and Writing Experiences

Regardless of the academic subject or grade you teach, one of your goals should be to help students not only become competent at reading and writing but also enjoy these activities. Think about your own past and current experiences in reading and writing:

1. What made learning to read enjoyable for you?
   _____
   _____

2. What made learning to read difficult or unenjoyable?
   _____
   _____

3. How do you feel about reading now?
   _____
   _____

4. Do you enjoy libraries? Why or why not?
   _____
   _____

5. Are there reading skills that you still need to improve?
   _____
   _____

6. What made learning to write enjoyable for you?
   _____
   _____

7. What made learning to write difficult or unenjoyable?
   _____
   _____

8. How do you feel about writing now?
   _____
   _____

9. Are there writing skills that you still need to improve?
   _____
   _____

Based on your own experience and ideas in this chapter, how could you make learning to read and write more successful and enjoyable for your students?

CONNECTING WITH STUDENTS: Best Practices
Strategies for Incorporating Writing into the Curriculum

You will have many opportunities to incorporate writing into the curriculum. Here are some examples (Bruning & Horn, 2001; Halonen, 2010):

1. *Nurture positive attitudes toward writing.* This can be done by making sure that many writing tasks ensure student success and giving students choices about what they will write.

2. *Foster student engagement through authentic writing tasks and contexts.* Encourage students to write about topics of personal interest, have students write for different audiences, and integrate writing into instruction in other disciplines, such as science, mathematics, and social studies.

3. *Provide a supportive context for writing.* Encourage students to set writing goals, plan how to reach the goals, and monitor their progress toward the goals. Assist students in creating goals that are neither too challenging nor too simple. Teach writing strategies and monitor their use by students. Give students feedback on their progress toward their writing goals. Use peers as writing partners in literacy communities.

4. *Have students write to learn.* This can work in any subject area. For example, in biology, after students have studied the adaptation of different species, ask them to write a summary of the main ideas and generate examples not described in class or the text.

5. *Use free-writing assignments.* In free writing, students write whatever they think about a subject. Such assignments are usually unstructured but have time limits. For example, one free-writing assignment in American history might be "Write about the American Revolution for five minutes." Free writing helps students discover new ideas, connections, and questions they might not have generated if they had not had this free-writing opportunity. They can then share these observations with the class to generate further discussion.

6. *Give students creative writing assignments.* These assignments give students opportunities to explore themselves and their world in creative, insightful ways. They might include poetry, short stories, or essays reflecting personal experiences. Publishing online via the Web or creating iBooks (for example, by using an app like Book Creator) provides additional realism and significance to writing assignments. Students often become more motivated to do their best work when they publish it for an audience that is larger than their teacher or classroom peers.

7. *Require formal writing assignments.* These involve giving students opportunities to express themselves using an objective point of view, precise writing style, and evidence to support their conclusions. Formal writing helps students learn how to make formal arguments. For example, high school students might construct a major paper on a topic such as "Global Warming: Real Fears or Hype?" or "An In-Depth Examination of Faulkner's Writing Style" or "Why People Are Prejudiced."

Such writing projects stimulate students to think analytically, learn how to use resources, and cite references. Work with students on generating topics for a paper, structuring the paper, using planning and time management skills for completing the paper in a timely manner, drafting and revising, and overcoming spelling and grammatical errors.

8. *Invite writers and authors to visit your classroom.* Look around your community—there likely are some good writers and possibly authors who would be willing to come to your classroom and talk with your students about their work. People who work in libraries and bookstores likely can give you information about local writers and authors. See *Through the Eyes of Teachers* to learn how third-grade teacher Beverly Gallagher incorporates this strategy into her classroom.

THROUGH THE EYES OF TEACHERS
Imagine the Possibilities

Beverly Gallagher, a third-grade teacher at Princeton Day School in New Jersey, created the Imagine the Possibilities program, which brings nationally known poets and authors to her school. She phones each student's parents periodically to describe their child's progress and new interests. She invites students from higher grades to work with small groups in her class so that she can spend more one-on-one time with students. Beverly also created poetry partnerships between eleventh-graders and her third-graders in which the older and younger students collaborate to create poems. Each of her students keeps a writer's notebook to record thoughts, inspirations, and words that intrigue them. Students get special opportunities to sit in an author's chair, where they read their writing to the class. (Source: "All-USA first teacher team," October 10, 2000, *USA Today*. © 2000)

Beverly Gallagher with students in her third grade class.
Beverly G. Gallagher

Review, Reflect, and Practice

③ Describe how writing develops and discuss some useful approaches to teaching writing.

REVIEW
- What skills are acquired in writing? At what ages are they commonly acquired?
- What cognitive processes are essential to effective writing?
- What are the key ideas in social constructivist approaches to writing?

REFLECT
- For the age group and subject you plan to teach, in what ways will the writing assignments you give to students likely be highly structured and specific? In what ways might they be flexible and open-ended?

PRAXIS™ PRACTICE

1. Which of the following is the best example of developmentally appropriate writing instruction for first-graders?
   a. Ms. Balboa's students are learning how to spell through the use of drill and practice of specific words.
   b. Ms. Donovan carefully corrects students' grammar and spelling errors on their papers and is critical of their errors.
   c. Ms. Figo's students use invented spelling in their work, and she provides them with correct spelling but she does not criticize their efforts.
   d. Ms. Lalas's students practice writing by copying stories that she has written on the blackboard.

2. Ms. Williams emphasizes the importance of prewriting activities to her students. Which aspect of the cognitive approach to writing does she emphasize?
   a. metacognitive strategies
   b. planning
   c. problem solving
   d. revising

3. Which of the following is the best example of a social constructivist approach to writing?
   a. Ms. Reddick's students write reports on various subjects, based on research they have completed.
   b. Ms. Duhon's students write about their personal experiences and meet with her regularly to discuss their work.
   c. Ms. Williams' students write responses to essay questions about material in their social studies text.
   d. Ms. Randolph's students choose the books they want to read and write book reports about each book that they complete.

Please see answer key at end of book . . . .

LG 4 Characterize how mathematical thinking develops and identify some issues related to teaching mathematics.

④ MATHEMATICS

In our examination of math education, we will explore these questions: What are some developmental changes in the way children think about mathematics and their math abilities at different grade levels? What is the biggest controversy in mathematics education today? What are the key cognitive and constructivist processes involved in math learning? What role should technology play in math education?

DEVELOPMENTAL CHANGES

The National Council of Teachers of Mathematics (NCTM, 2000) has described the basic principles and standards for school mathematics at different grade levels. We will survey these for all grade levels, beginning with prekindergarten through grade 2.

DEVELOPMENT

Prekindergarten Through Grade 2 Children already have a substantial understanding of numbers before they enter first grade (Van de Walle et al., 2016). Most kindergartners from middle-income families can count past 20, and many can count beyond 100; most can accurately count the number of objects in a set, can add and subtract single digits, and know the relative magnitudes of single-digit numbers (for example, that 8 is greater than 6) (Siegler & Robinson, 1982). However, there is a special concern about young children from economically disadvantaged families who lack opportunities to learn math in early childhood programs or through everyday activities at home and in the community. Leading experts recommend that young children learn two important aspects of math before they enter school: (1) basic aspects of numbers, and (2) basic aspects of geometry (Cross et al., 2009). Researchers have found that early number competencies are linked to future math success (Jordan et al., 2009). In an analysis of six longitudinal studies, school-entry math knowledge was one of three key predictors (along with reading and attention skills) of school achievement later in elementary school and middle school (Duncan et al., 2007).

Building Blocks for Math is a program for developing preschool children's early math skills (McGraw-Hill, 2015). The program embeds math learning in everyday activities, including circle and story time. Researchers have found that the Building Blocks program is effective in improving young children's math skills (Clements & Sarama, 2008).

RESEARCH

Children enter elementary school with different levels of mathematical understanding. Some children will need additional support for math learning. Early assessments should be used to obtain information for teaching and for potential early interventions.

Understanding basic aspects of number and geometry are critical in kindergarten through the second grade (NCTM, 2000). For example, at these grade levels, children need to learn the base-10 numeration system. They must recognize that the word *ten* may represent a single entity or 10 separate units (10 ones) and that these representations can be interchanged.

When they go to school, children learn many higher numerical skills (NCTM, 2007a). It is important to be aware that they are often doing something more than simply learning to calculate in a standard way. In fact, what children learn about mathematics and how to solve mathematical problems often reflects independent thinking as well as what they are being "taught." This can be true even in the case of learning the basic "facts" of addition and subtraction, which most of us ultimately memorize.

Grades 3 Through 5 Three key themes of mathematics in grades 3 through 5 are as follows:

- *Multiplicative reasoning.* The emphasis on multiplicative reasoning develops knowledge that children build on as they move to the middle grades, where the focus is on proportional reasoning. In multiplicative reasoning, children need to develop their understanding of fractions as part of a whole and as division.
- *Equivalence.* The concept of *equivalence* helps students to learn different mathematical representations and provides an avenue for exploring algebraic ideas.

What are some developmental changes in the basic mathematical principles children need to learn in elementary school?
Tim Pannell/Corbis RF/SuperStock

What are some developmental changes in the math principles students need to learn in middle school and high school?

Thomas Imo/Alamy Stock Photo

- *Computational fluency.* Students need to learn efficient and accurate methods of computing that are based on well-understood properties and number relationships. For example, 298 × 42 can be thought of as (300 × 42) − (2 × 42), or 41 × 16 is computed by multiplying 41 × 8 to get 328 and then doubling 328 to obtain 656.

Grades 6 Through 8 In middle school, students benefit from a balanced mathematics program that includes algebra and geometry. Teachers can help students understand how algebra and geometry are connected. Middle school mathematics also should prepare students to deal with quantitative solutions in their lives outside of school.

Students develop far more powerful mathematical reasoning when they learn algebra. A single equation can represent an infinite variety of situations. Even many students who get *A*'s and *B*'s in algebra classes, however, do so without understanding what they are learning—they simply memorize the equations. This approach might work well in the classroom, but it limits these students' ability to use algebra in real-world contexts (NCTM, 2007b).

Grades 9 Through 12 The NCTM (2000) recommends that all students study mathematics in each of the four years of high school. Because students' interests may change during and after high school, they will likely benefit from taking a range of math classes. They should experience the interplay of algebra, geometry, statistics, probability, and discrete mathematics (which involves the mathematics of computers). They should become adept at visualizing, describing, and analyzing situations in mathematical terms. They also need to be able to justify and prove mathematically based ideas.

> **Thinking Back/Thinking Forward**
>
> Common Core enthusiasts also argue that the Standards focus more on critical thinking, problem solving, communication, and technology than No Child Left Behind does. Connect to "Standardized Tests and Teaching."

CONTROVERSY IN MATH EDUCATION

Educators currently debate whether math should be taught using a cognitive, conceptual, and constructivist approach or a practice-oriented, computational approach. Some proponents of the cognitive approach argue against memorization and practice in teaching mathematics. Instead, they emphasize constructivist mathematical problem solving. Others assume that speed and automaticity are fundamental to effective mathematics achievement and argue that such skills can be acquired only through extensive practice and computation. In recent years, the constructivist approach has become increasingly popular. In this approach, effective instruction focuses on involving children in solving a problem or developing a concept and in exploring the efficiency of alternative solutions. This shift in mathematics teaching, away from the computational approach, has been supported by the Common Core Standards' emphasis on the cognitive, conceptual, and constructivist approach.

Gary Piercey, who teaches math to high school students in Houston, Texas, makes the classroom an exciting place for students. He sometimes dresses up for skits like the one shown here in which he plays Freeze, whose evil plans can be foiled only by students being able to successfully solve algebra problems.

Paul S. Howell

COGNITIVE PROCESSES

In our discussion of developmental changes and the controversy in math education, we mentioned several cognitive processes that help children learn math, such as problem-solving skills, understanding how math concepts are linked, and exploring alternative solutions. The National Research Council (2005) concluded that conceptual understanding, procedural fluency, effective organization of knowledge, and metacognitive strategies are important processes in learning math.

In our discussion of the controversy in math education, we saw that debate flourishes about whether conceptual understanding or procedural competences should be the main focus in math education. The National Research Council's (2005) conclusion is that both are important. Teaching math with only an emphasis on procedural competency results in students having too little conceptual understanding, and students who have too little knowledge of procedures often do not solve math problems competently.

As students move through elementary and secondary school and take increasingly complex math courses, new knowledge and competencies must build on, and be integrated with, previous knowledge (Posamentier & Smith, 2015). By the time students begin solving algebra problems, they must have a network of organized knowledge that they can engage to support new algebraic understanding. "The teacher's challenge, then, is to help students build and consolidate prerequisite competencies, understand new concepts in depth, and organize both concepts and competencies in a network of knowledge" (Fuson et al., 2005, p. 232).

Math instruction that supports students' use of metacognitive strategies also is recommended by the National Research Council (2005). Students can engage in metacognitive self-monitoring to assess their progress in solving individual math problems and their progress in a math course. "Metacognitive functioning is also facilitated by shifting from a focus on answers as just right or wrong to a more detailed focus on 'debugging' a wrong answer, that is, finding where the error is, why it is an error, and correcting it" (Fuson et al., 2005, p. 239).

Developing some effective general problem-solving strategies can also help students' math learning. Two of these strategies are making a drawing of a situation and asking oneself questions. Students can learn to use these strategies as part of their self-monitoring in math.

In a recent book, *Mathematical Mindsets,* Jo Boaler (2016) described her research on how children can enjoy and succeed in math. She says that society has traditionally valued the type of math student who is good at memorizing and calculating, but not valued the student who learns math more deeply, slower, and creatively. Boaler points out that too often students think that the most important aspect of learning math is to become able to solve problems quickly, creating pressure that leads to math anxiety. Also, students who think more deeply, slower, and creatively when solving math problems may get turned off by the subject because they are required to memorize shallow facts and rules. In one analysis, Boaler (2016) examined the math achievement of 13 million students in many countries and found that the lowest-achieving students were those whose main strategy was memorization. The highest-achieving students were more likely to perceive math as a combination of big ideas.

In teaching students math, Boaler emphasizes the importance of Carol Dweck's (2006, 2015a, b) concept of **mindset**, which Dweck defines as the cognitive view individuals develop for themselves. Dweck concludes that individuals have one of two mindsets: (1) a fixed mindset, in which they believe that their qualities are carved in stone and cannot change; or (2) a growth mindset, in which they believe their qualities can change and improve through their effort. Boaler's Stanford University Center—*youcubed*—provides free mindset math learning materials that have been used in more than 100,000 schools (see www.youcubed.org/). She also offers online materials that are designed to help teachers and parents work more effectively with students as well as resources to help students gain a deeper understanding of math concepts.

SOME CONSTRUCTIVIST PRINCIPLES

From a constructivist perspective, the principles discussed next can be followed when teaching math (Middleton & Goepfert, 1996). These include strategies for making math realistic and interesting, building on students' prior knowledge, and making the math curriculum socially interactive.

mindset Dweck's concept that refers to the cognitive view individuals develop for themselves; individuals have one of two mindsets: fixed or growth.

Make Math Realistic and Interesting Build your teaching of math around realistic and interesting problems. These problems might involve some kind of conflict, suspense, or crisis that motivates students' interest. The math problem-solving activities might center on the student, community issues, scientific discoveries, or historical events. Math games can provide a motivating context for learning math. Connecting math with other subject areas, such as science, geography, reading, and writing, also is recommended.

Consider the Students' Prior Knowledge In our discussion of cognitive processes, we indicated that building on the student's knowledge is an important aspect of math education (National Research Council, 2005). Evaluate what knowledge the students bring to the unit and the context in which instruction takes place. Make enough information available for students to be able to come up with a method for solving math problems but withhold enough information to ensure that students must stretch their minds to solve the problems.

Make the Math Curriculum Socially Interactive Develop math projects that require students to work together to come up with a solution (NCTM, 2007c). Build into the math curriculum opportunities for students to use and improve their communication skills. Generate math projects that engender discussion, argument, and compromise.

TECHNOLOGY AND MATH INSTRUCTION

One issue in math education is how technology intensive it should be (NCTM, 2007c). The NCTM's *Curriculum and Evaluation Standards* recommends that calculators be used at all levels of mathematics instruction and that some access to computers is also necessary if students are to be adequately educated for future careers. In many school systems, getting adequate funds for computers is a major issue.

TECHNOLOGY

DIVERSITY

Unlike U.S. teachers, Japanese and Chinese teachers do not allow the everyday use of calculators or computers in mathematics classes because they want to make sure that students understand the concepts and operations required to solve problems. Some critics argue that the American emphasis on the early use of technology prevents students from gaining experience in manipulating concrete objects—experience that is essential for learning mathematical concepts (Stevenson, 2001). Only at the high school level, after students have developed a clear understanding of mathematical concepts, are East Asian students allowed to use calculators for solving mathematical problems. In the National Assessment of Educational Progress, in the fourth grade, frequent calculator use was associated with lower national achievement test scores in mathematics, whereas in the eighth and twelfth grades, more frequent use of calculators was linked with higher national test scores (see Figure 3). Teachers can select online tools and apps that teach math concepts in an interactive way rather than selecting tools such as calculators that offload computational processes without

FIGURE 3 FREQUENCY OF CALCULATOR USE AT DIFFERENT GRADE LEVELS CORRELATED WITH NATIONAL MATHEMATICS ACHIEVEMENT TEST SCORES

Note: Scores on the National Mathematics Achievement Test can range from 0 to 500.

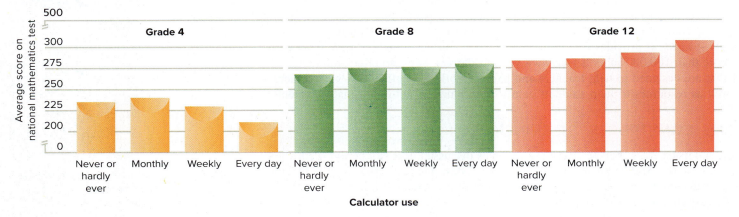

promoting conceptual understanding. For young students, this might include apps that teach number sense (for example, Pearl Diver HD) or interaction simulations that explore fractions or function (for example, PhET math simulations).

Some teachers were recently asked to describe their best strategies for teaching math. Following are their responses.

EARLY CHILDHOOD   For preschoolers, math is a natural. They constantly want to know how much, how long, or is it finished yet. We build on this inquisitiveness by helping children find the answers for themselves. In the classroom, we have scales for measuring blocks, liquid, counting bears, and more. We measure how tall they are throughout the year and show them in inches and centimeters. We sharpen their counting skills by having them count the number of steps to the bathroom, and have clocks, timers, rulers, calculators, and numbers in numerous places.

—VALARIE GORHAM, *Kiddie Quarters, Inc.*

ELEMENTARY SCHOOL: GRADES K–5   I find that math manipulatives (physical objects used to represent or model a problem situation) are extremely helpful in teaching my second-graders because they help bring students from concrete thinking to more abstract thinking. Instead of simply memorizing, manipulatives allow students to understand complicated mathematical concepts. This understanding helps them to apply mathematical knowledge to other problems and areas.

—SUSAN FROELICH, *Clinton Elementary School*

MIDDLE SCHOOL: GRADES 6–8   Math skills can be taught through any number of academic disciplines. In social studies, for example, I apply math skills by having students create timelines, placing historical events in chronological order. Graphing skills are also used when we locate different places on a map.

—CASEY MAASS, *Edison Middle School*

HIGH SCHOOL: GRADES 9–12   As a career and technical education teacher, I make it a point to show students how mathematical skills are applied to real-world situations. For example, I have my food services students create a gingerbread house in which they use rulers, measurements, and protractors—things some of them have not used since middle school. They also multiply and divide recipes. Having my students develop recipes that sometimes work and sometimes fail (often because of incorrect measurements or division) helps them to see the importance of mastering mathematical skills.

—SANDY SWANSON, *Menomonee Falls High School*

CONNECTING WITH STUDENTS: Best Practices
Strategies for Teaching Mathematics

What are some effective strategies for helping your students improve their math skills? Following are some recommendations:

1. *Teach students to become both procedurally and conceptually competent in math.* Students need to develop good computational skills, and they also need to understand math concepts.

2. *Help students to develop good math problem-solving skills.*

3. *Encourage students to use metacognitive strategies.* Guide students to monitor their progress in solving math problems and becoming more competent at math.

4. *Make math interesting for students.* For example, using real-world contexts and games can increase many

continued

CONNECTING WITH STUDENTS: Best Practices
Strategies for Teaching Mathematics

students' motivation for spending time on math, especially students who are not doing well in math. In *Through the Eyes of Teachers*, you can read about Henry Brown, who thinks it is important to teach real-world math skills.

THROUGH THE EYES OF TEACHERS
Never See Failure as Failure

Henry Brown was an at-risk student when his life was turned around by middle school teacher Cora Russell, and the experience inspired him to become a teacher. Brown, a Florida Teacher of the Year, teaches math at Hallandale Adult Alternative High School. In Brown's view, teachers should "never see failure as failure." Half of the students enter the school with math skills below the fifth-grade level. Brown believes it is important to teach real-world math skills. In one project, Brown devised a dummy corporation and had students play different roles in it, learning important math skills as they worked and made decisions in the corporation. He also created Helping Hands, which involves senior citizens in the classroom.

(Source: "All-USA first teacher team," October 10, 2001, *USA Today*. © 2001)

Henry Brown.
Andrew Itkoff

5. *Use technology effectively.* As indicated earlier, some research indicates that use of calculators and computers in math should be delayed until the middle school years. When using computers for math, target conceptual understanding.

6. *Connect with parents.* Family Math is a program that helps parents experience math with their children in a positive, supportive way. In addition to telling parents about Family Math, consider having Family Math nights, especially at the beginning of the school year. At the Family Math night, offer resources that parents can use at home to help their children learn math more effectively.

7. *If you teach math, one good active step is to join the NCTM and use its resources.* The NCTM has annual conferences, publishes an annual yearbook with stimulating chapters on recent developments in math education, and publishes journals such as *Mathematics Teacher*. For more information about the NCTM, call (800) 235-7566 or go to www.nctm.org.

Review, Reflect, and Practice

4 Characterize how mathematical thinking develops and identify some issues related to teaching mathematics.

REVIEW
- What are some developmental changes in mathematical skills?
- What is the main controversy in math education?
- What are some cognitive processes involving math?
- What are some constructivist principles in learning math?
- What role can technology play in math instruction?

REFLECT
- Do you think that teachers in Asia are wise not to allow young students to use calculators? Should the United States follow this example?

Review, Reflect, and Practice

PRAXIS™ PRACTICE

1. Ms. Carpenter's students are working on developing an understanding of place value. They are most likely to belong to which grade level?
   a. K–2
   b. 3–5
   c. 6–8
   d. 9–12

2. Malavi is very fast and accurate at doing multiplication and division. In the controversy on math education, he could be cited as an example of the importance of adopting which of these approaches?
   a. constructivist
   b. practice, computational
   c. conceptual
   d. cognitive

3. Joan is going over her math exam. She is examining her mistakes in an effort to find out what she did wrong. Then she corrects her mistakes and resubmits the exam. Her teacher, Mr. Ewing, allows students to receive credit for going through this process because he believes it helps students to learn from their errors. This is an example of:
   a. algebraic reasoning
   b. algorithms
   c. debugging
   d. rote memorization

4. Which of the following is the best example of application of constructivist principles to math teaching?
   a. Ms. Carmichael's students complete timed tests requiring mastery of basic math facts.
   b. Ms. Dodge's students play store, which allows them to add up their purchases, pay for them, and make change.
   c. Ms. Luker's students solve word problems but do not work on computation.
   d. Mr. Pinks' students complete problems on the board so he can determine whether they have grasped the concepts involved.

5. Based on the results of research on calculator use and math achievement, at which of the following grade levels should Ingrid start using a calculator in doing math?
   a. first
   b. third
   c. fifth
   d. eighth

Please see answer key at end of book . . . .

5 SCIENCE

LG 5 Identify some challenges and strategies related to teaching children how to think scientifically.

Our examination of science focuses on these questions: What are some key ideas in educating students about science? What are some constructivist strategies for teaching science?

SCIENCE EDUCATION

Scientists typically engage in certain kinds of thinking and behavior. For example, they regularly make careful observations; collect, organize, and analyze data; measure,

Thinking Back/Thinking Forward

Having a deep understanding of subject matter is an important aspect of being a competent teacher. Connect with "Educational Psychology: A Tool for Effective Teaching."

Pete Karpyk, who teaches chemistry in Weirton, West Virginia, uses an extensive array of activities that bring science alive for students. Here he has shrink-wrapped himself to demonstrate the effects of air pressure. He has some students give chemistry demonstrations at elementary schools and has discovered that in some cases students who don't do well on tests excel when they teach children. He also adapts his teaching based on feedback from former students and incorporates questions from their college chemistry tests as bonus questions on the tests he gives his high school students. (Source: Wong Briggs, 2005, p. 6D.)

Dale Sparks/All-Pro Photography

graph, and understand spatial relations; pay attention to and regulate their own thinking; and know when and how to apply their knowledge to solve problems (Lehrer & Schauble, 2015).

These skills, which are essential to the practice of science, are not routinely taught in schools, especially elementary schools. As a result, many students are not competent at them. Many scientists and educators argue that schools need to focus more attention on guiding students in learning how to use these skills (Chiappetta & Koballa, 2015; Edwards et al., 2017).

Children have many misconceptions that are incompatible with science and reality. They may go through mental gymnastics trying to reconcile seemingly contradictory new information with their previous beliefs. For example, after learning about the solar system, children sometimes conclude that there are two Earths—the seemingly flat world in which they live and the round ball floating in space that their teacher has just described.

Good teachers perceive and understand a child's underlying concepts, then use the concepts as a scaffold for learning (DeRosa & Abruscato, 2015). Effective science teaching helps children distinguish between fruitful errors and misconceptions, and detect plainly wrong ideas that need to be replaced by more accurate conceptions (Edwards et al., 2017).

CONSTRUCTIVIST TEACHING STRATEGIES

Many science teachers help their students construct their knowledge of science through guided discovery (DeRosa & Abruscato, 2015). Constructivist teaching emphasizes that children have to build their own scientific knowledge and understanding with guidance from the teacher. At each step in science learning, they need to interpret new knowledge in the context of what they already understand. Rather than putting fully formed knowledge into children's minds, in the constructivist approach teachers serve as guides and consultants as children construct scientifically valid interpretations of the world and provide students with feedback to help them correct their scientific misconceptions.

Critics of constructivist approaches argue that too much attention is given to inquiry skills and not enough is given to discipline-specific information. In response, advocates of the constructivist approach to biology argue that it creates more scientifically literate citizens who know how to think in scientific ways rather than just memorize scientific facts.

Keep in mind, though, that it is important that students not be left completely on their own to construct scientific knowledge independent of *science content*. Students' inquiry should be guided (Magnusson & Palincsar, 2005). Teachers at a minimum should initially scaffold students' science learning, extensively monitor their progress, and ensure that they are learning science content accurately. Thus, in pursuing science investigations, students need to "learn inquiry skills *and* science content" (Lehrer & Schauble, 2015).

CONNECTING WITH STUDENTS: Best Practices
Best Practices and Strategies for Teaching Science

Consider adopting the following strategies when teaching science:

1. *Help students learn how to think like scientists.* Create settings in which students are required to make careful observations, work effectively with data, and solve scientific problems.

2. *Monitor students' misconceptions about science and work with them to develop more accurate conceptions.*

3. *Guide students in developing inquiry skills.* When teaching inquiry skills, don't leave students completely to their own devices; use guided inquiry.

CONNECTING WITH STUDENTS: Best Practices
Best Practices and Strategies for Teaching Science

4. *Make science interesting by giving students opportunities to explore everyday science problems.* In *Through the Eyes of Teachers,* you can read about how Peggy Schweiger, a physics teacher at Klein Oak High School in Katy, Texas, does this.

THROUGH THE EYES OF TEACHERS
Dropping an Egg on a Teacher's Head

Peggy Schweiger uses hands-on projects, such as wiring a doll house and making replicas of a boat for a regatta, to improve students' understanding of physics. She especially works hard to create projects that will interest both female and male students. According to former student Alison Arnett, 19, "She taught us how to think and learn, not how to succeed in physics class. We were encouraged to stand on desks, tape things to the ceiling, and even drop an egg on her head to illustrate physics—anything to make us discover that we live with physics every day."

(Source: "All-USA First Teacher Team," October 10, 2001, *USA Today*.)

Peggy Schweiger with a student who is learning how to think and discover how physics works in people's everyday lives.
Patty Wood

Review, Reflect, and Practice

⑤ Identify some challenges and strategies related to teaching children how to think scientifically.

REVIEW
- What are key ideas in science education?
- What are some constructivist approaches to teaching science?

REFLECT
- How effectively did your elementary, middle, and high schools teach science to the typical student? If less than perfectly, how could their approach have been improved?

PRAXIS™ PRACTICE
1. Which of the following teachers is most likely to be successful in helping students to overcome scientific misconceptions?
   a. Ms. Coster finds out what her students' misconceptions are by carefully asking them questions and then explicitly combats their misconceptions via direct instruction.
   b. Ms. Quigley uses a science text and carefully tests her students over the content in the text.
   c. Mr. Jones sets up situations in which the students explore materials themselves to discover their misconceptions.
   d. Mr. Foster designs experiences that demonstrate to the students that their misconceptions are incorrect and point out the correct principles.

continued

> ### Review, Reflect, and Practice
>
> 2. Which of the following is the best example of constructivist teaching strategies in science?
>   a. Mr. Ricardo's students study the material in their science tests and take quizzes over each chapter.
>   b. Mr. Bunker's students have a "science bee" every Friday. He asks questions and the students respond. Students who give incorrect answers are out of the competition.
>   c. Ms. Mertz's students perform carefully designed experiments in a few areas that demonstrate scientific principles, helping them to learn in depth and to learn the process of scientific inquiry.
>   d. Ms. O'Connor's students keep science notebooks in which they take notes on her presentations, and she gives periodic tests on the material in the notebooks.
>
> *Please see answer key at end of book . . . .*

LG 6 Summarize how learning in social studies is becoming more constructivist.

6 SOCIAL STUDIES

What is the nature of social studies? What key themes characterize teaching and learning in social studies? How can constructivist approaches be applied to social studies?

WHAT IS SOCIAL STUDIES?

In general, the field of **social studies**, also called social sciences, seeks to promote civic competence. The goal is to help students make informed and reasoned decisions for the public good as citizens of a culturally diverse, democratic society in an interdependent world (Chapin, 2015). In schools, social studies draws from disciplines such as anthropology, economics, geography, history, law, philosophy, political science, psychology, religion, and sociology.

Social studies is taught in kindergarten through grade 12 in the United States. In elementary school, children often learn social studies that are integrated across several disciplines. This often takes the form of units constructed around broad themes that are examined in terms of time, continuity, and change (Parker & Beck, 2017). In middle schools and high schools, courses may be interdisciplinary—such as a history course drawing from geography, economics, and political science—or focused more on a single discipline, such as just history itself (Chapin, 2015).

The National Council for the Social Sciences (2000) emphasizes that ten themes should be stressed in social sciences:

- *Time, continuity, and change.* Students need to understand their historical roots and locate themselves in time. Knowing how to effectively read about and construct the past helps students to explore questions such as "How am I connected to the past?" and "How can my personal experience be viewed as part of the larger human story across time?" This theme typically appears in history courses. Rather than simply teaching history as lists of facts to be memorized, expert history teachers guide students in analyzing and reflecting about historical events, especially encouraging students to think about how events might be interpreted in different ways (Levstik, 2017). A number of expert history teachers also get students to engage in debate about the evidence pertaining to a particular historical circumstance.

social studies The field that seeks to promote civic competence with the goal of helping students make informed and reasoned decisions for the public good as citizens of a culturally diverse, democratic society in an interdependent world.

- *People, places, and environments.* The study of these topics helps students to develop spatial and geographic perspectives on the world. Armed with this knowledge, students are better equipped to make informed and competent decisions about the relationship of humans to their environment. In schools, this theme usually appears in units and courses linked to geography.
- *Individual development and identity.* A student's personal identity is shaped by culture, groups, and institutions. Students can explore such questions as "Who am I?" "How do people learn, think, and develop?" and "How do people meet their needs in a variety of contexts?" In schools, this theme usually appears in units and courses focused on psychology and anthropology.
- *Individuals, groups, and institutions.* Students need to learn about the ways in which schools, churches, families, government agencies, and the courts play integral roles in people's lives. Students can explore the roles of various institutions in the United States and other countries. In schools, this theme typically appears in units and courses on sociology, anthropology, psychology, political science, and history.
- *Power, authority, and governance.* Understanding the development of power, authority, and governance in the United States and other parts of the world is essential for developing civic competence. In this theme, students explore such topics as the following: What is power and what forms does it take? How do people gain power, use it, and justify it? How can people keep their government responsive to their needs and interests? How can conflicts within a nation and between nations be resolved? This theme typically appears in units and courses focused on government, political science, history, and other social sciences.
- *Production, distribution, and consumption.* People have needs and desires that sometimes exceed the limited resources that are available to them. As a result, questions such as these are raised: What is to be produced? How is production to be organized? How are goods and services distributed? What is the most effective allocation of production (land, capital, and management)? Increasingly, these questions are global in scope. In schools, this theme typically appears in units and courses focused on economics.
- *Science, technology, and society.* Modern life as we know it would be impossible without technology and the science that supports it. However, technology raises many questions: Is newer technology always better? How can people effectively cope with rapid technological advances? How are values related to technology? This theme appears in units and courses involving history, geography, economics, civics, and government.
- *Global connections.* The reality of increasing interdependence among nations requires an understanding of nations and cultures around the world. Conflicts between national and global priorities can involve health care, economic development, environmental quality, universal human rights, and other agendas. This theme typically appears in units and courses involving geography, culture, economics, and other social sciences.
- *Civic ideals and practices.* Understanding civic ideals and the practices of citizenship is important for full participation in society. Students focus on such questions as these: What is civic participation and how can I be involved? What is the balance between individual needs and community responsibilities? In schools, this theme typically appears in units and courses involving history, political science, and anthropology.
- *Culture.* The study of culture prepares students to ask and answer questions such as these: How are cultures similar and different? What is the best way to interact with people who are from cultures that are different from your own? How does religion influence the beliefs of people in different cultures? In schools, the theme of culture typically appears in units and courses that focus

What knowledge and perspectives do courses in geography help students to develop?
Glowimages/age fotostock

Thinking Back/Thinking Forward

Technological advances make it possible for students around the world to communicate through videoconferencing over the Internet. Connect with "Sociocultural Diversity."

TECHNOLOGY

DIVERSITY

DIVERSITY

on geography, history, and anthropology, as well as multicultural topics that cut across the curriculum. We further explore teaching about culture and cultural diversity by examining the study of UN Peacekeeping next.

One Canadian middle school social studies teacher developed a project on UN peacekeeping to encourage students to think more deeply and productively about respecting citizens in their own country and about the hardships that people in many countries continue to experience (Welshman, 2000). During the last 50 years, the United Nations has been involved in separating adversaries, maintaining cease-fires, delivering humanitarian relief, helping refugees, and creating conditions that promote democracy. Studying the UN initiatives became a way for students to examine various prosocial values such as kindness, empathy, cooperation, loyalty, equality, and responsibility. In this project, students used a variety of resources, including books and the Internet, over the course of several class periods.

In introducing the UN peacekeeping topic, the teacher asked the students if they'd ever had a disagreement with a friend or classmate at school. Students contributed comments and the teacher said that in many instances it takes a third party to sort things out and help solve the problem. The teacher then shifted attention to how such conflicts also characterize world politics between countries and different ethnic groups. Nations, regions, and small groups of people have disagreements, and there is no teacher present to help cool things down. This is where UN peacekeepers often step in to help solve a particular problem.

Then, students brainstormed about UN peacekeeping, during which they recalled any information they had previously learned about the topic and discussed their ideas with each other. The classroom had a world map on which to identify regions of the world where peacekeeping was taking place or had taken place.

Next, the students were organized into five small groups of five students each to explore questions they had about UN peacekeeping. The first group of students focused on the history of peacekeeping. They explored questions such as where the first peacekeeping mission occurred and how peacekeeping has changed since the end of the Cold War. Group two expressed an interest in the personal side of peacekeeping. Their questions included how much force peacekeepers can use in a mission and some of the dangers they face. The third group wanted to know about the organization of peacekeeping missions and asked questions such as these: Who provides funding for the mission? How are peacekeepers selected? The fourth group was interested in Canada's role in UN peacekeeping, asking these questions: When did Canada get involved in this? Have any Canadians commanded UN peacekeeping missions? The fifth group was intrigued by why peacekeeping occurs and asked questions such as these: What type of decision-making process is used to determine when to form a UN peacekeeping mission? How do people decide which world problems should be dealt with and which should not? After generating these questions, students researched and presented answers.

CONSTRUCTIVIST APPROACHES

Many social studies classes continue to be taught in a traditional manner of using a single textbook, with the teacher lecturing and using controlling question-and-answer strategies. However, some educators conclude that learning about social studies would benefit from constructivist strategies such as using varied sources of information, gathering student-generated questions to guide inquiry, and engaging in peer collaboration—the strategy used in the UN peacekeeping unit we just discussed. In the constructivist view, students should form their own interpretation of evidence and submit it for review. Allowing them

In the History Alive! program of the Teacher's Curriculum Institute, students work in cooperative groups of four to prepare one student to be the actor in a lively panel debate.
Teacher's Curriculum Institute

to do so should encourage greater reflection and deeper understanding of social issues (Levstik, 2017; Maxim, 2014).

Constructivist approaches also emphasize the meaningfulness of social studies (Odhiambo et al., 2016). Students benefit when they find that what they learned in social studies classes is useful both within and outside of school. Meaningful learning often takes place when classroom interaction focuses on sustained examination of a few important topics rather than superficial coverage of many.

Constructivist approaches to social studies also stress the importance of thinking critically about values. Ethical dimensions of topics and controversial issues provide an arena for reflective thinking and understanding. Effective teachers recognize opposing points of view, show respect for well-supported positions, demonstrate sensitivity to cultural similarities and differences, and are committed to social responsibility. From the constructivist perspective, teachers guide students to consider ethical dimensions of topics and address controversial issues rather than directly telling students what is or is not ethical.

Review, Reflect, and Practice

 Summarize how learning in social studies is becoming more constructivist.

REVIEW
- What does social studies instruction aim to accomplish? What themes are emphasized by the National Council for the Social Sciences?
- What are some constructivist approaches to teaching social studies?

REFLECT
- Think about a specific community in which you might teach one day. How might you tailor social studies instruction specifically for those children? How could you make it constructivist?

PRAXIS™ PRACTICE

1. Mr. Chen wants his students to understand that not all people live in the same way that they do. His students study the ways of life of different people around the world. Which theme of social studies does Mr. Chen emphasize?
   a. culture
   b. civic ideals and practice
   c. power, authority, and governance
   d. production, distribution, and consumption

2. Which is the best example of a constructivist approach to social studies?
   a. Mr. Ewing's students listen to his lectures and take notes on the content covered.
   b. Ms. Drexler's students color and label detailed maps to help them learn geography.
   c. Ms. Byrd's students learn the material in their textbooks and take tests covering the content on a regular basis.
   d. Mr. Jordan presents his students with a controversial issue, which they discuss and debate.

Please see answer key at end of book . . . .

7 TECHNOLOGY RESOURCES

In previous sections of this chapter, we have explored effective strategies for educating students in a number of content areas. Now we will describe some of the best ways to use technology in these and other content areas.

TECHNOLOGY

A wealth of content-specific technology resources is available for teachers (Mayer, 2017). Some of these resources are commercial products, while others are free.

In English language arts, there are many good programs for beginning readers, such as the *Reader Rabbit* series. For older students, Google Lit Trips (www.googlelittrips.org) has sources developed by teachers that allow students to explore many places referenced in literature for all ages. Project Gutenberg (www.gutenberg.org) gives the full texts of thousands of books whose copyright has expired. Many children's authors have Web sites that provide supplementary information about the authors and their books (see, for example, www.judyblume.com). There are good supports for writing in most word processing programs, as well as programs that read written text aloud to students, such as *Write: OutLoud,* thereby helping students to improve their writing. Further, the Puppet Pals app scaffolds characters and settings so that even young children can record stories. For actual book creation, the My Story Book Creator app is good for younger children and the Book Creator App allows teachers and students to produce attractive, polished books that can be published as iBooks or exported as PDF files.

There are many commercial programs that give students practice in arithmetic and algebra as well as interesting applications that support geometry explorations, such as the *Geometric Supposer.* Symbol manipulation programs, like Mathematica (www.wolfram.com/mathematica/?source=nav) or Maple (www.maplesoft.com), allow students to explore algebra and calculus in multiple representations. There are also large repositories of mathematics learning objects (see http://www.saab.org/moe/moe/collections.html or www.merlot.org/artifact/BrowseArtifacts.po?catcode=223&browsecat=223&sort=rating) for supporting the learning of specific mathematical concepts. Also, the Sim Calc projects (http://kaputcenter.org/products/software/simcalc-mathworlds-software/) provide simulations and activities that run on calculators, computers, and handheld devices; these are designed to help students explore change and variation. And the National Council for Teachers of Mathematics (www.nctm.org) provides a variety of digital objects for illustrating mathematical concepts for its members, called *Illuminations.*

Technological support for inquiry-based science includes the use of science probes, online access to science expeditions, online interactive activities for students (for example, www.exploratorium.edu), and virtual science laboratories such as those freely available at www.sciencecourseware.org. Vernier (www.vernier.com) and Pasco (www.pasco.com) offer a wide variety of hardware and software for supporting hands-on science activities. Online access to science expeditions can be found at Web sites such as the Jason Project (www.jason.org). There are also good online repositories of learning objects for teaching science, including the National Science Foundation's *Digital Library* (www.scilinks.org/) and the National Science Teachers Association's *SciLinks* (https://www.scilinks.org/).

In social studies, Tom Snyder Productions (http://teacher.scholastic.com/products/tomsnyder.htm) offers a variety of role-playing simulations that introduce students to decision making among competing stakeholders, as do *SimCity* and *Civilization* from Aspyr (www.aspyr.com) on a grander and more complex scale. My World GIS (www.myworldgis.org) is a geographic information system designed for use in educational settings that allows students to explore and analyze geographic data from around the world. There are also incredible sources of original documents (for example, see the Library of Congress *American Memory Collection* at http://memory.loc.gov/ammem or the *Congressional Record* at www.congress.gov/congressional-record, virtual tours of cities all over the world, world newspapers,

My World GIS allows students to explore geographic information from around the world. Teachers can use My World GIS software to create numerous projects for students.

Jackie Karsten/National Geographic Creative

and collections of maps, including the David Rumsey historical map collection (www.davidrumsey.com). Another terrific social studies application is Google Earth (http://earth.google.com), which allows students to bring up aerial views of landscapes all over the world at varying degrees of resolution.

There are also good resources for specialized content areas. For example, the *WebMuseum* is a good source of reproductions for teaching art history, especially the Impressionists. Indeed, museums around the world have good reproductions available. The *Afropop Worldwide* site has a wealth of information about African and world music, including music downloads.

And there is much, much more available over the Internet. For example, the digital objects available in the MERLOT (www.merlot.org) library. A blog called "Free Technology for Teachers" has good ideas for supporting learning and instruction using online tools and apps (www.freetech4teachers.com/).

To close our coverage of learning and cognition in the content areas, the following comments by former high school history teacher Robert Bain (2005, p. 209) capture many of the themes emphasized in this chapter, not only about social science education but also about education in other content areas:

> When my high school students began to study history, they tended to view the subject as a fixed entity, a body of facts that historians retrieved and placed in textbooks (or in the minds of history teachers) for students to memorize. The purpose of history, if it had one, was to somehow inoculate students from repeating past errors. The process of learning history was straightforward and, while not always exciting, relatively simple. Ironically, when I first entered a school to become a history teacher over 30 years ago, I held a similar view, often supported by my education and history courses. . . . I no longer hold such innocent and naïve views of learning or teaching history, and I try to disabuse my students of these views as well. Indeed, our experiences in my history courses have taught us that, to paraphrase Yogi Berra, it's not what we know that's the issue, it's what we know for sure that isn't so. . . . Learning and teaching history demands complex thinking by both teachers and students. It centers around interesting, generative, and organizing problems; critical weighing of evidence and accounts; suspension of our views to understand those of others; use of facts, concepts, and interpretations to make judgments; and later, if the evidence persuades, to changes in our views and judgments.

Connecting with the Classroom: Crack the Case

The Constructivist Math Curriculum

Connie teaches fourth grade in a middle-SES school district. Her district has adopted a new K–6 math curriculum for this year, based on constructivist principles. In attending the in-service devoted to training teachers in implementing the new curriculum, Connie discovers that many differences exist between what she has been teaching for the past 20 years and this new curriculum. The new curriculum focuses on the use of math in "real life." Instead of endless speed drills, the problems ask the students to think and make connections between their lives at home and what they are doing in math. What drill and practice there is takes place in the context of various games the children play together. Students are allowed, and even taught, to approach problems in a variety of ways rather than focusing on a single algorithm for a particular type of problem. Many of these approaches are completely alien to Connie and, she guesses, to other teachers and parents. "This is going to be a lot of work," she thinks. "I'm going to have to relearn math myself in order to teach this way."

As the school year begins, other teachers begin expressing their concerns over the new curriculum. It is just so different from anything they have ever done in the past. Most of the teachers are managing to stay just a lesson or two ahead of the students. The children in first and second grade seem to love the new math program. They are actively involved during math period, and many of them have said that math is fun. The students in fourth through sixth grade don't appear to be as enthusiastic about the new curriculum, however. Many of them are unable to complete their homework. They can't seem to grasp how to complete problems using the techniques taught in

continued

the new curriculum. They constantly fall back on the old algorithms they were taught when they were younger. This is frustrating Connie and her colleagues, as they have worked very hard to master the alternate ways of approaching problems themselves.

To make matters worse, parents are complaining. They can't help their children with their homework because they don't know how to use the new approaches, either. This has caused many parents to become angry. Several have threatened to remove their children from the school and take them "somewhere where they teach normal math." A group of parents will be addressing the board of education regarding this at their next meeting.

Adding fuel to the fire is one of the middle school math teachers, who insists that this new curriculum won't give the students the foundation they need for algebra. "They need to develop automaticity with their math facts. That just isn't going to happen with this program. It takes them in too many directions. They'll never make it back to normal in time for algebra."

Proponents answer the middle school teacher by indicating that the new curriculum will actually better prepare the students for higher math because they will have a better conceptual understanding of *why* they are doing things and how the traditional algorithms work. Connie feels caught in the middle. She understands what the curriculum is supposed to do. She even believes it might actually benefit the students in the long run. However, every day she has students in tears in her class because they don't understand what she is asking them to do. She has fielded her share of phone calls from angry parents as well.

1. What are the issues in this case?
2. The students in first and second grade seem to be flourishing in this curriculum, whereas the older students are struggling. Why might this be? Tie your answer to a constructivist principle.
3. How should the teachers address parental concerns regarding the new curriculum?
4. How should administrators address the concerns of the algebra teacher?
5. What can the teachers do to help their students at this point?

Connecting with Learning: Reach Your Learning Goals

① EXPERT KNOWLEDGE AND PEDAGOGICAL CONTENT KNOWLEDGE: Distinguish between expert knowledge and pedagogical content knowledge.

- Expert knowledge, also called *subject matter knowledge,* involves being an expert regarding the content of a discipline. Pedagogical content knowledge involves knowledge of how to effectively teach a particular discipline. Both types of knowledge are required of expert teachers.

② READING: Explain how reading develops and discuss some useful approaches to teaching reading.

A Developmental Model of Reading

- Chall's model proposes five stages in reading development: (0) from birth to first grade, identify letters of the alphabet and learn to write one's name; (1) in first and second grade, learn to sound out words and complete learning of letter names and sounds; (2) in second and third grade, become more fluent at retrieving individual words and other reading skills; (3) in fourth through eighth grade, increasingly obtain new information from print and shift from "learning to read" to "reading to learn"; and (4) in high school, become a fully competent reader and understand material from different perspectives.

Approaches to Reading

- Current debate focuses on the phonics approach versus the whole-language approach. The phonics approach emphasizes that reading instruction should focus on phonics and basic rules for translating written symbols into sounds and give children simplified materials for early reading instruction. The whole-language approach stresses that reading instruction should parallel children's natural language learning and give children whole-language materials, such as books and poems.
- Although both approaches can benefit children, the phonics approach needs to be emphasized especially in kindergarten and first grade. Research indicates that phonological awareness

- Cognitive Approaches
  - instruction is especially effective when it is combined with letter training and as part of a total literacy program.
  - Effective phonological awareness training mainly involves two skills: blending and segmentation. Children's reading also benefits from guided oral reading and instruction in reading strategies.
  - Cognitive approaches to reading emphasize decoding and comprehending words, building on prior knowledge, and developing expert reading strategies.
  - Metacognitive strategies and automatic processes are involved in decoding and comprehending words.
  - Prior knowledge about a topic can help students make correct inferences about material they read.
  - Transactional strategy instruction is one approach to helping students learn to read.

- Social Constructivist Approaches
  - Social constructivist approaches to reading stress that the social context plays an important part in helping children learn to read and that meaning is socially negotiated.
  - Reciprocal teaching can help students improve their reading.
  - Recognition of school/family/community connections to reading also reflects the social constructivist perspective.

❸ WRITING: Describe how writing develops and discuss some useful approaches to teaching writing.

- Developmental Changes
  - Children's writing follows a developmental timetable, emerging out of scribbling. Most 4-year-olds can print their name. Most 5-year-olds can reproduce letters and copy several short words.
  - Advances in children's language skills and cognitive development provide the foundation for improved writing.

- Cognitive Approaches
  - Cognitive approaches to writing emphasize many of the same themes as for reading, such as constructing meaning and developing strategies. Planning, problem solving, revising, and metacognitive strategies are thought to be especially important.

- Social Constructivist Approaches
  - Social constructivist approaches to writing focus on the social context in which writing is produced. This social context includes the importance of students participating in a writing community to understand author/reader relationships and grasp perspectives of others.
  - Social constructivist approaches to writing include writing of "real texts" about meaningful experiences, teacher-student writing conferences, peer collaboration in writing, and school-community connections.

❹ MATHEMATICS: Characterize how mathematical thinking develops and identify some issues related to teaching mathematics.

- Developmental Changes
  - Children have a substantial understanding of numerical concepts before they enter first grade. When they go to school, children learn more advanced numerical skills.
  - The National Council of Teachers of Mathematics has developed standards for learning mathematics at these grade levels: kindergarten through grade 2 (base-10 numeration system, for example); grades 3 through 5 (multiplicative reasoning, equivalence, and computational fluency); grades 6 through 8 (mathematical reasoning—algebra and geometry); and grades 9 through 12 (interplay of algebra, geometry, statistics, probability, and discrete mathematics).

- Controversy in Math Education
  - Currently, there is controversy in math education about whether math should be taught using a cognitive, conceptual, and constructivist approach or a practice-oriented, computational approach.
  - Students need to develop both a conceptual understanding of math and procedural competency in math.

continued

Cognitive Processes
- Among the cognitive processes involved in math are conceptual understanding, knowledge of math procedures, effective organization of knowledge, metacognitive strategies, and mindset.

Some Constructivist Principles
- Some constructivist principles include making math education more realistic and interesting, making connections to students' prior knowledge, and making the math curriculum socially interactive.

Technology and Math Instruction
- The NTCM's *Curriculum and Evaluation Standards* recommends that calculators be used at all levels of mathematical instruction and that students' access to computers also is necessary. However, some education experts argue that, as in East Asia, calculators should not be used prior to high school to improve students' ability to learn math concepts.

5 SCIENCE: Identify some challenges and strategies related to teaching children how to think scientifically.

Science Education
- There is a significant shortage of qualified science teachers in middle and high school education in the United States. Too often, the skills that scientists use, such as careful observation, graphing, self-regulatory thinking, and knowing when and how to apply one's knowledge to solve problems, are not routinely taught in schools.
- Children have many misconceptions that are incompatible with science and reality. Good teachers perceive and understand a child's underlying concepts, then use the concepts as a scaffold for learning.

Constructivist Teaching Strategies
- Constructivist teaching strategies include an emphasis on discovery learning—however, teachers need to supply guidance and feedback, and be consultants as children construct scientifically valid interpretations of the world.
- Effective science education emphasizes inquiry and science content knowledge.

6 SOCIAL STUDIES: Summarize how learning in social studies is becoming more constructivist.

What Is Social Studies?
- The field of social studies seeks to promote civic competence. In schools, social studies draws from disciplines such as anthropology, economics, geography, history, law, philosophy, political science, psychology, religion, and sociology.
- Ten themes are recommended to be used for units and courses in social studies by the National Council for the Social Sciences: time, continuity, and change; people, places, and environments; individual development and identity; individuals, groups, and institutions; power, authority, and governance; production, distribution, and consumption; science, technology, and society; global connections; civic ideals and practices; and culture.

Constructivist Approaches
- Many social studies classes continue to be taught in a traditional lecture format, but there is increasing interest in teaching these classes from a constructivist perspective. This perspective emphasizes use of varied sources of information, the importance of greater reflection, understanding, meaning, critical thinking about values, and sustained examination of a few important topics rather than superficial coverage of many topics.

7 TECHNOLOGY RESOURCES: Identify online resources for implementing constructivist approaches to content area teaching.

- A wealth of content-specific technology resources, including commercial and free products, is available for teachers online.

KEY TERMS

expert knowledge 357
mindset 375
pedagogical content knowledge 358
phonics approach 360
reciprocal teaching 362
social studies 382
transactional strategy instruction approach 362
whole-language approach 360

PORTFOLIO ACTIVITIES

Now that you have a good understanding of this chapter, complete these exercises to expand your thinking.

Independent Reflection

1. **The Cognitive and Socially Constructive Classroom.** For the grade level you plan to teach, create a summary of good ideas for making learning both cognitive and socially constructive. Draw ideas from this and other chapters. Add further ideas of your own. (INTASC: Principles *3, 8*)

Research/Field Experience

2. **Researching the Nuts and Bolts of Reading.** Read about current trends in teaching children to read. Evaluate these trends based on what you've learned in this chapter. Compare current trends with how you were taught to read. Which method do you think is most effective? Why? What do you think accounts for persistent low reading scores on nationwide standardized tests? (INTASC: Principles *4, 7*)

Collaborative Work

3. **Taking a Stand in the Math Controversy.** There is controversy in math education about whether math should be taught in a constructivist manner or in a more traditional manner. There is also controversy about whether calculators and computers should be used in math instruction in the elementary school years. Get together with several students and evaluate these controversies. Summarize your discussion. (INTASC: Principles *1, 4, 8*)

chapter 12
PLANNING, INSTRUCTION, AND TECHNOLOGY

chapter outline

① Planning

Learning Goal 1 Explain what is involved in classroom planning.

Instructional Planning
Time Frames and Planning

② Teacher-Centered Lesson Planning and Instruction

Learning Goal 2 Identify important forms of teacher-centered instruction.

Teacher-Centered Lesson Planning
Direct Instruction
Teacher-Centered Instructional Strategies
Evaluating Teacher-Centered Instruction

③ Learner-Centered Lesson Planning and Instruction

Learning Goal 3 Discuss important forms of learner-centered instruction.

Learner-Centered Principles
Some Learner-Centered Instructional Strategies
Evaluating Learner-Centered Strategies

④ Technology and Education

Learning Goal 4 Summarize how to effectively use technology to help children learn.

The Technology Revolution and the Internet
Standards for Technology-Literate Students
Teaching, Learning, and Technology

Education is the transmission of civilization.
—Ariel and Will Durant
American Authors and Philosophers, 20th Century

LWA/Dann Tardif/Blend Images/Corbis

Connecting with Teachers Lois Guest and Kevin Groves

In Lois Guest's fifth-grade classroom at Hesperian Elementary School in San Lorenzo, California, 30 students are working on their new laptop computers provided by the school district. A month after the computers arrived, outdated encyclopedias sit on shelves, and students no longer have to compete for time in the school's computer lab.

The new laptops mark a monumental shift in Guest's career. She has taught for 35 years at Hesperian Elementary and remembers when slide projectors were the height of high tech. Now, she is building a Web site for her class and learning how to use a digital camera and an optical scanner. Guest says that she is learning a lot about technology and that her students are also teaching her how to do things on the computer. Ten-year-old Bianca Gutierrez said that she enjoys working on her new laptop computer so much that it makes her look forward to coming to school.

When Kevin Groves took his fifth-grade class on a field trip to a botanical garden, his students insisted that they be allowed to bring their laptops. One of his students, Salvador Mata, sat on the grass with his mother and explained to her how to make a PowerPoint presentation. His mother is pleased about Salvador learning how to use a computer at such an early age, believing that it will help him get a good job later in his life. Groves commented that he researches every link he puts on his Web site to make sure it is educational and won't lead to something bad for his students. (Source: *USA Today*, October 10, 2001, pp. A1, A24)

Lois Guest (left) and Kevin Groves (right) working with students on their PowerPoint presentations.
(Left) Mark Costantini/San Francisco Chronicle/Polaris; (Right) Kevin Groves

Preview

This chapter builds on the discussions of learning and cognitive processes in other chapters and addresses instructional planning at the level of the overall lesson plan or unit. We explore teacher-centered lesson planning, building on the behavioral principles covered in the chapter on behavioral and social cognitive approaches, and learner-centered lesson planning, building on material covered in other chapters of this text. Finally, we explore important classroom applications of technology, such as use of the Internet.

1 PLANNING

LG 1 Explain what is involved in classroom planning.

It has been said that when people fail to plan, they plan to fail. Many successful people attribute their accomplishments to effective planning. Our introduction to planning describes what instructional planning is and the different time frames of planning.

INSTRUCTIONAL PLANNING

Planning is a critical aspect of being a competent teacher (Burden & Byrd, 2016). **Instructional planning** involves developing a systematic, organized strategy for lessons. Teachers need to decide what and how they are going to teach before they do it. Although some wonderful instructional moments are spontaneous, lessons still should be carefully planned (Borich, 2017).

instructional planning A systematic, organized strategy for planning lessons.

Instructional planning might be mandated by the school in which you teach. Many principals and instructional supervisors require teachers to keep written plans, and you may be asked to submit lesson plans several weeks in advance. When observing classroom teachers, supervisors check to see if the teacher is following the plan. If a teacher is absent, a substitute teacher can follow the plan.

Expectations for teacher planning have increased with the promulgation of state learning standards that specify what students need to know and be able to do (Guillaume, 2016). However, these standards usually do not state what the teacher should do in the classroom to reach these standards. When standards are in place, teachers must figure out how to plan and organize their curriculum around the most important dimensions implied by the standards and create a "sequence and set of learning activities for the particular students they teach" (Darling-Hammond et al., 2005, p. 184).

Many planning strategies are organized around four elements: "the nature of the subject matter, the learners, the context, and the teacher's role" (Darling-Hammond et al., 2005, p. 184). One effective planning strategy that many teachers use is *mapping backward* from "goals to desired performances to activities and elements of scaffolding needed to support student progress." Indeed, a good strategy is to begin your planning by thinking about what goals you want your students to reach by the end of the school year and then map backward from that point. In one analysis, many experienced teachers described how in the early years of their teaching they lacked a long-term vision in their curriculum planning; they strongly urged beginning teachers to think more about the big picture—the key things they want their students to learn this year—and how they can guide their students to get there (Kunzmann, 2003).

Linda Darling-Hammond and her colleagues (2005, pp. 185–186) described some important aspects of curriculum planning:

> Teachers must decide what is important to include, given their goals, and know how to make it accessible to a particular group of students. This requires thinking about how to give students a schema or conceptual map of the domain to be studied (National Research Council, 2000) as well as planning specific activities in light of students' levels of readiness for various kinds of learning experiences. It also requires consideration of the kinds of information, demonstrations, models, inquiry opportunities, discussion, and practice students need over time to understand particular concepts and develop particular skills. . . .

In sum, teachers need to "figure out which things students should do when, in what order, and how" to implement the big picture of their curricular vision.

TIME FRAMES AND PLANNING

As we just indicated, developing systematic time plans involves knowing what needs to be done and when to do it, or focusing on "task" and "time."

You will need to plan for different time spans, ranging from yearly to daily planning (Parkay, 2016). If school-wide planning or your own career planning is involved, the time frame likely will be a number of years. Robert Yinger (1980) identified five time spans of teacher planning: yearly planning, term planning, unit planning, weekly planning, and daily planning. Figure 1 illustrates these time frames and shows planning for them. Yinger also recommends that teachers attend to four areas when planning: goals, sources of information, the form of the plan, and criteria for the effectiveness of the planning.

Although planning is a key dimension of successful teaching, don't overplan to the point of becoming an automaton. Develop organized plans and try to carry them out, but be flexible; as a year, month, week, or day unfolds, adapt to changing

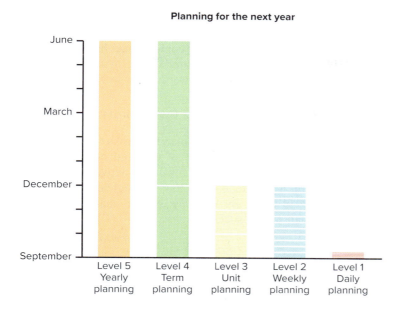

FIGURE 1 FIVE TIME SPANS OF TEACHING PLANNING AND THEIR OCCURRENCE OVER THE SCHOOL YEAR

Source: "A Study of Teacher Planning," by R. J. Yinger, 1980, *The Elementary School Journal, 80* (3), p. 113. University of Chicago Press.

circumstances. A controversial current event or necessary topic might emerge that you did not originally include. Monitor and rework your plans as the school year goes by to suit these changing circumstances (Borich, 2017).

A final comment needs to be made about planning. It is increasingly understood that teachers need to monitor and evaluate their curriculum planning in terms of how well students are making progress toward learning goals as they go through the term. Thus, time for assessment and feedback to students needs to be built into the planning process (Brookhart & Nitko, 2015; Popham, 2017).

A final consideration involves how much time schools allot to lesson planning in the United States compared with other countries. Recent cross-cultural comparisons reveal that lesson planning is given a much higher priority in Chinese than American schools (Shen et al., 2007; Shen et al., 2007). Many American teachers' schedules allow little time for lesson planning, in many cases 30 minutes or less, during the school day. By contrast, Chinese teachers teach only one or two hours a day, in a core subject area, and they spend extensive time on lesson planning: on average about two hours a week of formal collaboration and two hours a week of informal collaboration with colleagues in one core subject area. They also have one to two hours a day to correct homework and classwork, and 30 minutes a day to provide homework feedback to students.

What planning strategies do teachers use to make their teaching more effective? Following are their responses.

How does time allotted to lesson planning differ in Chinese and American schools?
Dwight Cendrowski/Alamy Stock Photo

Thinking Back/Thinking Forward

Think of integrated assessment planning in terms of three time frames: preinstruction, during instruction, and postinstruction. Connect to "Classroom Assessment and Grading"

DIVERSITY

EARLY CHILDHOOD Lesson planning for our preschoolers is done by a team of two at the beginning of the month. The team determines what will be covered by reviewing skills that need to be mastered and implementing appropriate activities. We also incorporate the children's interests in building our plans.

—VALARIE GORHAM, *Kiddie Quarters, Inc.*

ELEMENTARY SCHOOL: GRADES K–5 To prepare for my second-grade classes, I plan each week's (and sometimes two weeks') lessons the Thursday before. This way I can have all copies made, have the necessary materials, and be sure additional materials are available (library books, for example). I then map out the week and check that time is set aside to reteach and reinforce material.

—JANINE GUIDA POUTRE, *Clinton Elementary School*

MIDDLE SCHOOL: GRADES 6–8 When planning my lessons, I use the backward design method: I make a list of essential questions that I want my students to know when they finish the activity. These essential questions go on my whiteboard so that the students are aware of what they are going to learn. By knowing exactly what I want the students to learn, I can plan a successful lesson.

—CASEY MAASS, *Edison Middle School*

HIGH SCHOOL: GRADES 9–12 I get to school by 6:00 a.m. to plan and lay out what I need for the day. I need quiet time without others around and access to copy machines without a line. By 7:00 a.m. I have my activities for the day laid out and ready to go. Of course, I am a morning person!

—SANDY SWANSON, *Menomonee Falls High School*

Review, Reflect, and Practice

1 Explain what is involved in classroom planning.

REVIEW
- What is instructional planning? Why does instruction need to be planned?
- What planning needs to be done related to the use of time?

REFLECT
- In your own K–12 experiences, did you ever have a teacher who did not put enough effort into planning? What was that like for students?

PRAXIS™ PRACTICE
1. Ms. Swenson is planning for the school year. Which of the following strategies should she follow?
   a. Plan forward, starting with plans for the first week of school.
   b. Map backward, determining the goals she wants her students to reach by the end of the school year.
   c. Not spend too much time in planning but rather get a sense of where her students are in the first month of school.
   d. Engage in circular planning.
2. In planning, Mr. Tomasello considers the objectives established by the district and state-mandated standards and aligns his curriculum to them. After doing this, he considers what he wants to teach when, based on the sequence that makes the most sense. Finally, he reserves the necessary equipment and requests the appropriate materials to carry out his plans. At what level of planning is Mr. Tomasello most likely to be engaging?
   a. daily
   b. weekly
   c. term
   d. yearly

Please see answer key at end of book ....

2 TEACHER-CENTERED LESSON PLANNING AND INSTRUCTION

- Teacher-Centered Lesson Planning
- Direct Instruction
- Teacher-Centered Instructional Strategies
- Evaluating Teacher-Centered Instruction

LG 2 Identify important forms of teacher-centered instruction.

Traditionally, the focus in schools has been on teacher-centered lesson planning and instruction. In this approach, planning and instruction are highly structured and the teacher directs students' learning.

TEACHER-CENTERED LESSON PLANNING

Three general tools are especially useful in teacher-centered planning. These are behavioral objectives, task analysis, and instructional taxonomies (classifications), which we explore next.

Behavioral Objectives Behavioral objectives are statements about changes that the teacher wishes to see in students' performance. Behavioral objectives should be very specific and often have three parts (Mager, 1962):

- *Student's behavior.* Focus on what the student will learn or do.
- *Conditions under which the behavior will occur.* State how the behavior will be evaluated or tested.
- *Performance criteria.* Determine what level of performance will be acceptable.

For example, a teacher might develop a behavioral objective around the idea that the student will describe five causes of the decline of the British Empire (student's behavior). The teacher plans to give the student an essay test on this topic (conditions under which the behavior will occur). And the teacher decides that explaining four or five causes will be acceptable performance (performance criterion).

Task Analysis Another tool of teacher-centered planning is **task analysis**, which focuses on breaking down a complex task that students are to learn into its component parts (Alberto & Troutman, 2017). The analysis can proceed in three basic steps (Moyer & Dardig, 1978):

1. Determine what skills or concepts the student needs to have to learn the task.
2. List any materials that will be required in order to perform the task, such as paper, pencil, and calculator.
3. List all of the components of the task in the order in which they must be performed.

Instructional Taxonomies Instructional taxonomies also aid teacher-centered approaches. A **taxonomy** is a classification system. **Bloom's taxonomy** was developed by Benjamin Bloom and his colleagues (1956). It classifies educational objectives into three domains: cognitive, affective, and psychomotor. Bloom's taxonomy has been used by many teachers in their lesson planning to create goals and objectives (Tarman & Kuran, 2015; Yanchinda et al., 2016).

The Cognitive Domain Bloom's cognitive taxonomy has six objectives (Bloom et al., 1956):

- *Knowledge.* Students have the ability to remember information. For example, an objective might be to list or describe four main advantages of using a computer for word processing.

behavioral objectives Statements that communicate proposed changes in students' behavior to reach desired levels of performance.

task analysis Breaking down a complex task that students are to learn into its component parts.

taxonomy A classification system.

Bloom's taxonomy Developed by Benjamin Bloom and colleagues; classifies educational objectives into three domains—cognitive, affective, and psychomotor.

What objectives are involved in Bloom's cognitive taxonomy?
Hero Images/Getty Images

- *Comprehension.* Students understand the information and can explain it in their own words. For example, an objective might be to explain or discuss how a computer can effectively be used for word processing.
- *Application.* Students use knowledge to solve real-life problems. For example, an objective might be to apply what has been learned about using a computer for word processing to how this could be used in various careers.
- *Analysis.* Students break down complex information into smaller parts and relate information to other information. For example, an objective might be to compare one type of word-processing program with another for doing term papers.
- *Synthesis.* Students combine elements and create new information. For example, an objective might be to organize all that has been learned about the use of computers for writing.
- *Evaluation.* Students make good judgments and decisions. For example, an objective might be to critique different word-processing programs or to judge the strengths and weaknesses of a particular word-processing program.

The Affective Domain The affective taxonomy consists of five objectives related to emotional responses to tasks (Krathwohl et al., 1964). Each of the following five objectives requires the student to show some degree of commitment or emotional intensity:

- *Receiving.* Students become aware of or attend to something in the environment. For example, a guest comes to class to talk with students about reading. An objective might be for students to listen carefully to the speaker.
- *Responding.* Students become motivated to learn and display a new behavior as a result of an experience. An objective might be for students to become motivated to become better readers as a result of the guest speaker's appearance.
- *Valuing.* Students become involved in, or committed to, some experience. An objective might be for students to value reading as an important skill.
- *Organizing.* Students integrate a new value into an already existing set of values and give it proper priority. An objective might be to have students participate in a book club.
- *Value characterizing.* Students act in accordance with the value and are firmly committed to it. An objective might be that over the course of the school year, students increasingly value reading.

The Psychomotor Domain Most of us link motor activity with physical education and athletics, but many other subjects, such as handwriting and word processing, also involve movement. In the sciences, students have to manipulate complex equipment; the visual and manual arts require good hand-eye coordination. Bloom's psychomotor objectives include these:

- *Reflex movements.* Students respond involuntarily without conscious thought to a stimulus—for example, blinking when an object unexpectedly hurtles their way.
- *Basic fundamentals.* Students make basic voluntary movements that are directed toward a particular purpose, such as grasping a microscope knob and correctly turning it.
- *Perceptual abilities.* Students use their senses, such as seeing, hearing, or touching, to guide their skill efforts, such as watching how to hold an instrument in science, like a microscope, and listening to instructions on how to use it.

- *Physical abilities.* Students develop general skills of endurance, strength, flexibility, and agility, such as running long distances or hitting a softball.
- *Skilled movements.* Students perform complex physical skills with some degree of proficiency, such as effectively sketching a drawing.
- *Nondiscursive behaviors.* Students communicate feelings and emotions through bodily actions, such as doing pantomimes or dancing to communicate a musical piece.

Teachers can use Bloom's taxonomies for the cognitive, affective, and psychomotor domains to plan instruction. In the past, instructional planning has generally focused on cognitive or behavioral objectives. Bloom's taxonomy provides for a more expansive consideration of skills by also including affective and psychomotor domains.

A group of educational psychologists updated Bloom's knowledge and cognitive process dimensions in light of recent theory and research (Anderson & Krathwohl, 2001). In the update, the knowledge dimension has four categories, which lie along a continuum from concrete (factual) to abstract (metacognition):

- *Factual:* The basic elements students must know to be acquainted with a discipline or solve problems in it (technical vocabulary, sources of information)
- *Conceptual:* The interrelationships among the basic elements within a larger structure that allow them to function together (periods of geological time, forms of business ownership)
- *Procedural:* How to do something, methods of inquiry, and criteria for using skills (skills used in painting with watercolors, interviewing techniques)
- *Metacognitive:* Knowledge of cognition and awareness of one's own cognition (knowledge of outlining and strategies for remembering)

In the update of the cognitive process dimension, six categories lie along a continuum from less complex (remember) to more complex (create):

- *Remember.* Retrieve relevant knowledge from long-term memory. (Recognize the dates of important events in U.S. history.)
- *Understand.* Construct meaning from instruction that includes interpreting, exemplifying, classifying, summarizing, inferring, comparing, and explaining. (Explain the causes of important eighteenth-century events in France.)
- *Apply.* Carry out or use a procedure in a given situation. (Use a law in physics in situations in which it is appropriate.)
- *Analyze.* Break material into its component parts and determine how the parts relate to each other and to overall structure or purpose. (Distinguish between relevant and irrelevant numbers in a math word problem.)
- *Evaluate.* Make judgments based on criteria and standards. (Detect inconsistencies or fallacies in a product.)
- *Create.* Put elements together to form a coherent or functional whole; reorganize elements into a new pattern or structure. (Generate hypotheses to account for an observed phenomenon.)

direct instruction approach A structured, teacher-centered approach characterized by teacher direction and control, high teacher expectations for students' progress, maximum time spent by students on academic tasks, and efforts by the teacher to keep negative affect to a minimum.

DIRECT INSTRUCTION

Direct instruction is a structured, teacher-centered approach that is characterized by teacher direction and control, high teacher expectations for students' progress, maximum time spent by students on academic tasks, and efforts by the teacher

How have the objectives been modified in the update of Bloom's cognitive taxonomy?
Mel Yates/Photodisc/Getty Images

> **Thinking Back/Thinking Forward**
>
> A major curriculum controversy is whether teaching should mainly follow a direct instruction or constructivist approach. Connect to "Educational Psychology: A Tool for Effective Teaching."

DIVERSITY

RESEARCH

DEVELOPMENT

to keep negative affect to a minimum. The focus of direct instruction is academic activity; nonacademic materials (such as toys, games, and puzzles) tend not to be used; also deemphasized is nonacademically oriented teacher-student interaction (such as conversations about self or personal concerns) (Burden & Byrd, 2016).

Teacher direction and control take place when the teacher chooses students' learning tasks, directs students' learning of the tasks, and minimizes the amount of nonacademic talk. The teacher sets high standards for performance and expects students to reach these levels of excellence.

An important goal in the direct-instruction approach is maximizing student learning time (Borich, 2017). Time spent by students on academic tasks in the classroom is called *academic learning time*. Learning takes time. The more academic learning time students experience, the more likely they are to learn the material and achieve high standards. The premise of direct instruction is that the best way to maximize time on academic tasks is to create a highly structured, academically oriented learning environment.

Cross-cultural research about the amount of time students spend on math in different countries, as well as other comparisons across countries, reveals that students in many Asian countries spend more time and effort in learning than do U.S. students. Harold Stevenson, one of the leading experts on children's learning, conducted research on this topic for five decades. In the 1980s and 1990s, he turned his attention to discovering ways to improve children's learning by conducting cross-cultural comparisons of children in the United States with children in Asian countries, especially Japan, China, and Taiwan (Stevenson, 1992, 1995, 2000; Stevenson & Hofer, 1999; Stevenson et al., 1990). In Stevenson's research, Asian students consistently outperformed American students in mathematics. Also, the longer students were in school, the wider the gap became—the lowest difference was in first grade, the highest in eleventh grade (the highest grade studied).

To learn more about the reasons for these cross-cultural differences, Stevenson and his colleagues spent thousands of hours observing in classrooms, as well as interviewing and surveying teachers, students, and parents. They found that Asian teachers spent more of their time teaching math than American teachers did. For example, in Japan more than one-fourth of the total classroom time in first grade was spent on math instruction, compared with only one-tenth of the time in U.S. first-grade classrooms. Also, Asian students were in school an average of 240 days a year, compared with 178 days in the United States.

Also, differences were found between the Asian and American parents. American parents had much lower expectations for the children's education and achievement than did the Asian parents. Also, the American parents were more likely to say that their children's math achievement was due to innate ability; the Asian parents were more likely to say that their children's math achievement was the consequence of effort and training. The Asian students were more likely to do math homework than the American students, and the Asian parents were far more likely to help their children with their math homework than were the American parents (Chen & Stevenson, 1989).

In addition to maximizing student learning time, another emphasis in the direct-instruction approach is keeping negative affect to a minimum. Researchers have found that negative affect interferes with learning (Merrell et al., 2007). Advocates of

In Stevenson's research, Asian students scored considerably higher than U.S. students on math achievement tests. *What are some possible explanations for these findings?*
Amana Images Inc./DAJ/Alamy Stock Photo

direct instruction underscore the importance of keeping an academic focus and avoiding negative affect, such as the negative feelings that can often arise in both the teacher and students when a teacher overcriticizes (Sieberer-Nagler, 2016).

TEACHER-CENTERED INSTRUCTIONAL STRATEGIES

Many teacher-centered strategies reflect direct instruction. Here we will talk about orienting students to new material; lecturing, explaining, and demonstrating; questioning and discussing; mastery learning; seatwork; and homework.

Orienting   Before presenting and explaining new material, establish a framework for the lesson and orient students to the new material: (1) review the previous day's activities; (2) discuss the lesson's objective; (3) provide clear, explicit instructions about the work to be done; and (4) give an overview of today's lesson.

Advance organizers are teaching activities and techniques that establish a framework and orient students to material before it is presented. You can use advance organizers when you begin a lesson to help students see the "big picture" of what is to come and how information is meaningfully connected.

Advance organizers come in two forms: expository and comparative. **Expository advance organizers** provide students with new knowledge that will orient them to the upcoming lesson. The chapter-opening outline and learning goals in each chapter of this text are expository advance organizers. Another way to provide an expository advance organizer is to describe the lesson's theme and why it is important to study this topic. For example, in orienting students to the topic of exploring the Aztec civilization in a history class, the teacher says that they are going to study the Spanish invasion of Mexico and describes who the Aztecs were, what their lives were like, and their artifacts. To heighten student interest, she also says that they will study worlds in collision as Spain's conquistadors were filled with awe at sights of a spectacular Western civilization. There are Mexican American students in her class, and the teacher emphasizes how this information can help everyone in the class understand these students' personal and cultural identity.

Comparative advance organizers introduce new material by connecting it with what students already know. For example, in the history class just mentioned, the teacher says that the Spanish invasion of Mexico continued the transatlantic traffic that changed two worlds: Europe and the Americas. She asks students to think about how this discussion of the Aztecs connects with Columbus' journey, which they examined last week.

DIVERSITY

Lecturing, Explaining, and Demonstrating   Lecturing, explaining, and demonstrating are common teacher activities in the direct-instruction approach (Mowbray & Perry, 2015). Effective teachers spend more time explaining and demonstrating new material than their less-effective counterparts do.

On some occasions we sit through boring lectures, yet on other occasions we have been captivated by a lecturer and learned a great deal from the presentation. Let's explore some guidelines for when lecturing is a good choice and some strategies for delivering an effective lecture. Here are some goals that lecturing can accomplish (Henson, 1988):

1. Presenting information and motivating students' interest in a subject
2. Introducing a topic before students read about it on their own, or giving instructions on how to perform a task
3. Summarizing or synthesizing information after a discussion or inquiry
4. Providing alternative points of view or clarifying issues in preparation for discussion
5. Explaining materials that students are having difficulty learning on their own

advance organizers Teaching activities and techniques that establish a framework and orient students to material before it is presented.

expository advance organizers Organizers that provide students with new knowledge that will orient them to the upcoming lesson.

comparative advance organizers Organizers that introduce new material by connecting it with the students' prior knowledge.

CONNECTING WITH STUDENTS: Best Practices
Strategies for Lecturing

To ensure success when lecturing, follow these strategies:

1. *Be prepared.* Don't just "wing" a lecture. Spend time preparing and organizing what you will present.

2. *Make the lecture interesting and exciting by keeping it short and interspersing it with questions and activities.* For example, lecture for 10 or 15 minutes to provide the background information and framework for a topic, then place students in small discussion groups. Vary the pace of the lecture by interlacing it with related video clips, demonstrations, handouts, and/or activities for students. Think about what you can say that will motivate students' interest in a topic.

3. *Follow a designated sequence and include certain key components:*

   - Begin with advance organizers or previews of the topic.

   - Verbally and visually highlight any key concepts or new ideas (like the boldfaced key terms in this book). Use the blackboard, an overhead projector, or another large-display device.

   - Present new information in relation to what students already know about the topic.

   - Periodically elicit student responses to ensure that they understand the information up to that point and to encourage active learning.

   - At the end of the lecture, provide a summary or an overview of the main ideas.

   - Make connections to future lectures and activities.

Questioning and Discussing It is necessary but challenging to integrate questions and discussion in teacher-centered instruction (Jiang, 2014; Robitaille & Maldonado, 2015). Teachers should respond to each student's learning needs while maintaining the group's interest and attention. It also is important to distribute participation widely while also retaining the enthusiasm of eager volunteers. An additional challenge is allowing students to contribute while still maintaining the focus on the lesson. In a recent research review, asking a large number of questions and monitoring the responses of all students was one of the four specific practices linked to students' achievement (Coe et al., 2014).

CONNECTING WITH STUDENTS: Best Practices
Strategies for the Effective Use of Questions

Let's examine some effective strategies for using questions in the classroom:

1. *Use fact-based questions as entrées into thinking-based questions.* For example, in teaching a lesson on environmental pollution, the teacher might ask the fact-based question: "What are three types of environmental pollution?" Then she could follow with this thinking-based question: "What strategies can you think of for reducing one of these types of environmental pollution?" Don't overuse fact-based questions, because they tend to produce rote learning rather than learning for understanding.

2. *Avoid yes/no and leading questions.* Yes/no questions should be used only as a segue into more probing questions. For example, avoid questions like "Was environmental pollution responsible for the dead fish in the lake?" Keep these questions to a minimum, only occasionally using them as a warm-up for questions such as these: "How did the pollution kill the fish?" "Why do you think companies polluted the lake?" "What can be done to clean up environmental pollution?"

    Also avoid asking leading questions such as "Don't you agree?" or other rhetorical questions such as "You do want to read more about environmental pollution, don't you?" These types of questions don't produce meaningful responses and simply hand the initiative back to the teacher.

3. *Leave enough time for students to think about answers.* Too often when teachers ask questions, they don't give

CONNECTING WITH STUDENTS: Best Practices
Strategies for the Effective Use of Questions

What are some good teaching strategies for the effective use of questions?

students enough time to think. In one study, teachers waited less than one second, on average, before calling on a student to respond (Rowe, 1986)! In the same study, teachers waited only about one second, on average, for the student to respond before supplying the answer themselves. Such intrusions don't give students adequate time to construct answers. In the same study, teachers were subsequently instructed to wait three to five seconds to allow students to respond to questions. The increased wait time led to considerable improvements in responses, including better inferences about the materials and more student-initiated questions. Waiting three to five seconds or more for students to respond is not as easy as it might seem; it takes practice. But your students will benefit considerably from having time to think and construct responses.

4. *Ask clear, purposeful, brief, and sequenced questions.* Avoid being vague. Focus the questions on the lesson at hand. Plan ahead so that your questions are meaningfully tied to the topic. If your questions are long-winded, you run the risk that they will not be understood, so briefer is better. Also plan questions so that they follow a logical sequence, integrating them with previously discussed material before moving to the next topic.

5. *Monitor how you respond to students' answers.* What should you do after a student responds to your question? Many teachers just say "Okay" or "Uh-huh" (Sadker & Zittleman, 2016). Instead, use the student's response as a basis for follow-up questions and engage the student or other students in a dialogue. Provide feedback that is tailored to the student's existing level of knowledge and understanding.

6. *Be aware of when it is best to pose a question to the entire class or to a particular student.* Asking the entire class a question makes all students in the class responsible for responding. Asking a specific student a question can make other students less likely to answer it. Some reasons to ask a question to a particular student are: (a) to draw an inattentive student into the lesson, (b) to ask a follow-up question of someone who has just responded, and (c) to call on someone who rarely responds when questions are asked to the class as a whole. Don't let a small group of assertive students dominate the responses; talk with them independently about continuing their positive responses without monopolizing class time. One strategy for giving students an equal chance to respond is to pull names from a cookie jar or check names off a class list as students respond (Weinstein & Romano, 2015).

7. *Encourage students to ask questions.* Praise them for good questions. Ask them "How?" and "Why?" and encourage them to ask "How?" and "Why?"

Mastery Learning **Mastery learning** involves learning one concept or topic thoroughly before moving on to a more difficult one. A successful mastery learning approach involves these procedures (Bloom, 1971; Carroll, 1963):

- Specify the learning task or lesson. Develop precise instructional objectives. Establish mastery standards (this typically is where *A* students perform).
- Break the course into learning units that are aligned with instructional objectives.
- Plan instructional procedures to include corrective feedback to students if they fail to master the material at an acceptable level, such as 90 percent correct. The corrective feedback might take place through supplemental materials, tutoring, or small-group instruction.
- Give an end-of-unit or end-of-course test that evaluates whether the student has mastered all of the material at an acceptable level.

mastery learning Involves learning one topic or concept thoroughly before moving on to a more difficult one.

For the teacher

1. Keeping track of what the rest of the class is doing
2. Keeping students on-task
3. Dealing with the varying paces at which students work ("ragged" endings)
4. Selecting or creating seatwork that is clear and meaningful
5. Matching seatwork to students' varying levels of achievement
6. Collecting, correcting, recording, and returning seatwork assignments

For the student

1. Completing assigned work on their own
2. Understanding how and when to obtain the teacher's help
3. Understanding the norms for assisting peers
4. Learning how to be effective in obtaining help from peers

FIGURE 2 CHALLENGES OF SEATWORK FOR TEACHERS AND STUDENTS

DIVERSITY

RESEARCH

DEVELOPMENT

Mastery learning gets mixed reviews. Some studies indicate that mastery learning is effective in increasing the time that students spend on learning tasks (Lalley & Gentile, 2009; Mitee & Obaitan, 2015), but others find less support for mastery learning (Bangert et al., 1983). Outcomes of mastery learning depend on the teacher's skill in planning and executing the strategy (Joyce et al., 2015). One context in which mastery learning might be especially beneficial is remedial reading (Schunk, 2016). A well-organized mastery learning program for remedial reading allows students to progress at their own rates based on their skills, their motivation, and the time they have to learn.

Seatwork Seatwork refers to the practice of having all or a majority of students work independently at their seats. Teachers vary in how much they use seatwork as part of their instruction (Weinstein, 2015). Some teachers use it every day; others rarely use it. Figure 2 summarizes the challenges of seatwork for the teacher and the student. Learning centers are especially good alternatives to paper-and-pencil seatwork. Figure 3 provides some suggestions for learning centers. A computer station can be an excellent learning center.

Homework Another important instructional decision involves how much and what type of homework to give students (Fernandez-Alonso et al., 2015; Novak & Lynott, 2015; Valle et al., 2015). Comments by a leading researcher, Harris Cooper (2006, 2007, 2009), suggest that in the United States homework is the source of more friction between school and home than any other aspect of education. In the cross-cultural research discussed earlier that focused on Asian and American students, the time spent on homework was assessed (Chen & Stevenson, 1989). Asian students spent more time doing homework than American students did. For example, on weekends Japanese first-graders did an average of 66 minutes of homework, and American first-graders did only 18 minutes. Also, Asian students had a much more positive attitude about homework than American students did. And Asian parents were far more likely to help their children with their homework than American parents were.

In a research review, Cooper and his colleagues (2006) concluded that overall research indicates there is a positive influence of homework on students' achievement. The research review also indicated that the homework-achievement link is stronger in grades 7 to 12 than kindergarten to grade 6. In one study, Cooper (1998) collected data on 709 students in grades 2 through 4 and 6 through 12. In the lower grades, there was a significant negative relation between the amount of homework assigned and students' attitudes, suggesting that elementary school children resent having to do homework. But in grades 6 and higher, the more homework students completed, the higher their achievement. It is not clear which was the cause and which the effect, though. Were really good students finishing more assignments because they were motivated and competent in academic subjects, or was completing homework assignments causing students to achieve more?

A key aspect of the debate about whether elementary school children should be assigned homework is the type of homework assigned. What is good homework?

Science	Social studies	Mathematics	Art	Writing	Computer
Simple experiments with lab sheets	Recreating items used by different civilizations	Math "challenges" and puzzles	Holiday or thematic projects	Class story writing (e.g., add-on stories)	Content-related programs
Observations over time with recording forms	Creating charts or graphs of population trends	Manipulative activities	Crafts related to curriculum studies (quilting, quilling, origami, etc.)	Rewrites of literature	Simulations
Exploring properties of objects and classifying them	Map making			Writing plays or puppet shows	Story writing

FIGURE 3 SUGGESTIONS FOR LEARNING CENTERS

Especially for younger children, the emphasis should be on homework that fosters a love of learning and sharpens study skills. Short assignments that can be quickly completed should be the goal. With young children, long assignments that go uncompleted or completed assignments that bring a great deal of stress, tears, and tantrums should be avoided. Too often teachers assign homework that duplicates without reinforcing material that is covered in class. Homework should be an opportunity for students to engage in creative, exploratory activities, such as doing an oral history of one's family or determining the ecological effects of neighborhood business. Instead of memorizing names, dates, and battles of the Civil War as a homework assignment, students might write fictional letters from Northerners to Southerners, expressing their feelings about the issues dividing the nation. The homework assignments should be linked to the next day's class activities to emphasize to students that homework has meaning and is not just a plot to make them miserable. Homework also should have a focus. Don't ask students to write an open-ended theme from a novel the class is reading. Rather, ask them to select a character and explain why he or she behaved in a particular way.

RESEARCH

In Cooper and his colleagues' (2006) review of research, homework began to have a payoff in middle school. How can homework have little or no effect in elementary school yet be so beneficial in middle and high school? In the higher grades, it is easier to assign focused, substantive homework that requires students to integrate and apply knowledge—the type of homework that promotes learning (Corno, 1998). Also, by high school, students have resigned themselves to the routine of homework. Working hard after school and having good study skills are more accepted by middle and high school students.

Some educational psychologists argue that the main reason homework has not been effective in elementary school is that it has focused too much on subject matter and not enough on developing attitudes toward school, persistence, and responsible completion of assignments (Corno, 1998). They stress that it is not homework per se that benefits students but, rather, the opportunities it provides for the student to take responsibility. They think that teachers need to inform parents about guiding their children in these aspects of doing their homework: setting goals, managing their time, controlling their emotions, and checking their work, rather than playing avoidance games or leaving hard work for last. Teachers and parents can use homework in the early grades to help children wrestle with goal setting and follow-through.

Cooper and his colleagues (Cooper, 2009; Cooper & Patall, 2007; Cooper et al., 2006) also have found the following:

- Homework has more positive effects when it is distributed over a period of time rather than done all at once. For example, doing 10 math problems each night for five nights is better than doing 50 over the weekend.
- Homework effects are greater for math, reading, and English than for science and social studies.
- For middle school students, one or two hours of homework a night is optimal. High school students benefit from even more hours of homework, but it is unclear what a maximum number of hours ought to be.

Homework can be a valuable tool for increasing learning, especially in middle and high school (Cooper, 2006, 2007, 2009). However, it is important to make homework meaningful, monitor it, and give students feedback about it.

In the last decade, there has been increasing research interest in parents' roles in students' homework (Madjar et al., 2016; Moroni et al., 2015; Nunez et al., 2015; Silinskas et al., 2015). A recent research review concluded that positive achievement outcomes occur only when parents are directly involved in assisting their children during homework tasks (Aries & Cabus, 2015). In this review, positive outcomes especially occurred when the parental assistance involved engaging in meta-strategies or support for children's understanding of the homework. Also, in this review, when parents simply facilitated, structured, or emotionally supported their children's homework, achievement outcomes were either indecisive or negative.

RESEARCH

EVALUATING TEACHER-CENTERED INSTRUCTION

Research on teacher-centered instruction has contributed many valuable suggestions for teaching, including these:

- Be an organized planner, create instructional objectives, and spend initial time orienting students to a lesson.
- Have high expectations for students' progress and ensure that students have adequate academic learning time.
- Use lecturing, explaining, and demonstrating to benefit certain aspects of students' learning.
- Engage students in learning by developing good question-asking skills and getting them involved in class discussion.
- Have students do meaningful seatwork or alternative work to allow individualized instruction with a particular student or a small group.
- Give students meaningful homework to increase their academic learning time and involve parents in students' learning.

Advocates of the teacher-centered approach especially believe that it is the best strategy for teaching basic skills, which involve clearly structured knowledge and skills (such as those needed in English, reading, math, and science). Thus, in teaching basic skills, the teacher-centered approach might consist of a teacher explicitly or directly teaching grammar rules, reading vocabulary, math computations, and science facts.

Teacher-centered instruction has been criticized for several reasons, however. Critics say that teacher-centered instruction often leads to passive, rote learning and inadequate opportunities to construct knowledge and understanding (McCall, 2007). They also criticize teacher-centered instruction as producing overly structured and rigid classrooms, inadequate attention to students' socioemotional development, external rather than internal motivation to learn, too much reliance on paper-and-pencil tasks, few opportunities for real-world learning, and too little collaborative learning in small groups. Such criticisms often are leveled by advocates of learner-centered planning and instruction, a topic we will explore next.

Review, Reflect, and Practice

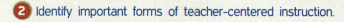 Identify important forms of teacher-centered instruction.

REVIEW
- What are some useful tools in teacher-centered lesson planning?
- What is direct instruction?
- What are some good teacher-centered instructional strategies?
- What are some pros and cons of teacher-centered instruction?

REFLECT
- As a student, have you ever wished that a teacher used more (or less) teacher-centered instruction? What lessons can you draw from this for your own work as a teacher?

PRAXIS™ PRACTICE
1. Mr. McGregor has assigned his students to write an essay explaining the impact of the use of the atomic bomb during World War II. Which cognitive level of Bloom's taxonomy is best illustrated by this assignment?
   a. analysis
   b. application
   c. comprehension
   d. knowledge

Review, Reflect, and Practice

2. A first grade teacher spends about a quarter of her instructional time on mathematics and assigns at least an hour of math homework each weekend. This math class is most typical of instructional methods in
   a. the United States
   b. France
   c. Japan
   d. Germany

3. Ms. Davidson is giving a lecture to introduce her students to a unit on the American Revolution. She begins with a little-known fact to pique her students' interest. She then distributes a brief outline of what her lesson will cover. She lectures from carefully prepared notes, using visual aids to help her students understand the material and keep their interest. Periodically during the lecture she asks questions to make sure her students are attending to, and understanding, the material. She calls on the first person to raise her hand to answer the question. If this person does not answer immediately, she supplies the answer herself so that the students do not become confused and the lesson does not drag on. What should Ms. Davidson do differently?
   a. Allow her students more time to answer questions.
   b. Avoid asking questions during the lecture.
   c. Be more spontaneous in her class presentations.
   d. Avoid using distracting visual aids.

4. Ms. Bancroft likes to lecture most of the time, makes sure that her students stay on task when they are in the classroom, and has students do meaningful seatwork. Ms. Bancroft is following which of these approaches?
   a. cognitive constructivist
   b. social constructivist
   c. direct instruction
   d. individualized

Please see answer key at end of book . . . .

3 LEARNER-CENTERED LESSON PLANNING AND INSTRUCTION

LG 3 Discuss important forms of learner-centered instruction.

Just as the behavioral approaches provide the conceptual underpinnings for teacher-centered lesson planning and instruction, the information processing and constructivist approaches form the theoretical backdrop for learner-centered lesson planning and instruction. In this section, we will explore the principles and strategies used in learner-centered instruction.

LEARNER-CENTERED PRINCIPLES

Learner-centered lesson planning and instruction move the focus away from the teacher and toward the student (McCombs, 2010, 2015). In one large-scale study, students' perceptions of a positive learning environment and interpersonal relationships with the teacher—factors associated with learner-centered instruction—were important in enhancing students' motivation and achievement (McCombs, 2001).

John Mahoney, teaching math to one of his students. Another student of Mahoney's, Nicole Williams, says, "He's not going to tell you the answer. He's going to make you think" (Wong Briggs, 2004, p. 6D). *What are some important cognitive and metacognitive factors in learner-centered instruction?*
John F. Mahoney

Increased interest in learner-centered principles of lesson planning and instruction has resulted in a set of guidelines called *Learner-Centered Psychological Principles: A Framework for School Reform and Redesign* (Presidential Task Force on Psychology and Education, 1992; Work Group of the American Psychological Association Board of Educational Affairs, 1995, 1997). The guidelines were constructed and are periodically revised by a prestigious group of scientists and educators from a wide range of disciplines and interests. These principles have important implications for the way teachers plan and instruct, as they are based on research on the most effective ways children learn.

The Work Group of the American Psychological Association Board of Educational Affairs (1997) stresses that research in psychology relevant to education has been especially informative, producing advances in our understanding of cognitive, motivational, and contextual aspects of learning. The work group states that the learner-centered psychological principles it has proposed are widely supported and are being increasingly adopted in many classrooms. The principles emphasize the active, reflective nature of learning and learners. According to the work group, education will benefit when the primary focus is on the learner.

The fourteen learner-centered principles can be classified in terms of four main sets of factors: cognitive and metacognitive, motivational and instructional, developmental and social, and individual differences (Work Group of the American Psychological Association Board of Educational Affairs, 1997). Figure 4 describes the 14 learner-centered principles.

SOME LEARNER-CENTERED INSTRUCTIONAL STRATEGIES

In other chapters we discussed a number of strategies that teachers can consider in developing learner-centered lesson plans. These especially include the teaching strategies based on the theories of Piaget and Vygotsky, constructivist and social constructivist aspects of thinking, and learning and cognition in the content areas. To provide you with a further sense of learner-centered strategies that you can incorporate into your lesson planning, we will examine problem-based learning, essential questions, and discovery learning.

Problem-Based Learning Problem-based learning emphasizes real-life problem solving (Barber et al., 2015; Winfrey et al., 2015). A problem-based curriculum exposes students to authentic problems like those that crop up in everyday life. Problem-based learning is a learner-centered approach that focuses on a problem to be solved through small-group efforts. Students identify problems or issues that they wish to explore, then locate materials and resources they need to address the issues or solve the problems. Teachers act as guides, helping students to monitor their own problem-solving efforts.

What are some learner-centered psychological principles?
Photodisc/SuperStock

Cognitive and Metacognitive Factors: These principles highlight learners' intellectual capacities and how the learning process is facilitated by contexts that support thinking strategies.

1. Nature of the learning process
   The learning of complex subject matter is most effective when it is an intentional process of constructing meaning from information and experience.
2. Goals of the learning process
   The successful learner, over time and with support and instructional guidance, can create meaningful, coherent representations of knowledge.
3. Construction of knowledge
   The successful learner can link new information with existing knowledge in meaningful ways.
4. Strategic thinking
   The successful learner can create a repertoire of thinking and reasoning strategies to achieve complex goals.
5. Thinking about thinking
   Higher-order strategies for selecting and monitoring mental operations facilitate creative and critical thinking.
6. Context of learning
   Learning is influenced by environmental factors, including culture, technology, and instructional practices.

Motivational and Instructional Factors: These principles highlight the roles of motivation and emotion in learning, focusing on how contexts can meet individual learners' needs for control and choice.

7. Motivational and emotional influences on learning
   What and how much is learned is influenced by the learner's motivation. Motivation to learn, in turn, is influenced by the learner's emotional states, beliefs, interests, goals, and habits of thinking.
8. Intrinsic motivation to learn
   The learner's creativity, higher-order thinking, and natural curiosity all contribute to motivation to learn. Intrinsic motivation is stimulated by tasks of optimal novelty and difficulty, relevant to personal interests and providing for personal choice and control.
9. Effects of motivation on effort
   Acquisition of complex knowledge and skills requires extended learner effort and guided practice. Without learners' motivation to learn, the willingness to exert this effort is unlikely without coercion.

Developmental and Social Factors: These principles focus on how learner development and interpersonal interactions can influence learning.

10. Developmental influences on learning
    As individuals develop, there are different opportunities and constraints for learning. Learning is most effective when development within and across physical, cognitive, and socioemotional domains is taken into account.
11. Social influences on learning
    Learning is influenced by social interactions, interpersonal relations, and communication with others.

Individual Difference Factors: These principles emphasize the importance of setting high standards and using assessment to adapt instruction to meet the needs of diverse learners.

12. Individual differences in learning
    Learners have different strategies, approaches, and capabilities for learning that are a function of prior experience and heredity.
13. Learning and diversity
    Learning is most effective when differences in learners' linguistic, cultural, and social backgrounds are taken into account.
14. Standards and assessment
    Setting appropriately high and challenging standards and assessing the learner as well as learning progress—including diagnostic, process, and outcome assessment—are integral parts of the learning process.

FIGURE 4   LEARNER-CENTERED PSYCHOLOGICAL PRINCIPLES

An example of a problem-based learning project involves sixth-grade students in exploring an authentic health problem in their local community: the causes, incidence, and treatment of asthma and its related conditions (Jones et al., 1997). Students learn how environmental conditions affect their health and share this understanding with others. The project integrates information from many subject areas, including health, science, math, and the social sciences. One study found that problem-based learning was positive associated with high school students' critical thinking skills in math courses (Widyatiningtyas et al., 2015).

In a recent meta-analysis that compared problem-based learning with traditional teaching methods, problem-based learning had a more positive effect on students' attitudes (Batdi, 2014). In one study, 20 eleventh-grade chemistry students were randomly assigned to either a teacher-centered or problem-based learning experience to learn about the effects of temperature, concentration, and pressure on cell potential (Tarhan & Acar, 2007). Interviews with the students following the instruction revealed that the students in both conditions were equally successful in gaining an understanding of the topic, but that students in the problem-based learning condition were more motivated, self-confident, and interested in solving problems.

RESEARCH

essential questions Questions that reflect the heart of the curriculum, the most important things that students should explore and learn.

discovery learning Learning in which students construct an understanding on their own.

guided discovery learning Learning in which students are encouraged to construct their understanding with the assistance of teacher-guided questions and directions.

Essential Questions Essential questions are questions that reflect the heart of the curriculum, the most important things that students should explore and learn. For example, in one lesson the initial essential question was "What flies?" Students explored the question by examining everything from birds, bees, fish, and space shuttles to the notion that time flies and ideas fly. The initial question was followed by other questions, such as "How and why do things fly in nature?" "How does flight affect humans?" and "What is the future of flight?"

Essential questions like these perplex students, cause them to think, and motivate their curiosity (Wiggins & Wilbur, 2015; Wilhelm, 2014). Essential questions are creative choices. With just a slight change, a lackluster question such as "What was the effect of the Civil War?" can become the thought-provoking question "Is the Civil War still going on?"

Discovery Learning Discovery learning is learning in which students construct an understanding on their own. Discovery learning stands in contrast to the direct-instruction approach discussed earlier, in which the teacher directly explains information to students. In discovery learning, students have to figure out things for themselves. Discovery learning meshes with the ideas of Piaget, who once commented that every time you teach a child something you keep the child from learning.

As teachers began to use discovery learning, they soon found that for it to be effective as a systematic instruction approach it needed to be modified. This led to the development of **guided discovery learning**, in which students are still encouraged to construct their understanding, but with the assistance of teacher-guided questions and directions (Janssen et al., 2014).

A research review indicated that guided discovery learning was superior to pure discovery learning in every case (Mayer, 2004). In this review, it also was concluded that constructivist learning is better supported by curricular focus than by pure discovery.

EVALUATING LEARNER-CENTERED STRATEGIES

The learner-centered approach to lesson planning and instruction is positive in many ways (McCombs, 2015). The fourteen learner-centered principles developed by the American Psychological Association task force can be very helpful in guiding students' learning. The principles

What is guided discovery learning?
Steve Debenport/Getty Images

encourage teachers to help students actively construct their understanding, set goals and plan, think deeply and creatively, monitor their learning, solve real-world problems, develop more positive self-esteem and control their emotions, be internally motivated, learn in a developmentally appropriate way, collaborate effectively with others (including diverse others), evaluate their learner preferences, and meet challenging standards.

Critics of learner-centered instruction argue that it gives too much attention to the process of learning (such as learning creatively and collaboratively, like through discovery learning) and not enough to academic content (such as the facts of history, like through lecture) (Hirsch, 1996). Some critics stress that learner-centered instruction works better in some subjects than in others (Feng, 1996). They say that in areas with many ill-defined problems, such as the social sciences and humanities, learner-centered instruction can be effective. However, they believe that in well-structured knowledge domains such as math and science, a teacher-centered structure works better. Critics also say that learner-centered instruction is less effective at the beginning level of instruction in a field because students do not have the knowledge to make decisions about what and how they should learn. And critics stress that there is a gap between the theoretical level of student-centered learning and its actual application (Airasian & Walsh, 1997). The consequences of implementing learner-centered strategies in the classroom are often more challenging than anticipated.

RESEARCH

In a recent study, the Minnesota New Country School (MNCS), a learner-centered school, was evaluated (Aslan & Reigeluth, 2015/2016). This school uses a self-directed, project-based learning approach with each student choosing an advisor until they graduate. The advisors and administrators in the school all said that the number one challenge in the school was changing students' mindsets from being directed by teachers to engaging in self-direction.

Although we have presented teacher-centered and learner-centered planning and instruction in separate sections, don't think of them as always being either/or approaches. Many effective teachers use some of both in making the classroom a positive learning environment for children (Yeh, 2009). Research on the choice and sequencing of learning activities in the classroom indicates that using both constructivist and direct instruction approaches is often more effective than using either approach alone (Darling-Hammond et al., 2005).

Consider high school history teacher Robert Bain's (2005) description of how students initially spent time in learner-centered instruction working on constructing accounts of Columbus' voyage to America and struggled with the question of how the anniversaries of the voyage were celebrated. Bain then used teacher-centered direct instruction by lecturing about leading historians' current thinking about the topic. Also, a study of a ninth-grade technology-enhanced classroom revealed that both student-centered and teacher-centered instruction promoted students' conceptual understanding and provided students with different opportunities to engage in learning (Wu & Huang, 2007).

Interactive whiteboards, a relatively new instructional technology, can be used in both teacher-centered and student-centered instruction (Swan et al., 2009). Interactive whiteboards are being used in many schools to replace the traditional blackboard and chalk. This new technology allows teachers and students to interact with content projected from a computer screen onto a whiteboard surface. Virtually anything that can be done on a computer can done on an interactive whiteboard, with the advantage that drawing, marking, and highlighting of computer-based output is supported. A whole class can follow interactions, and lessons can be saved and replayed.

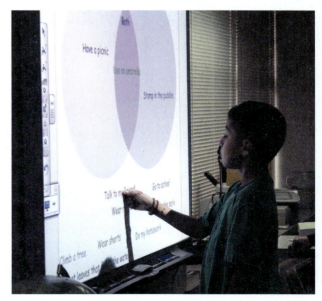

Students using interactive whiteboards at the Research Center for Educational Technology's AT&T classroom at Kent State University.
Research Center for Educational Technology, Kent State University

Some teachers were recently asked to describe their most effective learner-center strategies. Following are their responses.

EARLY CHILDHOOD Learner-centered strategies are common in my preschool classroom. For example, each morning children are given time for free play in which they play dress-up, pretend to cook in a mock kitchen, and build structures using Legos. Through these activities, children not only learn important skills, but they are also instilled with a love of school.

—MISSY DANGLER, *Suburban Hills School*

ELEMENTARY SCHOOL: GRADES K–5 I use guided discovery learning in almost all of my science classes. The children work in groups, are given guidance at the beginning of the lesson and then assigned a task to do in order to find the answer to a question. When students ask questions, I refer them to an instruction sheet I have given them or ask questions to guide their thinking. If a student asks, "Can we do this?" I reply, "Try it and see!" I also encourage students to count on other members of their group to uncover answers to questions and use phrases such as "Many heads are better than one."

—JANINE GUIDA POUTRE, *Clinton Elementary School*

MIDDLE SCHOOL: GRADES 6–8 In order to master new vocabulary, I often have my students quiz each other on vocabulary words. It is a noisy activity, but the students love it and learn at the same time.

—MARGARET REARDON, *Pocantico Hills School*

HIGH SCHOOL: GRADES 9–12 I prefer being the "guide on the side," not the "sage on the stage," when it comes to teaching. I did a writing workshop in which I presented a short mini-lesson each day, and my students chose how to spend the rest of the period. The students set their own goals, and their grade was partly based on achievement of those goals. I conferenced one-on-one with each student daily to monitor how they were doing; students loved the freedom.

—JENNIFER HEITER, *Bremen High School*

CONNECTING WITH STUDENTS: Best Practices
Strategies for Using Learner-Centered Instruction

Following are some effective ways to incorporate learner-centered instruction into your teaching:

1. *Become familiar with the learner-centered psychological principles and incorporate them in your lesson planning and teaching.*
2. *Focus on the whole child.* Pay attention to motivational and affective factors, and developmental and social factors, in addition to cognitive factors. In *Through the Eyes of Teachers,* you can read about elementary-school science teacher Luis Recalde and how he focuses on the whole child and makes learning fascinating for students.

THROUGH THE EYES OF TEACHERS
Fostering Learning, Unity, and Civic Pride

Luis Recalde, a fourth- and fifth-grade science teacher at Vincent E. Mauro Elementary School in New Haven, Connecticut, uses every opportunity to make science fascinating and

CONNECTING WITH STUDENTS: Best Practices
Strategies for Using Learner-Centered Instruction

motivating for students to learn. Recalde infuses hands-on science experiences with energy and enthusiasm. To help students get a better sense of what it is like to be a scientist, he brings lab coats to the classroom for students to wear. He holds science fair workshops for teachers and often gives up his vacation time to help students with science projects. He started soccer teams and gardens to foster unity and civic pride among African American and Latinx students. An immigrant himself, he knows the importance of fostering positive relations among students from different ethnic groups.

3. *Use problem-based learning, essential questions, and guided discovery learning in your teaching.*
4. *Remember that the most effective teachers don't use direct instruction or learner-centered instruction exclusively but instead use both to make the classroom a positive learning environment for students.*

Elementary school science teacher Luis Recalde holds up a seaweed specimen in one of the hands-on, high-interest learning contexts he creates for students.
Stan Godlewski

Review, Reflect, and Practice

 Discuss important forms of learner-centered instruction.

REVIEW
- What is learner-centered lesson planning? Summarize the APA's fourteen learner-centered principles.
- How do problem-based learning, essential questions, and discovery learning each embody learner-centered principles?
- What are some pros and cons of learner-centered instruction?

REFLECT
- As a student, have you ever wished that a teacher would use more (or less) learner-centered instruction? What lessons can you draw from this for your own work as a teacher?

PRAXIS™ PRACTICE
1. Joan just received a *D* on her science exam. "I knew it," she states, "I've never been any good at science." Which set of factors of the APA's learner-centered principles is best exemplified by Joan's statement?
   a. cognitive and metacognitive
   b. developmental and social
   c. individual differences
   d. motivational and emotional

continued

Review, Reflect, and Practice

2. Mr. Williams wants his third-grade students to understand the purpose of blubber in marine mammals. He sets up an experiment for his students using ice water, latex gloves, and lard. First, students put their gloved hands in ice water until they cannot keep them there any longer. Other students time how long they keep their hands submerged. Then, students put their gloved hands in bags of lard and submerge their hands again. Again, other students time how long they keep their hands submerged. All of the students are able to keep their hands in the ice water longer with their hands in the lard than they can when their hands are merely gloved. What learner-centered instructional strategy has Mr. Williams used?
   a. discovery learning
   b. essential questions
   c. guided discovery
   d. problem-based learning

3. Ms. Flanagan, who takes a teacher-centered approach, just observed Mr. Houston's constructivist teaching in his seventh-grade math class. Ms. Flanagan is likely to be most critical of which of the following she observed?
   a. Mr. Houston assigning students homework
   b. Mr. Houston encouraging students to construct their own math problem-solving strategies
   c. Mr. Houston having high expectations for student learning
   d. Mr. Houston using technology to help students learn

Please see answer key at end of book . . . .

LG 4 Summarize how to effectively use technology to help children learn.

TECHNOLOGY

Thinking Back/Thinking Forward

Technology and children's vocabulary development. Connect to "Cognitive and Language Development."

Technology connections with students around the world. Connect to "Sociocultural Diversity."

Computer-supported intentional learning environments. Connect to "Social Constructivist Approaches."

Content-specific applications of technology in reading, writing, math, science, and social studies. Connect to "Learning and Cognition in the Content Areas."

---

4 TECHNOLOGY AND EDUCATION

The Technology Revolution and the Internet | Standards for Technology-Literate Students | Teaching, Learning, and Technology

So far in this chapter we have described many aspects of planning and instruction. In contemporary society, technology plays important roles in planning and instruction. Three important ways that technology affects curriculum planning are: (1) as a learning goal for students to develop certain technology competencies; (2) as a resource for curriculum planning through the extensive materials that are available on the Internet; and (3) as tools that improve students' ability to learn through techniques such as simulation and visualization in science and text analysis in literature, as well as software that encourages reflection and provides models of good performance (Darling-Hammond et al., 2005).

Technology is such an important theme in education that it is woven throughout this book. In each chapter, you come across one or more discussions of technology related to the chapter's contents. In other chapters you have studied topics such as technology and children's vocabulary development, technology as a means of connecting with students around the world, computer-supported intentional learning environments and content-specific applications of technology in reading, writing, math, science, and social studies. Here we will explore the technology revolution and the Internet, standards for technology-literate students, and teaching and learning with technology.

THE TECHNOLOGY REVOLUTION AND THE INTERNET

Students today are growing up in a world that is far different technologically from the world in which their parents and grandparents were students. If students are to be adequately prepared for tomorrow's jobs, technology must be an integral part of schools and classrooms (Maloy et al., 2017; Roblyer, 2016).

The Internet The **Internet** is a system of computer networks that operates worldwide. As the core of computer-mediated communication, the Internet is playing an important role in the technology revolution, especially in schools. In many cases, the Internet has more current, up-to-date information than textbooks. Nearly 100 percent of public schools in the United States are now connected to the Internet, and schools are increasingly using **cloud computing**, where services such as servers, storage, and applications are delivered to an organization's computers and devices through the Internet.

The Internet did not become the common portal it is today until the introduction of the World Wide Web (the Web) in 1991. The **Web** is a system for browsing Internet sites. It is named the Web because it is made of many sites linked together. The Web presents the user with documents, called Web pages, full of links to other documents or information systems. Selecting one of these links, the user can access more information about a particular topic. Web pages include text as well as multimedia (images, video, animation, and sound—all of which can be accessed by students with a click or tap for interactions). Web indexes and search engines such as Google can help students find the information they are seeking by examining and collating a variety of sources.

The Internet can be a valuable tool for helping students learn. However, it has some potential drawbacks. To use it effectively with your students, you will have to know how to use it and feel comfortable with it, as well as have up-to-date equipment and software. In addition, concerns have been raised about students accessing pornographic material and biased Web sites, as well as the questionable accuracy of some information gleaned from the Internet. Many of these problems are solved by installing firewalls or blocking software on school servers.

When used effectively, however, the Internet expands access to a world of knowledge and people that students cannot experience in any other way. Here are some effective ways that the Internet can be used in classrooms:

- *Navigating and integrating knowledge.* Teachers can focus on authentic data for problem solving and inquiry, such as temperature records or census data. Also, it can be helpful to reconcile information from multiple sources as well as teaching and modeling evaluation of information, analysis of source credibility, and documentation of Internet resources.
- *Collaborative learning.* One of the most effective ways to use the Internet in your classroom is through project-centered activities. Blog publishing (allowing moderated comments) can be a good collaborative online activity. Another collaborative use of the Internet is to have a group of students conduct a survey on a topic, put it on the Internet, and hope to obtain responses from many parts of the world. They can organize, analyze, and summarize the data they receive, and then share them with other classes around the world. Yet another type of collaborative learning project involves sending groups of students on Internet "scavenger hunts" to find information and/or solve a problem. Online citizen science projects also are inherently collaborative with data being pooled online for analysis. In the classroom, Web publishing and online videos can be highly collaborative activities with activities with different groups assigned to different roles and responsibilities (for example, art department, script writers, technical team).
- Kent Innovation High School in Michigan extensively uses project-based learning and the Internet (Langel, 2015). Every student has a laptop and the entire school is invested in the use of Google Drive, where students can store designs, drawings, recordings, stories, videos, and so on. Teachers use Google Drive to introduce, trace, and plan projects with students, who use it for generating ideas, planning, and orchestrating their own projects.
- *Computer-mediated communications (CMC).* An increasing number of innovative educational projects include the use of computer-mediated communications.

A student creating a multimedia program in the Research Center for Educational Technology's AT&T classroom at Kent State University.
Research Center for Educational Technology, Kent State University

> **Thinking Back/Thinking Forward**
>
> Collaborative learning is reflected in teaching strategies such as the use of cooperative learning and small-group work. Connect to "Social Constructivist Approaches."

Internet The core of computer-mediated communication; a system of computer networks that operates worldwide.

cloud computing Delivery of services such as servers, storage, and applications to an organization's computers and devices through the Internet.

Web A system for browsing Internet sites that refers to the World Wide Web; named the Web because it is composed of many sites that are linked together.

For example, there are many online sites (such as www.studentsoftheworld.info and www.tesol.net/teslpnpl.html) set up to allow teachers and students to correspond with "pen pals" around the world. Some of these even provide safe access to more innovative CMC forms such as chats and blogs.

- *Improving teachers' knowledge and understanding.* Two excellent Internet resources for teachers are the Educational Resources Information Center (ERIC at https://eric.ed.gov/) and the Educators' Reference Desk (www.eduref.org), which provide free information about a wide range of educational topics. The ERIC database gives abstracts of more than 1 million journal and nonjournal educational papers going back to 1966 and the full text of over 100,000 papers from educational conferences. The Educators' Reference Desk gives easy access to over 2,000 lesson plans and over 3,000 links to online education information. Other excellent Internet resources for teachers include Harvard's Websites for Educators (https://www.gse.harvard.edu/library/educator-resources), a selective list of topically organized websites that support the practice of educators, and the PBS TeacherLine (http://teacherline.pbs.org/teacherline), which provides links to teaching resources and online professional development courses for teachers.
  - NASA for educators (www.nasa.gov/audience/foreducators/index.html) has an extensive set of resources geared to teachers at all levels and in all subject areas as well as professional development materials to help teachers use these resources effectively.

Increasing numbers of teachers are using social media as an important tool for professional networking and development. Many Twitter chats are devoted to teachers in certain areas, grade levels, or content areas. Teachers often report that this activity is a useful and meaningful source of professional support and ideas. A list of educator Twitter chats can be found at www.iste.org/explore/articleDetail?articleid=7.

Graphics and Presentation Graphics software and PowerPoint can improve many presentations by enhancing the content and attractiveness of the visual aids you use to teach students. Software graphics packages can be used to copy and create images, formulate charts and graphs, set the timing of material, and compose effective visual presentations. When used competently, PowerPoint and other graphics software packages can improve the organization of content and make it more dynamic.

STANDARDS FOR TECHNOLOGY-LITERATE STUDENTS

If students are to be adequately prepared for tomorrow's jobs, schools must take an active role in ensuring students become technologically literate. Most national standards recognize this. For example, the National Council of Teachers of English/International Reading Association Standards for the English Language Arts (NCTE/IRA, 1996) include the following: "Students use a variety of technological and information resources (such as libraries, databases, computer networks, and video) to gather and synthesize information and to create and communicate knowledge," and a major theme in the National Council for the Social Studies, Curriculum Standards for the Social Studies (NCSS, 1994) is "Science, Technology, and Society."

The International Society for Technology in Education (ISTE) has developed technology standards for students (ISTE, 2007, 2016)

A high school student creating a PowerPoint presentation in a math class.
Herwig Vergult/AFP/Getty Images

A student creating a bar graph on a computer.
Bill Aron/PhotoEdit

and educators (ISTE, 2017). Recently ISTE (2016) updated its technology standards for students. These standards now involve being a(an):

- *Empowered Learner.* Students actively use technology to reach learning goals.
- *Digital Citizen.* Students demonstrate responsibility and are ethical in their use of technology.
- *Knowledge Constructor.* Students use a variety of resources and digital tools to construct knowledge, become more creative, and engage in meaningful learning.
- *Innovative Designer.* Students use various technologies to solve problems and craft useful and imaginative solutions to these problems.
- *Computational Thinker.* Students develop strategies in using technology to create solutions and test them.
- *Creative Communicator.* Students communicate effectively and think creatively in their use of digital tools to attain goals.
- *Global Collaborator.* Students use technology to widen their perspectives and enhance their learning by connecting with others locally and globally.

In addition, ISTE provides performance indicators for achieving these standards at four levels: prekindergarten through grade 2, grades 3 through 5, grades 6 through 8, and grades 9 through 12. ISTE also includes examples and scenarios to illustrate how technology literacy can be integrated across the curriculum at each of these levels.

At the second level (grades 3 through 5), a teacher might make extensive use of Internet resources. She could use the Global Learning and Observations for a Better Environment (GLOBE) Web site (www.globe.gov) to engage students in making environmental observations around the school, reporting the data to a processing facility through GLOBE, and using global images created from their data to examine local environmental issues.

DEVELOPMENT

Population growth and urban planning are the focus of a social studies technology-based learning activity in grades 9 through 12. The activity challenges students to find sources online and elsewhere that describe real-world population dilemmas. The activity can be altered to address different cities and regions worldwide. In small groups in class, students can discuss problems that may occur as a result of a city being heavily populated. They can be asked to project what problems a city such as Tokyo is likely to face in terms of population growth in the year 2050.

TEACHING, LEARNING, AND TECHNOLOGY

A special concern is how technology can be used to improve teaching and learning (Maloy et al., 2017; Roblyer, 2016). Following are some effective strategies for using technology in the classroom.

Using Technology to Improve Students' Understanding In the last several decades at the Educational Technology Center at Harvard University, a number of educators have focused on developing ways to use technology to improve students' understanding. Martha Stone Wiske has especially been instrumental in creating ways to incorporate technology into classroom contexts that transform student learning. Wiske and her colleagues (2005) described how to more effectively use technology to teach for understanding by considering (1) the topics that are worth understanding, (2) what students should understand about

Students at Christopher Maddox High School in Park City, Utah, present a daily, live TV broadcast to more than 1,200 peers and 80 adults. The students create a program that highlights school news and events and have full responsibility for writing scripts, operating cameras, directing segments, and handling other aspects of producing a TV broadcast.
UrbancowE+/Getty Images

such topics, (3) how students develop and demonstrate understanding, (4) how students and teachers assess understanding, and (5) how students and teachers learn together. These five aspects of understanding are based on ideas developed at Harvard by David Perkins, Howard Gardner, and Vito Perrone. Following are Wiske and her colleagues' (2005) views of how to use technology to enhance understanding:

1. *Evaluate which topics are worth understanding.* Technology is especially appropriate for generating worthwhile and interesting learning topics. The Internet provides a wealth of information about virtually every topic imaginable that can be mined to generate new topics or expand what students are studying as part of the curriculum. The wide range of information provided by the Internet allows students to learn more about their own interests and ideas and carve a unique pathway in learning about a topic, instead of following cookie-cutter steps in a traditional textbook or workbook (Roblyer, 2016). Wiske and her colleagues (2005) also point out that technology can often be used effectively to teach where problem spots emerge every year. "Examples include heat and temperature or weight and density in science, ratios in mathematics, and stereotypes in history and social studies classes" (p. 28). These topics, which many students struggle to understand, are central to the subject matter and are frequently more easily understood through the use of technology.

2. *Think about what students should understand about a topic.* When teachers consider using technology in the classroom, it is important for them to think about the learning goals they have for their students. Goals might include learning a new concept or applying a key concept to relevant situations. A goal related to technology might be to understand how to find and critically examine information on the Internet that is relevant to a classroom topic. Generating goals in this manner reminds the teacher that "surfing the Web" is "not an end in itself" but rather a way to use "technology to accomplish meaningful work" (Wiske et al., 2005, p. 44).

3. *Pay attention to how students develop and demonstrate understanding.* Use technology to help students "stretch their minds" and understand something in ways that they never did before. In improving students' understanding, Wiske and her colleagues (2005) recommend that teachers use technology when it can "enhance and enrich their performances of understanding. . . . Word processors, digital audio and video technologies for creating Web sites allow students to express their understanding in a rich variety of media. These technologies also capture student work in forms that can be easily revised, combined, and distributed" (Wiske et al., 2005, pp. 65–66).

4. *Consider how students and teachers assess learning.* Use ongoing assessment instead of only using a final assessment. During ongoing assessment, you might guide students in understanding what quality work involves or use peer collaboration to help students analyze and improve their work. A helpful strategy is to also encourage students to assess their own learning progress and to monitor how effectively they are learning. Technology can be used in several ways to effectively assess learning.

"Digital technologies, including audio and video recorders and computers, can capture student work in forms that are easy to review. Interactive workspaces and software with multiple windows can help to keep assessment guidelines in view and even offer prompts and reminders. . . . Using networked technologies, students may post their work online where it can be readily reviewed and annotated by multiple advisors, including distant teachers and peers who cannot meet face-to-face. Technologies also provide easy means of preserving digital archives of student work. These may allow teachers and students to create individual portfolios to demonstrate and evaluate a student's work over time" (Wiske et al., 2005, pp. 84–85).

5. *Reflect on how students and teachers can learn together.* "Networked technologies provide multiple advantages for connecting learners with reflective, collaborative communities. . . ." For example, "E-mail permits users to send and receive many-to-many messages and to do so quickly. Students can share information and work with many other students all over the world, exchanging multiple rounds of reflective dialogue. The Web, with digital images, video and audio recordings, and videoconferencing, also allows students and their teachers to publish and collaborate on work, opening up the possibility of communicating with a wide range of audiences outside the classroom" (Wiske et al., 2005, pp. 100, 102). Social media also can be an important tool to accomplish these goals as well.

Students working on a GenYes project. *What are some characteristics of GenYes?*
Generation YES

In further considering the role of technology in learning, a technology program that is increasingly used in schools is the GenYes program. The goal of the GenYes program is to support the effective integration of technology in teaching and learning (GenYes, 2010). The program, created by Dennis Harper at the Northwest Regional Educational Laboratory, emphasizes that teachers and students are partners in creating lessons that use technology in ways students find meaningful and relevant. GenYes is available for both elementary and secondary school students, who learn by co-creating lessons with teachers while their teachers learn about technology from the students. Instead of teaching technology skills to teachers with the hope that they will use those skills in teaching students, GenYes works with students to help them form productive technology partnerships with their teachers. Students and their teacher-partners learn how to use telecommunication devices, the Internet, presentation tools, and other emerging technologies.

Among the technology units that GenYes students and teachers collaborate on are:

- *Online communications,* such as safety, e-mail, forums, blogs, messaging, and collaborative projects
- *Digital media,* such as graphics, animation, and video
- *Digital authoring,* including planning, creating, and delivering multimedia projects
- *Web publishing,* such as designing and constructing Web pages
- *Student leadership and community service*

In addition, a number of mini-units, such as podcasting, digital storytelling, handhelds, and video tutorials can be incorporated in the GenYes class or used by students when they are working on technology projects.

GenYes students are paired, either individually or in teams, with a partner-teacher. Initial meetings are held to determine a curriculum focus that could be enriched by an infusion of technology. The GenYes students are responsible for the nuts and bolts of the technology, and the teacher provides content accuracy and pedagogical strategies.

The GenYes program was initiated in Olympia, Washington, in 1996 and is now used in a number of classrooms across the United States. Teachers and students have consistently reported that GenYes has provided them with an excellent opportunity to improve their technology skills. The GenYes program reflects the learner-centered strategies we discussed earlier in this chapter and the social constructivist approaches described in the chapter on that topic.

Technological Pedagogical Content Knowledge (TPCK) *Technological Pedagogical Content Knowledge (TPCK)* is a model created by Matthew Koehler and Punya Mishra (2010; Mishra & Koehler, 2006) that emphasizes the importance of not looking at technology as a stand-alone entity but rather addressing links between technology, content knowledge, and pedagogy (see Figure 5). In their view, knowing how to use

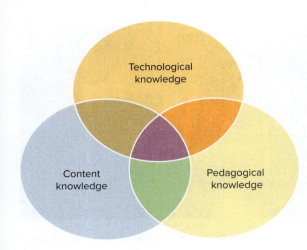

FIGURE 5 TECHNOLOGICAL PEDAGOGICAL CONTENT KNOWLEDGE

technology is not sufficient for instructional success in the classroom; you also need to know how to teach with it. They argue that teachers who are skilled in all three domains—technology, content knowledge, and pedagogy—have a level of expertise in teaching a particular topic using technology that differs from that of a technology expert (a computer scientist, for example), a content knowledge expert in a particular discipline (science, for example), or a pedagogical expert (an experienced educator, for example). TPCK has been adopted by the American Association of Colleges of Teacher Education, which sponsored a book by Koehler and Mishra (2010) on the integration of technology, content knowledge, and pedagogy to improve classroom instruction. Educators are showing continuing interest in using TPCK in their classroom teaching (Kennedy, 2015; Niess & Gillow-Wiles, 2014).

Stages of Integrating Technology into Classroom Teaching Integrating technology into your classroom teaching often takes place in the following sequence (Norris & Soloway, 1999):

Stage 1: Teacher is aware that a particular technology exists but hasn't used it; may be avoiding the technology.

Stage 2: Teacher is currently trying to learn the basic aspects of the technology but often becomes frustrated and still lacks confidence with this technology.

Stage 3: Teacher is beginning to see how to use a particular technology and thinks about specific situations in which to use it.

Stage 4: Teacher is gaining confidence in using the technology for certain tasks and feeling more comfortable in using it.

Stage 5: Teacher now thinks about this technology as something that helps him or her and no longer lacks confidence in using it; teacher perceives that the technology can be used in a number of instructional contexts.

Stage 6: Teacher can use this technology as an effective instructional tool across the curriculum to meet instructional objectives.

To further evaluate your technology skills and attitudes, complete *Self-Assessment 1*.

How do teachers use technology to help students learn? Following are their responses.

EARLY CHILDHOOD Technology helps preschoolers learn music—in addition to listening to music to learn a song, they can also see the written words projected on a screen along with appropriate clip art.

—CONNIE CHRISTY, *Aynor Elementary School (Preschool Program)*

ELEMENTARY SCHOOL: GRADES K–5 I often have my fifth-grade students research topics using Google and have them sift through the information. We discuss valid sources and try to determine ones that are questionable.

—CRAIG JENSEN, *Cooper Mountain Elementary School*

MIDDLE SCHOOL: GRADES 6–8 As a Spanish language teacher, I devised a plan with a teacher from Chile in which my students e-mailed her students in Spanish. In turn, her students e-mailed mine in English. This bilingual process helped both groups of students learn the respective languages of each country.

—MARGARET REARDON, *Pocantico Hills School*

SELF-ASSESSMENT 1
Evaluating My Technology Skills and Attitudes

How good are your technology skills? How positive are your attitudes about using technology and incorporating it into your classroom? For these items, consider the grade and subject(s) you are most likely to teach. Rate yourself from 1 to 5, with 1 = Not like me at all and 5 = Very much like me.

1. I'm reasonably proficient at using a computer, including installing and uninstalling software.
2. I am able to use tablets and mobile devices with relative ease.
3. I know when and how to use technology to improve students' understanding.
4. I have ideas for using word processing together with other language learning resources in the classroom and know the best apps to use in teaching.
5. I know how to search efficiently and thoroughly for information that interests me on the Internet.
6. I can vet the quality, accuracy, and sufficiency of information that I find on the Internet.
7. I have ideas about how to use the Internet in my classroom.
8. I'm proficient at using e-mail.
9. I know how to use PowerPoint.
10. I have been part of collaborative learning exercises that involve technology.
11. I can see how collaborative learning can be used with technology in my classroom.
12. I am aware of the sociocultural issues involved in technology and education.
13. I know some good Web sites, journals, and software catalogs that can help me learn how to use technology more effectively in the classroom.
14. I have a good understanding of social media as a tool for communication.
15. I have a good understanding of how to use social media (e.g., blogs, Instagram, Pintrest) for professional development.
16. I know what cloud computing is and how to use it.
17. I understand online safety and etiquette.
18. I know how to use online tools for assessment and student tracking.

SCORING AND INTERPRETATION

Look at your scores for each item and evaluate your technology strengths and weaknesses. By the time you step into your classroom for your first day of teaching, make it a goal to be able to confidently rate yourself on each of these items at the level of 4 or 5. On items on which you rated yourself 1, 2, and 3, try to take technology courses at your local college that will improve your knowledge and skills in those areas.

HIGH SCHOOL: GRADES 9-12 Because kids love technology so much, I like to display notes using PowerPoint slides instead of simply lecturing. Video clips and connection to the Internet are available, so it is easy to display visuals to reinforce topics. I also encourage my students to purchase a flash drive so that their work can be portable and all in one place.

—JENNIFER HEITER, *Bremen High School*

CONNECTING WITH STUDENTS: Best Practices
Strategies for Choosing and Using Technology in the Classroom

Technology will be a part of your classroom. Here are some guidelines for choosing and using it:

1. *Choose technology with an eye toward how it can help students actively explore, construct, and restructure information.* Look for software, apps, and online (cloud-based) tools and sites that let students directly manipulate the information. One review found that students' learning improved when information was presented in a multimedia fashion that stimulated them to actively select, organize, and integrate visual and verbal information (Mayer, 1997). You might want to consult with a school or district media specialist to find the software that best reflects these characteristics. An excellent resource for teachers that emphasize the use of technology to improve students' learning and understanding is the International Society for Technology in Education (ISTE) Web site (www.iste.org). Software catalogs and journals also are good sources of information.

2. *Look for ways to use technology as part of collaborative and real-world learning.* In Ann Brown and Joe Campione's (1996) words, education should be about "fostering a community of learners." Students often learn better when they work together to solve challenging problems and construct innovative projects (Kaendler et al., 2015). The term *computer-supported collaborative learning* (CSCL) has been coined to describe learning that occurs when students share and construct knowledge while interacting with others using a computer or the Internet (Kirschner et al., 2015; Rodriguez-Triana et al., 2015; Xiong et al., 2015). One example of CSCL is collaborative writing, which motivates students to generate ideas and share them with others to develop a better understanding of a topic. This might be accomplished using blogs, interactive whiteboards, and other communication tools. Also, think of technologies such as the Web, e-mail, social media, and the Cloud as tools for providing students with opportunities to engage in collaborative learning. In this way, students can reach outside the classroom to include the real world and communicate with people in locations that otherwise would be inaccessible to them.

3. *Choose technology that presents positive models for students.* Monitor technology for equity in ethnicity and culture, and be sure that the models presented are positive role models.

4. *Remember that your teaching skills are critical, regardless of the technology you use.* You don't have to worry that technology will replace you as a teacher. Technology becomes effective in the classroom only when you know how to use it, demonstrate it, guide and monitor its use, and incorporate it into a larger effort to develop students who are motivated to learn, actively learn, and communicate effectively. Even the most sophisticated digital tools will not benefit students much unless you appropriately orient students to it, ask them good questions about the material, orchestrate its use, and tailor it to their needs.

5. *Continue to learn about technology yourself and increase your technological competence.* Digital technology is still changing at an amazing pace. Make it a personal goal to be open to new technology, keep up with technological advances by reading educational journals, and take courses in educational computing to increase your skills. You will be an important model for your students in terms of your attitude toward technology, your ability to use it effectively yourself, and your ability to communicate how to use it effectively to your students.

TECHNOLOGY

Review, Reflect, and Practice

4 Summarize how to effectively use technology to help children learn.

REVIEW
- What characterizes the technology revolution and the Internet?
- What are some standards for technology-literate students?
- What are five things that teachers need to ask when considering the use of technology in the classroom to improve students' understanding?

REFLECT
- Would one or more of the ways that computers can be used to support learning and instruction be useful to the subject and grade level you plan to teach? How?

Review, Reflect, and Practice

PRAXIS™ PRACTICE

1. Ms. Carlson's students are working on assignments posted onto their school server through the internet. This delivery system is referred to as
   a. in-house intranet
   b. social media for kids
   c. cloud computing
   d. Web enhancement

2. Mr. Wilson's social studies students are examining various websites to research regional population growth and urban planning around the world. This activity is best aimed at which grade levels?
   a. PK–2
   b. 3–5
   c. 6–8
   d. 9–12

3. Which of the following examples best reflects the effective use of technology to promote student understanding?
   a. Roberto is playing an online multiplication facts game that provides points for correct answers and feedback indicating the correct answer when he is wrong.
   b. Patricia is using a word-processing program to type a paper for her English class after having written it out longhand.
   c. Deshawn is immersed in a technology simulation of the desert ecosystem.
   d. Carmine is texting his best friend during class regarding their plans for the evening.

Please see answer key at end of book . . . .

Connecting with the Classroom: Crack the Case

The Big Debate

Mrs. Rumer was new to teaching third grade at Hillside Elementary School. Before the school year began, she met with other new teachers and their mentors for planning sessions. The administration appeared to be aware of just how much planning was necessary for successful teaching. Mrs. Rumer openly shared her ideas with her mentor, Mrs. Humbolt, and the rest of the group.

"I really want to have a learner-centered classroom," she said. "I'd like to use aspects of problem-based learning, essential questions, and guided discovery. I think the students will learn so much more that way than if I use teacher-centered instruction."

Mrs. Humbolt smiled and said, "Well, they'd probably have more fun, but I doubt that their test scores would reflect much learning at all. We really need to prepare our students to meet state standards, Mrs. Rumer. To do that, you'd better throw in some good old-fashioned direct instruction." Several other teachers readily agreed. One commented, "That constructivist stuff is too much fluff; I want my students to be serious and learn what I teach them." Another said, "I use the computers in the classroom for drilling students to memorize material for the state tests they have to take, sort of like giving them electronic flash cards. I guess that wouldn't fit your scheme."

The other teachers' comments surprised Mrs. Rumer. She had learned in her education courses that learner-centered instruction is supposed to be the best way to teach children. She wanted her students to actively construct their knowledge, not merely have her pour information into their minds. The principal assured her that if she wanted to use a learner-centered approach, she would have that freedom.

continued

With this assurance, Mrs. Rumer began making lists of everything she would have to plan for in order to have an effective learner-centered classroom. She began by going through the district's curriculum guide for third grade. She made lists of all the objectives. Then she went through the learner-centered psychological principles from the APA. After doing this, she realized her job was going to be a daunting one.

1. What are the issues in this case?
2. Where should Mrs. Rumer go from here?
3. How can she take a curriculum that has been taught in a teacher-centered manner and convert it to a learner-centered curriculum? Should she? Why or why not?
4. How can she incorporate technology into the curriculum so that the computers don't become mere electronic flashcards?
5. Which of the following is an activity that would most likely appeal to Mrs. Rumer?
   a. The students will master their basic multiplication facts by completing a worksheet covering them each day.
   b. The students will master their basic multiplication facts by playing multiplication baseball.
   c. The students will master their basic multiplication facts by taking daily timed tests covering them.
   d. The students will master their basic multiplication facts by writing out their multiplication tables repeatedly.
6. Which of the following is an activity that would most likely appeal to Mrs. Rumer's colleagues?
   a. The students will learn the scientific process by completing several experiments.
   b. The students will learn the scientific process by focusing on essential questions in science.
   c. The students will learn the scientific process by reading about it in their science texts and listening to lectures.
   d. The students will learn the scientific process by testing the water in a nearby creek.

Connecting with Learning: Reach Your Learning Goals

1 PLANNING: Explain what is involved in classroom planning.

Instructional Planning
- Instructional planning involves developing a systematic, organized strategy for lessons. Planning is critically important to being a competent teacher, and instructional planning may be mandated by schools.

Time Frames and Planning
- Teachers need to make plans for different time frames, ranging from yearly planning to daily planning.
- Yinger identified five time frames of teacher planning: yearly, term, unit, weekly, and daily.

2 TEACHER-CENTERED LESSON PLANNING AND INSTRUCTION: Identify important forms of teacher-centered instruction.

Teacher-Centered Lesson Planning
- Teacher-centered lesson planning includes creating behavioral objectives, analyzing tasks, and developing instructional taxonomies (classifications).
- Behavioral objectives are statements that propose changes in students' behavior to reach desired performance levels.
- Task analysis focuses on breaking down a complex task that students are to learn into its component parts.
- Bloom's taxonomy classifies educational objectives into cognitive, affective, and psychomotor domains and is used by many teachers to create goals and objectives in lesson planning.

Direct Instruction
- Direct instruction is a structured, teacher-centered approach that involves teacher direction and control, high expectations for students' progress, maximum time spent by students on academic tasks, and efforts by the teacher to keep negative affect to a minimum. The teacher chooses students' learning tasks and directs students' learning of those tasks. The use of nonacademic materials is deemphasized, as is nonacademically oriented teacher-student interaction.

Teacher-Centered Instructional Strategies

- Teacher-centered instructional strategies include orienting students to new material; lecturing, explaining, and demonstrating; questioning and discussing; mastery learning (learning one topic or concept thoroughly before moving on to a more difficult one); seatwork (having students work independently at their seats); and homework.

Evaluating Teacher-Centered Instruction

- Teacher-centered instruction includes useful techniques, and its advocates especially believe it is the best strategy for teaching basic skills such as math computations, grammar rules, and reading vocabulary. Critics of teacher-centered instruction say that by itself it tends to lead to passive rote learning, overly rigid and structured classrooms, inadequate attention to socioemotional development, external rather than internal motivation, excessive use of paper-and-pencil tasks, too few opportunities for real-world learning, and too little collaborative learning in small groups.

3 LEARNER-CENTERED LESSON PLANNING AND INSTRUCTION: Discuss important forms of learner-centered instruction.

Learner-Centered Principles

- Learner-centered lesson planning and instruction move the focus away from the teacher and toward the student.
- The APA's learner-centered psychological principles emphasize the active, reflective nature of learning and learners. The fourteen principles involve cognitive and metacognitive factors (the nature of the learning process, goals of the learning process, the construction of knowledge, strategic thinking, thinking about thinking, and the context of learning); motivational and emotional factors (motivational and emotional influences on learning, intrinsic motivation to learn, and effects of motivation on effort); developmental and social factors (developmental influences on learning and social influences on learning); and individual difference factors (individual differences in learning, learning and diversity, and standards and assessments).

Some Learner-Centered Instructional Strategies

- Problem-based learning emphasizes real-world problem solving. A problem-based curriculum exposes students to authentic problems.
- Problem-based learning focuses on small-group discussion rather than lecture. Students identify issues they wish to explore, and teachers act as guides, helping students monitor their problem-solving efforts.
- Essential questions are questions that engagingly reflect the heart of the curriculum, cause students to think, and motivate their curiosity.
- Discovery learning is learning in which students construct an understanding on their own. Most discovery-learning approaches today involve guided discovery, in which students are encouraged to construct their understanding with the assistance of teacher-guided questions and directions.

Evaluating Learner-Centered Strategies

- The learner-centered model of planning and instruction has many positive features. The fourteen APA learner-centered principles are guidelines that can help teachers develop strategies that benefit student learning (such as encouraging students to actively construct knowledge, think deeply and creatively, be internally motivated, solve real-world problems, and collaboratively learn).
- Critics argue that learner-centered planning and instruction focuses too much on the process of learning and not enough on academic content; is more appropriate for social sciences and humanities than science and math; is not appropriate for beginning instruction when students have little or no knowledge about the topic; and is more challenging to implement than most teachers envision.
- Keep in mind that although we presented teacher-centered and learner-centered approaches separately, many teachers use aspects of both approaches.

continued

4 TECHNOLOGY AND EDUCATION: Summarize how to effectively use technology to help children learn.

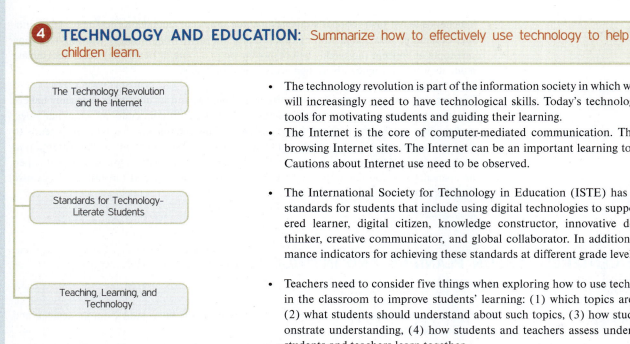

- The technology revolution is part of the information society in which we now live, and students will increasingly need to have technological skills. Today's technologies can be remarkable tools for motivating students and guiding their learning.
- The Internet is the core of computer-mediated communication. The Web is a system for browsing Internet sites. The Internet can be an important learning tool in many classrooms. Cautions about Internet use need to be observed.
- The International Society for Technology in Education (ISTE) has established technology standards for students that include using digital technologies to support being a(an) empowered learner, digital citizen, knowledge constructor, innovative designer, computational thinker, creative communicator, and global collaborator. In addition, ISTE provides performance indicators for achieving these standards at different grade levels.
- Teachers need to consider five things when exploring how to use technology more effectively in the classroom to improve students' learning: (1) which topics are worth understanding, (2) what students should understand about such topics, (3) how students develop and demonstrate understanding, (4) how students and teachers assess understanding, and (5) how students and teachers learn together.

KEY TERMS

advance organizers 401
behavioral
   objectives 397
Bloom's taxonomy 397
cloud computing 415
comparative advance
   organizers 401
direct instruction 399
discovery learning 410
essential questions 410
expository advance
   organizers 401
guided discovery learning 410
instructional planning 393
Internet 415
mastery learning 403
task analysis 397
taxonomy 397
Web 415

PORTFOLIO ACTIVITIES

Now that you have a good understanding of this chapter, complete these exercises to expand your thinking.

Independent Reflection

1. **Developing a Classroom Technology Plan.** Create a written plan for how you might use digital technologies for the subject(s) and grade level you plan to teach. How will you adapt your plan for students with little or no experience with digital technologies? How can your classroom benefit from students with advanced technology skills? (INTASC: Principles *1, 4, 8*)

Research/Field Experience

2. **Instructional Planning in Action.** Ask a teacher at the grade level you plan to teach to show you the materials he or she uses in planning lessons, units, the term, and the yearly curriculum for one or more subjects. Create samples for your own later use based on what the teacher shows you. Discuss the importance of planning at each of these levels. (INTASC: Principles *7, 9*)

Collaborative Work

3. **Evaluating Teacher-Centered and Learner-Centered Classrooms.** With three other students in the class, divide up the work of observing an early childhood, an elementary, a middle school, and a high school classroom. Reconvene after each of you has observed a classroom, and discuss the aspects of teacher-centered and learner-centered approaches the teachers were using. Evaluate how effective the approaches were. Write a comparative analysis. (INTASC: Principles *1, 2, 3, 4, 5, 6, 7, 8, 9*)

chapter 13
MOTIVATION, TEACHING, AND LEARNING

chapter outline

① Exploring Motivation

Learning Goal 1 Define motivation and compare the behavioral, humanistic, cognitive, and social perspectives on motivation.

What Is Motivation?
Perspectives on Motivation

② Achievement Processes

Learning Goal 2 Discuss the important processes in motivation to achieve.

Extrinsic and Intrinsic Motivation
Attribution
Mastery Motivation and Mindset
Self-Efficacy
Goal Setting, Planning, and Self-Monitoring
Expectations
Delay of Gratification
Values and Purpose

③ Motivation, Relationships, and Sociocultural Contexts

Learning Goal 3 Explain how relationships and sociocultural contexts can support or undercut motivation.

Social Motives
Social Relationships
Sociocultural Contexts

④ Exploring Achievement Difficulties

Learning Goal 4 Recommend how to help students with achievement difficulties.

Students Who Are Low Achieving and Have Low Expectations for Success
Students Who Protect Their Self-Worth by Avoiding Failure
Students Who Procrastinate
Students Who Are Perfectionists
Students with High Anxiety
Students Who Are Uninterested or Alienated

The art of teaching is the art of awakening the curiosity of young minds.

—Anatole France
French Novelist and Poet, 20th Century

Wavebreakmedia/Shutterstock

Connecting with Teachers: Jaime Escalante

An immigrant from Bolivia named Jaime Escalante became a math teacher at Garfield High School in East Los Angeles, a school largely populated by Latinx students from low-income families. When he began teaching at Garfield, many of the students had little confidence in their math abilities, and most of the teachers had low expectations for the students' success. Escalante took it as a special challenge to improve the students' math skills, even enable them to perform well on the Educational Testing Service Advanced Placement (AP) calculus exam.

The first year was difficult. Escalante's calculus class began at 8 a.m. He told the students the doors would be open at 7 a.m. and that instruction would begin at 7:30 a.m. He also worked with them after school and on weekends. He put together lots of handouts, told the students to take extensive notes, and required them to keep a folder. He gave them a five-minute quiz each morning and a test every Friday. He started with fourteen students, but in two weeks the number was cut in half. Only five students lasted through the spring. One of the boys who quit said, "I don't want to come at 7:00. Why should I?"

When Escalante was teaching, on the 5-point AP calculus test (with 5 highest, 1 lowest), a 3 or better meant that a student was performing at a college level and would receive credit for the course at most major universities. The AP calculus scores for Escalante's first five students were two 4's, two 2's, and one 1. This was better than the school had done in the past, but Escalante resolved to do better.

Three years later, the AP calculus test scores for Escalante's class of 15 students were one 5, four 4's, nine 3's, and one 2. Ten years after Escalante's first class, 151 students were taking calculus in the East Los Angeles high school.

Jaime Escalante in a classroom teaching math.
AP Images

Escalante's persistent, challenging, and inspiring teaching raised Garfield High, a school plagued by poor funding, violence, and inferior working conditions, to seventh place among U.S. schools in calculus. Escalante's commitment and motivation were transferred to his students, many of whom no one had believed in before Escalante came along. Escalante's contributions were portrayed in the film *Stand and Deliver*. Escalante, his students, and celebrity guests also introduce basic math concepts for sixth- to twelfth-grade students on *Futures 1 and 2 with Jaime Escalante*, a PBS series. Escalante has now retired from teaching but continues to work in a consulting role to help improve students' motivation to do well in math and improve their math skills. Escalante's story is testimony to how one teacher can make a major difference in students' motivation and achievement.

Preview

As we saw in the "Planning, Instruction, and Technology" chapter, motivation is a key component of the American Psychological Association's learner-centered psychological principles. Indeed, motivation is a critical aspect of teaching and learning. Unmotivated students won't expend the necessary effort to learn. As Jaime Escalante's teaching story shows, highly motivated students are eager to come to school and are absorbed in the learning process.

LG 1 Define motivation and compare the behavioral, humanistic, cognitive, and social perspectives on motivation.

A young Canadian, Terry Fox, did one of the great long-distance runs in history (McNally, 1990). Averaging a marathon (26.2 miles) a day for five months, he ran 3,359 miles across most of Canada. What makes his grueling feat truly remarkable is that Terry Fox had lost a leg to cancer before the run, so he was running with the aid of a prosthetic limb. Terry Fox clearly was a motivated person, but exactly what does it mean to be motivated?

WHAT IS MOTIVATION?

Motivation involves the processes that energize, direct, and sustain behavior. Why did Terry Fox do this run? When Terry was hospitalized with cancer, he told himself that if he survived he would do something to help fund cancer research. Thus, the motivation for his run was to give purpose to his life by helping other people with cancer.

Terry Fox's behavior was energized, directed, and sustained. Running across most of Canada, he encountered unforeseen hurdles: severe headwinds, heavy rain, snow, and icy roads. Because of these conditions, he averaged only eight miles a day after the first month, far below what he had planned. But he kept going and picked up the pace in the second month until he was back on track. His example stands as a testimonial to how motivation can help each of us prevail.

Terry Fox's story is portrayed in a good classroom film, *The Power of Purpose*. One sixth-grade teacher showed the film to her class and then asked her students to write down what they learned from it. One student wrote, "I learned that even if something bad happens to you, you have to keep going, keep trying. Even if your body gets hurt, it can't take away your spirit."

PERSPECTIVES ON MOTIVATION

Different psychological perspectives explain motivation in different ways. Let's explore four of these perspectives: behavioral, humanistic, cognitive, and social.

The Behavioral Perspective
The behavioral perspective emphasizes external rewards and punishments as keys in determining a student's motivation. **Incentives** are positive or negative stimuli or events that can motivate a student's behavior. Advocates of the use of incentives emphasize that they add interest or excitement to the class and direct attention toward appropriate behavior and away from inappropriate behavior (Emmer & Evertson, 2017; Evertson & Emmer, 2017).

Incentives that classroom teachers use include numerical scores and letter grades, which also provide feedback about the quality of the student's work, and checkmarks or stars for competently completing work. Other incentives include giving students recognition—for example, by displaying their work, giving them a certificate of achievement, placing them on the honor roll, and verbally mentioning their accomplishments. Another type of incentive focuses on allowing students to do something special—such as playing computer games or going on a field trip—as a reward for good work. Shortly, in our discussion of intrinsic and extrinsic motivation, we will look more closely at the issue of whether incentives are a good idea.

The Humanistic Perspective
The **humanistic perspective** stresses students' capacity for personal growth, freedom to choose their destiny, and positive qualities (such as being sensitive to others). This perspective is closely associated with Abraham Maslow's (1954, 1971) belief that certain basic needs must be met before higher needs can be satisfied. According to Maslow's **hierarchy of needs**, individuals' needs must be satisfied in this sequence (see Figure 1):

- *Physiological:* Hunger, thirst, sleep
- *Safety:* Ensuring survival, such as protection from war and crime
- *Love and belongingness:* Security, affection, and attention from others
- *Esteem:* Feeling good about oneself
- *Self-actualization:* Realization of one's potential

Thus, in Maslow's view, students must satisfy their need for food before they can achieve. His view also provides an explanation of why children who come from poor or abusive homes are less likely to achieve in school than children whose basic needs are met.

motivation The processes that energize, direct, and sustain behavior.

incentives Positive or negative stimuli or events that can motivate a student's behavior.

humanistic perspective A view that stresses students' capacity for personal growth, freedom to choose their destiny, and positive qualities.

hierarchy of needs Maslow's concept that individual needs must be satisfied in this sequence: physiological, safety, love and belongingness, esteem, and self-actualization.

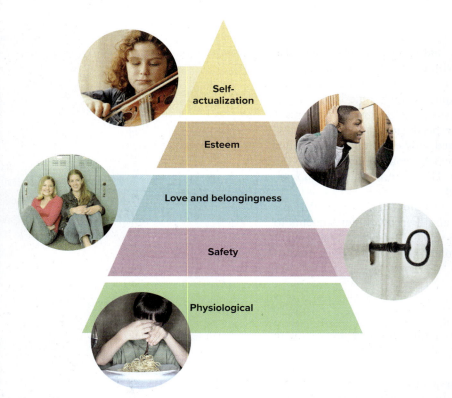

FIGURE 1 MASLOW'S HIERARCHY OF NEEDS

Abraham Maslow developed the hierarchy of human needs to show how we have to satisfy certain basic needs before we can satisfy higher needs. In the diagram, lower-level needs are shown toward the base of the pyramid, higher-level needs toward the peak.

(Top left) Mel Curtis/Photodisc/Getty Images; (Middle left) Andersen Ross/Photodisc/Getty Images; (Top right) Ken Karp/McGraw-Hill; (Bottom right) Ryan McVay/Photodisc/Getty Images; (Bottom left) Brooke Fasani/Corbis

Self-actualization, the highest and most elusive of Maslow's needs, is the motivation to develop one's full potential as a human being. In Maslow's view, self-actualization is possible only after the lower needs have been met. Maslow cautions that most people stop maturing after they have developed a high level of esteem and therefore never become self-actualized. Some characteristics of self-actualized individuals include being spontaneous, problem-centered rather than self-centered, and creative.

The idea that human needs are hierarchically arranged is appealing. However, not everyone agrees with Maslow's choice of key motives or ordering of motives. For example, for some students other needs/motives, such as the cognitive motivation to acquire and understand information and knowledge, might be stronger than Maslow's higher needs, such as esteem needs. Other students might meet their esteem needs even though they have not experienced love and belongingness.

The Cognitive Perspective According to the cognitive perspective on motivation, students' thoughts guide their motivation. In recent years, there has been a surge of interest in the cognitive perspective on motivation (Schunk, 2016; Wentzel & Miele, 2016). This interest focuses on ideas such as students' goal-setting, their attributions, their expectations for success, and their beliefs that they can effectively control their environment and the outcomes of their efforts (Graham & Taylor, 2016; Schunk & DiBenedetto, 2016).

Thus, whereas the behavioral perspective sees the student's motivation as a consequence of external incentives, the cognitive perspective argues that internal influences should be emphasized. The cognitive perspective recommends giving students more responsibility for controlling their own achievement outcomes (Miele & Scholer, 2016; Ryan & Deci, 2016).

The cognitive perspective on motivation fits with the ideas of R.W. White (1959), who proposed the concept of **competence motivation**, the idea that people are motivated to deal effectively with their environment, to master their world, and to process information efficiently. White said that people do these things because they are internally motivated to interact effectively with the environment. The concept of competence motivation explains why humans are motivated to achieve scientific and technological innovation, as well as contribute to society and not just to build their own competence.

The Social Perspective Are you the kind of person who is motivated to be around people a lot? Or would you rather stay home and read a book? The **need for affiliation or relatedness** is the motive to be securely connected with other people. This involves establishing, maintaining, and restoring warm, close personal relationships. Students' need for affiliation or relatedness is reflected in their motivation to spend time with peers, their close friendships, their attachment to their parents, and their desire to have a positive relationship with their teachers (Rowe et al., 2016; Wentzel, 2016; Wentzel & Ramani, 2016; Wubbels et al., 2016). Recent research indicates that relatedness support and satisfaction are associated with more effective engagement, learning, and achievement (Linnenbrink-Garcia & Patall, 2016).

---

self-actualization The highest and most elusive of Maslow's needs; the motivation to develop one's full potential as a human being.

competence motivation The idea that people are motivated to deal effectively with their environment, to master their world, and to process information efficiently.

need for affiliation or relatedness The motive to be securely connected with other people.

Recently, the concept of a *belonging mindset*, which describes the belief that people like you belong in your school (Rattan et al., 2015). Many students aren't sure whether they belong or are well-connected to their school, creating a sense of uneasiness that is especially likely to occur for students from negatively stereotyped groups. Such negative belonging concerns are associated with lower achievement. However, when underrepresented students feel they belong and are well connected to their school, they have better physical and mental health, and have greater academic success (Walton & Cohen, 2011; Walton et al., 2014). In a recent study, when underrepresented students participated in belonging discussions, their academic achievement increased (Stephens et al., 2014).

Students in schools with caring and supportive interpersonal relationships have more positive academic attitudes and values and are more satisfied with school (Wentzel, 2016). One study revealed that students' mastery motivation and engagement increased more over the school year when they had more emotionally-supportive teachers (Ruzek et al., 2016). In other research, the value that middle school students assigned to math increased when they had a teacher whom they perceived to be high in support (Eccles, 1993; Wang et al., 2017).

As you think about various perspectives on motivation, realize that you don't have to adopt just one perspective. All of the perspectives provide information that is relevant to children's education.

Meredith MacGregor, shown here as a senior at Fairview High School in Boulder, Colorado, was an aspiring scientist and one of Colorado's top high school long-distance runners. She maintained a 4.0 grade point average, participated in a number of school organizations, and cofounded the AfriAid Club. She was named a *USA Today* High School Academic All-Star and was awarded the Intel Foundation Young Scientist Award (Wong Briggs, 2007). *What are some factors that likely are involved in Meredith's motivation to achieve?*
Kevin Moloney

Review, Reflect, and Practice

① Define motivation and compare the behavioral, humanistic, cognitive, and social perspectives on motivation.

REVIEW
- What is motivated behavior?
- How would you briefly summarize the four main perspectives on motivation?

REFLECT
- Recall a situation in which you were highly motivated to accomplish something.
- How would you describe your motivation in terms of each of the four perspectives?

PRAXIS™ PRACTICE

1. Which of the following best exemplifies what motivation is?
   a. Robbie is emotional about the upcoming school year and wants to do well.
   b. Sherrie is energized, sets a high goal for doing well in her English class, persists with considerable effort, and makes an *A* in the class.
   c. Carmello is good at directing his attention to what he wants to accomplish.
   d. Latisha works hard, experiences positive feelings about her academic work, and enjoys working with others.

2. Which of the following best exemplifies the cognitive perspective on motivation?
   a. Mr. Davidson gives his students tickets when he "catches them being good" so that they will continue to behave appropriately.
   b. Mr. McRoberts wants his students to believe they can be successful in anything if they try, so he ensures success for those students who work hard.
   c. Ms. Boeteng believes that her students will be more motivated in school if they establish good relationships with both her and with their classmates, so she provides emotional support.
   d. Ms. Pocius keeps a supply of cereal in her desk drawer so that if one of her students is hungry, she can provide food.

Please see answer key at end of book . . . .

LG 2 Discuss the important processes in motivation to achieve.

2 ACHIEVEMENT PROCESSES

- Extrinsic and Intrinsic Motivation
- Mastery Motivation and Mindset
- Goal-Setting, Planning, and Self-Monitoring
- Delay of Gratification
- Attribution
- Self-Efficacy
- Expectations
- Values and Purpose

The current interest in motivation in school has been fueled by the cognitive perspective and an emphasis on discovering the most important processes involved in students' achievement (Linnenbrink-Garcia & Patall, 2016; Miele & Scholer, 2016; Roeser, 2016; Schunk & DiBenedetto, 2016). In this section, you will read about a number of effective cognitive strategies for improving students' motivation to achieve. We'll begin by exploring a crucial distinction between extrinsic (external) and intrinsic (internal) motivation. That will lead us to examine several other important cognitive insights about motivation. Then, we will study the role of expectations in students' motivation.

EXTRINSIC AND INTRINSIC MOTIVATION

Extrinsic motivation involves doing something to obtain something else (a means to an end). Extrinsic motivation is often influenced by external incentives such as rewards and punishments. For example, a student may study hard for a test in order to obtain a good grade in the course.

The behavioral perspective emphasizes the importance of extrinsic motivation in achievement; the humanistic and cognitive approaches stress the importance of intrinsic motivation in achievement. **Intrinsic motivation** involves the internal motivation to do something for its own sake (an end in itself). For example, a student may study hard for a test because he or she enjoys the content of the course.

Current evidence strongly favors establishing a classroom climate in which students are intrinsically motivated to learn (Ryan & Deci, 2009, 2016). For example, a study of third- through eighth-grade students found that intrinsic motivation was positively linked with grades and standardized test scores, whereas extrinsic motivation was negatively related to achievement outcomes (Lepper et al., 2005). When goals are framed only extrinsically, students show a lower level of independent motivation and lower persistence on achievement tasks (Vansteenkiste et al., 2008).

Parental use of intrinsic versus extrinsic motivational practices also is linked to children's motivation. In one study, children had higher intrinsic motivation in math and science from 9 to 17 years of age when their parents engaged in task-intrinsic practices (encouraging children's pleasure and engagement in learning) than when their parents engaged in task-extrinsic practices (providing external rewards and consequences contingent on children's performance) (Gottfried et al., 2009).

Students are more highly motivated to learn when they are given choices, become absorbed in challenges that match their skills, and receive rewards that have informational value but are not used for control. Praise also can enhance students' intrinsic motivation. To see why these things are so, let's first explore four types of intrinsic motivation: (1) self-determination and personal choice, (2) optimal experiences and flow, (3) interest, and (4) cognitive engagement and self-responsibility. Then we'll discuss how extrinsic rewards can either enhance or undermine intrinsic motivation. Next we will identify some developmental changes in intrinsic and extrinsic motivation as students move up the educational ladder. Finally, we will offer some concluding thoughts about intrinsic and extrinsic motivation.

Self-Determination and Personal Choice One view of intrinsic motivation emphasizes self-determination (Ryan & Deci, 2009, 2016). In this view, students want to believe that they are doing something because of their own will, not because of

RESEARCH

These students were given an opportunity to write and perform their own play. Such types of self-determining opportunities can enhance students' motivation to achieve.
Adam Taylor/Digital Vision/Getty Images

extrinsic motivation The external motivation to do something to obtain something else (a means to an end).

intrinsic motivation The internal motivation to do something for its own sake (an end in itself).

external success or rewards. The architects of self-determination theory, Richard Ryan and Edward Deci (2009, 2016) refer to teachers who create circumstances for students to engage in self-determination as *autonomy-supportive teachers.*

RESEARCH

Researchers have found that students' internal motivation and intrinsic interest in school tasks increase when students have some choice and some opportunities to take personal responsibility for their learning (Grolnick et al., 2009). In one study, teachers were encouraged to give the students more responsibility for their school programs (deCharms, 1984)—in particular, opportunities to set their own goals, plan how to reach the goals, and monitor their progress toward the goals. Students were given some choice in the activities they wanted to engage in and when they would do them. They also were encouraged to take personal responsibility for their behavior, including reaching the goals that they had set. Compared with a control group, students in this intrinsic motivation/self-determination group had higher achievement gains and were more likely to graduate from high school.

CONNECTING WITH STUDENTS: Best Practices
Strategies for Student Self-Determination and Choice

Following are some effective ways you can guide students' self-determination in your classroom:

1. *Take the time to talk* with students and discuss with them why the learning activity is important.
2. *Provide students opportunities to make choices* that are meaningful to them.
3. *Be attentive to students' feelings* when they are being asked to do something they don't want to do.
4. *Manage the classroom effectively, in a way that lets students make personal choices.* Let students select topics for book reports, writing assignments, and research projects. Let them decide how they want to report their work; for instance, let them report to you or to the class as a whole, individually or with a partner.
5. *Establish learning centers* where students can work individually or collaboratively with other students on different projects and can select their activities from a menu that you have developed.
6. *Create self-selected interest groups* and let students work on relevant research together.

Optimal Experiences and Flow Mihaly Csikszentmihalyi (1990, 1993; Csikszentmihalyi & Csikszentmihalyi, 2006) has proposed ideas that are relevant to understanding intrinsic motivation. He has studied the optimal experiences of people for more than two decades. People report that these optimal experiences involve feelings of deep enjoyment and happiness. Csikszentmihalyi uses the term *flow* to describe optimal experiences in life. He has found that flow occurs most often when people develop a sense of mastery and are absorbed in a state of concentration while they engage in an activity. He argues that flow occurs when individuals are engaged in challenges they find neither too difficult nor too easy. For example, flow is occurring when a student is deeply absorbed in working on a science project that her teacher has structured at a challenging level but not beyond the student's capability.

Perceived levels of challenge and skill can result in different outcomes (see Figure 2) (Brophy, 1998). Flow is most likely to occur in areas in which students are challenged and perceive themselves as having a high degree of skill. When students' skills are high but the activity provides little challenge, the result is boredom. When both the challenge and skill levels are low, students feel apathy. And when students face a challenging task that they don't believe they have adequate skills to master, they experience anxiety.

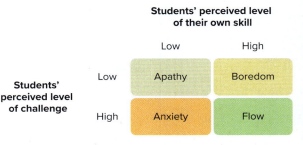

FIGURE 2 OUTCOMES OF PERCEIVED LEVELS OF CHALLENGE AND SKILL

CONNECTING WITH STUDENTS: Best Practices
Strategies for Helping Students Achieve Flow

How can you encourage students to achieve flow? Here are some strategies (Csikszentmihalyi, Rathunde, & Whalen, 1993):

1. *Be competent and motivated.* Become an expert about the subject matter, show enthusiasm when you teach, and present yourself as a model who is intrinsically motivated. In *Through the Eyes of Teachers*, Rhonda Nachamkin describes how expertise and enthusiasm come through as she turns the classroom into an exciting place for students to learn.

THROUGH THE EYES OF TEACHERS
Turning the Classroom into an Egyptian Tomb, New York City, and Mount Olympus

Rhonda Nachamkin, who teaches first grade at River Eves Elementary School in Roswell, Georgia, has a high-energy style and approaches each unit as if it were a Hollywood production. She turns the classroom into an Egyptian tomb, New York City, or Mount Olympus. She sends parents scurrying to learn who Anubis (Egyptian god) and Prometheus (Greek Titan who stole fire from the gods) were so they can converse about these topics with their 6-year-olds. Rhonda likes to use multiple versions of fairy tales to teach reading, spelling, and analytical concepts. (Source: USA Today, 1999.)

Rhonda Nachamkin helps one of her students, Patrick Drones, with his work.
Michael A. Schwarz

2. *Create an optimal match.* A good strategy is to develop and maintain an optimal match between what you challenge students to do and what their skills are. That is, encourage students to achieve challenging but reasonable goals.

3. *Remove distractions from the classroom.* It is difficult for students to get into a "flow" state if there are a lot of distractions.

4. *Raise confidence.* Provide students with both instructional and emotional support that encourages them to tackle learning with confidence and a minimum of anxiety.

Interest Educational psychologists also have examined the concept of *interest*, which has been proposed as more specific than intrinsic motivation (Alexander & Grossnickle, 2016; Linnenbrink-Garcia & Patall, 2016). A distinction has been made between *individual interest*, which is thought to be relatively stable, and *situational interest*, which is believed to be generated by specific aspects of a task activity. Individual interest might involve students' math ability that they bring to the course, such as the longstanding ability and success students have had in math. Situational interest might involve how interesting a particular teacher makes a math class.

Research on interest has focused mainly on its relationship to learning and cognitive processes, as well as its importance in various academic domains (Fox & Dinsmore, 2016). Interest is linked more closely to measures of deep learning, such as recall of main ideas and responses to more difficult comprehension questions, than to surface learning, such as responses to simple questions and verbatim recall of text (Wigfield et al., 2015). Researchers have found that that a number of contextual factors, such as autonomy support, instructor approachability, involvement opportunities, and course material relevance, are linked to situational interest and in turn may support individual interest (Linnenbrink-Garcia & Patall, 2016).

How can technology be used to stimulate students' interest? Authentic tasks approximate the real world or real life as closely as possible, and they can spark students' interest and curiosity. Students often perceive technology-based learning experiences as real-world activities. Indeed, as 21st-century learners and workers, they will use technology as an integrated method of accessing information, organizing their thinking, collaborating with others, and communicating with stakeholders.

Integrating technology into the classroom can increase students' motivation to learn and engagement in learning, especially when it is used to foster authentic learning. For example, researchers have documented improved motivation (Swan et al., 2005), engagement (Silvernail & Lane, 2004), learning (Hegedus et al., 2015), behavior (Apple

TECHNOLOGY

Computer, 1995), and school attendance (Apple Computer, 1995) among students involved in technology-rich initiatives. In addition, research indicates that such students are better organized and more independent learners (Zucker & McGhee, 2005). Also, research reveals that special needs students can achieve at the same levels as regular students in some situations when using technology (Swan et al., 2006).

Serious games are software applications developed using gaming technology and design principles whose primary purpose is for something other than pure entertainment, usually for training or education. The serious games movement in education takes as its framework situated and authentic learning. One example of serious games is *Quest Atlantis Remixed* (http://atlantisremixed.org/), a National Science Foundation–funded project that uses a three-dimensional multiuser environment to immerse 9- to 12-year-old children in educational tasks. Currently, thousands of registered users from five continents use *Quest Atlantis Remixed* in schools. Researchers have found that students who use *Quest Atlantis Remixed* improve their learning in science and social studies while enhancing their sense of academic efficacy (Gresalfi, 2015; Gresalfi et al., 2009).

A computer screen from *Quest Atlantis*, the 2007 version that preceded *Quest Atlantis Remixed*. Building on the model of online role-playing games, *Quest Atlantis* combines elements of the commercial gaming world with educational research on motivation and emotion. The core components include a 3D multi-user environment; an unfolding story involving a mythical Council and a set of social commitments; a customizable home page; various trajectories through which the player's character can develop; inquiry learning situations, including quests, missions, simulated worlds; and a global community of participants who log in from five continents.
Source: Quest Atlantis

Cognitive Engagement and Self-Responsibility Phyllis Blumenfeld and her colleagues (2006) proposed another variation on intrinsic motivation. They emphasize the importance of creating learning environments that encourage students to become cognitively engaged and take responsibility for their learning. The goal is to get students to become motivated to expend the effort to persist and master ideas rather than simply doing enough work to just get by and make passing grades. Especially important is to embed subject matter content and skills learning within meaningful contexts, especially real-world situations that mesh with students' interests (Gregory & Korth, 2016).

Extrinsic Rewards and Intrinsic Motivation Now that we have discussed a number of views of intrinsic motivation, let's examine whether classroom rewards might be useful in some situations and whether certain types of rewards might actually increase intrinsic motivation. As we saw in the chapter on behavioral and social cognitive approaches, external rewards can be useful in changing behavior. However, in some situations rewards can undermine learning. In a classic study, students who already had a strong interest in art and did not expect a reward spent more time drawing than did students who also had a strong interest in art but knew they would be rewarded for drawing (Lepper et al., 1973).

However, classroom rewards can be useful (Cameron & Pierce, 2008). Two uses are (1) as an incentive to engage in tasks, in which case the goal is to control the student's behavior; and (2) to convey information about mastery. When rewards are offered that convey information about mastery, students' feelings of competence are likely to be enhanced. Rewards used as incentives lead to perceptions that the student's behavior was caused by the external reward and not by the student's own motivation to be competent.

To better understand the difference between using rewards to control students' behavior and using them to provide information about mastery, consider this example (Schunk, 2016): A teacher puts a reward system in place in which the more work students accomplish, the more points they will earn. Students will be motivated to work to earn points because they are told that the points can be exchanged for privileges. However, the points also provide information about their capabilities. That is, the more points students earn, the more work they have accomplished. As they accumulate points, students are more likely to feel competent. In contrast, if points are provided simply for spending time on a task, the task might be perceived as a means to an end. In this case, because the points don't convey any information about capabilities, students are likely to perceive the rewards as controlling their behavior.

> **Thinking Back/Thinking Forward**
> One strategy for increasing desirable behaviors is to choose effective reinforcers. Connect to "Behavioral and Social Cognitive Approaches."

Thus, rewards that convey information about students' mastery can increase intrinsic motivation by increasing their sense of competence (Cameron & Pierce, 2008). On the other hand, extensive negative feedback, such as criticism, that carries information students are incompetent can undermine intrinsic motivation, especially if students doubt their ability to become competent (Stipek, 2002). However, this does not mean students should not be given critical/corrective feedback, because such critical/corrective feedback is a key aspect of educating students.

Judy Cameron (2001) argues that rewards do not always decrease a student's intrinsic motivation. In her analysis of approximately a hundred studies, she found that verbal rewards (praise and positive feedback) can be used to enhance students' intrinsic motivation. She also concluded that when tangible rewards (such as gold stars and money) were offered contingent on task performance or given unexpectedly, intrinsic motivation was maintained. Some critics argue that Cameron's analysis is flawed—for instance, that it does not adequately detect some of the negative effects of rewards on motivation (Deci et al., 2001).

In summary, it is important to examine what rewards convey about competence. When rewards are tied to competence, they tend to promote motivation and interest. When they are not, they are unlikely to raise motivation or may diminish it once the rewards are withdrawn (Schunk, 2016).

DEVELOPMENT

RESEARCH

Developmental Shifts in Intrinsic and Extrinsic Motivation Many psychologists and educators stress that it is important for children to develop greater internalization and intrinsic motivation as they grow older (Wigfield et al., 2015). However, researchers have found that as students move from the early elementary school years to the high school years, their intrinsic motivation decreases (Wigfield et al., 2015). In one research study, the biggest drop in intrinsic motivation and increase in extrinsic motivation occurred between sixth grade and seventh grade (Harter, 1981). In another study, as students moved from sixth through eighth grade, they increasingly said school was boring and irrelevant (Harter, 1996). In this study, however, students who were intrinsically motivated did much better academically than those who were extrinsically motivated.

Why the shift toward extrinsic motivation as children move to higher grades? One explanation is that school grading practices reinforce an external motivation orientation. That is, as students get older, they lock into the increasing emphasis on grades, and their internal motivation drops.

Jacquelynne Eccles and her colleagues (Eccles, 2004, 2007; Wigfield et al., 2015) have identified some specific changes in the school context that help to explain the decline in intrinsic motivation. Middle and junior high schools are more impersonal, more formal, more evaluative, and more competitive than elementary schools. Students compare themselves more with other students because they increasingly are graded in terms of their relative performance on assignments and standardized tests.

Proposing the concept of *person-environment fit,* Eccles (2004, 2007) argues that a lack of fit between the middle school/junior high environment and the needs of young adolescents produces increasingly negative self-evaluations and attitudes toward school. Her research has revealed that teachers became more controlling just at the time when adolescents are seeking more autonomy, and the teacher-student relationship becomes more impersonal at a time when students are seeking more independence from their parents and need more support from other adults. At a time when adolescents are becoming more self-conscious, an increased emphasis on grades and other competitive comparisons only makes things worse.

Recent research shows that students in grades 6 and 7 have better reading and mathematics outcomes when they remain in elementary school rather than transferring to middle school (Malone et al., 2019). Given that many elementary schools only go up to grades 5 or 6, how might teachers make school a more appealing environment for young adolescents? Perhaps by getting to know students better and linking their interests to academic content.

Thinking Back/Thinking Forward

The transition to middle or junior high school can be stressful because it coincides with many other developmental changes. Connect to "Social Contexts and Socioemotional Development."

Although there is less research on the transition to high school, the existing research suggests that, like the transition to middle school, it can produce similar problems (Eccles et al., 1998). High schools often are even larger and more bureaucratic than middle schools. In such schools, a sense of community usually is undermined, with little opportunity for students and teachers to get to know each other. As a consequence, distrust between students and teachers develops easily and there is little communication about students' goals and values. Such contexts can especially harm the motivation of students who are not doing well academically.

What lessons can be drawn from this discussion? Perhaps the single most important lesson is that middle school and junior high school students benefit when teachers think of ways to make their school settings more personal, less formal, and more intrinsically motivating.

Some Final Thoughts About Intrinsic and Extrinsic Motivation An overwhelming conclusion of motivation research is that teachers should encourage students to become intrinsically motivated. Similarly, teachers should create learning environments that promote students' cognitive engagement and self-responsibility for learning. That said, the real world includes both intrinsic and extrinsic motivation, and too often intrinsic and extrinsic motivation have been pitted against each other as polar opposites. In many aspects of students' lives, both intrinsic and extrinsic motivation are at work (Cameron & Pierce, 2008). Further, both intrinsic and extrinsic motivation can operate simultaneously. Thus, a student may work hard in a course because she enjoys the content and likes learning about it (intrinsic) and to earn a good grade (extrinsic) (Schunk, 2016). Keep in mind, though, that many educational psychologists recommend that extrinsic motivation by itself is not a good strategy.

Our discussion of extrinsic and intrinsic motivation sets the stage for introducing other cognitive processes involved in motivating students to learn. As we explore six additional cognitive processes, notice how intrinsic and extrinsic motivation continue to be important. The seven processes are (1) attribution; (2) mastery motivation and mindset; (3) self-efficacy; (4) goal setting, planning, and self-monitoring; (5) expectations; (6) delay of gratification; and (7) values and purpose.

ATTRIBUTION

Attribution theory states that individuals are motivated to discover the underlying causes of their own performance and behavior. Attributions are perceived causes of outcomes. In a way, attribution theorists say, students are like intuitive scientists, seeking to explain the cause behind what happens (Graham & Taylor, 2016; Graham & Williams, 2009). For example, a secondary school student asks, "Why am I not doing well in this class?" or "Did I get a good grade because I studied hard or the teacher made up an easy test, or both?" The search for a cause or explanation is most likely to be initiated when unexpected and important events end in failure, such as when a good student gets a low grade. Some of the most frequently inferred causes of success and failure are ability, effort, task ease or difficulty, luck, mood, and help or hindrance from others.

Bernard Weiner (1986, 1992) identified three dimensions of causal attributions: (1) *locus,* whether the cause is internal or external to the actor; (2) *stability,* the extent to which the cause remains the same or changes; and (3) *controllability,* the extent to which someone can control the cause. For example, a student might perceive his aptitude as located internally, stable, and uncontrollable. The student also might perceive chance or luck as external to himself, variable, and uncontrollable. Figure 3 lists eight possible combinations of locus, stability, and controllability and how they match up with various common explanations of failure.

attribution theory The theory that individuals are motivated to discover the underlying causes of their own behavior and performance.

Combination of causal attributions	Reason students give for failure
Internal-stable-uncontrollable	Low aptitude
Internal-stable-controllable	Never study
Internal-unstable-uncontrollable	Sick the day of the test
Internal-unstable-controllable	Did not study for this particular test
External-stable-uncontrollable	School has tough requirements
External-stable-controllable	The instructor is biased
External-unstable-uncontrollable	Bad luck
External-unstable-controllable	Friends failed to help

FIGURE 3 COMBINATIONS OF CAUSAL ATTRIBUTIONS AND EXPLANATIONS FOR FAILURE

When students fail or do poorly on a test or an assignment, they attribute the outcome to certain causes. The explanation reflects eight combinations of Weiner's three main categories of attributions: locus (internal-external), stability (stable-unstable), and controllability (controllable-uncontrollable). *Human Motivation: Metaphors, Theories, and Research* by Bernard Weiner, p. 253. Copyright 1992 by Sage Publications Inc. Books. Reproduced with permission of Sage Publications Inc Books in the format Textbook via Copyright Clearance Center.

Weiner, Bernard. *Human Motivation: Metaphors, Theories, and Research.* Sage Publications Inc., 1992, 253.

To see how attributions affect subsequent achievement strivings, consider two students, Jane and Susan. Both students fail a math test, but each attributes this negative outcome to a different set of causes (Graham & Weiner, 1996, p. 72):

> When Jane flunks her math test, she searches for the reasons for the failure. Her analysis leads her to attribute the failure to herself, not blaming her teacher or bad luck. She also attributes the failure to an unstable factor—lack of preparation and study time. Thus, she perceives that her failure was due to internal, unstable, and also controllable factors. Because the factors are unstable, Jane has a reasonable expectation that she can still succeed in the future. And because the factors are controllable, she also feels guilty. Her expectations for success enable her to overcome her deflated sense of self-esteem. Her hope for the future results in renewed goal setting and increased motivation to do well on the next test. As a result, Jane seeks tutoring and increases her study time.
>
> When Susan fails the test, she also searches for reasons for the failure. As it happens, her analysis leads her to attribute her failure to internal (lack of ability), stable, and uncontrollable factors. Because Susan perceives the cause of her failure to be internal, her self-esteem suffers. Because it is stable, she sees failure in her future and has a helpless feeling that she can't do anything about her situation. And because it is uncontrollable, she feels ashamed and humiliated. In addition, her parents and teacher tell her that they feel sorry for her but don't provide any recommendations or strategies for success, furthering her belief that she is incompetent. With low expectations of success, low self-esteem, and a depressed mood, Susan decides to drop out of school instead of studying harder.

What are the best strategies for teachers to use in helping students like Susan change their attributions? Educational psychologists often recommend providing students with a planned series of achievement experiences in which modeling, information about strategies, practice, and feedback are used to help them (1) concentrate on the task at hand rather than worrying about failing, (2) cope with failures by retracing their steps to discover their mistake or by analyzing the problem to discover another approach, and (3) attribute their failures to a lack of effort rather than lack of ability (Dweck & Elliott, 1983).

The current strategy is not to expose students to models who handle tasks with ease and demonstrate success but rather to expose them to models who struggle to overcome mistakes before finally succeeding (Brophy, 2004). In this way, students learn how to deal with frustration, persist in the face of difficulties, and constructively cope with failure.

MASTERY MOTIVATION AND MINDSET

Cognitive engagement and self-motivation for improvement characterize adolescents with a mastery motivation (Dweck & Master, 2009). These children also have a growth mindset—a sense of confidence that they can produce positive outcomes if they put forth the effort.

Mastery Motivation Developmental psychologists Valanne Henderson and Carol Dweck (1990) have found that children often show two distinct responses to difficult or challenging circumstances. Children who display **mastery orientation** are task-oriented; instead of focusing on their ability, they concentrate on learning strategies and the process of achievement rather than the outcome. Those with a **helpless orientation** seem trapped by the experience of difficulty and they attribute their difficulty to lack of ability. They frequently say such things as "I'm not very good at this," even though they might earlier have demonstrated their ability through many successes. And, once they view their behavior as failure, they often feel anxious, and their performance worsens even further. Figure 4 describes some behaviors that might reflect helplessness (Stipek, 2002).

The student:
- Says "I can't"
- Doesn't pay attention to teacher's instructions
- Doesn't ask for help, even when it is needed
- Does nothing (for example, stares out the window)
- Guesses or answers randomly without really trying
- Doesn't show pride in successes
- Appears bored, uninterested
- Is unresponsive to teacher's exhortations to try
- Is easily discouraged
- Doesn't volunteer answers to teacher's questions
- Maneuvers to get out of or to avoid work (for example, has to go to the nurse's office)

FIGURE 4 BEHAVIORS THAT SUGGEST HELPLESSNESS

mastery orientation A task-oriented response to difficult or challenging circumstances that focuses on learning strategies and the process of achievement rather than the outcome.

helpless orientation A response to challenges and difficulties in which the individual feels trapped by the difficulty and attributes the difficulty to a lack of ability.

In contrast, mastery-oriented children often instruct themselves to pay attention, to think carefully, and to remember strategies that have worked for them in previous situations. They frequently report feeling challenged and excited by difficult tasks, rather than being threatened by them (Anderman & Anderman, 2010).

Another issue in motivation involves whether to adopt a mastery or a performance orientation. Children with a **performance orientation** focus on winning rather than achievement, and they believe that success results from winning. Does this mean that mastery-oriented children do not like to win and that performance-oriented children are not motivated to experience the self-efficacy that comes from being able to take credit for one's accomplishments? No. A matter of emphasis or degree is involved, though. For mastery-oriented individuals, winning isn't everything; for performance-oriented individuals, skill development and self-efficacy take a backseat to winning.

Recall that the No Child Left Behind (NCLB) Act emphasizes testing and accountability. Although NCLB may motivate some teachers and students to work harder, motivation experts worry that it encourages a performance rather than a mastery motivational orientation on the part of students (Meece et al., 2006).

A final point needs to be made about mastery and performance goals: They are not always mutually exclusive. Students can be both mastery- and performance-oriented, and researchers have found that mastery goals combined with performance goals often benefit students' success (Schunk et al., 2008).

> **Thinking Back/Thinking Forward**
>
> Some critics contend that the No Child Left Behind legislation is harmful for students who are gifted and hampers students' creativity. Connect to "Learners Who Are Exceptional" and "Complex Cognitive Processes."

Mindset Carol Dweck's (2006, 2012, 2015, 2016) most recent analysis of motivation for achievement stresses the importance of children developing a **mindset**, which she defines as the cognitive view individuals develop for themselves. She concludes that individuals have one of two mindsets: (1) *fixed mindset,* in which they believe that their qualities are carved in stone and cannot change; or (2) *growth mindset,* in which they believe their qualities can change and improve through their effort. A fixed mindset is similar to a helpless orientation; a growth mindset is much like having mastery motivation.

In her book *Mindset,* Dweck (2006) argued that individuals' mindsets influence whether they will be optimistic or pessimistic, shape their goals and how hard they will strive to reach those goals, and affect many aspects of their lives, including achievement and success in school and sports. Dweck says that mindsets begin to be shaped as children interact with parents, teachers, and coaches, who themselves have either a fixed mindset or a growth mindset. She described the growth mindset of Patricia Miranda:

performance orientation A focus on winning rather than achievement outcome; success is believed to result from winning.

mindset Dweck's concept that refers to the cognitive view individuals develop for themselves; individuals have one of two mindsets: fixed or growth.

> [She] was a chubby, unathletic school kid who wanted to wrestle. After a bad beating on the mat, she was told, "You're a joke." First she cried, then she felt: "That really set my resolve . . . I had to keep going and had to know if effort and focus and belief and training could somehow legitimize me as a wrestler." Where did she get this resolve? Miranda was raised in a life devoid of challenge. But when her mother died of an aneurysm at age forty, ten-year-old Miranda . . . [thought] "If you only go through life doing stuff that's easy, shame on you." So when wrestling presented a challenge, she was ready to take it on.
>
> Her effort paid off. At twenty-four, Miranda was having the last laugh. She won a spot on the U.S. Olympic team and came home from Athens with a bronze medal. And what was next? Yale Law School. People urged her to stay where she was already on top, but Miranda felt it was more exciting to start at the bottom again and see what she could grow into this time. (Dweck, 2006, pp. 22–23)

Patricia Miranda (in blue) winning the bronze medal in the 2004 Olympics. *What characterizes her growth mindset, and how is it different from a fixed mindset?*
Hasam Sarbakhshian/AP Images

At a workshop for teachers and board members at Pennington School, Marva Collins encourages a participant who plays the role of a student.
Margaret Thomas/The Washington Post/Getty Images

Consider also the powerful role second-grade Chicago teacher Marva Collins has in creating a growth mindset in her students. She tells her students, many of whom are repeating the second grade,

> I know most of you can't spell your name. You don't know the alphabet, you don't know how to read . . . I promise you that you will. None of you has ever failed. School may have failed you. Well, goodbye to failure, children. Welcome to success. You will read hard books in here and understand what you read. You will write every day. . . . But you must help me to help you. If you don't give anything, don't expect anything. Success is not coming to you, you must come to it. (Dweck, 2006)

Her second-grade students usually have to start with the lowest level of reader available, but by the end of the school year, most of the students are reading at the fifth-grade level. Collins takes inner-city children living in low-income, often poverty, circumstances and challenges them to be all they can be. She won't accept failure by her students and teaches students to be responsible for their behavior every day of their lives. Collins tells students that being excellent at something is not a one-time thing but a habit, that determination and persistence are what move the world, and that thinking others will make you successful is a sure way to fail.

DIVERSITY

In recent research by Dweck and her colleagues, students from lower-income families were less likely to have a growth mindset than their counterparts from wealthier families (Claro et al., 2016). However, the achievement of students from lower-income families who did have a growth mindset was more likely to be protected from the negative effects of poverty.

Dweck and her colleagues (Blackwell & Dweck, 2008; Blackwell et al., 2007; Dweck, 2012, 2015, 2016; Dweck & Master, 2009) recently incorporated information about the brain's plasticity into their effort to improve students' motivation to achieve and succeed. In one study, they assigned two groups of students to eight sessions of either (1) study skills instruction or (2) study skills instruction plus information about the importance of developing a growth mindset (called incremental theory in the research) (Blackwell et al., 2007). One of the exercises in the growth mindset group, titled "You Can Grow Your Brain," emphasized that the brain is like a muscle that can change and grow as it gets exercised and develops new connections. Students were informed that the more you challenge your brain to learn, the more your brain cells grow. Both groups had a pattern of declining math scores prior to the intervention. Following the intervention, the group who received only the study skills instruction continued to decline. The group who received study skills instruction plus the growth-mindset emphasis on how the brain develops when it is challenged were able to reverse the downward trend and improve their math achievement. In a recent study conducted by Dweck and her colleagues (Paunesku et al., 2015), underachieving high school students read online modules about how the brain changes when people learn and study hard. Following the online exposure about the brain and learning, the underachieving students improved their grade point averages.

In other work, Dweck has been creating a computer-based workshop called "Brainology" to teach students that their intelligence can change (Blackwell & Dweck, 2008). Students experience six modules about how the brain works and how to make their brain improve. After the program was tested in 20 New York City schools, students strongly endorsed the value of the computer-based brain modules. Said one student, "I will try harder because I know that the more you try the more your brain knows" (Dweck & Master, 2009, p. 137).

Carol Dweck. *What does she emphasize as the most important aspects of students' achievement?*
Courtesy of Dr. Carol Dweck

Dweck and her colleagues also recently have found that a growth mindset can prevent negative stereotypes from undermining achievement. For example, believing that math ability can be learned helped to protect women from negative gender stereotyping about math (Good et al., 2012). And other research recently indicated that willpower is a virtually boundless mindset that predicts how long people will work and resist temptations during stressful circumstances (Dweck, 2012; Job et al., 2010; Miller et al., 2012). Also in a longitudinal study of university students, a nonlimited theory (i.e., a mindset that willpower is not a finite resource) predicted better self-regulation (improvements in time management and less procrastination, unhealthy eating, and impulsive spending) (Job et al., 2015). In this study, among students with a heavy course load, those who had a nonlimited theory got higher grades.

SELF-EFFICACY

In the chapter on behavioral and social cognitive approaches we introduced Albert Bandura's concept of **self-efficacy**, the belief that one can master a situation and produce positive outcomes. Bandura (1997, 2001, 2009, 2010a, 2012, 2015) emphasizes that self-efficacy is a critical factor in whether or not students achieve. Self-efficacy has much in common with mastery motivation and intrinsic motivation. Self-efficacy is the belief that "I can"; helplessness is the belief that "I cannot." Students with high self-efficacy agree with such statements as "I know that I will be able to learn the material in this class" and "I expect to be able to do well at this activity."

Dale Schunk (2008, 2016) has applied the concept of self-efficacy to many aspects of students' achievement. In his view, self-efficacy influences a student's choice of activities. Students with low self-efficacy for learning might avoid many learning tasks, especially those that are challenging, whereas students with high self-efficacy eagerly approach these learning tasks. Students with high self-efficacy are more likely to persist with effort at a learning task than are students with low self-efficacy (Schunk & DiBenedetto, 2016). One study revealed that high-self-efficacy adolescents had higher academic aspirations, spent more time doing homework, and were more likely to associate learning activities with optimal experience than their low-self-efficacy counterparts (Bassi et al., 2007).

Your self-efficacy as a teacher will have a major impact on the quality of learning that your students experience (Wyatt, 2016). Students learn much more from teachers with a sense of high self-efficacy than from those beset by self-doubts. However, students can benefit when teachers tell students about mistakes they have made themselves and how they learned from them. Teachers with low self-efficacy often become mired in classroom problems and are inclined to say that low student ability is the reason their students are not learning. Low-self-efficacy teachers don't have confidence in their ability to manage their classrooms, become stressed and angered at students' misbehavior, are pessimistic about students' ability to improve, take a custodial view of their job, often resort to restrictive and punitive modes of discipline, and say that if they had it to do all over again they would not choose teaching as a profession.

Efficacious schools are pervaded by high expectations and standards for achievement (Walsh, 2008). Teachers regard their students as capable of high academic achievement, set challenging academic standards for them, and provide support to help them reach these high standards. In contrast, in low-achieving schools not much is expected academically of students, teachers spend less time actively teaching and monitoring students' academic progress, and they tend to write off a high percentage of students as unteachable (Brookover et al., 1979). Not surprisingly, students in such schools have low self-efficacy and a sense of academic futility.

RESEARCH

Thinking Back/Thinking Forward

Bandura's social cognitive theory emphasizes reciprocal links between behavior, environment, and person/cognitive factors. Connect to "Behavioral and Social Cognitive Approaches."

What characterizes students, teachers, and schools with high self-efficacy?
Monashee Frantz/OJO Images/Getty Images

self-efficacy The belief that one can master a situation and produce positive outcomes.

CONNECTING WITH STUDENTS: Best Practices
Strategies for Improving Students' Self-Efficacy

Following are some effective strategies for improving students' self-efficacy (Stipek, 2002):

1. *Teach specific strategies.* Teach students specific strategies, such as outlining and summarizing, that can improve their ability to focus on their tasks.
2. *Guide students in setting goals.* Help them create short-term goals after they have made long-term goals. Short-term goals especially help students to judge their progress.
3. *Consider mastery.* Give students performance-contingent rewards, which are more likely to signal mastery, rather than rewarding them for merely engaging in a task.
4. *Combine strategy training with goals.* Schunk and his colleagues (Schunk, 2001; Schunk & Rice, 1989; Schunk & Swartz, 1993) have found that a combination of strategy training and goal setting can enhance students' self-efficacy and skill development. Give feedback to students on how their learning strategies relate to their performance.
5. *Provide students with support.* Positive support can come from teachers, parents, and peers. In *Through the Eyes of Teachers*, Joanna Smith, a high school English teacher, describes how she helps students who struggle with "failure syndrome."

THROUGH THE EYES OF TEACHERS
Helping Students Who Feel Like Failures Gain Confidence

I believe that encouragement can help students overcome "failure syndrome." Students with failure syndrome give up immediately when they sense any difficulty whatsoever. It is easy to feel frustrated when facing these students, but I have found success when I truly reach them. The only way for me to reach individual students is to get to know them and their families by giving journal assignments, choices about books they read, opportunities to tell me about themselves, and by opening myself up to them. These students also need a lot of encouragement. They need to know that you have noticed and are not happy with their failure, and then they need to know you believe in them. Only then will students with failure syndrome perform.

Joanna Smith

6. *Help students believe in their cognitive abilities.* You are likely to have some students in your class who have a history of being unsuccessful in academic settings. Talking to these students about your confidence in their abilities can improve their self-efficacy and can help them to become more motivated.

GOAL SETTING, PLANNING, AND SELF-MONITORING

Goal setting is increasingly recognized as a key aspect of achievement (Hofer & Fries, 2016; Martin & Collie, 2016; Senko, 2016). Researchers have found that self-efficacy and achievement improve when students set goals that are specific, proximal, and challenging (Bandura, 1997; Schunk, 2016). A nonspecific, fuzzy goal is "I want to be successful." A more concrete, specific goal is "I want to make the honor roll by the end of the semester."

Long-Term and Short-Term Goals Students can set both long-term (distal) and short-term (proximal) goals. It is okay to let students set some long-term goals, such as "I want to graduate from high school" or "I want to go to college," but if you do, make sure that they also create short-term goals as steps along the way. "Getting an *A* on the next math test" is an example of a short-term, proximal goal. So is "Doing all of my homework by 4 p.m. Sunday." As mentioned earlier, attention should focus mainly on short-term goals, which help students judge their progress better than do long-term goals. David McNally (1990), author of *Even Eagles Need a Push*, advises that when students set goals and make plans, they should be reminded to live their lives one day at a time. Have them make their commitments in bite-size chunks. As McNally says, a house is built one brick at a time, a cathedral one stone at a time. The artist paints one stroke at a time. The student should also work in small increments.

Challenging Goals Another good strategy is to encourage students to set challenging goals. A challenging goal is a commitment to self-improvement. Strong interest and involvement in activities is sparked by challenges. Goals that are easy to reach generate little interest or effort. However, goals should be optimally matched to the student's skill level. If goals are unrealistically high, the result will be repeated failures that lower the student's self-efficacy.

Developmental Changes and Goal-Setting Unfortunately, many of the changes involved in the transition to middle school are likely to increase students' motivation to achieve performance goals rather than mastery goals (Wigfield et al., 2015). Consider that these often include a drop in grades, a lack of support for autonomy, whole-class task organization and between-class ability groupings that likely increase social comparison, concerns about evaluation, and competitiveness.

DEVELOPMENT

In one research study, both teachers and students reported that performance-focused goals were more common and task-focused goals less common in middle school than in elementary school classrooms (Midgley et al., 1995). In addition, the elementary school teachers reported using task-focused goals more than middle school teachers did. At both grades, the extent to which the teachers were task-focused was linked with the students' and the teachers' sense of personal efficacy. Not unexpectedly, personal efficacy was lower for students in middle school than for those in elementary school. Thus, middle school teachers especially need to increasingly include task-focused goals in their instruction (Anderman et al., 2002). Also, a recent Japanese study revealed that in junior high and high school classrooms in which teachers created a mastery goal structure for their classroom, students were more intrinsically motivated and had a higher academic self-concept; by contrast, in performance-oriented goal structure classrooms students were less intrinsically motivated and had a lower academic self-concept (Murayama & Elliot, 2009).

RESEARCH

Planning and Self-Monitoring In the chapter on planning, instruction, and technology, we described the importance of planning for teachers. Planning is also important for students. It is not enough just to get students to set goals. It is also important to encourage them to plan how they will reach their goals. Being a good planner means managing time effectively, setting priorities, and being organized. Give students, especially at the middle school and high school levels, practice at managing their time, setting priorities, and being organized.

EXPECTATIONS

Expectations can exert a powerful influence on students' motivation. Let's examine students' expectations and teachers' expectations.

Students' Expectations How hard students will work can depend on how much they expect to accomplish. If they expect to succeed, they are more likely to work hard to reach a goal than if they expect to fail. Jacquelynne Eccles (1987, 1993) defined expectations for students' success as "beliefs about how well they will do on upcoming tasks, either in the immediate or long-term future" (Eccles & Wigfield, 2002, p. 119). Three aspects of ability beliefs, according to Eccles, are students' beliefs about how good they are at a particular activity, how good they are in comparison with other individuals, and how good they are in relation to their performance in other activities.

How hard students work also depends on the value they place on the goal (Wigfield et al., 2016). Indeed, for many decades the combination of expectancy and value has been the focus of a number of efforts to better understand students' achievement motivation (Atkinson, 1957; Eccles, 1993, 2007; Feather, 1966; Linnenbrink-Garcia & Patall, 2016; Wigfield et al., 2016). In Jacquelynne Eccles' (1993, 2007) model, "expectancies and values are assumed to directly influence performance, persistence, and task choice. Expectancies and values are . . . influenced by perceptions of competence, perceptions of the difficulty of different tasks, and individuals' goals" (Wigfield et al., 2006, pp. 938–939).

A student and teacher at Langston Hughes Elementary School in Chicago, a school whose teachers have high expectations for students. *How do teachers' expectations influence students' achievement?*
Ralf Finn Hestoft/Corbis Historical/Getty Images

Teachers' Expectations Teachers' expectations influence students' motivation and performance. "When teachers hold high generalized expectations for student achievement and students perceive these expectations, students achieve more, experience a greater sense of self-esteem and competence as learners, and resist involvement in problem behaviors both during childhood and adolescence" (Wigfield et al., 2006, p. 976). In an observational study of 12 classrooms, teachers with high expectations spent more time providing a framework for students' learning, asked higher-level questions, and were more effective in managing students' behavior than teachers with average and low expectations (Rubie-Davies, 2007).

Teachers often have more positive expectations for high-ability than for low-ability students, and these expectations are likely to influence their behavior toward them. For example, teachers require high-ability students to work harder, wait longer for them to respond to questions, respond to them with more information and in a more elaborate fashion, criticize them less often, praise them more often, are more friendly to them, call on them more often, seat them closer to the teachers' desks, and are more likely to give them the benefit of the doubt on close calls in grading than they are for students with low ability (Brophy, 2004). In a recent study, pre-service elementary school teachers had lower expectations for girls' than boys' math achievement (Mizala et al., 2015). However, for one ethnic group—African Americans—teachers have lower expectations for African American boys than African American girls (Rowley et al., 2014).

RESEARCH

delay of gratification Postponing immediate rewards in order to attain larger, more valuable rewards in the future.

An important teaching strategy is to monitor your expectations and be sure to have positive expectations for students with low abilities. Fortunately, researchers have found that with support teachers can adapt and raise their expectations for less advanced students or students with lower skill levels (Weinstein et al., 1995).

DELAY OF GRATIFICATION

Delaying gratification also is an important aspect of reaching goals—especially long-term goals (Imuta et al., 2014; Mischel, 2014; Schlam et al., 2013). **Delay of gratification** involves postponing immediate rewards in order to attain larger, more valuable rewards in the future. While it may be more attractive to adolescents to hang out with friends today than to work on a project that is due for a class assignment later in the week, their decision not to delay gratification can have negative consequences for their academic achievement.

Walter Mischel and his colleagues (Mischel et al., 1972; Mischel & Moore, 1973; Zayas et al., 2014) have conducted classic research on the delay of gratification with preschool children using the marshmallow task. In this research, young children were told the experimenter needed to leave the room to work on something and while he or she was gone they could

How did Walter Mischel and his colleagues study young children's delay of gratification? In their research, what later developmental outcomes were linked to the preschoolers' ability to delay gratification?
Amy Kiley Photography

choose to have one marshmallow immediately, or if they waited until the experimenter returned they could have two marshmallows. A majority of the children did wait a short while but only a subset of the young children waited the entire 15 minutes until the experimenter returned. On average, preschoolers succumbed to the temptation and ate the marshmallow within one minute.

In longitudinal research, Mischel and his colleagues have found that the preschool children who were able to delay gratification became more academically successful, had higher SAT scores and higher grade point averages at the end of college, and coped more effectively with stress as adolescents and emerging adults (Mischel, 2014). And as adults, they made more money in their careers, were more law-abiding, were more likely to have a lower body mass index, and were happier than individuals who were unable to delay gratification as preschoolers (Mischel, 2014; Moffitt, 2012; Moffitt et al., 2011; Schlam et al., 2013). Although the ability to delay gratification in preschool was linked to academic success and coping in adolescence and competence in adulthood, Mischel (2014) emphasizes that adolescents and adults can improve their ability to delay gratification.

VALUES AND PURPOSE

Students who have positive values and a sense of purpose are more likely to be able to delay gratification than those who don't. Also, in the discussion of expectations, we indicated that how hard students work is influenced by the value they place on the goal they have set. We also commented that the culture's achievement orientation influences students' values. Just what are "values"? *Values* are beliefs and attitudes about the way we think things should be. They involve what is important to individuals. Values can be attached to all sorts of things, such as religion, money, sex, helping others, family, friends, self-discipline, cheating, education, career, and so on. In the chapter on social contexts and socioemotional development, we described two moral education approaches that emphasize the importance of values in students' development: character education and values clarification.

It is important to note the integral role purpose plays in shaping students' values. In his book, *The Path to Purpose: Helping Our Children Find Their Calling in Life* (2008), William Damon defines *purpose* as an intention to accomplish something meaningful to oneself and contribute something to the world beyond the self. Finding purpose involves answering such questions as "*Why* am I doing this? *Why* does it matter? *Why* is it important for me and the world beyond me? *Why* do I strive to accomplish this end?" (Damon, 2008, pp. 33–34).

In interviews with 12- to 22-year-olds, Damon found that only about 20 percent had a clear vision of where they wanted to go in life, what they wanted to achieve, and why. The largest percentage—about 60 percent—had engaged in some potentially purposeful activities, such as service learning or fruitful discussions with a career counselor—but still did not have a real commitment or any reasonable plans for reaching their goals. And slightly more than 20 percent expressed no aspirations and in some instances said they didn't see any reason to have aspirations.

THROUGH THE EYES OF STUDENTS

Hari Prabhakar, Student on a Path to Purpose

Hari Prabhakar's ambition was to become an international health expert. Prabhakar graduated from Johns Hopkins University in 2006 with a double major in public health and writing. A top student (3.9 GPA), he took the initiative to pursue a number of activities outside the classroom in the health field. Toward the end of high school, Hari created the Tribal India Health Foundation, which provides assistance in bringing low-cost health care to rural areas in India. Juggling his roles as a student and as the foundation's director, Prabhakar spent about 15 hours a week leading Tribal India Health. In describing his work, Prabhakar said (Johns Hopkins University, 2006):

> I have found it very challenging to coordinate the international operation . . . . It takes a lot of work, and there's not a lot of free time. But it's worth it when I visit our patients and see how they and the community are getting better.

More recently, Prabhakar studied at Harvard Medical School and currently is an internist affiliated with Massachusetts General Hospital.

(Sources: Johns Hopkins University, 2006; Lunday, 2006; Marshall Scholarships, 2007; Prabhakar, 2007).

Hari Prabhakar (*in rear*) at a screening camp in India that he created as part of his Tribal India Health Foundation.
Hari Prabhakar

Thinking Back/Thinking Forward

Character education is a direct approach that involves teaching students basic moral literacy; values clarification emphasizes helping students to clarify what their lives are for and what is worth working for. Connect to "Social Contexts and Socioemotional Development."

DEVELOPMENT

Damon concludes that most teachers and parents communicate the importance of studying hard and getting good grades but rarely discuss what these behaviors might lead to—the purpose for studying hard and getting good grades. Damon emphasizes that too often students focus only on short-term goals and don't explore the big, long-term picture of what they want to do in life. These interview questions Damon (2008, p. 135) has used in his research are good springboards for getting students to reflect on their purpose:

What's most important to you in your life?

Why do you care about those things?

Do you have any long-term goals?

Why are these goals important to you?

What does it mean to have a good life?

What does it mean to be a good person?

If you were looking back on your life now, how would you like to be remembered?

What strategies do teachers use to help students achieve? Following are their responses.

EARLY CHILDHOOD Our preschoolers are given goals to achieve throughout the year. For example, weekly goals are to identify and write a new letter each week. To motivate children to achieve this goal, we ask them to bring in a special object from home that begins with the letter of the week and share it with the class. The children enjoy the weekly responsibility of bringing in special objects and feel involved in the learning process.

—MISSY DANGLER, *Suburban Hills School*

ELEMENTARY SCHOOL: GRADES K-5 I begin the school year by sharing my teaching goals with the students. After that, I ask the children to come up with a list of their goals for the year, and we display them next to the child's self-portrait. These goals and self-portraits are on display all year, so that we are all reminded of what is important. We also work on classroom rules that support the students, and my goals.

—YVONNE WILSON, *North Elementary School*

MIDDLE SCHOOL: GRADES 6-8 In this age of testing, it's important to motivate students to learn for learning's sake (not just to do well on a test). With that in mind, I intentionally identify material that will *not* be included in the assessment process. This material is usually high interest, trivia, or sometimes a wonderful story relevant to the material. Although this material won't be on the test, my students look forward to learning it.

—MARK FODNESS, *Bemidji Middle School*

HIGH SCHOOL: GRADES 9-12 My high school art students respond best to praise. Everyone loves to hear, "Wow, that looks fantastic; good job!" Another motivator for my students is that artworks that are well done may be entered in one of the many contests, shows, and exhibits we enter each year. Having a reward dangling out there is a great motivational tool.

—DENNIS FETERSON, *Deer River High School*

Review, Reflect, and Connect

 Discuss the important processes in motivation to achieve.

REVIEW
- What are extrinsic and intrinsic motivation? How are they involved in students' achievement?
- What characterizes attribution theory and an attribution approach to students' achievement?
- How does a mastery orientation compare with a helpless orientation and a performance orientation? Why is a growth mindset important in students' achievement?
- What is self-efficacy? What types of instructional strategies benefit students' self-efficacy?
- How are goal setting, planning, and self-monitoring important in improving students' motivation to achieve?
- How can students' and teachers' expectations affect students' motivation?
- What is delay of gratification and how does it relate to developmental outcomes?
- What do values and purpose mean? Why is it important for students to develop a sense of purpose?

REFLECT
- Sean and Dave both get cut from the basketball team. The next year, Sean tries out again but Dave does not. What causal attributions (and their effects) could explain the different behaviors of these two students?

PRAXIS™ PRACTICE
1. Which of the following is the best example of someone who is intrinsically motivated?
   a. Eric is reading a Harry Potter book because he wants to become a better reader.
   b. Jordan is reading a Harry Potter book because he can't wait to see what happens to Harry and his friends.
   c. Josh is reading a Harry Potter book so that he will have read enough pages to qualify for the class pizza party at the end of the month.
   d. Martynas is reading a Harry Potter book because his teacher assigned it and he wants to please his teacher.
2. Joan just failed a science test. "I knew it," she says. "I have never been any good at science, and I never will be." Which of the following categories best characterizes Joan's attribution for her failure?
   a. external-stable-controllable
   b. external-unstable-uncontrollable
   c. internal-stable-controllable
   d. internal-stable-uncontrollable
3. Which of the following is the best example of a performance goal orientation?
   a. Alicia competes with her best friend to see who can get the higher grade on every test, taking delight in receiving the high score.
   b. Cassandra hates math, does not believe that she can be successful, and gives up at the first sign of struggling.
   c. Ed struggles in math but wants very much to learn the material, so when he gets stuck on a problem, he asks for help.
   d. Martin does his work as requested and does a fair job on it, but he doesn't really care about his grades or about how much he learns.

continued

Review, Reflect, and Connect

4. Jacob is struggling in algebra and as a result is experiencing low self-efficacy. Which of the following people would provide the best role model?
   a. David, a local engineer, who tells the class how useful math will be in their future careers
   b. Jamal, a fellow student, who has also struggled in the course but is now grasping the concepts
   c. Mrs. Jackson, Jacob's algebra teacher, who has always loved math
   d. Suzanne, a fellow student, who is getting an *A* with minimal effort

5. Which student has the least appropriate goal?
   a. As Mark is choosing courses for his senior year in high school, he decides to take the more challenging of the two courses his counselor suggested to him.
   b. Sam is taking geometry in his senior year of high school because he has always struggled in math.
   c. Sylvia decides to take advanced placement calculus in her senior year, although she knows it is a difficult course.
   d. Zelda is a capable math student, but she chooses an easy math course in which she is almost certain to get an *A*.

6. Ms. Martin teaches eighth-grade history to an academically diverse class. DeMarcus is a gifted student who has always earned high marks. Joe has a learning disability. Ms. Martin does not believe it would be fair to expect the same performance from Joe as from DeMarcus. However, she knows that Joe can learn the material with proper scaffolding. Because of this, she seats Joe near her desk, praises him when he does something well, and gives him constructive criticism when needed. How are her expectations and behavior likely to affect the achievement of these students?
   a. Her expectations are likely to result in similar achievement from both students.
   b. Her expectations are likely to result in high achievement from DeMarcus and fairly high achievement from Joe.
   c. Her expectations are likely to result in high achievement from Joe and low achievement from DeMarcus.
   d. Her expectations are likely to result in low achievement from both students.

7. Which of the following is more likely to result in higher academic achievement, fewer problems in adolescence, better career success in adulthood, and better physical and mental health in adulthood?
   a. Giving children gold stars for their performance
   b. Guiding children to develop effective strategies for delaying gratification
   c. Getting children to rotely memorize content on a regular basis
   d. Working with children to get them to have realistic self-esteem

8. Which of the following questions that a teacher poses to Chase, a student in her eleventh-grade class, best reflects an inquiry about his purpose?
   a. Why did you not study harder for your test this week?
   b. What's most important to you in your life?
   c. What can you do the rest of the year to get a good grade in this course?
   d. How are you going to improve your chances of becoming a school leader?

Please see answer key at end of book . . . .

3 MOTIVATION, RELATIONSHIPS, AND SOCIOCULTURAL CONTEXTS

LG 3 Explain how relationships and sociocultural contexts can support or undercut motivation.

In addition to achievement motives, students also have social motives. Our coverage of the social dimensions of motivation focuses on students' social motives, relationships, and sociocultural contexts.

SOCIAL MOTIVES

Social motives are needs and desires that are learned through experiences with the social world. Students' social needs are reflected in their desires to be popular with peers and have close friends and the powerful attraction they feel to someone they love. Though each student has a need for affiliation or relatedness, some students have a stronger need than others. Some students like to be surrounded by lots of friends. In middle and high school, some students feel something is drastically missing from their lives if they don't have a girlfriend or boyfriend to date regularly. Others don't have such strong needs for affiliation. They don't fall apart if they don't have several close friends around all day and don't sit in class in an anxious state if they don't have a romantic partner.

Every school day, students work at establishing and maintaining social relationships. Researchers have found that students who display socially competent behavior are more likely to excel academically than those who do not (Kindermann, 2016; Wentzel & Muenks, 2016). Overall, though, researchers have given too little attention to how students' social worlds are related to their motivation in the classroom.

Both teacher approval and peer approval are important social motives for most students (Wentzel, 2016). In the elementary school years, students are motivated to please their parents more than their peers (Berndt, 1979). By the end of elementary school, parent approval and peer approval are about equally motivating for most students. By eighth or ninth grade, peer conformity outstrips conformity to parents. By twelfth grade, conformity to peers drops off somewhat as students become more autonomous and make more decisions on their own.

Adolescence can be an especially important juncture in achievement motivation and social motivation (Juvonen & Knifsend, 2016). New academic and social pressures force adolescents to take on new roles that involve more responsibility. As adolescents experience more intense achievement demands, their social interests might cut into the time they need for academic matters. Or ambitions in one area can undermine the attainment of goals in another area, as when academic achievement leads to social disapproval. In early adolescence, students face a choice between whether they will spend more of their time pursuing social goals or academic goals. The results of this decision have long-term consequences in terms of how far adolescents will go in their education and the careers they will pursue.

What are some aspects of students' social worlds that are linked to their motivation in the classroom?
Comstock/Getty Images

DEVELOPMENT

SOCIAL RELATIONSHIPS

Students' relationships with parents, peers, and friends have a tremendous impact on their lives. Their interactions with teachers, mentors, and others also can profoundly affect their achievement and social motivation.

Research has been conducted on links between parenting and students' motivation (Rowe et al., 2016). Studies have examined family demographic characteristics,

social motives Needs and desires that are learned through experiences with the social world.

child-rearing practices, and provision of specific experiences at home (Eccles et al., 1998).

Demographic Characteristics Parents with more education are more likely than less-educated parents to believe that their involvement in their child's education is important, to be active participants in their child's education, and to have intellectually stimulating materials at home (Schneider & Coleman, 1993). When parents' time and energy are largely consumed by other concerns or people other than the child, the child's motivation can suffer. Living in a single-parent family, having parents who are consumed by their work, and living in a large family can undercut children's achievement. Parental overinvolvement also can undermine students' achievement.

> **Thinking Back/Thinking Forward**
>
> Family management practices, such as maintaining a structured and organized family environment and effectively monitoring the child's behavior, are positively related to children's grades and self-responsibility. Connect to "Social Contexts and Socioemotional Development."

Child-Rearing Practices Even though demographic factors can affect students' motivation, more important are the parents' child-rearing practices (Wigfield et al., 2015). Here are some positive parenting practices that result in improved motivation and achievement:

- Knowing enough about the child to provide the right amount of challenge and the right amount of support
- Providing a positive emotional climate that motivates children to internalize their parents' values and goals
- Modeling motivated achievement behavior—working hard and persisting with effort at challenging tasks

RESEARCH

Provision of Specific Experiences at Home In addition to general child-rearing practices, parents provide various activities or resources at home that may influence students' interest and motivation to pursue various activities over time (Wigfield et al., 2015). For example, reading to one's preschool children and providing reading materials in the home are positively related to students' later reading achievement and motivation (Wigfield & Asher, 1984). Indeed, researchers have found that children's skills and work habits when they enter kindergarten are among the best predictors of academic motivation and performance in both elementary and secondary school (Entwisle & Alexander, 1993). The extent to which parents emphasize academic achievement or sports and provide opportunities and resources for their children to participate in these activities in the elementary school years influence whether the children are likely to continue to choose course work and extracurricular activities consistent with these activities in adolescence (Simpkins et al., 2004).

> **Thinking Back/Thinking Forward**
>
> Five different peer statuses of children are popular, average, neglected, rejected, and controversial. Connect to "Social Contexts and Socioemotional Development."

Peers Peers can affect a student's motivation in a number of ways (Grenhow & Askari, 2016; Wentzel & Muenks, 2016). In considering students' achievement, it is important to consider not only academic goals but social goals as well.

Students who are more accepted by their peers and who have good social skills often do better in school and have positive academic achievement motivation. In contrast, rejected students, especially those who are highly aggressive, are at risk for a number of achievement problems, including getting low grades and dropping out of school (Dodge, 2010). A recent study revealed that having aggressive-disruptive friends in adolescence was linked to a lower likelihood of graduating from high school (Veronneau et al., 2008). Having friends who are academically oriented is linked to higher achievement in adolescence (Crosnoe et al., 2008).

Teachers Teachers play an important role in students' achievement (Fox & Dinsmore, 2016; Wubbels et al., 2016). When researchers have observed classrooms, they have found that effective, engaging teachers provide support for students to make good progress, but encourage them to become self-regulated achievers (Martin & Collie, 2016). The encouragement takes place in a very positive environment, one in which students are constantly being guided to become motivated to try hard and develop self-efficacy.

Many children who do not do well in school consistently have negative interactions with their teachers (Stipek, 2002). They are frequently in trouble for not completing assignments, not paying attention, goofing off, or acting out. In many cases, they deserve to be criticized and disciplined, but too often the classroom becomes a highly unpleasant place for them.

Researchers have found that students who feel they have supportive, caring teachers are more strongly motivated to engage in academic work than students with unsupportive, uncaring teachers (Wentzel, 2016). One researcher examined students' views of the qualities of good relationships with a teacher by asking middle school students questions such as how they knew a teacher cared about them (Wentzel, 1997). As shown in Figure 5, students had favorable impressions of teachers who were attentive to them as human beings. Interestingly, students also considered teachers' instructional behaviors in evaluating how much their teachers cared about them. The students said that teachers convey that they care about their students when they make serious efforts to promote learning and have appropriately high standards.

What role do teachers play in students' motivation?
Photodisc Collection/EyeWire/Getty Images

Students' motivation is optimized when teachers provide them with challenging tasks in a mastery-oriented environment that includes good emotional and cognitive support, meaningful and interesting material to learn and master, and sufficient support for autonomy and initiative (Wentzel, 2016). Many researchers conclude that when academic work is meaningful, it sustains students' attention and interest, engages them in learning, and reduces the likelihood that students will feel alienated from school (Blumenfeld et al., 2006). Also, as we saw in our discussion of Bandura's ideas on self-efficacy earlier in the chapter, the motivation and achievement climate of the entire school affects students' motivation. Schools with high expectations and academic standards, as well as academic and emotional support for students, often have students who are motivated to achieve (Reksten, 2009).

RESEARCH

Teachers and Parents In the past, schools have given little attention to how teachers can enlist parents as partners with them in providing opportunities for students to achieve. Currently there is considerable interest in how to accomplish this partnership (Nitecki, 2015; Regional Educational Laboratory Mid-Atlantic, 2015). When teachers systematically and frequently inform parents of their children's progress and parents get involved in their children's learning, children often reach higher levels of academic achievement (Horvat & Baugh, 2015). And a recent longitudinal study found that collectively tenth-grade students' own positive expectations, their parents' expectations for their success, and their English and math teachers' expectations for their success predicted their postsecondary status (highest level of education) four years later (Gregory & Huang, 2013). In this study, these expectations together were a better predictor of postsecondary status than student characteristics such as socioeconomic status and academic performance.

> **Thinking Back/Thinking Forward**
>
> Joan Epstein has proposed a number of effective strategies for forging family-school linkages. Connect to "Social Contexts and Socioemotional Development."

	Teachers who care	Teachers who do not care
Teaching behaviors	Makes an effort to make class interesting; teaches in a special way	Teaches in a boring way, gets off-task, teaches while students aren't paying attention
Communication style	Talks to me, pays attention, asks questions, listens	Ignores, interrupts, screams, yells
Equitable treatment and respect	Is honest and fair, keeps promises, trusts me, tells the truth	Embarrasses, insults
Concern about individuals	Asks what's wrong, talks to me about my problems, acts as a friend, asks when I need help, takes time to make sure I understand, calls on me	Forgets name, does nothing when I do something wrong, doesn't explain things or answer questions, doesn't try to help me

FIGURE 5 STUDENTS' DESCRIPTIONS OF TEACHERS WHO CARE

SOCIOCULTURAL CONTEXTS

DIVERSITY

Diversity within ethnic minority groups is evident in their levels of achievement (Banks, 2015; Koppelman, 2017). For example, many Asian American students have a strong academic achievement orientation, but some do not (Golnick & Chinn, 2017).

In addition to recognizing the diversity that exists within every cultural group in terms of their achievement, it also is important to distinguish between difference and deficiency. Too often, the achievements of ethnic minority students—especially African American, Latinx, and Native American—have been interpreted according to middle-socioeconomic-status White standards as deficits when these students simply are culturally different and distinct.

RESEARCH

However, achievement differences are more closely related to socioeconomic status than to ethnicity (Ballentine & Roberts, 2009). Many studies have found that socioeconomic status predicts achievement better than ethnicity (Entwisle et al., 2010; Rowley et al., 2010). Regardless of their ethnic background, students from middle- and upper-income families fare better than their counterparts from low-income backgrounds in a host of achievement situations—expectations for success, achievement aspirations, and recognition of the importance of effort, for example. An especially important factor in the lower achievement of students from low-income families is lack of adequate resources, such as an up-to-date computer in the home (or even any computer at all) to support students' learning (Schunk, et al., 2008).

RESEARCH

Sandra Graham (1986, 1990) has conducted a number of studies that reveal not only a stronger role of socioeconomic status than of ethnicity in achievement but also the importance of studying ethnic minority student motivation in the context of general motivational theory. Her inquiries fall within the framework of attribution theory and focus on the causes African American students identify for their achievement orientation, such as why they succeed or fail. Graham has found that middle-income African American students, like their White middle-income counterparts, have high achievement expectations and understand that failure is usually due to a lack of effort rather than bad luck.

A special challenge for many ethnic minority students, especially those living in poverty, is dealing with racial prejudice, conflict between the values of their group and the majority group, and a lack of high-achieving adults in their cultural group who can serve as positive role models (Banks, 2015). The lack of high-achieving role models relates to the number of mentors in these students' lives. One study revealed that perceived racial discrimination by teachers was negatively related to African American and Caribbean adolescents' academic achievement (Thomas et al., 2009).

It is important to further consider the nature of the schools that primarily serve ethnic minority students (Wigfield et al., 2015). More than one-third of African American and almost one-third of Latinx students attend schools in the 47 largest city school districts in the United States, compared with only 5 percent of White and 22 percent of Asian American students. Many of these ethnic minority students come from low-income families (more than half are eligible for free or reduced-cost lunches). These inner-city schools are less likely than other schools to serve more-advantaged populations or to offer high-quality academic support services, advanced courses, and courses that challenge students' active thinking skills. Even students who are motivated to learn and achieve can find it difficult to perform effectively in such contexts.

A special concern among educators is to find ways to support the achievement efforts of ethnic minority students, many of whom come from low-income backgrounds (Zusho et al., 2015; Rowley et al., 2014). In the *Connecting with Teachers* segment that opened this chapter, you

UCLA educational psychologist Sandra Graham is shown talking with adolescent boys about motivation. She has conducted a number of studies which reveal that middle-socioeconomic-status African American students—like their White counterparts—have high achievement expectations and attribute success to internal factors such as effort rather than external factors such as luck.
Dr. Sandra Graham

read about Jaime Escalante, who made a major difference in the motivation of Latinx students to learn and excel at math in East Los Angeles.

Another individual has been exceptional in supporting the motivation of African American students in Washington, D.C. Henry Gaskins, a physician, began an after-school tutoring program for ethnic minority students. For four hours every week night and all day on Saturdays, 80 students receive study assistance from Gaskins, his wife, two adult volunteers, and academically talented peers. Those who can afford it contribute $5 to cover the cost of school supplies. In addition to tutoring them in various school subjects, Gaskins helps the tutees learn how to set academic goals and plan how to achieve these goals. Gaskins also encourages students to self-monitor their progress toward the goals. Many of the students being tutored have parents who are high school dropouts and either can't or aren't motivated to help their sons and daughters achieve.

Every community has people like Dr. Henry Gaskins who can help provide much-needed mentoring and tutoring for students from low socioeconomic backgrounds whose parents cannot help them achieve academically. Many of these potential mentors and tutors from the community have not been contacted by school personnel. If the need exists among your students, make a commitment to scour the community for talented, motivated, and concerned adults like Gaskins, who might only need to be asked to provide mentoring and tutoring support for disadvantaged students.

Dr. Henry Gaskins, here talking with three high school students, began an after-school tutorial program for ethnic minority students in 1983 in Washington, D.C. Volunteers like Dr. Gaskins can be especially helpful in developing a stronger sense of the importance of education in ethnic minority adolescents.

Joan Marcus Photography

Review, Reflect, and Practice

3 Explain how relationships and sociocultural contexts can support or undercut motivation.

REVIEW
- What are social motives and the need for affiliation?
- In what ways are students' school performances linked to relationships with parents, peers, friends, and teachers?
- How do ethnicity and socioeconomic status influence motivation to achieve in school?

REFLECT
- Suppose several children from low-income families in your elementary school classroom are struggling with achieving their potential. How would you work with them to improve their chances of being successful in school?

PRAXIS™ PRACTICE
1. Which of the following students is most likely to conform to peer expectations for academic achievement?
   a. Patrick, who is in second grade
   b. Ross, who is in fifth grade
   c. Sheldon, who is in eighth grade
   d. Rose, who is a senior in high school
2. Which classroom is likely to have the most positive impact on student motivation?
   a. Ms. Davidson is only concerned about her students' academic performance, not their personal lives. Her class is very challenging, though not terribly interesting.
   b. Mr. Nelson works hard to get to know his students on a personal level as well as an academic basis. Because he cares so much for them, he makes sure that his class is easy enough for all of his students to do well.

continued

Review, Reflect, and Practice

   c. Ms. Pagliuca works hard to get to know her students on a personal as well as an academic basis. She gives her students work that is challenging and interesting.
   d. Mr. Williams' class is very challenging and competitive. His students compete on a daily basis for points.
3. Which of the following students is *least* likely to have a strong achievement motivation?
   a. Lee, an African American student from a middle-income family
   b. Pedro, a Latino student from a middle-income family
   c. Ross, an African American student from an affluent family
   d. Sean, a White student from a low-income family

Please see answer key at end of book . . . .

LG 4 Recommend how to help students with achievement difficulties.

4 EXPLORING ACHIEVEMENT DIFFICULTIES

- Students Who Are Low Achieving and Have Low Expectations for Success
- Students Who Protect Their Self-Worth by Avoiding Failure
- Students Who Procrastinate
- Students Who Are Perfectionists
- Students with High Anxiety
- Students Who Are Uninterested or Alienated

Achievement problems can surface when students don't set goals, don't plan how to reach them, and don't adequately monitor their progress toward the goals (Senko, 2016). They also can arise when students are low achievers and have low expectations for success, try to protect their self-worth by avoiding failure, procrastinate, are perfectionists, become overwhelmed by anxiety, or become uninterested or alienated from school. Many of these obstacles to achievement surface during elementary school and then become more pronounced during middle school or high school. We will discuss a number of strategies that teachers, counselors, mentors, and parents can use to help students overcome obstacles to their achievement.

STUDENTS WHO ARE LOW ACHIEVING AND HAVE LOW EXPECTATIONS FOR SUCCESS

Jere Brophy (1998) provided the following description of low-achieving students with low expectations for success: These students need to be consistently reassured that they can meet the goals and challenges you have set for them and that you will give them the help and support they need to succeed. However, they need to be reminded that you will accept their progress only as long as they make a real effort. They might require individualized instructional materials or activities to provide an optimal challenge for their skill level. Help them set learning goals and give them support for reaching these goals. Require these students to put forth considerable effort and make progress, even though they might not have the ability to perform at the level of the class as a whole.

Failure syndrome refers to having low expectations for success and giving up at the first sign of difficulty. Failure syndrome students are different from low-achieving students who fail despite putting forth their best effort. Failure syndrome students don't put forth enough effort, often beginning tasks in a halfhearted manner and giving up quickly at the first hint of a challenge. Failure syndrome students often have low self-efficacy and a fixed mindset.

failure syndrome Having low expectations for success and giving up at the first sign of difficulty.

Training method	Primary emphasis	Main goals
Efficacy training	Improve students' self-efficacy perceptions	Teach students to set and strive to reach specific, proximal, and challenging goals. Monitor students' progress and frequently support students by saying things like "I know you can do it." Use adult and peer modeling effectively. Individualize instruction and tailor it to the student's knowledge and skills. Keep social comparison to a minimum. Be an efficacious teacher and have confidence in your abilities. View students with a failure syndrome as challenges rather than losers.
Strategy training	Improve students' domain- and task-specific skills and strategies	Help students to acquire and self-regulate their use of effective learning and problem-solving strategies. Teach students what to do, how to do it, and when and why to do it.

FIGURE 6 COGNITIVE RETRAINING METHODS FOR INCREASING THE MOTIVATION OF STUDENTS WHO DISPLAY FAILURE SYNDROME

A number of strategies can be used to increase the motivation of students who display failure syndrome. Especially beneficial are cognitive retraining methods such as efficacy training and strategy training, which are described in Figure 6.

STUDENTS WHO PROTECT THEIR SELF-WORTH BY AVOIDING FAILURE

Some individuals are so interested in protecting their self-worth and avoiding failure that they become distracted from pursuing goals and engage in ineffective strategies (De Castella et al., 2013). These strategies include the following behaviors (Covington & Dray, 2002):

- *Nonperformance.* The most obvious strategy for avoiding failure is to not try. In the classroom, nonperformance tactics include appearing eager to answer a teacher's question but hoping the teacher will call on another student, sliding down in the seat to avoid being seen by the teacher, and avoiding eye contact. These can seem like minor deceptions, but they might portend other, more chronic forms of noninvolvement such as dropping out and excessive absences.
- *Procrastination.* Individuals who postpone studying for a test until the last minute can blame failure on poor time management, thus deflecting attention away from the possibility that they are incompetent. A variation on this theme is to take on so many responsibilities that you have an excuse for not doing any one of them in a highly competent manner.
- *Setting unreachable goals.* By setting goals so high that success is virtually impossible, individuals can avoid the implication that they are incompetent, because virtually anyone would fail to reach such a challenging goal.

Efforts to avoid failure often involve *self-handicapping strategies* (Akin & Akin, 2014; Callan et al., 2014). That is, some individuals deliberately handicap themselves by not making an effort, by putting off a project until the last minute, by fooling around the night before a test, and so on so that if their subsequent performance is at a low level, these circumstances, rather than lack of ability, will be seen as the cause. A recent meta-analysis confirmed that self-handicapping is linked to students' lower achievement (Schwinger et al., 2014).

RESEARCH

Here are a few strategies to help students reduce preoccupation with protecting self-worth and avoiding failure (Covington & Teel, 1996):

- Guide students in setting challenging but realistic goals.
- Help students strengthen the link between their effort and self-pride. Tell them to take pride in their effort and minimize social comparison.
- Encourage students to have positive beliefs about their abilities but don't tell them they have high ability or praise them for high ability.

STUDENTS WHO PROCRASTINATE

Another way that students can fail to reach their potential is to regularly engage in procrastination (Ebadi & Shakoorzadeh, 2015; Grunschel & Schopenhauer, 2015). A meta-analysis of research studies revealed that procrastination is linked to low self-efficacy, low conscientiousness, distractibility, and low achievement motivation (Steel, 2007). Other reasons students procrastinate include poor time management, difficulty concentrating, fear and anxiety (being overwhelmed by the task and afraid of getting a bad grade, for example), negative beliefs, personal problems (financial problems, problems with a boyfriend or girlfriend, and so on), boredom, unrealistic expectations and perfectionism (believing you must read everything written on a subject before you begin to write a paper, for example), and fear of failure (thinking that if you don't get an *A,* you are a failure, for example) (University at Buffalo Counseling Services, 2016).

Procrastination can take many forms, including these (University of Illinois Counseling Center, 2016):

- Ignoring the task and hoping that it will go away
- Underestimating the work involved in the task or overestimating one's abilities and resources
- Spending endless hours on computer games and surfing the Internet
- Substituting a worthy but lower-priority activity, such as cleaning one's room instead of studying
- Believing that repeated minor delays won't hurt
- Persevering on only part of the task, such as writing and rewriting the first paragraph of a paper but never getting to the body of it
- Becoming paralyzed when having to choose between two alternatives—for example, agonizing over doing biology homework or English homework first with the outcome that neither is done

CONNECTING WITH TEACHERS: Best Practices
Strategies for Helping Students Conquer Procrastination

Here are some good strategies for helping students reduce or eliminate procrastination:

1. *Get them to acknowledge that procrastination is a problem.* Too often, procrastinators don't face up to their problem. When students admit that they procrastinate, this can sometimes get them to begin thinking about how to solve the problem.

2. *Encourage them to identify their values and goals.* Get them to think about how procrastination can undermine their values and goals.

3. *Help them manage their time more effectively.* Have students make yearly (or term), monthly, weekly, and daily plans. Then help them monitor how they use their time and find ways to use it more wisely.

4. *Have them divide the task into smaller parts.* Sometimes students procrastinate because they view the task as so large and overwhelming that they will never be able to finish it. When this is the case, get them to divide the task into smaller units and set subgoals for completing one unit at a time. This strategy can often make what seems to be a completely unmanageable task manageable.

5. *Teach them to use behavioral strategies.* Have them identify the diversions that might be keeping them from focusing on the most important tasks and activities. Get them to note when and where they engage in these diversions. Then have them plan how to diminish and control their use. Other behavioral strategies include having students make a contract with you, their parents, or a mentor, or having students build in a reward for themselves, which gives them an incentive to complete all or part of the task.

6. *Help them learn how to use cognitive strategies.* Encourage students to watch for mental self-seductions that can lead to behavioral diversions, such as "I will do it tomorrow," "What's the problem with watching an hour or two of TV now?" and "I can't do it." Help them learn how to dispute mental diversions. For example, get them to tell themselves, "I really don't have much time left and other things are sure to come up later," or "If I get this done, I'll be able to enjoy my time more."

STUDENTS WHO ARE PERFECTIONISTS

As mentioned earlier, perfectionism is sometimes the underlying reason for procrastinating. Perfectionists think that mistakes are never acceptable, that the highest standards of performance always have to be achieved. As indicated in Figure 7, healthy achievement and perfectionism differ in a number of ways. Perfectionists are vulnerable to decreased productivity, impaired health, relationship problems, and low self-esteem (Bonvanie et al., 2015; Harrison & Craddock, 2016). Depression, anxiety, and eating disorders are common outcomes of perfectionism (Teixeira et al., 2016). In a recent research study, parents' perfectionism was linked to their children's and adolescents' higher levels of anxiety (Affrunti & Woodruff-Borden, 2014).

STUDENTS WITH HIGH ANXIETY

Anxiety is a vague, highly unpleasant feeling of fear and apprehension. It is normal for students to be concerned or worried when they face school challenges, such as doing well on a test. Indeed, researchers have found that many successful students have moderate levels of anxiety (Bandura, 1997). However, some students have high levels of anxiety and worry constantly, which can significantly impair their ability to achieve (Ramirez et al., 2016). A recent study found that the worry component of text anxiety was linked to lower achievement in eleventh-grade students (Steinmayr et al., 2016).

Some students' high anxiety levels are the result of parents' unrealistic achievement expectations and pressure (Wigfield et al., 2015). For many students, anxiety increases across the school years as they encounter more frequent evaluation, engage in social comparison, and may experience failure (Wigfield et al., 2015). When schools create such circumstances, they likely increase students' anxiety.

A number of intervention programs have been created to reduce high anxiety levels (Garcia-Lopez et al., 2014). Some intervention programs emphasize relaxation techniques. These programs often are effective at reducing anxiety but do not always lead to improved achievement. Anxiety intervention programs linked to worrying emphasize modifying the negative, self-damaging thoughts of anxious students by getting them to engage in more positive, task-focused thoughts (Watson & Tharp, 2014). These programs have been more effective than the relaxation programs in improving students' achievement (Wigfield et al., 2006).

Perfectionist
- Sets standards beyond reach and reason
- Is never satisfied by anything less than perfection
- Becomes dysfunctionally depressed when experiences failure and disappointment
- Is preoccupied with fear of failure and disapproval—this can deplete energy levels
- Sees mistakes as evidence of unworthiness
- Becomes overly defensive when criticized

Healthy striver
- Sets high standards, but just beyond reach
- Enjoys process as well as outcome
- Bounces back from failure and disappointment quickly and with energy
- Keeps normal anxiety and fear of failure and disapproval within bounds—uses them to create energy
- Sees mistakes as opportunities for growth and learning
- Reacts positively to helpful criticism

FIGURE 7 DIFFERENCES BETWEEN PERFECTIONISTS AND HEALTHY STRIVERS

CONNECTING WITH STUDENTS: Best Practices
Strategies for Helping Students Overcome Their Perfectionist Tendencies

Following are some effective strategies for guiding students in reducing or eliminating perfectionist tendencies (University of Texas at Austin Counseling and Mental Health Center, 2016):

1. *Have students list the advantages and disadvantages of trying to be perfect.* When students do this, they may discover that the cost of trying to be perfect is too great.

2. *Guide students in becoming more aware of the self-critical nature of all-or-none thinking.* Help students learn how to substitute more realistic, reasonable thoughts for their habitual overly self-critical ones.

3. *Help students become realistic about what they can achieve.* By getting students to set more realistic goals, you can help them to gradually see that "imperfect" outcomes don't lead to the negative consequences they expect and fear.

4. *Talk with students about learning to accept criticism.* Perfectionists frequently view criticism as a personal attack and respond defensively to it. Guide students to become more objective about the criticism and about themselves.

STUDENTS WHO ARE UNINTERESTED OR ALIENATED

Jere Brophy (1998) argues that the most difficult motivation problem involves students who are apathetic, uninterested in learning, or alienated from school learning. Achieving in school is not an important value for them. To reach apathetic students requires sustained efforts to resocialize their attitudes toward school achievement (Murdock, 2009).

CONNECTING WITH STUDENTS: Best Practices
Strategies to Reach Uninterested or Alienated Students

Following are some ways you might use to try reach students who are uninterested or alienated (Brophy, 1998):

1. *Work on developing a positive relationship with the student.* If the uninterested or alienated student doesn't like you, it is hard to get the student to work toward any achievement goals. Show patience, but be determined to help the student and push for steady progress in spite of setbacks or resistance.

2. *Make school more intrinsically interesting.* To make school more intrinsically interesting for this type of student, find out the student's interests and if possible include those interests in assignments that you make.

3. *Teach strategies for making academic work more enjoyable.* Help students understand that they are causing their own problems, and find ways to guide them in taking pride in their work.

4. *Consider a mentor.* Think about enlisting the aid of a mentor in the community or an older student you believe the uninterested or alienated student will respect.

Several teachers recently were asked what strategies they use to help unmotivated students to get motivated. Following are their responses.

EARLY CHILDHOOD Sometimes children become unmotivated because they fear that they will do something wrong or not live up to the teacher's expectations. To combat this issue, we lavish our preschoolers with praise for any and all efforts.

—MISSY DANGLER, *Suburban Hills School*

ELEMENTARY SCHOOL: GRADES K–5 Unmotivated students are usually motivated by something that holds their interest. I once had a student who was withdrawn and would not participate in group discussions. I later found out about his interest in boats, specifically the *Titanic*. I then incorporated his interests into a few different activities, and he became a different learner. He was more involved in discussions, and his confidence in the group increased as he learned of other students in class who also shared his interests.

—HEATHER ZOLDAK, *Ridge Wood Elementary School*

MIDDLE SCHOOL: GRADES 6–8 An important aspect of motivation is to provide challenges for students. For example, I begin my Civil War unit by telling students that we'll be using this topic as an opportunity to see what it would be like to take a college freshman history course. Even though the material is extensive and more difficult than other units, the average grades on the final exam are higher than any other unit because students are motivated by the challenge of doing college-level work.

—MARK FODNESS, *Bemidji Middle School*

HIGH SCHOOL: GRADES 9–12 Building relationships with students based on their interests is a key to improving their motivation. For example, I recently talked with a student who didn't show much interest in class but loves clothes. I asked her about an outfit she had on with a cat on it (since I love cats). She explained that the outfit was Baby Phat and brought me all kinds of information on the clothing line and is even trying to get me to wear some of the clothes. More importantly, this student, who showed little interest in class, now participates and turns in assignments that are above average.

—SANDY SWANSON, *Menomonee Falls High School*

This chapter has focused on student motivation. It also is important for you to be motivated as a teacher as well. To evaluate your motivation, complete *Self-Assessment 1*.

Review, Reflect, and Practice

 Recommend how to help students with achievement difficulties.

REVIEW
- How can low-achieving students with low achievement expectations be described and how can teachers help them?
- What are some strategies students use to protect their self-worth by avoiding failure? How can these students be helped?
- What characterizes students who procrastinate, and what are some strategies to help them?
- What characterizes students who are perfectionistic, and how can teachers help students with these tendencies?
- What is anxiety, how does high anxiety interfere with achievement, and what type of programs can benefit students with high anxiety?
- How can teachers help students who are uninterested or alienated?

REFLECT
- Think about several of your own past schoolmates who showed low motivation in school. Why do you think they behaved the way they did? What teaching strategies might have helped them?

PRAXIS™ PRACTICE
1. Which of the following students is the best example of failure syndrome?
   a. Andrea, who does not do well in school and rarely tries anymore
   b. Marcy, who works very hard and manages to earn C's
   c. Samantha, who does very well in school but does not try very hard
   d. Vivi, who is never satisfied with her own performance
2. Scott slides down in his seat to avoid being called on by the teacher. His behavior reflects which of the following in an effort to protect his self-worth by avoiding failure?
   a. failure syndrome
   b. nonperformance
   c. procrastination
   d. setting unreachable goals

continued

Review, Reflect, and Practice

3. Which teaching strategy is most likely to help students overcome procrastination?
   a. assigning a large project to be done in parts, with each part due at a different time
   b. assigning many large projects in a semester to ensure that students will have to learn to manage their time
   c. assigning no work that must be done outside of class
   d. assigning students to list all of the things they would rather do than their homework
4. Becky gets very upset when she does not receive full credit on an assignment. She takes particular offense at any critical remarks that are made of her work. Which of the following strategies is most likely to help Becky overcome her perfectionism?
   a. Give Becky lots of constructive feedback, both positive and negative, and allow her to revise her work.
   b. Make sure that Becky is capable of earning full credit on every assignment you give her.
   c. Make sure that Becky is not capable of earning full credit on any assignments you give her so she will get used to it.
   d. Never give Becky any kind of feedback other than a grade, so you don't upset her.
5. Carmella has a great deal of anxiety about school, and it is interfering with her ability to concentrate in school. Which of the following is most likely to help her reduce her anxiety?
   a. helping her to replace her negative, self-damaging thoughts with more positive, task-focused thoughts
   b. encouraging her to set higher goals
   c. guiding her to reduce procrastination
   d. getting her to face the reality of concentrating better
6. Which of the following is most likely to help a teacher get an uninterested or alienated student to become more motivated to do well in school?
   a. stress how important going to college is
   b. find out the student's interests and include those in the student's assignments
   c. compare the student with other students who are more motivated
   d. describe some strategies for reducing perfectionism

Please see answer key at end of book . . . .

SELF-ASSESSMENT 1
Evaluating My Motivation

Here are 19 statements you can use to analyze your motivational makeup. Rate yourself from 1 (not like me at all) to 5 (very much like me) on each of the statements. Because your motivation may vary according to the task and context, please try to consider a specific scenario (e.g., learning in my educational psychology class, teaching in my internship) when rating these items.

1. I am aware of the hierarchy of motives in my life and which ones are the most important for me.
2. I am intrinsically motivated.
3. I have high expectations and standards for success.
4. I experience many moments of flow.
5. I am aware of the people in my life who have motivated me the most and what it is they did that motivated me.
6. I make achievement-related attributions that emphasize effort.
7. I have a mastery motivation orientation rather than a helpless or performance orientation.
8. I have a growth mindset, rather than a fixed mindset.
9. I am motivated to learn and succeed because of my success aspirations, not because I want to protect my self-worth or avoid failure.
10. I have high self-efficacy.
11. I regularly set goals, plan how to reach those goals, and systematically monitor my progress toward the goals.
12. I set specific, proximal, and challenging goals.
13. I am a good time manager, regularly doing weekly plans, monitoring my use of time, and making to-do lists.
14. I am very effective at delaying gratification rather than seeking immediate gratification.
15. I am good at learning from my mistakes to improve my future success.
16. I don't let anxiety or other emotions get in the way of my motivation.
17. I have a good support system for my motivation and have positive, close relationships with people who can help me sustain my motivation.
18. I do tasks in a timely manner and I don't procrastinate.
19. I'm not a perfectionist.

SCORING AND INTERPRETATION

Examine the pattern of your responses. If you rated yourself 4 or 5 on each of the items, you likely are getting your motivation to work to your advantage, and you likely will be a positive motivational model for your students. However, for any items on which you rated yourself 3 or below, spend some time thinking about how you can improve those aspects of your motivational life.

Connecting with the Classroom: Crack the Case

The Reading Incentive Program

Catherine teaches second grade in an economically disadvantaged elementary school. Many of her students read below grade level. Some of her students have had little exposure to reading outside of school, and most do not choose to read during their free time at school. Knowing that reading skills are important to future success in school, Catherine is justifiably concerned.

In an effort to entice her students to read more, Catherine develops a reading incentive program. She places a large chart on the classroom wall to track student progress. Each time a student completes a book, he or she tells Catherine, who then places a star next to the student's name on the chart. Each student who reads five books per month receives a small prize from the class prize box. The student who reads the most books in any given month receives a larger prize. When Catherine tells her students about the new incentive program, they are very excited.

"This is great!" says Joey. "I'm gonna get the most stars!"

"No, you won't," says Peter. "Sami will. She's always got her nose stuck in a book. She's the best reader in the class."

Sami is a very good reader. She is reading well above grade level and generally favors novels from the young adult section of the library. These books are rather lengthy and take her quite some time to finish. However, she really enjoys them. Catherine has brought her several from her own collection as well, since none of her classroom books seem to interest Sami.

The first week of the program is quite exciting. Every day students tell Catherine about the books they have read. The chart begins to fill with stars. By the end of the week, all the students have at least one star next to their name except Sami. During the last week of the month, many students choose reading as a free-time activity. The students are anxious to ensure that they will earn at least one prize, and many are devouring books in anticipation of being the month's "top reader." At the end of the month, 23 of Catherine's 25 students have 5 stars on the chart. The only exceptions are Sami, who has only 1 star, and Michael, who had chicken pox during the month. True to his word, Joey receives the most stars—15. The students excitedly choose their prizes.

The following month, the reading frenzy continues. This time Sami joins her classmates in their accumulation of stars and receives 30, making her the top reader. Joey is right behind her with 25. Every student in the class earns at least 5 stars, entitling all to a prize. Because they are all reading so much, Catherine gives them a Friday afternoon party, at which they watch an animated movie and eat popcorn.

A similar pattern is repeated over the next several months. The star chart fills quickly. Catherine believes that the students are reading enough that they will do quite well on the annual state achievement test. She is thrilled with their progress. She decides that after the test, she will drop the incentive program and just quietly keep track of how much her students read. After doing this, she notices that once again very few students are reading during their free time. Even Sami is no longer reading when she is finished with her other work. Now she draws instead.

1. What are the issues in this case?
2. Analyze the case from the perspective of extrinsic and intrinsic motivation.
3. Analyze the case from a goal-orientation perspective.
4. Why do you think Sami went from receiving 1 star the first month to receiving 30 stars the next? Why does she no longer read in her free time at school?
5. What are the problems with this type of incentive program? How might an incentive program be developed that does not undermine students' motivation to read?

Connecting with Learning: Reach Your Learning Goals

1 EXPLORING MOTIVATION: Define motivation and compare the behavioral, humanistic, cognitive, and social perspectives on motivation.

What Is Motivation?

Perspectives on Motivation

- Motivated behavior is behavior that is energized, directed, and sustained.
- The behavioral perspective on motivation emphasizes that external rewards and punishments are the key factors that determine a student's motivation. Incentives are positive or negative stimuli or events that can motivate a student's behavior.

- The humanistic perspective stresses our capacity for personal growth, freedom to choose our own destiny, and our positive qualities.
- According to Maslow's hierarchy of needs, individuals' needs must be satisfied in this sequence: physiological, safety, love and belonging, esteem, and self-actualization. Self-actualization, the highest and most elusive of the needs Maslow describes, involves the motivation to develop one's full potential as a human being.
- In the cognitive perspective on motivation, students' thoughts guide their motivation. The cognitive perspective focuses on the internal motivation to achieve; attributions; students' beliefs that they can effectively control their environment; and goal setting, planning, and monitoring progress toward a goal. The cognitive perspective meshes with R. W. White's concept of competence motivation.
- The social perspective emphasizes the need for affiliation, which is reflected in students' motivation to spend time with peers, their close friendships, attachment to parents, and their desire to have a positive relationship with teachers.

❷ ACHIEVEMENT PROCESSES: Discuss the important processes in motivation to achieve.

Extrinsic and Intrinsic Motivation

- Extrinsic motivation involves doing something to obtain something else (a means to an end) or to avoid an unpleasant consequence. Intrinsic motivation involves the internal motivation of doing something for its own sake (an end in itself). Overall, most experts recommend that teachers create a classroom atmosphere in which students are intrinsically motivated to learn.
- One view of intrinsic motivation emphasizes its self-determining characteristics. Giving students some choice and providing opportunities for personal responsibility increase intrinsic motivation.
- Csikszentmihalyi uses the term *flow* to describe life's optimal experiences, which involve a sense of mastery and absorbed concentration in an activity. Flow is most likely to occur in areas in which students are engaged in challenges that are neither too difficult nor too easy.
- Interest is conceptualized as more specific than intrinsic motivation, and interest is positively linked to deep learning.
- It is important for teachers to create learning environments that encourage students to become cognitively engaged and develop a responsibility for their learning.
- In some situations, rewards can actually undermine learning. When rewards are used, they should convey information about task mastery rather than external control.
- Researchers have found that as students move from the early elementary school years to high school, their intrinsic motivation drops, especially during the middle school years.
- The concept of person-environment fit calls attention to the lack of fit between adolescents' increasing interest in autonomy and schools' increasing control, which results in students' negative self-evaluations and attitudes toward school.
- Overall, the overwhelming conclusion is that it is a wise strategy to create learning environments that encourage students to become intrinsically motivated. However, in many real-world situations, both intrinsic and extrinsic motivation are involved, and too often intrinsic and extrinsic motivation have been pitted against each other as polar opposites.

Attribution

- Attribution theory states that individuals are motivated to discover the underlying causes of their own performance and behavior.
- Weiner identified three dimensions of causal attributions: (1) locus, (2) stability, and (3) controllability. Different combinations of these dimensions produce different explanations of failure and success.

Mastery Motivation and Mindset

- Students with a mastery orientation are challenged and excited by difficult tasks, and concentrate on learning strategies and the achievement process instead of on performance outcome.

continued

- **Self-Efficacy**
  - Students with a helpless orientation feel trapped by difficult tasks, are anxious, and feel they lack ability. Students with a performance orientation are focused on winning, not on achievement outcome. A mastery orientation is preferred over helpless or performance orientations in achievement situations.
  - Mindset is the cognitive view, either fixed or growth, that individuals develop for themselves. Dweck argues that a key aspect of promoting adolescents' development is guiding them to develop a growth mindset. Students with a growth mindset believe they can improve their abilities through effort.
  - Self-efficacy is the belief that one can master a situation and produce positive outcomes. Bandura stresses that self-efficacy is a critical factor in whether students will achieve. Schunk argues that self-efficacy influences a student's choice of tasks and that low-self-efficacy students avoid many learning tasks, especially those that are challenging. Instructional strategies that emphasize "I can do it" benefit students.
  - Low-self-efficacy teachers become mired in classroom problems.

- **Goal Setting, Planning, and Self-Monitoring**
  - Researchers have found that self-efficacy and achievement increase when students set goals that are specific, proximal, and challenging.
  - Being a good planner helps students manage time effectively, set priorities, and be organized. Giving students opportunities to develop their time management skills likely will benefit their learning and achievement.
  - Self-monitoring is a key aspect of learning and achievement.

- **Expectations**
  - Students' expectations for success and the value they place on what they want to achieve influence their motivation. The combination of expectancy and value has been the focus of a number of models of achievement motivation.
  - Teachers' expectations can have a powerful influence on students' motivation and achievement. Teachers often have higher expectations for high-ability students than for low-ability students. It is important for teachers to monitor their expectations and to have high expectations for all students.

- **Delay of Gratification**
  - Delay of gratification—the ability to postpone immediate rewards in order to attain larger rewards in the future—plays a very important role in children's and adolescents' ability to reach their goals.
  - Longitudinal research has shown that preschool children who delay gratification are more likely to have academic success and fewer problems in adolescence and to have greater career success as well as better physical and mental health in adulthood.

- **Values and Purpose**
  - Values are beliefs and attitudes about the way we think things should be—what is important to us as individuals.
  - Purpose is an intention to accomplish something meaningful to oneself and to contribute something to the world beyond the self. Damon has found that far too few students engage in purposeful reflection about what they want to do with their lives, and he concludes that parents and teachers need to ask students more questions, especially "Why" questions that will encourage them to think more deeply about their purpose in life.

3 MOTIVATION, RELATIONSHIPS, AND SOCIOCULTURAL CONTEXTS: Explain how relationships and sociocultural contexts can support or undercut motivation.

- **Social Motives**
  - Social motives are needs and desires that are learned through experiences with the social world.
  - The need for affiliation or relatedness involves the motive to be securely connected with people. Students vary in their need for affiliation—some like to be surrounded by many friends and date regularly, while others do not have such strong social needs.

Social Relationships

- In terms of achievement and social motivation, approval from teachers, peers, friends, and parents is important. Peer conformity peaks in early adolescence, a time of important decisions about whether to pursue academic or social goals.
- Understanding the parent's role in students' motivation focuses on demographic characteristics (for example, educational level, time spent at work, and family structure), child-rearing practices (for example, providing the right amount of challenge and support), and provision of specific experiences at home (for example, providing reading materials).
- Peers can affect students' motivation through social comparison, social competence, peer co-learning, and peer-group influences.
- Research shows that a teacher's support and caring can play a powerful role in students' motivation. A teacher's instructional style and socioemotional support also can play a role in a student's achievement. An important aspect of student motivation is enlisting parents as partners with the teacher in educating the student.

Sociocultural Contexts

- Teachers should recognize and value diversity within any cultural group and should be careful to distinguish the influences of socioeconomic status from those of ethnicity.
- Differences in achievement are more closely linked to socioeconomic status than to ethnicity. The quality of schools for many socioeconomically impoverished students is lower than for their middle-income counterparts.
- Everyday racial discrimination at school from teachers and peers is linked to a decline in grades of African American middle school students.

4 EXPLORING ACHIEVEMENT DIFFICULTIES: Recommend how to help students with achievement difficulties.

Students Who Are Low Achieving and Have Low Expectations for Success

- A student with low ability and low expectations for success often needs reassurance and support but also needs to be reminded that progress will be acceptable only when considerable effort is put forth.
- A student with failure syndrome (who has low expectations for success and gives up easily) likely will benefit from cognitive retraining methods such as efficacy training and strategy training.

Students Who Protect Their Self-Worth by Avoiding Failure

- Students who are motivated to protect self-worth and avoid failure often engage in one or more of these ineffective strategies: nonperformance, procrastination, or setting unreachable goals. These students likely need guidance in setting challenging but realistic goals, strengthening the link between their effort and self-worth, and developing positive beliefs about their abilities.

Students Who Procrastinate

- Procrastination can take many forms, including ignoring a task and hoping it will go away, underestimating the amount of work a task requires, spending endless hours on distracting activities, and substituting worthwhile but lower-priority activities.
- Strategies for helping students overcome procrastination include acknowledging they have a procrastination problem, encouraging them to identify their values and goals, helping them to manage their time more effectively, having them divide the task into smaller parts, and teaching them how to use behavioral and cognitive strategies.

Students Who Are Perfectionists

- Perfectionists think that mistakes are never acceptable and that the highest standards of performance always have to be achieved. Perfectionists are vulnerable to a number of physical and mental health problems.
- Teachers can help students with perfectionist tendencies by having them list the advantages and disadvantages of trying to be perfect, guiding students to become more aware of the self-critical nature of their all-or-none thinking, helping them to become more realistic about what they can achieve, and helping them to learn how to accept criticism.

continued

Students with High Anxiety

- Anxiety is a vague, highly unpleasant feeling of fear and apprehension. High anxiety can result from unrealistic parental expectations.
- Students' anxiety increases as they get older and face more evaluation, social comparison, and failure (for some students).
- Cognitive programs that replace students' self-damaging thoughts with positive, constructive thoughts have been more effective than relaxation programs in benefiting student achievement.

Students Who Are Uninterested or Alienated

- Strategies for helping an uninterested or alienated student include establishing a positive relationship with the student, making school more intrinsically interesting, using teaching strategies for making academic work more enjoyable, and finding a mentor in the community or an older student who can become a support person for the student.

KEY TERMS

attribution theory 437
competence motivation 430
delay of gratification 444
extrinsic motivation 432
failure syndrome 454

helpless orientation 438
hierarchy of needs 429
humanistic perspective 429
incentives 429
intrinsic motivation 432

mastery orientation 438
mindset 439
motivation 429
need for affiliation or relatedness 430

performance orientation 439
self-actualization 430
self-efficacy 441
social motives 449

PORTFOLIO ACTIVITIES

Now that you have a good understanding of this chapter, complete these exercises to expand your thinking.

Independent Reflection

1. **Motivate and Invigorate Your Students.** Design a motivationally rich classroom. What materials would be available? Describe your classroom walls and learning centers. How would teaching proceed? What types of activities would students participate in? Write a description of your classroom design. (INTASC: Principle *3*)

Research/Field Experience

2. **The Face of Student Motivation.** Observe a teacher at the grade level you plan to teach and note the strategie he or she uses to motivate students. Which strategies are most effective? Least effective? Why do you think this is so? Which students seem particularly difficult to motivate? Why do you think this is so? What would you do differently to foster student motivation in the classroom? (INTASC: Principles *3, 7, 9*)

Collaborative Work

3. **Case Studies in Motivation.** With three other students in the class, create a plan to improve the motivation of these students: (1) 7-year-old Tanya, who has low ability and low expectations for success; (2) 10-year-old Samuel, who works overtime to keep his self-worth at a high level but has a strong fear of failure; (3) 13-year-old Sandra, who is quiet in the classroom and underestimates her skills; and (4) 16-year-old Robert, who shows little interest in school and currently lives with his aunt (you have been unable to contact his parents). (INTASC: Principles *1, 2, 3*)

chapter 14
MANAGING THE CLASSROOM

chapter outline

1. Why Classrooms Need to Be Managed Effectively

Learning Goal 1 Explain why classroom management is both challenging and necessary.

Management Issues in Elementary and Secondary School Classrooms

The Crowded, Complex, and Potentially Chaotic Classroom

Getting Off to the Right Start

Emphasizing Instruction and a Positive Classroom Climate

Management Goals and Strategies

2. Designing the Physical Environment of the Classroom

Learning Goal 2 Describe the positive design of the classroom's physical environment.

Principles of Classroom Arrangement

Arrangement Style

3. Creating a Positive Environment for Learning

Learning Goal 3 Discuss how to create a positive classroom environment.

General Strategies

Creating, Teaching, and Maintaining Rules and Procedures

Getting Students to Cooperate

Classroom Management and Diversity

4. Being a Good Communicator

Learning Goal 4 Identify some good approaches to communication for both students and teachers.

Speaking Skills

Listening Skills

Nonverbal Communication

5. Dealing with Problem Behaviors

Learning Goal 5 Formulate some effective approaches that teachers can use to deal with problem behaviors.

Management Strategies

Dealing with Aggression

> *Precision in communication is more important than ever in our era of hair-trigger balances, when a false or misunderstood word may create as much disaster as a sudden thoughtless act.*
>
> —James Thurber
> American Essayist and Humorist, 20th Century

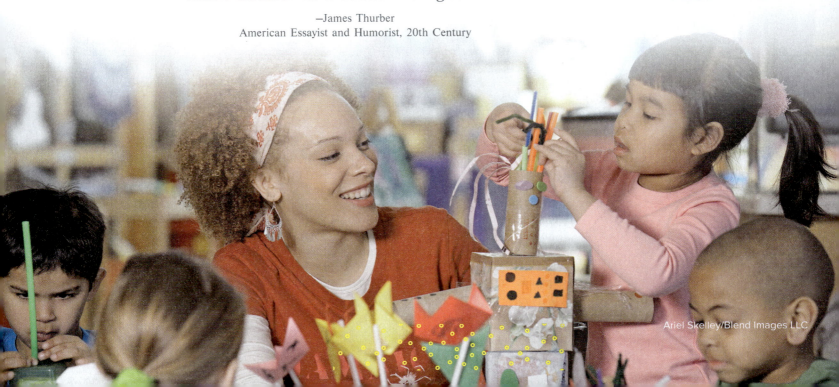

Ariel Skelley/Blend Images LLC

Connecting with Teachers: Adriane Lonzarich

Adriane Lonzarich owns and operates Heartwood, a small preschool in San Mateo, California. In the afternoons, she also holds art classes for 5- to 12-year-old children. She talks about her ideas for managing the classroom:

> The most valuable advice I ever received for managing the classroom is to approach a problem or area of difficulty with three questions in this order: (1) Is it the environment? (2) Is it the teacher? (3) Is it the child? For example, if the issue of concern is unfocused energy of the group, I would first ask myself, Is it the environment? Is it overstimulating? Is there not enough to do? Do I need to rearrange the classroom and create more intimate spaces for quiet activity, or do I need to let them have more time outside, and so on? In many cases, I don't need to go on to the next two questions.
>
> Is it the teacher? Am I tired? Nervous? Uninspiring? Have I not taken the time to demonstrate the activities? Have I not been consistent in presenting, monitoring, and enforcing basic classroom rules? Have I not paid enough attention to their needs that day?
>
> Is it the child? If I've addressed all the other possibilities and I'm convinced that the problem is the child's problem, not the environment's or the teacher's, I explore what might be going on. Is anything happening in the child's home that might be causing his or her problems? Is it time for a parent conference? Does the child need help in bonding with a friend? Is the child afraid of failure and avoiding meaningful learning for that reason?
>
> This approach is empowering because it is much easier to change the environment or oneself than to change someone else's behavior. It also is effective because it does not zero in on the problem as the child's until all other avenues have been explored.

Preview

In educational circles, it is commonly said that no one pays any attention to good classroom management until it is missing. When classrooms are effectively managed, they run smoothly and students are actively engaged in learning. When classrooms are poorly managed, they can become chaotic settings in which learning is a foreign activity. Our coverage begins by examining why classrooms need to be managed effectively, then turns to strategies for designing the classroom's physical environment. Next, we discuss the importance of creating a positive environment for learning and ways to be an effective communicator. The chapter concludes with information about what to do when students engage in problem behavior.

LG 1 Explain why classroom management is both challenging and necessary.

Effective classroom management maximizes children's learning opportunities (Evertson & Emmer, 2017). Experts in classroom management report that there has been a change in thinking about the best way to manage classrooms. The older view emphasized creating and applying rules to control students' behavior. The newer view focuses more on meeting students' needs for nurturing relationships and creating opportunities for self-regulation (Noddings, 2007). Classroom management that orients students toward passivity and compliance with rigid rules can undermine their engagement in active learning, higher-order thinking, and the social construction of knowledge (Jones & Jones, 2016). The new trend in classroom management places more emphasis on guiding students toward self-discipline and less on externally controlling the student (Emmer & Evertson, 2017). Historically in classroom management, the teacher was thought of as a director. In the current learner-centered approach to classroom management, the teacher is more of a guide, coordinator, and facilitator (Emmer & Evertson, 2017). The new classroom management model does not mean slipping into a permissive mode. Emphasizing caring and students' self-regulation does not mean that the teacher abdicates responsibility for what happens in the classroom.

As you explore various aspects of managing the classroom, realize the importance of consulting and working with other staff members on management issues. Also recognize that your class is part of the broader context of school culture and that in such areas as discipline and conflict management your policies will need to reflect and be consistent with the policies of the school and other teachers in the school. We will begin our tour of effective classroom management by exploring how management issues sometimes differ in elementary and secondary classrooms.

MANAGEMENT ISSUES IN ELEMENTARY AND SECONDARY SCHOOL CLASSROOMS

Elementary and secondary school classrooms have many similar management issues. At all levels of education, good managers design classrooms for optimal learning, create positive environments for learning, establish and maintain rules, get students to cooperate, effectively deal with problems, and use good communication strategies.

However, the same classroom management principles sometimes are applied differently in elementary and secondary schools because these two types of schools are structured differently (Emmer & Evertson, 2017; Evertson & Emmer 2017; Weinstein & Novodvorsky, 2015; Weinstein & Romano, 2015). In many elementary schools, teachers face the challenge of managing the same 20 to 25 children for the entire day. In middle and high schools, teachers face the challenge of managing five or six different groups of 20 to 25 adolescents for about 50 minutes each day. Compared with secondary school students, elementary school students spend much more time with the same students in the small space of a single classroom, and having to interact with the same people all day can breed feelings of confinement and boredom and other problems. However, with 100 to 150 students, secondary school teachers are likely to be confronted with a wider range of problems than elementary school teachers. Also, because secondary school teachers have less time with each student in the classroom, it can be more difficult for them to establish personal relationships with students. In addition, secondary school teachers need to get the classroom lesson moving quickly and manage time effectively because class periods are so short.

Secondary school students' problems can be more long-standing and more deeply ingrained, and therefore more difficult to address, than those of elementary school students. Also in secondary schools, discipline problems are frequently more severe, the students being potentially more unruly and even dangerous. Because most secondary school students have more advanced reasoning skills than elementary school students, they might demand more elaborate and logical explanations of rules and discipline. And in secondary schools, hallway socializing can carry into the classroom. Every hour there is another "settling down" process. Keep in mind these differences between elementary and secondary schools as we further explore how to effectively manage the classroom. As we see next, at both elementary and secondary school levels, classrooms can be crowded, complex, and potentially chaotic.

Carmella Williams Scott, a middle school English and law teacher at Fairmont Alternative School in Newman, Georgia, created Juvenile Video Court TV, a student-run judicial system, so that students could experience the "other side of the bench" as a judge, lawyer, bailiff, and camera operator. She especially targeted gang leaders for inclusion in the system because they ran the school. Carmella likes to use meaningful questions to guide students' critical thinking. She believes that mutual respect is a key factor in her success as a teacher and the lack of discipline problems she has in her classes (Wong Briggs, 1999).
Michael A. Schwarz

DEVELOPMENT

What are some different management issues in teaching elementary and secondary school students?
(Left) BananaStock/age fotostock; (right) Echo/Cultura/Getty Images

THE CROWDED, COMPLEX, AND POTENTIALLY CHAOTIC CLASSROOM

Carol Weinstein and Andrew Mignano (2007) used the title of this section, "The Crowded, Complex, and Potentially Chaotic Classroom," as an alert for potential problems and highlighted Walter Doyle's (1986, 2006) six characteristics that reflect a classroom's complexity and potential for problems:

- *Classrooms are multidimensional.* Classrooms are the setting for many activities, ranging from academic activities such as reading, writing, and math to social activities such as playing games, communicating with friends, and arguing. Teachers have to keep records and keep students on a schedule. Work has to be assigned, monitored, collected, and evaluated. Students have individual needs that are more likely to be met when the teacher takes them into account.
- *Activities occur simultaneously.* Many classroom activities occur simultaneously. One cluster of students might be writing at their desks, another might be discussing a story with the teacher, one student might be picking on another, others might be talking about what they are going to do after school, and so on.
- *Things happen quickly.* Events often occur rapidly in classrooms and frequently require an immediate response. For example, two students suddenly argue about the ownership of a notebook, a student complains that another student is copying her answers, a student speaks out of turn, a student marks on another student's arm with a felt-tip pen, two students abruptly start bullying another student, or a student is rude to you.
- *Events are often unpredictable.* Even though you might carefully plan the day's activities and be highly organized, events will occur that you never expect: A fire alarm goes off; a student gets sick; two students get into a fight; a computer won't work; a previously unannounced assembly takes place; the heat goes off in the middle of winter; and so on.
- *There is little privacy.* Classrooms are public places where students observe how the teacher handles discipline problems, unexpected events, and frustrating circumstances. Some teachers report that they feel like they are in a "fishbowl," or constantly onstage. Much of what happens to one student is observed by other students, and students make attributions about what is occurring. In one case, they might perceive that the teacher is being unfair in the way she disciplines a student. In another, they might appreciate her sensitivity to a student's feelings.
- *Classrooms have histories.* Students have memories of what happened earlier in their classroom. They remember how the teacher handled a discipline problem earlier in the year, which students have gotten more privileges than others, and

whether the teacher abides by his promises. Because the past affects the future, it is important for teachers to manage the classroom today in a way that will support rather than undermine learning tomorrow. This means that the first several weeks of the school year are critical for establishing effective management principles.

The crowded, complex nature of the classroom can lead to problems if the classroom is not managed effectively. Indeed, such problems are a major public concern about schools.

GETTING OFF TO THE RIGHT START

One key to managing the complexity of the classroom is to make careful use of the first few days and weeks of school. To accomplish this goal, you will need to engage in advance planning before the school year begins to determine how you are going to manage the classroom on the first day and beyond (Evertson & Poole, 2008; Sterling, 2009). At the beginning of the school year, you will want to (1) communicate your rules and procedures to the class and get student cooperation in following them, and (2) get students to engage effectively in all learning activities.

Taking the time in the first week of school to establish these expectations, rules, and routines will help your class run smoothly and set the tone for developing a positive classroom environment.

THROUGH THE EYES OF STUDENTS

First Week of School

Sept. 8: Well now that I know what my teacher is like, I wish I didn't. My best friend Annie got the good teacher, Ms. Hartwell. I got the witch Ms. Birdsong. The first thing she did was to read all of her rules to us. It must have taken half an hour. We will never get to do anything fun. Fifth grade is ruined.

Sept. 12: Ms. Birdsong is still strict but I'm starting to like her better. And she even is beginning to be a little funny sometimes. I guess she's just serious about wanting us to learn.

—*Brooke*
Fifth-Grade Student
St. Louis, Missouri

CONNECTING WITH STUDENTS: Best Practices
Strategies for a Good Beginning of the School Year

Following are some competent teaching strategies to adopt for the beginning of the school year (Emmer & Evertson, 2009, 2017):

1. *Establish expectations for behavior and resolve student uncertainties.* At the beginning of the school year, students will not be sure what to expect in your classroom. They might have expectations, based on their experiences with other teachers, that are different from what your classroom will be like. In the first few days of school, lay out your expectations for students' work and behavior. Don't focus just on course content in the first few days and weeks of school. Be sure to take the time to clearly and concretely spell out class rules, procedures, and requirements so that students know what to expect in your class. In *Through the Eyes of Teachers,* middle school history teacher Chuck Rawls describes what he does at the beginning of the school year.

THROUGH THE EYES OF TEACHERS
Establish Yourself in a Positive Manner

My first few days and weeks are highly structured—desks in straight rows, and daily assignments starting with Day One. I try to make the initial environment as businesslike, straightforward, and structured as I possibly can. The games and easy give-and-take come later, after it is firmly established who is in charge of the class, and also if the kids are capable of doing that. Sometimes they aren't.

I'm not saying to scare the kids—they still need to feel safe and comfortable. The main thing is to establish yourself, at least in the minds of the kids, as an organized, confident, firm but fair subject-matter expert.

Someone said the lasting impression is made in the first 15 or 45 seconds of the first introduction. This is true.

Chuck Rawls

2. *Make sure that students experience success.* In the first week of school, content, activities, and assignments should be designed to ensure that students succeed. This helps students develop a positive attitude and provides them with confidence to tackle more difficult tasks later.

3. *Be available and visible.* Show your students that they can approach you when they need information. During seatwork or group work, make yourself available instead of going to your desk and completing paperwork. Move around the room, monitor students' progress, and provide assistance when needed.

4. *Be in charge.* Even if you have stated your class rules and expectations clearly, some students will forget and others will test you to see if you are willing to enforce the rules, especially in the first several weeks of school. Continue to consistently establish the boundaries between what is acceptable and what is not acceptable in your classroom.

EMPHASIZING INSTRUCTION AND A POSITIVE CLASSROOM CLIMATE

Despite the public's belief that a lack of discipline is the number one problem in schools, educational psychology emphasizes ways to develop and maintain a positive classroom environment that supports learning (Jones & Jones, 2016). This involves using preventive, proactive strategies rather than becoming immersed in reactive disciplinary tactics.

RESEARCH

In a classic study, Jacob Kounin (1970) was interested in discovering how teachers responded to student misbehaviors. Kounin was surprised to find that effective and ineffective classroom managers responded in very similar ways to the misbehaviors. What the effective managers did far better than the ineffective managers was manage the group's activities. Researchers in educational psychology consistently find that teachers who competently guide and structure classroom activities are more effective than teachers who emphasize their disciplinary role (Panayiotou, et al., 2014; Wong et al., 2012).

Throughout this book we emphasize a vision of students as active learners engaged in meaningful tasks, who think reflectively and critically and often interact with other students in collaborative learning experiences. Historically, the effectively managed classroom has been described as a "well-oiled machine," but a more appropriate metaphor for today's effectively managed classroom is a "beehive of activity" (see Figure 1) (Randolph & Evertson, 1995). This does not imply that classrooms should be wildly noisy and chaotic. Rather, students should be actively learning and busily engaged in tasks that they are motivated to do rather than quietly and passively sitting in their seats. Often they will be interacting with each other and the teacher as they construct their knowledge and understanding.

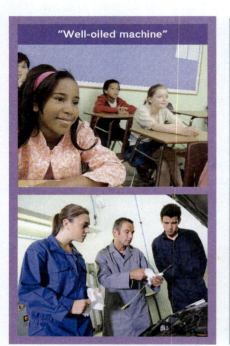
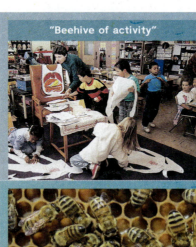

FIGURE 1 THE EFFECTIVELY MANAGED CLASSROOM

"Well-oiled machine" or "beehive of activity"? (Top left) Spencer Grant/PhotoEdit; (Top right) Elizabeth Crews; (Bottom left) Goodluz/Shutterstock; (Bottom right) Photo Luc Gilbert/Flickr/Getty Images

---

CONNECTING WITH STUDENTS: Best Practices
Strategies for Increasing Academic Learning Time

Strategies for increasing academic learning time include maintaining activity flow, minimizing transition time, and holding students accountable (Weinstein, 2007; Weinstein & Romano, 2015):

1. *Maintain activity flow.* In an analysis of classrooms, Jacob Kounin (1970) studied teachers' ability to initiate and maintain the flow of activity. Then he searched for links between activity flow and students' engagement and misbehavior. He found that some teachers engaged in "flip-flopping"—terminating an activity, starting another, and then returning to the first one. Others were distracted from an ongoing activity by a small event that really did not need attention. For example, in one situation a teacher who was explaining a math problem at the board noticed a student leaning on his left elbow while working on the problem. The teacher went over to the student and told him to sit up straight, interrupting the flow of the class. Some teachers "overdwell" on something that students already understand or go on at length about appropriate behavior. All of these

CONNECTING WITH STUDENTS: Best Practices
Strategies for Increasing Academic Learning Time

situations—flip-flopping, responding to distractions, and overdwelling—can interrupt the classroom's flow.

2. *Minimize transition time.* In transitions from one activity to another, there is more room for disruptive behavior to occur. Teachers can decrease the potential for disruption during transitions by preparing students for forthcoming transitions, establishing transition routines, and clearly defining the boundaries of lessons.

3. *Hold students accountable.* If students know they will be held accountable for their work, they are more likely to make good use of class time. Clearly communicating assignments and requirements encourages student accountability. Explain to students what they will be doing and why, how long they will be working on the activity, how to obtain help if they need it, and what to do when they are finished. Helping students establish goals, create plans, and monitor their progress also increases students' accountability. And maintaining good records can help you hold students accountable for their performance.

How do teachers create a positive classroom environment? Following are their responses.

EARLY CHILDHOOD We create positive classrooms for our preschoolers by frequently praising children, speaking with calm voices, following daily schedules, and setting clear rules that are expected to be followed.

—MISSY DANGLER, *Suburban Hills School*

ELEMENTARY SCHOOL: GRADES K–5 To create a positive classroom for my second-graders, I have a banner stretched across one of the walls of my classroom that reads: "This Is a Positive Learning Area"; this statement is the foundation for

everything I do. On the first day of class, I tell the students that they will learn from me, learn from each other, and I will learn from them. I work with them to establish our classroom as a community of learners in order to build feelings of trust, respect, and understanding. With these values in place, academic learning can begin.

—ELIZABETH FRASCELLA, *Clinton Elementary School*

MIDDLE SCHOOL: GRADES 6–8 One of the best ways to create a positive environment for my sixth-graders is to monitor classroom seating arrangements. I recognize who can sit next to each other and who can't. In middle school, when social cliques often form, I change seating arrangements every three weeks or so.

—MARGARET REARDON, *Pocantico Hills School*

HIGH SCHOOL: GRADES 9–12 I create a positive environment by keeping expectations high and consistently enforced. For example, I expect students to turn in their

homework on time. No late work is accepted—however, I do tell students that if they are up late and overwhelmed by an assignment, they can come to me and ask for an extension. I ask that these extensions be the exception, not the rule. My high school students respond well to clear rules and expectations.

—JOSEPH MALEY, *South Burlington High School*

MANAGEMENT GOALS AND STRATEGIES

Effective classroom management has two main goals: to help students spend more time on learning and less time on non-goal-directed activity, and to prevent students from developing academic and emotional problems.

Help Students Spend More Time on Learning and Less Time on Non-Goal-Directed Activity   In other chapters we discussed the importance of being a good time manager. Effective classroom management will help you maximize your instructional time and your students' learning time. Carol Weinstein and Ingrid Novodvorsky (2015) described the amount of time available for various classroom activities in a typical 42-minute secondary school class over the course of a school year. Actual yearly learning time is only about 62 hours, which is approximately half of the mandated school time for a typical class. Although their time figures are only estimates, they suggest that the hours available for learning are far less than would appear. And as we underscored in the chapter on planning, instruction, and technology, learning takes time.

> **Thinking Back/Thinking Forward**
>
> Managing the classroom includes effective planning and involves knowing what needs to be done and when to do it, or focusing on "task" and "time." Connect to "Planning, Instruction, and Technology."

Prevent Students from Developing Problems   A well-managed classroom not only fosters meaningful learning but also helps prevent academic and emotional problems from developing (Eisenman et al., 2015). Well-managed classrooms keep students busy with engaging, appropriately challenging tasks, have activities in which students become absorbed and motivated to learn, and establish clear rules and regulations students must abide by. In such classrooms, students are less likely to develop academic and emotional problems. By contrast, in poorly managed classrooms, students' academic and emotional problems are more likely to fester. The academically unmotivated student becomes even less motivated. The shy student becomes more reclusive. The bully becomes meaner.

TECHNOLOGY

Managing Instruction   Classroom management involves not only managing student behaviors but also managing instruction (Jones & Jones, 2016; Martella & Marchand-Martella, 2015). Ideally, the two go hand in hand—students who are engaged in learning tasks are less likely to develop behavior problems. Recently classroom response systems have been used as part of classroom management (Baumann et al., 2015; Brookhart, 2015).

Using student response systems, teachers have the ability to pose questions and give practice to whole classes of students, and to gather instant data on all of their students, which can be used to quickly assess comprehension (Miles & Soares da Costa, 2016). This true, formative assessment enables the teacher to identify students' misconceptions and errors and then correct them immediately. In addition, it encourages active student participation and helps students explore what they know and don't know—and hence take control of their own learning. Most student response systems also produce records of student responses, which can be automatically entered as grades.

A number of companies offer student response systems. Two of the most popular ones are TurningPoint's Audience Response System (www.turningtechnologies.com/higher-education), and Quizdom's Student Response System (https://qwizdom.com/education).

Student response systems that require a particular type of hardware are being used less than in past years; they are being replaced with systems that can be used regardless of the type of device the teacher has (computer, laptop, cell phone, and so on). Poll Everywhere (www.polleverywhere.com/) is a subscription-based example. One of the best solutions for K-12 students is surprisingly low-tech: Plickers (http://plickers.com/). To use this, teachers need a mobile device, such as a smartphone, that can scan

Using their wireless clickers, students can answer questions and record their responses with a simple click of a button. Classroom response systems such as the one shown here are increasingly used in classroom instruction and management.
Turning Technologies, LLC

cards students hold up to indicate their answer. The app is free, teachers already have the device, and the cards can be printed at school. Requiring no software or electronic devices at all, you also can ask students to make hand signals or hold up cards to indicate answers.

Numerous studies show that these relatively simple systems can be effective classroom management tools (Cohn et al. 2016; Hooker et al., 2016). Common outcomes include increases in student engagement, teacher awareness of student knowledge, and student understanding of content.

RESEARCH

Review, Reflect, and Practice

 1 Explain why classroom management is both challenging and necessary.

REVIEW

- Why must management principles be applied differently to elementary and secondary school classrooms?
- What are six reasons that classrooms are crowded, complex, and potentially chaotic?
- What strategies can help teachers get a school year off to the right start?
- What do experts say should be the basic approach to classroom management? What did Kounin find that effective teachers did differently from ineffective teachers in managing the classroom?
- What are the two main goals of effective classroom management?

REFLECT

- Which would probably be easier for you to manage—an elementary school classroom or a high school classroom? Why?

PRAXIS™ PRACTICE

1. Which characteristic of classrooms is best exemplified in the following scenario? Holly and Alex are having a conflict. Holly takes a black, permanent marker and makes a large mark on Alex's shirt. Mr. Bronson witnesses the incident and does nothing. Two weeks later, during another conflict, Alex makes a mark on the back of Holly's shirt with a pen. This time Mr. Bronson gives Alex a detention. Alex becomes upset at what he perceives as unfair treatment.
   a. Classrooms are multidimensional.
   b. Classrooms have histories.
   c. There is little privacy.
   d. Things happen quickly.
2. Mr. McClure wants to be certain that his students understand that he has high expectations for them. Therefore, he gives a very difficult exam during the first week of school. Which principle of getting off to the right start did Mr. McClure ignore?
   a. Be available and visible.
   b. Be in charge.
   c. Establish expectations for behavior and resolve student uncertainties.
   d. Make sure that students experience success.
3. Which teacher is most likely to have classroom management problems?
   a. Mr. Knight, who, in an effort to keep students from being bored, has numerous activities during the period, all of which require transitional time
   b. Mr. Quinn, whose students know that they have to accomplish a significant amount of work that will be collected at the end of the class period
   c. Ms. Leifeit, whose students are always actively engaged in activities that require students to work together

continued

> ### Review, Reflect, and Practice
>
> d. Ms. Jefferson, who establishes rules and procedures early in the school year and consistently enforces them
>
> 4. Which of the following teachers is likely to be most effective in maximizing academic learning time?
>   a. Ms. Chang, who focuses on classroom discipline. Her students are reprimanded every time she notices what she perceives to be off-task behavior.
>   b. Ms. George, who regularly starts one activity, stops it in favor of another, then returns to the first activity.
>   c. Ms. Lange, who informs her students how long they will have to complete an activity, warns them when there are five minutes left, and then plays a certain piece of music during transition time. At the end of the music, the students are expected to be ready for the next activity.
>   d. Ms. Purdy, who requires her students to sit up straight with both feet on the floor as a means of gaining their attention.
>
> *Please see answer key at end of book . . . .*

LG 2 Describe the positive design of the classroom's physical environment.

2 DESIGNING THE PHYSICAL ENVIRONMENT OF THE CLASSROOM

When thinking about effectively managing the classroom, inexperienced teachers sometimes overlook the physical environment. As you will see in this section, designing the physical environment of the classroom involves far more than arranging a few items on a bulletin board.

PRINCIPLES OF CLASSROOM ARRANGEMENT

Here are four basic principles that you can use when arranging your classroom (Evertson & Emmer, 2009, 2017):

- *Reduce congestion in high-traffic areas.* Distraction and disruption can often occur in high-traffic areas. These include group work areas, students' desks, the teacher's desk, the pencil sharpener, bookshelves, computer stations, and storage locations. Separate these areas from each other as much as possible and make sure they are easily accessible.
- *Make sure that you can easily see all students.* An important management task is to carefully monitor students. To do this, you will need to be able to see all students at all times. Make sure there is a clear line of sight between your desk, instructional locations, students' desks, and all student work areas. Stand in different parts of the room to check for blind spots.
- *Make often-used teaching materials and student supplies easily accessible.* This minimizes preparation and cleanup time, as well as slowdowns and breaks in activity flow.
- *Make sure that students can easily observe whole-class presentations.* Establish where you and your students will be located when whole-class presentations take place. For these activities, students should not have to move their chairs

or stretch their necks. To find out how well your students can see from their locations, sit in their seats in different parts of the room.

ARRANGEMENT STYLE

In thinking about how you will organize the classroom's physical space, you should ask yourself what type of instructional activity students will mainly be engaged in (whole-class, small-group, individual assignments, and so on). Consider the physical arrangements that will best support that type of activity (Weinstein, 2007).

Standard Classroom Arrangements Figure 2 shows five categories of classroom arrangement styles: auditorium, face-to-face, offset, seminar, and cluster (Renne, 1997). In traditional **auditorium style**, all students sit facing the teacher (see Figure 2A). This arrangement inhibits face-to-face student contacts, and the teacher is free to move anywhere in the room. Auditorium style often is used when the teacher lectures or someone is making a presentation to the entire class.

In **face-to-face style**, students sit facing each other (see Figure 2B). Distraction from other students is higher in this arrangement than in the auditorium style.

In **offset style**, small numbers of students (usually three or four) sit at tables but do not sit directly across from one another (see Figure 2C). This produces less distraction than face-to-face style and can be effective for cooperative learning activities.

In **seminar style**, larger numbers of students (ten or more) sit in circular, square, or U-shaped arrangements (see Figure 2D). This is especially effective when you want students to talk with each other or to converse with you.

In **cluster style**, small numbers of students (usually four to eight) work in small, closely bunched groups (see Figure 2E). This arrangement is especially effective for collaborative learning activities.

Clustering desks encourages social interaction among students. In contrast, rows of desks reduce social interaction among students and direct students' attention toward the teacher. Arranging desks in rows can benefit students when they are working on individual assignments, whereas clustered desks facilitate cooperative learning. In classrooms in which seats are organized in rows, the teacher is most likely to interact with students seated in the front and center of the classroom (Adams & Biddle, 1970) (see Figure 3). This area has been called the "action zone" because students in the front and center locations interact the most with the teacher. For example, they most often ask questions and are most likely to initiate discussion. If you use a row arrangement, move around the room when possible, establish eye contact with students seated outside the "action zone," direct comments to students in the peripheral seats, and periodically have students change seats so that all students have an equal opportunity to sit in the front and center seats.

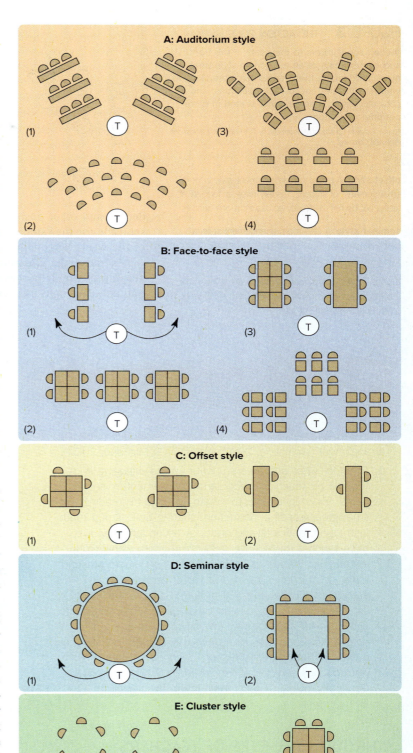

FIGURE 2 VARIATIONS OF CLASSROOM SEATING ARRANGEMENTS

auditorium style A classroom arrangement style in which all students sit facing the teacher.

face-to-face style A classroom arrangement style in which students sit facing each other.

FIGURE 3 THE ACTION ZONE

"Action zone" refers to the seats in the front and center seats of an auditorium-style arrangement. Students in these seats are more likely to interact with the teacher, ask questions, and initiate discussion than students seated in more peripheral locations.

Source: *Excellent Classroom Management,* by C.H. Rinne, 1997, Wadsworth Publishing Company.

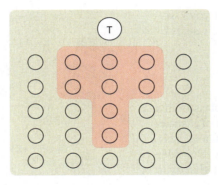

offset style A classroom arrangement style in which small numbers of students (usually three or four) sit at tables but do not sit directly across from one another.

seminar style A classroom arrangement style in which large numbers of students (ten or more) sit in circular, square, or U-shaped arrangements.

cluster style A classroom arrangement style in which small numbers of students (usually four to eight) work in small, closely bunched groups.

Personalizing the Classroom According to classroom management experts Carol Weinstein and Andrew Mignano (2007), classrooms too often resemble motel rooms—pleasant but impersonal, revealing nothing about the people who use the space. Such anonymity is especially true of secondary school classrooms, where six or seven different classes might use the space in a single day. To personalize classrooms, post students' photographs, artwork, written projects, charts that list birthdays (of early childhood and elementary school students), and other positive expressions of students' identities. A bulletin board can be set aside for the "student of the week" or be used to display each student's best work of the week, personally chosen by each student.

None of the classrooms we have described will exactly match yours. However, keeping in mind the basic principles we have described should help you create an optimal classroom arrangement for learning.

CONNECTING WITH STUDENTS: Best Practices
Strategies for Designing a Classroom Arrangement

Follow these steps to ensure success in designing a classroom arrangement (Weinstein, 2007; Weinstein & Mignano, 2007):

1. *Consider what activities students will be engaging in.* If you will be teaching kindergarten or elementary school students, you might need to create settings for reading aloud, small-group reading instruction, sharing time, group math instruction, and arts and crafts. A secondary school science teacher might have to accommodate whole-group instruction, "hands-on" lab activities, and media presentations. On the left side of a sheet of paper, list the activities your students will perform. Next to each activity, list any special arrangements that need to be taken into account—for instance, art and science areas need to be near a sink, and computers need to be near an electrical outlet. In *Through the Eyes of Teachers,* William Williford, who teaches science at Perry Middle School in Perry, Georgia, provides a recommendation for classroom arrangement.

THROUGH THE EYES OF TEACHERS
Hissing Cockroaches and Minicams

My classroom is set up with tables with about four students per table. This allows for individual or group activities without a lot of transition time or movement. Since my current subject is science, there is an aquarium with fish, a terrarium with a lizard or praying mantis, and a cage with Madagascar hissing cockroaches.

William Williford, teaching science at Perry Middle School.
William Williford, Perry Middle School, Perry, GA

There is a table with gadgets and mini-experiments. A Minicam may be focused on an earthworm or a spider with the image on the TV as students enter the classroom. The idea is to arrange the classroom so that it promotes inquiry, questioning, and thinking about science.

William Williford

2. *Draw up a floor plan.* Before you actually move any furniture, draw several floor plans and then choose the one that you think will work the best.

CONNECTING WITH STUDENTS: Best Practices
Strategies for Designing a Classroom Arrangement

3. *Involve students in planning the classroom layout.* You can do most of your environmental planning before school starts, but once it begins, ask students how they like your arrangement. If they suggest improvements that are reasonable, try them out. Students often report that they want adequate room and a place of their own where they can keep their things.

4. *Try out the arrangement and be flexible in redesigning it.* Several weeks into the school year, evaluate how effective your arrangement is. Be alert for problems that the arrangement might be generating.

Review, Reflect, and Practice

2 Describe the positive design of the classroom's physical environment.

REVIEW
- What are some basic principles of classroom design and arrangement?
- What are some standard styles of arrangement?

REFLECT
- How would you design and arrange your ideal classroom? How would you personalize it?

PRAXIS™ PRACTICE

1. Ms. Craig likes her students to work in small groups. Therefore, she arranges her students' desks in small circles or clusters. What is the problem with this arrangement for whole-class presentations?
   a. Ms. Craig will be unable to see all of her students.
   b. Some students will have to turn their chairs to see.
   c. The classroom will be too congested.
   d. There will be blind spots.

2. Mr. James wants his students to be able to talk to each other as well as to him. What type of classroom arrangement is best suited to his needs?
   a. auditorium style
   b. cluster style
   c. offset style
   d. seminar style

Please see answer key at end of book . . . .

3 CREATING A POSITIVE ENVIRONMENT FOR LEARNING

General Strategies | Creating, Teaching, and Maintaining Rules and Procedures | Getting Students to Cooperate | Classroom Management and Diversity

LG 3 Discuss how to create a positive classroom environment.

Students need a positive environment for learning. We will discuss some general classroom management strategies for providing this environment, ways to effectively establish and maintain rules, positive strategies for getting students to cooperate, and suggestions for managing diverse classrooms.

Thinking Back/Thinking Forward

In most instances, authoritative parenting is linked with more positive child outcomes than authoritarian, neglectful, or indulgent parenting. Connect to "Social Contexts and Socioemotional Development."

GENERAL STRATEGIES

General strategies include using an authoritative style and effectively managing classroom activities.

The **authoritative classroom management style** is derived from Diana Baumrind's (1971, 1996) parenting styles, which were discussed in the chapter on social contexts and socioemotional development. Like authoritative parents, authoritative teachers have students who tend to be self-reliant, delay gratification, get along well with their peers, and show high self-esteem. An authoritative strategy of classroom management encourages students to be independent thinkers and doers but still involves effective monitoring. Authoritative teachers engage students in considerable verbal give-and-take and show a caring attitude toward them. However, they still declare limits when necessary. Authoritative teachers clarify rules and regulations, establishing these standards with input from students.

The authoritative style contrasts with two ineffective strategies: authoritarian and permissive. The **authoritarian classroom management style** is restrictive and punitive. The focus is mainly on keeping order in the classroom rather than on instruction and learning. Authoritarian teachers place firm limits and controls on students and have little verbal exchange with them. Students in authoritarian classrooms tend to be passive learners, fail to initiate activities, express anxiety about social comparison, and have poor communication skills. The **permissive classroom management style** offers students considerable autonomy but provides them with little support for developing learning skills or managing their behavior. Not surprisingly, students in permissive classrooms tend to have inadequate academic skills and low self-control.

Overall, an authoritative style will benefit your students more than authoritarian or permissive styles. An authoritative style will help your students become active, self-regulated learners. In addition to adopting an authoritative style, the strategies described in *Connecting with Students* can benefit your classroom management.

CREATING, TEACHING, AND MAINTAINING RULES AND PROCEDURES

To function smoothly, classrooms need clearly defined rules and procedures. Students need to know specifically how you want them to behave. Without clearly defined classroom rules and procedures, the inevitable misunderstandings can breed chaos. For example, consider these procedures or routines: When students enter the classroom, are they supposed to go directly to their seats or may they socialize for a few minutes until you tell them to be seated? When students want to go to the library, do they need a pass? When students are working at their seats, may they help each other or are they required to work individually?

Both rules and procedures are stated expectations about behavior (Evertson & Emmer, 2009, 2017). *Rules* focus on general or specific expectations or standards for behavior. An example of a general rule is "Respect other persons." An example of a more specific rule is "Cell phones must always be turned off when you are in this classroom." *Procedures*, or routines, also communicate expectations about behavior, but they usually are applied to a specific activity, and their aim is to accomplish something rather than to prohibit a behavior or define a general standard (Evertson & Emmer, 2009, 2017). You might establish procedures for collecting homework assignments, turning in work late, using the pencil sharpener, or using equipment. You can develop procedures for beginning the day (for example, a procedure for "settling in" to the classroom—maybe a social item such as a riddle or brief note about school events), leaving the room (for example, to go to the bathroom), returning to the room (such as after lunchtime), and ending the day (for example, clearing off desks and leaving on time).

---

authoritative classroom management style A management style that encourages students to be independent thinkers and doers but still provides effective monitoring. Authoritative teachers engage students in considerable verbal give-and-take and show a caring attitude toward them. However, they still set limits when necessary.

authoritarian classroom management style A management style that is restrictive and punitive, with the focus mainly on keeping order in the classroom rather than instruction or learning.

permissive classroom management style A management style that allows students considerable autonomy but provides them with little support for developing learning skills or managing their behavior.

CONNECTING WITH STUDENTS: Best Practices
Strategies for Being an Effective Classroom Manager

Effective classroom managers:

1. *Show how they are "with it."* Jacob Kounin (1970), whose views were discussed earlier, used the term **withitness** to describe a management strategy in which teachers show students that they are aware of what is happening. These teachers closely monitor students' behavior on a regular basis. This allows them to detect inappropriate behavior early, before it gets out of hand. Teachers who are not "with it" are likely to be unaware of such misbehaviors until they gain momentum and spread.

2. *Cope effectively with overlapping situations.* Kounin observed that some teachers seem to have one-track minds, dealing with only one thing at a time. This ineffective strategy often led to frequent interruptions in the flow of the class. For example, one teacher was working with a reading group when she observed two boys on the other side of the room hitting each other. She immediately got up, went over to the other side of the room, harshly criticized them, and then returned to the reading group. However, by the time she returned to the reading group, the students in the reading group had become bored and were starting to misbehave themselves. In contrast, effective managers were able to deal with overlapping situations in less disruptive ways. For example, in the reading group situation, effective managers quickly responded to students from outside the group who came to ask questions but not in a way that significantly altered the flow of the reading group's activity. When moving around the room and checking each student's seatwork, they kept a roving eye on the rest of the class.

3. *Maintain smoothness and continuity in lessons.* Effective managers keep the flow of a lesson moving smoothly, maintaining students' interest and not giving them opportunities to be easily distracted. Earlier in the chapter, we mentioned some ineffective practices that can disrupt the flow of a lesson, including flip-flopping and overdwelling. Another teacher action that disrupts the lesson's flow is called "fragmentation," in which the teacher breaks an activity into components even though the activity could be performed as an entire unit. For example, a teacher might individually ask six students to do something, such as get out their art supplies, when all six could be asked to do this as a group.

4. *Engage students in a variety of challenging activities.* Kounin also found that effective classroom managers engage students in a variety of challenging but not overly hard activities. The students frequently worked independently rather than being directly supervised by a teacher who hovered over them. In *Through the Eyes of Teachers,* Mark Fodness, an award-winning seventh-grade social studies teacher in Bemidji, Minnesota, gives this advice on managing the classroom.

THROUGH THE EYES OF TEACHERS
Great Teachers Have Few Discipline Problems

The single best method of decreasing undesirable behaviors among students is by increasing the effectiveness of teaching methods. The best teachers have very few discipline problems, not because they are great disciplinarians, but because they are great teachers. To emphasize this point with one of my student teachers, I had her follow our class out the door and into their next classes. She later returned, amazed at what she had seen. Students who she had thought were very well behaved had been off-task or disruptive in other classrooms. In one room, where a substitute teacher was doing his best to fill in, she described students' behavior as "shocking." Yet in another class, where the teacher was presenting a riveting lesson on a novel, the same students once again were well behaved even though the teacher did not seem to be using any specific discipline strategy.

Many first-year teachers and veterans alike identify discipline as their number one teaching challenge. However, the best solution is to use exemplary teaching strategies. I asked my seventh-grade students to identify the characteristics of teachers who had well-behaved classes. Here is a sample of their responses: well prepared, interesting, funny, organized, fair, caring, nice, and energetic.

Mark Fodness

Mark Fodness, teaching students in his middle school social studies classroom.

Rules tend not to change because they address fundamental ways we deal with others, ourselves, and our work, such as having respect for others and their property, and keeping our hands and our feet to ourselves. On the other hand, procedures may change because routines and activities in classrooms change.

What is the best way to get students to learn about rules and procedures? Should the teacher make the rules and procedures, then inform the class about them? Should students be allowed to participate in generating rules and procedures?

Some teachers like to include students in setting rules in the hope that this will encourage them to take more responsibility for their own behavior (Emmer & Evertson, 2009, 2017). Student involvement can take many different forms, including a discussion of the reason for having rules and the meaning of particular rules. The teacher might begin by having students discuss why rules are needed and then move on to a number of individual rules. The teacher can clarify the rule by describing, or asking students to describe, the general area of behavior it involves. Students usually can contribute concrete examples of the rule.

Some teachers start with a whole-class discussion of classroom rules. During the discussion, the teacher and the students suggest possible rules for the classroom, and the teacher records these on an overhead projector, a chalkboard, or a large piece of chart paper. Then, the teacher and students arrange them into broad categories and develop titles for the categories. In some classrooms, this activity is followed by having students role-play each of the rules.

In some schools, students are allowed to participate in setting rules for the entire school. In some cases, student representatives from each room or grade level participate in generating school-wide rules with guidance from teachers and school administrators. However, within individual classrooms, especially in elementary schools, it is uncommon for students to participate in creating rules. Most teachers

withitness A management style described by Kounin in which teachers show students that they are aware of what is happening. Such teachers closely monitor students on a regular basis and detect inappropriate behavior early, before it gets out of hand.

CONNECTING WITH STUDENTS: Best Practices
Strategies for Establishing Classroom Rules and Procedures

Here are four principles to keep in mind when you establish rules and procedures for your classroom (Source: *Middle and Secondary Classroom Management* 3/E, by C.S. Weinstein, 2007, McGraw-Hill):

1. *Rules and procedures should be reasonable and necessary.* Ask yourself if the rules and procedures you are establishing are appropriate for this grade level. Also ask yourself if there is a good reason for the rule or procedure. For example, one secondary school teacher has a rule that students must come to class on time. Students are clearly told that if they are late, they will get a detention even on the first violation. She explains the rule to the students at the beginning of the school year and tells them the reason for the rule: If they are late, they might miss important material.

2. *Rules and procedures should be clear and comprehensible.* If you have general rules, make sure that you clearly specify what they mean. For example, one teacher has the rule "Be prepared." Instead of leaving the rule at this general level, the teacher specifies what it means to be prepared and describes specific procedures involving the rule: having your homework, notebook, pen or pencil, and textbook with you every day.

3. *Rules and procedures should be consistent with instructional and learning goals.* Make sure that rules and procedures do not interfere with learning. Some teachers become so concerned about having an orderly, quiet classroom that they restrict students from interacting with each other and from engaging in collaborative learning activities.

4. *Classroom rules should be consistent with school rules.* Know what the school's rules are, such as whether particular behaviors are required in the halls, in the cafeteria, and so on. Many schools have a handbook that spells out what is acceptable and what is not. Familiarize yourself with the handbook. Some teachers go over the handbook with students at the beginning of the school year so that students clearly understand the school's rules regarding absenteeism, truancy, fighting, smoking, substance abuse, abusive language, and so on.

prefer to create and present their rules, although as indicated earlier, they may encourage discussion of the rules. In secondary schools, especially high schools, greater student contribution to rule setting is possible because of their more-advanced cognitive and socioemotional knowledge and skills.

Many effective classroom teachers clearly present their rules to students and give explanations and examples of them. Teachers who set reasonable rules, provide understandable rationales for them, and enforce them consistently usually find that the majority of the class will abide by them.

GETTING STUDENTS TO COOPERATE

You want your students to cooperate with you and abide by classroom rules without always having to resort to discipline to maintain order. How can you get your students to cooperate? There are three main strategies: Develop a positive relationship with students, get students to share and assume responsibility, and reward appropriate behavior.

Develop a Positive Relationship with Students When most of us think of our favorite teacher, we think of someone who cared about us whether or not we learned. Showing that you genuinely care about students as individuals apart from their academic work helps to gain their cooperation (Jones & Jones, 2016). It is easy to get caught up in the pressing demands of academic achievement and classroom business and ignore the socioemotional needs of students.

One study found that in addition to having effective rules and procedures, successful classroom managers also showed a caring attitude toward students (Emmer et al., 1980). This caring was evidenced in part by a classroom environment in which students felt safe and secure and were treated fairly. The teachers were sensitive to their needs and anxieties (for example, they created enjoyable activities the first several days of the school year rather than giving them diagnostic tests) and had good communication skills (including listening skills), and they effectively expressed their feelings to students. The classroom atmosphere was relaxed and pleasant. For example, the focus was on academic work but teachers gave students breaks and allowed them free time to read, use the computer, or draw. Figure 4 presents some teaching guidelines for developing a positive relationship with students.

Get Students to Share and Assume Responsibility Earlier in this chapter, we discussed the importance of developing an authoritative atmosphere in the classroom and the issue of whether students should be allowed to participate in establishing class rules. Some experts on classroom management argue that sharing responsibility with students for making classroom decisions increases the students' commitment to the decisions (Blumenfeld et al., 2006).

Reward Appropriate Behavior We have discussed rewards extensively in the chapter on behavioral and social cognitive approaches. You might want to read the discussion of rewards in that chapter again, especially the section "Applied Behavior Analysis in Education," and think about how rewards can be used in effectively managing the classroom (Alberto & Troutman, 2017). The discussion of rewards in the chapter on motivation, teaching, and learning also is relevant to classroom management, especially the information about rewards and intrinsic motivation. Following are some guidelines for using rewards in managing the classroom.

> **Thinking Back/Thinking Forward**
>
> Using differential reinforcement to decrease undesirable behavior is a recommended first strategy by applied behavior analysts. Connect to "Behavioral and Social Cognitive Approaches."

1. Give a student a friendly "hello" at the door.
2. Have a brief one-on-one conversation about things that are happening in the student's life.
3. Write a brief note of encouragement to the student.
4. Use students' names in class more.
5. Show enthusiasm about being with students (even late in the day, week, or year).
6. Risk more personal self-disclosures, which help students see you as a real person. However, don't cross the line and go too far. Always take into account children's level of understanding and emotional vulnerability in disclosing information about yourself to them.
7. Be an active listener who carefully attends to what the student is saying, even if it is something trivial.
8. Let students know that you are there to support and help them.
9. Keep in mind that developing positive, trusting relationships takes time. This especially is the case for students from high-risk environments who might not initially trust your motives.

FIGURE 4 GUIDELINES FOR ESTABLISHING POSITIVE RELATIONSHIPS WITH STUDENTS

CONNECTING WITH STUDENTS: Best Practices
Strategies for Guiding Students to Share and Assume Responsibility

Following are some guidelines for getting students to share and assume responsibility in the classroom (Fitzpatrick, 1993):

1. *Involve students in the planning and implementation of school and classroom initiatives.* This participation helps to satisfy students' needs for self-confidence and belonging.

2. *Encourage students to judge their own behavior.* Rather than pass judgment on students' behavior, ask questions that motivate students to evaluate their own behavior. For example, you might ask, "Does your behavior reflect the class rules?" or "What's the rule?" Such questions place responsibility on the student. Initially, some students try to blame others or change the subject. In such situations, stay focused and guide the student toward accepting responsibility. Keep in mind that students don't develop responsibility overnight. Many student misbehaviors are ingrained habits that take a long time to break. Be patient one more time than the student expects—difficult to do, but good advice.

3. *Don't accept excuses.* Excuses just pass on or avoid responsibility. Don't even entertain a discussion about excuses. Rather, ask students what they can do the next time a similar situation develops.

4. *Let students participate in decision making by holding class meetings.* In his classic book, *Schools Without Failure,* William Glasser (1969) argued that class meetings can be used to deal with student behavior problems or virtually any issue that is of concern to teachers and students.

Choose Effective Reinforcers Find out which reinforcers work best with which students, and individualize reinforcement (Alberto & Troutman, 2017). For one student, the most effective reward might be praise; for another, it might be getting to do a favorite activity. Remember that pleasurable activities often are especially valuable in gaining students' cooperation. You might tell a student, "When you complete your math problems, you can go to the media area and play a computer game."

Use Prompts and Shaping Effectively Remember that if you wait for students to perform perfectly, they might never do so. A good strategy is to use prompts and shape students' behavior by rewarding improvement (Alberto & Troutman, 2017). Some prompts come in the form of hints or reminders, such as "Remember the rule about lining up." Shaping behavior involves rewarding a student for successive approximations to a specified target behavior. Thus, you might initially reward a student for getting 60 percent of her math problems right, then for 70 percent the next time, and so on.

Use Rewards to Provide Information About Mastery, Not to Control Students' Behavior Rewards that impart information about students' mastery can increase their intrinsic motivation and sense of responsibility (Vargas, 2009). However, rewards that are used to control students' behavior are less likely to promote self-regulation and responsibility. For example, a student's learning might benefit from being selected as student of the week because he or she engaged in a number of highly productive, competent activities. However, the student likely will not benefit from being given a reward for sitting still at a desk; such a reward is an effort by the teacher to control the student, and students in heavily controlled learning environments tend to act like "pawns."

> **Thinking Back/Thinking Forward**
> It is important to consider what rewards convey about competence. Connect to "Motivation, Teaching, and Learning."

DIVERSITY

CLASSROOM MANAGEMENT AND DIVERSITY

The growing diversity of students makes classroom management more challenging (Coronel & Gomez-Hurtado, 2015). Children of color, especially African American and Latinx children, and children from low-income backgrounds constitute a disproportionate number of referrals for discipline problems in schools (Rueda, 2015). A special concern is the high number of disciplinary actions that African American students, especially those who are male, experience (Simmons-Reed & Cartledge, 2014). African American male students are three times more likely to be suspended or expelled than their non-Latinx White male counterparts (Chatmon & Gray, 2015).

A number of scholars argue that miscommunication between teachers and students and teachers' lack of sensitivity to cultural and socioeconomic variations in students contribute to this disproportionate number of referrals (Banks, 2015; Koppelman, 2017). Cultural mismatches especially are likely to appear in schools where the teachers are overwhelmingly from non-Latinx White, middle-income backgrounds and the majority of the students are children of color from low-income backgrounds.

Engaging in culturally responsive teaching and demonstrating sensitivity to cultural and socioeconomic variations in students can help teachers to reduce discipline problems in their classroom (Holloway & Jonas, 2016). An increasing number of programs reveal that showing greater cultural sensitivity to socioculturally diverse students benefits those who are placed at risk for academic and emotional problems (Zusho et al., 2016). Weinstein, Tomlinson-Clarke, and Curran (2004) provided a conceptualization of culturally responsive classroom management that includes five essential components: teacher's "(a) recognition of one's own ethnocentrism; (b) knowledge of students' cultural backgrounds; (c) understanding of the broader social, economic, and political context; (d) ability and willingness to use culturally appropriate management strategies; and (e) commitment to building caring classrooms" (p. 25).

> **Thinking Back/Thinking Forward**
>
> Culturally responsive (or culturally relevant) teaching seeks to make connections with the learner's cultural background. Connect to "Educational Psychology: A Tool for Effective Teaching."

Review, Reflect, and Practice

③ Discuss how to create a positive classroom environment.

REVIEW
- What are some general strategies for creating a positive environment for learning?
- What are some hallmarks of good classroom rules?
- What are the best approaches for getting students to cooperate?
- What is important for teachers to know about classroom management and diversity?

REFLECT
- In your classroom, what standards of "good" behavior would be nonnegotiable? Would you be flexible about some things? Explain.

PRAXIS™ PRACTICE
1. Ms. Rockefeller has high expectations for her students' behavior. She is rather harsh with punishments when students do not live up to these expectations and accepts no explanations for noncompliance. Her standard response to excuses is "I don't want to hear it. You broke the rules. You know the consequences." Which management style does Ms. Rockefeller exemplify?
    a. authoritative
    b. authoritarian
    c. permissive
    d. neglectful
2. Which of the following is the best example of a clearly stated classroom procedure?
    a. Keep your hands to yourself.
    b. Put all homework in the homework folder when you come in.

continued

> ### Review, Reflect, and Practice
>
>   c. Respect other people's property.
>   d. Stay quietly in your seat with both feet flat on the floor.
> 3. Which teacher is most likely to gain the cooperation of students in following classroom rules and procedures?
>   a. Ms. Benes and her students developed a list of rules and procedures at the beginning of the school year; however, she does not enforce the rules and procedures she has established. There are no reinforcements for proper behavior and no consequences for inappropriate behavior.
>   b. Ms. Costanza wants her classroom to be very orderly. As a result, she punishes students for the slightest infractions.
>   c. Ms. Kramer's students participated in the development of classroom rules. They all agreed that each rule was necessary and that the procedures would make things run more smoothly. When students disobey a rule, she asks them if their behavior is appropriate.
>   d. Ms. Peterman has a long list of rules and procedures for students to follow. For instance, when they enter the classroom, they are to first put their homework in the proper folder, then change into their P.E. shoes. If students do these things in the opposite order, they are reprimanded.
> 4. During a class discussion in social sciences, a male African American high school student says that Mr. Smith, a non-Latinx White teacher, doesn't seem to understand the difficulties and discrimination that many ethnic minority groups have experienced. Which of the following is the most appropriate response of the non-Latinx White teacher?
>   a. Ignore what the student said rather than reinforcing what was said
>   b. Tell the student that he seems to be overreacting
>   c. Say that he appreciates the student's contribution to the discussion and that he hopes to better understand such difficulties and discrimination
>   d. State that he doesn't appreciate the student's lack of respect for his knowledge
>
> *Please see answer key at end of book . . . .*

LG 4 Identify some good approaches to communication for both students and teachers.

4 BEING A GOOD COMMUNICATOR

SPEAKING SKILLS

You and your students will benefit considerably if you have effective speaking skills and you work with your students on developing their speaking skills. Let's first explore some strategies for speaking with your class.

Speaking with the Class and Students In speaking with your class and with individual students, one of the most important things to keep in mind is to clearly communicate information (Grice et al., 2016; Hogan et al. 2017). *Clarity* in speaking is essential to good teaching.

Some good strategies for speaking clearly with your class include (Florez, 1999):

1. Selecting vocabulary that is understandable and appropriate for the level of your students

2. Speaking at an appropriate pace, neither too rapidly nor too slowly

3. Being precise in your communication and avoiding vagueness
4. Using good planning and logical thinking skills as underpinnings of speaking clearly with your class

Barriers to Effective Verbal Communication Barriers to effective verbal communication include (Gordon, 1970):

- *Criticizing.* Harsh, negative evaluations of another person generally reduce communication. An example of criticizing is telling a student, "It's your fault you flunked the test; you should have studied." Instead of criticizing, you can ask students to evaluate why they did not do well on a test and try to get them to arrive at an attribution that reflects lack of effort as the reason for the poor grade.
- *Name-calling and labeling.* These are ways of putting down the other person. Students engage in a lot of name-calling and labeling. They might say to another student, "You are a loser," or "You are stupid." Monitor students' use of such name-calling and labeling. When you hear this type of statement, intervene and talk with them about considering other students' feelings.
- *Advising.* Advising is talking down to others while giving them a solution to a problem. For example, a teacher might say, "That's so easy to solve. I can't understand why . . ."
- *Ordering.* Commanding another person to do what you want is often not effective because it creates resistance. For example, a teacher might yell at a student, "Clean up this space, right now!" Instead, a calm, firm reminder such as "Remember the rule of cleaning things up when we are finished" works better.
- *Threatening.* Threats are intended to control the other person by verbal force. For example, a teacher might say, "If you don't listen to me, I'm going to make your life miserable here." A better strategy is to approach the student more calmly and talk with the student about listening better.
- *Moralizing.* This means preaching to the other person about what he or she should do. For example, a teacher might say, "You know you should have turned your homework in on time. You ought to feel bad about this." Moralizing increases students' guilt and anxiety. A better strategy in this case is not to use words such as *should* and *ought* but, instead, to talk with the student in a less condemning way about why the homework was not turned in on time.

Giving an Effective Speech Not only will you be speaking in your class every day to your students in both formal and informal ways, but you also will have opportunities to give talks at educational and community meetings. Knowing some good strategies for giving a speech can significantly reduce your anxiety and help you deliver an effective speech (Pearson et al., 2017; Zarefsky, 2016).

Also, as most of us reflect on our experiences as students, we can remember few opportunities to give talks in class unless we took a specific class in speech. But not only can students be given speaking opportunities through formal presentations, they also can participate in panel discussions and debates. All these activities give students opportunities to improve their speaking, organizational, and thinking skills (Ford-Brown & Kindersley, 2017; Seiler et al., 2017).

The following guidelines for delivering an effective speech can benefit students as well as teachers (Alverno College, 1995):

- *Connect with the audience.* Talk directly to the audience; don't just read your notes or recite a memorized script.
- *State your purpose.* Keep this focus throughout the talk.
- *Effectively deliver the speech.* Use eye contact, supportive gestures, and effective voice control.
- *Use media effectively.* This can help the audience grasp key ideas and varies the pace of the talk.

Giving students opportunities to practice their speaking skills is a vastly underutilized aspect of elementary and secondary education. Fear of speaking in front of a group is consistently listed as the number one fear of adults. *How do you think you can help your students become more effective speakers?*

PeopleImages.com/Digital Vision/Getty Images

THROUGH THE EYES OF STUDENTS

Forensics Teacher Tommie Lindsey's Students

Tommie Lindsey teaches competitive forensics (public speaking and debate) at Logan High School in Union City, California. Forensics classes in most U.S. schools are mainly in affluent areas, but most of Lindsey's students come from impoverished or at-risk backgrounds. His students have won many public speaking honors.

The following comments by his students reflect Lindsey's outstanding teaching skills:

"He's one of the few teachers I know who cares so much. . . . He spends hours and hours, evenings, and weekends, working with us."

—Justin Hinojoza, 17

"I was going through a tough time. . . . Mr. Lindsey helped me out. I asked how I could pay back and he said, 'Just help someone the way I helped you.'"

—Robert Hawkins, 21

"This amazing opportunity is here for us students and it wouldn't be if Mr. Lindsey didn't create it."

—Michael Joshi, 17

As a ninth-grade student, Tommie Lindsey became a public speaker. He says that his English teacher doubted his ability, and he wanted to show her how good he could be at public speaking, preparing a speech that received a standing ovation. Lindsey remembers, "She was expecting me to fail, and I turned the tables on her. . . . And we do that with our forensic program. When we started, a lot of people didn't believe our kids could do the things they do."

For his outstanding teaching efforts, Tommie Lindsey was awarded a prestigious MacArthur Fellowship in 2005 (Source: Seligson, 2005).

Tommie Lindsey, working with his students on improving their public speaking and debate skills.
Tommie Lindsey

LISTENING SKILLS

Effectively managing your classroom will be easier if you and your students have good listening skills. Listening is a critical skill for making and keeping relationships (Devito, 2017; Manning, 2017). If you are a good listener, students, parents, other teachers, and administrators will be drawn to you. If your students are good listeners, they will benefit more from your instruction and will have better social relationships. Poor listeners "hog" conversations. They talk "to" rather than "with" someone. Good listeners actively listen (Beebe et al., 2016). They don't just passively absorb information. **Active listening** means giving full attention to the speaker, focusing on both the intellectual and the emotional content of the message.

Some good active listening strategies follow:

- Pay careful attention to the person who is talking, including maintaining eye contact.
- Paraphrase.
- Synthesize themes and patterns.
- Give specific feedback that describes the listener's feelings or provides some actionable suggestions to the speaker.

active listening A listening style that gives full attention to the speaker and notes both the intellectual and emotional content of the message.

NONVERBAL COMMUNICATION

In addition to what you say, you also communicate by how you fold your arms, cast your eyes, move your mouth, cross your legs, or touch another person. Indeed, many communication experts maintain that most interpersonal communication is nonverbal (Pearson et al., 2017). Even a person sitting in a corner, silently reading, is nonverbally communicating something, perhaps that he or she wants to be left alone. And when you notice your students blankly staring out the window, it likely indicates that they are bored. It is hard to mask nonverbal communication. Recognize that it can tell you how you and others really feel.

Let's further explore nonverbal communication by examining facial expressions, personal space, and silence. People's faces disclose emotions and telegraph what really matters to them (Alberts, et al., 2016). A smile, a frown, or a puzzled look all communicate.

Each of us has a personal space that at times we don't want others to invade. Not surprisingly, given the crowdedness of the classroom, students report that having their own space where they can put their materials and belongings is important to them. Make sure that all students have their own desks or spaces. Tell students that they are entitled to have this individual space, and that they should courteously respect other students' space.

In our fast-paced, modern culture we often act as if there is something wrong with anyone who remains silent for more than a second or two after something is said to them. After asking students a question, teachers need to remain silent long enough for students to think reflectively before giving an answer. By being silent, a good listener can observe the speaker's eyes, facial expressions, posture, and gestures for communication; think about what the other person is communicating; and consider what the most appropriate response is. Of course, silence can be overdone and is sometimes inappropriate. It is rarely wise to listen for an excessive length of time without making a verbal response.

Thinking Back/Thinking Forward

Waiting three to five seconds or more after asking a question can often produce better student responses. Connect to "Planning, Instruction, and Teaching."

Some specific technology tools that can used for classroom management and communication include the following:

- Class Dojo (www.classdojo.com) for tracking student behavior
- Faronics Insight (www.faronics.com/products/insight/) for managing student computers by controlling devices and access to them
- Remind (www.remind.com), a communication app for contacting parents and students

TECHNOLOGY

How would you describe the nonverbal behaviors of the teachers and the students in these two photographs?
(Left) Tim Pannell/Corbis/Getty Images; (right) F64/Photodisc/Getty Images

SELF-ASSESSMENT 1
Evaluating My Communication Skills

Good communication skills are critical for effectively managing a classroom. Read each of the statements and rate them on a scale from 1 (very much unlike me) to 5 (very much like me).

1. I know the characteristics of being a good speaker in class and with students.
2. I am good at public speaking.
3. I do not tend to dominate conversations.
4. I talk "with" people, not "to" people.
5. I don't criticize people very much.
6. I don't talk down to people or put them down.
7. I don't moralize when I talk with people.
8. I'm good at giving my full attention to someone when they are talking with me.
9. I maintain eye contact when I talk with people.
10. I smile a lot when I interact with people.
11. I know the value of silence in communication and how to practice it effectively.

1	2	3	4	5

SCORING AND INTERPRETATION

Look over your self-ratings. For any items on which you did not give yourself a 4 or 5, work on improving these aspects of your communication skills. Both you and your students will benefit.

We have discussed a number of communication skills that will help you manage your classroom effectively. To evaluate your communication skills, complete *Self-Assessment 1*.

Teachers were asked to describe communication skills that have been effective in their classrooms. Following are their responses.

EARLY CHILDHOOD At our preschool, we communicate in such a way that children know what they *can do,* not what they can't. For example, instead of telling children to "keep quiet," we tell them to "use their listening ears."

—HEIDI KAUFMAN, *MetroWest YMCA Child Care and Educational Program*

ELEMENTARY SCHOOL: GRADES K–5 I use a lot of call and response methods to get my second-graders' attention. For example, I say, "One, two, three, eyes on me," and the children respond, "One, two, eyes on you." On the first day of school, they are taught to stop what they are doing when they hear me say this and turn to me for new instructions or information.

—JANINE GUIDA POUTRE, *Clinton Elementary School*

MIDDLE SCHOOL: GRADES 6–8 One of the keys to communicating effectively is good listening skills. I teach my students to have respect for speakers by having them clear their desk of everything on it whenever someone, teacher or student, is presenting. This strategy assures that the class is listening and respecting the person making a presentation rather than doodling in notebooks or reading.

—MARK FODNESS, *Bemidji Middle School*

HIGH SCHOOL: GRADES 9–12 I show my students the importance of being an effective communicator by giving them a complicated set of directions verbally (such as how to properly fold a dinner napkin) and then asking them to do the task without talking to anyone or asking questions. After this activity, I hold a discussion on why it was impossible to do the task given the ineffective communication of instructions. This activity quickly shows students the value of communicating effectively.

—SANDY SWANSON, *Menomonee Falls High School*

Review, Reflect, and Practice

 4 Identify some good approaches to communication for both students and teachers.

REVIEW
- What are some barriers to effective speech? What are some principles of good speech? What is active listening and what can teachers and students do to develop active listening skills?
- What are some important aspects of nonverbal communication for teachers to understand?

REFLECT
- What are your own communication strengths and weaknesses? What might you do to improve your communication skills?

PRAXIS™ PRACTICE
1. Ms. Carmichael is upset with Zack, one of her fifth-grade students, because he has not turned in his homework for the third time in the past week. She is discussing the situation with him, trying to express the importance of turning in assignments on time. Which of the following is likely to be her best response to the situation?
   a. "Okay, Zack, you may turn it in tomorrow."
   b. "What is wrong with you, Zack? This is the third time in a week! I know you can do the work. Are you just plain lazy? Is that it? This is getting ridiculous. Do you want to fail?"
   c. "Zack, I know you can do the work. Are you trying to make things more difficult for me by not turning it in?"
   d. "Zack, I can't possibly assess your understanding of the material when you don't turn in your work. This can't continue. Please get it to me by the end of the day, and no more late work."
2. Edward and James are having a discussion about the best way to engage their students' interest in American history. Which of the following best exemplifies active listening?
   a. As Edward speaks about the importance of integrating electronic media into their courses, James interrupts with an argument that primary sources are much more useful and accurate.

continued

> ### Review, Reflect, and Practice
>
> b. As Edward speaks about the importance of integrating electronic media into their courses, James makes a rude noise and tells him that is a bunch of nonsense.
> c. As Edward speaks, James maintains eye contact and nods occasionally. However, James is really planning how he will counter Edward's assertion that electronic media will engage the students.
> d. As Edward speaks, James maintains eye contact, nods his head occasionally, and leans forward. When Edward has finished, James says, "So what you're saying is that if we used more electronic media, the kids would be more interested, right?"
>
> 3. As Edward is speaking about the importance of integrating electronic media into their American history courses, James checks his watch, looks toward the door, and drums his fingers on the desk. What message is James communicating?
>   a. anxiety
>   b. boredom
>   c. disdain
>   d. interest
>
> *Please see answer key at end of book . . . .*

LG 5 Formulate some effective approaches that teachers can use to deal with problem behaviors.

5 DEALING WITH PROBLEM BEHAVIORS

No matter how hard you have worked to plan and create a positive classroom environment, problem behaviors will emerge. It is important that you deal with them in a timely, effective manner.

MANAGEMENT STRATEGIES

Classroom management experts Carolyn Evertson and Edward Emmer (2009, 2017) distinguish between minor and moderate interventions for problem behaviors. Their approach is described in the following sections.

Minor Interventions Some problems require only minor interventions. These problems involve behaviors that, if infrequent, usually don't disrupt class activities and learning. For example, students might call out to the teacher out of turn, leave their seats without permission, engage in social talk when it is not allowed, or eat candy in class. When only minor interventions are needed for problem behaviors, these strategies can be effective (Evertson & Emmer, 2009, pp. 188–190):

- "*Use nonverbal cues.* Make eye contact with the student and give a signal such as a finger to the lips, a head shake, or a hand signal to issue a desist."
- *Keep the activity moving.* Sometimes transitions between activities take too long, or a break in activity occurs when students have nothing to do. In these situations, students might leave their seats, socialize, crack jokes, and begin to get out of control. A good strategy is not to correct students' minor misbehaviors in these situations but rather start the next activity in a more timely fashion. By effectively planning the day, you should be able to eliminate these long transitions and gaps in activity.

- *Move closer to students.* When a student starts misbehaving, simply moving near the student will often cause the misbehavior to stop.
- *"Redirect the behavior."* If students get off-task, let them know what they are supposed to be doing. You might say, "Okay, remember, everybody is supposed to be working on math problems."
- *"Provide needed instruction."* Sometimes students engage in minor misbehaviors when they haven't understood how to do the task they have been assigned. Unable to effectively do the activity, they fill the time by misbehaving. Solving this problem involves carefully monitoring students' work and providing guidance when needed.
- *Directly and assertively tell the student to stop.* Establish direct eye contact with the student, be assertive, and tell the student to stop the behavior. "Keep your comments brief and monitor the situation until the student complies. Combine this strategy with redirection to encourage desirable behavior."
- *"Give the student a choice."* Place responsibility in the student's hands by saying that he or she has a choice of either behaving appropriately or receiving a negative consequence. Be sure to tell the student what the appropriate behavior is and what the consequence is for not performing it.

Moderate Interventions Some misbehaviors require a stronger intervention than those just described—for example, when students abuse privileges, disrupt an activity, goof off, or interfere with your instruction or other students' work. Here are some moderate interventions for dealing with these types of problems (Evertson & Emmer 2009, pp. 177–178):

Carolyn Evertson (*center*, in red, shown in a COMP classroom), a leading expert on classroom management, created COMP, the Classroom Organization and Management Program, with Evelyn Harris. COMP includes many of the themes we have emphasized in developing a positive environment for learning. COMP emphasizes supporting students' learning and guiding students in taking responsibility for their own decisions, behavior, and learning. COMP also includes strategies for problem prevention, management and instruction integration, student involvement, and professional collaboration among teachers. The program is implemented through training workshops, classroom application, and collaborative reflection. Research has revealed that COMP results in positive changes in teacher and student behavior (Evertson & Harris, 1999).
Carolyn Everston

- *"Withhold a privilege or a desired activity."* Inevitably, you will have students who abuse privileges they have been given, such as being able to move around the classroom or to work on a project with friends. In these cases, you can revoke the privilege.
- *"Isolate or remove students."* In the chapter on behavioral and social cognitive approaches we discussed the time-out, which involves removing a student from positive reinforcement. If you choose to use a time-out, you have several options. You can (1) keep the student in the classroom, but deny the student access to positive reinforcement; (2) take the student outside the activity area or out of the classroom; or (3) place the student in a time-out room designated by the school. If you use a time-out, be sure to clearly identify the student's behavior that resulted in the time-out, such as "You are being placed in time-out for 30 minutes because you punched Derrick." If the misbehavior occurs again, reidentify it and place the student in time-out again. After the time-out, don't comment on how well the student behaved during the time-out; just return the student to the activity that was interrupted.
- *Impose a penalty.* A small amount of repetitious work can be used as a penalty for misbehavior. In writing, a student might have to write an extra page; in math, a student might have to do extra problems; in physical education, a student might have to run an extra lap. The problem with penalties is that they can harm the student's attitude toward the subject matter.

Students also can be made to serve a detention for their misbehaviors, at lunch, during recess, before school, or after school. Teachers commonly assign detentions for goofing off, wasting time, repeating rule violations, not completing assignments, and disrupting the class. Some detentions are served in the classroom; some schools have a detention hall where students can be sent. If the detention occurs in your classroom, you will have to supervise it. The length of the detention should initially be short—about 10 to 15 minutes—if the misbehavior is not severe. As when using the time-out, you will need to keep a record of the detention.

Using Others as Resources
Among the people who can help you get students to engage in more appropriate behavior are peers, parents, the principal or counselor, and mentors.

Peer Mediation Peers sometimes can be very effective at getting students to behave more appropriately. Peer mediators can be trained to help students resolve quarrels and change undesirable behaviors. For example, if two students have started to argue with each other, an assigned peer mediator can help to mediate the dispute, as described later in the chapter when we discuss conflict resolution.

Parent-Teacher Conference You can telephone the student's parents or confer with them in a face-to-face conference. Just informing them can sometimes get the student to improve behavior. Don't put the parents on the defensive or suggest that you are blaming them for their child's misbehavior in school. Just briefly describe the problem and say that you would appreciate any support that they can give you.

Enlist the Help of the Principal or Counselor
Many schools have prescribed consequences for particular problem behaviors. If you have tried unsuccessfully to deal with the behavior, consider asking the school's administration for help. This might involve referring the student to the principal or a counselor, which may result in a detention or warning to the student, as well as a parent conference with the principal. Letting the principal or counselor handle the problem can save you time. However, such help is not always practical on a regular basis in many schools.

Find a Mentor Earlier we underscored the importance of students having at least one person in their life who cares about them and supports their development. Some students, especially those from high-risk impoverished backgrounds, do not have that one person. A mentor can provide such students with the guidance they need to reduce problem behaviors (Pennanen et al., 2016; Roscoe, 2015). Another recent study indicated that the mentoring relationship was more likely to endure when youth initiated mentoring, such as when youth nominated mentors from the nonparental adults in their social network (such as teachers, family friends, extended family members) rather than when mentors were recommended by parents or program staff, and when mentors were of the same ethnic group as the youth (Schwartz et al., 2013). Also in this study, when the youth-initiated mentoring endured, the mentoring was linked to educational and vocational success three years later.

You likely will have some students in your class who can benefit from mentoring. Look around the community for potential mentors for students in high-risk, low-income circumstances or ask students to think of an individual that they would like to have as a mentor.

How do teachers handle student misbehavior in their classrooms? Following are their responses.

EARLY CHILDHOOD We teach our preschoolers that misbehavior always brings a consequence. We first speak to students about why the behavior is wrong and ways to conduct themselves next time. We also send notes home to parents when misbehavior occurs. A student will be placed in time-out as a last resort.

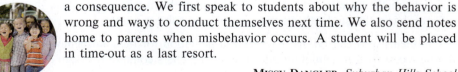

—MISSY DANGLER, *Suburban Hills School*

ELEMENTARY SCHOOL: GRADES K-5 I make it a point to call every parent during the first month of school to establish a nonthreatening rapport and to have a

good-natured telephone call be the first communication of the year between us. During the call, I introduce myself, say something positive about his or her child, and ask the parent if he or she has any questions for me. If and when there is a call to be made to a parent for student misbehavior, I have already made positive contact with the parent, and the parent may be more willing to help with the problem.

—JANINE GUIDA POUTRE, *Clinton Elementary School*

MIDDLE SCHOOL: GRADES 6-8 If a student presents a problem that may cause harm to other classmates, either remove that student or remove the entire class. Students look to adults for safety.

—FELICIA PETERSON, *Pocantico Hills School*

HIGH SCHOOL: GRADES 9-12 I treat all of my students with respect, even the ones that are misbehaving. For example, when I see signs of misbehavior, I meet with

the student individually outside of class and say something like "I get distracted when you talk to Sally while I'm speaking. Could you work on that for me? I don't want to stop class, because I think that would be embarrassing for you." Most students are receptive to the respect that I give them in these situations.

—JOSEPH MALEY, *South Burlington High School*

DEALING WITH AGGRESSION

Violence in schools is a major, escalating concern. In many schools, it now is common for students to fight, bully other students, or threaten each other and teachers verbally or with a weapon. These behaviors can arouse your anxiety and anger, but it is important to be prepared for their occurrence and handle them calmly. Avoiding an argument or emotional confrontation will help you to solve the conflict.

School Violence Let's now explore different types of aggressive behavior problems and teacher strategies for how to effectively deal with them.

Fighting Classroom management experts Carolyn Evertson and Edmund Emmer (2009, 2017) offer the following suggestions for dealing with students who are fighting. In elementary school, you can usually stop a fight without risking injury to yourself. If for some reason you cannot intervene, immediately get help from other teachers or administrators. When you intervene, give a loud verbal command: "Stop!" Separate the fighters, and as you keep them separated, tell other students to leave or return to what they are doing. If you intervene in a fight that involves secondary school students, you will probably need the help of one or two other adults. Your school likely will have a policy regarding fighting. If so, you should carry it out and involve the principal and/or parents if necessary.

Generally, it is best to let the fighters have a cooling-off period so that they can calm down. Then meet with the fighters and get their points of view on what precipitated the fight. Question witnesses if necessary. Have a conference with the fighters, emphasizing the inappropriateness of fighting, the benefits of taking each other's perspective, and the value of cooperation.

Bullying Significant numbers of students are victimized by bullies (Connell et al., 2015; Naidoo et al., 2016; Wang et al., 2016; Wu et al., 2016). In a national survey of more than 15,000 sixth- through tenth-grade students, nearly one of every three students said that they had experienced occasional or frequent involvement as a victim

RESEARCH

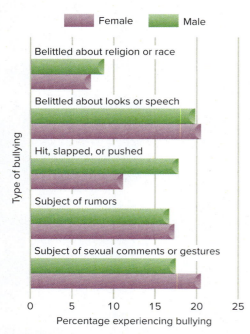

FIGURE 5 BULLYING BEHAVIORS AMONG U.S. YOUTH

This graph shows the types of bullying most often experienced by U.S. youth. The percentages reflect the extent to which bullied students said that they had experienced a particular type of bullying. In terms of gender, note that when they were bullied, boys were more likely to be hit, slapped, or pushed than girls were.

bystander someone who witnesses bullying occur electronically or in person; bystanders can play different roles; intervening in bullying can cause it to stop in less than 10 second in over half of incidences.

or perpetrator in bullying (Nansel et al., 2001). In this study, bullying was defined as verbal or physical behavior intended to disturb someone less powerful. As shown in Figure 5, being belittled about looks or speech is one of the most frequent types of bullying (Peets, et al., 2011). Boys are more likely to be bullies than girls, but gender differences regarding victims of bullies are less clear.

Who is likely to be bullied? In the study just described, boys and younger middle school students were most likely to be affected (Nansel et al., 2001). Children who said they were bullied reported more loneliness and difficulty in making friends, while those who did the bullying were more likely to have low grades and to smoke cigarettes and drink alcohol.

Researchers have found that anxious, socially withdrawn, and aggressive children are often the victims of bullying (Rubin et al., 2016). Anxious and socially withdrawn children may be victimized because they are nonthreatening and unlikely to retaliate if bullied, whereas aggressive children may be the targets of bullying because their behavior is irritating to bullies. Overweight and obese children are often bullied (Puhl & King, 2013).

Social contexts such as poverty, family, school, and peer groups also influence bullying (Prinstein & Giletta, 2016; Troop-Gordon & Ladd, 2015). A recent meta-analysis indicated that lack of positive parenting behavior (including having good communication, a warm relationship, being involved, and engaging in supervision of their children) and the presence of negative parenting behavior (including child maltreatment—physical abuse and neglect) was related to a greater likelihood of becoming either a bully or a victim at school (Lereya et al., 2013).

The social context of the peer group also plays an important role in bullying (Troop-Gordon & Ladd, 2015). Researchers have found that 70 to 80 percent of victims and their bullies are in the same school classroom (Salmivalli & Peets, 2009). Classmates are often aware of bullying incidents and in many cases witness bullying (Barhight et al., 2015). In many cases, bullies torment victims to gain higher status in the peer group and bullies need others to witness their power displays. Many bullies are not rejected by the peer group. These witnesses are referred to as **bystanders**. Recent research has focused on the different types of bystanders and their effects on bullying. Bystanders can play different roles: outsiders do not get involved, while reinforcers and assistants support or help the bully. Defenders, on the other hand, support the victim. Intervening in bullying can cause it to stop in less than 10 second in over half of incidences (Espalage et al., 2012). See this helpful website managed by the U.S. Department of Health and Human Services for more information: https://www.stopbullying.gov/research-resources/bystanders-are-essential/index.html.

What are the outcomes of bullying? A recent study revealed that peer victimization in the fifth grade was associated with worse physical and mental health in the tenth grade (Bogart et al., 2014). Researchers have found that children who are bullied are more likely to experience depression, engage in suicidal ideation, and attempt suicide than their counterparts who have not been the victims of bullying (Undheim, 2013; Yen et al., 2014). A recent study indicated that peer victimization during the elementary school years was a leading indicator of internalizing problems (depression, for example) in adolescence (Schwartz et al., 2015). Also, a longitudinal study found that children who were bullied at 6 years of age were more likely to have excess weight gain when they were 12 to 13 years of age (Sutin et al., 2016). And another recent study revealed that being a victim of bullying in childhood was linked to increased use of mental health services by the victims five decades later (Evans-Lacko et al., 2016).

Consider these cases in which bullying was linked to suicide: an 8-year-old jumped out of a two-story building in Houston; a 13-year-old hanged himself in Houston; and teenagers harassed a girl so mercilessly that she killed herself in Massachusetts. Further, a recent analysis concluded that bullying can have long-term effects, including difficulty in forming lasting relationships and resolving problems at work (Wolke & Lereya, 2015).

An increasing concern is peer bullying and harassment on the Internet (called *cyberbullying*) (Barlett, 2015; Vollink et al., 2016; Wolke et al., 2016). A study involving third- to sixth-graders revealed that engaging in cyber aggression was related to

CONNECTING WITH STUDENTS: Best Practices
Strategies for Reducing Bullying

Here are some suggestions to reduce bullying:

1. *Confront a bully in a firm manner.* It is usually a good idea to confront the bully in private when possible. If you need to confront the bully in public (classroom or playground when other students are present), approach the bully, describe what you saw, explain why it is not acceptable, and impose a consequence. A warning, time out, apology to victim, and loss of privileges are possible consequences.

2. *Get older peers to serve as monitors for bullying and intervene when they see it taking place.* Choose students who are respected by their peers when selecting these monitors.

3. *Be aware that bullying often occurs outside the classroom, so you may not actually see it taking place.* Also, many victims of bullying don't report the bullying to adults. Unsupervised areas such as the playground, bus, and school corridors are common places where students are bullied.

4. *If you observe bullying in your classroom or in other locations, you will need to make a decision about whether it is serious enough to report to school authorities or parents.* If you observe a student engaging in bullying on multiple occasions, set up a conference with the bully's parents and ask for their help in stopping the bullying.

5. *Get together with other teachers and the school administration to develop school-wide rules and sanctions against bullying and post them throughout the school.*

6. *Become educated about ways that your school and teachers can communicate effectively with students about cyberbullying.* Information about preventing cyberbullying can be found at www.stopcyberbullying.org/. Also, an excellent book to read on the topic is *Bullying Beyond the Schoolyard: Preventing and Responding to Cyberbullying* (Hinduja & Patchin, 2015).

What are some strategies for reducing bullying?
Lopolo/Shutterstock

loneliness, lower self-esteem, fewer mutual friendships, and lower peer popularity (Schoffstall & Cohen, 2011). Further, recent research found that cyberbullying was more strongly associated with suicidal ideation than traditional bullying (van Geel et al., 2014). Further, a longitudinal study found that adolescents experiencing social and emotional difficulties were more likely to be both cyberbullied and traditionally bullied than traditionally bullied only (Cross et al., 2015). In this study, adolescents targeted in both ways stayed away from school more than their counterparts who were traditionally bullied only.

TECHNOLOGY

Increasing interest is being directed to finding ways to prevent and treat bullying and victimization (Cantone et al., 2015; Flannery et al., 2016; Menesiniet et al., 2016; Olweus, 2013; Saarento, et al., 2014). School-based interventions vary greatly, ranging from involving the whole school in an antibullying campaign to providing individualized social skills training (Alsaker & Valanover, 2012). One of the most promising bullying intervention programs has been created by Dan Olweus (2003, 2013). This program focuses on 6- to 15-year-olds with the goal of decreasing opportunities and rewards for bullying. School staff are instructed in ways to improve peer relations and make schools safer. When properly implemented, the program reduces bullying by 30 to 70 percent (Ericson, 2001; Olweus, 2003, 2013). Information on how to implement the program can be obtained from the Center for the Prevention of Violence at the University of Colorado (https://cspv.colorado.edu/). A recent research review concluded that bullying interventions focused on the whole school, such as Olweus', are more effective than interventions involving classroom curricula or social skills training (Cantone et al., 2015). Also, a recent teacher intervention in elementary and secondary schools to decrease bullying that focused on increasing bullies' empathy and condemning their behavior was effective in increasing the bullies' intent to stop being a bully (Garandeau et al., 2016). In this study, blaming the bully had no effect.

Defiance or Hostility Toward the Teacher   Edmund Emmer and Carolyn Evertson (2009, 2017) discussed the following strategies for dealing with students who defy you or are hostile toward you. If students get away with this type of behavior, it likely will continue and even spread. Therefore, try to defuse the event by keeping it private and handling the student individually, if possible. If the defiance or hostility is not extreme and occurs during a lesson, try to depersonalize it and say that you will deal with it in a few minutes to avoid a power struggle. At an appropriate later time, meet with the student and spell out any consequence the misbehavior might merit.

In extreme and rare cases, students will be completely uncooperative, in which case you should send another student to the office for help. In most instances, though, if you stay calm and don't get into a power struggle with the student, the student will calm down, and you can talk with the student about the problem.

Review, Reflect, and Practice

 Formulate some effective approaches that teachers can use to deal with problem behaviors.

REVIEW
- What are some minor and moderate interventions for managing problem behaviors in the classroom environment? Who else can help?
- What can the teacher do about fighting, bullying, and defiance? What are some effective school-based bullying intervention programs?

REFLECT
- How worried are you about problem behaviors among the students you plan to teach? In view of your own current skills, personality, and values, what steps could you begin to take to prepare yourself for dealing with them?

PRAXIS™ PRACTICE

1. Mr. Martin is telling his students how to complete their assignment for tomorrow. While he talks, Sally and Shelly are discussing their after-school plans. Mr. Martin should:
   a. interrupt his instructions to say, "Listen up, girls or you'll be spending your after-school hours with me"
   b. interrupt his instructions to ask, "Is there something that you would like to share with the class, girls?"
   c. keep talking, but look directly at Sally and Shelly; if that doesn't work, slowly approach them
   d. stop his instructions and wait silently for the girls to stop talking, while looking directly at them, then say, "Thank you, ladies"

2. Ken is a fifth-grade student who is not well liked by his peers. They tease him about the way he looks, the way he dresses, his lack of coordination, and his lack of emotional self-regulation. The bulk of this belittling takes place on the playground during recess. The teasing often reduces Ken to tears, which seems to add fuel to the fire. Which of the following is most likely to reduce this bullying behavior?
   a. in-school suspensions for the bullies
   b. isolating Ken from his peers so he does not have to deal with the bullying
   c. removing the bullies' recess privileges
   d. social-skills training for both the bullies and Ken

Please see answer key at end of book . . . .

Connecting with the Classroom: Crack the Case

The Chatty Student

Mrs. Welch was a new middle school language-arts teacher. Prior to beginning her new position, she developed a classroom management plan that mirrored the code of conduct for the school. She expected the students to behave respectfully toward her and toward their classmates. She also expected them to respect school property and the learning environment. In addition, she expected them to keep their hands, feet, and possessions to themselves. Minor behavioral infractions were to result in a verbal warning. Further infractions would net more severe consequences in steps: a detention, a referral to the office, and a call to the students' parents. Mrs. Welch was pleased with her management plan. She distributed it to students on the first day of class. She also distributed it to parents at the annual Back-to-School Night during the first week of school.

Darius, a student in one of Mrs. Welch's seventh-grade classes, was what Mrs. Welch termed "chatty." He was very social and spent much of his class time talking to other students rather than working. Mrs. Welch tried moving him to different parts of the room and tried seating him next to students to whom she had never seen him talk, neither of which decreased his chattiness. He simply made new friends and continued chatting, sometimes disrupting the class in the process. She tried seating him next to girls, and this seemed to make things even worse.

Darius was very bright in addition to being very social. Although he was only in seventh grade, he was taking algebra with a group of mathematically advanced eighth-grade students. This was something of an anomaly in this school; in fact, it had never been done previously. The algebra teacher, Mrs. Zaccinelli, and Darius had a good relationship. He *never* disrupted her class or misbehaved in any way in her class. Mrs. Zaccinelli was amazed to hear that Darius did not always behave appropriately in his other classes.

Mrs. Zaccinelli served as Mrs. Welch's mentor. She had helped Mrs. Welch to write her classroom management plan and served as a sounding board when she had difficulties. At one point when Mrs. Welch was discussing her eighth-grade classes, Mrs. Zaccinelli referred to inclusion in the eighth-grade algebra class as "a privilege, not a right." She further told Mrs. Welch that she expected her students to behave appropriately at all times.

The next day, Darius was especially talkative in class. Mrs. Welch asked him to stop talking. He did, but he resumed his chatter within five minutes. When he began talking again, Mrs. Welch took him aside and told him loudly, "That's it, Darius. I'm going to have you removed from algebra class. You know taking that class is a privilege, not a right."

Darius was stunned. He sat quietly for the rest of the period but did not participate. He made no eye contact with Mrs. Welch or any other students. The rest of the day was something of a blur to him. He had no idea how he would explain this to his parents.

When Darius told his mother he was going to be removed from algebra for his behavior in language arts, she immediately went to see Mrs. Welch. She tried to tell Mrs. Welch that to remove Darius from algebra would be to deny him the free and appropriate public education to which he (and all other students) was entitled. Mrs. Welch held her ground and insisted that she could and would have his placement altered.

1. What are the issues in this case?
2. Is removal from algebra class an appropriate consequence for Darius? Why or why not?
3. Do you think removal from algebra class would have a positive effect on Darius' behavior? Why or why not?
4. What impact do you think this would have on his motivation in school?
5. How do you think this situation will affect the relationship between Mrs. Welch and Darius?
6. What do you think Darius' mother will do now?
7. How do you think Mrs. Zaccinelli will react when she hears about the situation?
8. How do you think the principal will react?
9. What should Mrs. Welch do?
10. How would Mrs. Welch's strategy of moving Darius to quiet him be characterized?
    a. This is an example of a minor intervention.
    b. This is an example of a moderate intervention.
    c. This is an example of a severe intervention.
    d. This is an example of an effective intervention.
11. Which of the following is likely to be the most effective way for Mrs. Welch to deal with Darius' chatty behavior?
    a. Make Darius write out a page of the dictionary.
    b. Put tape over Darius' mouth.
    c. Isolate Darius from his peers for the remainder of the period.
    d. Send Darius to the office for the principal to discipline.

Connecting with Learning: Reach Your Learning Goals

1 WHY CLASSROOMS NEED TO BE MANAGED EFFECTIVELY: Explain why classroom management is both challenging and necessary.

Management Issues in Elementary and Secondary School Classrooms

- Many management issues are similar across elementary and secondary school classrooms. However, differences in elementary and secondary classrooms have meaning for the way classrooms need to be managed.
- Elementary school teachers often see the same 20 to 25 students all day long; secondary school teachers see 100 to 150 students about 50 minutes a day. Confinement, boredom, and interaction with the same people all day in elementary school can create problems.
- Secondary school teachers have to get the lesson moving quickly. They also might see a greater range of problems, and their students can have more long-standing problems that are more difficult to modify. These problems can be more severe than those of elementary school students. Secondary school students might demand more elaborate and logical explanations of rules and discipline.

The Crowded, Complex, and Potentially Chaotic Classroom

- Six reasons that classrooms are crowded, complex, and potentially chaotic are (1) multidimensionality, (2) simultaneous activities going on, (3) events occurring at a rapid pace, (4) unpredictable events, (5) lack of privacy, and (6) classroom histories.

Getting Off to the Right Start

- Good strategies for getting off to the right start with students are to (1) establish expectations for behavior and resolve student uncertainties, (2) make sure that students experience success, (3) be available and visible, and (4) be in charge.

Emphasizing Instruction and a Positive Classroom Climate

- The focus in educational psychology used to be on discipline. Today it is on developing and maintaining a positive classroom environment that supports learning. This involves using proactive management strategies rather than being immersed in reactive discipline tactics.
- Historically, the well-managed classroom was conceptualized as a "well-oiled machine," but today it is more often viewed as a "beehive of activity." Kounin found that good classroom managers effectively manage the group's activities.

Management Goals and Strategies

- Goals and strategies for classroom management include (1) helping students spend more time on learning and less time on non-goal-directed activity (maintain activity flow, minimize transition times, and hold students accountable) and (2) preventing students from developing academic and emotional problems.

2 DESIGNING THE PHYSICAL ENVIRONMENT OF THE CLASSROOM: Describe the positive design of the classroom's physical environment.

Principles of Classroom Arrangement

- Basic principles of effective design of the classroom's physical environment include (1) reducing congestion in high-traffic areas, (2) making sure that you can easily see all students, (3) making often-used teaching materials and student supplies easily accessible, and (4) making sure that all students can see whole-class presentations.

Arrangement Style

- Classroom arrangement styles include auditorium, face-to-face, offset, seminar, and cluster. It is important to personalize the classroom, to consider what activities students will be engaging in, to draw up a floor plan, to involve students in classroom design, and to try out the arrangement and be flexible in redesigning it.

3 CREATING A POSITIVE ENVIRONMENT FOR LEARNING: Discuss how to create a positive classroom environment.

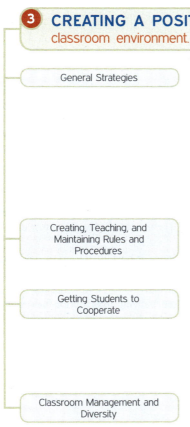

General Strategies

- Use an authoritative style of classroom management rather than an authoritarian or permissive style. The authoritative style involves engaging in considerable verbal give-and-take with students, having a caring attitude toward students, and placing limits on student behavior when necessary.
- Authoritative teaching is linked with competent student behavior. Also, being sensitive to ethnic and socioeconomic variations in students is an important aspect of managing the classroom effectively.
- Kounin's work revealed other characteristics that were associated with effective classroom management: exhibiting withitness, coping with overlapping situations, maintaining smoothness and continuity in lessons, and engaging students in a variety of challenging activities.

Creating, Teaching, and Maintaining Rules and Procedures

- Distinguish between rules and procedures and consider the appropriateness of including students in the discussion and generation of rules. Classroom rules should be (1) reasonable and necessary, (2) clear and comprehensible, (3) consistent with instructional and learning goals, and (4) consistent with school rules.

Getting Students to Cooperate

- Getting students to cooperate involves (1) developing a positive relationship with students; (2) getting students to share and assume responsibility (involve students in the planning and implementation of school and classroom initiatives, encourage students to judge their own behavior, don't accept excuses, and give the self-responsibility strategy time to work); and (3) rewarding appropriate behavior (choose effective reinforcers, use prompts and shaping effectively, and use rewards to provide information about mastery).

Classroom Management and Diversity

- The increasing diversity of students makes managing the classroom more complex. Too often teachers are not knowledgeable about the cultural background of their students and as a consequence miscommunicate with them.
- Cultural mismatches may especially occur in schools in which the teachers are overwhelmingly non-Latinx White and the students are mainly from ethnic minority groups. Engaging in culturally responsive teaching and classroom management can help teachers reduce discipline problems in the classroom.

4 BEING A GOOD COMMUNICATOR: Identify some good approaches to communication for both students and teachers.

Speaking Skills

- Some barriers to effective speech include being imprecise and vague, using vocabulary inappropriate for the students' level, and speaking too quickly or too slowly.
- You and your students will benefit considerably if you have effective speaking skills and you work with your students on developing their speaking skills.
- Speaking effectively with the class and students involves being a clear communicator, connecting with the audience, using media effectively, and avoiding barriers to verbal communication such as criticizing, name-calling, ordering, and threatening. Both teachers and students can benefit from knowing how to give speeches effectively.

Listening Skills

- Active listening occurs when a person gives full attention to the speaker, focusing on both the intellectual and the emotional content of the message. Some good active listening strategies are to (1) pay careful attention to the person who is talking, including maintaining eye contact; (2) paraphrase; (3) synthesize themes and patterns; and (4) give specific feedback.

Nonverbal Communication

- A number of communication experts stress that the majority of communication is nonverbal rather than verbal. It is hard to mask nonverbal communication, so a good strategy is to recognize that nonverbal communication usually reflects how a person really feels.
- Nonverbal communication involves facial expressions and eye communication, touch, space, and silence.

continued

⑤ DEALING WITH PROBLEM BEHAVIORS: Formulate some effective approaches that teachers can use to deal with problem behaviors.

Management Strategies

- Interventions can be characterized as minor or moderate.
- Minor interventions involve using nonverbal cues, keeping the activity moving, moving closer to students, redirecting the behavior, giving needed instruction, directly and assertively telling the student to stop the behavior, and giving the student a choice.
- Moderate interventions include withholding a privilege or a desired activity, isolating or removing students, and imposing a penalty or detention. A good management strategy is to have supportive resources. These include using peers as mediators, calling on parents for support, enlisting the help of a principal or counselor, and finding a mentor for the student.

Dealing with Aggression

- Violence is a major, escalating concern in schools. Be prepared for aggressive actions on the part of students so that you can calmly cope with them. Try to avoid an argument or emotional confrontation.
- Helpful guidelines for dealing with fighting, bullying, and defiance or hostility toward the teacher include developing and posting school-wide rules and sanctions against bullying, defusing the hostile event by keeping it private and handling the student individually, and if needed sending another student to the office for help. Two school-based bullying intervention programs are Olweus Bullying Prevention and Bully-Proofing Your School (for more information see the National Center for School Engagement's website on Bully-Proofing Your School).

KEY TERMS

active listening 488
auditorium style 477
authoritarian classroom
  management style 480
authoritative classroom
  management style 480
bystander 496
cluster style 477
face-to-face style 477
offset style 477
permissive classroom
  management style 480
seminar style 477
withitness 481

PORTFOLIO ACTIVITIES

Now that you have a good understanding of this chapter, complete the following exercises to expand your thinking.

Independent Reflection

1. **Cultivating Respectful Student-Teacher Relationships.** How self-disclosing and open should teachers be with students? It is important for teachers to develop positive relationships with students, but is there a point at which teachers become too close to their students? Write a personal reflection on this issue, incorporating thoughts about how it might relate to your future work as a teacher. (INTASC: Principle *3, 9*)

Research/Field Experience

2. **Researching School Discipline Policies.** Interview school counselors at an elementary, a middle, or a high school. Ask them to describe the discipline policies at their schools and to evaluate how well they work. Also ask them to describe the most difficult student problem they have ever dealt with. Write up that problem as a case study. (INTASC: Principles *3, 9*)

Collaborative Work

3. **Creating Classroom Rules.** List the rules you feel your students must follow. Describe how you might react when students break these rules. Then get together with three or four of your classmates and discuss each other's lists. Revise your rules based on their feedback. (INTASC: Principle *3*)

Design elements: Apple: Turnervisual/Getty Images; Magnifying Glass with Folders: ayax/Getty Images; Families: rangepuppies/Getty Images; Hands, Computer Screen, Pencil, Magnifying Glass with Book: McGraw-Hill; Early Childhood: Ariel Skelley/Brand X/Getty Images; Elementary School: Vetta/Getty Images; Middle School: Hill Street Studios/Getty Images; High School: Dean Mitchell/Getty Images

chapter 15

STANDARDIZED TESTS AND TEACHING

chapter outline

① The Nature of Standardized Tests

Learning Goal 1 Discuss the nature and purpose of standardized tests as well as the criteria for evaluating them.

Standardized Tests and Their Purposes
Criteria for Evaluating Standardized Tests

② Aptitude and Achievement Tests

Learning Goal 2 Compare aptitude and achievement tests and describe different types of achievement tests as well as some issues involved in these tests.

Comparing Aptitude and Achievement Tests
Types of Standardized Achievement Tests
High-Stakes State Standards-Based Tests
Standardized Tests of Teacher Candidates

③ The Teacher's Roles

Learning Goal 3 Identify the teacher's roles in standardized testing.

Preparing Students to Take Standardized Tests
Understanding and Interpreting Test Results
Using Standardized Test Scores to Plan and Improve Instruction

④ Issues in Standardized Tests

Learning Goal 4 Evaluate some key issues in standardized testing.

Standardized Tests, Alternative Assessments, and High-Stakes Testing
Diversity and Standardized Testing

People do not have equal talents. But all individuals should have an equal opportunity to develop their talents.

—John F. Kennedy
U.S. President, 20th Century

Ocean/Comstock Images/Corbis

Connecting with Teachers Barbara Berry

Barbara Berry teaches French and humanities at Ypsilanti High School in Ypsilanti, Michigan, where she also is chairperson of the foreign languages department. She offers this story related to standardized tests:

> I had a fourth-year French student who was a wonderful student and clearly had a gift for languages. A minority student, she had been recruited by a major state university and offered a "full-ride" scholarship, provided she met certain requirements on the Scholastic Assessment Test (SAT). She took the test and did well on the verbal part but not well enough on the math part to meet the scholarship requirements. She was taking her fourth year of math classes and receiving above-average grades but said she just didn't like math and didn't understand it.
>
> Although I was teaching French at the time, I knew that I enjoyed math and had done well in school and on standardized tests. I knew that the SAT math section includes a lot of algebra. I offered to tutor her before she retook the SAT. She accepted the offer. I obtained some algebra materials from the math department to help work with her. Mostly, though, she worked on her own, reading the book and doing problems, only coming to me when she encountered problems. We met about once a week. About six weeks later, she retook the test and improved her math SAT score by 110 points. She got the scholarship.
>
> I did not teach this student much math, although I did help her work through some of the more difficult problems. What I did most to help her were two things: (1) I communicated my own enthusiasm for math and expressed confidence in her ability to do it, and (2) I focused her efforts on the material that the test assesses. Since we related so well with each other in my French class, I felt that I could help her feel better about her ability to do math.

Preview

As Barbara Berry's story shows, standardized tests can have a major impact on students' lives. They are widely used to evaluate students' learning and achievement. Although they are increasingly used to compare students' performance in different schools, districts, states, and countries, they are not without controversy. A significant change in standardized testing in recent years is that there is much less emphasis on traditional standardized tests and more emphasis given to end-of-year standards based on tests that are created by states and used for teacher, school, and district accountability.

We begin our discussion in this chapter by examining some basic ideas about standardized tests and then distinguish aptitude and achievement tests. Then we explore what your role as a teacher is likely to be in regard to standardized testing and conclude the chapter by describing several important issues in standardized testing.

LG 1 Discuss the nature and purpose of standardized tests as well as the criteria for evaluating them.

1 THE NATURE OF STANDARDIZED TESTS

- Standardized Tests and Their Purposes
- Criteria for Evaluating Standardized Tests

Chances are, you have taken a number of standardized tests. In kindergarten, you may have taken a school readiness test, in elementary school some basic skills or achievement tests, and in high school the SAT or ACT test for college admission. But what does it mean to say that a test is "standardized"? And what purpose is served by standardized testing?

STANDARDIZED TESTS AND THEIR PURPOSES

Standardized tests have uniform procedures for administration and scoring and often allow a student's performance to be compared with the performance of other students at the same age or grade level on a national basis. Standardized tests can serve a number of purposes:

- *Provide information about students' progress.* Standardized tests are a source of information about how well students are performing. Students in one class might get *A*'s but perform at a mediocre level on a nationally standardized test, and students in another class might get *B*'s and do extremely well on the same nationally

standardized tests Tests with uniform procedures for administration and scoring. They assess students' performance in different domains and allow a student's performance to be compared with the performance of other students at the same age or grade level on a national basis.

standardized test. Without an external, objective marker such as a standardized test, individual classroom teachers have difficulty knowing how well their students are performing compared with students elsewhere in the state or nation. Standardized tests also are used to show growth in achievement across months or years.

- *Diagnose students' strengths and weaknesses.* Standardized tests also can provide information about a student's learning strengths or weaknesses. Different subscale scores can be compared to show strengths and weaknesses, and individually administered tests can be used to pinpoint the student's learning weaknesses.
- *Provide evidence for placement of students in specific programs.* Standardized tests can be used to make decisions about whether a student should be allowed to enter a specific program. In elementary school, a standardized test might be used to provide information for placing students in different reading groups. In high school, a standardized test might be used to determine which math classes a student should take. In some cases, standardized tests are used along with other information to evaluate whether a student might be allowed to skip a grade or to graduate. Students also might take standardized tests to determine their suitability for particular careers. One type of standardized test—the *benchmark* or *interim assessment*—is given quarterly to help teachers determine the areas of achievement that need further instruction.
- *Provide information for planning and improving instruction.* In conjunction with other information about students, scores from standardized tests can be used by teachers in making decisions about instruction. For example, students' scores on a standardized test of reading skills administered at the start of the school year can help teachers determine the level at which they need to gear their reading instruction. Students' scores on a standardized test at the end of the year might inform teachers about how effective their reading instruction has been, information that could be used to continue similar instruction or modify it accordingly.
- *Contribute to accountability.* Schools and teachers are increasingly being held accountable for students' learning. Although this application is controversial, standardized tests are being used to determine how effectively schools are using tax dollars. In Texas, principals can lose their jobs if their school's standardized test scores don't measure up. In Maryland, schools that don't do well forfeit thousands of dollars in reward money. Interest in accountability has led to the creation of **standards-based tests**, which assess skills that students are expected to have mastered before they can be promoted to the next grade or permitted to graduate. Schools that use standards-based tests often require students who do not pass the tests to attend special programs in the summer that will help them reach the minimum level of competency required by the school system. **High-stakes testing** is using tests in a way that will have important consequences for the student, affecting decisions such as whether the student will be promoted to the next grade or be allowed to graduate. Later in the chapter, we will discuss state-mandated tests, which are increasingly being used to make such "high-stakes" decisions. For now, though, note that an important theme throughout this chapter is that a standardized test should not be the only method for evaluating a student's learning. Nor should standardized tests by themselves be considered sufficient information in holding schools accountable for students' learning (McMillan, 2014; Popham, 2017).

DEVELOPMENT

> **Thinking Back/Thinking Forward**
> Teachers need to integrate assessment in their planning. Connect to "Classroom Assessment and Grading."

What are some of the most important purposes of standardized tests?
Stretch Photography/Blend Images/Getty Images

standards-based tests Tests that assess skills that students are expected to master before they can be promoted to the next grade or permitted to graduate.

high-stakes testing Using tests in a way that will have important consequences for the student, affecting such decisions as whether the student will be promoted or be allowed to graduate.

CRITERIA FOR EVALUATING STANDARDIZED TESTS

Among the ways to evaluate standardized tests are to understand whether the test is norm-referenced or criterion-referenced, and the extent to which the test score is valid, reliable, and fair. Let's begin our discussion by examining norm-referenced and criterion-referenced tests.

Norm-Referenced and Criterion-Referenced Tests Standardized tests can be norm-referenced or criterion-referenced. A **norm group** is the group of individuals previously tested that provides a basis for interpreting a test score. Thus, in **norm-referenced tests** a student's score is interpreted by comparing it with how others (the norm group) performed.

The norm-referenced test is said to be based on *national norms* when the norm group consists of a nationally representative group of students. For example, a standardized test for fourth-grade science knowledge and skills might be given to a national sample of fourth-grade students. The scores of the representative sample of thousands of fourth-grade students become the basis for comparison. This norm group should include students from urban, suburban, and rural areas; different geographical regions; private and public schools; boys and girls; and different ethnic groups. Based on an individual student's score on the standardized science test, the teacher can determine whether a student is performing above, on a level with, or below a national norm (Brookhart & Nieto, 2015). The teacher also can see how the class as a whole is performing in relation to the general population of students.

Unlike norm-referenced tests, **criterion-referenced tests** are standardized tests in which the student's performance is compared with established criteria or standards (McMillan, 2014). State standardized tests are typically criterion-referenced tests that do not use norms. For example, state criterion-referenced tests might assess whether a student has attained a level of achievement termed "proficient," or reached a certain percentage level, such answering 80 percent of the items correctly. These levels of achievement are set by the state and used to determine annual yearly progress (AYP) for No Child Left Behind requirements. Criterion-referenced tests are designed to assess students' skills and knowledge in specific areas, such as English, math, and science.

Validity, Reliability, and Fairness Whether the standardized test is norm-referenced or criterion-referenced, three important ways to evaluate the test involve determining whether it is valid, reliable, and fair. Let's explore how to evaluate a standardized test's validity first.

Validity Traditionally, validity has been defined as the extent to which a test measures what it is intended to measure. However, an increasing number of assessment experts in education argue that not just the characteristics of the test itself are valid or invalid—rather, it also is important to consider the inferences that are made about the test scores (McMillan, 2014, 2016). Thus, **validity** involves the extent to which a test measures what it is intended to measure and whether inferences about test scores are accurate and appropriate.

In terms of the test characteristics themselves—the substance of the test—three types of validity can be described: content validity, criterion validity, and construct validity. A valid standardized test should have good **content validity**, which is the test's ability to sample the content that is to be measured. This concept is similar to "content-related evidence." For example, if a standardized fourth-grade science test purports to assess both content information and problem-solving skills, then the test should include items that measure content information about science and items that measure problem-solving skills.

Another form of validity is **criterion validity,** which is the test's ability to predict a student's performance as measured by other assessments or criteria. How might criterion validity be assessed for the standardized science test? One method is to get a representative sample of fourth-grade teachers to evaluate the competence of the students in their science classes and then compare those competence ratings with the students' scores on the standardized tests. Another method is to compare the scores of students on the standardized test with the scores of the same students on a different test that was designed to test mastery of the same material.

Criterion validity can be either concurrent or predictive (Biggs & Colesante, 2015; Davison et al., 2015). **Concurrent validity** is the relation between the test's

---

norm group The group of individuals previously tested that provides a basis for interpreting a test score.

norm-referenced tests Standardized tests in which a student's score is interpreted by comparing it with how others (the norm group) performed.

criterion-referenced tests Standardized tests in which the student's performance is compared with established criteria.

validity The extent to which a test measures what it is intended to measure and whether inferences about the test scores are accurate and appropriate.

content validity A test's ability to sample the content that is to be measured.

criterion validity A test's ability to predict a student's performance as measured by other assessments or criteria.

concurrent validity The relation between a test's scores and other criteria that are currently (concurrently) available.

scores and other criteria that are currently (concurrently) available. For example, does the standardized fourth-grade science test correspond to students' grades in science this semester? If it does, we say that test has high concurrent validity. **Predictive validity** is the relation between test scores and the student's future performance. For example, scores on the fourth-grade science test might be used to predict how many science classes different students will take in high school, whether middle school girls are interested in pursuing a science career, or whether students will win an award in science at some point in the future.

A third type of validity is *construct validity*. A *construct* is an unobservable trait or characteristic of a person, such as intelligence, creativity, learning style, personality, or anxiety. **Construct validity** is the extent to which there is evidence that a test measures a particular construct. Construct validity is the broadest of the types of validity we have discussed and can include evidence from concurrent and predictive validity (Salvia et al., 2017). Judgments about construct validity might also rely on a description of the development of the test, the pattern of the relations between the test and other significant factors (such as high correlations with similar tests and low correlations with tests measuring different constructs), and any other type of evidence that contributes to understanding the meaning of test scores. Because a construct typically is abstract, a variety of evidence may be needed to determine whether a test validly measures a particular construct.

Earlier we indicated that we should consider not only the substance of the test in determining validity but also whether inferences about the test scores are accurate (McMillan, 2014, 2016). Let's look at an example of how this might work. A school superintendent decides to use test scores from a standardized test given to students each spring as an indicator of teacher competence. In other words, the test scores are being used to *infer* whether teachers are competent. These are the validity questions in this situation: How reasonable is it to use standardized test scores to measure teacher competence? Is it actually true (accurate) that teachers whose students score high are more competent than teachers whose students score low?

If it is stated that a test is valid and reliable, what does that mean? What are some different types of validity and reliability?
Christopher Futcher/iStockphoto/Getty Images

Reliability **Reliability** is the extent to which a test produces a consistent, reproducible score. To be called reliable, scores must be stable, dependable, and relatively free from errors of measurement (Popham, 2017). Reliability can be measured in several ways, including test-retest reliability, alternate-forms reliability, and split-half reliability.

Test-retest reliability is the extent to which a test yields the same performance when a student is given the same test on two occasions. Thus, if the standardized fourth-grade science test is given to a group of students today and then given to them again a month later, the test would be considered reliable if the students' scores were consistent across the two testings. There are two negative features of test-retest reliability: Students sometimes do better the second time they take the test because of their familiarity with it, and some students may have learned information in the time between the first test and the second test that changes their performance.

Alternate-forms reliability is determined by giving different forms of the same test on two different occasions to the same group of students and observing how consistent the scores are. The test items on the two forms are similar but not identical. This strategy eliminates the likelihood that students will perform better on the second test administration due to their familiarity with the items, but it does not eliminate a student's increase in knowledge and increased familiarity with the testing procedures and strategies.

Split-half reliability involves dividing the test items into two halves, such as the odd-numbered and even-numbered items. The scores on the two sets of items are compared to determine how consistently the students performed across each set. When split-half reliability is high, we say that the test is *internally consistent*. For

predictive validity The relation between test scores and the student's future performance.

construct validity The extent to which there is evidence that a test measures a particular construct. A construct is an unobservable trait or characteristic of a person, such as intelligence, learning style, personality, or anxiety.

reliability The extent to which a test produces a consistent, reproducible score.

test-retest reliability The extent to which a test yields the same performance when a student is given the same test on two or more occasions.

alternate-forms reliability Reliability judged by giving different forms of the same test on two different occasions to the same group of students to determine how consistent their scores are.

split-half reliability Reliability judged by dividing the test items into two halves, such as the odd-numbered and even-numbered items. The scores on the two sets of items are compared to determine how consistently the students performed across each set.

example, on the standardized fourth-grade science test, the students' scores on the odd-numbered and even-numbered items could be compared. If they scored similarly on the two sets of items, we could conclude that the science test had high split-half reliability.

Reliability is influenced by a number of errors in measurement. A student can have adequate knowledge and skill, yet still not perform consistently across several tests because of a number of internal and external factors. Internal factors include health, motivation, and anxiety. External factors include inadequate directions given by the examiner, ambiguously created items, poor sampling of information, and inefficient scoring. When students perform inconsistently across the same or similar tests of their knowledge and skill, careful analysis should be made of internal and external factors that may have contributed to the inconsistency.

Validity and reliability are related. A test score that is valid is reliable, but a test score that is reliable is not necessarily valid. People can respond consistently on a test, but the test might not be measuring what it purports to measure. To understand this, imagine that you have three darts to throw. If all three fall close together, you have reliability. However, you have validity only if all three hit the bull's-eye.

Fairness and Bias Fair tests are unbiased and nondiscriminatory (McMillan, 2014). They are not influenced by factors such as gender, ethnicity, or subjective factors such as the bias of a scorer. When tests are fair, students have the opportunity to demonstrate their learning so that their performance is not affected by their gender, ethnicity, disability, or other factors unrelated to the purpose of the test.

An unfair test is a test that puts a particular group of students at a disadvantage. This often occurs when there is something about the test that makes it more difficult for students with certain characteristics. For instance, suppose a test that is designed to assess writing skills asks students to write a short story about a boy who practices very hard to be good in football and makes the team. Clearly, this type of item will be easier for boys than girls because boys are generally more familiar with football, so the test will be unfair to girls as an assessment of their writing skills. Consider also an item that might be used to assess reading comprehension. The reading passage is about a sailing experience. Thus, students who have had experience in sailing are likely to have an easier time reading and understanding the passage than those who have not. It is impossible to completely eliminate all unfair aspects of a test for every student, but test-makers can do much to create tests that are as fair as possible.

For students with disabilities, fairness often requires adaptations in administering the test. Many of the adaptations depend on the particular disability (Turnbull et al., others, 2016). The goal is to lessen the negative influence of the disability on the trait being tested. For example, for students with a hearing disability, be sure that the directions are written; for students with a visual problem, be sure that directions are given orally.

Thinking Back/Thinking Forward

Establishing high-quality assessments that are valid, reliable, and fair is an important goal for teachers when they construct tests to evaluate students' learning and achievement. Connect to "Classroom Assessment and Grading."

Review, Reflect, and Practice

1 Discuss the nature and purpose of standardized tests as well as the criteria for evaluating them.

REVIEW
- What is meant by standardized test? What are the uses of standardized tests?
- What are norm-referenced and criterion-referenced tests? Why are validity, reliability, and fairness important in judging the quality of a standardized test?

REFLECT
- Give an example of test scores that are reliable but not valid.

Review, Reflect, and Practice

PRAXIS™ PRACTICE

1. Which of the following is NOT an example of using the results of a standardized test to provide information for planning and improving instruction?
   a. At Lincoln Elementary School, students take a standardized achievement test each year to help determine who is in need of specialized services.
   b. At Jefferson Elementary School, teacher salary increases are based in part on student performance on the state-mandated standardized test.
   c. Mr. Whitney uses the results of the social studies portion of the state-mandated standardized achievement test to help him to see how well his instruction is working to help his students meet state standards in history.
   d. Ms. Walker uses the results of a standardized reading test to place her students into small instructional reading groups. She gives the same test several times throughout the school year to gauge progress and regroup students.

2. Which of the following is the best example of the predictive validity of a test?
   a. Students who score well on the ACT taken in their junior year in high school tend to do better in their first year of college than those who score poorly.
   b. The reading portion of a standardized test is supposed to measure both reading comprehension and vocabulary knowledge. It contains a section related to vocabulary and a reading passage with questions that follow.
   c. Students who do well on the state-mandated standardized test also do well on a nationally normed standardized test.
   d. Students who do well on the reading section of the state-mandated standardized test also get good grades in reading.

Please see answer key at end of book . . . .

2 APTITUDE AND ACHIEVEMENT TESTS

LG 2 Compare aptitude and achievement tests and describe different types of achievement tests as well as some issues involved in these tests.

There are two main types of standardized tests: aptitude tests and achievement tests. First, we will define and compare these types of tests, then examine different types of achievement tests. Next, we'll describe high-stakes state standards-based tests, as well as standardized tests of teacher candidates.

COMPARING APTITUDE AND ACHIEVEMENT TESTS

An **aptitude test** is designed to predict a student's ability to learn a skill or accomplish something with further education and training. Aptitude tests include general mental ability tests such as the intelligence tests (Stanford-Binet, Wechsler scales, and so on) that we described in the chapter on individual variations. They also include tests used to predict success in specific academic subjects or occupational areas. For example, one aptitude test might be given to students to predict their future success in math, whereas another might be given to predict whether an individual is likely to do well in sales or medicine.

An **achievement test** is intended to measure what the student has learned or what skills the student has mastered. However, the distinction between aptitude and

> **Thinking Back/Thinking Forward**
> Controversy characterizes what intelligence is and how to assess it. Connect to "Individual Variations."

aptitude test A type of test that is used to predict a student's ability to learn a skill or accomplish something with further education and training.

achievement test A test that measures what the student has learned or what skills the student has mastered.

achievement tests is sometimes blurred. Both types of tests assess a student's current status, the questions they use are often quite similar, and usually the results of the two kinds of tests are highly correlated.

The SAT that you may have taken as part of your admission to college is usually described as an aptitude test, but the SAT can be an aptitude test or an achievement test, depending on the purpose for which it is used. If it is used to predict your success in college, it is an aptitude test. If it is used to determine what you have learned (such as vocabulary, reading comprehension, and math skills), it is an achievement test.

TYPES OF STANDARDIZED ACHIEVEMENT TESTS

There are numerous types of standardized achievement tests (Kara & Celikler, 2015; Osadebe, 2015). One common way to classify them is as survey batteries, specific subject tests, or diagnostic tests.

Survey Batteries A *survey battery* is a group of individual subject-matter tests that is designed for a particular level of students. Survey batteries are the most widely used national norm-referenced standardized tests (McMillan, 2008). Some common batteries are the California Achievement Tests, Iowa Tests of Basic Skills, Metropolitan Achievement Tests, and Stanford Achievement Test Series.

Many survey batteries also contain a number of subtests within a subject area. For example, the Metropolitan Achievement Tests include reading as one of the subject areas at each level. The reading subtests on the Metropolitan Tests include vocabulary, word recognition, and reading comprehension.

In their early years, survey batteries consisted of multiple-choice items to assess the student's content knowledge. However, recent editions have increasingly included open-ended items that evaluate the student's thinking and reasoning skills.

Tests for Specific Subjects Some standardized achievement tests assess skills in a particular area such as reading or mathematics. Because they focus on a specific area, they usually assess the skill in a more detailed, extensive way than a survey battery. Two examples of specific area tests that involve reading are the Woodcock Reading Mastery Tests and the Gates-McKillop-Horowitz Reading Diagnostic Test. Some standardized subject-area tests cover such topics as chemistry, psychology, or computer science that are not included in survey batteries.

Diagnostic Tests As we said earlier, diagnosis is an important function of standardized testing. *Diagnostic testing* consists of a relatively in-depth evaluation of a specific area of learning. Its purpose is to determine the specific learning needs of a student so that those needs can be met through regular or remedial instruction (Cil, 2015; Kim, 2015). Reading and mathematics are the two areas in which standardized tests are often used for diagnosis.

Test publishers of many national norm-referenced standardized achievement tests claim that their tests can be used for diagnosis (McMillan, 2008). However, for a test to be effective in diagnosis it should have several test items for each skill or objective that is measured, and many of these national tests fall short in this regard.

HIGH-STAKES STATE STANDARDS-BASED TESTS

As the public and government have demanded increased accountability of how effectively schools are educating our nation's children, state standards-based tests have taken on a more powerful role. Indeed, a recent trend in standardized testing is that much less attention is being given to traditional standardized tests and far more emphasis is placed on end-of-year standards based on tests created by states and used for accountability purposes. Most teachers today are much more concerned with these accountability tests than aptitude or more traditional standardized achievement tests.

State tests today tend to be standards based end-of-year tests that are required for states to receive federal education funds. In most cases, these tests serve multiple purposes, including making decisions about student remediation, promotion, and graduation, as well as holding teachers, schools, and districts accountable for providing high-quality standards-based instruction for all students. States have mandated tests for many years, but their emphasis has recently changed. Prior to the 1990s, their content often was not closely linked with what was actually taught and learned in the classroom. The early state-mandated assessments simply provided an overall view of how students in a state were performing in certain subject areas, especially reading and mathematics. This is similar to the National Assessment of Educational Progress (NAEP), which is the largest nationally representative, longitudinal assessment of what students in the U.S. know and can do in various subject areas.

In the 1990s, efforts were initiated to connect state-mandated testing to state-endorsed instructional objectives. Most states already have identified or are in the process of identifying objectives that every student in the state is expected to achieve. These objectives—often called standards—form the basis not only for these mandated standards-based tests but also for such activities as teacher education and curriculum decisions. Teachers are strongly encouraged to incorporate these objectives into their classroom planning and instruction. In many states, the objectives are reflected in the achievement tests that are given to every student in the state. Many school districts use pacing guides for curriculum to ensure that all students are adequately prepared for the state-mandated tests.

The Format of State Standards-Based Tests

State-standards-based tests contain mostly or only multiple-choice items. These types of items, however, do not support or promote constructivist learning. When constructivist-based assessments are included, they typically involve short-answer items or writing prompts. Very few states include a portfolio as part of their assessment. Almost all states use criterion-referenced scoring, which means that the student's score is evaluated against predetermined standards.

Possible Advantages and Uses of High-Stakes Testing

A number of policy makers argue that high-stakes state standards-based testing will have a number of positive effects:

- Improved student performance
- More time teaching the subjects tested
- High expectations for all students
- Identification of poorly performing schools, teachers, and administrators
- Improved confidence in schools as test scores increase

The widest uses of these tests for guiding the progress of individual students have to do with decisions regarding remediation, promotion, and graduation. Remediation consists of assigning students who do not do well on the tests to special classes. Such remediation usually occurs after school, on Saturday, or during the summer. State-level funding for remedial education is on the rise, though national level data is limited.

Many advocates of state standards-based tests argue that students should not be promoted to the next grade without reaching a certain standard of performance on the tests. In this regard, the goal is to end social promotion (promotion based on the idea that students should not be left behind their age-mates).

State standards-based tests are also being used in many states to determine whether a student should be allowed to graduate from high school. Such a decision can have a major impact on a youth's future. In addition, state standards-based tests are used to make decisions about school and staff accountability. Holding schools accountable means using test scores to place the schools in designated categories, such as watch/warning (which is publicly reported and implies that improvement is expected); probation (which usually requires the school to submit a comprehensive reform plan); failing/in crisis (which requires serious outside assistance in developing an improvement plan); accredited, accredited with warning, and nonaccredited. This puts considerable pressure on schools to do everything possible to obtain passing scores.

Criticism of State Standards-Based Tests Critics of the state standards-based tests argue that state-mandated tests lead to these negative consequences (McMillan, 2002):

- *Dumbing down the curriculum with greater emphasis on rote memorization than on problem-solving and critical-thinking skills.* In one analysis, most state tests focused on less-demanding knowledge and skills rather than more-complex cognitive skills (Quality Counts, 2001). This narrows the curriculum and focuses it on lower-order cognitive skills. Adhering to a test-driven curriculum often means superficial coverage of topics.
- *Teaching to the test.* Teachers increasingly teach knowledge and skills that are to be covered on the state tests. They spend inordinate amounts of time on test-like activities and practice tests, with less time for actual teaching of important content and skills.
- *Discriminating against low-socioeconomic-status (SES) and ethnic minority children.* This results when disproportionate percentages of these children do not meet the state standards, while higher-SES and non-Latinx White students do. Researchers have found that students who are placed in the lowest tracks or remedial programs—disproportionately low-income and minority students—are most likely to experience subsequent inferior teaching and reduced achievement (Zusho et al., 2016). There is evidence that high-stakes state standards-based testing that rewards or sanctions schools based on average student scores can create incentives for pushing low-scorers into special education, holding them back a grade, and encouraging them to drop out of school so that the schools' average scores will look better (Darling-Hammond, 2001).
- *Narrowing the curriculum.* Because of the potential negative consequence of poor performance on state-mandated tests, many schools limit the curriculum to only what is covered on the test. In some cases, non-tested subjects, such as foreign language or art, are deemphasized.

RESEARCH

For these reasons and others, the American Psychological Association, the American Educational Research Association, and the National Council on Measurement in Education have issued standards for the use of tests, noting that test scores are too limited and unstable to be used as the sole source of information for any major decision about student placement or promotion. Test scores should always be used in combination with other sources of information about student achievement when making important decisions about students (National Research Council, 2001).

There are a number of concerns about the way high-stakes testing currently is structured (National Council of Teachers of English, 2014; Sadker & Zittleman, 2016). One major concern involves the validity of the inferences that can be drawn from the results (National Research Council, 2001). Just documenting higher test scores does not mean that education has improved. Indeed, if the tests are assessing the wrong skills or are flawed, it could mean just the opposite. As yet, we do not know if the high-stakes testing is causing students to be better prepared for college and the workplace. Thus, high-stakes tests are not a panacea or quick fix for improving education.

Yet another concern is the extent to which high-stakes testing is useful for improving teaching and learning—the ultimate goal of educational reforms (Wei et al., 2015). Most current high-stakes tests provide very limited information for teachers and administrators about why students do not perform well or how they can modify instruction to improve student achievement. Most of the high-stakes tests provide only general information about where a student stands relative to peers (such as scoring at the 63rd percentile) or whether the students have not performed well in certain domains (such as performing below the basic level in mathematics). Such tests do not provide information about whether students are using misguided strategies to solve problems or identify specific concepts in a domain that students do not understand.

THROUGH THE EYES OF STUDENTS

It's As If a Test Score Is All There Is to a Person

Spend enough time in school and you start to think that standardized tests are the only things that matter in life. My standardized test scores are disappointing, but I take pride in being in the top 4 percent of my class. I have a 4.0 GPA. If I can pull off those kinds of grades in tough classes—including three Advanced Placement courses—I'm forced to wonder, what do these tests really prove?

It's as if a test score is all there is to a person. I enjoy all kinds of creative writing, and I spend long nights trying to understand school subjects, rather than just memorize formulas. But none of this matters for standardized tests.

—*Tania Garcia*
Twelfth-Grade Student
Oakland High School
Oakland, California

High-stakes tests, given their infrequent administration, propensity for producing anxiety, and requirements that they assess many standards, are not adequate on their own for diagnosing student learning needs or informing instructional planning in any great detail. More specialized, norm-referenced standardized testing (such as the Woodcock-Johnson III Diagnostic Reading Battery) and/or frequent, ongoing assessments, covered in the chapter on classroom assessment and grading, are needed for this.

In sum, most current high-stakes tests do not provide information about the types of interventions that would improve students' performance or even yield information about students' strengths and weaknesses. Moreover, the validity of the information that high-stakes tests can provide for evaluating the effectiveness of teachers and schools (for accountability purposes) has been called into question. The American Educational Research Association made a statement in 2015 cautioning against the use of value-added models (VAM) for high-stakes decisions, such as evaluation of educators and educator preparation programs. VAM, which is still used by a number of states to statistically estimate the amount of student learning attributable to the teacher based on annual high-stakes tests, has been challenged in a numerous lawsuits.

No Child Left Behind In the introductory chapter of this text we described the No Child Left Behind (NCLB) Act, the federal government's legislation that was signed into law in 2002. NCLB is the U.S. government's effort to hold schools and school districts accountable for the success or failure of their students. The legislation shifts responsibility to the states, with states being required to create their own standards for students' achievement in mathematics, English/language arts, and science. Reading and math assessments in grades 3 to 8 were required through 2006, and beginning in the 2007–2008 school year, science assessments were made in elementary, middle, and high schools. The goal was that by 2014 every U.S. student would test to proficiency in core math and literacy skills (Shaul, 2007). With the 2015 passage of the Every Student Succeeds Act (ESSA; the latest reauthorization of the Elementary and Secondary Education Act or ESEA), states are required to test students in reading and math annually in grades 3–8 and once in high school. Students must also be tested in science once during elementary school, once in middle school, and once in high school.

> **Thinking Back/Thinking Forward**
>
> Because of NCLB, standards-based instruction has become a major issue in U.S. education. Connect to "Educational Psychology: A Tool for Effective Teaching."

States are required to create an accountability system that ensures students are making adequate annual progress in the subject areas just mentioned. Schools that fail to make *adequate yearly progress (AYP)* for two consecutive years are labeled "underperforming." Underperforming schools are to be given special help, but they must give parents the option of moving their children to a better-performing school. If underperforming schools don't improve after four years, states are required to implement major staff and curriculum changes in the schools, and if progress is not made after five years, states must close the schools. A difficulty in achieving AYP is that it must be achieved not only for the entire school but certain subgroups of students as well, including those who are economically disadvantaged, students from ethnic minority groups, students with disabilities, and students with limited English proficiency (Hallahan et al., 2015; Smith et al., 2016).

RESEARCH

Also as part of the No Child Left Behind legislation, states and districts are required to provide report cards that show a school's performance level, so that the public is aware of which schools are underperforming. Another aspect of the No Child Left Behind legislation is that all teachers now are required to be "highly qualified," which means being licensed and having an academic major in the field in which they are teaching. Schools are required to notify parents if a teacher is not "highly qualified." One analysis revealed considerable variability across states in what constitutes a highly qualified teacher (Birman et al., 2007). The percentage of teachers who fell into the "not highly qualified category" was higher for special education teachers, teachers of limited proficiency English students, middle school teachers, and teachers in high-poverty and high ethnic minority schools.

Each state is allowed to have different criteria for what constitutes passing or failing grades on tests designated for NCLB inclusion. This has led to a number of problems. For example, an analysis of NCLB data indicated that almost every fourth-grade student in Mississippi knows how to read but only half of Massachusetts's students do (King, 2007). When these students take a common assessment, Massachusetts students' achievement is much higher than Mississippi students' achievement. Clearly, Mississippi's standard for passing the reading test is far below that of Massachusetts. In the recent analysis involving state-by-state comparisons, it was clear that many states had taken the safe route and were keeping the passing bar low. Thus, while one of NCLB's goals was to raise standards for achievement in U.S. schools, allowing states to set their own standards likely has lowered achievement.

A number of criticisms of No Child Left Behind have been made. Some critics argue that the NCLB legislation will do more harm than good (Lewis, 2007). One widely adopted criticism stresses that using a single score from a test as the sole indicator of students' and teachers' progress and competence represents a very narrow aspect of students' and teachers' skills. This criticism is similar to the one leveled at IQ testing, described in the chapter on individual variations.

To more accurately assess student progress and achievement, many psychologists and educators argue that a number of measures should be used—including tests, quizzes, projects, portfolios, and classroom observations—rather than a single score on a single test. Also, the tests schools are using to assess achievement and progress as part of NCLB don't measure such important skills as creativity, motivation, persistence, flexible thinking, and social skills. Critics point out that teachers and schools are spending far too much class time "teaching only to the test" by drilling students and having them memorize isolated facts at the expense of more student-centered constructivist teaching that focuses on higher-level thinking skills, which students need for success in life.

Another criticism is that the increased cost of carrying out standardized testing on a statewide basis, including creating tests, administering them, scoring them, and reporting their results to the federal government, comes at a time when most states are facing budget crunches. Having to spend so much more money on testing means that some existing resources and programs in other areas will have to be trimmed or eliminated.

Yet another criticism of NCLB is that high-stakes testing encourages test score inflation. Test score inflation occurs when over the course of several years scores rise but do not reflect actual improvements in student learning.

DIVERSITY

One goal of NCLB is to close the ethnic achievement gap that characterizes lower achievement by African American and Latinx students and higher achievement by Asian American and non-Latinx White students. However, leading expert Linda Darling-Hammond (2007) concluded that NCLB has failed to reach this goal. She criticizes NCLB for inappropriate assessment of English language learners and students with special needs, strong incentives to exclude low-achieving students from school to achieve test score targets, and the continued shortage of highly qualified teachers in high-need schools.

Other criticisms of NCLB have been voiced. Some individuals are concerned that in the era of No Child Left Behind policy there is a neglect of students who are gifted in the effort to raise the achievement level of students who are not doing well. So too is there mounting concern that No Child Left Behind legislation has harmed the development of students' creative thinking by focusing attention on the memorization of content. And there is concern that the No Child Left Behind policy encourages a performance rather than a mastery orientation to achievement.

Educators are increasingly interested in ways that technology can be used effectively in conjunction with standardized tests. The growing emphasis on accountability and data-driven decision making occasioned by the No Child Left Behind legislation has prompted educators to think differently about how standardized assessments and resulting data can inform classroom instruction and ultimately affect student achievement. Educators across the country, therefore, are working hard to develop strategies that provide standardized test data to stakeholders at all levels of the educational system and offer teachers technical assistance to administer assessments and use results effectively.

A good example is the state of New Mexico's early literacy program. A recipient of a federal Department of Education Reading First grant, the state recognized that Reading First offered them not only a unique opportunity to support literacy instruction, but also a way to collect and use data in a standardized fashion. State education officials contracted with Wireless Generation, a company that provides mobile software for early literacy assessments that teachers can use to administer assessments and record student data that are immediately made available in graphic form. This lets teachers view a student's assessment results as well as individual student data in relation to previous assessments or assessment data from other students in the same classroom (Good & Kaminski, 2003).

Teachers were asked about their opinions of the No Child Left Behind Act. Following are their responses.

A New Mexico teacher using technology to improve student assessment.

Martha McArthur, Reading First Program, NM

EARLY CHILDHOOD Our preschool receives state funding so that financially disadvantaged children receive a quality preschool experience that their parents would

not otherwise be able to afford. The No Child Left Behind Act is controversial and continues to be hotly debated; however, no matter what your opinion is, unless educational opportunities are created for the least financially able, the American educational system will never be equal for all. Everyone deserves a chance to shine, and a quality preschool education is a start.

—VALARIE GORHAM, *Kiddie Quarters, Inc.*

ELEMENTARY SCHOOL: GRADES K–5 The NCLB Act is an idealistic approach to measuring student growth and teacher effectiveness. Just as no one program works in every classroom, we cannot expect all children to meet the same standards regard-

less of their background or experiences. The stress of having to meet state benchmarks and increase scores on state and/or national tests has taken a toll on veteran teachers. For us, teaching is no longer fun—we are now required to teach so many test-specific skills that we are unable to instill a lifelong love of learning in our students.

—KAREN PERRY, *Cooper Mountain Elementary School*

MIDDLE SCHOOL: GRADES 6–8 NCLB is a typical example of how the education "pendulum" swings too far in any given direction. Although testing is important, NCLB makes testing the ultimate measuring tool. Many students who do not excel

at reading or math (or who struggle with standardized tests) are seen as failures, as are the schools they attend. Ironically, these students and schools spend so much time trying to remediate for the tests that they are not allowed to explore other options in which the student might thrive.

—MARK FODNESS, *Bemidji Middle School*

HIGH SCHOOL: GRADES 9–12 I find it somewhat ridiculous that teachers are graded by how well their students do. Are dentists judged by how many patients have zero cavities? On the other hand, NCLB does hold teachers accountable and raises the bar. In that sense, it is beneficial.

—JENNIFER HEITER, *Bremen High School*

> **Thinking Back/Thinking Forward**
>
> Criticisms of NCLB include neglect of children who are gifted, harm of children's development of creative thinking skills, and encouragement of a performance rather than a mastery achievement motivation. Connect to "Learners Who Are Exceptional" and "Motivation, Teaching, and Learning."

Common Core In 2009, the Common Core State Standards Initiative was endorsed by the National Governors Association in an effort to implement more rigorous state guidelines for educating students. The Common Core Standards specify what students should know and the skills they should develop at each grade level in various content areas (Common Core State Standards Initiative, 2016). Forty-six states initially agreed to implement the Standards, but they have generated considerable controversy. At least 10 states have now downgraded participation in Common Core (for example, substantially revising the standards and renaming them in Florida) or withdrawn from national tests associated with it. Some critics argue that the Standards are simply a further effort by the federal government to control education and that they emphasize a "one size fits all" approach that pays little attention to individual variations in students. Supporters say that the Standards provide much-needed detailed guidelines and important milestones for students to achieve. Common Core enthusiasts also argue that the Standards focus more on critical thinking, problem solving, communication, and technology than No Child Left Behind does.

Every Student Succeeds Act (ESSA)   The most recent initiative in U.S. education is the *Every Student Succeeds Act (ESSA)* that was passed into law in December 2015 and was to be fully implemented in the 2017–2018 school year (Rothman, 2016). The law replaced No Child Left Behind in the process of modifying but not completely eliminating standardized testing. ESSA retains annual testing for reading and writing success in grades 3 to 8, then once more in high school. The new law also allows states to scale back the role that tests have in holding schools accountable for student achievement. And schools must use at least one nonacademic factor—such as student engagement—when tracking schools' success.

Other aspects of the new law include still requiring states and districts to improve their lowest-performing schools and to ensure that they improve their work with historically underperforming students, such as English-language learners, ethnic minority students, and students with a disability. Also, states and districts are required to put in place challenging academic standards, although they can opt out of state standards involving Common Core.

World-Class Standards   Because U.S. students are assessed periodically on standardized tests in reading, math, and science, their achievement can be compared with that of students in many other countries. How are U.S. students faring versus students in other countries? Recent international assessments of student achievement in reading, math, and science include (1) Progress in International Reading Literacy Study (PIRLS), which assesses fourth-grade students' reading achievement every five years (first assessment in 2001); (2) Program for International Student Assessment (PISA), which tests reading, math, and science achievement of 15-year-old students every three years (first assessment in 2000); and (3) Trends in International Mathematics and Science Study (TIMSS), which assesses math and science achievement of fourth- and eighth-grade students every four years (the first assessment was in 1995).

- *Reading.* For PIRLS reading scores in 2011, the average U.S. reading score for fourth-grade students (556) was above the average score of 500 for the 45 countries in the study (Mullis et al., 2012a). From 2006 to 2011, fourth-grade U.S. students' reading achievement scores showed an impressive gain (540 to 556). The highest-scoring fourth-grade students were from Hong Kong China, Russia, Finland, Singapore, and Northern Ireland, with the U.S. average reading score in sixth place. For reading in the PISA assessment in 2012, 15-year-old U.S. students had an average score of 498, slightly above the average score of 496 for the 65 countries (Kelly et al., 2013). The highest-scoring 15-years-olds were from China Shanghai, Hong Kong China, Singapore, Japan, and Korea.
- *Math.* For TIMMS math scores in 2011, U.S. fourth- and eighth-grade students' scores (540 and 509, respectively) were above the average of 500 (Mullis et al., 2012b). Fourth-grade students in 10 of 50 countries scored higher

than their U.S. counterparts, while eighth-grade students in 8 of the 50 countries scored higher than their U.S. counterparts. The highest math scores for both fourth- and eighth-graders were attained by East Asian countries, with Singapore the highest in the fourth grade and South Korea the highest in the eighth grade. For PISA math scores in 2012, U.S. 15-year-old students' average math score (481) was below the average math score (494) of students in the 65 countries (Kelly et al., 2013). Fifteen-year-olds in Shanghai China, Singapore, Hong Kong China, Chinese Taipei, and Korea had the highest math scores. Fifteen-year olds in 35 of the 65 countries scored higher than the U.S. 15-year-olds.

- In the 2011 TIMMS science assessment, both fourth- and eighth-grade U.S. students were above the international average in science (539 for fourth-graders and 520 for eighth-graders, with 500 as the average score) (Martin et al., 2012). As in math comparisons, East Asian countries such as Singapore, Chinese Taipei, and Japan scored the highest on the international science comparisons. For the science scores of 15-year-olds in the 2012 PISA assessment, U.S. 15-year-old students scored below the average (497, compared with the average of 501), placing the U.S. students in the bottom one-third of students in the international comparisons (Kelly et al., 2013). Countries with the highest science scores for 15-year-olds in the 2012 assessment were Shanghai China, Hong Kong China, Singapore, Japan, and Finland.

Recent international comparisons indicate that students in many East Asian countries have significantly higher math and science achievement scores on standardized tests than U.S. students. Shown here is a 5-year-old girl from China working on complex math problems on a blackboard in her home.
Marie Dubrac/ANYONE/Amana Images/Getty Images

These international assessments indicate that the United States has made some improvement in the reading, math, and science achievement of elementary and secondary school students in recent years. Especially disconcerting, though, is that in most comparisons, the rankings for U.S. students in reading, math, and science when compared to students in other countries decline as they go from elementary school to high school. Also, U.S. students' achievement scores in math and science are still far below those of students in many East Asian countries.

STANDARDIZED TESTS OF TEACHER CANDIDATES

Not only do students have to take standardized tests, but as you are likely aware, so do teacher candidates. Many teacher candidates are required to take some version of the PRAXIS™ tests or a test created by an individual state.

The PRAXIS™ Tests and State Tests for Teachers

Most states now require teacher candidates to take a licensing exam. In some cases, this involves one or more PRAXIS™ tests published by Educational Testing Service or a test that is used only by a particular state. More than 40 states now use PRAXIS™ tests. The tests used by states for licensing of teacher candidates assess (1) basic skills or general academic ability; (2) subject-matter knowledge (such as math, English, science, or social studies); and/or (3) pedagogical knowledge. In many cases, there is little consistency across states in which specific tests are used.

The PRAXIS™ tests consist of PRAXIS I™, PRAXIS II™, and PRAXIS III™. The PRAXIS I™ test is a preliminary screening of basic skills that is often taken early in an undergraduate program or before a student is formally admitted to a teacher certification program.

PRAXIS II™ tests are essentially exit exams that typically are taken in the junior or senior year of undergraduate school to ensure that students know their specialty content areas and/or effective pedagogy before being awarded a preliminary teaching certificate. The PRAXIS II™ tests cover four main categories: (1) organizing content knowledge for student learning; (2) creating an environment for student learning; (3) teaching for student learning, and (4) teacher professionalism. They use a case-study approach to measure students' pedagogical knowledge.

DEVELOPMENT

The PRAXIS II™ tests are oriented toward specific age groups (elementary school—K-6; middle school—grades 5-9; and secondary school—grades 7-12).

The Praxis II™ pedagogy tests are based on job analysis research and the INTASC Principles noted at the end of each chapter in this book. The INTASC Principles are teaching standards defined by the Interstate New Teacher Assessment and Support Consortium, which is a national organization dedicated to reforming teacher preparation, licensing, and professional development.

PRAXIS III™ tests are assessments of classroom teaching performance. They are typically administered during the first year of teaching and can be used as part of a licensing decision. PRAXIS III™ tests include essays, oral response tests, listening tasks, portfolio reviews, video stimuli, and in-class observation.

Criticisms of the current PRAXIS™ and state licensure tests for teacher candidates have been made. Three such criticisms follow (Darling-Hammond & Baratz-Snowden, 2005, pp. 61–62):

- *Tests assess "low-level or marginally relevant knowledge and skills"* rather than "deep knowledge of subject matter and actual teaching skills."
- *The cutoff scores for the tests sometimes are low or not enforced.* If states are experiencing a shortage of teachers, "they often waive the testing requirement" and hire individuals who have failed the test.
- A lack of consistency across states has restricted teacher mobility. This is especially a problem because some states have teacher surpluses while others have teacher shortages.

Several teachers were asked about their experiences with the standardized tests for teacher certification. Following are their responses.

Teacher candidates at a two-day PRAXIS™ workshop at Western Kentucky University—Elizabethtown. *What are some characteristics of the PRAXIS™ tests?*
WKU-Elizabethtown/Radcliff/Fort Knox

EARLY CHILDHOOD Preschool teachers do not need to pass state-standardized tests. There are, however, certificate programs for those who choose to teach young children.

—VALARIE GORHAM, *Kiddie Quarters, Inc.*

ELEMENTARY SCHOOL: GRADES K-5 I honestly don't remember much about the test I took because it was over 19 years ago. What I do remember was that it was rigorous, and that I reviewed all I could think of in math, reading, and writing before the test. I also thought about and reflected on my education and what kind of philosophy I wanted to adopt as a teacher.

—CRAIG JENSEN, *Cooper Mountain Elementary School*

MIDDLE SCHOOL: GRADES 6-8 Taking the PRAXIS™ test was an extremely intense and stressful time for me. For the PRAXIS™ II, I bought a study guide. I worked with the guide for about two weeks before the test, which prepared me—however, the test was still difficult because either you know the information or you don't.

—CASEY MAASS, *Edison Middle School*

HIGH SCHOOL: GRADES 9-12 When taking these types of tests, it is important to be able to write with a clock blinking on the computer screen. I practiced for this particular scenario by playing video games so I got used to performing under the pressure of a blinking clock.

—SANDY SWANSON, *Menomonee Falls High School*

The Call for a National Test for Teacher Candidates Currently, no national test is required for teacher candidates, but the call for one has been made and a new test is currently being rolled out and made available for use. The National Academy of Education, which is made up of a distinguished group of educators, prepared *A Good Teacher in Every Classroom* (Darling-Hammond & Baratz-Snowden, 2005). The report states that the national test should assess a common core of knowledge for professional preparation, including how to create learning opportunities that make subjects accessible to all students. The National Academy of Education also recommended that the test results should be incorporated into state licensing requirements: Such a test, like those used to certify doctors, lawyers, and architects, should demonstrate not only what teachers *know* about their subjects and how to teach them but also what they can *do* in the classroom—for example, whether they can plan and implement lessons to teach standards, evaluate students' needs and design instruction to meet them, use a variety of teaching strategies, and maintain a purposeful, productive classroom. Fortunately, assessments that use videotapes of teaching and teachers' and students' work samples to evaluate what teachers actually do in the classroom have been developed by the National Board for Professional Teaching Standards (for use in certifying veteran accomplished teachers) and by states such as Connecticut for use in licensing beginning teachers (Darling-Hammond & Baratz-Snowden, 2005, pp. 62-63).

Recently, *ed*TPA (which stands for Education Teacher Performance Assessment) was developed by the Stanford Center for Assessment, Learning, and Equity (SCALE) (2013) with input from hundreds of teacher educators. The new national teacher test includes both written tests of subject knowledge and observations of teacher candidates in the classroom to determine whether they are effective in planning, teaching, and assessing student learning. Teacher candidates must submit a video recording of themselves teaching in a classroom as part of a portfolio of other teaching content that is scored by educators. The national teaching test is subject-specific for 27 different fields.

Review, Reflect, and Practice

 Compare aptitude and achievement tests and describe different types of achievement tests as well as some issues involved in these tests.

REVIEW
- How can aptitude and achievement tests be compared?
- What are survey batteries, specific subject tests, and diagnostic tests?
- What are some possible advantages to high-stakes state standards-based testing and what are some ways their results are being used? What are some criticisms of high-stakes state standards-based testing?
- How can standardized tests of teachers be characterized?

REFLECT
- What value do you see in the No Child Left Behind legislation? What problems? Should No Child Left Behind legislation be abolished or retained? Explain.

PRAXIS™ PRACTICE
1. Which of the following would be an appropriate use of an aptitude test?
   a. Josh takes a standardized test to help determine whether he is likely to be successful in medical school.
   b. Pete takes a standardized test to help determine what he has learned in his teacher preparation program.
   c. Stan takes a standardized test to determine to what degree he has met state mathematics standards.
   d. Penelope takes a standardized test to determine whether she can graduate from high school.

continued

Review, Reflect, and Practice

2. Ms. Jerovitz is reviewing the results of a standardized achievement test her students have taken. She carefully examines and charts the scores on each of the subtests included in the test. She has scores in mathematical reasoning, computation, vocabulary, reading comprehension, spelling, science, and social studies. What type of test did her students most likely take?
   a. diagnostic test
   b. aptitude test
   c. intelligence test
   d. survey battery

3. Ms. Comer is frustrated by the state standards-based tests she must give to her third-grade students. State funding for the district is now tied to performance on these tests. As a result, Ms. Comer and other teachers are under pressure from the administration and board of education to ensure that all students meet state standards. Which of the following is the most likely outcome of this scenario?
   a. Ms. Comer and other teachers will become better teachers so that their students will achieve at higher levels.
   b. Ms. Comer and other teachers will begin to teach only the things that will be covered on the state standards-based test, thus narrowing the curriculum and student learning opportunities.
   c. Ms. Comer and other teachers will ignore the pressure from administrators and the board of education, continue to teach as they always have, and hope for the best.
   d. Ms. Comer and other teachers will spend more time enriching their curriculum so that students will achieve at higher levels.

4. Sally is nervous about the test she will be taking as part of the teacher certification process. The test will cover information regarding educational psychology and child development. Which test is Sally most likely taking?
   a. PRAXIS I™
   b. PRAXIS II™
   c. PRAXIS III™
   d. National Teacher Certification Test

Please see answer key at end of book . . . .

LG 3 Identify the teacher's roles in standardized testing.

3 THE TEACHER'S ROLES

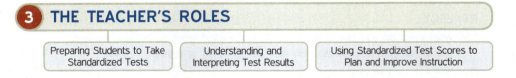

Preparing Students to Take Standardized Tests | Understanding and Interpreting Test Results | Using Standardized Test Scores to Plan and Improve Instruction

The teacher's roles in standardized testing include preparing students for the test, understanding and interpreting test results, and communicating test results to parents. Teachers also use test scores to plan and improve instruction.

PREPARING STUDENTS TO TAKE STANDARDIZED TESTS

All students need the opportunity to do their best. One way to do this is to make sure that students have good test-taking skills (Popham, 2017). You should communicate a positive attitude about the test to students. Explain the test's nature and purpose, and describe it as an opportunity and a challenge rather than an ordeal. For example, you can encourage students by telling them:

- The test provides an opportunity to show how much you have learned.
- While it might be challenging, remember you have learned so much more than is covered on the test, so you should be confident in your ability to do well.

Avoid saying anything that might cause students to feel nervous about the test. If you observe that anxiety in some students may hinder their performance, consider having a counselor talk with them about ways to reduce their test anxiety. Also, use challenging tasks that require critical thinking rather than the "drill and kill" approach that emphasizes rote memorization (Bonney & Sternberg, 2016). It is important not to teach to the test because if you do so, students will miss out on opportunities to become engaged in real world problems and higher level thinking that actually prepare them better for the exam!

Some don'ts regarding teachers preparing students for standardized tests include (McMillan, 2014): don't teach to the test, don't use the standardized test format for classroom tests, don't describe tests as a burden, don't tell students that important decisions will be made solely on the results of a single test, don't use previous forms of the same test to prepare students, and don't convey a negative attitude about the test.

How do teachers prepare students for standardized tests? Following are their responses.

EARLY CHILDHOOD A standard test is administered to our preschool children twice per school year. In September, it measures how much they know; in the spring, it measures how much they have learned. The test is hands-on; children manipulate materials and answer questions aloud. There is no preparation for this test.

—VALARIE GORHAM, *Kiddie Quarters, Inc.*

ELEMENTARY SCHOOL: GRADES K–5 We practice on sample tests, discussing the kinds of questions that will appear on the test, strategies for answers, and general good attitudes for test taking (for example, don't rush, read the whole question). We also reorganize the desks so that students get used to the testing configuration. I have students stretch, take deep breaths, and wriggle their fingers in order to warm up for the test. I also make a few cheerful comments before the test to relax them.

—KEREN ABRA, *Convent of the Sacred Heart Elementary School*

MIDDLE SCHOOL: GRADES 6–8 As a social studies teacher, I assist the language-arts and reading teachers in preparing students for the standardized exam by helping students build their writing skills. I assign essays after each unit and teach students to prepare the essays in the same way that they will need to do on the state test. The social studies department in my district meets monthly with the language-arts department so that we can work together to raise test scores.

—CASEY MAASS, *Edison Middle School*

HIGH SCHOOL: GRADES 9–12 In addition to going over the standard test-taking strategies, we also stress the importance of eating a filling breakfast the day of the test and getting a good night's sleep the night before the test.

—JENNIFER HEITER, *Bremen High School*

UNDERSTANDING AND INTERPRETING TEST RESULTS

Knowledge of some basic descriptive statistics will help you interpret standardized tests. Your ability to understand and interpret the results of standardized tests will come in handy when you have parent-teacher conferences regarding children in your class. We will discuss these basic statistics as well as some ways that test results are commonly reported.

Understanding Descriptive Statistics Our primary focus here is on **descriptive statistics**, which are mathematical procedures used to describe and summarize data (information) in a meaningful way. We will study frequency distributions, measures of central tendency, measures of variability, and the normal distribution.

Frequency Distributions The first step in organizing data involves creating a **frequency distribution**, a listing of scores, usually from highest to lowest, along with the number of times each score appears. Imagine that a test was given and 21 students received the following scores on the test: 96, 95, 94, 92, 88, 88, 86, 86, 86, 86, 84, 83, 82, 82, 82, 78, 75, 75, 72, 68, and 62. Figure 1(a) shows a frequency distribution for these scores. Frequency distributions often are presented graphically. For example, a **histogram** is a frequency distribution in the form of a graph. Vertical bars represent the frequency of scores per category. Figure 1(b) shows a histogram for the 21 scores. A histogram often is called a *bar graph*. Notice in the histogram that the horizontal axis (the *x*-axis) indicates the obtained scores and the vertical axis (the *y*-axis) indicates how often each score occurs.

Although representing a group of scores graphically can provide insight about students' performance, so can some statistical techniques that represent scores numerically. These techniques involve the concepts of central tendency and variability, each of which we will discuss.

Measures of Central Tendency A measure of **central tendency** is a number that provides information about the average, or typical, score in a set of data. There are three primary measures of central tendency: mean, median, and mode. The **mean** is the numerical average of a group of scores, commonly labeled as X or M by statisticians. The mean is computed by adding all the scores and then dividing the sum by the number of scores. Thus, the mean for the 21 students' test scores above is $1,740/21 = 82.86$. The mean often is a good indicator of the central tendency of a group of scores.

The **median** is the score that falls exactly in the middle of a distribution of scores after they have been arranged (or ranked) from highest to lowest. In our example of 21 test scores, the median is the 11th ranked score (10 above, 10 below it), so the median is 84.

descriptive statistics Mathematical procedures that are used to describe and summarize data (information) in a meaningful way.

frequency distribution A listing of scores, usually from highest to lowest, along with the number of times each score appears.

histogram A frequency distribution in the form of a graph.

central tendency A number that provides information about the average, or typical, score in a set of data.

mean The numerical average of a group of scores.

median The score that falls exactly in the middle of a distribution of scores after they have been arranged (or ranked) from highest to lowest.

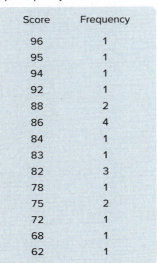
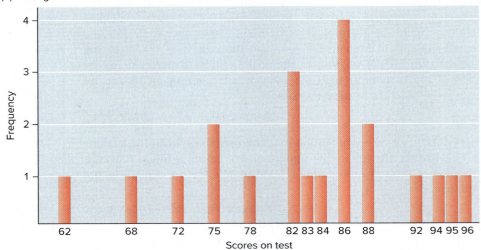

FIGURE 1 A FREQUENCY DISTRIBUTION AND HISTOGRAM

CONNECTING WITH STUDENTS: Best Practices
Strategies for Improving Students' Test-Taking Skills

Following are some important test-taking skills that you might want to discuss with your students (Waugh & Gronlund, 2013):

1. *Read the instructions carefully.*
2. *Read the items carefully.*
3. *Keep track of the time and work quickly enough to finish the test.*
4. *Skip difficult items and return to them later.*
5. *Make informed guesses instead of omitting items, if scoring favors doing so.*
6. *Eliminate as many answers as possible on multiple-choice items.*
7. *Follow directions carefully in marking the answer (such as darkening the entire space).* Make sure students know how to do this by modeling a sample answer for them.
8. *Check to be sure that the appropriate response was marked on the answer sheet.*
9. *Go back and check answers if time permits.*

In *Through the Eyes of Teachers,* Marlene Wendler, a fourth-grade teacher in New Ulm, Minnesota, describes her experiences with standardized tests that her students take.

THROUGH THE EYES OF TEACHERS
Make Sure You Evaluate Your Students on More than Just Tests

Standardized tests are just one very small, isolated picture of a child. A much fuller "video" comes from daily observations. Do not unfairly label a child based on a test. Rarely or never during the school year do my students encounter fill-in-the-oval items like those on standardized tests. Therefore, to be fair, before standardized testing I give them examples similar to the format of the test. If adults take a test with a special format, they prepare themselves by practicing in that format. Why should it be any different for children?

Marlene Wendler

The **mode** is the score that occurs most often. The mode can be determined easily by looking at the frequency distribution or histogram. In our example of 21 scores, the mode is 86 (the score occurring most often—four times). The measure of central tendency you choose should be based on the type of data you have. Medians and modes are used when you have ordinal/ranked data (like proficiency level on a scale of 1–5 on a state test). For categorical data, you have to use the mode. When you have continuous data (as many standardized test scores are), the mean is best unless the data are skewed (most scores at one extreme), in which case the median provides a clearer picture.

A set of scores may have more than one mode. For example, in our example of 21 students taking a test, if four students had scored 86 and four students had scored 75, then the set of scores would have two modes (86 and 75). A set of scores with two modes is called a *bimodal distribution.* It is possible for a set of scores to have more than two modes, in which case it is called a *multimodal distribution.*

Measures of Variability In addition to obtaining information about the central tendency of a set of scores, it also is important to know about their variability. **Measures of variability** tell us how much the scores vary from one another. Two measures of variability are range and standard deviation.

The **range** is the distance between the highest and lowest scores. The range of the 21 students' test scores in our example is 34 points (96 − 62 = 34). The range is a rather simple measure of variability and it is not used often. The most commonly used measure of variability is the standard deviation.

The **standard deviation** is a measure of how much a set of scores varies around the mean of the scores. In other words, it reveals how closely scores cluster around the mean (Frey, 2005). The smaller the standard deviation, the less the scores tend to vary from the mean. The greater the standard deviation, the more the scores tend to spread out from the mean. Calculating a standard deviation is not very difficult,

mode The score that occurs most often.

measures of variability Measures that tell how much scores vary from one another.

range The distance between the highest and lowest scores.

standard deviation A measure of how much a set of scores varies on average around the mean of the scores.

especially if you have a calculator that computes square roots. To calculate a standard deviation, follow these four steps:

1. Find the mean of the scores.
2. From each score, subtract the mean and then square the difference between the score and the mean. (Squaring the scores will eliminate any minus signs that result from subtracting the mean.)
3. Add the squares and then divide that sum by the number of scores.
4. Compute the square root of the value obtained in step 3. This is the standard deviation.

The formula for these four steps is

$$\sqrt{\frac{\Sigma(\chi - \overline{\chi})^2}{N}}$$

where χ = the individual score and $\overline{\chi}$ = the mean, N = the number of scores, and Σ means "the sum of." Apply this formula to the test scores of the 21 students as follows:

1. We already computed the mean of the scores and found that it was 82.86.
2. Subtract 82.86 from the first score: 96 − 82.86 = 13.14. Square 13.14 to get 172.66. Save the value and go on to do the same for the second score, the third score, and so on.
3. Add the 21 scores to get 1,543.28. Divide the sum by 21: 1,543.28/21 = 73.49.
4. Find the square root of 73.49. The result is 8.57, the standard deviation.

Calculators are very helpful in computing a standard deviation. To evaluate your knowledge of and skills in computing the various measures of central tendency and variability we have described, complete *Self-Assessment 1*. Mastering these kinds of descriptive statistics is useful not only for classroom work but also for understanding research results. The standard deviation is a better measure of variability than the range because the range represents information about only two bits of data (the highest and lowest scores), whereas the standard deviation represents combined information about all the data. It also usually is more helpful to know how much test scores are spread out or clustered together than to know the highest and lowest scores. If a teacher gives a test and the standard deviation turns out to be very low, it means the scores tend to cluster around the same value. That could mean that everyone in the class learned the material equally well, but it more likely suggests that the test was too easy and is not discriminating very effectively between students who mastered the material and those who did not.

The Normal Distribution In a **normal distribution**, most of the scores cluster around the mean. The farther above or below the mean we travel, the less frequently each score occurs. A normal distribution also is called a *normal curve, bell-shaped curve,* or *bell curve.* Many characteristics, such as human intelligence measured by intelligence tests, athletic ability, weight, and height, follow or approximate a normal distribution. Normal distributions are useful to know about because when testing a large number of students with a good standardized test, the graph of resulting scores will tend to resemble a normal curve (Bart & Kato, 2008).

We presented the normal distribution for standardized testing of intelligence in the chapter on individual variations. Here we provide a more detailed description of the normal distribution, including some important characteristics (see Figure 2). First, the normal distribution is symmetrical. Because of this symmetry, the mean, median, and mode are identical in a normal distribution. Second, its bell shape shows that the most common scores are near the middle. The scores become less frequent the farther away from the middle they appear (that is, as they become more extreme). Third, the normal distribution incorporates information about both

normal distribution A "bell-shaped curve" in which most of the scores are clustered around the mean and scores that are far above or below the mean are rare.

SELF-ASSESSMENT 1
Evaluating My Knowledge of and Skills in Computing Measures of Central Tendency and Variability

Examine each of these statements and place a check mark next to the statement if you feel confident of your knowledge of the concept and your skill in computing the measure or using the instrument.

_____ I know what a frequency distribution is.
_____ I can describe what a histogram is and know how to create one.
_____ I understand what a mean is and know how to compute it.
_____ I understand what a median is and know how to calculate it.
_____ I know what a mode is and am aware of how to compute it.
_____ I know what a range is and how to arrive at it.
_____ I can discuss what a standard deviation is and know how to compute it.
_____ I have a good calculator and know how to use it to compute basic descriptive statistics.

For any items that you did not check off, go back and study the concept again. If you are still not confident about computing the various measures, seek additional help from a college instructor, a math-skills tutor (many colleges have these available for students), or a capable friend. Practice the calculations in order to absorb the concepts.

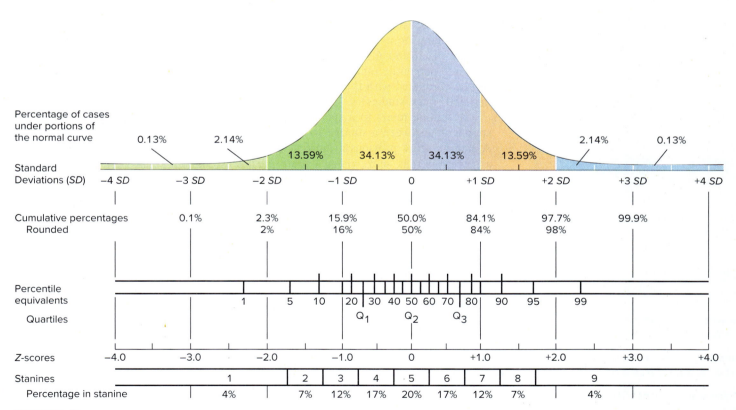

FIGURE 2 SOME COMMONLY REPORTED TEST SCORES BASED ON THE NORMAL CURVE

the mean and the standard deviation. The area on the normal curve that is 1 standard deviation above the mean and 1 standard deviation below it represents 68.26 percent of the scores. At 2 standard deviations above and below the mean, 95.42 percent of the scores are represented. Finally, at 3 standard deviations above and below the mean, 99.74 percent of the scores are included. If we apply this

Stanine Score	Percentile Rank Score
9	96 or Higher
8	89–95
7	77–88
6	60–76
5	40–59
4	23–39
3	11–22
2	4–10
1	Below 4

FIGURE 3 THE RELATION BETWEEN STANINE SCORE AND PERCENTILE-RANK SCORE

information to the normal distribution of IQ scores in the population, 68 percent of the population has an IQ between 85 and 115, 95 percent an IQ between 70 and 130, and 99 percent between 55 and 145.

Interpreting Test Results Understanding descriptive statistics provides the foundation for effectively interpreting test results. A **raw score** is the number of items the student answered correctly on the test. Raw scores, by themselves, are not very useful because they don't provide information about how easy or difficult the test was or how the student fared compared with other students. Test publishers usually provide teachers with many different kinds of scores that go beyond raw scores. These include percentile-rank scores, stanine scores, grade-equivalent scores, and standard scores.

Percentile-Rank Scores A **percentile-rank score** reveals the percentage of the distribution that lies at or below the score. It also provides information about the score's position in relation to the rest of the scores. Percentile ranks range from 1 to 99. If a student has a percentile rank of 81 on a test, it means that the student performed as well as or higher on the test than 81 percent of the sample who made up the norm group. Note that percentiles do not refer to percentages of items answered correctly on the test. Percentile rank for standardized tests is determined by comparison with the norm group distribution. Different comparison groups may be used in computing percentile ranks, such as urban norms or suburban norms.

Stanine Scores A **stanine score** describes a student's test performance on a 9-point scale ranging from 1 to 9. Scores of 1, 2, and 3 are usually considered to be below average; 4, 5, and 6 average; and 7, 8, and 9 above average. As in the case for a student's percentile rank score, a stanine score in one subject area (such as science) can be compared with the student's stanine score in other areas (such as math, reading, and social studies).

A stanine refers to a specific percentage of the normal curve's area. The correspondence between a stanine score and a percentile-rank score is shown in Figure 3. A stanine score provides a more general index of a student's performance, whereas a percentile rank score yields a more precise estimation.

Grade-Equivalent Scores A **grade-equivalent score** indicates a student's performance in relation to grade level and months of the school year, assuming a 10-month school year, to the norm group. Thus, a grade-equivalent score of 4.5 refers to fourth grade, fifth month in school. A grade equivalent of 6.0 stands for the beginning of the sixth grade. In some test reports, the decimal point is omitted so that 45 is the same as 4.5 and 60 is the same as 6.0.

Grade-equivalent scores should be used only to interpret a student's progress, not for grade placement. Because grade-equivalent scores are often misleading and misinterpreted, other types of scores, such as standard scores, are more appropriate.

Standard Scores A **standard score** is expressed as a deviation from the mean, which involves the concept of standard deviation that we discussed earlier. The term *standard* as used in *standard score* does not refer to a specific level of performance or expectation but rather to the standard normal curve (McMillan, 2002). Scores on state standards-based tests that we discussed earlier in our coverage of high-stakes testing are standard scores derived from raw score distributions, and they are unique to each state. For example, in Virginia, the standard score ranges from 0 to 600, with a score of 400 designated as "proficient." Actually, the stanine scores and grade-equivalent scores we already have profiled are standard scores. Two additional standard scores we will evaluate here are *z*-scores and *T*-scores (Peyton, 2005).

raw score The number of items a student answered correctly on the test.

percentile-rank score The percentage of a distribution that lies at or below the score.

stanine score A 9-point scale that describes a student's performance.

grade-equivalent score A score that indicates a student's performance in relation to grade level and months of the school year, assuming a 10-month school year.

standard score A score expressed as a deviation from the mean; involves the standard deviation.

A *z*-score provides information about how many standard deviations a raw score is above or below the mean. Calculation of a *z*-score is done using this formula:

$$z\text{-score} = \frac{\chi - \bar{\chi}}{SD}$$

where χ = any raw score, $\bar{\chi}$ = mean of the raw scores, and *SD* equals the standard deviation of the raw score distribution.

Consider again our example of 21 students taking a test. What would a student's *z*-score be if the student's raw score were 86? Using the formula just shown, it would be

$$\frac{86 - 82.6}{8.57} = .37$$

Thus, the raw score of 86 is .37 of a standard deviation above the mean. The *z*-score mean is 0 and the standard deviation is 1.

In addition to showing a student's relative placement on a test, standard scores also allow for comparisons across different types of tests. For example, a student may score 1 standard deviation above the mean on a math test and 1 standard deviation below the mean on a reading test. Comparisons of raw scores don't always allow for such comparisons.

Don't Overinterpret Test Results Use caution in interpreting small differences in test scores, especially percentile rank and grade-equivalent test scores. All tests have some degree of error. A good strategy is to think of a score not as a single number but as a location in a band or general range. Small differences in test scores are usually not meaningful.

Some test reports include percentile bands, a range of scores (rather than a single score) expressed in percentiles, such as 75th to 85th percentile for an obtained score of 80. This is referred to as the *standard error of measurement*. The Metropolitan Achievement Tests use percentile bands in reporting scores. A percentile rank of 6 to 8 points or a two- to five-month grade-equivalence difference between two students rarely indicates any meaningful difference in achievement.

When considering information from a standardized test, don't evaluate it in isolation (McMillan, 2014; Popham, 2017). Evaluate it in conjunction with other information you know about the student and your classroom instruction. Most manuals that accompany standardized tests warn against overinterpretation.

USING STANDARDIZED TEST SCORES TO PLAN AND IMPROVE INSTRUCTION

Teachers can use standardized test scores from the end of the previous year in planning their instruction for the next year and as a way to evaluate the effectiveness of instruction after content and skills have been taught (McMillan, 2007). Any use of standardized test results should be made in conjunction with information from other sources.

Prior to instruction, standardized test results may provide an indication of the general ability of the students in the class. This can help the teacher select the appropriate level of instruction and materials to begin the school year. A standardized test should not be used to develop a very low or very high expectation for a student or the entire class. Expectations should be appropriate and reasonable. If the results of a reading readiness test suggest that the class overall lacks appropriate reading skills, the teacher needs to carefully select reading materials that the students will be able to understand.

A very recent development involves test publishers and school districts developing items that correspond to the standards in state tests, then allowing schools or teachers to pull from an item bank to "test" progress toward meeting the standard, typically at each nine weeks of the school year (McMillan, 2014). The intent is to provide an evaluation of student learning that can be used to plan subsequent

z-score A score that provides information about how many standard deviations a raw score is above or below the mean.

teaching weekly or monthly. Usually these "benchmark" or "interim" tests are online, and information about them can be found on the Web sites of major testing companies, such as Educational Testing Service.

Standardized tests are sometimes used in grouping students. In cooperative learning, it is common to group students so that a wide range of abilities is reflected in the group. However, a single test score or single test should not be used by itself for any instructional purpose. It always should be used in conjunction with other information.

The subscales of tests (such as in reading and math) can be used to pinpoint strengths and weaknesses of incoming students in particular subject areas. This can help teachers to determine the amount of instruction to give in different areas. If students' achievement is considerably lower than what is expected on the basis of ability testing, they may need further testing, special attention, or counseling.

Standardized tests administered after instruction can be used to evaluate the effectiveness of instruction and the curriculum. Students should score well in the areas that have been emphasized in instruction. If they do not, then both the test itself and the instruction need to be analyzed to determine why this is the case.

In using standardized tests to plan and improve instruction, we emphasize again, it is important not to use a single test or test score to make decisions. This is especially relevant in placement decisions, which should be made on the basis of information from multiple sources, including prior teachers' comments, grades, systematic observations, and further assessments. It also is very important to guard against using a single test to develop an expectation for a student's ability and to make sure that the student's test scores reflect a fair assessment.

There likely will be times as a teacher when you will need to communicate test results that involve statistics to parents. In *Connecting with Students,* you can read about some strategies for communicating effectively with parents about test results.

CONNECTING WITH STUDENTS: Best Practices
Strategies for Communicating Test Results to Parents

Following are some good strategies for communicating test results to parents (McMillan, 2014):

1. *Don't report the test scores in isolation.* Report the scores in the context of the student's overall work and performance on other classroom assessments. This will help keep parents from placing too much importance on a score from a single standardized test.

2. *Try to use easy-to-understand language when you describe the student's test results to parents.* Don't get caught up in using obscure test language. Be able to report the information in your own words.

3. *Let parents know that the scores are approximate rather than absolute.* You might say something about how various internal and external factors can affect students' test scores.

4. *Recognize that percentile scores or bands are the easiest set of scores for parents to understand.*

5. *Prior to the conference, spend some time familiarizing yourself with the student's test report.* Make sure you know how to interpret each score you report to parents. It is not a good idea just to show parents the numbers on a test report. You will need to summarize what the scores mean.

6. *Be ready to answer questions that parents might have about their child's strengths, weaknesses, and progress.*

7. *Rather than talking "to" or lecturing parents, talk "with" them in a discussion format.* After you have described a test result, invite them to ask questions that will help you to further clarify for them what the test results mean.

To read one teacher's comments about effective ways to communicate with parents, see *Through the Eyes of Teachers.*

THROUGH THE EYES OF TEACHERS
The Importance of Parents' Support

Vicki Stone, a middle school language arts teacher in Huntington, West Virginia, says that parental support is vital to the success of her teaching strategy. She holds parent conferences to inform and enable parents to be partners in the student's educational program for the year. They discuss the student's strengths and weaknesses. Based on the Stanford Achievement Test and the parental input, her lesson plans take into account the student's weaknesses, identifying areas where targeted instruction is needed.

Review, Reflect, and Practice

 Identify the teacher's roles in standardized testing.

REVIEW

- What are effective ways to prepare students for standardized tests?
- What roles do frequency distributions, measures of central tendency and variability, and normal distributions play in describing standardized test results? What are some different types of scores? How should scores be interpreted?
- How can standardized tests be used in planning and improving instruction?

REFLECT

- Considering the grade level and subject(s) that you plan to teach, how might standardized test results be useful to you in your instructional planning?

PRAXIS™ PRACTICE

1. Mark, Jenny, Nicole, and Chris are all taking the SAT this year. Which student is preparing the most wisely?
   a. Chris, who has taken a test-taking skills test every year throughout high school
   b. Jenny, who has consistently taken relatively easy high school courses and has gotten straight A's
   c. Mark, who has enrolled in a specialized, expensive SAT preparation program
   d. Nicole, who has taken a rigorous high school program of studies and has reviewed some of the math she took in her early high school years
2. Ms. Scott has just received the standardized test scores for her class. As she reviews each of them, she notices that Pete scored at the 98th percentile on the reading portion of this nationally normed test. What does this mean?
   a. Pete did better than 98 percent of the norm group on the test.
   b. Pete's score is 1 standard deviation above the mean score of the norm group.
   c. Pete got 98 percent of the answers correct on the reading portion of the test.
   d. Pete's score is 3 standard deviations above the mean score of the norm group.
3. Which of the following is an example of best practices in using the results of standardized tests to plan and improve instruction?
   a. Ms. Carter uses only her students' standardized test scores to determine their placement in her class.
   b. Mr. Peabody decides that the standardized test scores are invalid when his students do not do well in an area he emphasized in class.
   c. Mr. Lemhert looks at the standardized test scores of each student and uses the information to help him identify relative strengths and weaknesses.
   d. Ms. Ziegler uses her students' standardized test scores to explain their classroom performance to their parents.

Please see answer key at end of book....

4 ISSUES IN STANDARDIZED TESTS

- Standardized Tests, Alternative Assessments, and High-Stakes Testing
- Diversity and Standardized Testing

LG 4 Evaluate some key issues in standardized testing.

As we have already mentioned, standardized testing is controversial. One debate concerns how standardized tests stack up against alternative methods of assessment, especially in high-stakes state standards-based testing. Another is about whether standardized tests discriminate against ethnic minority students and students from low-income backgrounds.

STANDARDIZED TESTS, ALTERNATIVE ASSESSMENTS, AND HIGH-STAKES TESTING

As we will explain in greater detail in the chapter on classroom assessment and grading, alternative assessments include assessments of student performance, such as assessments of oral presentations, real-world problems, projects, and portfolios (systematic and organized collections of the student's work that demonstrate the student's skills and accomplishments) (Burke, 2010). Which is the best way to assess student performance—standardized tests that mainly rely on multiple-choice questions, or alternative assessments?

Some experts argue that performance tests should be used, either instead of standardized tests that mainly include multiple-choice questions or at least as part of the student's total assessment (Wiggins, 2013/2014). The argument is that performance assessment is more meaningful, involves higher-level thinking skills, and fits better with current educational reform that emphasizes constructivist and social constructivist learning (Ernst & Glennie, 2015; Parsi & Darling-Hammond, 2015). In Kentucky and Vermont, the inclusion of problem solving in mathematics and the written communication of mathematical ideas on state-mandated tests led teachers to work more on these areas in their math instruction. However, use of performance assessments for large-scale assessments can be problematic because their reliability can be low, the amount of time and energy required is often too extensive, and performance assessments don't typically address a wide range of learning outcomes.

Standardized tests are especially helpful in providing information about comparability from a "big picture" perspective. Comparing their class with the one down the hall won't give teachers the information they need about where their students stand compared with the broader population of students. Standardized tests can provide better information about "big picture" questions: Are my fourth-grade students learning basic math? Can my seventh-grade students read at a predefined level of competency?

At the same time, teachers are urged to scrupulously avoid any misuses of tests or test results and to educate themselves about tests so that they understand their capabilities and limitations, not asking tests to do more than they can or are intended to do. Teachers also are reminded that standardized tests should be only one of a number of assessments used to evaluate students.

DIVERSITY AND STANDARDIZED TESTING

Earlier in this chapter, we raised the issue of fairness in standardized testing (McMillan, 2014). And in the chapter on individual variations, we discussed issues related to diversity and assessment. A special concern is cultural bias in tests and the importance of creating culturally responsive tests for diagnostic and instructional purposes (Banks, 2014; Gollnick & Chinn, 2017; Koppelman, 2017). Because of the potential for cultural bias in standardized tests, it is important to assess students using a variety of methods. As indicated earlier, some assessment experts emphasize that performance and portfolio assessments reduce some of the inequity that characterizes standardized tests for ethnic minority students and students from low-income backgrounds (Wiggins, 2013/2014).

In sum, portfolio assessment holds promise by focusing instruction on higher-level thinking skills, providing useful feedback to teachers about students' thinking skills, and emphasizing real-world problem solving (Popham, 2017). However, portfolio assessment is not currently used as part of NCLB or other large-scale standardized testing. As indicated earlier, using portfolio and performance assessment as part of large-scale standardized testing can be problematic.

> **Thinking Back/Thinking Forward**
> Performance assessments require students to create answers or products that demonstrate their knowledge or skill, such as writing an essay, conducting an experiment, carrying out a project, creating a portfolio, etc. Connect to "Classroom Assessment and Grading."

How might standardized tests discriminate against ethnic minority students?
Gary He/McGraw-Hill

DIVERSITY

Review, Reflect, and Practice

4 Evaluate some key issues in standardized testing.

REVIEW
- Why is it argued that performance assessments should accompany standardized tests in high-stakes testing? What are some problems in using performance assessments as part of large-scale standardized testing?
- What characterizes concern about diversity and standardized tests?

REFLECT
- In what situations would you rather be tested with standardized testing? With performance assessments? Why?

PRAXIS™ PRACTICE
1. Which of the following is the best example of a performance test used to issue a driver's license?
   a. a road test
   b. a written test covering the rules of the road
   c. a vision test
   d. a computerized test covering the meaning of road signs
2. What is a good test strategy to avoid cultural bias?
   a. Use a single, good standardized test to control for extraneous influences.
   b. Assess students using a variety of methods.
   c. Assume that ethnic differences are due to heredity.
   d. Avoid using portfolios for assessment purposes.

Please see answer key at end of book . . . .

> **Thinking Back/Thinking Forward**
> Creating culture-fair tests is very difficult—so difficult that Robert Sternberg concludes that there are no culture-fair tests, only culture-reduced tests. Connect to "Individual Variations."

Connecting with the Classroom: Crack the Case

The Standardized Test Pressure

Ms. Pryor teaches third grade at Pulaski Elementary School in Steelton. In her state, third grade is the first grade level at which students are tested using the statewide standardized test. The test, given in March of each year, is supposed to measure how well the school is doing at meeting state standards in math, science, reading, writing, and social studies. This test yields individual, classroom, school, and district scores, and compares these to state averages. The state uses district-level scores to address school funding. Schools that have a large percentage of students who do not meet or exceed state standards run the risk of losing a portion of their funding. In recent years, the Steelton School District has broadened the purpose of the state-mandated tests to include how well an individual teacher is doing at helping his or her students meet state standards.

Student scores have become part of the teacher evaluation process. Steelton teachers receive merit points based on the percentage of their class that meets or exceeds state standards. Those with more merit points are given greater consideration if they request an in-district transfer, reimbursement for attending conferences, or release time for other development activities. Ms. Pryor has always received merit points for her students' performance on this test.

In addition to the state test, the district uses a nationally normed test to assess achievement. This test yields individual scores as they relate to national norms. These scores are reported as percentile-rank scores and grade-equivalent scores. This test is generally given near the beginning of the school year. The district uses the results of these tests to identify students in need of special education services or enrichment programs.

continued

Ms. Pryor is not thrilled about giving her students so many standardized tests. She says, "Sometimes it seems all we do is prepare for these tests and take them." However, she makes sure she has taught her students appropriate test-taking strategies. She also tries to give her students some experiences that mirror the standardized tests, such as filling in bubbles on answer sheets, and having limited time in which to complete tests. She carefully goes over tests from previous years and uses them to write lesson plans. She makes sure to teach everything covered on previous state tests prior to the test in March, leaving the "fun stuff" for the end of the school year. The week before state testing, Ms. Pryor sends notes home to parents asking them to ensure that their children get adequate sleep and eat breakfast during testing weeks. After all, student performance on these tests impacts how the school is perceived and whether or not Ms. Pryor will receive merit points.

In the past, some groups of students have been excused from state testing. These students included those with learning disabilities and those who were not proficient at English. However, this year the rules have changed. The state now mandates that all students be tested regardless of ability or primary language. This concerns Ms. Pryor. If these students are included in the state testing, it is rather unlikely that her class will all meet or exceed state standards, resulting in no merit points for Ms. Pryor.

After receiving the results of the nationally normed tests, Ms. Pryor devises a strategy to ensure that more of her students will meet or exceed state standards on the state test in the spring. She begins by looking at her students' national percentile scores. She separates the students into three groups—those who scored above the 60th percentile, those who scored between the 40th and 60th percentiles, and those who scored below the 40th percentile. Her reasoning is that those who scored above the 60th percentile will meet state standards with no problem. In fact, many of them probably already have met state standards for third grade, given their grade-equivalent scores on the national test. She needn't worry about this group. Those who scored below the 40th percentile are not likely to meet state standards no matter what she does. Some may come close, but the return on her effort is not likely to be great. That leaves the middle group. She reasons that if she works intensively with this group, she has a chance of helping them to meet state standards—and that if they do, she will meet her goal in terms of merit points.

1. What testing issues are evident in this case?
2. What does Ms. Pryor do correctly in terms of preparing her students to take standardized tests?
3. What does Ms. Pryor do incorrectly in terms of preparing her students to take standardized tests?
4. What does it mean if a student's national percentile-rank score is 60?
   a. The student got 60 percent of the items correct.
   b. The student scored as well as or better than 60 percent of the students in the norm group.
   c. The student scored as well as or worse than 60 percent of the students in the norm group.
   d. The student scored as well as or better than 60 percent of the students in his class.
5. When Ms. Pryor uses percentile-rank scores on the nationally normed achievement test to evaluate likely performance on the state-mandated test, what is she likely expecting from the nationally normed test?
   a. She expects the nationally normed test to have predictive validity for the state-mandated test.
   b. She expects the nationally normed test to have concurrent validity.
   c. She expects the nationally normed test to have test-retest reliability.
   d. She expects the nationally normed test to have split-half reliability.
6. In what ways is it evident that the state-mandated test is a high-stakes test?
7. Why do you think Ms. Pryor decided only to concentrate her efforts at the middle of her class?
8. To what extent do you agree with her strategy? Why?

Connecting with Learning: Reach Your Learning Goals

 THE NATURE OF STANDARDIZED TESTS: Discuss the nature and purpose of standardized tests as well as the criteria for evaluating them.

| Standardized Tests and Their Purposes |

- Standardized tests have uniform procedures for administration and scoring.
- Many standardized tests allow a student's performance to be compared with the performance of other students at the same age or grade level on a national basis.

Criteria for Evaluating Standardized Tests

- The purposes of standardized tests include providing information about students' progress, diagnosing students' strengths and weaknesses, providing evidence for placement of students in specific programs, providing information for planning and improving instruction, and contributing to accountability.
- Interest in accountability has led to the creation of state standards-based high-stakes benchmark testing. Important decisions about students should be made not on the basis of a single standardized test but rather on the basis of information from a variety of assessments.
- The most important ways to evaluate standardized tests involve whether the correct interpretations are being made based on the type of test (norm-referenced or criterion-referenced), and the extent to which they yield valid, reliable, and fair scores.
- Norm-referenced tests involve comparing a student's performance with scores for a group of individuals previously tested that provides a basis for interpreting the student's score. National norms are based on a nationally representative group of students.
- Criterion-referenced tests are standardized tests in which the student's performance is compared to established criteria rather than norms. State standardized tests are typically criterion-referenced, and criterion-referenced tests are designed to assess skills and knowledge in specific areas, such as English, math, and science.
- Validity is the extent to which a test measures what it is intended to measure and the extent to which inferences about test scores are accurate and appropriate. Three important types of validity are content validity, criterion validity (which can be either concurrent or predictive), and construct validity.
- Reliability is the extent to which a test produces a consistent, reproducible measure of performance. Reliable measures are stable, dependable, and relatively free from errors of measurement. Reliability can be measured in several ways, including test-retest reliability, alternate-forms reliability, and split-half reliability.
- Fair tests are unbiased and nondiscriminatory, uninfluenced by irrelevant factors such as gender, ethnicity, or bias on the part of the scorer.

2 APTITUDE AND ACHIEVEMENT TESTS: Compare aptitude and achievement tests and describe different types of achievement tests as well as some issues involved in these tests.

Comparing Aptitude and Achievement Tests

- An aptitude test predicts a student's ability to learn, or what the student can accomplish with further education and training.
- An achievement test measures what the student has learned, or the skills the student has mastered.
- Aptitude tests include general mental ability tests, such as intelligence tests, and specific tests used to predict success in an academic subject or occupational area. The SAT test can be used as an aptitude test or as an achievement test.

Types of Standardized Achievement Tests

- Standardized achievement tests include survey batteries (individual subject matter tests that are designed for a particular level of students), specific subject tests (assess a skill in a more detailed, extensive way than a survey battery), and diagnostic tests (given to students to pinpoint specific learning needs so those needs can be met with regular or remedial instruction).

High-Stakes State Standards-Based Tests

- Some possible advantages of high-stakes state standards-based testing: improved student performance; more time teaching subjects being tested; high expectations for all students; identification of poorly performing schools, teachers, and administrators; and increased confidence in schools as test scores improve.
- High-stakes state standards-based tests are being used in decisions about remediation, promotion, and graduation. High-stakes state standards-based tests are criticized for dumbing down and narrowing the curriculum, promoting rote memorization, encouraging teachers to teach to the test, and discriminating against students from low-income and minority backgrounds.

continued

Standardized Tests of Teacher Candidates

- International comparisons on standardized tests show that the United States has made some improvement compared with other countries in recent years, although it is disconcerting that U.S. students' rankings in reading, math, and science are higher in elementary school but not nearly as good in secondary school. Also, U.S. students lag considerably behind East Asian countries in math and science achievement.
- Most teacher candidates have to take one or more standardized tests as part of licensure to teach in a particular state. Many states use one or more of the PRAXIS™ tests created by Educational Testing Service, although some states create their own tests.
- Criticisms of the current tests of teacher candidates have been made, and a call for a national test of teacher candidates has been made. In 2013, a national teacher test, *ed*TPA, was developed; the test includes both written knowledge about subject matter as well as a classroom observation of a teacher candidate.

3 THE TEACHER'S ROLES: Identify the teacher's roles in standardized testing.

Preparing Students to Take Standardized Tests

- Teachers can prepare students to take standardized tests by making sure that students have good test-taking skills; communicating a positive attitude about the test to students; describing the test as an opportunity, not an ordeal; and avoiding comments that might raise students' anxiety.

Understanding and Interpreting Test Results

- Descriptive statistics are math procedures used to describe and summarize data in a meaningful way.
- A frequency distribution is a listing of scores, usually from highest to lowest, along with the number of times each score appears. A histogram is one way to present a frequency distribution.
- Measures of central tendency include the mean, median, and mode.
- Measures of variability tell how much scores vary and include the range and standard deviation.
- The normal distribution is also called a bell-shaped curve in which most scores cluster around the mean. A normal distribution is symmetrical and incorporates information about both the mean and the standard deviation.
- A raw score is the number of items a student gets right on a test, which typically is not as useful as many other types of scores.
- Percentile-rank scores reveal the percentage of the distribution that lies at or below the particular score. Stanine scores describe a student's performance on a 9-point scale ranging from 1 to 9. Grade-equivalent scores indicate a student's performance in relation to grade level and months of the school year.
- Standard scores are expressed as a deviation from the mean and involve the concept of standard deviation (z-scores are examples of standard scores).
- Avoid overinterpreting test results. A good strategy is to think of a score not as a single number but as a general range. Don't evaluate standardized test results in isolation from other information about the student, such as classroom performance and the nature of instruction.

Using Standardized Test Scores to Plan and Improve Instruction

- Standardized test scores can be used to plan and improve instruction either prior to instruction or after instruction. Standardized tests sometimes are used in grouping students, but it is important to guard against having unrealistic expectations for students based on test scores.
- The subscales of tests can be used to pinpoint students' strengths and weaknesses in particular subject areas, which can help teachers determine the amount of instruction to give in different areas. Standardized tests should always be used in conjunction with other information about students and the appropriateness and fairness of the tests should be considered.

4 ISSUES IN STANDARDIZED TESTS: Evaluate some key issues in standardized testing.

Standardized Tests, Alternative Assessments, and High-Stakes Testing

- There is disagreement about the value of standardized tests versus alternative assessments such as performance tests and portfolio assessments. When used correctly, standardized tests have value but provide only part of the assessment picture and do have limits.
- Some assessment experts and teachers emphasize that high-stakes state standards-based testing should include more alternative assessments. However, using performance assessments in large-scale standardized testing can be problematic.

Diversity and Standardized Testing

- Cultural bias is of special concern in standardized testing. Some assessment experts believe that performance assessments have the potential to reduce bias in testing.

KEY TERMS

achievement test 509
alternate-forms reliability 507
aptitude test 509
central tendency 522
concurrent validity 506
construct validity 507
content validity 506
criterion validity 506
criterion-referenced tests 506

descriptive statistics 522
frequency distribution 522
grade-equivalent score 526
high-stakes testing 505
histogram 522
mean 522
measures of variability 523
median 522
mode 523

norm group 506
normal distribution 524
norm-referenced tests 506
percentile-rank score 526
predictive validity 507
range 523
raw score 526
reliability 507
split-half reliability 507

standard deviation 522
standard score 525
standardized tests 503
standards-based tests 504
stanine score 525
test-retest reliability 506
validity 505
z-score 526

PORTFOLIO ACTIVITIES

Now that you have a good understanding of this chapter, complete the following exercises to expand your thinking.

Independent Reflection

1. **Find a Frequency Distribution.** Create a frequency distribution and histogram for the following scores: 98, 96, 94, 94, 92, 90, 90, 88, 86, 86, 86, 82, 80, 80, 80, 80, 80, 78, 76, 72, 70, 68, 64. (INTASC: Standard 6)

Research/Field Experience

2. **What Do the Critics Say About Standardized Testing?** In a short essay, evaluate each of the following criticisms of standardized tests. State whether you agree with the criticism and then explain your reasoning. (1) High-stakes multiple-choice tests will lead to a "dumbing down" of teaching and learning. (2) Establishing national tests will undermine new educational programs at the state and local levels. (INTASC: Principle 6)

Collaborative Work

3. **Calculate and Interpret Test Results.** With a partner in your class, calculate the mean, median, and mode of the 23 scores just listed. Compute the range and standard deviation for these scores. What do these figures mean? (INTASC: Principle 6)

chapter 16

CLASSROOM ASSESSMENT AND GRADING

chapter outline

① The Classroom as an Assessment Context

Learning Goal 1 Discuss the classroom as an assessment context.

Assessment as an Integral Part of Teaching
Making Assessment Compatible with Contemporary Views of Learning and Motivation
Creating Clear, Appropriate Learning Targets
Establishing High-Quality Assessments
Current Trends

② Traditional Tests

Learning Goal 2 Provide some guidelines for constructing traditional tests.

Selected-Response Items
Constructed-Response Items

③ Alternative Assessments

Learning Goal 3 Describe some types of alternative assessments.

Trends in Alternative Assessment
Performance Assessment
Portfolio Assessment

④ Grading and Reporting Performance

Learning Goal 4 Construct a sound approach to grading.

The Purposes of Grading
The Components of a Grading System
Reporting Students' Progress and Grades to Parents
Some Issues in Grading

I call my tests "opportunities" to give students a different way of thinking about them.

—Bert Moore
Contemporary American Psychologist

FatCamera/E+/Getty Images

Connecting with Teachers   Vicky Farrow

Vicky Farrow is a former high school teacher who currently teaches educational psychology at Lamar University in Beaumont, Texas. She reflects on the ongoing process of assessment in the classroom and what to do and what not to do in constructing tests:

> Assessment is an ongoing process. It is more than giving tests or assigning grades. It is everything a teacher does to determine if his or her students are learning. It may be asking students questions, monitoring their understanding as you circulate through the room during an activity, and noticing the frown on the face of a student who is confused or the smile of a student who has grasped the concept. Without this ongoing assessment, a teacher can never know if instruction is effective or needs to be modified. Done effectively, assessment provides a teacher with valuable information for providing an optimal learning experience for every child.
>
> When you do give tests, every item on a test should relate back to the objectives. This helps the teacher avoid "gotcha" questions—those questions that may be trivial or unimportant to the intended learning outcomes. If it is not important enough to spend valuable class time on, it probably is not important enough to test the student over.
>
> Be careful that test items are written at an appropriate level. The test should be testing students' understanding of the unit content, not their reading skills (unless, of course, it is reading skills that are being tested). I remember as a student taking an analogies test that was intended to assess my ability to identify relationships between concepts. However, the vocabulary was so difficult that I missed some items because the words were too difficult for that level of schooling.
>
> If an essay question is on an examination, write a model answer *before* grading the exam. Would you make your answer key for a multiple-choice test from a student's paper, wrong answers and all? Of course not! It does not make any more sense to do that with an essay item. If an essay item is well written and a model answer is constructed in advance, the grade a student receives will more accurately reflect the level of that student's understanding of the material being tested.

Preview

Assessment of students' learning has recently generated considerable interest in educational circles. This interest has focused on issues such as the extent to which teachers should incorporate state standards into their teaching and assessment, as well as the degree to which teachers should use traditional tests or alternative assessments. Our coverage of classroom assessments begins with an examination of the varied features of the classroom as an assessment context. Then we contrast traditional tests and alternative assessments, and we conclude with a discussion of the role of grading in education.

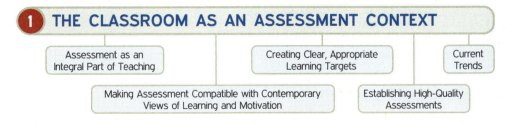

LG 1 Discuss the classroom as an assessment context.

When you think of assessment, what comes to mind? Probably tests. However, as we discuss the classroom as a context for assessment, you will discover that contemporary assessment strategies involve far more than testing.

ASSESSMENT AS AN INTEGRAL PART OF TEACHING

Teachers spend more time in assessment than you might imagine. The high-stakes testing required by No Child Left Behind has meant that teachers have to integrate this testing in their assessment planning (McMillan, 2014). For example, many teachers spend considerable time prepping students for such tests. In a recent U.S. survey of K-12 teachers, most of the teachers said that too much time is spent on testing (Grunwald & Associates, 2014). Seventy percent of the teachers reported that state-mandated accountability tests take too much time away from student learning. Following are additional findings in the national survey:

- Educators and students both value assessment, but say that assessment should support learning.
- Teachers use assessment results frequently to inform their teaching.
- Teachers state that students' performance on classroom tests provides better feedback for students and more instructional support than state accountability tests.

With so much time spent on assessment, it should be done well (Popham, 2017). Assessment expert James McMillan (2014) stresses that competent teachers frequently evaluate their students in relation to learning goals and adapt their instruction accordingly. Assessment not only documents what students know and can do but also affects their learning and motivation. These ideas represent a change in the way assessment is viewed: away from the concept of assessment as an isolated outcome done only after instruction is finished and toward the concept of integrating assessment with instruction.

Think of integrating instruction and assessment in terms of three time frames: preinstruction, during instruction (formative), and postinstruction (summative) (O'Shea, 2009). The Standards for Teacher Competence in Educational Assessment, developed jointly in the early 1990s by the American Federation of Teachers, National Council on Measurement in Education, and National Education Association, describe the teacher's responsibility for student assessment in these three time frames (see Figure 1).

Preinstruction Assessment Imagine that you want to know how well your students can solve a certain level of math problem before you begin formal instruction on a more advanced level. You might look at your students' prior grades and their scores on standardized math tests, as well as observe your students for several days to see how well they perform. These assessments are designed to answer this question: What math skills are my students able to demonstrate? If the results of your assessment

FIGURE 1 TEACHER DECISION MAKING BEFORE, DURING, AND AFTER INSTRUCTION

These are questions a teacher can answer to improve assessment before, during, and after instruction.

Source: *Essential Assessment Concepts for Teachers and Administrators* (p. 3), by J. McMillan, 2001, Corwin Press, 2001.

Preinstruction	During instruction (formative assessment)	Postinstruction (summative assessment)
Do my students have the prerequisite knowledge and skills to be successful?	Are students paying attention to me?	How much have my students learned?
What will interest my students?	Are students understanding the material?	What should I do next?
What will motivate my students?	To which students should I direct questions?	Do I need to review anything the class didn't understand?
How long should I plan to cover each unit?	What type of questions should I ask?	What grades should I give?
What teaching strategies should I use?	How should I respond to student questions?	What should I tell my students?
How should I grade students?	When should I stop lecturing?	How should I change my instruction next time?
What type of group learning should I use?	Which students need extra help?	Do the test scores really reflect what my students know and can do?
What are my learning objectives or targets?	Which students should be left alone?	Is there anything that students misunderstood?

indicate that students lack prerequisite knowledge and skills, you will decide to begin with materials that are less difficult for them. If they do extremely well on your pre-instruction assessment, you will move your level of instruction to a higher plane. Without this preinstruction assessment, you run the risk of having a class that is overwhelmed (if your instruction level is too advanced) or bored (if your instruction level is too low).

Much of preinstruction assessment is informal observation. In the first several weeks of school, you will have numerous opportunities to observe students' characteristics and behavior. Be sensitive to whether a student is shy or outgoing, has a good or weak vocabulary, speaks and listens effectively, is considerate of others or is egocentric, engages in appropriate or inappropriate behavior, and so on. Also focus on the student's nonverbal behavior for cues that might reveal nervousness, boredom, frustration, or a lack of understanding.

In preinstruction assessments, guard against developing expectations that will distort your perception of a student. It is virtually impossible not to have expectations about students. Because teacher expectations are potentially powerful influences on student learning, some teachers don't even want to look at a student's prior grades or standardized test scores. Whether you do or do not examine such assessment information, work on making your expectations realistic. If you err, err in the direction of having overly positive expectations for students.

A good strategy is to treat your initial impressions of students as hypotheses to be supported or modified by subsequent observation and information. Some of your initial observations will be accurate; others will need to be revised. As you try to get a sense of what your students are like, refrain from believing hearsay information, from making enduring judgments based on only one or two observations, and from labeling students.

Some teachers also administer diagnostic pretests in subject areas to examine a student's level of knowledge and skill. And many schools are increasingly collecting samples of students' work in portfolios, which can accompany a student from grade to grade. The portfolios provide teachers with a far more concrete, less biased set of information to evaluate than other teachers' hearsay comments. We will describe portfolios in much greater depth later in the chapter.

Thinking Back/Thinking Forward

Reading and mathematics are the two areas in which standardized tests are often used for diagnostic purposes. Connect to "Standardized Tests and Teaching."

Assessment During Instruction One of the most significant trends in classroom assessment is the increasing use of **formative assessment**, which is assessment during the course of instruction rather than after it is completed. Formative assessment has become a buzzword with its emphasis on assessment for learning rather than assessment of learning (Loughland & Kilpatrick, 2015; Mandinach & Lash, 2016). An important aspect of being an effective teacher is assessing students' understanding, and formative assessment is extremely important in this regard. Your ongoing observation and monitoring of students' learning while you teach informs you about what to do next (Decristan et al., 2015; Shirley & Irving, 2015). Assessment during instruction helps you set your teaching at a level that challenges students and stretches their thinking. It also helps you to detect which students need your individual attention.

Assessment during instruction takes place at the same time as you make many other decisions about what to do, say, or ask next to keep the classroom running smoothly and help students actively learn. It requires listening to student answers, observing other students for indications of understanding or confusion, framing the next question, and looking around the class for misbehavior (McMillan, 2014). Simultaneously, the teacher needs to monitor the pace of the activity, decide which students to call on, evaluate answer quality, and structure the sequence of content. With small groups, the teacher might need to be aware of several different activities simultaneously.

formative assessment Assessment during the course of instruction rather than after it is completed.

What is formative assessment? Why is it such an important aspect of assessment?
Hero/Corbis/Glow Images

> **Thinking Back/Thinking Forward**
>
> High-achieving students are often self-regulatory learners. Connect to "Behavioral and Social Cognitive Approaches."
>
> Metacognitive regulation involves learning a number of strategies that result in solutions to learning problems. Monitoring how well one is performing on a task is an important aspect of metacognition. Connect to "The Information-Processing Approach."

Oral questions are an especially important aspect of assessment during instruction. Some teachers ask as many as 300 to 400 questions a day, not only to stimulate students' thinking and inquiry but also to assess their knowledge and skill levels.

When you ask questions, remember to avoid overly broad, general questions; involve the whole class in questioning instead of calling on the same students all of the time; allow sufficient "wait time" after asking a question; probe students' responses with follow-up questions; and highly value students' own questions.

An increasing trend in formative assessment is to get students to assess their own progress on a day-to-day basis (Brown, et al., 2015). An important goal of student self-assessment is for students to become deeply involved in evaluating their schoolwork so they can more quickly determine how they are progressing. In a recent study with community college students, those who were in self-assessment courses showed greater self-regulation and greater likelihood of continuing their college education than their counterparts in traditional assessment courses (Mahlberg, 2015).

Encouraging students to assess their own progress also can increase their self-confidence and motivation to learn. Getting students to be reflective and monitor their progress is a key aspect of student self-assessment. Self-monitoring relates to our discussion of self-regulation in the chapter on behavioral and social cognitive approaches and our coverage of metacognition in the chapter on the information-processing approach. One of the biggest challenges of incorporating student self-assessment in classroom assessment is getting students used to doing it. A good teaching strategy is to create student self-assessment worksheets, checklists, and other prepared material to facilitate their evaluation of their progress.

Providing effective feedback is an essential aspect of formative assessment and has always been an integral aspect of good teaching (Mandinach & Lash, 2016). The idea is not only to continually assess students as they learn but to provide informative feedback so that students' focus is appropriate. Researchers have found that positive feedback during formative assessment increases students' self-regulation of learning (Boud, et al., 2015). As part of providing feedback in formative assessment, instructional "correctives" are used to help students make progress. The idea is to provide assessment, feedback, and then more instruction (McMillan, 2014). Among the important aspects of feedback in formative assessment is that it should be immediate, specific, and individualized. Figure 2 describes some dos and don'ts in giving praise as a part of feedback.

Postinstruction Assessment **Summative assessment** (or formal assessment) is assessment after instruction is finished, with the purpose of documenting student performance. Assessment after instruction provides information about how well your students have mastered the material, whether students are ready for the next unit, what grades they should be given, what comments you should make to parents, and how you should adapt your instruction (McMillan, 2014).

MAKING ASSESSMENT COMPATIBLE WITH CONTEMPORARY VIEWS OF LEARNING AND MOTIVATION

Throughout this book, we have encouraged you to view students as active learners who discover and construct meaning; set goals, plan, and reach goals; associate and link new information with existing knowledge in meaningful ways; think reflectively, critically, and creatively; develop self-monitoring skills; have positive expectations for learning and confidence in their skills; are enthusiastically and internally motivated to learn; apply what they learn to real-world situations; and communicate effectively.

Assessment plays an important role in effort, engagement, and performance (Doe, 2015; San, 2016). Your informal observations can provide information about how motivated students are to study a subject. If you have a good relationship with the student, direct oral questioning in a private conversation can often produce valuable insight about the student's motivation. In thinking about how assessment and

Do
Focus on specific accomplishments.
Attribute success to effort and ability.
Praise spontaneously.
Refer to prior achievement.
Individualize and use variety.
Give praise immediately.
Praise correct strategies leading to success.
Praise accurately with credibility.
Praise privately.
Focus on progress.

Don't
Focus on general or global achievement.
Attribute success to luck or other's help.
Praise predictably.
Ignore prior achievement.
Give the same praise to all students.
Give praise much later.
Ignore strategies and focus only on outcomes.
Praise for undeserving performance.
Praise publicly.
Focus solely on current performance.

FIGURE 2 DO'S AND DON'TS OF USING PRAISE WHEN GIVING FEEDBACK IN FORMATIVE ASSESSMENTS

Source: *Classroom Assessment* (p. 143, Table 5.5), by J.H. McMillan, 2007, Pearson Education, Inc.

summative assessment Assessment after instruction is finished to document student performance; also called formal assessment.

motivation are linked, ask yourself if your assessments will encourage students to become more meaningfully involved in the subject matter and more intrinsically motivated to study the topic. Assessments that are challenging but fair should increase students' enthusiasm for learning. Assessments that are too difficult will lower students' self-esteem and self-efficacy, as well as raise their anxiety. Assessing students with measures that are too easy will bore them and not motivate them to study hard enough.

Susan Brookhart (1997, 2008) developed a model of how classroom assessment helps motivate students. She argues that every classroom environment hosts a series of repeated assessment events. In each assessment event, the teacher communicates with the students through assignments, activities, and feedback about performance. Students respond according to their perceptions of these learning opportunities and how well they think they will be able to perform. Brookhart argues that this view of classroom assessment suggests that teachers should evaluate students using a variety of performances, especially performances that are meaningful to students.

Similarly, many other classroom assessment experts emphasize that if you view motivated, active learning as an important goal of instruction, you should create alternative assessments that are quite different from traditional tests, which don't evaluate how students construct knowledge and understanding, set and reach goals, or think critically and creatively (McMillan, 2014; Popham, 2017). Later in the chapter, we will explore how alternative assessments can be used to examine these aspects of students' learning and motivation.

> **Thinking Back/Thinking Forward**
>
> Teachers' expectations play an important role in students' achievement. Connect to "Motivation, Teaching, and Learning."

CREATING CLEAR, APPROPRIATE LEARNING TARGETS

Tying assessment to current views on learning and motivation also involves developing clear, appropriate learning goals, or targets. A *learning target* consists of what students should know and be able to do. You should establish criteria for judging whether students have attained the learning target (McMillan, 2014). Figure 3 provides some examples of unit learning targets.

Students will be able to explain how various cultures are different and how cultures influence people's beliefs and lives by answering orally a comprehensive set of questions about cultural differences and their effects.
Students will demonstrate their knowledge of the parts of a plant by filling in words or a diagram for all parts studied.
Students will demonstrate their understanding of citizenship by correctly identifying whether previously unread statements about citizenship are true or false. A large number of items is used to sample most of the content learned.
Students will be able to explain why the American Constitution is important by writing an essay that indicates what would happen if we abolished our Constitution. The papers would be graded holistically, looking for evidence of reasons, knowledge of the Constitution, and organization.
Students will show that they know the difference between components of sentences by correctly identifying verbs, adverbs, adjectives, nouns, and pronouns in seven of eight long, complex sentences.
Students will be able to multiply fractions by correctly computing eight of ten fraction problems. The problems are new to the students; some are similar to "challenge" questions in the book.
Students will be able to use their knowledge of addition, subtraction, division, and multiplication to solve word problems that are similar to those used in the sixth-grade standardized test.
Students will demonstrate their understanding of how visual art conveys ideas and feelings by correctly indicating, orally, how examples of art communicate ideas and feelings.

FIGURE 3 EXAMPLES OF UNIT LEARNING TARGETS

ESTABLISHING HIGH-QUALITY ASSESSMENTS

Another important goal for the classroom as an assessment context is achieving high-quality assessment. Like standardized testing, assessment reaches a high level of quality when it yields valid and reliable information about students' performance. High-quality assessments also are fair (McMillan, 2014).

Validity As indicated in the chapter on standardized tests and teaching, *validity* refers to the extent to which assessment measures what it is intended to measure and the appropriateness of inference from and uses of the information (McMillan, 2014). *Inferences* are conclusions that teachers draw from information.

You can't assess everything a student learns. Thus, your assessment of a student will necessarily be a sample of the student's learning. The most important source of information for validity in your classroom, then, will be *content-related evidence*, the extent to which the assessment reflects what you have been teaching (McMillan, 2014).

Adequately sampling content is clearly an important goal of valid assessment. Use your best professional judgment when sampling content. Thus, you wouldn't want to use just one multiple-choice question to assess a student's knowledge of a chapter on geography. An increasing trend is to use multiple methods of assessment, which can provide a more comprehensive sampling of content. Thus, the teacher might assess students' knowledge of the geography chapter with some multiple-choice questions, several essay questions, and a project to complete. Always ask yourself whether your assessments of students are adequate samples that accurately reflect their knowledge and understanding.

Linking instruction and assessment in the classroom leads to the concept of **instructional validity**: the extent to which the assessment is a reasonable sample of what actually went on in the classroom (McMillan, 2014). For example, a classroom assessment should reflect both what the teacher taught and students' opportunity to learn the material. Consider a math class in which the teacher gives students a test on their ability to solve multiplication problems. For instructional validity, it is important that the teacher competently instructed students in how to solve the problems and gave students adequate opportunities to practice this skill.

An important strategy for validity in classroom assessment is to systematically link learning targets, content, instruction, and assessment (McMillan, 2014). Imagine that you are a science teacher and that one of your learning targets is to get students to think more critically and creatively in designing science projects. Ask yourself what content is important to achieve this learning target. For instance, will it help students to read biographies of famous scientists that include information about how they came up with their ideas? Also ask yourself what learning targets you will emphasize in instruction. For your target regarding students' science projects, it will be important for you to carry through in your instruction on the theme of helping students to think critically and creatively about science.

Reliability As indicated in the chapter on standardized tests and teaching, *reliability* is the extent to which a test produces consistent, reproducible scores. Reliable scores are stable, dependable, and relatively free from errors of measurement. Consistency depends on circumstances involved in taking the test and student factors that vary from one test to another (McMillan, 2011).

Reliability is not about the appropriateness of the assessment information but about determining how consistently an assessment measures what it is designed to measure (Suen, 2008). If a teacher gives students the same test in a math class on two occasions and the students perform in a consistent manner on the tests, this indicates that the test was reliable. However, the consistency in students' performance (with high-scorers being high both times the test was given, middle-scorers performing similarly across the two assessments, and low-scorers doing poorly on

instructional validity The extent to which the assessment is a reasonable sample of what went on in the classroom.

both assessments) says nothing about whether the test actually measured what it was designed to measure (for example, being an accurate, representative sample of questions that measured the math content that had been taught). Thus, reliable assessments are not necessarily valid.

Reliability is reduced by errors in measurement. A student can have adequate knowledge and skill and still not perform consistently across several assessments because of a number of factors. Internal factors can include health, motivation, and anxiety. External factors can include inadequate directions given by the teacher, ambiguously created items, poor sampling of information, and inefficient scoring of the student's responses. For example, a student might perform extremely well on the first test a teacher gives to assess the student's reading comprehension but considerably lower on the second test in this domain. The student's lack of knowledge and skill could be the reason for the low reliability across the two assessments, but the low reliability also could be due to any number of measurement errors. In classroom assessment there typically is no statistical measure of reliability. Rather, teachers rely on their observations and judgments about whether possible influences of error have occurred.

Thinking Back/Thinking Forward

Validity, reliability, and fairness not only are important aspects of teacher-constructed tests but also are important aspects of standardized tests. Connect to "Standardized Tests and Teaching."

Fairness High-quality classroom assessment is not only valid and reliable but also fair (McMillan, 2014). Assessment is fair when all students have an equal opportunity to learn and demonstrate their knowledge and skill. Assessment is fair when teachers have developed appropriate learning targets, provided competent content and instruction to match those targets, and chosen assessments that reflect the targets, content, and instruction.

Assessment bias includes offensiveness and unfair penalization (Popham, 2008). An assessment is biased if it is offensive to a subgroup of students. This occurs when negative stereotypes of particular subgroups are included in the test. For example, consider a test in which the items portray males in high-paying and prestigious jobs (doctors and business executives) and females in low-paying and less prestigious jobs (clerks and secretaries). Because some females taking the test likely will be offended by this gender inequality, and appropriately so, the stress this creates may produce a less-successful outcome for females on the test.

An assessment also may be biased if it unfairly penalizes a student based on the student's group membership, such as ethnicity, socioeconomic status, gender, religion, and disability. For example, consider an assessment that focuses on information that students from affluent families are far more likely to be familiar with than students from low-income families (Popham, 2017). A teacher decides to see how well students can collaboratively solve problems in groups. The content of the problem to be discussed is a series of locally presented operas and symphonies likely to have been attended only by those who can afford the high ticket prices. Even if the affluent students didn't attend these musical events themselves, they may have heard their parents talk about them. Thus, students from low-income families might perform less effectively on the collaborative problem-solving exercise pertaining to musical events not because they are less skilled at such problem solving but because they are unfamiliar with the events.

DIVERSITY

Some assessment experts believe it is important to create a philosophy of *pluralistic assessment,* which includes being responsive to cultural diversity in the classroom and at school. This usually includes performance assessments during instruction and after instruction.

Geneva Gay (1997, pp. 215–216, 218) evaluated the role of ethnicity and culture in assessment and recommended a number of culturally responsive strategies in assessing students. She advocates (1) modifying the Eurocentric nature of current U.S. instruction and achievement assessments; (2) using a wider variety of assessment methods that take into account the cultural styles of students of color; (3) evaluating students against their own records; and (4) assessing students in ways that serve culturally appropriate diagnostic and developmental functions.

Gay notes that achievement assessments "are designed to determine what students know. Presumably they reflect what has been taught in schools." She argues that "although progress has been made in the last three decades to make school curricula more inclusive of ethnic and cultural diversity, most of the knowledge taught, and consequently the achievement tests, continue to be Eurocentric." She points out that even mastery of skills tends to be "transmitted through Eurocentric contexts. For instance, achievement tests may embed skills in scenarios that are not relevant to the cultural backgrounds and life experiences of students of color," as when a teacher asks "immigrant students from the Caribbean who have never experienced snow to engage in problem solving" by evaluating the challenges and dilemmas presented by a blizzard. The students might have the problem-solving skill to respond to this request, but their unfamiliarity with cold winters can interfere with their ability to perform the task effectively.

This does not mean that students of color should not be assessed or that they should not be expected to meet high achievement standards. They should. However, "to avoid perpetuating educational inequality through assessment procedures, these students should not always be expected to demonstrate" knowledge and skills in terms of contexts with which they are not familiar. A good strategy is to use a variety of assessment methods to ensure that no single method gives an advantage to one ethnic group over another. These methods should include socioemotional measures as well as measures of academic content. Teachers also should carefully observe and monitor students' performance for verbal and nonverbal information in the assessment context.

Gay stresses that assessment should always "serve diagnostic and developmental functions and be culturally responsible. . . . Narrative reports, developmental profiles, student-teacher-parent conferences, and anecdotal records should always be included in reporting students' progress."

CURRENT TRENDS

Here are some current trends in classroom assessment (Hambleton, 1996; McMillan, 2014; National Research Council, 2001):

- *Using at least some performance-based assessment.* Historically, classroom assessment has emphasized the use of **objective tests**, such as multiple-choice, which have relatively clear, unambiguous scoring criteria. In contrast, **performance assessments** require students to create answers or products that demonstrate their knowledge or skill. Examples of performance assessment include writing an essay, conducting an experiment, carrying out a project, solving a real-world problem, and creating a portfolio (Stiggins, 2008).
- *Examining higher-level cognitive skills.* Rather than assess only content knowledge, as many objective tests do, a current trend is to evaluate a student's higher-level cognitive skills, such as problem solving, critical thinking, decision making, drawing of inferences, and strategic thinking.

  There are a number of online assessment tools that can be used to assess students' higher-level thinking. Among the best online assessment tools for this purpose are Kahoot! and Socrative, which can deploy your multiple-choice, true–false, or short answer questions. Note that the thinking level assessed depends on the way you ask your questions. Case-based questions are more likely to require thinking at levels greater than recalling facts, as are items like those in the Praxis™ practice sections of this book, which require application and evaluation.
- *Using multiple assessment methods.* In the past, assessment meant using a test—often a multiple-choice test—as the sole means of assessing a student. A current trend is to use multiple methods to assess students. Thus, a teacher might use any number of these methods: a multiple-choice test, an essay, an interview, a project, a portfolio, and student evaluations of themselves. Multiple assessments provide a broader view of the child's learning and achievement than a single measure.

Thinking Back/Thinking Forward

Complex cognitive processes include reasoning, critical thinking, decision making, problem solving, and creative thinking. Connect to "Complex Cognitive Processes."

---

objective tests Tests that have relatively clear, unambiguous scoring criteria, usually multiple-choice tests.

performance assessment Assessment that requires creating answers or products that demonstrate knowledge and skill; examples include writing an essay, conducting an experiment, carrying out a project, solving a real-world problem, and creating a portfolio.

- *Using more multiple-choice items to prepare students for taking high-stakes state standards-based tests.* Just when a trend in assessment that was more compatible with cognitive, constructivist, and motivational approaches (performance assessment, use of portfolios, and student self-assessment) had developed, teachers returned to using objective formats for assessment, in many cases more than before. In assessment expert James McMillan's (2007, p. 19) view, many teachers need to balance the demands of tests mandated by No Child Left Behind "with what they know about best practices of teaching and assessment that maximize student learning and motivation. Clearly, classroom assessment must be considered in the current climate that emphasizes high-stakes testing."
- *Having high performance standards.* Another trend is the demand for high performance standards, even world-class performance standards, for interpreting educational results. World-class performance standards can benefit contemporary classroom assessment by providing goals, or targets, to attain. However, questions arise about who should set these standards and whether they should be set at all.
- *Using computers as part of assessment.* Traditionally, computers have been used to score tests, analyze test results, and report scores. Today, computers increasingly are being used to construct and administer tests, as well as to present different assessment formats to students in a multimedia environment (Greenhow, 2015). With coming advances in technology, assessment practices are likely to be very different from traditional paper-and-pencil tests.

The two students here are demonstrating their knowledge and understanding of nutrition. *What are some other examples of performance assessment?*
Fuse/Corbis/Getty Images

TECHNOLOGY

Many school systems are turning to *Web-based assessment*—assessment available on the Internet—because of its potential for greater accuracy and cost reduction. A number of testing firms, including Educational Testing Service, are developing tests to be administered on computers in the classroom, school, or district, but those are not Web-based assessments. If an assessment is Web-based, students use a computer and the assessment takes place on the Internet (Ibrahim et al., 2015).

Some of the best Web-based assessments can be easily adapted to the curriculum you use in your classroom. Some of the assessments focus on recording and evaluating student behavior, some involve academic progress, and others include all of these areas. The best Web-based assessments let teachers "develop their own tests or forms and usually include a databank of questions or other assessment tools. Most are aligned with various state and national standards," or No Child Left Behind.

Trends in assessment also include emphasizing integrated rather than isolated skills, involving students in all aspects of assessment, giving students more feedback, and making standards and criteria public rather than private and secretive.

What are some ways that computers are being used in the assessment of students?
Creatas/PunchStock

Review, Reflect, and Practice

1 Discuss the classroom as an assessment context.

REVIEW
- Describe assessment before, after, and during instruction.
- How can assessment be brought into line with contemporary views of learning and motivation?
- What are learning targets?
- What standards can be used to judge the quality of classroom assessments?
- What are some current trends in assessing students' learning?

continued

Review, Reflect, and Practice

REFLECT
- Think of one of the better teachers that you had as a K–12 student. In retrospect, how would you describe the teacher's classroom as an "assessment context"?

PRAXIS™ PRACTICE
1. Which of the following is the best example of formative assessment?
   a. Mr. Harrison's students write a paper at the conclusion of a unit of instruction. This allows him to assess to what degree his students understand the content of the unit.
   b. Mr. Shockey asks his students open-ended questions during instruction. This way he can determine to what degree his students understand the content of his lesson.
   c. Ms. Manning plays a game of *Jeopardy!* at the end of her unit of instruction to assess student understanding of the content of the unit.
   d. Ms. Walker gives her students a brief assessment prior to beginning a unit of instruction, so she knows what her students are already capable of doing. This allows her to gear her instruction to her students' zones of proximal development.

2. Which of the following assessments will most likely enhance student motivation to study and learn?
   a. Mr. Ditka assigns his students a project that requires knowledge from the unit of instruction to complete successfully.
   b. Mr. Payton gives periodic tests that are easy enough for all of his students to earn high scores if they have attended class.
   c. Mr. Rivera puts two or three tricky questions in each test so he can determine which of his students read the items carefully before responding.
   d. Mr. Singletary constructs very challenging exams to ensure that only those students who have studied the material carefully will be successful.

3. Ms. Ramirez has assigned her students to analyze the water in a nearby stream, determine the level of pollution in the stream, and develop a solution to the pollution problem. What type of learning target has she created?
   a. affect
   b. knowledge
   c. product
   d. reasoning

4. Ms. Vick has created an assessment to measure the degree to which her students have mastered the content of her unit on the U.S. Constitution. Included in the test are items about the Bill of Rights, other constitutional amendments, the American Revolution, and World War II. What is the best description of this assessment?
   a. It is likely to yield both valid and reliable scores.
   b. The scores are unlikely to be valid or reliable.
   c. While the scores may be reliable, they will not be valid.
   d. While the scores may be valid, they will not be reliable.

5. Ms. Krzyzewski is teaching a science unit on anatomy. Students have been studying the anatomy of various animals. Which of the following is the best example of a performance assessment of this material?
   a. Students answer oral questions regarding the structures present in different animals.
   b. Students write an essay comparing and contrasting the anatomy of frogs and pigs.
   c. Students dissect animals and identify their anatomical parts.
   d. Students take a multiple-choice test covering the material in the unit.

Please see answer key at end of book . . . .

2 TRADITIONAL TESTS

- Selected-Response Items
- Constructed-Response Items

LG 2 Provide some guidelines for constructing traditional tests.

Traditional tests are typically paper-and-pencil tests in which students select from choices, calculate numbers, construct short responses, or write essays. Our coverage of traditional tests focuses on two main types of item formats in assessment: (1) selected-response items and (2) constructed-response items.

SELECTED-RESPONSE ITEMS

Selected-response items have an objective format that allows students' responses to be scored quickly. A scoring key for correct responses is created and can be applied by an examiner or by a computer. Multiple-choice, true/false, and matching items are the most widely used types of items in selected-response tests.

Multiple-Choice Items A **multiple-choice item** consists of two parts: the stem plus a set of possible responses. The stem is a question or statement. Incorrect alternatives are called *distractors*. The student's task is to select the correct answer rather than choosing one of the distractors—for example:

What is the capital of Vermont? (Stem)
   a. Boston (distractor)
   b. Montpelier (answer)
   c. Portland (distractor)
   d. Weston (distractor)

Susan Brookhart (2015) recent described two advantages that multiple-choice items provide: (1) They only require choice, not extensive written or spoken answers, which means that students who do not have well-developed written or oral language skills can still display their thinking skills, and (2) by using multiple-choice items teachers can ask and students answer far more multiple-choice questions than open-ended questions in a specified period of time. This allows teachers to ask questions about more aspects of the content that students are learning.

Students below the fourth grade probably should answer questions on the test page rather than on a separate answer sheet. Young elementary school students tend to respond slowly and lose their place easily when they have to use a separate answer sheet. Using a separate answer sheet with older students often reduces scoring time because the answers usually can fit on only one page. Many school districts have commercially printed answer sheets that teachers can order for their classes. If you hand-score multiple-choice tests, consider preparing a scoring stencil by cutting or punching holes in the answer sheet in the locations of the correct answers.

For most classroom requirements, simply count the number of answers marked correctly. Some teachers penalize students for guessing by deducting for wrong answers, but assessment experts say that this probably is not worth the extra bother and frequently leads to mistakes in scoring.

Strengths and limitations of multiple-choice items are listed in Figure 4.

selected-response items Test items with an objective format in which student responses can be scored quickly. A scoring guide for correct responses is created and can be applied by an examiner or a computer.

multiple-choice item An objective test item consisting of two parts: a stem plus a set of possible responses.

Strengths
1. Both simple and complex learning outcomes can be measured.
2. The task is highly structured and clear.
3. A broad sample of achievement can be measured.
4. Incorrect alternatives provide diagnostic information.
5. Scores are less influenced by guessing than true/false items.
6. Scoring is easy, objective, and reliable.

Limitations
1. Constructing good items is time consuming.
2. It is frequently difficult to find plausible distractors.
3. The multiple-choice format is ineffective for measuring some types of problem solving and the ability to organize and express ideas.
4. Score can be influenced by reading ability.

FIGURE 4 STRENGTHS AND LIMITATIONS OF MULTIPLE-CHOICE ITEMS

Source: *Assessment of Student Achievement* (p. 60), by N.E. Gronlund, 1998, Allyn & Bacon.

CONNECTING WITH STUDENTS: Best Practices
Strategies for Writing Multiple-Choice Items

Some good strategies for writing high-quality multiple-choice items include the following (Gronlund & Waugh, 2009; McMillan, 2014):

1. *Write the stem as a question.*
2. *Give three or four possible alternatives from which to choose.*
3. *State items and options positively when possible.* Elementary school students especially find negatives confusing. If you use the word *not* in the stem, *italicize* or underline it*—*for example:

    Which of the following cities is *not* in New England?
    a. Boston
    b. Chicago
    c. Montpelier
    d. Providence

4. *Include as much of the item as possible in the stem, thus making the stem relatively long and the alternatives relatively short*—for example:

    Which U.S. president wrote the Gettysburg Address?
    a. Thomas Jefferson
    b. Abraham Lincoln
    c. James Madison
    d. Woodrow Wilson

5. *Alternatives should grammatically match the stem so that answers are grammatically correct.* For example, the first item is better than the second:

    Orville and Wilbur Wright became famous because of which type of transportation?
    a. airplane
    b. automobile
    c. boat
    d. train

    Orville and Wilbur Wright became famous because of an
    a. airplane
    b. automobile
    c. boat
    d. train

6. *Write items that have a clearly defensible correct or best option.* Unless you give alternative directions, students will assume that there is only one correct or best answer to an item.
7. *Vary the placement of the correct option.* Students who are unsure of an answer tend to select the middle options and avoid the extreme options. Alphabetizing response choices (by the first letters in the response) will help to vary the placement of the correct option.
8. *Beware of cues in the length of the options.* Correct answers tend to be longer than incorrect ones because of the need to include specifications and qualifications that make it true. Lengthen the distractors (incorrect responses) to approximately the same length as the correct answer.
9. *Don't expect students to make narrow distinctions among answer choices.* For example, the first item is better than the second:

    The freezing point of water is
    a. 25°F
    b. 32°F
    c. 39°F
    d. 46°F

    The freezing point of water is
    a. 30°F
    b. 31°F
    c. 32°F
    d. 33°F

10. *Do not overuse "None of the above" and "All of the above."* Also avoid using variations of "(a) and (b)" or "(c) and (d) but not (a)."
11. *Don't use the exact wording in a textbook when writing a question.* Struggling students might recognize the correct answer but not really understand its meaning.
12. *Write at least some items that encourage students to engage in higher-level thinking.* As we indicated earlier, a current trend is to use more multiple-choice items in classroom assessment because of the demands imposed on teachers by high-stakes state standards-based tests. An important issue in the return to using more multiple-choice items is the cognitive level demanded by the items. Many teachers report that they use "higher-level" test items, but in reality they mainly are using lower-level recall and recognition items (McMillan, 2014).

    How can you write higher-level thinking multiple-choice items? Here are some recommendations (Center for Instructional Technology, 2006):

    - Don't write more than three or four items a day that involve higher-level thinking because they are more difficult to write and take more time than simple, straightforward items.

CONNECTING WITH STUDENTS: Best Practices
Strategies for Writing Multiple-Choice Items

- Write one or two items after a class (a good idea for writing any test items) and then simply assemble them at a later time when making up a test.
- Use some analogy-based items (see the discussion of analogies in the chapter on complex cognitive processes). An example of a multiple-choice item using an analogy is:

  Bandura is to social cognitive theory as _____ is to social constructivist theory:
  a. Piaget
  b. Siegler
  c. Vygotsky
  d. Skinner

- Write some case-study items. You already have encountered many of these in this textbook. Many of the PRAXIS™ Practice features at the end of main sections in a chapter and all of the *Crack the Case* multiple-choice items at the end of chapters involve case studies.
- Write items in which students have to select what is missing or needs to be changed in a scenario you provide.

True/False Items   A true/false item asks a student to mark whether a statement is true or false—for example:

Montpelier is the capital of Vermont.   True   False

The ease with which true/false items can be constructed has a potential drawback. Teachers sometimes take statements directly from a text or modify them slightly when making up true/false items. Avoid this practice, because it tends to encourage rote memorization with little understanding of the material.

The strengths and limitations of true/false items are described in Figure 5.

Matching Items   Used by many teachers with younger students, matching requires students to connect one group of stimuli correctly with a second group of stimuli. Matching is especially well suited for assessing associations or links between two sets of information. In a typical matching format, a teacher places a list of terms on the left side of the page and a description or definition of the terms on the right side of the page. The student's task is to draw lines between the columns that correctly link terms with their definitions or descriptions. In another format, a space is left blank next to each term, in which the student writes the correct number or letter of the description/definition. When using matching, limit the number of items to be matched to no more than eight or ten. Using no more than five or six items per set is a good strategy.

Matching tests are convenient for teachers in that (1) their compact form requires little space, thus making it easy to assess quite a lot of information efficiently, and (2) they can be easily scored by using a correct-answer template (Popham, 2017).

But matching tests may tend to ask students to connect trivial information. Also, most matching tasks require students to connect information they have simply memorized, although items can be constructed that measure more complex cognitive skills.

CONSTRUCTED-RESPONSE ITEMS

Constructed-response items require students to write out information rather than select a response from a menu. Short-answer and essay items are the most commonly used forms of traditional constructed-response items. In scoring, many constructed-response items require judgment on the part of the examiner.

Short-Answer Items   A **short-answer item** is a constructed-response format in which students are required to write a word, a short phrase, or several sentences in response to a prompt. For example, a student might be asked, "Who discovered penicillin?"

Strengths

1. The item is useful for outcomes where there are only two possible alternatives (for example, fact or opinion, valid or invalid).
2. Less demand is placed on reading ability than in multiple-choice items.
3. A relatively large number of items can be answered in a typical testing period.
4. Scoring is easy, objective, and reliable.

Limitations

1. It is difficult to write items at a high level of knowledge and thinking that are free from ambiguity.
2. When a student indicates correctly that a statement is false, that response provides no evidence that the student knows what is correct.
3. No diagnostic information is provided by the incorrect answers.
4. Scores are more influenced by guessing than with any other item type.

FIGURE 5   STRENGTHS AND LIMITATIONS OF TRUE/FALSE ITEMS

Source: *Assessment of Student Achievement* (p. 79), by N.E. Gronlund, 1998, Pearson Education, Inc.

constructed-response items   Items that require students to write out information rather than select a response from a menu.

short-answer item   A constructed-response format in which students are required to write a word, a short phrase, or several sentences in response to a prompt.

The short-answer format allows recall and could provide a problem-solving assessment of a wide range of material. The disadvantages of short-answer questions are that they can require judgment in scoring and typically measure rote learning.

Sentence completion is a variation of the short-answer item in which students express their knowledge and skill by completing a sentence. For example, a student might be asked to complete this sentence stem: The name of the person who discovered penicillin is _____.

Essays Essay items allow students more freedom of response to questions but require more writing than other formats. Essay items are especially good for assessing students' understanding of material, higher-level thinking skills, ability to organize information, and writing skills. Here are some examples of high school essay questions:

What are the strengths and weaknesses of a democratic approach to government?
Describe the main themes of the novel you just read.
Argue that the United States is a gender-biased nation.

Essay items can require students to write anything from a few sentences to several pages. In some cases, teachers ask all students to answer the same essay question(s). In others, teachers let students select from a group of items the item(s) they want to write about, a strategy that makes it more difficult to compare different students' responses.

Suggestions for writing good essay items include these (Sax, 1997):

- *Specify limitations.* Be sure to specify the length of the desired answer and the weight that will be given to each item in determining scores or judgments.
- *Structure and clarify the task.* Make clear what your students are supposed to write about. A poorly worded item is "Who was George Washington?" This could be answered in six words: "First president of the United States." In cases like this, ask yourself what more you want the student to tell. This more-structured essay item requires more thinking on the part of the student:

    Discuss several events in the life of George Washington that confirm or disprove the claim that "he never told a lie." Use the events to support a claim of your own about how truthful Washington was.

- *Ask questions in a direct way.* Don't get too tricky. You might hear the term *rubric* used in regard to scoring students' responses on essays and other tests. In this context, rubric simply means a scoring system. Figure 6 lists some strengths and limitations of essay questions.

FIGURE 6 STRENGTHS AND LIMITATIONS OF ESSAY QUESTIONS

Strengths
1. The highest level of learning outcomes (analysis, synthesis, evaluation) can be measured.
2. The integration and application of ideas can be emphasized.
3. Preparation time is usually less than for selection-type formats.

Limitations
1. Achievement may not be adequately sampled due to the time needed to answer each question.
2. It can be difficult to relate essay responses to intended learning outcomes because of freedom to select, organize, and express ideas.
3. Scores are raised by writing skill and bluffing, and lowered by poor handwriting, misspelling, and grammatical errors.
4. Scoring is time consuming, subjective, and possibly unreliable.

Source: *Assessment of Student Achievement.* (p. 103), by N.E. Gronlund, 1998, Pearson Education, Inc.

essay item Test item that requires more writing than other formats but allows more freedom of response to questions.

CONNECTING WITH STUDENTS: Best Practices
Strategies for Scoring Essay Questions

Here are some good strategies for scoring essays (Sax, 1997):

1. *Outline a plan for what constitutes a good or acceptable answer prior to administering or scoring students' responses* (McMillan, 2011). Essays can be scored holistically or analytically. *Holistic scoring* means making an overall judgment about the student's answer and giving it a single number or letter. You might make this judgment based on your overall impression of the essay or base it on several criteria that you have generated. Holistic scoring is often used when essays are long. *Analytic scoring* means scoring various criteria separately, then adding up the points to produce an overall score for the essay. Analytic scoring can be time consuming, so avoid having more than three or four criteria for an essay.

2. *Devise a method by which you can score the essays without knowing which students wrote them.* You might do this by having students write their name beside a number on a separate sheet, then write only their number on the essay.

CONNECTING WITH STUDENTS: Best Practices
Strategies for Scoring Essay Questions

When you record the grade, you can match up the student's number and name. This reduces the chance that your positive or negative expectations for the student will enter into your evaluation of the responses.

3. *Evaluate all answers to the same questions together.* Read and score all students' responses to one item before moving on to the next item. It is easier for you to remember the criteria for evaluating an answer to a single essay item than to remember the criteria for all essay items. Also, if you read all of one student's responses together, your evaluation of the first few items will tend to influence your evaluation of the remaining items.

4. *Decide on a policy for handling irrelevant or incorrect responses.* Some students try to bluff their way through essays. Other students write everything they know about a topic without taking the time to zero in on what the item is asking for. Still other students might use poor grammar, misspell words, or write illegibly. Decide ahead of time whether and how much you will penalize such responses.

5. *If possible, reread papers before handing them back to students.* This helps you guard against any flaws or oversights in your scoring.

6. *Write comments on the paper.* An essay, especially a long one, with only a number or letter grade on it does not give adequate feedback to a student. And if you only circle or correct spelling errors and grammar, you are not giving students insight about the content of their essay responses. A good strategy is to write a number of brief comments at appropriate places throughout the essay, such as "Expand this idea more," "Unclear," or "Needs an example," in addition to making overall comments about the essay at its beginning or end.

Review, Reflect, and Practice

2 Provide some guidelines for constructing traditional tests.

REVIEW
- What are some important ideas to remember when creating multiple-choice, true/false, and matching items?
- What are constructed-response items and how do short-answer items differ from essay items?

REFLECT
- Why do you think traditional testing has survived so long in K–12 classrooms?

PRAXIS™ PRACTICE

1. Mr. Brown, a college instructor, includes the following item in a test about the impact of the family on children: What parenting style does Homer Simpson exhibit? Mr. Brown's possible answers are authoritative, authoritarian, neglectful, and permissive. Which of the following is the most appropriate criticism of Mr. Brown's question and answers?
    a. It is too easy to eliminate options because they are not all parenting styles.
    b. Parenting style has nothing to do with the impact of family on children.
    c. The question is biased in favor of people who watch *The Simpsons*.
    d. There is more than one clearly correct response.

2. Mr. Dent has just returned Marcia's graded essay to her. Notations of spelling and grammar errors, and the grade, 42/50—B, are all he has written on the test. What is the most appropriate criticism of this assessment?
    a. An essay should never be worth this many points on a test.
    b. Essays should not be graded numerically, providing a letter grade is sufficient.
    c. There are no comments about what she did well and where she lost points.
    d. Spelling and grammar errors should not be marked on an essay.

Please see answer key at end of book . . . .

LG 3 Describe some types of alternative assessments.

3 ALTERNATIVE ASSESSMENTS

There are alternatives to the traditional assessments that we just discussed (McMillan, 2014; Popham, 2017). Let's examine some trends in this regard.

TRENDS IN ALTERNATIVE ASSESSMENT

One current trend is to require students to solve some type of authentic problem or to perform in terms of completing a project or demonstrating other skills outside the context of a test or an essay (Chai et al., 2015; Cirit, 2015). Another trend is to have students create a learning portfolio to demonstrate what they have learned (Cote & Emmett, 2015; Qvortrup & Keiding, 2015). Such alternative assessments are needed to make instruction compatible with contemporary views of learning and motivation.

Alternative assessments offer students more choices than they would have in taking a test or writing an essay (Hoachlander, 2015; Kim & Covino, 2015). Consider several alternative assessments that a middle school language-arts teacher devised (Combs, 1997). She gave students a menu of options to choose from that included book reports, artwork, videos, and models. For example, in a unit on mystery, students might choose to write a report on an author of mystery stories, write an original mystery, make a children's mystery book, or conduct an interview with a private investigator. Each of these options came with a detailed set of instructions and a scoring guide for quality control. Figure 7 shows the directions and scoring guide for alternative assessments that focus on the Middle Ages and family history.

FIGURE 7 EXAMPLES OF ALTERNATIVE ASSESSMENT IN A MIDDLE-SCHOOL LANGUAGE-ARTS CLASS

Middle Ages option model

Directions:
Make a model of a creature or character from the Middle Ages. Write a one-half to one page description of your character (tell who or what it is and its importance in the Middle Ages). Your model must portray the creature or character through the use of appropriate costume, props, or other attributes.

Scoring Guide
- 25 Model portrays the character or creature and time period through the use of attire, props, and other attributes
- 10 Artistic quality
- 15 Model shows evidence of effort
- 50 A one-half to one page written description of the character is included

Family history option: family tree poster

Directions:
Make a poster of your family tree, going back at least three generations. Provide as much information about the family members as possible, including, but not limited to, birthdate, death date (if not living), occupation, place of birth, accomplishments, and so on. In addition, provide at least two anecdotes about your family's history (for example, how they came to live in our town, special notoriety, honors, awards, medals). You must *write out* your family tree! (You may not make a copy of a commercially prepared family tree and paste it on the poster.) Make your poster attractive and neat!

Scoring Guide
- 25 Family tree includes at least three generations prior to you
- 25 In addition to names, most entries include information such as birth, death, and place of birth
- 25 Poster includes at least two anecdotes about interesting or well-known family members
- 15 Poster is neatly and attractively typed or written by you
- 10 Mechanics, spelling, usage

Authentic assessment means evaluating a student's knowledge or skill in a context that approximates the real world or real life as closely as possible. Traditional assessment has involved the use of paper-and-pencil tests that are often far removed from real-world contexts. An increasing trend is to assess students with items that more closely reflect reality. In some circles, the terms *performance assessment* and *authentic assessment* have been used interchangeably. However, not all performance assessments are authentic (McMillan, 2014).

Critics of authentic assessment argue that such assessments are not necessarily superior to more conventional assessments, such as multiple-choice and essay tests (Terwilliger, 1997). They say that the proponents of authentic assessment rarely present data in support of the validity of authentic assessments. They also point out that authentic assessments don't adequately examine knowledge and basic skills.

PERFORMANCE ASSESSMENT

Moving from traditional assessment with objective tests to performance assessment has been described as going from "knowing" to "showing" (Burz & Marshall, 1996). Performance assessments include what is commonly thought of as students' actual performances (such as in dance, music, art, and physical education), as well as papers, projects, oral presentations, experiments, and portfolios. Figure 8 shows an example of a performance assessment in science (Solano-Flores & Shavelson, 1997).

authentic assessment Evaluating a student's knowledge or skill in a context that approximates the real world or real life as closely as possible.

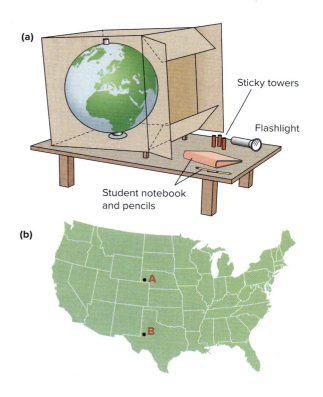

Observation/results	score
Tower C is in eastern United States	1
Tower C is in northeastern United States	1
Tower C is somewhere between Pennsylvania and Maine	1

Data gathering/modeling		score
Flashlight Position	Points flashlight at Equator	2
Flashlight Motion	Moves flashlight from E to W	2
Globe Rotation	Rotates globe	1
	Rotates globe from W to E	2
Towers	Moves Tower C around on the map/globe until shadow is matched	1
	Moves Tower C around on the map/globe in the E/NE region until shadow is matched	2
Shadows	Uses shadows of Towers A and B as reference	1

FIGURE 8 A PERFORMANCE-BASED ASSESSMENT IN SCIENCE

(a) The equipment consists of a spinning Earth globe inside a carton box, three sticky towers, and a flashlight; the students stick Towers A and B at two specific U.S. locations on the globe and are told what Tower C's shadow looks like when it is noon for Towers A and B. They have to find out where Tower C is within the United States. The solution requires modeling the sunlight by using the flashlight to project the towers' shadows onto the globe. (b) Students are asked to draw a dot on the map to show where they think Tower C is. The response format involves having students record in notebooks their solutions, the actions they carried out, and the reasoning behind their actions. (c) Students' performances are scored for the accuracy of their results and the accuracy of their modeling, reasoning, and observations.

Some disciplines, such as art, music, and physical education, have been using performance assessments for many years. The major change in performance assessment has involved introducing these forms of assessment into the traditional "academic areas." Indeed, recently there has been increased interest in including performance assessments in state assessment of students' learning and progress (Darling-Hammond & Falk, 2013; Parsi & Darling-Hammond, 2015).

Features of Performance Assessment Performance assessments often include an emphasis on "doing" open-ended activities for which there is no correct, objective answer and that may assess higher-level thinking (Peterman et al., 2015). Examples of open-ended activities include conducting an experiment, developing a plan for a new park, analyzing government or school policies to make the case for or against, and reimagining a novel through a new medium like a painting or play. Performance assessment tasks sometimes also are realistic. Evaluating performance often includes direct methods of evaluation, self-assessment, assessment of group performance as well as individual performance, and an extended period of time for assessment.

Traditional tests emphasize what students know. Performance assessments are designed to evaluate what students know and can do. In many cases, there is no correct, objective answer. For example, there is no one "correct answer" when a student gives a talk in class, creates a painting, performs a gymnastic routine, or designs a science project. Many performance assessments give students considerable freedom to construct their own responses rather than narrowing their range of answers. Although this makes scoring more difficult, it provides a context for evaluating students' higher-level thinking skills, such as the ability to think deeply about an issue or a topic.

Performance assessments use direct methods of evaluation, such as evaluating writing samples to assess writing skills and judging oral presentations to assess speaking skills. Observing a student give an oral presentation is a more direct assessment than asking the student a series of questions about speaking skills on a paper-and-pencil test.

Some performance assessments also involve having students evaluate their own performance. This emphasis shifts responsibility away from teachers and places it more squarely on the student's shoulders. Rubrics are useful aids to students in conducting self-assessments. A **rubric** is a guide that lists specific criteria for grading and scoring academic papers, projects, or tests. For example, students might be required to evaluate a scrapbook that they have created. One criterion for evaluation might be "Gives enough details?" with the following possible responses: excellent ("Yes, I put enough details to give the reader a sense of time, place, and events"), good ("Yes, I put in some details, but some key details are missing"), minimal ("No, I did not put in enough details but did include a few"), and inadequate ("No, I had almost no details").

Some performance assessments evaluate how effectively a group of students perform, not just how the students perform individually. Thus, a group of students might be assigned to create a science project rather than having each student do a project individually. Evaluation of the student can include both the individual's contribution and the group's product. Group projects are often complex and allow for the assessment of cooperative skills, communication skills, and leadership skills.

Finally, as we noted, performance assessments may take place over an extended period of time. In traditional assessment, assessment occurs in a single time frame. For example, a teacher gives a multiple-choice test and students are allowed an hour to take it. By contrast, it is not unusual for performance assessments to involve sustained work over days, weeks, and even months. For example, a student might be evaluated once a month on the progress the student is making on a science project, then receive a final evaluation when the project is completed.

Guidelines for Performance Assessment Guidelines for performance assessment cover four general issues (Russell & Airasian, 2012): (1) establishing a clear purpose,

rubric A guide that lists specific criteria for grading and scoring academic papers, projects, or tests.

(2) identifying observable criteria, (3) providing an appropriate setting, and (4) judging or scoring the performance.

Make sure that any performance assessment has a clear purpose and that a clear decision can be made from the assessment. The purposes can be diverse: to assign a grade, to evaluate a student's progress, to recognize the important steps in a performance, to generate products to be included in a learning portfolio, to provide concrete examples of students' work for admission to college or other programs, and so forth.

Performance criteria are specific behaviors that students need to perform effectively as part of the assessment. Establishing performance criteria helps the teacher to go beyond general descriptions (such as "Do an oral presentation" or "Complete a science project") in specifying what the student needs to do. Performance criteria help you make your observations more systematic and focused. As guidelines, they direct your observations. Without such criteria, your observations can be unsystematic and haphazard. Communicating these performance criteria to students at the beginning of instruction lets students know how to focus their learning.

What might be some guidelines for creating performance criteria for evaluating the art creations of these elementary school students?
BananaStock/age fotostock

Once you have clearly outlined the performance criteria, it is important to specify the setting in which you will observe the performance or product. You may want to observe behaviors directly in the regular flow of classroom activity, in a special context you create in the classroom, or in a context outside the classroom. As a rule of thumb it is a good idea to observe the student on more than one occasion, because a single performance might not fairly represent the student's knowledge or skill.

Finally, you will need to score or rate the performance. *Scoring rubrics* involve the criteria that are used to judge performance, what the range in the quality of the performance should look like, what score should be given and what that score means, and how the different levels of quality should be described and differentiated from one another.

In preparing a rubric, you may want to (Re: Learning by Design, 2000):

1. *Include a scale of possible points to be assigned in scoring work.* High numbers usually are assigned to the best work. Scales typically use 4, 5, or 6 as the highest score, down to 1 or 0 for the lowest score.

2. *Provide descriptors for each performance criterion to increase reliability and avoid biased scoring.*

3. *Decide whether the rubric will be generic, genre-specific, or task-specific.* If generic, the rubric can be used to judge a broad performance, such as communication or problem solving. If genre-specific, the rubric applies to a more specific type of performance, such as an essay, a speech, or a narrative as a form of communication; open-ended or closed-end problems as kinds of problems solved. A task-specific rubric is unique to a single task, such as a single math problem or a speech on a specific topic.

4. *Decide whether the rubric should be longitudinal.* This type of rubric assesses progress over time toward mastery of educational objectives. One strategy for developing rubrics is to work backward from *exemplars*—examples of student work (McMillan, 1997, p. 218). "These exemplars can be analyzed to determine what descriptors distinguish them. The examples can also be used as *anchor* papers for making judgments, and can be given to students to illustrate the dimensions." An *anchor* is a sample of work or performance used to set the specific performance standard for a rubric level. Thus, attached to a paragraph describing a six-level performance in writing might be two or three samples of writing to illustrate

performance criteria Specific behaviors that students need to perform effectively as part of an assessment.

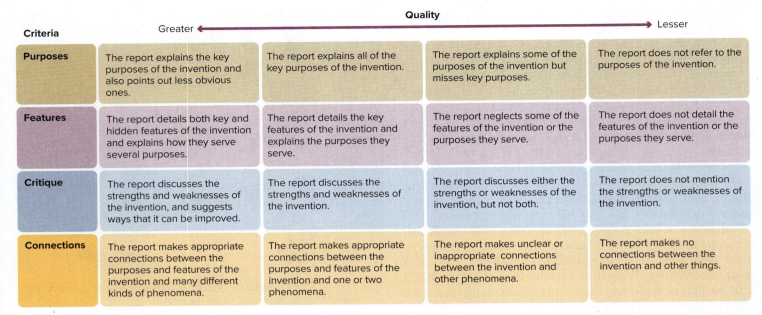

FIGURE 9 SCORING RUBRIC FOR A REPORT ON AN INVENTION

Note: A teacher might assign each of the columns a score and/or label, such as column 1: 4 (Excellent), column 2: 3 (Good), column 3: 2 (Minimal), and column 4: 1 (Inadequate).

several levels (Re: Learning by Design, 2000). Figure 9 shows a scoring rubric for scoring a report on an invention. Figure 10 indicates the importance of clarity in creating rubrics.

Evaluating Performance Assessment Many educational psychologists support the increased use of performance-based assessment (McMillan, 2014; Parsi & Darling-Hammond, 2015; Popham, 2017). They contend that performance assessments involve students more in their learning, encourage higher-level thinking skills, can measure what is really important in the curriculum, and can tie assessment more to real-world, real-life experiences.

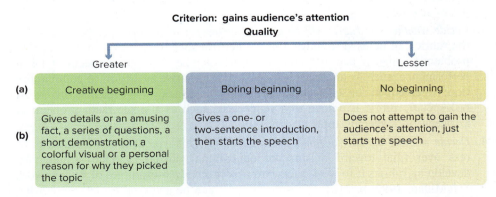

FIGURE 10 CREATING CLARITY IN A RUBRIC FOR ONE DIMENSION OF AN ORAL PRESENTATION

The descriptions on top (a) are rather vague and do not clearly specify what students need to do to be evaluated very positively on the criterion. The descriptions on the bottom (b) provide more detailed specifications of how the criterion will be rated, a recommended strategy.

CONNECTING WITH STUDENTS: Best Practices
Strategies for Developing Scoring Rubrics

Following are some helpful strategies for incorporating scoring rubrics in performance assessments (McMillan, 2014; Relearning by Design, 2000):

1. *Match the type of rating with the purpose of the assessment.* If your purpose is global and you need a general judgment, use a holistic scale. If your purpose is to provide specific feedback on different aspects of a performance, use a more analytical approach.

2. *Share the criteria with students prior to instruction.* This encourages students to incorporate the descriptions as standards to guide their work.

3. *Build your rubrics from the top, starting from a description of an exemplary performance.* Even if no student can perform at an exemplary level, the rubric should be built from a picture of excellence to establish an anchor for scoring. A good strategy is to use two or three examples of excellence rather than a single example so that students are not limited in their thinking about what an excellent performance is. After you have described the best level of quality, describe the worst; then fill in the middle levels.

4. *Carefully construct the rubric language for each criterion or score.* Use words such as *excellent* and *good,* and carefully describe what each term means. Typically, you will have a paragraph for each criterion or score that includes concrete indicators of when the criterion or score has been met.

5. *Make rubrics more authentic.* Criteria should validly, not arbitrarily, distinguish different degrees of performance. For example, criteria often used in assessing writing in large-scale performance tests include: organization, usage/word choice, focus, sentence construction, mechanics, and voice. However, the following criteria are more authentic in that they relate more clearly to the impact of the writing (and they include the previously mentioned criteria without restricting the writer to conventions and rules): clarity, memorability, persuasiveness, and enticingness.

6. *Show students models.* Let students look at examples of work that meets expectations and work that does not. Identify what's good or bad about the models.

7. *Take appropriate steps to minimize scoring error.* A scoring system should be objective and consistent. Some types of errors, in particular, should be avoided in scoring rubrics. The most common errors involve personal bias and halo effects of the person making the judgment. Personal bias occurs when teachers tend to give students higher scores (such as mostly 5 and 6 on a 1- to 6-point scale), lower scores (1 or 2), or scores in the middle (3 or 4). A halo effect occurs when a teacher's general impression of the student influences the score given on a particular performance.

However, "although support for performance-based assessment is high in many parts of the United States and Canada, effective implementation" faces several hurdles (Hambleton, 1996, p. 903). Performance assessments often "take considerably more time to construct, administer, and score than objective tests." Also, many performance tests do not meet the standards of validity and reliability advocated by many educational psychologists. Moreover, the research base for performance tests is not well established.

Still, even the strongest supporters of traditional tests acknowledge that these tests do not measure all of what schools expect students to learn (Hambleton, 1996). Although planning, constructing, and scoring performance tests is challenging, teachers should make every effort to include performance assessments as an important aspect of their teaching.

Several teachers were asked how they use performance assessment in the classroom. Following are their responses.

EARLY CHILDHOOD Most of the assessments in early childhood classrooms are based on a performance assessment model. Teachers observe and record information that the child presents as part of play and participation in classroom activities. For example, a teacher might date a paper that a child used to write her full phone number for the first time, demonstrating the knowledge of identity, ability to write the specific numbers, sequencing, memory, and more. This piece of information would be kept in the child's portfolio record to be shared with the family as part of the assessment process.

—HEIDI KAUFMAN, *Metro West YMCA Child Care and Educational Program*

ELEMENTARY SCHOOL: GRADES K–5 I set up an assignment that students prepare in class and for homework. For example, they can memorize and perform a poem or write and perform a speech about a human rights activist. I assess the student's performance, research, content, language, effort, and care.

—KEREN ABRA, *Convent of the Sacred Heart Elementary School*

MIDDLE SCHOOL: GRADES 6–8 One project I give my students is a decades project. The students get to choose a decade that interests them and present their findings to the class. They can do this like a news report and dress up like people from that decade. They can also bring in music from their decade and mementoes as well. This is a lot of fun and a great learning experience for students.

—CASEY MAASS, *Edison Middle School*

HIGH SCHOOL: GRADES 9–12 In sophomore English, students give four speeches. One demonstrates a method, one uses PowerPoint as a visual aid, one shares a personal story, and one is videotaped and reflected on formally. We also do extemporaneous speeches where a student will choose a topic and speak for two minutes. Speeches are often very stressful for many high school students, but I usually see growth with each speech.

—JENNIFER HEITER, *Bremen High School*

PORTFOLIO ASSESSMENT

Interest in portfolio assessment has increased dramatically in recent years (Qvortrup & Keiding, 2015; Ugodulunwa & Wakjissa, 2015). Portfolios represent a significant departure from traditional tests of learning. Figure 11 summarizes the contrast between portfolios and traditional testing.

A **portfolio** consists of a systematic and organized collection of a student's work that demonstrates the student's skills and accomplishments. A portfolio is a purposeful collection of work that tells the story of the student's progress and achievements. It is much more than a compilation of student papers stuffed into a manila folder or a collection of memorabilia pasted into a scrapbook. To qualify for inclusion in a portfolio, each piece of work should be created and organized in a way that demonstrates progress and purpose. Portfolios can include many different types of work, such as writing samples, journal entries, videotapes, art, teacher comments, posters, interviews, poetry, test results, problem solutions, recordings of foreign language communication, self-assessments, and any other expression of the student that the teacher believes demonstrates the student's skills and accomplishments. Portfolios can be collected on paper, in photographs, and on audiotape, video, computer disk, or CD-ROM. Today, portfolios can be created using cloud-based portfolio tools.

Four classes of evidence that can be placed in students' portfolios are artifacts, reproductions, attestations, and productions (Barton & Collins, 1997):

- *Artifacts* are documents or products, such as student papers and homework, that are produced during normal academic work in the classroom. Artifacts can be digitized via image files, video files, and audio files; then the files can be saved online in cloud repositories. Apps are available for digitizing students' work, with one of the best for this purpose being Three Ring (https://edshelf.com/tool/three-ring/).

portfolio A systematic and organized collection of a student's work that demonstrates the student's skills and accomplishments.

Traditional tests	Portfolios
• Separate learning, testing, and teaching	• Link assessment and teaching to learning
• Fail to assess the impact of prior knowledge on learning by using short passages that are often isolated and unfamiliar	• Address the importance of the student's prior knowledge as a critical determinant to learning by using authentic assessment activities
• Rely on materials requesting only literal information	• Provide opportunities to demonstrate inferential and critical thinking that are essential for constructing meaning
• Prohibit collaboration during the assessment process	• Represent a collaborative approach to assessment involving both students and teachers
• Often treat skills in isolated contexts to determine achievement for reporting purposes	• Use multifaceted activities while recognizing that learning requires integration and coordination of communication skills
• Assess students across a limited range of assignments that may not match what students do in classrooms	• Represent the full range of instructional activities that students are doing in their classrooms
• Assess students in a predetermined situation where the content is fixed	• Can measure the student's ability to perform appropriately in unanticipated situations
• Assess all students on the same dimensions	• Measure each student's achievements while allowing individual differences
• Address only achievement	• Address improvement, effort, and achievement
• Seldom provide vehicles for assessing students' abilities to monitor their own learning	• Implement self-assessment by having students monitor their learning
• Are mechanically scored or scored by teachers who have little input into the assessment	• Engage students in assessing their progress and/or accomplishments and establishing ongoing learning goals
• Rarely include items that assess emotional responses to learning	• Provide opportunities to reflect upon feelings about learning

FIGURE 11 CONTRASTING TRADITIONAL TESTS AND PORTFOLIOS

Source: *Portfolios*, by N.J. Johnson and L.M. Rose, 1997, Rowman & Littlefield Education.

- *Reproductions* consist of documentation of a student's work outside the classroom, such as special projects and interviews. For example, a student's description of an interview with a local scientist in the community about the scientist's work is a reproduction.
- *Attestations* represent the teacher's or other responsible person's documentations of the student's progress. For example, a teacher might write evaluative notes about a student's oral presentation and place them in the student's portfolio.
- *Productions* are documents the student prepares especially for the portfolio. Productions consist of three types of materials: goal statements, reflections, and captions. Students generate goal statements about what they want to accomplish with their portfolio, write down their reflections about their work and describe their progress, and create captions that describe each piece of work in the portfolio and its importance.

Using Portfolios Effectively Effective use of portfolios for assessment requires (1) establishing the portfolio's purpose, (2) involving the student in decisions about it, (3) reviewing the portfolio with the student, (4) setting criteria for evaluation, (5) scoring and judging the portfolio, and (6) student self-reflection.

Establishing Purpose Portfolios can be used for different purposes. Two broad types of purposes are to document growth and to show best work. A **growth portfolio** consists of the student's work over an extended time frame (throughout the school year or even longer) to reveal the student's progress in meeting learning targets. Growth portfolios

growth portfolio A portfolio of work over an extended time frame (throughout the school year or longer) to reveal the student's progress in meeting learning targets.

also are sometimes referred to as "developmental portfolios." Growth portfolios are especially helpful in providing concrete evidence of how much a student has changed or learned over time. As students examine their portfolios, they can see for themselves how much they have improved. One example of a growth portfolio is the Integrated Language Arts Portfolio used in the elementary school grades in Juneau, Alaska (Arter, 1995). It is designed to replace report cards and grades as a way to demonstrate growth and accomplishments. Growth is tracked along a developmental continuum for levels of skills in reading, writing, speaking, and listening. A student's status on the continuum is marked at several designated times during the year. Samples of the student's work are used as the basis for judgments about the student's developmental level.

A **best-work portfolio** showcases the student's most outstanding work. Sometimes it even is called a "showcase portfolio." Best-work portfolios are more selective than developmental portfolios and often include the student's latest product. Best-work portfolios are especially useful for parent-teacher conferences, students' future teachers, and admission to higher education levels.

"Passportfolios," or "proficiency portfolios," are sometimes used to demonstrate competence and readiness to move on to a new level of work. For example, the Science Portfolio was an optional aspect of the Golden State Evaluation in California (California State Department of Education, 1994). Under No Child Left Behind, a number of states used portfolios as alternative proficiency assessments for students with severe disabilities who were unable to participate in standardized testing. However, with the passage of ESSA, student assessments for accountability cannot solely be delivered as portfolios (Samuels, 2018). States are now developing new alternate assessments that include standardized tasks. Regardless of the format of alternate assessments, ESSA restricts the number of students in a state who can take them to only 1% of students. High schools in California, however, have been adding portfolios for a different purpose–to demonstrate students have the skills they need for college or work after graduation. Some schools have even made the defense of their portfolio a graduation requirement (Hopkins, 2017).

Involving Students in Selecting Portfolio Materials Many teachers let students make at least some of the decisions about the portfolio's contents. When students are allowed to choose the contents for their own portfolios, a good strategy is to encourage self-reflection by having them write a brief description of why they chose each piece of work.

Reviewing with Students Explain to students at the beginning of the year what portfolios are and how they will be used. You also should have a number of student-teacher conferences throughout the year to review the student's progress and help the student to plan future work for the portfolio (McMillan, 2014).

Setting Criteria for Evaluation Clear and systematic performance criteria are essential for effectively using portfolios. Clear learning targets for students make developing performance criteria much easier. Ask yourself what knowledge and skills you want your students to have. This should be the focus of your teaching and your performance criteria.

Scoring and Judging It takes considerable time to score and judge portfolios. Teachers must evaluate not only each individual item but also the portfolio as a whole. When the portfolio's purpose is to provide descriptive information about the student for the teacher at the next grade level, no scoring or summarizing of the portfolio might be necessary. However, when its purpose is to diagnose, reflect improvement, provide evidence for effective instruction, motivate students to reflect on their work, or give grades to students, summary scoring and judgments are needed. Checklists and rating scales are commonly used for this purpose. As with other aspects of portfolio assessment, some teachers give students the opportunity to evaluate and critique their own work.

best-work portfolio A portfolio that showcases the student's most outstanding work.

Evaluating the Role of Portfolios in Assessment Learning portfolios have several strengths: Their comprehensive nature captures the complexity and completeness of the student's work and accomplishments. They provide opportunities for encouraging student decision making and self-reflection. They motivate students to think critically and deeply. And they provide an excellent mechanism for evaluating student progress and improvement.

Learning portfolios also have several weaknesses. They take considerable time to coordinate and evaluate. Their complexity and uniqueness make them difficult to evaluate, and their reliability is often much lower than that of traditional tests. And their use in large-scale assessments (such as statewide evaluation) is expensive. However, even with these weaknesses in mind, most educational psychology experts and educational organizations, such as the National Education Association, support the use of portfolios.

How do teachers use portfolios in their classrooms? Following are their responses.

EARLY CHILDHOOD We use portfolios to collect specific work done by our children—such as sample writing and pictures—three times during the year. We arrange these portfolios similarly so that we can assess and compare the child's development over the year. Parents are shown the portfolios during conferences to demonstrate how their child has progressed. We also use portfolios as a tool to assess possible developmental delays.

—VALARIE GORHAM, *Kiddie Quarters, Inc.*

ELEMENTARY SCHOOL: GRADES K–5 My fourth-graders do a "Best Work" writing portfolio and a "Draft" writing portfolio. The process of gathering materials for both of these portfolios takes roughly five weeks, with writing lessons mixed in. By the end of the year, students see their writing progress by examining both their Draft and Best Work portfolios.

—SHANE SCHWARZ, *Clinton Elementary School*

MIDDLE SCHOOL: GRADES 6–8 I have my students keep portfolios with their tests, quizzes, reports, projects, essays, and other important assignments. A key part of the portfolio process is when I instruct students to take their portfolios home, evaluate their work with their parents or guardians, and then come back to school with a set of goals to improve their work in class.

—CASEY MAASS, *Edison Middle School*

HIGH SCHOOL: GRADES 9–12 I use portfolios for my work-experience students. Four times a year, they include evaluations from supervisors at their job assignments, their own reflections on the job itself, completed job applications, and feedback on interviews that they have gone on. I encourage students to assemble their portfolios professionally for use when seeking their next job.

—SANDY SWANSON, *Menomonee Falls High School*

Now that you've read about many types of assessment, this is a good time to think about what your classroom assessment philosophy will be. *Self-Assessment 1* gives you this opportunity.

SELF-ASSESSMENT 1
Planning My Classroom Assessment Practices

With the subject matter and grade level at which you plan to teach in mind, examine the following list of assessments that we have discussed in this chapter. Rate each of the assessments on this scale: 1 = I don't plan to use this at all, 2 = I plan to use this occasionally, 3 = I plan to use this moderately, 4 = I plan to use this often, and 5 = This will be one of the most important assessments I will use.

	1	2	3	4	5

1. Informal observations in preinstruction assessment
2. Structured exercises in preinstruction assessment
3. Observation during instruction
4. Questions during instruction
5. Student self-assessment
6. Assessments of students' motivation, effort, and participation
7. True/false items
8. Multiple-choice items
9. Matching
10. Short-answer items
11. Essays
12. Authentic assessment
13. Experiments
14. Projects
15. Oral presentations
16. Interviews
17. Performances
18. Exhibitions
19. Portfolios

Look back through your responses and then use this information to help you formulate your classroom assessment philosophy here. If you need more space, do this outside the book or on the student website.

_____
_____
_____
_____
_____
_____

Review, Reflect, and Practice

3 Describe some types of alternative assessments.

REVIEW

- What makes an assessment "authentic"? What are some criticisms of authentic assessments?
- What are some of the features of performance assessment? What are some guidelines for using them?
- What is a portfolio and how can portfolios be used in assessment? What are some strengths and weaknesses of portfolios?

REFLECT

- Suppose that you were teaching this course in educational psychology. How would you go about creating rubrics for assessing answers to the preceding three items?

PRAXIS™ PRACTICE

1. Nicole has just been told that as part of her teacher certification process, there will be a performance assessment. Which of the following is the best performance assessment of Nicole's teaching skills?
   a. a multiple-choice exam
   b. an essay exam
   c. an exam based on case studies
   d. direct observation of classroom teaching

2. Kyle is working on his portfolio for journalism class. Included in the portfolio are his teacher's evaluation notes regarding articles he has written for the school newspaper. These notes are examples of which of the following:
   a. artifacts
   b. attestations
   c. productions
   d. reproductions

Please see answer key at end of book....

4 GRADING AND REPORTING PERFORMANCE

LG 4 Construct a sound approach to grading.

Grading means translating descriptive assessment information into letters, numbers, or other marks that indicate the quality of a student's learning or performance.

THE PURPOSES OF GRADING

Grading is carried out to communicate meaningful information about a student's learning and achievement. In this process, grades serve four basic purposes (Russell & Airasian, 2012):

- *Administrative.* Grades help determine students' class rank, credits for graduation, and whether a student should be promoted to the next grade.
- *Informational.* Grades can be used to communicate with students, parents, and others (such as admissions officers for subsequent schooling) about a student's

grading Translating descriptive assessment information into letters, numbers, or other marks that indicate the quality of a student's learning or performance.

work. A grade represents the teacher's overall conclusion about how well a student has met instructional objectives and learning targets.
- *Motivational.* Many students work harder because they are extrinsically motivated by a desire for high grades and a fear of low grades.
- *Guidance.* Grades help students, parents, and counselors to select appropriate courses and levels of work for students. They provide information about which students might require special services and what levels of future education students will likely be able to handle.

THE COMPONENTS OF A GRADING SYSTEM

Grades reflect teachers' judgments. Three main types of teacher judgments underlie a teacher's grading system (Russell & Airasian, 2012): (1) What standard of comparison will I use for grading? (2) What aspects of students' performance will I use to establish grades? and (3) How will I weight different kinds of evidence in giving grades?

Standards of Comparison A student's performance can be graded by comparing it with the performance of other students or to predefined standards of performance.

Comparing Performance Across Students **Norm-referenced grading** is a grading system based on comparison of a student's performance with that of other students in the class or of other classes and other students. In such a system, students get high grades for performing better than most of their classmates, and students get low grades for performing worse. Norm-referenced grading is commonly referred to as *grading on the curve.* In norm-referenced grading, the grading scale determines what percentages of students get particular grades. In most instances, the scale is created so that the largest percentage of students get *C*'s.

This is a typical breakdown of grades: 15 percent *A*'s, 25 percent *B*'s, 40 percent *C*'s, 15 percent *D*'s, and 5 percent *F*'s. In assigning grades, instructors often look for gaps in the range of scores. If six students score 92 to 100 and ten students score 81 to 88, and there are no scores between 88 and 92, the teacher would assign a grade of *A* to the 92 to 100 scores and a *B* to the 81 to 88 scores. Norm-referenced grading has been criticized for reducing students' motivation, increasing their anxiety, increasing negative interactions among students, and hindering learning. Consequently, norm-referenced grading is not widely used.

Comparing Performance with a Predetermined Standard **Criterion-referenced grading** is being used when students receive a certain grade for a certain level of performance, regardless of any comparison with the work of other students. Sometimes criterion-referenced grading is called *absolute grading.* Typically, criterion-referenced grading is based on the proportion of points attained on a test or the level of mastery reached in a performance skill, such as giving an oral presentation and meeting all the predetermined criteria. Criterion-referenced grading is recommended over norm-referenced grading.

In theory, the standard established is supposed to be absolute, but in practice it doesn't always work out that way (McMillan, 2014). For example, a school system often develops a grading system that goes something like this: $A = 94$ to 100 percent correct, $B = 87$ to 93 percent, $C = 77$ to 86 percent, $D = 70$ to 76 percent, and $F =$ below 70 percent. Although this system is absolute in the sense that every student must get 94 points to get an *A* and every student who does not get at least 70 points gets an *F,* teachers and classrooms vary enormously in what constitutes mastery of material to get a 94, an 87, a 77, or a 70. One teacher might give very hard tests, another very easy tests.

norm-referenced grading A grading system based on comparing a student's performance with that of other students in the class or of other classes and other students.

criterion-referenced grading A grading system that assigns a certain grade for a certain level of performance, regardless of the performance of other students.

Many teachers use different cutoff scores than the ones just mentioned. Some teachers argue that low grades discourage student motivation and refuse to give *D's* or *F's*; others won't fail students unless their scores fall below 50.

Standards-based grading is a recent development based on criterion-referenced grading. It involves basing grading on standards that students are expected to achieve in a course. In some cases, national associations, such as the National Council of Teachers of Mathematics (NCTM), have developed standards that students should achieve. Thus, in one form of standards-based grading, a mathematics teacher might tie students' grades to how well they meet these national standards.

Rubrics are often used in standards-based grading to indicate the degree to which students have met standards. Grades are based on what level of the rubric is reached (McMillan, 2011). For example, grades might be assigned based on these categories: below basic, basic, proficient, and advanced.

Aspects of Performance Over the course of a grading period, students will likely have created many products that can be evaluated and used as a basis for grading. These can include test and quiz results, as well as various alternative assessments such as oral reports, projects, interviews, and homework. Increasingly, portfolios are used as the complete collection of materials to be graded or a portion of the work on which an overall grade is based. Some educators argue that grades should be based only on academic performance. In the view of other educators, grades should be based mainly on academic performance, but teacher ratings of motivation, effort, and participation can be factored in as well.

Many teachers use tests as the main, or even sole, basis for assigning grades. However, many assessment experts recommend basing an overall grade on a series of tests and other types of assessments (McMillan, 2014). Thus, a semester grade in geography might be based on two major tests and a final, eight quizzes, homework, two oral reports, and a project. Basing a grade on a series of tests and different types of assessment helps to balance out students' strengths and weaknesses, as well as compensate for a poor performance or two because of internal and external sources of measurement error.

Some educators advocate factoring characteristics such as motivation, effort, and participation into grades, especially by giving borderline students a plus or minus. Thus, a teacher might convert a student's *B* to a *B+* if the student was highly motivated, put forth considerable effort, and actively participated in the class—or to a *B−* if the student was poorly motivated, made little effort, and did not actively participate. However, other educators stress that grades should be based only on academic performance. One of the problems with including factors such as effort in grades is the difficulty in determining the reliability and validity of evaluations of effort. Measures of effort or improvement can be made more systematic and reliable by developing scoring rubrics and examples (McMillan, 2014).

Weighting Different Kinds of Evidence You will need to determine how much weight to give the different components of a student's grade. For example, the teacher might arrive at a weighting system that looks something like this:

Major tests (2):	20 percent
Final test:	25 percent
Quizzes:	20 percent
Homework:	5 percent
Oral report:	10 percent
Project:	20 percent

THROUGH THE EYES OF STUDENTS

Accepting Responsibility

Our teacher tells us that our grades are our responsibility. Nobody else's. "Don't blame anybody else but yourself if you don't make good grades," she says. At the beginning of the year, she said she would help us every way she could to help us make good grades and she has been good about that.

—*Cassandra*
Middle School Student
Atlanta, Georgia

Many teachers don't use homework as a component for a grade. One reason for this is that when a student's grade depends on homework or other work done outside class, parents might be tempted to do their child's work to ensure a high grade. Another reason is that including homework as a component of grading favors students from more supportive home environments. As with other aspects of classroom assessment, your judgment is involved in how you synthesize information to arrive at a student's grade. If a student fails to turn in a certain number of homework assignments, some teachers lower the student's grade. Another option is to grade homework for completion rather than correctness and/or use completed homework as a ticket for the opportunity to retake a test.

REPORTING STUDENTS' PROGRESS AND GRADES TO PARENTS

Grades are the most common method of informing parents about a child's progress and performance in the classroom. Especially important in reporting students' progress is the report card.

The Report Card   The report card is a standard method of reporting students' progress and grades to parents (McMillan, 2014). The form of judgments on report cards varies from one school system to another, and, in many cases, from one grade level to another. Some report cards convey letter grades (typically *A, B, C, D,* and *F,* sometimes also allowing pluses and minuses). Some report cards convey numerical scores (such as 91 in math, 85 in English, and so on). Other report cards have a pass/fail category in one or more subjects. Yet other report cards have checklists indicating skills or objectives the student has attained. Some report cards have categories for affective characteristics, such as effort, cooperation, and other appropriate and inappropriate behaviors.

Checklists of skills and objectives are mainly used in elementary schools or kindergartens. In the higher elementary school grade levels and secondary schools, letter grades are mainly used, although these might be accompanied by other information such as written comments.

Written Progress Reports   Another reporting strategy is to provide parents with a weekly, biweekly, or monthly report of the student's progress and achievement (McMillan, 2014). These written reports can include the student's performance on tests and quizzes, projects, oral reports, and so on. They also can include information about the student's motivation, cooperation, and behavior, as well as suggestions for how parents can help students improve their performance.

Parent-Teacher Conferences   Parent-teacher conferences are another way to communicate information about grades and assessment. Such conferences are both a responsibility and an opportunity. Parents have a right to know how their child is doing in school and how their child might improve. Conferences provide an opportunity for teachers to give parents helpful information about how they can be partners with the teacher in helping the child learn more effectively.

SOME ISSUES IN GRADING

Should a zero be given to a missed assignment or paper? Should teachers go strictly by the numbers when assigning a grade? Should grading be abolished? Is there too much grade inflation? These are important issues that concern many educators today.

Should a Missed Assignment or Paper Receive a Zero?   One grading issue is whether a student should be given a zero or at least some points for a missed assignment or paper. Including a zero with other scores badly skews the mean of the scores. Many experts on assessment recommend not using a zero in this manner because it weights the assignment or paper more than what was intended because the interval between 0 and 65 or 70 is

CONNECTING WITH STUDENTS: Best Practices
Best Strategies for Parent-Teacher Conferences Related to Grades and Assessment

Following are some effective strategies for meeting with parents about their child's progress and grades (Payne, 2003):

1. *Be prepared.* Review the student's performance prior to the meeting with parents. Think about what you are going to say to the parents.
2. *Be positive.* Even if the student has performed poorly, try to find at least some areas to discuss in which the student has performed well. This does not mean glossing over and ignoring a student's lack of achievement; it means including positive areas in addition to the negative ones. Don't say: "Your child has Cs in all her subjects. She might benefit from a tutor." Instead say: "Your child has mastered writing simple sentences, but is struggling with compound sentences. She has lots of great ideas, and I look forward to working with her to combine them in more complex ways."
3. *Be objective.* Even as you provide positive aspects of the student's record to communicate to parents, also be objective and honest about what needs to improve. Don't give parents false hopes if the student has low ability in a particular subject area. Don't say: "Your child mastered almost all the material in this course!" Instead say, "Your child understands most of the content well, but he could take more time to write out his steps legibly and check his work to avoid mistakes."
4. *Practice good communication skills.* Good communication means being an active listener and giving parents adequate opportunities to contribute to the conversation. Make sure that parents and students understand your grading criteria. Don't say: "Here are your child's scores. Do you have any questions?" Instead say: "Here are your child's scores on the rubric for the final paper. What questions or concerns do you have?" In *Through the Eyes of Teachers*, Lynn Ayres, an English teacher at East Middle School, Ypsilanti, Michigan, provides her thoughts about this topic.

THROUGH THE EYES OF TEACHERS
Some Grading Strategies

I think it is extremely important that parents and students clearly know what is expected of students if they are to succeed in my class. I try to help students understand that they are in control of the grade they get. If students think a grading system is capricious or unknowable, it creates frustration, anxiety, and is of little use in motivating students. By getting them to see that their grades are in their own hands, I move to the position of "facilitator" in the classroom. The students see me as someone who is there to help them achieve rather than someone who sits in judgment of their work and gives them a grade.

Lynn Ayres

5. *Don't talk about other students.* The focus of the parent-teacher conference should be on the parent's child. Don't compare the child with other students. Don't say: "Your child has the highest grade in the class." Instead say: "Your child's scores demonstrate she has mastered all of the learning objectives."

---

more than the intervals between the scores for other grades (McMillan, 2014). Using a score of 60 for a missed assignment or paper is considered more reasonable.

Should Teachers Go Strictly by the Numbers in Grading? A concern in making out grades is that too many teachers engage in "mindless" number crunching, which is now more likely to occur with grading software available. No matter how objective the process is for averaging scores and grades, grading is a matter of professional judgment. Going strictly by the numbers can result in a grade that is not consistent with the actual knowledge and skill of the student, especially if pulled down by minor assignments and homework, or a later paper. In the end, it is important for teachers to be confident that the grade they give reflects what the student knows, understands, and is able to do in relation to standards of performance (McMillan, 2014).

Should Grading Be Abolished? Occasionally there are calls to abandon grades, usually based on the belief that evaluation of students is necessary but that competitive grading deemphasizes learning in favor of judging. Critics argue that grading discourages the vast majority of students, especially those who receive below-average grades. The critics often call for more constructive evaluation that encourages students to engage in maximum effort by underscoring their strengths, identifying concrete ways to improve, and providing positive feedback. Critics also point out that grading often motivates students to study only the material that will be on the test.

As classroom assessment experts Michael Russell and Peter Airasian (2012) concluded, grades are powerful symbols in our society that are taken seriously by students, teachers, and the public. Regardless of whether you like the way grading is currently conducted or think it should be drastically changed, in the foreseeable future it is important for you to take grading your students seriously and do it in a way that is fair to your students. Never use grades to reward or punish students because you like them or don't like them. Always base students' grades on how well they have learned the subject matter, based on objective evidence of learning.

Is There Too Much Grade Inflation? Some teachers do not like to give low grades because they point out that they diminish the student's motivation to learn. However, some critics argue that grade inflation, especially in the form of giving high grades for mediocre performance, gives students a false belief that they are learning and achieving more than they actually are. The result is that many students discover that they can perform well below their ability and still achieve high grades.

In a longitudinal study, the College Board found that graduating seniors in 1996 had a grade point average (GPA) of 2.64 but by 2006 their GPA had increased approximately one-fourth of a letter grade to 2.90, despite SAT scores remaining relatively unchanged (Godfrey, 2011–12). In another study conducted by ACT, high school grade average showed little evidence of overall grade change from 2004 to 2011 (Zhang & Sanchez, 2013). However, in this study, there were significant variations in grade inflation/deflation among high schools that were not related to poverty or ethnic minority enrollment.

Review, Reflect, and Practice

 Construct a sound approach to grading.

REVIEW
- What are the purposes of grading?
- What types of judgments underlie a teacher's grading system? Comment about each type. What are some choices in reporting students' progress to parents?
- What are some issues in grading?

REFLECT
- What criteria would you adopt for deciding whether a teacher is doing an excellent job in grading?

PRAXIS™ PRACTICE

1. Amaal brings home her school report card. On the card are letter grades indicating that Amaal has earned A's in math, reading, and social studies, and B's in science and P.E. Her parents look over her grades, sign the card, and return it to the school. What purpose did these grades serve?
   a. administrative
   b. guidance
   c. informational
   d. motivational

2. Mr. Walker teaches algebra. On the first day of class, he tells students that of the 25 students in the class, 5 would receive A's, 6 would receive B's, 7 would receive C's, 4 would receive D's, and 3 would receive F's. What type of grading system is Mr. Walker using?
   a. criterion-referenced
   b. norm-referenced
   c. standards-based
   d. weighted

Review, Reflect, and Practice

3. Isabella brings home her quarterly school report card. On the card are letter grades indicating that Isabella has earned *A*'s in math, language arts, and social studies, and *B*'s in science and P.E. Which of the following is a valid criticism of such a grading system?
   a. It gives parents too much information about the student's performance.
   b. It is too specific.
   c. Letter grades are unfair.
   d. It does not provide enough information to allow parents to evaluate their child's performance.

4. Ms. Gregory and Ms. Templeton are discussing grading issues. Which of the following comments made by Ms. Gregory and Ms. Templeton is the *least* likely to be supported by educational psychologists?
   a. Many students are being rewarded with high grades for mediocre performance.
   b. In the last several decades, grades have been increasing, while SAT scores have been going down.
   c. Some teachers don't like to give low grades because they believe the low grades decrease students' motivation.
   d. Grades should be abolished.

Please see answer key at end of book . . . .

Connecting with the Classroom: Crack the Case

The Case of the Project

Mr. Andrews generally was using traditional, multiple-choice tests in his sixth-grade class on ancient history, but the students seemed bored with studying for these tests and with his lectures. Therefore, for the unit on ancient Mesopotamia, he decided to allow the students to complete a project instead of taking a test. He gave these choices:

- Construct a test covering the chapter on Mesopotamia.
- Create a game about Mesopotamia.
- Create a diorama about Mesopotamia.
- Write a play about life in Mesopotamia.
- Create artifacts from Mesopotamia that an archaeologist might find.

Mr. Andrews' co-teacher, Ms. Benjamin, told the children that they could not use a computer to complete their projects.

Sally decided to write a test for her project. She carefully read the chapter and constructed questions as she went along. She used short-answer questions because she was worried about constructing good multiple-choice questions. It had been her experience that the distractors used in these questions were often confusing. She felt the same way about true/false questions. She wanted to make her questions as clear as possible because she didn't want her classmates to be mad at her when they took her test.

Sally carefully printed each question by hand because of the ban on using a computer. She then created a key, which she intended to use to grade her classmates' tests. The final product consisted of 25 short-answer questions. She was very proud of her work the day she turned it in.

Mr. Andrews looked at her test and told her, "This isn't acceptable. Why didn't you type it?"

"Ms. Benjamin told us we couldn't use computers."

"That isn't what she meant. She meant you couldn't use the Internet," responded Mr. Andrews. "Take it home and type it. Turn it in tomorrow."

Sally left the room, very upset. She took her test home and carefully typed both the test and the key. She turned them in the next day. Three days later, Sally received these marks:

Content: **B** Did not include a question on religion (actually Sally did have a question regarding polytheism). Should have included a variety of question types, such as multiple-choice, matching, and true/false.

Mechanics: **A** Nicely typed. Correct spelling used. Accuracy: **B**

Effort: **C**

Overall Grade: C

continued

Sally was upset with her grade. "A *C* for effort? I worked really hard on this! I even had to do it twice, 'cause of stupid Ms. Benjamin!" She took her grade sheet and test home and showed it to her mother. Sally's mother was equally upset, particularly about the low grade for effort. She called Mr. Andrews, asking to see the guidelines for the project and the grading rubric. Mr. Andrews was unable to provide either. She asked him the difference between content and accuracy. He could not tell her. She also asked him how he had measured effort, to which he responded, "I consider what I expect from students and then what they give me."

"So you're telling me that you graded content three times. Once you gave her a *B*, once a *B*, and once a *C*, right?"

Mr. Andrews did not know how to respond to her question.

1. What are the issues involved in this situation?
2. What did Mr. Andrews do wrong?
3. How should he have gone about developing his alternative assessments?
4. How should he have developed his grading guide?
5. What do you think of the practice of including an effort grade on students' projects? Why?

Connecting with Learning: Reach Your Learning Goals

① THE CLASSROOM AS AN ASSESSMENT CONTEXT: Discuss the classroom as an assessment context.

Assessment as an Integral Part of Teaching

- Preinstruction assessment, assessment during instruction, and postinstruction assessment should be integral to teaching. Much of preinstruction assessment involves informal observations, which require interpretation. In informal observations, watch for nonverbal cues that give insights about the student. Structured exercises also can be used in preinstruction assessment.
- Guard against expectations that will distort your perception of a student. Treat your initial perceptions as hypotheses to be confirmed or modified by subsequent observation and information. Some teachers also administer pretests in subject areas.
- An increasing trend is to examine students' learning portfolios from previous grades. Formative assessment is assessment during instruction with an emphasis on assessment for learning instead of assessment of learning.
- An increasing trend is to have students engage in self-assessment of their progress on a day-to-day basis as part of formative assessment.
- Summative assessment, or formal assessment, is assessment after instruction is finished in order to document student mastery of the material, whether students are ready for the next unit, how your teaching should be adapted, and what grades the students should get.

Making Assessment Compatible with Contemporary Views of Learning and Motivation

- To bring assessment into line with contemporary views of motivation and learning, it is important to focus on the following: active learning and constructing meaning; the use of planning and goal setting; reflective, critical, and creative thinking; positive student expectations for learning and confidence in skills; degree of motivation; the ability to apply what is learned to real-world situations; and effective communication.
- Consider the role that assessment (especially alternative assessment) plays in effort, engagement, and performance.

Creating Clear, Appropriate Learning Targets

- A learning target, much like an instructional objective, consists of what students should know and be able to do.

Establishing High-Quality Assessments

- High-quality assessments are valid, reliable, and fair. Validity is the extent to which an assessment measures what it is intended to measure, as well as how accurate and useful a teacher's inferences are. Reliability is the extent to which assessments produce consistent, reproducible scores. Assessment is fair when all students have an equal opportunity to learn and demonstrate their knowledge and skills. Having a pluralistic assessment philosophy, including being sensitive to cultural diversity, also contributes to fairness.

Current Trends

- Current trends in assessment include using at least some performance-based assessments, examining higher-level skills, using multiple assessment methods, having high performance standards, and using computers as a part of assessment.
- Other trends focus on assessing an integration of skills, giving students considerable feedback, and making standards and criteria public.

2 TRADITIONAL TESTS: Provide some guidelines for constructing traditional tests.

Selected-Response Items

- A multiple-choice item has two parts: a stem and a number of possible options or alternatives. Incorrect alternatives are called distractors.
- True/false items can seem easy to construct but can encourage rote memorization.
- Matching items often are used with younger students.

Constructed-Response Items

- Constructed-response items require students to write out information rather than select it from a menu. Short-answer and essay items are the most commonly used constructed-response items. Short-answer items require students to write a word, a short phrase, or several sentences in response to a task and often encourage rote memorization.
- Essay questions allow students more freedom of response than the other item formats. Essay questions are especially good for assessing students' understanding of concepts, higher-level thinking skills, organizational skills, and writing skills.

3 ALTERNATIVE ASSESSMENTS: Describe some types of alternative assessments.

Trends in Alternative Assessment

- Authentic assessment is evaluating a student's knowledge or skill in a context that approximates the real world or real life as closely as possible. Critics argue that authentic assessments are not necessarily better than more conventional assessments, that there is little data to support their validity, and that they don't adequately examine knowledge and basic skills.

Performance Assessment

- Performance assessments of higher-level thinking often emphasize "doing": performing open-ended activities for which there is no one correct answer. The tasks are sometimes realistic, and many, but not all, performance assessments are authentic (approximate the real world or real life).
- Evaluating performance often includes direct methods of evaluation, self-assessment, assessment of group performance as well as individual performance, over an extended period of time.
- There are four main guidelines in using performance assessments: (1) establishing a clear purpose, (2) identifying observable criteria, (3) providing an appropriate setting, and (4) judging or scoring the performance.

Portfolio Assessment

- A portfolio is a systematic and organized collection of a student's work to demonstrate skills and accomplishments. Four classes of evidence can be included: artifacts, reproductions, attestations, and productions.
- Using a portfolio for assessment requires (1) establishing the portfolio's purpose, (2) involving the student in decisions about it, (3) reviewing the portfolio with the student, (4) setting criteria for evaluation, and (5) scoring and judging the portfolio.
- Two broad purposes of portfolios are to document growth through a growth portfolio and to showcase the student's most outstanding work through a best-work portfolio.
- Learning portfolios have strengths—such as capturing the complexity and completeness of the student's work and accomplishments, as well as encouraging student decision making and self-reflection—and weaknesses—such as the time required to coordinate and evaluate them and the difficulty of evaluating them.

continued

4. GRADING AND REPORTING PERFORMANCE: Construct a sound approach to grading.

The Purposes of Grading
- Grading purposes include administrative (help determine students' class rank, credits); informational (communicate with parents, teachers, students); motivational (students' desire for higher grades); and guidance (select appropriate courses and levels for students).

The Components of a Grading System
- Three main types of teacher judgments underlie a grading system: (1) standard of comparison to use for grading (norm-referenced or criterion-referenced—criterion-referenced grading is recommended over norm-referenced); (2) aspects of students' performance (a good strategy is to base an overall grade on a series of assessments, including tests and other assessments); and (3) weighting of different kinds of evidence (judgment is involved in how teachers synthesize information to arrive at a student's grade).

Reporting Students' Progress and Grades to Parents
- Report cards are the standard method of reporting. Checklists of skills and objectives are sometimes used in kindergarten and elementary school. Letter grades are standard in the higher elementary grades and secondary schools. Reporting also includes written progress reports and parent-teacher conferences.

Some Issues in Grading
- Issues in grading include (1) whether teachers should assign a zero for a missed assignment or paper; (2) whether teachers should go strictly by the numbers in grading; (3) whether grading should be abolished (although the form of grading might change in the future, judgments about students' performance will still be made and communicated to students, parents, and others); and (4) whether grade inflation is a problem.

KEY TERMS

authentic assessment 553
best-work portfolio 560
constructed-response items 549
criterion-referenced grading 564
essay item 550
formative assessment 539
grading 563
growth portfolio 559
instructional validity 542
multiple-choice item 547
norm-referenced grading 564
objective tests 544
performance assessment 544
performance criteria 555
portfolio 558
rubric 554
selected-response items 547
short-answer item 549
summative assessment 540

PORTFOLIO ACTIVITIES

Now that you have a good understanding of this chapter, complete the following exercises to expand your thinking.

Independent Reflection

1. **State Your Views on Assessment.** Think about the following statements and decide whether you agree or disagree with each.
   (1) Multiple-choice tests should not be used to assess students' learning. (2) A teacher should never use a single measure to assess learning. (3) Performance-based assessment is too subjective. (INTASC: Principle 6) Explain your positions.

Research/Field Experience

2. **Balancing Traditional and Alternative Assessments.** Consider a course you took in grade school or high school in which your performance was assessed using traditional methods. In a brief position statement, explain how students could have been evaluated using alternative assessments or some combination of traditional and alternative assessments. What would have been gained (or lost) by using alternative assessments? (INTASC: Principle 6)

Collaborative Work

3. **Develop an Assessment Plan.** Get together with a classmate who plans to teach the same subject(s) and grade level. Select a subject and construct a plan for assessment throughout the course. (INTASC: Principles 4, 6)

Glossary

A

accommodation Piagetian concept of adjusting schemas to fit new information and experiences.

achievement test A test that measures what the student has learned or what skills the student has mastered.

action research Research used to solve a specific classroom or school problem, improve teaching and other educational strategies, or make a decision at a specific location.

active listening A listening style that gives full attention to the speaker and notes both the intellectual and emotional content of the message.

advance organizers Teaching activities and techniques that establish a framework and orient students to material before it is presented.

algorithms Strategies that guarantee a solution to a problem.

alternate-forms reliability Reliability judged by giving different forms of the same test on two different occasions to the same group of students to determine how consistent their scores are.

altruism An unselfish interest in helping another person.

amygdala The seat of emotions in the brain.

analogy A correspondence in some respects between otherwise dissimilar things.

androgyny The presence of positive masculine and feminine characteristics in the same individual.

applied behavior analysis Application of the principles of operant conditioning to change human behavior.

aptitude test A type of test that is used to predict a student's ability to learn a skill or accomplish something with further education and training.

articulation disorders Problems in pronouncing sounds correctly.

Asperger syndrome A relatively mild autism spectrum disorder in which the child has relatively good verbal language, milder nonverbal language problems, a restricted range of interests and relationships, and often engages in repetitive routines.

assimilation Piagetian concept of the incorporation of new information into existing knowledge (schemas).

associative learning Learning that two events are connected (associated).

Atkinson-Shiffrin model A model of memory that involves a sequence of three stages: sensory memory, short-term memory, and long-term memory.

attention The focusing of mental resources.

attention deficit hyperactivity disorder (ADHD) A disability in which children consistently show one or more of the following characteristics over a period of time: (1) inattention, (2) hyperactivity, and (3) impulsivity.

attribution theory The theory that individuals are motivated to discover the underlying causes of their own behavior and performance.

auditorium style A classroom arrangement style in which all students sit facing the teacher.

authentic assessment Evaluating a student's knowledge or skill in a context that approximates the real world or real life as closely as possible.

authoritarian classroom management style A management style that is restrictive and punitive, with the focus mainly on keeping order in the classroom rather than instruction or learning.

authoritarian parenting A restrictive and punitive parenting style in which there is little verbal exchange between parents and children; this style is associated with children's social incompetence.

authoritative classroom management style A management style that encourages students to be independent thinkers and doers but still provides effective monitoring. Authoritative teachers engage students in considerable verbal give-and-take and show a caring attitude toward them. However, they still set limits when necessary.

authoritative parenting A positive parenting style that encourages children to be independent but still places limits and controls on their actions, allows extensive verbal give-and-take, and is associated with children's social competence.

autism spectrum disorders (ASD) Also called pervasive developmental disorders, they range from the severe disorder labeled autistic disorder to the milder disorder called Asperger syndrome. Children with these disorders are characterized by problems in social interaction, verbal and nonverbal communication, and repetitive behaviors.

autistic disorder A severe developmental autism spectrum disorder that has its onset in the first three years of life and includes deficiencies in social relationships, abnormalities in communication, and restricted, repetitive, and stereotyped patterns of behavior.

automaticity The ability to process information with little or no effort.

B

backward-reaching transfer Occurs when the individual looks back to a previous situation for information to solve a problem in a new context.

behavioral objectives Statements that communicate proposed changes in students' behavior to reach desired levels of performance.

behaviorism The view that behavior should be explained by observable experiences, not by mental processes.

belief perseverance The tendency to hold on to a belief in the face of contradictory evidence.

best-work portfolio A portfolio that showcases the student's most outstanding work.

between-class ability grouping (tracking) Grouping students based on their ability or achievement.

Big Five factors of personality Openness, conscientiousness, extraversion, agreeableness, and neuroticism (emotional stability).

Bloom's taxonomy Developed by Benjamin Bloom and colleagues; classifies educational objectives into three domains—cognitive, affective, and psychomotor.

bystander Someone who witnesses bullying occur electronically or in person; bystanders can play different roles; intervening in bullying can cause it to stop in less than 10 second in over half of incidences.

C

care perspective A moral perspective that focuses on connectedness and relationships among people; Gilligan's approach reflects a care perspective.

case study An in-depth look at an individual.

central tendency A number that provides information about the average, or typical, score in a set of data.

centration Focusing, or centering, attention on one characteristic to the exclusion of all others; characteristic of preoperational thinking.

cerebral palsy A disorder that involves a lack of muscle coordination, shaking, or unclear speech.

character education A direct approach to moral education that involves teaching students basic moral literacy to prevent them from engaging in immoral behavior and doing harm to themselves or others.

children who are gifted Children with above-average intelligence (usually defined as an IQ of 130 or higher) and/or superior talent in some domain such as art, music, or mathematics.

chunking Grouping, or "packing," information into "higher-order" units that can be remembered as single units.

classical conditioning A form of associative learning in which a neutral stimulus becomes associated with a meaningful stimulus and acquires the capacity to elicit a similar response.

cloud computing Delivery of services such as servers, storage, and applications to an organization's computers and devices through the Internet.

cluster style A classroom arrangement style in which small numbers of students (usually four to eight) work in small, closely bunched groups.

cognitive apprenticeship A relationship in which an expert stretches and supports a novice's understanding and use of a culture's skills.

cognitive moral education An approach to moral education based on the belief that students should value things such as democracy and justice as their moral reasoning develops; Kohlberg's theory has served as the foundation for many cognitive moral education efforts.

cognitive-behavioral approaches Changing behavior by getting individuals to monitor, manage, and regulate their own behavior rather than letting it be controlled by external factors.

collectivism A set of values that support the group.

comparative advance organizers Organizers that introduce new material by connecting it with the students' prior knowledge.

competence motivation The idea that people are motivated to deal effectively with their environment, to master their world, and to process information efficiently.

concept map A visual presentation of a concept's connections and hierarchical organization.

concepts Ideas that group objects, events, and characteristics on the basis of common properties.

concrete operational stage Piaget's third cognitive developmental stage, occurring between about 7 and 11 years of age. At this stage, the child thinks operationally, and logical reasoning replaces intuitive thought but only in concrete situations; classification skills are present, but abstract problems present difficulties.

concurrent validity The relation between a test's scores and other criteria that are currently (concurrently) available.

confirmation bias The tendency to search for and use information that supports our ideas rather than refutes them.

conservation The idea that some characteristic of an object stays the same even though the object might change in appearance; a cognitive ability that develops in the concrete operational stage, according to Piaget.

construct validity The extent to which there is evidence that a test measures a particular construct. A construct is an unobservable trait or characteristic of a person, such as intelligence, learning style, personality, or anxiety.

constructed-response items Items that require students to write out information rather than select a response from a menu.

constructivist approach A learner-centered approach to learning that emphasizes the importance of individuals actively constructing knowledge and understanding with guidance from the teacher.

content validity A test's ability to sample the content that is to be measured.

continuity-discontinuity issue The issue regarding whether development involves gradual, cumulative change (continuity) or distinct stages (discontinuity).

contracting Putting reinforcement contingencies into writing.

control group In an experiment, a group whose experience is treated in every way like the experimental group except for the manipulated factor.

conventional reasoning The second, or intermediate, level in Kohlberg's theory of moral development. At this level, individuals abide by certain standards (internal), but they are the standards of others such as parents or the laws of society (external). The conventional level consists of two stages: mutual interpersonal expectations, relationships, and interpersonal conformity (stage 3) and social systems morality (stage 4).

convergent thinking Thinking with the aim of producing one correct answer. This is usually the type of thinking required on conventional intelligence tests.

cooperative learning Learning that occurs when students work in small groups to help each other learn.

corpus callosum The brain region where fibers connect the left and right hemispheres.

correlational research Research that describes the strength of the relation between two or more events or characteristics.

creativity The ability to think about something in novel and unusual ways and come up with unique solutions to problems.

criterion validity A test's ability to predict a student's performance as measured by other assessments or criteria.

criterion-referenced grading A grading system that assigns a certain grade for a certain level of performance, regardless of the performance of other students.

criterion-referenced tests Standardized tests in which the student's performance is compared with established criteria.

critical thinking Thinking reflectively and productively and evaluating the evidence.

cross-cultural studies Studies that compare what happens in one culture with what happens in one or more other cultures; they provide information about the degree to which people are similar and to what degree behaviors are specific to certain cultures.

cue-dependent forgetting Retrieval failure caused by a lack of effective retrieval cues.

culture The behavior patterns, beliefs, and all other products of a particular group of people that are passed on from generation to generation.

culture-fair tests Tests of intelligence that are intended to be free of cultural bias.

D

decay theory The theory that new learning involves the creation of a neurochemical "memory trace," which will eventually disintegrate. Thus, decay theory suggests that the passage of time is responsible for forgetting.

decision making Evaluating alternatives and making choices among them.

declarative memory The conscious recollection of information, such as specific facts or events that can be verbally communicated.

deductive reasoning Reasoning from the general to the specific.

deep/surface styles Involve the extent to which students approach learning materials in a way that helps them understand the meaning of the materials (deep style) or as simply what needs to be learned (surface style).

delay of gratification Postponing immediate rewards in order to attain larger, more valuable rewards in the future.

dependent variable The factor that is measured in an experiment.

descriptive statistics Mathematical procedures that are used to describe and summarize data (information) in a meaningful way.

development The pattern of biological, cognitive, and socioemotional processes that begins at conception and continues through the life span. Most development involves growth, although it also eventually involves decay (dying).

developmentally appropriate education Education that focuses on the typical developmental patterns of children (age appropriateness) and the uniqueness of each child (individual appropriateness).

differentiated instruction Involves recognizing individual variations in students' knowledge, readiness, interests, and other characteristics, and taking these differences into account when planning curriculum and engaging in instruction.

difficult child A temperament style in which the child tends to react negatively, cries frequently, engages in irregular routines, and is slow to accept new experiences.

direct instruction approach A structured, teacher-centered approach characterized by teacher direction and control, high teacher expectations for students' progress, maximum time spent by students on academic tasks, and efforts by the teacher to keep negative affect to a minimum.

discovery learning Learning in which students construct an understanding on their own.

divergent thinking Thinking with the aim of producing many answers to the same question. This is characteristic of creativity.

divided attention Concentrating on more than one activity at a time.

domain theory of moral development Theory that moral development includes the domains of social knowledge and reasoning.

Down syndrome A genetically transmitted form of intellectual disability due to an extra (47th) chromosome.

dual-process model States that decision-making is influenced by two systems—one analytical and one experiential—that compete with each other; in this model, it is the experiential system—monitoring and managing actual experiences—that benefits adolescent decision making.

dyscalculia Also known as developmental arithmetic disorder, this learning disability involves difficulty in math computation.

dysgraphia A learning disability that involves difficulty in handwriting.

dyslexia A severe impairment in the ability to read and spell.

early-later experience issue Involves the degree to which early experiences (especially infancy) or later experiences are the key determinants of the child's development.

E

easy child A temperament style in which the child is generally in a positive mood, quickly establishes regular routines, and easily adapts to new experiences.

ecological theory Bronfenbrenner's theory that development is influenced by five environmental systems: microsystem, mesosystem, exosystem, macrosystem, and chronosystem.

educational psychology The branch of psychology that specializes in understanding teaching and learning in educational settings.

elaboration The extensiveness of information processing involved in encoding.

emotional and behavioral disorders Serious, persistent problems that involve relationships, aggression, depression, fears associated with personal or school matters, and other inappropriate socioemotional characteristics.

emotional intelligence The ability to perceive and express emotion accurately and adaptively, to understand emotion and emotional knowledge, to monitor one's own and others' emotions and feelings, to discriminate among them, and to use this information to guide one's thinking and action.

emotions Feelings, or affect, that occur when an individual is engaged in an interaction that is important to him or her, especially to his or her well-being.

empowerment Providing people with intellectual and coping skills to succeed and make this a more just world.

encoding The process by which information gets into memory.

encoding specificity principle The principle that associations formed at the time of encoding or learning tend to be effective retrieval cues.

epigenetic view Development is seen as an ongoing, bidirectional interchange between heredity and the environment.

epilepsy A neurological disorder characterized by recurring sensorimotor attacks or movement convulsions.

episodic memory The retention of information about the where and when of life's happenings.

equilibration A mechanism that Piaget proposed to explain how children shift from one stage of thought to the next. The shift occurs as children experience cognitive conflict, or disequilibrium, in trying to understand the world. Eventually, they resolve the conflict and reach a balance, or equilibrium, of thought.

essay item Test item that requires more writing than other formats but allows more freedom of response to questions.

essential questions Questions that reflect the heart of the curriculum, the most important things that students should explore and learn.

ethnicity A shared pattern of characteristics such as cultural heritage, nationality, race, religion, and language.

ethnographic study In-depth description and interpretation of behavior in an ethnic or a cultural group that includes direct involvement with the participants.

executive attention Involves planning actions, allocating attention to goals, detecting and compensating for errors, monitoring progress on tasks, and dealing with novel or difficult circumstances.

executive function An umbrella-like concept that encompasses a number of higher-level cognitive processes linked to the development of the brain's prefrontal cortex. Executive function involves managing one's thoughts to engage in goal-directed behavior and exercise self-control.

experimental group The group whose experience is manipulated in an experiment.

experimental research Research that allows the determination of the causes of behavior and involves conducting an experiment, which is a carefully regulated procedure in which one or more of the factors believed to influence the behavior being studied is manipulated and all others are held constant.

expert knowledge Also called *subject matter knowledge*; means excellent knowledge about the content of a particular discipline.

expository advance organizers Organizers that provide students with new knowledge that will orient them to the upcoming lesson.

expressive language The ability to use language to express one's thoughts and communicate with others.

extrinsic motivation The external motivation to do something to obtain something else (a means to an end).

F

face-to-face style A classroom arrangement style in which students sit facing each other.

failure syndrome Having low expectations for success and giving up at the first sign of difficulty.

far transfer The transfer of learning to a situation that is very different from the one in which the initial learning took place.

fixation Using a prior strategy and thereby failing to examine a problem from a fresh, new perspective.

fluency disorders Disorders that often involve what is commonly referred to as "stuttering."

formal operational stage Piaget's fourth cognitive developmental stage, which emerges between about 11 and 15 years of age; thought becomes more abstract, idealistic, and logical.

formative assessment Assessment during the course of instruction rather than after it is completed.

forward-reaching transfer Occurs when the individual looks for ways to apply learned information to a future situation.

frequency distribution A listing of scores, usually from highest to lowest, along with the number of times each score appears.

fuzzy trace theory States that memory is best understood by considering two types of memory representations: (1) verbatim memory trace and (2) fuzzy trace, or gist. In this theory, older children's better memory is attributed to the fuzzy traces created by extracting the gist of information.

G

gender The characteristics of people as males and females.

gender role A set of expectations that prescribes how females or males should think, act, and feel.

gender schema theory States that gender typing emerges as children gradually develop gender schemas of what is gender-appropriate and gender-inappropriate in their culture.

gender stereotypes Broad categories that reflect impressions and beliefs about what behavior is appropriate for females and males.

gender typing Acquisition of a traditional masculine or feminine role.

goodness of fit The match between a child's temperament and the environmental demands the child must cope with.

grade-equivalent score A score that indicates a student's performance in relation to grade level and months of the school year, assuming a 10-month school year.

grading Translating descriptive assessment information into letters, numbers, or other marks that indicate the quality of a student's learning or performance.

gratitude A feeling of thankfulness and appreciation, especially in response to someone doing something kind or helpful.

growth portfolio A portfolio of work over an extended time frame (throughout the school year or longer) to reveal the student's progress in meeting learning targets.

guided discovery learning Learning in which students are encouraged to construct their understanding with the assistance of teacher-guided questions and directions.

H

helpless orientation A response to challenges and difficulties in which the individual feels trapped by the difficulty and attributes the difficulty to a lack of ability.

heuristics Strategies or rules of thumb that can suggest a solution to a problem but don't ensure that it will work.

hidden curriculum Dewey's concept that every school has a pervasive moral atmosphere even if it does not have a program of moral education.

hierarchy of needs Maslow's concept that individual needs must be satisfied in this sequence: physiological, safety, love and belongingness, esteem, and self-actualization.

high-road transfer Applying information from one situation to another in a way that is conscious and effortful.

high-stakes testing Using tests in a way that will have important consequences for the student, affecting such decisions as whether the student will be promoted or be allowed to graduate.

hindsight bias The tendency to falsely report, after the fact, having accurately predicted an event.

histogram A frequency distribution in the form of a graph.

hostile environment sexual harassment Occurs when students are subjected to unwelcome sexual conduct that is so severe, persistent, or pervasive that it limits the students' ability to benefit from their education.

humanistic perspective A view that stresses students' capacity for personal growth, freedom to choose their destiny, and positive qualities.

hypothetical-deductive reasoning Piaget's formal operational concept that adolescents can develop hypotheses to solve problems and systematically reach a conclusion.

I

identity achievement The identity status in which individuals have explored meaningful alternatives and made a commitment.

identity diffusion The identity status in which individuals have neither explored meaningful alternatives nor made a commitment.

identity foreclosure The identity status in which individuals have made a commitment but have not explored meaningful alternatives.

identity moratorium The identity status in which individuals are in the midst of exploring alternatives but have not yet made a commitment.

impulsive/reflective styles Involves a student's tendency either to act quickly and impulsively or to take more time to respond and reflect on the accuracy of the answer.

incentives Positive or negative stimuli or events that can motivate a student's behavior.

inclusion Educating children with special education needs full-time in the regular classroom.

independent variable The manipulated, influential, experimental factor in an experiment.

individualism A set of values that give priority to personal rather than to group goals.

individualized education plan (IEP) A written statement that spells out a program specifically tailored for the student with a disability.

Individuals with Disabilities Education Act (IDEA) This act spells out broad mandates for services to all children with disabilities, including evaluation and determination of eligibility, appropriate education and an individualized education plan (IEP), and education in the least restrictive environment (LRE).

inductive reasoning Reasoning from the specific to the general.

indulgent parenting A parenting style that includes parental involvement but places few limits or restrictions on children's behavior; linked with children's social incompetence.

information-processing approach A cognitive approach in which children manipulate information, monitor it, and strategize about it. Central to this approach are cognitive processes such as attention, memory, and thinking.

instructional planning A systematic, organized strategy for planning lessons.

instructional validity The extent to which the assessment is a reasonable sample of what went on in the classroom.

intellectual disability A condition with an onset before age 18 that involves low intelligence (usually below 70 on a traditional individually administered intelligence test) and difficulty in adapting to everyday life.

intelligence Problem-solving skills and ability to adapt to and learn from experiences.

intelligence quotient (IQ) A person's mental age (MA) divided by chronological age (CA), multiplied by 100.

interference theory The theory that we forget not because we actually lose memories from storage but because other information gets in the way of what we are trying to remember.

Internet The core of computer-mediated communication; a system of computer networks that operates worldwide.

intrinsic motivation The internal motivation to do something for its own sake (an end in itself).

intuitive thought substage The second substage of preoperational thought, lasting from about 4 to 7 years of age. Children begin to use primitive reasoning and want to know the answer to all sorts of questions. They seem sure about their knowledge in this substage but are unaware of how they know what they know.

J

jigsaw classroom A classroom in which students from different cultural backgrounds cooperate by doing different parts of a project to reach a common goal.

Joplin plan A standard nongraded program for instruction in reading.

justice perspective A moral perspective that focuses on the rights of the individual; Kohlberg's theory is a justice perspective.

L

laboratory A controlled setting from which many of the complex factors of the real world have been removed.

language A form of communication, whether spoken, written, or signed, that is based on a system of symbols.

language disorders Significant impairments in a child's receptive or expressive language.

lateralization Specialization of functions in each hemisphere of the brain.

learning A relatively permanent influence on behavior, knowledge, and thinking skills, which comes about through experience.

learning and thinking styles Individuals' preferences in how they use their abilities.

learning disability Difficulty in learning that involves understanding or using spoken or written language; the difficulty can appear in listening, thinking, reading, writing, and spelling. A learning disability also may involve difficulty in doing mathematics. To be classified as a learning disability, the learning problem is not primarily the result of visual, hearing, or motor disabilities; intellectual disability; emotional disorders; or due to environmental, cultural, or economic disadvantage.

least restrictive environment (LRE) A setting that is as similar as possible to the one in which children who do not have a disability are educated.

levels of processing theory The theory that processing of memory occurs on a continuum from shallow to deep, with deeper processing producing better memory.

limbic system Brain region that is the seat of emotions and in which rewards are experienced.

long-term memory A type of memory that holds enormous amounts of information for a long period of time in a relatively permanent fashion.

low-road transfer The automatic, often unconscious, transfer of learning to another situation.

M

mastery learning Involves learning one topic or concept thoroughly before moving on to a more difficult one.

mastery orientation A task-oriented response to difficult or challenging circumstances that focuses on learning strategies and the process of achievement rather than the outcome.

mean The numerical average of a group of scores.

means-end analysis A heuristic in which one identifies the goal (end) of a problem, assesses the current situation, and evaluates what needs to be done (means) to decrease the difference between the two conditions.

measures of variability Measures that tell how much scores vary from one another.

median The score that falls exactly in the middle of a distribution of scores after they have been arranged (or ranked) from highest to lowest.

memory The retention of information over time, which involves encoding, storage, and retrieval.

memory span The number of digits an individual can report back without error in a single presentation.

mental age (MA) An individual's level of mental development relative to others.

mental processes Thoughts, feelings, and motives that cannot be observed by others.

mental set A type of fixation in which an individual tries to solve a problem in a particular way that has worked in the past.

metacognition Cognition about cognition, or "knowing about knowing."

metalinguistic awareness Knowledge of language.

mindfulness Being alert, mentally present, and cognitively flexible while going through life's everyday activities and tasks. Mindful students maintain an active awareness of the circumstances in their lives.

mindset Dweck's concept that refers to the cognitive view individuals develop for themselves; individuals have one of two mindsets: fixed or growth.

mixed methods research Involves research that blends different research designs or methods.

mode The score that occurs most often.

Montessori approach An educational philosophy in which children are given considerable freedom and spontaneity in choosing activities and are allowed to move from one activity to another as they desire.

moral development Development with respect to the rules and conventions of just interactions between people.

morphology Refers to the units of meaning involved in word formation.

motivation The processes that energize, direct, and sustain behavior.

multicultural education Education that values diversity and includes the perspectives of a variety of cultural groups on a regular basis.

multiple-choice item An objective test item consisting of two parts: a stem plus a set of possible responses.

myelination The process of encasing many cells in the brain with a myelin sheath that increases the speed at which information travels through the nervous system.

N

naturalistic observation Observation conducted in the real world rather than in a laboratory.

nature-nurture issue Nature refers to an organism's biological inheritance, nurture to environmental influences. The "nature" proponents claim biological inheritance is the most important influence on development; the "nurture" proponents claim environmental experiences are the most important.

near transfer The transfer of learning to a situation that is similar to the one in which the initial learning took place.

need for affiliation or relatedness The motive to be securely connected with other people.

negative reinforcement Reinforcement based on the principle that the frequency of a response increases because an aversive (unpleasant) stimulus is removed.

neglectful parenting A parenting style of uninvolvement in which parents spend little time with their children; associated with children's social incompetence.

neo-Piagetians Developmental psychologists who believe that Piaget got some things right but that his theory needs considerable revision; they emphasize information processing through attention, memory, and strategies.

network theories Theories that describe how information in memory is organized and connected; they emphasize nodes in the memory network.

neuroconstructivist view Emphasizes that brain development is influenced by both biological processes and environmental experiences; the brain has plasticity and depends on experience; and brain development is linked closely with cognitive development.

nongraded (cross-age) program A variation of between-class ability grouping in which students are grouped by their ability in particular subjects, regardless of their age or grade level.

norm group The group of individuals previously tested that provides a basis for interpreting a test score.

norm-referenced grading A grading system based on comparing a student's performance with that of other students in the class or of other classes and other students.

norm-referenced tests Standardized tests in which a student's score is interpreted by comparing it with how others (the norm group) performed.

normal distribution A "bell-shaped curve" in which most of the scores are clustered around the mean and scores that are far above or below the mean are rare.

O

objective tests Tests that have relatively clear, unambiguous scoring criteria, usually multiple-choice tests.

observational learning Learning that involves acquiring skills, strategies, and beliefs by observing others.

offset style A classroom arrangement style in which small numbers of students (usually three or four) sit at tables but do not sit directly across from one another.

operant conditioning A form of learning in which the consequences of behavior produce changes in the probability that the behavior will occur.

optimistic/pessimistic styles Involves having either positive (optimistic) or negative (pessimistic) expectations for the future.

organization Piaget's concept of grouping isolated behaviors into a higher-order, more smoothly functioning cognitive system; the grouping or arranging of items into categories.

orthopedic impairments Restricted movements or lack of control of movements, due to muscle, bone, or joint problems.

overconfidence bias The tendency to have more confidence in judgments and decisions than we should have, based on probability or past experience.

P

participant observation Observation conducted while the teacher-researcher is actively involved as a participant in the activity or setting.

pedagogical content knowledge Knowledge about how to effectively teach a particular discipline.

percentile-rank score The percentage of a distribution that lies at or below the score.

performance assessment Assessment that requires creating answers or products that demonstrate knowledge and skill; examples include writing an essay, conducting an experiment, carrying out a project, solving a real-world problem, and creating a portfolio.

performance criteria Specific behaviors that students need to perform effectively as part of an assessment.

performance orientation A focus on winning rather than achievement outcome; success is believed to result from winning.

permissive classroom management style A management style that allows students considerable autonomy but provides them with little support for developing learning skills or managing their behavior.

person-situation interaction The view that the best way to conceptualize personality is not in terms of personal traits or characteristics alone, but also in terms of the situation involved.

personality Distinctive thoughts, emotions, and behaviors that characterize the way an individual adapts to the world.

phonics approach An approach that emphasizes that reading instruction should teach phonics and its basic rules for translating written symbols into sounds; early reading instruction should use simplified materials.

phonology A language's sound system.

portfolio A systematic and organized collection of a student's work that demonstrates the student's skills and accomplishments.

positive reinforcement Reinforcement based on the principle that the frequency of a response increases because it is followed by a rewarding stimulus.

postconventional reasoning The third and highest level in Kohlberg's theory of moral development. At this level, morality is more internal. The postconventional level consists of two stages: social contract or utility and individual rights (stage 5) and universal ethical principles (stage 6).

pragmatics The appropriate use of language in different contexts.

preconventional reasoning The lowest level in Kohlberg's theory. At this level, morality is often focused on reward and punishment. The two stages in preconventional reasoning are punishment and obedience orientation (stage 1) and individualism, instrumental purpose, and exchange (stage 2).

predictive validity The relation between test scores and the student's future performance.

prefrontal cortex The front region of the frontal lobes; involved in reasoning, decision making, and self-control.

prejudice An unjustified negative attitude toward an individual because of the individual's membership in a group.

Premack principle The principle that a high-probability activity can serve as a reinforcer for a low-probability activity.

preoperational stage The second Piagetian stage, lasting from about 2 to 7 years of age, when symbolic thought increases and operational thought is not yet present.

problem solving Finding an appropriate way to attain a goal.

problem-based learning Learning that emphasizes authentic problems like those that occur in daily life.

procedural memory Nondeclarative knowledge in the form of skills and cognitive operations. Procedural memory cannot be consciously recollected, at least not in the form of specific events or facts.

program evaluation research Research designed to make decisions about the effectiveness of a particular program.

project-based learning Learning in which students work on real, meaningful problems and create tangible products.

prompt An added stimulus or cue that is given just before a response that increases the likelihood the response will occur.

prototype matching Deciding whether an item is a member of a category by comparing it with the most typical item(s) of the category.

Public Law 94-142 The Education for All Handicapped Children Act, which required that all students with disabilities be given a free, appropriate public education and also provided the funding to help implement this education.

punishment A consequence that decreases the probability that a behavior will occur.

Q

qualitative research Involves obtaining information using descriptive measures such as interviews, case studies, personal journals and diaries, and focus groups, as well as using thematic analysis rather than statistics to analyze textual data.

quantitative research Employs numerical calculations in an effort to discover information about a particular topic.

quid pro quo sexual harassment Occurs when a school employee threatens to base an educational decision (such as a grade) on a student's submission to unwelcome sexual conduct.

R

random assignment In experimental research, the assignment of participants to experimental and control groups by chance.

range The distance between the highest and lowest scores.

raw score The number of items a student answered correctly on the test.

receptive language The reception and understanding of language.

reciprocal teaching A learning arrangement in which students take turns leading a small-group discussion; can also involve teacher-scaffolded instruction.

rehearsal The conscious repetition of information over time to increase the length of time information stays in memory.

reinforcement (reward) A consequence that increases the probability that a behavior will occur.

reliability The extent to which a test produces a consistent, reproducible score.

response cost Taking a positive reinforcer away from an individual.

rubric A guide that lists specific criteria for grading and scoring academic papers, projects, or tests.

S

scaffolding A technique that involves changing the level of support for learning. A teacher or more advanced peer adjusts the amount of guidance to fit the student's current performance.

schedules of reinforcement Partial reinforcement timetables that determine when a response will be reinforced.

schema Information—concepts, knowledge, information about events—that already exists in a person's mind.

schema theories Theories that when we construct information, we fit it into information that already exists in our mind.

schemas In Piaget's theory, actions or mental representations that organize knowledge.

script A schema for an event.

selected-response items Test items with an objective format in which student responses can be scored quickly. A scoring guide for correct responses is created and can be applied by an examiner or a computer.

selective attention Focusing on a specific aspect of experience that is relevant while ignoring others that are irrelevant.

self-actualization The highest and most elusive of Maslow's needs; the motivation to develop one's full potential as a human being.

self-efficacy The belief that one can master a situation and produce positive outcomes.

self-esteem Also called *self-image* and *self-worth*, the individual's overall conception of herself or himself.

self-instructional methods Cognitive-behavioral techniques aimed at teaching individuals to modify their own behavior.

self-regulatory learning The self-generation and self-monitoring of thoughts, feelings, and behaviors in order to reach a goal.

semantic memory An individual's general knowledge about the world, independent of the individual's identity with the past.

semantics The meaning of words and sentences.

seminar style A classroom arrangement style in which large numbers of students (ten or more) sit in circular, square, or U-shaped arrangements.

sensorimotor stage The first Piagetian stage, lasting from birth to about 2 years of age, when infants construct an understanding of the world by coordinating sensory experiences with motor actions.

sensory memory Memory that holds information from the world in its original form for only an instant.

serial position effect The principle that recall is better for items at the beginning and the end of a list than for items in the middle.

seriation A concrete operation that involves ordering stimuli along some quantitative dimension.

service learning A form of education that promotes social responsibility and service to the community.

shaping Teaching new behaviors by reinforcing successive approximations to a specified target behavior.

short-answer item A constructed-response format in which students are required to write a word, a short phrase, or several sentences in response to a prompt.

short-term memory A limited-capacity memory system in which information is retained for as long as 30 seconds, unless the information is rehearsed, in which case it can be retained longer.

situated cognition The idea that thinking is located (situated) in social and physical contexts, not within an individual's mind.

slow-to-warm-up child A temperament style in which the child has a low activity level, is somewhat negative, and displays a low intensity of mood.

social cognitive theory Bandura's theory that social and cognitive factors, as well as behavior, play important roles in learning.

social constructivist approach Emphasizes the social contexts of learning and that knowledge is mutually built and constructed; Vygotsky's theory exemplifies this approach.

social conventional reasoning Focuses on conventional rules that have been established by social consensus to control behavior and maintain the social system.

social motives Needs and desires that are learned through experiences with the social world.

social studies The field that seeks to promote civic competence with the goal of helping students make informed and reasoned decisions for the public good as citizens of a culturally diverse, democratic society in an interdependent world.

socioeconomic status (SES) A grouping of people with similar occupational, educational, and economic characteristics.

specific language impairment (SLI) Involves problems in language development that are not accompanied by other obvious physical, sensory, or emotional problems; in some cases, the disorder is called developmental language disorder.

speech and language disorders A number of speech problems (such as articulation disorders, voice disorders, and fluency disorders) and language problems (difficulties in receiving information and expressing language).

splintered development The circumstances in which development is uneven across domains.

split-half reliability Reliability judged by dividing the test items into two halves, such as the odd-numbered and even-numbered items. The scores on the two sets of items are compared to determine how consistently the students performed across each set.

standard deviation A measure of how much a set of scores varies on average around the mean of the scores.

standard score A score expressed as a deviation from the mean; involves the standard deviation.

standardized tests Tests with uniform procedures for administration and scoring. They assess students' performance in different domains and allow a student's performance to be compared with the performance of other students at the same age or grade level on a national basis.

standards-based tests Tests that assess skills that students are expected to master before they can be promoted to the next grade or permitted to graduate.

stanine score A nine-point scale that describes a student's performance.

stereotype threat Anxiety regarding whether one's behavior might confirm a negative stereotype about one's group.

strategy construction Creation of a new procedure for processing information.

subgoaling The process of setting intermediate goals that place students in a better position to reach the final goal or solution.

summative assessment Assessment after instruction is finished to document student performance; also called formal assessment.

sustained attention Maintaining attention over an extended period of time; also called vigilance.

symbolic function substage The first substage of preoperational thought, occurring between about 2 and 4 years of age; the ability to represent an object not present develops and symbolic thinking increases; egocentrism is present.

syntax The ways that words must be combined to form acceptable phrases and sentences.

systematic desensitization A method based on classical conditioning that reduces anxiety by getting the individual to associate deep relaxation with successive visualizations of increasingly anxiety-provoking situations.

T

task analysis Breaking down a complex task that students are to learn into its component parts.

taxonomy A classification system.

teacher-as-researcher Also called teacher-researcher, this concept involves classroom teachers conducting their own studies to improve their teaching practice.

temperament A person's behavioral style and characteristic ways of responding.

test-retest reliability The extent to which a test yields the same performance when a student is given the same test on two or more occasions.

theory of mind Awareness of one's own mental processes and the mental processes of others.

thinking Manipulating and transforming information in memory, which often is done to form concepts, reason, think critically, make decisions, think creatively, and solve problems.

time-out Removing an individual from positive reinforcement.

transactional strategy instruction approach A cognitive approach to reading that emphasizes instruction in strategies, especially metacognitive strategies.

transfer Applying previous experiences and knowledge to learning or problem solving in a new situation.

transitivity The ability to reason and logically combine relationships.

triarchic theory of intelligence Sternberg's view that intelligence comes in three main forms: analytical, creative, and practical.

validity The extent to which a test measures what it is intended to measure and whether inferences about the test scores are accurate and appropriate.

values clarification An approach to moral education that emphasizes helping people clarify what their lives are for and what is worth working for; students are encouraged to define their own values and understand the values of others.

voice disorders Disorders producing speech that is hoarse, harsh, too loud, too high-pitched, or too low-pitched.

W

Web A system for browsing Internet sites that refers to the World Wide Web; named the Web because it is composed of many sites that are linked together.

whole-language approach An approach that stresses that reading instruction should parallel children's natural language learning. Reading materials should be whole and meaningful.

within-class ability grouping Placing students in two or three groups within a class to take into account differences in students' abilities.

withitness A management style described by Kounin in which teachers show students that they are aware of what is happening. Such teachers closely monitor students on a regular basis and detect inappropriate behavior early, before it gets out of hand.

working memory A three-part system that holds information temporarily as a person performs a task. A kind of "mental workbench" that lets individuals manipulate, assemble, and construct information when they make decisions, solve problems, and comprehend written and spoken language.

Z

z-score A score that provides information about how many standard deviations a raw score is above or below the mean.

zone of proximal development (ZPD) Vygotsky's term for the range of tasks that are too difficult for children to master alone but can be mastered with guidance and assistance from adults or more-skilled children.

Praxis™ Practice Answer Key

CHAPTER 1

Historical Background
1. b
2. c

Effective Teaching
1. d
2. b

Research in Educational Psychology
1. a   3. c
2. d   4. c

CHAPTER 2

An Overview of Child Development
1. d   3. a
2. c   4. d

Cognitive Development
1. b
2. d
3. c

Language Development
1. a
2. b
3. b

CHAPTER 3

Contemporary Theories
1. b
2. c

Social Contexts of Development
1. b
2. d
3. a

Socioemotional Development
1. c
2. b
3. b

CHAPTER 4

Intelligence
1. a   4. b
2. b   5. b
3. d

Learning and Thinking Styles
1. b
2. d
3. a

Personality and Temperament
1. b
2. b

CHAPTER 5

Culture and Ethnicity
1. c   3. a
2. c   4. c

Multicultural Education
1. d   3. a
2. d   4. a

Gender
1. c   4. a
2. c   5. a
3. b

CHAPTER 6

Children with Disabilities
1. c   5. c
2. b   6. b
3. a   7. b
4. b   8. d

Educational Issues Involving Children with Disabilities
1. b
2. c

Children Who Are Gifted
1. d
2. b
3. b

CHAPTER 7

What Is Learning?
1. b
2. b

Behavioral Approach to Learning
1. d
2. b

Applied Behavior Analysis in Education
1. a   3. d
2. a   4. d

Social Cognitive Approaches to Learning
1. b   3. a
2. a   4. b

CHAPTER 8

The Nature of the Information-Processing Approach
1. b
2. a
3. a

Attention
1. a
2. a

Memory
1. a   3. a
2. b   4. d

Expertise
1. b
2. a
3. b

Metacognition
1. d
2. c
3. a

CHAPTER 9

Conceptual Understanding
1. b
2. c

Thinking
1. c   4. a
2. d   5. a
3. c

Problem Solving
1. b   3. b
2. a   4. a

Transfer
1. b
2. c

CHAPTER 10

Social Constructivist Approaches to Teaching
1. a
2. b

Teachers and Peers as Joint Contributors to Students' Learning
1. b 3. a
2. b 4. a

Structuring Small-Group Work
1. b
2. d
3. d

CHAPTER 11

Expert Knowledge and Pedagogical Content Knowledge
1. b

Reading
1. c 3. c
2. b 4. b

Writing
1. c
2. b
3. b

Mathematics
1. a 4. b
2. b 5. d
3. c

Science
1. d
2. c

Social Studies
1. a
2. d

CHAPTER 12

Planning
1. b
2. d

Teacher-Centered Lesson Planning and Instruction
1. a 3. a
2. c 4. c

Learner-Centered Lesson Planning and Instruction
1. d
2. c
3. b

Technology and Education
1. c
2. d
3. a

CHAPTER 13

Exploring Motivation
1. b
2. b

Achievement Processes
1. b 5. d
2. d 6. b
3. a 7. b
4. b 8. b

Motivation, Relationships, and Sociocultural Contexts
1. c
2. c
3. d

Students with Achievement Problems
1. a 5. a
2. b 6. b
3. a
4. a

CHAPTER 14

Why Classrooms Need to Be Managed Effectively
1. b 3. a
2. d 4. c

Designing the Physical Environment of the Classroom
1. b
2. d

Creating a Positive Environment for Learning
1. b 3. c
2. b 4. c

Being a Good Communicator
1. d
2. d
3. b

Dealing with Problem Behaviors
1. c
2. d

CHAPTER 15

The Nature of Standardized Tests
1. b
2. a

Aptitude and Achievement Tests
1. a 3. b
2. d 4. b

The Teacher's Roles
1. d
2. a
3. c

Issues in Standardized Tests
1. a
2. b

CHAPTER 16

The Classroom as an Assessment Context
1. b 4. c
2. a 5. c
3. d

Traditional Tests
1. c
2. c

Alternative Assessments
1. d
2. b

Grading and Reporting Performance
1. c 3. d
2. b 4. d

Interstate Teacher Assessment and Support Consortium (InTASC)

MODEL CORE TEACHING STANDARDS

"These standards outline the common principles and foundations of teaching practice that cut across all subject areas and grade levels and that are necessary to improve student achievement" (CCSSO, 2011, p. 3).

1. **Learner Development:** The teacher considers the growth and development patterns of their learners in order to create appropriately challenging learning experiences.
2. **Learning Differences:** The teacher aims for an inclusive learning environment in which individual differences and cultures are respected and used to support students' growth.
3. **Learning Environments:** The teacher collaborates with learners, their families, and colleagues to foster a positive space for students to cooperate with each other and develop ownership of their learning.
4. **Content Knowledge:** The teacher uses a variety of methods, processes of inquiry, and academic understanding of the discipline to help learners connect with and master the content.
5. **Application of Content:** The teacher is able to engage learners in solving authentic problems by encouraging creativity and critical thinking to connects concepts and consider different perspectives.
6. **Assessment:** The teacher uses different assessment approaches to monitor students' growth, engage students in evaluating their own learning, and inform decision making.
7. **Planning for Instruction:** The teacher supports each student to meet the learning goals by planning instruction that considers content areas, cross-disciplinary skills, learning theory, human development, and curriculum in a manner that works in the community context.
8. **Instructional Strategies:** The teacher creates connections and builds skills by using different strategies to encourage students to make connections and apply their knowledge.
9. **Professional Learning and Ethical Practice:** The teacher aims to continually develop their own knowledge and skills and adjust their practices to meet the needs of each learner.
10. **Leadership and Collaboration:** The teacher takes the lead on collaborating with other school professionals and learners' families to ensure learner growth and development.

Source: Adapted from *Interstate Teacher Assessment and Support Consortium (InTASC) Model Core Teaching Standards: A Resource for State Dialogue,* by Council of Chief State School Officers (CCSSO), 2011 (https://ccsso.org/sites/default/files/2017-11/InTASC_Model_Core_Teaching_Standards_2011.pdf).

References

A

Abbassi, E., & others (2015). Emotional words can be embodied or disembodied: The role of superficial vs. deep types of processing. *Frontiers in Psychology, 6,* 975.

ABC News. (2005). *Larry Page and Sergey Brin.* Retrieved December 12, 2005, from http://abcnews.go.com?Entertainment/12/8/05

Abrami, P.C., & others (2015). Strategies for teaching students to think critically: A meta-analysis. *Review of Educational Research, 85,* 275–314.

Achieve, Inc. (2005). *Rising to the challenge: Are high school graduates prepared for college and work?* Washington, DC: Author.

Adams, A. (2015). A cultural historical theoretical perspective of discourse and design in the science classroom. *Cultural Studies of Science Education, 10,* 329–338.

Adams, R., & Biddle, B. (1970). *Realities of teaching.* New York: Holt, Rinehart & Winston.

Affrunti, N.W., & Woodruff-Borden, J. (2014). Perfectionism in pediatric anxiety and depression. *Clinical Child and Family Psychology Review, 17,* 299–317.

Ahrons, C. (2007). Family ties after divorce: Long-term implications for children. *Family Process, 46,* 53–65.

Airasian, P., & Walsh, M.E. (1997, February). Constructivist cautions. *Phi Delta Kappan,* pp. 444–450.

Akcay, N.O. (2016). Implementation of cooperative learning model in preschool. *Journal of Education and Learning, 5,* 83–93.

Akin, A., & Akin, U. (2014). Examining the relationship between authenticity and self-handicapping. *Psychology Reports, 115,* 795–804.

Alba-Fisch, M. (2016). Collaborative divorce: An effort to reduce the damage of divorce. *Journal of Clinical Psychology, 72,* 444–457.

Alberto, P.A., & Troutman, A.C. (2017). *Applied behavior analysis for teachers* (9th ed.). Upper Saddle River, NJ: Pearson.

Alberts, J.K., Nakayama, T.K., & Martin, J.N. (2016). *Human communication in society* (4th ed.). Upper Saddle River, NJ: Pearson.

Alderson-Day, B., & Fernyhough, C. (2014). More than one voice: Investigating the phenomenological properties of inner speech requires a variety of methods. *Consciousness and Cognition, 24,* 113–114.

Aleven, V., McLaughlin, E.A., Glenn, R.A., & Koedinger, K.R. (2017). Instruction based on adaptive learning technologies. In R.E. Mayer & P.A. Alexander (Eds.), *Handbook of research on learning and instruction* (2nd ed.). New York: Routledge.

Alexander, B.T., Dasinger, J.H., & Intapad, S. (2015). Fetal programming and cardiovascular pathology. *Comprehensive Physiology, 5,* 997–1025.

Alexander, P.A. (2003). The development of expertise. *Educational Researcher, 32*(8), 10–14.

Alexander, P.A., & Grossnickle, E.M. (2016). Positioning interest and curiosity within a model of academic development. In K. Wentzel & D. Miele (Eds.), *Handbook of motivation at school* (2nd ed.). New York: Routledge.

All Kinds of Minds. (2009). *Learning Base: Self-regulating learning.* Retrieved August 15, 2009, from www.allkindsofminds.org/learning

Allington, R.L. (2015). *What really matters for middle school readers.* Upper Saddle River, NJ: Pearson.

Allyn, P. (2016). *Core ready lesson sets for grades 6–8.* Upper Saddle River, NJ: Pearson.

Al-Qawabeh, R. H., & Aljazi, A. A. (2018). The effectiveness of using PQ4R strategy in teaching reading comprehension in Arabic language subject among ninth grade students' achievement in Jordan. *World Journal of Educational Research, 5,* 159–171. doi: 10.22158/wjer.v5n2p159

Alsaker, F.D., & Valanover, S. (2012). The Bernese Program Against Victimization in Kindergarten and Elementary School. *New Directions in Youth Development, 133,* 15–28.

Alverno College. (1995). *Writing and speaking criteria.* Milwaukee, WI: Alverno Productions.

Amabile, T.M. (1993). Commentary. In D. Goleman, P. Kaufman, & M. Ray, *The creative spirit.* New York: Plume.

Ambrose, D., & Sternberg, R.J. (2016). *Creative intelligence in the 21st century.* Rotterdam, The Netherlands: Sense Publishers.

Ambrose, D., & Sternberg, R.J. (2016a). *Giftedness and talent in the 21st century.* Rotterdam, The Netherlands: Sense Publishers.

Ambrose, D., & Sternberg, R.J. (2016b). Previewing a collaborative exploration of giftedness and talent in the 21st century. In D. Ambrose & R.J. Sternberg (Eds.), *Giftedness and talent in the 21st century.* Rotterdam, The Netherlands: Sense Publishers.

Ambrose, L., & Machek, G.R. (2015). Identifying creatively gifted students: Necessity of a multi-method approach. *Contemporary School Psychology, 19,* 121–127.

American Psychiatric Association. (2013). *DSM-V.* Arlington, VA: Author.

An, D., & Carr, M. (2017). Learning styles theory fails to explain learning and achievement: Recommendations for alternative approaches. *Personality and Individual Differences, 116,* 410–416.

Anastasi, A., & Urbino, S. (1997). *Psychological testing* (11th ed.). Upper Saddle River, NJ: Prentice-Hall.

Anderman, E.M., & Anderman, L.H. (2010). *Classroom motivation.* Upper Saddle River, NJ: Merrill.

Anderman, E.M., Austin, C.C., & Johnson, D.M. (2002). The development of goal orientation. In A. Wigfield & J.S. Eccles (Eds.), *Development of achievement motivation.* San Diego: Academic Press.

Anderman, L.H., & Klassen, R.M. (2016). Being a teacher: Efficacy, emotions, and interpersonal relationships in the classroom. In L. Corno & E.A. Anderman (Eds.), *Handbook of educational psychology* (3rd ed.). New York: Routledge.

Anderson, L.W., & Krathwohl, D.R. (Eds.). (2001). *A taxonomy for learning, teaching, and assessing.* New York: Longman.

Anderson, S.B., & Guthery, A.M. (2015). Mindfulness-based psychoeducation for parents of children with attention-deficit/hyperactivity disorder: An applied clinical project. *Journal of Child and Adolescent Psychiatric Nursing, 28,* 43–49.

Anglin, D.M., & others (2016). Ethnic identity, racial discrimination, and attenuated psychotic symptoms in an urban population of emerging adults. *Early Intervention in Psychiatry.* doi:10.1111/eip.12314

Annas, J., Narváez, D., & Snow, N. (Eds.) (2016). *Advances in virtue development.* New York: Oxford University Press.

Ansary, N.S., McMahon, T.J., & Luthar, S.S. (2012). Socioeconomic context and emotional-behavioral achievement links: Concurrent and prospective associations among low- and high-income youth. *Journal of Research on Adolescence, 22,* 14–30.

Ansary, N.S., McMahon, T.J., & Luthar, S.S. (2016). Trajectories of emotional-behavioral difficulty and academic competence: A 6-year, person-centered, prospective study of affluent suburban adolescents. *Development and Psychopathology.* doi:10.1017/S0954579416000110

Appel, M., & Kronberger, N. (2012). Stereotypes and the achievement gap: Stereotype threat prior to test taking. *Educational Psychology Review, 24,* 609–635.

Apple Computer. (1995). *Changing the conversation about teaching, learning and technology: A report on 10 years of ACOT research.* Retrieved April 8, 2005, from http://images.apple.com/education/k12/leadership/acot/pdf/10yr.pdf

Applebee, A., & Langer, J. (2006). *The partnership for literacy: A study of professional development, instructional change and student growth.* Retrieved August 5, 2008, from http://cela.albany.edu/publication/IRAResearch

Arends, R.I. (2004). *Learning to teach* (6th ed.). New York: McGraw-Hill.

Aries, R.J., & Cabus, S.J. (2015). Parental homework involvement improves test scores? A review of the literature. *Review of Education, 3,* 179–199.

Arkes, J. (2015). The temporal effects of divorces and separations on children's academic achievement and problem behavior. *Journal of Divorce and Remarriage, 56,* 25–42.

Arnett, J.J. (2006). Emerging adulthood: Understanding the new way of coming of age. In J.J. Arnett & J.L. Tanner (Eds.), *Emerging adults in America.* Washington, DC: American Psychological Association.

Arnett, J.J. (Ed.). (2012). *Adolescent psychology around the world.* New York: Psychology Press.

Arnett, J.J. (2015). *Emerging adulthood* (2nd ed.). New York: Oxford University Press.

Aronson, B., & Laughter, J. (2016). The theory and practice of culturally relevant education: A synthesis of research across content areas. *Review of Educational Research, 86,* 163–206.

Aronson, E.E. (1986, August). *Teaching students things they think they already know about: The case of prejudice and desegregation.* Paper presented at the meeting of the American Psychological Association, Washington, DC.

Aronson, E.E., Blaney, N., Stephan, C., Sikes, J., & Snapp, M. (1978). *The jigsaw classroom.* Thousand Oaks, CA: Sage.

Aronson, E.E., & Patnoe, S. (1997). *The jigsaw classroom* (2nd ed.). Boston: Addison-Wesley.

Aronson, J. (2002). Stereotype threat: Contending and coping with unnerving expectations. *Improving academic achievement.* San Diego: Academic Press.

Arter, J. (1995). *Portfolios for assessment and instruction.* ERIC Document Reproduction Service No. ED388890.

Ashcraft, M.H., & Radvansky, G.A. (2016). *Cognition* (6th ed.). Upper Saddle River, NJ: Pearson.

Aslan, S., & Reigeluth, C.M. (2015/2016). Examining the challenges of learner-centered education. *Phi Delta Kappan, 97,* 65–70.

Aspen Institute (2013). *Two generations, one future.* Washington, DC: Aspen Institute.

Atkinson, J.W. (1957). Motivational determinants of risk-taking behavior. *Psychological Review, 64,* 359–372.

Atkinson, R.C., & Shiffrin, R.M. (1968). Human memory: A proposed system and its control processes. In K.W. Spence & J.T. Spence (Eds.), *The psychology of learning and motivation* (Vol. 2). San Diego: Academic Press.

Audesirk, G., Audesirk, T., & Byers, B.E. (2017). *Biology* (11th ed.). Upper Saddle River, NJ: Pearson.

Azmitia, M. (2015). Reflections on the cultural lenses of identity development. In K.C. McLean & M. Syed (Eds.), *Oxford handbook of identity development.* New York: Oxford University Press.

B

Babbie, E.R. (2017). *The basics of social research* (7th ed.). Boston: Cengage.

Baddeley, A. (2000). Short-term and working memory. In E. Tulving & F.I.M. Craik (Eds.), *The Oxford handbook of memory.* New York: Oxford University Press.

Baddeley, A.D. (2007). *Working memory, thought and action.* Oxford: Oxford University Press.

Baddeley, A.D. (2012). Prefatory. *Annual Review of Psychology* (Vol. 63). Palo Alto, CA: Annual Reviews.

Baddeley, A.D. (2013). On applying cognitive psychology. *British Journal of Psychology, 104,* 443–456.

Baer, J. (2015). The importance of domain-specific expertise in creativity. *Roeper Review, 37,* 165–178.

Baer, J. (2016). Creativity doesn't develop in a vacuum. *New Directions in Child and Adolescent Development, 151,* 9–20.

Bain, R.B. (2005). "They thought the world was flat?": Applying the principles of *How People Learn* in teaching high school history. In M.S. Donovan & J.D. Bransford (Eds.), *How students learn.* Washington, DC: National Academies Press.

Ballentine, J.H., & Roberts, K.A. (2009). *Our social world* (2nd ed.). Thousand Oaks, CA: Sage.

Bandura, A. (1965). Influence of models' reinforcement contingencies on the acquisition of imitative responses. *Journal of Personality and Social Psychology, I,* 589–596.

Bandura, A. (1986). *Social foundations of thought and action.* Englewood Cliffs, NJ: Prentice Hall.

Bandura, A. (1997). *Self-efficacy: The exercise of control.* New York: W.H. Freeman.

Bandura, A. (2001). Social cognitive theory. *Annual Review of Psychology* (Vol. 51). Palo Alto, CA: Annual Reviews.

Bandura, A. (2009). Social and policy impact of social cognitive theory. In M. Mark, S. Donaldson, & B. Campbell (Eds.), *Social psychology and program/policy evaluation.* New York: Guilford.

Bandura, A. (2010). Self-efficacy. In D. Matsumoto (Ed.), *Cambridge dictionary of psychology.* Cambridge, UK: Cambridge University Press.

Bandura, A. (2010). Self-reinforcement. In D. Matsumoto (Ed.), *Cambridge dictionary of psychology.* Cambridge, UK: Cambridge University Press.

Bandura, A. (2012). Social cognitive theory. *Annual Review of Clinical Psychology* (Vol. 8). Palo Alto, CA: Annual Reviews.

Bandura, A. (2015). *Moral disengagement.* New York: Worth.

Bangert, K., Kulik, J., & Kulik, C. (1983). Individualized systems of instruction in secondary schools. *Review of Educational Research, 53,* 143–158.

Banks, J.A. (2003). *Teaching strategies for ethnic studies* (7th ed.). Boston: Allyn & Bacon.

Banks, J.A. (2006). *Cultural diversity and education* (5th ed.). Boston: Allyn & Bacon.

Banks, J.A. (2008). *Introduction to multicultural education* (4th ed.). Boston: Allyn & Bacon.

Banks, J.A. (2014). *Introduction to multicultural education* (5th ed.). Upper Saddle River, NJ: Pearson.

Banks, J.A. (2015). *Cultural diversity and education* (6th ed.). Upper Saddle River, NJ: Pearson.

Banks, J.A., & others (2005). Teaching diverse learners. In L. Darling-Hammond & J. Bransford (Eds.), *Preparing teachers for a changing world.* San Francisco: Jossey-Bass.

Barbarin, O.A., Chinn, L., & Wright, Y.F. (2014). Creating developmentally auspicious school environments for African American boys. *Advances in Child Development and Behavior, 47,* 333-365.

Barber, W., King, S., & Buchanan, S. (2015). Problem-based learning and authentic assessment in digital pedagogy: Embracing the role of collaborative communities. *Electronic Journal of e-Learning, 13,* 59-67.

Barbot, B., & Tinio, P.P. (2015). Where is the "g" in creativity? A specialization-differentiation hypothesis. *Frontiers of Human Neuroscience.* doi:10.3389/fnhym.2014.01041

Barhight, L.R., Hubbard, J.A., Grassetti, S.N., & Morrow, M.T. (2015). Relations between actual group norms, perceived peer behavior, and bystander children's intervention to bullying. *Journal of Clinical Child and Adolescent Psychology.* doi:10.1080/15374416.2015.1046180.

Barlett, C.P. (2015). Predicting adolescents' cyberbullying behavior: A longitudinal risk analysis. *Journal of Adolescence, 41,* 86-95.

Barron, A.E., Dawson, K., & Yendol-Hoppey, D. (2009). Peer coaching and technology integration: An evaluation of the Microsoft Peer Coaching Program. *Mentoring and Tutoring: Partnership in Learning, 17,* 83-102.

Bart, W.M., & Kato, K. (2008). Normal curve. In N.J. Salkind (Ed.), *Encyclopedia of educational psychology.* Thousand Oaks, CA: Sage.

Bart, W.M., & Peterson, D.P. (2008). Stanford-Binet test. In N.J. Salkind (Ed.), *Encyclopedia of educational psychology.* Thousand Oaks, CA: Sage.

Bartlett, J. (2015, January). Personal conversation. Richardson, TX: Department of Psychology, University of Texas at Dallas.

Barton, J., & Collins, A. (1997). Starting out: Designing your portfolio. In J. Barton & A. Collins (Eds.), *Portfolio assessment: A handbook for educators.* Boston: Addison-Wesley.

Bassi, M., Steca, P., Della Fave, A., & Caprara, G.V. (2007). Academic self-efficacy beliefs and quality of experience on learning. *Journal of Youth and Adolescence, 36,* 301-312.

Batdi, V. (2014). The effects of a problem-based learning approach on students' attitude levels: A meta-analysis. *Educational Research and Reviews, 9,* 272-276.

Bates, J.E. (2012a). Behavioral regulation as a product of temperament and environment. In S.L. Olson & A.J. Sameroff (Eds.), *Biopsychosocial regulatory processes in the development of childhood behavioral problems.* New York: Cambridge University Press.

Bates, J.E. (2012b). Temperament as a tool in promoting early childhood development. In S.L. Odom, E.P. Pungello, & N. Gardner-Neblett (Eds.), *Infants, toddlers, and families in poverty.* New York: Guilford.

Bates, J.E., & Pettit, G.S. (2015). Temperament, parenting, and social development. In J.E. Grusec & P.D. Hastings (Eds.), *Handbook of socialization* (2nd ed.). New York: Guilford.

Bauer, P.J. (2009). Neurodevelopmental changes in infancy and beyond: Implications for learning and memory. In O.A. Barbarin & B.H. Wasik (Eds.), *Handbook of child development and early education.* New York: Guilford.

Bauer, P.J., & Larkina, M. (2016). Predicting remembering and forgetting of autobiographical memories in children and adults: A prospective study. *Memory, 24,* 1345-1368.

Baumann, Z.D., Marchetti, K., & Soltoff, B. (2015). What's the payoff? Assessing the efficacy of student response systems. *Journal of Political Science Education, 11,* 249-263.

Bauman-Waengler, J. (2016). *Articulation and phonology in speech sound disorders* (5th ed.). Upper Saddle River, NJ: Pearson.

Baumeister, R.F., Campbell, J.D., Krueger, J.I., & Vohs, K.D. (2003). Does high self-esteem cause better performance, interpersonal success, happiness, or healthier lifestyles? *Psychological Science in the Public Interest, 4*(1), 1-44.

Baumrind, D. (1971). Current patterns of parental authority. *Developmental Psychology Monographs, 4*(1, Pt. 2).

Baumrind, D. (1996, April). Unpublished review of J.W. Santrock's *Children* (5th ed.). New York: McGraw-Hill.

Bear, D.R., & others (2016). *Words their way* (6th ed.). Upper Saddle River, NJ: Pearson.

Beaty, J.J., & Pratt, L. (2015). *Early literacy in preschool and kindergarten* (4th ed.). Upper Saddle River, NJ: Pearson.

Becker, D.R., Miao, A., Duncan, R., & McClelland, M.M. (2014). Behavioral self-regulation and executive function both predict visuomotor skills and early academic achievement. *Early Childhood Research Quarterly, 29,* 411-424.

Bednar, R.L., Wells, M.G., & Peterson, S.R. (1995). *Self-esteem* (2nd ed.). Washington, DC: American Psychological Association.

Beebe, S.A., Beebe, S.J., & Ivy, D.K. (2016). *Communication* (6th ed.). Upper Saddle River, NJ: Pearson.

Beebe, S.A., Beebe, S.J., & Redmond, M. (2017). *Interpersonal communication* (8th ed.). Upper Saddle River, NJ: Pearson.

Beghetto, R.A., & Kaufman, J.C. (Eds.). (2017). *Nurturing creativity in the classroom* (2nd ed.). New York: Cambridge University Press.

Belsky, J., & Pluess, M. (2016). Differential susceptibility to context: Implications for developmental psychopathology. In D. Cicchetti (Ed.), *Developmental psychopathology* (3rd ed.). New York: Wiley.

Bem, S.L. (1977). On the utility of alternative procedures for assessing psychological androgyny. *Journal of Consulting and Clinical Psychology, 45,* 196-205.

Bendixen, L. (2016). Teaching for epistemic change in elementary school classrooms. In J. Greene & others (Eds.), *Handbook of epistemic change.* New York: Routledge.

Benner, A.D., Boyle, A.E., & Sadler, S. (2016). Parental involvement and adolescents' educational success: The roles of prior achievement and socioeconomic status. *Journal of Youth and Adolescence, 45,* 1053-1064.

Bennett, K., & Dorjee, D. (2016). The impact of a mindfulness-based stress reduction course (MBSR) on well-being and academic achievement of sixth-form students. *Mindfulness, 7,* 105-114.

Benson, P.L., Scales, P.C., Hamilton, S.F., & Sesma, A. (2006). Positive youth development. In W. Damon & R. Lerner (Eds.), *Handbook of child psychology* (6th ed.). New York: Wiley.

Berg, A.T., Rychlik, K., Levy, S.R., & Testa, F.M. (2014). Complete remission of childhood-onset epilepsy: Stability and prediction over two decades. *Brain, 137,* 3213-3222.

Berger, I., Remington, A., Leitner, Y., & Leviton, A. (2015). Brain development and the attention spectrum. *Frontiers in Human Neuroscience, 9,* 23.

Berk, L.E. (1994). Why children talk to themselves. *Scientific American, 271*(5), 78-83.

Berk, L.E., & Spuhl, S.T. (1995). Maternal interaction, private speech, and task performance in preschool children. *Early Childhood Research Quarterly, 10,* 145-169.

Berko, J. (1958). The child's learning of English morphology. *Word, 14,* 150-177.

Berko Gleason, J. (2009). The development of language: An overview. In J. Berko Gleason & N. Ratner (Eds.), *The development of language* (7th ed.). Boston: Allyn & Bacon.

Berko Gleason, J., & Ratner, N.B. (Eds.). (2009). *The development of language* (7th ed.). Boston: Allyn & Bacon.

Berndt, T.J. (1979). Developmental changes in conformity to peers and parents. *Developmental Psychology, 15,* 608–616.

Bernier, R., & Dawson, G. (2016). Autism spectrum disorders. In D. Cicchetti (Ed.), *Developmental psychopathology* (3rd ed.). New York: Wiley.

Berninger, V.W. (2006). A developmental approach to learning disabilities. In W. Damon & R. Lerner (Eds.), *Handbook of child psychology* (6th ed.). New York: Wiley.

Berninger, V., Nagy, W., Tanimoto, S., Thompson, R., & Abbott, R. (2015). Computer instruction on handwriting, spelling, and composing for students with specific learning disabilities in grades 4 to 9. *Computers and Education, 81,* 154–168.

Berninger, V.W., Raskind, W., Richards, T., Abbott, R., & Stock, P. (2008). A multidisciplinary approach to understanding developmental dyslexia within working-memory architecture: Genotypes, phenotypes, brain, and instruction. *Developmental Neuropsychology, 33,* 707–744.

Berninger, V.W., Richards, T., & Abbott, R.D. (2015). Differential diagnosis of dysgraphia, dyslexia, and OWL LD: Behavioral and neuroimaging evidence. *Reading and Writing, 8,* 1119–1153.

Bernthal, J.E., Bankson, N.W., & Flipsen, P. (2017). *Articulation and phonological disorders* (8th ed.). Upper Saddle River, NJ: Pearson.

Best, D.L. (2010). Gender. In M.H. Bornstein (Ed.), *Handbook of developmental cultural science.* New York: Psychology Press.

Betts, J., McKay, J., Maruff, P., & Anderson, V. (2006). The development of sustained attention in children: The effect of age and task load. *Child Neuropsychology, 12,* 205–221.

Bialystok, E. (2001). *Bilingualism in development: Language, literacy, and cognition.* New York: Cambridge University Press.

Bialystok, E. (2007). Acquisition of literacy in preschool children. A framework for research. *Language Learning, 57,* 45–77.

Bialystok, E. (2011, April). *Becoming bilingual: Emergence of cognitive outcomes of bilingualism in immersion education.* Paper presented at the meeting of the Society for Research in Child Development, Montreal.

Bialystok, E. (2014). Language experience changes language and cognitive ability: Implications for social policy. In B. Spolsky, O. Inbar-Lourie, & M. Tannenbaum (Eds.), *Challenges for language education and policy.* New York: Routledge.

Bialystok, E. (2015). The impact of bilingualism on cognition. In R. Scott & S. Kosslyn (Eds.), *Emerging trends in the social and behavioral sciences.* New York: Wiley.

Bianco, F., Lecce, S., & Banerjee, R. (2016). Conversations about mental states and theory of mind development during middle childhood: A training study. *Journal of Experimental Child Psychology, 149,* 41–61.

Biggs, D.A., & Colesante, R.J. (2015). The moral competence tests: An examination of samples in the United States. *Journal of Moral Education, 44,* 497–515.

Bigler, R.S., Hayes, A.R., & Liben, L.S. (2014). Analysis and evaluation of the rationales for single-sex schooling. *Advances in Child Development and Behavior, 47,* 225–260.

Bigorra, A., Garolera, M., Guijarro, S., & Hervas, A. (2016). Long-term far-transfer effects of working memory training in children with ADHD: A randomized controlled trial. *European Child and Adolescent Psychiatry, 25,* 853–867.

Bilen, D., & Tavil, Z.M. (2015). The effects of cooperative learning strategies on vocabulary skills of fourth-grade students. *Journal of Education and Training Studies, 6,* 151–165.

Bill and Melinda Gates Foundation. (2008). *Report gives voice to dropouts.* Retrieved July 5, 2008, from www.gatesfoundation.org/UnitedStates/Education/TransformingHighSchools/Related.

Bill and Melinda Gates Foundation. (2016). *College-ready education.* Retrieved January 6, 2016, from www.gatesfoundation.org

Birman, B.F., & others (2007). State and local implementation of the "No Child Left Behind Act." In *Volume II—Teacher quality under "NCLB": Interim report.* Jessup. MD: U.S. Department of Education.

Bjorklund, D.F. (2012). *Children's thinking* (5th ed.). Boston: Cengage.

Bjorklund, D.F., & Rosenblum, K. (2000). Middle childhood: Cognitive development. In A. Kazdin (Ed.), *Encyclopedia of psychology.* Washington, DC, & New York: American Psychological Association and Oxford University Press.

Blackwell, L.S., & Dweck, C.S. (2008). *The motivational impact of a computer-based program that teaches how the brain changes with learning.* Unpublished manuscript, Department of Psychology, Stanford University, Palo Alto, CA.

Blackwell, L.S., Trzesniewski, K.H., & Dweck, C.S. (2007). Implicit theories of intelligence predict achievement across an adolescent transition: A longitudinal study and an intervention. *Child Development, 78,* 246–263.

Blair, C., & Raver, C.C. (2015). School readiness and self-regulation: A developmental psychobiological approach. *Annual Review of Psychology* (Vol. 66). Palo Alto, CA: Annual Reviews.

Blair, C., Raver, C.C., & Finegood, E.D. (2016). Self-regulation and developmental psychopathology: Experiential canalization of brain and behavior. In D. Cicchetti (Ed.), *Developmental psychopathology* (3rd ed.). New York: Wiley.

Blakely-McClure, S.J., & Ostrov, J.M. (2016). Relational aggression, victimization, and self-concept: Testing pathways from middle childhood to adolescence. *Journal of Youth and Adolescence, 45,* 376–390.

Blakemore, J.E.O., Berenbaum, S.A., & Liben, L.S. (2009). *Gender development.* New York: Psychology Press.

Blankenship, T.L., & others (2015). Working memory and recollection contribute to academic achievement. *Learning and Individual Differences, 43,* 164–169.

Blood, J.D., & others (2015). The variable heart: High frequency and very low frequency correlates of depressive symptoms in children and adolescents. *Journal of Affective Disorders, 186,* 119–126.

Bloom, B. (1985). *Developing talent in young people.* New York: Ballantine.

Bloom, B.S. (1971). Mastering learning. In J.H. Block (Ed.), *Mastery learning.* New York: Holt, Rinehart & Winston.

Bloom, B.S., Engelhart, M.D., Frost, E.J., Hill, W.H., & Krathwohl, D.R. (1956). *Taxonomy of educational objectives.* New York: David McKay.

Bloom, L. (1998). Language acquisition in its developmental context. In W. Damon (Ed.), *Handbook of child psychology* (5th ed., Vol. 2). New York: Wiley.

Blumenfeld, P.C., Kempler, T.M., & Krajcik, J.S. (2006). Motivation and cognitive engagement in learning environments. In R.K. Sawyer (Ed.), *Cambridge handbook of learning sciences.* New York: Cambridge University Press.

Blumenfeld, P.C., Krajcik, J.S., & Kempler, T.M. (2006). Motivation in the classroom. In W. Damon & R. Lerner (Eds.), *Handbook of child psychology* (6th ed.). New York: Wiley.

Blumenfeld, P.C., Pintrich, P.R., Wessels, K., & Meece, J. (1981, April). *Age and sex differences in the impact of classroom experiences on self-perceptions.* Paper presented at the biennial meeting of the Society of Research in Child Development, Boston.

Boaler, J. (2016). *Mathematical mindsets.* San Francisco: Jossey-Bass.

Bodrova, E., & Leong, D.J. (2007). *Tools of the mind* (2nd ed.). Upper Saddle River, NJ: Prentice Hall.

Bodrova, E., & Leong, D.J. (2015). Vygotskian and post-Vygotskian views of children's play. *American Journal of Play, 7,* 371–388.

Boekaerts, M. (2009). Goal-directed behavior in the classroom. In K.R. Wentzel & A. Wigfield (Eds.), *Handbook of motivation at school.* New York: Routledge.

Bogart, L.M., & others (2014). Peer victimization in the fifth grade and health in the tenth grade. *Pediatrics, 133,* 440–447.

Bonney, C.R., & Sternberg, R.J. (2017). Learning to think critically. In R.E. Mayer & P.A. Alexander (Eds.), *Handbook of learning and instruction* (2nd ed.). New York: Routledge.

Bonvanie, I.J., & others (2015). Short report: Functional somatic symptoms are associated with perfectionism in adolescents. *Journal of Psychosomatic Research, 79,* 328–330.

Borich, G.D. (2017). *Effective teaching methods* (9th ed.). Upper Saddle River, NJ: Pearson.

Bostic, J.Q., & others (2015). Being present at school: Implementing mindfulness in schools. *Child and Adolescent Clinics of North America, 24,* 245–259.

Boud, D., Lawson, R., & Thompson, D.G. (2015). The calibration of student adjustment through self-assessment: Disruptive effects of assessment patterns. *Higher Education Research and Development, 34,* 45–59.

Boutot, E.A. (2017). *Autism spectrum disorder* (2nd ed.). Upper Saddle River, NJ: Pearson.

Bowman-Perrott, L. (2009). Classwide peer tutoring: An effective strategy for students with emotional and behavioral disorders. *Intervention in School and Clinic, 44,* 259–267.

Boyatzis, R.E., Batista-Foguet, J.M., Fernandez-I-Marin, X., & Truninger, M. (2015). EI competencies as a related but different characteristic than intelligence. *Frontiers in Psychology, 6,* 72.

Boyles, N.S., & Contadino, D. (1997). *The learning differences sourcebook.* Los Angeles: Lowell House.

Boynton, P.M. (2017). *Research companion.* New York: Routledge.

Bradley, R. H., Corwyn, R. F., McAdoo, H. P., et al. (2001). The home environments of children in the United States part I: Variations by age, ethnicity, and poverty status. *Child Development, 72,* 1844–1867.

Brainerd, C.J., Forrest, T.J., Karibian, D., & Reyna, V.F. (2006). Fuzzy-trace theory and memory development. *Developmental Psychology, 42,* 962–979.

Brainerd, C.J., & Reyna, V.E. (2014). Dual processes in memory development: Fuzzy-trace theory. In P. Bauer & R. Fivush (Eds.), *Wiley-Blackwell handbook of children's memory.* New York: Wiley.

Brainerd, C.J., & others (2015). Episodic memory does not add up: Verbatim-gist superposition predicts violation of the additive law of probability. *Journal of Memory and Language, 84,* 224–245.

Brams, H., Mao, A.R., & Doyle, R.L. (2009). Onset of efficacy of long-lasting psychostimulants in pediatric attention-deficit/hyperactivity disorder. *Postgraduate Medicine, 120,* 69–88.

Branscum, P., & Crowson, H.M. (2016). The association between environmental and psychosocial factors toward physical activity and screen time of children: An application of the Integrative Behavioral Model. *Journal of Sports Science.* doi: 10.1080/02640414.2016.1206666

Bransford, J., Darling-Hammond, L., & LePage, P. (2005). Introduction. In L. Darling-Hammond & J. Bransford (Eds.), *Preparing teachers for a changing world.* New York: Jossey-Bass.

Bransford, J., Derry, S., Berliner, D., Hammerness, K., & Beckett, K.L. (2005). Theories of learning and their role in teaching. In L. Darling-Hammond & J. Bransford (Eds.), *Preparing teachers for a changing world.* San Francisco: Jossey-Bass.

Bransford, J.D., & Stein, B.S. (1993). *The IDEAL problem solver.* New York: W.H. Freeman.

Bransford, J., & others (2006). Foundations and opportunities for an interdisciplinary science. In R.K. Sawyer (Ed.), *The Cambridge handbook of the learning sciences.* New York: Cambridge University Press.

Bredekamp, S. (2017). *REVEL for effective practices in early childhood education* (3rd ed.). Upper Saddle River, NJ: Pearson.

Brenner, J.D. (2016). Traumatic stress from a multi-level developmental psychopathology perspective. In D. Cicchetti (Ed.), *Developmental psychopathology* (3rd ed.). New York: Wiley.

Brewer, M.B., & Campbell, D.I. (1976). *Ethnocentrism and intergroup attitudes.* New York: Wiley.

Bridgeland, J.M., Dilulio, J.J., & Wulsin, S.C. (2008). *Engaged for success.* Washington, DC: Civic Enterprises.

Briggs, T.W. (1999, October 14). Honorees find keys to unlocking kids' minds. Retrieved March 10, 2000, from www.usatoday.com/education

Brock, R.L., & Kochanska, G. (2016). Interparental conflict, children's security with parents, and long-term risk of internalizing problems: A longitudinal study from ages 2 to 10. *Development and Psychopathology, 28,* 45–54.

Brody, N. (2000). Intelligence. In A. Kazdin (Ed.), *Encyclopedia of psychology.* Washington, DC, & New York: American Psychological Association and Oxford University Press.

Brody, N. (2007). Does education influence intelligence? In P.C. Kyllonen, R.D. Roberts, & L. Stankov (Eds.), *Extending intelligence.* Mahwah, NJ: Erlbaum.

Bronfenbrenner, U. (1995). Developmental ecology through space and time: A future perspective. In P. Moen, G.H. Elder, & K. Luscher (Eds.), *Examining lives in context.* Washington, DC: American Psychological Association.

Bronfenbrenner, U., & Morris, M.A. (2006). The ecology of developmental processes. In W. Damon & R. Lerner (Eds.), *Handbook of child psychology* (6th ed.). New York: Wiley.

Brookhart, S.M. (1997). A theoretical framework for the role of classroom assessment in motivating student effort and achievement. *Applied Measurement in Education, 10,* 161–180.

Brookhart, S.M. (2008). *Assessment and grading in classrooms.* Upper Saddle River, NJ: Prentice Hall.

Brookhart, S.M. (2015). Making the most of multiple choice. *Educational Leadership, 73,* 36–39.

Brookhart, S.M., & Nitko, A.J. (2015). *Educational assessment of students* (7th ed.). Upper Saddle River, NJ: Pearson.

Brookover, W.B., Beady, C., Flood, P., Schweitzer, U., & Wisenbaker, J. (1979). *School social systems and student achievement: Schools make a difference.* New York: Praeger.

Brooks, J.G., & Brooks, M.G. (1993). *The case for constructivist classrooms.* Alexandria, VA: Association for Supervision and Curriculum Development.

Brooks, J.G., & Brooks, M.G. (2001). *In search of understanding: The case for constructivist classrooms.* Upper Saddle River, NJ: Merrill.

Brophy, J. (1998). *Motivating students to learn.* New York: McGraw-Hill.

Brophy, J. (2004). *Motivating students to learn* (2nd ed.). Mahwah, NJ: Erlbaum.

Brown, A.L., & Campione, J.C. (1996). Psychological learning theory and the design of innovative environments. In L. Schauble & R. Glaser (Eds.), *Contributions of instructional innovation to understanding learning.* Mahwah, NJ: Erlbaum.

Brown, G.T.L., Andrade, H.L., & Chen, F. (2015). Accuracy in student self-assessment: Directions and cautions for research. *Assessment in Education: Principles, Policy, and Practice, 22,* 444–457.

Bruning, R., & Horn, C. (2001). Developing motivation to write. *Educational Psychologist, 35,* 25–37.

Bryce, C.I., Goble, P., Swanson, J., Fabes, R.A., Hanish, L.D., & Martin, C.L. (2018). Kindergarten school engagement: Linking early temperament and academic achievement at the transition to school. *Early Education and Development, 29,* 780–796.

Bucher, R.D. (2015). *Diversity consciousness* (4th ed.). Upper Saddle River, NJ: Pearson.

Burchinal, M.R., & others (2015). Early child care and education. In R.M. Lerner (Ed.), *Handbook of child psychology and developmental science* (7th ed.). New York: Wiley.

Burden, P.R., & Byrd, D.M. (2016). *Methods for effective teaching* (7th ed.). Upper Saddle River, NJ: Pearson.

Burkart, J.M., Schubiger, M.N., & van Schaik, C.P. (2016). The evolution of general intelligence. *Behavioral and Brain Sciences.* doi:10.1017/S0140525X16000959

Burke, K. (2010). *How to assess authentic learning* (5th ed.). Thousand Oaks, CA: Sage.

Burkham, D.T., Lee, V.E., & Smerdon, B.A. (1997). Gender and science learning early in high school: Subject matter and laboratory experiences. *American Educational Research Journal, 34,* 297–331.

Bursuck, W.D., & Damer, M. (2015). *Teaching reading to students who are at risk or have disabilities* (3rd ed.). Upper Saddle River, NJ: Pearson.

Burt, K.B., Coatsworth, J.D., & Masten, A.S. (2016). Competence and psychopathology in development. In D. Cicchetti (Ed.), *Developmental psychopathology* (3rd ed.). New York; Wiley.

Burz, H.L., & Marshall, K. (1996). *Performance-based curriculum for mathematics: From knowing to showing.* ERIC Document Reproduction Service No. ED400194.

Busching, R., & Krahe, B. (2015). The girls set the tone: Gendered classroom norms and the development of aggression in adolescence. *Personality and Social Psychology Bulletin. 41,* 659–676.

Buss, D.M. (2012). *Evolutionary psychology* (4th ed.). Boston: Allyn & Bacon.

Buss, D.M. (2015). *Evolutionary psychology* (5th ed.). Upper Saddle River, NJ: Pearson.

Busso, D.S., & Pollack, C. (2015). No brain left behind: Consequences of neuroscience discourse for education. *Learning, Media, and Technology, 40,* 168–186.

Butcher, K.R., & Jameson, J.M. (2016). Computer-based instruction (CBI) within special education. In J.K. Luiselli & A.J. Fischer (Eds.), *Computer-assisted instruction and web-based innovations in psychology, special education, and health.* New York: Elsevier.

C

Cain, M.S., Leonard, J.A., Gabrieli, J.D., & Finn, A.S. (2016). Media multitasking in adolescence. *Psychonomic Bulletin & Review.* doi: 10.3758/s13423-016-1036-3

Cairncross, M., & Miller, C.J. (2016). The effectiveness of mindfulness-based therapies for ADHD: A meta-analytic review. *Journal of Attention Disorders.* doi:10.1177/1087054715625301

Calet, N., Gutierrez-Palma, N., & Defior, S. (2015). A cross-sectional study of fluency and reading comprehension in Spanish primary school children. *Journal of Research in Reading, 38,* 272–285.

California State Department of Education (1994). *Golden State examination science portfolio.* Sacramento: California State Department of Education.

Calkins, S.D., & Perry, N.B. (2016). The development of emotion regulation. In D. Cicchetti (Ed.), *Developmental psychopathology* (3rd ed.). New York: Wiley.

Callan, M.J., Kay, A.C., & Dawtry, R.J. (2014). Making sense of misfortune: Deservingness, self-esteem, and patterns of self-defeat. *Journal of Personality and Social Psychology, 107,* 142–162.

Calvert, S.L. (2015). Children and digital media. In R.M. Lerner (Ed.), *Handbook of child psychology and developmental science* (7th ed.). New York: Wiley.

Camacho, D.E., & Fuligni, A.J. (2015). Extracurricular participation among adolescents from immigrant families. *Journal of Youth and Adolescence, 44,* 1251–1262.

Cameron, J.R. (2001). Negative effects of reward on intrinsic motivation—A limited phenomenon. *Review of Educational Research, 71,* 29–42.

Cameron, J.R., & Pierce, D. (2008). Intrinsic versus extrinsic motivation. In N.J. Salkind (Ed.), *Encyclopedia of educational psychology.* Thousand Oaks, CA: Sage.

Campbell, D.T., & LeVine, D.T. (1968). Ethnocentrism and intergroup relations. In R. Abelson & others (Eds.), *Theories of cognitive consistency.* Chicago: Rand McNally.

Campbell, L., Campbell, B., & Dickinson, D. (2004). *Teaching and learning through multiple intelligences* (3rd ed.). Boston: Allyn & Bacon.

Cantone, E., & others (2015). Interventions on bullying and cyberbullying in schools: A systematic review. *Clinical Practice and Epidemiology in Mental Health, 11* (Suppl. 1), S58–S76.

Capar, G., & Tarim, K. (2015). Efficacy of the cooperative learning method on mathematics achievement and attitude: A meta-analysis research. *Educational Sciences: Theory and Practice, 15,* 553–559.

Cardelle-Elawar, M. (1992). Effects of teaching metacognitive skills to students with low mathematics ability. *Teaching and Teacher Education, 8,* 109–121.

Carey, D.P. (2007). Is bigger really better? The search for brain size and intelligence in the twenty-first century. In S. Della Sala (Ed.), *Tall tales about the mind and brain: Separating fact from fiction.* Oxford, UK: Oxford University Press.

Carlson, S.M., & White, R. (2013). Executive function and imagination. In M. Taylor (Ed.), *Handbook of imagination.* New York: Oxford University Press.

Carlson, S.M., Zelazo, P.D., & Faja, S. (2013). Executive function. In P.D. Zelazo (Ed.), *Oxford handbook of developmental psychology.* New York: Oxford University Press.

Carnegie Council on Adolescent Development. (1995). *Great transitions.* New York: Carnegie Foundation.

Carnegie Foundation. (1989). *Turning points: Preparing youth for the 21st century.* New York: Author.

Carpendale, J.I., & Chandler, M.J. (1996). On the distinction between false belief understanding and subscribing to an interpretive theory of mind. *Child Development. 67,* 1686–1706.

Carrell, S.E., Malmstrom, F.V., & West, J.E. (2008). Peer effects in academic cheating. *Journal of Human Resources, 43,* 173–207.

Carroll, J.B. (1963). A model of school learning. *Teachers College Record, 64,* 723–733.

Cartmill, E., & Goldin-Meadow, S. (2016). Gesture. In D. Matsumoto, H.C. Hwang, & M.G. Frank (Eds.), *APA handbook of nonverbal communication.* Washington, DC: American Psychological Association.

Carver, C.S., & Scheier, M.F. (2017). *Perspectives on personality* (8th ed.). Upper Saddle River, NJ: Pearson.

Case, R. (2000). Conceptual structures. In M. Bennett (Ed.), *Developmental psychology.* Philadelphia: Psychology Press.

CASEL. (2016). *Collaborative for Academic, Social, and Emotional Learning.* Retrieved August 12, 2016, from www.casel.org

Casey, B.J. (2015). The adolescent brain and self-control. *Annual Review of Psychology* (Vol. 66). Palo Alto, CA: Annual Reviews.

Casey, B.J., Galvan, A., & Somerville, L.H. (2016). Beyond simple models of adolescence to an integrated circuit-based account: A commentary. *Developmental Cognitive Neuroscience, 17,* 128-130.

Casey, E.C., & others (2016). Promoting resilience through executive function training for homeless and highly mobile preschoolers. In S. Prince-Embury & D. Saklofske (Eds.), *Resilience intervention for diverse populations.* New York: Springer.

Cassidy, A.R. (2016). Executive function and psychosocial adjustment in healthy children and adolescents: A latest variable modeling investigation. *Child Neuropsychology, 22,* 292-317.

Ceci, S.J., & Williams, W.M. (1997). Schooling, intelligence, and income. *American Psychologist, 52,* 1051-1058.

Celio, C.I., Durlak, J., Dymnicki, A. (2011). A meta-analysis of the impact of service-learning on students. *Journal of Experiential Education, 34*(2), 164-181. doi: 10.1177/105382591103400205

Center for Instructional Technology. (2006). Writing multiple-choice questions that demand critical thinking. Retrieved January 12, 2006, from http://cit.necc.mass.edu/atlt/TestCritThink.htm

Centers for Disease Control and Prevention. (2007). *Autism and developmental disabilities monitoring (ADDM) network.* Atlanta: Author.

Centers for Disease Control and Prevention. (2012). CDC estimates 1 in 88 children in the United States has been identified as having an autism spectrum disorder. *CDC Division of News & Electronic Media, 404,* 639-3286.

Centers for Disease Control and Prevention. (2016). *ADHD.* Retrieved January 12, 2016, from www.cdc.gov/ncbddd/adhd/data.html

Cerillo-Urbina, A.J., & others (2015). The effects of physical exercise in children with attention deficit hyperactivity disorder: A systematic review and meta-analysis of randomized controlled trials. *Child Care, Health, and Development, 41,* 779-788.

Chai, C.S., & others (2015). Assessing multi-dimensional students' perceptions of twenty-first century learning practices. *Asia Pacific Education Review, 16,* 389-398.

Chall, J.S. (1979). The great debate: Ten years later with a modest proposal for reading stages. In L.B. Resnick & P.A. Weaver (Eds.), *Theory and practice of early reading.* Mahwah, NJ: Erlbaum.

Chance, P. (2014). *Learning and behavior* (7th ed.). Boston: Cengage.

Chang, M., Choi, N., & Kim, S. (2015). School involvement of parents of linguistic and racial minorities and their children's mathematics performance. *Educational Research and Evaluation, 21,* 209-231.

Chao, R.K. (2005, April). *The importance of Guan in describing control of immigrant Chinese.* Paper presented at the meeting of the Society for Research in Child Development, Atlanta.

Chao, R.K. (2007, March). *Research with Asian Americans: Looking back and moving forward.* Paper presented at the meeting of the Society for Research in Child Development, Boston.

Chapin, J.R. (2015). *Practical guide to middle and secondary social studies* (4th ed.). Upper Saddle River, NJ: Pearson.

Chaplin, T.M. (2015). Gender and emotion expression: A developmental contextual perspective. *Emotion Review, 7,* 14-21.

Chaplin, T.M., & Aldao, A. (2013). Gender differences in emotion in children: A meta-analytic review. *Psychological Bulletin, 139,* 735-765.

Chappuis, J., Stiggins, R.J., Chappuis, S., & Arter, J.A. (2017). *Classroom assessment for student learning.* Upper Saddle River, NJ: Pearson

Charney, R.S. (2005). *Exploring the first "R": To reinforce.* Retrieved October 26, 2006, from www.nea.org/classmanagement/ifc050201.html

Chatmon, C., & Gray, R. (2015). Lifting up our kings: Developing Black males in a positive and safe place. *Voices in Urban Education, 42,* 50-56.

Chavarria, M.C., & others (2014). Puberty in the corpus callosum. *Neuroscience, 265,* 1-8.

Checa, P., & Fernandez-Berrocal, P. (2015). The role of intelligence quotient and emotional intelligence in cognitive control processes. *Frontiers in Psychology, 6,* 1853.

Chen, C., & Stevenson, H.W. (1989). Homework: A cross-cultural comparison. *Child Development, 60,* 551-561.

Chen, X., & Liu, C. (2016). Culture, peer relationships, and developmental psychopathology. In D. Cicchetti (Ed.), *Developmental psychopathology* (3rd ed.). New York: Wiley.

Chess, S., & Thomas, A. (1977). Temperamental individuality from childhood to adolescence. *Journal of Child Psychiatry, 16,* 218-226.

Chevalier, N., & others (2015). Myelination is associated with processing speed in early childhood: Preliminary insights. *PLoS One, 10,* e139897

Chi, M.T.H. (1978). Knowledge structures and memory development. In R.S. Siegler (Ed.), *Children's thinking: What develops?* Hillsdale, NJ: Erlbaum.

Chiang, H.L., & others (2015). Altered white matter tract property related to impaired focused attention, sustained attention, cognitive impulsivity, and vigilance in attention-deficit/hyperactivity disorder. *Journal of Psychiatry and Neuroscience, 40,* 140106.

Chiappetta, E.L., & Koballa, T.R. (2015). *Science instruction in the middle and secondary schools* (8th ed.). Upper Saddle River, NJ: Pearson.

Child Trends Data Bank. (2015, October). *Participation in school athletics.* Washington, DC: Child Trends.

Children's Defense Fund. (1992). *The state of America's children.* Washington, DC: Author.

Chiou, W.B., Chen, S.W., & Liao, D.C. (2014). Does Facebook promote self-interest? Enactment of indiscriminate one-to-many communication on online social networking sites decreases prosocial behavior. *Cyberpsychology, Behavior, and Social Networking, 17,* 68-73.

Chomsky, N. (1957). *Syntactic structures.* Hague: Mouton.

Choukas-Bradley, S., & Prinstein, M.J. (2016). Peer relationships and the development of psychopathology. In M. Lewis & D. Rudolph (Eds.), *Handbook of developmental psychopathology* (3rd ed.). New York: Springer.

Cianciolo, A.T., & Sternberg, R.J. (2016). Practical intelligence and tacit knowledge: A prototype view of expertise. In K.A. Ericsson & others (Eds.), *Cambridge handbook on expertise and expert performance.* New York: Cambridge University Press.

Cicchetti, D., & Toth, S.L. (2015). A multi-level perspective on child maltreatment. In R.M. Lerner (Ed.), *Handbook of child psychology and developmental science* (7th ed.). New York: Wiley.

Cicchetti, D., & Toth, S.L. (2016). Child maltreatment and developmental psychopathology: A multi-level perspective. In D. Cicchetti (Ed.), *Developmental psychopathology* (3rd ed.). New York: Wiley.

Cil, E. (2015). Effect of two-tier diagnostic tests on promoting learners' conceptual understanding of variables in conducting scientific experiments. *Applied Measurement in Education, 28,* 253-273.

Cirit, N.C. (2015). Assessing ELT pre-service teachers via Web 2.0 tools: Perceptions toward traditional, online, and alternative assessment. *Turkish Online Journal of Educational Technology, 14*(3), 9-19.

Clark, B. (2008). *Growing up gifted* (7th ed.). Upper Saddle River, NJ: Prentice Hall.

Clark, D.A., Donnellan, M.B., Robins, R.W., & Conger, R.D. (2015). Early adolescent temperament, parental monitoring, and substance use in Mexican-origin adolescents. *Journal of Adolescence, 41,* 121-130.

Clark, E.V. (2014). Pragmatics in acquisition. *Journal of Child Language, 41* (Suppl. 1), S105–S116.

Clark, E.V. (2017). *Language in children.* New York: Psychology Press.

Clark, K.B., & Clark, M.P. (1939). The development of the self and the emergence of racial identification in Negro preschool children. *Journal of Social Psychology, 10,* 591–599.

Clark, L. (Ed.). (1993). *Faculty and student challenges in facing cultural and linguistic diversity.* Springfield, IL: Charles C. Thomas.

Clarke, A.J., Burgess, A., Menezes, A., & Mellis, C. (2015). Senior students' experience as tutors of their junior peers in the hospital setting. *BMC Research Notes, 8,* 743.

Clarke-Stewart, A.K., & Parke, R.D. (2014). *Social development* (2nd ed.). New York: Wiley.

Claro, S., Paunesku, D., & Dweck, C.S. (2016). Growth mindset tempers the effect of poverty on academic achievement. *Proceedings of the National Academy of Sciences USA, 113,* 8664–8868.

Clements, D.H., & Sarama, J. (2008). Experimental evaluation of the effects of a research-based preschool mathematics curriculum. *American Educational Research Journal, 45,* 443–494.

Cloud, J. (2007, August 27). Failing our geniuses. *Time,* 40–47.

Coe, R., Aloisi, C., Higgins, S., & Major, L.E. (2014). *What makes great teaching? Review of the underpinning research.* London: Sutton Trust.

CogMed. (2013). *CogMed: Working memory is the engine of learning.* Upper Saddle River, NJ: Pearson.

Cohen, G.L., Garcia, J., Apfel, N., & Master, A. (2006). Reducing the racial achievement gap: A social–psychological intervention. *Science, 313,* 1307–1310. doi: 10.1126/science.1128317.

Cohn, S.T., & Fraser, B.J. (2016). Effectiveness of student response systems in terms of learning environment, attitudes, and achievement. *Learning Environments Research, 19,* 153–167.

Colangelo, N.C., Assouline, S.G., & Gross, M.U.M. (2004). *A nation deceived: How schools hold back America's brightest students.* Retrieved October 16, 2006, from http://nationdeceived.org/

Colby, A., Kohlberg, L., Gibbs, J., & Lieberman, M. (1983). A longitudinal study of moral judgment. *Monograph: The Society for Research in Child Development, 48* (21, Serial No. 201).

Colby, S.L., & Ortman, J.M. (2015, March). Projections of the size and composition of the U.S. population: 2014 to 2060. *Current Population Reports.* Washington, DC: United States Census Bureau.

Cole, M. (2006). Culture and cognitive development in phylogenetic, historical, and ontogenetic perspective. In W. Damon & R. Lerner (Eds.), *Handbook of child psychology* (6th ed.). New York: Wiley.

Cole, M.W., Yarkoni, T., Repovs, G., Anticevic, A., & Braver, T.S. (2012). Global connectivity of prefrontal cortex predicts cognitive control and intelligence. *Journal of Neuroscience, 32,* 8988–8999.

Cole, P.M. (2016). Emotion and the development of psychopathology. In D. Cicchetti (Ed.), *Developmental psychopathology* (3rd ed.). New York: Wiley.

Cole, P.M., & Tan, P.Z. (2015). Emotion socialization from a cultural perspective. In J.E. Grusec & P.D. Hastings (Eds.), *Handbook of socialization* (2nd ed.). New York: Wiley.

College Board. (2015). *SAT.* Princeton, NJ: Educational Testing Service.

Collins, M. (1996, Winter). The job outlook for 96 grads. *Journal of Career Planning,* pp. 51–54.

Combs, D. (1997, September). Using alternative assessment to provide options for student success. *Middle School Journal,* pp. 3–8.

Comer, J.P. (1988). Educating poor minority children. *Scientific American, 259,* 42–48.

Comer, J.P. (2004). *Leave no child behind.* New Haven, CT: Yale University Press.

Comer, J.P. (2006). Child development: The underweighted aspect of intelligence. In P.C. Kyllonen, R.D. Roberts, & L. Stankov (Eds.), *Extending intelligence.* Mahwah, NJ: Erlbaum.

Comer, J.P. (2010). Comer School Development Program. In J. Meece & J. Eccles (Eds.), *Handbook of research on schools, schooling, and human development.* New York: Routledge.

Committee for Children. (2016). *Second Step.* Retrieved August 12, 2016, from www.cfchildren.org/second-step

Common Core State Standards Initiative. (2016). *Common Core.* Retrieved February 25, 2016, from www.core standards.org/

Condition of Education. (2015). *Participation in education.* Washington, DC: U.S. Department of Education.

Conley, M.W. (2008). *Content area literacy: Learners in context.* Boston: Allyn & Bacon.

Conn, K.M., Fisher, S.G., & Rhee, H. (2016). Parent and child independent report of emotional responses to asthma-specific vignettes: The relationship between emotional states, self-management behaviors, and symptoms. *Journal of Pediatric Nursing, 31,* e83–e90.

Connell, N.M., Morris, R.G., & Piquero, A.R. (2016). Predicting bullying: Exploring the contribution of negative life experiences in predicting adolescent bullying behavior. *International Journal of Offender Therapy and Comparative Criminology, 60,* 1082–1096.

Conti, E., & others (2015). The first 1000 days of the autistic brain: A systematic review of diffusion imaging studies. *Frontiers in Human Neuroscience, 9,* 159.

Cooper, H. (1998, April). *Family, student, and assignment characteristics of positive homework experiences.* Paper presented at the meeting of the American Educational Research Association, San Diego.

Cooper, H. (2006). *The battle over homework.* Thousand Oaks, CA: Corwin.

Cooper, H. (2007). *The battle over homework: Common ground for administrators, teachers, and parents* (3rd ed.). Thousand Oaks. CA: Corwin Press.

Cooper, H. (2009). Homework. In T. Bidell (Ed.), *Chicago companion to the child.* Chicago: University of Chicago Press.

Cooper, H., & Patall, E.A. (2007). Homework. In S. Mathison & E.W. Ross (Eds.), *Battleground schools* (pp. 319–326). Westport, CT: Greenwood Press.

Cooper, H., Robinson, J.C., & Patall, E.A. (2006). Does homework improve academic achievement? A synthesis of research, 1987–2003. *Review of Educational Research, 76,* 1–62.

Copeland, L. (2003, December). Science teacher just wanted to do some good, and he has. *USA Today.* Retrieved December 12, 2003, from www.usatoday.com/news/education/2003-12-30-laster-usal_x.htm

Corno, L. (1998, March 30). Commentary. *Newsweek,* p. 51.

Cornoldi, C., Carretti, B., Drusi, S., & Tencati, C. (2015). Improving problem solving in primary school students: The effect of a training program focusing on metacognition and working memory. *British Journal of Educational Psychology, 85,* 424–439.

Coronel, J.M., & Gomez-Hurtado, I. (2015). Nothing to do with me! Teachers' perceptions of cultural diversity in Spanish secondary schools. *Teachers and Teaching: Theory and Practice, 21,* 400–420.

Cossentino, J. (2008). Montessori schools. In N.J. Salkind (Ed.), *Encyclopedia of educational psychology.* Thousand Oaks, CA: Sage.

Cote, J.E. (2015). Identity-formation research from a critical perspective: Is a social science developing? In K.C. McLean & M. Syed (Eds.), *Oxford handbook of identity development.* New York: Oxford University Press.

Cote, K., & Emmett, T. (2015). Effective implementation of e-portfolios: The development of e-portfolios to support online learning. *Theory Into Practice, 54,* 352–363.

Council of Chief State School Officers (2005). *Marilyn Jachetti Whirry.* Retrieved February 8, 2006, from www.cesso.org

Courage, M.L. (2015). Translational science and multitasking: Lessons from the lab and everyday world. *Developmental Review, 35,* 1–4.

Courage, M.L., Bakhtiar, A., Fitzpatrick, C., Kenny, S., & Brandeau, K. (2015). Growing up multitasking: The costs and benefits for cognitive development. *Developmental Review, 35,* 5–41.

Covington, M.V., & Dray, E. (2002). The development course of achievement motivation: A need-based approach. In A. Wigfield & J.S. Eccles (Eds.), *Development of achievement motivation.* San Diego: Academic Press.

Covington, M.V., & Teel, K.T. (1996). *Overcoming student failure.* Washington, DC: American Psychological Association.

Cracolice, M.S., & Busby, B.D. (2015). Preparation for college general chemistry: More than just a matter of content knowledge acquisition. *Journal of Chemical Education, 92,* 1790–1797.

Craig, F., & others (2016). A review of executive function deficits in autism spectrum disorder and attention-deficit/hyperactivity disorder. *Neuropsychiatric Disease and Treatment, 12,* 1191–1202.

Craik, F.I.M., & Lockhart, R.S. (1972). Levels of processing: A framework for memory research. *Journal of Verbal Learning and Verbal Behavior, 11,* 671–684.

Crain, T.L., Schonert-Reichl, K.A., & Roeser, R.W. (2016). Cultivating teacher mindfulness: Effects of a randomized controlled trial on work, home, and sleep outcomes. *Journal of Occupational Health Psychology.* doi:10.1037/ocp0000043

Crone, L.A. (2017). *The adolescent brain.* New York: Routledge.

Crosnoe, R. (2011). *Fitting in, standing out.* New York: Cambridge University Press.

Crosnoe, R., & Benner, A.D. (2015). Children at school. In R.M. Lerner (Ed.), *Handbook of child psychology and developmental science* (7th ed.). New York: Wiley.

Crosnoe, R., Bonazzo, C., & Wu, N. (2015). *Healthy learners: A whole child approach to disparities in early education.* New York: Teachers College Press.

Crosnoe, R., Riegle-Crumb, C., Field, S., Frank, K., & Muller, C. (2008). Peer group contexts of girls' and boys' academic experiences. *Child Development, 79,* 139–155.

Cross, C.T., Woods, T.A., & Schweingruber, H. (Eds.). (2009). *Mathematics learning in early childhood: Paths toward excellence and equity.* Washington, DC: National Academies Press.

Cross, D., Lester, L., & Barnes, A. (2015). A longitudinal study of the social and emotional predictors and consequences of cyber and traditional bullying victimization. *International Journal of Public Health, 60,* 207–217.

Crouter, A.C. (2006). Mothers and fathers at work. In A. Clarke-Stewart & J. Dunn (Eds.), *Families count.* New York: Cambridge University Press.

Crowley, K., Callahan, M.A., Tenenbaum, H.R., & Allen, E. (2001). Parents explain more to boys than to girls during shared scientific thinking. *Psychological Science, 12,* 258–261.

Csikszentmihalyi, M. (1990). *Flow.* New York: Harper & Row.

Csikszentmihalyi, M. (1993). *The evolving self.* New York: Harper & Row.

Csikszentmihalyi, M. (1996). *Creativity.* New York: HarperCollins.

Csikszentmihalyi, M. (2000). Creativity: An interview. In A. Kazdin (Ed.), *Encyclopedia of psychology.* Washington, DC, & New York: American Psychological Association and Oxford University Press.

Csikszentmihalyi, M., & Csikszentmihalyi, I.S. (Eds.). (2006). *A life worth living.* New York: Oxford University Press.

Csikszentmihalyi, M., Rathunde, K., & Whalen, S. (1993). *Talented teenagers: The roots of success and failure.* Cambridge, UK: Cambridge University Press.

Cucina, J.M., Peyton, S.T., Su, C., & Byle, K.A. (2016). Role of mental abilities and mental tests in explaining school grades. *Intelligence, 54,* 90–104.

Cuevas, J. (2015). Is learning styles-based instruction effective? A comprehensive analysis of recent research on learning styles. *Theory and Research in Education, 13,* 308–333.

Cummings, E.M., & Miller, L.M. (2015). Emotional security theory: An emerging theoretical model for youths' psychological and physiological responses across multiple developmental contexts. *Current Directions in Psychological Science, 24,* 208–213.

Cummings, E.M., & Valentino, K.V. (2015). Developmental psychopathology. In R.M. Lerner (Ed.), *Handbook of child psychology and developmental science* (7th ed.). New York: Wiley.

Cunningham, B., Hoyer, K.M., & Sparks, D. (2015, February). Gender differences in science, technology, engineering, and mathematics (STEM) interest, credits earned, and NAEP performance in the 12th grade. *Stats in Brief,* National Center for Education Statistics 2015-075, pp. 1–27.

Cunningham, P.M. (2017). *Phonics they use* (7th ed.). Upper Saddle River, NJ: Pearson.

Cunningham, P.M., & Allington, R.L. (2016). *Classrooms that work* (6th ed.). Upper Saddle River, NJ: Pearson.

Curran, K., DuCette, J., Eisenstein, J., & Hyman, I.A. (2001, August). *Statistical analysis of the cross-cultural data: The third year.* Paper presented at the meeting of the American Psychological Association, San Francisco, CA.

Curtis, L.A., & Bandy, T. (2016). *The Quantum Opportunities Program: A randomized controlled evaluation.* Washington, DC: Milton S. Eisenhower Foundation.

Curtis, M.E., & Longo, A.M. (2001, November). *Teaching vocabulary development to adolescents to improve comprehension.* Retrieved April 26, 2006, from www.readingonline.org/articles/curtis

D

Dahl, R.E. (2004). Adolescent brain development: A period of vulnerabilities and opportunities. *Annals of the New York Academy of Sciences, 1021,* 1–22.

Dale, B., & others (2014). Utility of the Stanford-Binet Intelligence Scales, Fifth Edition, with ethnically diverse preschoolers. *Psychology in the Schools, 51,* 581–590.

Damasio, A.R. (1994). Descartes' error and the future of human life. *Scientific American, 271,* 144.

Damon, W. (2008). *The path to purpose: Helping our children find their calling in life.* New York: Free Press.

Dansereau, D.F. (1988). Cooperative learning strategies. In C.E. Weinstein, E.T. Goetz, & P.A. Alexander (Eds.), *Learning and study strategies.* Orlando, FL: Academic Press.

Dariotis, J.K., & others (2016). A qualitative evaluation of student learning and skills use in a school-based mindfulness and yoga program. *Mindfulness, 7,* 76–89.

Darling-Hammond, L. (2001, August). *What's at stake in high-stakes testing?* Paper presented at the meeting of the American Psychological Association, San Francisco.

Darling-Hammond, L. (2007). Race, inequality and educational accountability: The irony of "No Child Left Behind." *Race, Ethnicity, and Education, 10,* 245–260.

Darling-Hammond, L., & Baratz-Snowden, J. (Eds.). (2005). *A good teacher in every classroom: Preparing the highly qualified teachers our children deserve.* San Francisco: Jossey-Bass.

Darling-Hammond, L., & Bransford, J. (Eds.). (2005). *Preparing teachers for a changing world.* San Francisco: Jossey-Bass.

Darling-Hammond, L., & Falk, B. (2013). *Teacher learning through assessment.* Washington, DC: Center for American Progress.

Darling-Hammond, L., & others (2005). Educational goals and purposes: Developing a curricular vision for education. In L. Darling-Hammond & J. Bransford (Eds.), *Preparing teachers for a changing world.* San Francisco: Jossey-Bass.

Davies, J., & Brember, I. (1999). Reading and mathematics attainments and self-esteem in years 2 and 6—an eight-year cross-sectional study. *Educational Studies, 25,* 145–157.

Davies, P.T., Martin, M.J., & Sturge-Apple, M.L. (2016). Emotional security theory and developmental psychopathology. In D. Cicchetti (Ed.), *Developmental psychopathology* (3rd ed.). New York: Wiley.

Davison, M.L., & others (2015). Criterion-related validity: Assessing the value of subscores. *Journal of Educational Measurement, 52,* 263–279.

De Castella, K., Byrne, D., & Covington, M. (2013). Unmotivated or motivated to fail? A cross-cultural study of achievement motivation, fear of failure, and student disengagement. *Journal of Educational Psychology, 105,* 861–880.

de Haan, M., & Johnson, M.H. (2016). Typical and atypical human functional brain development. In D. Cicchetti (Ed.), *Developmental psychopathology* (3rd ed.). New York: Wiley.

De La Paz, S., & McCutchen, D. (2017). Learning to write. In R.E. Mayer & P.A. Alexander (Eds.), *Handbook of research on learning and instruction* (2nd ed.). New York: Routledge.

Deary, I. (2012). Intelligence. *Annual Review of Psychology* (Vol. 63). Palo Alto, CA: Annual Reviews.

Deary, I.J., Strand, S., Smith, P., & Fernandes, C. (2007). Intelligence and educational achievement. *Intelligence, 35,* 13–21.

Decety, J., & Cowell, J. (2016). Developmental social neuroscience. In D. Cicchetti (Ed.), *Developmental psychopathology* (3rd ed.). New York: Wiley.

deCharms, R. (1984). Motivation enhancement in educational settings. In R. Ames & C. Ames (Eds.), *Research on motivation in education* (Vol. 1). Orlando: Academic Press.

Deci, E.I., Koestner, R., & Ryan, R.M. (2001). Extrinsic rewards and intrinsic motivation in education: Reconsidered once again. *Review of Educational Research, 71,* 1–28.

Decristan, J.K., & others (2015). Embedded formative assessment and classroom process quality: How do they interact in promoting science understanding? *American Educational Research Journal, 52,* 1133–1159.

Del Campo, L., Buchanan, W.R., Abbott, R.D., & Berninger, V.W. (2015). Levels of phonology related to reading and writing in middle and late childhood. *Reading and Writing, 28,* 183–198.

Delisle, J.R. (1987). *Gifted kids speak out.* Minneapolis: Free Spirit Publishing.

Dell, A.G., Newton, D.A., & Petroff, J.G. (2017). *Assistive technology in the classroom* (3rd ed.). Upper Saddle River, NJ: Pearson.

Demby, S.L. (2016). Parenting coordination: Applying clinical thinking to the management of post-divorce conflict. *Journal of Clinical Psychology.* doi:10.1002/jclp.22261

Dempster, F.N. (1981). Memory span: Sources of individual and developmental differences. *Psychological Bulletin, 89,* 63–100.

DeNavas-Walt, C., & Proctor, B.D. (2015). *Income and poverty in the United States: 2014.* Washington, DC: U.S. Census Bureau.

Deng, Y., & others (2016). Gender differences in emotional response: Inconsistency between experience and expressivity. *PLoS One, 11*(6), e0158666.

Denham, S.A., Bassett, H.H., & Wyatt, T. (2015). The socialization of emotional competence. In J.E. Grusec & P.D. Hastings (Eds.), *Handbook of socialization* (2nd ed.). New York: Guilford.

Derman-Sparks, L., & The Anti-Bias Curriculum Task Force (1989). *Anti-bias curriculum.* Washington, DC: National Association for the Education of Young Children.

DeRosa, D.A., & Abruscato, J.A. (2015). *Teaching children science* (8th ed.). Upper Saddle River, NJ: Pearson.

DeRosier, M.E., & Marcus, S.R. (2005). Building friendships and combating bullying: Effectiveness of S.S. GRIN at one-year follow-up. *Journal of Clinical Child and Adolescent Psychology, 34,* 140–150.

Devito, J.A. (2017). *Essentials of human communication* (9th ed.). Upper Saddle River, NJ: Pearson.

Dewey, J. (1933). *How we think.* Lexington, MA: D.C. Heath.

DeZolt, D.M., & Hull, S.H. (2001). Classroom and school climate. In J. Worell (Ed.), *Encyclopedia of women and gender.* San Diego: Academic Press.

Diamond, A. (2013). Executive functions. *Annual Review of Psychology* (Vol. 64). Palo Alto, CA: Annual Reviews.

Diamond, A., & Lee, K. (2011). Interventions shown to aid executive function development in children 4 to 12 years old. *Science, 333,* 959–964.

Diaz, C. (2005). Unpublished review of J.W. Santrock's *Educational psychology* (3rd ed.). New York: McGraw-Hill.

Dickinson, D. (1998). *How technology enhances Howard Gardner's eight intelligences.* Retrieved February 15, 2002, from www.america-tomorrow.com/ati/nhl80402.htm

Dickinson, D., Wolf, M., & Stotsky, S. (1993). "Words Move": The interwoven development of oral and written language in the school years. In Jean Berko Gleason (Ed.), *The development of language* (3rd ed.). New York: Macmillan.

Ding, X.P., & others (2014). Elementary school children's cheating behavior and its cognitive correlates. *Journal of Experimental Child Psychology, 121,* 85–95.

Dodge, K.A. (2010). *Current directions in child psychopathology.* Boston: Allyn & Bacon.

Doe, C. (2015). Student interpretation of diagnostic feedback. *Language Assessment Quarterly, 12,* 110–135.

Dohla, D., & Heim, S. (2016). Developmental dyslexia and dysgraphia: What can we learn from one about the other? *Frontiers in Psychology, 6,* 2045.

Doll, J.J., Eslami, Z., & Walters, L. (2013). Understanding why students drop out of high school, according to their own reports: Are they pushed or pulled, or do they fall out? A comparative analysis of seven nationally representative studies. *SAGE Open, 3*(4). doi: 10.1177/2158244013503834

Domjan, M. (2015). *Principles of learning and behavior* (6th ed.). Boston: Cengage.

Donndelinger, S. J. (2005). Integrating comprehension and metacognitive reading strategies. In S. E. Isreal, C. C. Block, K. L. Bauserman, & K. Kinnucan-Welsch (Eds.), *Metacognition in literacy learning: Theory, assessment, instruction, and professional development* (pp. 241–260). Mahwah, NJ: Lawrence Erlbaum Associates.

Dovis, S., Van der Oord, S., Wiers, R.W., & Prins, P.J. (2015). Improving executive functioning in children with ADHD: Training multiple executive functions within the context of a computer game. A randomized double-blind placebo controlled trial. *PLoS One, 10 (4),* e0121651.

Doyle, W. (1986). Classroom organization and management. In M.C. Wittrock (Ed.), *Handbook of research on teaching* (3rd ed.). New York: Macmillan.

Doyle, W. (2006). Ecological approaches to classroom management. In C.M. Evertson & C.S. Weinstein (Eds.), *Handbook of classroom management.* Mahwah, NJ: Erlbaum.

Duan, X., Dan, Z., & Shi, J. (2013). The speed of information processing of 9- to 13-year-old intellectually gifted children. *Psychology Reports, 112,* 20-32.

Duff, D., Tomblin, J.B., & Catts, H. (2015). The influence of reading on vocabulary growth: A case for a Matthew effect. *Journal of Speech, Language, and Hearing Research, 58,* 853-864.

Duggan, K.A., & Friedman, H.S. (2014). Lifetime biopsychosocial trajectories of the Terman gifted children: Health, well-being, and longevity. In D.K. Simonton (Ed.), *Wiley-Blackwell handbook of genius.* New York: Oxford University Press.

Duncan, G.J., Magnuson, K., & Votruba-Drzal, E. (2015). Children and socioeconomic status. In M.H. Bornstein & T. Leventhal (Eds.), *Handbook of child psychology and developmental science* (7th ed., Vol. 4). New York: Wiley.

Duncan, G.J., & others (2007). School readiness and later achievement. *Developmental Psychology, 43,* 1428-1446.

Dunlosky, J., & others (2013). Improving students' learning with effective learning techniques: Promising directions from cognitive and educational psychology. *Psychological Science in the Public Interest, 14,* 4-58.

Dupere, V., & others (2015). Stressors and turning points in high school and dropout: A stress process, life course framework. *Review of Educational Research, 85,* 591-629.

Durston, S., & Casey, B.J. (2006). What have we learned about cognitive development from neuroimaging. *Neuropsychologia, 44,* 2149-2157.

Durston, S., & others (2006). A shift from diffuse to focal cortical activity with development. *Developmental Science, 9,* 1-8.

Dweck, C.S. (2006). *Mindset.* New York: Random House.

Dweck, C.S. (2012). Mindsets and human nature: Promoting change in the Middle East, the school yard, the racial divide, and willpower. *American Psychologist, 67,* 614-622.

Dweck, C.S. (2015a, September 23). Carol Dweck revisits the "growth mindset." *Education Week, 35*(5), 24-26.

Dweck, C.S. (2015b, December). The remarkable reach of "growth mindsets." *Scientific American, 27,* 36-41.

Dweck, C.S. (2016, March 11). *Growth mindset revisited.* Invited presentation at Leaders to Learn From. Washington, DC: Education Week.

Dweck, C.S., & Elliott, E. (1983). Achievement motivation. In P. Mussen (Ed.), *Handbook of child psychology* (4th ed., Vol. 4). New York: Wiley.

Dweck, C.S., & Master, A. (2009). Self-theories and motivation: Students' beliefs about intelligence. In K.R. Wentzel & A. Wigfield (Eds.), *Handbook of motivation at school.* New York: Routledge.

E

Eagly, A.H. (2012). Women as leaders: Paths through the labyrinth. In M.C. Bligh & R. Riggio (Eds.), *When near is far and far is near: Exploring distance in leader-follower relationships.* New York: Wiley Blackwell.

Eagly, A.H. (2013). Science and politics: A reconsideration. In M.K. Ryan & N.R. Branscombe (Eds.), *Sage handbook of gender and psychology.* Thousand Oaks, CA: Sage.

Eagly, A.H., & Crowley, M. (1986). Gender and helping behavior: A meta-analytic review of the social psychological literature. *Psychological Bulletin, 100,* 283-308.

Eagly, A.H., & Steffen, V.J. (1986). Gender and aggressive behavior: A meta-analytic review of the social psychological literature. *Psychological Bulletin, 100,* 309-330.

Ebadi, S., & Shakoorzadeh, R. (2015). Investigation of academic procrastination prevalence and its relationship with academic self-regulation and achievement motivation among high-school students in Tehran city. *International Education Studies, 8*(10), 193-199.

Eccles, J.S. (1987). Gender roles and women's achievement-related decisions. *Psychology of Women Quarterly, 11,* 135-172.

Eccles, J.S. (1993). School and family effects on the ontogeny of children's interests, self-perceptions, and activity choice. In J. Jacobs (Ed.), *Nebraska symposium on motivation, 1992; Developmental perspectives on motivation.* Lincoln, NE: University of Nebraska Press. https://www.ncbi.nlm.nih.gov/pmc/articles/PMC5481391/.

Eccles, J.S. (2004). School, academic motivation, and stage-environment fit. In R. Lerner & L. Steinberg (Eds.), *Handbook of adolescent psychology* (2nd ed.). New York: Wiley.

Eccles, J.S. (2007). Families, schools, and developing achievement-related motivations and engagement. In J.E. Grusec & P.D. Hastings (Eds.), *Handbook of socialization.* New York: Guilford.

Eccles, J.S., & Roeser, R.W. (2015). School and community influences on human development. In M.H. Bornstein & M.E. Lamb (Eds.), *Developmental science* (7th ed.). New York: Psychology Press.

Eccles, J. S., & Wigfeld, A. (2002). Motivational beliefs, values, and goals. *Annual Review of Psychology, 53,* 109-132.

Eccles, J.S., Wigfield, A., & Schiefele, U. (1998). Motivation to succeed. In W. Damon (Ed.), *Handbook of child psychology* (5th ed., Vol. 4). New York: Wiley.

Echevarria, J.J., Richards-Tutor, C., & Vogt, M.J. (2015). *Response to intervention (RTI) and English learners: Using the SIOP model* (2nd ed.). Upper Saddle River, NJ: Pearson.

Educational Cyber Playground (2006). *Ringleader Alan Haskvitz.* Retrieved July 1, 2006, from http://www.edu-cyberpg.com/ringleaders/al.html

Edwards, A.R., Esmonde, I., Wagner, J.F., & Beattie, R.C. (2017). Learning science. In R.E. Mayer & P.A. Alexander (Eds.), *Handbook of research on learning and instruction* (2nd ed.). New York: Routledge.

Egalite, A.J., Kisida, B., & Winters, M.A. (2015). Representation in the classroom: The effect of own-race teachers on student achievement. *Economics of Education Review, 44*(April), 44-52.

Eisenberg, N., Duckworth, A., Spinrad, L., & Valiente, C. (2014). Conscientiousness and healthy aging. *Developmental Psychology, 50,* 1331-1349.

Eisenberg, N., Fabes, R.A., & Spinrad, T.L. (2006). Prosocial development. In W. Damon & R. Lerner (Eds.), *Handbook of child psychology* (6th ed.). New York: Wiley.

Eisenberg, N., Smith, C.L., & Spinrad, T.L. (2016). Effortful control: Relations with emotion regulation, adjustment, and socialization in childhood. In K.D. Vohs & R.F. Baumeister (Eds.), *Handbook of self-regulation* (3rd ed.). New York: Guilford.

Eisenberg, N., & Spinrad, T.L. (2016). Multidimensionality of prosocial behavior: Rethinking the conceptualization and development of prosocial behavior. In L. Padilla-Walker & G. Carlo (Eds.), *Prosocial behavior.* New York: Oxford University Press.

Eisenberg, N., Spinrad, T.L., & Knafo-Noam, A. (2015). Prosocial development. In R.M. Lerner (Ed.), *Handbook of child psychology and developmental science* (7th ed.). New York: Wiley.

Eisenberg, N., Spinrad, T.L., & Valiente, C. (2016). Emotion-related self-regulation and children's social, psychological, and academic functioning. In L. Balter & C.S. Tamis-LeMonda (Eds.), *Child psychology* (3rd ed.). New York: Routledge.

Eisenhower Foundation. (2010). *Quantum Opportunities program.* Retrieved June 26, 2010, from http://www.eisenhowerfoundation.org/qop.php

Eisenman, G., Edwards, S., & Cushman, C.A. (2015). Bringing reality to classroom management in teacher education. *Professional Educator, 39*(1).

Eklund, K., Tanner, N., Stoll, K., & Anway, L. (2015). Identifying emotional and behavioral risk among gifted and nongifted children: A multi-gate, multi-informant approach. *School Psychology Quarterly, 30,* 197–211.

Elam, K.K., Sandler, I., Wolchik, S., & Tein, J.Y. (2016). Non-residential father-child involvement, interparental conflict, and mental health of children following divorce: A person-focused approach. *Journal of Youth and Adolescence, 45,* 581–593.

Elkind, D. (1976). *Child development and education: A Piagetian perspective.* New York: Oxford University Press.

Elkind, D. (1978). Understanding the young adolescent. *Adolescence, 13,* 127–134.

Ellis, S., Klahr, D., & Siegler, R.S. (1994, April). *The birth, life, and sometimes death of good ideas in collaborative problem-solving.* Paper presented at the meeting of the American Educational Research Association, New Orleans.

Emmer, E.T., & Evertson, C. (2009). *Classroom management for middle and secondary teachers* (8th ed.). Boston: Allyn & Bacon.

Emmer, E.T., & Evertson, C.M. (2017). *Classroom management for middle and high school teachers* (10th ed.). Upper Saddle River, NJ: Pearson.

Emmer, E.T., Evertson, C.M., & Anderson, L.M. (1980). Effective classroom management at the beginning of the school year. *Elementary School Journal, 80,* 219–231.

Engler, B. (2009). *Personality theories* (8th ed.). Belmont, CA: Wadsworth.

Enright, M.S., Schaefer, L.V., Schaefer, P., & Schaefer, K.A. (2008). Building a just adolescent community. *Montessori Life, 20,* 36–42.

Entwisle, D.R., & Alexander, K.L. (1993). Entry into the school: The beginning school transition and educational stratification in the United States. *Annual Review of Sociology, 19,* 401–423.

Entwisle, D.R., Alexander, K.L., & Olson, L. (2010). The long reach of socioeconomic status in education. In J. Meece & J. Eccles (Eds.), *Handbook of research on schools, schooling, and human development.* New York: Routledge.

Epstein, J. (1998, April). *Interactive homework: Effective strategies to connect home and school.* Paper presented at the meeting of the American Educational Research Association, San Diego.

Epstein, J.L. (2001). *School, family, and community partnerships.* Boulder, CO: Westview Press.

Epstein, J.L. (2009). *School, family, and community partnerships* (3rd ed.). Thousand Oaks, CA: Corwin Press.

Ericson, N. (2001, June). *Addressing the problem of juvenile bullying.* Washington, DC: Office of Juvenile Justice and Delinquency Prevention, Office of Justice Programs, U.S. Department of Justice.

Ericsson, K.A. (2014). A view from the expert-performance approach. In D.K. Simonton (Ed.), *Wiley handbook of genius.* New York: Wiley.

Ericsson, K.A., Krampe, R.T., & Tesch-Romer, C. (1993). The role of deliberate practice in acquisition of expert performance. *Psychological Review, 100,* 363–406.

Ericsson, K.A., & Moxley, J.H. (2013). Experts' superior memory: From accumulation of chunks to building memory skills that mediate improved performance and learning. In T.J. Perfect & D.S. Lindsay (Eds.), *SAGE handbook of applied memory.* Thousand Oaks, CA: Sage.

Ericsson, K.A., & others (Eds.). (2016). *Cambridge handbook of expertise and expert performance.* New York: Cambridge University Press.

Erikson, E.H. (1968). *Identity: Youth and crisis.* New York: W.W. Norton.

Ernst, J.V., & Glennie, E. (2015). Redesigned high schools for transformed STEM learning: Performance assessment pilot outcome. *Journal of STEM Education: Innovations and Research, 16*(4), 27–35.

Espelage, D.L., & Colbert, C.L. (2016). School-based interventions to prevent bullying and promote social behaviors. In K.R. Wentzel & G.B. Ramani (Eds.), *Handbook of social influences in school contexts.* New York: Routledge.

Estes, T.H., & Mintz, S.L. (2016). *Instruction* (7th ed.). Upper Saddle River, NJ: Pearson.

Evans, G.W. (2004). The environment of childhood poverty. *American Psychologist, 59,* 77–92.

Evans, G.W., & Cassells, R.C. (2014). Childhood poverty, cumulative risk exposure, and mental health in emerging adults. *Clinical Psychological Science, 2,* 287–296.

Evans, G.W., & English, K. (2002). The environment of poverty: Multiple stressor exposure, psychophysiological stress, and socioeconomic disadvantage. *Child Development, 73,* 1238–1248.

Evans, S.Z., Simons, L.G., & Simons, R.L. (2016). Factors that influence trajectories of delinquency throughout adolescence. *Journal of Youth and Adolescence, 45,* 156–171.

Evans-Lacko, S., & others (2016). Childhood bullying victimization is associated with the use of mental health services over five decades: A longitudinal nationally representative study. *Psychological Medicine.* doi:10.1017/S0033291716001719

Evertson, C.M., & Emmer, E.T. (2009). *Classroom management for elementary teachers* (8th ed.). Boston: Allyn & Bacon.

Evertson, C.M., & Emmer, E.T. (2017). *Classroom management for elementary teachers* (10th ed.). Upper Saddle River, NJ: Pearson.

Evertson, C.M., & Harris, A.H. (1999). Support for managing learning-centered classrooms: The classroom organization and management program. In H.J. Freiberg (Ed.), *Beyond behaviorism: Changing the classroom management paradigm.* Boston: Allyn & Bacon.

Evertson, C.M., & Poole, I.R. (2008). Proactive classroom management. In T. Good (Ed.), *Twenty-first century education: A reference handbook.* Los Angeles, CA: Sage.

F

Fahey, P.F., Wu, H.C., & Hoy, W.K. (2010). Individual academic optimism of teachers: A new concept and its measure. In W.K. Hoy & M. DiPaola (Eds.), *Analyzing school contexts.* Greenwich, CT: Information Age.

Fakhoury, M. (2015). Autistic spectrum disorders: A review of clinical features, theories, and diagnosis. *International Journal of Neuroscience, 43,* 70–77.

Fazio, L.K., DeWolf, M., & Siegler, R.S. (2016). Strategy use and strategy choice in fraction magnitude comparison. *Journal of Experimental Psychology, 42,* 1–16.

Feather, N.T. (1966). Effects of prior success and failure on expectations of success and subsequent performance. *Journal of Personality and Social Psychology, 3,* 287–298.

Feeney, S., Moravcik, E., & Nolte, S. (2016). *Who am I in the lives of children?* (10th ed.). Upper Saddle River, NJ: Pearson.

Feng, Y. (1996). Some thoughts about applying constructivist theories to guide instruction. *Computers in the Schools, 12,* 71–84.

Fenzel, L.M., Blyth, D.A., & Simmons, R.G. (1991). School transitions, secondary. In R.M. Lerner, A.C. Petersen, & J. Brooks-Gunn (Eds.), *Encyclopedia of adolescence* (Vol. 2). New York: Garland.

Ferguson, C.J. (2013). Spanking, corporal punishment, and negative long-term outcomes: A meta-analytic review of longitudinal studies. *Clinical Psychology Review, 33,* 196–208.

Fernandez-Alonso, R., Suarez-Alvarez, J., & Muniz, J. (2015). Adolescents' homework performance in mathematics and science: Personal factors and teaching practice. *Journal of Educational Psychology, 107,* 1075–1085.

Fernandez-Berrocal, P., & Checa, P. (2016). Editorial: Emotional intelligence and cognitive abilities. *Frontiers in Psychology, 7,* 955.

Fernandez-Jaen, A., & others (2015). Cortical thickness differences in the prefrontal cortex in children and adolescents with ADHD in relation to dopamine transporter (DAT1) genotype. *Psychiatry Research., 233,* 409–417.

Ferrer, E., & others (2013). White matter maturation supports the development of reasoning ability through its influence on processing speed. *Developmental Science, 16,* 941-951.

Fidalgo, R., Harris, K.R., & Braaksma, M. (2016). *Design principles for teaching effective writing.* Leiden, The Netherlands: Brill.

Fields, R.D. (2015). A new mechanism of neural plasticity: Activity-dependent myelination. *Nature Reviews: Neuroscience, 16,* 756-767.

Finion, K.J., & others (2015). Emotion-based preventive intervention: Effectively promoting emotion knowledge and adaptive behavior among at-risk preschoolers. *Development and Psychopathology, 27,* 1353-1365.

Fiorella, L., & Mayer, R.E. (2015). *Learning as thinking and thinking as learning.* Washington, DC: American Psychological Association.

Fischer, K.W., & Immordino-Yang, M.H. (2008). Introduction: The fundamental importance of the brain and learning for education. In *The Jossey-Bass reader on the brain and learning.* San Francisco: Jossey-Bass.

Fischer, P., Krueger, J.I., Greitemeyer, T., Vogrincic, C., Kastenmüller, A., Frey, D, Heene, M., Wicher, M., & Kainbacher M. (2011). The bystander-effect: A meta-analytic review on bystander intervention in dangerous and non-dangerous emergencies. *Psychological Bulletin, 137*(4), 517-537. doi: http://dx.doi.org/10.1037/a0023304

Fischhoff, B., Bruine de Bruin, W., Parker, A.M., Millstein, S.G., & Halpern-Felsher, B.L. (2010). Adolescents' perceived risk of dying. *Journal of Adolescent Health, 46,* 265-269.

Fisher, B.W., Gardella, J.H., & Teurbe-Tolon, A.R. (2016). Peer cybervictimization among adolescents and the associated internalizing and externalizing problems: A meta-analysis. *Journal of Youth and Adolescence, 45,* 1727-1743.

Fisher, D., & Frey, N. (2016). *Improving adolescent literacy* (4th ed.). Upper Saddle River, NJ: Pearson.

Fitzpatrick, J. (1993). *Developing responsible behavior in schools.* South Burlington, VT: Fitzpatrick Associates.

Fives, H., & Buehl, M.M. (2016). Teaching motivation: Self-efficacy and goal orientation. In K. Wentzel & D. Miele (Eds.), *Handbook of motivation at school* (2nd ed.). New York: Routledge.

Flannery, D.J., & others (2016). Bullying prevention: A summary of the report of the National Academies of Sciences, Engineering, and Medicine: Committee on the Biological and Psychological Effects of Peer Victimization: Lessons for bullying prevention. *Prevention Science, 17,* 1044-1053.

Flavell, J.H. (2004). Theory-of-mind development: Retrospect and prospect. *Merrill-Palmer Quarterly, 50,* 274-290.

Flavell, J.H., Friedrichs, A., & Hoyt, J. (1970). Developmental changes in memorization processes. *Cognitive Psychology, 1,* 324-340.

Flavell, J.H., Green, F.L., & Flavell, E.R. (1995). The development of children's knowledge about attentional focus. *Developmental Psychology, 31,* 706-712.

Flavell, J.H., Green, F.L., & Flavell, E.R. (1998). The mind has a mind of its own: Developing knowledge about mental uncontrollability. *Cognitive Development, 13,* 127-138.

Flavell, J.H., Miller, P.H., & Miller, S. (2002). *Cognitive development* (4th ed.). Upper Saddle River. NJ: Prentice Hall.

Florez, M.A.C. (1999). Improving adult English language learners' speaking skills. *ERIC Digest,* EDO-LE-99-01, 1-5.

Flower, L.S., & Hayes, J.R. (1981). Problem-solving and the cognitive processes in writing. In C. Frederiksen & J.F. Dominic (Eds.), *Writing: The nature, development, and teaching of written communication.* Mahwah, NJ: Erlbaum.

Flynn, J.R. (1999). Searching for justice: The discovery of IQ gains over time. *American Psychologist, 54,* 5-20.

Flynn, J.R. (2007). The history of the American mind in the 20th century: A scenario to explain gains over time and a case for the irrelevance of g. In P.C. Kyllonen, R.D. Roberts, & L. Stankov (Eds.), *Extending intelligence.* Mahwah, NJ: Erlbaum.

Flynn, J.R. (2011). Secular changes in intelligence. In R.J. Sternberg & S.B. Kaufman (Eds.), *Cambridge handbook of intelligence.* New York: Cambridge University Press.

Flynn, J.R. (2013). *Are we getting smarter?* New York: Cambridge University Press.

Fogarty, R. (Ed.). (1993). *The multiage classroom.* Palatine, IL: IRI/Skylight.

Ford, D.Y. (2014). Why education must be multicultural: Addressing a few misperceptions with counterarguments. *Gifted Child Today, 37,* 59-62.

Ford, D.Y. (2015a). Multicultural issues: Recruiting and retaining Black and Hispanic students in gifted education: Equality versus equity in schools. *Gifted Child Today, 38,* 187-191.

Ford, D.Y. (2015b). Culturally responsive gifted classrooms for culturally different students: A focus on invitational learning. *Gifted Child Today, 38,* 67-69.

Ford-Brown, L.A., & Kindersley, D.K.D. (2017). *DK communication.* Upper Saddle River, NJ: Pearson.

Fox, E., & Alexander, R.A. (2017). Learning to read. In R.E. Mayer & P.A. Alexander (Eds.), *Handbook of research on learning and instruction* (2nd ed.). New York: Routledge.

Fox, E., & Dinsmore, D.L. (2016). Teacher influences on the development of students' personal interest in academic domains. In K.R. Wentzel & G.B. Ramani (Eds.), *Handbook of social influences in school contexts.* New York: Routledge.

Francks, C. (2016). Exploring human brain lateralization with molecular genetics and genomics. *Annals of the New York Academy of Sciences.* doi: 10.1111/nyas.12770

Frankenberg, E., & Orfield, G. (Eds.). (2007). *Lessons in integration.* Charlottesville, VA: University of Virginia Press.

Frederikse, M., Lu, A., Aylward, E., Barta, P., Sharma, T., & Perlsons, G. (2000). Sex differences in inferior lobule volume in schizophrenia. *American Journal of Psychiatry, 157,* 422-427.

Freeman, J., & Garces-Bascal, R.M. (2015). Gender differences in gifted children. In M. Neihart & others (Eds.), *Social and emotional development of gifted children.* Waco, TX: Prufrock Press.

Frey, B. (2005). Standard deviation. In S.W. Lee (Ed.), *Encyclopedia of school psychology.* Thousand Oaks. CA: Sage.

Friedman, H.S., & Schustack, M.W. (2016). *REVEL for personality* (6th ed.). Upper Saddle River, NJ: Pearson.

Friedman, N.P., & others (2007). Greater attention problems during childhood predict poorer executive functioning in late adolescence. *Psychological Science, 18,* 893-900.

Fritz, K.M., & O'Connor, P.J. (2016). Acute exercise improves mood and motivation in young men with ADHD symptoms. *Medicine and Science in Sports and Exercise, 48,* 1153-1160.

Fuchs, D., Fuchs, L.S., & Burish, P. (2000). Peer-assisted strategies: An empirically-supported practice to promote reading. *Learning Disabilities Research and Practice, 9,* 203-212.

Fuchs, D., Fuchs, L.S., Mathes, P.G., & Simmons, D.C. (1997). Peer-assisted learning strategies: Making classrooms more responsive to diversity. *American Educational Research Journal, 34,* 174-206.

Fuchs, L.S., & others (2016a). Effects of intervention to improve at-risk fourth-graders' understanding, calculations, and word problems with fractions. *Elementary School Journal, 116,* 625-651.

Fuchs, L.S., & others (2016b). Pathways to third-grade calculation versus word-reading competence: Are they more alike or different? *Child Development, 87,* 558-567.

Fuchs, L.S., & others (2016c). Supported self-explaining during fraction intervention. *Journal of Educational Psychology.*

Fuhs, M.W., Nesbitt, K.T., Farran, D.C., & Dong, N. (2014). Longitudinal associations between executive functioning and academic skills across content areas. *Developmental Psychology, 50,* 1698–1709.

Fuligni, A.J., & Tsai, K.M. (2015). Developmental flexibility in the age of globalization: Autonomy and identity development among immigrant adolescents. *Annual Review of Psychology* (Vol. 66). Palo Alto, CA: Annual Reviews.

Furth, H.G., & Wachs, H. (1975). *Thinking goes to school.* New York: Oxford University Press.

Fuson, K.C., Kalchman, M., & Bransford, J.D. (2005). Mathematical understanding: An introduction. In M.S. Donovan & J.D. Bransford (Eds.), *How students learn.* Washington, DC: National Academies Press.

G

Galambos, N.L., Berenbaum, S.A., & McHale, S.M. (2009). Gender development in adolescence. In R.M. Lerner & L. Steinberg (Eds.), *Handbook of adolescent psychology.* New York: Wiley.

Galdiolo, S., & Roskam, I. (2016). From me to us: The construction of family alliance. *Infant Mental Health, 37,* 29–44.

Galinsky, E. (2010). *Mind in the making.* New York: Harper Collins.

Gallant, S.N. (2016). Mindfulness meditation practice and executive functioning: Breaking down the benefit. *Consciousness and Cognition, 40,* 116–130.

Gallo, E.F., & Posner, J. (2016). Moving towards causality in attention-deficit/hyperactivity disorder: Overview of neural and genetic mechanisms. *Lancet Psychiatry, 3,* 555–567.

Galloway, M.K. (2012). Cheating in advantaged high schools: Prevalence, justifications, and possibilities for change. *Ethics & Behavior, 22,* 378–399. doi: 10.1080/10508422.2012.679143

Galvan, A., & Tottenham, N. (2016). Adolescent brain development. In D. Cicchetti (Ed.), *Developmental psychopathology* (3rd ed.). New York: Wiley.

Gambrari, I.A., Yusuf, M.O., & Thomas, D.A. (2015). Effects of computer-assisted STAD, LTM, and ICI cooperative learning strategies on Nigerian secondary school students' achievement, gender, and motivation in physics. *Journal of Education and Practice, 19,* 16–28.

Gambrell, L.B., Morrow, L.M., & Pressley, M. (Eds.). (2007). *Best practices in literacy instruction.* New York: Guilford.

Gandara, P. (2002). *Peer group influence and academic aspirations across cultural/ethnic groups of high school students.* Santa Cruz, University of California, Center for Research on Education, Diversity & Excellence.

Garandeau, C.F., Vartio, A., Poskiparta, E., & Salmivalli, C. (2016). School bullies' intention to change behavior following teacher interventions: Effects of empathy arousal, condemning of bullying, and blaming the perpetrator. *Prevention Science, 17,* 1034–1043.

Garcia-Lopez, L.J., Diaz-Castela, M.D., Muela-Martinez, J.A., & Espinosa-Fernandez, L. (2014). Can parent training for parents with high levels of expressed emotion have a positive effect on their child's social anxiety improvement? *Journal of Anxiety Disorders, 28,* 812–822.

Gardner, H. (1983). *Frames of mind.* New York: Basic Books.

Gardner, H. (1993). *Multiple intelligences.* New York: Basic Books.

Gardner, H. (1998). Multiple intelligences: Myths and messages. In A. Woolfolk (Ed.), *Readings in educational psychology* (2nd ed.). Boston: Allyn & Bacon.

Gardner, H. (2002). The pursuit of excellence through education. In M. Ferrari (Ed.), *Learning from extraordinary minds.* Mahwah, NJ: Erlbaum.

Gardner, M., Brooks-Gunn, J., & Chase-Lansdale, P.L. (2016). The two-generation approach to building human capital: Past, present, and future. In E. Votruba-Drzal & E. Dearing (Eds.), *Handbook of early childhood development programs, practices, and policies.* New York: Wiley.

Gardner, M., & Steinberg, L. (2005). Peer influence and risk taking, risk preference, and psychology, *Developmental Psychology, 41,* 625–635.

Garmon, A., Nystrand, M., Berends, M., & LePore, P.C. (1995). An organizational analysis of the effects of ability grouping. *American Educational Research Journal, 32,* 687–715.

Gasser, L., Grutter, J., Buholzer, A., & Wettstein, A. (2018). Emotionally supportive classroom interactions and students' perceptions of their teachers as caring and just. *Learning and Instruction, 54,* 82–92.

Gates, W. (1998, July 20). Charity begins when I'm ready [interview]. *Fortune* magazine.

Gauvain, M. (2016). Peer contributions to cognitive development. In K. Wentzel & G.B. Ramani (Eds.), *Handbook of social influences in school contexts.* New York: Routledge.

Gay, G. (1997). Educational equality for students of color. In J.A. Banks & C.M. Banks (Eds.), *Multicultural education* (3rd ed.). Boston: Allyn & Bacon.

Gay, G. (2013). Teaching to and through cultural diversity. *Curriculum Inquiry, 43,* 48–70.

Gelman, R. (1969). Conservation acquisition: A problem of learning to attend to relevant attributes. *Journal of Experimental Child Psychology, 7,* 67–87.

Gelman, S.A., & Opfer, J.E. (2004). Development of the animate-inanimate distinction. In U. Goswami (Ed.), *Blackwell handbook of childhood cognitive development.* Malden, MA: Blackwell.

Genesee, F., & Lindholm-Leary, K. (2012). The education of English language learners. In K. Harris, S. Graham, & T. Urdan (Eds.), *APA educational psychology handbook.* Washington, DC: American Psychological Association.

GenYes (2010). Retrieved January 14, 2010, from http: genyes.com

Gershoff, E.T. (2013). Spanking and development: We know enough now to stop hitting our children. *Child Development Perspectives, 7,* 133–137.

Gershoff, E.T., & Grogan-Kaylor, A. (2016). Spanking and child outcomes: Old controversies and new meta-analyses. *Journal of Family Psychology, 30,* 453–469.

Gerst, E.H., & others (2016). Cognitive and behavioral rating measures of executive function as predictors of academic outcomes in children. *Child Neuroscience.* doi:10.1080/09297049.2015.1120860

Geurten, M., Lejeune, C., & Meulemans, T. (2016). Time's up! Involvement of metamemory knowledge, executive functions, and time monitoring in children's prospective memory performance. *Child Neuropsychology, 22,* 443–457.

Gilligan, C. (1982). *In a different voice.* Cambridge, MA: Harvard University Press.

Gilligan, C. (1992, May). *Joining the resistance: Girls' development in adolescence.* Paper presented at the symposium on development and vulnerability in close relationships, Montreal, Quebec.

Gilligan, C. (1998). *Minding women: Reshaping the education realm.* Cambridge, MA: Harvard University Press.

Gilligan, C., Spencer, R., Weinberg, M.K., & Bertsch, T. (2003). On the listening guide: A voice-centered relational model. In P.M. Carnic & J.E. Rhodes (Eds.), *Qualitative research in psychology.* Washington, DC: American Psychological Association.

Ginsburg-Block, M. (2005). Peer tutoring. In S.W. Lee (Ed.), *Encyclopedia of school psychology.* Thousand Oaks, CA: Sage.

Glasser, W. (1969). *Schools without failure.* New York: Harper & Row.

Gleichgerrcht, E., & others (2015). Educational neuromyths among teachers in Latin America. *Mind, Brain, and Education, 9,* 170–178.

Glesne, C. (2016). *Becoming qualitative researchers* (5th ed.). Upper Saddle River, NJ: Pearson.

Gliner, J.A., Morgan, G.A., & Leech, N.L. (2017). *Research methods in applied settings.* New York; Routledge.

Globallab (2016). *Global student laboratory.* Retrieved August 21, 2016, from https://globallab.org/en/project/catalog/#.V7nsGal08kw

Gluck, M.A., Mercado, E., & Myers, C.E. (2016). *Learning and memory* (3rd ed.). New York: Worth.

Goddings, A-L., & Mills, K. (2017). *Adolescence and the brain.* New York: Routledge.

Godfrey, H.K., & Grimshaw, G.M. (2016). Emotional language is all right: Emotional prosody reduces hemispheric asymmetry for linguistic processing. *Laterality.* doi 10.1080/1357650X.2015.1096940

Godfrey, K.E. (2011-12). *Investigating grade inflation and non-equivalence.* New York: College Board.

Goffin, S.G., & Wilson, C.S. (2001). *Curriculum models and early childhood education.* Upper Saddle River, NJ: Prentice Hall.

Gold, J., & Lanzoni, M. (Eds.). (1993). [Video] *Graduation by portfolio—Central Park East Secondary School.* New York: Post Production, 29th St. Video, Inc.

Goldberg, J.S., & Carlson, M.J. (2015). Patterns and predictors of coparenting after unmarried parents part. *Journal of Family Psychology, 29,* 416-426.

Goldberg, W.A., & Lucas-Thompson, R. (2008). Maternal and paternal employment, effects. In M.M. Haith & J.B. Benson (Eds.), *Encyclopedia of infant and early childhood development.* Oxford, UK: Elsevier.

Goldman-Rakic, P. (1996). *Bridging the gap.* Presentation at the workshop sponsored by the Education Commission of the States and the Charles A. Dana Foundation, Denver.

Goldner, L. (2016). Protégés' personality traits, expectations, the quality of the mentoring, and relationships and adjustment: A Big Five analysis. *Child & Youth Forum, 45,* 85-105.

Goleman, D. (1995). *Emotional intelligence.* New York: Basic Books.

Goleman, D., Kaufman, P., & Ray, M. (1993). *The creative spirit.* New York: Plume.

Gollnick, D.M., & Chinn, P.C. (2017). *Multicultural education in a pluralistic society* (10th ed.). Upper Saddle River, NJ: Pearson.

Gomez, K., & Lee, U-S. (2015). Situated cognition and learning environments: Implications for teachers online and offline in the new digital media age. *Interactive Learning Environments, 23,* 634-652.

Gong, Y., Ericsson, K.A., & Moxley, J.H. (2015). A refined technique for identifying chunk characteristics during recall of briefly presented chess positions and their relations to chess skill. *PLoS One, 10,* e0118756.

Gonzales, N.A., & others (2016). Culturally adapted preventive interventions for children and adolescents. In D. Cicchetti (Ed.), *Developmental psychopathology* (3rd ed.). New York: Wiley.

González, N., & Moll, L.C., & Amanti, C. (Eds.). (2005). *Funds of knowledge: Theorizing practices in households, communities, and classrooms.* Mahwah, NJ: Erlbaum.

Good, C., Rattan, A., & Dweck, C.S. (2012). Why do women opt out? Sense of belonging and women's representation in mathematics. *Journal of Personality and Social Psychology, 102,* 700-717.

Good, R.H., & Kaminski, R.A. (2003). Dynamic indicators of basic early literacy skills (6th ed.). Longmont, CO: Sopris West Educational Services.

Goodkind, S. (2013). Single-sex public education for low-income youth of color: A critical theoretical review. *Sex Roles, 69,* 363-381.

Goodlad, S., & Hirst, B. (1989). *Peer tutoring: A guide to learning by teaching.* New York: Nichols.

Gordon, T. (1970). *Parent effectiveness training.* New York: McGraw-Hill.

Gottfried, A.E., Marcoulides, G.A., Gottfried, A.W., & Oliver, P.H. (2009). A latent curve model of motivational practices and developmental decline in math and science academic intrinsic motivation. *Journal of Educational Psychology, 101,* 729-739.

Gottlieb, R., Jahner, E., Immordino-Yang, M.H., & Kaufman, S.B. (2017). How social-emotional imagination facilitates deep learning and creativity in the classroom. In R.A. Beghetto & J.C. Kaufman (Eds.), *Nurturing creativity in the classroom.* New York: Cambridge University Press.

Graham, S. (1986, August). *Can attribution theory tell us something about motivation in Blacks?* Paper presented at the meeting of the American Psychological Association, Washington, DC.

Graham, S. (1990). Motivation in African Americans. In G.L. Berry & J.K. Asamen (Eds.), *Black students.* Newbury Park, CA: Sage.

Graham, S. (2005, February 16). Commentary in *USA Today,* p. 2D.

Graham, S. (2017). Writing research and practice. In D. Lapp & D. Fisher (Eds.), *Handbook of research on teaching the English language arts* (2nd ed.). New York: Routledge.

Graham, S., & Harris, K.R. (2016). Evidence-based practice and writing instruction. In C. MacArthur, S. Graham, & J. Fitzgerald (Eds.), *Handbook of writing research* (2nd ed.). New York: Guilford.

Graham, S., & Harris, K.R. (2017). Self-regulated strategy development: Theoretical bases, critical instruction elements, and future research. In R. Fidalgo, K.R., Harris, & M. Braaksma (Eds.), *Design principles for teaching effective writing.* Hershey, PA: Brill.

Graham, S., Harris, K.R., McArthur, C., & Santangelo, T. (2017). Self-regulation and writing. In D. Schunk & J. Greene (Eds.), *Handbook of self-regulation of learning and performance* (2nd ed.). New York: Routledge.

Graham, S., & Perin, D. (2007). A meta-analysis of writing instruction for adolescent students. *Journal of Educational Psychology, 99,* 445-476.

Graham, S., Rouse, A., & Harris, K.R. (2017). Scientifically supported writing practices. In A. O'Donnell (Ed.), *Oxford handbook of educational psychology.* New York: Oxford University Press.

Graham, S., & Taylor, A.Z. (2016). Attribution theory and motivation in school. In K. Wentzel & D. Miele (Eds.), *Handbook of motivation at school* (2nd ed.). New York: Routledge.

Graham, S., & Weiner, B. (1996). Theories and principles of motivation. In D.C. Berliner & R.C. Calfee (Eds.), *Handbook of educational psychology.* New York: Macmillan.

Graham, S., & Williams, C. (2009). An attributional approach to motivation in school. In K. Wentzel & A. Wigfield (Eds.), *Handbook of motivation at school.* New York: Routledge.

Gravetter, F.J., & Forzano, L.B. (2016). *Research methods for the behavioral sciences* (5th ed.). Boston: Cengage.

Gravetter, F.J., & Wallnau, L.B. (2017). *Statistics for the behavioral sciences* (10th ed.). Boston: Cengage.

Gray, J. (1992). *Men are from Mars, women are from Venus.* New York: HarperCollins.

Gredler, M. (2009). *Learning and instruction* (6th ed.). Upper Saddle River, NJ: Merrill.

Green, C.G., Landry, O., & Iarocci, G. (2016). Developments in the developmental approach to intellectual disability. In D. Cicchetti (Ed.), *Developmental psychopathology* (3rd ed.). New York: Wiley.

Greenhow, M. (2015). Effective computer-aided assessment of mathematics: Principles, practice, and results. *Teaching Mathematics and Its Applications, 34,* 117-137.

Greenough, W.T. (1997, April 21). Commentary in article, "Politics of biology." *U.S. News & World Report,* p. 79.

Greenough, W.T. (2000). Brain development. In A. Kazdin (Ed.), *Encyclopedia of psychology.* Washington, DC, & New York: American Psychological Association and Oxford University Press.

Gregorson, M., Kaufman, J.C., & Snyder, H. (Eds.). (2013). *Teaching creativity and teaching creatively.* New York: Springer.

Gregory, A., & Huang, F. (2013). It takes a village: The effects of 10th grade college-going expectations of students, parents, and teachers four years later. *American Journal of Community Psychology, 52,* 41-55.

Gregory, A., & Korth, J. (2016). Teacher-student relationships and behavioral engagement in the classroom. In K.R. Wentzel & G.B. Ramani (Eds.), *Handbook of social influences in school contexts.* New York: Routledge.

Gregory, R.J. (2016). *REVEL for psychological testing* (7th ed.). Upper Saddle River, NJ: Pearson.

Grenell, A., & Carlson, S.M. (2016). Pretense. In D. Couchenour & K. Chrisman (Eds.), *Encyclopedia of contemporary early childhood education.* Thousand Oaks, CA: Sage.

Grenhow, C., & Askari, E. (2016). Peers and social media networks: Exploring adolescents' social functioning and academic outcomes. In K.R. Wentzel & G.B. Ramani (Eds.), *Handbook of social influences in school contexts.* New York: Routledge.

Gresalfi, M. (2015). Designing to support critical engagement with statistics. *ZDM: The International Journal of Mathematics Education, 47,* 933-946.

Gresalfi, M., Barab, S.A., Siyahhan, S., & Christensen, T. (2009). Virtual worlds, conceptual understanding, and me: Designing for consequential engagement. *On the Horizon, 17*(1), 21-34.

Grice, G.L., Skinner, J.F., & Mansson, D.H. (2016). *Mastering public speaking* (9th ed.). Upper Saddle River, NJ: Pearson.

Griffen, R. (2013). An analysis of student academic performance at Advancement Via Individual Determination (AVID) national demonstration schools and AVID schools. *ERIC,* #ED561515.

Griffin, J.A., Freund, L.S., & McCardle, P. (Eds.). (2015). *Executive function in preschool age children.* Washington, DC: American Psychological Association.

Griffiths, H., & Fazel, M. (2016). Early intervention crucial in anxiety disorders in children. *Practitioner, 260,* 17-20.

Grigg, W.S., Lauko, M.A., & Brockway, D.M. (2006). *The nation's report card: Science, 2005* (NCES 2006-466). U.S. Department of Education, DC: U.S. Government Printing Office.

Grigorenko, E.L., & others (2016). The trilogy of G x E. Genes, environments, and their interactions: Conceptualizations, operationalization, and application. In D. Cicchetti (Ed.), *Developmental psychopathology* (3rd ed.). New York: Wiley.

Grindal, M., & Nieri, T. (2016). The relationship between ethnic-racial socialization and adolescent substance abuse: An examination of social learning as a causal mechanism. *Journal of Ethnicity in Substance Abuse, 15,* 3-24.

Grindstaff, K., & Richmond, G. (2008). Learners' perceptions of the roles of peers in a research experience: Implications for the apprenticeship process, scientific inquiry, and collaborative work. *Journal of Research in Science Teaching, 45,* 251-272.

Grolnick, W.S., Friendly, R.W., & Bellas, V.M. (2009). Parenting and children's motivation at school. In K.R. Wentzel & A. Wigfield (Eds.), *Handbook of motivation at school.* New York: Routledge.

Gronlund, N.E., & Waugh, C.K. (2009). *Assessment of student achievement* (9th ed.). Upper Saddle River, NJ: Prentice Hall.

Groppe, K., & Elsner, B. (2016). Executive function and weight status in children: A one-year prospective investigation. *Child Neuropsychology.* doi:10.1080/09297049.2015.1089981

Grunschel, C., & Schopenhauer, L. (2015). Why are students (not) motivated to change academic procrastination? An investigation based on the transtheoretical model of change. *Journal of College Student Development, 56,* 187-200.

Grunwald & Associates (2014). *Make assessment matter.* Bethesda, MD: Author.

Guastello, D.D., & Guastello, S.J. (2003). Androgyny, gender role behavior, and emotional intelligence among college students and their parents. *Sex Roles, 49,* 663-673.

Guilford, J.P. (1967). *The structure of intellect.* New York: McGraw-Hill.

Guillaume, A.M. (2016). *K-12 classroom teaching* (5th ed.). Upper Saddle River, NJ: Pearson.

Gur, R.C., & others (1995). Sex differences in regional cerebral glucose metabolism during a resting state. *Science, 267,* 528-531.

Gurol, M., & Kerimgil, S. (2010). Academic optimism. *Procedia–Social and Behavioral Sciences, 9,* 929-932.

Gurwitch, R.H., Silovksy, J.F., Schultz, S., Kees, M., & Burlingame, S. (2001). *Reactions and guidelines for children following trauma/disaster.* Norman, OK: Department of Pediatrics, University of Oklahoma Health Sciences Center.

Gyabak, K., Ottenbriet-Leftwich, A., & Ray, J. (2015). Teachers using designerly thinking in K-12 online course design. *Journal of Online Learning Research, 1,* 253-274.

H

Haines, S.J., & others (2015). Fostering family-school and community-school partnerships in inclusive schools: Using practice as a guide. *Research and Practice for persons with severe disabilities, 40,* 227-239.

Hakuta, K. (2001, April 5). *Key policy milestones and directions in the education of English language learners.* Paper prepared for the Rockefeller Foundation Symposium, Leveraging change: An emerging framework for educational equity, Washington, DC.

Hakuta, K. (2005, April). *Bilingualism at the intersection of research and public policy.* Paper presented at the meeting of the Society for Research in Child Development, Atlanta.

Hakuta, K., Butler, Y.G., & Witt, D. (2000). *How long does it take English learners to attain proficiency?* Berkeley, CA: The University of California Linguistic Minority Research Institute Policy Report 2000-1.

Hale-Benson, J.E. (1982). *Black children: Their roots, culture, and learning styles.* Baltimore: Johns Hopkins University Press.

Hall, G.S. (1904). *Adolescence* (Vols. 1 & 2). Englewood Cliffs, NJ: Prentice Hall.

Hallahan, D.P., Kauffman, J.M., & Pullen, P.C. (2015). *Exceptional learners* (13th ed.). Upper Saddle River, NJ: Pearson.

Halonen, J. (2010). Express yourself. In J.W. Santrock & J. Halonen, *Your guide to college success* (6th ed.). Belmont, CA: Wadsworth.

Halonen, J.A., & Santrock, J.W. (2013). *Your guide to college success* (7th ed.). Boston: Cengage.

Halpern, D.F. (2012). *Sex differences in cognitive abilities* (2nd ed.). New York: Psychology Press.

Halpern, D.F., & others (2011). The pseudoscience of single-sex schooling. *Science, 333,* 1706-1717.

Hambleton, R.K. (1996). Advances in assessment models, methods, and practices. In D.C. Berliner & R.C. Calfee (Eds.), *Handbook of educational psychology.* New York: Macmillan.

Hamilton, R., & Duschi, R. (2017). Teaching science. In R.E. Mayer & P.A. Alexander (Eds.), *Handbook of research on learning and instruction* (2nd ed.). New York: Routledge.

Hamilton, S.F., & Hamilton, M.A. (2004). Contexts for mentoring: Adolescent-adult relationships in workplaces and communities. In R. Lerner & L. Steinberg (Eds.), *Handbook of adolescent psychology* (2nd ed.). New York: Wiley.

Han, M. (2015). An empirical study on the application of cooperative learning to English listening classes. *English Language Teaching, 8,* 177-184.

Harley, T.A. (2017). *Talking the talk* (2nd ed.). New York: Routledge.

Harris, J., Golinkoff, R.M., & Hirsh-Pasek, K. (2011). Lessons from the crib for the classroom: How children really learn vocabulary. In S.B. Neuman & D.K. Dickinson (Eds.), *Handbook of early literacy research.* New York: Guilford.

Harris, K.R., & Graham, S. (2017). Self-regulated strategy development: Theoretical bases, critical instructional elements, and future research. In R. Fidalgo, K.R. Harris, & M. Braaksma (Eds.), *Design principles for teaching effective writing.* Leiden, The Netherlands: Brill.

Harris, K.R., Graham, S., & Adkins, M. (2015). Practice-based professional development and self-regulated strategy development for tier 2, at-risk writers in second grade. *Contemporary Educational Psychology, 40,* 5-16.

Harris, K.R., Graham, S., Mason, L., & Friedlander, B. (2008). *Powerful writing strategies for all students.* Baltimore: Paul H. Brookes.

Harris, K.R., & others (2017). Self-regulated strategy development in writing: A classroom example of developing executive functioning and future directions. In L. Meltzer (Ed.), *Executive functioning in education* (2nd ed.). New York: Guilford.

Harris, P.L. (2006). Social cognition. In W. Damon & R. Lerner (Eds.), *Handbook of child psychology* (6th ed.). New York: Wiley.

Harrison, F., & Craddock, A.E. (2016). How attempts to meet others' unrealistic expectations affect health: Health-promoting behaviors as a mediator between perfectionism and physical health. *Psychology, Health, and Medicine, 21,* 386-400.

Hart, B., & Risley, T.R. (1995). *Meaningful differences.* Baltimore: Paul H. Brookes.

Hart, C.H., Yang, C., Charlesworth, R., & Burts, D.C. (2003, April). *Early childhood teachers' curriculum beliefs, classroom practices, and children's outcome: What are the connections?* Paper presented at the biennial meeting of the Society for Research in Child Development, Tampa, FL.

Hart, D., Matsuba, M.K., & Atkins, R. (2014). The moral and civic effects of learning to serve. In L. Nucci, T. Krettenauer, & D. Narváez (Eds.), *Handbook of moral and character education* (2nd ed.). New York: Routledge.

Harter, S. (1981). A new self-report scale of intrinsic versus extrinsic orientation in the classroom: Motivational and informational components. *Developmental Psychology, 17,* 300-312.

Harter, S. (1996). Teacher and classmate influences on scholastic motivation, self-esteem, and level of voice in adolescents. In J. Juvonen & K.R. Wentzel (Eds.), *Social motivation.* New York: Cambridge University Press.

Harter, S. (2006). The self. In W. Damon & R. Lerner (Eds.), *Handbook of child psychology* (6th ed.). New York: Wiley.

Harter, S. (2016). I-self and me-self processes affecting developmental psychopathology and mental health. In D. Cicchetti (Ed.), *Developmental psychopathology.* New York: Wiley.

Hartshorne, H., & May, M.S. (1928-1930). *Moral studies in the nature of character: Studies in deceit, Vol. 1; Studies in self-control, Vol. 2; Studies in the organization of character, Vol. 3.* New York: Macmillan.

Hartup, W.W. (1983). The peer system. In P.H. Mussen (Ed.), *Handbook of child psychology* (4th ed., Vol. 4). New York: Wiley.

Hastings, P.D., Miller, J.G., & Truxel, N.R. (2015). Making good: The socialization of children's prosocial development. In J.E. Grusec & P.D. Hastings (Eds.), *Handbook of socialization* (2nd ed.). New York: Guilford.

Hawkins, G.E., Hayes, B.K., & Heit, E. (2016). A dynamic model of reasoning and memory. *Journal of Experimental Psychology: General, 145,* 155-180.

Hayes, J.R., & Flower, L.S. (1986). Writing research and the writer. *American Psychologist, 41,* 1106-1113.

Heath, S.B. (1989). Oral and literate traditions among Black Americans living in poverty. *American Psychologist, 44,* 367-373.

Heiman, G.W. (2015). *Behavioral sciences STAT* (2nd ed.). Boston: Cengage.

Heller, C., & Hawkins, I. (1994). Spring, Teaching tolerance. *Teachers College Record,* p. 2.

Helles, A., Gillberg, C.L., Gillberg, C., & Bilistedt, E. (2015). Asperger syndrome in males over two decades: Stability and predictors of diagnosis. *Journal of Child Psychology and Psychiatry, 56,* 711-718.

Henderson, V.L., & Dweck, C.S. (1990). Motivation and achievement. In S.S. Feldman & G.R. Elliott (Eds.), *At the threshold: The developing adolescent.* Cambridge, MA: Harvard University Press.

Hendricks, C.C. (2017). *Improving schools through action research* (4th ed.). Upper Saddle River, NJ: Pearson.

Hennessey, B. (2017). Intrinsic motivation and creativity: Have we come full circle? In R.A. Beghetto & J.C. Kaufman (Eds.), *Nurturing creativity in the classroom* (2nd ed.). New York: Cambridge University Press.

Henson, K. (1988). *Methods and strategies for teaching in secondary and middle schools.* New York: Longman.

Hertzog, N.B. (1998, January/February). Gifted education specialist. *Teaching Exceptional Children,* pp. 39-43.

Hetherington, E.M. (1995, March). *The changing American family and the well-being of others.* Paper presented at the meeting of the Society for Research in Child Development, Indianapolis.

Hetherington, E.M. (2006). The influence of conflict, marital problem solving, and parenting on children's adjustment in nondivorced, divorced, and remarried families. In A. Clarke-Stewart & J. Dunn (Eds.), *Families count.* New York: Oxford University Press.

Heward, W.L., Alber-Morgan, S., & Konrad, M. (2017). *Exceptional children* (11th ed.). Upper Saddle River, NJ: Pearson.

Hickok, G., & Small, S. (Eds.). (2016). *Neurobiology of language.* New York: Elsevier.

Hiebert, E.H., & Raphael, T.E. (1996). Psychological perspectives on literacy and extensions to educational practice. In D.C. Berliner & R.C. Calfee (Eds.), *Handbook of educational psychology.* New York: Macmillan.

Higgins, A., Power, C., & Kohlberg, L. (1983, April). *Moral atmosphere and moral judgment.* Paper presented at the biennial meeting of the Society for Research in Child Development, Detroit.

Hilgard, E.R. (1996). History of educational psychology. In D.C. Berliner & R.C. Calfee (Eds.), *Handbook of educational psychology.* New York: Macmillan.

Hill, E.M. (2016). The role of narcissism in health-risk and health-protective behaviors. *Journal of Health Psychology, 21,* 2021-3032.

Hill, K., & Roth, T.L. (2016). Epigenetic mechanisms in the development of behavior. In D. Cicchetti (Ed.), *Developmental psychopathology* (3rd ed.). New York: Wiley.

Hillman, C.H., & others (2014). Effects of the FITKids randomized controlled trial on executive control and brain function. *Pediatrics, 134,* e1063-e1071.

Hinduja, S.K., & Patchin, J.W. (2015). *Bullying beyond the schoolyard: Preventing and responding to cyberbullying* (2nd ed.). Thousand Oaks, CA: Corwin.

Hirsch, E.D. (1996). *The schools we need: And why we don't have them.* New York: Doubleday.

Hirsch, J.K., Wolford, K., Lalonde, S.M., Brunk, L., & Parker-Morris, A. (2009). Optimistic explanatory style as a moderator of the association between negative life events and suicide ideation. *Crisis, 30,* 48-53.

Hirsh-Pasek, K., & Golinkoff, R.M. (2016). Early language and literacy: Six principles. In S. Gilford (Ed.), *Head Start teacher's guide.* New York: Teacher's College Press.

Hirsh-Pasek, K., & others (2015). Putting education in educational apps: Lesson for the science of learning. *Psychological Science in the Public Interest, 16,* 3-34.

Hirsh-Pasek, K., & others (2015). The contribution of early communication to low-income children's language success. *Psychological Science, 26,* 1071-1083.

Hmelo-Silver, C.E., & Chinn, C.A. (2016). Collaborative learning. In L. Corno & E.M. Anderman (Eds.), *Handbook of educational psychology* (3rd ed.). New York: Routledge.

Hoachlander, G. (2014/2015). Integrating S, T, E, and M. *Educational Leadership, 72,* 74-78.

Hocutt, A.M. (1996). Effectiveness of special education: Is placement the critical factor? *Future of Children, 6*(1), 77-102.

Hofer, M., & Fries, S. (2016). A multiple goal perspective on academic motivation. In K. Wentzel & D. Miele (Eds.), *Handbook of motivation at school* (2nd ed.). New York: Routledge.

Hoff, E. (2015). Language development. In M.H. Bornstein & M.E. Lamb (Eds.), *Developmental science: An advanced textbook* (7th ed.). New York: Psychology Press.

Hoff, E., & others (2014). Expressive vocabulary development in children from bilingual homes: A longitudinal study from two to four years. *Early Childhood Research Quarterly, 29,* 433-444.

Hofmeister, P., & Vasishth, S. (2014). Distinctiveness and encoding effects in online sentence comprehension. *Frontiers in Psychology, 5,* 1237.

Hogan, J.M., Andrews, P.H., Andrews, J.R., & Williams. G. (2017). *Public speaking and civic engagement* (4th ed.). Upper Saddle River, NJ: Pearson.

Hogeveen, J., Salvi, C., & Grafman, J. (2016). 'Emotional intelligence': Lessons from lesions. *Trends in Neurosciences, 39,* 694-705. doi: 10.1016/j.tins.2016.08.007

Hollingworth, L.S. (1916). Sex differences in mental tests. *Psychological Bulletin, 13,* 377-383.

Holloway, S.D., & Jonas, M. (2016). Families, culture, and schooling: A critical review of theory and research. In K.R. Wentzel & G.B. Ramani (Eds.), *Handbook of social influences in school contexts.* New York: Routledge.

Holmes, C.J., Kim-Spoon, J., & Deater-Deckard, K. (2016). Linking executive function and peer problems from early childhood through middle adolescence. *Journal of Abnormal Child Psychology, 44,* 31-42.

Holzman, L. (2017). *Vygotsky at work and play* (2nd ed.). New York: Routledge.

Homa, D. (2008). Long-term memory. In N.J. Salkind (Ed.), *Encyclopedia of educational psychology.* Thousand Oaks, CA: Sage.

Hooker, J.F., Derker, K.J., Summers, M.E., & Parker, M. (2016). The development and validation of the Student Response System Benefit Scale. *Journal of Computer Assisted Learning, 32,* 120-127.

Hooper, S., Ward, T.J., Hannafin, M.J., & Clark, H.T. (1989). The effects of aptitude composition on achievement during small group learning. *Journal of Computer-Based Instruction, 16,* 102-109.

Horowitz, F.D., & others (2005). Educating teachers for developmentally appropriate practice. In L. Darling-Hammond & J. Bransford (Eds.), *Preparing teachers for a changing world.* San Francisco: Jossey-Bass.

Horvat, E.M., & Baugh, D.E. (2015). Not all parents make the grade in today's schools. *Phi Delta Kappan, 96*(7), 8-13.

Howe, M.L. (2015). An adaptive view of memory development. In R.M. Lerner (Ed.), *Handbook of child psychology and developmental science* (7th ed.). New York: Wiley.

Howell, D.C. (2017). *Fundamental statistics for the behavioral sciences* (9th ed.). Boston: Cengage.

Howes, C., & Ritchie, S. (2002). *A matter of trust: Connecting teachers and learners in the early childhood classroom.* New York: Teachers College Press.

Howland, S.M., & others (2015). Educational technology research journals: "International Journal of Computer-Supported Collaborative Learning," 2006-2014. *Educational Technology, 55,* 42-47.

Hoy, A.W., Hoy, W.K., & Kurtz, N.M. (2008). Teacher's academic optimism: The development and test of a new construct. *Teaching and Teacher Education, 24,* 821-832.

Hoy, W.K., Tarter, C.J., & Hoy, A.W. (2006). Academic optimism in schools: A force for student achievement. *American Educational Research Journal, 43,* 425-446.

Huang, Y-M. (2015). Exploring the factors that affect the intention to use collaborative technologies: The differing perspectives of sequential/global learners. *Australasian Journal of Educational Technology, 31,* 278-292.

Huerta, J., & Watt, K.M. (2015). Examining the college preparation and intermediate outcomes of college success of AVID graduates enrolled in universities and community colleges. *American Secondary Education, 43,* 20-35.

Huerta, J., Watt, K.M., & Butcher, J.T. (2013). Examining Advancement Via Individual Determination (AVID) and its impact on middle school rigor and student preparedness. *American Secondary Education, 41,* 24-37.

Hughes, C., & Devine, R.T. (2015). Individual differences in theory of mind: A social perspective. In R.M. Lerner (Ed.), *Handbook of child psychology and developmental science* (7th ed.). New York: Wiley.

Hughes, C., Marks, A., Ensor, R., & Lecce, S. (2010). A longitudinal study of conflict and inner state talk in children's conversations with mothers and younger siblings. *Social Development, 19,* 822-837.

Hulme, C., & Snowling, M.J. (2016). Reading disorders and dyslexia. *Current Opinion in Pediatrics.* doi:10.1097/MOP.0000000000000411

Humphrey, N., Curran, A., Morris, E., Farrell, P., & Woods, K. (2007). Emotional intelligence and education: A critical review. *Educational Psychology, 27,* 235-254.

Hunt, E. (2006). Expertise, talent, and social encouragement. In K.A. Ericsson, N. Charness, P.J. Feltovich, & R.R. Hoff man (Eds.), *The Cambridge handbook of expertise and expert performance.* New York: Cambridge University Press.

Hunt, E.B. (1995). *Will we be smart enough? A cognitive analysis of the coming work force.* New York: Russell Sage.

Huston, A.C. (2015). Thoughts on "Probability values and human values in evaluating single-sex education." *Sex Roles, 72,* 446-450.

Huston, A.C., & Ripke, M.N. (2006). Experiences in middle childhood and children's development. In A.C. Huston & M.N. Ripke (Eds.), *Developmental contexts in middle childhood.* New York: Cambridge University Press.

Huttenlocher, P.R., & Dabholkar, A.S. (1997). Regional differences in synaptogenesis in human cerebral cortex. *Journal of Comparative Neurology, 37*(2), 167-178.

Hwang, Y. S., Goldstein, H., Medvedev, O. N., Singh, N. N., Noh, J. E., & Hand, K. (2019). Mindfulness-based intervention for educators: Effects of a school-based cluster randomized controlled study. *Mindfulness, 10,* 1417-1436.

Hyde, J.S. (2007). *Half the human experience* (7th ed.). Boston: Houghton Mifflin.

Hyde, J.S. (2014). Gender similarities and differences. *Annual Review of Psychology* (Vol. 66). Palo Alto, CA: Annual Reviews.

Hyde, J.S., Lindberg, S.M., Linn, M.C., Ellis, A.B., & Williams, C.C. (2008). Gender similarities characterize math performance. *Science, 321*, 494-495.

Hyman, I., Eisenstein, J., Amidon, A., & Kay, B. (2001, August 28). An update on the cross-cultural study of corporal punishment and abuse. In F. Farley (Chair), *Cross cultural aspects of corporal punishment and abuse: A research update.* Symposium presented at the 2001 Annual Convention of the American Psychological Association, San Francisco, CA.

Hyson, M., Copple, C., & Jones, J. (2006). Early childhood development and education. In W. Damon & R. Lerner (Eds.), *Handbook of child psychology* (6th ed.). New York: Wiley.

I

Ibrahim, W., Atif, Y., Shualb, K., & Sampson, D. (2015). A web-based course assessment tool with direct mapping to student outcomes. *Educational Technology & Society, 18*(2), 46-59.

IDRA. (2013, October). *The Valued Youth Program newsletter.* San Antonio, TX: IDRA.

Ikram, U.Z., & others (2016). Perceived ethnic discrimination and depressive symptoms: The buffering effects of ethnic identity, religion, and ethnic social network. *Social Psychiatry and Psychiatric Epidemiology, 51*, 679-688.

Imuta, K., Hayne, H., & Scarf, D. (2014). I want it all and I want it now: Delay of gratification in preschool children. *Developmental Psychobiology, 56*, 1541-1552.

International Montessori Council. (2006). *Larry Page and Sergey Brin, founders of Google.com, credit their Montessori education for much of their success on prime-time television.* Retrieved March 24, 2006, from www.Montessori.org/enews/barbara_walters.html

Irvine, J.J. (1990). *Black students and school failure.* New York: Greenwood Press.

ISTE. (2007a). *National educational technology standards for students* (2nd ed.). Eugene, OR: Author.

ISTE. (2007b). *National educational technology standards for teachers.* Eugene, OR: Author.

ISTE. (2016, June). *Redefining learning in a technology-driven world.* Arlington, VA: ISTE.

Izard, C.E., & others (2008). Accelerating the development of emotional competence in Head Start children: Effects on adaptive and maladaptive behavior. *Development and Psychopathology, 20*, 369-397.

J

Jachyra, P., Atkinson, M., & Washiya, Y. (2015). "Who are you, and what are you doing here?": Methodological considerations in ethnographic health and physical education research. *Ethnography and Education, 10*, 242-261.

Jackson, S.L. (2016). *Research methods* (5th ed.). Boston: Cengage.

Jacoby, N., Overfeld, J., Brinder, E.B., & Heim, C.M. (2016). Stress neurobiology and developmental psychopathology. In D. Cicchetti (Ed.), *Developmental psychopathology* (3rd ed.). New York: Wiley.

James, W. (1899/1993). *Talks to teachers.* New York: W.W. Norton.

Janssen, F.J., Westbroek, H.B., & van Driel, J.H. (2014). How to make guided discovery learning practical for student teachers. *Instructional Science, 42*, 67-90.

Jarjour, I.T. (2015). Neurodevelopmental outcome after extreme prematurity: A review of the literature. *Pediatric Neurology, 52*, 143-152.

Jaroslawska, A.J., & others (2016). Following instructions in a virtual school: Does working memory play a role? *Memory and Cognition, 44*, 580-589.

Jenkins, J., & Jenkins, L. (1987). Making peer tutoring work. *Educational Leadership, 44*, 68-74.

Jenkins, J.M., & Astington, J.W. (1996). Cognitive factors and family structure associated with theory of mind development in young children. *Developmental Psychology, 32*, 70-78.

Jennings, P.A. (2015). *Mindfulness for teachers.* New York: Norton.

Jeong, H., & Hmelo-Silver, C.E. (2016). Seven affordances of Computer-Supported Collaborative Learning: How to support collaborative learning? How can technologies help? *Educational Psychologist, 51*, 247-265.

Jiang, Y. (2014). Exploring teacher questioning as a formative assessment strategy. *RELC Journal, 45*, 287-304.

Jin, H., & Wong, K.Y. (2015). Mapping conceptual understanding of algebraic concepts: An exploratory investigation involving grade 8 Chinese students. *International Journal of Science and Mathematics Education, 13*, 683-703.

Job, V., Bernecker, K., Miketta, S., & Friese, M. (2015). Implicit theories about willpower predict the activation of a rest goal following self-control exertion. *Journal of Personality and Social Psychology, 109*, 694-706.

Job, V., Dweck, C.S., & Walton, G.M. (2010). Ego-depletion—Is it all in your head? Implicit theories about willpower affect self-regulation. *Psychological Science, 21*, 1686-1693.

Johns Hopkins University. (2006). *Research: Tribal connection.* Retrieved January 31, 2008, from http://www.krieger.jhu.edu/research/spotlight/prabhakar.html

Johnson, D.W., & Johnson, R.T. (2002). *Multi-cultural and human relations.* Boston: Allyn & Bacon.

Johnson, D.W., & Johnson, R.T. (2009). *Joining together* (10th ed.). Upper Saddle River, NJ: Pearson.

Johnson, D.W., & Johnson, R.T. (2015). Cooperation and competition and intercultural competence. In J. Bennett (Ed.), *Encyclopedia of intercultural competence.* Thousand Oaks, CA: Sage.

Johnson, D.W., & others (2014). The relationship between motivation and achievement in interdependent situations. *Journal of Applied Social Psychology, 44*, 622-633.

Johnson, J.S., & Newport, E.L. (1991). Critical period effects on universal properties of language: The status of subjacency in the acquisition of a second language. *Cognition, 39*, 215-258.

Johnson, M.H. (2016). Developmental neuroscience, psychophysiology, and genetics. In M.H. Bornstein & M.E. Lamb (Eds.), *Developmental science* (7th ed.). New York: Psychology Press.

Johnson-Laird, P.N. (2008). Mental models and deductive reasoning. In J.E. Adler & L.J. Rips (Eds.), *Reasoning.* New York: Cambridge University Press.

Jonassen, D.H. (2006). *Modeling with technology: Mindtools for conceptual change.* Columbus, OH: Merrill/Prentice-Hall.

Jonassen, D.H. (2010). *Mindtools.* Retrieved February 11, 2010, from http://web.missouri.edu/jonassend/mindtools.html

Jonassen, D.H., & Grabowski, B.L. (1993). *Handbook of individual differences, learning, and instruction.* Mahwah, NJ: Erlbaum.

Jones, B.F., Rasmussen, C.M., & Moffitt, M.C. (1997). *Real-life problem solving.* Washington, DC: American Psychological Association.

Jones, S.M., Bub, K.L., & Raver, C.C. (2013). Unpacking the black box of the CSRP intervention: The mediating roles of teacher-child relationship quality and self-regulation. *Early Education Development, 24*, 1043-1064.

Jones, V., & Jones, L. (2016). *Comprehensive classroom management* (11th ed.). Upper Saddle River, NJ: Pearson.

Jordan, N.C., Glutting, J., & Ramineni, C. (2010). The importance of number sense to mathematics achievement in first and third grades. *Learning and Individual Differences, 20,* 82-88.

Joseph, L. M., Alber-Morgan, S., Cullen, J., & Rouse, C. (2016). The effects of self-questioning on reading comprehension: A literature review. *Reading & Writing Quarterly, 32*(2), 152-173, DOI: 10.1080/10573569.2014.891449

Josephson Institute of Ethics. (2008). *The ethics of American youth, 2008.* Los Angeles: Josephson Institute.

Jouriles, E.N., McDonald, R., & Kouros, C.D. (2016). Interparental conflict and child adjustment. In D. Cicchetti (Ed.), *Developmental psychopathology* (3rd ed.). New York: Wiley.

Joyce, B.R., Weil, M., & Calhoun, E. (2015). *Models of teaching* (9th ed.). Upper Saddle River, NJ: Pearson.

Jung, I., & Suzuki, Y. (2015). Scaffolding strategies for Wiki-based collaboration: Action research in a multicultural Japanese language program. *British Journal of Educational Technology, 46,* 829-838.

Jurkowski, S., & Hanze, M. (2015). How to increase the benefits of cooperation: Effects of training in transactive communication on cooperative learning. *British Journal of Educational Psychology, 85,* 357-371.

Juvonen, J., & Knifsend, C. (2016). School-based peer relationships and achievement motivation. In K. Wentzel & D. Miele (Eds.), *Handbook of motivation at school* (2nd ed.). New York: Routledge.

K

Kaderavek, J.N. (2015). *Language disorders in children* (2nd ed.). Upper Saddle River, NJ: Pearson.

Kaendler, C., Wiedmann, M., Rummel, N., & Spada, H. (2015). Teacher competencies for the implementation of collaborative learning in the classroom: A framework and research review. *Educational Psychology Review, 27,* 505-536.

Kagan, J. (1965). Reflection-impulsivity and reading development in primary grade children. *Child Development, 36,* 609-628.

Kagan, J. (2002). Behavioral inhibition as a temperamental category. In R.J. Davidson, K.R. Scherer, & H.H. Goldsmith (Eds.), *Handbook of affective sciences.* New York: Oxford University Press.

Kagan, J. (2010). Emotions and temperament. In M.H. Bornstein (Ed.), *Handbook of developmental cultural science.* New York: Psychology Press.

Kagan, J. (2013). Temperamental contributions to inhibited and uninhibited profiles. In P.D. Zelazo (Ed.), *Oxford handbook of developmental psychology.* New York: Oxford University Press.

Kagan, S. (1992). *Cooperative learning.* San Juan Capistrano, CA: Resources for Teachers.

Kagitcibasi, C. (2007). *Family, self, and human development across cultures.* Mahwah, NJ: Erlbaum.

Kahn, S., & Ginther, D. (2017). Women and STEM. No 23525. NBER Working Papers, National Bureau of Economic Research. Retrieved from: https://EconPapers.repec.org/RePEc:nbr:nberwo:23525

Kail, R.V. (2007). Longitudinal evidence that increases in processing speed and working memory enhance children's reasoning. *Psychological Science, 18,* 312-313.

Kamii, C. (1985). *Young children reinvent arithmetic: Implications of Piaget's theory.* New York: Teachers College Press.

Kamii, C. (1989). *Young children continue to reinvent arithmetic.* New York: Teachers College Press.

Kamps, D.M., & others (2008). The efficacy of ClassWide peer tutoring in middle schools. *Education and Treatment of Children, 31,* 119-152.

Kana, R.K., & others (2016). Aberrant functioning of the theory-of-mind network in children and adolescents with autism. *Molecular Autism.* doi:10.1186/s13229-015-0052-x

Kara, F., & Celikler, D. (2015). Development achievement test: Validity and reliability study for achievement test on matter changing. *Journal of Education and Practice, 6*(24), 21-26.

Karmiloff-Smith, A. (2017). *Thinking developmentally from constructivism to neuroconstructivism.* New York: Routledge.

Karniol, R., Grosz, E., & Schorr, I. (2003). Caring, gender-role orientation, and volunteering. *Sex Roles, 49,* 11-19.

Katz, L. (1999). Curriculum disputes in early childhood education. *ERIC Clearinghouse on Elementary and Early Childhood Education,* Document EDO-PS-99-13.

Kauffman, J.M., & Landrum, T.J. (2009). *Characteristics of emotional and behavioral disorders of children and youth* (9th ed.). Boston: Allyn & Bacon.

Kauffman, J.M., McGee, K., & Brigham, M. (2004). Enabling or disabling? Observations on changes in special education. *Phi Delta Kappan, 85,* 613-620.

Kavanaugh, R.D. (2006). Pretend play and theory of mind. In L.L. Balter & C.S. Tamis-LeMonda (Eds.), *Child psychology* (2nd ed.). New York: Psychology Press.

Kayaoglu, M.N. (2015). Teacher researchers in action research in a heavily centralized education system. *Educational Action Research, 23,* 140-161.

Kazdin, A.E. (2017). *REVEL for research design in clinical psychology* (5th ed.). Upper Saddle River, NJ: Pearson.

Keating, D.P. (1990). Adolescent thinking. In S.S. Feldman & G.R. Elliott (Eds.), *At the threshold: The developing adolescent.* Cambridge, MA: Harvard University Press.

Kellogg, R.T. (1994). *The psychology of writing.* New York: Oxford University Press.

Kelly, D., & others (2013). *Performance of U.S. 15-year-old students in mathematics, science, and reading literacy in an international context.* Washington, DC: National Center for Education Statistics.

Kelly, S. (2008). Tracking. In N.J. Salkind. (Ed.), *Encyclopedia of educational psychology.* Thousand Oaks, CA: Sage.

Kennedy, J. (2015). Using TPCK as a scaffold to self-assess the novice online teaching experience. *Distance Education, 36,* 148-154.

Keogh, B.K. (2003). *Temperament in the classroom.* Baltimore: Paul H. Brookes.

Kharitonova, M., Winter, W., & Sheridan, M.A. (2015). As working memory grows: A developmental account of neural bases of working memory capacity in 5- to 8-year-old children and adults. *Journal of Cognitive Neuroscience, 27,* 1775-1788.

Killen, M., & Smetana, J.G. (2015). Morality: Origins and development. In R.M. Lerner (Ed.), *Handbook of child psychology and developmental science* (7th ed.). New York: Wiley.

Kim, A-Y. (2015). Exploring ways to provide diagnostic feedback with ESL placement test: Cognitive diagnostic assessment of L2 reading ability. *Language Testing, 2,* 227-258.

Kim, H.J., Yang, J., & Lee, M.S. (2015). Changes in heart rate variability during methylphenidate treatment in attention deficit hyperactivity disorder children: A 12-week prospective study. *Yonsei Medical Journal, 56,* 1365-1371.

Kim, K.H. (2010, May). Unpublished data. School of Education, College of William & Mary, Williamsburg, VA.

Kim, M., & Covino, K. (2015). When stories don't make sense: Alternative ways to assess young children's narratives in social contexts. *Reading Teacher, 68,* 357-361.

Kindermann, T.A. (2016). Peer group influences on students' academic motivation. In K.R. Wentzel & G.B. Ramani (Eds.), *Handbook of social influences in school contexts.* New York: Routledge.

King, C.T., Chase-Lansdale, P.L., & Small, M. (Eds.). (2015). *Two generations, one future: An anthology from the Ascend Fellowship.* Washington, DC: Ascend at the Aspen Institute.

King, L. (2007, June 7). The standards complaint. *USA Today*, p. 11D.

Kirschner, P.A., Kreijns, K., Phielix, C., & Fransen, J. (2015). Awareness of cognitive and social behavior in a CSCL environment. *Journal of Computer Assisted Learning, 31,* 59-77.

Kitsantas, A., & Cleary, T.J. (2016). The development of self-regulated learning in secondary school: A social cognitive instructional perspective. In K. Wentzel & D. Miele (Eds.), *Handbook of motivation at school* (2nd ed.). New York: Routledge.

Kivel, P. (1995). *Uprooting racism: How White people can work for racial justice.* Philadelphia: New Society.

Klein, A. (2019). States, districts tackle the tough work of making ESSA a reality. *Education Week, 38*(27), 4-6.

Klein, S. (2012). *State of public school segregation in the United States, 2007-2010.* Washington, DC: Feminist Majority Foundation.

Klimstra, T.A., Luyckx, K., Germeijs, V., Meeus, W.H., & Goossens, L. (2012). Personality traits and educational identity formation in late adolescents: Longitudinal associations and academic progress. *Journal of Youth and Adolescence, 41,* 346-361.

Klug, J., & others (2016). Secondary school students' LLL competencies and their relation with classroom structure and achievement. *Frontiers in Psychology, 7,* 680.

Kluhara, S.A., Graham, S., & Hawken, L.S. (2009). Teaching writing to high school students: A national survey. *Journal of Educational Psychology, 101,* 136-160.

Kobak, R.R., & Kerig, P.K. (2015). Introduction to the special issue: Attachment-based treatments for adolescents. *Attachment and Human Development, 17,* 111-118.

Koehler, M.J., & Mishra, P. (2010). Introducing technological pedagogical content knowledge (TPCK), AACTE's Committee on Innovation and Technology (Eds.), *The handbook of technological pedagogical content knowledge for educators.* New York: Routledge.

Koenig, M.A., & others (2015). Reasoning about knowledge: Children's evaluations of generality and verifiability. *Cognitive Psychology, 83,* 22-39.

Kohlberg, L. (1976). Moral stages and moralization: The cognitive-developmental approach. In T. Lickona (Ed.), *Moral development and behavior.* New York: Holt, Rinehart & Winston.

Kohlberg, L. (1986). A current statement of some theoretical issues. In S. Modgil & C. Modgil (Eds.), *Lawrence Kohlberg.* Philadelphia: Falmer.

Koppelman, K.L. (2017). *Understanding human differences* (5th ed.). Upper Saddle River, NJ: Pearson.

Kormi-Nouri, R., & others (2015). Academic stress as a health measure and its relationship to patterns of emotion in collectivist and individualist cultures: Similarities and differences. *International Journal of Higher Education, 4,* 92-104.

Kostons, D., & van der Werf, G. (2015). The effects of activating prior topic and metacognitive knowledge on text comprehension scores. *British Journal of Educational Psychology, 85,* 264-275.

Kounin, J.S. (1970). *Discipline and management in classrooms.* New York: Holt, Rinehart & Winston.

Kozol, J. (1991). *Savage inequalities.* New York: Crown.

Kozol, J. (2005). *The shame of the nation.* New York: Crown.

Krajcik, J.S., & Blumenfeld, P.C. (2006). Project-based learning. In R.K. Sawyer (Ed.), *The Cambridge handbook of learning sciences.* New York: Oxford University Press.

Krathwohl, D.R., Bloom, B.S., & Masia, B.B. (1964). *Taxonomy of educational objectives. Handbook II: Affective domain.* New York: David McKay.

Kreutzer, L.C., & Flavell, J.H. (1975). An interview study of children's knowledge about memory. *Monographs of the Society for Research in Child Development, 40* (1, Serial No. 159).

Kroger, J. (2015). Identity development through adulthood: The move toward "wholeness." In K.C. McLean & M. Syed (Eds.), *Oxford handbook of identity development.* New York: Oxford University Press.

Kucian, K., & von Aster, M. (2015). Developmental dyscalculia. *European Journal of Pediatrics, 174,* 1-13.

Kuebli, J. (1994, March). Young children's understanding of everyday emotions. *Young Children,* pp. 36-48.

Kuhn, D. (2009). Adolescent thinking. In R.M. Lerner & L. Steinberg (Eds.), *Handbook of adolescent psychology* (3rd ed.). New York: Wiley.

Kuhn, D., & Franklin, S. (2006). The second decade: What develops (and how)? In W. Damon & R. Lerner (Eds.), *Handbook of child psychology* (6th ed.). New York: Wiley.

Kuhn, D., Katz, J., & Dean, D. (2004). Developing reason. *Thinking & Reasoning, 10*(2), 197-219.

Kuhn, S., & Lindenberger, U. (2016). Research on human plasticity in adulthood: A lifespan agenda. In K.W. Schaie & S.L. Willis (Eds.), *Handbook of the psychology of aging* (8th ed.). New York: Elsevier.

Kunzmann, R. (2003). From teacher to student: The value of teacher education for experienced teachers. *Journal of Teacher Education, 54,* 241-253.

Kyllonen, P.C. (2016). Human cognitive abilities. In L. Corno & E.M. Anderman (Eds.), *Handbook of educational psychology* (6th ed.). New York: Routledge.

L

Ladd, G.W., Birch, S.H., & Buhs, E.S. (1999). Children's social and scholastic lives in kindergarten: Related spheres of influence? *Child Development, 70*(6), 1373-1400.

Ladson-Billings, G. (1995). But that's just good teaching! The case for culturally relevant pedagogy. *Theory into Practice, 34*(3), 159-165. DOI: HYPERLINK "http://dx.doi.org/10.1080/00405849509543675" HYPERLINK "http://dx.doi.org/10.1080/00405849509543675" 10.1080/00405849509543675

Ladson-Billings, G. (2006). From the achievement gap to the education debt: Understanding achievement in U.S. schools. *Educational Researcher, 35*(7), 3-12.

Lai, Y., & others (2015). Effects of mathematics anxiety and mathematical metacognition on word problem solving in children with and without mathematical learning difficulties. *PLoS One, 10,* e0130570.

Laible, D., Thompson, R.A., & Froimson, J. (2015). Early socialization. In J.E. Grusec & P.D. Hastings (Eds.), *Handbook of socialization* (2nd ed.). New York: Guilford.

Lalley, J.P., & Gentile, J.R. (2009). Classroom assessment and grading to assure mastery. *Theory Into Practice, 48,* 28-35.

Lamela, D., Figueiredo, B., Bastos, A., & Feinberg, M. (2016). Typologies of post-divorce coparenting and parental well-being, parenting quality, and children's psychological adjustment. *Child Psychiatry and Human Development, 47,* 716-728.

Lanciano, T., & Curci, A. (2014). Incremental validity of emotional intelligence ability in predicting academic achievement. *American Journal of Psychology, 127,* 447-461.

Landa, S. (2000, Fall). If you can't make waves, make ripples. *Intelligence Connections Newsletter of the ASCD, X* (1), 6-8.

Lane, J.D., Evans, E.M., Brink, K.A., & Wellman, H.M. (2016). Developing concepts of ordinary and extraordinary communication. *Developmental Psychology, 52,* 19-30.

Langbeheim, E. (2015). A project-based course on Newton's laws for talented junior high-school students. *Physics Education, 50,* 410-415.

Langel, N. (2015). Kent Intermediate School District, Kent Innovation High School. In S. Page (Ed.), *Connect* (Issue 2). Philadelphia: Center on Innovations in Learning, Temple University.

Langer, E. (1997). *The power of mindful learning.* Reading, MA: Addison-Wesley.

Langer, E. (2005). *On becoming an artist.* New York: Ballantine.

Lansford, J.E. (2013). Single- and two-parent families. In J. Hattie & E. Anderman (Eds.), *International guide to student achievement.* New York: Routledge.

Laranjo, J., Bernier, A., Meins, E., & Carlson, S.M. (2010). Early manifestations of theory of mind: The roles of maternal mind-mindedness and infant security of attachment. *Infancy, 15,* 300-323.

Larson, R.W. (2007). Development of the capacity for teamwork in youth development. In R.K. Silbereisen & R.M. Lerner (Eds.), *Approaches to positive youth development.* Thousand Oaks, CA: Sage.

Larson, R.W. (2014). Studying experience: Pursuing the "something more." In R.W. Lerner & others (Eds.), *The developmental science of adolescence: History through autobiography.* New York: Springer.

Larson, R.W., & Dawes, N.P. (2015). How to cultivate adolescents' motivation: Effective strategies employed by the professional staff of American youth programs. In S. Joseph (Ed.), *Positive psychology in practice.* New York: Wiley.

Larson, R.W., & Verma, S. (1999). How children and adolescents spend time across the world: Work, play, and developmental opportunities. *Psychological Bulletin, 125,* 701-736.

Larson, R., Wilson, S., & Rickman, A. (2009). Globalization, societal change, and adolescence across the world. In R.M. Lerner & L. Steinberg (Eds.), *Handbook of adolescent psychology* (3rd ed.). New York: Wiley.

Larzelere, R.E., & Kuhn, B.R. (2005). Comparing child outcomes of physical punishment and alternative discipline tactics: A meta-analysis. *Clinical Child and Family Psychology Review, 8,* 1-37.

Leaper, C. (2013). Gender development during childhood. In P.D. Zelazo (Ed.), *Oxford handbook of developmental psychology.* New York: Oxford University Press.

Leaper, C. (2015). Gender development from a social-cognitive perspective. In R.M. Lerner (Ed.), *Handbook of child psychology and developmental science* (7th ed.). New York: Wiley.

Leaper, C., & Brown, C.S. (2008). Perceived experiences with sexism among adolescent girls. *Child Development, 79,* 685-704.

Leaper, C., & Brown, C.S. (2015). Sexism in schools. In L.S. Liben & R.S. Bigler (Eds.), *Advances in Child Development and Behavior.* San Diego: Elsevier.

Leaper, C., & Farkas, T. (2015). The socialization of gender during childhood and adolescence. In J.E. Grusec & P.D. Hastings (Eds.), *Handbook of socialization* (2nd ed.). New York: Guilford.

Leary, M.R. (2017). *REVEL for introduction to behavioral research methods* (7th ed.). Upper Saddle River, NJ: Pearson.

Lee, C.D., & Slaughter-Defoe, D. (1995). Historical and sociocultural influences of African American education. In J.A. Banks, & C.M. Banks (Eds.), *Handbook of research on multicultural education.* New York: Macmillan.

Lee, R., Zhai, F., Brooks-Gunn, J., Han, W.J., & Waldfogel, J. (2014). Head Start participation and school readiness: Evidence from the Early Childhood Longitudinal Study-Birth Cohort. *Developmental Psychology, 50,* 202-215.

Lee, T-W., Wu, Y-T., Yu, Y., Wu, H-C., & Chen, T-J. (2012). A smarter brain is associated with stronger neural interaction in healthy young females: A resting EEG coherence study. *Intelligence, 40,* 38-48.

Lehr, C.A., Hanson, A., Sinclair, M.F., & Christensen, S.I. (2003). Moving beyond dropout prevention towards school completion. *School Psychology Review, 32,* 342-364.

Lehrer, R., & Schauble, L. (2015). The development of scientific thinking. In R.M. Lerner (Ed.), *Handbook of child psychology and developmental science* (7th ed.). New York: Wiley.

Lepper, M.R., Corpus, J.H., & Iyengar, S.S. (2005). Intrinsic and extrinsic orientations in the classroom: Age differences and academic correlates. *Journal of Educational Psychology, 97,* 184-196.

Lepper, M.R., Greene, D., & Nisbett, R. (1973). Undermining children's intrinsic interest with intrinsic rewards: A test of the over-justification hypothesis. *Journal of Personality and Social Psychology, 28,* 129-137.

Lereya, S.T., Samara, M., & Wolke, D. (2013). Parenting behavior and the risk of becoming a victim and a bully/victim: A meta-analysis study. *Child Abuse and Neglect, 37*(12), 1091-1098.

Lerner, R.M., Boyd, M., & Du, D. (2008). Adolescent development. In I.B. Weiner & C.B. Craighead (Eds.), *Encyclopedia of psychology* (4th ed.). New York: Wiley.

Lesaux, N., & Siegel, L. (2003). The development of reading in children who speak English as a second language. *Developmental Psychology, 39,* 1005-1019.

Leslie, S.J., Cimpian, A., Meyer, M., & Freeland, E. (2015). Expectations of brilliance underlie gender distributions across academic disciplines. *Science, 347,* 262-265.

Leu, D.J., & Kinzer, C.K. (2017). *Phonics, phonemic awareness, and word analysis for teachers* (10th ed.). Upper Saddle River, NJ: Pearson.

Leung, K.C. (2015). Preliminary empirical model of crucial determinants of best practices for peer tutoring on academic achievement. *Journal of Educational Psychology, 107,* 558-579.

Lever-Duffy, J., & McDonald, J. (2015). *Teaching and learning with technology* (5th ed.). Upper Saddle River, NJ: Pearson.

Levin, J. (1980). *The mnemonics 80s: Key-words in the classroom.* Theoretical paper No. 86. Wisconsin Research and Development Center for Individualized Schooling, Madison.

Levin, J.A., Fox, J.A., & Forde, D.R. (2015). *Elementary statistics in social research* (12th ed.). Upper Saddle River, NJ: Pearson.

Levstik, L. (2017). Learning history. In R.E. Mayer & P.A. Alexander (Eds.), *Handbook of research on learning and instruction* (2nd ed.). New York: Routledge.

Lewanda, A.F., & others (2016). Preoperative evaluation and comprehensive risk assessment for children with Down syndrome. *Pediatric Anesthesia, 26,* 356-362.

Lewis, A.C. (2007). Looking beyond NCLB. *Phi Delta Kappan, 88,* 483-484.

Lewis, K.M., & others (2013). Problem behavior and urban, low-income youth: A randomized controlled trial of Positive Action in Chicago. *American Journal of Prevention, 44,* 622-630.

Lewis, M. (2016). Self-conscious emotions: Embarrassment, pride, shame, guilt, and hubris. In L.F. Barrett, M. Lewis, & J.M. Haviland-Jones (Eds.), *Handbook of emotion* (4th ed.). New York: Guilford.

Lewis, R.B., Wheeler, J.J., & Carter, S.L. (2017). *Teaching students with special needs* (9th ed.). Upper Saddle River, NJ: Pearson.

Liben, L.S. (1995). Psychology meets geography: Exploring the gender gap on the national geography bee. *Psychological Science Agenda, 8,* 8-9.

Liben, L.S. (2015). Probability values and human values in evaluating single-sex education. *Sex Roles, 72,* 401-426.

Lillard, A.S. (2017). *Montessori* (3rd ed.). New York: Oxford University Press.

Linnenbrink-Garcia, L., & Patall, E.A. (2016). Motivation. In L. Corno & E.M. Anderman (Eds.), *Handbook of educational psychology* (3rd ed.). New York: Routledge.

Lipsitz, J. (1984). *Successful schools for young adolescents.* New Brunswick, NJ: Transaction Books.

Litton, E.F. (1999). Learning in America: The Filipino-American sociocultural perspective. In C. Park & M.M. Chi (Eds.), *Asian-American education: Prospects and challenges.* Westport, CT: Bergin & Garvey.

Lockl, K., & Schneider, W. (2007). Knowledge about the mind: Links between theory of mind and later metamemory. *Child Development, 78,* 147-167.

Logan, J. (1997). *Teaching stories.* New York: Kodansha International.

Logie, R.H., & Cowan, N. (2015). Perspectives on working memory: Introduction to the special issue. *Memory and Cognition, 43,* 315-324.

Los, B. (2015). *A historical syntax of English.* New York: Oxford University Press.

Loughland, T., & Kilpatrick, L. (2015). Formative assessment in primary science. *Education 3-13, 43,* 128-141.

Lozano, E., & others (2015). Problem-based learning supported by semantic techniques. *Interactive Learning Environments, 23,* 37-54.

Lubinski, D. (2009). Exceptional cognitive ability: The phenotype. *Behavior Genetics, 39,* 350-358.

Luders, E., Narr, K.L., Thompson, P.M., & Toga, A.W. (2009). Neuroanatomical correlates of intelligence. *Intelligence, 37,* 156-163.

Luiselli, J.K., & Fischer, A.J. (Eds.). (2016). *Computer-assisted and web-based instruction in psychology, special education, and health.* New York: Elsevier.

Lunday, A. (2006). *Two Homewood seniors collect Marshall, Mitchell scholarships.* Retrieved January 31, 2008, from http://www.jhu.edu/~gazette/2006/04dec06/04schol.html

Luria, A., & Herzog, E. (1985, April). *Gender segregation across and within settings.* Paper presented at the biennial meeting of the Society for Research in Child Development, Toronto.

Luthar, S.S. (2006). Resilience in development: A synthesis of research across five decades. In D. Cicchetti & D.J. Cohen (Eds.), *Developmental psychopathology* (2nd ed.). Hoboken, NJ: Wiley.

Luthar, S.S., Barkin, S.H., & Crossman, E.J. (2013). "I can, therefore I must": Fragility in the upper-middle classes. *Development and Psychopathology, 25,* 1529-1549.

Luthar, S.S., Crossman, E.J., & Small, P.J. (2015). Resilience in the face of adversities. In R.M. Lerner (Ed.), *Handbook of child psychology and developmental science* (7th ed.). New York: Wiley.

Lyon, T.D., & Flavell, J.H. (1993). Young children's understanding of forgetting over time. *Child Development, 64,* 789-800.

Lyytinen, H., & others (2015). Dyslexia—early identification and prevention: Highlights from the Jyvaskyla Longitudinal Study of Dyslexia. *Current Developmental Disorders Reports, 2,* 330-338.

M

Maccoby, E.E. (1998). *The two sexes: Growing up apart, coming together.* Cambridge, MA: Harvard University.

Maccoby, E.E. (2007). Historical overview of socialization research and theory. In J.E. Grusec & P.D. Hastings (Eds.), *Handbook of socialization.* New York: Guilford.

Maccoby, E.E., & Jacklin, C.N. (1974). *The psychology of sex differences.* Palo Alto, CA: Stanford University Press.

Madjar, N., Shklar, N., & Moshe, L. (2016). The role of parental attitudes in children's motivation toward homework assignments. *Psychology in the Schools, 53,* 173-188.

Mager, R. (1962). *Preparing instructional objectives* (2nd ed.). Palo Alto, CA: Fearon.

Magnusson, S.J., & Palincsar, A.S. (2005). Teaching to promote the development of scientific knowledge and reasoning about light at the elementary school level. In *How students learn.* Washington, DC: National Academies Press.

Mahlberg, J. (2015). Formative self-assessment college classes improves self-regulation and retention in first/second year community college students. *Community College Journal of Research and Practice, 39,* 772-783.

Mahoney, J., Parente, M.E., & Zigler, E. (2010). After-school program engagement and in-school competence: Program quality, content, and staffing. In J. Meece & J. Eccles (Eds.), *Handbook of schools, schooling, and human development.* New York: Routledge.

Malinin, L.H. (2016). Creative practices embodied, embedded, and enacted in architectural settings: Toward a model of creativity. *Frontiers in Psychology, 6,* 1978.

Malone, M., Cornell, D. G., & Shukla, K. (2019). Grade configuration is associated with school-level standardized test pass rates for sixth-, seventh-, and eighth-grade students. *School Effectiveness and School Improvement, 1.* DOI: 10.1080/09243453.2019.1654526.

Maloy, R.W., Verock, R-E., Edwards, S.A., & Woolf, B.P. (2017). *Transforming learning with new technologies* (3rd ed.). Upper Saddle River, NJ: Pearson.

Mammarella, I.C., Hill, F., Devine, A., Caviola, S., & Szucs, D. (2015). Math anxiety and developmental dyscalculia: A study of working memory processes. *Journal of Clinical and Experimental Neuroscience, 37,* 878-887.

Mandinach, E.B., & Lash, A.A. (2016). Assessment illuminating paths of learning. In L. Corno & E.M. Anderman (Eds.), *Handbook of educational psychology* (3rd ed.). New York: Routledge.

Mandler, G. (1980). Recognizing: The judgment of previous occurrence. *Psychological Review, 87,* 252-271.

Manis, F.R., Keating, D.P., & Morrison, F.J. (1980). Developmental differences in the allocation of processing capacity. *Journal of Experimental Child Psychology, 29,* 156-169.

Manning, J. (2017). *Practical approach to communication.* Upper Saddle River, NJ: Pearson.

Marchel, M.A., Fischer, T.A., & Clark, D.M. (2015). *Assistive technology for children and youth with disabilities.* Upper Saddle River, NJ: Pearson.

Marcia, J.E. (1980). Identity in adolescence. In J. Adelson (Ed.), *Handbook of adolescent psychology.* New York: Wiley.

Marcia, J.E. (1998). Optimal development from an Eriksonian perspective. In H.S. Friedman (Ed.), *Encyclopedia of mental health* (Vol. 2). San Diego: Academic Press.

Mares, M-L., & Pan, Z. (2013). Effects of *Sesame Street:* A meta-analysis of children's learning in 15 countries. *Journal of Applied Developmental Psychology, 34,* 140-151.

Margolis, A., & others (2013). Using IQ discrepancy scores to examine neural correlates of specific cognitive abilities. *Journal of Neuroscience, 33,* 14135-14145.

Marino, C., & others (2016). Modeling the contribution of personality, social identity, and social norms to problematic Facebook use in adolescents. *Addictive Behaviors, 63,* 51-56.

Marklein, M.B. (1998, November 24). An eye-level meeting of the minds. *USA Today,* p. 9D.

Marks, A.K., Ejesi, K., McCullough, M.B., & Garcia Coll, C. (2015). Developmental implications of discrimination. In R.M. Lerner (Ed.), *Handbook of child psychology and developmental science* (7th ed.). New York: Wiley.

Marshall Scholarships. (2007). *Scholar profiles: 2007.* Retrieved January 31, 2008, from http://www.marshallscholarship.org/profiles2007.html

Marshall, P.S., Hoelzle, J.B., Hyederdahl, D., & Nelson, D.W. (2016). The impact of failing to identify suspect effort in patients undergoing adult attention-deficit/hyperactivity disorder (ADHD) assessment. *Psychological Assessment.* doi:10.1037/pas0000340

Martella, R.C., & Marchand-Martella, N.E. (2015). Improving classroom behavior through effective instruction: An illustrative example using SRA FLEX literacy. *Education and Treatment of Children, 38,* 241-271.

Martin, A.J., & Collie, R.J. (2016). The role of teacher-student relationships in unlocking students' academic potential: Exploring motivation, engagement, resilience, adaptability, goals, and instruction. In K.R. Wentzel & G.B. Ramani (Eds.), *Handbook of social influences in school contexts.* New York: Routledge.

Martin, C.L., & Ruble, D.N. (2010). Patterns of gender development. *Annual Review of Psychology* (Vol. 31). Palo Alto, CA: Annual Reviews.

Martin, C.L., & others (2013). The role of sex of peers and gender-typed activities in young children's peer affiliative networks: A longitudinal analysis of selection and influence. *Child Development, 84,* 921-937.

Martin, M.O., Mullis, I.V.S., Foy, P., & Stanco, G.M. (2012). *TIMSS 2011 international results in science.* TIMSS & PIRLS International Study Center, Boston College.

Marton, F., Hounsell, D.J., & Entwistle, N.J. (1984). *The experience of learning.* Edinburgh: Scottish Academic Press.

Mary, A., & others (2016). Executive and attentional contributions to theory of mind deficit in attention deficit/hyperactivity disorder (ADHD). *Child Neuropsychology, 22,* 345-365.

Maslow, A.H. (1954). *Motivation and personality.* New York: Harper & Row.

Maslow, A.H. (1971). *The farther reaches of human nature.* New York: Viking Press.

Maslowsky, J., Owotomo, O., Huntley, E. D., & Keating, D. (2019). Adolescent risk behavior: Differentiating reasoned and reactive risk-taking. *Journal of Youth and Adolescence, 48,* 243-255.

Masten, A.S. (2013). Risk and resilience in development. In P.D. Zelazo (Ed.), *Oxford handbook of developmental psychology.* New York: Oxford University Press.

Masten, A.S. (2014a). Global perspectives on resilience in children and youth. *Child Development, 85,* 6-20.

Masten, A.S. (2014b). *Ordinary magic: Resilience in development.* New York: Guilford.

Masten, A.S. (2016). Pathways to integrated resilience science. *Psychological Inquiry.* doi:10.1080/1047840X.2015.1012041

Masten, A.S., & Cicchetti, D. (2016). Resilience in development: Progress and transformation. In D. Cicchetti (Ed.), *Developmental psychopathology* (3rd ed.). New York: Wiley.

Masten, A.S., & Labella, M.H. (2016). Risk and resilience in child development. In L. Balter & C.S. Tamis-LeMonda (Eds.), *Child psychology* (3rd ed.). New York: Taylor and Frances.

Masten, A.S., & others (2008). School success in motion: Protective factors for academic achievement in homeless and highly mobile children in Minneapolis. *Center for Urban and Regional Affairs Reporter, 38,* 3-12.

Mathes, P.G., Torgesen, J.K., & Allor, J. H. (2001). The effects of peer-assisted literacy strategies for first-grade readers with and without additional computer-assisted instruction in phonological awareness. *American Educational Research Journal, 38,* 371-410.

Matsumoto, D., & Juang, L. (2017). *Culture and psychology* (6th ed.). Boston: Cengage.

Matusov, E., Bell, N., & Rogoff, B. (2001). *Schooling as a cultural process: Working together and guidance by children from schools differing in collaborative practices.* Unpublished manuscript, Department of Psychology, University of California at Santa Cruz.

Maxim, G.W. (2014). *Dynamic social studies for constructivist classrooms* (10th ed.). Upper Saddle River, NJ: Pearson.

Maxwell, L.A. (2014, 08/20). U.S. school enrollment hits majority-minority milestone. *Education Week,* 1-7.

Mayer, R.E. (1997). Multimedia learning: Are we asking the right questions? *Educational Psychologist, 32,* 1-19.

Mayer, R.E. (2004). Should there be a three-strike rule against pure discovery learning? *American Psychologist, 59,* 14-19.

Mayer, R.E. (2004). Teaching of subject matter. *Annual Review of Psychology* (Vol. 55). Palo Alto, CA: Annual Reviews.

Mayer, R.E. (2008). *Learning and instruction* (2nd ed.). Upper Saddle River, NJ: Prentice Hall.

Mayer, R.E., & Alexander, P.A. (Eds.). (2017). *Handbook of research on learning and instruction* (2nd ed.). New York: Routledge.

McAllum, R. (2014). Reciprocal teaching: Critical reflection on practice. *Kairaranga, 15,* 26-35.

McCall, A. (2007). Supporting exemplary social studies teaching in elementary schools. *Social Studies, 97,* 161-167.

McClelland, M.M., Acock, A.C., Piccinin, A., Rhea, S.A., & Stallings, M.C. (2013). Relations between preschool attention span-persistence and age 25 educational outcomes. *Early Childhood Research Quarterly, 28,* 314-324.

McClelland, M.M., Diaz, G., & Lewis, K. (2016). Self-regulation. *In SAGE encyclopedia of contemporary early childhood education.* Thousand Oaks, CA: Sage.

McClelland, M.M., Wanless, S.B., & Lewis, K.W. (2016). Self-regulation. In H. Friedman (Ed.), *Encyclopedia of mental health* (2nd ed.). New York: Elsevier.

McCombs, B.L. (2001, April). https://www.ncbi.nlm.nih.gov/pmc/articles/PMC5298258/

McCombs, B.L. (2010). Learner-centered practices: Providing the context for positive learner development. In J. Meece & J. Eccles (Eds.), *Handbook of research on schools, schooling, and human development.* New York: Routledge.

McCombs, B.I. (2015). Learner-centered online instruction. *New Directions for Teaching and Learning, 144,* 57-71.

McDonald, B.A., Larson, C.D., Dansereau, D., & Spurlin, J.E. (1985). Cooperative dyads: Impact on text learning and transfer. *Contemporary Educational Psychology, 10,* 369-377.

McDonnell, C.G., & others (2016). Mother-child reminiscing at risk: Maternal attachment, elaboration, and child autobiographical memory specificity. *Journal of Experimental Child Psychology, 143,* 65-84.

McFarland, J., Cui, J., Rathbun, A., & Holmes, J. (2018). Trends in High School Dropout and Completion Rates in the United States: 2018 (NCES 2019-117). U.S. Department of Education. Washington, DC: National Center for Education Statistics. Retrieved from http://nces.ed.gov/pubsearch

McGraw-Hill (2015). *Building blocks 2015.* New York: McGraw-Hill Higher Education.

McKay, R. (2008). Multiple intelligences. In N.J. Salkind (Ed.), *Encyclopedia of educational psychology.* Thousand Oaks, CA: Sage.

McKeown, M., & Beck, I.L. (2010). The role of metacognition in understanding and supporting reading comprehension. In D.J. Hacker, J. Dunlosky, & A.C. Graesser (Eds.), *Handbook of metacognition in education.* New York: Psychology Press.

McKown, C., Gumbiner, L. N., & Johnson, J. (2011). Diagnostic efficiency of several methods of identifying socially rejected children and effect of participation rate on classification accuracy. *Journal of School Psychology, 49,* 573-595. doi: https://doi.org/10.1016/j.jsp.2011.06.002

McLean, K.C., & Breen, A.V. (2009). Processes and content of narrative identity development in adolescence: Gender and well-being. *Developmental Psychology, 45,* 702-710.

McLoyd, V., Purtell, K.M., & Hardaway, C.R. (2015). Race, class, and ethnicity as they affect emerging adulthood. In R.M. Lerner (Ed.),

Handbook of child psychology and developmental science (7th ed.). New York: Wiley.

McMillan, J.H. (1997). *Classroom assessment.* Boston: Allyn & Bacon.

McMillan, J.H. (2002). *Essential assessment concepts for teachers and administrators.* Thousand Oaks, CA: Corwin Press.

McMillan, J.H. (2007). *Classroom assessment* (4th ed.). Boston: Allyn & Bacon.

McMillan, J.H. (2008). *Educational research: Fundamentals for the consumer* (5th ed.). Boston: Allyn & Bacon.

McMillan, J.H. (2011). *Classroom assessment* (5th ed.). Boston: Allyn & Bacon.

McMillan, J.H. (2014). *Classroom assessment* (6th ed.). Upper Saddle River, NJ: Pearson.

McMillan, J.H. (2016). *Fundamentals of educational research* (7th ed.). Upper Saddle River, NJ: Pearson.

McNally, D. (1990). *Even eagles need a push.* New York: Dell.

Meece, J.L., Anderman, E.M., & Anderman, L.H. (2006). Classroom goal structure, student motivation, and academic achievement. *Annual Review of Psychology* (Vol. 57). Palo Alto, CA: Annual Reviews.

Meichenbaum, D., Turk, D., & Burstein, S. (1975). The nature of coping with stress. In I. Sarason & C. Spielberger (Eds.), *Stress and anxiety:* Washington, DC: Hemisphere.

Meins, E., & others (2013). Mind-mindedness and theory of mind: Mediating processes of language and perspectival symbolic play. *Child Development, 84,* 1777–1790.

Memari, A., Ziaee, V., Mirfazeli, F., & Kordi, R. (2012). Investigation of autism comorbidities and associations in a school-based community sample. *Journal of Child and Adolescent Psychiatric Nursing, 25,* 84–90.

Menesini, E., Palladino, B.E., & Nocentini, A. (2016). Let's not fall into the trap: Online and school based program to prevent cyberbullying among adolescents. In T. Vollink, F. DeHue, & C. McGuckin (Eds.), *Cyberbullying.* New York: Psychology Press.

Merenda, P. (2004). Cross-cultural adaptation of educational and psychological testing. In R.K. Hambleton, P.F. Merenda, & C.D. Spielberger (Eds.), *Adapting educational and psychological tests for cross-cultural assessment.* Mahwah, NJ: Erlbaum.

Merrell, K.W., Carrizales, D., Feuerborn, L., Gueldner, B.A., & Tran, O.K. (2007). *Strong kids–grades 6-8: A social and emotional learning curriculum.* Baltimore: Brookes.

Metzger, M. (1996, January). Maintaining a life. *Phi Delta Kappan, 77,* 346–351.

Michaels, S. (1986). Narrative presentations: An oral presentation for literacy with first graders. In J. Cook-Gumperz (Ed.), *The social construction of literacy.* New York: Cambridge University Press.

Middleton, J., & Goepfert, P. (1996). *Inventive strategies for teaching mathematics.* Washington, DC: American Psychological Association.

Midgley, C., Anderman, E., & Hicks, L. (1995). Differences between elementary school and middle school teachers and students: A goal theory approach. *Journal of Early Adolescence, 15,* 90–113.

Miele, D.B., & Scholer, A.A. (2016). Self-regulation of motivation. In K. Wentzel & D. Miele (Eds.), *Handbook of motivation at school* (2nd ed.). New York: Routledge.

Miles, N.G., & Soares da Costa, T.P. (2016). Acceptances of clickers in a large multimodal biochemistry class as determined by student evaluations of teaching: Are they just an annoying distraction for distance students? *Biochemistry and Molecular Biology Education, 44,* 99–108.

Miller, A.D., Murdock, T. B., & Grotewiel, M. M. (2017). Addressing academic dishonesty among the highest achievers. *Theory Into Practice, 56*(2), 121–128.

Miller, E.B., Farkas, G., & Duncan, G.J. (2016). Does Head Start differentially benefit children with risk by the program's service model? *Early Child Research Quarterly, 34,* 1–12.

Miller, E.B., Farkas, G., Vandell, D.L., & Duncan, G.J. (2014). Do the effects of Head Start vary by parental preacademic stimulation? *Child Development, 85,* 1385–1400.

Miller, E.M., & others (2012). Theories of willpower affect sustained learning. *PLoS One, 7*(6),

Miller, G.A. (1956). The magical number seven, plus or minus two: Some limits on our capacity for information processing. *Psychological Review, 48,* 337–442.

Miller-Jones, D. (1989). Culture and testing. *American Psychologist, 44,* 360–366.

Mills, D., & Mills, C. (2000). *Hungarian kindergarten curriculum translation.* London: Mills Production.

Mills, G.E., & Gay, L.R. (2016). *Educational research* (11th ed.). Upper Saddle River, NJ: Pearson.

Mills, M.T. (2015). Narrative performance of gifted African American school-aged children from low-income backgrounds. *American Journal of Speech-Language Pathology, 24,* 36–46.

Miltenberger, R.G. (2016). *Behavior modification* (6th ed.). Boston: Cengage.

Minuchin, P.P., & Shapiro, E.K. (1983). The school as a context for social development. In P.H. Mussen (Ed.), *Handbook of child psychology* (4th ed., Vol. 4). New York: Wiley.

Mischel, W. (2014). *The marshmallow test: Mastering self-control.* Boston: Little Brown.

Mischel, W., Ebbesen, E.B., & Zeiss, A.R. (1972). Cognitive and attentional mechanisms in delay of gratification. *Journal of Personality and Social Psychology, 21,* 204–218.

Mischel, W., & Moore, B. (1973). Effects of attention to symbolically presented rewards on self-control. *Journal of Personality and Social Psychology, 28,* 172–179.

Mishra, P., & Koehler, M.J. (2006). Technological pedagogical content knowledge: A new framework for teacher knowledge. *Teachers College Record, 108,* 1017–1054.

Mitchell, A.B., & Stewart, J.B. (2013). The efficacy of all-male academies: Insights from critical race theory (CRT). *Sex Roles, 69,* 382–392.

Mitee, T.L., & Obaitan, G.N. (2015). Effect of mastery learning on senior secondary school students' cognitive learning outcome in quantitative chemistry. *Journal of Education and Practice, 6*(5), 34–38.

Mizala, A., Martinez, F., & Martinez, S. (2015). Pre-service elementary school teachers' expectations about student performance: How their beliefs are affected by their mathematics anxiety and student's gender. *Teaching and Teacher Education, 50,* 70–78.

Moffitt, T.E. (2012). *Childhood self-control predicts adult health, wealth, and crime.* Paper presented at the Symposium on Symptom Improvement in Well-Being, Copenhagen.

Moffitt, T.E., & others (2011). A gradient of childhood self-control predicts health, wealth, and public safety. *Proceedings of the National Academy of Sciences U.S.A., 108,* 2693–2698.

Mohammadjani, F., & Tonkaboni, F. (2015). A comparison between the effect of cooperative learning teaching method and lecture teaching method on students' learning and satisfaction level. *International Education Studies, 9,* 107–112.

Mohammadzadeh, A., & others (2016). Understanding intentionality in children with attention-deficit/hyperactivity disorder. *Attention Deficit and Hyperactivity Disorders, 8,* 73–78.

Molinero, C., & others (2016). Usefulness of the WISC-IV in determining intellectual giftedness. *Spanish Journal of Psychology.* doi:10.1017/sjp.2015.63

Moll, L.C., & González, N. (2004). Engaging life: A funds of knowledge approach to multicultural education. In J.A. Banks & C.A.M. Banks (Eds.), *Handbook of research on multicultural education* (2nd ed.). San Francisco: Jossey-Bass.

Monahan, K.C., & others (2016). Integration of developmental neuroscience and contextual approaches to the study of adolescent development. In D. Cicchetti (Ed.), *Developmental psychopathology* (3rd ed.). New York: Wiley.

Moore, D.S. (2013). Behavioral genetics, genetics, and epigenetics. In P.D. Zelazo (Ed.), *Handbook of developmental psychology*. New York: Oxford University Press.

Moore, D. (2015). *The developing genome.* New York: Oxford University Press.

Moore, M.W., Brendel, P.C., & Fiez, J.A. (2014). Reading faces: Investigating the use of a novel face-based orthography in acquired alexia. *Brain and Language, 129C,* 7-13.

Moran, S., & Gardner, H. (2006). Extraordinary achievements. In W. Damon & R. Lerner (Eds.), *Handbook of child psychology* (6th ed.). New York: Wiley.

Moriguchi, Y., Chevallier, N., & Zelazo, P.D. (2016). Editorial: Development of executive function during childhood. *Frontiers in Psychology, 7,* 6.

Moroni, S., & others (2015). The need to distinguish quantity and quality in research on parental involvement: The example of parental help with homework. *Journal of Educational Research, 108,* 417-431.

Morris, A., Cui, L., & Steinberg, L. (2013). Arrested development: The effects of incarceration on the development of psychosocial maturity. *Development and Psychopathology, 24*(3), 1073-1090.

Morris, A.S., & others (2013). Effortful control, behavioral problems, and peer relations: What predicts academic adjustment in kindergartners from low-income families? *Early Education and Development, 24,* 813-828.

Morrison, G.S. (2017). *Fundamentals of early childhood education* (8th ed.). Upper Saddle River, NJ: Pearson.

Mowbray, R., & Perry, B. (2015). Improving lecture quality through training in public speaking. *Innovations in Education and Teaching International, 52,* 207-217.

Moyer, J.R., & Dardig, J.C. (1978). Practical task analysis for teachers. *Teaching Exceptional Children, 11,* 16-18.

Mudigoudar, B., Weatherspoon, S., & Wheless, J.W. (2016). Emerging antiepileptic drugs for severe pediatric epilepsies. *Seminars in Pediatric Neurology, 23,* 167-179.

Müller, U., & Kerns, K. (2015). Development of executive function. In R.M. Lerner (Ed.), *Handbook of child psychology and developmental science* (7th ed.). New York: Wiley.

Mullis, I.V.S., Martin, M.O., Foy, P., & Arora, A. (2012). *TIMSS 2011 international results in mathematics.* TIMSS & PIRLS International Study Center, Boston College.

Mullis, I.V.S., Martin, M.O., Foy, P., & Drucker, K.T. (2012a). *PIRLS 2011: International results in reading.* Boston: TIMSS & PIRLS International Study Center, Boston College.

Mulvey, K.L., & Killen, M. (2016). Keeping quiet just wouldn't be right: Children and adolescents' evaluations of challenges to peer relational and physical aggression. *Journal of Youth and Adolescence, 45,* 1824-1835.

Murawska, J.M., & Zollman, A. (2015). Taking it to the next level: Students using inductive reasoning. *Mathematics Teaching in the Middle School, 20,* 416-422.

Murayama, K., & Elliott, A.J. (2009). The joint influence of personal achievement goals and classroom goal structures on achievement-relevant outcomes. *Journal of Educational Psychology, 101,* 432-447.

Murdock, T.B. (2009). Achievement motivation in racial and ethnic context. In K.R. Wentzel & A. Wigfield (Eds.), *Handbook of motivation at school.* New York: Routledge.

Murry, V.M., Hill, N.E., Witherspoon, D., Berkel, C., & Bartz, D. (2015). Children in diverse social contexts. In R.M. Lerner (Ed.), *Handbook of child psychology and developmental science* (7th ed.). New York: Wiley.

Myers, D.G. (2010). *Psychology* (9th ed). New York: Worth.

Myerson, J., Rank, M.R., Raines, F.Q., & Schnitzler, M.A. (1998). Race and general cognitive ability: The myth of diminishing returns in education. *Psychological Science, 9,* 139-142.

N

National Association for the Education of Young Children. (1996). NAEYC Position statement: Responding to linguistic and cultural diversity—Recommendations for effective early childhood education. *Young Children, 51,* 4-12.

National Association of Secondary School Principals. (1997). Students say: What makes a good teacher? *Schools in the Middle, 6*(5), 15-17.

Nagel, M., & Scholes, L. (2017). *Understanding development and learning.* New York: Oxford University Press.

Naidoo, S., Satorius, B.K., de Vines, H., & Taylor, M. (2016). Verbal bullying changes among students following an educational intervention using the integrated model for behavior change. *Journal of School Health, 86,* 813-822.

Nam, C.S., Li, Y., Yamaguchi, T., & Smith-Jackson, T.L. (2012). Haptic user interfaces for the visually impaired: Implications for haptically enhanced science learning systems. *International Journal of Human-Computer Interaction, 28,* 784-798.

Nansel, T.R., & others (2001). Bullying behaviors among U.S. youth: Prevalence and association with psychosocial adjustment. *Journal of the American Medical Association, 285,* 2094-2100.

Narváez, D. (2014). *The neurobiology and development of human morality.* New York: Norton.

Narváez, D. (2015). The neurobiology of moral sensitivity: Evolution, epigenetics, and early experience. In D. Mowrer & P. Vanderberg (Eds.), *The art of morality.* New York: Routledge.

Narváez, D. (2016). The ontogenesis of moral becoming. In A. Fuentes & A. Visala (Eds.), *Verbs, bones, and brains.* Notre Dame, IN: University of Notre Dame Press.

Nash, J.M. (1997, February 3). Fertile minds. *Time,* pp. 50-54.

NASSPE. (2012). *Single-sex schools/schools with single-sex classrooms/what's the difference?* Retrieved from www.singlesexschools.org/schools-schools.com

Nathan, M.J., & Petrosino, A.J. (2003). Expert blind spot among preservice teachers. *American Educational Research Journal, 40*(4), 905-928.

National Assessment of Educational Progress. (2000). *Reading achievement.* Washington in National Center for Education Statistics.

National Assessment of Educational Progress. (2007). *The nation's report card.* Washington, DC: National Center for Education Statistics.

National Assessment of Educational Progress. (2015). *Nation's report card.* Washington, DC: U.S. Department of Education.

National Association for the Education of Young Children. (1996). NAEYC position statement: Responding to linguistic and cultural diversity—Recommendations for effective early childhood education. *Young Children, 51,* 4-12.

National Association for the Education of Young Children (NAEYC). (2009). *Developmentally appropriate practice in early childhood programs serving children from birth through age 8.* Washington, DC: NAEYC.

National Center for Education Statistics. (2008). *Children and youth with disabilities in public schools.* Washington, DC: U.S. Department of Education.

National Center for Education Statistics. (2014). *School dropouts.* Washington, DC: Author.

National Center for Education Statistics. (2015). *The condition of education.* Washington, DC: U.S. Department of Education.

National Center for Education Statistics. (2016). *School dropouts.* Washington, DC: Author.

National Center for Education Statistics. (2016). *Students with disabilities.* Washington, DC: U.S. Department of Education.

National Center for Learning Disabilities. (2006). *Learning disabilities.* Retrieved March 6, 2006, from http://www.ncld.org/

National Council for the Social Studies. (1994). *Expectations of excellence: Curriculum standards for social studies.* Waldorf, MD: NCSS.

National Council for the Social Studies. (2000). *National standards for social studies teachers.* Baltimore: Author.

National Council of Teachers of English/International Reading Association. (1996). *Standards for the English Language Arts.* Urbana, IL: NCTE/IRA.

National Council of Teachers of English. (2014). How standardized tests shape—and limit—student learning. A policy research brief. *ERIC,* #ED556345.

National Council of Teachers of Mathematics. (2000). *Principles and standards for school mathematics.* Reston, VA: NCTM.

National Council of Teachers of Mathematics. (2007a). *Navigating through number and operations in grades 3–5.* Reston, VA: NCTM.

National Council of Teachers of Mathematics. (2007b). *Mathematics teaching today: Professional standards for teaching mathematics, revision.* Reston, VA: NCTM.

National Council of Teachers of Mathematics. (2007c). *Making sense of mathematics: Children sharing and comparing solutions to challenging problems.* Reston, VA: NCTM.

National Institute of Mental Health. (2016). *Autism spectrum disorder (ASD).* Retrieved January 7, 2016, from http://www.nimh.nih.gov/health/topics/autism-spectrum-disorders-asd/index.shtml

National Institutes of Health. (1993). *Learning disabilities* NIH publication (No. 93-3611). Bethesda, MD: Author.

National Joint Committee on Learning Disabilities. (2005). *Responsiveness to Intervention and Learning Disabilities.*

National Reading Panel. (2000). *Teaching children to read.* Washington, DC: National Institute of Child Health and Human Development.

National Research Council. (1999). *How people learn.* Washington, DC: National Academies Press.

National Research Council. (2001). *Knowing what students know.* Washington, DC: National Academies Press.

National Research Council. (2005). *How students learn.* Washington, DC: National Academies Press.

Navsaria, D., & Sanders, L.M. (2015). Early literacy promotion in the digital age. *Pediatric Clinics of North America, 62,* 1273–1295.

Nel, N.M., Romm, N.R.A., & Tiale, L.D.N. (2015). Reflections on focus group sessions regarding inclusive education: Reconsidering focus group research possibilities. *Australian Educational Researcher, 42,* 35–53.

Nelson, C.A. (2011). Brain development and behavior. In A.M. Rudolph, C. Rudolph, L. First, G. Lister, & A.A. Gersohon (Eds.), *Rudolph's pediatrics* (22nd ed.). New York: McGraw-Hill.

Nesbitt, K.T., Farran, D.C., & Fuhs, M.W. (2015). Executive function skills and academic gains in prekindergarten: Contributions of learning-related behaviors. *Developmental Psychology, 51,* 865–878.

Neugarten, B.L. (1988, August). *Policy issues for an aging society.* Paper presented at the meeting of the American Psychological Association, Atlanta.

Neumann, N., Lotze, M., & Eickhoff, S.B. (2016). Cognitive expertise: An ALE meta-analysis. *Human Brain Mapping, 37,* 262–272.

Neville, H.J. (2006). Different profiles of plasticity within human cognition. In Y. Munakata & M.H. Johnson (Eds.), *Attention and Performance XXI: Processes of change in brain and cognitive development.* Oxford. UK: Oxford University Press.

NICHD Early Child Care Research Network. (2005). Predicting individual differences in attention, memory, and planning in first graders from experiences at home, child care, and school. *Developmental Psychology, 41,* 99–114.

Nichols, J.D., & Miller, R.B. (1994). Co-operative learning and student motivation. *Contemporary Educational Psychology, 19,* 167–178.

Niess, M., & Gillow-Wiles, H. (2014). Transforming science and mathematics teachers' technological pedagogical knowledge using a learning trajectory instructional approach. *Journal of Technology and Teacher Education, 22,* 497–520.

Nikola-Lisa, W., & Burnaford, G.E. (1994). A mosaic: Contemporary schoolchildren's images of teachers. In P.B. Joseph & G.E. Burnaford (Eds.), *Image of schoolteachers in twentieth century America.* New York: St. Martin's Press.

Nilsson, K.K., & de Lopez, K.J. (2016). Theory of mind in children with specific language impairment: A systematic review and meta-analysis. *Child Development, 87,* 143–153.

Ning, L.F., & others (2015). Meta-analysis of differentially expressed genes in autism based on gene expression data. *Genetics and Molecular Research, 14,* 2146–2155.

Nisbett, R.E., & others (2012). Intelligence: New findings and theoretical developments. *American Psychologist, 67,* 130–159.

Nitecki, E. (2015). Integrated school-family partnerships in preschool: Building quality involvement through multidimensional relationships. *School Community Journal, 25,* 195–219.

Noddings, N. (2007). *When school reform goes wrong.* New York: Teachers College Press.

Noddings, N. (2008). Caring and moral education. In L. Nucci & D. Narváez (Eds.), *Handbook of moral and character education.* Clifton, NJ: Psychology Press.

Nolen-Hoeksema, S. (2011). *Abnormal psychology* (5th ed.). New York: McGraw-Hill.

Norris, K. & Soloway, E. (1999). *Teachers and technology: A snapshot survey.* Denton, TX: University of North Texas, Texas Center for Educational Technology.

North American Montessori Teachers' Association. (2016). *Montessori schools.* Retrieved January 6, 2016, from www.montessori-namta.org

Novak, B.E., & Lynott, F.J. (2015). Homework in physical education: Benefits and implementation. *Strategies: A Journal for Physical and Sports Educators, 28,* 22–26.

Nucci, L. (2006). Education for moral development. In M. Killen & J. Smetana (Eds.), *Handbook of moral development.* Mahwah, NJ: Erlbaum.

Nunez, J.C., & others (2015). Relationships between perceived parental involvement in homework, student homework behaviors, and academic achievement: Differences among elementary, junior high, and high school students. *Metacognition and Learning, 10,* 375–406.

O

O'Brien, M., & others (2014). Women's work and child care: Perspectives and prospects. In E.T. Gershoff, R.S. Mistry, & D.A. Crosby (Eds.), *Societal contexts of child development.* New York: Oxford University Press.

O'Connor, T.G. (2016). Developmental models and mechanisms for understanding the effects of early experience on psychological development. In D. Cicchetti (Ed.), *Developmental psychopathology* (3rd ed.). New York: Wiley.

O'Shea, M. (2009). *Assessment throughout the year.* Upper Saddle River, NJ: Merrill.

Oakes, J., & Saunders, M. (2002). *Access to textbooks, instructional materials, equipment, and technology: Inadequacy of California's schools.* Los Angeles: Department of Education, UCLA.

Oakhill, J., Berenhaus, M.S., & Cain, K. (2016). Children's reading comprehension and comprehension difficulties. In A. Pollastek & R. Treiman (Eds.), *Oxford handbook of reading.* New York: Oxford University Press.

Obel, C., & others (2016). The risk of attention deficit hyperactivity disorder in children exposed to maternal smoking during pregnancy—a re-examination using a sibling design. *Journal of Clinical Psychology and Psychiatry, 57,* 532–537.

Odhiambo, E.A., Nelson, L.E., & Chrisman, K. (2016). *Social studies and young children.* Upper Saddle River, NJ: Pearson.

Ogbu, J., & Stern, P. (2001). Caste status and intellectual development. In R.J. Sternberg & E.L. Grigorenko (Eds.), *Environmental effects on cognitive abilities.* Mahwah, NJ: Erlbaum.

Olszewski-Kubilius, P., & Thomson, D. (2015). Talent development as a framework for gifted education. *Gifted Child Today, 38,* 49–59.

Oluo, I. (2018). *So you want to talk about race.* NY: Seal Press.

Olweus, D. (2003). Prevalence estimation of school bullying with the Olweus bully/victim questionnaire. *Aggressive Behavior, 29*(3), 239–269.

Olweus, D. (2013). School bullying: Development and some important challenges. *Annual Review of Clinical Psychology* (Vol. 9). Palo Alto, CA: Annual Reviews.

Oostdam, R., Blok, H., & Boendermaker, C. (2015). Effects of individualized and small-group guide oral reading interventions on reading skills and reading attitudes of poor readers in grades 2-4. *Research Papers in Education, 30,* 427–450.

Ornstein, P.A., Coffman, J.L., & Grammer, J.K. (2007, April). *Teachers' memory-relevant conversations and children's memory performance.* Paper presented at the biennial meeting of the Society for Research in Child Development, Boston.

Ornstein, P.A., Coffman, J.L., Grammer, J.K., San Souci, P.P., & McCall, L.E. (2010). Linking the classroom context and the development of children's memory skills. In J. Meece & J. Eccles (Eds.), *Handbook of research on schools, schooling, and human development.* New York: Routledge.

Orpinas, P., McNicholas, C., & Nahapetyan, L. (2015). Gender differences in trajectories of relational aggression perpetration and victimization from middle to high school. *Aggressive Behavior, 41,* 401–412.

Orth, U., Robins, R.W., & Widaman, K.F. (2012). Life-span development of self-esteem and its effects on important life outcomes. *Journal of Personality and Social Psychology, 102,* 1271–1288. doi: 10.1037/a0025558

Orrock, J., & Clark, M.A. (2016). Using systems theory to promote academic success of African American males. *Urban Education.* doi:10.1177/0042085915613546

Osadebe, P.U. (2015). Construction of valid and reliable test for assessment of students. *Journal of Education and Practice, 6,* 51–66.

Ostrov, J.M., Keating, C.F., & Ostrov, J.M. (2004). Gender differences in preschool aggression during free play and structured interactions: An observational study. *Social Development, 13,* 255–277.

Owens, R.E., Farinella, K.A., & Metz, D.E. (2015). *Introduction to communication disorders* (5th ed.). Upper Saddle River, NJ: Pearson.

Pace, A., Hirsh-Pasek, K., & Golinkoff, R.M. (2016). How high quality language environments create high quality learning environments. In S. Jones & N. Lesaux (Eds.), *The leading edge of early childhood education.* Cambridge, MA: Harvard University Press.

Pace, A., Levine, D., Morini, G., Hirsh-Pasek, K., & Golinkoff, R.M. (2016). The story of language acquisition: From words to world and back again. In L. Balter & C. Tamis-LeMonda (Eds.), *Child psychology* (3rd ed.). New York: New York University Press.

Pahlke, E., Hyde, J.S., & Allison, C.M. (2014). The effects of single-sex compared with coeducational schooling on students' performance and attitudes: A meta-analysis. *Psychological Bulletin, 140,* 1042–1072.

Paivio, A. (1971). *Imagery and verbal processes.* Fort Worth, TX: Harcourt Brace.

Paivio, A. (1986). *Mental representations: A dual coding approach.* New York: Oxford University Press.

Paivio, A. (2013). Dual-coding theory, word abstractness, and emotion: A critical review of Kousta et al. (2011). *Journal of Experimental Psychology: General, 142,* 282–287.

Palincsar, A.S., & Brown, A.L. (1984). Reciprocal teaching of comprehension-fostering and comprehension-monitoring activities. *Cognition and Instruction, 1,* 117–175.

Pan, B.A., & Uccelli, P. (2009). Semantic development. In J. Berko Gleason & N. Ratner (Eds.), *The development of language* (7th ed.). Boston: Allyn & Bacon.

Pan, C.Y., & others (2016). Effects of physical exercise intervention on motor skills and executive functions with ADHD: A pilot study. *Journal of Attention Disorders.* doi:10.1177/1087054715569282

Panayiotou, A., & others (2014). Teacher behavior and student outcomes: Results of a European study. *Educational Assessment, Evaluation, and Accountability, 26,* 73–93.

Pang, V.O. (2005). *Multicultural education.* (3rd ed.). New York: McGraw-Hill.

Papert, S. (1980). *Mindstorms, children, computers, and powerful ideas.* New York: Basic Books.

Park, K.M., & Park, H. (2015). Effects of self-esteem improvement program on self-esteem and peer attachment in elementary school children with observed problematic behaviors. *Asian Nursing Research, 9,* 53–59.

Parkay, F.W. (2016). *Becoming a teacher* (10th ed.). Upper Saddle River, NJ: Pearson.

Parker, W.C., & Beck, T.A. (2017). *Social studies in elementary education* (15th ed.). Upper Saddle River, NJ: Pearson.

Parsi, A., & Darling-Hammond, L. (2015). *Performance assessments: How state policy can advance assessments for 21st century learning.* White paper. ERIC, #ED562629.

Pascual, A., Extebarria, I., Ortega, I., & Ripalda, A. (2012). Gender differences in adolescence in emotional variables relevant to eating disorders. *International Journal of Psychology and Psychological Therapy, 12,* 59–68.

Patton, G.C., & others (2011). A prospective study of the effects of optimism on adolescent health risks. *Pediatrics, 127,* 308–316.

Paunesku, D., & others (2015). Mind-set interventions are a scaleable treatment for academic underachievement. *Psychological Science, 26,* 784–793.

Paus, T., & others (2008). Morphological properties of the action-observation cortical network in adolescents with low and high resistance to peer influence. *Social Neuroscience, 3,* 303–316.

Pavlov, I.P. (1927). *Conditioned reflexes.* New York: Dover.

Pawluk, D., & others (2015). Guest editorial: Haptic assistive technology for individuals who are visually impaired. *IEE Trans Haptics, 8,* 245–247.

Payne, D.A. (2003). *Applied educational assessment* (2nd ed.). Belmont, CA: Wadsworth.

Pearson, J., Nelson, P., Titsworth, S., & Hosek, A. (2017). *Human communication* (6th ed.). New York: McGraw-Hill.

Peets, K., Hodges, E.V.E., & Salmivalli, C. (2011). Actualization of social cognitions into aggressive behavior toward disliked targets. *Social Development, 20,* 233–250.

Peng, P., & Fuchs, D. (2016). A meta-analysis of working memory deficits in children with learning difficulties: Is there a difference between the verbal domain and numerical domain? *Journal of Learning Disabilities, 49,* 3-20.

Pennanen, M., & others (2016). What is "good" mentoring? Understanding mentoring practices of teacher induction through case studies of Finland and Australia. *Pedagogy, Culture, and Society, 24,* 27-53.

Pennington, C.R., Heim, D., Levy, A.R., & Larkin, D.T. (2016). Twenty years of stereotype threat research: A review of psychological mediators. *PLoS One, 11*(1), E0146487.

Perry, D.G., & Pauletti, R.E. (2011). Gender and adolescent development. *Journal of Research on Adolescence, 21,* 61-74.

Persky, H.R., Daane, M.C., & Jin, Y. (2003). *The nation's report card: Writing 2002.* Washington. DC: U.S. Department of Education.

Peter D. Hart Research Associates. (2006). How should colleges prepare students to succeed in today's global economy? Washington, DC: The Association of American Colleges and Universities. Retrieved from http://www.aacu.org/leap/documents/Re8097abcombined.pdf. NACE. (2013). Job Outlook 2014. Retrieved from https://web.iit.edu/sites/web/files/departments/career-services/pdfs/nace%20job-outlook-2014.pdf.

Peterman, K., Cranston, K.A., Pryor, M., & Kermish-Allen, R. (2015). Measuring primary students' graph interpretation skills via a performance assessment: A case study in instrument development. *International Journal of Science Education, 37,* 2787-2808.

Peters-Burton, E.E., & others (2015). The effect of cognitive apprenticeship-based professional development on teacher self-efficacy of science teaching, motivation, knowledge, calibration, and perceptions of inquiry-based teaching. *Journal of Science Teacher Education, 26,* 525-548.

Peterson, E.R., Rayner, S.G., & Armstrong, S.J. (2009). Researching the psychology of cognitive style and learning style: Is there really a future? *Learning and Individual Differences, 19,* 518-523.

Philipsen, N.M., Johnson, A.D., & Brooks-Gunn, J. (2009). Poverty, effects on social and emotional development. *International Encyclopedia of Education* (3rd ed.). St. Louis: Elsevier.

Phye, G.D., & Sanders, C.E. (1994). Advice and feedback: Elements of practice for problem solving. *Contemporary Educational Psychology, 19,* 286-301.

Piaget, J. (1954). *The construction of reality in the child.* New York: Basic Books.

Piaget, J., & Inhelder, B. (1969). *The child's conception of space.* New York: Norton.

Pianta, R.C. (2016). Classroom processes and teacher-student interaction: Integrations with a developmental psychopathology perspective. In D. Cicchetti (Ed.), *Developmental psychopathology* (3rd ed.). New York: Wiley.

Pisani, F., & Spagnoli, C. (2016). Neonatal seizures: A review of outcomes and outcome predictors. *Neuropediatrics, 47,* 12-19.

Plucker, J. (2010, July 19). Commentary in P. Bronson & A. Merryman, The creativity crisis. *Newsweek,* 45-46.

Pluess, M., & Bartley, M. (2015). Childhood conscientiousness predicts the social gradient of smoking in adulthood: A life course analysis. *Journal of Epidemiology and Community Health, 69,* 330-338.

Poehlmann-Tynan, J., & others (2016). A pilot study of contemplative practices with economically disadvantaged preschoolers: Children's empathic and self-regulatory behaviors. *Mindfulness, 7,* 46-58.

Pollack, W. (1999). *Real boys.* New York: Owl Books.

Polson, D. (2001). Helping children learn to make responsible choices. In B. Rogoff, C.G. Turkanis, & L. Lartlett (Eds.), *Learning together.* New York: Oxford University Press.

Popham, W.J. (2008). *Classroom assessment* (5th ed.). Boston: Allyn & Bacon.

Popham, W.J. (2017). *Classroom assessment* (8th ed.). Upper Saddle River, NJ: Pearson.

Poropat, A.E. (2016). The role of personality and temperament in learning. In L. Corno & E.M. Anderman (Eds.), *Handbook of educational psychology* (3rd ed.). New York: Routledge.

Posamentier, A.S., & Smith, B.S. (2015). *Teaching secondary mathematics* (9th ed.). Upper Saddle River, NJ: Pearson.

Posner, M.I., & Rothbart, M.K. (2007). *Educating the human brain.* Washington, DC: American Psychological Association.

Poulos, A.M., & Thompson, R.F. (2015). Localization and characterization of essential associative memory trace in the mammalian brain. *Brain Research, 1621,* 252-259.

Powell, R.A., Honey, P.L., & Symbaluk, D.G. (2017). *Introduction to learning and behavior* (5th ed.). Boston: Cengage.

Powers, C.J., Bierman, K.L., & Coffman, D.L. (2016). Restrictive educational placements increase adolescent risks for students with early-starting conduct problems. *Journal of Child Psychology and Psychiatry, 57,* 899-908.

Powers, K.E., Chavez, R.S., & Heatherton, T.F. (2016). Individual differences in response of dorsomedial prefrontal cortex predict daily social behavior. *Social Cognitive and Affective Neuroscience, 11,* 121-126.

Prabhakar, H. (2007). Hopkins Interactive Guest Blog: *The public health experience at Johns Hopkins.* Retrieved January 31, 2008, from http://hopkins.typepad.com/guest/2007/03/the_public_heal.html

Presidential Task Force on Psychology and Education (1992). *Learner-centered psychological principles: Guidelines for school redesign and reform* (draft). Washington, DC: American Psychological Association.

Pressley, M. (1983). Making meaningful materials easier to learn. In M. Pressley & J.R. Levin (Eds.), *Cognitive strategy research: Educational applications.* New York: Springer-Verlag.

Pressley, M. (2007). Achieving best practices. In L.B. Gambrell, L.M. Morrow, & M. Pressley (Eds.), *Best practices in literary instruction.* New York: Guilford.

Pressley, M., Allington, R., Wharton-McDonald, R., Block, C.C., & Morrow, L.M. (2001). *Learning to read: Lessons from exemplary first grades.* New York: Guilford.

Pressley, M., Borkowski, J.G., & Schneider, W. (1989). Good information processing: What it is and what education can do to promote it. *International Journal of Educational Research, 13,* 857-867.

Pressley, M., Cariligia-Bull, T., Deane, S., & Schneider, W. (1987). Short-term memory, verbal competence, and age as predictors of imagery instructional effectiveness. *Journal of Experimental Child Psychology, 43,* 194-211.

Pressley, M., & Harris, K.R. (2006). Cognitive strategies instruction: From basic research to classroom instruction. In P.A. Alexander & P.H. Winne (Eds.), *Handbook of educational psychology* (2nd ed.). Mahwah, NJ: Erlbaum.

Pressley, M., & Hilden, K. (2006). Cognitive strategies. In W. Damon & R. Lerner (Eds.), *Handbook of child psychology* (6th ed.). New York: Wiley.

Pressley, M., Levin, J.R., & McCormick, C.B. (1980). Young children's learning of a foreign language vocabulary: A sentence variation of the keyword. *Contemporary Educational Psychology, 5,* 22-29.

Pressley, M., & McCormick, C.B. (2007). *Child and adolescent development for educators.* New York: Guilford.

Pressley, M., Mohan, L., Fingeret, L., Reffitt, K., & Raphael Bogaert, L. (2007). Writing instruction in engaging and effective elementary settings. In S. Graham, C.A. MacArthur, & J. Fitzgerald (Eds.), *Best practices in writing instruction.* New York: Guilford.

Pressley, M., Raphael, L., Gallagher, D., & DiBella, J. (2004). Providence-St. Mel School: How a school that works for African-American students works. *Journal of Educational Psychology, 96,* 216-235.

Pressley, M., Schuder, T., SAIL Faculty and Administration, German, J., & El-Dinary, P.B. (1992). A researcher-educator collaborative interview study of transactional comprehension strategies instruction. *Journal of Educational Psychology, 84,* 231-246.

Pressley, M., & others (2001). A study of effective first grade literacy instruction. *Scientific Studies of Reading, 15,* 35-58.

Pressley, M., & others (2003). *Motivating primary grades teachers.* New York: Guilford.

Pressley, T., Roehrig, A.D., & Turner, J.E. (2018). Elementary teachers' perceptions of a reformed teacher evaluation system. *Teacher Educator, 53,* 21-43.

Price, K.W., Meisinger, E.S., Louwerse, M.M., & D'Mello, S. (2016). The contributions of oral and silent reading fluency to reading comprehension. *Reading Psychology, 37,* 167-201.

Prinstein, M.J., & Giletta, M. (2016). Peer relations and developmental psychopathology. In D. Cicchetti (Ed.), *Developmental psychopathology* (3rd ed.). New York: Wiley.

PSU. (2006). Anchored instruction. Retrieved January 6, 2006, from www.ed.psu.edu/nasa/achrtxt.html

Puhl, R.M., & King, K.M. (2013). Weight discrimination and bullying. *Best Practice and Research: Clinical Endocrinology and Metabolism, 27,* 117-127.

Putallaz, M., & others (2007). Overt and relational aggression and victimization: Multiple perspectives within the school setting. *Journal of School Psychology, 45,* 523-547.

Q

Qu, Y., & Pomerantz, E.M. (2015). Divergent school trajectories in early adolescence in the United States and China: An examination of underlying mechanisms. *Journal of Youth and Adolescence, 44,* 2095-2109.

Quality Counts. (2001). *A better balance: Standards, tests, and the tools to succeed.* Bethesda, MD: Education Week on the Web.

Quinn, P.C. (2016). What do infants know about cats, dogs, and people? Development of a "like-people" representation for non-human animals. In L. Freund & others (Eds.), *Social neuroscience and human-animal interaction.* Washington, DC: American Psychological Association.

Quinn, P.C., & Bhatt, R.S. (2016). Development of perceptual organization in infancy. In J. Wagemans (Ed.), *Oxford handbook of perceptual organization.* New York: Oxford University Press.

Qvortrup, A., & Keiding, T.B. (2015). Portfolio assessment: Production and reduction in complexity. *Assessment & Evaluation in Higher Education, 40,* 407-419.

R

Rabiner, D.L., Murray, D.W., Skinner, A.T., & Malone, P.S. (2010). A randomized trial of two promising computer-based interventions for students with attention difficulties. *Journal of Abnormal Child Psychology, 38,* 131-142.

Raeff, C. (2017). *Exploring the dynamics of human development.* New York: Oxford University Press.

Raffaelli, M., & Ontai, L.L. (2004). Gender socialization in Latino families: Results from two retrospective studies. *Sex Roles, 50,* 287-299.

Rajiah, K., & Saravanan, C. (2014). The effectiveness of psychoeducation and systematic desensitization to reduce test anxiety among first-year pharmacy students. *American Journal of Pharmacy Education, 78,* 163.

Rakoczy, H., Warneken, F., & Tomasello, M. (2007). "This way!", "No! That way!"—3-year-olds know that two people can have mutually incompatible desires. *Cognitive Development, 22,* 47-68.

Ramey, C.T., Bryant, D.M., Campbell, F.A., Sparling, J.J., & Wasik, B.H. (1988). Early intervention for high-risk children. The Carolina Early Intervention Program. In R.H. Price, E.L. Cowen, R.P. Lorion, & J. Ramos-McKay (Eds.), *14 ounces of prevention.* Washington, DC: American Psychological Association.

Ramey, S.L., Ramey, C.T., & Lanzi, R.G. (2009). Early intervention: Background, research findings, and future directions. In J.W. Jacobson, J.A. Mulick, & J. Rojahn (Eds.), *Handbook of intellectual and developmental disabilities.* New York: Springer.

Ramirez, G., & others (2016). On the relationship between math anxiety and math achievement in early elementary school: The role of problem solving strategies. *Journal of Experimental Child Psychology, 141,* 83-100.

Randolph, C.H., & Evertson, C.M. (1995). Managing for learning: Rules, roles, and meanings in a writing class. *Journal of Classroom Instruction, 30,* 17-25.

Rapin, I. (2016). Dyscalculia and the calculating brain. *Pediatric Neurology, 61,* 11-20.

Rattan, A., Savani, K., Chugh, D., & Dweck, C.S. (2015). Leveraging mindsets to promote academic achievement: Policy recommendations. *Perspectives on Psychological Science, 10,* 721-726.

Rawson, K., Thomas, R.C., & Jacoby, L.L. (2015). The power of examples: Illustrative examples enhance concept learning of declarative concepts. *Educational Psychology Review, 27,* 483-504.

Razza, R.A., Martin, A., & Brooks-Gunn, J. (2012). The implications of early attentional regulation for school success among low-income children. *Journal of Applied Developmental Psychology, 33,* 311-319.

Re: Learning by Design. (2000). *Design resource center.* Re: Learning by Design. Retrieved July 16, 2002, from http://www.relearning.org

Regalado, M., Sareen, H., Inkelas, M., Wissow, L.S., & Halfon, N. (2004). Parents' discipline of young children: Results from the National Survey of Early Childhood Health. *Pediatrics, Supplement, 113,* 1952-1958.

Regional Educational Laboratory Mid-Atlantic. (2015). Engaging families in partnership programs to promote student success: Q & A for Dr. Joyce L. Epstein. ERIC Number: ED562603.

Reid, G., Fawcett, A., Manis, F., & Siegel, L. (2009). *The SAGE handbook of dyslexia.* Thousand Oaks, CA: Sage.

Reis, S.M., & Renzulli, J.S. (2014). Challenging gifted and talented learners with a continuum of research-based intervention strategies. In M.A. Bray & T.J. Kehle (Eds.), *Oxford handbook of school psychology.* New York: Oxford University Press.

Reksten, L.E. (2009). *Sustaining extraordinary student achievement.* Thousand Oaks, CA: Corwin Press.

Renne, C.H. (1997). *Excellent classroom management.* Belmont, CA: Wadsworth.

Renzulli, J.S. (1998). A rising tide lifts all ships: Developing the gifts and talents of all students. *Phi Delta Kappan, 80,* 1-15.

Renzulli, J.S. (2017). Developing creativity across all areas of the curriculum. In R.A. Beghetto & J.C. Kaufman (Eds.), *Nurturing creativity in the classroom* (2nd ed.). New York: Cambridge University Press.

Reyna, V.F., & Rivers, S.F. (2008). Current theories of risk and rational decision making. *Developmental Review, 28,* 1-11.

Reyna, V.F., Weldon, R.B., & McCormick, M.J. (2015). Educating intuition: Reducing risky decisions using fuzzy-trace theory. *Current Directions in Psychological Science, 24,* 392-398.

Reyna, V.F., & Zayas, V. (Eds.). (2014). *Neuroscience of risky decision making.* Washington, DC: American Psychological Association.

Reynolds, G.D., & Romano, A.C. (2016). The development of attention systems and memory in infancy. *Frontiers in Systems Neuroscience, 10,* 15.

Rhodes, J.E., & Lowe, S.R. (2009). Mentoring in adolescence. In R.M. Lerner & L. Steinberg (Eds.), *Handbook of adolescent psychology* (3rd ed.). New York: Wiley.

Ricco, R.B. (2015). The development of reasoning. In R.M. Lerner (Ed.), *Handbook of child psychology* (7th ed.). New York: Wiley.

Riener, C.R., & Willingham, D. (2010). The myth of learning styles. *Change: The Magazine of Higher Learning, 42*(5), 32-35.

Ristic, J., & Enns, J.T. (2015). Attentional development: The past, the present, and the future. In R.M. Lerner (Ed.), *Handbook of child psychology and developmental science.* New York: Wiley.

Rittle-Johnson, B. (2006). Promoting transfer: Effects of self-explanation and direct instruction. *Child Development, 77,* 1-15.

Roberts, B.W., Wood, D., & Caspi, A. (2008). Personality development. In O.P. John, R.W. Robins, & L.A. Pervin (Eds.), *Handbook of personality* (3rd ed.). New York: Guilford.

Robins, R.W., Trzesniewski, K.H., Tracey, J.L., Potter, J., & Gosling, S.D. (2002). Age differences in self-esteem from age 9 to 90. *Psychology and Aging, 17,* 423-434.

Robinson-Zanartu, C., Doerr, P., & Portman, J. (2015). *Teaching 21 thinking skills for the 21st century.* Upper Saddle River, NJ: Pearson.

Robitaille, Y.P., & Maldonado, N. (2015). Teachers' experiences relative to successful questioning and discussion techniques. *American Journal of Contemporary Research, 5,* 7-16.

Roblyer, M.D. (2016). *Integrating educational technology into teaching* (7th ed.). Upper Saddle River, NJ: Pearson.

Roche, S. (2016). Education for all: Exploring the principle and process of inclusive education. *International Review of Education, 62*(2), 131-137.

Rodriguez-Triana, M.J., & others (2015). Scripting and monitoring meet each other: Aligning learning analytics and learning design to support teachers in orchestrating CSCL situations. *British Journal of Educational Psychology, 46,* 330-343.

Roeser, R.W. (2016). Beyond all splits: Mindfulness in students' motivation, learning, and self/identity development in school. In K.R. Wentzel & D.B. Miele (Eds.), *Handbook of motivation at school* (2nd ed.). New York: Routledge.

Roeser, R.W., & Eccles, J.S. (2015). Mindfulness and compassion in human development: Introduction to the special section. *Developmental Psychology, 51,* 1-6.

Roeser, R.W., & Zelazo, P.D. (2012). Contemplative science, education and child development. *Child Development Perspectives, 6,* 143-145.

Roeser, R.W., & others (2014). Contemplative education. In L. Nucci & others (Eds.), *Handbook of moral and character education.* New York: Routledge.

Rogoff, B. (2003). *The cultural nature of human development.* New York: Oxford University Press.

Rogoff, B. (2015). Human teaching and learning involve cultural communities, not just individuals. *Behavioral and Brain Sciences, 38,* e60.

Rogoff, B., Turkanis, C.G., & Bartlett, L. (Eds.). (2001). *Learning together: Children and adults in a school community.* New York: Oxford University Press.

Rohrbeck, C.A., Ginsburg-Block, M.D., Fantuzzo, J.W., & Miller, T.R. (2003). Peer-assisted learning interventions with elementary school students: A meta-analytic review. *Journal of Educational Psychology, 95,* 240-257.

Rommel, A.S., & others (2015). Is physical activity causally associated with symptoms of attention-deficit/hyperactivity disorder? *Journal of the American Academy of Child and Adolescent Psychiatry, 54,* 565-570.

Rosander, P., & Backstrom, M. (2014). Personality traits measured at baseline can predict academic performance in upper secondary school three years later. *Scandinavian Journal of Psychology, 55,* 611-618.

Rosch, E.H. (1973). On the internal structure of perceptual and semantic categories. In T.E. Moore (Ed.), *Cognition and the acquisition of language.* New York: Academic Press.

Roscoe, J.L. (2015). Advising African American and Latino students. *Research and Teaching in Developmental Education, 31*(2), 48-60.

Roscoe, R.D., & Chi, M.T.H. (2008). Tutor learning: The role of explaining and responding to questions. *Instructional Science, 36,* 321-350.

Rosenblum, G.D., & Lewis, M. (2003). Emotional development in adolescence. In G. Adams & M. Berzonsky (Eds.), *Blackwell handbook of adolescence.* Malden, MA: Blackwell.

Roseth, C.J. (2016). Character education, moral education, and moral-character education. In L. Corno & E.M. Anderman (Eds.), *Handbook of educational psychology* (6th ed.). New York: Routledge.

Roth, B., & others (2015). Intelligence and school grades: A meta-analysis. *Intelligence, 53,* 118-137.

Rothbart, M.K. (2004). Temperament and the pursuit of an integrated developmental psychology. *Merrill-Palmer Quarterly, 50,* 492-505.

Rothbart, M.K., & Bates, J.E. (2006). Temperament. In W. Damon & R. Lerner (Eds.), *Handbook of child psychology* (6th ed.). New York: Wiley.

Rothbart, M.K., & Posner, M.I. (2015). The developing brain in a multitasking world. *Developmental Review, 35,* 42-63.

Rothman, R. (2016). Accountability for what matters. *State Education Standard, 16,* 10-13.

Rouse, A., & Graham, S. (2017). Teaching writing to adolescents: The use of evidence-based practices. In K. Hinchman & D. Appelman (Eds.), *Adolescent literacy.* New York: Guilford.

Rowe, M. (1986). Wait time: Slowing down may be a way of speeding up! *Journal of Teacher Education, 37,* 43-50.

Rowe, M., Ramani, G., & Pomerantz, E.M. (2016). Parental involvement and children's motivation and achievement: A domain-specific perspective. In K. Wentzel & D. Miele (Eds.), *Handbook of motivation at school* (2nd ed.). New York: Routledge.

Rowell, L.L., Polush, E.Y., Riel, M., & Bruewer, A. (2015). Action researchers' perspectives about the distinguishing characteristics of action research: A Delphi and learning circles mixed-methods study. *Educational Action Research, 23,* 243-270.

Rowley, S.J., Kurtz-Costes, B., & Cooper, S.M. (2010). The role of schooling in ethnic minority achievement and attainment. In J. Meece & J. Eccles (Eds.), *Handbook of research on school, schooling, and human development.* New York: Routledge.

Rowley, S.J., & others (2014). Framing Black boys: Parent, teacher, and student narratives of the academic lives of Black boys. *Advances in Child Development and Behavior, 47,* 301-332.

Rubie-Davies, C.M. (2007). Classroom interactions: Exploring the practices of high-and low-expectation teachers. *British Journal of Educational Psychology, 77,* 289-306.

Rubin, K.H., Bukowski, W.M., & Bowker, J. (2015). Children in peer groups. In R.M. Lerner (Ed.), *Handbook of child psychology and developmental science* (7th ed.). New York: McGraw-Hill.

Rubin, K.H., & others (2016). Peer relationships. In M.H. Bornstein & M.E. Lamb (Eds.), *Developmental science* (7th ed.). New York: Psychology Press.

Rueda, E. (2015). The benefits of being Latino: Differential interpretations of student behavior and the social construction of being well behaved. *Journal of Latinos and Education, 14,* 275-290.

Rumberger, R., Addis, H., Allensworth, E., Balfanz, R., Bruch, J., Dillon, E., Duardo, D., Dynarski, M., Furgeson, J., Jayanthi, M., Newman-Gonchar, R., Place, K., & Tuttle, C. (2017). *Preventing dropout in secondary schools* (NCEE 2017-4028). Washington, DC: National Center for Education Evaluation and Regional Assistance (NCEE), Institute of Education Sciences, U.S. Department of Education. https://whatworks.ed.gov

Rumberger, R.W. (1995). Dropping out of middle school: A multilevel analysis of students and schools. *American Education Research Journal, 3,* 583–625.

Runco, M.A. (2016). Commentary: Overview of developmental perspectives on creativity and the realization of potential. *New Directions in Child and Adolescent Development, 151,* 97–109.

Russell, M.K., & Airasian, P.W. (2012). *Classroom assessment* (7th ed.). New York: McGraw-Hill.

Ryan, R.M., & Deci, E.L. (2009). Promoting self-determined school engagement, motivation, learning, and well-being. In K.R. Wentzel & A. Wigfield (Eds.), *Handbook of motivation at school.* New York: Routledge.

Ryan, R.M., & Deci, E.L. (2016). Facilitating and hindering motivation, learning, and well-being in schools: Research and observations from self-determination theory. In K.R. Wentzel & D.B. Miele (Eds.), *Handbook of motivation at school* (2nd ed.). New York: Routledge.

S

Saarento, S., Boulton, A.J., & Salmivalli, C. (2015). Reducing bullying and victimization: Student- and classroom-level mechanisms of change. *Journal of Abnormal Child Psychology, 43,* 61–76.

Saarni, C. (1999). *The development of emotional competence.* New York: Guilford.

Saarni, C., Campos, J., Camras, L.A., & Witherington, D. (2006). Emotional development. In W. Damon & R. Lerner (Eds.), *Handbook of child psychology* (6th ed.).

Sabers, D.S., Cushing, K.S., & Berliner, D.C. (1991). Differences among teachers in a task characterized by simultaneity, multi-dimensionality, and immediacy. *American Educational Research Journal, 28,* 63–88.

Sackett, P.R., Borneman, M.J., & Connelly, B.S. (2009). Responses to issues raised about validity, bias, and fairness in high-stakes testing. *American Psychologist, 64,* 285–287.

Sadker, D.M., & Zittleman, K. (2015). *Teachers, schools, and society* (4th ed.). New York: McGraw-Hill.

Sadker, M.P., & Sadker, D.M. (1994). *Failing at fairness: How America's schools cheat girls.* New York: Scribner.

Saenz, L.M., Fuchs, L.S., & Fuchs, D. (2005). Peer-assisted learning strategies for English language learners with learning disabilities. *Exceptional Children, 71,* 231–247.

Saleh, M., Lazonder, A. W., & De Jong, T. (2005). *Instructional Science, 33*(2), 105–119. DOI: 10.1007/s11251-004-6405-z.

Salk, R.H., Petersen, J.L., Abramson, L.Y., & Hyde, J.S. (2016). The contemporary face of gender differences and similarities in depression throughout adolescence: Development and chronicity. *Journal of Affective Disorders, 205,* 28–35.

Salkind, N.J. (2017). *Exploring research, books a la carte* (9th ed.). Upper Saddle River, NJ: Pearson.

Salmivalli, C., & Peets, K. (2009). Bullies, victims, and bully-victim relationships in middle childhood and adolescence. In K.H. Rubin, W.M. Bukowski, & B. Laursen (Eds.), *Handbook of peer interactions, relationships, and groups.* New York: Guilford.

Salomon, G., & Perkins, D. (1989). Rocky roads to transfer: Rethinking mechanisms of a neglected phenomenon. *Educational Psychologist, 24,* 113–142.

Salovey, P., & Mayer, J.D. (1990). Emotional intelligence. *Imagination, Cognition, and Personality, 9,* 185–211.

Salvia, J., Ysseldyke, J.E., & Witmer, S. (2017). *Assessment in special and inclusive education* (13th ed.). Boston: Cengage.

Samovar, L.A., Porter, R.E., McDaniel, E.R., & Roy, C.S. (2017). *Communication between cultures* (9th ed.). Boston: Cengage.

San, I. (2016). Assessment for learning: Turkey case. *Universal Journal of Educational Research, 4,* 137–143.

Sanger, M.N. (2008). What we need to prepare teachers for the moral nature of their work. *Journal of Curriculum Studies, 40,* 169–185.

Sanson, A.V., & Rothbart, M.K. (2002). Child temperament and parenting. In M.H. Bornstein (Ed.), *Handbook of parenting* (2nd ed.). Mahwah, NJ: Erlbaum.

Santarnecchi, E., Rossi, S., & Rossi, A. (2015). The smarter, the stronger: Intelligence level correlates with brain resilience to systematic insults. *Cortex, 64,* 293–309.

Santos, C.G., & others (2016). The heritable path of human physical performance from single polymorphisms to the "next generation." *Scandinavian Journal of Medicine and Science in Sports, 26,* 600–612.

Santrock, J.W., & Halonen, J.A. (2009). *Your guide to college success* (6th ed.). Belmont, CA: Wadsworth.

Sarraj, H., Bene, K., Li, J., & Burley, H. (2015). Raising cultural awareness of fifth-grade students through multicultural education: An action research study. *Multicultural Education, 22*(2), 39–45.

Sax, G. (1997). *Principles of educational and psychological measurement and evaluation* (4th ed). Belmont, CA: Wadsworth.

Say, G.N., Karabekirogiu, K., Babadagi, Z., & Yuce, M. (2016). Maternal stress and perinatal factors in autism and attention deficit/hyperactivity disorder. *Pediatrics International, 58,* 265–269.

Scarr, S., & Weinberg, R.A. (1983). The Minnesota Adoption Studies: Genetic differences and malleability. *Child Development, 54,* 253–259.

Schaefer, R.T. (2015). *Racial and ethnic groups* (14th ed.). Upper Saddle River, NJ: Pearson.

Schaie, K.W., & Willis, S.L. (Eds.). (2016). *Handbook of the psychology of aging* (8th ed.). New York: Elsevier.

Schauble, L., Beane, D.B., Coates, G.D., Martin, L.M.W., & Sterling, P.V. (1996). Outside classroom walls: Learning in informal environments. In L. Schauble & R. Glaser (Eds.), *Innovations in learning.* Mahwah, NJ: Erlbaum.

Schlam, T.R., Wilson, N.L., Shoda, Y., Mischel, W., & Ayduk, O. (2013). Preschoolers' delay of gratification predicts their body mass 30 years later. *Journal of Pediatrics, 162*(1), 90–93.

Schmidt, J., Shumow, L., & Kackar-Carm, H. (2007). Adolescents' participation in service activities and its impact on academic, behavioral, and civic outcomes. *Journal of Youth and Adolescence, 36,* 127–140.

Schneider, B., & Coleman, J.S. (1993). *Parents, their children, and schools.* Boulder, CO: Westview Press.

Schneider, W. (2004). Memory development in childhood. In U. Goswami (Ed.), *Blackwell handbook of childhood cognitive development.* Malden, MA: Blackwell.

Schneider, W. (2015). *Memory development from early childhood through emerging adulthood.* Zurich, Switzerland: Springer International Switzerland.

Schneider, W., & Pressley, M. (1997). *Memory development between 2 and 20* (2nd ed.). Mahwah, NJ: Erlbaum.

Schoffstall, C.L., & Cohen, R. (2011). Cyber aggression: The relation between online offenders and offline social competence. *Social Development, 20*(3), 587–604.

Schonert-Reichl, K.A., & others (2015). Enhancing cognitive and socio-emotional development through a simple-to-administer mindfulness-based school program for elementary school children: A randomized controlled trial. *Developmental Psychology, 51,* 52–56.

Schrum, L., & Berenfeld, B. (1997). *Teaching and learning in the information age: A guide to telecommunications.* Boston: Allyn & Bacon.

Schunk, D.H. (2001). Social cognitive theory and self-regulated learning. In B.J. Zimmerman & D.H. Schunk (Eds.), *Self-regulated learning and achievement* (2nd ed.). Mahwah, NJ: Erlbaum.

Schunk, D.H. (2008). *Learning theories: An educational perspective* (5th ed.). Upper Saddle River, NJ: Prentice Hall.

Schunk, D.H. (2016). *Learning theories: An educational perspective* (7th ed.). Upper Saddle River, NJ: Pearson.

Schunk, D.H., & DiBenedetto, M.K. (2016a). Expectancy-value theory. In K. Wentzel & D. Miele (Eds.), *Handbook of motivation at school* (2nd ed.). New York: Routledge.

Schunk, D.H., & DiBenedetto, M.K. (2016b). Self-efficacy theory in education. In K.R. Wentzel & D.B. Miele (Eds.), *Handbook of motivation at school* (2nd ed.). New York: Routledge.

Schunk, D.H., Pintrich, P.R., & Meece, J.L. (2008). *Motivation in education: Theory, research, and applications* (3rd ed.). Upper Saddle River, NJ: Prentice Hall.

Schunk, D.H., & Rice, J.M. (1989). Learning goals and children's reading comprehension. *Journal of Reading Behavior, 23,* 351–364.

Schunk, D.H., & Swartz, C.W. (1993). Goals and progressive feedback: Effects on self-efficacy and writing achievement. *Contemporary Educational Psychology, 18,* 337–354.

Schunk, D.H., & Zimmerman, B.J. (2006). Competence and control beliefs: Distinguishing the means and ends. In P.A. Alexander & P.H. Winne (Eds.), *Handbook of educational psychology* (2nd ed.). Mahwah, NJ: Erlbaum.

Schwartz, D.L., Bransford, J.D., & Sears, D. (2005). Efficiency and innovation in transfer. In J. Mestre (Ed.), *Transfer of learning: Research and perspectives.* Greenwich, CT: Information Age Publishing.

Schwartz, S.E., Rhodes, J.E., Spencer, R., & Grossman, J.B. (2013). Youth initiated mentoring: Investigating a new approach to working with vulnerable adolescents. *American Journal of Community Psychology, 52,* 155–169.

Schwartz, S.J., & others (2015). Trajectories of cultural stressors and effects on mental health and substance use among Hispanic immigrant adolescents. *Journal of Adolescent Health, 56,* 433–439.

Schwartz-Mette, R.A., & Rose, A.J. (2016). Depressive symptoms and conversational self-focus in adolescents' friendships. *Journal of Abnormal Child Psychology, 44,* 87–100.

Schwinger, M., Wirthwein, L., Gunnar, L., & Steinmayr, R. (2014). Academic self-handicapping and achievement: A meta-analysis. *Journal of Educational Psychology, 106,* 744–761.

Scott, S.V., & Rodriquez, L.F. (2015). "A fly in the ointment": African American male pre-service teachers' experiences with stereotype threat in teacher education. *Urban Education, 50,* 689–717.

Sears, D.A. (2006, June). Effects of innovation versus efficiency tasks on recall and transfer in individual and collaborative learning contents. In *Proceedings of the 7th International Conference on Learning Sciences,* pp. 681–687.

Sears, D.A. (2008). Unpublished review of J.W. Santrock's *Educational Psychology* (4th ed.). New York: McGraw-Hill.

Seesjarvi, E., & others (2016). The nature and nurture of melody: A twin study of musical pitch and rhythm perception. *Behavior Genetics, 46,* 506–515.

Seiler, W.J., Beall, M.L., & Mazer, J.P. (2017). *Communication* (10th ed.). Upper Saddle River, NJ: Pearson.

Seligman, M.E.P. (2007). *The optimistic child.* New York: Mariner.

Seligson, T. (2005, February 20). They speak for success. *Parade Magazine.*

Selkie, E.M., Fales, J.L. & Moreno, M.A. (2016). Cyberbullying prevalence among U.S. middle and high school-aged adolescents: A systematic review and quality assessment. *Journal of Adolescent Health, 58,* 125–133.

Senden, M.G., Sikstrom, S., & Lindholm, T. (2015). "She" and "he" in news media messages: Pronoun use reflects gender biases in semantic contexts. *Sex Roles, 72,* 40–49.

Senko, C. (2016). Achievement goal theory: A story of early promises, eventual discords, and future possibilities. In K.R. Wentzel & D.B. Miele (Eds.), *Handbook of motivation at school* (2nd ed.). New York: Routledge.

Stenmark, J., Thompson, V., & Cassey, R. (1986). *Family math.* Berkeley, CA: University of California, Lawrence Hall of Science.

Serry, T., Rose, M., & Liamputtong, P. (2014). Reading Recovery teachers discuss Reading Recovery: A qualitative investigation. *Australian Journal of Learning Difficulties, 19,* 61–73.

Sezgin, F., & Erdogan, O. (2015). Academic optimism, hope, and zest for work as predictors of teacher self-efficacy and perceived success. *Educational Sciences: Theory and Practice, 15,* 7–19.

Shakeshaft, N.G., & others (2015). Thinking positively: The genetics of high intelligence. *Intelligence, 48,* 123–132.

Shapiro, J. R., Williams, A. M., & Hambarchyan, M. (2013). Are all interventions created equal? A multi-threat approach to tailoring stereotype threat interventions. *Journal of Personality and Social Psychology, 104*(2), 277–288. doi: 10.1037/a0030461

Sharan, S. (1990). Cooperative learning and helping behavior in the multi-ethnic classroom. In H.C. Foot, M.J. Morgan, & R.H. Shute (Eds.), *Children helping children.* New York: Wiley.

Sharan, S., & Sharan, S. (1992). *Expanding cooperative learning through group investigation.* New York: Teachers College Press.

Sharan, S., & Shaulov, A. (1990). Cooperative learning, motivation to learn, and academic achievement. In S. Sharan (Ed.), *Cooperative learning.* New York: Praeger.

Shaul, M.S. (2007). *No Child Left Behind Act: States face challenges measuring academic growth that education's initiatives may help address.* Washington, DC: Government Accountability Office.

Shaw, P., & others (2007). Attention-deficit/hyperactivity disorder is characterized by a delay in cortical maturation. *Proceedings of the National Academy of Sciences, 104*(49), 19649–19654.

Shaywitz, S.E., Morris, R., & Shaywitz, B.A. (2008). The education of dyslexic children from childhood to young adulthood. *Annual Review of Psychology* (Vol. 59). Palo Alto, CA: Annual Reviews.

Shen, J., Poppink, S., Cui, Y., & Fan, G. (2007). Lesson planning: A practice of professional responsibility and development. *Educational Horizons, 85,* 248–258.

Shen, J., Zhen, J., & Poppink, S. (2007). Open lessons: A practice to develop a learning community for teachers. *Educational Horizons, 85,* 181–191.

Shenhav, A., & Greene, J.D. (2014). Integrative moral judgment: Dissociating the roles of the amygdala and the ventromedial prefrontal cortex. *Journal of Neuroscience, 34,* 4741–4749.

Shields, P.M., & others (2001). *The status of the teaching profession, 2001.* Santa Cruz, CA: The Center for the Future of Teaching and Learning.

Shields, S.A. (1991). Gender in the psychology of emotion: A selective research review. In K.T. Strongman (Ed.), *International review of studies on emotion* (Vol. 1). New York: Wiley.

Shiraev, E., & Levy, D.A. (2010). *Crosscultural psychology* (4th ed.). Boston: Allyn & Bacon.

Shirley, M.L., & Irving, K.E. (2015). Connected classroom technology facilitates multiple components of formative assessment practice. *Journal of Science Education and Technology, 24,* 56–68.

Shirts, R.G. (1997). *BaFa, BaFa, a crosscultural simulation.* Del Mar, CA: SIMILE II.

Sieberer-Nagler, K. (2016). Effective classroom–management and positive teaching. *English Language Learning, 9,* 163–172.

Siegel, L.S. (2003). Learning disabilities. In I.B. Weiner (Ed.), *Handbook of psychology* (Vol. 7). New York: Wiley.

Siegler, R.S. (1998). *Children's thinking* (3rd ed.). Upper Saddle River, NJ: Prentice Hall.

Siegler, R.S. (2016a). Continuity and change in the field of cognitive development and in the perspective of one cognitive developmentalist. *Child Development Perspectives, 10,* 128–133.

Siegler, R.S. (2016b). How does change occur? In R. Sternberg, S. Fiske, & D. Foss (Eds.), *Scientists make a difference: One hundred eminent behavioral and brain scientists talk about their most important contributions.* Cambridge, UK: Cambridge University Press.

Siegler, R.S., & Braithwaite, D.W. (2017). Numerical development. *Annual Review of Psychology* (Vol. 68). Palo Alto, CA: Annual Reviews.

Siegler, R.S., & Robinson, M. (1982). The development of numerical understandings. In H.W. Reese & L.P. Lipsitt (Eds.), *Advances in child development and behavior* (Vol. 12). New York: Academic Press.

Silinskas, G., & others (2015). The development of dynamics of children's academic performance and mothers' homework-related affect and practices. *Developmental Psychology, 51,* 419–433.

Silva, C. (2005, October 31). When teen dynamo talks, city listens. *Boston Globe,* pp. B1, B4.

Silva, K., Shulman, E., Chein, J., & Steinberg, L. (2016). Peers increase late adolescents' exploratory behavior and sensitivity to positive and negative feedback. *Journal of Research on Adolescence.* doi:10.1111/jora.12219

Silvernail, D.L., & Lane, D.M.M. (2004). *The impact of Maine's one-to-one laptop program on middle school teachers and students.* (Report #1). Gorham, ME: Maine Education Policy Research Institute, University of Southern Maine Office.

Simmons, E.S., Lanter, E., & Lyons, M. (2014). Supporting mainstream educational success. In F.R. Volkmer & others (Eds.), *Handbook of autism and pervasive developmental disorders.* New York: Wiley.

Simmons-Reed, E.A., & Cartledge, G. (2014). School discipline disproportionality: Culturally competent interventions for African American males. *Interdisciplinary Journal of Teaching and Learning, 4,* 95–109.

Simons, J., Finlay, B., & Yang, A. (1991). *The adolescent and young adult fact book.* Washington, DC: Children's Defense Fund.

Simpkins, S.D., Fredricks, J.A., Davis-Kean, P.E., & Eccles, J.S. (2004). Healthy mind, healthy habits: The influence of activity involvement in middle childhood. In A.C. Huston & M.N. Ripke (Eds.), *Middle childhood: Contexts of development.* New York: Cambridge University Press.

Simpkins, S.D., Fredricks, J.A., & Eccles, J.S. (2015). Families, schools, and developing achievement-related motivation. In J.E. Grusec & P.D. Hastings (Eds.), *Handbook of socialization* (2nd ed.). New York; Guilford.

Singh, N.N., & others (2016). Effects of Samatha meditation on active academic engagement and math performance of students with attention/deficit/hyperactivity disorder. *Mindfulness, 7,* 68–75.

Sinha, S.R., & others (2015). Collaborative learning engagement in a computer-supported inquiry learning environment. *International Journal of Computer-Supported Collaborative Learning, 10,* 273–307.

Skiba, M.T., Sternberg, R.J., & Grigorenko, E.L. (2017). Roads not taken, new roads to take. In R.A. Beghetto & J.C. Kaufman (Eds.), *Nurturing creativity in the classroom* (2nd ed.). New York: Cambridge University Press.

Skinner, B.F. (1938). *The behavior of organisms.* New York: Appleton-Century-Crofts.

Skinner, B.F. (1954). The science of learning and the art of teaching. *Harvard Educational Review, 24,* 86–97.

Skinner, B.F. (1957). *Verbal behavior.* New York: Appleton-Century-Crofts.

Skinner, B.F. (1958). Teaching machines. *Science, 128,* 969–977.

Skotko, B.G., Levine, S.P., Macklin, E.A., & Goldstein, R.D. (2016). Family perspectives about Down syndrome. *American Journal of Medical Genetics A, 170A,* 930–941.

Slavin, R.E. (1995). *Cooperative learning: Theory, research, and practice* (2nd ed.). Boston: Allyn & Bacon.

Slavin, R.E. (2015). Cooperative learning in elementary schools. *Education, 43,* 5–14.

Slavin, R.E., Madden, N.A., Chambers, B., & Haxby, B. (2009). *2 million children* (2nd ed.). Thousand Oaks, CA: Sage.

Slavin, R.E., Madden, N.A., Dolan, L.L., & Wasik, B.A. (1996). *School: Success for all.* Newbury Park, CA: Corwin Press.

Sloutsky, V. (2015). Conceptual development. In R.M. Lerner (Ed.), *Handbook of child psychology and developmental science* (7th ed.). New York: Wiley.

Smith, A., Steinberg, L., Strang, N., & Chein, J. (2015). Age differences in the impact of peers on adolescents' and adults' neural responses to reward. *Developmental Cognitive Neuroscience, 11,* 75–82.

Smith, R.A., & Davis, S.F. (2016). *REVEL for the psychologist as a detective* (6th ed.). Upper Saddle River, NJ: Pearson.

Smith, R.L., Rose, A.J., & Schwartz-Mette, R.A. (2010). Relational and overt aggression in childhood and adolescence: Clarifying mean-level gender differences and associations with peer acceptance. *Social Development, 19,* 243–269.

Smith, T.E., & others (2016). *Teaching students with special needs in inclusive settings* (7th ed.). Upper Saddle River, NJ: Pearson.

Snell, M.E., & Janney, R.E. (2005). *Practices for inclusive schools: Collaborative teaming* (2nd ed.). Baltimore: Brookes.

Snow, C.E., & Kang, J.Y. (2006). Becoming bilingual, biliterate, and bicultural. In W. Damon & R. Lerner (Eds.), *Handbook of child psychology* (6th ed.). New York: Wiley.

Snow, R.E., Como, L., & Jackson, D. (1996). Individual differences in affective and conative functions. In D.C. Berliner & R.C. Calfee (Eds.), *Handbook of educational psychology.* New York: Macmillan.

Sobel, D.M., & Letourneau, S.M. (2016). Children's developing knowledge of and reflection about teaching. *Journal of Experimental Child Psychology, 143,* 111–122.

Soderqvist, S., & Bergman, N.S. (2015). Working memory training is associated with long-term attainments in math and reading. *Frontiers in Psychology, 6,* 1711.

Solano-Flores, G., & Shavelson, R.J. (1997, Fall). Development of performance assessments in science: Conceptual, practical, and logistical issues. *Educational Measurement,* pp. 16–24.

Soloman, H.J., & Anderman, E.M. (2017). Learning with motivation. In R.E. Mayer & P.A. Alexander (Eds.), *Handbook of research on learning and instruction* (2nd ed.). New York: Routledge.

Sommer, T.E., Sabol, T.J., Chase-Lansdale, P.L., & Brooks-Gunn, J. (2016). Two-generation education programs for parents and children. In S. Jones & N. Lesaux (Eds.), *The leading edge of early childhood education.* Cambridge, MA: Harvard Education Press.

Soravia, L.M., & others (2016). Prestimulus default mode activity influences depth of processing and recognition in an emotional memory task. *Human Brain Mapping*. doi:10.1002/hbm.23076

Sousa, D.A. (1995). *How the brain learns: A classroom teacher's guide*. Reston, VA: National Association of Secondary School Principals.

Spence, J.T., & Buckner, C.E. (2000). Instrumental and expressive traits, trait stereotypes, and sexist attitudes: What do they signify? *Psychology of Women Quarterly, 24,* 44-62.

Spence, J.T., & Helmreich, R. (1978). *Masculinity and femininity: Their psychological dimensions*. Austin: University of Texas Press.

Spencer, S.J., Logel, C., & Davies, P.G. (2016). Stereotype threat. *Annual Review of Psychology* (Vol. 67), 415-437.

Spiegler, M.D. (2016). *Contemporary behavior therapy* (6th ed.). Boston: Cengage.

Sporer, N., Brunstein, J.C., & Kieschke, U. (2009). Improving students' reading comprehension skills: Effects of strategy instruction and reciprocal teaching. *Learning and Instruction, 19,* 272-286.

Spring, J. (2014). *American education* (16th ed.). New York: McGraw-Hill.

Sroufe, L.A., Cooper, R.G., DeHart, G., & Bronfenbrenner, U. (1992). *Child development: Its nature and course* (2nd ed.). New York: McGraw-Hill.

Stahl, S. (2002, January). *Effective reading instruction in the first grade*. Paper presented at the Michigan Reading Recovery conference. Dearborn, MI.

Stanford Center for Assessment, Learning, and Equity (SCALE). (2013). *edTPA*. Palo Alto, CA: Author.

Stanovich, K.E. (2013). *How to think straight about psychology* (10th ed.). Upper Saddle River, NJ: Pearson.

Starr, C. (2015). An objective look at early sexualization and the media. *Sex Roles, 72,* 85-87.

Steel, P. (2007). The nature of procrastination: A meta-analytic and theoretical review of quintessential self-regulatory failure. *Psychological Bulletin, 133,* 65-94.

Steele, C.M., & Aronson, J.A. (2004). Stereotype threat does not live by Steele and Aronson (1995) alone. *American Psychologist, 59,* 47-48.

Steinberg, L. (2015a). How should the science of adolescent brain pathology inform legal policy? In J. Bhabha (Ed.), *Coming of age*. Philadelphia: University of Pennsylvania Press.

Steinberg, L. (2015b). The neural underpinnings of adolescent risk-taking: The roles of reward-seeking, impulse control, and peers. In G. Oettigen & P. Gollwitzer (Eds.), *Self-regulation in adolescence*. New York: Cambridge University Press.

Steinberg, L.D. (2014). *Age of opportunities*. Boston: Houghton Mifflin Harcourt.

Steinmayr, R., Crede, J., McElvany, N., & Wirthwein, L. (2016). Subjective well-being, test anxiety, academic achievement: Testing for reciprocal effects. *Frontiers in Psychology, 6,* 1994.

Stephens, J.M. (2008). Cheating. In N.J. Salkind (Ed.), *Encyclopedia of educational psychology*. Thousand Oaks, CA: Sage.

Stephens, N.M., Hamedani, M.G., & Destin, M. (2014). Closing the social-class achievement gap: A difference-education intervention improves first-generation students' academic performance and all students' college transition. *Psychological Science, 25,* 943-953.

Sterling, D.R. (2009). Classroom management: Setting up the classroom for learning. *Science Scope, 32,* 29-33.

Sternberg, R.J. (1986). *Intelligence applied*. San Diego: Harcourt Brace Jovanovich.

Sternberg, R.J. (2004). Individual differences in cognitive development. In U. Goswami (Ed.), *Blackwell handbook of childhood cognitive development*. Malden, MA: Blackwell.

Sternberg, R.J. (2010). Componential models of creativity. In M. Runco & S. Spritzker (Eds.), *Encyclopedia of creativity*. New York: Elsevier.

Sternberg, R.J. (2012). Human intelligence. In V.S. Ramachandran (Ed.), *Encyclopedia of human behavior* (2nd ed.). New York: Elsevier.

Sternberg, R.J. (2013). Contemporary theories of intelligence. In I.B. Weiner & others (Eds.), *Handbook of psychology* (2nd ed., Vol. 7). New York: Wiley.

Sternberg, R.J. (2014). Teaching about the nature of intelligence. *Intelligence, 42,* 176-179.

Sternberg, R.J. (2015a). Competence versus performance models of people and tests: A commentary on Richardson and Norgate. *Applied Developmental Science, 19,* 170-175.

Sternberg, R.J. (2015b). Styles of thinking and learning: Personal mirror or personal image: A review of the malleability of intellectual styles. *American Journal of Psychology, 128,* 115-122.

Sternberg, R.J. (2016). Multiple intelligences in the new age of thinking. In S. Goldstein, D. Princiotta, & J. Naglieri (Eds.), *Handbook of intelligence*. New York: Springer.

Sternberg, R.J. (2016a). What does it mean to be intelligent? In R.J. Sternberg & others (Eds.), *Scientists making a difference*. New York: Cambridge University Press.

Sternberg, R.J. (2016b). Theories of intelligence. In S. Pfeiffer (Ed.), *APA handbook of giftedness and talent*. Washington, DC: American Psychological Association.

Sternberg, R.J. (2016c). Wisdom. In S.J. Lopez (Ed.), *Encyclopedia of positive psychology* (2nd ed.). New York: Wiley.

Sternberg, R.J. (2017). Teaching for creativity. In R.A. Beghetto & J.C. Kaufman (Eds.), *Cambridge companion in nurturing creativity* (2nd ed.). New York: Cambridge University Press.

Sternberg, R.J., Jarvin, L., & Grigorenko, E.L. (2009). *Teaching for intelligence, creativity, and success*. Thousand Oaks, CA: Corwin.

Sternberg, R.J., & Spear-Swerling, P. (1996). *Teaching for thinking*. Washington, DC: American Psychological Association.

Sternberg, R.J., & Sternberg, K. (2017). *Cognitive psychology* (7th ed.). Boston: Cengage.

Stevenson, H.W. (1992, December). Learning from Asian schools. *Scientific American,* pp. 6, 70-76.

Stevenson, H.W. (1995). Mathematics achievement of American students: First in the world by 2000? In C.A. Nelson (Ed.), *Basic and applied perspectives in learning, cognition, and development*. Minneapolis: University of Minnesota Press.

Stevenson, H.W. (2000). Middle childhood: Education and schooling. In A. Kazdin (Ed.), *Encyclopedia of psychology*. Washington, DC, & New York: American Psychological Association and Oxford University Press.

Stevenson, H.W. (2001). *Commentary on NCTM standards*. Department of Psychology, University of Michigan, Ann Arbor.

Stevenson, H.W., & Hofer, B.K. (1999). Education policy in the United States and abroad: What we can learn from each other. In G.J. Cizek (Ed.), *Handbook of educational policy*. San Diego: Academic Press.

Stevenson, H.W., Lee, S., Chen, C., Stigler, J.W., Hsu, C., & Kitamura, S. (1990). Contexts of achievement. *Monographs of the Society for Research in Development, 55* (Serial No. 221).

Stiggins, R. (2008). *Introduction to student-involved assessment for learning* (5th ed.). Upper Saddle River, NJ: Prentice Hall.

Stipek, D.J. (2002). *Motivation to learn* (4th ed.). Boston: Allyn & Bacon.

Stipek, D.J. (2005, February 16). Commentary in *USA TODAY,* p. 1D.

Stipek, D.J., Feiler, R., Daniels, D., & Milburn, S. (1995). Effects of different instructional approaches on young children's achievement and motivation. *Child Development, 66,* 209-223.

Straus, M.A. (1991). Discipline and deviance: Physical punishment of children and violence and other crimes in adulthood. *Social Problems, 38,* 133–154.

Strentze, T. (2007). Intelligence and socioeconomic success: A meta-analytic review of longitudinal research. *Intelligence, 35,* 401–426.

Suad Nasir, N., Rowley, S.J., & Perez, W. (2016). Cultural, racial/ethnic, and linguistic diversity and identity. In L. Corno & E.M. Anderman (Eds.), *Handbook of educational psychology* (3rd ed.). New York: Routledge.

Sue, D., Sue, D.W., & Sue, D.M. (2016). *Understanding abnormal behavior* (11th ed.). Boston: Cengage.

Sue, D., Sue, D.W., & Sue, D.M. (2017). *Essentials of understanding abnormal behavior* (3rd ed.). Boston: Cengage.

Suen, H.K. (2008). Measurement. In N.J. Salkind (Ed.), *Encyclopedia of educational psychology*. Thousand Oaks, CA: Sage.

Sullivan, A.L., & Simonson, G.R. (2016). A systematic review of school-based social-emotional interventions for refugee and war-traumatized youth. *Review of Educational Research, 86,* 503–530.

Sutin, A.R., Robinson, E., Daly, M., & Terracciarno, A. (2016). Parent-reported bullying and child weight gain between 6 and 15. *Child Obesity.* doi:10.1089/chi.2016.0185.

Swan, K., Kratcoski, A., Schenker, J., & van't Hooft, M. (2009). Interactive whiteboards and student achievement. In M. Thomas & E.C. Schmid (Eds.), *Interactive whiteboards for education and training: Emerging technologies and applications.* Hershey, PA: IGI Global.

Swan, K., van't Hooft, M., Kratcoski, A., & Unger, D. (2005). Uses and effects of mobile computing devices in K-8 classrooms: A preliminary study. *Journal of Research on Technology and Education, 38*(1), 99–112.

Swan, K., & others (2006). Ubiquitous computing: Rethinking teaching, learning and technology integration. In S. Tettegah & R. Hunter (Eds.), *Education and technology: Issues in applications, policy, and administration.* New York: Elsevier.

Swanberg, A.B., & Martinsen, O.L. (2010). Personality, approaches to learning and achievement. *Educational Psychology, 30,* 75–88. DOI: 10.1080/01443410903410474

Swanson, H.L. (1999). What develops in working memory? A life-span perspective. *Developmental Psychology, 35,* 986–1000.

Swanson, H.L. (2016). Cognition and cognitive disabilities. In L. Corno & E.M. Anderman (Eds.), *Handbook of educational psychology* (3rd ed.). New York: Routledge.

Sweller, J. (2012). Human cognitive architecture: Why some instructional procedures work and others do not. In K.R. Harris, S. Graham, T. Urdan, C.B. McCormick, G.M. Sinatra, & J. Sweller (Eds.), *Educational psychology handbook, Volume 1: Theories, constructs, and critical issues* (pp. 295–325). Washington, DC: American Psychological Association.

T

Tamis-LeMonda, C.S., & others (2008). Parents' goals for children: The dynamic coexistence of individualism and collectivism in cultures and individuals. *Social Development, 17,* 183–209.

Tannen, D. (1990). *You just don't understand: Women and men in conversation.* New York: Ballantine.

Tarhan, L., & Acar, B. (2007). Problem-based learning in an eleventh-grade chemistry class: "Factors affecting cell potential." *Research in Science & Technological Education, 25,* 351–369.

Tarman, B., & Kuran, B. (2015). Examination of the cognitive level of questions in social studies textbooks and the views of teachers based on Bloom taxonomy. *Educational Sciences: Theory and Practice, 15,* 213–222.

Taylor, B.G., & Mumford, E.A. (2016). A national descriptive portrait of adolescent relationship abuse: Results from the National Survey on Teen Relationships and Intimate Violence. *Journal of Interpersonal Violence, 31,* 963–988.

Taylor, B.K. (2015). Content, process, and product: Differentiated instruction. *Kappa Delta Pi Record, 51,* 13–17.

Taylor, C., & others (2016). Examining ways that a mindfulness-based intervention reduces stress in public school teachers: A mixed-methods study. *Mindfulness, 7,* 115–129.

Teixeira, M.D., & others (2016). Eating behaviors, body image, perfectionism, and self-esteem in a sample of Portuguese girls. *Revista Brasileira de psiquiatria, 38,* 135–140.

Tenenbaum, H.R., Callahan, M., Alba-Speyer, C., & Sandoval, L. (2002). Parent-child science conversations in Mexican-descent families: Educational background, activity, and past experience as moderators. *Hispanic Journal of Behavioral Science, 24,* 225–248.

Tennyson, R., & Cocchiarella, M. (1986). An empirically based instructional design theory for teaching concepts. *Review of Educational Research, 56,* 40–71.

Terman, D.L., Larner, M.B., Stevenson, C.S., & Behrman, R.E. (1996). Special education for students with disabilities: Analysis and recommendations. *Future of Children, 6*(1), 4–24.

Terwilliger, J. (1997). Semantics, psychometrics, and assessment reform: A close look at "authentic" assessments. *Educational Researcher, 26,* 24–27.

Theunissen, M.H., Vogels, A.G., & Reijneveld, S.A. (2015). Punishment and reward in parental discipline for children aged 5 to 6 years: Prevalence and groups at risk. *Academic Pediatrics, 15,* 96–102.

Thillay, A., & others (2015). Sustained attention and prediction: Distinct brain maturation trajectories during adolescence. *Frontiers in Human Neuroscience, 9,* 519.

Thomas, A., & Chess, S. (1991). Temperament in adolescence and its functional significance. In R.M. Lerner, A.C. Petersen, & J. Brooks-Gunn (Eds.), *Encyclopedia of adolescence* (Vol. 2). New York: Garland.

Thomas, M.S.C., & Johnson, M.H. (2008). New advances in understanding sensitive periods in brain development. *Current Directions in Psychological Science, 17,* 1–5.

Thomas, O.N., Caldwell, C.H., Fiason, N., & Jackson, J.S. (2009). Promoting academic achievement: The role of racial identity in buffering perceptions of teacher discrimination on academic achievement among African American and Caribbean Black adolescents. *Journal of Educational Psychology, 101,* 420–431.

Thomas, R.M. (2005). *Teachers doing research: An introductory guidebook.* Boston: Allyn & Bacon.

Thompson, P.A., & others (2015). Developmental dyslexia: Predicting individual risk. *Journal of Child Psychology and Psychiatry, 56,* 976–987.

Thompson, R.A. (2015). Relationships, regulation, and development. In R.M. Lerner (Ed.), *Handbook of child psychology* (7th ed.). New York: Wiley.

Tobias, E.S., Campbell, M.R., & Greco, P. (2015). Bringing curriculum to life. Enacting project-based learning in music programs. *Music Education Journal, 102,* 39–47.

Toldson, I.A., & Lewis, C.W. (2012). *Challenge the status quo: Academic success among school-age African-American males.* Washington, DC: Congressional Black Caucus Foundation.

Tompkins, G.E. (2015). *Literacy in the early grades* (4th ed.). Upper Saddle River, NJ: Pearson.

Tompkins, G.E. (2016). *Language arts* (9th ed.). Upper Saddle River, NJ: Pearson.

Trahan, L.H., Stuebing, K.K., Fletcher, J.M., & Hiscock, M. (2014). The Flynn effect: A meta-analysis. *Psychological Bulletin, 140,* 1332–1360.

Tran, T.D., Luchters, S., & Fisher, J. (2016). Early childhood development: Impact of national human development, family poverty, parenting practices, and access to early childhood education. *Child Care and Human Development*. doi: 10.1111/cch.12395

Trochim, W., Donnelly, J.P., & Arora, K. (2016). *Research methods: The essential knowledge base* (2nd ed.). Boston: Cengage.

Troop-Gordon, W., & Ladd, G.W. (2015). Teachers' victimization-related beliefs and strategies: Associations with students' aggressive behavior and peer victimization. *Journal of Abnormal Child Psychology, 43,* 45–60.

Trzesniewski, K.H., & others (2006). Low self-esteem during adolescence predicts poor health, criminal behavior, and limited income prospects during adulthood. *Developmental Psychology, 42,* 381–390.

Tsal, Y., Shalev, L., & Mevorach, C. (2005). The diversity of attention deficits in ADHD. *Journal of Learning Disabilities, 38,* 142–157.

Tsang, C.L. (1989). Bilingual minorities and language issues in writing. *Written Communication, 9*(1), 1–15.

Tulving, E. (2000). Concepts of memory. In E. Tulving & F.I.M. Craik (Eds.), *The Oxford handbook of memory*. New York: Oxford University Press.

Turiel, E. (2015). Moral development. In R.M. Lerner (Ed.), *Handbook of child psychology and developmental science* (7th ed.). New York: Wiley.

Turnbull, A., Rutherford-Turnbull, H., Wehmeyer, M.L., & Shogren, K.A. (2016). *Exceptional lives* (8th ed.). Upper Saddle River, NJ: Pearson.

Tzeng, J-Y. (2014). Mapping for depth and variety: Using a "six W's" scaffold to facilitate concept mapping for different history concepts with different degrees of freedom. *Educational Studies, 40,* 253–275.

U

U.S. Department of Education. (2000). *To assure a free and appropriate education of all children with disabilities.* Washington, DC: U.S. Office of Education.

U.S. Office for Civil Rights. (2016). *Frequently asked questions about sexual harassment, including sexual violence.* Retrieved August 21, 2016, from www2.ed.gov/about/offices/list/ocr/qa-sexharass.html

U.S. Office of Education. (1998). *The benchmark study.* Washington, DC: Office of Education & Minority Affairs.

Ugodulunwa, C., & Wakjissa, S. (2015). Use of portfolio assessment technique in teaching map sketching and location in secondary school geography in Jos, Nigeria. *Journal of Education and Practice, 6*(17), 23–30.

Underwood, M.K. (2011). Aggression. In M.K. Underwood & L. Rosen (Eds.), *Social development*. New York: Guilford.

Undheim, A.M. (2013). Involvement in bullying as predictor of suicidal ideation among 12- to 15-year-old Norwegian adolescents. *European Child and Adolescent Psychiatry, 22,* 357–265.

Ungar, M. (2015). Practitioner review: Diagnosing childhood resilience: A systematic diagnosis of adaption in diverse social ecologies. *Journal of Child Psychology and Psychiatry, 56,* 4–17.

UNICEF. (2016). *The state of the world's children 2016.* Geneva, Switzerland: Author.

University of Buffalo Counseling Services. (2016). *Procrastination.* Buffalo, NY: Author.

University of Illinois Counseling Center. (2016). *Overcoming procrastination.* Urbana-Champaign, IL: Department of Student Affairs.

University of Texas at Austin Counseling and Mental Health Center. (2016). *Perfectionism versus healthy striving: Coping strategies.* Austin, TX: Author.

Updegraff, K.A., & Umana-Taylor, A.J. (2015). What can we learn from the study of Mexican-origin families in the United States? *Family Process, 54,* 205–216.

USA Today. (1999). All-USA TODAY Teacher Team. Retrieved January 15, 2004, from www.usatoday.com/news/education/1999

USA Today. (2000, October 10). All-USA first teacher team. Retrieved November 15, 2004, from http://www.usatoday.com/life/teacher/teach/htm

USA Today. (2003, October 15). From kindergarten to high school, they make the grade. Retrieved April 22, 2006, from www.usatoday.com/news/education/2003-10-15-2003-winners

V

Valle, A., & others (2015). Multiple goals and homework involvement in elementary school students. *Spanish Journal of Psychology, 18,* E81.

Vallone, R.P., Griffin, D.W., Lin, S., & Ross, L. (1990). Overconfident prediction of future actions and outcomes by self and others. *Journal of Personality and Social Psychology, 58,* 582–592.

Van de Walle, J.A., Karp, K.S., & Bay-Williams, J.M. (2016). *Elementary and middle school mathematics* (9th ed.). Upper Saddle River, NJ: Pearson.

Van der Graaff, J., Carlo, G., Crocetti, E., Koot, H. M., & Branje, S. (2018). Prosocial behavior in adolescence: Gender differences in development and links with empathy. *Journal of Youth and Adolescence, 47,* 1086–1099. doi: 10.1007/s10964-017-0786-1

Van Geel, M., Vedder, P., & Tanilon, J. (2014). Relationship between peer victimization, cyberbullying, and suicide in children and adolescents: A meta-analysis. *JAMA Pediatrics, 168,* 435–442.

Van Lamsweerde, A.E., Beck, M.R., & Johnson, J.S. (2016). Visual working memory organization is subject to top-down control. *Psychonomic Bulletin and Review, 23,* 1181–1189.

Van Tassel-Baska, J. (2015). Theories of giftedness: Reflections on James Gallagher's work. *Journal for the Education of the Gifted, 38,* 18–23.

Vandell, D.L., Larson, R.W., Mahoney, J.L., & Watts, T. (2015). Children in organized activities. In R.M. Lerner (Ed.), *Handbook of child psychology and developmental science* (7th ed.). New York: Wiley.

Vansteenkiste, M., Timmermans, T., Lens, W., Soenens, B., & Van den Broeck, A. (2008). Does extrinsic goal framing enhance extrinsic goal-oriented individuals' learning and performance? An experimental test of the match perspective versus self-determination theory. *Journal of Educational Psychology, 100,* 387–397.

Vargas, J. (2009). *Behavior analysis for effective teaching.* New York: Routledge.

Veenman, M.V.J. (2017). Learning to self-monitor and self-regulate. In R.E. Mayer & P.A. Alexander (Eds.), *Handbook of research on learning and instruction* (2nd ed.). New York: Routledge.

Veira, J.M., & others (2016). Parents' work-family experiences and children's problem behaviors: The mediating role of parent-child relationship. *Journal of Family Psychology, 30,* 419–430.

Verhagen, J., & Leseman, P. (2016). How do verbal short-term memory and working memory relate to the acquisition of vocabulary and grammar? A comparison between first and second language learners. *Journal of Experimental Child Psychology, 141,* 65–82.

Vernon-Feagans, L., Garrett-Peters, P., De Marco, A., & BratschHines, M. (2012). Children living in rural poverty: The role of chaos in early development. In V. Maholmes & R. B. King (Eds.), *The Oxford handbook of poverty and child development* (pp. 448–466). New York, NY: Oxford University Press.

Veronneau, M-H., Vitaro, F., Pedersen, S., & Tremblay, R.E. (2008). Do peers contribute to the likelihood of secondary graduation among disadvantaged boys? *Journal of Educational Psychology, 100,* 429–442.

Vollink, T., Dehue, F., & McGuckin, C. (Eds.). (2016). *Cyberbullying.* New York: Psychology Press.

Vukelich, C., Christie, J., Enz, B.J., & Roskos, K.A. (2016). *Helping young children learn language and literacy* (4th ed.). Upper Saddle River, NJ: Pearson.

Vygotsky, L.S. (1962). *Thought and language.* Cambridge, MA: MIT Press.

Vysniauske, R., Verburgh, L., Oosteriaan, J., & Molendijk, M.L. (2016). The effects of physical exercise on functional outcomes in the treatment of ADHD. *Journal of Attention Disorders.* doi:10.1177/1087054715627489

W

Wadsworth, M.E., & others (2016). Poverty and the development of psychopathology. In D. Cicchetti (Ed.), *Developmental psychopathology* (3rd ed.). New York: Wiley.

Wagner, R.K., & Sternberg, R.J. (1986). Tacit knowledge and intelligence in the everyday world. In R.J. Sternberg & R.K. Wagner (Eds.), *Practical intelligence.* Cambridge, UK: Cambridge University Press.

Waiter, G.D., & others (2009). Exploring possible neural mechanisms of intelligence differences using processing speed and working memory tasks. *Intelligence, 37,* 199–206.

Walsh, J. (2008). Self-efficacy. In N.J. Salkind (Ed.), *Encyclopedia of educational psychology.* Thousand Oaks, CA: Sage.

Walton, G.M., & Cohen, G.I. (2011). A brief social-belonging intervention improves academic and health outcomes of minority students. *Science, 331,* 1447–1451.

Walton, G.M., & others (2014). Two brief interventions to mitigate a "chilly climate" transform women's experience, relationships, and achievement in engineering. *Journal of Educational Psychology, 107,* 468–485.

Wang, C., & others (2016). Longitudinal relationships between bullying and moral disengagement among adolescents. *Journal of Youth and Adolescence.* doi:10.1007/s10964-016-0577-0

Wang, M. T., & Degol, J. L. (2017). Gender gap in science, technology, engineering, and mathematics (STEM): Current knowledge, implications for practice, policy, and future directions. *Educational Psychology Review, 29*(1), 119–140. doi:10.1007/s10648-015-9355-x

Wang, M. -T., & Eccles, J. S. (2013). School context, achievement motivation, and academic engagement: A longitudinal study of school engagement using a multidimensional perspective. *Learning and Instruction, 28,* 12–23. doi: https://doi.org/10.1016/j.learninstruc.2013.04.002

Wang, Q., & Pomerantz, E.M. (2009). The motivational landscape of early adolescence in the United States and China: A longitudinal study. *Child Development, 86,* 1272–1287.

Wang, Z., Devine, R.T., Wong, K.K., & Hughes, C. (2016). Theory of mind and executive function during middle school across cultures. *Journal of Experimental Child Psychology, 149,* 6–22.

Wardlow, L., & Harm, E. (2015). Using appropriate digital tools to overcome barriers to collaborative learning in classrooms. *Educational Technology, 55,* 32–35.

Wasserberg, M.J. (2014). Stereotype threat effects on African American children in an urban elementary school. *Journal of Experimental Education, 82,* 502–517.

Waterman, A.S. (2015). Identity as internal processes: How the "I" comes to define the "me." In K.C. McLean & M. Syed (Eds.), *Oxford handbook of identity development.* New York: Oxford University Press.

Watson, D.L., & Tharp, R.G. (2014). *Self-directed behavior* (10th ed.). Boston: Cengage.

Waugh, C.K., & Gronlund, N.E. (2013). *Assessment of student achievement* (10th ed.). Upper Saddle River, NJ: Pearson.

Weaver. J.M., & Schofield, T.J. (2015). Mediation and moderation of divorce effects on children's behavior problems. *Journal of Family Psychology, 29,* 39–48.

Webb, L.D., & Metha, A. (2017). *Foundations of American education* (8th ed.). Upper Saddle River, NJ: Pearson.

Webb, N.M., & Palincsar, A.S. (1996). Group processes in the classroom. In D.C. Berliner & R.C. Calfee (Eds.), *Handbook of educational psychology.* New York: Macmillan.

Wei, R.C., Pecheone, R.L., & Wilczak, K.L. (2015). Measuring what really matters. *Phi Delta Kappan, 97*(1), 8–13.

Weiler, L.M., & others (2015). Time-limited, structured youth mentoring and adolescent problem behaviors. *Applied Developmental Science, 19,* 196–205.

Weiner, B. (1986). *An attributional theory of motivation and emotion.* New York: Springer.

Weiner, B. (1992). *Human motivation: Metaphors, theories, and research.* Newbury Park, CA: Sage.

Weinstein, C.S. (2007). *Middle and secondary classroom management* (3rd ed.). Boston: McGraw-Hill.

Weinstein, C.S. (2015). *Middle and secondary school classroom management* (5th ed.). New York: McGraw-Hill.

Weinstein, C. S., Tomlinson-Clarke, S., & Curran, M. (2004). Toward a conception of culturally responsive classroom management. *Journal of Teacher Education, 55*(1), 25–38. DOI: 10.1177/0022487103259812.

Weinstein, C.S., & Mignano, A. (2007). *Elementary classroom management* (4th ed.). Boston: McGraw-Hill.

Weinstein, C.S., & Novodvorsky, I. (2015). *Middle and secondary classroom management* (5th ed.). New York: McGraw-Hill.

Weinstein, C.S., & Romano, M. (2015). *Elementary classroom management* (6th ed.). New York: McGraw-Hill.

Weinstein, R.S. (2004). *Reaching higher: The power of expectations in schooling.* Cambridge, MA: Harvard University Press.

Weinstein, R.S., Madison, S.M., & Kuklinski, M.R. (1995). Raising expectations in schooling: Obstacles and opportunities for change. *American Educational Research Journal, 32*(1), 121–159.

Wellman, H.M. (2011). Developing a theory of mind. In U. Goswami (Ed.), *Wiley-Blackwell handbook of childhood cognitive development* (2nd ed.). New York: Wiley.

Wellman, H.M. (2015). *Making minds.* New York: Oxford University Press.

Wellman, H.M., Cross, D., & Watson, J. (2001). Meta-analysis of theory-of-mind development: The truth about false belief. *Child Development, 72,* 655–684.

Welshman, D. (2000). *Social studies resources.* St. Johns, Newfoundland: Leary Brooks Jr. High School.

Wendelken, C., Gerrer, E., Whitaker, K.J., & Bunge, S.A. (2016). Fronto-parietal network reconfiguration supports the development of reasoning ability. *Cerebral Cortex, 26,* 2178–2190.

Wenglinsky, H. (2002). The link between teacher classroom practices and student academic performance. *Education Policy Analysis Archives, 10,* 12.

Wentzel, K.R. (1997). Student motivation in middle school: The role of perceived psychological caring. *Journal of Educational Psychology, 89,* 411–419.

Wentzel, K.R. (2016). Teacher-student relationships. In K.R. Wentzel & D.B. Miele (Eds.), *Handbook of motivation at school* (2nd ed.). New York: Routledge.

Wentzel, K.R., Barry, C.M., & Caldwell, K.A. (2004). Friendships in middle school: Influences on motivation and school adjustment. *Journal of Educational Psychology, 96,* 195–203.

Wentzel, K.R., & Erdley, C.A. (1993). Strategies for making friends: Relations to social behavior and peer acceptance in early adolescence. *Developmental Psychology, 29,* 819–826.

Wentzel, K.R., & Miele, D.B. (Eds.). (2016). *Handbook of motivation at school.* New York: Routledge.

Wentzel, K.R., & Muenks, G.B. (2016). Peer influence on students' motivation, academic achievement, and social behavior. In K.R. Wentzel & G.B. Ramani (Eds.), *Handbook of social influences in school contexts.* New York: Routledge.

Wentzel, K.R., & Ramani, G.B. (Eds.). (2016). *Handbook of social influences in school contexts.* New York: Routledge.

What Works Clearinghouse. (2007). *Peer-assisted learning strategies.* Rockville, MD: Author.

What Works Clearinghouse. (2009, August). *Success for All.* Washington, DC: Institute of Education Sciences. Also available on ERIC, #ED506157.

What Works Clearinghouse. (2012). *Success for All. What Works Clearinghouse intervention report.* Princeton, NJ: What Works Clearinghouse.

What Works Clearinghouse. (2012). https://ies.ed.gov/ncee/wwc/Docs/InterventionReports/wwc_pals_050112.pdf.

What Works Clearinghouse. (2014). *WWC review of the report "Evaluation of the i3 scale-up of Reading Recovery year one report, 2011-2012." What Works Clearinghouse single study review.* Princeton, NJ: What Works Clearinghouse.

What Works Clearinghouse. (2017). https://ies.ed.gov/ncee/wwc/Docs/InterventionReports/wwc_sfa_032817.pdf.

Wheeler, J.J., Mayton, M.R., & Carter, S.L. (2015). *Methods of teaching students with autism spectrum disorders.* Upper Saddle River, NJ: Pearson.

White, R.W. (1959). Motivation reconsidered: The concept of confidence. *Psychological Review, 66,* 297-333.

Widyatiningtyas, R., Kusumah, Y.S., Sumamo, U., & Sabandar, J. (2015). The impact of problem-based learning approach to senior high school students' mathematics critical thinking ability. *Indonesian Mathematical Society Journal on Mathematics Education, 6,* 30-38.

Wigfield, A., & Asher, S.R. (1984). Social and motivational influences on reading. In P.D. Pearson, R. Barr, M.L. Kamil, & P. Mosenthal (Eds.), *Handbook of reading research.* New York: Longman.

Wigfield, A., Tonks, S.M., & Klauda, S.L. (2016) Expectancy-value theory. In K.R. Wentzel & D.B. Miele (Eds.), *Handbook of motivation at school* (2nd ed.). New York: Routledge.

Wigfield, A., & others (2015). Development of achievement motivation and engagement. In R.M. Lerner (Ed.), *Handbook of child psychology and developmental science* (7th ed.). New York: Wiley.

Wiggins, G. (2013/2014). How good is good enough? *Educational Leadership, 71*(4), 10-16.

Wiggins, G., & Wilbur, D. (2015). How to make your questions essential. *Educational Leadership, 73,* 10-15.

Wilhelm, J.D. (2014). Learning to love the questions: How essential questions promote creativity and deep learning. *Knowledge Quest, 42,* 36-41.

Wilkinson, I.A.G., & Gaffney, J.S. (2016). Literacy for schooling. In L. Corso & E.M. Anderman (Eds.), *Handbook of educational psychology* (3rd ed.). New York: Routledge.

Williams, P., Sullivan, S., & Kohn, L. (2012). Out of the mouths of babes: What do secondary students believe about outstanding teachers? *American Secondary Education, 40*(2), 104-119.

Willingham, D.T., Hughes, E.M., & Dobolyi, D.G. (2015). The scientific status of learning styles theories. *Teaching of Psychology, 42,* 266-271.

Willoughby, M.T., & others (2016). Developmental delays in executive function from 3 to 5 years of age predict kindergarten academic readiness. *Journal of Learning Disabilities.* doi:10.1177/0022219415619754

Winfrey Avant, D., & Bracy, W. (2015). Teaching note—using problem-based learning to illustrate the concepts of privilege and oppression. *Journal of Social Work Education, 51,* 604-614.

Winn, I.J. (2004). The high cost of uncritical teaching. *Phi Delta Kappan, 85,* 496-497.

Winne, P.H. (2001). Self-regulated learning viewed from models of information processing. In B.J. Zimmerman & D.H. Schunk (Eds.), *Self-regulated learning and academic achievement.* Mahwah, NJ: Erlbaum.

Winne, P.H. (2005). Key issues in modeling and applying research on self-regulated learning. *Applied Psychology: An International Review, 54,* 232-238.

Winner, E. (1986, August). Where pelicans kiss seals. *Psychology Today,* pp. 24-35.

Winner, E. (1996). *Gifted children: Myths and realities.* New York: Basic Books.

Winner, E. (2006). Development in the arts. In W. Damon & R. Lerner (Eds.), *Handbook of child psychology* (6th ed.). New York: Wiley.

Winner, E. (2014). Child prodigies and adult genius: A weak link. In D.K. Simonton (Ed.), *Wiley-Blackwell handbook of genius.* New York: Wiley.

Winsler, A., Carlton, M.P., & Barry, M.J. (2000). Age-related changes in preschool children's systematic use of private speech in a natural setting. *Journal of Child Language, 27,* 665-687.

Wiske, M.S., Franz, K.R., & Breit, L. (2005). *Teaching for understanding with technology.* New York: Wiley.

Witelson, S.F., Kigar, D.L., & Harvey, T. (1999). The exceptional brain of Albert Einstein. *The Lancet, 353,* 2149-2153.

Wittmer, D.S., & Honig, A.S. (1994). Encouraging positive social development in young children. *Young Children, 49,* 4-12.

Wolfers, T., & others (2016). Quantifying patterns of brain activity: Distinguishing unaffected siblings from participants with ADHD and healthy individuals. *Neuroimage: Clinical, 12,* 227-233.

Wolke, D., & Lereya, S.T. (2015). Long-term effects of bullying. *Archives of Disease in Childhood, 100,* 879-885.

Wolke, D., Lereya, S.T., & Tippett, N. (2016). Individual and social determinants of bullying and cyberbullying. In T. Vollink, F. Dehue, & C. McGuckin (Eds.), *Cyberbullying.* New York: Psychology Press.

Wong, H., Wong, R., Rogers, K., & Brooks, A. (2012). Managing your classroom for success. *Science and Children, 49*(9), 60-64.

Wong, M.D., & others (2014). Successful schools and risky behaviors among low-income adolescents. *Pediatrics, 134,* e389-e396.

Wong Briggs, T. (1999, October 14). *Honorees find keys to unlocking kids' minds.* Retrieved March 10, 2000, from www.usatoday.com/education

Wong Briggs, T. (2004, October 14). Students embrace vitality of *USA Today's* top 20 teachers. *USA Today,* p. 7D.

Wong Briggs, T. (2005). Math teacher resets the learning curve. Retrieved March 6, 2006, from www.usatoday.com/news/education/2005-04-05-math-teacher_x.htm

Wong Briggs, T. (2007, October 18). An early start for learning. *USA Today,* p. 6D.

Work Group of the American Psychological Association Board of Educational Affairs. (1997). *Learner-centered psychological principles: A framework for school reform and redesign.* Washington, DC: American Psychological Association.

Wood, D.J., Bruner, J.S., & Ross, G. (1976). The role of tutoring in problem solving. *Journal of Child Psychiatry and Psychology, 17*(2), 89-100.

Write: Outloud. (2009). Retrieved January 16, 2009, from *USA Today* www.donjohnston.com/products/write_outloud/index.html

Wu, H-K., & Huang, Y-L. (2007). Ninth-grade student engagement in teacher-centered and student-centered technology-enhanced learning environments. *Science Education, 91,* 727–749.

Wu, L., Sun, S., He, Y., & Jiang, B. (2016). The effect of interventions targeting screen time reduction: A systematic review and meta-analysis. *Medicine, 95*(27), e4029.

Wu, W.C., Luu, S., & Luh, D.L. (2016). Defending behaviors, bullying roles, and their associations with mental health in junior high school students: A population-based study. *BMC Public Health, 16*(1), 1066.

Wubbels, T., & others (2016). Teacher-student relationships and student achievement. In K.R. Wentzel & G.B. Ramani (Eds.), *Handbook of social influences in school contexts.* New York: Routledge.

Wyatt, M. (2016) "Are they becoming more reflective and/or efficacious?" A conceptual model mapping how teachers' self-efficacy beliefs might grow. *Educational Review, 68,* 114–137.

X

Xing, S., & others (2016). Right hemisphere gray matter structure and language outcomes in chronic left hemisphere stroke. *Brain, 139*(Pt. 1), 227–241.

Xiong, Y., So, H-J., & Toh, Y. (2015). Assessing learners' perceived readiness for computer-supported collaborative learning (CSCL): A study on initial development and validation. *Journal of Computing in Higher Education, 27,* 215–239.

Xu, Y. (2015). Examining the effects of adapted peer tutoring on social and language skills of young English language learners. *Early Child Development and Care, 185,* 1587–1600.

Y

Yanchinda, J., Yodmongkol, P., & Chakpitak, N. (2016). Measurement of learning process by semantic association technique on Bloom's taxonomy vocabulary. *International Education Studies, 9,* 107–122.

Yasnitsky, A., & Van der Veer, R. (Eds.). (2016). *Revisionist revolution in Vygotsky studies.* New York: Psychology Press.

Yeh, Y-C. (2009). Integrating e-learning into the direction-instruction model to enhance the effectiveness of critical-thinking instruction. *Instructional Science, 37,* 185–203.

Yen, C.F., & others (2014). Association between school bullying levels/types and mental health problems among Taiwanese adolescents. *Comprehensive Psychiatry, 55,* 405–413.

Yeung, W.J. (2012). Explaining the black-white achievement gap: An international stratification and developmental perspective. In K.R. Harris, S. Graham, & T. Urdan (Eds.), *APA handbook of educational psychology.* Washington, DC: American Psychological Association.

Yinger, R.J. (1980). Study of teacher planning. *Elementary School Journal, 80,* 107–127.

Z

Zarefsky, D. (2016). *Public speaking* (8th ed.). Upper Saddle River, NJ: Pearson.

Zayas, V., Mischel, W., & Pandey, G. (2014). Mind and brain in delay of gratification. In V.F. Reyna & V. Zayas (Eds.), *The neuroscience of decision making.* Washington, DC: American Psychological Association.

Zelazo, P.D., & Lyons, K.E. (2012). The potential benefits of mindfulness training in early childhood: A developmental social cognitive neuroscience perspective. *Child Development Perspectives, 6,* 154–160.

Zelazo, P.D., & Muller, U. (2011). Executive function in typical and atypical children. In U. Goswami (Ed.), *Wiley-Blackwell handbook of childhood cognitive development* (2nd ed.). New York: Wiley.

Zeng, R., & Greenfield, P.M. (2015). Cultural evolution over the last 40 years in China: Using the Google Ngram viewer to study implications of social and political change for cultural values. *International Journal of Psychology, 50,* 47–55.

Zhang, L-F., & Sternberg, R.J. (2012). Learning in cross-cultural perspective. In T. Husen & T.N. Postlethwaite (Eds.), *International encyclopedia of education* (3rd ed.). New York: Elsevier.

Zhang, Q., & Sanchez, E.I. (2013). High school grade inflation from 2004 to 2011. *ACT Research Report Services 2013* (3). Iowa City, IA: ACT.

Zhong, P., Liu, W., & Yan, Z. (2016). Aberrant regulation of synchronous network activity by the attention deficit hyperactivity disorder-associated human dopamine D4 receptor variation D4.7 in the prefrontal cortex. *Journal of Physiology, 594,* 135–147.

Zhou, Q., Lengua, L.J., & Wang, Y. (2009). The relations of temperament reactivity and effortful control to children's adjustment problems in the United States and China. *Developmental Psychology, 45,* 724–239.

Zimmer-Gembeck, M.J., & Skinner, E. A. (2011). The development of coping across childhood and adolescence: An integrative review and critique of research. *International Journal of Behavioral Development, 35,* 1–17. doi: 10.1177/0165025410384923

Zimmerman, B.J., Bonner, S., & Kovach, R. (1996). *Developing self-regulated learners.* Washington, DC: American Psychological Association.

Zirpoli, T.J. (2016). *Behavior management* (7th ed.). Upper Saddle River, NJ: Pearson.

Zohar, A., & Ben David, A. (2008). Explicit teaching of meta-strategic knowledge in authentic classroom situations. *Metacognition Learning, 3,* 59–82. doi: 10.1007/s11409-007-9019-4

Zosuls, K.M., Lurye, L.E., & Ruble, D.N. (2008). Gender: Awareness, identity, and stereotyping. In M.M. Haith & J.B. Benson (Eds.), *Encyclopedia of infancy and early childhood.* New York: Oxford University Press.

Zuberer, A., Brandeis, D., & Drechsler, R. (2015). Are treatments for neurofeedback training in children with ADHD related to successful regulation of brain activity? A review on the learning of regulation of brain activity and a contribution to the discussion on specificity. *Frontiers in Human Neuroscience, 9,* 135.

Zucker, A.A., & McGhee, R. (2005). *A study of one-to-one computer use in mathematics and science instruction at the secondary level in Henrico County Public Schools.* Washington, DC: SRI International.

Zusho, A., Daddino, J., & Garcia, C-B. (2016). Culture, race, ethnicity, and motivation. In K.R. Wentzel & G.B. Ramani (Eds.), *Handbook of social influences in school contexts.* New York: Routledge.

Name Index

A

Abbassi, E., 265
Abbott, R. D., 7, 58, 187, 188
ABC News, 86
Abra, K., 23, 71, 120, 242, 368, 521, 558
Abrami, P. C., 306
Abruscato, J. A., 380
Acar, B., 410
Achieve, Inc., 365
Adams, A., 54, 336
Adams, R., 477
Adkins, M., 367
Affrunti, N. W., 457
Ahrons, C., 79
Airasian, P., 411
Airasian, P. W., 554, 563, 564, 568
Akcay, N. O., 343
Akin, A., 455
Akin, U., 455
Alba-Fisch, M., 80
Alber-Morgan, S., 186, 204, 205
Alberto, P. A., 195, 228, 230, 231, 235, 260, 397, 483, 484
Alberts, J. K., 489
Aldao, A., 172
Alderson-Day, B., 52
Aleven, V., 11
Alexander, K. L., 450, 452
Alexander, P. A., 6, 257, 280, 358, 434
Alexander, R. A., 361
Allington, R. L., 360–362, 366
Allison, C. M., 176
Allor, J. H., 341
Allyn, P., 360, 361
Aloisi, C., 402
Alsaker, F. D., 497
Alverno College, 487
Amabile, T. M., 316, 333
Amanti, C., 162
Ambrose, D., 208–210, 212, 313, 316, 317
Ambrose, L., 280
Anastasi, A., 117
Anderman, E. M., 8, 89, 100, 439, 443
Anderman, L. H., 6, 12, 14, 100, 439
Anderson, L. M., 483
Anderson, L. W., 399
Anderson, S. B., 192
Andrade, H. L., 540
Anglin, D. M., 97
Annas, J., 102
Ansary, N. S., 148
Anti-Bias Curriculum Task Force, 164

Appel, M., 127
Applebee, A., 366
Apple Computer, 435
Arends, R. I., 322
Aries, R. J., 405
Aristotle, 30, 219, 334
Arkes, J., 79
Armstrong, S. J., 135
Arnett, J. J., 30
Arnoux, D., 156
Aronson, E. E., 162, 345, 358
Aronson, J., 127
Aronson, J. A., 127
Arora, K., 16
Arter, J., 560
Ashcraft, M. H., 221, 235, 257, 265, 270, 319
Asher, S. R., 450
Askari, E., 450
Aslan, S., 411
Assouline, S. G., 212
Astington, J. W., 287
Atkins, R., 103
Atkinson, J. W., 443
Atkinson, M., 19
Atkinson, R. C., 269
Audesirk, G., 32
Audesirk, T., 32
Austin, C. C., 443
Ayres, L., 263, 567
Azmitia, M., 96

B

Babbie, E. R., 16
Baddeley, A., 267
Baer, J., 277, 316
Bain, R. B., 387, 411
Ballentine, J. H., 452
Bandura, A., 221, 237, 238, 239, 248, 249, 253, 441, 442, 457, 464
Bandy, T., 150
Banerjee, R., 287
Bangert, R., 404
Banks, J. A., 129, 153, 158, 159, 161, 165, 166, 452, 485, 530
Bankson, N. W., 197, 198
Baratz-Snowden, J., 518, 519
Barbarin, O. A., 176
Barber, W., 408
Barbot, B., 313
Barhight, L. R., 496
Barkin, S. H., 148

Barlett, C. P., 496
Barnes, A., 497
Barron, A. E., 342
Barry, C. M., 83
Barry, M. J., 52
Bart, W. M., 116, 524
Bartlett, J., 269
Bartlett, L., 29
Barton, J., 558
Bassett, H. H., 105
Bassi, M., 436
Batdi, V., 410
Bates, J. E., 137–139
Bauer, P. J., 256, 274
Baugh, D. E., 451
Baumann, Z. D., 474
Bauman-Waengler, J., 197
Baumeister, R. F., 93
Baumrind, D., 78, 480
Bay-Williams, J. M., 6, 358, 373
Beall, M. L., 487
Bear, D. R., 360
Beaty, J. J., 62
Beck, I. L., 367
Beck, M. R., 272
Beck, T. A., 382
Becker, D. R., 302
Bednar, R. L., 95
Beebe, S. A., 8, 488
Beebe, S. J., 8, 488
Beghetto, R. A., 313, 316
Bell, N., 336
Bellas, V. M., 433
Belsky, J., 31
Bem, S. L., 173
Bendixen, L., 6
Benner, A. D., 79, 148
Bennett, K., 306
Benson, P. L., 103
Berenbaum, S. A., 99, 169, 170, 175
Berenfeld, B., 164
Berenhaus, M. S., 361
Berg, A. T., 196
Berger, I., 107, 191
Bergman, N. S., 268
Berk, L. E., 52
Berko, J., 60
Berko Gleason, J., 58, 63
Berliner, D. C., 278
Berndt, T. J., 449
Bernier, R., 199
Berninger, V., 7
Berninger, V. W., 186, 187
Bernthal, J. E., 197, 198
Berry, B., 504

Berry, L., 240
Best, D. L., 169, 174
Betti, U., 92
Betts, J., 260
Bhatt, R. S., 49, 296, 297
Bialystok, E., 154, 155
Bianco, F., 287
Bickford, L., 256
Biddle, B., 477
Bierman, K. L., 200
Biggs, D. A., 506
Bigler, R. S., 176
Bigorra, A., 268
Bilen, D., 343
Bill and Melinda Gates Foundation, 90
Binet, A., 115
Birch, S. H., 82
Birman, B. F., 513
Bjorklund, D. F., 258, 286
Blackwell, L. S., 440
Blair, C., 104, 245, 302
Blakely-McClure, S. J., 172
Blakemore, J. E. O., 99, 169, 170, 175
Blankenship, K., 229
Blankenship, T. L., 268
Blok, H., 360
Blood, J. D., 18
Bloom, B., 4, 209, 211
Bloom, B. S., 397, 403
Bloom, L., 60
Blumenfeld, P. C., 88, 323, 346, 435, 451, 483
Blyth, D. A., 88
Boaler, J., 375
Bodrova, E., 55, 303
Boendermaker, C., 360
Bogart, L. M., 496
Bonazzo, C., 90
Bonner, S., 245
Bonney, C. R., 305, 307, 521
Bonvanie, I. J., 457
Borich, G. D., 5, 6, 88, 393, 395, 400
Borkowski, J. G., 288
Borneman, M. J., 128
Bostic, J. Q., 305
Boud, D., 540
Boulton, A. J., 497
Boutot, E. A., 199
Bowker, J., 168
Bowman-Perrott, L., 341
Boyatzis, R. E., 123
Boyd, M., 39
Boyle, A. E., 79
Boyles, N. S., 195
Boynton, P. M., 16

I-1

Braaksma, M., 367
Bracy, W., 322
Bradburn, S., 14
Brainerd, C. J., 272
Braithwaite, D. W., 257
Brams, H., 191
Brandeis, D., 192
Branscum, P., 11
Bransford, J., 7, 222, 278–280, 283, 326, 358
Bransford, J. D., 319, 326, 375
Bredekamp, S., 7, 85, 86, 126
Breen, A. V., 93
Breit, L., 418, 419
Brember, I., 93
Brendel, P. C., 38
Brenner, J. D., 106
Brewer, M. B., 146
Bridgeland, J. M., 103
Briggs, T. W., 310
Brigham, M., 200
Brin, S., 86
Brock, R. L., 80
Brody, N., 123, 124, 127
Bronfenbrenner, U., 44, 71, 72
Brookhart, S. M., 10, 395, 474, 506, 541, 547
Brookover, W. B., 441
Brooks, J. G., 306, 309, 332
Brooks, M. G., 306, 309, 332
Brooks-Gunn, J., 148, 149, 260
Brophy, J., 284, 433, 438, 444, 454, 458
Brown, A. L., 363, 422
Brown, C. S., 175, 178
Brown, G. T. L., 540
Brown, H., 378
Bruning, R., 371
Brunstein, J. C., 363
Bub, K. L., 245
Buchanan, S., 408
Bucher, R. D., 9, 153
Buckner, C. E., 173
Buehl, M. M., 12
Buhs, E. S., 82
Bukowski, W. M., 168
Burchinal, M. R., 85
Burden, P. R., 6, 7, 357, 393, 400
Burish, P., 341
Burke, K., 530
Burkham, D. T., 170
Burkhart, J. M., 123
Burnaford, G. E., 13
Burstein, S., 244
Bursuck, W. D., 188
Burt, K. B., 32
Burz, H. L., 553
Busby, B. D., 304
Busching, R., 172
Buss, D. M., 32, 172
Busso, D. S., 38
Butcher, J. T., 129
Butcher, K. R., 207
Butler, Y. G., 155
Byers, B. E., 32
Byrd, D. M., 6, 7, 357, 393, 400
Byrne, D., 455

C

Cabus, S. J., 405
Cagle, M., 212
Cain, K., 361
Cain, M. S., 11
Cairncross, M., 192
Caldwell, K. A., 83
Calet, N., 361
Calhoun, E., 6, 404
California State Department of Education, 560
Calkins, S. D., 104
Callan, M. J., 455
Calvert, S. L., 11
Camacho, D. E., 91
Cameron, J. R., 435–437
Campbell, B., 118, 121
Campbell, D. I., 146
Campbell, D. T., 146
Campbell, L., 118, 121
Campbell, M. R., 322
Campione, J. C., 422
Cantone, E., 497
Capar, G., 343
Carey, D. P., 124
Carlson, M. J., 79
Carlson, S. M., 221, 303
Carlton, M. P., 52
Carnegie Council on Adolescent Development, 150
Carnegie Foundation, 88
Carpendale, J. I., 287
Carrell, S. E., 100
Carroll, J. B., 403
Carter, S. L., 189, 196, 199, 205
Cartledge, G., 485
Cartmill, E., 59
Carver, C. S., 137
Case, R., 50
CASEL Collaborative for Academic, Social, and Emotional Learning, 105
Casey, B. J., 37, 256–257, 303
Casey, E. C., 302
Caspi, A., 136
Cassidy, A. R., 302
Cassidy, K., 310
Catts, H., 59
Ceci, S. J., 126
Celikler, D., 510
Center for Instructional Technology, 548
Centers for Disease Control and Prevention, 199
Cerillo-Urbina, A. J., 192
Chai, C. S., 552
Chakpitak, N., 397
Chall, J. S., 359
Chance, P., 224, 231
Chandler, M. J., 287
Chang, M., 80
Chao, R. K., 78, 79
Chapin, J. R., 382
Chaplin, T. M., 172, 173
Chappuis, J., 10
Charney, R. S., 220

Chase-Lansdale, P. L., 148, 149
Chatmon, C., 485
Chavarria, M. C., 37
Chavez, R. S., 200
Checa, P., 123
Chen, C., 400, 404
Chen, F., 540
Chen, S. W., 47
Chen, X., 146
Chess, S., 137, 139
Chevalier, N., 257
Chevallier, N., 302
Chi, M. T. H., 278, 340
Chiang, H. L., 191
Chiappetta, E. L., 380
Children's Defense Fund, 148
Child Trends Data Bank, 176
Chinn, C. A., 54, 335
Chinn, L., 176
Chinn, P. C., 9, 152, 158, 160, 161, 165, 452, 530
Chiou, W. B., 48
Choi, N., 80
Chomsky, N., 59
Choukas-Bradley, S., 85
Chrisman, K., 385
Christy, C., 48, 53, 63, 315, 420
Cianciolo, A. T., 277
Cicchetti, D., 235, 303
Cil, E., 510
Cirit, N. C., 552
Clark, A. J., 80
Clark, B., 211
Clark, D. M., 11, 207
Clark, E. V., 58–60
Clark, K. B., 3, 4
Clark, L., 327
Clark, M. A., 72
Clark, M. P., 3, 4
Clarke, A. J., 340
Clarke-Stewart, A. K., 78, 79
Claro, S., 440
Cleary, T. J., 8, 245
Clements, D. H., 373
Cloud, J., 210, 211
Coatsworth, J. D., 32
Cocchiarella, M., 297
Coe, R., 402
Coffman, D. L., 200
Coffman, J. L., 275
Cohen, G. I., 431
Cohen, R., 497
Cohn, S. T., 475
Colangelo, N. C., 212
Colbert, C. L., 83
Colby, A., 98
Colby, S. L., 152
Cole, M. W., 124
Cole, P. M., 50, 104, 146
Coleman, J. S., 450
Colesante, R. J., 506
College Board, 170, 171
Collie, R. J., 88, 442, 450
Collins, A., 558
Collins, M., 328, 440
Combs, D., 552
Comer, J. P., 165

Committee for Children, 105
Common Core State Standards Initiative, 516
Como, L., 133
Condition of Education, 185, 186, 197, 199, 205
Confucius, 242
Conley, M. W., 366
Conn, K. M., 123
Connell, N. M., 495
Connelly, B. S., 128
Contadino, D., 195
Conti, E., 199
Cooper, H., 404, 405
Cooper, S. M., 452
Copeland, L., 329
Copple, C., 55, 86
Corno, L., 405
Cornoldi, C., 268
Coronel, J. M., 484
Corpus, J. H., 432
Cossentino, J., 86
Cote, K., 75, 552
Coulter, D. L., 194
Council of Chief State School Officers, 296
Courage, M. L., 11, 260
Covington, M., 455
Covington, M. V., 455
Covino, K., 552
Cowan, N., 267
Cowell, J., 30
Cracolice, M. S., 304
Craddock, A. E., 457
Craig, F., 191
Craik, F. I. M., 265
Crain, T. L., 306
Crone, L. A., 36
Crosnoe, R., 89, 90, 148, 450
Cross, C. T., 373, 497
Cross, D., 287
Crossman, E. J., 148
Crouter, A. C., 79
Crowley, K., 16
Crowley, M., 173
Crowson, H. M., 11
Csikszentmihalyi, I. S., 433
Csikszentmihalyi, M., 313–316, 433, 434
Cucina, J. M., 124
Cuevas, J., 135
Cui, L., 105, 139
Cummings, E. M., 80
Cunningham, B., 170
Cunningham, P. M., 358, 360–362, 366
Curci, A., 123
Curran, K., 234
Curtis, L. A., 150
Cushing, K. S., 278
Cushman, C. A., 474

D

Daane, M. C., 365
Dabholkar, A. S., 36
Daddino, J., 73, 153, 162, 452, 485, 512

Dahl, R. E., 37
Dale, B., 127
Damasio, A. R., 99
Damer, M., 188
Damon, W., 445, 446
Dan, Z., 125
Dangler, M., 74, 93, 134, 192, 211, 232, 273, 308, 342, 346, 412, 446, 458, 473, 494
Dansereau, D. F., 345, 349
Dardig, J. C., 397
Dariotis, J. K., 306
Darling-Hammond, L., 7, 279, 394, 411, 414, 512, 514, 518, 519, 530, 554, 556
Davies, J., 93
Davies, P. G., 127
Davies, P. T., 80
Davis, S. F., 15
Davison, M. L., 506
Dawes, N. P., 147
Dawson, G., 199
Dawson, K., 342
Dawtry, R. J., 455
Dean, D., 304
Deary, I. J., 124
Deater-Deckard, K., 303
De Castella, K., 455
Decety, J., 30
deCharms, R., 433
Deci, E. I., 436
Deci, E. L., 4, 430, 432, 433
Decristan, J. K., 539
Defior, S., 361
de Haan, M., 18, 30, 35, 37-39, 257
Dehue, F., 496
De La Paz, S., 366, 367
Del Campo, L., 58, 188
Delisle, J. R., 210
Dell, A. G., 207
de Lopez, K. J., 286
Demby, S. L., 80
Dempster, F. N., 267
DeNavas-Walt, C., 148
Deng, Y., 172
Denham, S. A., 105
Derman-Sparks, L., 164
DeRosa, D. A., 380
DeRosier, M. E., 83
Descartes, R., 295
Destin, M., 431
Devine, R. T., 286
Devito, J. A., 488
Dewey, J., 2-4, 6, 25, 49, 101
DeWolf, M., 50, 57
DeZolt, D. M., 171, 175
Diamond, A., 302, 303
Diaz, C., 12, 166
Diaz, G., 245
DiBenedetto, M. K., 8, 430, 432, 441
Dickinson, D., 118, 119, 121
Ding, X. P., 100
Dinsmore, D. L., 434, 450
Dodge, K. A., 450
Doe, C., 540
Doerr, P., 6

Dohla, D., 187
Domjan, M., 221, 225
Donnelly, J. P., 16
Dorjee, D., 306
Dovis, S., 191
Downing, N., 190
Doyle, R. L., 191
Doyle, W., 470
Dray, E., 455
Drechsler, R., 192
Du, D., 39
Duan, X., 125
Duckworth, E., 356
Duff, D., 59
Duggan, K. A., 209
Duncan, G. J., 87, 126, 148, 373
Dunlosky, J., 275
Dupere, V., 90
Durant, A., 392
Durant, W., 392
Durston, S., 37
Duschi, R., 6
Dweck, C. S., 375, 438-441, 464

E

Eagly, A. H., 172, 173
Ebadi, S., 456
Ebbesen, E. B., 445
Eccles, J. S., 88-90, 305, 306, 431, 436, 443, 450
Echevarria, J. J., 155
Edison, T., 313
Educational Cyber Playground, 310
Edwards, A. R., 380
Edwards, S., 474
Egalite, A. J., 152
Eickhoff, S. B., 277
Eisenberg, N., 100, 101, 103, 104, 171, 245
Eisenhower Foundation, 150
Eisenman, G., 474
Eklund, K., 209
Elam, K. K., 80
Elkind, D., 44, 47
Elliot, A. J., 443
Elliott, E., 438
Ellis, S., 344
Elsner, B., 302
Emmer, E. T., 8, 429, 468, 469, 471, 476, 480, 482, 483, 492, 493, 495, 498
Emmett, T., 552
Engler, B., 136
English, K., 149
Enns, J. T., 260, 261
Enright, M. S., 102
Entwisle, D. R., 450, 452
Entwistle, N. J., 133
Epicurus, 184
Epstein, J., 451
Epstein, J. L., 80, 82
Erdley, C. A., 84
Erdogan, O., 134
Ericson, N., 497

Ericsson, K. A., 209, 277, 279, 280, 283, 320, 357
Erikson, E., 70-76, 94
Ernst, J. V., 530
Escalante, J., 428, 453
Espelage, D. L., 83
Estes, T. H., 5
Evans, G. W., 149
Evans, M., 206
Evans, S. Z., 85
Evans-Lacko, S., 496
Evertson, C., 471, 482, 498
Evertson, C. M., 8, 429, 468, 469, 471, 472, 476, 480, 482, 492, 493, 495

F

Fabes, R. A., 8, 101
Fahey, P. F., 134
Faja, S., 303
Fakhoury, M., 199
Fales, J. L., 11
Falk, B., 554
Farinella, K. A., 197, 198
Farkas, G., 87
Farkas, T., 168
Farran, D. C., 302
Farrow, V., 537
Fazel, M., 200
Fazio, L. K., 50, 56
Feather, N. T., 443
Feeney, S., 7, 85, 86
Feng, Y., 411
Fenzel, L. M., 88
Ferguson, C. J., 235
Fernandez-Alonso, R., 404
Fernandez-Berrocal, P., 123
Fernandez-Jaen, A., 191
Fernyhough, C., 52
Ferrer, E., 258
Fidalgo, R., 367
Fields, R. D., 36
Fiez, J. A., 38
Finegood, E. D., 104, 245
Finion, K. J., 104
Finlay, B., 341
Fiorella, L., 288
Fischer, A. J., 207
Fischer, K. W., 39
Fischer, T. A., 11, 207
Fischhoff, B., 47
Fisher, B. W., 11
Fisher, D., 359, 366
Fisher, J., 148
Fisher, S. G., 123
Fitzpatrick, J., 484
Fives, H., 12
Flannery, D. J., 497
Flavell, E. R., 286
Flavell, J. H., 50, 258, 285, 286
Flipsen, P., 197
Florez, M. A. C., 486
Flower, L. S., 367
Flynn, J. R., 126

Fodness, M., 48, 64, 81, 103, 274, 346, 364, 446, 458, 481, 491, 515
Fogarty, R., 129
Ford, D. Y., 211
Ford-Brown, L. A., 487
Forde, D. R., 19
Forzano, L. B., 20
Fox, E., 361, 434, 450
Fox, J. A., 19
Fox, T., 428, 429
France, A., 427
Francks, C., 38
Frankenberg, E., 163
Franklin, S., 305
Franz, K. R., 417, 418
Frascella, E., 160, 307, 328, 342, 346, 364, 473
Fraser, B. J., 475
Frederikse, M., 169
Fredricks, J. A., 89
Freeman, J., 175
Freund, L. S., 302
Frey, B., 523
Frey, N., 359, 366
Friedman, H. S., 137, 209
Friedman, N. P., 261
Friedrichs, A., 286
Friendly, R. W., 433
Fries, S., 442
Fritz, K. M., 191
Froelich, S., 17, 53, 75, 377
Froimson, J., 235
Fucher, K., 166
Fuchs, D., 268, 340, 341
Fuchs, L. S., 56, 341
Fuhs, M. W., 302, 303
Fuligni, A. J., 91, 153
Furlow, J., 350
Furth, H. G., 44
Fuson, K. C., 375

G

Gaffney, J. S., 52, 340
Galambos, N. L., 171
Galdiolo, S., 79
Galinsky, E., 62, 303
Gallagher, B., 371
Gallant, S. N., 303
Gallo, E. F., 191
Galvan, A., 18, 36, 302
Gambrari, I. A., 344
Gambrell, L. B., 289
Gandara, P., 162
Garandeau, C. F., 498
Garces-Bascal, R. M., 175
Garcia, C. B., 73, 153, 162, 452, 485, 512
Garcia-Lopez, L. J., 457
Gardella, J. H., 11
Gardner, H., 114, 118-123, 130, 208, 243, 316, 418
Gardner, M., 148, 149, 312
Garmon, A., 130
Gaskins, H., 453
Gates, B., 209, 211

Gauvain, M., 4, 6, 50, 56, 221, 335, 336
Gay, G., 161, 543, 544
Gay, L. R., 18
Gelman, R., 43
Gelman, S. A., 50
Genesee, F., 156
Gentile, J. R., 404
GenYes, 419
Gershoff, E. T., 235
Gerst, E. H., 268
Giles, L., 323
Giletta, M., 496
Gilligan, C., 99
Gillow-Wiles, H., 420
Ginsburg-Block, M., 341
Glasser, W., 484
Gleichgerrcht, E., 38
Glennie, E., 530
Glesne, C., 5, 22
Gliner, J. A., 16
Globallab, 164
Gluck, M. A., 257, 271
Glutting, J., 373
Goddings, A-L., 35
Godfrey, H. K., 38
Godfrey, K. E., 568
Goepfert, P., 375
Goffin, S. G., 86
Goldberg, J. S., 79
Goldberg, W. A., 79
Goldin-Meadow, S., 59
Goldman-Rakic, P., 39
Goleman, D., 121
Golinkoff, R. M., 59, 61
Gollnick, D. M., 9, 152, 158, 160, 161, 162, 165, 530
Gomez, K., 337
Gomez-Hurtado, I., 484
Gong, Y., 277, 280
Gonzales, N. A., 32, 73
González, N., 162
Good, C., 441
Good, R. H., 515
Goodkind, S., 176
Goodlad, S., 343
Gordon, T., 487
Gorham, V., 17, 81, 103, 160, 177, 188, 261, 328, 364, 377, 395, 515, 518, 521, 561
Gottfried, A. E., 432
Gottlieb, R., 316
Grabowski, B. L., 132
Graham, S., 4, 95, 365–367, 430, 437, 438, 452
Grammer, J. K., 275
Gravetter, F. J., 19, 20
Gray, J., 172
Gray, R., 485
Greco, P., 322
Gredler, M., 55
Green, C. G., 194
Green, F. L., 287
Greene, D., 435
Greene, J. D., 99
Greenfield, P. M., 146
Greenhow, M., 545
Greenough, W. T., 126

Gregorson, M., 314
Gregory, A., 435, 451
Gregory, R. J., 18
Grenell, A., 221
Grenhow, C., 450
Gresalfi, M., 435
Grice, G. L., 486
Griffen, R., 129
Griffin, J. A., 302
Griffiths, H., 200
Grigorenko, E. L., 18, 33, 125, 316
Grimshaw, G. M., 38
Grindal, M., 97
Grindstaff, K., 338
Grogan-Kaylor, A., 235
Grolnick, W. S., 433
Gronlund, N. E., 547, 548
Groppe, K., 302
Gross, M. U. M., 212
Grossnickle, E. M., 434
Grosz, E., 173
Groves, K., 393
Grunschel, C., 456
Grunwald & Associates, 537
Guastello, D. D., 173
Guastello, S. J., 173
Guest, L., 393
Guilford, J. P., 313
Guillaume, A. M., 6, 394
Gur, R. C., 169
Gurol, M., 134
Gurwitch, R. H., 107
Guthery, A. M., 192
Gutierrez-Palma, N., 361

H

Haines, S. J., 72
Hakuta, K., 156
Hall, G. S., 105
Hall, J., 47
Hallahan, D. P., 186, 187, 194, 199, 513
Halonen, J. A., 246, 281, 367, 371
Halpern, D. F., 170, 171, 176
Hambleton, R. K., 544, 557
Hamedani, M. G., 431
Hamilton, M. A., 339
Hamilton, R., 6
Hamilton, S. F., 339
Han, M., 343
Hanze, M., 343
Hardaway, C. R., 148
Harley, T. A., 59
Harm, E., 336
Harper, D., 419
Harris, A. H., 493
Harris, J., 60
Harris, K. R., 286–288, 361, 366, 367
Harris, P. L., 289
Harrison, F., 457
Hart, B., 363
Hart, C. H., 85
Hart, D., 103
Harter, S., 92, 93, 95, 436
Hartshorne, H., 100

Hartup, W. W., 83
Harvey, T., 124
Haskvitz, A., 309, 310
Hastings, P. D., 171
Hawken, L. S., 366
Hawkins, G. E., 304
Hawkins, I., 165
Hayes, A. R., 176
Hayes, B. K., 304
Hayes, J. R., 367
Hayne, H., 444
Heatherton, T. F., 200
Heim, S., 187
Heiman, G. W., 19
Heit, E., 304
Heiter, J., 23, 75, 81, 94, 104, 121, 177, 193, 274, 364, 369, 412, 515, 521, 558
Heller, C., 165
Helles, A., 199
Helmreich, R., 173
Henderson, V. L., 438
Hendricks, C. C., 21
Hennessey, B., 316
Henson, K., 401
Hertzog, N. B., 210
Herzog, E., 168
Hetherington, E. M., 80
Heward, W. L., 186, 204, 205
Hickok, G., 59
Hicks, L., 443
Hiebert, E. H., 362, 368
Higgins, A., 102
Higgins, S., 402
Hilden, K., 288
Hilgard, E. R., 4
Hill, E. M., 93
Hill, K., 18
Hill, P. L., 8, 136
Hillman, C. H., 303
Hinduja, S. K., 497
Hirsch, E. D., 411
Hirsch, J. K., 134
Hirsh-Pasek, K., 59, 60, 88
Hirst, B., 343
Hitchcock, A. M., 197
Hmelo-Silver, C. E., 54, 335, 337
Hoachlander, G., 552
Hocutt, A. M., 186
Hodges, E. V. E., 496
Hofer, B. K., 400
Hofer, M., 442
Hoff, E., 58, 155
Hofmeister, P., 266
Hogan, J. M., 486
Hollingworth, L. S., 4
Holloway, S. D., 146, 485
Holmes, C. J., 303
Holmes, Z., 240
Holzman, L., 50, 53
Homa, D., 274
Honey, P. L., 221
Honig, A. S., 101
Hooker, J. F., 475
Hooper, S., 348
Horn, C., 371
Horowitz, F. D., 34, 43, 51, 52

Horvat, E. M., 451
Hounsell, D. J., 133
Howe, M. L., 264
Howell, D. C., 19
Howes, C., 88
Howland, S. M., 337
Hoy, A. W., 134
Hoy, W. K., 134
Hoyer, K. M., 170
Hoyt, J., 286
Huang, Y-L., 411
Huang, Y-M., 336
Huerta, J., 129
Hughes, C., 286
Hull, S. H., 171, 175
Hulme, C., 187
Humphrey, N., 123
Hunt, E., 283
Hunt, E. B., 124
Huston, A. C., 148, 176
Huttenlocher, P. R., 36
Huxley, T., 113
Hyde, J. S., 169, 170, 172
Hyman, I., 234
Hyson, M., 55, 86

I

Iarocci, G., 194
Ibrahim, W., 545
IDRA, 341
Ikram, U. Z., 96
Immordino-Yang, M. H., 39
Imuta, K., 444
Inhelder, B., 42
International Center for Academic Integrity, 100
International Montessori Council, 86
Irving, K. E., 539
ISTE, 10
Ivy, D. K., 488
Iyengar, S. S., 432
Izard, C. E., 104

J

Jachyra, P., 19
Jacklin, C. N., 171
Jackson, D., 133
Jackson, S. L., 16
Jacoby, L. L., 298
Jacoby, N., 18
James, W., 2–4, 6, 49
Jameson, J. M., 207
Janney, R. E., 205
Janssen, F. J., 410
Jarjour, I. T., 188
Jaroslawska, A. J., 268
Jarvin, L., 126
Jenkins, J., 343
Jenkins, J. M., 287
Jenkins, L., 343
Jennings, P. A., 310

Jensen, C., 64, 103, 177, 274, 315, 369, 420, 518
Jeong, H., 337
Jiang, Y., 402
Jin, H., 298
Jin, Y., 365
Job, V., 441
Johns Hopkins University, 445
Johnson, A. D., 149
Johnson, D. M., 443
Johnson, D. W., 344–346
Johnson, J. S., 154, 272
Johnson, M. H., 18, 30, 35, 37–39, 66, 154, 257
Johnson, R. T., 344–346
Johnson-Laird, P. N., 305
Jonas, M., 146, 485
Jonassen, D. H., 132, 307
Jones, B. F., 410
Jones, J., 55, 85
Jones, L., 8, 468, 472, 474, 483
Jones, S. M., 245
Jones, V., 8, 468, 472, 474, 483
Jordan, N. C., 373
Josephson Institute of Ethics, 100
Jouriles, E. N., 80
Joyce, B. R., 6, 404
Juang, L., 146, 174
Jung, I., 338
Jurkowski, S., 343
Juvonen, J., 449

K

Kackar-Carm, H., 103
Kaderavek, J. N., 193, 198
Kagan, J., 132, 138, 139, 142, 349
Kail, R. V., 258
Kalchman, M., 375
Kamii, C., 51
Kaminski, R. A., 515
Kamps, D. M., 341
Kana, R. K., 286
Kang, J. Y., 156
Kara, F., 510
Karmiloff-Smith, A., 35
Karniol, R., 173
Karp, K. S., 6, 358, 373
Karpyk, P., 380
Kato, K., 524
Katz, J., 304
Katz, L., 87
Kauffman, J., 206
Kauffman, J. M., 186, 187, 194, 199, 205, 513
Kauffman, W. N., 357
Kaufman, H., 22, 120, 242, 369, 490, 558
Kaufman, J. C., 313, 314, 316
Kavanaugh, R. D., 286
Kay, A. C., 455
Kayaoglu, M. N., 21
Kazdin, A. E., 18
Keating, C. F., 171
Keating, D. P., 261, 307

Keiding, T. B., 552, 558
Kellogg, R. T., 367
Kelly, D., 516, 517
Kelly, S., 129
Kempler, T. M., 346, 451, 483
Kennedy, J., 420
Kennedy, J. F., 503
Keogh, B. K., 138
Kerig, P. K., 80
Kerimgil, S., 134
Kerns, K., 50, 302
Kharitonova, M., 268
Kieschke, U., 363
Kigar, D. L., 124
Killen, M., 99, 172
Kilpatrick, L., 539
Kim, A-Y., 510
Kim, H. J., 18
Kim, K. H., 314
Kim, M., 552
Kim, S., 80
Kim-Spoon, J., 303
Kindermann, T. A., 82, 449
Kindersley, D. K. D., 487
King, C. T., 149
King, K. M., 496
King, L., 514
King, S., 408
Kinzer, C. K., 360
Kirschner, P. A., 422
Kirton, J., 73
Kisida, B., 152
Kitsantas, A., 8, 245
Kivel, P., 165
Klahr, D., 344
Klassen, R. M., 6, 12
Klauda, S. L., 84, 443
Klein, S., 176
Klug, J., 171
Kluhara, S. A., 366
Knafo-Noam, A., 100–102, 171
Knifsend, C., 449
Kobak, R. R., 80
Koballa, T. R., 380
Kochanska, G., 80
Koehler, M. J., 419, 420
Koenig, M. A., 285
Koestner, R., 436
Kohlberg, L., 97–99, 102, 107, 108, 111
Konrad, M., 186, 204, 205
Koppelman, K. L., 4, 9, 152, 158, 160, 452, 485, 530
Kormi-Nouri, R., 146
Korth, J., 435
Kostons, D., 361
Kounin, J. S., 472, 475, 481, 482
Kouros, C. D., 80
Kovach, R., 245, 248
Kozol, J., 149, 150, 153
Krahe, B., 172
Krajcik, J. S., 323, 346, 451
Krampe, R. T., 209, 283
Krathwohl, D. R., 398, 399
Kreutzer, L. C., 286
Kroger, J., 75
Kronberger, N., 127

Kucian, K., 187
Kuebli, J., 105
Kuhn, B. R., 235
Kuhn, D., 37, 50, 287, 303, 304, 305, 306, 307, 313
Kuhn, S., 33
Kuklinski, M. R., 444
Kulik, C., 404
Kulik, J., 404
Kunzmann, R., 394
Kuran, B., 397
Kurtz, N. M., 134
Kurtz-Costes, B., 452
Kyllonen, P. C., 124

L

Labella, M. H., 303
Ladd, G. W., 82, 496
Laible, D., 235
Lalley, J. P., 404
Lamela, D., 80
Lanciano, T., 123
Landa, S., 114
Landrum, T. J., 200
Landry, O., 194
Lane, D. M. M., 434
Lane, J. D., 286
Langbeheim, E., 323
Langel, N., 415
Langer, E., 305
Langer, J., 366
Lansford, J. E., 80
Lanter, E., 199
Lanzi, R. G., 125
Laranjo, J., 286
Larkin, A., 8
Larkina, M., 256
Larson, R., 147
Larson, R. W., 147
Larzelere, R. E., 235
Lash, A. A., 539, 540
Laster, C., 329
Lawrence, D. H., 92
Lawson, R., 540
Leaper, C., 168, 171, 172, 175, 178
Learning by Design, 555–557
Leary, M. R., 17
Lecce, S., 287
Lee, C. D., 327
Lee, K., 296
Lee, M. S., 18
Lee, R., 87
Lee, T-W., 124
Lee, U-S., 337
Lee, V. E., 167
Leech, N. L., 16
Lehr, C. A., 90
Lehrer, R., 380
Lejeune, C., 254
Lengua, L. J., 139
Leong, D., 55
Leong, D. J., 303
LePage, P., 358
Lepper, M. R., 432, 435

Lereya, S. T., 496
Lerner, R. M., 39
Lesaux, N., 156
Leseman, P., 268
Leslie, S. J., 127
Lester, L., 497
Letourneau, S. M., 258, 285
Leu, D. J., 360
Leung, K. C., 340
Lever-Duffy, J., 11
Levin, J., 275
Levin, J. A., 19
Levin, J. R., 266
LeVine, D. T., 146
Levstik, L., 382, 385
Levy, D. A., 72
Lewanda, A. F., 195
Lewis, A. C., 514
Lewis, C. W., 240
Lewis, K., 245
Lewis, K. M., 150
Lewis, K. W., 245
Lewis, M., 104, 105
Lewis, R. B., 189, 196, 205
Liamputtong, P., 339
Liao, D. C., 47
Liben, L. S., 99, 169, 170, 175, 176
Lillard, A. S., 86
Lindbloom, E., 211
Lindenberger, U., 33
Lindholm, T., 168
Lindholm-Leary, K., 156
Lindsey, T., 488
Linnenbrink-Garcia, L., 430, 432, 434, 443
Lipsitz, J., 369
Liu, C., 146
Liu, W., 191
Lively, A., 150
Lockhart, R. S., 265
Lockl, K., 286
Logan, J., 95
Logel, C., 127
Logie, R. H., 267
Longfellow, H. W., 28
Longworth, M., 145
Lonzarich, A., 468
Los, B., 58
Lotze, M., 277
Loughland, T., 539
Lowe, S. R., 343
Lozano, E., 322
Lubinski, D., 124
Lucas-Thompson, R., 79
Luchters, S., 148
Luders, E., 124, 125, 169
Luh, D. L., 495
Luiselli, J. K., 207
Luria, A., 168
Lurye, L. E., 169
Luthar, S. S., 148
Luu, S., 495
Lynott, F. J., 404
Lyon, T. D., 286
Lyons, K. E., 305, 306
Lyons, M., 199
Lyytinen, H., 188

Name Index

M

Maass, C., 17, 53, 94, 120, 160, 177, 193, 211, 242, 261, 309, 328, 369, 377, 396, 518, 521, 558, 561
Maccoby, E. E., 168, 171
Machek, G. R., 208
Madison, S. M., 444
Madjar, N., 405
Mager, R., 397
Magnuson, K., 126, 148
Magnusson, S. J., 380
Mahlberg, J., 540
Mahoney, J., 54, 91, 408
Major, L. E., 402
Maldonado, N., 402
Maley, J., 309, 473, 495
Malinin, L. H., 332
Malmstrom, F. V., 100
Maloy, R. W., 10, 11, 415, 417
Mammarella, I. C., 187
Mandinach, E. B., 539, 540
Mandler, G., 266
Manis, F. R., 261
Manning, B. H., 245
Manning, J., 488
Mansson, D. H., 486
Mao, A. R., 191
Marchand-Martella, N. E., 474
Marchel, M. A., 11, 207
Marchetti, K., 474
Marcia, J. E., 94, 95, 111
Marcus, S. R., 83
Mares, M-L., 242
Margolis, A., 124
Marino, C., 11
Marks, A. K., 153
Marshall, K., 553
Marshall, P. S., 191
Martella, R. C., 474
Martin, A., 260
Martin, A. J., 88, 442, 450
Martin, C. L., 166, 168, 517
Martin, J. N., 489
Martin, M. J., 80
Martinez, F., 444
Martinez, S., 444
Marton, F., 133
Mary, A., 191
Masia, B. B., 398
Maslow, A. H., 430
Masten, A. S., 33, 106, 303
Master, A., 438, 440
Mathes, P. G., 341
Matsuba, M. K., 103
Matsumoto, D., 146, 174
Matusov, E., 336
Maxim, G. W., 385
Maxwell, L. A., 152
May, M. S., 100
Mayer, J., 123
Mayer, R. E., 6, 257, 288, 358, 359, 362, 386, 410, 422
Mayton, M. R., 199
Mazer, J. P., 487
McAllum, R., 363
McAuliffe, C., 1, 2

McCall, A., 406
McCardle, P., 302
McClelland, M. M., 245, 260
McCombs, B. L., 407, 410
McCormick, C. B., 266, 289
McCormick, M. J., 312
McCutchen, D., 366, 367
McDonald, B. A., 345
McDonald, J., 11
McDonald, R., 80
McDonnell, C. G., 265
McGee, K., 206
McGhee, R., 435
McGraw-Hill, 373
McGuckin, C., 496
McKay, R., 119
McKeown, M., 367
McLean, K. C., 93
McLoyd, V., 148
McMahon, T. J., 148
McMillan, J. H., 10, 16, 20, 22, 505–508, 510, 512, 521, 526, 527, 528, 530, 537–545, 548, 550, 552, 553, 555–557, 560, 564–567
McNally, D., 428, 442
McNicholas, C., 172
Mead, M., 144
Meece, J. L., 439, 453
Meichenbaum, D., 244
Meins, E., 286
Memari, A., 199
Menesini, E., 497
Mercado, E., 257, 271
Merenda, P., 127
Merrell, K. W., 400
Metha, A., 3
Metz, D. E., 197, 198
Metzger, M., 2
Mevorach, C., 189
Michaels, S., 327
Middleton, J., 375
Midgley, C., 443
Miele, D. B., 8, 171, 245, 430, 432
Mignano, A., 470, 478
Miles, N. G., 474
Miller, C. J., 192
Miller, E. B., 87
Miller, E. M., 441
Miller, G. A., 267
Miller, J. G., 171
Miller, L. M., 80
Miller, P. H., 50
Miller, R. B., 344
Miller, S., 50
Miller-Jones, D., 127
Mills, C., 262
Mills, D., 262
Mills, G. E., 18
Mills, K., 35
Mills, M. T., 211
Miltenberger, R. G., 226, 228, 244, 249
Mintz, S. L., 5
Minuchin, P. P., 85
Miranda, P., 439
Mirkovich, K., 5
Mischel, W., 444, 445
Mishra, P., 419, 420
Mitchell, A. B., 176

Mitee, T. L., 404
Mizala, A., 444
Moffitt, M. C., 410
Moffitt, T. E., 445
Mohammadjani, F., 343
Mohammadzadeh, A., 286
Molinero, C., 208
Moll, L. C., 162
Monahan, K. C., 30, 35, 37, 39, 40, 49, 257, 312
Montessori, M., 86
Moore, B., 444, 536
Moore, D., 32
Moore, D. S., 32
Moore, M., 35, 255
Moore, M. W., 38
Moore, R., 233, 275
Moran, S., 123
Moravcik, E., 7, 85, 86
Moreno, M. A., 11
Morgan, G. A., 16
Moriguchi, Y., 302
Moroni, S., 405
Morris, A., 105
Morris, A. S., 139
Morris, M. A., 71
Morris, R., 188
Morris, R. G., 495
Morrison, F. J., 261
Morrison, G. S., 7, 85, 126
Morrow, L. M., 289
Moshe, L., 405
Mowbray, R., 401
Moxley, J. H., 277, 279, 280
Moyer, J. R., 397
Mudigoudar, B., 196
Muenks, G. B., 82, 83, 239, 449, 450
Müller, U., 50, 302
Mullis, I. V. S., 511, 512
Mulvey, K. L., 172
Mumford, E. A., 178
Muniz, J., 404
Murawska, J. M., 304
Murayama, K., 443
Murdock, T. B., 458
Murry, V. M., 148
Myers, C. E., 257, 271
Myers, D. G., 33
Myerson, J., 127

N

NAASP, 6, 12
Nachamkin, R., 434
Nagel, M., 38
Nahapetyan, L., 172
Naidoo, S., 495
Nakamura, J., 151
Nakayama, T. K., 489
Nam, C. S., 197
Nansel, T. R., 496
Narváez, D., 99, 101, 102
NASSPE, 175
Nathan, M. J., 357
National Assessment of Educational Progress, 170, 171, 361, 376, 511

National Association for the Education of Young Children (NAEYC), 34, 85, 87, 156
National Center for Education Statistics, 89, 185, 186, 240
National Center for Learning Disabilities, 184
National Council for the Social Sciences, 382, 385
National Council for the Social Studies, 416
National Council of Teachers of English, 61, 512
National Council of Teachers of English/International Reading Association, 416
National Council of Teachers of Mathematics, 373, 374, 376, 378, 379, 386, 565
National Governors Association, 10
National Institute of Mental Health, 199
National Institutes of Health, 188
National Reading Panel, 360
National Research Council, 277–279, 283, 327, 358, 374–376, 394, 512, 544
Navsaria, D., 363
Nel, N. M., 19
Nelson, C., 37
Nelson, L. E., 385
Nesbitt, K. T., 303
Neugarten, B. L., 75
Neumann, N., 277
Neville, H. J., 154
Newport, E. L., 154
Newton, D. A., 207
NICHD Early Child Care Research Network, 260
Nichols, J. D., 344
Nieri, T., 97
Niess, M., 420
Nikola-Lisa, W., 13
Nilsson, K. K., 286
Ning, L. F., 199
Nisbett, R., 435
Nisbett, R. E., 125, 127
Nitecki, E., 451
Nitko, A. J., 10, 395
Nocentini, A., 497
Noddings, N., 102, 468
Nolen-Hoeksema, S., 105
Nolte, S., 7, 85, 86
Norris, K., 420
North American Montessori Teachers' Association, 86
Novak, B. E., 404
Novodvorsky, I., 469, 474
Nucci, L., 103
Nunez, J. C., 405

O

Oakes, J., 153
Oakhill, J., 361
Obaitan, G. N., 404

Obel, C., 191
O'Brien, M., 79
O'Connor, P. J., 33, 191
Odhiambo, E. A., 385
Ogbu, J., 127
Olejniczak, T., 76, 133
Olson, L., 452
Olszewski-Kubilius, P., 208
Olweus, D., 497
Ontai, L. L., 174
Oostdam, R., 360
Opfer, J. E., 50
Orfield, G., 163
Ornstein, P. A., 275
Orpinas, P., 172
Orrock, J., 72
Ortman, J. M., 152
Osadebe, P. U., 510
O'Shea, M., 538
Ostrov, J. M., 171, 172
Owens, R. E., 197

P

Pace, A., 59
Page, L., 86
Pahlke, E., 176
Paivio, A., 266
Palincsar, A. S., 363, 368, 380
Palladino, B. E., 497
Pan, B. A., 64
Pan, C. Y., 192
Pan, Z., 242
Panayiotou, A., 472
Pandey, A., 444
Pang, V. O., 9, 162
Papert, S., 48
Parente, M. E., 91
Park, H., 93
Park, K. M., 93
Parkay, F. W., 5, 6, 394
Parke, R. D., 78, 79
Parker, W. C., 382
Parsi, A., 530, 554, 556
Pascual, A., 172
Patall, E. A., 405, 430, 432, 434, 443
Patchin, J. W., 497
Patnoe, S., 350
Patton, G. C., 134
Pauletti, R. E., 171
Paunesku, D., 440
Paus, T., 39
Pavlov, I., 223, 224
Pawluk, D., 197
Payne, B. D., 241
Payne, D. A., 567
Pearson, J., 487, 489
Pecheone, R. L., 512
Peets, K., 96
Peng, P., 268
Pennanen, M., 494
Pennington, C. R., 127
Perez, W., 127
Perin, D., 366, 367
Perkins, D., 326, 327, 418

Perrone, V., 418
Perry, B., 401
Perry, D. G., 171
Perry, K., 515
Perry, N., 40
Perry, N. B., 104
Persky, H. R., 365
Peterman, K., 486, 554
Peters-Burton, E. E., 338
Peterson, D., 48, 53, 134, 160, 316
Peterson, D. P., 116
Peterson, E. R., 135
Peterson, F., 134, 188, 233, 495
Peterson, S. R., 95
Petroff, J. G., 207
Petrosino, A. J., 357
Pettit, G. S., 137, 139
Philipsen, N. M., 149
Phye, G. D., 329
Piaget, J., 5, 35, 40–54, 56, 67, 72, 335, 336, 337, 408
Pianta, R. C., 32
Pierce, D., 435–437
Piercey, G., 374
Pintrich, P. R., 88, 439, 441
Piquero, A. R., 495
Pisani, F., 195
Plucker, J., 314
Pluess, M., 32
Poehlmann-Tynan, J., 306
Pollack, C., 38
Pollack, W., 173
Polson, D., 29
Pomerantz, E. M., 4, 77, 80, 146, 430, 449
Poole, I. R., 471
Popham, W. J., 9, 10, 18, 395, 505, 507, 520, 527, 530, 538, 541, 543, 549, 552, 556
Poppink, S., 395
Portman, J., 6
Posamentier, A. S., 375
Posner, J., 191
Posner, M. I., 259, 260, 262
Poulos, A. M., 225
Poutre, J. G., 48, 93, 192, 232, 396, 412, 490, 495
Powell, R. A., 221
Power, C., 102
Powers, C. J., 200
Powers, K. E., 286
Prabhakar, H., 445
Pratt, L., 62
Premack, D., 228
Presidential Task Force on Psychology and Education, 408
Pressley, M., 18, 266, 287–290, 293, 329, 360, 361, 362, 366, 368
Price, K. W., 362
Price, P., 188
Prinstein, M. J., 85, 496
Proctor, B. D., 148
PSU, 337
Puhl, R. M., 496
Pullen, P. C., 186, 187, 194, 199, 205, 513
Purtell, K. M., 148
Putallaz, M., 172

Q

Qu, Y., 146
Quality Counts, 512
Quinn, P. C., 49, 296, 297
Qvortrup, A., 552, 558

R

Rabiner, D. L., 262
Radvansky, G. A., 221, 235, 257, 265, 270, 319
Raeff, C., 33
Raffaelli, M., 174
Rajiah, K., 225
Rakoczy, H., 287
Ramani, G., 4, 77, 80, 146, 430, 449
Ramani, G. B., 430
Ramey, C. T., 125
Ramey, S. L., 125
Ramineni, C., 373
Ramirez, G., 457
Randolph, C. H., 472
Ransleben, S., 51
Raphael, T. E., 362, 368
Rasmussen, C. M., 410
Rathunde, K., 434
Ratner, N. B., 58
Rattan, A., 431, 441
Raver, C. C., 104, 245, 302
Rawls, C., 12, 335, 471
Rawson, K., 298
Rayner, S. G., 135
Razza, R. A., 260
Reardon, M., 75, 316, 412, 420, 473
Recalde, L., 412, 413
Redmond, M., 8
Regalado, M., 234
Regional Educational Laboratory Mid-Atlantic, 451
Reid, A., 32
Reid, G., 188
Reigeluth, C. M., 411
Reijneveld, S. A., 235
Reis, S. M., 210
Reksten, L. E., 451
Renne, C. H., 477
Renzulli, J. S., 210, 313, 316
Reyna, V. F., 47, 272, 312
Reynolds, G. D., 257, 260
Rhee, H., 123
Rhodes, J. E., 340
Ricco, R. B., 304
Rice, J. M., 442
Richards, T., 187
Richards-Tutor, C., 155
Richmond, G., 338
Rickman, A., 147
Rinne, Carl H., 478
Ripke, M. N., 148
Risley, T. R., 363
Ristic, J., 260, 261
Ritchie, S., 87
Rittle-Johnson, B., 329
Rivers, S. F., 47

Roberts, B. W., 8, 136
Roberts, K. A., 452
Robins, R. W., 93, 175
Robinson, J. C., 405
Robinson, M., 373
Robinson-Zanartu, C., 6
Robitaille, Y. P., 402
Roblyer, M. D., 10, 415, 417, 418
Roche, S., 148
Rodriguez-Triana, M. J., 422
Rodriquez, L. F., 127
Roeser, R. W., 89, 90, 305, 306, 432
Rogoff, B., 29, 336, 338
Rohrbeck, C. A., 341
Rollins Hayes, V., 185
Romano, A. C., 127, 257, 260
Romano, M., 403, 469, 472
Romm, N. R. A., 19
Rommel, A. S., 192
Rosch, E. H., 299
Roscoe, J. L., 494
Roscoe, R. D., 340
Rose, A. J., 200
Rose, L. M., 559
Rose, M., 339
Rosenblum, G. D., 105
Rosenblum, K., 286
Roseth, C. J., 99, 101, 103
Roskam, I., 79
Rossi, A., 124
Rossi, S., 124
Roth, B., 124
Roth, T. L., 18
Rothbart, M. K., 138, 139, 142, 259, 260, 262
Rothman, R., 10, 516
Rouse, A., 366, 367
Rowe, M., 4, 77, 80, 146, 403, 430, 449
Rowell, L. L., 21
Rowley, S. J., 444, 452
Rubie-Davies, C. M., 444
Rubin, K. H., 83, 168, 496
Ruble, D. N., 168
Rueda, E., 485
Rumberger, R. W., 90
Runco, M. A., 316
Russell, M. K., 554, 563, 564, 568
Ryan, R. M., 4, 284, 430, 432, 433

S

Saarento, S., 497
Saarni, C., 106
Sabers, D. S., 278
Sackett, P. R., 128
Sadker, D. M., 175, 512
Sadker, M. P, 175
Sadler, S., 79
Saenz, L. M., 341
Salkind, N. J., 16
Salmivalli, C., 496, 497
Salomon, G., 326, 327
Salovey, P., 123
Salvia, J., 507
Samara, M., 496
Samovar, L. A., 146

San, I., 540
Sanchez, E. I., 568
Sanchez, G., 3, 4
Sanders, C. E., 329
Sanders, L. M., 363
Sanger, M. N., 101
Sanson, A. V., 138
Santarnecchi, E., 124
Santayana, G., 29
Santos, C. G., 283
Santrock, J. W., 154, 246, 281, 282, 323, 367
Sarama, J., 373
Saravanan, C., 225
Sarraj, H., 9
Saunders, M., 153
Sax, G., 550
Say, G. N., 191
Scarf, D., 444
Scarr, S., 127
Schaefer, R. T., 152
Schaie, K. W., 72
Schauble, L., 323, 380
Scheier, M. F., 137
Schiefele, U., 437, 450
Schlam, T. R., 444, 445
Schmidt, J., 103
Schneider, B., 450
Schneider, W., 264, 266, 272, 286, 287
Schoffstall, C. L., 497
Schofield, T. J., 79
Scholer, A. A., 245, 430, 432
Scholes, L., 38
Schonert-Reichl, K. A., 306
Schopenhauer, L., 456
Schorr, I., 173
Schrum, L., 164
Schunk, D. H., 5, 8, 235, 237, 239, 244, 245, 248, 326, 329, 404, 430, 435, 436, 437, 439, 441, 442, 452, 464
Schustack, M. W., 137
Schwartz, D. L., 326
Schwartz, S. E., 494
Schwartz, S. J., 496
Schwartz-Mette, R. A., 172, 200
Schwarz, S., 188, 561
Schweiger, P., 381
Schweingruber, H., 373
Schwinger, M., 455
Scott, C. W., 469
Scott, S. V., 127
Sears, D., 326
Sears, D. A., 326, 344
Seesjarvi, E., 283
Seiler, W. J., 487
Seligman, M. E. P., 134
Seligson, T., 488
Selkie, E. M., 11
Senden, M. G., 168
Senko, C., 442, 454
Serry, T., 339
Sezgin, F., 134
Shakeshaft, N. G., 123
Shakoorzadeh, R., 456
Shalev, L., 189

Shapiro, E. K., 85
Sharan, S., 344, 345
Shaul, M. S., 513
Shaulov, A., 344
Shavelson, R. J., 553
Shaw, P., 191
Shaywitz, B. A., 188
Shaywitz, S. E., 188
Shen, J., 395
Shenhav, A., 99
Sheridan, M. A., 268
Shi, J., 125
Shields, P. M., 153
Shields, S. A., 173
Shiffrin, R. M., 269
Shiraev, E., 72
Shirley, M. L., 539
Shirts, R. G., 163
Shklar, N., 405
Shumow, L., 103
Sieberer-Nagler, K., 401
Siegel, L., 156
Siegel, L. S., 188
Siegler, R. S., 50, 57, 217, 50, 56, 257, 258, 288, 291, 344, 373
Sikstrom, S., 168
Silinskas, G., 405
Silva, K., 102, 312
Silvernail, D. L., 434
Simmons, E. S., 199
Simmons, R. G., 88
Simmons-Reed, E. A., 485
Simon, T., 115
Simons, J., 341
Simons, L. G., 85
Simons, R. L., 85
Simonson, G. R., 107
Simpkins, S. D., 91, 450
Singh, N. N., 306
Sinha, S. R., 335
Skiba, M. T., 316
Skinner, B. F., 4, 225, 229, 234, 249, 252
Skinner, J. F., 486
Skotko, B. G., 195
Slaughter-Defoe, D., 327
Slavin, R. E., 339, 345, 346
Sloutsky, V., 298
Small, M., 149
Small, P. J., 148
Small, S., 59
Smerdon, B. A., 170
Smetana, J. G., 99
Smith, A., 312
Smith, B. S., 375
Smith, C. L., 101
Smith, J., 121, 196, 442
Smith, R. A., 15
Smith, R. L., 172
Smith, T. E., 186, 204, 205, 513
Snell, M. E., 205
Snow, C. E., 156
Snow, R. E., 133
Snowling, M. J., 187
Snyder, H., 314
Snyder, T., 386
So, H-J., 337, 422

Soares da Costa, T. P., 474
Sobel, D. M., 258, 285
Soderqvist, S., 268
Solano-Flores, G., 553
Soloman, H. J., 8, 89
Soloway, E., 420
Soltoff, B., 474
Somerville, L. H., 303
Sommer, T. E., 149
Soravia, L. M., 265
Sousa, D. A., 38
Spagnoli, C., 195
Sparks, D., 170
Spear-Swirling, P., 309
Spence, J. T., 173
Spencer, S. J., 127
Spiegler, M. D., 228, 237, 244, 249
Spinrad, T. L., 101, 104
Sporer, N., 363
Spring, J., 3
Spuhl, S. T., 52
Sroufe, L. A., 44
Stahl, S., 358
Stanovich, K. E., 311
Starr, C., 168
Steel, P., 456
Steele, C. M., 127
Steffen, V. J., 172
Stein, B. S., 319
Steinberg, L., 37, 105, 312
Steinberg, L. D., 78
Steinmayr, R., 457
Stephens, J. M., 100
Stephens, N. M., 431
Sterling, D. R., 471
Stern, P., 127
Stern, W., 115
Sternberg, K., 305, 313, 317
Sternberg, R. J., 7, 8, 115, 118, 123–128, 131, 132, 208–210, 212, 221, 277, 305, 307, 309, 313, 316, 317, 521, 531
Stevenson, H. W., 376, 400, 404
Stewart, J. B., 176
Stiggins, R., 544
Stipek, D. J., 85, 95, 436, 438, 442, 451
Stone, V., 528
Straus, M. A., 234
Strentze, T., 124
Sturge-Apple, M. L., 80
Suad Nasir, N., 127
Suarez-Alvarez, J., 404
Sue, D., 153
Sue, D. M., 153
Sue, D. W., 153
Suen, H. K., 542
Sullivan, A. L., 107
Sutin, A. R., 496
Suzuki, Y., 338
Swan, K., 164, 411, 435
Swanson, H. L., 198, 268, 269
Swanson, S., 17, 64, 189, 212, 233, 262, 328, 342, 347, 377, 396, 459, 491, 518, 561
Swartz, C. W., 442
Symbaluk, D. G., 221

T

Tamis-LeMonda, C. S., 146, 147
Tan, P. Z., 146
Tanilon, J., 497
Tannen, D., 172
Tarhan, L., 410
Tarim, K., 343
Tarman, B., 397
Tarter, C. J., 134
Tavil, Z. M., 343
Taylor, A. Z., 4, 430, 437
Taylor, B. G., 178
Taylor, B. K., 9
Taylor, C., 306
Teel, K. T., 455
Teixeira, M. D., 457
Tenebaum, H. R., 16
Tennyson, R., 297
Terman, D. L., 194
Terwilliger, J., 553
Tesch-Romer, C., 209, 283
Teurbe-Tolon, A. R., 11
Tharp, R. G., 457
Theunissen, M. H., 235
Thillay, A., 260
Thomas, A., 137
Thomas, D. A., 344
Thomas, M. S. C., 154
Thomas, O. N., 452
Thomas, R. C., 298
Thomas, R. M., 22
Thompson, D. G., 540
Thompson, P. A., 187
Thompson, R. A., 105, 172, 235
Thompson, R. F., 225
Thomson, D., 208
Thorndike, E. L., 2, 3, 6
Thurber, J., 467
Tiale, L. D. N., 19
Tinio, P. P., 313
Tippett, N., 496
Tobias, E. S., 322
Toh, Y., 337, 422
Toldson, I. A., 240
Tomasello, M., 287
Tomblin, J. B., 59
Tompkins, G. E., 62, 154, 361, 365, 367
Tonkaboni, F., 343
Tonks, S. M., 85, 433
Torgesen, J. K., 341
Toth, S. L., 235
Tottenham, N., 18, 36
Trahan, L. H., 126
Tran, T. D., 148
Trochim, E., 16
Troop-Gordon, W., 496
Troutman, A. C., 195, 228, 230, 231, 235, 397, 483, 484
Truxel, N. R., 171
Trzesniewski, K. H., 92, 93, 440
Tsai, K. M., 153
Tsal, Y., 189
Tsang, C. L., 327
Tulving, E., 270
Turiel, E., 99, 101

Turk, D., 244
Turkanis, C. G., 29
Turnbull, A., 189, 191, 204, 508
Tzeng, J-Y., 298

U

Uccelli, P., 64
Ugodulunwa, C., 558
Umana-Taylor, A. J., 96
Underwood, M. K., 171
Undheim, A. M., 496
Ungar, M., 107
University of Buffalo Counseling Services, 456
University of Illinois Counseling Center, 456
University of Texas at Austin Counseling and Mental Health Center, 457
Updegraff, K. A., 96
Urbino, S., 117
U.S. Office for Civil Rights, 178
U.S. Office of Education, 19
USA Today, 8, 371, 378, 381, 393, 434

V

Valanover, S., 497
Valentino, K. V., 80
Valiente, C., 104
Valle, A., 404
Vallone, R. P., 311
Vandell, D. L., 80, 85
Van der Veer, R., 50, 53, 222, 336
van der Werf, G., 361
Van de Walle, J. A., 6, 53, 358, 373
van Driel, J. H., 410
van Geel, M., 497
van Lamsweerde, A. E., 272
Vansteenkiste, M., 432
Van Tassell-Baska, J., 8
Vargas, J., 484
Vasishth, S., 266
Vedder, P., 497
Veenman, M. V. J., 10
Veira, J. M., 79
Verhagen, J., 268
Verma, S., 147
Veronneau, M-H., 450
Vogels, A. G., 235
Vogt, M. J., 155

Vollink, T., 496
von Aster, M., 187
von Neumann, J., 257
Votruba-Drzal, E., 126, 148
Vukelich, C., 62
Vygotsky, L. S., 5, 28, 29, 35, 50, 52–57, 67, 68, 115, 141, 335–338, 351, 353, 408
Vysniauske, R., 192

W

Wachs, H., 45
Wadsworth, M. E., 126, 148
Wagner, R. K., 124
Waiter, G. D., 125
Wakjissa, S., 558
Wallnau, L. B., 19
Walsh, J., 441
Walsh, M. E., 411
Walters, B., 86
Walton, G. M., 431, 441
Wang, C., 495
Wang, Q., 146
Wang, Y., 139
Wanless, S. B., 245
Wardlow, L., 336
Warneken, F., 287
Washiya, Y., 19
Wasserberg, M. J., 127
Waterman, A. S., 94
Watson, D. L., 457
Watson, J., 287
Watt, K. M., 129
Waugh, C. K., 548
Weatherspoon, S., 196
Weaver, J. M., 79
Webb, L. D., 3
Webb, N. M., 363, 368
Wechsler, D., 116
Wei, R. C., 512
Weil, M., 6, 404
Weiler, L. M., 339
Weinberg, R. A., 127
Weiner, B., 437, 438
Weinstein, C. S., 117, 403, 404, 444, 469, 472, 474, 477, 478, 485
Weldon, R. B., 312
Wellman, H. M., 286, 287
Wells, M. G., 95
Welshman, D., 384
Wendelken, C., 36
Wendler, M., 163, 166, 243, 523
Wenglinksy, H., 159

Wentzel, K. R., 4, 8, 82–84, 88, 171, 239, 430, 431, 449, 451
West, J. E., 100
Westbroek, H. B., 410
Whalen, S., 434
What Works Clearinghouse, 339–341
Wheeler, J. J., 189, 196, 199, 205
Wheless, J. W., 196
Whirry, M., 296
White, R., 303
White, R. W., 430
Widyatiningtyas, R., 410
Wigfield, A., 78, 80, 85, 88, 171, 434, 436, 443, 444, 450, 452, 457
Wiggins, G., 410, 530
Wilbur, D., 410
Wilczak, K. L., 512
Wilhelm, J. D., 410
Wilkinson, I. A. G., 52, 340
Williams, C., 437
Williams, T., 264
Williams, W. M., 126
Williford, W., 478
Willingham, D. T., 135
Willis, S. L., 72
Willoughby, M. T., 302
Wilson, C. S., 86
Wilson, S., 147
Wilson, Y., 446
Winfrey Avant, D., 322
Winn, I. J., 306
Winne, P. H., 245
Winner, E., 42, 123, 208–212, 217
Winsler, A., 52
Winters, M. A., 152
Wiske, M. S., 417, 418
Witelson, S. F., 124
Witmer, S., 507
Witt, D., 155
Wittmer, D. S., 101
Wolfers, T., 191
Wolke, D., 496
Wong, H., 472
Wong, K. Y., 298
Wong Briggs, T., 8, 9, 51, 54, 151, 212, 408, 431, 469
Wood, D., 51, 136
Woodruff-Borden, J., 457
Woods, T. A., 373
Work Group of the American Psychological Association Board of Educational Affairs, 408
Wright, Y. F., 176
Wu, H. C., 134
Wu, H-K., 411
Wu, L., 11

Wu, N., 90
Wu, W. C., 495
Wubbels, T., 430, 450
Wulsin, S. C., 103
Wyatt, M., 441
Wyatt, T., 105

X

Xing, S., 38
Xiong, Y., 337, 422
Xu, Y., 340

Y

Yanchinda, J., 397
Yang, A., 341
Yang, J., 18
Yasnitsky, A., 50, 53, 222, 336
Yeh, Y-C., 411
Yen, C. F., 496
Yendol-Hoppey, D., 342
Yeung, W. J., 127
Yinger, R. J., 394
Yodmongkol, P., 397
Ysseldyke, J. E., 507
Yusuf, M. O., 344

Z

Zarefsky, D., 8, 487
Zayas, V., 312, 444
Zeiss, A. R., 444
Zelazo, P. D., 302, 305, 306
Zeng, R., 146
Zhang, L-F., 128
Zhang, Q., 568
Zhen, J., 395
Zhong, P., 191
Zhou, Q., 139
Zimmerman, B. J., 245, 248
Zirpoli, T. J., 199
Zittleman, K., 403, 512
Zoldak, H., 22, 82, 134, 458
Zollman, A., 304
Zosuls, K. M., 169
Zuberer, A., 192
Zucker, A. A., 435
Zusho, A., 73, 153, 162, 452, 485, 512

Subject Index

A

ability grouping, 128–130
acclimation, 271
accommodation, 40
accountability, standardized tests for, 18, 510–511, 513
achievement difficulties
  apathy or alienation, 458
  avoiding failure, 455
  ethnicity and, 452–453
  high anxiety, 457
  low expectations, 454–455
  perfectionism, 457
  procrastination, 456
achievement processes. See also motivation
  attribution, 437
  delay of gratification, 444–445
  expectations, 443–444
  goal setting, 442–443
  mastery motivation, 438–439
  mindset, 439–441
  planning and self-monitoring, 443
  self-efficacy, 238, 441–442
  values and purpose, 445–446
achievement tests, 509–510
action research, 21
active listening, 488
adaptive expertise, 279–280
adolescence, 260. See also high school; middle school
  brain development in, 36, 37, 39
  critical thinking in, 307
  culture and time use by, 147
  decision making in, 311–312
  as development period, 30
  egocentrism in, 47
  formal operational stage, 41, 45–48
  identity versus identity confusion stage, 74, 75
  language development in, 62–64
  self-esteem decline in, 93
  theory of mind in, 287
  transition to middle school, 88–89
Advancement Via Individual Determination (AVID), 129
advance organizers, 401
advising, 487
affective domain, 398
affiliation, need for, 430
African Americans. See also diversity; ethnicity
  achievement and, 453
  culturally relevant teaching for, 161–162

educational psychology pioneers, 2–3
intelligence tests and, 126, 127
NCLB Act and, 513–515
parenting styles of, 78–79
aggression, 495–498
  bullying, 495–498
  defiance or hostility toward teachers, 498
  with emotional and behavioral disorders, 199–200
  fighting, 492
  gender and, 171–172
  school violence, 495
algorithms, 320
alienated students, 458
alphabetic principle, 62
alternate-forms reliability, 507
alternative assessments, 552–562
  authentic assessment, 553
  performance assessment, 230, 544, 553–558
  portfolio assessment, 558–561
  standardized tests and, 529–530
  trends in, 552–553
altruism, 100
amygdala, 37, 38
analogies, 304–305
analytical intelligence, 117
androgyny, 173
anxiety, 200
apathetic students, 458
applied behavior analysis, 228–235
  contracting in, 230
  decreasing undesirable behaviors, 231–235
  differential reinforcement in, 231
  evaluating, 235
  explanation of, 232
  extinction in, 231–232
  increasing desirable behaviors, 228–231
  prompts in, 230–231, 484
  punishment in, 234–235
  removing desirable stimuli in, 232
  shaping in, 231, 484
  teaching strategies using, 232–233, 235–236
aptitude tests, 509
articulation disorders, 197
artifacts in portfolios, 558
Asian Americans. See also diversity; ethnicity
  achievement and, 452
  culturally relevant teaching for, 162–163
  diversity of, 152

increase in U.S., 152
parenting styles of, 78–79
Asperger syndrome, 198–199
assessments. See classroom assessment; standardized tests
assessment skills of teachers, 9–10
assimilation, 40
assisted practice, 362
assistive technology, 207
associative learning, 221
athletics, gender and, 177
Atkinson-Shiffrin model, 269
attention, 259–264
  developmental changes in, 260–261
  divided, 260
  executive, 260
  explanation of, 259–260
  in observational learning, 238
  selective, 260
  sustained, 260
  teaching strategies for, 261–263
  working memory and, 269
attention deficit hyperactivity disorder (ADHD), 189–193
attestations in portfolios, 559
attribution theory, 437–438
auditorium style classroom arrangement, 477
authentic assessment, 553
authentic tasks, 434
authoritarian classroom management style, 480
authoritarian parenting, 78–79
authoritative classroom management style, 480
authoritative parenting, 78, 80
autism spectrum disorders (ASD), 198–199
autistic disorder, 198, 199
automaticity, 258
autonomy-supportive teachers, 433
autonomy versus shame and doubt stage, 73, 74
average children, 83
aversive stimuli, 234–235

B

backward-reaching transfer, 327
Bandura's social cognitive theory, 237–238
bar graphs (histograms), 522
behavior
  problems, classroom, 492–498
  in social cognitive theory, 237–238

behavioral and emotional disorders, 199–200
behavioral approach to learning
  applied behavior analysis, 228–235
  classical conditioning in, 221, 223–225
  operant conditioning in, 221, 225–227
  other approaches compared to, 222
  overview, 4, 221
behavioral objectives, 397
behavioral perspective on motivation, 429
behaviorism, 221, 257
belief perseverance, 311
best-work portfolios, 560
between-class ability grouping, 129–131
bias
  in classroom assessment, 543
  confirmation, 311
  cultural, 128–129
  in decision making, 311
  ethnicity and, 153
  gender, 175–177, 179
  hindsight, 311
  in multicultural education, 166
  overconfidence, 311
  in standardized tests, 508, 531
  tracking and, 128–130
"Big Five" factors of personality, 136–137
bilingualism, 154–158
Binet tests, 115–116
bioecological theory, 72
biological influences on language development, 59
biological processes, 30
blindness, 196
Bloom's taxonomy, 397–399
Bobo doll study, 239
bodily-kinesthetic skills, 119, 120
brain
  ADHD and, 191
  gender and, 170
  intelligence and, 124–125
  learning disabilities and, 188
  lobes of, 26
  mental retardation from damage, 195
  myelination in, 36
  regions of, 36
  synaptic density in, 36
brain development, 35–40
  in adolescence, 37, 39
  education and, 38–40
  lateralization, 38
  in middle and late childhood, 36–37

I-10

Subject Index

neuron and brain region, 36
plasticity in, 38
Bronfenbrenner's ecological theory, 71–73
bullying, 495–498

C

care perspective, 99
caring by teachers, 11–13
case studies, 18–19
cause
  correlation versus, 19–20
  explanation of, 20
central executive for working memory, 267
central tendency, 522–523
centration, 42
cerebral palsy, 196
challenging goals, 442–443
change, mechanisms of, 258
character education, 102, 108
cheating, 99–100
child development. *See* development
child-rearing practices, 450
children who are gifted, 208–212
  characteristics of, 280–290
  developmental changes in, 209
  domain-specific giftedness, 209
  education of, 210–212
  explanation of, 208
  interviews with, 210
  nature-nurture issue and, 209
  NCLB Act and, 211, 514
children with disabilities, 185–207
  ADHD, 188–193
  autism spectrum disorders, 198–199
  classroom assessment and, 543
  emotional and behavioral disorders, 199–201
  intellectual disabilities, 193–195
  learning disabilities, 186–190
  legal issues regarding, 204–206
  percentages of students, 185
  physical disorders, 196
  self-assessment of experience with, 200, 201
  sensory disorders, 196–197
  speech and language disorders, 197–198
  technology supporting, 207
chronosystem, 72
chunking, 267
class cooperation, 344
classical conditioning, 221, 223–225
classification, 44, 50
classroom aides, 339
classroom arrangement, 476–479
classroom assessment, 536–573
  alternative assessments, 552–562
  compatibility with learning and motivation, 540–541
  current trends in, 544–545
  fairness of, 543–544
  high-quality, 542–544

during instruction, 538–540
learning targets for, 541
NCLB Act and, 537–538
as part of teaching, 537–540
pluralistic, 543
postinstruction, 538, 540
preinstruction, 538–539
self-assessment of practices, 562
time spent on, 537–538
traditional tests, 547–551
validity of, 542
classroom management, 467–502
  authoritarian style, 480
  authoritative style, 480
  characteristics of effective managers, 481
  communication and, 486–491
  complexity and potential for problems, 470–471
  creating a positive learning environment, 479–485
  diversity and, 484–485
  goals and strategies for, 474–475
  issues in elementary and secondary schools, 469–470
  need for, 468–469
  permissive style, 480
  of physical environment, 476–479
  positive climate for, 472–473
  for problem behaviors, 492–498
  right start for, 471
  rules and procedures for, 480, 482–483
  student cooperation in, 483–484
  teachers' skills in, 8
cloud computing, 415
cluster style classroom arrangement, 477
cognition
  explanation of, 221
  in social cognitive theory, 237
cognitive apprenticeship, 338
cognitive approaches
  beginnings of, 4
  to learning, 221–222
  to reading, 361–362
  to writing, 367–368
cognitive behavior approaches to learning, 244–245
cognitive constructivist approach, 221, 222
cognitive control, 37
cognitive development
  brain and, 35–40
  information-processing approach, 56–58
  Piaget's and Vygotsky's theories compared, 52, 53, 55, 335–336
  Piaget's theory, 40–51, 54
  Vygotsky's theory, 50–57
cognitive domain, 397–398
cognitive engagement, 435
cognitive moral education, 102
cognitive perspective on motivation, 430
cognitive processes
  explanation of, 30
  in learner-centered approach, 409
  of mathematics, 374–375

other processes and, 30
in Piaget's theory, 40–41
of reading, 560
cognitive psychology, 257
collaboration, 6
Collaborative for Academic, Social, and Emotional Learning (CASEL), 105–106
collaborative learning, 336–337, 368, 415
collaborative teaming, 205–207
collectivism, 146
collectivistic cultures, 146–147
Comer Project for Change, 165
commitment of teachers, 11–13
Common Core State Standards Initiative (2009), 10, 515–516
communication, 486–491. *See also* language
  effective, barriers to, 487
  listening skills, 488
  nonverbal, 489
  self-assessment of, 490
  speaking skills, 486–487
  teachers' skills, 8
community
  reading and, 363
  teamwork with schools, 165
community-service programs, 210
comparative advance organizers, 401
competence motivation, 430
comprehending words, 361–363
computational fluency, 374
computer-mediated communications (CMC), 415
Computer-Supported Collaborative Learning (CSCL), 336–337
computer-supported intentional learning environments, 414
concept maps, 298–299
concepts, 296–301
concrete operational stage, 41, 44–46, 50
concurrent validity, 506–507
conditioned response, 223–225
conditioned stimulus, 223–225
confirmation bias, 311
conservation, 42, 56
constructed-response items, 549–550
constructivist approaches. *See also* Piaget's cognitive development theory; social constructivist approaches
  cognitive apprenticeship in, 338
  collaboration in, 6
  cooperative learning in, 342–347
  direct instruction with, 6–7
  to early childhood education, 86–87
  explanation of, 6
  to learning, 222
  to mathematics, 376–377, 387
  Piaget's theory and, 48–49
  scaffolding in, 338
  to science, 380
  situated cognition in, 337

small-group work in, 348–351
to social studies, 384–386
teachers and peers as joint contributors, 339–342
tutoring in, 338–342
Vygotsky's social constructivism, 53
construct validity, 507
content validity, 506
continuity-discontinuity issue, 33
contracting, 230
control group, 20
conventional reasoning, 97
convergent thinking, 313
cooperative communities, 344–346
cooperative learning, 342–347
cooperative scripting, 344
cooperative students, 483–484
coparenting, 79
corpus callosum, 37, 38
correlational research, 19–20
cortisol, 18
counselors, help from, 494
counterconditioning, 225
creative intelligence, 117–118
creative thinking, 313–317
creative writing, 371
creativity, explanation of, 313
criterion-referenced grading, 564
criterion-referenced tests, 506
criterion validity, 506
critical thinking, 305–308
  in adolescence, 307
  in constructivist approaches, 385
  explanation of, 7, 305
  mindfulness, 305–306
  in schools, 306–307
  skills of teachers, 7
  teaching strategies for, 308–309, 357
  technology and, 307–308
criticism, 487
cross-age program, 129
cross-cultural studies, 146
cue-dependent forgetting, 273
culture, 146–147. *See also* diversity; ethnicity; gender; multicultural education; socioeconomic status (SES)
  adolescents' time use and, 147
  Asian and U.S. education compared, 400, 404
  bilingualism, 154–156
  classroom management and, 484–485
  cross-cultural studies, 146
  culturally relevant teaching, 161–162
  explanation of, 146
  gender and, 173–175
  individualist versus collectivist, 146–147
  intelligence and, 127–128
  intelligence tests and, 127–128
  as mesosystem, 72
  multicultural education, 158–165
  teachers' skills for working with, 9
  transfer and, 327–328
culture-fair tests, 127–128

curriculum. *See also* instructional planning
   early childhood education controversy, 86–87
   gender and, 176
   hidden, 101
   mathematics, 376
   standardized tests and, 512
   technology's role in, 414
   writing, 371
cyberbullying, 496–497

D

deafness, 196
decay theory, 273
decision making, 330–313
declarative memory, 269–270
decoding words, 361–362
deductive reasoning, 305
deep processing, 265
deep/surface styles, 133
defiance, 498
delay of gratification, 444–445
deliberate practice, 283
demographic characteristics, motivation and, 450
demonstrating, 401–402
dependent variable, 20
depression, 200
descriptive statistics, 522–523
development. *See also* cognitive development
   attention and, 260–261
   brain development, 35–40
   ecological theory, 71–73
   education and, 33–34
   Erikson's life-span theory, 73–76
   explanation of, 29
   giftedness and, 209
   goal setting and, 443
   identity development, 94–97
   issues in, 31–33
   language development, 58–65
   mathematics and, 373–374
   memory and, 268, 269
   metacognition and, 285–287
   moral, 97–104
   problem solving and, 321–322
   processes and periods of, 29–31
   reading and, 359–360
   social contexts of, 77–91
   socioemotional, 71–76, 92–94
   splintered, 34
   writing and, 366
developmental cognitive neuroscience, 30
developmentally appropriate practice (DAP), 7–8, 85, 87
developmental portfolios, 559–560
developmental social neuroscience, 30
diagnostic testing, 510
diaries, 19
difference reduction, 320
differential reinforcement, 231
differentiated instruction, 9

difficult child, 138
direct instruction, 6–7, 86–87, 399–400
disabilities. *See* children with disabilities
discovery learning, 410
discrimination, prejudice and, 153
discrimination in conditioning, 224, 226
discussing, 402
disequilibrium, 40–41
divergent thinking, 313
diversity. *See also* culture; ethnicity; gender; socioeconomic status (SES)
   bilingualism, 154–155
   classroom assessment and, 543–544
   classroom management and, 484–485
   differentiated instruction for, 9
   early educational psychology and, 3–4
   in ethnic groups, 151–153
   standardized testing and, 530–531
   teachers' skills for working with, 9
divided attention, 260
divorced families, 79–80
domain-specific giftedness, 209
domain theory of moral development, 99
Down syndrome, 195
dual-language education, 155–156
dual-process model, 312
dyscalculia, 187
dysgraphia, 187
dyslexia, 187

E

early childhood
   attention in, 261
   as development period, 30
   emotional development in, 104
   initiative versus guilt stage, 73–74
   language development in, 59–62
   literacy in, 62
   metamemory in, 286
   preoperational stage, 42–45
   school-family linkages, 81
   theory of mind in, 286–287
early childhood education. *See also* teaching strategies
   curriculum controversy, 86–87
   developmentally appropriate practice, 85–87
   initiative versus guilt stage, 74
   low-income families and, 87
   mathematics in, 373, 376
   Montessori approach, 86
   performance assessment, 557–558
   positive classroom climate, 471
   reading in, 359, 363
   standards for technology-literate students, 417
   technology-literate students, 420
   transition to elementary school, 87–88
early-later experience issue, 33
easy child, 137
ecological theory, 71–73
editing, 367, 368

education. *See also* early childhood education; schools; teaching strategies
   bilingual, 155–156
   brain development and, 38–40
   of children who are gifted, 210–212
   concerns about writing in, 365–366
   development and, 33–34
   gender and achievement, 177
   issues-centered, 163
   moral, 101–103, 162
   multicultural, 158–166
   SES and, 87, 148–150
educationally blind children, 194
educational psychology, 2–4
effect of a cause, 20
efficacy training, 455
effortful control, 139
egocentrism
   adolescent, 47
   in Piaget's theory, 41, 47
elaboration, 265–266, 313
elementary school. *See also* middle and late childhood; teaching strategies
   classroom management in, 469
   industry versus inferiority stage, 75
   male teachers in, 240
   mathematics in, 373–374
   performance assessment in, 558
   reading in, 359
   standards for technology-literate students, 417
   technology-literate students, 420
   transition from, 88–89
   transition to, 87–88
emotion
   explanation of, 104
   gender and, 172, 174
   problem solving and, 321
emotional and behavioral disorders, 199–201
emotional development, 104–107
   in early childhood, 104
   in high school, 105
   in middle and late childhood, 104–105
   socio-emotional educational programs, 105–106
   stress, coping with, 106–107
emotional disturbance (ED), 199, 200
emotional intelligence, 121, 123
emotional swings, 105
Emotion-Based Prevention Program (EBP), 104
empowerment of students, 160–161
encoding, 258, 264–267
encoding specificity principle, 273
English-language learners (ELL), 155–156
environmental influences. *See also* nature-nurture issue
   in development, 18
   on language development, 59
   on mental retardation, 104
   in social cognitive theory, 237–238
environmental systems, 71–72
epigenetic view, 32
epilepsy, 196

episodic memory, 270
equilibration, 40–41
equilibrium, 40–41
equity pedagogy, 159
equivalence, 373
Erikson's life-span theory, 73–76
essay items, 550
essential questions, 410
ethnic identity, 96–97
ethnicity, 151–154. *See also* culture; diversity; socioeconomic status (SES); *specific groups*
   achievement and, 452–453
   classroom assessment and, 543–544
   diversity in groups, 152, 154
   explanation of, 151–154
   gender and, 173
   gifted students and, 221
   high school dropout rate and, 90
   immigration and, 152–153
   improving relations, 162–165
   intelligence and, 127
   interethnic relations, 145
   multicultural education, 158–166
   NCLB Act and, 514
   parenting styles and, 78–79
   prejudice, discrimination, and bias, 153
   schools and, 153
   small-group work and, 349
   special education and, 207
   transfer and, 327–328
ethnographic studies, 19
Every Student Succeeds Act (ESSA), 10, 516
exceptional learners. *See* children who are gifted; children with disabilities
executive attention, 260
executive function, 302–303
exercise, 192
exosystem, 72
expectations
   students', 443, 454–455
   teachers', 444
experimental group, 20
experimental research, 20–21
expert blind spots, 357
expertise, 277–284
   acquiring, 283
   adaptive, 279–280
   learning and, 277–282
   strategies in understanding, 280–282
   teaching and, 283–284
expert knowledge, 357
expert teachers, 358
explaining, 401–402
expository advance organizers, 401
expressive language, 198
extraversion/surgency, 138
extinction
   in applied behavior analysis, 231–232
   in classical conditioning, 224
   in operant conditioning, 226–227
extrinsic motivation, 432, 436–437
extrinsic rewards, 435–436

F

face-to-face style classroom arrangement, 477
failure syndrome, 454
fairness
	of classroom assessment, 543-544
	culture-fair tests, 127-128
	of standardized tests, 508
families, 77-82. See also parents
	in changing society, 79-80
	coparenting, 79
	divorced, 79-80
	parenting styles, 78-79
	reading and, 363
	school-family linkages, 80-82
	single-parent, 79
	working parents, 79
far transfer, 326
fear, 200-201
fighting, 495
fixation, 321
fixed-interval schedules, 229, 230
fixedmindset, 439-441
fixed-ratio schedules, 229, 230
flow, 433
fluency disorders, 197
fluent retrieval, 279-280
Flynn effect, 126
focus groups, 19
forgetting, 273
formal assessment, 540
formal operational stage, 41, 45-48
formative assessment, 539-540
forward-reaching transfer, 327
frequency distributions, 522
friendships, 83
functional behavioral assessment, 205
functional magnetic resonance imaging (fMRI), 18
fuzzy trace theory, 272

G

Gardner's frames of mind, 119-123
gender, 168-178. See also culture; diversity
	autism spectrum disorders and, 198-199
	bias, 175-177, 179
	classroom assessment and, 543
	controversies, 173
	culture and, 175
	explanation of, 168
	helping behavior and emotion and, 173-174
	science explanations and, 16
	self-assessment of, 174
	sexual harassment, 178
	similarities and differences, 169-172
	small-group work and, 349
	teachers and, 240
	views of, 168-177
gender identity, 168
gender-role classification, 172-173
gender roles, 168
gender schema theory, 168-169
gender stereotypes, 169
gender typing, 168
general intelligence, 123
generalization, 224, 226
generativity versus stagnation stage, 74
genetic factors
	in development, 18
	intellectual disabilities and, 194
genetics-environment issue. See nature-nurture issue
GenYes program, 419
giftedness. See children who are gifted
Global Student Laboratory Project, 164
goal setting
	achievement and, 442-443
	by teachers, 7
	unreachable goals, 455
Good Information-Processing model, 287-288
goodness of fit, 139
grade-equivalent scores, 522
grade inflation, 568
grading, 563-568
	aspects of performance and, 565
	criterion-referenced, 564
	explanation of, 563
	issues in, 566-568
	norm-referenced, 564
	purposes of, 563-564
	reporting to parents, 566-567
	rubrics for, 565
	standards-based, 565
	standards of comparison for, 564-565
	system components, 564-566
	weighting different kinds of evidence, 565-566
graphics software, 416-417
gratification, delay of, 444-445
gratitude, 100
group intelligence tests, 117
group investigation approach, 344
growth mindset, 439-441
growth portfolios, 559-560
guided discovery learning, 410
guided oral reading, 360

H

hearing impairments, 197
helping behavior, gender and, 173
helpless orientation, 438
heredity-environment issue. See nature-nurture issue
heterogeneous ability groups, 348-349
heuristics, 320
hidden curriculum, 101
hierarchy of needs, 429-430
high-road transfer, 326-327
high school. See also adolescence; teaching strategies
	classroom management in, 569-570
	dropout rates, 90
	emotional development in, 105
	extracurricular activities, 90-91
	identity versus identity confusion stage, 75
	improving, 89-91
	mathematics in, 373
	performance assessment in, 557
	reading in, 359
	standards for technology-literate students, 417
	technology-literate students, 422
high-stakes testing, 510-517
	advantages and uses of, 511
	alternative assessments, 530
	changing emphasis of, 510-511
	criticisms of, 512-513
	explanation of, 505
	format of state tests, 511
	international assessments, 516-517
	NCLB Act and, 513-515
hindsight bias, 311
histograms, 522
homework, 404-405
hormones, 18
hostile environment sexual harassment, 177, 178
hostility, 498
humanistic perspective on motivation, 429-430
humor, teachers' sense of, 12-13
hypothesis testing, 299
hypothetical-deductive reasoning, 4, 46-47

I

identity achievement, 95
identity development, 94-97
identity diffusion, 94
identity foreclosure, 94
identity moratorium, 94
identity statuses, 94-95
identity versus identity confusion stage, 74, 75
image construction, 266
immigration, 152-153
impulsive/reflective styles, 132-133
incentives, 429
inclusion, 205
independent variable, 20
individual intelligence tests, 115-117
individual interest, 434-435
individualism, 146
individualistic cultures, 146-147
individualized education plan (IEP), 204-205
Individuals with Disabilities Education Act (IDEA), 204-205
individual variations. See also intelligence
	accounting for, 8-9
	in learner-centered approach, 409
	learning and thinking styles, 132-134
	personality, 136-137
	temperament, 137-138
inductive reasoning, 304-305
indulgent parenting, 78
industry versus inferiority stage, 74, 75
infancy
	autonomy versus shame and doubt stage, 73, 74
	as development period, 30
	language development in, 59-60
	sensorimotor stage, 42
	trust versus mistrust stage, 73, 74
inferences, 542
information-processing approach
	attention in, 259-263
	to cognitive development, 56-57
	cognitive resources and, 257-258
	expertise in, 277-284
	explanation of, 256
	to learning, 221, 222
	mechanisms of change and, 258
	memory in, 264-276
	metacognition in, 287-288
initiative versus guilt stage, 73-74
instructional planning, 393-422
	elements of, 394
	explanation of, 393
	learner-centered, 407-413
	mandated by schools, 393
	state standards and, 393-394
	teacher-centered, 397-399
	teachers' skills in, 7
	technology's role in, 414
	time frames and, 394-395
instructional strategies. See also teaching strategies
	constructivist approach, 6, 7
	direct instruction, 6-7, 87, 399-401
	teacher-centered, 401-402
instructional taxonomies, 397-399
instructional validity, 542
instruction management, 474-475
instrumental conditioning. See operant conditioning
integrity versus despair stage, 74
intellectual disability, 193-194
intelligence
	controversies and issues, 125-130
	definitions of, 114-115
	gender and, 170
	multiple intelligences theories, 117-124
	neuroscience of, 124-125
	worldwide increase in, 125-126
intelligence quotient (IQ), 115
intelligence tests
	Binet tests, 115-116
	culture-fair, 127-128
	group tests, 117
	individual tests, 115-117
	strategies for interpreting, 117
	Wechsler scales, 116-117
interclass cooperation, 345
interdependence, 344
interest, 434-435
interference theory, 273
international assessments, 516-517
Internet, 414-417
interpersonal skills, 119, 120

Subject Index

interventions
  for bullying, 497
  for learning disabilities, 188
  minor, 492–493
  moderate, 493–494
interviews, 17–18
intimacy versus isolation stage, 74
intrapersonal skills, 119, 120
intrinsic motivation
  choices and, 432, 433
  cognitive engagement and self-responsibility for, 435
  developmental shifts in, 436–437
  explanation of, 432
  extrinsic rewards and, 435–436
  flow and, 433–434
  interest and, 434–435
  optimal experiences and, 433
  parental practices linked to, 432
  in real-world situations, 437
  self-determination and, 432–433
intuitive thought substage, 43–44
issues-centered education, 162

J

jigsaw classroom, 162–163, 344
Joplin plan, 129
journals, 19
junior high school. *See* middle school
justice perspective, 99

K

knowledge. *See also* teachers' knowledge and skills
  depth of, organization and, 278–279
  expert (subject matter), 357
  pedagogical content knowledge, 283–284, 357–358
  prior, mathematics and, 376
  prior, reading and, 362
  teachers' skills and, 6–14
  Technological Pedagogical Content Knowledge (TPCK), 419–420
Kohlberg's moral development theory, 97–99

L

labeling and name-calling, 487
laboratories, 16
language
  bilingualism, 154–156
  brain and processing of, 38, 39
  explanation of, 58
  metalinguistic awareness, 63
  morphology, 58, 60
  phonology, 58, 60
  pragmatics, 59, 61
  rule systems of, 58–61
  second, learning, 154
  semantics, 59, 61
  syntax, 58, 60–61
language development, 58–65
  in adolescence, 63
  in early childhood, 60–62, 64
  in infancy, 59–60
  in middle and late childhood, 62–63
  in Piaget's theory, 52
  teaching strategies for, 64
  in Vygotsky's theory, 52
language disorders, 197–198
lateralization of brain, 38
Latinos. *See also* diversity; ethnicity
  achievement and, 452–453
  diversity of, 152
  gender and, 174–175
  high school dropout rate of, 90
  increase in U.S., 152
  intelligence tests and, 127
  NCLB Act and, 514
learner-centered approach
  discovery learning in, 410–411
  essential questions in, 408
  evaluating, 410–411
  principles of, 407–408
  problem-based learning in, 322, 408
  teaching strategies for, 412–413
learning. *See also specific approaches*
  approaches to, 221–222
  classroom assessment compatibility with, 540–541
  expertise and, 277–282
  explanation of, 220
  scope of, 220–222
  spreading out and consolidating, 280
learning and thinking styles, 133–136
learning disabilities, 186–190
learning targets, 541
learning together approach, 344
least restrictive environment (LRE), 205–207
lecturing, 401
legal issues for children with disabilities, 204–207
lesson planning. *See* instructional planning
levels of processing theory, 265
life-span theory, 73–76
limbic system, 37, 38
listening skills, 488
literacy in early childhood, 62
long-term goals, 442
long-term memory, 269–270
Lorge-Thorndike Intelligence Tests, 117
low-road transfer, 326–327
low vision, 196

M

macrosystem, 72
maladjusted children, 199
mastery learning, 403–404
mastery motivation, 438–439
mastery orientation, 439
matching tests, 549
mathematics, 372–378
  Asian and U.S. education compared, 400, 404
  calculator use in, 376
  children with disabilities and, 188
  cognitive processes of, 374–375
  constructivist principles for, 375–376, 387
  controversy in education, 374
  developmental changes in, 373–374
  in Gardner's frames of mind, 118
  gender and skills in, 170
  international assessments, 516
  teaching strategies for, 377–378
  technology for instruction in, 376
  technology resources for, 385–386
mean, 522
meaning
  reading and, 362
  as socially negotiated, 362
  social studies and, 385
  writing and, 368
means-end analysis, 320
measures of variability, 522–523
media, models in, 242
median, 522
memory, 264–277
  Atkinson-Shiffrin model, 269
  declarative, 269
  encoding of, 264–267
  episodic, 270
  explanation of, 264
  forgetting, 273
  fuzzy trace theory of, 272
  long-term, 269–270
  mnemonic strategies, 274–275
  network theories of, 270–271
  procedural, 270
  retrieval of, 264, 272–273
  schema theories of, 271
  self-assessment of, 282
  semantic, 270
  sensory, 270
  short-term, 267–270
  storage of, 258, 267–272
  strategies for improving, 272–275
  working, 267–269
memory span, 267
mental age (MA), 115
mental processes, 221
mental set, 321
mentors, 210, 240, 241, 339–340, 342, 494
mesosystem, 72
metacognition, 285–289
  developmental changes in, 285–287
  explanation of, 258
  Good Information–Processing model, 287
  in learner-centered approach, 409
  mathematics and, 374–375
  as mechanism of change, 258
  metamemory, 285–286
  reading and, 361
  strategies and metacognitive regulation, 288–289
  teaching strategies for, 289
  theory of mind, 286–287
metacognitive knowledge, 285
metalinguistic awareness, 63
metamemory, 285–286
metaphor, 63
microsystem, 72
middle and late childhood. *See also* elementary school
  attention in, 262
  brain development in, 36–37
  concrete operational stage, 41, 45–46
  as development period, 30–31
  emotional development in, 104–105
  Gardner's frames of mind, 120
  industry versus inferiority stage, 74, 75
  language development in, 62–63
  preoperational stage, 42–45
  theory of mind in, 287
middle school. *See also* adolescence; teaching strategies
  classroom management in, 469–470
  effective schools, 88–89
  identity versus identity confusion stage, 75
  mathematics in, 374
  performance assessment in, 558
  reading in, 359
  standards for technology-literate students, 416–417
  technology-literate students, 420
  transition to, 88
milestones. *See also* stages of development
  adolescence, 30, 37, 39, 63
  in attention focus and control, 260–261
  brain development, 36–37
  early childhood, 30, 60–62
  infancy, 30, 59–60
  language development, 59–60, 62–63
  in mathematics, 373–374
  middle and late childhood, 31, 36–37, 62–63
  in reading, 359
  in theory of mind, 286–287
  in writing, 366–367
mindfulness, 305–306
mindfulness training, 192
mindset, 375, 439–441
minor interventions, 492–493
minorities. *See* culture; diversity; ethnicity; socioeconomic status (SES)
mixed methods research, 22
mnemonic strategies, 274–275
mode, 523
modeled demonstrations, 239
moderate interventions, 493–494
Montessori approach, 86
moral development, 97–104
  cheating, 99–100
  domains of, 97
  explanation of, 97
  Kohlberg's theory of, 97–99

moral education and, 100–103
prosocial behavior, 100, 101, 103
teaching strategies for, 103
moral education, 100–103, 162
moralizing, 487
morphology, 58, 60
motivation, 428–446, 449–453
behavioral perspective on, 429
classroom assessment compatibility with, 540–541
cognitive perspective on, 430
competence, 430
cooperative learning and, 344
for expertise, 283
explanation of, 429
extrinsic, 432, 436–437
failure syndrome and, 454
humanistic perspective on, 429–430
incentives for, 429
intrinsic, 432–437
in learner-centered approach, 409
mastery, 439
in observational learning, 239
as problem-solving obstacle, 321
self-assessment of, 461
skills of teachers, 8
social motives, 449
social perspective on, 430–431
social relationships and, 449–451
sociocultural contexts, 452–453
teachers' effect on, 450–451
teachers' need for, 11–13
teaching strategies for, 433, 434
multicultural education, 158–165
characteristics of multicultural schools, 158–159
culturally relevant teaching, 161–162
empowering students, 159–160
explanation of, 158
improving ethnic relations, 162–165
issues-centered education, 162
teaching strategies for, 160–161, 165–166
multiple-choice items, 547–549, 551
multiple intelligences theories, 117–124
comparison of, 123
emotional intelligence, 121, 123
evaluating, 122–123
Gardner's frames of mind, 118–122
Sternberg's triarchic theory, 117–118
multiplicative reasoning, 373
musical skills, 119, 120
myelination, 36

N

name-calling, 487
naturalistic observation, 16
naturalist skills, 119, 120
nature-nurture issue
evaluating, 31
explanation of, 31
giftedness and, 209
intelligence and, 125–126

language development and, 59
overview, 31–33
near transfer, 326
negative affectivity, 138–139
negative reinforcement, 225–226, 230
neglected children, 83
neglectful parenting, 78
neo-Piagetians, 50
network theories of memory, 270–271
neuroconstructivist view, 35
neurofeedback, 192
No Child Left Behind Act (NCLB), 513–515
accountability issues, 513
classroom assessment and, 537–538
classroom instruction and, 514–515
criticisms of, 514–515
giftedness and, 211, 514
motivation and, 439
standards-based instruction with, 10
teachers' opinions on, 514–515
No Child Left Behind (NCLB), 205
nongraded program, 129
nonperformance, 455
nonverbal communication, 489
normal distribution, 115, 116, 524–526
norm group, 506
norm-referenced grading, 564
norm-referenced tests, 506
note taking, 281

O

objective tests, 544
observation
research method, 16
teaching strategies using, 17
observational learning, 238–243
explanation of, 238
models in the classroom, 239–240
models in the media, 241
processes in, 238–239
self-assessment of, 241
teaching strategies using, 242–244
offset style classroom arrangement, 477, 478
online peer tutoring, 342
operant conditioning, 225–227
in applied behavior analysis, 228–235
associative learning in, 221
evaluating, 235
explanation of, 225
generalization, discrimination, and extinction in, 226–227
reinforcement and punishment in, 225–226
optimal experiences, 433
optimistic/pessimistic styles, 134
organization
depth of knowledge and, 278–279
detecting patterns of, 277–278
memory and, 265–267
in Piaget's theory, 40
orienting, 401
orthopedic impairments, 196

Otis-Lennon School Ability Test (OLSAT), 117
out-of-control behaviors, 200
overconfidence bias, 311

P

parents. *See also* families
communicating test results to, 528
coparenting, 79
motivation and, 432, 449–450
parenting styles, 78–79
reporting progress and grades to, 566–567
single-parent families, 79
teacher/parent partnership, 451
working parents, 79
parent-teacher conferences, 494, 566, 567
participant observation, 16
pass portfolios, 560
pedagogical content knowledge, 283–284, 357–358
technological (TPCK), 419–420
Peer-Assisted Learning Strategies (PALS), 340–341
peer mediation, 494
peers
bullying and, 495–498
as joint contributors with teachers, 339–342
motivation affected by, 450
as social context of development, 82–83
writing collaboration with, 358
peer statuses, 82–83
peer tutoring, 340–342
percentile-rank scores, 526
perfectionism, 457
performance assessment, 553–558
diversity and, 530
evaluating, 556–557
explanation of, 544
features of, 554
guidelines for, 554–556
scoring rubrics for, 555–557
uses for, 553–554, 557–558
performance criteria, 555
performance orientation, 439
performance tests, 530
permissive classroom management style, 480
persistence in problem solving, 321
personal goals, 443
personality, 136–137
personal journals and diaries, 19
person-environment fit, 436
person-situation interaction, 137–138
perspective taking in multicultural education, 163
phonics approach to reading, 360
phonological loop, 267
phonology, 58, 60
physical disorders, 196
physical performance, gender and, 169–170

physiological measures, 18
Piaget's cognitive development theory, 40–50
accommodation in, 40
assimilation in, 40
cognitive processes in, 40–41
concrete operational stage in, 41, 45–46
constructivism and, 48–49
equilibration in, 40–41
evaluating, 49–50
formal operational stage in, 41, 45–48
intuitive thought substage in, 42, 43
language development in, 52
neo-Piagetians, 50
organization in, 41
preoperational stage in, 42–45
schemas in, 40
sensorimotor stage in, 42
stages of development in, 40–47
symbolic function substage in, 42
teaching strategies using, 45–47, 51, 54
technology and, 48–49
Vygotsky's theory compared to, 52, 53, 55–56, 335–336
planning. *See also* instructional planning
achievement and, 443
standardized tests used for, 505, 527–528
strategies for, 395
technology's role in, 414
time frames and, 394–395
for writing, 366, 367
plasticity of brain, 38
pluralistic assessment, 543
popular children, 82–83
portfolio assessment, 530, 558–561
portfolios
best-work, 560
effective use of, 559–560
explanation of, 558
growth, 559–560
items in, 558–559
passportfolios, 560
proficiency, 560
role in assessment, 563
showcase, 560
traditional tests versus, 559
positive behavioral support, 205
positive learning environment, 478–485
general strategies for, 480
positive climate for, 472–473
rules and procedures for, 480, 482–483
student cooperation in, 483–484
positive reinforcement, 225
positive relationship with students, 483
postconventional reasoning, 98
postinstruction assessment, 538, 540
post-traumatic stress disorder, 107–108
poverty, 148–151. *See also* socioeconomic status (SES)
PQ4R study system, 280–282
practical intelligence, 117–118
pragmatics, 59, 61

Subject Index

PRAXIS tests, 517–518
preconventional reasoning, 97
predictive validity, 507
prefrontal cortex, 37, 38
preinstruction assessment, 538–539
prejudice, 153
prejudice reduction, 159
Premack principle, 228–229
preoperational stage, 41–45, 50
preschool years. *See* early childhood
presentation software, 416–417
prewriting, 367–368
principal, help from, 494
prior knowledge, 362, 376
private speech, 52, 55
problem-based learning, 322, 408
problem classroom behaviors, 492–498
   aggression, 495–498
   minor interventions for, 492–493
   moderate interventions for, 493–494
   teaching strategies for, 494–495
   using others as resources for, 494
problem solving, 319–329
   developmental changes in, 321–322
   explanation of, 319
   obstacles to, 321
   problem-based learning and, 322
   project-based learning and, 322–323
   self-assessment of, 324
   steps in, 319–321
   teaching strategies for, 323
   for writing, 366–367
procedural memory, 269–270
procedures, classroom, 480, 482–483
procrastination, 455, 456
production in observational learning, 238–239
productions in portfolios, 559
proficiency portfolios, 560
program evaluation research, 21
progress reports, 566
project-based learning, 322–323
prompts, 230–231, 484
prosocial behavior, 100, 101, 103, 171
prototype matching, 299–300
psychomotor domain, 398
puberty, 18
Public Law 94-142, 204
punishment, 225–226, 234–235
purpose, values shaped by, 445–446

Q

qualitative research, 22
quantitative research, 22
Quantum Opportunities Program, 149–150
Quest Atlantis Remixed, 435
questioning
   essential questions, 408
   instructional strategy, 402–403
   self-questioning, 280–281
questionnaires, 17–18
quid pro quo sexual harassment, 178

R

random assignment, 20–21
range, 523
Raven's Progressive Matrices Test, 128
raw score, 526
reading, 358–364
   children with disabilities and, 187
   cognitive approaches to, 361–362
   cognitive processes of, 359
   developmental model of, 359–360
   developmental stages of, 359
   goals of instruction in, 358
   guided oral reading, 360
   international assessments, 516
   phonics approach to, 360
   self-assessment of, 370
   social constructivist approaches to, 362–363
   teaching strategies for, 363–364
   technology resources for, 385–386
   whole-language approach to, 360
reasoning, 304–305, 373. *See also* thinking and thought
receptive language, 198
reciprocal determinism model, 237–238
reciprocal teaching, 362–363
rehearsal, 265
reinforcement
   contingent and timely, 229
   contracting in, 230
   differential, 231
   effective reinforcers, 228–229, 484
   negative, 225–226, 230
   in operant conditioning, 225–226
   positive, 225
   schedules of, 229–230
   terminating (extinction), 224, 226–227, 231–232
rejected children, 83
relatedness, need for, 430
relational aggression, 172
relationship skills, gender and, 171
reliability
   of classroom assessment, 542–543
   explanation of, 504, 542
   of standardized tests, 507–508
   validity and, 504
report cards, 566
reproductions in portfolios, 559
research, 15–24
   action, 21
   on cooperative learning, 343–344
   correlational, 19–20
   cross-cultural studies, 146
   experimental, 20–21
   importance of, 15–16
   influence on teachers, 22–23
   methods of, 16–21
   mixed methods, 22
   program evaluation, 21
   qualitative, 22
   quantitative, 22
   strategies for consuming, 23
   teacher-as-researcher, 21–22
   teaching strategies using, 22–23
response cost, 232–233
retention in observational learning, 238
retrieval, fluent, 279–280
retrieval of memory, 264, 272–273
revising, writing and, 367
rewards. *See also* reinforcement
   for appropriate behavior, 484
   extrinsic, 435–436
rubrics
   developing, 557
   for grading, 565
   for performance assessment, 554–556
rule-example strategy, 297
rules, classroom, 480, 482–483
rule systems of language, 58–61

S

scaffolding, 51–52, 55, 338
schedules of reinforcement, 229–230
schemas
   explanation of, 271
   gender, 168–169
   in Piaget's theory, 40
schema theories of memory, 271
school-community connections, writing and, 368
school/family/community connections, reading and, 363
school-family linkages, 80–82
school-neighborhood cooperation, 346
school-parent cooperation, 346
schools, 85–91. *See also* education; teaching strategies; specific kinds
   critical thinking in, 306–307
   ethnicity and, 153
   gender and achievement, 171
   multicultural, 158–159
   SES and, 148–149
   teamwork with community, 165
   violence in, 495
school-wide cooperation, 345–346
Schoolwide Enrichment Model (SEM), 210
science, 379–381
   constructivist approaches to, 380
   education of skills in, 379–381
   gender and skills in, 170
   international assessments, 516–517
   teaching strategies for, 380–381
   technology resources for, 385–386
scoring rubrics, 555–557
scripts, 271
seatwork, 404
second-language learning, 154–155
Second Step, 105
segregation, educational, 153
seizure disorders, 196
selected-response items, 547–549
selective attention, 260
self
   identity development and, 94–97
   self-esteem and, 92
self-actualization, 430
self-assessments
   assessment practices, 562
   central tendency and variability, 525
   classroom application of Piaget and Vygotsky, 54
   communication skills, 490
   creative thinking, 314
   Gardner's eight types of intelligence, 122–123
   gender-role orientation, 174
   identity, exploring, 96
   memory and study strategies, 282
   models and mentors, 241
   motivation, 461
   people with disabilities and disorders, experience with, 200
   problem-solving and thinking strategies, 324
   reading and writing, 370
   reading and writing experiences, 370
   self-monitoring, 246
   social constructivist approaches, 351
   social constructivist experiences, 351
   teacher characteristics, 13
   technology skills and attitudes, 421
self-determination, 432–433
self-efficacy, 238, 441–443, 455
self-esteem, 88, 92–94
self-handicapping strategies, 455
self-instructional methods, 244–245
self-monitoring, 443
self-monitoring assessment, 246
self-questioning, 281
self-regulation
   gender and, 172
   temperament and, 137
self-regulatory learning, 245–249
self-responsibility, 435
self-talk, 244–245
self-worth, avoiding failure and, 455
semantic memory, 270
semantics, 59, 61
seminar style, 477
seminar style classroom arrangement, 477
sensorimotor stage, 42
sensory disorders, 196–198
sensory memory, 267
sentence combining, 368
serial position effect, 272
seriation, 45
serious games, 435
service learning, 102–103
sexual harassment, 177
shaping, 231, 484
short-answer items, 549–550
short-term goals, 442
short-term memory, 267–270
showcase portfolios, 560
single-parent families, 79
situated cognition, 337
situational interest, 434
skills of teachers. *See* teachers' knowledge and skills
slow-to-warm-up child, 137–138
small-group work, 348–349

Subject Index

social cognitive approaches to learning
  Bandura's, 237–238
  cognitive behavior approaches, 242
  evaluating, 249
  observational learning, 338–342
  other approaches compared to, 221, 222
  self-regulatory learning, 245–250
social cognitive theory, 237–238
social constructivist approaches. *See also*
    Vygotsky's cognitive development theory
  explanation of, 335–336
  to learning, 221, 222
  to reading, 362–363
  self-assessment of, 351
  to teaching, 335–337
  Vygotsky's theory as, 53
  to writing, 367–368
social contexts of development, 77–91
  families, 77–82
  in learner-centered approach, 409
  peers, 82–83
  schools, 83–91
  writing and, 367–368
social conventional reasoning, 99
social-emotional education programs, 105–106
social media, 416
social motives, 449
social perspective on motivation, 430–431
social promotion, 511
social relationships, motivation and, 449–451
social skills improvement, 85
social studies, 382–387, 416
sociocultural cognitive theory. *See*
    Vygotsky's cognitive development theory
sociocultural contexts for motivation, 452–453
sociocultural diversity. *See* culture;
    diversity; ethnicity; gender;
    socioeconomic status (SES)
socioeconomic status (SES), 147–151.
    See also diversity
  affluence, challenges of, 147–148
  classroom assessment and, 543
  early childhood education and, 87
  explanation of, 147
  language experiences and, 363
  low, education and, 148–149
  overview, 147–148
  poverty in America, 148
  small-group work and, 349
  standardized tests and, 512
  stressors and, 148
socioemotional development
  coping with stress, 106–107
  ecological theory of, 71–73
  life-span theory of, 73–76
  moral development, 97–103
  of the self, 92–97
socioemotional processes, 30
spatial skills, 118
speaking skills, 486–487
special education. *See* children with disabilities

specific language impairment (SLI), 198
speech and language disorders, 198–199
speeches, delivering, 487
splintered development, 33
split-half reliability, 507–508
SQ3R study system, 281
STAD (Student-Teams-Achievement Divisions), 344
stages of development
  in Erikson's life-span theory, 73–74
  in Kohlberg's moral development theory, 97–99
  in Piaget's theory, 40–48
  in reading, 360
standard deviation, 523–524
standardized tests, 503–535
  achievement tests, 509–510
  alternative assessments, 530–531
  aptitude tests, 509
  criteria for evaluating, 505–508
  criterion-referenced, 506
  descriptive statistics and, 521–526
  diversity and, 530
  explanation of, 18, 504
  fairness and bias of, 508, 530
  high-stakes testing, 505, 510–517
  international assessments, 516–517
  interpreting results of, 526–527
  nature of, 504–508
  norm-referenced, 506
  planning and improving instruction using, 527–528
  preparing students to take, 520–521
  purposes of, 205, 504–505, 508–510, 533
  reliability of, 504–505
  research using, 18
  of teacher candidates, 517–519
  validity of, 506–507
standards-based grading, 565
standards-based instruction, 10
standards-based tests, 505, 511–513
standard scores, 526
standards for technology-literate students, 416
Stanford-Binet tests, 115–116, 124
stanine scores, 526
statistics, 521–522
statuses
  identity, 96
  peer, 83
stereotype threat, 127
Sternberg's triarchic theory, 117–118
storage of memory, 267–272
strategy construction, 258
strategy training, 455
stress, 104, 106–107, 149
student cooperation, 483–484
students' expectations, 443, 454–455
student-teacher writing conferences, 368
study systems, 280–282
subgoaling, 320
subject-matter competence of teachers, 6, 12
subject matter knowledge, 357
Success for All (SFA), 339
summarization, in writing, 368
summative assessment, 540

survey batteries, 510
surveys, 17–18
sustained attention, 260
symbolic function substage, 42
synapses and synaptic density, 36
syntax, 58, 60–61
systematic desensitization, 224–225

T

talent, 283
task analysis, 397–398
taxonomies, instructional, 397–400
teacher-as-researcher, 21–23
teacher-centered instructional strategies, 401–405
  direct instruction, 6–7, 87, 400–405
  evaluating, 406
  homework, 404–405
  lecturing, explaining, and demonstrating, 401
  mastery learning, 403
  orienting, 401–402
  questioning and discussing, 402–403
  seatwork, 404
teacher-centered lesson planning, 397–399
teachers. *See also* self-assessments
  autonomy-supportive, 433
  characteristics of best and worst, 12, 13
  commitment, motivation, and caring in, 11–13
  defiance or hostility toward, 498
  expectations of, 444
  importance of, 87
  as joint contributors with peers, 339–342
  as partners with parents, 451
  standardized certification tests for, 517–519
  student achievement and, 450–451
teachers' knowledge and skills, 6–14
  accounting for individual variations, 8–9
  assessment skills, 9–10
  classroom management skills, 8
  communication skills, 8
  for culturally diverse students, 9
  developmentally appropriate practices, 7–8
  expert knowledge, 357
  goal setting and instructional planning, 7
  instructional strategies, 6–7
  motivational skills, 8
  pedagogical content knowledge, 283–284, 357–358
  subject-matter competence, 6, 12
  Technological Pedagogical Content Knowledge (TPCK), 419–420
  technological skills, 10–11, 416
  thinking skills, 7
teacher-student interaction, gender and, 175–176

teaching
  art and science of, 4–5
  classroom assessment and, 537–539
  creative thinking and, 313–316
  culturally relevant, 161–162
  effective, 14
  expertise and, 283–284
  how to learn, 2
  reciprocal, 362–363
teaching strategies. *See also* classroom management
  for achievement, 446
  for applied behavior analysis, 232–233, 235
  attention-related, 261–263
  with Bronfenbrenner's theory, 73
  for bullying reduction, 497
  for children in poverty, 151
  for children who are gifted, 211–212
  for children with disabilities, 188, 190, 192, 198, 206
  classroom arrangements and, 477–478
  for communicating standardized test results to parents, 528–529
  communication skills, 490–491
  for concept formation, 300–301
  cooperative learning and, 346–347
  for creative thinking, 315–317
  for critical thinking, 310, 357
  for decision making, 312
  for frames of mind, 121–122
  for gender bias reduction, 177–180
  for handling misbehavior, 494–495
  for increasing learning time, 405
  intelligence test interpretation, 117
  for language development, 64
  for learner-centered approach, 412
  for learning and thinking styles, 134–135
  for lecturing, 401
  for lesson planning, 395
  with life-span theory, 74–76
  for linguistically and culturally diverse students, 156–157
  for mathematics, 377–378
  for memory improvement, 273–275
  for metacognition strategies, 289
  for moral development, 103
  for multicultural education, 160–161, 165–166
  for observational learning, 240, 242–244
  for parent-teacher conferences, 567
  peer tutoring and, 342–343
  for perfectionist students, 457
  with Piaget's theory, 45–48, 51, 54
  for planning, 395
  for portfolio assessment, 561
  for positive classroom climate, 473
  for problem solving, 323
  for procrastinating students, 456
  for prosocial behavior, 101
  for questioning, 402–403
  for reading, 360–361, 363–364
  research use, 16, 22–23
  for school-family linkages, 81–82
  for science, 380–381

teaching strategies—Cont
for scoring essay questions, 550
for scoring rubrics, 557
for self-determination, 433
for self-efficacy, 442
for self-esteem, 93–94
for self-regulatory learning, 249
for small-group work, 350
for social skills improvement, 85
for starting out right, 471
teacher-centered, 401–405
for teaching mathematics, 473
for technology use, 420–422
temperament and, 138
time-out use, 232
for tracking use, 130
for transfer facilitation, 328–329
for unmotivated students, 458
with Vygotsky's theory, 54–55
for writing, 357, 371–372
for writing multiple-choice items, 548–549
team-building skills, 349
Technological Pedagogical Content Knowledge (TPCK), 419–420
technology, 414–416
for children with disabilities, 207
for collaborative learning, 336–337
content-specific resources, 385–386
for creative thinking, 317
critical thinking and, 307–308
graphics and presentation, 416–417
for improving students' understanding, 417–420
integrating into classroom, stages of, 420
Internet, 414–416
for language development, 60–61
for math instruction, 376
for multicultural education, 164
for multiple intelligences and learning, 119–120
Piaget's theory and, 48–49
self-assessment of, 421
skills of teachers, 10–11, 416
stages of integrating into classroom teaching, 420
standards for technology-literate students, 416
teaching strategies using, 420–422
Technological Pedagogical Content Knowledge (TPCK), 419–420
television shows, 242
temperament, 137–139
terminating reinforcement. See extinction

test-retest reliability, 507
tests. See classroom assessment; standardized tests
theory of mind, 286–287
with Vygotsky's theory, 29, 54–55
for writing, 357, 369, 371
for writing multiple-choice items, 548–549
team-building skills, 349
Technological Pedagogical Content Knowledge (TPCK), 419–420
technology, 414–416
for children with disabilities, 207
for collaborative learning, 336–337
content-specific resources, 385–386
for creative thinking, 317
critical thinking and, 307–308
graphics and presentation, 416–417
for improving students' understanding, 416–420
integrating into classroom, stages of, 420
Internet, 414–416
for language development, 61
for math instruction, 376
for multicultural education, 164
for multiple intelligences and learning, 119–120
Piaget's theory and, 48–79
self-assessment of, 421
skills of teachers, 10–11, 415
stages of integrating into classroom teaching, 420
standards for technology-literate students, 416
teaching strategies using, 420–422
Technological Pedagogical Content Knowledge (TPCK), 419–420
television shows, 242
temperament, 137–139
terminating reinforcement. See extinction
test-retest reliability, 507
tests. See classroom assessment; standardized tests
theory of mind, 286–287
thinking and thought, 302–317
conceptual understanding, 296–301
convergent thinking, 313
creative thinking, 313–317
critical thinking, 7, 305–308
decision making, 310–313
divergent thinking, 313
hypothetical-deductive reasoning, 46
in Kohlberg's moral development theory, 97–99

learning and thinking styles, 132–134
problem solving, 319
reasoning, 304–305
skills of teachers, 7
theory of mind, 286–287
thinking, explanation of, 302
in Vygotsky's theory, 52
threats, 487
time frames, planning and, 394–395
time-out strategy, 232, 233
tolerance, increasing, 165
Tools of the Mind curriculum, 55
top-dog phenomenon, 88
tracking, 128–131
traditional tests, 547–561
constructed-response items on, 549–561
essay items on, 550
multiple-choice items, 547–549, 561
portfolios versus, 559
selected-response items on, 547–551
short-answer items on, 549–550
true/false items on, 549
transactional strategy instruction approach, 362
transfer, 326–329
transitivity, 45
trauma, 106–107
triarchic theory of intelligence, 117–118
true/false items on tests, 549
trust versus mistrust stage, 73, 74
tutoring, 338–342
classroom aides in, 339
mentors in, 339–340, 342
peer tutoring, 340–342
volunteers in, 339

unconditioned response, 223, 225
unconditioned stimulus, 223–224
uninterested students, 458

validity
of classroom assessment, 542
explanation of, 506, 542
reliability and, 508
of standardized tests, 506–507
values, achievement and, 445–446
values clarification, 102, 162
variability, measures of, 523–524

variable-interval schedules, 229–230
variable-ratio schedules, 229–230
verbal skills
in Gardner's frames of mind, 118
gender and, 170
speaking skills, 486–487
violence in schools, 495. See also aggression
visual impairments, 196
visuospatial working memory, 267–268
vocabulary development, 60–62
voice disorders, 197
volunteers, 339
Vygotsky's cognitive development theory, 50–57
evaluating, 53, 55
language and thought in, 52
Piaget's theory compared to, 52, 53, 56, 335–336
scaffolding in, 51–52, 55
teaching strategies using, 29, 54–55
zone of proximal development in, 50–51, 54

Web, explanation of, 415
Web-based assessment, 545
Wechsler scales, 116–117
whole-language approach to reading, 360
within-class ability grouping, 130
withitness, 481
working memory, 267–269
working parents, 79
work/study programs, 210
writing, 365–371
children with disabilities and, 188
cognitive approaches to, 367–368
concerns about education in, 365–366
developmental changes in, 366–367
self-assessment of, 370
self-evaluations of, 368
social constructivist approaches to, 367–368
teaching strategies for, 357, 369, 371
technology resources for, 386
written progress reports, 566

Z

zone of proximal development (ZPD), 50–51, 54
z-score, 527

This beautiful volume has been made possible through the generosity and support of the following sponsors:

Big Horn Federal

Buffalo Bill Historical Center

City of Cody

Margaret S. Coe

First Bank

William C. Garlow

Marathon Oil Company

James Nielson

Shoshone First Bank

Micheal and Michelle Thompson

Western Bank of Cody

Wilder Enterprises

BUFFALO BILL'S TOWN IN THE ROCKIES

A PICTORIAL HISTORY OF CODY, WYOMING

by
Jeannie Cook
Lynn Johnson Houze
Bob Edgar
Paul Fees

THE DONNING COMPANY PUBLISHERS

Survey Party. (AHC/UW)

Copyright © 1996 by Jeannie Cook, Lynn Johnson Houze, Bob Edgar, and Paul Fees

All rights reserved, including the right to reproduce this work in any form whatsoever without permission in writing from the publisher, except for brief passages in connection with a review.

The Donning Company/Publishers
184 Business Park Drive, Suite 106
Virginia Beach, VA 23462

Steve Mull, General Manager
Barbara Bolton, Project Director
Tracey Emmons-Schneider, Director of Research
Richard A. Horwege, Editor
Chris Decker, Graphic Designer
Dawn V. Kofroth, Production Manager
Tony Lillis, Director of Marketing
Teri S. Arnold, Marketing Assistant

Library of Congress Cataloging-in-Publication Data:

Buffalo Bill's town in the Rockies : a pictorial history of Cody, Wyoming / by Jeannie Cook . . . [et. al].
    p. cm.
  Includes bibliographical references (p.) and index.
  ISBN 0-89865-967-1 (hardcover : alk. paper)
1. Cody (Wyo.)—History—Pictorial works. 2. Cody (Wyo.)—History. I. Cook, Jeannie.
F769.C6B84   1996
978.7'42—dc20

Printed in the United States of America

96-747
CIP

Contents

Foreword — 7

Preface — 9

Acknowledgments — 11

Chapter 1 Buffalo Bill: Town Builder — 13

Chapter 2 Big Horn Basin and the Cody Country — 19

Chapter 3 1896–1905 — 51

Chapter 4 1906–1915 — 73

Chapter 5 1916–1925 — 91

Chapter 6 1926–1935 — 107

Chapter 7 1936–1945 — 117

Chapter 8 1946–1955 — 129

Chapter 9 1956–1965 — 141

Chapter 10 1966–1975 — 149

Chapter 11 1976–1985 — 157

Chapter 12 1986–1995 — 167

Bibliography — 180

Index — 182

About the Authors — 191

Al and Pete Simpson, circa 1942. (Kershaw/Leibel Collection/PCHSA)

Foreword

by Alan and Peter Simpson

Our first memories of Cody are tied to the days when we were just "little guys." Our dear Dad used to sing us an old Civil War song before we would go to bed at night. We can still hear his beautiful tenor voice as he performed this lovely bedtime ritual. He would sing, "There were two little boys with two little toys—each was a wooden horse." It was so long ago, yet now, in our minds and in our hearts, it feels as if it were yesterday. In fact, we two can still sing every word of that powerful old tune. The song told the story of two friends growing up and sharing life's adventures, mysteries and troubles—very much like we two brothers. We couldn't have been raised with more nurturing and caring parents, or in a more magical place than Cody, Wyoming.

Dad came to Cody from Meeteetse and Thermopolis. He had experienced an exciting and adventurous time as he traveled "back East" for law school. Dad loved both the law and semipro baseball, which he played for a while with the Gebo Miners. Still, he never regretted his decision to "hang up his spikes" when he put a shingle on the door and entered private practice in Thermopolis. Of course, he had an added incentive to put his bachelor days behind him for he had met and fallen in love with a magnificent woman of great beauty (inside and out!)—Lorna Helen Kooi of Sheridan, Wyoming—our Mother. The folks moved to Cody right after their marriage on June 29, 1929.

Cody was a great place for children to grow up. There was a splendid prairie dog town nearby, canals, ditches, livestock, cowboys, fox farms (all things cherished by boys!), and all sorts of mischief and adventure around to tempt two curious chaps. There were those big yellow buses going back and forth to Yellowstone Park. And we were right in the middle of it all, digging in caves under the Southfork Hill and dipping in DeMaris Springs; exploring Cedar Ridge and Frost Cave; and climbing all the hills near town. We always found a "precious place" to sit and look at the clouds, and brag and play "mumblety-peg," and just enjoy being with our young friends.

On special summer evenings, you would find us on the shores of Yellowstone Lake, setting up the grill and helping to get the fire going so Mom and Pop could fry up some steaks—with fried potatoes and a big can of stewed tomatoes on the side! And we would sing around the fire "In the Evening by the Moonlight" and "There's a Long, Long Trail A'winding" and "Red Sails in the Sunset." What warm, wonderful memories they are!

The charm and power of Cody is simple, but irresistible. Young people revel in it. Old people find their way back to be rejuvenated by its splendor. It has always been the perfect place to invest one's youth or the later years—or both!

Wherever we go, whatever course life takes, wherever we have lived, inevitably someone will ask the eternal question "Where are you from?" Our hearts swell with pride and excited eyes reveal a special glint and there is a lilt in our voices as we chuckle and say "We're from Cody, Wyoming, the Athens of the West—out where the canary bird sings bass and a cowboy is not a male calf!" After another smile and a wink we add with all the honesty and sincerity there is to muster, that this hometown of Cody is a wonderful, caring, forgiving, and loving town.

So those two little boys who found so much happiness and enchantment in Cody, Wyoming, are grown men now. And even today, when people ask if we've lived in Cody, Wyoming, all our lives, we are always swift to say—"Not yet!"

Hunting Camp. (AHC/UW)

Preface

The town of Cody is one hundred years old in 1996 which is not very old compared to other towns in the country. We should have had an easy time collecting photos and documenting the town history, but the "early" years posed a problem. The first settlers of this area had a hard time making a living when they arrived. In fact, they had a hard time getting here. Until 1901, the nearest railhead was Red Lodge, Montana, after which a long wagon ride ensued before the settlers reached Cody. The region is high desert country and was very desolate, until the Cody Canal brought water to the town, and area farms, at the turn of the century.

The town's early residents had to spend so much time surviving, that there was little time for recording their experiences, let alone preserving them. Many personal recollections were written well after the fact and copies of early newspapers, which could clarify events, are scarce.

The fact that Buffalo Bill was a famous entertainer, known worldwide, both helped and hindered our research. He was so popular that those early Cody residents were more inclined to remember their experiences with him. However, while there was a lot written about him, it often stretched the truth in order to make a better story.

We have worked hard to sort out the facts from the stories about Cody's early days, while resources are still available. The original settlers are gone and we have lost almost all of the next generation. We have tried to pick a representative sample of photos that depict Cody's history. There are hundreds of photos that could have been used, and many stories that could have been told, to help us celebrate our town's centennial and Buffalo Bill's one hundred and fiftieth birthday.

Cody, 1903. (Stimpson/Wyoming State Museum)

Acknowledgments

This book has been a "work in progress" for many years, starting with the first photographers and historians, who recorded Cody's early days. We thank the members of the Park County Historical Society, who recognized how unique these records were and collected and preserved them. Without their foresight, this book may never have been written. We were fortunate to be able to build upon the earlier works of Lucille Nichols Patrick and Dave Wasden.

Historical Society Archives research assistant Carmela Conning did a wonderful job in tracking down land records, city records, newspaper articles, plus any required research at the Park County Library. Her research was essential to this project. Christina Stopka and Frances Clymer of the Buffalo Bill Historical Center's McCracken Research Library and associate registrar Elizabeth Holmes found photos and allowed access to the collections. Rick Ewig and D. C. Thompson at the University of Wyoming's American Heritage Center researched collections of early Cody families. Christy Cook found the first Cody plat map and photocopied many items from the collections of the American Heritage Center and the Coe Library. Jean Brainerd and staff at the State Archives in Cheyenne, were most helpful.

Mike Cook spent many hours typing, proofreading, and editing. Ester Johannson Murray and Altamae Markham also proofread, checking for historical accuracy. Bob Florida surveyed and identified the locations of early Cody buildings.

Photo Credits

We thank the photographers separately because this is a pictorial history and without them, there would be no book. Special recognition to the Cody photographers of the past: F. J. Hiscock, Hetty and Harold Sturm, Stanley Kershaw, Andy Anderson, William Bates, and Jack Richard. Mike Cook and Dewey Vanderhoff provided recent Cody photographs. Devendra Shrikhande, Larry Leibel, and Mike Cook's reprint work brought to life photographs we thought were beyond hope. Pete Lovelace reprinted many photographs from his Sturm collection. Dave Richard did last minute developing and printing. Mark Bagne provided photographs from the *Cody Enterprise* files. Cody families searched their albums for photos, and many "old-timers" helped with photo identifications, their names are too numerous to mention.

The following abbreviations identify sources that are used repeatedly:

American Heritage Center, University of Wyoming (AHC/UW)

Buffalo Bill Historical Center (BBHC)

Cody Enterprise (CE)

Park County Historical Society Archives (PCHSA)

The photographer, if known, is listed first, followed by the collection name, then the institution which owns the photograph. When photographs are privately owned, the family or individual is listed.

Buffalo Bill always referred to his production as the "Wild West" but over time it has evolved to "Buffalo Bill's Wild West Show." Originally the Garlow Photograph Collection belonged to William F. Cody.

Buffalo Bill Town Builder

by Paul Fees

1

The Major came in just in time to start the paper off in a big way. The Major knew more adjectives than anyone else. They were big, very intensifying and glowing adjectives, and were just what was wanted to properly describe such a new country as ours. He was editor-in-chief.

—Charles Hayden reminiscing about the founding of Cody, and its first newspaper fifty years before.

"Major" John M. Burke was called "the prince of press agents." He was a close friend and confidant of Buffalo Bill Cody and longtime publicist for the Wild West show. Burke was never at a loss for words, but all of his powers of elaboration were called for when he first described this dusty townsite. There was very little on which to elaborate.

In a way, words, especially printed words, created and built the town of Cody. The early speculators and first settlers found a dry, treeless plain downwind from the sulphur springs on the aptly named Stinking Water River. In agreeing to name the new village Cody in 1896, the founders assured two things: that the fifty-year-old showman would commit the rest of his life and much of his fortune to his namesake community; and, perhaps more important, that the whole world would hear of it.

The town and its promoters seemed to reflect Buffalo Bill's personality. Naturalist and Cody taxidermist Will Richard said, "We should be showman enough to sell our country and our town to the world." In grand ads in newspapers and Wild West show programs a picture of an expansive and welcoming Buffalo Bill was flanked with the words "FINE LAND WAITS THE PLOW" and "UNLIMITED WATER WAITS THE CULTIVATOR." Of course, in 1896, they were fine and unlimited mostly in the imaginations of the readers.

Cody probably first saw the Basin at least from a distance in 1874 while guiding Lieutenant Anson Mills on a military expedition into the Big Horn Mountains. But it seems likely that his first visit to his future home took place in 1894 when he accompanied his son-in-law, Horton Boal, and George Beck on a horseback trip from Sheridan, Wyoming. He immediately fell in love with what he saw and began buying property, including a ranch on the South Fork of the Stinking Water River. He soon acquired a herd of horses from his old friend Mike Russell of Deadwood and registered their brand—TE—in Wyoming as his own. Within a year he led a group of investors which included Buffalo (New York) businessmen George Bleistein, Bronson Rumsey, and Henry Gerrans; Horace Alger, of Sheridan; Wild West show partner Nate Salsbury; William Sweeney, director of the show's Cowboy Band; and Nebraska's Lincoln Land Company.

In the fall of 1895, while his eastern friends went on a hunting trip, Cody took a long ride up the North Fork of the Stinking Water. When he returned, according to Charles Hayden, "he reported a very feasible east Park entrance," a new gateway to Yellowstone. Within a few years, outfitters and guides would establish tours to Yellowstone over the Sylvan Pass trail he blazed, and Cody himself would be poised to build on the potential for tourism.

Buffalo Bill seemed to know what it took to make a town. At a time when the regional boom town was Meeteetse, he predicted that the two towns which would anchor the business of the Big Horn Basin were Worland and Cody.

Left: **Buffalo Bill in his Wild West show costume, circa 1900. (BBHC)**

Major John Burke, press agent for the Wild West show, about 1890. (BBHC)

Both served potential agricultural hinterlands and both had likelier access to rail transportation. With its hot springs and its proximity to hunting, fishing, and Yellowstone National Park, Cody also had the makings of a tourist spa.

The western town in nineteenth-century America preceded settlement of the surrounding countryside. With its establishment and a commitment to growth by its founders, a town could attract investment and begin to lay out the networks of incentives that would assure continued expansion and permanence. Not only did the place need to attract visitors, they had to be persuaded to stay. It was important not only to provide farmers with land, it was necessary to give them access to markets and to satisfy their first need in a dry country—a reliable supply of water.

The Shoshone Irrigation Company, established by Cody's founding partners and managed by George Beck, sought to capitalize on federal and state government incentives to bring water to potentially fertile farmland. Buffalo Bill and his partners at first hoped to profit from the sale of land and of water rights to help fund the Cody Canal. Continuing demands for the bales of cash required to build the canal proved too much for the investors. As realization of the impossibility of succeeding through traditional private means began to dawn, Colonel Cody seems to have been the first of the partners to understand the need to change course, to give up hope of profit from selling irrigation rights and to seek federal help.

Cody in fact recognized the desirability of giving whatever incentives necessary to assure settlement. In April 1900, he persuaded his partner, Nate Salsbury, to join him in relinquishing claim to certain irrigable lands in order to assist Mormon farmers. Salsbury had insisted upon selling the rights for $20,000. According to pioneer Charles Welch, Cody replied: "When you die it will be said of you, 'Here lies Nate Salsbury, who made a million dollars in the show business and kept it,' but when I die people will say, 'Here lies Bill Cody who made a million dollars in the show business and distributed it among his friends.'"

In addition to encouraging Mormon colonizers, Cody acted as agent for European groups, particularly from Germany, who expressed interest in immigrating to the West. He also surrendered the rest of his irrigation rights to the federal government which in turn created an irrigation district, built the necessary canals and dams (including the huge Buffalo Bill Dam), and opened the area to homesteading. There would be no direct profit for Buffalo Bill, but his town continued to grow.

The importance of adequate transportation was, of course, transcendent. Buffalo Bill opened a livery, advocated the building of good roads, invested in stagecoaches (and, eventually, in the grand White Steamer touring cars), and most important, used all of his influence to persuade railroads to build to Cody. Not long after demonstrating the practicality of an east entrance to Yellowstone, he entertained representatives of the Chicago, Burlington, and Quincy line on the North Fork. In 1901, the CB&Q opened a spur to Cody, apparently honoring a commitment made to Buffalo Bill by its president, Charles Perkins. For a time the railroad considered pushing track up the North Fork to the Park itself.

Meanwhile Buffalo Bill, who had spent much of his adult life living in hotels, had begun planning a grand hotel for Cody. When the Irma Hotel opened in November 1902, it represented the largest financial commitment any individual would make to the young town. It may not have been as grand as Buffalo Bill had hoped, but it was billed as the most impressive hotel between St. Louis and the Pacific Coast. It could not turn a profit during its founder's lifetime, but as an investment in the future it fulfilled all of his hopes for it. Certainly it represented permanence and prosperity. It was (and is) a destination for travelers and a centerpiece of the town's activities. To ensure its success, Buffalo Bill established farms nearby to supply eggs, butter, and fresh produce. He opened a coal mine east of town to provide fuel. And he insisted on and invested in modernity. The town of Cody was so sparsely settled with so few trees and the buildings so far apart that it may have

Buffalo Bill with (left to right) Dr. George Powell, Dr. Will Powell, and Dr. Frank "White Beaver" Powell. Frank Powell oversaw the construction of Pahaska Tepee and Wapiti Inn for Colonel Cody. (BBHC)

Buffalo Bill, with his Wild West show troupe on tour in 1913. (BBHC)

seemed even more desolate than it was. "I think it blew harder then than it does now," wrote his niece Josephine Goodman Thurston in 1946. The Irma opened as an up-to-date oasis, she recalled: "It truly was luxurious when one stops to think what it meant to make things modern in this country at that time. Water was hauled in barrels from the river. The lighting system was acetylene gas. The telephones were in the rooms, but not yet in running order."

Buffalo Bill put his money into anything that seemed likely to make Cody prosper, from subscribing to the building of the Masonic Lodge to bottling the mineral waters of DeMaris Hot Springs. But his greatest investment was in the dissemination of words. When he started Cody's first "newspaper" in 1896, he was not aiming so much at keeping the locals informed. There were few enough that they all knew each other's business anyway, and there was not much space for reprinting outside news. His objectives were, rather, first to promote Cody to the world outside; and, second to assist local advertising and commerce.

When Colonel Cody persuaded Colonel J. H. Peake, a real newspaperman from Washington, D.C., to come to Wyoming in 1899 as editor, he was telling the world that his namesake community had matured. He bought a steam-driven Babcock printing press originally purchased for the *Duluth (Minnesota) Press* which had been run by his sister and her husband. It was not that the new *Cody Enterprise* would be any less an organ for local boosters, but now it would have the look and feel of a city newspaper. Peake's wife remarked that Cody seemed like a stagecoach stop on the way to somewhere else. But Colonel Peake believed like his employer that words could make progress real.

Buffalo Bill tirelessly promoted his new home in other ways as well. He lobbied for hunting laws to prevent what he feared would be the decline of the area's big game herds. Then each year he organized hunting trips for notables and those who could invest or at least carry word of Wyoming's beauties and opportunities back east. One of Mrs. Peake's first houseguests, for example, was General of the Army Nelson A. Miles, hero of the Civil War and Indian Wars, who with Buffalo Bill stopped in town on the way to the mountains.

The Wild West show in later years was a vast promotional canvas for the Cody country. Besides advertising and interviews in which he almost inevitably guided the interviewer to questions about Wyoming, Buffalo Bill painted the covered wagons in the show with slogans such as "Cody or Bust," and he introduced acts to the show bringing the cowboys (and cowgirls) and Indians together in celebrations called "Ranch Life in the West" or "Holiday at TE."

"I am a far-gazer," he said. Though in his life and work he personified the Old West to millions of Americans and Europeans, he never failed to look forward. "All of my interests are still with the West," he wrote, "the modern West." The sad irony is that he was able to spend so little time there; and when he was home, he felt a weight of responsibility which usually kept him from the rest he sought.

Legends have always circulated in his home town, started by those who did not know him but thought they should, that Buffalo Bill was a carouser and philanderer. In fact, from not long after the first time he visited the Big Horn Basin, Cody was, for health reasons, a teetotaler. He may have bought drink rounds for others, but he could not touch the stuff himself. Besides, as he wrote wearily but proudly to a friend in 1912, "being the father of the town, when I am there they expect me to lead."

More than just words, Buffalo Bill Cody was his own best advertisement for the West. He represented not only wilderness values and the romance of the wild but also the practical vision of the town builder. Shortly before his death in Denver in 1917, he responded to an interviewer's question with what could have been an epitaph:

"I don't want to die and have people say, 'Oh, there goes another old showman.' When I die I want the people of Wyoming who are living on the land that has been made fertile by my work and expenditure to remember me. I would like people to say, 'This is the man who opened up Wyoming to the best of civilization.'"

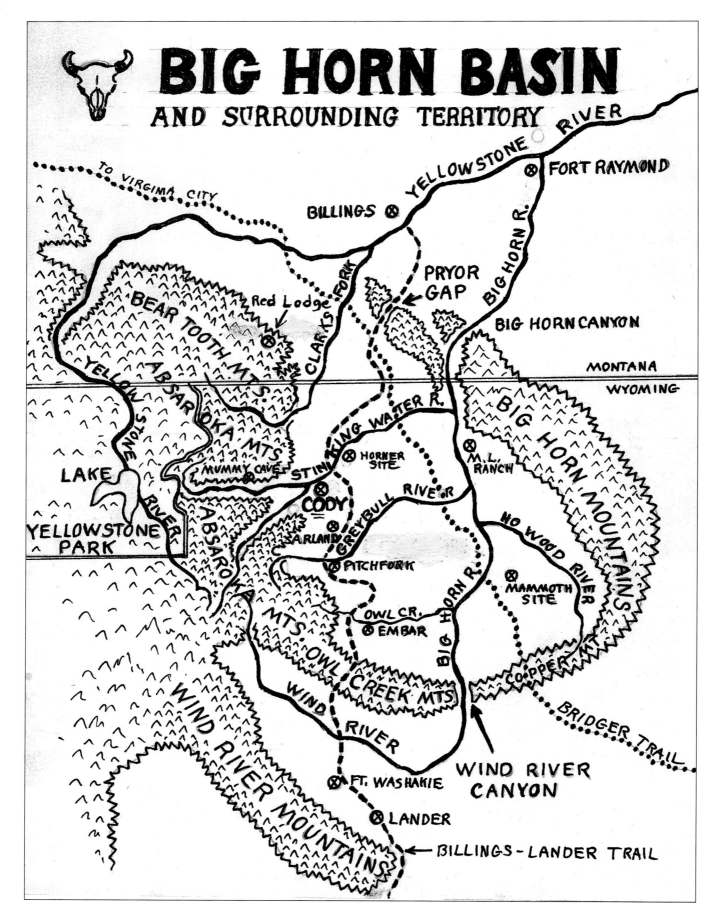

Big Horn Basin and the Cody Country

by Bob Edgar

2

Buffalo Bill Cody told this story near the turn of the century:

A great many years ago, it fell to my lot to be in charge of a large party of Arapaho Indians who, with permission of their agent, had left their reservation for the purpose of indulging in a winter's hunt upon the plains of the unsettled Indian territory. The popular guide and interpreter, Ben Clark, was of the party, game of every description was abundant and it seemed as if little remained to be desired.

A week later, I received a letter from the agent saying that he was aware that a number of Indians in my party were dissatisfied with their southern home and wished to go to some of the more northern agencies; that he had learned these Indians contemplated availing themselves of the opportunity then offered to accomplish their purpose. He charged me to use every effort to prevent any such movements which would undoubtedly result in general trouble.

Soon afterwards, I was rudely awakened about midnight by an Indian who informed me that 200 Indians had made their escape some hours earlier and that they were on their way northward. I at once started in pursuit and brought them back without bloodshed.

It was not easy for me, at that period, to understand why they showed such a preference for the country to the north and west, and I made several unsuccessful attempts to learn. One day a young warrior came to my tent to ask for a little tobacco.

Surely, I said to him, you could not find a more beautiful spot than this (we were camped on Wolf Creek near Antelope Peaks). The stream is full of excellent fish, grazing is good, game is abundant and the weather is delightful.

He listened to what I said in sullen silence, then uttered a guttural "ugh" and without attempting to conceal his disgust, turned away. I directed Clark to call him back and ask him if the country to the north was really more desirable.

This question acted like an invigorating tonic. He drew himself up to his full height and his eyes blazed as he answered:

"The land to the north and west, beneath the shadow of the giant mountains, is the country of the great medicine man of Tel-va-ki-v. Tis the land of plenty. There the buffalo grows larger and their coats are darker. There the region is covered with the short curly grass our ponies like. There grow the great wild plums that are good for my people in the summer or winter. There are medicine man's springs, that to bathe in is to give new life to one; to drink their waters is a cure for every ill. Our own medicine man, Minkutin, has tasted these waters. He is big and strong and great, he will never die. In the mountain beyond the river whose water is blue, there is gold and silver, the metals that the white man loves. In the beds of the streams, the gold is there too.

"In those mountains live the eagle, the only bird that gives us feathers for war bonnets. There the sun always shines. Tis the Ijis (Heaven) of the red man. My heart cries for it. The hearts of my people are not happy when away from Eithity-Yugala."

Where is this wonderful tract he speaks of?, I asked Clark.

He responded, "It is the Big Horn Basin, and if I had my choice of going there I should, without a moment's hesitation, go. For years I have heard of its wonders from different Indians."

That was in 1875. Since then I have found the Big Horn Basin and have made it my home.

The Big Horn Basin lies east of Yellowstone National Park. Approximately 100 by 125 miles in diameter, it comprises over 12,000 square miles. The basin is semiarid with an annual precipitation of about eight inches. The rugged Absaroka Mountains on the

A map drawn by Bob Edgar, reminiscent of the early maps, shows the Big Horn Basin and several of the sites discussed in this chapter. (Bob Edgar)

The remains of one of seven mammoths killed by ancient Indian hunters 11,200 years ago, five miles east of Worland, Wyoming. (Edgar Collection)

west, and the Big Horn Mountains on the east, each have at least one peak that is over thirteen thousand feet. The Bridger, Copper and Owl Creek Mountains enclose the southern portion of the basin. At the northern end, the Beartooth and Pryor Mountains border the broad valley of the Clarks Fork River, which flows on to its junction with the larger Yellowstone River, near Laurel, Montana.

The Wind River flows from the southwest into Wind River Canyon, then becomes the Big Horn River as it exits the canyon into the Big Horn Basin. All of the streams and rivers of the basin, with the exception of the Clarks Fork, drain into the Big Horn River, which exits the northeast corner of the basin through Big Horn Canyon and flows into the Yellowstone River east of Billings, Montana.

This northern opening was the easiest way into the Big Horn Basin. The route was used by Indians for thousands of years, and by the first American explorers, the fur traders, at the beginning of the nineteenth century.

The earliest date for human occupation in the basin was found at the "Colby" site, five miles east of the Big Horn River near Worland, in 1973. The site, which was excavated by the University of Wyoming, contained the remains of one mature and six immature mammoths. Among the remains were the finely flaked and fluted spear points that killed them and the tools that butchered them, approximately 11,200 years ago. The hairy mammoth, some of which stood fourteen feet at the shoulders, roamed the basin during the postglacial period.

The "Hanson" site, near Beaver Creek, north of Shell, was a folsom campsite. The radiocarbon date from the site indicated that ancient people occupied the site about 10,500 years ago. The packed, red-stained floors of two lodges, were unearthed along with examples of folsom-style projectile points in various stages of manufacture. Tools, and bones of mountain sheep were also found. In other folsom sites in the region, extinct bison and camel bones were also found.

The "Horner" site, which was discovered about four miles east of Cody in 1949, was an ancient bison trap. Princeton University and the Smithsonian Institution excavated the site from 1949 to 1953. Later excavations were done by the University of Wyoming. The remains of over four hundred bison were excavated, along with beautifully made Eden and Scottsbluff–style spear points and other tools. Radiocarbon dates indicate the trap was in use about nine thousand years ago.

Between 1963 and 1967, Mummy Cave, on the North Fork of the Shoshone River, between Cody and Yellowstone Park, was excavated. The work was done through the Buffalo Bill Historical Center, with grants from the National Geographic Society.

Mummy Cave contained thirty-eight levels of prehistoric Indian occupation, the earliest of which was almost forty feet below the surface. The radiocarbon dates on the occupation levels were from about three hundred years old, near the surface, to about ninety-two hundred years old at the deepest level.

In one of the levels, dated at about thirteen hundred years old, one of the ancient hunters was found, mummified, still wrapped in his robe of mountain sheep skin. A vast amount of information about the early inhabitants of the region was gleaned from Mummy Cave.

About one hundred years after the most recent occupation level at Mummy Cave, the horse made its appearance on the High Plains and

The Indian tribes of the northern plains and mountains were primarily nomadic hunters. These women are tanning buffalo hides and drying meat. (Edgar Collection)

Mummy Cave, prior to excavation. The shelter contained thirty-eight levels of prehistoric Indian occupation dating back over nine thousand years. (Edgar Collection)

mountains. Horses were gradually finding their way north with Indians who traded for, or stole them, from tribes on the southern Plains. These were descendants of horses introduced to the Americas two hundred years earlier by the Spaniards.

It appears that by the mid 1700s, the tribes of the northern Plains and mountains had horses in sufficient numbers to greatly aid themselves in warfare, hunting, and transporting their possessions, as they followed the buffalo and other game animals which were essential for their survival.

By 1800, Crow Indian country extended roughly from what is now south central Montana, down through was is now west central Wyoming. The Big Horn Basin was in the center of Crow territory.

Two members of the Lewis and Clark Expedition (1804–1806), John Colter and George Drouillard, have been given credit for being the first white Americans to enter the Big Horn

John Colter's name and the date "1810" was discovered on a sandstone cliff along the Yellowstone River. (Edgar Collection)

Basin and draw rough maps of the area where Cody is now located.

Colter was with Lewis on the return trip down the Missouri River. August 12, 1806, near the Mandan villages, they met Joseph Dixon and Forrest Hancock, two free trappers, who had been trapping on the river for a couple of years. Colter was given permission to be dismissed from the expedition and go back up the river to further explore the mountains with Dixon and Hancock. After exploring and trapping in the region, it is believed that they spent the winter of 1806–1807 in the vicinity of the Clarks Fork Canyon. When spring came, Colter left to go back down the river and in June of 1807, met Manuel Lisa at the mouth of the Platte River. Lisa and forty-two men were on their way up the river to build a fort and open a trading venture with the Indians. Colter joined Lisa's party.

They built a post, Fort Raymond, at the mouth of the Big Horn River in the fall of 1807. Lisa sent out scouts to contact the Indians for trade. Colter was sent into the Big Horn Basin. Traveling on foot with a pack and a flintlock rifle, he didn't return until early summer of 1808.

Colter's trek took him up Pryor Creek from the Yellowstone River, through Pryor Gap into the Big Horn Basin, then up the Stinking Water (Shoshone) River, to the locality of present-day Cody. He made a rough map, which showed the boiling springs on the Stinking Water River. The map showed the location of Cedar and Rattlesnake Mountains, along with Heart Mountain, which was called "Hart Butte."

It appears Colter went up the South Fork of the Shoshone River, through part of Yellowstone Park (Colter's Hell), then back through the Clarks Fork country, down the Stinking Water River, through Pryor Gap, back down to the Yellowstone River and the fort at the mouth of the Big Horn River.

In the winter of 1807, Drouillard left Lisa's fort and followed the Yellowstone River to the mouth of the Clarks Fork. He then followed the Clarks Fork to the mouth of Rock Creek, just below the canyon, where he found a Crow camp. He then traveled south over Skull Creek Pass, to the Stinking Water River, near the present site of Cody. Here he found a Crow camp on the north side of the river, above the hot springs. Drouillard made a map of the area which had translated Crow names for some of the landmarks. Cedar Mountain was "Spirit Mountain." Pat O'Hara Mountain was "Blue Bead" Mountain. On this mountain, the Indians obtained a clear, solid substance which they made into pipes. The North Fork of the Shoshone River was "Grass House River," which he described as having much beaver and otter. Heart Mountain was shown, however the spelling by both Colter and Drouillard was apparently incorrect. In an interpreted interview, a Crow Indian, Two Leggings, many years later referred to the mountain as "Buffalo Heart Mountain," a sacred mountain to the Crows. Crow medicinemen and leaders, including Two Leggings, had fasted, seeking visions on "Buffalo Heart Mountain."

On Drouillard's return trip, he traveled down the Stinking Water River, then up Sage Creek, through Pryor Gap, on to the Yellowstone River and back to Lisa's fort, arriving in the spring of 1808.

In the summer of 1808, Lisa and Drouillard went down the Missouri and gave Clark the map and information about the country they had explored. Clark published the material, making it available for anyone interested in the fur trade, to follow it right up the Missouri to the Yellowstone, then up the Clarks Fork into the Big Horn Basin.

While in St. Louis, Lisa formed the Missouri Fur Company. In the spring of 1809, Lisa led an expedition up the Missouri, but turned back to St. Louis at the Hidatsa village, leaving Pierre Menard in command. The party arrived at Lisa's fort in late fall and spent the winter trapping and trading. In March of 1810, Drouillard and thirty-two men under Menard, started for the Three Forks of the Missouri to establish another fort and trading post. Colter was their guide, as he had just explored the region. When they reached the Three Forks, they began constructing the fort and started trapping. Before the fort was finished, twenty men, including Drouillard, had been killed by the Blackfeet. Menard then gave up the venture and returned to Fort Lisa.

After this expedition, Menard went down the river with thirty packs of furs. Colter also left the mountains about this time, believing that if he stayed any longer, he would be killed, as his companions had been. Andrew Henry took some of the trappers and crossed the Continental Divide to the Snake River country. A hard winter and little success by spring, found the party ready to split up. Henry returned to St. Louis in the summer of 1811. Fort Lisa was abandoned and the Missouri Fur Company dissolved in January of 1812. A number of trappers were abandoned in the mountains.

Papypo Butte is located on the Greybull River, about thirty miles south of Cody. Stories passed down by Crow Indians, told of a desperate battle by a small party of Crow men, women, and children. They were attacked by a Blackfeet war party and forced to climb the butte for protection. When night came, there were casualties on both sides. The darkness was broken only by the light of Blackfeet fires, built to illuminate the east slope of the cliff-sided butte.

The Crows tied blankets, ropes and clothing together and lowered a girl off the dark side of the butte, praying she could find her way to the Crow camp and bring help. Morning came and the fight continued. No one knows how long the siege lasted, but finally Crow

Crow Indian "Bear in the Middle." The Mountain Crows roamed over a vast region, which included the Big Horn Basin. (Montana Historical Society)

Jim Bridger, in later years. Bridger was one of the foremost frontiersmen of the American West. (Kansas State Historical Society)

reinforcements killed and drove off the Blackfeet.

The Crow dead were placed on burial scaffolds on top of the butte. The posts were supported with sandstone slabs. Before the Blackfeet left, they had begun burying their dead in the nearby hills.

Among the scattered sandstone slabs still partly buried in the grass and sagebrush on Papypo Butte, a few stones with writing on them were found 161 years later. The writing was in English. One said "Here lies a man of Battle." Another said "Here sleep Alice Bear 1811." Another said "Here lay the son of Black Bear May 1811." The last two said "Born 1810–Died 1811" and "Joe is Dead 1811." Obviously there was at least one, possible two, white men with the Crows. Were these two of Lisa's abandoned trappers?

The War of 1812 and a depression in the country, nearly stopped the western fur trade until about 1822. Then another push was made into the mountains of the Yellowstone country. Clark's map led many parties directly into the Big Horn Basin.

The golden years of the beaver trade were 1822 to 1843. During that period various company traders and trappers, along with free trappers, roamed the region. Their colorful and wild experiences with both friendly and hostile Indians, rugged mountain passes, dangerous river crossings, winters of forty below with deep snow and grizzly bear confrontations would fill volumes. Although many stories of those times were recorded, many more have been lost to the eternal winds that blow over the prairies, mountains, and lost graves of the unfortunate.

During this period, Jim Bridger was probably the most knowledgeable frontiersman and trapper in the northern Plains and mountains. In 1830 Bridger had become so proficient in his calling and was considered so competent by the Rocky Mountain Fur Company, that he was sent with two hundred men to scout for fur in the Big Horn Basin. The party crossed the Yellowstone River and circled to the northwest. It is claimed that on this trip, Bridger first saw the wonders of what is now Yellowstone Park.

In one of Bridger's battles in the Blackfeet country, he was wounded in the back with two arrows. The iron point of one remained imbedded in a vertebra for nearly three years, before it was removed.

By the late 1830s, the beaver trade was dwindling. The American Fur Company bought out the Rocky Mountain Fur Company, then continued to operate until 1864.

In February of 1848, a group of free trappers led by William Hamilton had a battle with some Blackfeet in the Pryor Mountains, killing seven. Hamilton stated he moved up the South Fork of the Stinking Water River about thirty miles to a place called Beaver Swamp. Besides a large number of beaver skins, several otter were taken and hunters brought in twelve bear and four mountain lions. The party was visited by Chief Iron Bull, leader of a band of Crows, who had come from the Greybull. The chief inspected the Indian scalps the trappers carried and pronounced them "genuine" Blackfeet. He was made a present of two scalps. A ritual was immediately conducted, with warriors chanting and dancing around the scalps all night.

During the same time, Hamilton related that Blackfeet had killed two trappers on Gray Bull Creek (Greybull River) and had stolen five horses. The trappers killed were some distance from camp, looking after their traps, when Indians surprised them. The others heard the shots and hurried to camp to secure what horses they could, but the

Pat O'Hara and young Walt Hoffman. The photo was taken by Mrs. Hoffman at the Walter Hoffman homestead in 1914. O'Hara was about eighty-five years old and on his way to Oregon. (Hoffman Collection/PCHSA)

Indians ran off five head and also captured two rifles. One of the trappers went down the gulch and found his two dead friends, scalped and mutilated in a horrible manner.

Six years later, in 1854, Pat O'Hara came into the Big Horn Basin. He was employed by the American Fur Company as a trapper and hunter. Sixty years later, he rode up to the Hoffman Ranch, twenty miles northwest of Cody. By then the Crow name, "Blue Bead Mountain" had been changed to Pat O'Hara Mountain. Pat was about eighty-five years old and had decided to leave for Oregon. He was headed towards the Sunlight country when he stopped at the Hoffman's. Mrs. Hoffman and four-year-old Walt, were at the cabin. The following was written by Mrs. Hoffman:

He appeared one day in the fall of 1914 at our ranch on Blaine Creek, a tributary of Pat O'Hara Creek. He was tall, thin and straight, soft spoken and shy. He was loathe to speak much of his past, but reminisced a little. He recalled that he had lived in a cave on Pat O'Hara Creek, just above where the George Heald Ranch buildings were located. He had accumulated a nice assortment of pelts and was making ready to take them out, when one morning, as he moved the buffalo hide which served as a door, several arrows penetrated the hide. He remained in the cave until dark, then crept away, leaving the pelts behind. Another time he and two other trappers made ready to camp on Bald Ridge. He advised the other men to leave their saddles cinched because he had noticed that the "deer were running" (an indication that the Indians were on the move), but they failed to heed his advice. They were just ready to eat when Indians appeared and they had to mount their horses hurriedly and flee. One man's saddle came loose, and as he tried to mount, he was killed. As Pat looked back, the second man's saddle turned, due to the loose cinch, and he was killed. Pat alone escaped.

The next morning he prepared to leave our ranch on his trek to Oregon, which he hoped to reach. Pat rode his horse like an Indian, with a rope tied around the jaw. His equipment consisted of a frying pan and a coffee pot, a blanket and a slicker. We offered him some provisions, but he would accept only some coffee. As we reluctantly said good-bye, he rode slowly down the creek toward his final camp.

O'Hara was never seen again.

The discovery of gold at Gold Creek in 1862 and Alder Gulch in the spring of 1863, triggered a gold rush bringing several thousand prospectors and miners to the area. It was also the beginning of a decade of prospecting in the mountains of the Big Horn Basin, creating serious resentment among the Indians. Many of the fur trappers started prospecting for gold.

In the spring of 1864, Jim Bridger pioneered a wagon road through the Big Horn Basin to the gold camps at Virginia City, Montana Territory. On April 30, Bridger was released as post scout at Fort Laramie, to guide sixty-two wagons and three hundred people to the gold fields. They left the Oregon Trail near the Red Buttes on the Platte River and started off. The route that Bridger chose went through a pass east of Wind River Canyon on the southern portion of the Big Horn Mountains and into the Big Horn Basin. They built a ferry boat at the Big Horn River to carry the wagons across. They then traveled north across the basin and crossed the Clarks Fork River near present-day Bridger, Montana. A portion of that trail is still visible about thirty miles east of Cody. After crossing the Clarks Fork, the group traveled to the Yellowstone River and built another ferry, then over Bozeman Pass and down to Virginia City, where they arrived July 10, 1864, 510 miles from their starting point.

Bridger returned to Fort Laramie with a wagon train of discouraged prospectors, and September 18, left the Red Buttes with a second wagon train to Virginia City. On December 18, some of the party arrived at Virginia City on horseback, after leaving the wagons snowed in on the upper Yellowstone River. That season, the sixty-year-old Bridger rode horseback approximately two thousand miles, working on the trails, building ferrys and dealing with livestock. Bridger's trail was safer from Indian attacks, but never became popular because of the scarcity of water and grass.

In 1867 the Union Pacific reached Cheyenne. That same year, gold had been discovered near South Pass, and South Pass City sprang up almost overnight, with a population of over five thousand. Prospectors who had bad luck at South Pass moved into the Indian country of the Big Horn and Absaroka Mountains, which they believed were full of gold.

The United States government set up a treaty council at Fort Laramie for April and May of 1868. Couriers were sent to notify area tribes and request their representation at the meeting. Here they could discuss grievances and boundaries.

Crows from the Big Horn Basin and the upper Yellowstone River were well represented. Three of the chiefs that spoke to the government commissioners were "Blackfoot," "Wolf Bow," and "The Bears Tooth." All expressed concern over the en- croachment of the miners, and game being killed. The Bears Tooth ended his speech saying in part, "The Crows have made the long journey to Fort Laramie to speak at the great council. There is but little grass on the hills and many of our horses, that were already weak from the winter, have died on the way. On our return to the mountains, more will die." He took off his beaded moccasins, carried them up to the commissioners and presented them saying, "Here, take my moccasins too, for we have nothing left to give." The Crow chiefs signed the 1868 Treaty, not realizing that the Big Horn Basin had been taken from them. The Wyoming-Montana Territory line became the southern boundary of the Crow reserve. Was this done because the government suspected that the mountains of the Big Horn Basin were rich with gold?

Five years later, at a government meeting at Crow Agency on Mission Creek, on the upper Yellowstone River, Chief Blackfoot spoke to the commissioners. Following are comments from his speech:

The Treaty of 1868 is all lies, we do not want to hear it any more. Wrap it up and throw it away. We will not have that treaty. We wanted to know what was in that treaty and my friend has told us. The first time I went to Fort Laramie and met the Peace Commissioners, to what was said, we said yes. The second time we went, we signed the treaty, but neither my white friends, nor the Indian chiefs, said yes to what was in that treaty. We owned Horse Creek, Stinking Water and Heart Mountain. Many of these Indians were born there. The land we used to own, we do not think of taking pay for. They send us tin kettles, we go to get water to carry to our lodges, but it all runs out again. This is what we got for our land.

The Peace Commissioners traveled to Fort Bridger to meet with the Shoshonis, arriving June 4, 1868, to hold what was officially known as the "Fort Bridger Treaty Council of 1868." At this council, the boundary of the new Shoshoni Reservation was established farther to the north, out of the Bridger Valley, away from the surveyed route of the Union Pacific Railroad. The new Shoshoni Reservation consisted of about 2,774,400 acres.

In November of 1868, after the government abandoned the forts along the Bozeman Trail, the Sioux and Cheyenne came to a treaty council at Fort Laramie. Here they were allowed to keep the land along the east side of the Big Horn Mountains. Also, whites were specifically barred from the land north of the Platte River. Consequently, the Indian Treaty of 1868 made legal access into the Big Horn Basin impossible from any direction, even though it was no longer considered Indian Land. However, the Crows and Shoshonis continued to use the basin for quite a few more years.

The gold discovery at South Pass, and stories of more gold in the country to the north, drove gold hunters crazy. They were frustrated beyond words, by the Indian barrier surrounding the unprospected mountains of the Big Horn Basin.

In the winter of 1869–1870 an expedition was organized in Cheyenne, called the Big Horn Expedition. Their intent was to go through the Indian Reserve, into the Big Horn Basin. This expedition consisted of 130 well-armed men, under the leadership of W. L. Kuykendall. The expedition started for the basin in the spring of 1870 with wagons and equipment, including a cannon called the Big Horn gun, that fired a six-pound ball.

They got past the army, which was stationed at the recently established "Camp Brown" on the Wind River near present-day Lander. The expedition followed the Indian travois trail over the

Harry Yount, trapper and hunter. Yount was hired as the "Government Gamekeeper" of Yellowstone National Park. (Edgar Collection)

Owl Creek Mountains and into the Big Horn Basin. When the prospectors got to the Wood River west of Meeteetse in July, they set up a base camp on a bluff, where they could see in all directions. The valley was full of buffalo, elk, and deer. A young man named John Henry left to kill a buffalo for camp meat. He was found on a mountainside twelve days later, apparently killed by Indians, and partly eaten by wolves.

The men split into small parties and prospected up the river and several streams. Some gold was found near the head of Wood River. The prospecting party was soon upset in it's gold searching plans when soldiers appeared and informed the prospectors that they were infringing upon a treaty arrangement between the government and the Indians. They disbanded, leaving their wagons and heavy supplies behind. The ruins of their camp can be seen today. Part of the expedition turned back from Wood River, but a greater number continued north to the Yellowstone River, where the expedition dissolved.

In the fall of 1869, Jack Crandall and a partner discovered gold near the head of the Clarks Fork River, on one of it's tributaries. They wished to prospect longer, but snowstorms drove them out of the mountains. Crandall showed up in Bozeman and showed samples of tracer gold to his friend Horn Miller. Miller set about forming a small party to prospect the area in the spring.

Crandall and Daugherty headed into the mountains, planning to meet the rest of the party on the Clarks Fork about July 1. Miller's party traveled through part of present-day Yellowstone Park, Sunlight Creek, and the North Fork of the Shoshone River. In the vicinity of Sunlight Basin, they were attacked by Indians, who ran off all their horses. Traveling on foot by night, they abandoned most of their equipment and began a retreat through the rough country. Dissension broke out among the group and matters were not made any better by a wolf attack at the mouth of Miller Creek (named after Horn Miller), and another close call with the Indians. Several days after, they reached the Crow Agency, near Livingston, Montana Territory.

The failure of Crandall and Daugherty to join the main party was explained the next year when a hunter, Hank Bottler, found their bodies near a creek southeast of Cooke City. Their heads had been chopped off and stuck on upright mining picks, a coffee cup placed in front of each head. It was believed that the prospectors were killed by Crows or Arapahos. The creek was then named Crandall Creek.

Also in 1870, the Washburn Expedition made its way into the region of present-day Yellowstone National Park. This was a government expedition to find out if the fantastic stories of the mountain men about this wild region were true. Two years later, on March 1, 1872, upon passage by Congress and the Act of Dedication, this large region became Yellowstone National Park, "set apart for a public park or pleasuring ground, for the benefit and enjoyment of the people." Nathaniel Langford became the first superintendent of Yellowstone, and in 1880, Harry Yount, trapper, hunter, and guide, was hired as "Government Gamekeeper," to keep out poachers. This was, for all practical purposes, impossible at the time. Indians still hunted the region and white trappers and market hunters recognized no law in the mountains. Yount resigned after the first year, realizing he was ineffective. Younts Peak and Younts Creek, on the upper South Fork of the Shoshone River, were named for this mountain man.

During the summer of 1873, Captain William Jones of the Corps of Engineers, made a reconnaissance trip through northwestern Wyoming Territory, to name and map various streams and landmarks along the route. The following entries were made in his journal as the expedition passed through the western Big Horn Basin, with Shoshoni Indian guides who were changing some of the Crow names to their own, or names they made up at the moment.

Wednesday, July 23, 1873. We camped on Beaver Creek, which we renamed to Gooseberry. Some Shoshonee [sic] *Indians came in from Washakie's camp near the Stinking Water River. They report immense herds of buffalo down in the valley, and the village is having a grand hunt. We have seen a number of buffalo in the past few days and several have been killed.*

Saturday, July 26, 1873. Marched 18.8 miles to the North Fork of the Stinking Water River, crossing the South Fork or Ishawooa River. I have given this stream the Indian name of a peculiar shaped rock by means of which they could distinguish it. It is a remarkable finger shaped column of volcanic rock, standing alone in the valley about three miles above our crossing. [The Indian name for the South Fork of the Shoshone River was "Rock in the Valley" River, referring to Castle Rock.] Just below the junction of the two forks and about a mile below our crossing, the river, by a deep and rugged but short canyon, cut off the point of a sharp and high anticlinal ridge of yellow limestone which stands vertical along the summit, leaving a high bold peak which the Indians use as a landmark. The Shoshonis referred to it as the "Mountain with many cedars." I have therefore called it Cedar Mountain. [The Crow name was "Spirit Mountain."]

Near the head of the North Fork, the expedition went up Jones Creek, named after Captain Jones, and on into Yellowstone.

Four years later, in the late summer of 1877, Chief Joseph and the Nez Perce were following the Bannock Trail through Yellowstone Park, with General Howard and the U.S. Army in pursuit.

During the last week of August, the George Cowan Party, consisting of about ten men and women, were in the Lower Geyser Basin, viewing the wonders of the park. The party was discovered by some Nez Perce who proceeded to plunder their camp, wreck the wagons, and take their horses. Cowan was shot in the head with a cap

John "Liver Eating" Johnston ("Jeremiah Johnson" in the movie) at the age of fifty-three. Photo taken at Fort Keogh, Montana, in 1877. (Edgar Collection)

and ball revolver, which knocked him out, and his leg was shattered by another bullet. Albert Oldham was shot through the cheek, the bullet coming out under his jaw. The Indians captured a man and woman. The party was later reunited and by some miracle, the wounded men eventually recovered.

A few days later the Andrew Weikert Party was attacked by the Nez Perce. Weikert was creased across the shoulder by a bullet. Charles Steward was wounded in the leg. Charles Kenck and Richard Dietrict were killed. Their camp was pillaged.

The Nez Perce continued on their way, taking a route around the north shore of Yellowstone Lake, up Pelican Creek and over the divide to the upper Clarks Fork. They followed the south side of the Clarks Fork, crossing Crandall and Sunlight Creeks. Then took the zig-zag trail to the pass, a few miles south of the Clarks Fork Canyon. When they reached the summit, an aged Nez Perce asked to be left behind as he was too weak to travel. He was sitting under a pine tree as his people moved on toward Bald Ridge. When the Bannock Indian scouts, in advance of Howard's soldiers, reached the summit, they spotted the old Nez Perce under the tree and killed him. The place has since been referred to as "Dead Indian Hill."

When the Nez Perce started down the east slope of the mountain, little did they know what was waiting below. Colonel Sturgis and six companies of the Seventh Cavalry were camped south of the Clarks Fork Canyon.

Following is part of a letter that "Liver Eating" Johnston wrote to the *Billings Gazette* in 1884, as a rebuttal to something written earlier by a second lieutenant of the Seventh Cavalry. Johnston stated:

He says that when I was guiding the Seventh through the Heart Mountain region, I showed the white feather when I struck the Nez Perce trail. Some of these days I shall publish what I know about the march of the Nez Perce from Bald Ridge to the Bear Paws. I shall add some reminiscences of great interest to himself and some of his brother officers, who I know are much braver in attacking a beef steak than a hostile camp.

When the Seventh was in the region of Clarks Fork Canyon, I discovered the Nez Perce on Bald Ridge. I told the Lieutenant in charge of the detachment that I had found the Indians we were looking for. He looked through his field glass, but said that he could not see them. He didn't want to. He hadn't lost any hostile Indians I guess. The Crow scouts present at this time also saw the Nez Perce and told the brave officer so, but he wasn't open to conviction. None so blind as those who do not wish to see!

When the Nez Perce were discovered at Clarks Fork Canyon, Colonel Sturgis asked my opinion as to the best route to overtake them. I advised him strongly to remain where we were as, from the lay of the country, the Nez Perce must pass close to our encampment and they then could be attacked to advantage and the campaign ended. Colonel Sturgis saw the truth of my reasoning and agreed with me, as did Captains French and Benteen. All the other officers present demurred and overruled these three officers. They did so because they were afraid to fight and I told them so at the time in the presence of the command.

This bluntness on my part offended some of these suckling warriors and one of them has undoubtedly never forgiven me. The result of the council was that we moved on to Stinking Water and the Nez Perce passed by our rear and went on their march to the Bear Paws, thanks to blundering and arrant cowardice. During the balance of the campaign, I was the leading scout and guide of Sturgis' command, and part of the time for Howard's. Both these officers gave me the highest praise for my knowledge of the country, skill in guiding troops and bravery in a hostile country. So far as "sand" goes, I don't need to go to any Second Lieutenant for it. I have been in forty different Indian fights.

Chief Joseph surrendered at the Battle of the Bear Paw Mountains, October 5, 1877, about one day's travel from Canada.

Colonel Nelson Miles was also at the Battle of the Bear Paws, with four companies of the Second Cavalry, three of the Seventh and four of the Fifth. After the surrender, he turned his forces on the Sioux and Cheyenne, who were in their winter camps in the vicinity of the Wolf Mountains near the Wyoming-Montana line, east of the Little Big Horn Battleground. Johnston was hired as one of the head scouts.

Miles' command marched into the Tongue River country and the Wolf Mountains about the end of December 1877. The north wind howled and the

Bannock Indians that were captured at the Bennett Battle and taken to Fort Custer. (S. J. Morrow Collection, W. H. Over Museum)

temperature was far below zero. They were wearing buffalo coats, caps, and mittens. Miles had two howitzers inside canvas-covered wagons.

After several desperate battles, the Sioux, under Crazy Horse, and the Cheyenne, under Two Moons, were driven from their winter food supply. Forty below zero weather, drifted snow, no food, and pursuit by the army made victory impossible and survival unlikely. Two Moons and Little Chief surrendered three hundred Cheyenne on April 22, 1878. A few days later, Crazy Horse and two thousand Sioux surrendered at Red Cloud Agency.

For the Big Horn Basin, the year 1878 marked the beginning of change. The Indian barriers were removed and the basin was now open for white settlement.

The first to seek permanent holdings were those wishing to establish cattle ranches. The cattle market was booming in the West and, with thousands of acres of free grass, attracted both domestic and foreign investors. In the summer of 1878 John Chapman, a young cowboy from Oregon, was exploring for a ranch location in the Big Horn Basin, when he decided on a site on what is now Pat O'Hara Creek, about fifteen miles northwest of present-day Cody. In the early summer of 1879, he left Oregon with twelve hundred cows and eighty horses. Chapman and his cowboys trailed the stock through western Montana, arriving on Pat O'Hara Creek that fall.

Judge William Carter, the sutler at Fort Bridger for several years, learned about the opportunities in the Big Horn Basin from the post trader at Fort Washakie. He contracted Peter McCullough to hire cowboys and trail two thousand cows and some bulls into the Big Horn Basin. They arrived on the Stinking Water in October of 1879. They then located a ranch headquarters about sixteen miles southwest of present-day Cody, on what became known as Carter Creek. The McCullough Peaks, east of Cody, are named after McCullough, who operated the Carter Ranch for many years.

Oregon Basin, south of Cody, got it's name from when the Carter cattle were trailed into the area. A bull was lost that fall and was thought to have perished during the winter. However, it was found in good shape in the spring. The cowboys called the region, "the basin where the Oregon bull wintered." It was later shortened to "Oregon Basin."

Alice Bulltail, a Crow woman from Pryor, Montana, said when she was a young girl, about 1918, she came to Cody with her family. They took a ride through the canyon to the reservoir. She said her grandfather, "Comes Up Red," looked across the lake and called the rugged mountain in the distance "White Bear Mountain." This may be the Crow name for Carter Mountain.

In the spring of 1878, Count Otto Franc von Lichtenstein came West to look into starting a cattle ranch in the Big Horn Basin. As his health was not good, his doctor had suggested that he seek a drier climate. With this incentive and the financial backing of his two brothers in New York, he came West. Franc and his guide, who may have been Jack Wiggins, finally picked the location for the ranch headquarters in a valley of the upper Greybull River. That fall he contracted to buy fifteen hundred head of Hereford cattle in the Gallatin Valley of western Montana. The following spring, Wiggins began trailing the cattle to the newly established Pitchfork Ranch. To avoid the Indian country on the Yellowstone River, they trailed through Idaho, back over South Pass, across the Wind River and Owl Creek Mountains, into the Big Horn Basin and the Greybull River, arriving in the fall of 1879.

Over the next two decades many ranches were established in the Big Horn Basin. In the beginning the ranchers ran their cattle on the open range, with joint roundups in the spring to separate their cattle and brand calves. Another roundup occurred in the fall to separate cattle that would be shipped to market. The cattle were trailed to the railroad at various points on the Yellowstone River, for shipment east.

An unfortunate occurrence took place near the Clarks Fork Canyon September 4, 1878. Bannock Indians, whose reservation was at Fort Hall, Idaho, had been allowed to go on annual buffalo hunts east of the mountain ranges in the Big Horn Basin. They were starving on the reservation and their agent allowed the hunts to dry buffalo meat. The Bannock Trail came through Idaho and crossed Yellowstone Park, down the Clarks Fork, through

Arland and Corbett Trading Post established on Trail Creek in 1880. Taken in the early 1900s the photo shows a portion of the abandoned remains. (Edgar Collection)

Sunlight Basin, over Dead Indian Hill, and off the mountain south of the Clarks Fork Canyon.

As the party of about sixty Bannock men, women, and children passed through the park, some of the young men thought it fun to scare tourists by riding close and shooting their guns. Later they shot close to a survey crew. This created a panic and the army was notified. Soldiers from Fort Ellis were sent to watch for the Bannocks if they came out of the mountains on Rose Bud Creek. General Buell, at Fort Custer, was ordered to send a pack train to the mouth of the Clarks Fork Canyon. The cavalry was to go up the north side of the Yellowstone, then up the Clarks Fork with General Buell.

As this was going on, General Miles was coming up the Yellowstone with a party of officers, their wives, the Fifth Infantry Band and a pack train, on a vacation trip to Yellowstone. Miles' party was intercepted just north of Absarokee Agency, by a half-breed called Little Rock, who had been with the Bannocks, but had a falling out with them. He told Miles where the Bannocks would come out of the mountains. Miles left the women at the agency and, with his soldiers, a few Crow Indians and Little Rock, started around the Beartooth Mountains to the Clarks Fork Canyon.

It wasn't long until a scout spotted the Bannocks zig-zagging their way off the mountain, south of the canyon. The Indians crossed the river, went down a creek, and set up their lodges. Just before dawn September 4, the soldiers crept up to the Bannock camp. They were laying in the sagebrush with their 45-70 Springfield rifles. Captain Bennett was on horseback and gave the order to fire into the lodges. Several Bannocks were killed or wounded in the first volley. The others came out trying to run and fight, but were at a great disadvantage.

When the Bannocks surrendered, eleven had been killed, several escaped and thirty-one were captured. Captain Bennett and Little Rock had been killed. Two soldiers were wounded and the Crow scouts were driving the Bannock horses toward Absarokee Agency.

General Buell and his soldiers arrived shortly after the fight. Buell was furious with Miles. He said that he had sent Miles a courier the evening before, that the whole Indian camp could have been captured without a single shot and he would hold Miles responsible for the death of Bennett.

Bennett's body was taken back to Fort Keogh. Little Rock was buried on a hill which stood out in the Clarks Fork valley. The Bannock dead were buried in nearby hills. Little Rock and Bennett Creeks were named for two of the dead. So ended the last Indian conflict in the Big Horn Basin.

By 1878 the buffalo herds of the southern Plains had been mostly wiped out by hide hunters, only six years after the market for dried hides had been established in the East. For the fifty years prior to 1872 the Indian robe trade monopolized the buffalo hide market, on the southern and northern Plains. The fur companies, especially in the north, had been doing a big business trading for soft, tanned Indian robes. This market was larger and lasted longer than the market for beaver pelts. Some of the early fur company records show that in 1829–1830, 20,000 Indian tanned robes were shipped from Fort Tecumseh; 1834–1835, 9,000 from Fort McKenzie and 11,500 from Fort Union; and in 1843–1844, 10,000 from Fort Laramie.

In an article in an Eastern magazine in 1868, a trader on the upper Missouri River stated that 750,000 Indian tanned buffalo robes were freighted down the river that year. For the Indians, the buffalo robes were money at the trading houses. Several accounts stated that the best quality robes were those traded by the Crow.

In 1878 the white buffalo hunters from the southern Plains were looking for new range. The northern Plains of Wyoming, Montana, and the Dakotas became their destination. The most ideal country was the vast rolling hills and prairies, north and south of the Yellowstone River, north to the tributaries of the Missouri and between the Big Horn Mountains and the Black Hills. In these regions the terrain was such that the heavy hides could be freighted by wagon to the big rivers, where they could be loaded on steamboats for shipment.

The Big Horn Basin was different. Surrounded by mountains and containing a rough and broken interior, it was nearly impossible to hunt with wagons. Also it seems that the buffalo in the Big Horn Basin were not part of the large migratory herds of the plains, but localized, smaller herds that moved from the interior of the basin in the winter, to the mountains in the summer. So, as far as the robe trade was concerned, the Big Horn Basin was better suited for Indian hunters, than it was for the white hunters.

However, several white hunters did come into the Basin. Though the records are scanty, it seems that these hunters were more active in the eastern portion of the basin, near the Big Horn Mountains. Frank Sykes, Riley Kane, Oliver Hanna, and Jim White were among this group. White and Hanna hunted buffalo north of the Yellowstone River during the winter of 1879–1880. In the spring of 1880, they shipped forty-five hundred buffalo hides from Miles City, Montana Territory. They came into the Big Horn Basin through Pryor Gap in the late summer of 1880, setting up a hunting camp and cabin on Shell Creek, at the foot of the Big Horn Mountains.

White was a professional hunter who hunted the southern Plains until the buffalo were gone. He came to Wyoming in 1878 where he and Hanna became partners. Hanna asked White once how many buffalo he had killed. White got out an old greasy book that he kept records in and read the numbers he had sold. Hanna said he quit counting at sixteen thousand. White was killed by outlaws at his camp in October of 1880, while Hanna was gone. The desperadoes took their horses, mules, wagons, guns, and supplies. Hanna wrapped White in a buffalo hide and buried him on a sagebrush flat above Shell Creek.

In the spring of 1880, Vic Arland and John Corbett came into the Big Horn Basin to build the first trading post. They picked a site on Trail Creek, at the foot of Rattlesnake Mountain, a few miles northwest of present-day Cody. The site was appropriate because it was on the Indian trail into the mountains of the upper Clarks Fork River, one of the great hunting grounds of the region. Arland had come to the New World from Veincennes, France, in

The ranch headquarters that Vic Arland built on Trail Creek in 1882. He sold it to another Frenchman, Count Ivan Du Dore, that year. (Montana Historical Society)

The main building at the Arland and Corbett Trading Post established on Cottonwood Creek in 1883. The photo was taken shortly after Arland sold the location to Frenchman Count De Mailly. The two men on the left appear to be Frenchmen who came to the American West on a hunting trip. Arland moved south to Meeteetse Creek to establish another business in 1884. (Montana Historical Society)

Count De Mailly's branding corrals on Cottonwood Creek, circa 1886. (Montana Historical Society)

The "subscription" bridge built across the Stinking Water River in 1883. John Corbett established a new business near the bridge in 1884. (Montana Historical Society)

John Corbett's establishment just below the new Stinking Water bridge, circa 1885. (Montana Historical Society)

1870. About 1872 Arland traveled up the Mississippi River, arriving at Spotted Tail Agency, Dakota territory, in 1874, where he spent about a year. Arland wrote a letter from the agency telling about Indians on the war path and of a company of cavalry stationed there to keep the gold prospectors from going into the Indian treaty land of the Black Hills. In 1877, he came to Wyoming Territory, prospecting for gold in the Big Horn and Owl Creek Mountains, as far south as Fort Washakie, afterward going to Fort Custer at the mouth of the Little Bighorn River. The fort was under construction when he arrived. Here he worked a year with Corbett, hunting buffalo to supply meat for the garrison.

Arland and Corbett formed a partnership in a trading post venture in the Big Horn Basin. The Crow Indians around Fort Custer may have told them about the region. The establishment of the first cattle ranches in the area was, no doubt, another reason for the Trail Creek site.

Arland wrote a number of letters to Camille Dadant at Hamilton, Illinois. Fortunately, these letters survived and in 1961 were sent to the Buffalo Bill Historical Center. Following are portions of the letters:

Trail Creek, Wyoming Territory. March 1, 1882. Since the country where I now am is excellent for the raising of cattle, last summer I built a ranch about 5 miles below on the creek where I live, for a cattle raiser who has not been able to come take possession of it, according to what he told me. Since the construction of this ranch (Trail Creek Ranch), cost me $200 in labor, I was forced to remain until I can dispose of it.

Lately a Frenchman, Count Ivan Du Dore, who had come to America to hunt, was struck by the great advantages that the raising of cattle has to offer. Since he is very enterprising, he bought a large number of cows and entrusted his brother, who has come with him, to return to France to bring back some capital. Since the ranch that I built pleased him, he bought it from me for $600, the price that I was asking for it. You have no doubt heard tell of the great number of cattle that are being raised in the far west, and of the great profit the cattle raisers get. The land near the mountains is excellent for grazing. When in 1877 I left to prospect in the mountains, I pushed across an

Jesse and Elizabeth Frost and son Jack. (Frost Collection/PCHSA)

The settlement of Marquette, at the confluence of the North Fork and South Fork of the Shoshone River. (Gerber Family)

immense country not yet explored. Today, hundreds of thousands of cattle and horses cover the same country.

When in September 1880, my partner, J. Corbett and I came to Trail Creek, we were very far from civilization. Next summer, the Northern Pacific will be on the Yellowstone, up to Coulson [Billings, Montana] 125 miles direct from our place.

Now we are running a little store to supply the needs of the hunters and trappers of the region and of the Indians, Crows and Shoshonis, who are hunting in this vicinity. Since this little business promises to do well, I am going to remain here for some time. We harvested 6,000 lbs. of potatoes, 600 lbs. of onions, a large number of cabbages, carrots and other vegetables. And I can assure you that antelope, elk and mountain sheep are delicious fixed with vegetables.

Trail Creek, Wyoming Territory. July 24, 1883. They are going to build a bridge over Stinking Water. $5,000 have been raised by subscription for it, given by the cattle raisers, the businessmen of Billings, and the Northern Pacific. We are going to move our store close to the bridge, about 10 miles from our present location, which will increase our business considerably.

Cottonwood Creek Dec. 20, 1883. Since we have been established at Cottonwood, our business has increased considerably for we are on the road from Camp Brown (Lander) to Billings.

Cottonwood March 16, 1884. We are going to build a new store on the Meeteetse, about 35 miles to the south, and in the center of the cattle raisers of this area. We are going to sell our place on Cottonwood. It is a very good location. We have done considerable business this winter with the whites and Crow Indians. From March 4–14, our place was crowded from morning till evening with whites and Indians. These Indians were camped about 500 steps from our store. I am leaving for Meeteetse tomorrow, where

Red Lodge, Montana, about the time Vic Arland was killed while playing poker in Dunnivan's Saloon. (Edgar Collection)

I am going to build a temporary cabin.

Meeteetse, June 17, 1884. There are at the present time, about 30,000 head of cattle between Stinking Water and Grey Bull. In a radius of 20 miles from here, there are about 15 cattle ranches. We have a coach from Fort Washakie twice a week. We hope the coach will come directly from Billings to Fort Washakie the first of July, passing right by our place. This is one of the most game-filled regions of the far west. Buffalo, elk, deer, antelope, mountain sheep and bears are in abundance.

Meeteetse, Dec 5, 1884. The buffalo have entirely disappeared from the surrounding areas, and consequently the skins are very rare and very expensive.

Meeteetse, Feb 14, 1885. There are about 30 lodges of Crow and Snake Indians around our place. Consequently, game is rare. Lately a band of Crow Indians came to camp close to our place. They thought that they were giving me a great gift in giving me two scalps of Blackfeet, killed by them. I must tell you that I am far from putting the same value on these scalps as those Indians do.

Although Corbett kept an interest in the business with Arland, he established another business at the new bridge on the Stinking Water River in 1884. This became known as "Corbett" and soon consisted of a store, saloon, post office, and accommodations for travelers. Although whiskey and gambling often led to trouble, no accounts of anyone being killed there have been found.

Another new resident of the Stinking Water was another Frenchman, Charles DeMaris, who settled at the mineral springs in the canyon, in 1883. DeMaris was a cattleman from Montana and had run cattle on the Crow Reservation. DeMaris built a cabin and corral near the hot springs and soon got title to the springs and land on both sides of the river. He later built a two-story hotel and developed the springs as a health spa, also bottling and selling the mineral water as medicine. For generations, Indians of the region had camped on the river near the springs, treating their ailments with the healing water. Numerous teepee rings can still be seen on both sides of the river. The Crow and Shoshoni Indians returned to the springs into the early 1900s.

The Mahlon Frost family arrived in the Big Horn Basin during the spring of 1885. After getting acquainted with the area, they spent the winter on the South Fork of the Stinking Water, hunting and trapping, their nearest neighbors were four lodges of Shoshoni Indians.

In the fall of 1886, Mahlon, his wife Nancy, and their younger children, Ned and Daisy, took the train from Billings back to Minnesota for a visit. They left nineteen-year-old Jesse and Elliot Barnes to care for their possessions and livestock. Jesse paid $50 for relinquishment of a land claim on Sage Creek. He was aware of proposals to establish a stage line from the Northern Pacific's branch leading to the coal mines at Red Lodge, south through the Big Horn Basin to Fort Washakie, then on to the Union Pacific Railroad. He thought the Sage Creek location, on the established freight road, to be a good one. In the spring of 1887, the Frosts, along with their younger children, were met at the Billings railroad station by Jesse. They returned to Sage Creek and went about transforming a one-room, dirt-roof-and-floor log cabin into a home, livestock ranch, and stage station. They built buildings, put in hay and grain fields, and raised teams. They supplemented their income trapping furs and killing game for the meat markets during the winter, when the meat would keep. The meat was hauled to Billings, sold and shipped East on the railroad. Jesse got into the freighting business, hauling supplies to area ranches. Ned became one of the top hunting guides of the region.

Another well-known figure in the region was George Marquette, who came to the basin in 1878. Among his skills were constructing log buildings and playing the fiddle at area dances. In 1882, he built a log house for Richard Ashworth at the Z-T Ranch on the Greybull River. He built other log houses in the area and may have helped in the construction of some of the buildings at Arland, on Meeteetse Creek, in 1884.

His first homestead was on Marquette Creek. He later moved to the South Fork and built a log building that served as his residence and a dance hall. Other buildings included barns, corrals and the log building occupied by the Houx family. Frank Houx, later Cody's first mayor and governor of Wyoming, operated the dance hall.

Marquette was justice of the peace for Fremont County, Marquette Precinct, and first postmaster of "Old" Marquette, from April 1891 to March 31, 1903, when the post office moved four miles and George Payne became postmaster. "Old" Marquette had a store, one or more saloons, and stables and corrals for teams. "New" Marquette had a store, one or more saloons, rooming house, livery stables, corrals, and residential cabins. Marquette died November 29, 1906, while visiting friends at the Marquette store. Marquette ceased to exist after completion of the Shoshone Dam in 1910.

While developments were taking place in the Stinking Water Country, Arland was having his share of problems at his new town on Meeteetse Creek.

The devastating winter of 1886–1887 took its toll of cattle from the ranches in the Big Horn Basin. As a result, a good many ranchhands found themselves out of work. Desperate men were roaming the country looking for work, horses to steal, or someone to rob. There was no government welfare in the 1880s. Survival was accomplished by your wits and, sometimes, with a gun and a fast horse.

Montana had problems with outlaws earlier than Wyoming. In 1884–1885, Granville Stuart's Vigilantes hunted down and killed a substantial number of horse thieves, stage coach bandits, and murderers along the Yellowstone and Missouri Rivers. By 1885–1886, many of these desperadoes rode south to the Big Horn Basin to get away from the law. Arland attracted these characters like a moth to a flame. There was no resident law in the town. Arland had to enforce his own rules in the saloon and gambling hall. In a letter, Arland expressed a hint of the frustration of trying to keep order.

Meeteetse Creek, Dec 5, 1884. All the cowboys are singular characters, very violent and without equal in their spirit of independence, but they appreciate a man of courage and energy. In the towns of the west, they are getting a deplorable reputation for their audacity and lack of restraint.

In 1886, Arland got into an argument with Joe Crow, horse breaker and associate of Black Jack Miller, well-known horse thief from the Yellowstone River country. Crow was drunk when he fired his revolver at Arland. Arland dodged, jumped over the counter, and tried to get his own gun. Crow emptied his gun, grazing Arland's head and blowing a hole in the sugar scoop. In 1887, Arland was almost killed in the gambling hall. In a letter Arland said:

A man named Thomas Brady, a rascal of the worst sort, fired a revolver at me point blank, because I hadn't wanted to lend him some money to gamble. Fortunately, I was quick enough to thrust his gun aside with my hand. The sleeve of my shirt was burned and I was singed on the wrist.

February 22, 1888, at a George Washington birthday dance at Arland, a conflict between Arland and a cowboy named Andy Jackson took place. Arland hit Jackson with a bottle and pushed him out the door. Bill Landon, who was outside, convinced Jackson to get Landon's gun and kill Arland. Arland was warned and waiting, with a Sharps rifle, when Jackson came toward the saloon with a Colt .45 revolver. Arland killed Jackson, after ordering him three times to "drop his gun." Landon was furious and swore to kill Arland at the "least provocation." The time came on the night of April 24, 1890, in Dunnivan's Saloon in Red Lodge, Montana. Arland, John Dyer, and Lum Wilson took the stage from Arland to Red Lodge to "get away" for a while, gamble, and visit. The night they arrived, they ran into Landon, who had spent the winter there. At about 12:30 that night, Arland was killed, as he played cards, by a shot fired through the window by Bill Landon. However, at the trial two days later, Landon was acquitted as no one saw him fire the shot, and he would not admit to it. Arland was buried in the Red Lodge cemetery.

After Arland's death, Corbett moved to Arland to take over operation of his, and his late partner's interests. It seems that Corbett was easier going than Arland and the town became even more attractive to the outlaw element, men like Bill Gallagher, Blind Bill Hoolihan, Ed Nye, Robert (Butch Cassidy) Parker, Al Hainer, Jack Bliss, Jack Bedford, Dab Burch, Al Durant, and others. In 1890 Belle Drewry, a shady but attractive woman with a criminal record, came to town from the Fort Fetterman-Douglas area. There was also Rose Williams, Sagebrush Nancy, and others that followed the frontier settlements.

The January 2, 1892 *Billings Times* stated:

J. R. Weaver went out from Red Lodge to brand some colts and discovered that another big haul had been made by rustlers. The principle losers are as follows,

Frost stage station on Sage Creek, about 1890. (Frost Collection/PCHSA)

Dilworth Cattle Company, 150 head . . . Chapman Bros., 80 head . . . J. R. Weaver, 75 head, besides horses belonging to other ranches and cowboys, making an aggregate of about 400 or 500 head. The rustlers, who appear to be thoroughly organized, have had four or five men occupying a deserted shack on Alkali Creek, north of Heart Mountain.

Billings Gazette, March 10, 1892:

Separate and distinct from organized cattle rustlers on the border of Wyoming, is a horse rustling gang who have been operating on an extensive scale in that section of country at the head of Wood River. This gang is snowbound now and safe in their retreat. Since the days of Teton Jackson, there has been no such gang in the Big Horn Basin. Their depredations have been far reaching and wonderfully successful. The opening spring may be more red than green for the horse and cattle thieves of Wyoming.

Two members of the gang were apprehended in Star Valley April 8, 1892. They were Al Hainer and Robert (Butch Cassidy) Parker. The following is an excerpt written by William Simpson on May 5, 1939:

At the time of his [Cassidy's] arrest by Bob Calverly for stealing horses from John Chapman, an old-time resident on the Pat O'Hara district north of Cody, I was County and Prosecuting Attorney of Fremont County. I prosecuted Cassidy myself, not Judge J. L. Torrey. I knew John Ward [Sheriff of Uinta County] and Calverly well and have talked to Calverly about the arrest. I talked to Chapman, who was there, about it, and I will say Chapman had a high regard for Cassidy and assisted in taking care of his wounds at the time Bob hit him over the head with a 45 Colt.

In 1892 the stockmen of northern Wyoming and southern Montana raised a substantial amount of money to hire range detectives, often times nothing more than outlaws themselves. Nevertheless, over the next two or three years, the outlaw threat was greatly reduced.

Robert Leroy Parker, alias "Butch Cassidy," taken during his stay at the Wyoming State Penitentiary. (Gene Plambeck)

George Spencer and Mike Burnett were killed in a gunfight with a posse in Jackson Hole April 15, 1892. They had in their possession fifty-three stolen horses. Jack Bliss, leader of the Wood River horse thief gang, was killed near the head of the South Fork of the Shoshone River in mid-June 1892. Bliss and another outlaw, Irwin Collier, were busted out of the Lander jail by some of their friends. In the escape, a running gunfight occurred and a deputy sheriff was killed. Albert Nard, an ex-member of the Bliss gang, and David Shuck were deputized to trail Bliss and bring him back, dead or alive. The two hired killers followed his trail into the Big Horn Basin, past Arland, the Frost stage station, around Carter Mountain, up the South Fork trail (often referred to as the Horse Thief Trail) to a small meadow near the head of the river. At dusk they found Bliss's camp. Nard and Shuck tied their horses in the timber and sneaked toward the campfire. When they saw Bliss, one called out, "throw up your hands." Bliss reached for his gun. Nard fired two shots, Shuck fired three. Bliss ran about twenty feet and fell dead in the grass.

Nard and Shuck rode back down the river and told their story to Justice of the Peace George Marquette. Marquette appointed three other men for a coroner's jury and the six made the ride back to Bliss's camp. There Marquette viewed the body of Bliss, confirming his identity. He told the men to dig a grave and bury the outlaw where he fell. Later that summer, Nard and another deputy hunted down Allen Moore, alias Ed Hinkly, a horse thief and murderer, and killed him at a cabin in the Wind River Mountains

October 1, 1892, ML ranchhand Joe Rogers, Pitchfork ranchhand John Wickham and H. B. Peverly, believed to be a range detective for the Wyoming Cattlemen's Association, murdered David Burch and Jack Bedford, two accused horse thieves. They were shot in cold blood, while tied to their horses. The horses were also shot. The murders occurred near Bonanza, on No Wood Creek. Two members of the horse thief gang were killed in 1894. William Gallagher was shot by another gang member, Bill Wheaton, March 14, and Blind Bill Hoolihan was shot in the back and killed April 5. These killings were a result of jealousy over Belle Drewry, a woman at Arland. Rose Williams was also involved. About two months after the murder trial, Rose mysteriously died. Belle was killed a while later in revenge for killing Jesse Conway. After being convicted in the spring session of court in Lander, Wheaton and Cassidy were sent to the Wyoming State Prison.

While the outlaws were getting thinned out in the Big Horn Basin, men of vision were looking at the basin with other thoughts in mind. One such man was George Beck. Following, in part, is his story:

I lived on Big Goose Creek, about ten miles west of Sheridan. I had prospected in the Big Horn Mountains and finally was engaged in hydraulic work, and started a town on Bald Mountain, called Bald Mountain City, where I built a cabin and the men lived. Looking west from Bald Mountain, across the Big Horn Basin, we could easily see Cedar Mountain and a canyon made by the Stinking Water River.

An old man named Laban Hillberry, came to Bald Mountain and told me that there was a big river running through that canyon and that river could be taken around south of the mountain and cover a large area of land. The idea rather struck me, but before I determined to go there myself, I sent Jerry Ryan. He had a team, and he took Hillberry and went to see if he thought this report was correct. He came back that fall and told me that he thought it could be done, so next spring, when I

George Marquette with his fiddle, circa 1892. (Ebert Collection, PCHSA)

had finished my hydraulic work, I concluded to make a party to go there and survey the country.

Mr. Elwood Mead was then State Engineer, and I employed him to go with me. I made a surveying party of ten and had seven guests. We started across the mountains on the trail that was a short distance below Buffalo. We came out near Tensleep and crossed the Big Horn River near Lovell by ferry, which was the only means of crossing it during high water. We made it to Sage Creek and camped for a day or two at the bend where Sant Watkins later had his sheep corrals.

We started to run a few lines from there, but concluded it would be better to move up nearer the mountains and from there ran a line of levels up to the place where the headgate is now located, then coming back to our stake in the divide, ran lines eastward and covered in our preliminary survey practically 400,000 acres, taking in lands on both sides of the river. While doing this work, after having the headgate located, I took several trips with my guests into the mountains westward, mostly up the South Fork. Later in the summer we returned to Sheridan. I paid all expenses and disbanded the party. Mr. Mead made the maps of our preliminary survey.

I had as one of my guests, Horton Boal, the son-in-law of Col. Cody. As the Colonel had the Sheridan Inn, and Mr. George Canfield ran it, he came to Sheridan after his season closed in the Wild West Show. Boal and his wife, Arta Cody, lived at the Sheridan Inn, and he told Cody what he had seen over in the Big Horn Basin with me. Cody became very interested, came to see me and wanted to go into the enterprise. I told him that I had taken my friend, Horace Alger, who was cashier of the Bank of Commerce in Sheridan in with me, and would have to see him and talk it over.

Horace and I had a talk and concluded that as Cody was probably the best advertised man in the world, we might organize a company and make him president of it. As I had done all the work and put up all the money to date, I arranged it, and made Cody the president, Alger the treasurer and I would be secretary and manager. That was

Cody Canal headgate on the South Fork, 1895–1896. (Gerber Family)

satisfactory to Cody and we took in his partners Nate Salsbury, George Bleistein, Bronson Rumsey and H. M. Gerrans, all from Buffalo, New York. That was the company as organized. But no one had put up any money. I was left carrying it until the following spring, when I went east to meet Cody at Pittsburgh, and George Bleistein was there and handed me a check for $5,000. This was the first cash put into the company besides my own. Later, each of the directors came through with the same amount.

I found a contractor who had some good teams and an outfit, and started him to work on the ditch near a point opposite the Marion Williams Ranch on the South Fork. I also contracted another party as to building a headgate and others to riprap a thousand feet of river bank on the southeast side. The Williams Ranch soon became a popular place. Many a dinner was shared with the people involved with the canal work. There were occasional dances with George Marquette playing lively tunes on the fiddle. Frank Grouard, the Indian war scout and ex-U.S. Marshal, was working on the canal and also a regular guest.

When the ditch got around to the land on the east side of Sulfur Creek the next year, Colonel Cody went in with Hymer, Charles DeMaris and H. P. Arnold and located a townsite on the south side of the river near what is now known as DeMaris Springs.

In a letter that Cody wrote to Beck from Wilmington, North Carolina, on October 6, 1895, he suggested that they name the streets in the townsite after Civil War Generals and that Cody supply the Union names and Beck the Confederates.

Charles Hayden, an engineer at the time, stated in his memoirs:

Arrangements were made with H. P. Arnold to start a general store. Arnold was a genuine Yankee. He kept everything in stock and really was quite an acquisition to the community. A blacksmith came along and set up shop and before the winter was over, a full dozen buildings were occupied in the new town.

"Breaking ground" for the Cody Canal, 1894. (AHC/UW)

One of the dances held at the Williams Ranch. Bill Cody is second from left. Frank Williams, who performed in the Wild West Show, is at the far right. (Gerber Family)

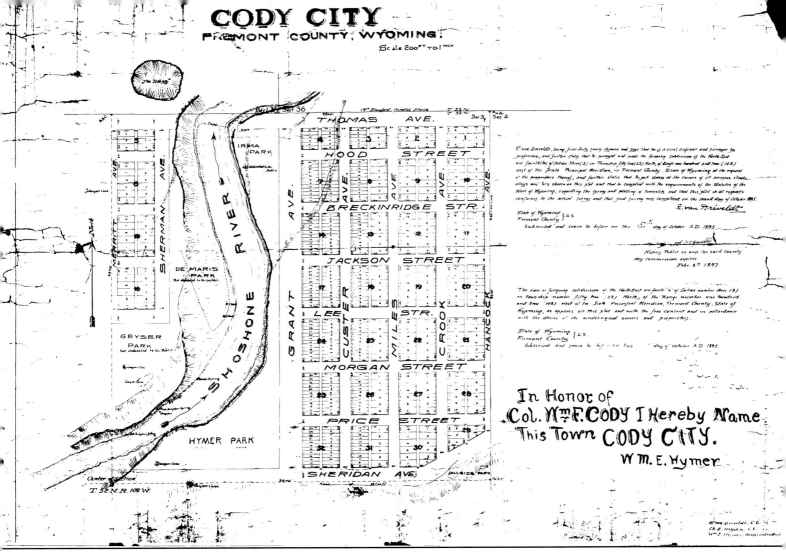

Cody City was platted in October of 1895 by Charles Hayden and E. van Dreveldt. The town was laid out on both sides of the river, but the only building done was near where the Cody Stampede grounds are today. (Edgar Collection)

The H. P. Arnold and Company, General Merchandise store, Cody City, 1895. (Williams Collection, PCHSA)

"Buildings at Cody City" looking across the canyon of the Stinking Water River from the west side in 1895. (Garlow Collection, PCHSA)

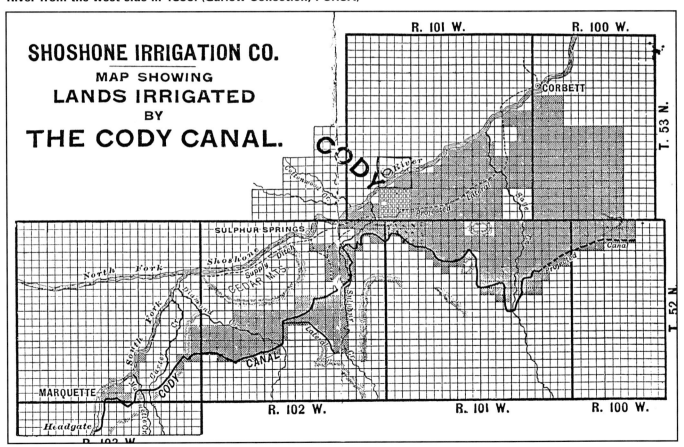

The first settlers on the Cody Canal, arrived May 7, 1895, to establish the village of Irma and farm today's Irma Flat. Of the original group of sixty to seventy German colonists, everyone but the Joe Vogel family had moved on by the following spring. (PCHSA)

A view of Cody taken in 1899 from the top of the Greybull hill, in line with Sixteenth Street. The house in the foreground, built by the Schwoobs that year, still stands. Newton's cabin across the street may be the oldest home in Cody. The buildings on the right are the Buffalo Bill Barn, the Schwoob blacksmith shop and the first *Cody Enterprise* building, all located on the site of the IGA store today. Beck's first house can be seen on the western boundary of town. The buildings in the center include Chapman's Council Saloon and a restaurant, on the site of the present Shoshone Bank. Water from the Cody Canal can be seen flowing along the base of the hill. (Garlow Collection/PCHSA)

George T. Beck didn't like the location, or financial arrangements, for Cody City and went forward with plans for a new townsite which would benefit the Shoshone Land and Irrigation Company.

Cody was founded at its present site in May 1896. Beck and Charles Hayden drove the first stake in the intersection that is now Thirteenth Street and Sheridan Avenue, after making certain the streets would run exactly north-south and east-west. George Russell built the first frame buildings on the northeast corner of that intersection. Beck's Shoshone Land and Irrigation Company office, also housing a commissary and post office, was first. Next to it was Cody's first boarding house, later called the Cody Hotel. Then Jerry Ryan built his residence on Alger and the first rooms of Beck's house on the west side of town, using sandstone quarried from what is now Beck Lake. Initially Cody had more tents than buildings. Gradually frame structures replaced tents as settlers were drawn by the promise of cheap land and irrigation water from the Cody Canal.

A turning point for the town came in 1901 when the Burlington Railroad finished its line to Cody. For choosing Cody as a terminus, the Lincoln Land Company, a subsidiary of the railroad, claimed ownership of half the town lots. Cody was incorporated in 1901, boasting a population of 550. All the development to sustain a new settlement was in place; access to water, lumber mills, coal mines, a stone quarry, brick yard, mercantile, telephone and telegraph service, freight companies, and the railroad.

By 1903 Cody had two churches, a school, and a city water system. In 1904 Beck built a power plant, the first wagon road to Yellowstone Park opened and work began on the Shoshone Reclamation Project. By 1905 services included hotels, boarding houses, bakeries, meat markets, dairy, newspapers, clothing stores, mercantile companies, livery stables, blacksmith shops, banks, doctors, dentists, attorneys, lumber yards, bottling company, carpenters, masons, saloons, drug stores, jewelers, photographers, engineers, camping and hunting companies with guides, realtors, dressmakers, brothels, and police and fire departments.

The agricultural base of the community grew from livestock and crops produced by area farms and ranches. Visitors were coming to enjoy Yellowstone Park, hunt, fish, bathe at the DeMaris Springs, and relocate to the country they had heard so much about from Buffalo Bill's Wild West Show.

1896-1905

by Jeannie Cook

3

Beck's company office and boarding house were the first buildings in town. They were located on the northeast corner of what is now Sheridan and Thirteenth Street, which was the center of town. The streets in Cody have been renumbered since the first plat was filed. (Gerber Family)

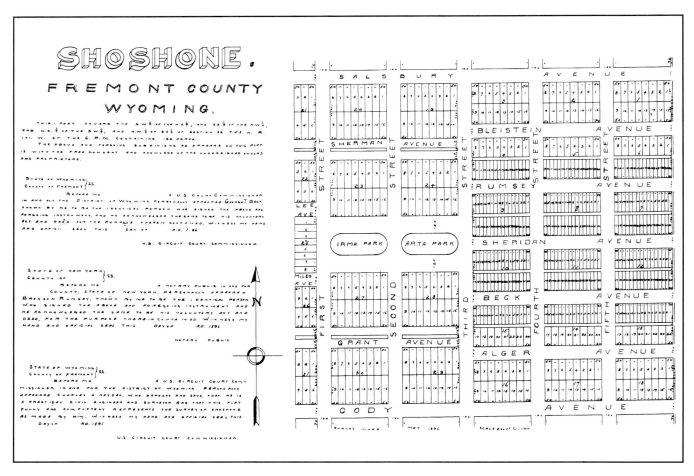

Cody was laid out in the spring of 1896 by George Beck and surveyor Charles Hayden. Six of the seven directors of the Shoshone Land and Irrigation Company, Cody, Beck, Alger, Salsbury, Rumsey, and Bleistein, had a street named in his honor. A street was finally named for Gerrans when the Canyon View subdivision was created in 1928. The plat map was first filed as "Shoshone" in Fremont County. The postmaster general would not give them a post office, since "Shoshone Agency" already existed in Fremont County. Colonel Cody gave up the name of *Cody City* at the DeMaris site and sent his foreman to Washington to request the name *Cody* for the new town. Cody's request was granted and according to Beck it highly pleased the Colonel. Cody, Wyoming, was on the map!(Coe Library/UW)

Cody town founders, standing left to right, are George Bleistein, H. M. Gerrans, and Bronson Rumsey. Seated are William F. Cody and George T. Beck. This photograph was probably taken at a Board of Directors' meeting in the East. (AHC/UW)

Shown is a turn-of-the-century Fourth of July celebration along Sheridan Avenue. Nate Salsbury, Colonel Cody's business manager and an investor in the Shoshone Land and Irrigation Company, was on hand to celebrate the Fourth of July in 1896. Beck gave the address and Salsbury claimed the town was exactly six weeks old on that day. (AHC/UW)

Bessie Nuckols, Betty and Jane Beck, and Camille Powers playing with their dolls at the Beck home. (Gerber Family)

TO BIG HORN COUNTY.

At a meeting of the Honorable Board of County Commissioners, held on the 7th day of September, A. D., 1896, at Hyattville, Big Horn County, Wyoming, the following proposition was submitted to said Board for the use and benefit of the people of Big Horn County:

KNOW ALL MEN BY THESE PRESENTS: That Geo. T. Beck, Agent of the Cody Townsite Company, of Big Horn County, State of Wyoming, party of the first part, does hereby agree for himself and for the Cody Townsite Company, as its Agent, to deed to the Honorable Board of County Commissioners, of Big Horn County, State of Wyoming, Trustees, party of the second part, for the use and benefit of the people of Big Horn County, State of Wyoming, all the following parts and parcels of land, situated and being in the County of Big Horn, State of Wyoming, to wit:

Block 25 (twenty-five) and Irma Park in the Town of Cody as the same is shown and designated on the official plat of said Town, which said plat is filed in the office of the said Cody Townsite Company, at Cody, Big Horn County, State of Wyoming.

The party of the first part hereby further agrees to erect, or cause to be erected on the above described real-estate, county buildings of the value of $5,000 (five thousand dollars), which said buildings shall be erected and constructed at the expense of the party of the first part, under the supervision, and according to the plans of the party of the second part, and when erected, said party of the first part hereby agrees to deed and transfer said above described buildings free of all encumbrance, to the said party of the second part.

Provided, however, that these presents are upon these express conditions, that the above mentioned deeds shall not be made unless the county seat of Big Horn County, shall be, at the General ensuing Election to be held on the 3rd day of November, A. D., 1896, located at the Town of Cody, County of Big Horn, State of Wyoming, in which case the said deed shall be made at once; otherwise, These Presents to be null and void, and of no effect.

IN WITNESS WHEREOF, I have hereunto set my hand and seal on the 7th day of September, A. D., 1896.

GEORGE T. BECK, Agent.

Attest:
C. A. GILLETTE.

State of Wyoming. } ss
County of Fremont.

Be it known that on the 7th day of September, A. D., 1896, before Charles A. Gillette, a U. S. Circuit Court Commissioner, in and for the said county and state, appeared George T. Beck, agent, to me personally known to be the identical person who signed the above and foregoing instruments, and that he acknowledged the same to be his voluntary act and deed.

WITNESS my hand and seal this 7th day of September, A. D. 1896.

CHARLES A. GILLETTE,
U. S. Circuit Court Commissioner,
Dist. of Wyoming.

[SEAL]

Any comments on the proposition here submitted to the people of Big Horn County are surely unnecessary as the benefits of the offer on the part of Cody, Wyoming, accruing to the people of Big Horn County, are plainly set forth in the proposition itself. Not only does it present to the people of Big Horn County buildings of the value of $5,000 (five thousand dollars,) but it saves them an equal amount of expenditure, being in reality a net saving to the tax-payers of $10,000. When one considers the heavy debt which the County will have to assume, the offer above made cannot but appeal to the good sense of each and every tax-payer and voter in the County.

Cody, Wyoming is situated on the Shoshone River, in what promises to be one of the finest agricultural sections of the State, not only on account of the immense amount of land capable of irrigation, but the unlimited amount of water carried by the Shoshone River as well. A recent report made by State Engineer Mead showed that this River exceeded, in volume, the total of all water carried by all of the Rivers of Eastern Colorado combined.

The town itself has already become the leading market of the County, the demands far exceeding the supply of the season just past, such an argument showing to the farmers and ranchmen the advantage to them of supporting and promoting the market for their produce. Not only has the Town become the present market of the County but it bids fair to become a manufacturing center of no little magnitude. The water power produced by the fall of the ditch of the Shoshone Irrigation Company around Cedar Mountain just above the Town, exceeds the power at Great Falls, Montana, which has made that Town the great manufacturing center of our sister State. An abundance of coal is found at a distance of three miles from the Town, thus forming an economical fuel.

The official survey of the B. & M. R. R. passing up the Shoshone River, gives this Town the advantage of a promised Railroad connection with the outside world, as well as making it, in a very short time, the business and commercial center of Big Horn County.

As a pleasure and health resort, the Town has advantages equal or superior to any in the County. The Hot Springs, situated on the banks of the Shoshone River, at a distance of three miles above the Town, contain medicinal properties of great value, bidding fair to make them as famous as any in the County, thus inducing many outside parties to locate here to obtain their benefits.

The proposed road to the National Park, to be built this coming season, will induce many excursionists to make the journey through the Basin by way of this Town, thus saving to this State the money which is now obtained by Montana.

The Town of Cody is situated in the center of Section 32, Tp. 53 N. R. 101 West of 6th Prin. M., and as laid out, covers 240 acres. The streets are 100 feet wide, and alleys through the business portion, 20 feet.

Business lots are 25x140 feet; residence lots, 50x150 feet. All lots will be sold with water to irrigate the same. The Cody Townsite Company offers all lots situated in Blocks 1, 2, 3, 17, 32, 33, 34, 39, 44, 47, 48, 49, at $5 (five dollars) each. All residence lots in Blocks 4, 5, 6, 13, 14, 15, 35, 36, 45, 46, for $10 (ten dollars) each, and business lots in these same blocks for $25 (twenty-five dollars) each. Payment, half cash, remainder in six months.

(The above prices subject to change at any time.)

This brochure was circulated throughout the Big Horn Basin by Beck to convince people to choose Cody as the seat for the newly organized Big Horn County. Beck and Cody thought the promise of a county building, commercial center, and railroad terminus would be attractive. Basin was chosen as the county seat, but the Cody group was told they could form a new county when the population warranted it. (AHC/UW)

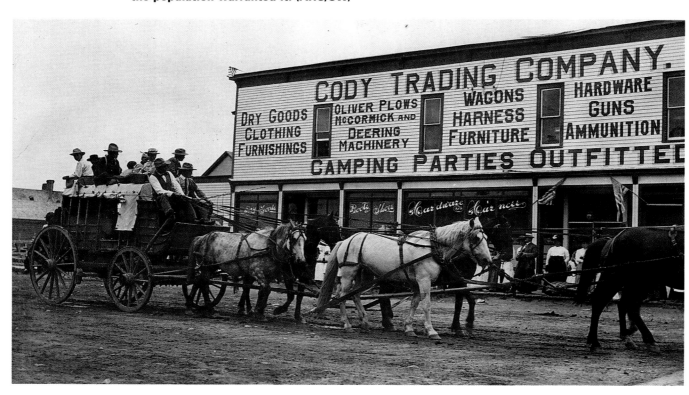

Beck's first home in Cody, showing his wife Daisy, daughters Betty and Jane, and Grandma Hurd. Before their marriage, Daisy had taught school at Marquette and was later secretary for the Shoshone Land and Irrigation Company, run by Beck. The Beck family was very involved in the business and social affairs of the town for many years. (AHC/UW)

Left: The first commissary operated where the Pioneer Building stands today. By 1898 a wood frame building was constructed on the south side of the street for the business. Jakie Schwoob took over management of what he called the Cody Trading Company. By 1920 Schwoob was the sole owner of the business bankrolled by Gerrans, Rumsey, and Bleistein. Schwoob went on to be called the "Merchant Prince of the Big Horn Basin" and was highly thought of by all who knew him. (Vawter Collection/PCHSA)

The Buffalo Bill Barn was built by Colonel Cody and was the first livery barn in Cody. He bought the entire block where the IGA store is located today. By 1899 the *Cody Enterprise* operated out of a drafty, wood-frame building west of the barn. The Schwoob Blacksmith Shop was on the south side of the complex. (Dunrud Collection/PCHSA)

By August of 1899 Buffalo Bill's friend, Colonel Peake and family, had moved from Washington, D.C., to Cody to run the *Cody Enterprise*, Cody's oldest business. The press was brought in from Duluth, Minnesota, where Cody's sister had operated a paper. The *Cody Enterprise* was the mouthpiece for Cody's colonization efforts and helped build a sense of community for the new settlers on the Cody Canal and in the town. The Peakes are standing in the center of the photograph. (Maier Collection/PCHSA)

Left: Agnes Chamberlin and her dog Dewey pose in front of the Hart Mountain Inn after a successful fishing trip. Agnes worked for the *Cody Enterprise* and later operated the Chamberlin Hotel. She played the piano for many of the early gatherings and was a public-spirited individual. (Daly Family)

Aurilla McFall and her husband, "Bad-Land" Dave, built the Hart Mountain Inn around 1898 and operated it for several years. Agnes Chamberlin described her in the following way: "Mrs. McFall used to get herself up with fluffy gray hair, long train, bright colors and all sorts of ornaments until she looked like an animated Christmas tree. She had bright black eyes and used lots of powder and rouge long before the rest of the women thought of using it." (Hiscock/Richard Collection/PCHSA)

At the turn of the century, J. W. Chapman owned the Council Saloon which was a favorite hangout for the local businessmen, farmers, and ranchers. Lawman Carl Hammitt, in the center, can be seen tipping a beer. Chapman later lost his saloon to Jess Frost in a poker game. In 1901 Cody's population was 550 souls with no church and at least ten saloons. (PCHSA)

Frank Houx became Cody's first mayor when the town was incorporated in 1901. Houx had the best interests of the community at heart and proclaimed, "It is of the utmost importance that we start right, and lay a broad and substantial foundation upon which to build, as the needs of our city may demand in the future." Houx went on to serve several terms as mayor and later became governor of the state of Wyoming from 1917 to 1919. (Patrick Collection/PCHSA)

George Beck, standing in the center of the back row, organized the Cody Club in the fall of 1900. An organization for sportsmen, it was joined by General Nelson Miles, Colonel Cody, A. A. Anderson, William Pickett, well-to-do Easterners, and local businessmen and ranchers. The only officers were Cody, first vice-president, and Pickett, second vice-president. The Cody Club was not successful as a hunting club, but would come into its own as a businessman's organization. The current Chamber of Commerce can trace its origins to the Cody Club. (AHC/UW)

This wooden foot bridge, shown in 1900, handled the pedestrian traffic across the Shoshone River. It was probably possible to lead a horse over the bridge, but wagons would have to ford the river. By 1901 a new bridge was built by the railroad to handle the traffic from the Burlington Depot into town, along what is now Twelfth Street. (Frost Collection/PCHSA)

In early November of 1901 the first train from Billings, over the Toluca route, full of dignitaries and guests, pulled into the Cody Depot. A parade formed at the Buffalo Bill Barn, led by the Billings Brass Band, with Colonel Cody and Mayor Houx riding in a carriage. According to the *Cody Enterprise*, "In the afternoon a monster ox was served to the crowds. Plenty of coffee, bread, beer and pickles were also furnished." The crowd numbered more than a thousand. In the evening the group was treated to a fireworks display, followed by Mayor Houx's welcome. Next Colonel Cody told of his plans for future development of this "wonderful Cody country." The Cody Trading Company storeroom was opened for dancing and the Cody Club served a midnight supper before the exhausted guests departed early the next morning. (Garlow Collection/PCHSA)

By July of 1901 construction of the Irma was underway. Architect Alfred Woods designed the hotel. Materials and tradesmen were brought from Nebraska. Fireplaces were built out of unusual local rock. Expensive furnishings were ordered and western art was purchased for decoration. Buffalo Bill's "Hotel in the Rockies" cost $80,000 according to advertisements in area papers. (Garlow Collection/PCHSA)

Colonel Cody sent out invitations, embossed with a golden buffalo, for the opening of the Irma Hotel held November 18, 1902. The hotel was named for his daughter Irma, whose engagement was announced before an elegant dinner was served. On behalf of the citizens of Cody, Beck presented Colonel Cody with a solid silver loving cup in appreciation for his contribution to the town. At least five hundred guests turned out for the party, "cowboys in chaps, men in full dress suits and ladies in evening gowns," according to the Colonel's niece, Josephine Goodman. The hotel was decorated with roses, carnations, fern leaves, smilax, and chrysanthemums, shipped in from Lincoln, Nebraska. The Lincoln Orchestra played for the dance, which continued until nearly daylight. As the night wore on, Mike Russell bought a round for the house and by some reports, old-timer Dad Pearce was trampled in the "stampede to the bar." Standing left to right on the Irma Hotel balcony are Cody Boal, Irma Cody, Lieutenant Clarence Stott, and Arta Clara Boal. Colonel Cody is standing in the center of the group in front of the Irma in this photograph, which was taken around the time of the opening. (BBHC)

A group of lady riders traveling down Sheridan Avenue towards the Irma Hotel. There were no stone or brick buildings in the business district except the Irma and Judge Wall's office. (Garlow Loan/BBHC)

A view of Beck Avenue looking west showing William Webster's log home and post office. The Commercial Saloon is in the center. Down the street is Cody Lumber and to the left is the Hart Mountain Inn. (Garlow Collection/PCHSA)

Pictured is a freight outfit coming into Cody. Cody's Main Street was so wide an outfit like this could turn around. Most of the freight came over the Red Lodge–Meeteetse Trail, or the Billings Freight Trail, until the Burlington Railroad line was completed in 1901. (Garlow Collection/PCHSA)

Beck and Cody at hunting camp in 1902. For all their differences, Cody and Beck remained good friends through the years. They were key people in the development of the town and the surrounding area. Cody's name was used to promote the town, while Beck managed the canal company. They both had their own business interests as well.
(AHC/UW)

Colonel Cody's friends enjoying the waters at DeMaris Hot Springs in the winter of 1902. Cody had invited guests to the Irma Hotel opening, with a hunt to follow the festivities. As was his usual custom, the group made a visit to the springs. (AHC/UW)

Jack Stilwell was a friend of Colonel Cody's and spent his last years in Cody. He was famous for his part in the Beecher Island fight in 1868. He was seventeen when he rode through hundreds of Cheyenne Indians to get help for Colonel Forsyth's trapped men. Stilwell became an attorney and was U.S. commissioner at the time of his death in 1903. He is buried at Trail Town in Cody. Stilwell is wearing a coat valued at $450, given to him by Cody. (PCHSA)

Katie Primm, "Cattle Queen of Nevada," was a proficient horsewoman and reportedly owned six thousand head of cattle. She came to Cody to run the Cody Hotel, where she met and married saloon owner Fred Primm in 1903. She took over ownership from Beck and ran the hotel until 1932. (Hall Collection/PCHSA)

During the off-season of the Wild West Show, Colonel Cody would bring famous friends to Cody to hunt and relax. Cody is pictured in front of the Irma Hotel getting ready to leave on one of these hunts. George Beck is shaking his hand and Chief Iron Tail, whose likeness is on the buffalo nickel, is standing in the group to the right. He was in charge of the Indians in the show and made frequent visits to Cody. Guides for the hunt were Ned Frost, second from the left, and John "Reckless" Davis, mounted on a horse to the right. (Hiscock/BBHC)

Circuit riders, traveling ministers of various denominations, held services in Cody before there were any churches. One day Beck, Cody, two cattlemen, and saloon owner Tom Purcell, became involved in a poker game. As a joke, the group agreed that the winner should donate the pot to the church of his choice. Beck won the $550 pot and chose the Episcopal Church, from which he was later expelled. That church is still used today and is known as the "poker church." Mrs. Beck is shown standing on the front steps of the church where she played the organ. (Gerber Family)

A group of well-known local men in front of the Cody Post Office. Webster was the postmaster then and had just moved his office from his log home on Beck Avenue. By 1904 both the owner of the Exchange Saloon, Ben Primm (far right on horseback), and forest ranger Frank Hammitt (standing in front of door) had died. Primm died of a sudden illness and Hammitt was found at the bottom of a cliff between Sunlight Basin and Crandall. (AHC/UW)

Etta Feeley was one of Cody's earliest madams and owned many properties around town. In 1904 business was thriving, in one month alone, she paid out over $300 in fines to the city. Etta's legal name was Alice Leach. She died in obscurity in Cody in 1960, at the age of ninety. Her husband Thomas had years before absconded with their life savings. (Patrick Collection/PCHSA)

Tryouts for performers and livestock in Colonel Cody's Wild West Show were held on the back lot of the Irma Hotel. A number of locals, who took part in Cody's show, were discovered in this manner. A group always gathered to view the action and Charles Hayden's young sons could watch the excitement from their front yard on Alger. The house on the right was built to provide living quarters for the hotel's domestic help, but later became known as Colonel Cody's home in Cody. (Anderson, Jensen Collection/PCHSA)

The stone school in the foreground was built at Beck's request and was one of the first buildings in Cody. It was originally the Jerry Ryan family residence. Due to a surveying error, the building extended forty feet into Alger Avenue, leaving only sixty feet for the street. Even today the western portion of Alger is narrower because of that error. Streets in the town were laid out by Beck to be one hundred feet wide to cut down on the danger from fire. (Murray Collection/PCHSA)

The interior of the stone school in 1903. The Newton, Goodman, Watkins, Robertson, and Vogel families had students enrolled in school then. Earlier locations for classes were the Cody Hotel and a back room of the Primm saloon. (BBHC)

Four of the five buildings on this section of Sheridan Avenue were saloons, including the Black Diamond, Cody Exchange, and Council. A freight outfit hauling wool was moving down the street. Buyers from all around would come to the Irma Hotel to make their deals. In 1904, more than 2 million pounds of wool were produced in the area. (Lovelace Collection/PCHSA)

Dr. Frank Powell, known as White Beaver, came to help Cody with his building projects. Powell oversaw the construction of Pahaska Tepee and Wapiti Inn on the North Fork. The resorts were completed in time for the opening of the wagon road through the east entrance of Yellowstone National Park in 1904. Dr. Powell also managed the Irma Hotel and stayed in Colonel Cody's private suite. (BBHC)

Dr. and Mrs. Chamberlin, with their Democrat wagon, were the first of 454 visitors through the East Gate in 1904. They are shown traveling up Sylvan Pass. To the right in the photograph are military cannons used to "shoot the pass" and clear avalanches. Until 1916, the U.S. Army managed and patrolled the park. (Daly Family)

Below: In 1904 George Beck, with help from a Philadelphia investor, began a power plant on the Shoshone River. Being a surveyor, Beck knew where the river would produce the most power, so he built his plant just upstream from the depot bridge on the south side of the river. Within six months the plant began to pay its $30,000 debt. Beck's Shoshone Electric Light and Power Company was authorized by the city, which had the option to buy the plant. (BBHC)

In order to begin work on the Shoshone Dam, a road had to be built through the canyon. A mix of foreigners, locals, and men from across the country made up the work crews. The work was dangerous and difficult. Some blasting was accomplished by rappelling down sheer cliff faces to set the charges. Local people became a nuisance when they rode out to the site to watch the work progress. (Hiscock/PCHSA)

On October 31, 1904, three strangers entered the First National Bank in the Walls Building to rob it. Cashier I. O. Middaugh made a run for help, but was shot dead in the street as the outlaws escaped empty handed. A posse was immediately formed but the assailants were not captured. The men believed to be involved in this incident were later sentenced to twenty-five years in prison for their part in a train robbery. Standing, left to right: John Kearns, unknown, John Thompson, William Kissick, Dr. Howe, Charles Hensley, Mrs. Walls, and Mark Chamberlin. (Maier Collection/PCHSA)

Brundage Hardware was one of Cody's early businesses. Like several buildings in town, Brundage Hardware and Richard Roth's business next door, shared a common interior wall. Roth died before construction was completed and it was rumored he was poisoned. This was never proven, because his "innards" were lost in the mail. (VanArsdall Collection/PCHSA)

STORY OF THE YEAR!

Improvements in Cody During 1905 Reach the Magnificent Sum of $200,000.00

After all there's nothing like facts and figures to demonstrate any great truth, and facts are what the Stockgrower always aims to give.

No hasty canvass of a growing town can be made without missing some one, but the writer has aimed to show in the following statement all the buildings which have been erected during the year 1905 in this rapidly growing young city.

That the figures show a grand total of $200,000 will be a surprise to many, but such is the fact. A fact which must certainly be a source of pride and satisfaction to every citizen.

The increased lot values do not enter into the following table of building operations:

J. E. Kearns, stone building	$ 3,600
G. A. Pulley stone building	5,000
J. K. Calkins stone building	2,500
McGuffey Bros. & Co. stone and brick bldg.	5,000
H. J. Luce residence	1,800
W. L. Walls stone building	3,700
I. C. Spencer residence	2,000
Walter Wiley "	2,500
H. A. Weston "	1,800
E. F. Neff "	2,500
C. M. Conger "	650
G. A. Pulley store building	650
G. A. Pulley improvements on old bldg.	400
G. A. Pulley cottage	400
" " wash house	750
M. A. Pulley	1,000
J. B. Neff "	1,500
J. G. Dewel "	1,400
A. S. Wyant "	1,500
L. H. Neff "	1,500
Miss Lockhart two residences	1,200
Walter Braten residence	150
Loren Marlow barn	1,200
C. B. Marlow residence	
Wm Lenninger stone bakery	3,000
M. Alfred Heimer residence	2,000
Mrs. Ella D. Watkins three residences	3,000
Mrs. E. A. Hooker restaurant	1,500
W. W. Yager addition	250
H. W. Darrah two offices, warehouse, sheds, etc	5,000
Mrs. Julia C. Goodman residence	4,000
Geo. T. Beck, Pres. Electric Light Co., plant	4,000
Cody Lumber Co., additions and improvements	3,000
F. J. Hiscock photo gallery	1,000
Miss Elizabeth Schart business building	1,000
Lyman Hatton cottage	400
Dr. F. A. Waples hospital	800
J. S. Dillon addition	350
John Smith residence	700
Ed Island cottage	400
W. H. Brundage addition	700
Roth & Brundage stone building	4,000
L. D. Hager cottage	500
F. A. Hawley residence	1,300
Arthur Evans cottage	800
Mr. Underwood cottage	450
C. J. Williams residence	800
Hugh Patchell dwelling	500
Miss Fletcher cottage	550
Geo. Hank cottage	350
Geo. Russell dwelling	550
Stanley Burns residence	1,000
J. A. Kelly "	1,000
Mr. Jones "	1,000
Mrs. Wurst improvements	150
Mrs. McGhan addition	500
B. Cowgill residence	1,000
Wm. Walters residence	1,000
Mr. Kitchens dwelling	
D. R. Hotsenpiller residence	1,000
Mrs. G. B. Grupp double dwelling	1,500
The City firemen's hall	1,000
Mr. Lowrey three cottages	375
Mrs. O. Archer dwelling	500
J. J. Deper "	
Chas. Pauling "	250
A. F. Kroeurle "	500
Geo. Sheets cottage	650
O. C. Tunnicliff cottage	125
Gus Long cottage	125
D. H. Rhodes dwelling	650
Cody Trading Co. brick office	750
Cody Trading Co. improvements	300
Mr. Stigers two cottages	600
H. H. Schwoob dwelling	800
H. H. Schwoob barn and granary	
J. T. Carpenter house and shop	2,500
Walter Oeland house and shop	1,500
Andrew Martin cottage	500
J. Y. Smith residence	1,500
H. Hansen dwelling	500
O. Carnogan "	600
F. H. Welch residence	2,500
S. C. Parks "	3,000
F. C. Barnett "	2,500
J. H. VanHorn "	2,000
G. T. Beck barn	500
John Johnson residence	2,000
Drs. Bradbury & Lane hospital	2,500
H. A. Munsterman house etc	1,500
C. P. Holt kitchen	300
Jeff Chapman residence	1,500
F. L. Pollock residence	1,400
Roy Pollock addition	200
L. C. Reif residence	2,000
A. Holm "	1,400
Thos. Archibald dwelling	600
John Hook barn	1,000
Mrs. Lowrey improvements	1,200
C. F. Scholes, shop	600
Other smaller buildings	3,225
	$161,000

UNDER CONSTRUCTION.

Odd Fellows' stone building	7,000
H. B. Robertson laundry	2,000
J. M. Schwoob stone building	5,000
G. A. Pulley stone building	5,000
Shoshone National Bank stone building	10,000
J. M. Schwoob residence	10,000
	$39,000
Grand Total	$200,000

Construction of the Pioneer Building began after George Beck's office was moved across the street. This building was erected for the Newton Company's general merchandise store, utilizing stone quarried from what is now Beck Lake. The benchmark for the town is etched on the west side of the building, showing an elevation of 4,990.83 feet above sea level at that point. Shown in the photograph are workers Fred Gail, Carl Hammitt, and Algott Johnson. (Hiscock/Hoge Collection/PCHSA)

Tobias and Prestley Riddle farming at Marquette. Agriculture was the mainstay of Cody's economy and the reason many people moved to the area. Without the Cody Canal irrigation project, the area would still be desert land. (Patrick Collection/PCHSA)

Left: In 1905 the *Cody Enterprise* reported improvements in Cody reaching $200,000. Apparently the residents of Cody had enough faith in the continued progress of their town to put down roots. They made substantial monetary commitments by erecting stone and brick buildings for their businesses and by building comfortable homes with additions. (Shaw Collection/PCHSA)

This photograph, taken in 1905, shows the growth of Cody. By that year the population had grown to about a thousand, doubling the total in 1900. The two-story building on the right is the Nearby Ranch, located on Alger Avenue. (Anderson/JensenCollection/ PCHSA)

This view of the land on top of the Greybull Hill was taken about 1905 and shows an irrigation ditch and a man working. A few structures can be seen in the distance but the development of this area would be slow in coming and it remained pasture until after World War II. (Anderson/Jensen Collection/PCHSA)

A view of the 1200 block of Sheridan Avenue before the fire of 1907. This devastating fire wiped out most of the block and if it had not been for the wide streets, the Cody Trading Company building on the next block would have been lost as well. The early buildings destroyed in this fire were of wood construction, built before people had much faith in the town. Subsequent buildings would be more substantial. (Richard Collection/PCHSA)

Cody's population peaked about 1908 when reclamation projects reached their zenith. In 1910, the population leveled off at 1,132, Park County opened for business in Cody in 1911, and the First Addition was added to the northern boundary of town in 1913. Building continued in the town with the addition of two hospitals, a library, fire hall, Masonic Temple, Presbyterian and Catholic Churches, Shoshone Bank, First National Bank, Courthouse, flour mill, sulfur plant, creamery, and brickyard.

Dave Jones held his opening in 1906, a Thanksgiving night fire burned most of the south side of the 1200 block on Sheridan Avenue in 1907, and Charles Workman won the *Denver Post* Endurance Race in 1908. In 1909 a new gambling law was enacted and four slot machines and two roulette wheels were confiscated, Doc Ash was killed from the blast of a single-barrel shotgun, rigged to go off when he opened his door. In 1910 Colonel and Mrs. Cody were reunited after a long separation, author Owen Wister visited the Aldrich Ranch and the Lakeview Canal was completed. In 1911 Mrs. Volkmer opened her millinery shop and 669 game licenses were issued in Cody for the season. The first Park County Fair was held in 1912, a new jail was built, and convicts came to Cody to work on road projects. In 1913 a poor farm was established, the first automobile "tags" arrived and four thousand trees were planted. In 1915 a celebration was held at the Irma Hotel for Colonel Cody's sixty-ninth birthday, Richard and Prante started a skunk and beaver fur business, and 270 tons of sulphur were shipped from Cody in the month of June.

Promoters worked hard to attract tourists and settlers. Tourism-related businesses were off to a good start, stock raising and farming were still the leading industries, while oil development was in its infancy.

Cody was moving into a new era with the "passing of the old West." The introduction of motorized vehicles to Cody hastened this process and would change the way merchants did business and families enjoyed their leisure time.

1906–1915

by Jeannie Cook

4

An early Independence Day parade on Beck Avenue showing the Methodist Church, Scholes Blacksmith Shop, and John Burns Family Liquor Store. Several of Burns' sons rode in the Wild West Show and later gained fame in silent movies. (Anderson/Jensen Collection/PCHSA)

Above: The Lane-Bradbury Hospital was built on Bleistein Avenue in 1906 after "Lady Doctor" Frances Lane and her associate, Dr. James Bradbury, won the contract to provide medical services for workers employed on the Shoshone Reclamation Project. Local folks supported the hospital, but it was rumored that the sick and injured construction workers received inadequate care. Caroline Lockhart tried to make a case against Dr. Lane and later wrote a book that maligned Lane and the town. Dr. Lane is shown in hunting attire. (Gerber Family)

Cody's first fire hall on Salsbury Avenue still stands. Volunteers Dr. Bradbury, Gus Holm, George Taylor, Andy Larson, Barney Cone, Walter Schwoob, Archie Abbott, Roy McGinnis, Carl Hammitt, Colonel Peake, and Nick Noble, are shown with their equipment. The wagons and carts were drawn by hand when fires were close by. (Dunrud Collection/PCHSA)

More than two hundred students were enrolled in Cody's "graded" schools during the time E. B. Rossiter was principal from 1906 to 1909. Usually five teachers, including Rossiter, handled the class load. The frame school seen here was built in 1904 at the site now occupied by the Wynona Thompson Auditorium. It had four large rooms, a basement, slate blackboards, and a school bell, which was quite a luxury. (Anderson/Jensen Collection /PCHSA)

Shown on the boardwalk in front of the Irma Hotel are Ruth Wiley, unknown, Bessie Hitchcock, Josie Thurston, Katherine Wiley, and Jessie Hitchcock. These young women were well known in the social circles of the day and attended parties together. (Harrison Collection/PCHSA)

Photographer Fay Hiscock came to Cody in 1904. Dubbed "the picture man" by Colonel Cody, Hiscock captured the history of Cody in photographs. Hiscock, who was an avid hunter and guide, is pictured here with his dogs. (VanArsdall Collection/PCHSA)

Ned Frost discovered the caverns on Cedar Mountain in the winter of 1908–1909 while hunting with his dogs. Frost followed as the dogs chased a bobcat into the caverns, then went back to town to tell his friends and organize an exploration party. Besides Frost, Will Richard, Fred Richard, Ray Pulley, Art Owens, Billy Lieb, Fay Hiscock, and George Mull returned to the caves the next day. The mountain was honeycombed with caverns and had been called "Spirit Mountain" by the Indians. During the Taft administration, Frost Cave was listed as a national monument and renamed Shoshone Caverns. (Tait Collection/PCHSA)

Cody, Beck, Gerrans, Bleistein, and Rumsey were busy filing placer mining claims on locations near Cody. They held shares in the Cody Oil and Development Company and the Shoshone Oil Company. Geologist Thomas Harrison, claimed the Oregon Basin dome held "unusual prospects to the seekers of oil." He located that field in 1911 and founded the Enalpac Oil Company, a forerunner to Ohio Oil and Marathon. (Buffalo Bill Memorial Museum/ Denver Colorado)

Joe Isham and Tom Kane were Cody's entire police force from 1906 to 1909. They were the first law officers in Cody to wear official uniforms. Their 1906 salary was $83.50 a month. Among their duties were road repair, fire code inspection, fence building, and collecting fines. (Hiscock/Richard Collection/PCHSA)

Little Joe Newell's birthday party was attended by his many friends. Joe is standing in the center of the group of children, all wearing their party clothes. His parents, Pearl and Kid Newell, operated the Irma Hotel for many years. Pearl was the daughter of Cody's first mayor. (Greenway Collection/PCHSA)

It took five years to complete the Shoshone Dam. The construction work was dangerous due to extreme conditions, which made it difficult to keep laborers on the job. As a joke, a group of local boys stuffed brush into the vents on Cedar Mountain. When the brush was lit on fire, the mountain began to smoke and looked like it might erupt. With the 1906 Vesuvius eruption fresh on their minds, the Italian work force, which was four hundred strong in 1908 became quite concerned and many left. (Nalls Collection/PCHSA)

Left: Around 1908 the CB&Q Railroad had a derailment near Cody. The stockcars had been carrying cattle to market. Many cattle were killed or injured and the railroad cars had extensive damage. Curious townspeople went to investigate the accident. (Larson Collection/PCHSA)

Above: The first library was built in 1906 with money raised by the Cody Women's Club. It was a tiny stone building located on the same lot where the library is today. Leonard Horr, the first librarian, is standing on the right, next to Charlie Workman. (Park County Library)

Palace Meat Market owners Armistead and Edelman advertised the best quality beef, mutton, and pork; fresh and salt meat. Chickens were wanted at all times and cash was paid for hides and pelts. (Hayden Collection/PCHSA)

Incinerators and outhouses were built along the alleys all over town. The ones shown were in the business district of downtown Cody, near the Irma Hotel. (Eskildson Collection/PCHSA)

Charles Hayden was Speaker of the House for the Tenth Wyoming Legislature, held in 1909, which authorized the establishment of Park County. Seated second from left, it was the slam of Hayden's gavel that made it official. The county's value was assessed at $4,000,000 and the town of Cody at $1,003,000. Cody was chosen county seat in the May election and billed as "the city of destiny in the county of opportunity." (Hayden Collection/PCHSA)

Buffalo Bill is shown leading a parade down Sheridan Avenue past the Holm Building. The billboard on the fence advertised Dave Jones Men's Store. "Buy it of Dave Jones," was a slogan recognized throughout the Northwest. Jones was noted for his contribution of time and money to community projects. (Holm Family)

Above: Cody changed from an undisciplined frontier town where, at the turn of the century, every other business was a bar, to a town with schools, churches, and ladies societies. This 1908 panoramic view shows considerable growth and improvements in Cody. By that time many of the Sheridan Avenue wooden structures had burned or been replaced by stone and brick buildings made possible by the money spent on irrigation projects and the growing agricultural base in the community. (Hiscock/Garlow Collection/PCHSA)

Above: W. B. Edwards, clerk for the Big Horn Basin Development Company, is shown coming up the old South Fork hill with Cody in the distance. The car he is driving was brought to Cody for the 1908 opening of the Wiley Irrigation Project. Due to financial and engineering problems, the project failed to open up new farmland, but did bring jobs and thousands of dollars to the Cody area. (Edwards Collection/PCHSA)

This row of residences and carriage houses is on Eleventh Street, looking north. The photograph, taken about 1910, shows the stone mansion of George and Daisy Beck. Unfortunately, the Beck home, which was the social and cultural center of the town, was later torn down. The next two houses belonged to R. C. Hargraves and Sant Watkins, both wealthy wool growers. Their homes are still in good repair. (Gerber Family)

Colonel Cody inspecting his Hereford cattle and horse herds on the TE Ranch. Cody came home to his favorite ranch each winter after the show season closed, to rest and entertain friends. Park County livestock totals for 1911 were 20,104 cattle, 7,382 horses and 130,833 sheep. (Buffalo Bill Memorial Museum/Denver Colorado)

Cody's Cowboy Band in front of the Presbyterian Church at Eleventh and Beck. The band was organized at the turn of the century to copy Colonel Cody's Wild West Show Cowboy Band. Frank Williams played in both bands and convinced the Colonel to buy uniforms for the home town group. This band represented Cody when the Wild West Show played in Billings in 1910. (BBHC)

The Cody Trading Company burned to the ground in February 1913. The fire started in the dry goods department. Even though the fire was discovered early, firemen were unable to save the store. The Newton Company and Cody Hotel, across the street, had damage to their windows due to the intense heat. Jakie Schwoob relocated to the Iowa Store, until he could rebuild. (AHC/UW)

Tex Holm and Buck Buckingham, guides from the Holm Lodge Dude Ranch, on the North Fork, took this party of tourists through Yellowstone Park in 1913. Most trips took eighteen days and covered four hundred miles. Guests could hunt small game, fish, ride horseback, pick wild flowers, and go snowballing. There were three Holm Lodges, one on the North Fork and two in Yellowstone Park, to handle groups of tourists and hunters. (Buckingham Collection/PCHSA)

Colonel Cody posed for a photograph with his family in front of the Irma Hotel in the fall of 1913. Cody is mounted on a white horse, holding his grandson Bill Garlow. To his right are Irma and Mrs. Cody. Fred Garlow is driving the car with George Walliker and Jane Garlow on the seat next to him and Fred Jr. in the back seat. Old friend "Bad-Land" Dave McFall is astride his horse on the right. (Richard Collection/BBHC)

According to an article in a September 1913 *Cody Enterprise*, "Prince of Monaco views parade from Irma Balcony and formally opens festivities at the fair grounds this afternoon. The cowboys and girls rode two abreast into the fair grounds. The Prince rode in J. M. Schwoob's car." Some of the riders were Mr. and Mrs. Fred Garlow, Colonel Cody, Hillis Jordon, May Edick, Mr. and Mrs. Gus Thompson, Mrs. Schwoob, Mr. and Mrs. Glen Downing, Dudley Smith, and the Newton women. (Lattrell Collection/PCHSA)

Charles Gates came to Cody in his Pullman car to join the hunting party of the Prince of Monaco. The Prince had already gone out with Fred Richard and Colonel Cody, so Ned Frost outfitted the Gates group. Gates was a very wealthy man and was said to have doubled his father's fortune before he set out to spend it. Charles was known as "Spend a Million Gates" while his Texas millionaire father was called "Bet a Million Gates." When the hunt was over Gates spent thousands of dollars in Cody. To celebrate, he treated his friends to $1,000 worth of liquor in one wild night on the town. Unfortunately Gates, who was only thirty-eight, took ill and died of heart failure, in spite of the best efforts of his personal physician, who traveled with him. Gates is standing second from the right. (Frost Collection/PCHSA)

The 1914 Park County Fair was held at the fairgrounds, where the LDS Church, Eastside School, and Circle Drive are today. The three-day event drew large crowds to see the agricultural products and bet on the races. Fay Hiscock made a hot air balloon ascent from the fairgrounds and captured this aerial view of Cody. (Hiscock/AHC/UW)

According to a Cody newspaper, Cassie McGann, alias Cassie LeFay, was wanted by Park County on four warrants in 1915. The charges were keeping a disorderly house, inmate of a disorderly house, vagrancy, and selling liquor without a license. For many years she operated a house of ill-repute and sold liquor on the premises. The people who knew Cassie well, saw her in a different light because of her many acts of kindness to the needy. (Jiter Collection/PCHSA)

According to Wyoming Guard records in 1908, nearly half of the men in Company E at Cody were over six feet tall and were considered hardy, self-reliant soldiers. Clarence Williams held the rank of lieutenant of Company E and was in charge of a detail that was ordered to Basin to guard the jail where prisoners of the Spring Creek Raid were held in 1909. This photo shows Company E at a training camp about 1914. (Williams Collection/PCHSA)

The Mikado, the second annual play put on by Cody High School in 1915, was a comic opera featuring seventy-five players. The play was elaborately staged and costumed and held in the Temple Theater of the Masonic Hall. The building had finally been completed in 1913 after several walls had blown down in a heavy windstorm. (Hiscock/Fell Collection/PCHSA)

The first auto entrance day into Yellowstone Park from the East Gate was in 1915. Jakie Schwoob and Gus Holm's [sic] were in the first vehicle and were responsible for getting the roads in order and promoting the Cody route by establishing the Black and Yellow Trail. This trail originated in Chicago and came through the Black Hills of South Dakota on through Wyoming into Yellowstone Park. Stones were painted yellow and left beside the road to mark the route. Cody merchants had high hopes that more tourists would come their way. The *Cody Enterprise* announced that an average of fifteen autos per day were arriving, representing every state in the Union but Rhode Island. (Hiscock/Richard Collection/BBHC)

Cody Sylvan Pass Motor Company's buses leaving from the Irma Hotel for an excursion to Yellowstone. Manager Kid Wilson made the run from Cody to Lake Hotel. He would leave Cody by eight in the morning and drive fifty-three miles to Pahaska for lunch. Wilson had to average ten mph to make Lake Junction by 4:30 that afternoon. Motor vehicles were required to stop and let horse drawn rigs pass, so schedules were seldom met. F. Jay Haynes was president of the bus line and took this photograph in 1916. (Haynes/Montana State Historical Society)

Cody was slowly gaining population with only an increase of 110 people over the previous census. New buildings included the Carnegie Library, Methodist Church, Cody Inn, Cody High School, and Rialto Theater. Other area improvements were the Sage Creek Community Club, fish hatchery, Hayden Arch Bridge, and a new airfield. Life went on in Cody, but the focus changed to community events, such as the Trappers Ball, Buffalo Bill Birthday Ball, Entrance Day to Yellowstone Park, the Cody Stampede, Chautauquas, and the fair.

By 1916, the people of Cody were bracing for World War I. Every church group and organization in town got into the spirit of giving to the war effort. Dances, raffles, and War Bond drives were held to raise money. In 1917 Cody's young men went off to war in France; most joined Company K. Returning servicemen brought back the Spanish flu and by 1918 influenza deaths were reported in the *Cody Enterprise*. Kissing was banned in Cody.

Cody saloons were closed in January of 1919 and servicemen were welcomed home in March. This was a wild era for Cody law enforcement. Illegal alcohol, gambling, prostitution, and game violations were prevalent. Two red lights were placed on top of the Pioneer Building to call out police.

The Park to Park Road, which linked three National Parks, opened in August of 1920 and the Black and Yellow Trail was finally, officially, opened by Yellowstone Park Superintendent Horace Albright in 1925. The North Fork route to Yellowstone became one of the "most scenic drives" in America. Oil and gas development was accelerating and silent films were being made in the Cody area. During this decade the last of the Cody family passed away. Colonel Cody died in 1917, his daughter Irma in the 1918 flu epidemic, and his wife in 1921.

1916–1925

by Jeannie Cook

5

Below: **The Park garage owned by Glen Newton and Dudley Watkins was opened to accommodate tourists and locals alike. It was the first service station in Cody and in front of the buildings is the first wrecker. The garage was located west of the Walls Building on Sheridan Avenue. (Irwin Collection/PCHSA)**

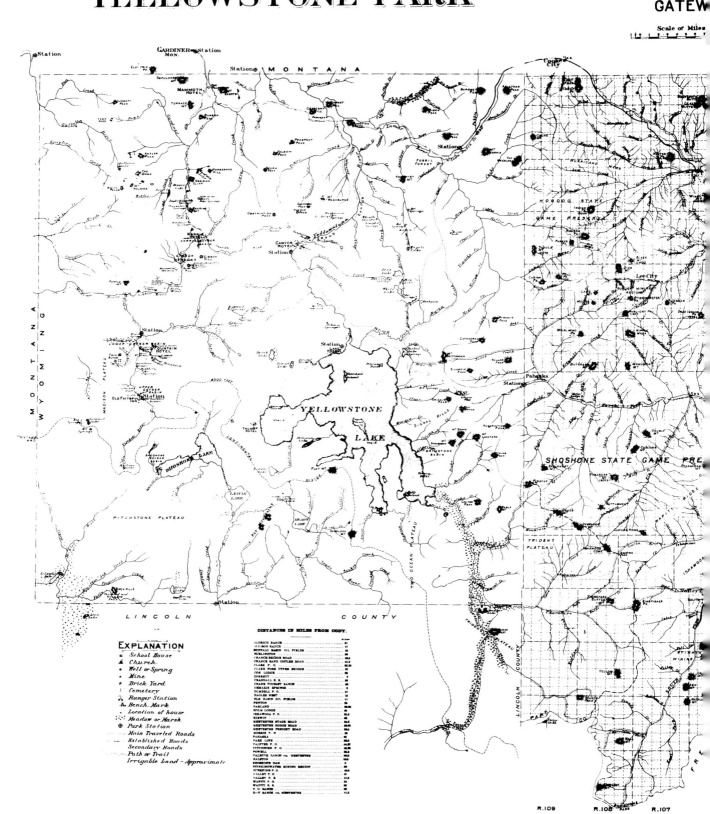

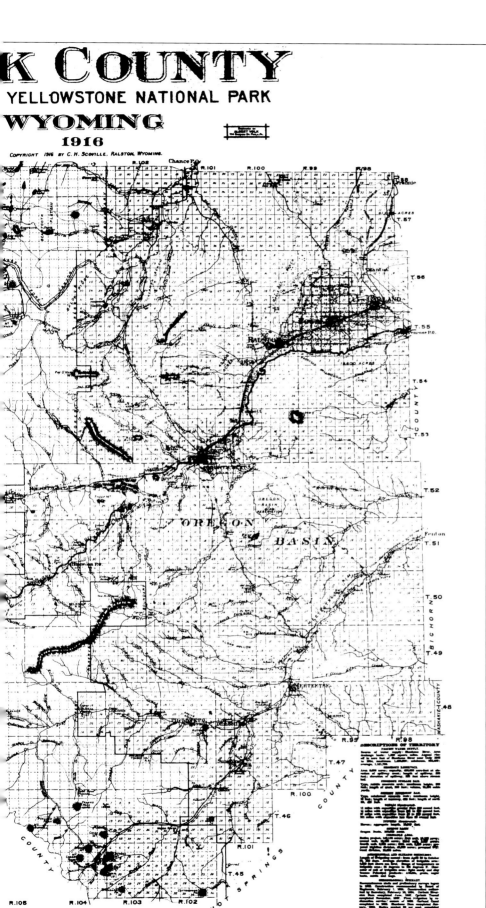

This 1916 map of Park County was drawn by surveyor Charles Scoville. It shows the location of many interesting sites associated with the history of Cody. (PCHSA)

With the advent of motor vehicle travel through Yellowstone Park, camping villages in Cody became a necessity. Camps were located at various sites around the town, voted on by the City Council. In 1924, the Buffalo Bill Campground was permanently located on forty acres on the east end of town. Tourists were advised that camping was part of a "real west" vacation. (Shaw Collection/PCHSA)

Cody's Boy Scout troop No. 1 was founded in 1911 by L. L. Newton and Reverend Haight for the boys in their Sunday school classes. There were fifteen charter members. In 1913 the City Council voted to assist the scouts in building an ice skating rink. In 1916 the boys shown in this photograph put on a fundraising play for the town. (Gerber Family)

A red brick addition was added to the frame school by 1910. This 1916 group of students includes Stanley Howell, Milward Simpson, Olive Fell, Meyer Rankin, Fern Isham, Frank Siggins, Lorraine Martin, Lizzy Martin, Frances Hill, Irene Bates, and Pearl Beam. (Daly Collection/PCHSA)

The Campfire Girls was a popular organization for young girls in the teens and twenties. In 1916, they had a ceremonial meeting at Eagle Creek, on the North Fork, which was attended by George Beck's daughters. (Gerber Family)

Company K of the Wyoming National Guard was mustered on Sheridan Avenue for service in World War I. This photograph shows the unit leaving from the Cody Depot, August 3, 1917. Company K merged with the 148th Field Artillery and became one of the first volunteer regiments ready for overseas duty. The 148th was on the fighting lines in France for 134 days and saw heavy action. They were mustered out of the service in June of 1919. (PCHSA)

Sawmills and lumber companies played a major role in the development of the Cody area. Major Hoopes and owners Mr. and Mrs. H. B. Robertson are shown in the yard of the Cody Lumber Company. Workers were getting ready to make a delivery. (Nordquist Collection/PCHSA)

The home of Cody's first mayor, Frank Houx, was built in 1909. Later Houx went on to become governor of Wyoming. Walter Kepford, who had ranched on the South Fork, bought the property in 1916. It is his family that is shown seated on the porch. The house, which has been converted to a restaurant, is located across the street from the Chamber of Commerce. (Berkshire Family)

Beck's daughters, Betty and Jane, as they appeared in their Red Cross headdress in 1917. Another group, called the Sammy Girls, also helped support the war effort. Cody women knitted socks and sweaters, collected books, rolled bandages, and raised money for the War Hospital Fund. (Gerber Family)

In 1917 the Cody Club lined up on the steps of the Irma Hotel. P. E. Markham was mayor then and is in the group, front row, fourth from the right. Also pictured are Paul Greever, Dave Shelley, Dave Jones, E. V. Robertson, Reverend Blaske, Fred Gail, and city law officers Harry Wiard, Tom Kane, Joe Isham, and Carl Hammitt. (Hoge Collection/PCHSA)

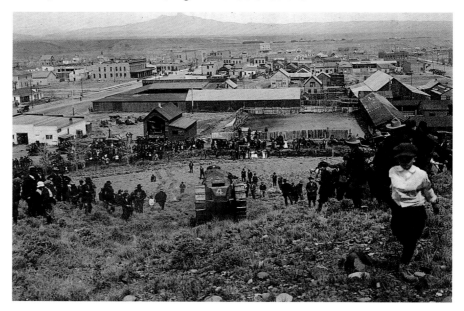

Several Liberty War Bond drives were undertaken in Cody. To gather interest for the drive and the war effort, this tank was brought to Cody and is shown moving up the hill south of town. Bonds sold in Cody reached $106,800 by April of 1918. (Shaw Collection/PCHSA)

Prohibition became law in 1918 and created an enforcement nightmare for Sheriff Bill Loomis. Moonshiners did a brisk business in the area. Governor Nellie Tayloe Ross was forced to remove Loomis from office when it was discovered he was taking bribes. *Cody Enterprise* editor Caroline Lockhart ran a column called "Water Wagon" in which she ridiculed efforts to control illegal alcohol. Caroline is leaning on the bar, entertaining her guests. (AHC/UW)

Geraldine Farrar was in Cody late in the summer of 1918 to star in the silent film *Hellcat*. Appearing with her were Milton Sills and Tom Sanchee. This Western film was produced by Goldwyn Pictures. Several scenes were shot at the Hargraves Ranch, four miles north of town. At least seventy-five locals were given parts as Indians, cowboys, and lawmen. Clarence Williams, second from the right; Jimmy Tuff, second from the left; and Pete Nordquist played cowboys, while George Inman was head scout. (Williams Collection/PCHSA)

The interior of the Cody Trading Company, as it appeared in about 1918. Jakie Schwoob had completed his new brick building in 1915 and held a housewarming party, which was attended by seven hundred people. Schwoob carried a full line of merchandise and had one of the best-stocked mercantile stores in the Big Horn Basin. His motto was, "We Sell Everything." Each department had a station where the customer's transaction was sent in a spring loaded tube to a balcony office, at the back of the store, where a clerk made change and sent the tube back. Schwoob was very advanced in his business practices. (Shaw Collection/PCHSA)

Furs displayed in the window of the Cody Trading Company were worth $10,000 to trappers Max Wilde, Phonograph Jones, and Ed Holmquist. These men spent the winter of 1919–1920 trapping in the mountains near Cody. In 1915, the state of Wyoming set up game districts and hunting seasons to regulate the wild game population, but these regulations did not apply to fur-bearing animals. (Hiscock/Pfrangle Collection/PCHSA)

An "Entrance Day" rodeo, organized by Clarence Williams, was held in 1919. The next year the event became known as the Cody Stampede and was held over the Fourth of July. Caroline Lockhart, local author and editor of the *Cody Enterprise*, was the first president of the Board of Directors. This rodeo view was taken about 1919 and shows the rodeo grounds where Circle Drive is today. (Williams Collection/PCHSA)

In 1922 the Beck power plant was replaced by a vastly improved new plant located in the Shoshone Canyon, below the dam. It was capable of generating fifty-four hundred horsepower. Town founder George Beck continued to hold the franchise. (Shaw Collection/PCHSA)

The Cody Stampede became a yearly event in 1920. People came from all over the Big Horn Basin and parts of Montana to attend the festivities. The Cody Band always played at the rodeo, in the parade, and at Wolfville, where merrymakers could dance and gamble. There were many good local cowboys and the Crow Indians from Chief Plenty Coups' tribe joined in. The balcony of the Irma Hotel was a favorite spot from which to watch the parade. (Richard Collection/BBHC)

Crops grown on lands irrigated by the Cody Canal were the pride of the community in years when water was abundant. Farmers were learning the hard way that they could expect some dry years and some wet years, which made farming a risky business. Livestock ownership and "hiring out" to do contract labor helped fill the financial gap. (Pearson Collection/PCHSA)

A gathering of Cody area people enjoying a summer day. During this decade outings like this were popular as people attended Independence Day celebrations, Chautauquas, agricultural fairs, church picnics, and baseball games. (Shaw Collection/PCHSA)

Joe Vogel, at left, and his cronies enjoying homemade beer in his Shady Rest Beer Gardens during Prohibition. Vogel, a German immigrant, was in the first group of pioneers to settle on the Irma Flat, and the only one to stay. He decided to come to Cody, after having seen the Wild West Show more than thirteen times. (Smallwood Family)

As early as 1918 work was progressing on a new sewer system for Cody. On several occasions that year, Mayor P. E. Markham ordered people to boil their drinking water because typhoid deaths had been linked to poor sanitation. William R. Coe purchased the bonds for a new water plant in 1922, and a reservoir was built south of town. Basic services in the town were improving and a Public Health Department was organized. This 1924 photograph shows work on a sewer main. (Landgren Collection/PCHSA)

On July 4, 1924, the equestrian statue of Buffalo Bill was dedicated as part of the Stampede celebration. A crowd of over one thousand spectators was on hand to witness the event. Colonel Cody had passed on in January of 1917 and was buried on Lookout Mountain near Denver. For years rumors persisted that the citizens of Cody were "coming for Buffalo Bill" who had chosen a gravesite on Cedar Mountain near Cody. (Fell Collection/PCHSA)

Dudley Watkins was known locally as a great exhibition aviator and barnstormer. He had served in the Aviation Corps as a pilot during World War I and was one of Cody's earliest aviators. After the war, Watkins and Prante Transportation was in service. It later became the Red Top Service Station and Cody Air Transport. The aircraft shown here was a World War I surplus Curtis Jenny JN4. (PCHSA)

In the winter of 1925 Bill Loewer made a picture jaunt across the country to promote Cody. He gave out postcards and posters and showed moving pictures to interest would-be tourists in the Cody country. He is shown here, first on the left, with his panel wagon covered with advertisements. (PCHSA)

Within two months of the death of William F. Cody in 1917, the Buffalo Bill Memorial Association was incorporated and the legislature of Wyoming allocated $5,000 for the erection of a suitable monument to his memory. Construction of the Buffalo Bill Museum began in 1926, with groundbreaking ceremonies featuring baseball stars Ty Cobb and Tris Speaker. The main building, modeled after the TE Ranch Building, was finished in June of 1927 and opened to the public July 4. Estimated upon completion to be worth $35,000, the building was built for $18,000.

The dedication was conducted by Milward Simpson and E. V. Robertson and attended by every major Wyoming politician. Other luminaries who spoke included Yellowstone Park Superintendent Horace Albright, Major Gordon Lillie (Pawnee Bill), and Crow Indian Chief Plenty Coups. In August, President Calvin Coolidge (the only President to visit Cody while in office), toured the museum and the west door became known as the "Coolidge Door." During the 1930s several buildings were added to the complex which, until 1967, served as the home of the Buffalo Bill Museum and its related collections. (Hiscock/Wilson Collection/PCHSA)

1926–1935

by Jeannie Cook

Some of the first subdivisions were added to Cody in the late 1920s and included Second Addition, Canyon View, Trueblood, and First Addition East. The population of the town reached eighteen hundred by 1930, an increase of more than five hundred people in ten years.

In 1926 Cody's dance and pool halls were ordered to close by midnight on Saturdays and the county fair was moved to Powell. In 1927, the Federal Building, which housed the post office, was completed and the Buffalo Bill Museum opened its doors to greet President Coolidge. By 1927 most of the town had access to natural gas. A new townsite was developed in Oregon Basin in 1928, to keep workers near their jobs in the oil field, and a warning was issued by the city government that liquor sales, gambling, and prostitution must stop. In 1929 the streets of Cody were renumbered and four blocks of Sheridan Avenue were paved. By 1930, Cody homes had a total of 660 telephones. The movie *Dude Wrangler* was shown in Cody and attended by author Caroline Lockhart.

In the early 1930s Cody began to feel the effects of the Depression. Relief organizations collected clothing for needy children and urged people to grow gardens. Wild game was given for county relief and people were urged to share jobs. Sheridan Avenue properties sold at "rock bottom" prices, but Cody never experienced a bank failure. In 1933 School District 6 cut its budget by 15 percent, beer was finally available again and, even though a whole carload arrived, the town felt it had little to celebrate.

In 1934 the Taggart Construction Company was awarded the contract to build a new road through the Shoshone Canyon. Yellowstone travel was double the previous year, and Park County was designated as a primary drought area. WPA (Works Progress Administration), CWA (Civil Works Administration), and CCC (Civilian Conservation Corps) projects brought money to the area by creating jobs, which helped Cody's economy. In 1935, the city of Cody purchased the power plant from George Beck, saloons were welcomed back to Cody, and in December, 125 Cody children got airplane rides for Christmas.

Below: Baseball greats Ty Cobb and Tris Speaker, after a successful hunt in the mountains west of Cody in 1926. Left to right are guide Carl Downing, Cobb, outfitter Max Wilde, and Speaker. Both Cobb and Speaker bagged a bull elk, a mountain sheep, and a buck deer. In addition, Speaker killed a brown bear, while Cobb added a grizzly bear and moose to his list of trophies during the twenty-six-day hunt. (Richard Collection/BBHC)

6

Irma and Larry Larom at Valley Ranch. Larom and Winthrop Brooks purchased the ranch, forty-three miles from Cody on the South Fork of the Shoshone River, in June of 1915. Larom developed the first ranch winter school in the northwest, with a college prep course for young men. The school had six instructors and an average annual enrollment of about thirty-five boys. In 1925 Larom helped organize the Dude Ranchers Association of America and was elected its first president. One year later, Larom bought out Brooks' interests in the ranch, which had become one of the premier "dude ranches" in the west. (PCHSA)

The 1927 performance of a *Womanless Wedding* presented at the Temple Theater in Cody was a big hit, according to the May 4, 1927 edition of the *Cody Enterprise*. The comedy was presented on two nights and the all-male cast included: Paul Sweitzer, Frank Blackburn, Roy Holm, Sam VanArsdall, Frank Siggins, Ernest Goppert, Ernie Shaw, Walter and Loren Schwoob, Major Hoopes, Fay Hiscock, and many more leaders of the Cody community. (Hiscock/Shaw Collection/PCHSA)

Above: Holders of early Oregon Basin oil leases, photographed on the lawn of the Park County Courthouse in 1927, with the Catholic Church in the background, left to right: Bertha Rousseau, Dick Rousseau, Ora Sonners, Judge Walter Owens, Carl Cox, Otto Koenig, Howard Bell, and Charles Stump. The Oregon Basin oil field had been withdrawn from entry by the federal government and was reopened in 1920. At midnight on February 25, 1920, these Cody residents were camped out in Oregon Basin preparing to file claims. A 1936 account of the experience in the *Park County Enterprise* recalls: "It was plenty cold with a lot of snow; Otto Koenig froze his toes, Dick Rousseau frosted his cheeks and Walter Owens stood around and joked." (Richard Collection/BBHC)

The 1927–1928 Cody School faculty and staff, left to right: Barney Goff, Superintendent Ray Robertson, Paul Sweitzer, Maevis Hughes, Gaylord Chamberlin, Lois Kurtz, Craig Thomas, Clarice Clemons, Geneva McFarland, Gracia Perry, Marguerite Kent, A. A. Hampshire, Margaret Pyron, Constance Willis, Margaret Avant, Grace Fite, Bess Sweitzer, Marge Thomas, Dorothy Krueger, and Helen Abramson. (McClellan Collection/PCHSA)

In 1928 the Texas Refining Company constructed its Cody plant which only operated for a few years. The Depression came in 1929 and the Oregon Basin field shut down because there was no market for heavy crude oil. The plant reopened about 1936. The Celotex plant is located on the old Texas refinery site today. (Hiscock/Shaw Collection/PCHSA)

The Oregon Basin field was booming with activity in the mid-1920s. A number of different companies were drilling for oil and gas. In 1924 Paul Stock brought the first rotary drilling rig in, to drill on Ora Sonners' claim. By 1927 the Illinois Pipeline Company finished their pipeline to Cody. Earlier, oil had been trucked to Cody and loaded into tank cars. This string of tank cars is hauling the first oil refined at the Texas Refining Company on February 24, 1928. (Hiscock/Frisby Collection/PCHSA)

Conditions such as this prompted the city fathers in early 1929, to begin planning a street-paving project. Although there was some initial opposition, the project was gaining favor by March of 1930. The first bid was let in August 1930 for $91,000, to pave four blocks of Sheridan Avenue. Paving started in early September and was completed November 5. Pat Greever Manning, daughter of then mayor Paul Greever, remembers leading the parade held to celebrate completion of Cody's first paved street. (Rankin Collection/PCHSA)

A view of Sheridan Avenue, looking west, taken about 1930, after the street was paved. Identifiable businesses are the Cody Trading Company, Dave Jones Clothiers, the Grocerteria, Cody Drug, and Kurtz Plumbing and Hardware. Note the location of the "C" at that time, which several of Cody's senior citizens can remember building and whitewashing. (Daly Collection/PCHSA)

Right: Cody Peak was dedicated July 4, 1932, honoring the memory of Colonel William Cody. The peak was dedicated by Cody's grandson, Bill Garlow, before a crowd of over 250 people. The marker, the work of Lawrence Tenney Stevens of New York City, was unveiled by Cody's granddaughter, Jane Garlow. The marker which was later destroyed by vandals, was covered with a robe from a buffalo that Cody had killed. It was located on the North Fork, near Pahaska Tepee. (Kershaw/Leibel Collection/PCHSA)

The 1930 Big Horn Basin track champions from Cody High School. The members of the team, identified in 1995 by team member Louis Moore were, standing, left to right: Coach Paul Sweitzer, for whom Sweitzer Gym was named, Vernon Skinner, John "Jock" Wiley, Paul Hindman, Ray Kepford, Hale Brundage, Frank Walters, Moore, James King, and George Downing. Seated, left to right: Roger Cook, Blen Holman, Don Newton, and Carl Learned. (Huss Collection/PCHSA)

Cedar Chapter 14, Order of Eastern Star in 1931. Front row, left to right: Jennie Gawthrop, Edith Williams, Irene Prante, Jessie Kepford, Jennie Vogel, Margaret Holm, Worthy Matron Mable Lieb, Edna Scholes, and Margaret Owens. Middle row, left to right: Minnie Lenninger, Ella Watkins, Harriet Robertson, and Minnie Williams. Back row, left to right: Effie Shaw, Jennie Wilson, Anna Spencer, and Agnes Chamberlin. (Williams Collection/PCHSA)

George Beck planting a Chinese elm tree in City Park on George Washington's bicentennial birthday in 1932. To the left is Paul Greever and to the right are Jane Garlow, Daisy Beck, Betty Beck, and T. Beck. George Beck was a descendant of the Washington family. The building in the background is the Green Gables, which was moved from Wiley Town in 1923. (Shaw Collection/PCHSA)

July 4, 1931. Left to right: Johnny Kirkpatrick, known as the "dean of Cody cowboys" who was still roping competitively at the age of seventy-three, Barbara Nichols, Lucille Nichols, and their father Kid Nichols. Nichols served as the arena director for the Cody Stampede Rodeo. In 1926 he donated all the logs for construction of the Buffalo Bill Museum. (Patrick Collection /PCHSA)

In 1931 Thomas Molesworth moved to Cody and operated a furniture store in the Pioneer Building. Later he established a Western furniture business, designing and building a full line of furniture which could be seen in hotels, lodges, private homes, and ranches all over Wyoming. His rustic furniture was also purchased by famous and wealthy people worldwide. Molesworth worked with Edward Grigware and other well-known artists on various projects around the country. Pictured is a typical arrangement of Molesworth furniture. His shop and factory, at the west end of Sheridan Avenue, was later occupied by Cedar Mountain Lodge. (Kershaw/Leibel Collection/PCHSA)

Right: George Beck's "Green Front Club" was the first business building in Cody. Constructed in 1896, it was moved from its original location to a spot just north of the Shoshone Bank, on Thirteenth Street. Here, Beck entertained his male business associates and friends, playing cards, etc. The Cody Club also met there. Beck's "Club" was the inspiration for today's "Directors Club." (Sturm/Lovelace Collection/PCHSA)

The 1935 Buffalo Bill Birthday celebration. Seated on the ground in a semicircle, Harry Thurston at left, Larry Larom as Custer, three Indian chiefs, and Finley Goodman as Buffalo Bill. Clarence Williams, dressed as Wild Bill Hickock, is standing in the back. (Williams Collection/PCHSA)

An aerial photograph of Cody, taken about 1940, looking southeast. The road leading across the river, coming into town on Twelfth Street is in the bottom left corner. The road leading up the Thirteenth Street hill is in the middle of the picture. Beck and Alkali Lakes can be seen at the top of the picture. Note the lack of development yet on top of the hill and in the area below where the hospital is now located. (Kershaw/Leibel Collection/PCHSA)

1936–1945

by Jeannie Cook

7

During Cody's fifth decade the Depression ended and World War II came and went, restoring prosperity to the country. By 1940, Cody's population reached 2,536. The Grandview, Terrace, and Cowgill Subdivisions were added in an attempt to keep up with the expanding needs of the community. A housing shortage developed and became acute during the war, when trailer houses were brought in to ease the shortage.

Eastside School was built in 1937 to handle the growing student population of the town and the Cody Theater opened its doors. In 1938 Husky Oil started its operations in Cody. In 1939 the library added Adolph Hitler's *Mein Kampf* to its shelves, a new town hall was dedicated, Congress approved funding for the Heart Mountain Division of the Shoshone Project and Carley Downing, who had performed in Buffalo Bill's Wild West Show, started the Cody Night Rodeo. Earl Durand, the so-called Tarzan of the Tetons went on a killing spree in Park County which started with his arrest for a game violation, and was finally ended when he was killed in an attempted bank robbery in Powell, in March of 1939.

In October of 1940, the first draft registrations began, Cody men started signing up for military service and the first blackout of Cody was attempted. The whole town was dark except for the "owl eyes" on the Vogel Building because no one knew how to shut them off. Also that year, Shoshone Bank deposits reached a ten-year high, Agnes Chamberlin donated land for an airport expansion, and Wolfville burned to the ground. A new hospital was completed, serving one thousand patients before it was a year old, and Cody girls were trained as nurses aides to help with staff shortages.

In 1941 a dance and dedication were held for the opening of the Cody Auditorium. The bombing of Pearl Harbor, December 7, 1941, had immediate repercussions in Cody. More men turned out to join all branches of the military and civilian work forces. There were shortages of all kinds and rationing was the order of the day for Cody people. Scrap metal drives were held and waste paper was the number one salvage item. Cody participated in seven War Bond drives. The Red Cross was active in war relief work, and the community sent a wide variety of items to men in uniform. In 1942 the *Cody Enterprise* began a column titled "War Rumblings" and the war relocation camp was built to detain Japanese-Americans. Men and women from all over the area worked building and staffing the camp. The Heart Mountain Camp became Wyoming's third largest city with a population of over ten thousand people.

In 1944 the public was advised to put off vacation trips to conserve gasoline and the Victory ship S.S. *Cody*, named in honor of Buffalo Bill, was launched in Long Beach, California, in December. Also that year, Westside School (the old Red School) started a hot lunch program and the Town Council enacted a 9:30 p.m. curfew for children under sixteen. In 1945 the *Cody Enterprise* announced a shortage of Coca-Cola in Cody. Both V-E Day, which came May 8, 1945, and V-J Day, September 2, 1945, were marked in Cody as a "Day of Reverence and Prayer." Armistice Day featured a parade of men in uniform, just returned from the war, and rationing was finally ended November 28. All of the churches in Cody sponsored memorial services honoring Cody's war dead, December 26, 1945, at the Cody Auditorium. Military men, and civilian workers who had died on Wake Island, and those still missing, were remembered.

This photograph, staged by Log Cabin Bar owner Bill DeMaris in 1936, was made into a postcard, which is available still. Seated around the table, left to right: George Inman, Snake River Bill, Morris Sanderson, John Kirkpatrick, and Two Dog Johnson. Standing, left to right: Soo Foo, Cigarette Charley, George Gentner, Bill Jones, Harry Vreeland, DeMaris, and bartender Red Felsheim. DeMaris purchased the Log Cabin Bar and a saddle shop next to it in 1933, paying $1,000 for each building. (Hiscock/PCHSA)

Christmas about 1936, with the S. P. VanArsdall family. Identified are Althea and S. P., first and second from the right; Bob, JoAnn, and Sam, fifth, sixth, and seventh from the right; VanArsdall's mother Lannie, third from the left; and Althea's mother, Mrs. Armes, to the left of "Santa." S. P. and Althea first came to Cody in 1916 to demonstrate Majestic ranges at the Cody Trading Company. They returned in 1917 to manage the Hardware Department of the Cody Trading Company and later ran Brundage Hardware. (VanArsdall Collection/PCHSA)

In August of 1936, pilot Bill Monday and rancher-photographer Charles Belden flew out of the Cody Airport with twenty-three baby antelope, destined for zoos as far away as Germany. The two-month-old antelope had been raised on the Belden Ranch. The antelope were bound for Chicago; Washington, D.C.; Philadelphia; and Newark, New Jersey, with two boarding the zeppelin *Hindenberg* in New Jersey for their trip on to Germany. Belden is standing next to Monday's Ryan monoplane. (Richard/Richard Collection/BBHC)

Henry Sayles was moving E. V. Robertson's sheep across the Twelfth Street depot bridge from their winter home at the Hoodoo Ranch, south of Cody, to summer pasture in the Beartooth Mountains. Robertson came to Cody in 1912 and became manager of the Hoodoo for his cousin W. R. Coe, eventually buying out Coe's interests in the ranch. From 1942 to 1948, Robertson served as Wyoming's U.S. senator. (Kershaw/Leibel Collection/PCHSA)

The Civilian Conservation Corps Camp on the North Fork of the Shoshone River, where the Clearwater Campground is today, was in operation from 1934 to 1942. The CCC was established in 1933 by President Franklin Roosevelt to help alleviate unemployment of unmarried men between the ages of seventeen and twenty-three. CCC volunteers worked on forest and park conservation projects throughout the United States and were also used fighting forest fires. The Blackwater fire, which started August 20, 1937, claimed fifteen lives, including those of ten CCC volunteers. Another thirty-nine men were injured during the blaze, which burned about seventeen thousand acres. A stone memorial, located where Blackwater Creek meets the highway between Cody and Yellowstone Park, lists the names of those men. It was dedicated August 20, 1939, two years to the day after the tragedy. (Richard/Richard Collection/BBHC)

Right: Ada and Paul Greever enjoying a visit to their cabin on the North Fork in 1938. The Greevers had just returned from four years in Washington, where Paul served in Congress and was instrumental in getting legislation passed to fund the Heart Mountain Division of the Shoshone Project. This irrigation division had been pending for nearly thirty years and had been included in some of the early surveys at the turn of the century. Greever resumed his law practice in Cody and was active in community affairs. (Kershaw/Leibel Collection/PCHSA)

A Bar Association dinner, for the Fifth Judicial District, held at the Irma Hotel about 1937. Cody people identified are: Frank Blackburn and Sally and Oliver Steadman, seated in the first seats on the right side of the first table. Estelle and Ernie Goppert standing, second and third from the right. Hazel Kerper and Mid and Meyer Rankin, are seated at the second table, third, fifth and sixth from the left. Bill Doezal and Bill Fell are standing, fourth and sixth from the left. (Lucier/Dicks Collection/PCHSA)

The "Cody Play Readers Club" dressed in Chinese costumes, held a benefit at the Beck residence in September 1938. From left to right: Jane Beck Johnson, Eugenia Jones, Ada Greever, Trude Burke, Stella Kershaw, Beth Bellamy, Mary Hogg, and Blanche Trimmer. Mrs. Johnson, wife of the U.S. ambassador to China, hosted the event to raise money for refugee children displaced by the Japanese invasion of China. When Ambassador Nelson Johnson returned to the states, he brought with him a letter from Madame Chiang Kai-shek, thanking the group for the $151 they raised. (Kershaw/Greever Collection/PCHSA)

Park County officials, on the front steps of the Park County Courthouse, in 1939. Back row: Wesley Kerper, Percy Metz, George Chase, and Sam Aldrich. Middle row: Morris Star, Chris Fesenbeck, Colonel Wright, William Wilkins, and Robert Phillips. Front row: Tom Osborne, Mrs. Fesenbeck, Mildred Anderson, Eva Larson, Molly Routt, Hazel Kerper, Orilla Hollister, Mrs. Phillips, Joe Freeborg, Frank Blackburn, and Dave Freeborg. (Kinkade Collection/PCHSA)

Cody old-timers Billy Howell and A. C. Newton, leading the Cody Stampede Parade down Sheridan Avenue past the Irma Hotel, in the early forties. This was one of the last parades held prior to World War II. During the war, the Stampede was put on hold. (PCHSA)

Taken during the summer of 1942 in front of the Eastside School, this shows the office crew responsible for the start of construction at the Heart Mountain Relocation Center located between Cody and Powell. Construction took less than three months and employed many area men and women. The camp was occupied from the fall of 1942 through November of 1945 and housed more than ten thousand Japanese-Americans, making it the third-largest city in Wyoming at that time. Ester Johansson Murray is seated in the front row, third from the right. (Murray Collection/PCHSA)

Local artist Olive Fell, photographed about 1939. Her log home and art studio were located at her Four Bear Ranch on the North Fork. Born in Montana in 1902, Fell graduated from Cody High School in the same class as former Governor and United States Senator Milward Simpson. Her best-known works were sketches of bear cubs, which were available locally and throughout Yellowstone and other national parks. (Fell Collection/ PCHSA)

Taken in 1940, this photograph shows the Park County Courthouse, completed in 1912, before any additions. Half the building behind the Courthouse served as quarters for the sheriff and his family, with the other half serving as the jail. The Civil War cannon on the lawn was sold as scrap metal during the early years of World War II. (Sturm/Lovelace Collection/PCHSA)

Milward, Alan, Pete, and Lorna Simpson "getting around" during gas rationing in 1942. Besides their own business interests during the war, the Simpsons managed businesses for men called into the service, and Lorna worked as a Red Cross volunteer. (Richard/Simpson Family)

The 1942 Cody High School band, sporting brand-new uniforms, in the Armistice Day parade. The Cody football team played Powell, and a dance was held later in the evening. The view of the north side of Sheridan Avenue, between Eleventh and Twelfth Streets, shows Mary Frost's Curio Shop, along with Ned Frost's Packard dealership and garage. The building on the west side of Eleventh Street is the Carnegie Library, which opened May 5, 1916, and served the area for many years. The Park County Library occupies that site today. (Sturm/Lovelace Collection/PCHSA)

Three teenage girls enjoying sodas in front of the Taylor-Made Ice Cream Shop, operated by Elsie Jensen and Martha Kinkade in 1943. Identified are Barbara Lasher, Shirley Sowards, and Rae Hall. In 1944, Edwin and Goldie Henderson bought the shop, which they managed for nearly twenty years. (Sturm/Lovelace Collection/PCHSA)

A photograph from Fred Garlow's album, taken when he was employed on the construction of the Alcan Highway. The highway, which was considered important to the war effort, spanned sixteen hundred miles and was designed and built by the U.S. Army Corps of Engineers. Among the other Cody civilian workers involved in the project were Jim Wilson, Earl Hayner, S. P. VanArsdall, Bill Pfrangle, Monte Jones, Virgil Ballow, Bill Bosler, Slim Waggoner, Kirk Hill, Alby Russell, and Ernie Shaw. The sign refers to the Diamond Bar in Cody, operated by "Frenchy" Sanders. (Garlow Collection/PCHSA)

Three Cody women, Ruth and Marjorie Taggart and Margaret Coe, kept Cody servicemen up on happenings back home during much of World War II. Their mimeographed paper, *San Francisco Clearing House for Cody Cowhands*, reached a monthly circulation of over 350. More than 10 percent of the Cody-Meeteetse population was in the service during the war, and all of them kept up on the happenings at home and with each other, through the paper. The three ladies also entertained Cody servicemen traveling through San Francisco, where they worked during the war years. (Elizabeth Frost)

Dick Frost, Nancy and John Allen, Ruth Taggart, Louis and Mary Cobb, and Elizabeth Frost at a party at Charlie Low's Forbidden City nightclub in San Francisco near the end of World War II. Allen and Cobb had just returned from overseas duty, while Frost was stationed in San Francisco. (Elizabeth Frost)

Milward Simpson was governor of Wyoming from 1955 to 1959. (Simpson Family)

1946-1955

by Lynn J. Houze

8

The end of World War II brought about the same positive changes to Cody as it did to the rest of the country, only a little more slowly. The year 1946 saw a year-long celebration of Buffalo Bill's one hundredth birthday and the moving of the Stampede grounds into a beautiful new arena.

On "top of the hill," new housing developments started with the Dacken Subdivision, located east of the Greybull Highway and south of Stampede Avenue, in 1949 as the returning soldiers needed homes for their families. Sunset School was built in 1954 where another housing area had developed.

Buffalo Bill's name began to appear on more and more landmarks and businesses as the town was anxious to honor him. By an act of Congress, both the Shoshone Reservoir and the Dam were named after him in 1946. The Buffalo Bill Boy Scout Camp began construction in 1948 and was completed two years later.

Challenger Airlines started both passenger and airmail service to Cody in 1947. By 1953, the airport had a new runway and lights so that planes could use the airport at night. One of the most memorable events during this time was the crash of oilman Paul Stock's business plane which occurred during a storm in January 1951. It was enroute from Denver to Cody when it crashed near Casper killing the four passengers, including Stock's well-liked secretary, Mabel Overly, and the pilot, Ralph Meyer. Sixteen Cody pilots were involved in the search which really didn't end until May 18 when the plane was found.

Our first radio station, KODI, began broadcasting and a new paper, the *Cody Times*, was started by two returning veterans, hometown boys and cousins, Jesse Frost and Jack Richard. The Buffalo Bill Museum was returned to private hands in 1948 after the town had administered it during the War. Westside School was built in 1948 followed by a new high school in 1952 and favorite son, Milward Simpson, was elected governor in 1954 but we lost a lot of our early pioneers who had done so much to build the town of Cody.

By 1955, the population had increased to approximately forty-two hundred and not only were oil and gas production up but the sheep and cattle industries were doing well. New ranching was being tried (turkeys) and more tourists were beginning to drive their cars to Yellowstone Park for their vacations creating a demand for more gas stations, new campgrounds, and the drive-up hotel or motel. The railroad was the obvious loser in this scenario and the Cody Burlington Inn, near the depot, was closed.

Cody's first radio station went on the air on February 28, 1947. Owned by Bill Garlow, Breck Moran, and Harry Moore, the station has since changed hands half a dozen times. Moran is interviewing Nelson Johnson, U.S. ambassador to Australia at the time and husband of George T. Beck's daughter, Jane. The Johnsons had previously lived in China where Nelson served as ambassador to that government until 1937 when the political climate (war) forced their return home. (Gerber Family)

In late July 1946, two of America's outstanding naval officers and their staff stopped in Cody to visit E. V. Robertson and to fish in Yellowstone. This dinner was held at the Burlington Inn with Fleet Admiral Nimitz seated to the right of an unidentified Army officer at the head of the table. Robertson is to the right of Nimitz and directly across from Nimitz is Wyoming Governor Lester Hunt with Rear Admiral Byrd on his left. Artist Ed Grigware, who served under Nimitz during World War II, and Milward Simpson presented the Admiral with his portrait painted by Grigware. (Richard/Richard Collection/BBHC)

The Cody Inn, located north of the Shoshone River near the Burlington Railroad Depot, had ninety-plus rooms with a dining room that could seat between four hundred and five hundred people. It became a favorite dining spot for Cody residents and tourists especially during the 1920s and 1930s when it was the scene of many dinner dances. Upwards of fifty buses were seen parked there daily waiting for the arrival of tourists on the "The Buffalo Bill Special." (Kershaw/Leibel Collection/PCHSA)

Katie and Claud Brown, owners of the Buffalo Bill Fur Salon, started a turkey farm north of Riverside Cemetery in 1949 and ran it for at least ten years. This amphibious jeep, known affectionately as the "amphib" but formally as the "Sea Horse," was Claud's pride and joy and evidently the turkeys thought so, too. (Sanzenbacher Collection/PCHSA)

The Buffalo Bill Scout Camp is located forty-four miles west of Cody on the North Fork. Financed by a trust composed of oil operators headed by Glenn Nielson and Paul Stock and constructed by Carl Forgey, the camp has been used by many different groups throughout the years. (Richard/Richard Collection/BBHC)

Mrs. Anna "Granny" Peake is shown here on her ninety-fifth birthday on September 19, 1951. She and her husband, Col. John H. Peake, came to Cody in August 1899, at the request of Buffalo Bill to start the *Cody Enterprise*. Mrs. Peake, whose home was where the Park County Courthouse parking lot is now, lived for two more years. Well-known and beloved in Cody, she outlived both her husband (1905) and her daughter. (VanArsdall Collection/PCHSA)

Right: Edward Grigware came to Cody in 1937 to start the "Frontier School of Western Art" with Stanley Kershaw, an internationally known photographer, under the auspices of the Buffalo Bill Museum Association. This began Cody's position as a leading center of Western American art. In 1950, Grigware was asked to paint a mural for the LDS Church on Wyoming Avenue. The *Cody Enterprise* said that this work, entitled *Lest We Forget*, is "so heroic in size, so masterfully painted, so inspirational in treatment that if Ed Grigware had never painted anything else in his lifetime, he would have justified his existence and earned his reputation with this one work alone." (Kershaw/Leibel Collection/PCHSA)

The Paul Stock residence was built in 1947, three years before this photo was taken. It sits above the Shoshone River with a gorgeous view of Cedar and Rattlesnake Mountains. Today the house and grounds belong to the BBHC and are used for receptions, for Larom Summer Institute instructors and for museum guests. (Stock Collection/BBHC)

The early settlers of the Cody area organized the Pioneers of the Cody Country in 1948. They were an off-shoot of a larger, older group known as the Big Horn County Pioneer Association, founded on July 4, 1904, in Cody. At their annual picnic held at the Elk Fork Campgrounds on the North Fork in August 1951, are left to right, front row: Monte Jones, Mrs. Andy Martin, Nellie White, Roxie Britton, Simon Snyder, A. C. Newton, Walt Owens, Lawrence Waggoner. Middle row: M. L. Austin, Greybull, Brownie Newton, Ned Frost, Lizzie Martin Stambaugh, and Lorraine Martin French. Back row: Andy Martin, Bob Rumsey, John Dahlem, Clarence Williams, Frank Williams, and Ed Null. (CE/PCHSA)

Husky Oil Company was founded January 1, 1938, by Glenn Nielson with nineteen loyal employees and was soon producing nine hundred barrels of oil per day. This is the main office and refinery which were located near the railroad depot north of Cody until late 1979. (Richard/Richard Collection/BBHC)

In 1952, construction began on the main part of Cody High School with an addition added in 1957. The "Little Red School House," seen in the background, was torn down in July 1958, much to the dismay of the town. (Richard/Richard Collection/BBHC)

Right: Evidence of Cody's improving economy is seen in this photo. Keystone Court (now Ponderosa Campground) was ready to house the ever increasing number of tourists who came through town on their way to Yellowstone; houses were being built in the Brown Subdivision; Paul Stock's house sits out on the point above the Shoshone River; and St. Anthony's Catholic Church can be seen in the background. (Richard/ Richard Collection/BBHC)

When electricity came to the North Fork in the early 1950s, the easiest and quickest way to get the poles up and the lines strung was to use helicopters!(Richard/Richard Collection/BBHC)

This photo of Harry and Josephine Thurston was taken just weeks prior to Harry's death in May 1952. Harry came to Cody in 1901 and his first job was as the teacher at Marquette School. The following year he became a Forest Service ranger and, subsequently, superintendent of the Shoshone National Forest from 1907 to 1912. Harry owned and operated a Ford dealership from 1912 tp 1926. Josie, who died in 1961, was the daughter of Julia Cody Goodman, Buffalo Bill's older sister and ran Elephant Head Lodge, on the North Fork, for many years. A well-liked, well-respected couple, they are now buried under the lone ponderosa pine at the Wapiti Ranger Station which Harry helped build in the winter of 1904–1905. (AHC/UW)

A typing class in the "new" Cody High School with Miss Ruby Kreinbrook teaching. This photo was taken sometime after the school opened in 1953. (Richard/Richard Collection/PCHSA)

This Frank Lloyd Wright–designed house of Quin and Ruth Blair was built in 1951 by Carl Forgey, a local Cody builder and is the only Wright house in Wyoming. At the time of construction, the forty-acre site was completely desolate and Cedar and Rattlesnake Mountains were visible behind the house. Today, with the trees and landscaping well established, the house is secluded and well hidden from the nearby highway. (Blair Family)

Known as the German Band, this group of Cody Elks played for informal gatherings as well as the 1953 State Elks Convention in Cody, lending an air of fun to any occasion. Standing, left to right: Bob Holm, Dean Kells, Louis Moore, Harold Stump, and A. G. Erickson. Sitting: Max Thompson, Jack Yule, and Paul Smith. (Richard/Zinn Collection/PCHSA)

Greeting visiting dignitaries in the Western way are members of the Buffalo Bill Museum's Board of Trustees and the mayor of Cody. Authors of a Buffalo Bill biography, Henry Sell and Victor Weybright, are seated next to the driver. Standing between the carriage and the airplane are Mary Jester Allen, Larry Larom (with cane), and Mayor Hugh Smith. The gentlemen on the stairs are executives of Marshall Field's Department Store in Chicago. (Richard/Richard Collection/BBHC)

Above: The Budweiser Clydesdales came to Cody in 1955 and Bud Webster "stabled" them in his Chevrolet dealership for the night. To the right of the horses are: Rudy Mork, bartender at the Diamond Bar; Frank James, owner of the bar (also known as "Frenchy's"); and Red Issacs. Among the spectators are "Brownie," standing in front of Merle Ranck's barber shop; Bill DeMaris, in the white shirt wearing his hat cocked; and Frank James Jr., on his bicycle behind the wagon! (Richard/Fran Swope)

Dedication of the Cody Memorial Hospital took place in July 1955, to honor the memory of W. R. Coe, longtime Cody philanthropist. Speaking at the ceremony were, left to right: Glenn Nielson, Milward Simpson, W. R. (Bill) Coe II and C. E. (Bud) Webster. (Richard/Bud Webster)

Progress continued for Cody during the next decade with either new schools or facilities being built (Junior High and Sweitzer Gym) or enlarged (High School). A Cody institution, the Cody Trading Company, went out of business and Shoshone Bank bought out the First National Bank. Dick Steck opened an IGA grocery store which is still known as Steck's today though owned by the McArtors. The Presbyterian Church moved to the Dacken Subdivision because it couldn't expand at its Beck Avenue location. When rock slides near the Buffalo Bill Dam made travel to Yellowstone dangerous and sometimes "iffy," three new tunnels were built. Big Horn Gypsum opened a $3 million plant but two years later was bought out by Celotex Corporation.

Tourists were coming to Cody in ever increasing numbers and the community responded with more and more motels, restaurants, gift shops, etc. The Whitney Gallery of Art was built on land near the Gertrude Vanderbilt Whitney statue with a magnanimous gift from that family, opening in early spring 1959, and had the support of many local philanthropically minded families: Coes, Taggarts, Nielsons, Laroms, Gopperts, and Stocks. Dr. Harold McCracken was named director. The fine art collection was started with generous gifts from the Coes, the Weisses, and Armand Hammer. The original Buffalo Bill Museum, crowded and in need of major repair, was closed and the collection moved to the Whitney Gallery. Mary Jester Allen, Buffalo Bill's niece, due to ill health and her age (eighty-four), stepped down.

Drag racing became a popular activity in 1963, starting with unsanctioned events held nine miles out the South Fork which had to be broken up by the police because they were taking place on a state highway. Later that summer, Ford dealer Dick Soll sponsored a group of Cody men in drag races in Montana, Wyoming, and Nebraska.

Winter gave the town an early Christmas present December 16, 1964, when the temperature reached at least -32 degrees F. and was known as "the night Cody froze." Wyoming's seventy-fifth birthday was in 1965 and there was a great deal of pride and spirit evident in the town throughout the year. While both the Cody Stampede and the Cody Nite Rodeo were at low points, this summer was a confidence-building season that foretold prosperous years ahead.

1956–1965

by Lynn J. Houze

9

Left: **Many new drivers didn't feel as though they could really drive until they had successfully navigated the "dam" hill! (Sturm/Lovelace Collection/PCHS)**

Above: Park County Country Club, located east of Cody just past the Sage Creek crossing on Greybull Highway, was the scene of the annual Fourth of July fireworks in the mid-1950s and attracted viewers from around the Big Horn Basin. One year an errant spark landed in the storage pit, igniting all the fireworks at once! The thirty-minute program was over sooner than expected and never again was a fireworks display held at the club. The PCCC also offered golf, trap shooting, swimming, dinners, and dances for its members. Its predecessor, the "Cody Golf Club," founded about 1928, was located between Newton Lake and the Heart Mountain Canal, north of town on Bureau of Reclamation land. Sparse vegetation and few amenities probably contributed to the move to Sage Creek in 1949. (Richard/Richard Collection/BBHC)

Above: The Good Neighbors, a women's extension club founded in January 1942, also included other family members for special occasions such as birthdays or the annual Christmas party. About 1956, left to right, back row: Cash Kelley, Carl Baier, Carl Forgey, and Orrin Kaiser. Middle: Nellie Borner, Frances Forgey, Nell Kelley, Gladys Wilson, Edith Vawter, Peg Huegli, Rachel Gosney, Vera Baier, Evelyn Kaiser, Nellie Follensbee, and Thelma Spiegelberg. Front: Hale Spiegelberg, Ted Huegli, and Betty Spiegelberg. (Spiegelberg Family)

Above: These "spirited" civic-minded citizens in front of Spirit Mountain Caverns (also known as Frost Cave) planned to turn these caves into a tourist attraction complete with electricity and an elevator! The caves extend far into Cedar Mountain and are so deep underground that no one has ever been able to explore them all. Left to right: Bill Bragg, Jeannette Miller, Dick Frost, Katie Brown, Claud Brown, Hugh Smith, Tom Cowgill, Ned Frost, the guide, Lorna Simpson, and Milward Simpson. (Richard/ Richard Collection/PCHSA)

A severe rock slide (see arrow) onto the highway near the Buffalo Bill Dam in 1958 pushed ahead the State Highway Department's timetable for the Shoshone Canyon Highway Project. Two small tunnels had been widened and paved in the 1920s to accommodate cars but they did not offer much protection from rock slides and the roadbed itself was as narrow as twelve feet in some places, reducing traffic to one lane. Construction of the three tunnels, the bridge, and the roadbed improvement took almost two years to complete. The dedication was held May 6, 1961. (Richard/Richard Collection, BBHC)

Left: When Park County Sheriff Frank Blackburn retired in January 1959, after thirty-two years, having been sheriff longer than anyone else in Wyoming, there were two other county officials who also had held office since the 1920s. Congratulating him are Eva Larson (left), county clerk from 1929 to 1975, and Orilla Hollister (right), clerk of court from 1922 to 1964. (Park County Sheriff's Collection/ PCHSA)

There's always room for one more! Clark Stafford is bathing his dog in ever diminishing water as his pet deer quenches his thirst. It's not uncommon for our pets to have to share their food with the area's wildlife or for our cars to have to share the streets with bear, deer, and elk! (Richard/Richard Collection/BBHC)

Memorial Day, about 1960, being celebrated by local military personnel and scouts at the War Memorial in City Park which had been erected in 1951 by the Rotary Club and Paul Stock. (Richard/Richard Collection/BBHC)

Elizabeth Frost and Henry Coe are riding in his 1910 Velie in the Fourth of July parade, about 1960. She is a longtime resident of Cody while her husband, Dick, was the grandson of early Cody rancher Mahlon Frost. Henry Coe had spent many summers in Cody before moving here permanently in the early thirties. He and Peg Shaw were married in 1943, bought Buffalo Bill's hunting lodge, Pahaska Tepee, and continued the philanthropic work of his father, W. R. Coe. The Buffalo Bill Museum (now BBHC) and the W. R. Coe Memorial Hospital (West Park) are two of the beneficiaries of four generations of the Coe family. (Richard/Richard Collection/BBHC)

The Methodist Church, on the northeast corner of Beck Avenue and Fourteenth Street, was dedicated in October 1916, and rededicated in 1939 after a fire had destroyed the church's interior, including the pipe organ. By 1961, the building was too small for the size of the congregation so it was torn down and a larger, more modern church was built on the same site. During the interim, the Methodists used the vacant Presbyterian Church, three blocks to the west. (Hiscock/Stringari Collection/PCHSA)

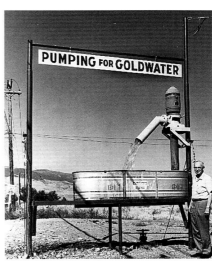

Marlin Kurtz, Cody representative to the State House from 1951 to 1965 and Speaker for those last two years, is seen here "campaigning" for Republican presidential candidate Barry Goldwater in 1964. This water pump is located in front of Pawnee Irrigation Supply, the first sprinkler irrigation business in the county and is still owned by the family today. A former teacher and state supervisor of distributive education, Kurtz worked at the Heart Mountain Relocation Camp during World War II. (Richard/Richard Collection, BBHC)

Gordon Way is showing Athalyn Worrall Husemann and her daughter, Harriet, Husky's newly acquired product, Dominion Briquettes, in front of his service station, about 1963. His station was in operation from October 1954 until July 1977, when Husky closed it. The Ways continue to own and operate Gordon's Oil Company, delivering fuel oil throughout the Big Horn Basin. (Richard/Richard Collection/BBHC)

Wyoming's 75th anniversary of statehood and Buffalo Bill's 119th birthday were celebrated jointly at the Irma Hotel on February 26, 1965. Period costume was encouraged by chairman Ruth Blair in order to create an authentic atmosphere while the dinner was the same menu served in 1915 to celebrate the Colonel's 69th. Sitting at the front table, left to right: Ernie Goppert, Angelyn McCracken, Harold McCracken, Louis Kousoulos, and Frank Blackburn. At the rear table, clockwise from the left: Fred Garlow, Thyra Thompson, Alice Messick, Lloyd Taggart, Cliff Hansen, Martha Hansen, and Peg Garlow. (Richard/Richard Collection/BBHC)

Left: When the Cody Trading Company closed its doors in 1963, the town lost its earliest business. Two years later, Woolworth's opened for business in the same building where it became a fixture on the southeast corner of Sheridan Avenue for the next twenty-five years. Subsequently, Tim Deroche renovated "The Cody Trading Company Building" which now houses a variety of shops. (Richard/Richard Collection/BBHC)

This aerial shot of Cody, looking east, shows how much the town has grown since the end of World War II. The area on top of the hill, to the east of the Greybull Highway, at the center of the photo, developed first. The Presbyterian Church (Sunday School building only) is visible (right, center) as is the Highland Manor Park area (center). (Richard/Richard Collection/BBHC)

Cody continued to grow in population and by 1970 had increased by approximately seventeen hundred residents since the last census. Direct telephone dialing began in 1966 and Frontier Airlines added more flights the following year.

Oil money continued to play a very important role in Cody's economic development. Paul Stock was named "Wyoming Oilman of the Year" for 1967 and the following year was Glenn Nielson's turn for that honor. In 1966, the Paul Stock Foundation gave the town the band shell in City Park and two years later, the Natatorium. Husky Oil continued to have record annual earnings and Mr. and Mrs. Nielson gave land for the Olive Glenn Country Club in 1970.

The slogan "Cody, Wyoming—Rodeo Capital of the World" was started in 1968 and is still in use today. The Stampede was very successful which carried over to the Cody Nite Rodeo. In 1969 a new road was built past the Buffalo Bill Dam as well as a four-lane road from the end of the Meeteetse road on into Cody.

Changes occurred all the time as Senator Milward Simpson retired from politics and George T. Beck Jr. retired as Cody postmaster. Fred Garlow took on a new appearance as he portrayed his famous grandfather, Buffalo Bill, on quiz shows, news shows, and in parades, in order to raise money to build a new Buffalo Bill Museum near the Whitney Gallery of Art. Sheriff Frank Blackburn died in 1970.

1966–1975

by Lynn J. Houze

10

Left: "Cody" Bill Smith, seen here at the Cody Stampede, won his first saddle bronc world championship in 1969 and went on to win it two more times. He is a local boy who started his career at the Cody Nite Rodeo and rode professionally for twenty years. (Wyoming State Museum)

Bob Moore, seated at the head of the table, is instructing these young scouts in knot-tying lessons in order to complete a badge requirement. On his immediate right, mostly hidden, is his son, Doug. (Buswell Collection/PCHSA)

Above: Over the years, fires have been responsible for the loss of several of Cody's historic buildings including the Bronze Boot, formerly known as the DeMaris Hotel and located at DeMaris Springs. After World War II, it became a restaurant/nightclub under the management of Nick Knight and was a favorite dining spot of Codyites. The name came from the boot worn by Knight's boyhood friend and rodeo star, Fritz Truan, who had been killed in the war. Truan's mother had the boot bronzed and then gave it to Knight. A year before the fire Hilda Ratliff, Knight's sister and manager of the Boot, moved the club into a new building across the river on the southern rim of the canyon where the building is today. The cause of this fire on April 10, 1968, was determined to be arson. (Tom Knapp drawing/Hilda Ratliff)

Right: The new construction in the area around Cody City Park is evident in this photo. On the left, near the middle, is the new Cody High School built in 1952. Below that is the Junior High, built in 1964, and next to it is Sweitzer Gym, built in 1958. The gym was named for longtime agricultural teacher and athletic coach Paul Sweitzer and dedicated in April 1958. The bandshell in the Park, a gift from Paul Stock, was dedicated on May 22, 1966. Just off to the right is the construction site of the new Buffalo Bill Museum which joined with the Whitney Gallery of Art to become the Buffalo Bill Historical Center. (Richard/ Richard Collection/BBHC)

A group of Park County Historical Society members erected a seventy-pound metal marker on top of Red Butte on September 29, 1967, to mark the site where Dr. Frank Powell's ashes had been scattered after his death in 1906. A longtime friend and business partner of Buffalo Bill's, "White Beaver" as he was also known, shared with his friend a desire to have his spirit overlook the town of Cody. The PCHS was formed in 1955 as an offshoot of the Pioneers of the Cody Country to continue the historical work of that group. Left to right: Senius Nielsen, Ellen Waggoner, Elsie Jensen, Mary Nielsen, Anne Fendrich, Alice Stafford, Jean Lupher, Henry Burrier, Dorthy Burgener, and Gertrude Burrier. (Richard/Mary Nielsen)

To raise funds for the new Buffalo Bill Museum over 117,000 Buffalo Bill Winchester Commemorative rifles were sold. This large replica of the rifle appeared in the Fourth of July parade, courtesy of Husky Oil and the Winchester Company, and a year later wound up on the roof of Jack's Sports and Hardware, the building where Big A Auto Parts is now. (Richard/Richard Collection/BBHC)

This buffalo represents the spirit of Buffalo Bill which was transferred from his burial site on Lookout Mountain, near Denver, Colorado, to the top of Cedar Mountain in an elaborate Indian ceremony of smoke signals. Held in conjunction with the annual Fourth of July Stampede, the laying of the cornerstone of the new wing of the Buffalo Bill Museum, a Pony Express ride from Cheyenne to Cody, and celebrities in attendance, this event was supposed to put an end to the feud between Cody and Denver as well as to have a part of Buffalo Bill back in Cody where he had wanted to be. (Richard/Richard Collection/BBHC)

In 1969, the old Buffalo Bill Museum, which had been purchased through the generosity of the Coe Foundation, the Paul Stock Foundation, Husky Oil, and Ernie Goppert, became available for community purposes only. An agreement was reached between the City of Cody and the Cody Country Art League, the Chamber of Commerce, and the Park County Historical Society for the use of the building. The Art League began in the spring of 1964, as a direct result of Adolph Spohr holding art classes for a group of Cody women calling themselves "The Painting Grandmothers." While the PCHS moved into the Courthouse in 1985, the other two groups remain providing an invaluable service to Codyites and tourists alike. Greeting guests at the Stock Center "Open House" are, left to right: Mayor and Mrs. Carl Krueger, Paul Stock, Eloise Stock, Mel Fillerup, Lucille Patrick, Hank Dais, Harold McCracken, and Goppert. (Stock Collection/BBHC)

The Fire Control Dispatch Center opened in June 1970, at the E. E. Faust Regional Airport in order to patrol the surrounding 3.5 million acres of National Forests and Wyoming State Park and Forest lands from the air. Dispatch Officer Leonard Foxworthy was in charge of assessing the fires and deploying the men, the smoke jumpers and/or the slurry bombers for the quickest possible suppression. Two B-17 bombers were converted each to carry a maximum of two thousand gallons of slurry, a fire retardant mixture of chemical phosphate and water. In 1986, this operation ceased when the federal "No-Burn" policy was discontinued. (Irene Foxworthy)

Sheridan Avenue, looking east, prior to Christmas 1972. It appears as though the whole town is concentrated in one block and everyone is doing their last-minute shopping! (Dewey Vanderhoff)

The Rotary Club of Cody began March 18, 1949, and three years later held their first "Rotary Club Show" in order to raise money for worthwhile projects. That first year they pledged $1,000 towards building of a new city pool which is located between the Convention Center and the Elks Club. Many projects have followed including the fitness course near the high school field, the shelter at Hugh Smith Park, and annual college scholarships to Cody youth. Other service organizations have helped Cody, notably the Lions Club (Beck Lake Park), the Elks Club, the Knights of Columbus, the Eagles, the Boy Scouts and the Girl Scouts, etc. The twenty-second Annual Rotary Club Show of 1973 was entitled: "AIRPORT-OR-The Next Time You Fly, Go By Air!" with first-year members strutting their stuff. Left to right: Ray Olson, Buddy Duval, Ed Goetz, Bill Rohrbach, Gene Stringari, and Jerry Troy. (Mike Cook)

In order to make way for a parking lot, Buffalo Bill's house was moved from its location on Beck Avenue between Eleventh and Twelfth Streets to the corner of Robertson Street and Southfork Road, south of Cody in the Valley View subdivision. This house had been built by Buffalo Bill about 1904 and was occupied by his wife, Louisa, and his daughter, Irma, and her family, the Garlows. (CE/PCHSA)

High school sports have always been a popular community activity in Cody and one of the most popular coaches was Spike Vannoy. He coached both basketball and football and when he died of cancer at the young age of fifty-three the students suffered a great loss. The high school football field was renamed in his honor at the beginning of the 1983 season. Left to right, first row: assistant coach and Junior High science teacher Jim Wallwork, Spike Vannoy, Scott Moore, and Kirk Winterholler. Back row: Bob Moncur, Ron LeMasters, Phil Ready (glasses), and Phil Guinn. (Mike Cook)

A fire that started in a shed in the alley behind the *Cody Enterprise* office on Sunday, May 19, spread to the roof of that building, smoldering throughout the night and the next morning until a full fire broke out around noontime. Despite heroic efforts by the Cody Volunteer Fire Department, two men died in the fire. Fireman Bob Moore was attempting to rescue reporter Eric Olson, who was in the basement darkroom, when the ceiling partially collapsed on Moore, knocking him to the floor and snapping his oxygen line, causing him to inhale smoke. He died five days later. Olson died from smoke inhalation, never getting out of the basement. Dewey Vanderhoff, *Enterprise* photographer, was working in the darkroom with Olson but escaped. In October 1977, Charles Gentner, a thirty-seven-year-old drifter, confessed to setting the original fire and was sentenced to two life sentences, twenty years for arson, and the recommendation that he never be granted parole. (Mick Hanson)

The Class of '49's twenty-fifth reunion was held in June at the 7-D Ranch in Sunlight Basin, north of Cody. The forty-nine class members were very close in school and they have remained so in part by holding a reunion every five years instead of the usual ten. In addition, a pledge made at graduation to hold their fortieth reunion in Hawaii was kept. Front row, left to right: Pat Davies Harres, Cathy Adix Moses, Darlene Knapp Noble, Betty Brown Meabon, Nita Jensen Hill, Nancy Stafford Shaw, and Jackie McNeil Hensley. Back row: Bob Borron, Pat Skaggs, Jim Nielson, Jerry Lanchberry, Al Simpson, Ralph Newell, Dick Black, Ken Nelson, Don Kurtz, Bob Hockley, and Dick Thompson. (Richard/Richard Collection/BBHC)

Reburial of John "Liver Eating" Johnston (1824–1900), a trapper, hunter, Army scout, and Civil War veteran among other things, took place at Bob Edgar's Old Trail Town on June 8, 1974. Over two thousand people watched Bob, Robert Redford, who had portrayed Johnston in the movie *Jeremiah Johnson*, Reverend Buswell, and various mountain men honor Johnston's memory. The speaker is Dr. Dewey Dominick, local family practitioner and BBHC trustee. (Dewey Vanderhoff/Bob Edgar Collection)

Harley Kinkade and Nic Patrick led this group of Girl Scouts over Dead Indian Pass into the Sunlight-Crandall area, carrying all the necessities of life including the "port-a-potties"! They came from throughout the United States to participate in Wyoming's first National Trek: "Long Tales–Lost Trails" and to Cody to celebrate the Fourth of July. (Bettie Daniels Collection/PCHSA)

Who better to help Cody celebrate the Fourth of July than John Wayne! Not only was this Fourth the Bicentennial of the U.S.A., but it was also the opening of the new Winchester Arms Museum at the Buffalo Bill Historical Center. The "Duke" was grand marshal of the parade, helped dedicate the WAM, and awarded prizes at the Cody Stampede to winning cowboys, making this celebration one that the town will long remember. (Dewey Vanderhoff)

1976–1985

by Lynn J. Houze

11

What a wonderful ten years this was for Cody! The oil boom brought good economic times to the town and the people, with new buildings and new businesses to show for it. The growth of the town spread out farther in all directions. Livingston Elementary School was built on top of the hill, replacing Westside School which was converted to administrative offices. In 1982, the West Cody Strip area and Valley View Subdivision on the hill south of the Strip were annexed by the town just six years after the Stampede grounds moved to its present location.

The Buffalo Bill Historical Center added two more museums to its complex. The Winchester Arms Museum opened in 1976 and a new wing was built to house the Plains Indian Museum in 1979, bringing the number of museums to four. The resulting increase in tourism helped the town.

In 1979, a new favorite son, but with the same last name, made the switch from state to national politics when Alan Simpson was elected senator from Wyoming, where he still serves today. One of our longest residents, Judge "Jack" Stilwell, changed his address from Riverside Cemetery to Old Trail Town when he was reburied there. We lost two of our favorite residents in 1985 when Buffalo Bill's grandson, Fred Garlow, and renowned artist, Nick Eggenhofer, both died.

In 1984, Husky Oil's Cody operation was purchased by Marathon Oil Company ending a relationship with the town that went back some forty-six years. Included in that purchase was the office building on Stampede Avenue which Marathon moved into the following June.

The pool at DeMaris Springs was a part of every Codyite's life, for at some point they would head there for swimming, picnicking, or sunbathing. The river rafting companies used the bank as a staging area for some of their trips down the lower Shoshone River. In 1978, several years after this photo was taken, Susan Thorne painted a two-hundred-foot mural, whimsically depicting a unicorn in a forest, that covered two of the walls. The 1981 flood took down the north wall and later flooding wiped out all but the west wall. Today, while the pool has been restored and a gazebo built, the area is closed to the public. (Dewey Vanderhoff)

158

Whether it took Cody a long time to adjust to motorized traffic or this sign was a unique way to get the tourists to "stop and shop" remains to be seen, but it certainly caught everyone's attention! (CE)

Another fire made news over Labor Day weekend in 1977 when a power line went down in Shoshone Canyon on Sunday morning, quickly igniting the dry brush. The five to ten acres that were burning on Rattlesnake Mountain when the firemen got there eventually spread to over one thousand. Two slurry bombers and about two hundred men fought the fire that wasn't controlled until the wind switched direction to the southwest. (CE)

Roberta Schultz, daughter of Irene and Bert Schultz, was born and raised in Cody. In 1978, she was Miss Cody Stampede and the following year was named Miss Rodeo Wyoming, representing our state in the PRCA finals in Oklahoma City, Oklahoma. (Dewey Vanderhoff)

With the growth of the residential area on top of the hill near the Olive Glenn Country Club came the overcrowding of Westside School, located near the High School and the Junior High. To alleviate that problem, Glenn E. Livingston Elementary School was built in 1979 and was dedicated in 1980. However, on the first day of classes that August the school was already overcrowded! (Richard/Richard Collection/BBHC)

Hugh Smith, mayor of Cody from 1948 to 1952 and again from 1954 to 1968, was a well-known Cody old-timer who, upon retirement, kept several unofficial offices throughout the town. If he wasn't in his chair at the Irma Hotel answering questions then he might be found at the Holiday Inn or at the Shoshone Bank, all places which he visited twice daily during his three-mile walk around town. Former Mayor Frank Houx and Vern Spencer were other old-timers who preceded Smith at the Irma, swapping stories with their friends. (Dewey Vanderhoff)

The Yellowstone Mountain Men of Cody held a rendezvous on Trail Creek, north of the Shoshone River near Indian encampments of earlier times. Patterned after events held in the 1800s, the "buckskinners" and their families came from several states to participate in black powder rifle shooting, mountain men contests, and primitive living. (Mike Cook)

The Plains Indian Museum of the BBHC was dedicated on June 16, 1979, with these three special men in attendance: Cody artist Nick Eggenhofer, the "dean of Western illustrators," "Slim" Pickens of Hollywood fame, who was present also when the buffalo was placed on top of Cedar Mountain, and Dick Frost, the curator of the Buffalo Bill Museum. Seen in the second row between "Slim" and Dick, is PIM curator George Horsecapture's daughter, Daylight. (Elizabeth Frost)

Once the Stampede grounds moved from the top of the hill to its present location, the area vacated saw the construction of several new buildings. In 1980, Husky Oil moved into their building (center of photo) on land that took up most of the former rodeo grounds. The U.S. Post Office, in need of space, moved into its building on the northeast corner of Stampede and Heart Mountain Street in the spring of 1981. Still under construction in this photo, about 1982, is the Sunshine Office Building (bottom). (Richard/Richard Collection/BBHC)

Right: The original plans for the new Park County Courthouse called for the existing building to be torn down so no attempt was made to make the two architectural styles compatible. When the residents (voters!) of Park County realized the fate of the old building they raised a fuss. Consequently, the old and the new buildings were connected to each other and the 1912 building was remodeled for other county offices, including the Park County Historical Society Archives which moved in in 1985. (Richard/Collection/BBHC)

Shootings and/or killings very rarely happen in Cody so when one does occur it becomes big news. On April 25, 1983, when Charles Pote fired an errant shot into the Silver Dollar Bar, killing Ron Jensen of Cody, the town talked of nothing else for weeks. Pote, Steve Alloway, and Connie Pote took off towards Yellowstone, hiding in a cabin on Pagoda Creek but were caught the next day. Mick Hanson is manning the road block west of the tunnels in between bites of breakfast. (CE)

In June 1983, Cody celebrated the centennial of Buffalo Bill's Wild West Show. The three-day event honored not only the pageantry but also the memory of the founder who brought America's west to millions of people throughout the world. (Weiglein/BBHC)

Valley School, a one-room schoolhouse thirty-seven miles southwest of Cody, was built in 1918 and has operated continuously since then. At one time, there were a dozen or more one-room schools in the Cody area but economics has forced consolidation with the larger town schools. (Jones Collection/PCHSA)

The Cody Unit of Marathon Oil Company's Big Horn Basin operation is located in Sage Creek near Beacon Hill Road within sight of Heart Mountain. The first well was drilled in 1976 by Husky Oil and unitized by them the following year. In 1984, Marathon Oil Company bought out Husky's properties including this unit. (Marathon Oil Company)

The Wyoming Vietnam Veterans Memorial was dedicated on November 11, 1986, after years of hard work by many Cody people including Rob Landes, Paul Clymer, Chriss and Meredith Peart, Jeff Smith, Diane and Gordon Russell, Gary Smith, and Linda Childs. This memorial, inspired by "The Wall" in Washington, D.C., contains the 137 names of Wyoming's soldiers who died in that war. Speakers at the ceremony included: Mayor Dorse Miller, Governor Ed Herschler, and State Representative Phil Robertson. The three helicopters performing the flyover are from the Army National Guard/Cheyenne Unit. (Weiglein/Vietnam Vets Collection/PCHSA)

1986–1995

by Lynn J. Houze

12

People continued to move into Cody and by 1990 the population was 7,897, an increase of almost 600 people from 1980. The economy had started to slow down as we followed the nation as a whole. Cody had a lot to celebrate, however, beginning with Wyoming's Centennial in 1990, followed by the Shoshone National Forest's one hundredth, the opening of the Cody Firearms Museum in a new wing of the Buffalo Bill Historical Center, and the seventy-fifth Cody Stampede. New school buildings rose at a tremendous rate: Cody Middle School (1994), Eastside School (1994), and the High School (completion expected 1996). In addition, expansion and renovations were made to both Wapiti and Sunset Schools and to the Stock Natatorium.

Cody continued to add new businesses, some successful and some not. Fast-food restaurants now number eight and many new motels have opened, as well. A number of older homes have been renovated as bed-and-breakfast establishments bringing to mind the early days of Cody when boarding houses were popular. Oil and gas production, ranching, farming and tourism continue to be very important to our economy. The 1988 fires in Yellowstone are still talked about and Cody had its second bank robbery of the century on April 11, 1995.

We begin our next one hundred years looking forward to the challenges but respectful of our past and appreciative of Cody's founders who had the foresight to realize that this area was a wonderful place for a town and had the knowledge to give us a good start. To those generations who came in between, we also say "thank you" for without their hard work and effort, Cody would not be ready for the twenty-first century.

On June 6, 1988, a fifteen-cent stamp honoring Buffalo Bill Cody was issued at the BBHC. This stamp was designed by Jack Rosenthal, member of the Citizen's Advisory Committee, and longtime proponent of a stamp to honor Buffalo Bill. Participants at the "First day of issue" ceremony included Rosenthal, Wyoming Governor Sullivan, Senator Alan Simpson, and Mayor Dorse Miller. (Fleetwood)

The Cody Search and Rescue Squad has been saving people since January 8, 1970. Some of the members attending a rappelling class are: Bob Pyle, Bob Newsome, and Marty Stennard. (CE)

As the fires in Yellowstone National Park became larger and spread nearer to Cody, this view, taken from the Eleventh Street hill, was a daily sight and the smell of smoke was ever present. (CE)

The 1988 fires in Yellowstone spread to the Crandall and Sunlight area northwest of Cody and burned over a million acres. Civilian firefighters from around the country were brought in as were military units. "R&R" for these soldiers was in Cody and the town showed their appreciation by donating baked goods, reading materials, and warm clothing for the unexpected, but very welcome, cold weather that came, bringing with it the snow that helped put out the fires. (CE)

Wyoming celebrated one hundred years of statehood throughout 1990 with many events but one of the most popular was the Centennial Wagon Train which began in Casper on June 2, with over fifty covered wagons and 340 people and ended in Cody on July 2 having almost doubled in size. Seen here are, left to right: Pete Lovelace, Kayne Pyatt (organizer), Governor Mike Sullivan, unknown, Ann Simpson, Senator Al Simpson, and Nancy Shaw. (CE)

A late spring snow made for wonderful sledding for Mickey and Robbie Neihart who are being pulled by their mom, Brenda, near Glendale Park. (CE)

The Cody Fire School, an annual event since 1974, has firefighters from all over the Rocky Mountain region participating. In 1986, a new training facility opened south of town on land near the municipal waterworks. Between four hundred and five hundred men attend each year with specialists from as far away as Louisiana, Colorado, Los Angeles, and Houston (the renowned Boots and Coots firefighters) acting as instructors. Seen here is Denver fireman Mike Parker (pointing) giving instruction on basic airpack operations. (CE)

A new Shoshone River Bridge begins to take shape in October 1991. This is at least the fourth bridge at this site and was completed late the following summer. The first bridge was a little farther upstream and each new bridge has moved downstream from its predecessor. (CE)

Watching football in Cody is always an adventure weather-wise as Joyce Skoric, John and Ryan Cowger, and Jim and McKenzie Landers can attest to, though its easier when Cody wins (37–13 over Riverton)! (CE)

Above: Twenty-four motorcyclists from the Cody-Powell area participated in a Christmas toy run down Sheridan Avenue in late October 1991. Over seven hundred toys were then given to the Cody Fire Department for distribution to needy children. Leading the parade is organizer Mike Cook (left), Rick "Wolf" Collins (Santa), Danny Miner (Elf), and Rocky Trojanowski (right). (CE)

Third grade Brownies from Troop No. 690 joined other local Girl Scouts in making decorations for the Children's Department Christmas tree in the Cody Library. Left to right, front row: Kristina Teaker, Stevie Goddard, Kera Washburn, and Jessica Cowles; second row: Crystal Davis, Melanie Teaker, and Shamie Young; third row: Stacy Schroeder, Anna Julien, Erin Copeland, Julie Gautsch, and Jolene Teten; and fourth row: Debbie Gautsch, Robin Washburn, and Kathy Julien. (CE)

Prince Albert of Monaco, great-grandson of the first Prince Albert, came to Cody in August 1993 to commemorate his great-grandfather's hunting trip with Buffalo Bill held eighty years ago. Among the crowd are: Jane Sanders, Peg Coe (chairman of the BBHC Board of Trustees), Peter Hassrick (director, BBHC) Mayor Jack Skates, and, in front of Prince Albert, Meghan Cranfill. (CE)

This corner recently housed Shoshone First National Bank and its parking lot until they moved a block east in 1994. New owners, Si and Corky Cathcart, decided to restore the building to the way it looked in 1910 and today the Sheridan Building houses retail stores and offices and has become a wonderful example of what restoration can do for a town. (Mike Cook)

May 24, 1995, was the "Grand Opening" of Albertson's Food Center and the reopening of Eastgate Center on "top of the hill." Owners, Marge and Dick Wilder of Wilder Enterprises, are seen here with Mayor Jack Skates cutting the ribbon to officially reopen the Center. Cody's Ambassadors, in the blazers, are, left to right: Kelly Jensen-Webster, Jerry Posey, Craig Robison (with plaque), Doreen Skates, Bob Richard, Colette Taggart, Hilda Ratliff, and Gladys Price. (Wilder Enterprises)

Frances Purvis has lived in Cody all her life though her mother went back to Montana briefly for Frances' birth in 1900. Her father, "Lute" Jones, was the first postmaster at Ishawooa on the South Fork. To celebrate her ninety-fifth birthday, both of her children, Grace and Paul, and all of their nine children between them, came to this first family reunion/birthday party. Additionally, there was at least one representative from each of the families of Frances' four sisters. Members came from as far away as Alaska, New York, and Texas. (CE/Frances Purvis)

The Buffalo Bill Dam was raised twenty-five feet in a $132 million project completed in 1993. Judging by how high the water rose the summer of 1995, it was just in time. At the same time, the Visitor Center was built to explain the historic role of water and irrigation throughout the Big Horn Basin. (CE)

The Buffalo Bill Art Show, founded in 1982 to promote Western art and artists, was the scene this year of the unveiling of *An Eagle's View* by Reid Christie. Pink Way (left) and Gerri Richard announced that this winning oil painting will be used throughout 1996 to promote Cody's Centennial and will be auctioned off at next year's show. (CE)

The Western Design Conference was started in 1993, by the Master Artisans Guild, headed by Mike Patrick. As Cody has been an art colony since the mid-1930s, the conference aimed to expand that area to furniture, interior design, and related fields, creating a "school of Western design" with Cody as the center. Other objectives of the conference included educating the public about Western furniture and showcasing the work of artisans from around the country. All this has happened with the result that the conference has achieved national participation in just three years. Seen here is Wardi Reber, representing "Different Hat Design." (Mike Cook)

Cody as it looks in 1995 from the same vantage point as the 1905 photo, seen earlier. The Nearby Ranch is in the lower right and the Courthouse near the center. The Cody *C*, the symbol of each Cody High graduating class, is also visible just in front of Rattlesnake Mountain. Hard work and patience have produced the trees which hide a number of early landmarks. (Mike Cook)

Bibliography

Books

Andren, Gladys. *Life Among the Ladies by the Lake.* Cody: By the author, 1984.

Bartlett, Richard A. *From Cody to the World.* Cody: Buffalo Bill Historical Center, 1992.

Billings Gazette Staff. *Wagons Across Wyoming.* Billings, Mont.: *Billings Gazette*, 1990.

Brininstool, E. A. *Fighting Indian Warriors.* New York: Bonanza Books, 1953.

Chamberlin, Agnes B. *The Cody Club 1900–1940.* New York: J. J. Little and Ives Company, 1940.

Churchill, Beryl G. *Dams, Ditches, and Water.* Cody: Rustler Printing and Publishing, 1979.

Cody High School Annual. *The Bronc. 1941, 1942, 1943,* and *1945.* Casper: Prairie Publishing.

Cook, Jeannie. *Wiley's Dream of Empire: The Wiley Irrigation Project.* Cody: Yellowstone Printing, 1990.

Denig, Edwin Thompson. *Five Indian Tribes of the Upper Missouri.* Norman: University of Oklahoma Press, 1958.

Dunraven, Earl of. *The Great Divide.* Lincoln: University of Nebraska Press, 1874.

Frison, George. *Prehistoric Hunters of the High Plains.* New York: Academic Press, 1978.

Furman, Necah Stewart. *Caroline Lockhart: Her Life and Legacy.* Cody: BBHC and Seattle: University of Washington Press, 1994

Glidden, Ralph. *Exploring the Yellowstone High Country.* Cooke City: Artcraft Printers, 1976.

Hamilton, William. *Sixty Years on the Plains and Mountains.* Alexandria, Va.: Time-Life Books, 1982.

Husted, Wilfred and Edgar, Bob. *The Archaeology of Mummy Cave, Wyoming.* Washington, D.C.: Smithsonian Publications, 1967.

Journals and Letters of Major John Owen 1850-1871. New York: Edward Eberstadt, 1927.

Kensel, W. Hudson. *Pahaska Tepee.* Cody: Buffalo Bill Historical Center, 1987.

Langford, Nathaniel Pitt. *The Discovery of Yellowstone Park: Journal of the Washburn Expedition 1870.* Lincoln: University of Nebraska Press, 1972.

Larson, T. A. *History of Wyoming.* 2nd. ed. rev. Lincoln: University of Nebraska Press, 1978.

Larson, T. A. *Wyoming's War Years, 1941–1945.* Reprint. Cheyenne: Wyoming Historical Foundation, 1993.

Lindsay, Charles. *The Big Horn Basin.* Lincoln: University of Nebraska Press, 1932.

Lucier, A. G. *Pictorial Souvenir of Cody, Wyoming.* Powell, Wyo.: By the author, n.d.

Murray, Ester Johannson. *Red Lodge–Meeteetse Trail.* N.p.: By the author, 1985.

National Guard of the State of Wyoming. *Historical and Pictorial Review.* Baton Rouge: Army and Navy Publishing Company, 1940.

Nielson, Glenn. *Episodes in My Life.* Cody: By the author, 1992.

Nobokov, Peter. *Two Leggings.* New York: Thomas Y. Crowell, 1967.

Patrick, Lucille Nichols. *The Best Little Town by a Dam Site.* 3rd ed. Cheyenne: Pioneer Printing, 1984.

Patrick, Lucille Nichols, ed. *The Park County Story.* Dallas: Taylor Publishing, 1980.

Russell, Don. *Lives and Legends of Buffalo Bill.* Norman, Okla.: University of Oklahoma Press, 1960.

Sell, Henry Blackman and Weybright, Victor. *Buffalo Bill and the Wild West.* New York: Signet Press, 1959.

Skarsten, M O. *George Drouillard.* Spokane, Wash.: Arthur H. Clark Company, 1964.

Stock, Margaret Reynolds. *Stock Family History.* Cody: Rustler Printing and Publishing, 1972.

Trenholm, Virginia Cole, ed. *Wyoming Blue Book.* 3 vols. Cheyenne: Wyoming State Archives and Historical Dept., 1974.

Trenholm, Virginia Cole and Carley, Maurine. *The Shoshonis Sentinels of the Rockies.* Norman: University of Oklahoma Press, 1964.

U.S. Government. *1868 Indian Treaty Records.* Washington, D.C.

U.S. Government Report. *Journals of the Captain Jones Expedition 1873.* Washington, D.C.

Walker, Tacetta B. *Stories of Early Days in Wyoming.* Casper: Prairie Publishing, 1936.

Walsh, Richard. *The Making of Buffalo Bill.* Kissimmee, Fla.: The International Cody Family Association, 1978.

Wasden, David J. *From Beaver to Oil.* Cheyenne: Pioneer Printing, 1973.

Welch, Charles A. *A History of the Big Horn Basin.* Salt Lake City: Deseret News Press, 1940.

Wishart, David J. *The Fur Trade of the American West.* Lincoln: University of Nebraska Press, 1979.

Yost, Nellie Snyder. *Buffalo Bill.* Chicago: Sage Books, 1979.

Business Directories

Cody Wyoming City Directory 1963. Chillicothe, Ohio: Mullin-Kille Con Survey Company.

Rocky Mountain Bell Telephone Company, Wyoming Division. *Official Directory, March 1, 1904.* Salt Lake City, 1904.

Wyoming State Business Directory. 1901–02, 1906–07, 1908–09, 1916, 1921, 1929, 1930, 1931, and *1941–42.*

Newspapers

Basin Republican Rustler
Billings Gazette
Cody Enterprise
Cody Times
Duluth Press
Livingston Enterprise
Northern Wyoming Herald
Park County Enterprise
Red Lodge Pickett
Shoshone Valley News
Wyoming Dispatch
Wyoming Stockgrower and Farmer

Periodicals

Cody Stampede Program. 1979, 1994.

McLaird, James D. "Building the Town of Cody: George T. Beck, 1894–1943." *Annals of Wyoming* 40 (April 1968): 73-105.

Russell, Don, ed. Julia Cody Goodman's "Memoirs of Buffalo Bill." Topeka: *Kansas Historical Quarterly* 4, Winter 1962.

Towne, Charles Wayland. "Preacher's Son on the Loose With Buffalo Bill Cody." *Montana: The Magazine of Western History* 18 (Autumn 1968): 40–55.

Unpublished Manuscripts

Beck, George T. "Personal Reminiscences of the Beginning of Cody, 1895–1896."

Daly, Judith Bost. "Memoirs of Agnes Chamberlin." 1993.

City of Cody. "City Council Minutes, 1901-1995."

Frost, Mary. "Frost Ranch on Sage Creek, Stinking Water River, Wyoming."

Fremont County, Wyoming. "County Records."

Hayden, Charles. "Building the Cody Canal, Location of the Town, and the First Settlers."

Hoffman, Manuelle. Untitled, 1914.

Houx, Frank. "Journal of Frank Houx." 1900(?).

Park County, Wyoming. "Land Records, County Clerk's Office."

Roberson, Betty Beck, and Johnson, Jane Beck, eds. "Beckoning Frontiers Footnote to American History." 1985.

Thurston, Josephine Goodman. "Col. Wm. F. Cody, Natural Promoter, Builds Cody Area."

Williams, Frank. "Reminiscences of Frank M. Williams."

Williams, Minnie. "Reminiscences of Minnie Williams—'Cody in the Making.'"

Wilson, E. D. "The Kid Wilson Chronicles."

Collections

American Heritage Center, University of Wyoming, Laramie. Collections of George T. Beck, Harry W. Thurston, Jacob Schwoob, and William F. Cody.

Harold McCracken Library, Buffalo Bill Historical Center, Cody. Collections of Mary Jester Allen, Garlow Family, William F. Cody, and others.

Park County Historical Society Archives, Cody. Manuscript and biographical files.

Wyoming State Archives, Cheyenne. Files on Cody, William F. Cody, Thurston, Schwoob, Coe, Garlow, Goppert, and Simpson.

Index

A

Abbott, Archie, 74
Abramson, Helen, 109
Absaroka Mountains, 19, 26
Absarokee Agency, 34
Act of Dedication, 29
Albertson's Food Center, 176
Albright, Horace, 91, 106
Alcan Highway, 126
Alder Gulch, 26
Aldrich Ranch, 73
Aldrich, Sam, 122
Alger Avenue, 64, 71, 179
Alger, Horace, 13, 45, 52
Alkali Creek, 43
Alkali Lake, 116
Allen, John, 127
Allen, Mary Jester, 138, 141
Allen, Nancy, 127
Alloway, Steve, 163
American Fur Company, 24, 25
American Heritage Center, 11
Anderson, A. A., 58
Anderson, Andy, 11
Anderson, Mildred, 122
Arapaho Indians, 19, 29
Arland and Corbett Trading Post, 33, 36
Arland, Victor, 35, 38, 40, 42
Armistice Day, 117, 125
Arnold, H. P., 46, 48
Ash, Doc, 73
Ashworth, Richard, 41
Austin, M. L., 133
Avant, Margaret, 109

B

Bagne, Mark, 11
Baier, Carl, 142
Baier, Vera, 142
Bald Mountain, 44
Bald Mountain City, 44
Ballow, Virgil, 126
Bandshell, 150
Bannock Indians, 31, 32, 33, 34
Bannock Trail, 33
Basin, 54, 88
Bates, Irene, 95
Bates, William, 11
Beam, Pearl, 95
Bear in the Middle, 23
Bear Paw Mountains, 31
Bears Tooth, The, Chief, 26, 27
Beartooth Mountains, 20, 34, 119
Beaver Swamp, 24
Beck Avenue, 61, 63, 73, 145, 153
Beck, Betty, 53, 55, 95, 97, 113
Beck, Daisy, 55, 63, 83, 113
Beck, George T., 15, 44, 46, 51, 52, 53, 54, 58, 60, 61, 63, 64, 67, 70, 77, 83, 101, 107, 113, 114
Beck, George T., Jr., 113, 149
Beck, Jane (Johnson), 53, 55, 95, 97, 121, 130
Beck Lake, 51, 70, 116
Beck Lake Park, 152
Bedford, Jack, 42, 44
Beecher Island, 62
Belden, Charles, 118
Bell, Howard, 109
Bellamy, Beth, 121
Bennett Battle, 32
Bennett, Captain, 34
Big A Auto Parts, 151
Big Horn Basin, 13, 14, 19, 21, 22, 23, 24, 25, 26, 27, 28, 29, 32, 33, 34, 35, 38, 41, 42, 43, 44, 45, 54, 55, 100, 101, 112, 142, 177
Big Horn Basin Development Company, 82
Big Horn Canyon, 20

Big Horn County, 54
Big Horn County Pioneer Association, 133
Big Horn Expedition, 27
Big Horn Gypsum, 141
Big Horn Mountains, 13, 20, 26, 27, 35, 38
Big Horn River, 20, 45
Billings Freight Trail, 61
Billings, Montana, 41, 59, 84
Black and Yellow Trail, 89, 91
Black Diamond (saloon), 65
Black, Dick, 154
Black Hills, 35
Blackburn, Frank, 108, 121, 122, 143, 146, 149
Blackfeet Indians, 23, 24
Blackfoot, Chief, 26, 27
Blackwater Memorial, 120
Blair, Quin, 136
Blair, Ruth Taggart, 127, 136, 146
Blaske, Reverend, 98
Bleistein Avenue, 74
Bleistein, George, 13, 46, 52, 55, 77
Bliss, Jack, 42, 44
Blue Bead Mountain, 23, 25
Boal, Arta Clara, 60
Boal, Cody, 60
Boal, Horton, 13, 45
Borner, Nellie, 142
Borron, Bob, 154
Bosler, Bill, 126
Bottler, Hank, 28
Boy Scouts, 94, 129, 131, 144, 149, 152
Bozeman Trail, 27
Bradbury, James, Dr., 74
Brady, Thomas, 42
Bragg, Bill, 142
Brainerd, Jean, 11
Bridger, Jim, 24, 26
Bridger, Montana, 26
Bridger Mountains, 20
Britton, Roxie, 133
Bronze Boot, 150
Brooks, Winthrop, 108
Brown, Claud, 131, 142
Brown, Katie, 131, 142
Brownie (O. W. Browne), 139
Brundage, Hale, 112
Brundage Hardware, 69, 118
Buckingham, Buck, 85
Budweiser Clydesdales, 139
Buell, General, 34
Buffalo Bill Art Show, 178
Buffalo Bill Barn, 50, 56, 59
Buffalo Bill Birthday Ball, 91, 115
Buffalo Bill Boy Scout Camp, 129, 131
Buffalo Bill Campground, 94
Buffalo Bill Dam (Shoshone Dam), 15, 41, 68, 79, 129, 141, 143, 149, 177
Buffalo Bill Historical Center, 20, 38, 132, 144, 150, 155, 156, 157, 161, 167, 168, 175
Buffalo Bill Memorial Association, 106, 132
Buffalo Bill Museum, 106, 107, 113, 129, 138, 141, 144, 149, 150, 151, 161
Buffalo Bill Visitor Center, 177
Buffalo Heart Mountain, 23
Buffalo hunters, 35, 38, 40
Bulltail, Alice, 33
Burch, David, 42, 44
Burgener, Dorothy, 150
Burke, John M., Major, 13, 14
Burke, Trude, 121
Burlington Railroad, 15, 51, 61, 79, 129, 130
Burnett, Mike, 44
Burns, John, 73
Burrier, Gertrude, 150
Burrier, Henry, 150
Buswell, Reverend, 155
Byrd, Rear Admiral, 130

C

Campfire Girls, 95
Canfield, George, 45
Canyon View Subdivision, 52, 107
Carter Creek, 33
Carter Mountain, 33, 44
Carter, William, Judge, 32
Cassidy, Butch, 42, 43
Castle Rock, 29
Cathcart, Corky, 175
Cathcart, Si, 175
Catholic Church, 73, 109. 134
Cedar Mountain, 23, 29, 44, 76, 79, 104, 132, 136, 142, 151, 161
Cedar Mountain Lodge, 114
Celotex Corporation, 110, 141
Challenger Airlines, 129
Chamberlin, Agnes, 57, 67, 112, 117
Chamberlin, Gaylord, 109
Chamberlin Hotel, 57
Chamberlin, Mark, 67, 69
Chapman, J. W., 57
Chapman, John, 32, 43
Charley, Cigarette, 118
Charlie Low's Forbidden City, 127
Chase, George, 122
Cheyenne Indians, 27, 31, 32, 62
Childs, Linda, 166
Christie, Reid, 178
Christmas, 118, 141, 142, 152, 174
City Park, 113, 144, 149, 150
Civil Works Administration, 107
Civilian Conservation Corps, 107, 120
Clark, William, 23
Clarks Fork Canyon, 22, 30, 31, 33, 34
Clarks Fork River, 20, 26, 28, 33, 35
Class of '49, 154
Clearwater Campground, 120
Clemons, Clarice, 109
Clymer, Frances, 11
Clymer, Paul, 166
Cobb, Louis, 127
Cobb, Mary, 127
Cobb, Ty, 106, 107
Cody Air Transport, 104
Cody Airport, 118
Cody, Arta, 45
Cody Auditorium, 117
Cody Burlington Depot, 58, 59, 96, 134
Cody Burlington Inn, 91, 129, 130
Cody Canal, 9, 15, 46, 47, 49, 50, 56, 70, 102
Cody Centennial, 178
Cody Chamber of Commerce, 58, 97, 151
Cody City, 48, 49, 50, 51, 52, 53, 54, 61, 64, 70, 71, 73, 80, 81, 82, 83, 84, 85, 91, 103, 107, 111, 116, 117, 123, 129, 141, 147, 149, 152, 157, 167, 179
Cody City Council, 94, 117
Cody Club, 58, 59, 98, 114
Cody Country Art League, 151
Cody Cowboy Band, 84, 101
Cody Drug, 111
Cody Elks Band, 137
Cody Enterprise, 11, 16, 50, 56, 57, 59, 99, 101, 117, 132, 154
Cody Exchange (saloon), 63, 65
Cody Fire School, 172
Cody Firearms Museum, 167
Cody Golf Club, 142
Cody Hotel, 51, 62, 65, 84
Cody, Irma, 60, 85, 86, 91, 153
Cody Library, 11, 80, 91, 125, 174
Cody, Louisa, 73, 91, 153
Cody Lumber Company, 61, 96
Cody Memorial Hospital, 139
Cody Nite Rodeo, 117, 141, 149
Cody Oil and Development Company, 77
Cody Peak, 112
Cody Play Readers Club, 121
Cody Police, 77, 91
Cody Search and Rescue Squad, 169
Cody Stampede, 91, 101, 104, 113, 123, 141, 149, 151, 156, 159, 167
Cody Sylvan Pass Motor Company, 90
Cody Theater, 117
Cody Times, 129
Cody Town Council, 117
Cody Trading Company, 55, 59, 72, 84, 100, 111, 118, 141, 146
Cody Volunteer Fire Department, 154, 174
Cody, William F., 9, 15, 16, 17, 19, 45, 46, 47, 51, 52, 53, 54, 55, 56, 58, 59, 60, 61, 62, 63, 64, 66, 73, 75, 77, 81, 82, 83, 84, 85, 86, 87, 91, 104, 106, 112, 129, 132, 135, 144, 146, 149, 150, 151, 153, 157, 168, 175
Coe family, 141, 144
Coe Foundation, 151
Coe, Henry, 144
Coe, Margaret Shaw, 127, 144, 175
Coe, W. R. (Bill), II, 139
Coe, W. R., Memorial Hospital, 144
Coe, William R., 103, 119, 139, 144
Colby site, 20
Collier, Irwin, 44
Collins, Rick "Wolf," 174
Colter, John, 21, 22, 23
Colter's Hell, 22
Commercial Saloon, 61
Company E, 88
Company K, 91, 96
Cone, Barney, 74
Conning, Carmela, 11
Conway, Jesse, 44
Cook, Christy, 11
Cook, Mike, 11, 174
Cook, Roger, 112
Cooke City, 28
Coolidge, Calvin, 106, 107
Coolidge Door, 106
Copeland, Erin, 174
Copper Mountain, 20
Corbett, John, 35, 37, 38, 39, 40, 42
Cottonwood Creek, 36, 39
Council Saloon, 50, 57, 65
Cowan, George, 29
Cowger, John, 173
Cowger, Ryan, 173
Cowgill Subdivision, 117
Cowgill, Tom, 142
Cowles, Jessica, 174
Cox, Carl, 109
Crandall Creek, 29, 30
Crandall, Jack, 28
Cranfill, Meghan, 175
Crazy Horse, 32
Crow Agency, 27, 28
Crow Indians, 21, 23, 24, 26, 27, 29, 33, 34, 38, 39, 40, 41
Crow, Joe, 42

D

Dacken Subdivision, 129, 141
Dahlem, John, 133
Dais, Hank, 151
Dave Jones Men's Store, 81, 111
Davis, Crystal, 174
Davis, John "Reckless," 63
De Mailly, Count, 36
Dead Indian Hill, 31, 34
Dead Indian Pass, 155
DeMaris, Bill, 118, 139
DeMaris, Charles, 40, 46
DeMaris Hotel, 150
DeMaris Springs, 7, 16, 46, 51, 52, 62, 150, 157
Depression, 107, 110, 117

Deroche, Tim, 146
Diamond Bar (Frenchy's), 126, 139
Directors Club, 114
Dixon, Joseph, 22
Doezal, Bill, 121
Dominick, Dewey, Dr., 155
Downing, Carley, 107, 117
Downing, George, 112
Downing, Glen, 86
Drewry, Belle, 42, 44
Drouillard, Frank, 22, 23
Drouillard, George, 21
Du Dore, Count Ivan, 35, 38
Dude Ranchers Association of America, 108
Dude Wrangler, 107
Durand, Earl, 117
Durant, Al, 42
Duval, Buddy, 152

E

E. E. Faust Regional Airport, 152
Eagle Creek, 95
Eagles, 152
East Gate, 66, 67, 89
Eastgate Center, 176
Eastside School, 87, 117, 123, 167
Edgar, Bob, 155
Edwards, W. B., 82
Eggenhofer, Nick, 157, 161
Elephant Head Lodge, 135
Eleventh Street, 83, 84, 153, 169
Elks Club, 137, 152
Enalpac Oil Company, 77
Entrance Day, 91, 101
Episcopal Church, 63, 84
Erickson, A. G., 137
Ewig, Rick, 11

F

Farming, 51, 70, 71, 73, 102, 120, 167
Farrar. Geraldine, 99
Feeley, Etta, 64
Fell, Bill, 121
Fell, Olive, 95, 124
Felsheim, Red, 118
Fendrich, Anne, 150
Fesenbeck, Chris, 122
Fesenbeck, Mrs. 122
Fillerup, Mel, 151
Fire, 72, 74, 79, 85, 120, 145, 150, 154, 158, 167, 169, 172
Fire Control Dispatch Center, 152
First Addition, 73, 107
First National Bank, 69, 73, 141
Fite, Grace, 109
Florida, Bob, 11
Follensbee, Nellie, 142
Foo, Soo, 118
Forest Service, 135
Forgey, Carl, 131, 136, 142
Forgey, Frances, 142
Forsyth, Colonel, 62
Fort Bridger, 27, 32
Fort Custer, 32, 34, 38
Fort Ellis, 34
Fort Hall, 33
Fort Keogh, 34
Fort Laramie, 26, 27, 34
Fort McKenzie, 34
Fort Raymond, 22
Fort Tecumseh, 34
Fort Union, 34
Fort Washakie, 33, 38, 40, 41
Fourteenth Street, 145
Fourth of July, 53, 72, 73, 101, 102, 142, 144, 151, 155, 156

Foxworthy, Leonard, 152
Frame school, 74
Freeborg, Dave, 122
Freeborg, Joe, 122
Freemont County, 41, 52
French, Lorraine Martin, 133
Frontier Airlines, 149
Frontier School of Western Art, 132
Frost Cave (Spirit Mountain Caverns), 7, 76, 142
Frost, Daisy, 41
Frost, Dick, 127, 142, 161
Frost, Elizabeth, 38
Frost, Elizabeth Freeman (Mrs. Dick), 127, 144
Frost, Jack, 38
Frost, Jesse, 38, 41, 57, 129
Frost, Mahlon, 41, 144
Frost, Mary, 125
Frost, Nancy, 41
Frost, Ned, 41, 63, 76, 87, 125, 133, 142
Frost stage station, 43
Frost's Curio Shop, 125
Frost's Packard, 125
Fur trade, 24, 34

G

Gail, Fred, 70, 98
Gallagher, William, 42, 44
Garlow, Bill, 85, 112, 130
Garlow, Fred, 86, 126, 146, 149, 157
Garlow, Fred, Jr., 85
Garlow, Irma Cody, 60, 85, 86, 91, 153
Garlow, Jane, 85, 112
Garlow, Peg, 146
Gas and oil, 73, 77, 91, 107, 109, 110, 129, 131, 134, 145, 149, 151, 157, 162, 165, 167
Gates, Charles, 87
Gautsch, Debbie, 174
Gautsch, Julie, 174
Gawthrop, Jennie, 112
Gentner, Charles, 154
Gentner, George, 118
Gerrans, Henry M., 13, 46, 52, 55, 77
Girl Scouts, 152, 155, 174
Goddard, Stevie, 174
Goetz, Ed, 152
Goff, Barney, 109
Gold Creek, 26
Good Neighbors Club, 142
Goodman, Finley, 115
Goodman, Julia Cody, 135
Goppert, Ernest, 108, 121, 146, 151
Goppert, Estelle, 121
Goppert family, 141
Gosney, Rachel, 142
Grandview Subdivision, 117
Grass House River, 23
Green Front Club, 114
Green Gables, 113
Greever, Ada, 120, 121
Greever, Paul, 98, 111, 113, 120
Greybull, 133
Greybull Hill, 50, 71
Greybull (Grey Bull) River, 24, 33, 40, 41
Grigware, Edward, 114, 130, 132
Grocerteria, 111
Grouard, Frank, 46
Guinn, Phil, 153

H

Haight, Reverend, 94
Hainer, Al, 42, 43
Hamilton, William, 24
Hammer, Armand, 141
Hammitt, Carl, 57, 70, 74, 98
Hammitt, Frank, 63
Hampshire, A. A., 109

Hancock, Forrest, 22
Hanna, Oliver, 35
Hansen, Cliff, 146
Hansen, Martha, 146
Hanson, Mick, 163
Hanson site, 20
Hargraves, R. C., 83
Hargraves Ranch, 99
Harres, Pat Davies, 154
Harrison, Thomas, 77
Hart Mountain Inn, 57, 61
Hassrick, Peter, 175
Hayden Arch Bridge, 91
Hayden, Charles, 13, 46, 48, 51, 52, 64, 81
Hayner, Earl, 126
Haynes, F. Jay, 90
Heart Mountain, 22, 23, 27, 31, 43
Heart Mountain Division, 117, 120
Heart Mountain Relocation Center, 117, 123, 145
Hellcat, 99
Henderson, Goldie, 126
Henry, Andrew, 23
Henry, John, 28
Hensley, Charles, 69
Hensley, Jackie McNeil, 154
Herschler, Ed, 166
High School, 88, 91, 112, 124, 125, 129, 134, 136, 141, 150, 153, 154, 159, 167, 173, 178
Highland Manor Park, 147
Hill, Frances, 95
Hill, Kirk, 126
Hill, Nita Jensen, 154
Hillberry, Laban, 44
Hindmann, Paul, 112
Hiscock, Fay J., 11, 75, 76, 87, 108
Hitchcock, Bessie, 75
Hitchcock, Jessie, 75
Hockley, Bob, 154
Hoffman, Walt, 25
Hogg, Mary, 121
Holiday Inn, 160
Holister, Orilla, 122, 143
Holm, Bob, 137
Holm Building, 81
Holm, Margaret, 112
Holm, Roy, 108
Holm, Tex, 85
Holman, Blen, 112
Holmes, Elizabeth, 11
Holmquist, Ed., 100
Holm's, Gus, 74, 89
Hoodoo Ranch, 119
Hoolihan, Blind Bill, 42, 44
Hoopes, Major, 96, 108
Horner site, 20
Horr, Leonard, 80
Horse Thief Trail, 44
Houx, Frank, 41, 58, 59, 97, 160
Howe, Dr., 69
Howell, Billy, 123
Howell, Stanley, 95
Huegli, Peg, 142
Huegli, Ted, 142
Hugh Smith Park, 152
Hughes, Maevis, 109
Hunt, Lester, 130
Hurd, Grandma, 55
Husemann, Athalyn Worrall, 145
Husemann, Harriet, 145
Husky Oil Company, 117, 134, 149, 151, 157, 162, 165

I
Illinois Pipeline Company, 110
Inman, George, 99, 118
Iowa Store, 84
Irma Flat, 49

Irma Hotel, 15, 16, 59, 60, 62, 63, 64, 65, 73, 75, 78, 80, 85, 86, 90, 101, 121, 123, 146, 160
Iron Bull, Chief, 24
Iron Tail, Chief, 63
Isham, Fern, 95
Isham, Joe, 77, 98
Ishawooa River, 29
Issacs, Red, 139

J
Jack's Sports and Hardware, 151
Jackson, Andy, 42
Jackson Hole, 44
Jackson, Teton, 43
James, Frank, 139
James, Frank, Jr., 139
Japanese-Americans, 117, 123
Jensen, Elsie, 126, 150
Jensen, Ron, 163
Jensen-Webster, Kelly, 176
Jeremiah Johnson, 30, 155
Johnson, Algott, 70
Johnson, Jane Beck, 53, 55, 95, 97, 121, 130
Johnson, Nelson, 121, 130
Johnson, Two Dog, 118
Johnston, John "Liver Eating," 30, 31, 155
Jones, Bill, 118
Jones Creek, 29
Jones, Dave, 73, 98
Jones, Eugenia, 121
Jones, Lute, 176
Jones, Monte, 126, 133
Jones, Phonograph, 100
Jones, William, Captain, 29
Joseph, Chief, 29, 31
Julien, Anna, 174
Julien, Kathy, 174
Junior High School, 141, 150, 159

K
Kai-Shek, Chiang, Madame, 121
Kaiser, Evelyn, 142
Kaiser, Orrin, 142
Kane, Riley, 35
Kane, Tom, 77, 98
Kearns, John, 69
Kelley, Cash, 142
Kelley, Nell, 142
Kells, Dean, 137
Kent, Marguerite, 109
Kepford, Jessie, 112
Kepford, Ray, 112
Kepford, Walter, 97
Kerper, Hazel, 121, 122
Kerper, Wesley, 122
Kershaw, Stanley, 11, 132
Kershaw, Stella, 121
Keystone Court, 134
King, James, 112
Kinkade, Harley, 155
Kinkade, Martha, 126
Kirkpatrick, John, 113, 118
Kissick, William, 69
Knight, Nick, 150
Knights of Columbus, 152
KODI, 129, 130
Koenig, Otto, 109
Kousoulos, Louis, 146
Kreinbrook, Ruby, 136
Krueger, Carl, 151
Krueger, Dorothy (Mrs. Carl), 109, 151
Kurtz, Don, 154
Kurtz, Lois, 109
Kurtz, Marlin, 145
Kurtz Plumbing and Hardware, 111
Kuykendall, W. L., 27

L

Lake Junction, 90
Lakeview Canal, 73
Lanchberry, Jerry, 154
Landers, Jim, 173
Landers, McKenzie, 173
Landes, Rob, 166
Landon, Bill, 42
Lane, Frances, Dr., 74
Lane-Bradbury Hospital, 74
Langford, Nathaniel, 29
Larom family, 141
Larom, Irma, 108
Larom, Larry, 108, 115, 138
Larom Summer Institute, 132
Larson, Andy, 74
Larson, Eva, 122, 143
Lasher, Barbara, 126
LDS Church, 87, 132
Leach, Thomas, 64
Learned, Carl, 112
Leibel, Larry, 11
LeMasters, Ron, 153
Lenninger, Minnie, 112
Lewis and Clark Expedition, 21
Lieb, Billy, 76
Lieb, Mable, 112
Lillie, Gordon, Major, (Pawnee Bill), 106
Lincoln Land Company, 13, 51
Lincoln, Nebraska, 60
Lincoln Orchestra, 60
Lions Club, 152
Liquor Store, 73
Lisa, Manuel, 22, 23
Little Big Horn Battleground, 31
Little Bighorn River, 38
Little Chief, 32
Little Rock, 34
Livingston Elementary School, Glenn E., 157, 159
Lockhart, Caroline, 74, 99, 101, 107
Loewer, Bill, 105
Log Cabin Bar, 118
Lookout Mountain, 104, 151
Lovelace, Pete, 11, 170
Lupher, Jean, 150

M

Manning, Pat Greever, 111
Maps, 18, 48, 49, 52, 92–93
Marathon Oil Company, 77, 157, 165
Markham, Altamae, 11
Markham, P. E., 98, 103
Marquette, 39, 55, 70
Marquette Creek, 41
Marquette, George, 41, 44, 45, 46
Marquette School, 135
Marshall Field's Department Store, 138
Martin, Andy, 133
Martin, Andy, Mrs., 133
Martin, Lizzy, 95
Martin, Lorraine, 95
Masonic Lodge, 16
Masonic Temple, 73, 88, 108
McArtor family, 141
McCracken, Angelyn, 146
McCracken, Harold, Dr., 141, 146, 151
McCracken Research Library, 11
McCullough Peaks, 33
McCullough, Peter, 33
McFall, Aurilla, 57
McFall, "Bad-Land" Dave, 57, 85
McFarland, Geneva, 109
McGann, Cassie, 88
McGinnis, Roy, 74
Meabon, Betty Brown, 154

Mead, Elwood, 45
Meeteetse, 28, 39, 40
Meeteetse Creek, 36, 41, 42
Memorial Day, 144
Menard, Pierre, 23
Messick, Alice, 146
Methodist Church, 73, 91, 145
Metz, Percy, 122
Meyer, Ralph, 129
Middaugh, I. O., 69
Middle School, 167
Mikado, The, 88
Miles, Nelson A., 17, 31, 32, 34, 58
Miller, Black Jack, 42
Miller Creek, 28
Miller, Dorse, 166, 168
Miller, Horn, 28
Miller, Jeannette, 142
Mills, Anson, 13
Miner, Danny, 174
Miss Rodeo Wyoming, 159
Missouri Fur Company, 23
Molesworth, Thomas, 114
Moncur, Bob, 153
Monday, Bill, 118
Moore, Allen, 44
Moore, Bob, 149, 154
Moore, Harry, 130
Moore, Louis, 137
Moore, Scott, 153
Moran, Breck, 130
Mork, Rudy, 139
Moses, Cathy Adix, 154
Mull, George, 76
Mummy Cave, 20, 21
Murray, Ester Johansson, 11, 123

N

Nancy, Sagebrush, 42
Nard, Albert, 44
Nearby Ranch, 71, 178
Nelson, Ken, 154
Newell, Joe, 78
Newell, Kid, 78
Newell, Pearl, 78
Newell, Ralph, 154
Newsome, Bob, 169
Newton, A. C., 123, 133
Newton, Brownie, 133
Newton Company, 70, 84
Newton, Don, 112
Newton family, 50, 86
Newton, Glen, 91
Newton, L. L., 94
Nez Perce Indians, 30, 31
Nichols, Barbara, 113
Nichols, Kid, 113
Nichols, Lucille, 113
Niehart family, 171
Nielsen, Mary, 150
Nielsen, Senius, 150
Nielson family, 141
Nielson, Glenn, 131, 134, 139, 149
Nielson, Jim, 154
Nimitz, Fleet Admiral, 130
No Wood Creek, 44
Noble, Darlene Knapp, 154
Noble, Nick, 74
Nordquist, Pete, 99
North Fork, 13, 15, 20, 23, 28, 29, 39, 66, 85, 91, 95, 112, 120, 124, 133, 135
Northern Pacific Railroad, 39, 41
Nuckols, Bessie, 53
Null, Ed, 133
Nye, Ed, 42

O

O'Hara, Pat, 25, 26
Oil and gas, 73, 77, 91, 107, 109, 110, 129, 131, 134, 145, 149, 151, 157, 162, 165, 167
Oldham, Albert, 30
Olive Glenn Country Club, 149, 159
Olson, Eric, 154
Olson, Ray, 152
Order of Eastern Star, 112
Oregon Basin, 33, 77, 107, 109, 110
Oregon Trail, 26
Osborne, Tom, 122
Overly, Mabel, 129
Owens, Art, 76
Owens, Margaret, 112
Owens, Walter, Judge, 109, 133
Owl Creek Mountains, 20, 28, 33, 38

P

Pahaska Tepee, 15, 66, 90, 112, 144
Palace Meat Market, 80
Papypo Butte, 23, 24
Park County, 81, 83, 92, 93, 107, 122, 124, 162
Park County Country Club, 142
Park County Courthouse, 73, 109, 122, 124, 132, 151, 162
Park County Fair, 73, 87
Park County Historical Society, 11, 150, 151; Archives, 162
Park Garage, 91
Parker, Robert Leroy (Butch Cassidy), 42, 43
Pat O'Hara Creek, 25, 32
Pat O'Hara Mountain, 23, 25
Patrick, Lucille Nichols, 11, 151
Patrick, Mike, 178
Patrick, Nic, 155
Paul Stock Foundation, 149, 151
Pawnee Irrigation Supply, 145
Peake, Anna "Granny," 17, 132
Peake, John H., Colonel, 16, 17, 56, 74, 132
Pearce, Dad, 60
Peart, Chriss, 166
Peart, Meredith, 166
Perry, Gracia, 109
Peverly, H. B., 44
Pfrangle, Bill, 126
Phillips, Mrs., 122
Phillips, Robert, 122
Pickens, Slim, 161
Pickett, William, 58
Pioneer Building, 55, 70, 91, 114
Pioneers of the Cody Country, 133, 150
Pitchfork Ranch, 33
Plains Indian Museum, 157, 161
Plenty Coups, Chief, 101, 106
"Poker church," 63
Ponderosa Campground, 134
Pony Express, 151
Poor farm, 73
Population, 51, 57, 71, 73, 91, 107, 117, 129, 149, 167
Posey, Jerry, 176
Pote, Charles, 163
Pote, Connie, 163
Powell, 107, 117, 123, 125
Powell, Frank, Dr., (White Beaver), 15, 66, 150
Powell, George, Dr., 15
Powell, Will, Dr., 15
Powers, Camille, 53
Prante, Irene, 112
Presbyterian Church, 73, 84, 141, 145, 147
Price, Gladys, 176
Primm, Ben, 63
Primm, Fred, 62
Primm, Katie, 62
Prince Albert, 175
Prince of Monaco, 86, 87
Prohibition, 99, 103, 107
Pryor Creek, 22
Pryor Gap, 23, 35
Pryor Montana, 33
Pryor Mountains, 20, 24
Public Health Department, 103
Pulley, Ray, 76
Purcell, Tom, 63
Purvis, Frances, 176
Pyatt, Kayne, 170
Pyle, Bob, 169
Pyron, Margaret, 109

R

Ranching, 51, 65, 73, 83, 108, 119, 129, 167
Ranck, Merle, 139
Rankin, Meyer, 95, 121
Rankin, Mid, 121
Ratliff, Hilda, 150, 176
Rattlesnake Mountain, 22, 35, 132, 136, 158, 178
Ready, Phil, 153
Reber, Wardi, 178
Red Brick School, 95, 134
Red Cloud Agency, 32
Red Cross, 97, 117, 125
Red Lodge, 9, 40, 41, 42
Red Lodge–Meeteetse Trail, 61
Red Top Service, 104
Redford, Robert, 155
Rialto Theater, 91
Richard, Bob, 176
Richard, Dave, 11
Richard, Fred, 76, 87
Richard, Gerri, 178
Richard, Jack, 11, 129
Richard, Will, 13, 76
Riddle, Prestley, 70
Riddle, Tobias, 70
River rafting, 157
Riverside Cemetery, 131, 157
Robertson, E. V., 98, 106, 119, 130
Robertson, Harriet, 96, 112
Robertson, Phil, 166
Robertson, Ray, 109
Robison, Craig, 176
Rocky Mountain Fur Company, 24
Rogers, Joe, 44
Rohrbach, Bill, 152
Rosenthal, Jack, 168
Ross, Nellie Tayloe, 99
Rossiter, E. B., 74
Rotary Club, 144, 152
Roth, Richard, 69
Rousseau, Bertha, 109
Rousseau, Dick, 109
Routt, Molly, 122
Rumsey, Bob, 133
Rumsey, Bronson, 13, 46, 52, 55, 77
Russell, Alby, 126
Russell, Diane, 166
Russell, George, 51
Russell, Gordon, 166
Russell, Mike, 13, 60
Ryan, Jerry, 44, 51, 64

S

S.S. *Cody*, 117
Sage Creek, 23, 41, 43, 45, 142, 165
Sage Creek Community Club, 91
Salsbury, Nate, 13, 15, 46, 52, 53
Sammy Girls, 97
San Francisco Clearing House for Cody Cowhands, 127
Sanchee, Tom, 99
Sanders, Frenchy, 126, 139
Sanders, Jane, 175

Sanderson, Morris, 118
Sayles, Henry, 119
Scholes Blacksmith Shop, 73
Scholes, Edna, 112
School District 6, 107
Schroeder, Stacy, 174
Schultz, Bert, 159
Schultz, Irene, 159
Schultz, Roberta, 159
Schwoob Blacksmith Shop, 50, 56
Schwoob, Jakie, 55, 84, 86, 89, 100
Schwoob, Loren, 108
Schwoob, Walter, 74, 108
Scoville, Charles, 93
Second Addition, 107
7-D Ranch, 154
Shady Rest Beer Gardens, 103
Shaw, Effie, 112
Shaw, Ernie, 108, 126
Shaw, Nancy Stafford, 154, 170
Shell Creek, 35
Shelley, Dave, 98
Sheridan Avenue, 51, 53, 60, 65, 72, 73, 81, 82, 91, 96, 101, 107, 111, 114, 123, 125, 146, 152, 174
Sheridan Building, 175
Shoshone, 52
Shoshone Bank, 50, 73, 117, 141, 160, 175
Shoshone Canyon, 101, 107, 158
Shoshone Canyon Highway Project, 143
Shoshone Dam (Buffalo Bill Dam), 15, 41, 68, 79, 129, 143, 149, 177
Shoshone Electric Light and Power Company, 67
Shoshone Land and Irrigation Company, 15, 51, 52, 53, 55
Shoshone National Forest, 135, 167
Shoshone Reclamation Project, 51, 74, 117, 120
Shoshone Reservoir, 129
Shoshone River, 39, 44, 58, 67, 108, 120, 132, 134, 157, 161
Shoshone River Bridge, 173
Shoshoni Indians, 27, 29, 39, 41
Shoshoni Reservation, 27
Shrikhande, Devendra, 11
Shuck, David, 44
Siggins, Frank, 95, 108
Sills, Milton, 99
Silver Dollar Bar, 163
Simpson, Alan, 6, 7, 125, 154, 157, 168, 170
Simpson, Ann, 170
Simpson, Lorna Helen Kooi, 7, 125, 142
Simpson, Milward, 7, 95, 106, 124, 125, 128, 129, 130, 139, 142, 149
Simpson, Peter, 6, 7, 125
Simpson, William, 43
Sioux Indians, 27, 31, 32
Skaggs, Pat, 154
Skates, Doreen, 176
Skates, Jack, 175, 176
Skinner, Vernon, 112
Skoric, Joyce, 173
Skull Creek Pass, 23
Slurry bombers, 152, 158
Smith, "Cody" Bill, 149
Smith, Dudley, 86
Smith, Gary, 166
Smith, Hugh, 138, 142, 160
Smith, Jeff, 166
Smith, Paul, 137
Snake Indians, 40
Snake River Bill, 118
Snyder, Simon, 133
Soll, Dick, 141
Sonners, Ora, 109, 110
South Fork, 13, 22, 29, 39, 41, 44, 45, 46, 97
South Fork Hill, 82
South Pass, 27, 33
South Pass City, 26
Sowards, Shirley, 126
Speaker, Tris, 106, 107
Spencer, Anna, 112
Spencer, George, 44
Spencer, Vern, 160
Spiegelberg family, 142
Spirit Mountain, 23, 29, 76
Spirit Mountain Caverns, 7, 76, 142
Spohr, Adolph, 151
Spring Creek Raid, 88
Stafford, Alice, 150
Stafford, Clark, 144
Stambaugh, Lizzie Martin, 133
Stampede Avenue, 157
Stampede grounds, 48, 129, 157, 162
Star, Morris, 122
Steadman, Oliver, 121
Steadman, Sally, 21
Steck, Dick, 141
Stennard, Marty, 169
Stevens, Lawrence Tenney, 112
Stilwell, Jack, 62, 157
Stinking Water River, 13, 22, 23, 27, 29, 31, 33, 37, 39, 40, 41, 44, 49
Stock, Eloise, 151
Stock family, 141
Stock Natatorium, 149, 167
Stock, Paul, 110, 131, 132, 134, 144, 150, 151
Stone school, 64, 65
Stopka, Christina, 11
Stott, Clarence, 60
Stringari, Gene, 152
Stuart, Granville, 42
Stump, Charles, 109
Stump, Harold, 137
Sturm, Harold, 11
Sturm, Hetty, 11
Sulfur Creek, 46
Sullivan, Mike, 168, 170
Sunlight Basin, 28, 34, 63, 154, 170
Sunlight-Crandall, 155
Sunlight Creek, 28, 30
Sunset School, 129
Sweeney, William, 13
Sweitzer, Bess, 109
Sweitzer Gym, 141, 150
Sweitzer, Paul, 108, 109, 112, 150
Sykes, Frank, 35
Sylvan Pass, 13, 67

T

Taggart, Colette, 176
Taggart Construction Company, 107
Taggart family, 141
Taggart, Lloyd, 146
Taggart, Marjorie, 127
Taylor, George, 74
Taylor-Made Ice Cream Shop, 126
TE Ranch, 83, 106
Teaker, Kristina, 174
Teaker, Melanie, 174
Terrace Subdivision, 117
Teten, Jolene, 174
Texas Refining Company, 110
Thirteenth Street, 51, 114, 116
Thomas, Craig, 109
Thomas, Marge, 109
Thompson, D. C., 11
Thompson, Dick, 154
Thompson, Gus, 86
Thompson, John, 69
Thompson, Max, 137
Thompson, Thyra, 146
Thorne, Susan, 157
Thurston, Harry, 115, 135

Thurston, Josephine Goodman, 16, 60, 75, 135
Toluca, 59
Tourism, 51, 66, 85, 86, 89, 91, 105, 107, 124, 130, 134, 141, 158, 167
Trail Creek, 33, 35, 38, 39, 161
Trail Town, 62, 155, 157
Trappers Ball, 91
Treaty of 1868, 27
Trimmer, Blanche, 121
Trojanowski, Rocky, 174
Troy, Jerry, 152
Trueblood Subdivision, 107
Tuff, Jimmy, 99
Turkeys, 131
Twelfth Street, 58, 116, 119, 153
Two Leggings, 23
Two Moons, 32

U
U.S. Post Office, 63, 107, 162
Union Pacific Railroad, 26, 27, 41

V
Valley Ranch, 108
Valley School, 165
Valley View, 153, 157
van Dreveldt, E., 48
VanArsdall family, 118
VanArsdall, S. P., 108, 126
Vanderhoff, Dewey, 11, 154
Vannoy, Spike, 153
Vawter, Edith, 142
V-E Day, 117
V-J Day, 117
Vogel Building, 117
Vogel, Jennie, 112
Vogel, Joe, 49, 103
Volkmer, Mrs., 73
von Lichtenstein, Count Otto Franc, 33
Vreeland, Harry, 118

W
Waggoner, Ellen, 150
Waggoner, Lawrence, 133
Waggoner, Slim, 126
Wagon Train, Centennial, 170
Wake Island, 117
Walliker, George, 85
Walls Building, 69, 91
Walls, Mrs., 69
Walls, William, 60
Wallwork, Jim 153
Walters, Frank, 112
Wapiti Inn, 15, 66
Wapiti Ranger Station, 135
War Bond drives, 91, 98, 117
War Hospital Fund, 97
War Memorial, 144
War of 1812, 24
War Rumblings, 117
Wasden, Dave, 11
Washburn Expedition, 29
Washburn, Kera, 174
Washburn, Robin, 174
"Water Wagon," 99
Watkins and Prante Transportation, 104
Watkins, Dudley, 91, 104
Watkins, Ella, 112
Watkins, Sant, 45, 83
Way, Gordon, 145
Way, Pink, 178
Wayne, John, 156
Weather, 170
Weaver, J. R., 42
Webster, C. E., (Bud), 139
Webster, William, 61, 63

Weikert, Andrew, 30
Weiss family, 141
Welch, Charles, 15
West Cody Strip, 157
West Park Hospital, 144
Western Design Conference, 178
Westside School, 117, 129, 157, 159
Wheaton, Bill, 44
White Bear Mountain, 33
White, Jim, 35
White, Nellie, 133
Whitney Gallery of Art, 141, 149, 150
Whitney, Gertrude Vanderbilt, 141
Wiard, Harry, 98
Wickham, John, 44
Wiggins, Jack, 33
Wild West Show, 11, 13, 14, 16, 17, 45, 47, 51, 63, 64, 73, 84, 103, 117, 164; Cowboy Band, 13, 84
Wilde, Max, 100, 107
Wilder, Dick, 176
Wilder, Marge, 176
Wiley Irrigation Project, 82
Wiley, John "Jock," 112
Wiley, Katherine, 75
Wiley, Ruth, 75
Wiley Town, 113
Wilkins, William, 122
Williams, Clarence, 88, 99, 101, 115, 133
Williams, Edith, 112
Williams, Frank, 47, 84, 133
Williams, Marion, 46
Williams, Minnie, 112
Williams Ranch, 46, 47
Williams, Rose, 42, 44
Willis, Constance, 109
Wilson, Gladys, 142
Wilson, Jennie, 112
Wilson, Jim, 126
Wilson, Kid, 90
Winchester Arms Museum, 156, 157
Winchester Company, 151
Wind River, 20
Wind River Canyon, 26
Wind River Mountains, 33, 44
Winterholler, Kirk, 153
Wister, Owen, 73
Wolf Bow, Chief, 26
Wolf Mountains, 31
Wolfville, 101, 117
Womanless Wedding, 108
Wood River, 28, 44
Woods, Alfred, 59
Woolworth's, 146
Workman, Charles, 73, 80
Works Progress Administration, 107
World War I, 91, 96, 97, 104
World War II, 117, 123, 124, 125, 126, 127, 129, 130, 147, 150
Wright, Colonel, 122
Wright, Frank Lloyd, 136
Wynona Thompson Auditorium, 74
Wyoming Centennial, 167, 170
Wyoming State Archives, 11
Wyoming Vietnam Veterans Memorial, 166

Y
Yellowstone Mountain Men, 161
Yellowstone National Park, 7, 13, 14, 15, 24, 28, 29, 33, 34, 51, 66, 85, 89, 90, 91, 92, 94, 107, 120, 124, 129, 130, 134, 167, 169, 170
Yellowstone River, 20, 22, 23, 26, 28, 33, 34, 35, 42
Young, Shamie, 174
Yount, Harry, 28, 29
Younts Creek, 29
Younts Peak, 29
Yule, Jack, 137

Left to right: Bob Edgar, Jeannie Cook, Paul Fees, and Lynn Houze, photo taken at Trail Town, near the site of Cody City. (Photo by Mike Cook)

About the Authors

JEANNIE COOK

A Wyoming native, Jeannie Cook was born in Greybull and raised on the family farm thirty-five miles east of Cody. She grew up hearing stories about the Cody country from her grandfather, W. B. Edwards, who came west in 1908.

Genealogical research has been her hobby for the past twenty years. She is a charter member of the Park County Genealogy Society and has served on the Board of the Park County Historical Society. Jeannie is a graduate of the University of Wyoming and has been employed as the curator of the Park County Historical Society Archives for the past seven years. For Wyoming's Centennial, She authored the book *Wiley's Dream of Empire*, which told the history of irrigation in the Big Horn Basin.

Jeannie and her husband Mike have made their home in Cody since 1969 and are the parents of two children, Christina and Billy.

LYNN JOHNSON HOUZE

Lynn Johnson Houze is the assistant curator of the Park County Historical Society Archives in Cody. A native of New Jersey, Lynn received her A.B. degree in history from Hood College in Frederick, Maryland, and her Master's of Library Science from George Peabody College, Vanderbilt University, in Nashville, Tennessee. She moved to Cody in 1983 after living in Baltimore; Hamilton, Ontario; and the Chicago area. She has three children: Jennifer, Alec, and Andrew.

Lynn inherited her love of history from both her father, whose family has lived in New Jersey since before the Revolutionary War, and her mother, the family genealogist, whose Scots-Irish ancestors came to New York City after the Civil War.

BOB EDGAR

Bob Edgar was born in the Big Horn Basin in 1939. He spent his early years in Oregon Basin, between Cody and Meeteetse, where he developed an early interest in archaeology, history, and collecting.

In 1960, Bob began work for Dr. Harold McCracken at the Buffalo Bill Historical Center to explore for, and record, prehistoric Indian sites in the mountain country of northwestern Wyoming.

In 1963 he was instrumental in initiating the Mummy Cave excavation west of Cody. Bob spent the next four years in charge of the excavation, which was sponsored by the National Geographic Society, through the Historical Center. The last year was in conjunction with the Smithsonian Institution, where he spent part of the year as coauthor of the scientific report of Mummy Cave.

Upon returning to Cody, he turned his efforts toward collecting frontier buildings and historical memorabilia of northwest Wyoming, which resulted in the creation of Old Trail Town in Cody.

PAUL FEES

Paul Fees was born in Arizona, where he spent his early years. He received his A.B. in history from Stanford University and his M.A. and Ph.D. in American Civilization from Brown University. Fees joined the staff of the Buffalo Bill Historical Center in Cody, Wyoming, in 1981 as curator of history and is currently the BBHC's senior curator. Additionally, Fees serves on the Wyoming Council for the Humanities, the Wyoming State Historical Records Advisory Board, the Museum of the Mountain Men Advisory Board, and is a panelist for the NEH Museums and Historical Organizations. He has published many papers and books on Western history including: *Frontier America* with Sarah Boehme in 1988, *Interior West* with Wally Reber in 1989, and *Myth of the West* with Chris Bruce in 1990. Fees, his wife Nancy and their two children reside in Cody.